A SURVEY OF FINANCIAL AND MANAGERIAL
ACCOUNTING

James Don Edwards, Ph.D., CPA
J. M. Tull Professor of Accounting
University of Georgia

Roger H. Hermanson, Ph.D., CPA
Ernst & Whinney Alumni Professor
Regents' Professor of Accounting
Georgia State University

R. F. Salmonson, Ph.D., CPA
Professor Emeritus
Michigan State University

1989   Fifth Edition

Homewood, IL   60430
Boston, MA 02116

The previous editions of this book were published
under the title, *A Survey of Basic Accounting*.

© RICHARD D. IRWIN, INC., 1973, 1977, 1981, 1985, and 1989

Sponsoring editor: Elizabeth Storey
Project editor: Rita McMullen
Production manager: Bette Ittersagen
Designer: Jeanne Wolfgeher
Compositor: Beacon Graphics Corporation
Typeface: 10/12 Palatino
Printer: R. R. Donnelley & Sons Company

Library of Congress Cataloging-in-Publication Data

Edwards, James Don.
    A survey of financial and managerial accounting/James Don
Edwards, Roger H. Hermanson, R. F. Salmonson.—5th ed.
        p.   cm.
    Rev. ed. of: A survey of basic accounting/R. F. Salmonson, James
Don Edwards, Roger H. Hermanson. 4th ed. 1985.
    Includes index.
    ISBN 0-256-06976-X
    1. Accounting. I. Hermanson, Roger H. II. Salmonson, R. F.
(Roland Frank), 1922–   Survey of basic accounting. III. Title.
HF5635.S17 1989
657—dc19   88–19835
                                                                         CIP

Printed in the United States of America
    2   3   4   5   6   7   8   9   0   DO   5   4   3   2   1   0

PREFACE

This fifth edition of *A Survey of Financial and Managerial Accounting* is designed for use by those who wish to obtain a basic understanding of financial and managerial accounting. Accounting topics are introduced and discussed on the assumption that the reader has no prior knowledge of accounting.

We have sought in this book to introduce topics in a manner that emphasizes the output of the accounting process. While some attention is directed toward procedures and techniques used to accumulate accounting information, the major emphasis is on the content of accounting reports and on the interpretation and possible uses of this information.

This edition has been thoroughly updated and substantially revised. Changes that resulted largely due to users' and reviewers' comments and to recent developments include:

1. A chapter on the statement of cash flows has been substituted for the old chapter on statement of changes in financial position. The Financial Accounting Standards Board mandated this new statement in late 1987.
2. The theory chapter now contains the conceptual framework material within the chapter rather than in the chapter appendix. International accounting appears as an appendix to the theory chapter rather than as an appendix at the end of the book.
3. Inflation accounting has been moved from the theory chapter to an appendix at the end of the text because the Financial Accounting Standards Board has made inflation accounting completely optional. Thus, its importance has diminished significantly.
4. Job order and process costing are now covered in two chapters rather than one as in the fourth edition.
5. The tax discussion in Chapter 21 incorporates the latest tax changes through the end of 1987.

Many improvements in the format of the book were made to further increase the students' ability to learn from the text. Some of these improvements include:

1. Learning objectives appear at the beginning of each chapter and also throughout the chapter.
2. At least one demonstration problem and solution appear in each chapter.

3. A description of each exercise and problem is located beside each one in the left-hand margin. These descriptions let both the instructor and students know the topic and requirements of an exercise or problem at a glance.
4. Each chapter contains a glossary of new terms with references to the pages on which the terms were first defined and discussed.
5. From one to three business decision problems appear at the end of each chapter to give the book more of a decision orientation.
6. The Study Guide and Working Papers booklet contains a section entitled "Understanding the Learning Objectives" for each chapter. Students can determine if they really have achieved the learning objectives.
7. The glossary for each chapter is repeated in the Study Guide and Working Papers booklet as a convenience to students and to emphasize the importance of understanding the terminology of accounting.
8. Additional illustrations have been added to further communicate and summarize key points.

The first 12 chapters are devoted to a discussion of financial accounting topics that relate largely to the determination and reporting of net income and financial position and to the basic theory underlying the financial statements of business corporations. Here again we have deliberately sought to emphasize certain subject matter because we believe that knowledge of it is crucial in gaining an understanding of financial accounting and financial reporting. For example, we direct attention to the alternative approaches to accounting for inventories and plant assets since these approaches may produce substantially different measurements of net income and of financial position. We also discuss such matters as the theory underlying accounting statements, the appraisal of financial position and the adequacy of earnings, stockholders' equity, debt financing and investments, and the new statement of cash flows. We omit largely procedural matters, such as payroll accounting and specialized journals.

The remaining nine chapters deal with managerial accounting topics that are likely to be of concern to management in directing the internal affairs of a business. The topics discussed include cost concepts, cost systems in manufacturing companies, standard cost systems, responsibility accounting and segment analysis, the budget, cost-volume-profit analysis, short-term decisions, tax considerations, and capital budgeting. We believe that knowledge of the topics included is essential to every reader who aspires to an executive position in business if he or she expects to understand accounting reports, to plan and control the operations of a business, and to communicate with other executives.

There are five appendixes in the text that you and your students may find useful. They are as follows: Appendix A: Inflation Accounting; Appendix B: Financial Statements Contained in the Annual Report of AMR Corporation (American Airlines); Appendix C: Future and Present Value Tables; Appendix D: The Use of the Microcomputer in Accounting; and Appendix E: The Computer: Basic Concepts.

We have designed this text for use at either the undergraduate or masters level. It will provide students who have no prior knowledge of accounting with the background necessary for further courses dealing with the accumulation, interpretation, and use of accounting information.

Various approaches may be taken in using this book in a one-quarter or a one-semester course. For a primarily "financial" course, one could focus attention on the first 12 chapters. If management accounting is to be emphasized, one could cover Chapters 1–4 and then concentrate on the last nine chapters. Alternatively, a balanced approach could be taken by covering all the chapters (in two quarters) or by covering selected chapters from both groupings.

Questions, exercises, and problems are provided at the end of each chapter in sufficient quantity for use in classroom discussion and for assignment as homework. A Solutions Manual is available for instructors using this text. A combination Study Guide and Working Papers booklet is available for students. The student booklet has been strengthened considerably with the addition of a section on understanding the learning objectives and a glossary of terms for each chapter. The student booklet also contains "completion and exercises" questions and multiple-choice questions for each chapter (with answers).

We are indebted to a number of members of the faculties of our respective universities for helpful comments on the organization and content of this book. In addition, we would like to acknowledge specifically the assistance of Martin A. Bubley, Northern Illinois University; V. Bruce Irvine, University of Saskatchewan; Gerald L. Johnson, California State University, Fresno; Peter Kenyon, Humboldt State University; Larry N. Killough and Rosalind Cranor, both of Virginia Polytechnic and State University; Richard D. Lamb, University of New Hampshire; Lawrence Rittenberg, University of Wisconsin; Victoria S. Rymer, George Mason University; G. A. Swanson, Tennessee Tech University; James Trebly, Marquette University; Deborah A. Wheless, James Madison University; V. Joyce Yearley, New Mexico State University.

Barbara Howard and Dianne Hermanson provided capable and efficient service in typing the manuscript. But we, of course, bear full responsibility for any deficiencies in the text.

James Don Edwards
Roger H. Hermanson
R. F. Salmonson

CONTENTS

Accounting Process Summarized. The Classified Balance Sheet:
*Current Assets. Long-Term Investments. Property, Plant, and Equipment.
Intangible Assets. Current Liabilities. Long-Term Liabilities. Stockholders'
Equity.* Appendix: The Worksheet for a Service Company

Assets or Other Nonmonetary Assets. Exchanges of Dissimilar Plant Assets. Exchanges of Similar Plant Assets. Removal Costs. Natural Resources: *Depletion.* Intangible Assets: *Acquisition of Intangible Assets. Amortization of Intangible Assets. Patents. Copyrights. Franchises. Trademarks; Trade Names. Leases. Leasehold Improvements. Goodwill. Reporting Amortization.*

Cost Driver. Accounting for Manufacturing Overhead. Job Order Costing—an Example.

Differential Analysis. Absorption versus Direct Costing: *Absorption Costing. Direct Costing. Comparing the Two Methods.*

INTRODUCTION: THE ACCOUNTING ENVIRONMENT

LEARNING OBJECTIVES

After studying this introduction, you should be able to:

1. Define accounting.
2. Describe the functions performed by accountants.
3. Describe employment opportunities in accounting.
4. Differentiate between financial and managerial accounting.
5. Identify the five organizations that have a role in the development of financial accounting standards.
6. Define and use correctly the new terms in the glossary.

You have embarked on the challenging and rewarding study of accounting—an old and time-honored discipline.[1] History indicates that all developed societies require certain accounting records, and record-keeping in an accounting sense is thought to have begun about 4000 B.C.

The record-keeping, control, and verification problems encountered in the ancient world had many characteristics similar to those encountered today. For example, ancient governments also kept records of receipts and disbursements. And in ancient accounting systems, it was just as necessary as it is today to have internal controls to check on the honesty and reliability of employees.

---

[1]When first studying any discipline, new terms are encountered. Usually these terms are set in boldface and defined at their first occurrence. However, sometimes it is more feasible not to define a term at its first occurrence. The boldface terms are also listed and defined at the end of this Introduction, or in the case of the chapters, at the end of the chapter. After the definition of the term in the terms list, a page number is given in parentheses indicating where the term is discussed in the chapter.

A study of the evolution of accounting suggests that accounting processes are reactive because they have developed primarily in response to business needs. Also, the development of accounting processes has been related to economic progress. History shows that the higher the level of civilization, the more elaborate the accounting methods.

The emergence of double-entry bookkeeping was a crucial event in accounting history. In 1494, a Franciscan monk, Luca Pacioli, described the double-entry "Method of Venice" system in his text called *Summa de Arithmetica, Geometric, Proportion et Proportionalite* (Everything about Arithmetic, Geometry, and Proportion). Pacioli's *Summa* is considered by many to be a reworked version of a manuscript that circulated among teachers and pupils of the Venetian schools of commerce and arithmetic.

In accounting, the name "Luca Pacioli" will always be important for the contribution he made to accounting systems. At the age of 20, Pacioli became a tutor to three sons of a rich merchant; later he lectured on mathematics and traveled throughout Italy. He also authored several books. Pacioli's friend Leonardo da Vinci helped prepare the drawings for one of Pacioli's books, and Pacioli is said to have calculated the amount of bronze needed for Leonardo's huge statue of the Duke.

Since Pacioli's days, the roles of accountants and professional accounting organizations have expanded in society and business. As professionals, accountants are expected to hold a responsibility to public service above their commitment to personal economic gain. Some accountants recognize that they are obligated to work for the improvement of society. Complementing their obligation to society, accountants have analytical and evaluative skills needed in the solution of the ever-growing problems of the world. The special abilities of accountants, as well as their independence and ethical standards, permit them to make a significant and unique contribution in such areas as protecting the public interest, preserving environmental interests, and controlling and improving public programs.

As a background for studying accounting, this Introduction will define accounting and list the functions performed by accountants. You will learn about the employment opportunities in accounting and be able to differentiate between financial and managerial accounting. You will be introduced to the five prominent organizations that have contributed to certain standards to which accountants must conform. You will realize that you are frequently exposed to accounting information in your everyday life. As you continue your study of accounting in the chapters ahead, it is the authors' hope that the language of business will become your own.

ACCOUNTING DEFINED

Objective 1:
Define accounting

Accounting is defined by the American Accounting Association—one of the prominent accounting authorities discussed later in this Introduction—as "the process of identifying, measuring, and communicating economic information to permit informed judgments and decisions by the users of the information."[2] This information is primarily financial and is generally stated in money terms. Accounting, then, is fundamentally a measurement and communication process (or information system) used to report on the activity of profit-seeking business organizations and not-for-profit organizations. As a measurement and communication process for business, accounting supplies information that permits informed judgments and decisions by users of the data.

The accounting process provides financial data for a wide range of individuals whose objectives in studying the data vary widely. For example, a bank official may study a company's financial statements to evaluate the company's ability to repay a loan, while a prospective investor may compare accounting data from several companies to decide which company appears to represent the best investment. Accounting also supplies management with significant financial and economic data that are useful for decision making.

Reliable information is necessary before a sound decision involving the allocation of scarce resources can be made. In decision making there are always alternatives—even if one of the alternatives is to take no action or to delay taking action. Accounting information is valuable because it can be used to predict the financial consequences of each alternative. Rather than depend on a "crystal ball" to estimate the future, accountants can use professional judgment in quantifying the future financial impact of various alternatives. Thus, the uncertainty of the financial results of an action is reduced.

Not only does accounting information play a significant role within the organization in reducing uncertainty, but it also provides the financial data required by law, either directly or indirectly, for external purposes. To do this, accountants provide information about a company's financial performance during a time period. This information tells how a company's management has discharged its stewardship responsibility for the company's resources. Owners have the right to know how their investments are managed. In fulfilling this obligation, accountants prepare financial statements such as an income statement and a balance sheet. In addition, they prepare tax returns for federal and state governments as well as fulfill the Securities and Exchange Commission's filing requirements.

Accounting is often confused with bookkeeping. Bookkeeping involves the routine recording of economic activities and is a mechanical process. Accounting includes bookkeeping but goes well beyond it in scope. Accountants analyze and interpret financial information, prepare financial statements, conduct audits, design accounting systems, prepare special business and financial studies, prepare forecasts and budgets, and provide tax services.

---

[2]American Accounting Association, *A Statement of Basic Accounting Theory* (Evanston, Ill., 1966), p. 1.

Specifically, the accounting process (also called the accounting cycle) consists of the following groups of functions (see Illustration 0.1):

Illustration 0.1
ACCOUNTING FUNCTIONS PERFORMED BY ACCOUNTANTS

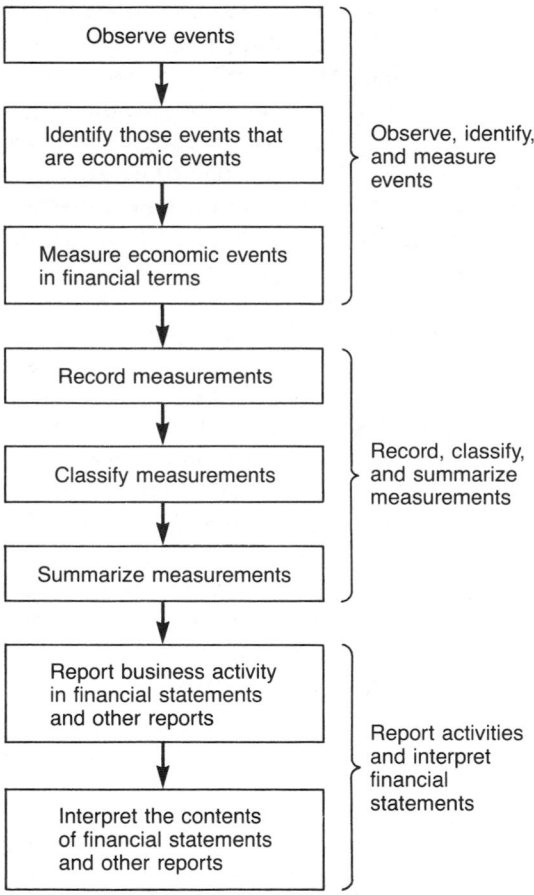

Observe events

Identify those events that are economic events

Measure economic events in financial terms

Observe, identify, and measure events

Record measurements

Classify measurements

Summarize measurements

Record, classify, and summarize measurements

Report business activity in financial statements and other reports

Interpret the contents of financial statements and other reports

Report activities and interpret financial statements

Objective 2:
Describe the functions performed by accountants

1. Accountants *observe* many events and *identify* and *measure* in financial terms (dollars) those events considered evidence of economic activity. (These three functions are often collectively referred to as *analyze.*) The purchase and sale of goods and services are examples of economic activities.
2. Next, the economic events are *recorded, classified* into meaningful groups, and *summarized* for conciseness.
3. Accountants *report* on business activity by preparing financial statements and special reports. Accountants are often asked to *interpret* these statements and reports for various groups such as management and

creditors. Interpretation may involve determining how the business is performing compared to prior years and other similar businesses.

EMPLOYMENT OPPORTUNITIES IN ACCOUNTING

Objective 3: Describe employment opportunities in accounting

As stated earlier, accounting is an old profession; records of business transactions have been prepared for centuries. However, it was only during the last half-century that accounting as a profession was accepted with the same importance as the medical and legal professions. Today, in the United States, well over a million people are employed as accountants, and several million are employed in accounting-related positions. Typically, accountants are employed in public accounting, private or industrial accounting, and governmental or other not-for-profit accounting.

Public Accounting

The **public accounting** profession offers accounting and related services for a fee to companies, other organizations, and the general public. An accountant may become a **certified public accountant (CPA).** A CPA is an accountant who has passed an examination prepared and graded by the American Institute of Certified Public Accountants (AICPA) and has met certain other requirements, including being licensed by the state. These requirements vary by state, but states typically require a CPA to have completed certain courses in accounting, worked a certain number of years in public accounting, and lived in that state a certain length of time before taking the examination. When all requirements are met, the accountant may be licensed by the state to practice as an independent professional. Generally, CPAs provide services in auditing, taxes, and management advising (or consulting).

Auditing. When a business seeks a loan or attempts to have its securities traded on a stock exchange, it is usually required to provide statements concerning its financial affairs. Users of a company's statements are more assured that the statements are presented fairly when the company has been audited by a CPA. A CPA firm is hired by the company to conduct an examination **(independent audit)** of its accounting and related records. The independent auditor verifies some of these records by contacting external sources. For example, the accountant may contact a bank to verify cash balances of the client. **Independent auditors** of the CPA firm perform an audit of a business to enable them to give an **independent auditor's opinion or report** as to whether or not the financial statements fairly (equitably) report the economic performance of the business. As you will learn in the section "Private or Industrial Accounting," auditors *within* a business also conduct audits, but these audits are not independent audits.

Tax Services. CPAs often provide expert advice on the preparation of federal, state, and local tax returns, as well as on tax planning. The objective in preparing tax returns is to use legal means to minimize the amount of taxes paid. Since almost every major business decision has a tax impact, clients also need tax planning so they know the tax effects of each financial decision.

Management Advisory (or Consulting) Services. CPAs often are engaged to provide a wide range of advisory or consulting services. The auditing services provided by CPAs often result in suggestions to clients on how to improve their operations. For example, CPAs might suggest improvements in the design and installation of an accounting system, the electronic processing of accounting data, inventory control, budgeting, or financial planning.

Private or Industrial Accounting

In contrast to public accountants, who provide services for many clients, **private or industrial accountants** provide services for a single business. Some companies employ only one private accountant, while other companies employ many. In a company with many accountants, the executive officer in charge of the accounting activity is often called a **controller.**

Private accountants may or may not be CPAs. If these accountants pass an examination prepared and graded by the Institute of Certified Management Accountants, an affiliate of the National Association of Accountants, and meet certain other requirements, they become **Certified Management Accountants (CMAs).** The National Association of Accountants is an organization primarily consisting of management accountants employed in private industry.

Private accountants may specialize in one particular job or task. For example, some may specialize in measuring and controlling costs, others in budgeting—the development of plans relating to future operations. Many private accountants become specialists in the design and installation of accounting data processing systems; others are **internal auditors** employed to conduct **internal audits** to see that the policies and procedures established by the business are followed in its divisions and departments. This last group of private accountants may earn the designation of **certified internal auditor (CIA).** The CIA certificate is granted by the Institute of Internal Auditors (IIA) after the accountant has successfully completed an examination prepared and graded by the Institute and has met certain other requirements.

Governmental and Other Not-for-Profit Accounting

Many accountants, including CPAs, are employed in **governmental or other not-for-profit accounting.** These accountants have essentially the same educational background and training as accountants in public and private (or industrial) accounting.

Governmental accountants are employed by government agencies at the federal, state, and local levels. Often they perform accounting duties relating to the control of tax revenues and expenditures. Government agencies that regulate business activity—such as the regulation of public utilities by a state public service commission—employ governmental accountants. FBI agents who have training as accountants find their accounting background useful in investigating criminals involved in illegal business activities, such as gambling.

Not-for-profit organizations such as churches, charities, fraternities, and universities need the services of accountants to record and account for funds received and disbursed. The academic segment of the accounting profession also employs accountants (including CPAs, CMAs, and CIAs). These accountants teach accounting to students and conduct research on accounting issues.

FINANCIAL ACCOUNTING VERSUS MANAGERIAL ACCOUNTING

Objective 4: Differentiate between financial and managerial accounting

An accounting information system provides data to help the decision-making process of individuals outside the business as well as inside the business. The decision-making individuals *outside* the business *are affected in some way by the performance of the business,* while the decision-making individuals *inside* the business *are responsible for the performance of the business.* For this reason, accounting is often divided into two categories: financial accounting and managerial accounting. This section discusses the distinction between financial and managerial accounting. Note, however, that financial accounting information is used both in financial accounting and managerial accounting.

Financial Accounting

Financial accounting information is meant primarily for external use, while managerial accounting information is meant for internal use. Stockholders and creditors are examples of people outside a company who want and need financial accounting information. These outside people make decisions on matters pertaining to the entire company, such as whether to extend credit to a company or to invest in a company. Consequently, financial accounting information relates to the company as a whole, while managerial accounting focuses on the parts or segments of the company.

There are several different groups of external users of accounting information. Each group has different interests in the company and wants answers to different questions. The groups and their possible questions are:

1. Owners and prospective owners. Has the company had satisfactory income on its total investment? Should an investment be made in this company? Should the present investment be increased, decreased, or retained at the same level? Can the company install costly pollution control equipment and still remain profitable?

2. Creditors and lenders. Should a loan be granted to the company? Will the company be able to pay its debts as they become due?
3. Employees and their unions. Does the company have the ability to pay increased wages? Is the company financially able to provide permanent employment?
4. Customers. Does the company offer useful products at fair prices? Will the company survive long enough to honor its product warranties?
5. Governmental units. Is the local public utility charging a fair rate for its services?
6. General public. Is the company providing useful products and gainful employment for citizens without causing serious environmental problems?

General-purpose financial statements provide most of the information needed by external users of financial accounting. These **financial statements** are formal reports providing information on a company's financial position (solvency), changes in this position, and the results of operations (profitability). Many companies publish these statements in an annual report. The **annual report** (see Appendix B at the end of the text) also contains the independent auditor's opinion as to the fairness of the financial statements, as well as information about the company's activities, products, and plans.

Financial accounting information is historical in nature, reporting on what has happened in the past. To facilitate comparisons between companies, this information must conform to certain standards or methods of presentation called **generally accepted accounting principles (GAAP).** These generally accepted accounting principles for business firms or for governmental organizations have been developed through accounting practice or have been established by an authoritative organization. You will learn about five of these authoritative organizations in a later section.

Managerial Accounting

Managerial accounting is meant for internal use; it provides special information for the managers of a company. The kind of information used by managers may range from broad, long-range planning data to detailed explanations of why actual costs varied from cost estimates.

Managerial accounting information should:

1. Relate to that part of the company which the manager oversees. For example, a production manager will want information on costs of production but not on advertising.
2. Involve planning for the future. For instance, a budget may be prepared that shows financial plans for the coming year.
3. Meet two tests: the information must be useful, and it must not cost more to gather than it is worth.

The purpose of managerial accounting is to generate information that a manager can use to make sound internal decisions. Internal management decisions can be classified into four major types:

1. Financing decisions—deciding what amounts of capital (funds) are needed to run the business and whether these funds are to be secured from owners or creditors. *Capital* used in this sense means *money* to be used by the company to purchase resources such as machinery and buildings and to pay expenses of conducting the business.
2. Resource allocation decisions—deciding how the total capital of a company is to be invested, such as the amount to be invested in machinery.
3. Production decisions—deciding what products are to be produced, by what means, and when.
4. Marketing decisions—setting selling prices and advertising budgets; determining where a company's markets are and how they are to be reached.

THE DEVELOPMENT OF FINANCIAL ACCOUNTING STANDARDS

Objective 5: Identify the five organizations that have a role in the development of financial accounting standards

The five organizations most influential in the establishment of generally accepted accounting principles (GAAP) for business firms or for governmental organizations are the American Institute of Certified Public Accountants, the Financial Accounting Standards Board, the Governmental Accounting Standards Board, the Securities and Exchange Commission, and the American Accounting Association. Each of these organizations has contributed in a different way to the development of GAAP.

American Institute of Certified Public Accountants (AICPA)

The **American Institute of Certified Public Accountants (AICPA)** is a professional organization of certified public accountants, many of whom are in public accounting. In addition, the AICPA has been the dominant organization in the development of accounting standards over the past half-century. In a 20-year period ending in 1959, the AICPA Committee on Accounting Procedure issued 51 *Accounting Research Bulletins* recommending certain principles or practices. The **Accounting Principles Board (APB)** was created in 1959 by the AICPA and was empowered to speak for it on matters of accounting principles. During the 14-year life of the APB it has issued 31 numbered *Opinions* that CPAs generally are required to follow. The AICPA continues to influence the development of accounting standards and practices through its monthly magazine, the *Journal of Accountancy*, its research division, and its other divisions and committees.

Financial Accounting Standards Board (FASB)

The Accounting Principles Board (APB) was replaced in 1973 by an independent, seven-member, full-time **Financial Accounting Standards Board**

(FASB). The FASB has issued numerous *Statements of Financial Accounting Standards* and interpretations of those standards. The FASB is widely accepted as the major influence *in the private sector* in the development of new financial standards.

Governmental Accounting Standards Board (GASB)

The **Governmental Accounting Standards Board (GASB)** was established in 1984 with a full-time chairman and four part-time members. The GASB has issued several statements on accounting and financial reporting in the governmental area. This organization is widely accepted as the major influence *in the private sector* in the development of new governmental accounting concepts and standards. The GASB also has the authority to issue interpretations of these standards.

Securities and Exchange Commission (SEC)

Created under the Securities and Exchange Act of 1934, the **Securities and Exchange Commission (SEC)** administers a number of important acts dealing with the interstate sale of securities (stocks and bonds). The SEC has the power to prescribe accounting practices to be followed by companies under its jurisdiction. This includes virtually every major U.S. business corporation. But rather than exercise this power, the SEC has adopted a policy of working closely with the accounting profession, especially the FASB, in the development of accounting standards. The SEC indicates to the FASB the accounting topics it believes should be addressed.

American Accounting Association (AAA)

Consisting largely of accounting educators, the **American Accounting Association (AAA)** has sought to encourage research and study at a theoretical level into the concepts, standards, and principles of accounting. In recent years, its journals, *The Accounting Review, Accounting Horizons*, and *Issues in Accounting Education* have carried many articles reporting on accounting issues.

SUMMARY

Accounting is fundamentally a measurement and communication process used to report on the activity of profit-seeking and not-for-profit organizations. This process is performed by accountants who *observe* many events and *identify* and *measure* those events considered evidence of economic activity; *record, classify,* and *summarize* these events; *report* on business activity by preparing statements and special reports; and *interpret* these statements and reports for internal and external decision making.

An accountant may be employed in public, private, or governmental and not-for-profit accounting, including the academic segment of the accounting profession. Today, in the United States, well over a million people are employed as accountants, and several million are employed in accounting-related positions.

An accounting information system provides data to help the decision-making process of individuals outside the business as well as inside the business. Financial accounting information is primarily meant for external use, while managerial accounting information is meant for internal use.

External users include actual and potential stockholders and creditors and their professional advisers, employees and their unions, customers, suppliers, governmental agencies, and the public at large. Internal users of accounting information include various levels of management personnel.

Financial accounting information must conform to certain standards or principles called generally accepted accounting principles (GAAP). These principles have been developed through accounting practice or have been established or influenced by five accounting organizations: American Institute of Certified Public Accountants (AICPA), Financial Accounting Standards Board (FASB), Governmental Accounting Standards Board (GASB), Securities and Exchange Commission (SEC), and American Accounting Association (AAA).

The first chapter shows you how to analyze business transactions and accumulate the information so that financial statements can be prepared. The process is based on the accounting equation.

Objective 6: Define and use correctly the new terms in the glossary

NEW TERMS USED IN THIS INTRODUCTION

Accounting "The process of identifying, measuring, and communicating economic information to permit informed judgments and decisions by the users of the information" (2).

Accounting Principles Board (APB) An organization created in 1959 by the AICPA and empowered to speak for it on matters of accounting principle; replaced in 1973 by the Financial Accounting Standards Board (9).

American Accounting Association (AAA) A professional organization of accountants, many of whom are college or university professors of accounting (10).

American Institute of Certified Public Accountants (AICPA) A professional organization of certified public accountants, many of whom are in public accounting practice (9).

Annual report A pamphlet or document of varying length containing audited financial statements and other information about a company, distributed annually to its owners (8).

Audit (independent) Performed by independent auditors to determine whether the financial statements of a business fairly reflect the economic performance of the business (5).

Audit (internal) Performed by accounting employees of a company to determine if company policies and procedures are being followed (6).

Certified Internal Auditor (CIA) An accountant who has passed an examination prepared and graded by the Institute of Internal Auditors and who has met certain other requirements (6).

Certified Management Accountant (CMA)   Awarded to accountants who pass an examination prepared and graded by the Institute of Certified Management Accountants, an affiliate of the National Association of Accountants, and meet certain other requirements (6).

Certified Public Accountant (CPA)   An accountant who has passed an examination prepared and graded by the American Institute of Certified Public Accountants (AICPA) and has met certain other requirements, such as work experience in accounting and specified courses in accounting. The accountant is then awarded a CPA certificate and may be licensed by the state to practice as an independent professional (5).

Controller   The executive officer in charge of a company's accounting activity (6).

Financial accounting   Relates to the process of supplying financial information to parties external to the reporting entity (7).

Financial Accounting Standards Board (FASB)   The highest ranking nongovernmental authority on the development of accounting standards or principles (9).

Financial statements   Formal reports providing information on a company's financial position (solvency), changes in this position, and the results of operations (profitability) (8).

Generally Accepted Accounting Principles (GAAP)   Accounting standards and principles that have been developed largely in accounting practice or have been established by an authoritative organization (8).

Governmental Accounting Standards Board (GASB)   This body issues statements on accounting and financial reporting in the governmental area (10).

Governmental or other not-for-profit accounting   Governmental accountants are employed by government agencies at the federal, state, and local levels. Other not-for-profit accountants record and account for receipts and disbursements for churches, charities, fraternities, and universities. Accountants in the academic segment of the accounting profession teach accounting to students and conduct research on accounting issues (6).

Independent audit   See Audit (independent).

Independent auditors   Certified public accountants who perform audits to determine whether the financial statements of businesses fairly reflect the economic performance of these businesses (5).

Independent auditor's opinion or report   The formal written statement by a certified public accountant that states whether or not the client's financial statements fairly reflect the economic performance of the business (5).

Internal audit   See Audit (internal).

Internal auditors   Private accountants employed to see that the policies and procedures established by the business are followed in its divisions and departments (6).

Managerial accounting   Relates to the process of supplying financial information for internal management use (8).

Private or industrial accountants   Accountants who provide accounting services for a single business and are employees of that business (6).

Public accounting   Relates to accounting and related services offered for a fee to companies, other organizations, and the general public (5).

Securities and Exchange Commission (SEC) A governmental agency created by Congress to administer acts dealing with interstate sales of securities and having the authority to prescribe the accounting and reporting practices of firms under its jurisdiction (10).

QUESTIONS

1. Define accounting.

2. What is the relationship between accounting as an information system and economic resources?

3. What is a CPA? What are some of the services usually provided by a CPA?

4. What is the role of the accountant in private industry? What are some of the services provided by the industrial accountant?

5. Describe the difference between financial accounting and managerial accounting.

6. Name five organizations that have played or are playing an important role in the development of accounting standards. Describe each briefly.

1 ACCOUNTING— A SOURCE OF FINANCIAL INFORMATION

LEARNING OBJECTIVES

After studying this chapter, you should be able to:

1. Identify and describe the three basic forms of business organizations.
2. Distinguish among the three types of business activities performed by business organizations.
3. Describe the content and purposes of the balance sheet, income statement, and statement of retained earnings.
4. State the basic accounting equation and describe its relationship to the balance sheet.
5. Analyze business transactions and determine their effects on items in the financial statements.
6. Prepare a balance sheet and income statement.
7. Define and use correctly the new terms in the glossary.

The Introduction provided a background for your study of accounting. You now know how to define accounting and know the functions accountants perform. After reading about the employment opportunities in accounting, you may have already chosen a field of accounting employment to pursue as a career. Even if you do not become an accountant, accounting information will be useful throughout your lifetime.

Now you are ready to learn about the forms of business organizations and the types of business activities they perform. Three of the financial statements used by these businesses are presented. Then you will learn about the accounting process (or accounting cycle) used to prepare those financial statements. In this accounting process, financial data—such as your daily personal purchases from businesses—are analyzed, recorded, classified, summarized, and finally reported in the financial statements of those businesses. Hopefully, as you study this chapter, you will recognize the unique, systematic nature of accounting—the language of business.

FORMS OF BUSINESS ORGANIZATIONS

Objective 1: Identify and describe the three basic forms of business organizations

There are three basic forms of organization for a business enterprise. They are the *single proprietorship, partnership,* and *corporation.* Accounting serves all forms of business organizations, but this book will use the corporation in its illustrations of basic accounting concepts. The corporation is the most significant in terms of volume of business. Virtually the same accounting concepts, however, apply to all three forms of organization.

Single Proprietorship

A **single proprietorship** is an unincorporated business owned by an individual and often managed by that same individual. Many individuals in small service-type businesses (such as physicians, lawyers, barbers, and electricians) and retail establishments (such as clothing stores, antique shops, and novelty stores) do business as single proprietorships. There are no legal formalities in organizing such a business, and usually only a limited amount of money is required to begin operations. There is no legal distinction between the business and its owner, since the owner is responsible for both personal and business debts. However, there is an accounting distinction. The financial activities of the business, such as selling services to the public, are kept separate from the personal financial activities, such as making a payment on an auto used exclusively for nonbusiness purposes. The business is considered an **entity** separate from the owner.

Partnership

A **partnership** is a business owned by two or more persons associated as partners and is often managed by those same persons. The partnership is created by an agreement setting forth the terms of the partnership. Preferably, the agreement should be in writing, but it may be oral. Included in the agreement will be such things as the initial investment of each partner, duties of each partner, means of dividing income (profits) or losses between the partners each year, and settlement to be made upon the death or withdrawal of a partner. A partnership often evolves out of one or more single proprietorships. For instance, Mr. X and Ms. Y, both CPAs, may each operate single proprietorships. Each sees the need to have another CPA to serve clients during vacations. Also, there may be a need to combine their strong points (X is a tax person, and Y is an auditor) to improve service to their clients. They may decide to combine their single proprietorships into a partnership. Partnerships, like single proprietorships, are commonly found in the service and retail fields.

Corporation

A **corporation** is a business that may be owned by a few persons or by thousands of persons and is incorporated under the laws of one of the 50 states. A corporation often is managed by persons other than the owners, although major owners sometimes serve as officers (managers) of the corporation. Ownership in a corporation is divided into units known as shares of stock. Thus, the owners are called **stockholders** or **shareholders.** Ownership interest is easily transferred by selling one's shares of stock to another person. Organized exchanges (such as the New York Stock Exchange) exist for this purpose. Corporations may evolve from single proprietorships or partnerships, although sometimes they are formed directly. The corporate form is more likely to appear where substantial money is needed to start the business, where a wide range of talents is needed to manage the business, and where the owners desire to limit their personal liability for debts. Unlike the single proprietorship and partnership forms, the corporation is a *legal entity* separate from its owners. The owners are *not* personally responsible for the debts of the corporation beyond the amounts they have invested in the corporation.

TYPES OF BUSINESS ACTIVITIES PERFORMED BY BUSINESS ORGANIZATIONS

Objective 2: Distinguish among the three types of business activities performed by business organizations

The forms of business entities discussed in the previous section are classified according to the type of ownership of the business entity. Single proprietors have one owner, partnerships have two or more owners, and corporations usually have many owners. We can also group business entities by the type of business activities they perform—service companies, merchandising companies, and manufacturing companies.

1. Service companies. **Service companies** perform services for a fee. This group includes companies such as accounting firms, law firms, repair shops, dry cleaning establishments, and many others. Accounting for service companies is illustrated in the early chapters of this text.
2. Merchandising companies. **Merchandising companies** purchase goods that are ready for sale and then sell them to customers. Merchandising companies include companies such as auto dealerships, clothing stores, and supermarkets. Accounting for merchandising companies is first illustrated in Chapter 4.
3. Manufacturing companies. **Manufacturing companies** buy materials, convert them into products, and then sell the products to other companies or to final customers. Examples of manufacturing companies are steel mills, auto manufacturers, and clothing manufacturers.

All these companies produce financial statements as the final end product of their accounting process. As you learned in the Introduction, these financial statements provide relevant financial information both to those inside the company—management—and those outside the company—

creditors, stockholders, and other interested parties. In the next section, you will learn about the three most common financial statements: the balance sheet, the income statement, and the statement of retained earnings.

FINANCIAL STATEMENTS OF BUSINESS ENTERPRISES

Objective 3:
Describe the content
and purposes of the
balance sheet,
income statement,
and statement of
retained earnings

Although a modern business firm has many objectives or goals, the two primary objectives of every business firm are profitability and solvency. Unless a firm can produce satisfactory income (profit) and pay its debts when they are due, any other objectives a firm may have will never be realized simply because the firm will not survive. The financial statements that reflect a firm's solvency (the balance sheet), its profitability (the income statement), and its changes in retained earnings (the statement of retained earnings) are illustrated and discussed below. A fourth financial statement, the statement of cash flows, is discussed in Chapter 10.

The Balance Sheet

The **balance sheet** (often called the **statement of financial position**) shows the assets, liabilities, and stockholders' equity of a business firm at a specific moment in time. The balance sheet is like a still photograph; it only captures reality as of a particular point in time. The balance sheet shows the **solvency** (the ability to pay debts as they come due) of a company.

Assets are things of value; they constitute the resources of the firm. They have value to the firm because of the uses to which they can be put or the things that can be acquired by exchanging them. In Illustration 1.1, the assets of the Ross Company, which performs delivery services, amount to $38,700. The assets consist of cash, **accounts receivable** (amounts due from customers for services previously rendered), delivery equipment, and office equipment.

Illustration 1.1

ROSS COMPANY
Balance Sheet
July 31, 1990

Assets		Liabilities and Stockholders' Equity	
Cash	$15,500	Liabilities:	
Accounts receivable	700	Accounts payable	$ 600
Delivery equipment	20,000	Notes payable	6,000
Office equipment	2,500	Total liabilities	$ 6,600
		Stockholders' equity:	
		Capital stock	$30,000
		Retained earnings	2,100
		Total stockholders' equity	$32,100
		Total liabilities and	
Total assets	$38,700	stockholders' equity	$38,700

Liabilities are the debts owed by a firm. Typically, they must be paid at certain known moments in time. Ross Company's liabilities consist of **accounts payable** (amounts owed to suppliers for previous purchases) and **notes payable** (written promises to pay a specific sum of money) totaling $6,600.

The Ross Company is a corporation. It is customary to refer to the owners' interest in a corporation as **stockholders' equity.** Ross Company's stockholders' equity consists of $30,000 paid for shares of capital stock and retained earnings of $2,100. **Capital stock** shows the amount of investment in a corporation by its owners. **Retained earnings** generally consists of the accumulated income of the corporation minus dividends distributed to stockholders. All of these items will be discussed in detail later in the text. At this point, simply note that the balance sheet heading includes the name of the organization and the title and date of the statement. Also note that the dollar amount of the total assets is equal to the claims on (or interests in) those assets.

The Income Statement

The purpose of the **income statement** (often called the **earnings statement**) is to report the profits of a business organization for a stated period of time. **Periodicity** is the assumption that an entity's life can be subdivided into time periods for purposes of reporting the economic activities. In accounting, **profitability** is measured by comparing revenues generated in a given period with expenses incurred to produce those revenues. **Revenues** are the inflows of assets from the sale of products or the rendering of services to customers. **Expenses** are the sacrifices made or the costs incurred to produce revenues. Expenses are measured by the assets surrendered or consumed in serving customers. If revenues exceed expenses, **net income** results. If the reverse is true, the business is said to be operating at a **net loss.** Illustration 1.2 contains the income statement of the Ross Company for the month of July 1990.

Illustration 1.2

ROSS COMPANY Income Statement For the Month Ended July 31, 1990		
Service revenues.		$5,700
Expenses:		
Wages	$2,600	
Rent	400	
Gas and oil	600	
Total expenses.		3,600
Net income		$2,100

The income statement shows that revenues (or delivery fees) of $5,700 were generated by serving customers during the month. Expenses for the month totaled $3,600, resulting in net income for July of $2,100. The major difference in the heading of the income statement from that of the balance sheet is that it expresses a period of time covered rather than a specific date or point in time.

The Statement of Retained Earnings

The purpose of the **statement of retained earnings** is to explain the changes in retained earnings that occurred between two balance sheet dates. Usually, these changes consist of the addition of net income (or deduction of net loss) and the deduction of dividends. Dividends are the means by which a corporation rewards its stockholders for providing it with investment funds. A **dividend** is a payment (usually of cash) to the owners of the business; it is a distribution of income to the owners rather than an expense of doing business. Since dividends are not an expense, they do not appear on the income statement.

The effect of a dividend is to reduce cash and retained earnings by the amount paid out. In effect, the income (earnings) is no longer "retained" but has been passed on to the stockholders (owners). And, of course, earning a return in the form of dividends is one of the primary reasons why people invest in corporations.

The statement of retained earnings for the Ross Company for the month of July 1990 is quite simple (see Illustration 1.3). Since the company was organized on June 1 and did not earn any revenues or incur any expenses during June, the beginning retained earnings balance on July 1 is zero. Net income for July of $2,100 would be added. Since no dividends were paid, the $2,100 would be the ending balance.

Illustration 1.3

ROSS COMPANY Statement of Retained Earnings For the Month Ended July 31, 1990	
Retained earnings, July 1	$ –0–
Add: Net income for July	2,100
Retained earnings, July 31	$2,100

To provide a more effective illustration, assume that the Ross Company's net income for August was $1,500 (revenues of $5,600 less expenses of $4,100) and that the company declared and paid dividends of $1,000. Its statement of retained earnings for August would be as shown in Illustration 1.4.

Illustration 1.4

ROSS COMPANY Statement of Retained Earnings For the Month Ended August 31, 1990	
Retained earnings, July 31	$2,100
Add: Net income for August	1,500
Total	$3,600
Less: Dividends	1,000
Retained earnings, August 31	$2,600

THE FINANCIAL ACCOUNTING PROCESS

We have introduced three principal financial statements: the balance sheet, income statement, and statement of retained earnings. Attention is now directed to the process of accumulating the data to include in the financial statements.

The Accounting Equation

*Objective 4:
State the basic accounting equation and describe its relationship to the balance sheet*

In the balance sheet presented in Illustration 1.1, total assets of the Ross Company were equal to total liabilities plus stockholders' equity. Another way of stating this relationship is that the assets of a business are equal to the equities in those assets; that is, Assets = Equities. Assets have already been defined simply as things of value. They are further defined as those economic resources which are owned by a business and which can be measured. All desired things, except those available in unlimited quantity without cost or effort, are economic resources.

Equities are interests in, or claims upon, assets. For example, assume that you purchased a new automobile for $10,000 by withdrawing $1,000 from your savings account and borrowing $9,000 from your credit union. Your equity in the automobile is $1,000 and that of your credit union is $9,000. The $9,000 can be further described as a liability. Your $1,000 equity could be described as the owner's equity or interest in the asset. Since, in the case of a corporation, the owners are stockholders, the basic **accounting equation** becomes:

$$\text{Assets} = \text{Liabilities} + \text{Stockholders' Equity}$$

Resources, or assets, must always be provided by someone—either a creditor or an owner (stockholders); therefore, this equation must always be in balance.

The right side of the above equation is also viewed in another manner—namely, it shows the sources of the existing group of assets. Thus, liabilities are not only claims against assets; they are also sources of assets. In a corporation, all assets are provided by either creditors (liability holders) or owners (stockholders).

As a business engages in economic activities, the dollar amounts and composition of its assets, liabilities, and stockholders' equity change. But the equality of the basic equation holds true.

Accounting Assumptions

Some underlying assumptions or concepts are used by the accountant in recording business transactions. A **transaction** is an event that affects the assets, liabilities, stockholders' equity, revenues, and/or expenses of an entity. Most transactions are the result of exchanges between entities. Our society is characterized by exchange. That is, the bulk of goods and services are exchanged rather than consumed by their producers. Exchange transactions provide much of the raw data entered into the accounting system. There are several reasons why this is true. First, an exchange is an observable event providing evidence of activity. Second, an exchange takes place at an agreed-upon price, and this price provides an objective measure of the economic activity that has occurred.

Before transactions can be recorded, however, certain basic accounting assumptions must be made. For instance, the data gathered in an accounting system are assumed to relate to a specific business firm or entity. The **business entity concept** assumes that a company has an existence separate and apart from its owners, creditors, employees, and other interested parties. Also, every transaction has a two-sided, or dual, effect upon each of the parties engaging in it; this is referred to as **duality.** Consequently, if information is to be complete, both sides or effects of every transaction must be included in the accounting system. Economic activity is recorded and reported in terms of a common unit of measure—the dollar. This is referred to as **money measurement.** Since most of the numbers entered in an accounting system are the bargained prices of exchange transactions, the result is that most assets (excluding cash and receivables) are recorded and reported at their acquisition costs, often referred to as historical costs. (**Cost** refers to the amount of cash or resources given up to acquire some desired thing.)

Unless strong evidence exists to the contrary, the accountant assumes that the entity will *continue* operations into the indefinite future. This is referred to as the **continuity (going-concern)** assumption. Consequently, assets that will be used up or consumed in future operations need not be reported at their current liquidation values (the amount that could be received from their sale). The underlying assumptions or basic concepts of accounting will be discussed further in Chapter 10.

Transaction Analysis

Objective 5: Analyze business transactions and determine their effects on items in the financial statements

A **source document** is any written or printed evidence of a business transaction that describes the essential facts of that transaction. Since each transaction that affects a business entity needs to be recorded in the accounting records, the analysis of transactions is an important part of financial accounting. To illustrate the analysis of transactions and their effects upon the basic accounting equation, the activities of the Ross Company that led to the statements in Illustrations 1.1, 1.2, and 1.3 are presented below. The numbers 1*a*, 2*a*, and so on refer to the summary of transactions found in Illustration 1.5.

Transactions affecting only the balance sheet.

1*a. Investment of owners' capital.* Assume that Ross Company was organized as a corporation on June 1, 1990. In its first transaction it issued shares of capital stock to John Ross for $30,000 cash. The transaction increased the assets (cash) of the Ross Company by $30,000 and increased its equities (the capital stock element of stockholders' equity) by $30,000. Consequently, the transaction yields a basic accounting equation containing the following:

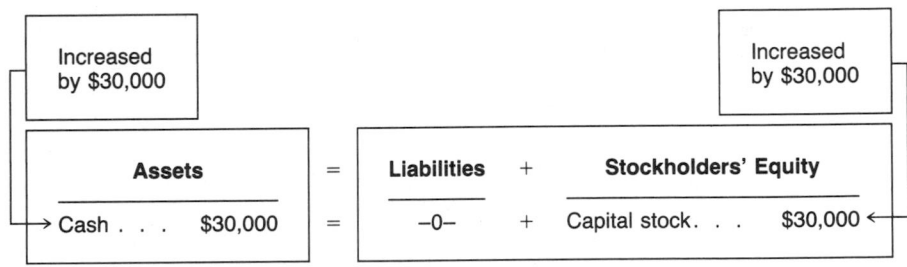

2*a. Borrowing of money.* As its second transaction, the company borrowed $6,000 from Ms. Ross' father, giving its written promise to repay (called a *note payable*) the amount within one year. The basic equation after the effects of this transaction is:

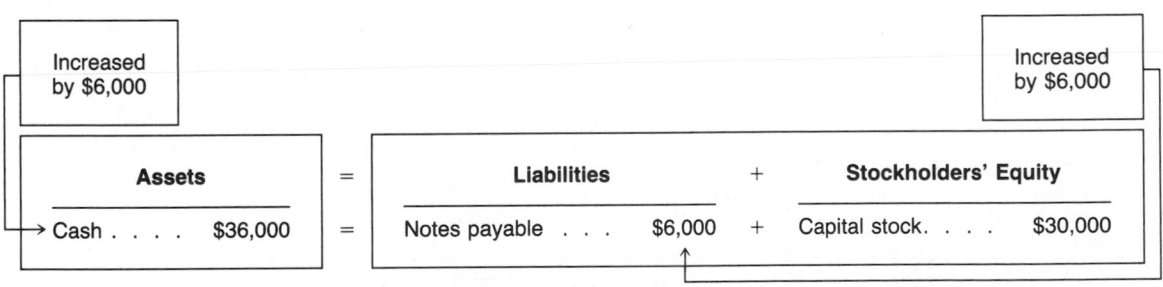

3*a. Purchase of assets for cash.* As its third transaction, the Ross Company spent $20,000 for three delivery trucks and $1,500 for some office equipment. In this transaction, the Ross Company received delivery equipment priced at $20,000 and office equipment priced at $1,500. It gave up cash of $21,500. This transaction does not change the totals in the basic equation; it merely changes the composition of the assets. The equation is now as follows:

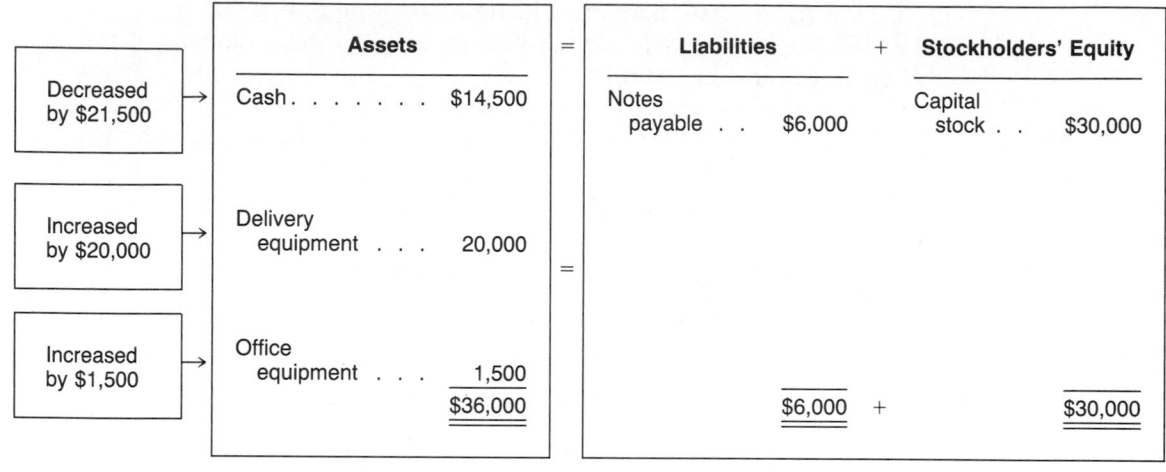

4a. *Purchase of an asset and incurring a liability.* In its fourth transaction in June, the Ross Company purchased an additional $1,000 of office equipment, agreeing to pay for it within 10 days after it receives a bill from the supplier. This transaction increases liabilities in the form of *accounts payable* by $1,000. (If merely an order for the equipment had been placed, no transaction would be recorded since the exchange had not yet been completed.) The items making up the totals in the accounting equation now appear as follows:

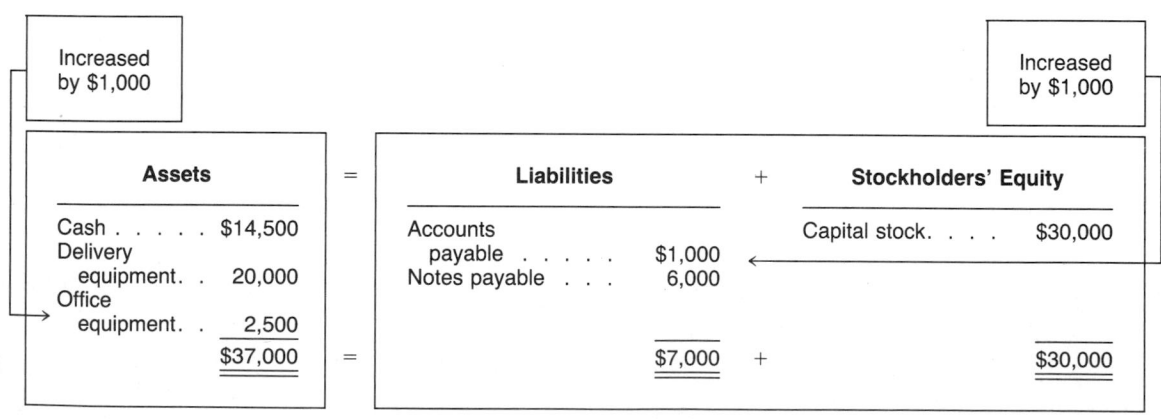

5a. *Payment of an account payable.* Next, the company paid the $1,000 balance due on the purchase of the office equipment. This transaction reduced cash by $1,000 and reduced the debt owed to the equipment supplier by $1,000. Thus, assets and liabilities are both decreased by $1,000. After this transaction, the totals in the accounting equation are as follows:

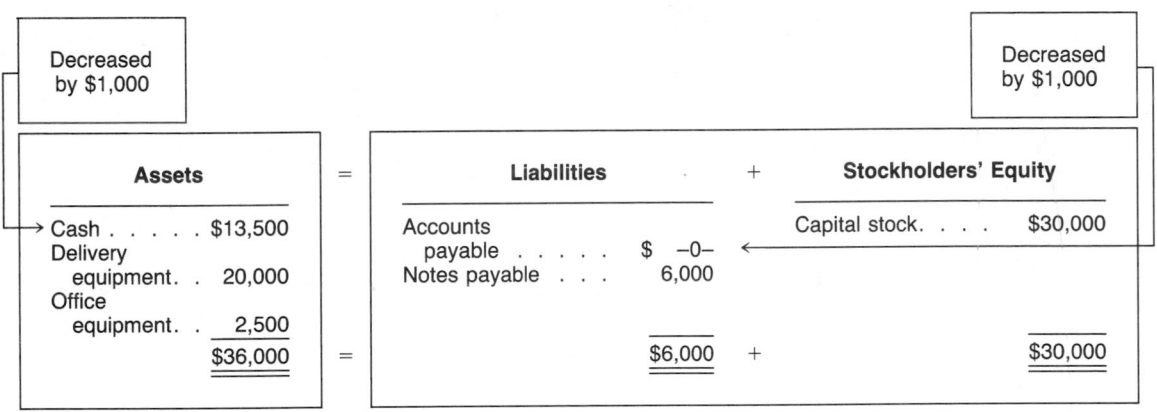

A summary of transactions prepared for the month of June appears in Illustration 1.5 in accounting equation form. You can see how the totals at the bottom tie into the balance sheet shown in Illustration 1.6. The balance sheet in Illustration 1.6 is dated June 30, 1990. These totals become the beginning totals for the month of July 1990.

Transactions affecting the income statement and/or the balance sheet. Thus far all transactions have consisted of exchanges or acquisitions of assets either by borrowing or by owner investment. This procedure was used so that you could focus on the accounting equation as it relates to the balance sheet. But a business is not formed merely to hold present assets. Rather, *a business seeks to use its assets to generate greater amounts of assets.* A business increases its assets by providing goods or services to customers. The expectation is that the value of the assets received from customers will exceed the cost of the assets consumed in serving those customers. The assets received are usually in the form of cash or accounts receivable.

Assume that the company engaged in the following transactions in July 1990.

1b. Earning of revenue for cash. Delivery services were performed for a customer for $4,800 cash. The cash balance increases by $4,800, and the stockholders' equity increases by $4,800 because revenues increase stockholders' equity.

Illustration 1.5
SUMMARY OF TRANSACTIONS

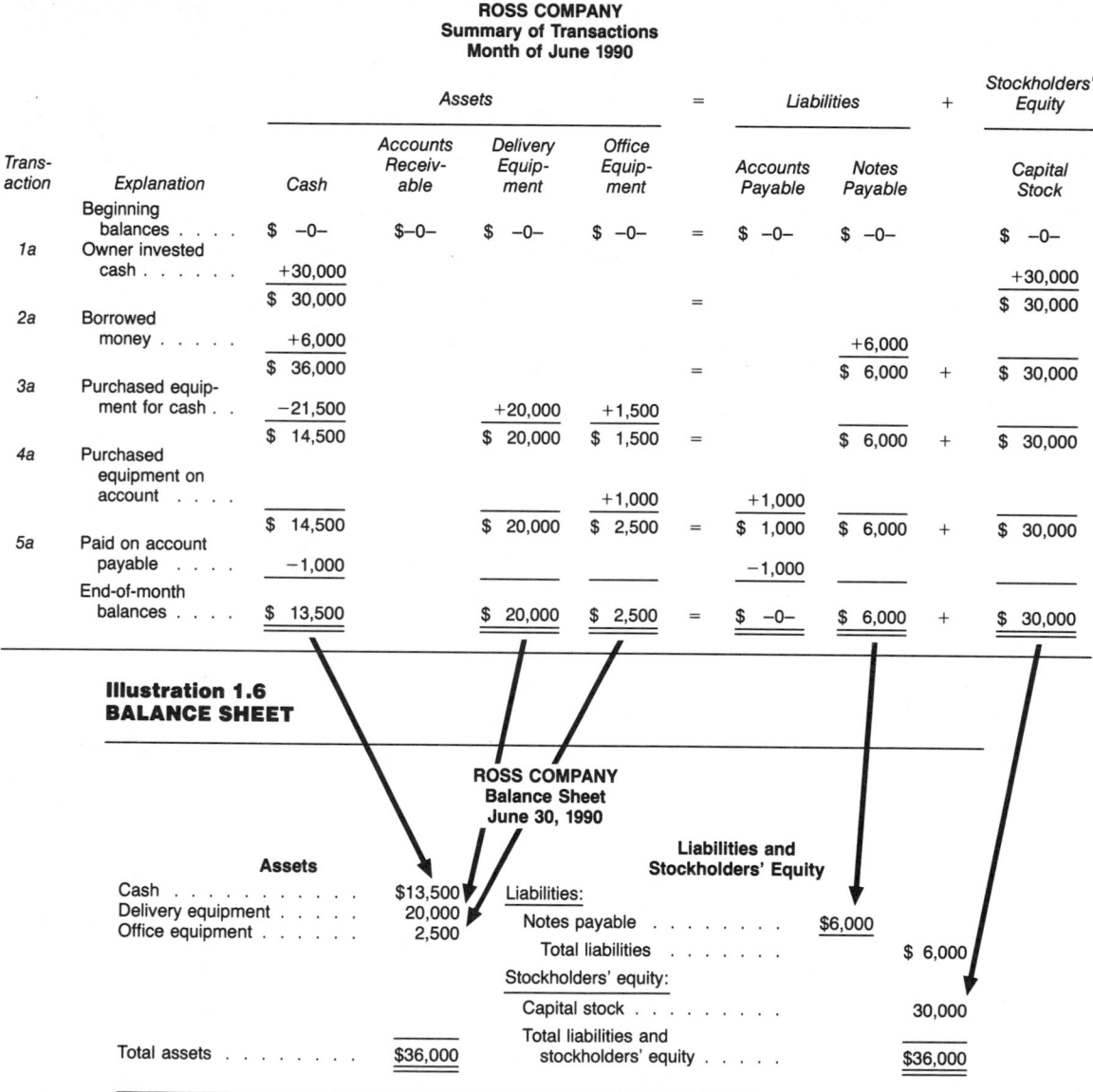

ROSS COMPANY
Summary of Transactions
Month of June 1990

Trans-action	Explanation	Cash	Accounts Receiv-able	Delivery Equip-ment	Office Equip-ment	=	Accounts Payable	Notes Payable	+	Capital Stock
				Assets		=	*Liabilities*		+	*Stockholders' Equity*
	Beginning balances	$ –0–	$–0–	$ –0–	$ –0–	=	$ –0–	$ –0–		$ –0–
1a	Owner invested cash	+30,000								+30,000
		$ 30,000				=				$ 30,000
2a	Borrowed money	+6,000						+6,000		
		$ 36,000				=		$ 6,000	+	$ 30,000
3a	Purchased equip-ment for cash . .	–21,500		+20,000	+1,500					
		$ 14,500		$ 20,000	$ 1,500	=		$ 6,000	+	$ 30,000
4a	Purchased equipment on account				+1,000		+1,000			
		$ 14,500		$ 20,000	$ 2,500	=	$ 1,000	$ 6,000	+	$ 30,000
5a	Paid on account payable	–1,000					–1,000			
	End-of-month balances	$ 13,500		$ 20,000	$ 2,500	=	$ –0–	$ 6,000	+	$ 30,000

Illustration 1.6
BALANCE SHEET

ROSS COMPANY
Balance Sheet
June 30, 1990

Assets		**Liabilities and Stockholders' Equity**		
Cash	$13,500	Liabilities:		
Delivery equipment	20,000	Notes payable	$6,000	
Office equipment	2,500	Total liabilities		$ 6,000
		Stockholders' equity:		
		Capital stock		30,000
Total assets	$36,000	Total liabilities and stockholders' equity		$36,000

Including the effects of the revenue transaction upon the financial status of the Ross Company yields the following basic equation:

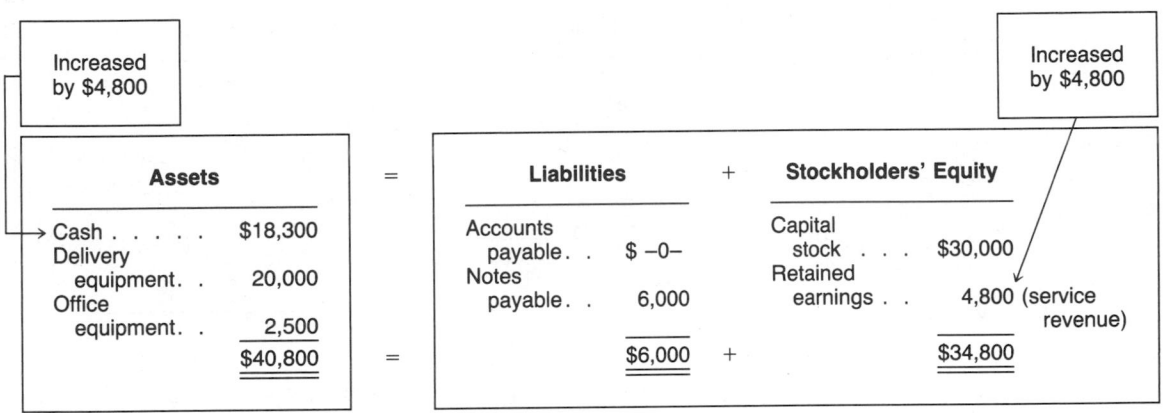

Increased by $4,800					

Assets		=	**Liabilities**	+	**Stockholders' Equity**
Cash	$18,300		Accounts payable. . $ –0–		Capital stock . . . $30,000
Delivery equipment. .	20,000		Notes payable. . 6,000		Retained earnings . . 4,800 (service revenue)
Office equipment. .	2,500				
	$40,800	=	$6,000	+	$34,800

Increased by $4,800

Note that the increase in stockholders' equity brought about by the revenue transaction is recorded as a separate item, "retained earnings." It cannot be recorded as capital stock. No additional shares of stock were issued. The expectation is that revenue transactions will yield net income. If net income is not distributed to stockholders, it is in fact retained. Later chapters will show that because of complexities in handling large numbers of transactions, revenues will be shown as affecting retained earnings only at the end of an accounting period. The procedure presented above is a shortcut used to explain why the accounting equation remains in balance.

2b. Earning of revenue on account. As its second transaction in July, the Ross Company performed services for a customer who agreed to pay $900 at a later date. The transaction consists of an exchange of services for a promise by the customer to pay later. It is similar to the preceding transaction in that stockholders' equity is increased because revenues have been earned. It differs because cash has not been received. A different asset, or item of value, has been received. This is the claim upon the customer—the right to collect from him or her at a later date. Technically, such claims are called accounts receivable. The important point is that accounting recognizes such claims as assets and records them. (If merely an *order* for service had been received, but the service had not yet been performed, no transaction would have been recorded since the revenue would not have been earned.) The accounting equation, including this item, is as follows:

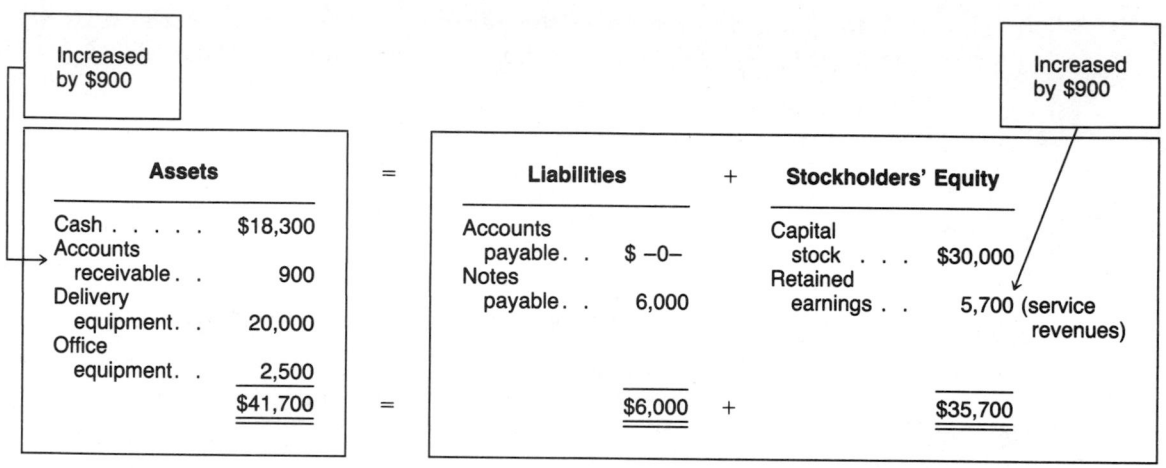

3b. *Collection of an account receivable.* Assume that $200 was collected from a customer who purchased services "on account." The transaction consists of the giving up of a claim upon the customer in exchange for cash. The effects of the transaction are to increase cash by $200 to $18,500 and to decrease accounts receivable by $200 to $700. Note that because one asset (cash) increased while another asset (accounts receivable) decreased, there was no change in the amount of total assets. There was instead a change in the composition of the assets.

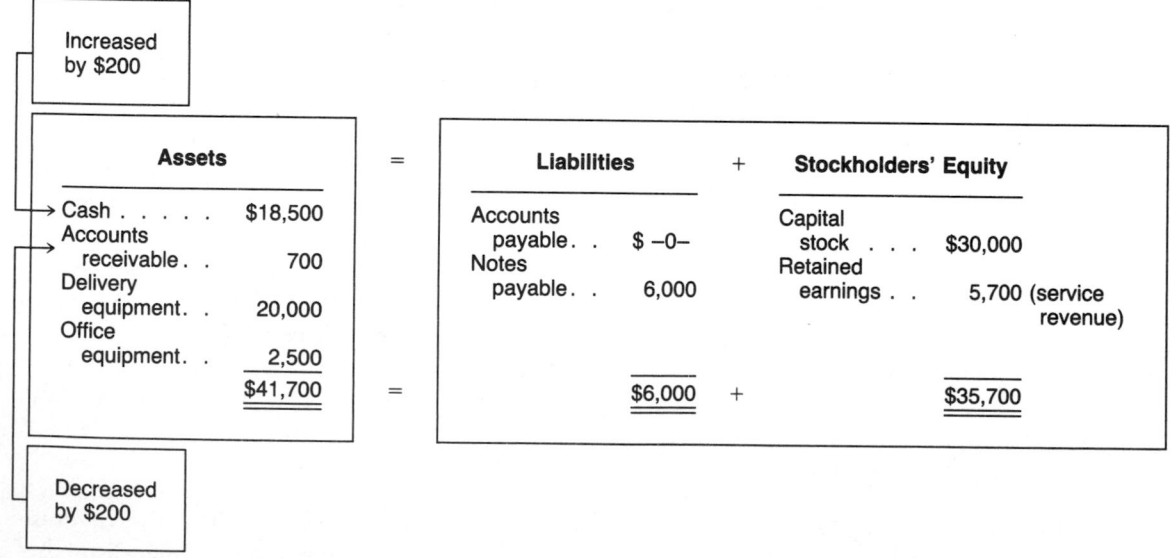

4b. *Payment of wages.* Ross Company paid wages of $2,600. The payment of wages consists of an exchange of cash for employee services.

Typically, the employee services will have already been received by the time payment is made (at week's end of month's end). Thus, the accountant treats the transaction as a decrease in an asset (cash) and a decrease in stockholders' equity, because an expense has been incurred.

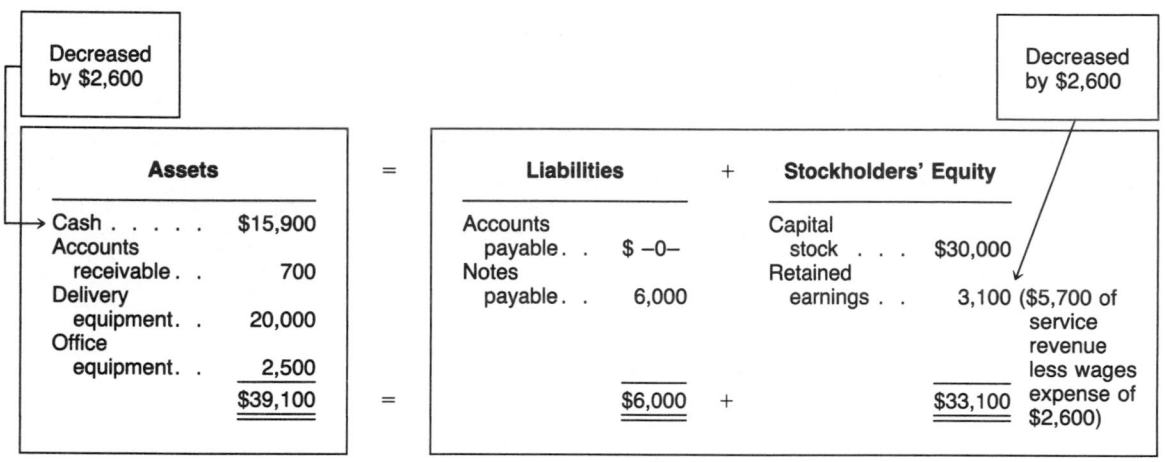

5b. *Payment of rent.* The Ross Company paid $400 cash as rent for office space in July. This transaction causes a decrease in the asset, cash, of $400 and a similar decrease in stockholders' equity. Including all of the above items in our accounting equation, it now reads:

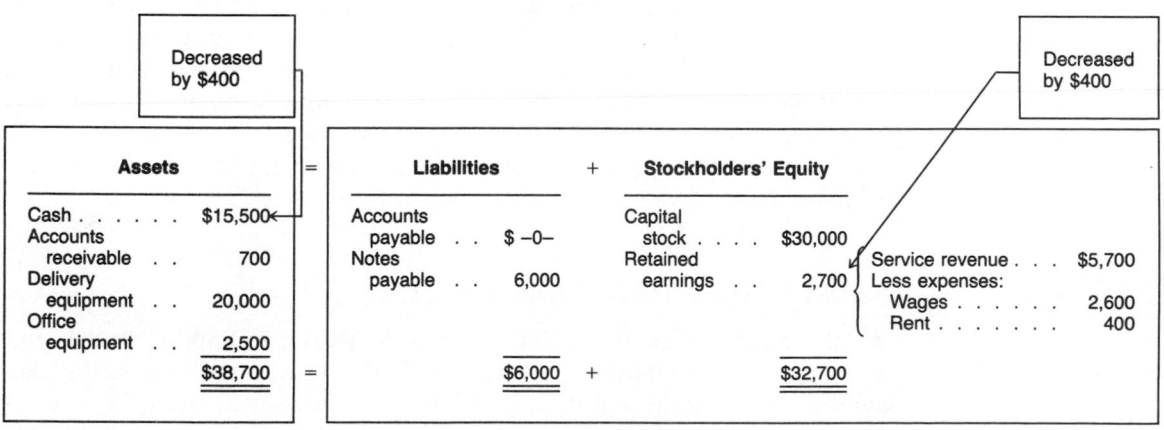

6b. *Incurring gas and oil expense.* The company received a bill for gasoline and oil used during the month in the amount of $600. This transaction involves an increase in a liability, accounts payable, and a decrease in stockholders' equity because of the incurrence of an expense. The accounting equation of the Ross Company now reads:

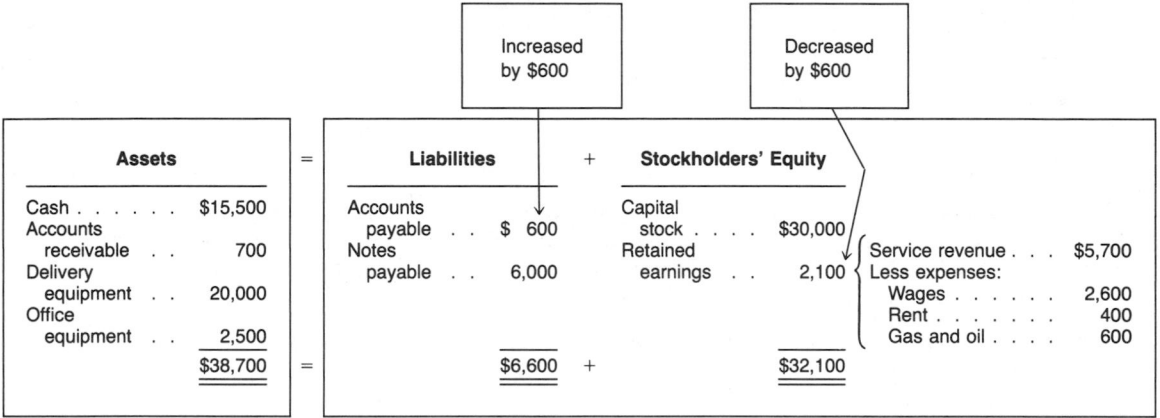

Summary of Transactions

The effects of all of the preceding transactions on the assets, liabilities, and stockholders' equity of the Ross Company in the month of July are summarized in Illustration 1.7. This summary shows how the basic equation of Assets = Equities is subdivided into three major elements of financial accounting: *assets, liabilities,* and *stockholders' equity*. The ending balances in each of the columns in Illustration 1.7 are the dollar amounts in Illustration 1.8 and those reported earlier in the balance sheet in Illustration 1.1. The itemized data in the Retained Earnings column are the revenue and expense items in Illustration 1.9 and those reported earlier in the income statement in Illustration 1.2. The beginning balance in the Retained Earnings column ($0) plus net income for the month ($2,100) is equal to the ending balance in retained earnings ($2,100) as shown earlier in Illustration 1.3.

DIVIDENDS PAID TO OWNERS

We have seen that stockholders' equity is increased by capital contributed by the stockholders and by revenues earned through operations. We also saw that stockholders' equity is decreased by expenses incurred in producing revenues. Withdrawals of cash or other assets in the form of dividends also reduce stockholders' equity. Thus, if the owners receive a dividend in the form of cash, the effect would be to reduce cash and stockholders' equity by that amount. It would reduce the retained earnings part of stockholders' equity. This amount is not an expense but is instead a distribution of income.

Illustration 1.7
SUMMARY OF TRANSACTIONS

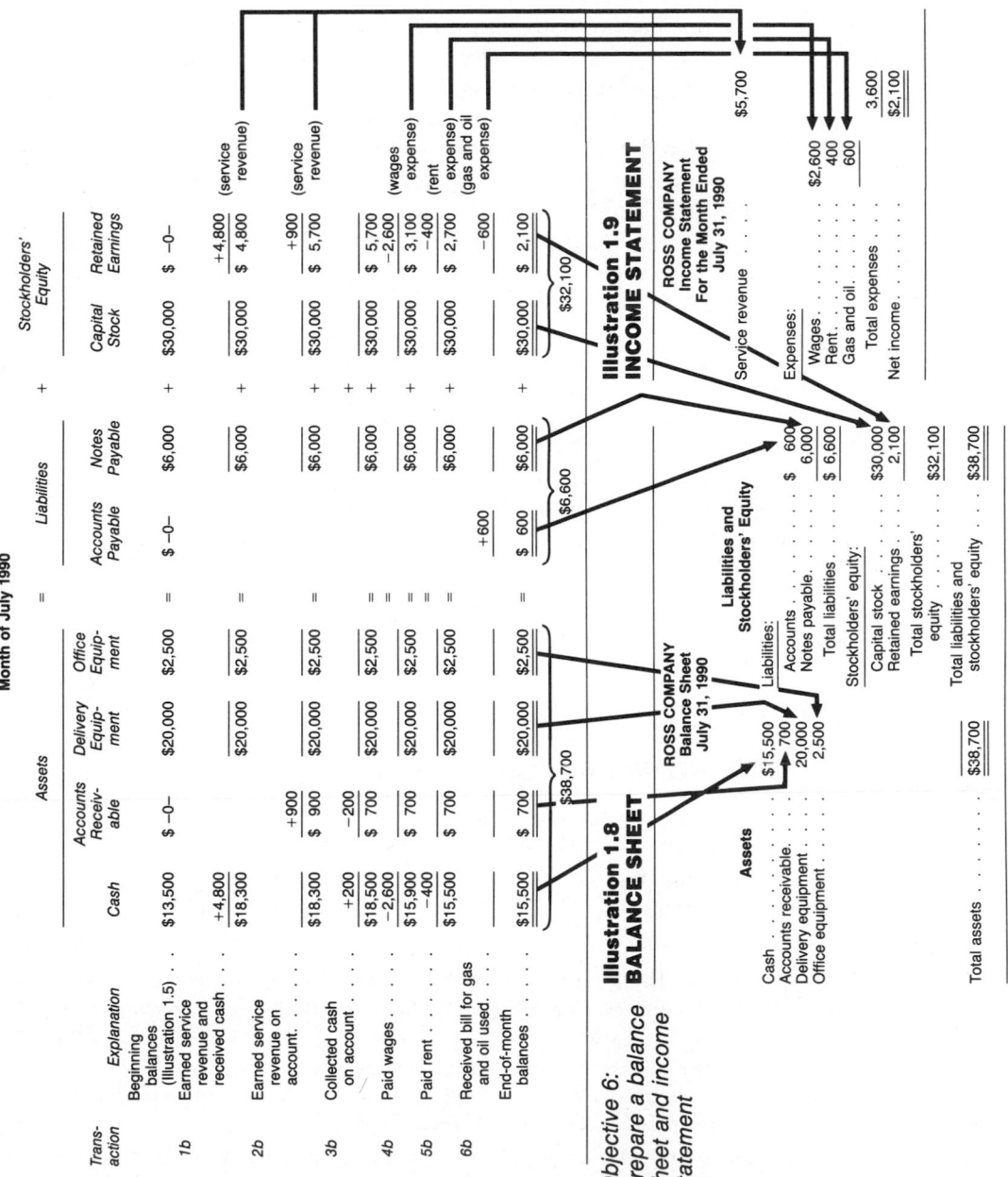

ROSS COMPANY
Summary of Transactions
Month of July 1990

		Assets				=	Liabilities		+	Stockholders' Equity	
Trans-action	Explanation	Cash	Accounts Receiv-able	Delivery Equip-ment	Office Equip-ment		Accounts Payable	Notes Payable		Capital Stock	Retained Earnings
	Beginning balances (Illustration 1.5)	$13,500	$ –0–	$20,000	$2,500	=	$ –0–	$6,000	+	$30,000	$ –0–
1b	Earned service revenue and received cash	+4,800									+4,800 (service revenue)
		$18,300		$20,000	$2,500	=		$6,000	+	$30,000	$ 4,800
2b	Earned service revenue on account		+900								+900 (service revenue)
		$18,300	$ 900	$20,000	$2,500	=		$6,000	+	$30,000	$ 5,700
3b	Collected cash on account	+200	–200								
		$18,500	$ 700	$20,000	$2,500	=		$6,000	+	$30,000	$ 5,700
4b	Paid wages	–2,600									–2,600 (wages expense)
		$15,900	$ 700	$20,000	$2,500	=		$6,000	+	$30,000	$ 3,100
5b	Paid rent	–400									–400 (rent expense)
		$15,500	$ 700	$20,000	$2,500	=		$6,000	+	$30,000	$ 2,700
6b	Received bill for gas and oil used						+600				–600 (gas and oil expense)
	End-of-month balances	$15,500	$ 700	$20,000	$2,500	=	$ 600	$6,000	+	$30,000	$ 2,100
		$38,700					$6,600			$32,100	

Objective 6:
Prepare a balance
sheet and income
statement

Illustration 1.8
BALANCE SHEET

ROSS COMPANY
Balance Sheet
July 31, 1990

Assets		Liabilities and Stockholders' Equity	
Cash	$15,500	**Liabilities:**	
Accounts receivable	700	Accounts	$ 600
Delivery equipment	20,000	Notes payable	6,000
Office equipment	2,500	Total liabilities	$ 6,600
		Stockholders' equity:	
		Capital stock	$30,000
		Retained earnings	2,100
		Total stockholders' equity	$32,100
Total assets	$38,700	Total liabilities and stockholders' equity	$38,700

Illustration 1.9
INCOME STATEMENT

ROSS COMPANY
Income Statement
For the Month Ended
July 31, 1990

Service revenue		$5,700
Expenses:		
Wages	$2,600	
Rent	400	
Gas and oil	600	
Total expenses		3,600
Net income		$2,100

31

SUMMARY

The three basic forms of business organization are the single proprietorship, partnership, and corporation. This text uses the corporation in its illustrations of accounting concepts.

Business organizations are also classified by the types of business activities they perform: service companies, merchandising companies, and manufacturing companies. Service companies perform services for a fee; merchandising companies purchase goods that are ready for sale and then sell them to customers; and manufacturing companies buy materials, convert them into products, and then sell the products to other companies or to final customers.

The end products of the financial accounting process are the balance sheet, income statement, statement of retained earnings, and statement of cash flows. Discussion of the statement of cash flows is deferred until Chapter 10.

Most of the information reported in these statements is found originally in the transactions entered into by an entity. These transactions are analyzed and their effects are recorded as increases or decreases in assets, liabilities, stockholders' equity, revenues, and expenses—the five basic elements of accounting. The framework for analysis is the basic equation of Assets = Equities, expanded to Assets = Liabilities + Stockholders' Equity. Revenues and expenses will create income (or loss) which affects the Retained Earnings account and, therefore, stockholders' equity.

Accounts and journal entries are discussed and illustrated in the next chapter. Accurate accumulation of financial data is necessary for the preparation of correct financial statements.

Objective 7: Define and use correctly the new terms in the glossary

NEW TERMS INTRODUCED IN CHAPTER 1

Accounting equation   Basically, Assets = Equities; in slightly expanded form for a corporation, Assets = Liabilities + Stockholders' Equity (21).

Accounts payable   Amounts owed to suppliers for goods or services purchased on credit (19).

Accounts receivable   Amounts owed to a business by its customers (18).

Assets   Things of value; they constitute the resources of the firm. Examples include money, machines, and buildings. Assets possess service potential or utility to their owners that can be measured and expressed in money terms (18).

Balance sheet   Financial statement that lists a company's assets, liabilities, and stockholders' equity (including dollar amounts) as of a specific moment in time. Also called a statement of financial position (18).

Business entity concept   The separate existence of the business organization (22).

Capital stock   The title given to an equity account showing the investment in a business corporation by its stockholders (19).

Continuity (going concern) The assumption by the accountant that unless specific evidence exists to the contrary, a business firm will continue to operate into the indefinite future (22).

Corporation Business that may be owned by a few persons or by thousands of persons and is incorporated under the laws of 1 of the 50 states (17).

Cost The sacrifice made or the resources given up to acquire some desired thing; the basis of valuation of the bulk of the assets of a business (22).

Dividend Payment (usually of cash) to the owners of the business; it is a distribution of income to owners rather than an expense of doing business (20).

Duality The two-sided effect of every transaction (22).

Entity A unit that is deemed to have an existence separate and apart from its owners, creditors, employees, and other interested parties and for which accounting records are maintained (16).

Equities Broadly speaking, all claims to or interests in assets (21).

Expenses The sacrifice made, usually measured in terms of the cost of the assets surrendered or consumed, to generate revenues (19).

Income statement (earnings statement) Financial statement showing the revenues and expenses of an organization for a specified period of time (19).

Liabilities Debts or obligations that usually possess a known or determinable amount, maturity date, and party to whom payment is to be made (19).

Manufacturing companies Companies that buy materials, convert them into products, and then sell the products to other companies or to final customers (17).

Merchandising companies Companies that purchase goods that are ready for sale and then sell them to customers (17).

Money measurement Expression of a property of an object in terms of a number of units of a standard monetary medium, such as the dollar (22).

Net income The amount by which the revenues of a period exceed the expenses of the same period (19).

Net loss The amount by which the expenses of a period exceed the revenues of the same period (19).

Notes payable Written promises to pay to other parties definite sums of money at certain or determinable dates, usually with interest at a specified rate (19).

Partnership Business owned by two or more persons associated as partners (16).

Periodicity An assumption that an entity's life can be subdivided into time periods for purposes of reporting its economic activities (19).

Profitability Ability to generate income. The income statement reflects a company's profitability (19).

Retained earnings Accumulated net income less dividend distributions to stockholders (19).

Revenues The inflows of assets resulting from the sale of goods or the providing of services to customers (19).

Service companies Companies that perform services (such as accounting firms, law firms, repair shops, or dry cleaning establishments) for a fee (17).

Single proprietorship Business owned by an individual and often managed by that same individual (16).

Solvency Ability to pay debts as they become due. The balance sheet reflects a company's solvency (18).

Source document Any written or printed evidence of a business transaction that describes the essential facts of that transaction (22).

Statement of retained earnings Statement used to explain the changes in retained earnings that occurred between two balance sheet dates (20).

Stockholders or shareholders Owners of the corporation; they buy shares of stock, which are units of ownership in the corporation (17).

Stockholders' equity The owners' interest in a corporation (19).

Transactions Recordable happenings or events (usually exchanges) that affect the assets, liabilities, stockholders' equity, revenues, or expenses of an entity (20).

DEMONSTRATION PROBLEM 1–1

On June 1, 1990, the Green Hills Riding Stable, Incorporated, was organized. The following transactions occurred during June:

Transactions:

June 1 Shares of capital stock were issued for $10,000 cash.
　4 A horse stable and riding equipment were rented (and paid for) for the month at a cost of $1,200.
　8 Horse feed for the month was purchased on credit, $800.
　15 Boarding fees of $3,000 for the month of June were charged to those owning horses that were boarded at the stable. (This amount is due on July 10.)
　20 Miscellaneous expenses of $600 were paid.
　29 Land was purchased from a savings and loan association by borrowing $40,000 from that association. The loan is due to be repaid in five years. Interest payments are due at the end of each month beginning July 31.
　30 Salaries of $700 for the month were paid.
　30 Riding and lesson fees were billed to customers in the amount of $2,400. (They are due on July 10.)

Required:

a. Prepare a summary of the above transactions. Use columns headed—Cash, Accounts Receivable, Land, Accounts Payable, Notes Payable, Capital Stock, and Retained Earnings. Determine balances after each transaction to show that the basic equation is in balance.

b. Prepare an income statement for the month of June 1990.

c. Prepare a statement of retained earnings for the month of June 1990.

d. Prepare a balance sheet as of June 30, 1990.

Solution to demonstration problem 1–1

a.

GREEN HILLS RIDING STABLE, INCORPORATED
Summary of Transactions
Month of June 1990

		Assets			=	Liabilities		+	Stockholders' Equity	
Date	Explanation	Cash	Accounts Receivable	Land		Accounts Payable	Notes Payable		Capital Stock	Retained Earnings
June 1	Capital stock issued	$10,000			=				$10,000	
4	Rent expense	−1,200								$−1,200
		$ 8,800			=				$10,000	$−1,200
8	Feed expense					$+800				−800
		$ 8,800			=	$ 800		+	$10,000	$−2,000
15	Boarding fees		$+3,000							+3,000
		$ 8,800	$ 3,000		=	$ 800		+	$10,000	$ 1,000
20	Miscellaneous expenses	−600								−600
		$ 8,200	$ 3,000		=	$ 800		+	$10,000	$ 400
29	Purchased land by borrowing . . .			$+40,000			$+40,000			
		$ 8,200	$ 3,000	$ 40,000	=	$ 800	$ 40,000	+	$10,000	$ 400
30	Salaries paid	−700								−700
		$ 7,500	$ 3,000	$ 40,000	=	$ 800	$ 40,000	+	$10,000	$ −300
30	Riding and lesson fees billed.		+2,400							+2,400
		$ 7,500	$ 5,400	$ 40,000	=	$ 800	$ 40,000	+	$10,000	$ 2,100

b.

GREEN HILLS RIDING STABLE, INCORPORATED
Income Statement
For the Month Ended June 30, 1990

Revenues:
Horse boarding fees $3,000
Riding and lesson fees 2,400
Total revenues $5,400

Expenses:
Rent expense $1,200
Feed expense 800
Salaries expense 700
Miscellaneous expenses 600
Total expenses 3,300
Net income $2,100

c.

GREEN HILLS RIDING STABLE, INCORPORATED
Statement of Retained Earnings
For the Month Ended June 30, 1990

Retained earnings, June 1 . . . . . . $ –0–
Add: Net income for June 2,100
Total $2,100
Less: Dividends . . . . –0–
Retained earnings, June 30 . . . . . $2,100

d.

GREEN HILLS RIDING STABLE, INCORPORATED
Balance Sheet
June 30, 1990
Assets

Cash	$ 7,500
Accounts receivable	5,400
Land	40,000
Total assets	$52,900

Liabilities and Stockholders' Equity

Liabilities:		
Accounts payable		$ 800
Notes payable		40,000
Total liabilities		$40,800
Stockholders' equity:		
Capital stock	$10,000	
Retained earnings	2,100	
Total stockholders' equity		12,100
Total liabilities and stockholders' equity		$52,900

QUESTIONS

1. Accounting has often been called the language of business. In what respects would you agree with this designation? How might it be argued that it is deficient?

2. Define asset, liability, and stockholders' equity.

3. How do liabilities and stockholders' equity differ? In what respects are they similar?

4. How do accounts payable and notes payable differ? How are they similar?

5. Define revenue. How is revenue measured?

6. Define expense. How is expense measured?

7. What is a balance sheet? This statement generally seeks to provide information relative to what aspect of a business?

8. What is an income statement? This statement generally provides information on what aspect of a business?

9. What information does the statement of retained earnings provide?

10. What is a transaction? What use does the accountant make of transactions? Why?

11. What is the accounting equation? Why must it always balance?

12. Give an example from your personal life that you believe illustrates your use of accounting information in reaching a decision.

13. Identify some of the underlying assumptions or concepts used by the accountant in recording business transactions.

EXERCISES

Analyze transactions

1. Give examples of transactions that would have the following effects upon the elements in a firm's accounting system:
  a. Increase cash; decrease some other asset.
  b. Decrease cash; increase some other asset.
  c. Increase an asset; increase a liability.
  d. Increase an expense; decrease an asset.
  e. Increase an asset other than cash; increase revenue.
  f. Decrease an asset; decrease a liability.

Compute net income and revenue

2. Assume that retained earnings increased by $24,000 from June 30, 1989, to June 30, 1990. A cash dividend of $2,000 was declared and paid during the year.
  a. Compute the net income for the year.
  b. Assume that expenses for the year were $60,000. Compute the revenue for the year.

Compute retained earnings

3. On December 31, 1989, Star Company had assets of $720,000, liabilities of $520,000, and capital stock of $160,000. During 1990, it earned revenues of $240,000 and incurred expenses of $180,000. Dividends declared and paid amounted to $16,000.
  a. Compute the company's retained earnings on December 31, 1989.
  b. Compute the company's retained earnings on December 31, 1990.

Analyze transactions

4. For each of the happenings below, determine if it has an effect upon the basic elements of accounting. For those that do, present an analysis of the transaction showing clearly its two sides or dual nature.
  a. Purchased equipment for cash, $1,200.
  b. Purchased a truck for $14,000, payment to be made later in the month.
  c. Paid $400 cash for the current month's utilities.
  d. Paid for the truck purchased in *(b)*.
  e. Employed Jack Lovgren as a salesperson at $3,000 per month. He is to start work next week.
  f. Signed an agreement with a bank in which the bank agreed to lend the company up to $150,000 any time within the next two years.

Identify transactions that increase expenses

5. Which of the following transactions results in an increase in an expense? Why?
  a. Cash of $80,000 was paid to employees for services received during the month.
  b. Cash of $400,000 was paid to acquire land.
  c. Paid a $40,000 note payable. No interest was involved.

Compute retained earnings and total assets at beginning of year

6. At the start of a year, a company had liabilities of $36,000 and capital stock of $100,000. At the end of the year, retained earnings amounted to $90,000. Net income for the year was $30,000, and $10,000 of dividends were declared and paid. Compute retained earnings and total assets at the beginning of the year.

Compute net income

7. Selected data for the Denver Company for the year 1990 are as follows (including all income statement data):

Revenue from services rendered on account.	$110,000
Revenue from services rendered for cash	30,000
Cash collected from customers on account	84,000
Stockholders' equity, January 1, 1990	160,000
Expenses incurred on account	60,000
Expenses incurred for cash	40,000
Dividends declared and paid	10,000
Capital stock issued for cash	20,000
Stockholders' equity, December 31, 1990	210,000

Compute net income for 1990.

Determine effect of transactions on stockholders' equity

8. Indicate the immediate amount of change (if any) in the stockholders' equity balance based on each of the following transactions:

a. The owner invested $45,000 cash in the business by purchasing capital stock.

b. Land costing $10,000 was purchased by paying cash.

c. The company performed services for a customer who agreed to pay $12,000 in one month.

d. Paid wages for the month, $9,000.

e. Paid $1,200 on an account payable.

Indicate effect of transactions on items in the accounting equation

9. Martin Company, engaged in a service business, completed the following selected transactions during the month of July 1990.

a. Purchased office equipment on account.

b. Paid an account payable.

c. Earned service revenue on account.

d. Borrowed money by signing a note at the bank.

e. Paid wages for month to employees.

f. Received cash on account from a charge customer.

g. Received gas and oil bill for month.

h. Purchased a truck for cash.

i. Paid a cash dividend.

Using a tabular form similar to that used in Illustration 1.7, indicate the effect of each transaction on the equation using (+) for increase and (−) for decrease. No dollar amounts are needed, and you need not fill in the Explanation column.

Prepare balance sheet

10. The column totals of a summary of transactions for the Stillwagon Company as of December 31, 1990, were as follows (listed in alphabetical order):

Accounts payable.	$ 30,000
Accounts receivable. . . .	60,000
Capital stock	100,000
Cash	40,000
Land	160,000
Notes payable	20,000
Retained earnings	?

Prepare a balance sheet.

Prepare income statement

11. Assume that the following items made up the total of the $155,000 ending balance in the Retained Earnings column in the summary of transactions for the Trask Company for the month of July 1990:

Wages expense	$40,000
Service revenue	80,000
Gas and oil expense	9,000
Rent expense	16,000
Dividends paid	10,000

Prepare an income statement for the month of July 1990.

Prepare statement of retained earnings

12. Given the following facts, prepare a statement of retained earnings for the Kent Company for the month of August 1990:

Balance in retained earnings at end of July, $80,000
Dividends paid in August, $30,000
Net income for August, $50,000

PROBLEMS

Prepare summary of transactions

1–1. Hunt Company completed the following transactions in September 1990:

Transactions:

Sept. 1 The company was organized and received $40,000 cash from the issuance of capital stock.
5 The company bought equipment for cash at a cost of $10,800.
7 The company performed services for a customer who agreed to pay $4,000 in one week.
14 The company received the $4,000 from the transaction of September 7.
20 Equipment costing $1,600 was acquired today; payment was postponed until September 28.
28 $1,200 was paid on the liability incurred on September 20.
30 Employee services for the month, $1,400, were paid.
30 Placed an order for new equipment advertised at $10,000.

Required:

Prepare a summary of transactions (see Illustration 1.7) for the company for the above transactions. Use money columns headed—Cash, Accounts Receivable, Equipment, Accounts Payable, Capital Stock, and Retained Earnings. Determine balances after each transaction to show that the basic equation balances.

Prepare summary of transactions and balance sheet

1–2. The Springfield Company completed the following transactions in June 1990:

Transactions:

June 1 The company was organized and received $80,000 cash from the issuance of capital stock.
4 The company paid $64,000 cash for equipment.
7 The company borrowed $12,000 cash from one of its suppliers by giving two notes, one for $5,400 and the other for $6,600. Neither note bears interest.
9 Cash received for services performed for a customer, $6,000.
12 Employee wages were paid in cash, $4,200.
18 Services performed for a customer who agreed to pay within a month amounted to $7,200.
25 The company paid the $5,400 note of June 7th.
30 Employee wages of $5,100 were paid in cash.
30 An order was received from a customer for services to be performed tomorrow, which will be billed at $4,000.

Required:

a. Prepare a summary of transactions (see Illustration 1.7). Include money columns for—Cash, Accounts Receivable, Equipment, Notes Payable, Capital Stock, and Retained Earnings.

b. Prepare a balance sheet as of June 30, 1990.

Prepare income statement

1–3. The following transactions are for the Daniels Company:

Transactions:

May	1	Paid May rent on the parking structure, $20,000.
	8	Received cash from James Company for parking services provided for its employees, $9,680.
	15	Received cash from James Company for week's parking services, $12,080.
	15	Wages paid for first half of May, $4,800.
	17	Received cash for shares of capital stock issued, $10,000.
	19	Paid advertising expenses for May, $1,600.
	22	Received cash from James Company for week's parking services, $15,840.
	31	Wages paid for last half of May, $6,000.
	31	Cash received from James Company for nine days' parking services, $14,080.
	31	Purchased motorized sweeper to clean parking structure, $12,000 cash.

Required:

Prepare an income statement for the month of May 1990.

Prepare income statement

1–4. Following are summarized transaction data for the Ewing Company for the year ending June 30, 1990:

Rent revenue from building owned	$640,000
Building repairs.	20,000
Building cleaning, labor cost	22,400
Property taxes on the building	15,240
Insurance on the building	9,600
Commissions paid to rental agent	24,000
Legal fees (for preparation of tenant leases)	9,200
Heating	21,000
Electricity	34,200
Cost of new awnings installed	24,800

Of the $640,000 of rent revenue above, $40,000 was not collected in cash until July 5, 1990.

Required:

Prepare an income statement for the year ended June 30, 1990.

Prepare summary of transactions, income statement, statement of retained earnings, and balance sheet

1–5. The following data are for the Davis Corporation:

DAVIS CORPORATION
Balance Sheet
October 1, 1990
Assets

Cash	$68,000
Accounts receivable	6,000
Total assets	$74,000

Liabilities and Stockholders' Equity

Accounts payable	$18,000
Capital stock	44,000
Retained earnings	12,000
Total liabilities and stockholders' equity	$74,000

Transactions:

Oct. 1   The account payable owed as of October 1 ($18,000) was paid.
1   The company paid rent for the premises for October, $6,400.
7   The company received cash of $1,400 from Thomas Company for parking by its employees during the week.
10   The company collected an account receivable of $4,800.
14   Cash received from Thomas Company for parking by its employees was $2,200.
15   Parking revenue earned but not yet collected from a fleet customer was $1,000.
16   The company paid wages of $800 for the period October 1–15.
19   The company paid advertising expenses of $400 for October.
21   Cash received from Thomas Company for parking service was $2,400.
24   The company incurred miscellaneous expenses of $280, which will be due November 10.
31   Cash received from Thomas Company for parking services $2,800.
31   The company paid wages of $1,000 for the period October 16–31.
31   A bill was sent to a large customer for parking services for October, $7,200.
31   Paid cash dividends of $8,000.

Required:

a. Prepare a summary of transactions (see Illustration 1.7) using column headings as given in the above balance sheet.

b. Prepare an income statement for October 1990.

c. Prepare a statement of retained earnings for October 1990.

d. Prepare a balance sheet as of October 31, 1990.

State causes of balance sheet changes

1–6. Given below are balance sheets for May and June and the income statement for June of the Harris Company:

HARRIS COMPANY
Balance Sheets

	May 31, 1990	June 30, 1990
Assets		
Cash	$40,000	$28,000
Accounts receivable.	–0–	16,000
Land	24,000	24,000
Total assets	$64,000	$68,000
Liabilities and Stockholders' Equity		
Liabilities	$16,000	$ 8,000
Capital stock	40,000	40,000
Retained earnings	8,000	20,000
Total liabilities and stockholders' equity	$64,000	$68,000

41

HARRIS COMPANY
Income Statement
For the Month Ended June 30, 1990

Revenue from services rendered		$64,000
Expenses:		
Salaries	$32,000	
Supplies bought and used	16,000	48,000
Net income		$16,000

A cash dividend of $4,000 was declared and paid in June.

Required:

State the probable causes of the changes in each of the balance sheet accounts from May 31 to June 30, 1990.

Identify information needed to make decision

1–7. Upon graduation from high school, Wayne Burke went to work for a builder of houses and small apartment buildings. During the next six years, Wayne earned a reputation as an excellent employee—hard working, dedicated, and dependable—and as a very capable all-around employee in the light construction industry. He could handle almost any job requiring carpentry, electrical, or plumbing skills.

Wayne then decided to go into business for himself under the name of Burke's Repair Shop, Inc. He invested cash, some power tools, and a used truck in his business. He completed many repair and remodeling jobs for both homeowners and apartment owners. The demand for his services was so large that he had more work than he could handle. He operated out of his garage which he had converted into a shop, adding several new pieces of power woodworking equipment.

Two years after going into business for himself, Wayne is faced with a decision of whether to continue in his own business or to accept a position as construction supervisor for a home builder. He has been offered an annual salary of $50,000 and a package of "fringe benefits" (medical and hospitalization insurance, pension contribution, vacation and sick pay, and life insurance) worth approximately $7,500 per year. The offer is very attractive to Wayne. But he dislikes giving up his business since he has thoroughly enjoyed "being his own boss," even though it has led to an average workweek well in excess of the standard 40 hours.

Wayne now comes to you for assistance in gathering the information needed to help him make a decision. Adequate accounting records have been maintained for his business by an experienced accountant.

Required:

Indicate the nature of the information Wayne needs if he is to make an informed decision. Pay particular attention to the information likely to be found in the accounting records for his business that would be useful. Does the accounting information available enter directly into the decision? Explain. Would you expect that Wayne could sell his business assets for more or less than their recorded amounts? Why?

BUSINESS DECISION PROBLEM 1–1

Prepare income statement and balance sheet; judge profitability of company

The Sunset Drive-In Theater, Inc. opened for business on June 1, 1990. Analysis of the transactions for the month of June 1990 discloses the following:

Ticket revenue.	$71,000
Rent expense for premises and equipment	9,000
Film rental expense paid	17,800
Revenue received from operators of candy and popcorn concessions.	10,000
Advertising expense	8,400
Wages and salaries expense	15,600
Utilities expense	5,000

Asset and liability amounts as of June 30 which the accountant has calculated include the following:

Cash	$100,000
Land	16,000
Accounts payable.	20,800

The balance in the Capital Stock account on June 1 was $70,000.

Required:

a. Prepare an income statement for the month of June 1990.

b. Prepare a balance sheet as of June 30, 1990.

c. Did the month of June seem to be a profitable month for this company?

2

THE BASIC ACCOUNTING SYSTEM

LEARNING OBJECTIVES

After studying this chapter, you should be able to:

1. Use the account as the basic classifying and storage unit for information.
2. Express the effects of business transactions in terms of debits and credits to six different types of accounts.
3. Record the effects of business transactions in a journal.
4. Post journal entries to the accounts in the ledger.
5. Prepare a trial balance to test the equality of debits and credits in the journalizing and posting process.
6. Define and use correctly the new terms in the glossary.

As you learned in Chapter 1, there are three forms of business organizations—single proprietorships, partnerships, and corporations—performing three types of business activities—service, merchandising, and manufacturing. The two most common financial statements produced by these business organizations are the balance sheet (which indicates the solvency of the business) and the income statement (which indicates the profitability of the business). These statements are the end products of the financial accounting process (or cycle), which has as its foundation the accounting equation.

The raw data of accounting are the business transactions. In Chapter 1, transactions were recorded as increases or decreases in accounting equation items. However, as you probably noticed when working through the sample transactions given in Chapter 1, listing all business transactions under three categories would become most cumbersome in actual practice. Most businesses, even small ones, enter into many transactions every day. Chapter 2 teaches you how business transactions are actually recorded in the accounting process.

To understand the dual procedure of recording business transactions with debits and credits, you begin by using the T-account, which classifies and summarizes the measurements of business activity. Then you learn about the ledger—a collection of accounts. You will follow a company through its various business transactions using these new tools. The need for a journal is explained, and soon you will be "journalizing." The recording of transactions must be checked for the equality of debits and credits. The trial balance is useful in doing this.

THE ACCOUNT

Objective 1: Use the account as the basic classifying and storage unit for information

An **account** is a storage unit used to classify and summarize money measurements of business activity of a similar nature. An account will be established whenever the data to be recorded in it are believed to be useful to some party having a valid interest in the business. Thus, every business will have a Cash account in its accounting system simply because knowledge of the amount of cash owned is useful information. An account title should indicate, as concisely as possible, the item of information being accumulated within it.

An account may take on a variety of forms, from a printed format in which entries are written by hand to an invisible encoding on a piece of magnetic computer tape. Every account format must provide for increases and decreases and computation of a balance.

The number of accounts in a given accounting system will depend upon the information needs of those interested in the business. The primary requirement is that each account provide useful information. Thus, one account may be established for cash rather than separate accounts for cash in the form of coins, cash in the form of currency, and cash in the form of deposits in banks, simply because the amount of cash may be useful information while the form of cash usually is not important.

The T-Account

Objective 2: Express the effects of business transactions in terms of debits and credits to six different types of accounts

The way an account functions may be shown by use of a T-account. It is used in texts for illustrative purposes only (it is not a replica of a form of account actually used in business). A **T-account** resembles the letter T. The name of the item accounted for (such as cash) is written across the top of the T. Increases are recorded on one side and decreases on the other side of the vertical line of the T.

Recording changes in assets and equities. Increases in *assets* are recorded on the left side of the account, decreases on the right side. The process is reversed for *equities* so that increases are recorded on the right side and decreases on the left side. Thus, a corporation would record the receipt of $10,000 for shares of its capital stock as follows (the figure in parentheses refers to the number of the transaction and ties the two sides of the transaction together):

Cash		Capital Stock	
(1) 10,000			(1) 10,000

The transaction involves an increase in the asset, cash, which is recorded on the left side of the Cash account, and an increase in stockholders' equity in the form of capital stock, which is recorded on the right side of the Capital Stock account.

Because liabilities are a subset of equities, changes in them are recorded in the same manner as for equities—increases on the right side, decreases on the left side.

To help remember which side of a T-account increases in assets and equities are shown on, simply remember the accounting equation given in the last chapter, Assets = Equities. Increases in the T-accounts are shown for each element on the same side that the element appears in the accounting equation. Assets appear on the left side of the equation, and increases in assets appear on the left side of the T-account. The opposite is true for equity items.

Recording changes in expenses and revenues. To understand the logic behind the recording of changes in expense and revenue accounts, recall that all expenses and revenues could be recorded directly in the Retained Earnings account, as was shown in Chapter 1. Since Retained Earnings is an equity account, increases are shown on the right side of the T-account and decreases are shown on the left side. Expenses and revenues are significant amounts to a business organization, so rather than place all of these changes within the Retained Earnings account, separate accounts are maintained for each expense and revenue item. The recording rules for expenses and revenues are as follows:

1. Since expenses decrease stockholders' equity (and decreases in stockholders' equity are recorded on the left side of a T-account), it follows that increases in expenses should be recorded on the left side of a T-account. Therefore, increases in expenses are recorded on the left, decreases in expenses on the right.
2. Similarly, since revenues increase stockholders' equity (and increases in stockholders' equity are recorded on the right side), it follows that increases in revenues should be recorded on the right side, decreases on the left side.

Thus, the payment of $600 of cash to employees as wages (transaction 2) would be recorded as follows:

Cash		Wages Expense	
	(2) 600	(2) 600	

A collection of $1,000 of cash from customers for services rendered (transaction 3) would be recorded in the following manner:

Cash		Service Revenue	
(3) 1,000			(3) 1,000

Recording changes in dividends. Since dividends decrease stockholders' equity, the Dividends account is treated similarly to expense accounts; increases are shown on the left side and decreases on the right side. Thus, the payment of a $2,000 cash dividend (transaction 4) would be recorded as follows:

Cash		Dividends	
	(4) 2,000	(4) 2,000	

At the end of the accounting period, the balances in the expense, revenue, and Dividends accounts are transferred to the Retained Earnings account. This transfer occurs only after the information in these accounts has been used to prepare the income statement. This step is discussed and illustrated in the next chapter.

Debits and credits. The accountant uses the term **debit** in lieu of saying "place an entry on the left side of the account" and **credit** for "place an entry on the right side of an account." Debit (abbreviated Dr.) means simply left side; credit (abbreviated Cr.), right side. A **debit entry** is an entry on the left side of an account, while a **credit entry** is an entry on the right side of an account.

Note that since assets and expenses are increased by debits, these accounts normally have **debit** (or left side) **balances.** Conversely, liability, stockholders' equity, and revenue accounts are increased by credits and normally have **credit** (or right side) **balances.**

The balance of any account is obtained by summing the debits to the account, summing the credits to the account, and subtracting the smaller sum from the larger. If the sum of the debits exceeds the sum of the credits, the account has a debit balance. For example, the Cash account below has a debit balance of $8,400, computed as total debits of $11,000 less total credits of $2,600:

(Dr.)		Cash	(Cr.)
(1)	10,000	(2)	600
(3)	1,000	(4)	2,000
Bal.	8,400		

Similarly, the following Accounts Payable account has a credit balance of $3,000:

(Dr.)	Accounts Payable		(Cr.)
10,000			7,000
			6,000
	Bal.		3,000

For the most part, amounts entered into the accounts are found in the transactions entered into by the business. Business transactions are first analyzed to determine the effects (increase or decrease) that they have upon the assets, liabilities, stockholders' equity, revenues, expenses, or dividends of the business. Then these increases or decreases are translated into debits and credits. For example, an increase in an asset is recorded as a debit in the proper asset account. (A synonym for "debit an account" is "**charge** an account.") When an asset account is debited, there may be any of five credits:

1. Another asset account may be credited (decreased).
2. A liability account may be credited (increased).
3. A stockholders' equity account may be credited (increased).
4. A revenue account may be credited (increased).
5. An expense account may be credited (decreased).

This **double-entry procedure** keeps the accounting equation in balance. Every transaction can be analyzed similarly into debits and credits, always of equal amounts.

The rules of debit and credit (rules of *double entry*) may be presented in account form as follows:

Debits *AE*	Credits *LI*
1. Increase assets.	1. Decrease assets.
2. Decrease liabilities.	2. Increase liabilities.
3. Decrease stockholders' equity.	3. Increase stockholders' equity.
4. Increase dividends.	4. Decrease dividends.
5. Decrease revenues.	5. Increase revenues.
6. Increase expenses.	6. Decrease expenses.

These rules may also be summarized as shown below. Note the treatment of expense and Dividends accounts as if they were merely subsets of the debit side of the Retained Earnings account. Increases in expenses and dividends do tend to reduce what would otherwise be a larger growth in Retained Earnings; and if expenses and dividends are reduced, Retained Earnings will increase. The exact reverse holds true for revenues.

Assets = Liabilities + Stockholders' Equity

Asset Accounts		=	Liability Accounts		+	Stockholders' Equity Accounts	
Debit*	Credit		Debit	Credit*		Debit	Credit*
+	−		−	+		−	+
Increases	Decreases		Decreases	Increases		Decreases	Increases

Expense Accounts and Dividends Account		Revenue Accounts	
Debit*	Credit	Debit	Credit*
+	−	−	+
Increases	Decreases	Decreases	Increases

*Normal balance.

THE LEDGER

Accounts are classified into two general groups: (1) balance sheet accounts or **real accounts** (assets, liabilities, and stockholders' equity); and (2) income statement accounts or **nominal accounts** (revenues and expenses). Balance sheet accounts are called *real* accounts since they are *not* subsets or subdivisions of any other account. Income statement accounts are called *nominal* accounts because they *are* merely subsets of the Retained Earnings account. The accounts are collectively referred to as the **ledger,** whether kept in a bound volume, handwritten in loose-leaf form, or magnetically encoded on plastic computer tape.

The list of the names of the accounts is known as the **chart of accounts.** Each account typically has an identification number as well as a name. For example, assets might be numbered from 100 to 199, liabilities from 200 to 299, stockholders' equity items from 300 to 399, revenues from 400 to 499, and expenses from 500 to 599. (Although any logical numbering may be used, the accounts usually appear in this order in the ledger.) The accounts would then be arranged in numerical sequence in the ledger. The use of account numbers helps to identify and locate accounts when recording data.

Having completed this introduction to accounts and the recording process, attention is now directed to the journal and to journal entries as the means whereby data are entered into an accounting system.

THE JOURNAL

Under double-entry accounting, every business transaction has a dual effect on the accounts of the business entity. With the rare exception of transactions such as an exchange of land for land, every recorded business transaction will affect at least two ledger accounts. Since each ledger account shows only the increases and decreases in the item for which it was established, the entire effects of a single business transaction will not appear in any one account. For example, the Cash account contains only data on changes in cash and does not show the exact accounts credited for receipts of cash or the exact accounts debited for cash disbursements.

Therefore, if transactions are recorded directly in the accounts, it is difficult to see the entire effect of any transaction upon an entity by looking at the accounts. To remedy this deficiency, the accountant employs a book or a record known as a journal. A **journal** contains a chronological record of the transactions of a business. Because each transaction is initially recorded in a journal before being entered in the ledger, a journal is called a book of *original entry.* Here every business transaction is analyzed for its effects upon the entity. These effects are expressed in terms of debit and credit—the inputs of the accounting system.

The functions and other advantages of using a journal are summarized below. The journal:

1. Sets forth transactions of each day.
2. Records transactions in chronological order.
3. Shows the analysis of each transaction in terms of debit and credit effects.
4. Supplies an explanation of each transaction.
5. Serves as a source for future reference to accounting transactions.
6. Removes lengthy explanations from the ledger accounts.
7. Makes posting the ledger at convenient times possible.
8. Assists in keeping the ledger in balance.
9. Aids in tracing errors.
10. Promotes the division of labor (for example, one person may enter the journal entries and another may post them).

The general journal.   The general journal is illustrated and discussed in this chapter. It is the most commonly used form of journal. The term *general* means all-purpose or for recording all types of transactions. Other types of special-purpose journals, however, also may be used. These special journals are not discussed in this text. As shown in Illustration 2.1, a general journal contains the following columns:

Illustration 2.1

	GENERAL JOURNAL		*Page 1*

Date		Account Titles and Explanation	Post. Ref.	Debit	Credit
1990 Jan.	1	Cash	100	5 0 0 0	
		Capital Stock	300		5 0 0 0
		Capital stock issued for cash.			
	5	Office Equipment	110	1 2 0 0	
		Accounts Payable	201		1 2 0 0
		Equipment purchased for the office on account.			

1. Date column. The first column on each general journal page is for the date. For the first journal entry on a page, the year, the month, and the day are entered here. For other entries on that page, only the day of the month is shown unless the month changes.
2. Account Titles and Explanation column. The names of the account to be debited, the account to be credited, and the explanation are given in this column. The debit is shown on the first line, and the credit is shown on the following line, indented to the right. The explanation of the transaction appears on the line(s) below the transaction, indented halfway between the debit and credit entry.
3. Posting Reference (Post. Ref.) column. This column shows the account number of the account that has been debited or credited. For instance, the number 100 in the first entry means that the Cash account number is 100. No number appears in the column until the information is posted to the appropriate ledger account.
4. Debit column. This column shows the monetary amount of the debit; it is on the same line as the name of the account debited.
5. Credit column. This column shows the monetary amount of the credit; it is on the same line as the name of the account credited.

A blank line separates the entries for individual transactions.

Journalizing

Journalizing is the process of entering a transaction in a journal. Information to be journalized originates on source materials or documents such as invoices, cash register tapes, timecards, and checks. The activity recorded on these documents must be analyzed to determine whether a recordable transaction has occurred. If so, the specific accounts affected, the dollar amounts of the changes, and the direction of the changes (whether increases or decreases) must also be determined. Then all of these changes must be translated into terms of debits and credits and entered in the journal.

A **journal entry** is the entire analysis of a business transaction, including when it occurred, what accounts were affected (debited or credited), and what the amount of the increase or decrease was. The explanation of a journal entry should be complete enough to fully describe the transaction and to prove the entry's accuracy and at the same time be concise. If a journal entry is self-explanatory, the explanation is often omitted in practice.

Compound Journal Entries

The analysis of a transaction often shows that more than two accounts are directly affected. In such cases, the journal entry involves more than one debit and/or credit. Such a journal entry is a **compound journal entry.** An entry with one debit and one credit is a simple journal entry.

As an illustration of a compound journal entry, assume that Beck Company purchased $8,000 of machinery from Taylor Company, paying $2,000 cash with the balance due in 30 days. The journal entry for Beck is as follows:

Machinery	8,000	
Cash.		2,000
Accounts Payable, Taylor Company		6,000
Machinery purchased from Taylor Company.		

POSTING

Objective 4: Post journal entries to the accounts in the ledger

In a sense, a journal entry is a set of instructions. It directs the entry of a certain dollar amount as a debit in a specific account. It also directs entry of a certain dollar amount as a credit in a specific account. The carrying out of these instructions is known as posting. **Posting** is the process of transferring information recorded in the journal to the proper place in the ledger. In Illustration 2.2, the first entry directs that $10,000 be posted as a debit to the Cash account and as a credit to the Capital Stock account. (The arrows in the illustration show how these amounts have been posted to the correct accounts.) The three-column balance type of account is shown in this illustration and is the more common form of ledger account. In contrast to the two-sided T-account format shown so far, the three-column format has columns for debit, credit, and balance. One advantage of this form is that the balance of the account is shown after each item has been posted.

Postings to the ledger accounts may be made (1) at the time the transaction is journalized; (2) at the end of the day, week, or month; or (3) as each journal page is filled. The time of posting is determined by such things as the need for ledger account balances to be completely up to

Illustration 2.2

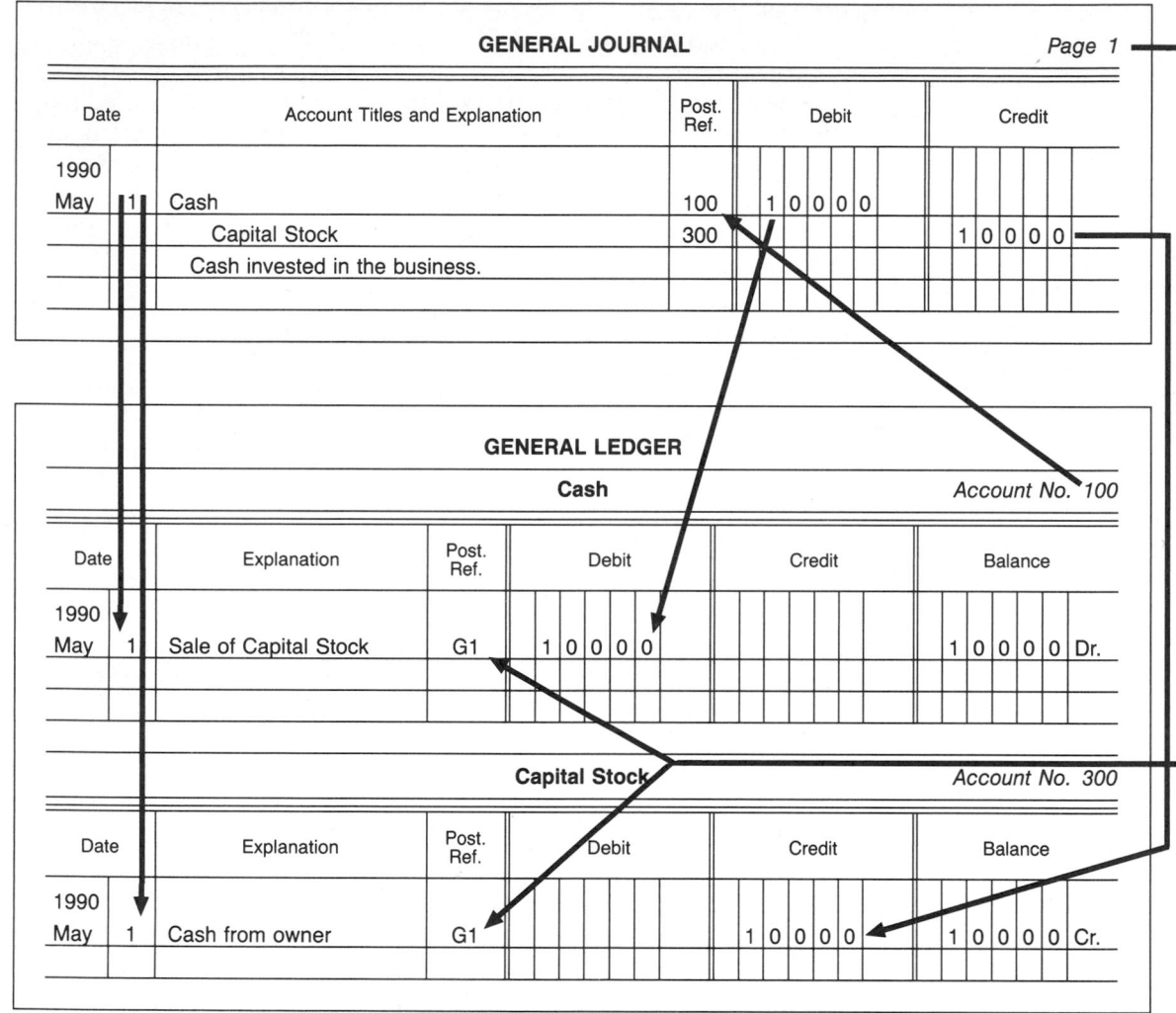

date, type of accounting system in use, number of people working in the accounting area, and number of business transactions recorded.

Cross-Indexing

The number of the ledger account to which the posting was made is placed in the Posting Reference (Post. Ref.) column (sometimes called Folio column) of the journal (see the arrow from Account No. 100 to the debit in the entry in the general journal). The number of the journal page *from* which the entry was posted is placed in the Post. Ref. column of the ledger account (see the arrow from page 1 in the general journal to G1 in the Post. Ref. column of the general ledger). The date of the transaction is also shown in the general ledger (see the arrows from the date in the general journal to the dates in the general ledger). Posting is always *from* the journal *to* the ledger account. **Cross-indexing** is the placing of the account number in the journal and the placing of the journal page number in the ledger account, as shown in Illustration 2.2.

Cross-indexing aids the tracing of any recorded transaction, either from the journal to the ledger or from the ledger to the journal. Cross-reference numbers should not be placed in the Post. Ref. column of the journal until the entry is posted; thereafter, the presence of cross-reference numbers indicates that the entry has been posted.

An understanding of the posting and cross-indexing process can be obtained by tracing the entries from the journal to the ledger. The ledger accounts might not contain explanations of all the entries since the explanations can be obtained from the journal.

THE ACCOUNTING SYSTEM ILLUSTRATED

Presented below is an illustration of an accounting system that might be employed by a small decorating service company, the Morgan Company. The company's balance sheet at December 31, 1989, is as follows:

MORGAN COMPANY
Balance Sheet
December 31, 1989

Assets		Liabilities and Stockholders' Equity		
Cash	$15,000	Liabilities:		
Accounts receivable	4,500	Accounts payable		$ 2,000
Furniture and equipment	6,000	Stockholders' equity:		
Office fixtures	10,000	Capital stock	$30,000	
		Retained earnings	3,500	
		Total stockholders' equity		33,500
		Total liabilities and		
Total assets	$35,500	stockholders' equity		$35,500

The balance sheet reflects ledger account balances as of the close of business on December 31, 1989. These are, of course, the opening balances on January 1, 1990, and are shown as such in the illustrated ledger accounts. The furniture, equipment, and office fixtures were purchased on December 31, 1989.

The Morgan Company's chart of accounts is as follows:

	Account No.	Account Title
Assets	100	Cash
	101	Accounts Receivable
	103	Furniture and Equipment
	104	Office Fixtures
Liability	200	Accounts Payable
Stockholders' equity	300	Capital Stock
	301	Retained Earnings
	302	Dividends
Revenue	400	Service Revenue
Expenses	500	Advertising Expense
	501	Salaries Expense
	502	Rent Expense
	504	Supplies Expense
	505	Miscellaneous Expense

Now assume that the following is a complete list and analysis of the transactions entered into by the Morgan Company in January 1990.

1. Jan. 2   Paid January rent for office, $1,000.

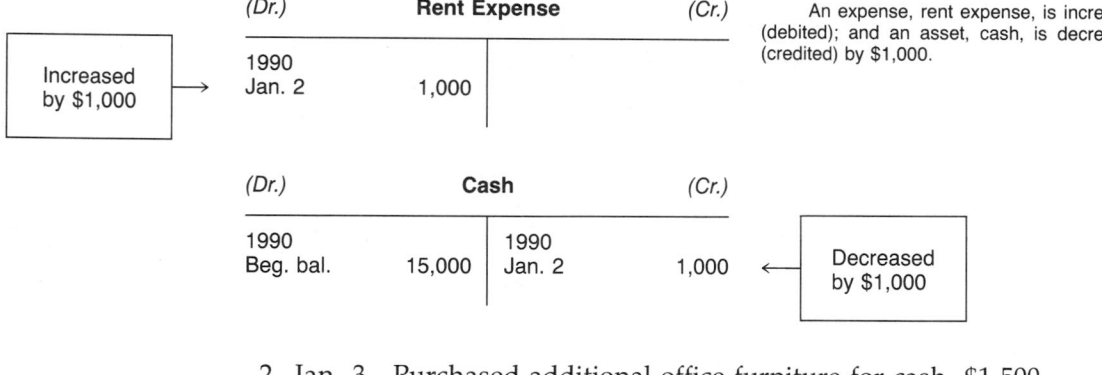

An expense, rent expense, is increased (debited); and an asset, cash, is decreased (credited) by $1,000.

2. Jan. 3   Purchased additional office furniture for cash, $1,500.

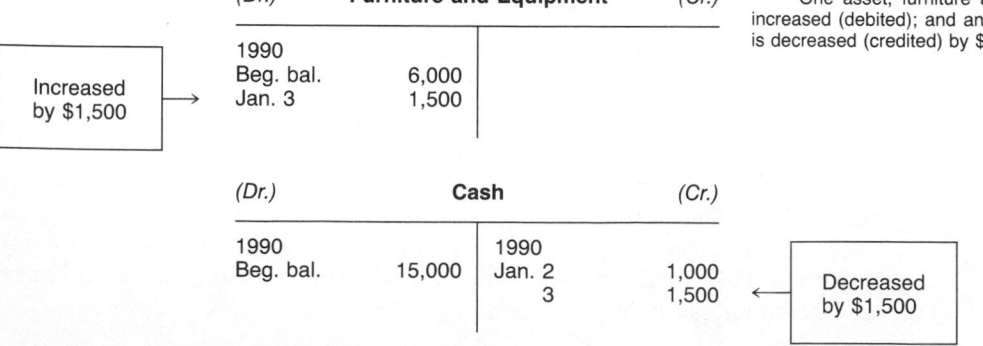

One asset, furniture and equipment, is increased (debited); and another asset, cash, is decreased (credited) by $1,500.

3. Jan. 4   Received a $200 invoice from the Burk Agency for planning January's advertising.

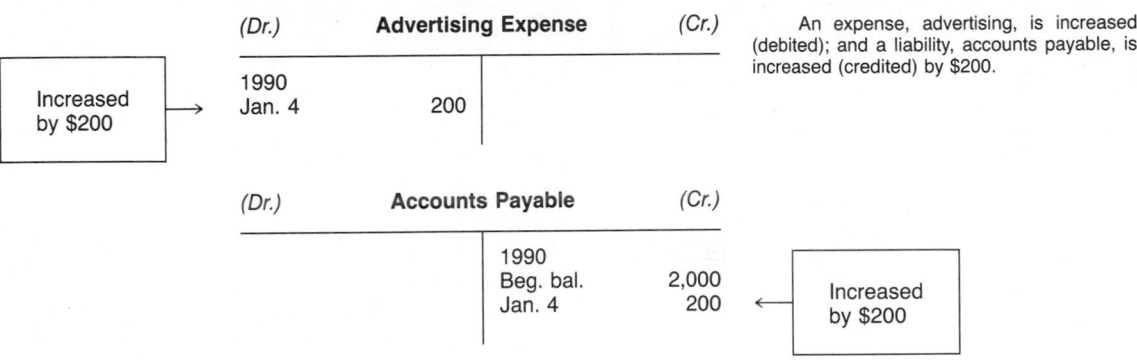

(Dr.)	**Advertising Expense**	(Cr.)
1990		
Jan. 4	200	

Increased by $200

An expense, advertising, is increased (debited); and a liability, accounts payable, is increased (credited) by $200.

(Dr.)	**Accounts Payable**	(Cr.)
	1990	
	Beg. bal.	2,000
	Jan. 4	200

Increased by $200

Sometimes prepaid expenses such as advertising, insurance, rent, and supplies are bought and will be fully used up within the current accounting period as in the first and third entries above. For instance, the company may buy supplies during the first part of the month that it intends to fully consume during that month. If supplies will be fully consumed during the period of purchase, it is best to debit Supplies Expense rather than an asset account such as Supplies on Hand, at time of purchase. This same advice applies to insurance and rent. If insurance is purchased that will be fully consumed during the current period, Insurance Expense rather than Prepaid Insurance should be debited at the time of purchase. If rent is paid that applies only to the current period, Rent Expense rather than Prepaid Rent should be debited at the time of payment. Following this advice simplifies the procedures at the end of the accounting period, as illustrated in the next chapter.

4. Jan. 6   Paid a $2,000 account payable.

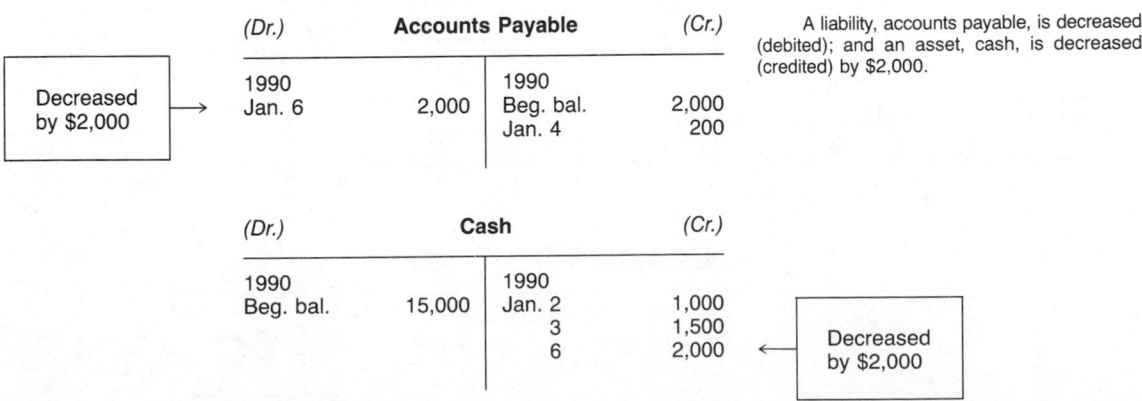

(Dr.)	**Accounts Payable**	(Cr.)
1990		1990
Jan. 6	2,000	Beg. bal.	2,000
		Jan. 4	200

Decreased by $2,000

A liability, accounts payable, is decreased (debited); and an asset, cash, is decreased (credited) by $2,000.

(Dr.)	**Cash**	(Cr.)
1990		1990
Beg. bal.	15,000	Jan. 2	1,000
		3	1,500
		6	2,000

Decreased by $2,000

5. Jan. 8   Paid the $200 advertising bill received on January 4.

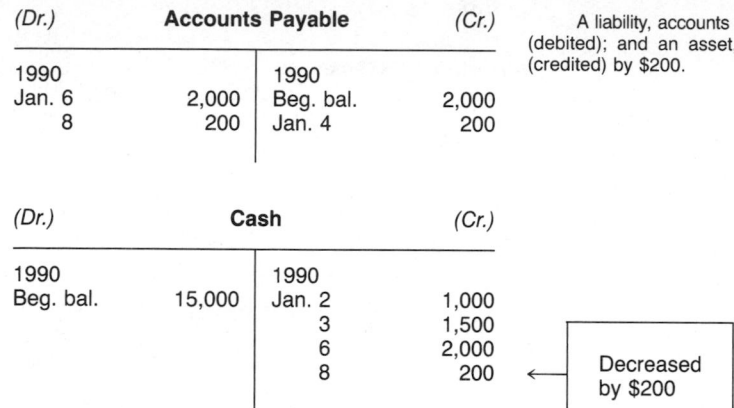

A liability, accounts payable, is decreased (debited); and an asset, cash, is decreased (credited) by $200.

6. Jan. 9   Purchased, for $200 cash, supplies to be used in January.

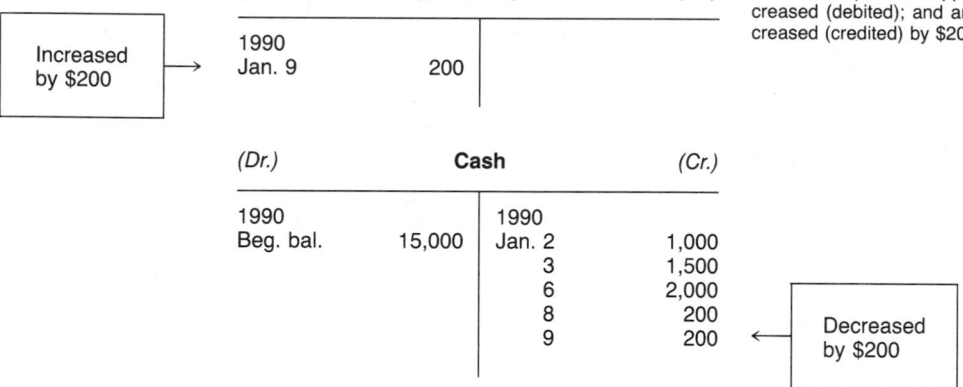

An expense, supplies expense, is increased (debited); and an asset, cash, is decreased (credited) by $200.

7. Jan. 10   Received $4,500 cash on an account receivable.

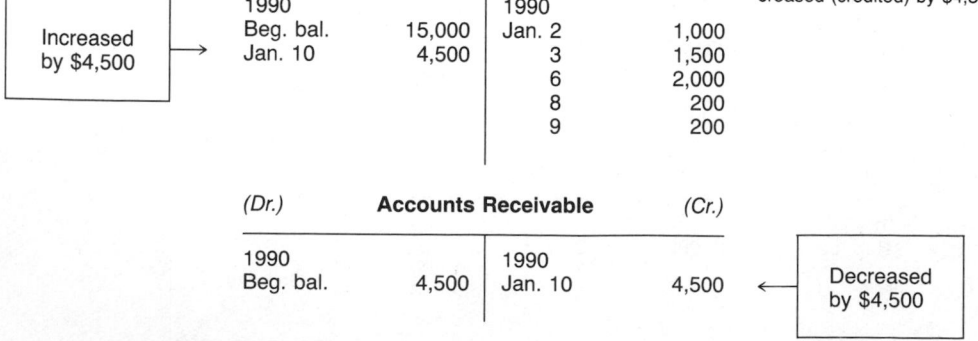

An asset, cash, is increased (debited); and another asset, accounts receivable, is decreased (credited) by $4,500.

8. Jan. 15   Performed services on account for a customer, $7,600.

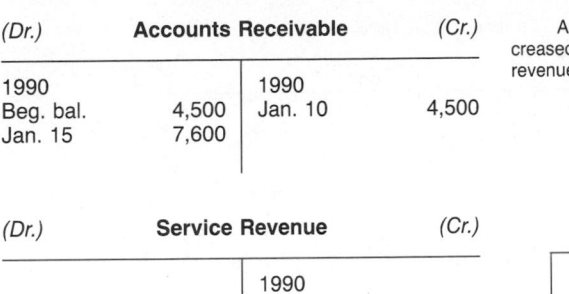

(Dr.)	**Accounts Receivable**		(Cr.)
1990		1990	
Beg. bal.	4,500	Jan. 10	4,500
Jan. 15	7,600		

An asset, accounts receivable, is increased (debited); and a revenue, service revenue, is increased (credited) by $7,600.

(Dr.)	**Service Revenue**		(Cr.)
		1990	
		Jan. 15	7,600

Increased by $7,600

9. Jan. 17   Paid a miscellaneous expense, $1,000.

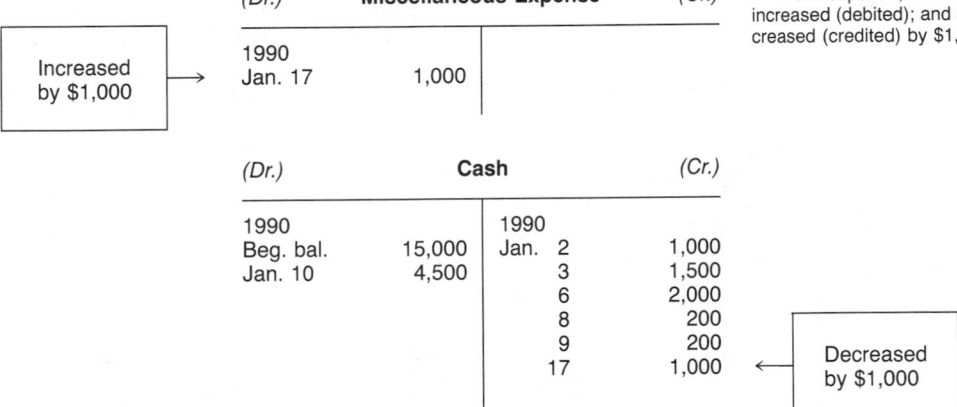

(Dr.)	**Miscellaneous Expense**		(Cr.)
1990			
Jan. 17	1,000		

An expense, miscellaneous expense, is increased (debited); and an asset, cash, is decreased (credited) by $1,000.

(Dr.)	**Cash**		(Cr.)
1990		1990	
Beg. bal.	15,000	Jan. 2	1,000
Jan. 10	4,500	3	1,500
		6	2,000
		8	200
		9	200
		17	1,000

Decreased by $1,000

10. Jan. 23   Received a $300 invoice from the *New York News* for advertising in the first half of January.

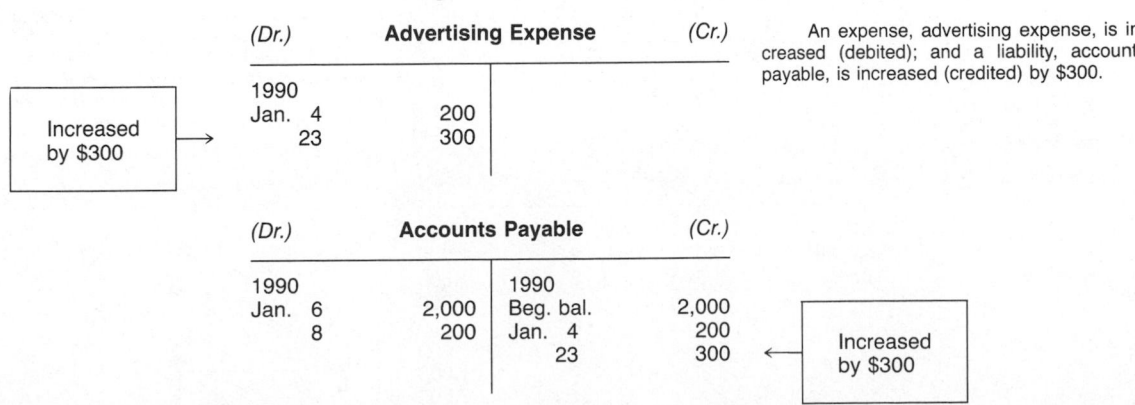

(Dr.)	**Advertising Expense**		(Cr.)
1990			
Jan. 4	200		
23	300		

An expense, advertising expense, is increased (debited); and a liability, accounts payable, is increased (credited) by $300.

(Dr.)	**Accounts Payable**		(Cr.)
1990		1990	
Jan. 6	2,000	Beg. bal.	2,000
8	200	Jan. 4	200
		23	300

Increased by $300

11. Jan. 31   Performed services on account, $3,000.

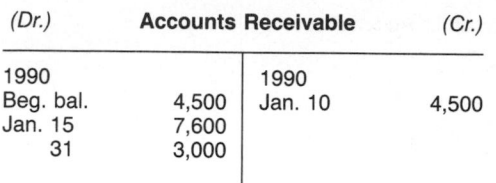

(Dr.)	Accounts Receivable		(Cr.)
1990		1990	
Beg. bal.	4,500	Jan. 10	4,500
Jan. 15	7,600		
31	3,000		

An asset, accounts receivable, is increased (debited); and a revenue, service revenue, is increased (credited) by $3,000.

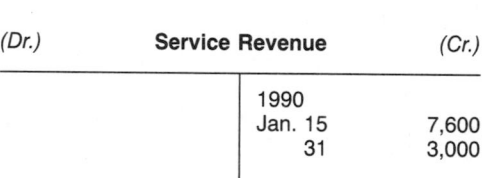

(Dr.)	Service Revenue		(Cr.)
		1990	
		Jan. 15	7,600
		31	3,000

12. Jan. 31   Paid salaries of $7,800 for the month.

(Dr.)	Salaries Expense		(Cr.)
1990			
Jan. 31	7,800		

An expense, salaries expense, is increased (debited); and an asset, cash, is decreased (credited) by $7,800.

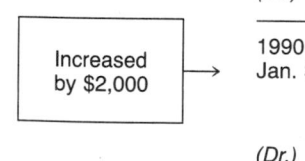

(Dr.)	Cash		(Cr.)
1990		1990	
Beg. bal.	15,000	Jan. 2	1,000
Jan. 10	4,500	3	1,500
		6	2,000
		8	200
		9	200
		17	1,000
		31	7,800

13. Jan. 31   Paid a cash dividend to stockholders, $2,000.

(Dr.)	Dividends		(Cr.)
1990			
Jan. 31	2,000		

A stockholders' equity account, Dividends, is increased (debited); and an asset, cash, is decreased (credited) by $2,000. Remember that dividends reduce the amount of Retained Earnings—which carries a credit balance—so dividends are debited for increases.

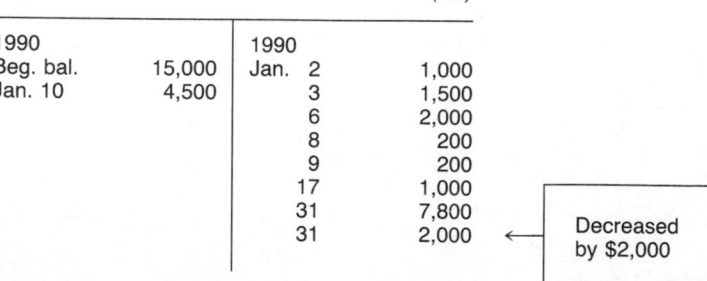

(Dr.)	Cash		(Cr.)
1990		1990	
Beg. bal.	15,000	Jan. 2	1,000
Jan. 10	4,500	3	1,500
		6	2,000
		8	200
		9	200
		17	1,000
		31	7,800
		31	2,000

The T-accounts shown in the list of transactions were used only for analysis purposes. In the accounting records, the transactions would first be entered in a journal and then posted to a ledger.

The transactions presented have been entered in the general journal of the Morgan Company for January 1990. Remember that the Posting Reference column normally would not be filled in until after the entries have been posted to the ledger.

GENERAL JOURNAL   *Page 1*

Date		Account Titles and Explanation	Post. Ref.	Debit	Credit
1990					
Jan.	2	Rent Expense	502	1 0 0 0	
		Cash	100		1 0 0 0
		Rent for January 1990.			
	3	Furniture and Equipment	103	1 5 0 0	
		Cash	100		1 5 0 0
		Purchased additional furniture.			
	4	Advertising Expense	500	2 0 0	
		Accounts Payable	200		2 0 0
		Advertising expense on account.			
	6	Accounts Payable	200	2 0 0 0	
		Cash	100		2 0 0 0
		Payment on account.			
	8	Accounts Payable	200	2 0 0	
		Cash	100		2 0 0
		Paid invoice of January 4.			
	9	Supplies Expense	504	2 0 0	
		Cash	100		2 0 0
		Supplies purchased and used.			
	10	Cash	100	4 5 0 0	
		Accounts Receivable	101		4 5 0 0
		Collection on account.			
	15	Accounts Receivable	101	7 6 0 0	
		Service Revenue	400		7 6 0 0
		Performed services on account.			

GENERAL JOURNAL *(continued)*   Page 1

Date		Account Titles and Explanation	Post. Ref.	Debit	Credit
1990					
Jan.	17	Miscellaneous Expense	505	1 0 0 0	
		Cash	100		1 0 0 0
		Paid other selling expenses.			
	23	Advertising Expense	500	3 0 0	
		Accounts Payable	200		3 0 0
		Advertising expense on account.			

GENERAL JOURNAL   Page 2

Date		Account Titles and Explanation	Post. Ref.	Debit	Credit
1990					
Jan.	31	Accounts Receivable	101	3 0 0 0	
		Service Revenue	400		3 0 0 0
		Performed services on account.			
	31	Salaries Expense	501	7 8 0 0	
		Cash	100		7 8 0 0
		Paid salaries for January.			
	31	Dividends	302	2 0 0 0	
		Cash	100		2 0 0 0
		Paid a dividend to stockholders.			

Posting the journal entries to the ledger produces the following accounts for the Morgan Company. Be sure to trace the posting of at least a few of the journal entries to make sure you understand how it was done.

GENERAL LEDGER

Cash   *Account No. 100*

Date		Explanation	Post. Ref.	Debit	Credit	Balance	
1990 Jan.	1	Balance				1 5 0 0 0	Dr.
	2		G1		1 0 0 0	1 4 0 0 0	Dr.
	3		G1		1 5 0 0	1 2 5 0 0	Dr.
	6		G1		2 0 0 0	1 0 5 0 0	Dr.
	8		G1		2 0 0	1 0 3 0 0	Dr.
	9		G1		2 0 0	1 0 1 0 0	Dr.
	10		G1	4 5 0 0		1 4 6 0 0	Dr.
	17		G1		1 0 0 0	1 3 6 0 0	Dr.
	31		G2		7 8 0 0	5 8 0 0	Dr.
	31		G2		2 0 0 0	3 8 0 0	Dr.

Accounts Receivable   *Account No. 101*

Date		Explanation	Post. Ref.	Debit	Credit	Balance	
1990 Jan.	1	Balance				4 5 0 0	Dr.
	10		G1		4 5 0 0	– 0 –	
	15		G1	7 6 0 0		7 6 0 0	Dr.
	31		G2	3 0 0 0		1 0 6 0 0	Dr.

Furniture and Equipment   *Account No. 103*

Date		Explanation	Post. Ref.	Debit	Credit	Balance	
1990 Jan.	1	Balance				6 0 0 0	Dr.
	3		G1	1 5 0 0		7 5 0 0	Dr.

GENERAL LEDGER *(continued)*

Office Fixtures   *Account No. 104*

Date		Explanation	Post. Ref.	Debit	Credit	Balance
1990 Jan.	1	Balance				1 0 0 0 0 Dr.

Accounts Payable   *Account No. 200*

Date		Explanation	Post. Ref.	Debit	Credit	Balance
1990 Jan.	1	Balance				2 0 0 0 Cr.
	4		G1		2 0 0	2 2 0 0 Cr.
	6		G1	2 0 0 0		2 0 0 Cr.
	8		G1	2 0 0		– 0 –
	23		G1		3 0 0	3 0 0 Cr.

Capital Stock   *Account No. 300*

Date		Explanation	Post. Ref.	Debit	Credit	Balance
1990 Jan.	1	Balance				3 0 0 0 0 Cr.

Retained Earnings   *Account No. 301*

Date		Explanation	Post. Ref.	Debit	Credit	Balance
1990 Jan.	1	Balance				3 5 0 0 Cr.

Dividends   *Account No. 302*

Date		Explanation	Post. Ref.	Debit	Credit	Balance
1990 Jan.	31		G2	2 0 0 0		2 0 0 0 Dr.

GENERAL LEDGER *(continued)*

Service Revenue — *Account No. 400*

Date		Explanation	Post. Ref.	Debit	Credit	Balance
1990						
Jan.	15		G1		7 6 0 0	7 6 0 0 Cr.
	31		G2		3 0 0 0	1 0 6 0 0 Cr.

Advertising Expense — *Account No. 500*

Date		Explanation	Post. Ref.	Debit	Credit	Balance
1990						
Jan.	4		G1	2 0 0		2 0 0 Dr.
	23		G1	3 0 0		5 0 0 Dr.

Salaries Expense — *Account No. 501*

Date		Explanation	Post. Ref.	Debit	Credit	Balance
1990						
Jan.	31		G2	7 8 0 0		7 8 0 0 Dr.

Rent Expense — *Account No. 502*

Date		Explanation	Post. Ref.	Debit	Credit	Balance
1990						
Jan.	2		G1	1 0 0 0		1 0 0 0 Dr.

Supplies Expense — *Account No. 504*

Date		Explanation	Post. Ref.	Debit	Credit	Balance
1990						
Jan.	9		G1	2 0 0		2 0 0 Dr.

	GENERAL LEDGER *(concluded)*						

		Miscellaneous Expense				*Account No. 505*	
Date		Explanation	Post. Ref.	Debit	Credit	Balance	
1990 Jan. 17			G1	1 0 0 0		1 0 0 0	Dr.

Control of the Recording Process

Earlier in the chapter, it was stated that accountants record increases in assets, expenses, and dividends as debits and increases in equities and revenues as credits. It would be possible to devise a scheme whereby all accounts were increased by entries on the debit side. At the end of any given period, then, all accounts would have positive debit balances. Under such a scheme, however, accountants would not know whether the basic equation of Assets = Equities was being maintained in the records. Furthermore, a valuable automatic check for arithmetic errors would be missing. If accountants wished to check upon the arithmetic accuracy of their work, they would have to repeat virtually every step in the initial recording process. Fortunately, there is an easier way.

Increases in assets, expenses, and dividends are recorded as debits and increases in equities and revenues as credits. This yields two sets of accounts—those with debit balances and those with credit balances. If the totals of these two groups are equal, the accountant has *some* assurance that the arithmetic part of the recording process has been properly carried out. The double-entry system of accounting requires that debits must equal credits in the entry to record every transaction. This equality of debits and credits for each transaction will always hold because both sides of every transaction are recorded. It is the equality of debits and credits, not of increases and decreases, that provides the important control device. If every transaction is recorded in terms of equal debits and credits, it follows that the total of the debit-balanced accounts must equal the total of the credit-balanced accounts.

THE TRIAL BALANCE

Objective 5: Prepare a trial balance to test the equality of debits and credits in the journalizing and posting process

The arithmetic accuracy of the recording process is generally tested by preparing a trial balance. A **trial balance** is a listing of the accounts and their debit or credit balances. The trial balance for the Morgan Company is shown in Illustration 2.3. Note the listing of the account titles on the

Illustration 2.3
A TRIAL BALANCE

MORGAN COMPANY Trial Balance January 31, 1990	Debits	Credits
Cash	$ 3,800	
Accounts receivable	10,600	
Furniture and equipment	7,500	
Office fixtures	10,000	
Accounts payable		$ 300
Capital stock		30,000
Retained earnings		3,500
Dividends	2,000	
Service revenue		10,600
Advertising expense	500	
Salaries expense	7,800	
Rent expense	1,000	
Supplies expense	200	
Miscellaneous expense	1,000	
	$44,400	$44,400

left (account numbers could be included, if desired), the column for debit balances, the column for credit balances, and the equality of the two totals.

Any inequality in the totals of the debits and credits columns would automatically signal the presence of an error. To find the cause of such an error, the accountant should work backwards through the accounting process by performing the following steps:

1. Re-add the trial balance.
2. Compare the trial balance figures with the account balances, and determine if the account balances are in the appropriate money columns.
3. Verify the balance of each ledger account.
4. Verify postings to the ledger.
5. Verify journal entries.
6. Review the transactions.

The equality of the two totals does not mean that the accounting has been error free. Serious errors may still have been made. Such errors might include the complete omission of an important transaction or the recording of an entry in the wrong account (for example, the recording of an asset as an expense, or vice versa). In these instances, the trial balance would have equal debit and credit totals but would be incorrect.

A trial balance may be prepared at any time—at the end of a day, a week, a month, a quarter, or a year. Typically, one is prepared whenever financial statements are to be prepared. Thus, the trial balance provides a listing of the accounts for statement preparation. A trial balance that is out of balance will also indicate the period in which an error was made.

FINANCIAL STATEMENTS

The financial statements desired by the management of the Morgan Company are presented in Illustrations 2.4, 2.5, and 2.6. As shown by the income statement in Illustration 2.4, the company earned net income of $100.

Illustration 2.4
AN INCOME STATEMENT

MORGAN COMPANY
Income Statement
For Month Ended January 31, 1990

Revenues:		
Service revenue		$10,600
Expenses:		
Advertising expense	$ 500	
Salaries expense	7,800	
Rent expense	1,000	
Supplies expense	200	
Miscellaneous expense	1,000	10,500
Net income		$ 100

In Illustration 2.5, the net income is added to the beginning balance in retained earnings. Then the dividends are deducted from that total to arrive at the ending balance in retained earnings. This ending balance of retained earnings appears in the balance sheet in Illustration 2.6, along with the ending balances in the other balance sheet accounts.

Illustration 2.5
A STATEMENT OF RETAINED EARNINGS

MORGAN COMPANY
Statement of Retained Earnings
For Month Ended January 31, 1990

Retained earnings, December 31, 1989	$3,500
Add: Net income for January	100
Total	$3,600
Less: Dividends	2,000
Retained earnings, January 31, 1990	$1,600

Illustration 2.6
A BALANCE SHEET

MORGAN COMPANY
Balance Sheet
January 31, 1990
Assets

Cash	$ 3,800
Accounts receivable	10,600
Furniture and equipment	7,500
Office fixtures	10,000
Total assets	$31,900

Liabilities and Stockholders' Equity

Liabilities:		
Accounts payable		$ 300
Stockholders' equity:		
Capital stock	$30,000	
Retained earnings	1,600	
Total stockholders' equity		31,600
Total liabilities and stockholders' equity		$31,900

SUMMARY

This chapter introduced the basic components of an accounting system and the manner in which data are entered in the system.

An account is a means employed to classify and summarize changes in assets, liabilities, stockholders' equity items, revenues, expenses, and dividends. By agreement, asset, expense, and Dividend accounts are increased by entries on the left side of the account (called the debit side) and decreased by entries on the right (credit) side. Liability, stockholders' equity, and revenue accounts are increased by entries on the credit side and decreased by entries on the debit side. As a result, assets, expenses, and dividends usually have debit balances, and the others usually have credit balances.

Recording increases and decreases in accounts in a manner that provides two groups of accounts—those with debit balances and those with credit balances—gives an automatic check upon the arithmetic accuracy of the accounting process.

Collectively, the accounts are referred to as the ledger. The chart of accounts is a list of the names and numbers of the accounts in an accounting system.

All data are entered in an accounting system by means of a journal, which is a chronological record of business transactions analyzed in terms of debit and credit. Business activity is analyzed and certain transactions are recorded in the journal in a process known as journalizing. The amounts journalized are then posted to the accounts. A trial balance is a listing of all of the accounts in the ledger together with their debit or credit balances which, in total, must be equal. Then, financial statements can be prepared.

The next chapter completes the discussion of the accounting cycle. Adjusting and closing entries are needed to prepare accurate financial statements.

Objective 6: Define and use correctly the new terms in the glossary

NEW TERMS INTRODUCED IN CHAPTER 2

Account   An element in an accounting system that is used to classify and summarize measurements of business activity. The three-column account is normally used. It contains columns for debit, credit, and balance (46).

Charge   Means the same as the word *debit* (49).

Chart of accounts   The complete listing of titles and account numbers of all of the accounts in the ledger; somewhat comparable to a table of contents (50).

Compound journal entry   A journal entry with more than one debit and/or credit (53).

Credit   The right side of any account; when used as a verb, to enter a dollar amount on the right side of an account; credits increase liability, stockholders' equity, and revenue accounts and decrease asset, expense, and dividends accounts (48).

Credit balance   The balance in an account when the sum of the credits to the account exceeds the sum of the debits to that account (48).

Credit entry   An entry on the right side of an account (48).

Cross-indexing   The placing of the account number in the journal and the placing of the journal page number in the ledger account (55).

Debit   The left side of any account; when used as a verb, to enter a dollar amount on the left side of an account; debits increase asset, expense, and dividends accounts and decrease liability, stockholders' equity, and revenue accounts (48).

Debit balance   The balance in an account when the sum of the debits to the account exceeds the sum of the credits to that account (48).

Debit entry   An entry on the left side of an account (48).

Double-entry procedure   The accounting requirement that every transaction be recorded in an entry that has equal debits and credits (49).

Journal   A chronological (arranged in order of time) record of business transactions; the simplest form of journal is the two-column general journal (51).

Journal entry   Shows all of the effects of a business transaction as expressed in terms of debit(s) and credit(s) and may include an explanation of the transaction (53).

Journalizing   A step in the accounting recording process that consists of entering a transaction in a journal (52).

Ledger   The complete collection of all of the accounts of a company; often referred to as the general ledger (50).

Nominal accounts   Income statement accounts—revenues and expenses (50).

Posting   Recording in the ledger the information contained in the journal (53).

Real accounts   Balance sheet accounts (assets, liabilities, and stockholders' equity) (50).

T-account   An account resembling the letter *T*, which is used for illustrative purposes only. Debits are entered on the left side of the account and credits are entered on the right side of the account (46).

Trial balance   A listing of the ledger accounts and their debit or credit balances to determine that debits equal credits in the recording process (66).

DEMONSTRATION PROBLEM 2–1

The Green Hills Riding Stable, Incorporated, had the following balance sheet on June 30, 1990:

GREEN HILLS RIDING STABLE, INCORPORATED
Balance Sheet
June 30, 1990

Assets

Cash	$ 7,500
Accounts receivable	5,400
Land	40,000
Total assets	$52,900

Liabilities and Stockholders' Equity

Liabilities:		
Accounts payable		$ 800
Notes payable		40,000
Total liabilities		$40,800
Stockholders' equity:		
Capital stock	$10,000	
Retained earnings	2,100	
Total stockholders' equity		12,100
Total liabilities and stockholders' equity		$52,900

Transactions for the month of July 1990 were as follows:

Transactions:

July 1   Additional shares of capital stock were issued for $25,000.
  1   Paid for a prefabricated building constructed on the land at a cost of $24,000.
  8   Paid the accounts payable of $800.
  10   Collected the accounts receivable of $5,400.
  12   Horse feed to be used in July was purchased on credit for $1,100.
  15   Boarding fees for July were charged to customers in the amount of $4,500. (This amount is due on August 10.)
  24   Miscellaneous expenses of $800 for July were paid.
  31   Paid interest expense on the notes payable of $200.
  31   Salaries of $1,400 for the month were paid.
  31   Riding and lesson fees were billed to customers in the amount of $3,600. (They are due on August 10.)

Required:

a. Prepare the journal entries to record the transactions for July 1990.

b. Post the journal entries to the ledger accounts after entering the beginning balances in those accounts. Insert cross-indexing references in the journal and ledger. Use the following chart of accounts.

Cash.	100	Retained Earnings	301
Accounts Receivable.	101	Horse Boarding Fees Revenue	400
Land	112	Riding and Lesson Fees Revenue . . .	401
Building	114	Feed Expense	501
Accounts Payable	200	Salaries Expense	502
Notes Payable	205	Interest Expense	504
Capital Stock	300	Miscellaneous Expense	510

c. Prepare a trial balance.

Solution to demonstration problem 2–1

a.

		GENERAL JOURNAL				*Page 1*

Date		Account Titles and Explanation	Post. Ref.	Debit	Credit
1990					
July	1	Cash	100	2 5 0 0 0	
		Capital Stock	300		2 5 0 0 0
		Additional capital stock issued.			
	1	Building	114	2 4 0 0 0	
		Cash	100		2 4 0 0 0
		Paid for building.			
	8	Accounts Payable	200	8 0 0	
		Cash	100		8 0 0
		Paid accounts payable.			
	10	Cash	100	5 4 0 0	
		Accounts Receivable	101		5 4 0 0
		Collected accounts receivable.			
	12	Feed Expense	501	1 1 0 0	
		Accounts Payable	200		1 1 0 0
		Purchased feed on credit.			
	15	Accounts Receivable	101	4 5 0 0	
		Horse Boarding Fees Revenue	400		4 5 0 0
		Billed boarding fees for July.			

GENERAL JOURNAL *(continued)*   *Page 1*

Date		Account Titles and Explanation	Post. Ref.	Debit	Credit
1990 Jan.					
	24	Miscellaneous Expense	510	8 0 0	
		Cash	100		8 0 0
		Paid miscellaneous expense for July.			
	31	Interest Expense	504	2 0 0	
		Cash	100		2 0 0
		Paid interest.			
	31	Salaries Expense	502	1 4 0 0	
		Cash	100		1 4 0 0
		Paid salaries for July.			
	31	Accounts Receivable	101	3 6 0 0	
		Riding and Lesson Fees Revenue	401		3 6 0 0
		Billed riding and lesson fees for July.			

b.

GENERAL LEDGER

Cash   *Account No. 100*

Date		Explanation	Post. Ref.	Debit	Credit	Balance
1990 June	30	Balance				7 5 0 0 Dr.
July	1	Stockholders' investment	G1	2 5 0 0 0		3 2 5 0 0 Dr.
	1	Building	G1		2 4 0 0 0	8 5 0 0 Dr.
	8	Accounts payable	G1		8 0 0	7 7 0 0 Dr.
	10	Accounts receivable	G1	5 4 0 0		1 3 1 0 0 Dr.
	24	Miscellaneous expense	G1		8 0 0	1 2 3 0 0 Dr.
	31	Interest expense	G1		2 0 0	1 2 1 0 0 Dr.
	31	Salaries expense	G1		1 4 0 0	1 0 7 0 0 Dr.

GENERAL LEDGER *(continued)*

Accounts Receivable   *Account No. 101*

Date		Explanation	Post. Ref.	Debit	Credit	Balance
1990 June	30	Balance				5 4 0 0 Dr.
July	10	Cash	G1		5 4 0 0	– 0 –
	15	Horse boarding fees	G1	4 5 0 0		4 5 0 0 Dr.
	31	Riding and lesson fees	G1	3 6 0 0		8 1 0 0 Dr.

Land   *Account No. 112*

Date		Explanation	Post. Ref.	Debit	Credit	Balance
1990 June	30	Balance				4 0 0 0 0 Dr.

Building   *Account No. 114*

Date		Explanation	Post. Ref.	Debit	Credit	Balance
1990 July	1	Cash	G1	2 4 0 0 0		2 4 0 0 0 Dr.

Accounts Payable   *Account No. 200*

Date		Explanation	Post. Ref.	Debit	Credit	Balance
1990 June	30	Balance				8 0 0 Cr.
July	8	Cash	G1	8 0 0		– 0 –
	12	Feed expense	G1		1 1 0 0	1 1 0 0 Cr.

Notes Payable   *Account No. 205*

Date		Explanation	Post. Ref.	Debit	Credit	Balance
1990 June	30	Balance				4 0 0 0 0 Cr.

GENERAL LEDGER *(continued)*

Capital Stock   Account No. 300

Date		Explanation	Post. Ref.	Debit	Credit	Balance
1990						
June	30	Balance				1 0 0 0 0 Cr.
July	1	Cash	G1		2 5 0 0 0	3 5 0 0 0 Cr.

Retained Earnings   Account No. 301

Date		Explanation	Post. Ref.	Debit	Credit	Balance
1990						
June	30	Balance				2 1 0 0 Cr.

Horse Boarding Fees Revenue   Account No. 400

Date		Explanation	Post. Ref.	Debit	Credit	Balance
1990						
July	15	Accounts receivable	G1		4 5 0 0	4 5 0 0 Cr.

Riding and Lesson Fees Revenue   Account No. 401

Date		Explanation	Post. Ref.	Debit	Credit	Balance
1990						
July	31	Accounts receivable	G1		3 6 0 0	3 6 0 0 Cr.

Feed Expense   Account No. 501

Date		Explanation	Post. Ref.	Debit	Credit	Balance
1990						
July	12	Accounts payable	G1	1 1 0 0		1 1 0 0 Dr.

GENERAL LEDGER *(concluded)*

Salaries Expense   *Account No. 502*

Date		Explanation	Post. Ref.	Debit	Credit	Balance
1990 July	31	Cash	G1	1 4 0 0		1 4 0 0 Dr.

Interest Expense   *Account No. 504*

Date		Explanation	Post. Ref.	Debit	Credit	Balance
1990 July	31	Cash	G1	2 0 0		2 0 0 Dr.

Miscellaneous Expense   *Account No. 510*

Date		Explanation	Post. Ref.	Debit	Credit	Balance
1990 July	24	Cash	G1	8 0 0		8 0 0 Dr.

c.

GREEN HILLS RIDING STABLE, INCORPORATED
Trial Balance
July 31, 1990

	Debits	Credits
Cash	$10,700	
Accounts Receivable	8,100	
Land	40,000	
Building	24,000	
Accounts Payable		$ 1,100
Notes Payable		40,000
Capital Stock		35,000
Retained Earnings		2,100
Horse Boarding Fees Revenue		4,500
Riding and Lesson Fees Revenue		3,600
Feed Expense	1,100	
Salaries Expense	1,400	
Interest Expense	200	
Miscellaneous Expense	800	
	$86,300	$86,300

QUESTIONS

1. Define debit and credit. Name the types of accounts that are:

   a. Increased by debits.

   b. Decreased by debits.

   c. Increased by credits.

   d. Do you think this system makes sense? Can you conceive of other possible methods for recording changes in accounts?

2. Describe a ledger and a chart of accounts. How do these two compare with a book and its table of contents?

3. Why are expense and revenue accounts used when all revenues and expenses could be shown directly in the Retained Earnings account?

4. What types of accounts appear in the trial balance? What are the purposes of the trial balance?

5. You have found that the total of the debits column of the trial balance of the Burns Company is $100,000 while the total of the credits column is $90,000. What are some of the possible causes of this difference?

6. Store equipment was purchased for $1,500. Instead of debiting the Store Equipment account, the debit was made to Delivery Equipment. Of what help will the trial balance be in locating this error? Why?

7. Differentiate between the trial balance, chart of accounts, balance sheet, and income statement.

8. A student remembered that the side toward the window in the classroom was the debit side of an account. The student took an examination in a room where the windows were on the other side of the room and became confused and consistently reversed debits and credits. Would the student's trial balance have equal debits and credits totals? If there were no existing balances in any of the accounts to begin with, would the error prevent the student from preparing correct financial statements? Why?

9. Are the following possibilities conceivable in an entry involving only one debit and one credit? Why?

   a. Increase a liability and increase an expense.

   b. Increase an asset and decrease a liability.

   c. Increase a revenue and decrease an expense.

   d. Decrease an asset and increase another asset.

   e. Decrease an asset and increase a liability.

   f. Decrease a revenue and decrease an asset.

   g. Decrease a liability and increase a revenue.

10. Describe the nature and purposes of the general journal. What does "journalizing" mean? Give an example of a compound entry in the general journal.

11. Describe the act of posting. What difficulties could arise if no cross-indexing existed between the general journal and the ledger accounts?

12. Which of the following cash payments would involve the recording of an expense? Why?

    a. Paid vendors for office supplies previously purchased on account.

    b. Paid an automobile dealer for a new company auto.

    c. Paid the current month's rent.

    d. Paid salaries for the last half of the current month.

EXERCISES

Fill in diagram

1. Below is a diagram of the various types of accounts. Indicate where pluses (+) or minuses (−) should be inserted to indicate what effect debits and credits have on each account.

Asset Accounts = **Liability Accounts** + **Stockholders' Equity Accounts**

Debit	Credit		Debit	Credit		Debit	Credit

Expense Accounts and Dividends Accounts **Revenue Accounts**

Debit	Credit		Debit	Credit

Determine debit and credit

2. What debit and credit would be required for each of the following transactions?

    a. Cash was received for services performed for a customer, $1,000.

    b. Services were performed for a customer on open account, $2,000.

Prepare journal entries

3. Give the entry required for each of the following transactions:

    a. Capital stock was issued for $200,000 cash.

    b. Purchased machinery for cash, $60,000.

Show entries using T-accounts

4. Using T-accounts, show how the following transactions would be recorded.

    a. Capital stock was issued for $35,000.

    b. Wages for the period were paid to employees, $4,000.

    c. Services were performed for a customer on account, $7,000.

Prepare journal entries

5. Give the journal entry required for each of the following transactions:

    a. Capital stock was issued for $45,000.

    b. A $30,000 loan was arranged with a bank. The bank increased the company's checking account by $30,000 after management of the company signed a written promise to return the money in 30 days.

    c. Cash was received for services performed for a customer, $900.

    d. Services were performed for a customer on account, $1,000.

Explain sets of debits and credits

6. Explain each of the sets of debits and credits existing in the accounts below. There are 10 transactions to be explained. Each set is designated by the small letters to the left of the amount. For example, the first transaction is the issuance of capital stock for cash and is denoted by the letter (*a*).

	Cash		
(a)	70,000	(e)	50,000
(d)	600	(f)	200
		(g)	1,200
		(i)	10,000
Bal.	9,200		

	Delivery Fee Revenue		
		(c)	600
		(j)	4,700
		Bal.	5,300

	Accounts Receivable		
(c)	600	(d)	600
(j)	4,700		
Bal.	4,700		

	Rent Expense	
(f)	200	

	Land	
(b)	50,000	
(i)	10,000	
Bal.	60,000	

	Delivery Expense	
(h)	400	

	Accounts Payable		
(e)	50,000	(b)	50,000
		(h)	400
		Bal.	400

	Salaries Expense	
(g)	1,200	

	Capital Stock	
		(a) 70,000

Prepare trial balance

7. Assume that the ledger accounts given in Exercise 6 are those of the Conrad Company as they appear at December 31, 1990. Prepare the trial balance as of that date.

Prepare income statement and balance sheet

8. Prepare the income statement for 1990 and the balance sheet as of the end of 1990 assuming that the data given in Exercise 6 are for the Conrad Company.

Prepare journal entries

9. Prepare journal entries to record each of the following transactions for the Tom King Company. Use the letter of the transaction in place of the date. Include an explanation for each entry.

a. Capital stock was issued for cash, $100,000.

b. Purchased delivery equipment on account, $70,000.

c. Earned (but did not yet receive) delivery fee revenue, $3,000.

d. Collected the account receivable for the delivery fee, $3,000.

e. Paid the account payable for the delivery equipment purchased, $70,000.

    f. Paid utilities for the month in the amount of $1,000.

    g. Paid salaries for the month in the amount of $4,500.

    h. Incurred delivery expenses in the amount of $800, but did not yet pay for them.

    i. Purchased more delivery equipment for cash, $25,000.

    j. Performed delivery services for a large retail store on account, $10,000.

Record transactions in T-accounts

10. Using the data in Exercise 9 record the transactions in T-accounts. Write the letter of the transaction in the T-account before the dollar amount. Determine a balance for each account.

Prepare trial balance

11. Using your answer for Exercise 10, prepare a trial balance. Assume the date of the trial balance is March 31, 1990.

Give journal entries

12. Give the entry (without dollar amounts) of a transaction that would involve the following combinations of types of accounts:

    a. An asset and a liability.

    b. An expense and an asset.

    c. A liability and an expense.

    d. Stockholders' equity and an asset.

    e. Two asset accounts.

    f. An asset and a revenue.

Determine trial balance errors

13. Ray Braxton owns and manages a bowling center called Tri-Angle Lanes. He also maintains his own accounting records and was about to prepare financial statements for the year 1990. When he prepared the trial balance from the ledger accounts, the total of the debits column was $990,200 and the total of the credits column was $985,200. What are the possible reasons why the totals of the debits and credits are out of balance? How would you proceed to find the error?

PROBLEMS

Record transactions in T-accounts and prepare trial balance

2–1. The Cole Company had the following transactions in August 1990:

Transactions:

Aug. 1   Issued capital stock for cash, $25,000.
       3   Borrowed $10,000 from the bank on a note.
       4   Purchased a truck for $9,500 cash.
       6   Performed services for a customer who promised to pay later, $5,000.
       7   Paid employee wages, $2,000.
     10   Partial collection was made for the services performed on August 6, $1,250.
     14   Supplies were purchased for use this month, $1,000. They will be paid for next month.
     17   A bill for $250 was received for gas and oil used to date.
     25   Services were performed for a customer who paid immediately, $8,000.
     31   Paid employee wages, $3,000.
     31   Paid dividend, $1,000.

Required:

a. Open T-accounts for the Cole Company and enter therein transactions given. Place the date of each transaction in the account.

b. Prepare a trial balance as of August 31, 1990.

Record transactions in T-accounts and prepare trial balance

2–2. The Robin Company had the following transactions for July 1990.

Transactions:

July 2 Cash of $10,000 was received for capital stock issued to the owners.
3 The company paid rent for July, $500.
5 Office furniture was purchased for $6,000 cash.
9 A bill for $1,000 for advertising for July was received and paid.
14 Cash of $1,400 was received for services to a customer.
15 Wages of $400 for the first half of July were paid in cash.
20 The company sold services on account to a customer, $800. The account is to be paid August 10.
22 Office furniture was acquired on account from the Mason Company; the price was $800.
30 Cash of $4,500 was received for services to a customer.
31 Wages of $400 for the second half of July were paid in cash.

Required:

a. Open proper T-accounts for the Robin Company and enter therein the transactions given. Place the date of each transaction in the accounts.

b. Prepare a trial balance as of July 31, 1990.

Prepare journal entries

2–3. Presented below are the transactions of the Tate Company (partially summarized for the sake of brevity) for the month of March 1990.

Transactions:

a. The company was organized and issued capital stock for cash of $150,000.
b. Paid $3,500 as the rent for March on a completely furnished building.
c. Paid cash for delivery trucks, $60,000.
d. Paid $2,000 as the rent for March on two forklift trucks.
e. Paid $900 for supplies received and used in March.
f. Performed delivery services for a customer who promised to pay $32,000 at a later date.
g. Collected cash of $28,000 from a customer on account (see [f] above).
h. Received a bill for $750 in advertising in the local newspaper in March.
i. Paid cash for gas and oil consumed in March, $174.
j. Paid $3,100 to employees for services provided in March.
k. Received an order for services at $30,000. The services will be performed in April.
l. Paid cash dividend, $4,500.

Required:

Prepare the general journal entries that would be required to record the above transactions in the records of the Tate Company.

Prepare an income statement, statement of retained earnings, and balance sheet

2–4. The trial balance prepared as of the end of the Guyson Company's calendar-year accounting period is as follows:

GUYSON COMPANY
Trial Balance
December 31, 1990

	Debits	Credits
Cash	$ 16,000	
Accounts receivable	50,000	
Land	146,000	
Accounts payable		$ 36,000
Notes payable		40,000
Capital stock		52,000
Retained earnings, January 1, 1990		31,600
Service revenue		132,000
Rent expense	4,800	
Supplies expense	2,800	
Advertising expense	4,000	
Salaries expense	68,000	
	$291,600	$291,600

Required:

a. Prepare an income statement for the year ended December 31, 1990.

b. Prepare the statement of retained earnings for the year ended December 31, 1990.

c. Prepare the balance sheet as of December 31, 1990.

Prepare ledger accounts, journalize transactions, post to ledger accounts, and prepare trial balance

2–5. Remco, Inc., was organized July 1, 1990. The following account numbers and titles constitute the chart of accounts for the company:

Account No.	Account Title
101	Cash
102	Accounts Receivable
111	Office Equipment
112	Cleaning Equipment
113	Service Truck
221	Accounts Payable
222	Notes Payable
331	Capital Stock
332	Retained Earnings
333	Dividends
441	Cleaning Service Revenue
551	Salaries Expense
552	Insurance Expense
553	Service Truck Expense
554	Rent Expense
555	Utilities Expense
556	Cleaning Supplies Expense

Transactions for July are:

Transactions:

July 1 The company issued $130,000 of capital stock for cash.
5 Office space was rented for July, and $2,500 cash was paid for the rental.
8 Desks and chairs were purchased for the office on account, $15,000.
10 Cleaning equipment was purchased for $16,800; a note was given, to be paid in 30 days.

15 Purchased a service truck for $60,000, paying $40,000 cash and giving a 60-day note to the dealer for $20,000.
18 Paid for cleaning supplies received and already used, $1,200.
23 Received $7,500 cash from a customer as cleaning service revenue.
27 Insurance expense for July was paid, $1,800 cash.
30 Paid for gasoline and oil used by the service truck in July, $270.
31 Billed a customer for cleaning services rendered, $17,000.
31 Paid salaries for July, $21,800.
31 Paid utilities bills for July, $2,400.
31 Paid cash dividend, $5,000.

Required:

a. Prepare ledger accounts for all of the above accounts except Retained Earnings.

b. Journalize the transactions given for July 1990.

c. Post the journal entries to the ledger accounts.

d. Prepare a trial balance as of July 31, 1990.

Prepare journal entries, post to ledger accounts, prepare trial balance, income statement, statement of retained earnings, and balance sheet

2–6. Moss Company is a lawn care company. Thus, it earns its revenue from sending its trucks to customers' residences and certain commercial establishments to care for lawns and shrubbery. Moss Company's trial balance at the end of the first 11 months of the year is presented below.

MOSS COMPANY
Trial Balance
November 30, 1990

Account No.	Account Title	Debits	Credits
1	Cash	$ 98,320	
2	Accounts receivable	104,800	
11	Office equipment	11,200	
12	Trucks	137,200	
21	Accounts payable		$ 44,800
31	Capital stock		40,000
32	Retained earnings, January 1, 1990		40,720
40	Lawn care revenue		360,000
41	Shrubbery care revenue		134,680
51	Salaries expense	87,800	
52	Chemical supplies expense	99,200	
53	Advertising expense	24,400	
54	Truck operating expense	29,200	
55	Rent expense	20,000	
56	Office supplies expense	1,600	
57	Telephone and utilities expense	3,080	
58	Customer entertainment expense	3,400	
		$620,200	$620,200

Transactions for December are:

Transactions:

Dec. 2 Paid rent for December, $4,000.
5 Paid an account payable of $44,800.
8 Paid advertising for the month of December, $1,600.
10 Purchased a new office desk on account, $1,400.
13 Purchased $320 of office supplies for December use on account.
15 Collected cash from a customer on account, $94,400.
20 Paid for customer entertainment, $100.
24 Collected $8,000 from a customer on account.

26 Paid for gasoline used in the trucks in December, $360.
28 Billed a commercial customer for services; lawn care, $63,000, and shrubbery care, $43,000.
30 Paid for December chemical supplies, $26,400.
31 Paid December salaries, $20,400.
31 Paid a $4,000 dividend. (The Dividends account is #33.)

Required:

a. Open three-column ledger accounts for each of the accounts in the trial balance under the date of December 1, 1990. Place the word *Balance* in the explanation space of each account.

b. Prepare general journal entries for the transactions given above for December 1990.

c. Post the journal entries to the general ledger accounts.

d. Prepare a trial balance as of December 31, 1990.

e. Prepare an income statement for the year ended December 31, 1990.

f. Prepare a statement of retained earnings for the year ended December 31, 1990.

g. Prepare the balance sheet as of December 31, 1990.

Prepare a written appraisal and an approximate income statement

2–7. A friend of yours, Frank Lane, is quite excited over the opportunity he has to purchase the land and several miscellaneous assets of the Farley Bowling Lanes Company for $250,000. Frank tells you that Mr. and Mrs. Farley (the sole stockholders in the company) are moving due to Mr. Farley's ill health. The annual rent on the building and equipment is $36,000.

Mr. Farley reports that the business earned a profit of $50,000 in 1990 (last year). Frank believes that an annual profit of $50,000 on an investment of $250,000 is a really good deal. But before completing the deal, he asks you to look it over. You agree and discover the following:

1. Mr. Farley has computed his annual profit for 1990 as the sum of his cash dividends plus the increase in the Cash account: dividends of $30,000 + increase in Cash account of $20,000 = $50,000 profit.

2. As buyer of the business, Frank will take over responsibility for repayment of a $200,000 loan (plus interest) on the land. The land was acquired at a cost of $416,000 seven years ago.

3. An analysis of the Cash account shows the following for 1990:

Rental revenues received		$280,000
Cash paid out in 1990 for:		
Wages paid to employees in 1990	$160,000	
Utilities paid for 1990	12,000	
Advertising expenses paid	10,000	
Supplies purchased and used in 1990	16,000	
Interest paid on loan	12,000	
Loan principal paid	20,000	
Cash dividends	30,000	260,000
Increase in cash balance for the year		$ 20,000

4. You also find that the annual rent of $36,000 and a December utility bill of $2,000 and an advertising bill of $3,000 have not been paid.

Required:

a. Prepare a written report for Frank giving your appraisal of the offer to sell the Farley Bowling Lanes Company. Comment on Mr. Farley's method of computing the annual "profit" of the business.

b. Include in your report an approximate income statement for 1990.

BUSINESS DECISION PROBLEM 2–1

Prepare journal entries, post to T-accounts, and judge profitability

Steve Gunnells lost his job as a carpenter with a contractor when a recession hit the construction industry. Steve had been making $50,000 per year. He decided to form his own company, a small corporation, and do home repairs.

The following is a summary of the transactions of the business during the first three months of operations in 1990:

Transactions:

Jan. 15 Stockholders invested $20,000 in the business.
Feb. 25 Received payment of $4,400 for remodeling a basement into a recreation room. The homeowner purchased all of the building materials.
Mar. 5 Paid cash for an advertisement that appeared in the local newspaper, $110.
Apr. 10 Received $6,400 for converting a room over a garage into an office for a college professor. The professor purchased all of the materials for the job.
11 Paid gas and oil expenses for automobile, $700.
12 Miscellaneous business expenses were paid, $450.
15 Paid dividends of $4,000.

Required:

a. Prepare journal entries for the above transactions.

b. Post the journal entries to T-accounts.

c. Prepare an income statement to determine how Steve is doing in this new venture. Should he stay in this business?

3

ADJUSTING ENTRIES AND COMPLETION OF THE ACCOUNTING CYCLE

After studying this chapter, you should be able to:

1. Identify why adjusting entries must be made.
2. Describe the basic characteristics of the cash basis and the accrual basis of accounting.
3. Identify the classes and types of adjusting entries.
4. Prepare adjusting entries.
5. Prepare closing entries.
6. Prepare a classified balance sheet.
7. Prepare a work sheet for a service company (Appendix 3-A).
8. Define and use correctly the new terms in the glossary.

Chapters 1 and 2 introduced the accounting process (or cycle) of analyzing, classifying, and summarizing business transactions into accounts. You learned how these transactions are entered into journals and ledgers. The trial balance was shown as a way to test the equality of debits and credits in the journalizing and posting process. The purpose of the entire accounting process is to produce accurate financial statements. At this point in your study of accounting, you are concentrating on two financial statements—the balance sheet and the income statement.

As you learned in Chapter 1 when you first began to analyze business transactions, the evidence of the transaction is usually a source document.

A source document is any written or printed evidence of a business transaction that describes the essential facts of that transaction, for example, receipts for cash paid or received, checks written or received, bills sent to customers, or bills received from suppliers, and so on. You should be familiar with some or all of these source documents by now. The journal entries made in Chapter 2 were triggered by the giving, receiving, or creating of a source document. Source documents are used to prepare journal entries during an accounting period.

The journal entries we will discuss in this chapter are called adjusting entries. Adjusting entries are triggered by the arrival of the end of the accounting period rather than the giving, receiving, or creating of a source document; their purpose is to bring the accounts to their proper balances before financial statements are prepared. In this chapter, you will learn about the classes and types of adjusting entries and how to record them.

THE NEED FOR ADJUSTING ENTRIES

Objective 1: Identify why adjusting entries must be made

The income statement of an entity for a certain period should report all of the entity's revenues for the period and all of the expenses incurred to generate those revenues. If it does not, it is incomplete, inaccurate, and may be misleading to users. Similarly, a balance sheet that does not report all of an entity's assets, liabilities, and stockholders' equities at the end of a period may also be misleading.

Adjusting entries are journal entries made to bring the accounts to their proper balances before financial statements are prepared. That is, adjusting entries are needed to convert the amounts that are actually in the accounts to the amounts that should be in the accounts for proper financial reporting. Accountants make this conversion by analyzing the accounts and determining which ones need adjustment. For example, assume a three-year insurance policy costing $600 was purchased at the beginning of the year and debited to Prepaid Insurance. At year-end it is obvious that $200 of the cost should be removed from the asset and recorded as an expense. Failure to do so misstates assets and net income on the financial statements.

Events such as the using up of insurance coverage that has been prepaid are known as *continuous events*. Most adjusting entries are the result of continuous events. The need for adjusting entries is based on the matching principle. The **matching principle** requires that expenses incurred in producing revenues be deducted from the revenues they generated during the accounting period. This matching of expenses and revenues is necessary for the income statement to present an accurate picture of the profitability of a business.

Objective 2: Describe the basic characteristics of the cash basis and the accrual basis of accounting

Some relatively small business firms, such as those engaged in rendering services, may account for their revenues and expenses on a cash basis. The **cash basis of accounting** means that, in most instances, expenses and revenues are not recorded until cash is paid out or received. Thus, for example, services rendered to clients in 1989 for which cash was collected in 1990 would be treated as 1990 revenues. Similarly, expenses incurred in 1989 that were paid for in 1990 would be treated as 1990 expenses. Because of potential mismatching of revenues and expenses, the cash basis of accounting is generally considered deficient. It is acceptable only in those circumstances where its results approximate those obtained under the accrual basis of accounting.

The **accrual basis of accounting** recognizes revenues when sales are made or services are rendered, whether or not cash has been received. Expenses are recognized as incurred, whether or not cash has been paid out. The accrual basis is more generally accepted than the cash basis because the accrual basis provides a better measure of an entity's income due to proper *matching* of revenues and expenses.

Since interested parties seek timely information, periodic financial statements must be prepared. In order to prepare such statements, the accountant must arbitrarily divide an entity's life into time periods and attempt to assign economic activity to specific periods. An **accounting period** may be one month, one quarter, or one year long. An accounting period of one year is called an **accounting year** or fiscal year. A **fiscal year** is any 12 consecutive months; it may or may not coincide with the **calendar year,** ending on December 31. Periodic reporting necessitates the preparation of adjusting entries.

Adjusting entries record economic activity that has taken place, but which has not yet been recorded. Some economic activity may be continuous in nature, such as the use of supplies during a month. It is not feasible to make an entry each time a pencil or pen is taken from a supply cabinet for use. The use of one pencil is hardly a recordable event. However, by the end of the month, many supplies have been used and it is then feasible to record their usage. Adjusting entries update certain account balances to record such continuous, previously unrecorded activities. Many adjusting entries are based in part upon estimates of future events. Estimation is necessary in order to provide timely information to users of financial statements.

Adjusting entries must be prepared whenever financial statements are to be prepared. Thus, if monthly financial statements are prepared, monthly adjusting entries are required. By custom, and in some instances by law, business firms report to their stockholders at least annually. Thus, adjusting entries will be required to be made at least once each year.

CLASSES OF ADJUSTING ENTRIES

Objective 3: Identify the classes and types of adjusting entries

Adjusting entries can be grouped into two broad classes. One class, **deferred items,** consists of those entries that relate to data previously recorded in the accounts. Adjusting entries in this class normally involve moving data from asset and liability accounts to expense and revenue accounts. (Sometimes the direction is reversed.) The two types of adjustments within this deferred items class are asset/expense adjustments and liability/revenue adjustments.

The other major class of adjusting entries, **accrued items,** consists of entries relating to activities on which no data have been previously recorded in the accounts. These entries involve the initial recording of assets and liabilities and the related revenues and expenses. The two types of adjustments within this accrued items class are asset/revenue adjustments and liability/expense adjustments. Illustration 3.1 shows the two major classes—deferred items and accrued items—and the four types of adjusting entries.

Illustration 3.1
CLASSES OF ADJUSTING ENTRIES

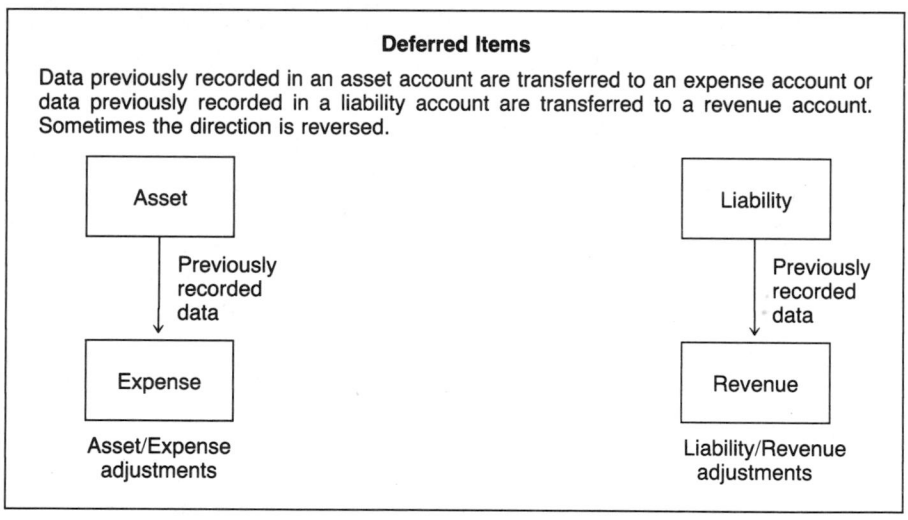

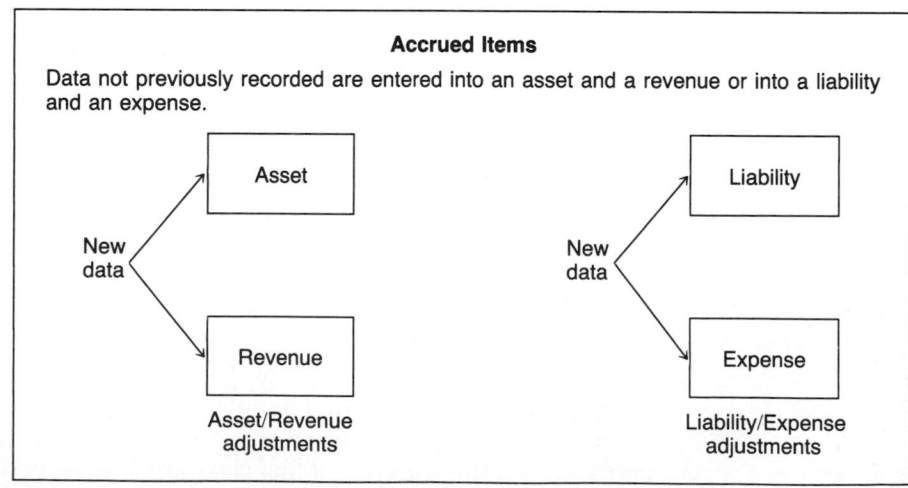

ADJUSTMENTS FOR DEFERRED ITEMS

The two types of adjustments within the deferred items class are prepaid expenses and unearned revenues. Prepaid expense (asset/expense) adjustments are discussed first.

Asset/Expense Adjustments—Prepaid Expenses and Depreciation

A **prepaid expense** is an asset awaiting assignment to expense. An adjusting entry for a prepaid expense involves recognition of the complete or partial expiration of the ability of such an asset to render future services because it has been used in generating current revenues. This makes the asset less valuable to its owners. Because of its relative importance, several examples of this type of adjusting entry are presented below.

Objective 4: Prepare adjusting entries

Prepaid insurance. When the premium on an insurance policy is paid in advance of the period covered by the policy, an asset is created. With the passage of time, the value of this asset expires and part of its cost becomes an expense. To illustrate, advance payment of the $7,200 premium on a one-year insurance policy that covers the period from August 1, 1990, to July 31, 1991, creates an asset called prepaid (or unexpired) insurance. An asset exists because benefits—insurance protection—will be received in the future. *The future services that an asset can render are what make the asset "a thing of value" to a business.* The journal entry to record this transaction is:

```
1990
Aug. 1  Prepaid Insurance . . . . . . . . . . . . . . . . . . . .    7,200
            Cash   . . . . . . . . . . . . . . . . . . . . . . . .          7,200
        To record payment in advance of annual insurance
        premium.
```

There are two accounts that relate to insurance, Prepaid Insurance (an asset) and Insurance Expense. After posting this entry, the Prepaid Insurance account has a $7,200 debit balance and the Insurance Expense account has a zero balance:

(Dr.)	Prepaid Insurance	(Cr.)	(Dr.)	Insurance Expense	(Cr.)
1990 Aug. 1 7,200			Bal. –0–		

If the company making this insurance payment has a calendar-year accounting period and records adjusting entries only at the end of the year, by December 31 a part of the period covered by the insurance policy has expired. Therefore, a part of the **service potential** (or benefits embodied in the asset) also has expired. The asset now provides less future benefits than when acquired, and this reduction of the asset's ability to provide services must be recognized. The cost of the services used up is treated as an expense. Since the policy provides the same services for every month

---

of its one-year life, it seems logical to assign an equal amount of the initial cost to each month. Thus, with 5 of the 12 months of coverage provided by payment of the premium having elapsed, 5/12 of the annual premium is charged to expense on December 31. The journal entry and the accounts after posting appear as follows:

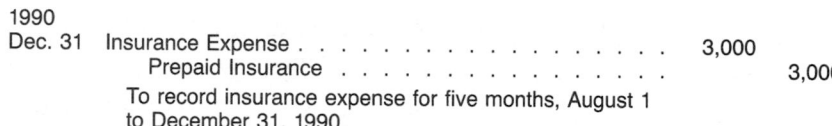

1990			
Dec. 31	Insurance Expense	3,000	
	Prepaid Insurance		3,000
	To record insurance expense for five months, August 1 to December 31, 1990.		

Adjustment 1—Insurance

In T-account format, the accounts would appear as follows after posting the two entries:

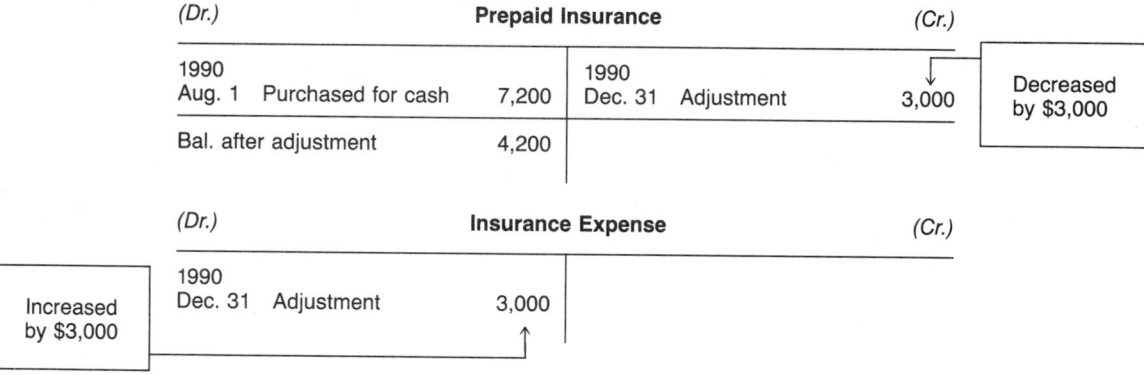

Decreased by $3,000

Increased by $3,000

The three-column ledger accounts after posting the two entries above appear as follows:

Prepaid Insurance — Account No. 103

Date	Explanation	Post. Ref.	Debit	Credit	Balance
1990					
Aug. 1	Purchased on Account	G63*	7 2 0 0		7 2 0 0 Dr.
Dec. 31	Adjustment	G75*		3 0 0 0	4 2 0 0 Dr.

Insurance Expense — Account No. 504

Date	Explanation	Post. Ref.	Debit	Credit	Balance
1990					
Dec. 31	Adjustment	G75*	3 0 0 0		3 0 0 0 Dr.

* Note: These posting references are assumed.

Before the adjusting entry was made, the entire $7,200 was a prepaid expense (an asset). The adjusting entry transferred $3,000 of the $7,200 to insurance expense. The insurance expense of $3,000 is reported in the income statement for the year ended December 31, 1990, as one of the expenses incurred in generating that year's revenues. The remaining amount of the prepaid expense, $4,200, is reported on the balance sheet as an asset. The $4,200 prepaid expense is a measure of the cost of the remaining asset, prepaid insurance. Prepaid insurance is an asset because it provides future benefits; in this case, there is insurance coverage for 7 more months.

In initially recording the purchase of the $7,200 of insurance, the accountant could have followed an alternative procedure. The debit could have been to Insurance Expense rather than Prepaid Insurance, as shown below. If this were the case, the adjusting entry would have been a debit to Prepaid Insurance (setting up the asset on the books) and a credit to Insurance Expense for $4,200 (reducing the period's expense). This would have resulted in a balance of $4,200 in the asset account and $3,000 in the expense account as shown in the T-accounts below. Thus, the end result is the same either way, and either method is correct. The adjusting entry, however, will depend on which account was originally debited for the prepayment. This same comment applies to many of the other adjustments that are illustrated in this chapter.

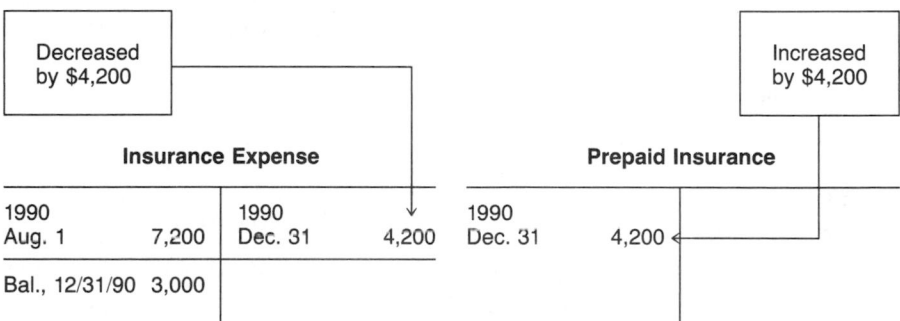

Prepaid rent. Prepaid rent is another example of the continuous incurrence of an expense that results from using up a previously recorded asset. When rent is paid in advance for any substantial period of time, the prepayment is debited to the Prepaid Rent account (an asset) at the date it is paid. Because the benefits resulting from the expenditure are yet to be received, the expenditure creates an asset. Services from the facilities being rented are received *continuously* through time. The expense is incurred *continuously* as time elapses. An entry could be made frequently, even daily, to record the expense incurred. But typically the entry is not made until financial statements are to be prepared. At that time, an entry is made transferring the cost of that portion of the asset that has expired from the asset account to an expense account.

The measurement of rent expense usually presents no problems. Generally, the rental contract specifies the amount of rent per unit of time.

If the contract states an annual rental, 1/12 of this annual rental is charged to expense each month. This may be the case even though there are varying numbers of days in some months. Normally, the variations are not considered significant enough to be taken into consideration.

To illustrate, assume that rent was paid in advance in the amount of $12,000 on September 1, 1990, for one year beginning on that date. The entry made at that time was:

```
1990
Sept. 1   Prepaid Rent . . . . . . . . . . . . . . . . . . . . . .    12,000
               Cash   . . . . . . . . . . . . . . . . . . . . . .             12,000
          To record advance payment of one year's rent.
```

The two accounts relating to rent are Prepaid Rent and Rent Expense. After this entry has been posted, the Prepaid Rent account has a $12,000 balance and the Rent Expense account has a zero balance:

(Dr.)	**Prepaid Rent**	*(Cr.)*	*(Dr.)*	**Rent Expense**	*(Cr.)*
1990 Sept. 1 12,000			Bal. –0–		

Assuming the company has a calendar-year accounting period ending December 31, 1990, an adjusting entry must be prepared. Since one third of the period covered by the prepaid rent (4 of 12 months) has elapsed, one third of the $12,000, or $4,000, of prepaid rent is charged to expense. The required adjusting entry and the accounts after posting appear as follows:

```
1990
Dec. 31   Rent Expense . . . . . . . . . . . . . . . . . . . . . .    4,000
               Prepaid Rent   . . . . . . . . . . . . . . . . . . .            4,000
          To record rent expense for four months.
```

The T-accounts would appear as follows after posting the adjusting entry:

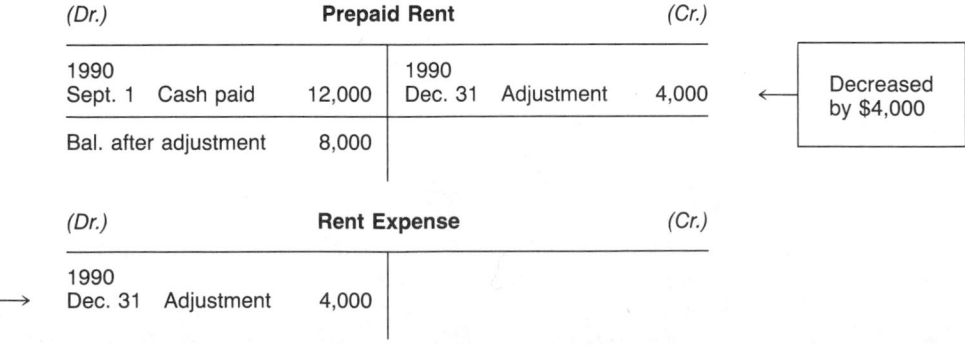

(Dr.)	**Prepaid Rent**		*(Cr.)*
1990 Sept. 1 Cash paid 12,000		1990 Dec. 31 Adjustment 4,000	
Bal. after adjustment 8,000			

Decreased by $4,000

(Dr.)	**Rent Expense**	*(Cr.)*
1990 Dec. 31 Adjustment 4,000		

Increased by $4,000

The $4,000 rent expense would appear in the income statement for the year ended December 31, 1990. The remaining $8,000 of prepaid rent is reported as an asset in the balance sheet for December 31, 1990.

Supplies on hand. Almost every business uses assets referred to as supplies in its operations. Supplies may be classified as office supplies (paper, stationery, carbon paper, pencils) or selling supplies (gummed tape, string, paper bags or cartons, wrapping paper) or, possibly, as cleaning supplies (soap, disinfectants). Supplies are frequently bought in bulk. The asset account may be called Supplies on Hand or Supplies Inventory.

To illustrate, assume that on December 4, 1990, a company purchased supplies for $1,400 and recorded the transaction as follows:

```
1990
Dec. 4   Supplies on Hand . . . . . . . . . . . . . . . . .   1,400
             Cash   . . . . . . . . . . . . . . . . . . . . .          1,400
         To record the purchase of supplies for future use.
```

After this entry has been posted, the Supplies on Hand account shows a debit balance of $1,400 and the Supplies Expense account has a zero balance as shown:

(Dr.)	Supplies on Hand	(Cr.)	(Dr.)	Supplies Expense	(Cr.)
1990 Dec. 4 1,400			Bal. –0–		

An actual physical inventory (a count of the supplies on hand) at the end of the month showed that only $900 of supplies were on hand. Thus, $500 of supplies must have been used in December. An adjusting journal entry is required to bring the accounts to their proper balances. The entry recognizes the reduction in the asset and the incurrence of an expense through the using up of supplies. From the information given, the asset balance should be $900 and the expense incurred, $500. By making the following adjusting entry, the accounts will be adjusted to those balances:

Adjustment 3— Supplies

```
1990
Dec. 31   Supplies Expense  . . . . . . . . . . . . . . . . .   500
              Supplies on Hand  . . . . . . . . . . . . . . .          500
          To record supplies used during December.
```

The T-accounts after posting the entry would appear as follows:

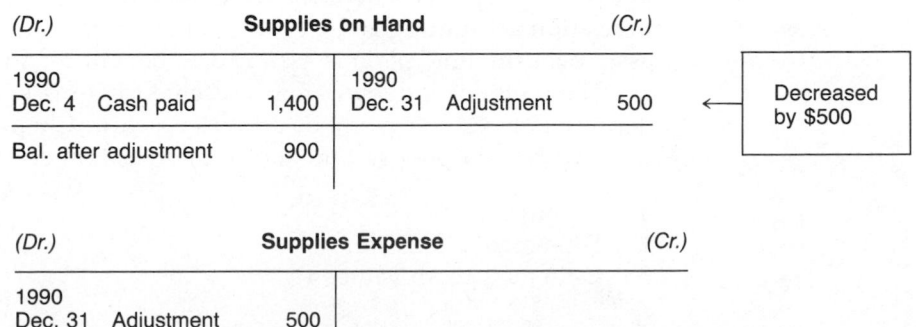

Increased by $500

While the entry to record the usage of supplies could be made when the supplies are issued from the storeroom, it is usually not worth the cost to account so carefully for such small items each time they are issued.

Supplies expense will appear in the income statement. Supplies on hand will be reported as an asset in the balance sheet.

Sometimes prepaid expenses such as insurance, rent, supplies, and advertising are bought and fully used up within one accounting period (usually one month or one year). If so, it is easier to debit an expense rather than an asset at the time of purchase. This procedure avoids having to make an adjusting entry at the end of the accounting period.

Depreciation. Depreciation is another example of the continuous incurrence of an expense that results from the gradual using up of a previously recorded asset. Assets such as buildings, machinery, and equipment will not continue to provide benefits or services indefinitely. Wear and tear resulting from their use will eventually cause them to be disposed of. The overall period of time involved in using up such assets is, however, less definite than in the case of an insurance premium or prepaid rent. The life of such assets (called **depreciable assets**) must be estimated in advance by the accountants or managers of a business.

In addition to estimating the life of a depreciable asset, the accountant must estimate the **scrap** (or salvage) **value** that the asset may have at the time of disposal in the future. For example, if you plan to dispose of your car three years after you purchase it, you can estimate the "trade-in" value that it will have at that time. Trade-in value is very similar to scrap value. The difference between the cost of an asset and its estimated scrap value is sometimes referred to as an asset's **depreciable cost.** This difference is the net cost of using the asset during its useful life. The **useful life** is the estimated number of periods that a company can make use of an asset.

Even though depreciable assets involve the use of estimates (for scrap value and life), the pattern of incurring an expense because of the expiration of service potential of an asset is basically the same as it was for a prepaid insurance premium. The cost of the asset less its scrap value is divided by the estimated number of years of life to find the amount of asset cost to be charged as an expense to each time period. **Depreciation expense** is the cost of a depreciable asset assigned to any time period. **Depreciation accounting** is the process of allocating the cost of a depreciable asset over the time periods assumed to benefit by that asset's usage.

The method of depreciation presented here is known as straight-line depreciation. (Other methods are discussed in Chapter 6.) The three factors involved in the computation of depreciation are:

1. Asset cost.
2. Estimated useful life.
3. Estimated scrap value.

The **depreciation formula** is as follows:

$$\text{Annual depreciation} = \frac{\text{Asset cost} - \text{Estimated scrap value}}{\text{Number of years of useful life}}$$

If a depreciable asset is used for less than a full annual period, only a fraction of the annual cost should be assigned to the expense account. In other words, if the asset has been used for only three months of a year, only 3/12 (or 1/4) of the annual amount should be recorded as an expense in that year.

Depreciation is sometimes expressed as an annual percentage rate determined by dividing the annual amount of depreciation by the cost of the asset. For instance, $1,000 ÷ $10,000 = 10 percent depreciation rate.

The accumulated depreciation account. The amount of an asset that expires in a period is not credited directly to the asset account itself but to an account called Accumulated Depreciation. The **Accumulated Depreciation account** is a type of contra account. A **contra account** is an account that is directly related to another account, but it carries the opposite type of balance. The accumulated depreciation account is a **contra asset account.** Since assets generally carry debit balances, a contra asset carries a credit balance.

Why is a contra asset account used to account for depreciation? Asset accounts such as prepaid insurance or rent may be credited directly when their values expire due to their short-term nature and the fact that it is known exactly what periods of time are benefited by them. Depreciable assets, on the other hand, require the use of estimates for both life and scrap value. Therefore, the recorded amounts of depreciation are really quite tentative. To provide more complete information on the balance sheet, depreciable asset accounts are shown at their original acquisition cost and the related accumulated depreciation is shown separately. The difference between the cost and the accumulated depreciation for any depreciable asset is called **book value,** or the cost not yet allocated as an expense. The balance in the accumulated depreciation account increases each year by the amount of depreciation recorded. Eventually, the accumulated depreciation account reaches the amount originally calculated as the depreciable cost of the asset (cost − estimated scrap value).

Depreciation accounting illustrated. To illustrate the accounting for depreciation, assume that at December 31, 1990, a company owns one delivery truck that cost $9,200. The truck was purchased on January 1, 1990. It is expected to have a useful life of five years; scrap value is estimated at $1,200. Therefore, the depreciation expense for one year equals ($9,200 − $1,200) ÷ 5, or $1,600. This amount of depreciation expense is allocated to 1990.

Depreciation for 1990 is recorded by the following entry:

Adjustment 4—
Depreciation
	1990
	Dec. 31 Depreciation Expense—Delivery Truck 1,600
	            Accumulated Depreciation—Delivery Truck 1,600
	       To record the depreciation expense for the year.

The T-accounts would appear as follows after posting the adjusting entry:

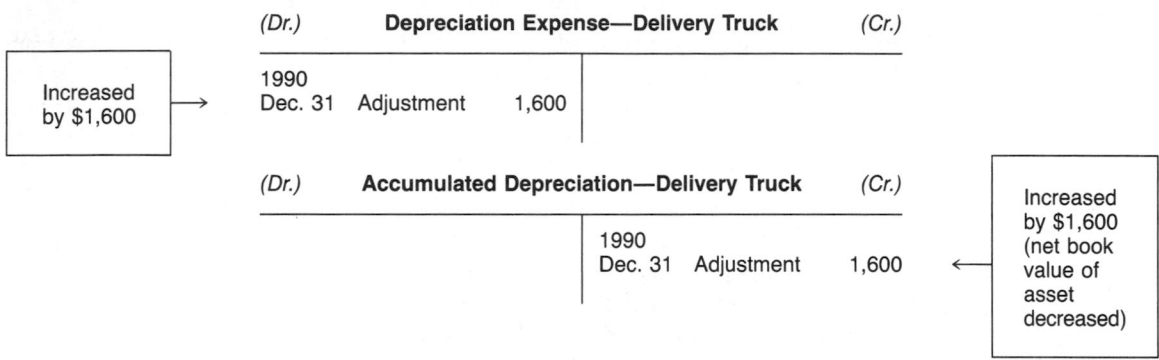

(Dr.)   **Depreciation Expense—Delivery Truck**   (Cr.)

Increased by $1,600	→

1990
Dec. 31   Adjustment   1,600

(Dr.)   **Accumulated Depreciation—Delivery Truck**   (Cr.)

1990
Dec. 31   Adjustment   1,600   ←   Increased by $1,600 (net book value of asset decreased)

The ledger accounts involving the delivery truck, after adjustment, will appear as follows:

Delivery Truck   *Account No. 130*

Date	Explanation	Post. Ref.	Debit	Credit	Balance
1990 Jan. 1	Purchased one truck	G8*	9 2 0 0		9 2 0 0 Dr.

Accumulated Depreciation—Delivery Truck   *Account No. 131*

Date	Explanation	Post. Ref.	Debit	Credit	Balance
1990 Dec. 31	Adjustment	G14*		1 6 0 0	1 6 0 0 Cr.

Depreciation Expense—Delivery Truck   *Account No. 418*

Date	Explanation	Post. Ref.	Debit	Credit	Balance
1990 Dec. 31	Adjustment	G14*	1 6 0 0		1 6 0 0 Dr.

*These posting references are assumed.

In the balance sheet at December 31, 1990, the asset accounts include the following:

Assets

Delivery truck	$9,200	
Less: Accumulated depreciation—delivery truck	1,600	$7,600

The portion of the cost of the asset not yet charged to expense at the end of the first year is $7,600. Since expected scrap value is $1,200, only $6,400 is expected to be charged to expense in future years. Since another $1,600 of depreciation would be recorded at the end of each of the next four years, the balance sheet at the end of the fifth year would show the following:

Assets

Delivery truck	$9,200	
Less: Accumulated depreciation—delivery truck	8,000	$1,200

Depreciation expense is reported in the income statement with all other expenses.

Liability/Revenue Adjustments—Unearned Revenues

The second type of adjusting entry under deferred items involves unearned revenues. An adjustment involving unearned revenues covers those situations where the customer has transferred assets, usually cash, to a company prior to the receipt of merchandise or services. When assets are received before being earned, a liability called **unearned revenue** is created. Such receipts are debited to Cash and credited to a liability account called Unearned Fees, Revenue Received in Advance, Advances by Customers, or some similar title. The seller is obligated either to provide the goods or services or return the customer's money. By providing the merchandise or performing the services, revenue is earned and the liability is canceled.

Advance payments are received for many items such as delivery services, tickets, rent, and magazine or newspaper subscriptions. While only advance receipt of delivery fees will be illustrated and discussed, the other items are treated similarly.

Unearned delivery fees. On December 7, a company received $4,500 from a customer in payment for future delivery services. The entry was recorded as follows:

1990			
Dec. 7	Cash	4,500	
	Unearned Delivery Fees		4,500
	To record the receipt of cash from a customer in payment for future delivery services.		

The two T-accounts relating to delivery fees are Unearned Delivery Fees (a liability) and Delivery Service Revenue. These accounts appear as follows after this entry has been posted.

(Dr.)	Unearned Delivery Fees	(Cr.)	(Dr.)	Delivery Service Revenue	(Cr.)
		1990 Dec. 7 4,500		Bal. —0—	

The liability established when the cash was received will be converted into revenue as the delivery services are performed. An adjusting entry is required in order to recognize the earning of revenue and the reduction of the related liability. Assuming that one third of the delivery services paid for in advance have been performed by the end of December, the required adjusting entry is:

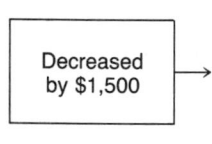

Adjustment 5—
Previously
unearned
revenue

```
1990
Dec. 31   Unearned Delivery Fees  . . . . . . . . . . . . . . . . .    1,500
                Delivery Service Revenue . . . . . . . . . . . . . .            1,500
            To transfer a portion of delivery fees from the liability
            account to the revenue account.
```

The T-accounts would appear as follows after the adjusting entry has been posted:

(Dr.)	Unearned Delivery Fees	(Cr.)

1990			1990		
Dec. 31	Adjustment	1,500	Dec. 7	Cash received	4,500
			Dec. 31	Bal. after adjustment	3,000

Decreased
by $1,500

(Dr.)	Delivery Service Revenue	(Cr.)

			1990		
			Dec. 31	Adjustment	1,500

Increased
by $1,500

Delivery service revenue is reported in the income statement for 1990. The $3,000 balance in the Unearned Delivery Fees account is reported as a liability in the balance sheet. In 1991, the $3,000 will be earned and transferred to a revenue account.

ADJUSTMENTS FOR ACCRUED ITEMS

The two types of adjustments within the accrued items class are accrued assets and accrued liabilities. Accrued assets are discussed first.

Asset/Revenue Adjustments—Accrued Assets

Accrued assets are those assets that exist at the end of an accounting period but have not yet been recorded. They represent rights to receive payments that are not legally due at the balance sheet date. At the end of an accounting period, any such rights must be recognized by preparing an adjusting entry. An example of this type of adjustment includes revenues earned that have not been billed or collected.

Interest revenue.   The interest received periodically on investments such as bonds and savings accounts is literally earned moment by moment.

Rarely is payment of the interest made on the last day of the accounting period. Thus, the accounting records normally will not show the amount of interest revenue earned nor the total assets owned by the investor unless an adjusting entry is made. An entry at the end of the accounting period is needed that debits a receivable account (an asset) and credits a revenue account to record the asset owned and the interest earned.

For example, assume that a company deposits some money in a savings account. The interest is received twice a year, on May 1 and November 1, in the amount of $1,800 on each date. Interest, then, is being earned at the rate of $300 per month ($1,800 ÷ 6). If the account was opened on May 2, 1990, Interest Revenue is credited with the $1,800 of cash received on November 1. At December 31, 1990, an additional two months' interest has been earned, although no money will be received until May 1, 1991. An entry must be made to show the amount of interest earned and the asset (the right to receive this interest) at December 31, 1990. The entry to record the accrual of interest revenue is:

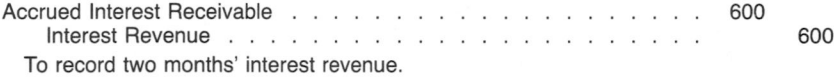

Accrued Interest Receivable	600	
Interest Revenue		600
To record two months' interest revenue.		

Adjustment 6—
Interest

The T-accounts relating to interest would appear as follows:

Accrued Interest Receivable

1990			
Dec. 31	Adjustment	600	

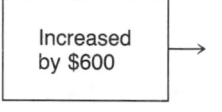

Increased
by $600

Interest Revenue

	1990		
	Nov. 1	Cash received	1,800
	Bal. before adjustment		1,800
	Dec. 31	Adjustment	600
	Bal. after adjustment		2,400

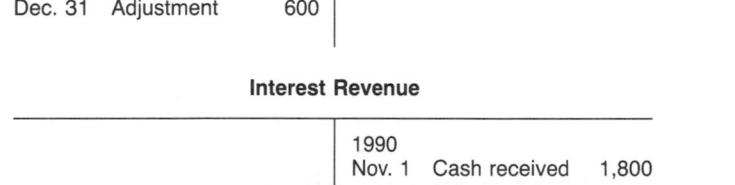

Increased
by $600

The $600 debit balance in Accrued Interest Receivable is reported as an asset in the December 31, 1990, balance sheet. The term **accrued** refers to a claim that comes into existence over time. The claim accumulates gradually with the passage of time. The $2,400 credit balance in Interest Revenue is the interest earned during the year. Recall that *under accrual basis accounting, it does not matter whether cash was collected during the year or not.* The interest revenue earned is reported in the income statement for the year.

Unbilled service fees. Services may be performed for customers in one accounting period while the billing for those services is in a different accounting period. Assume a company performed $1,000 of delivery services on account for clients in the last few days of December. Because it takes time to do the paper work, the clients will be billed for the services in January. The necessary adjusting entry at December 31, 1990, is:

Adjustment 7—
Unbilled
revenues

```
1990
Dec. 31   Accounts Receivable (or Accrued Fees Receivable) . . .   1,000
              Delivery Service Revenue . . . . . . . . . . . . .           1,000
          To record unbilled services performed in December.
```

After posting the adjusting entry the T-acounts will appear as follows:

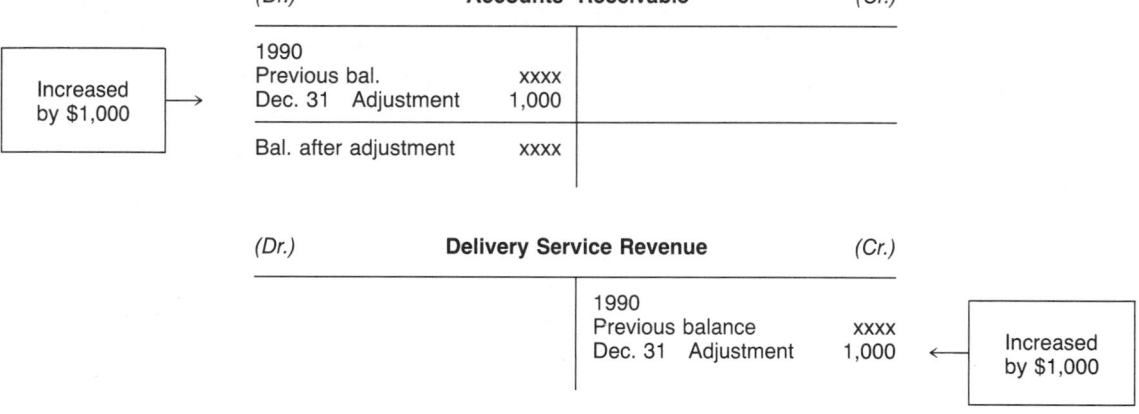

Increased
by $1,000

(Dr.)	Accounts Receivable		(Cr.)
1990			
Previous bal.	xxxx		
Dec. 31 Adjustment	1,000		
Bal. after adjustment	xxxx		

(Dr.)	Delivery Service Revenue		(Cr.)
		1990	
		Previous balance	xxxx
		Dec. 31 Adjustment	1,000

Increased
by $1,000

The delivery service revenue will appear in the income statement, and the accounts receivable will appear in the balance sheet.

Liability/Expense Adjustments—Accrued Liabilities

Accrued liabilities are those liabilities that exist at the end of an accounting period, but that have not yet been recorded. They represent obligations to make payments that are not legally due at the balance sheet date. At the end of an accounting period, any such obligations and the related expenses must be recognized in an adjusting entry. Accrued salaries, for example, are accrued liabilities that require adjustment.

Salaries. The recording of the payment of employee salaries (or wages) usually involves a debit to an expense account and a credit to cash. Unless salaries are paid on the last day of the accounting period for a pay period ending on that date, an adjusting entry will be required to record any salaries incurred but not yet paid.

Assume that a company paid $3,600 of salaries on Friday, December 28, 1990, to cover the first four weeks of December. The entry made at that time was:

```
1990
Dec. 28   Salaries Expense  . . . . . . . . . . . . . . . . . .      3,600
              Cash . . . . . . . . . . . . . . . . . . . . . . .            3,600
          Paid salaries for the first four weeks of December.
```

If salaries are $3,600 for four weeks, they are $900 per week. Assuming a five-day workweek, daily salaries are $180. Since the last day of December 1990 is a Monday, the expense account does not show salaries earned by employees for the last day of the month. Nor does the account show the employer's obligation to pay these salaries. The accounts pertaining to salaries appear as follows before adjustment:

(Dr.)	Salaries Expense	(Cr.)	(Dr.)	Salaries Payable	(Cr.)
1990 Dec. 28 3,600				Bal. –0–	

The following adjusting entry is needed on December 31:

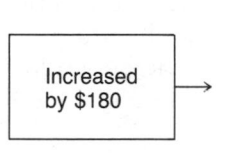

Adjustment 8—
Accrued
salaries

```
1990
Dec. 31   Salaries Expense  . . . . . . . . . . . . . . . . . . . . . . . .    180
              Salaries Payable . . . . . . . . . . . . . . . . . . . . . . .          180
          To accrue one day's salaries that were earned but are unpaid.
```

The two accounts involved appear as follows after adjustment:

(Dr.)	Salaries Expense	(Cr.)
1990 Dec. 28	3,600	
Dec. 31 Adjustment	180	
Bal. after adjustment	3,780	

Increased
by $180 →

(Dr.)	Salaries Payable	(Cr.)
	1990 Dec. 31 Adjustment	360

← Increased
by $180

The debit in the adjusting journal entry brings the month's salaries expense up to its correct $3,780 amount for income statement purposes. The credit records the $180 salary liability to employees. The salaries payable is shown as a liability in the balance sheet.

Failure to prepare proper adjusting entries causes net income to be in error. The following diagram shows the effect on net income of failing to record each of the major types of adjusting entries:

Failure to Recognize	Effect on Net Income	Effect on Balance Sheet Items
1. Consumption of the benefits of an asset (prepaid expense)	Overstates	Overstates assets Overstates retained earnings
2. Earning of previously unearned revenues	Understates	Overstates liabilities Understates retained earnings
3. Accrual of assets	Understates	Understates assets Understates retained earnings
4. Accrual of liabilities	Overstates	Understates liabilities Overstates retained earnings

This chapter has discussed and illustrated many, but not all, of the typical adjusting entries that companies must make at the end of an accounting period. Other types of adjusting entries are covered in later chapters.

CLOSING ENTRIES

Objective 5: Prepare closing entries

One step remains in our illustration of the financial accounting process—a step known as "closing the books." As illustrated, after adjusting entries have been prepared and posted, the accounts contain basically two types of information: (1) information relating to the activities for the period just ended (reported in the income statement) and (2) information on financial condition (reported in the balance sheet).

The first type of information is found in the expense and revenue accounts. As already indicated, these accounts are temporary subdivisions of the Retained Earnings account. They help the accountant fulfill a most important task—the determination of periodic net income. But after the financial statements for the period have been prepared, these temporary accounts have served their purpose. They must now be brought to a zero balance, or be "closed," to use accounting jargon. In this way, information pertaining to the next period can be gathered in them.

The balance in each expense and revenue account is transferred to an account called **Income Summary.** This is a *clearing* account used only at the end of the accounting period. It summarizes the expenses and revenues for the period, with the difference between these two being either net income or a net loss. Since revenue accounts have credit balances, they are debited and Income Summary credited. Conversely, expense accounts have debit balances, so they are credited and Income Summary debited.

The Income Summary now contains either a debit (net loss) or a credit (net income) balance; it is then debited or credited to bring it to a zero balance. Retained Earnings is credited or debited to keep the entry in balance. With the making of this last entry, the books are closed. Note carefully that only expense and revenue accounts and the Income Summary account are closed. If dividends are recorded by debiting Retained Earnings and crediting Cash, no closing entry for that item is required. But, if dividends are recorded by debiting a separate Dividends account and crediting Cash, the Dividends account must be credited and Retained Earnings debited as part of the closing process.

The closing process, using T-accounts and assuming there is net income for the period, is as shown below.

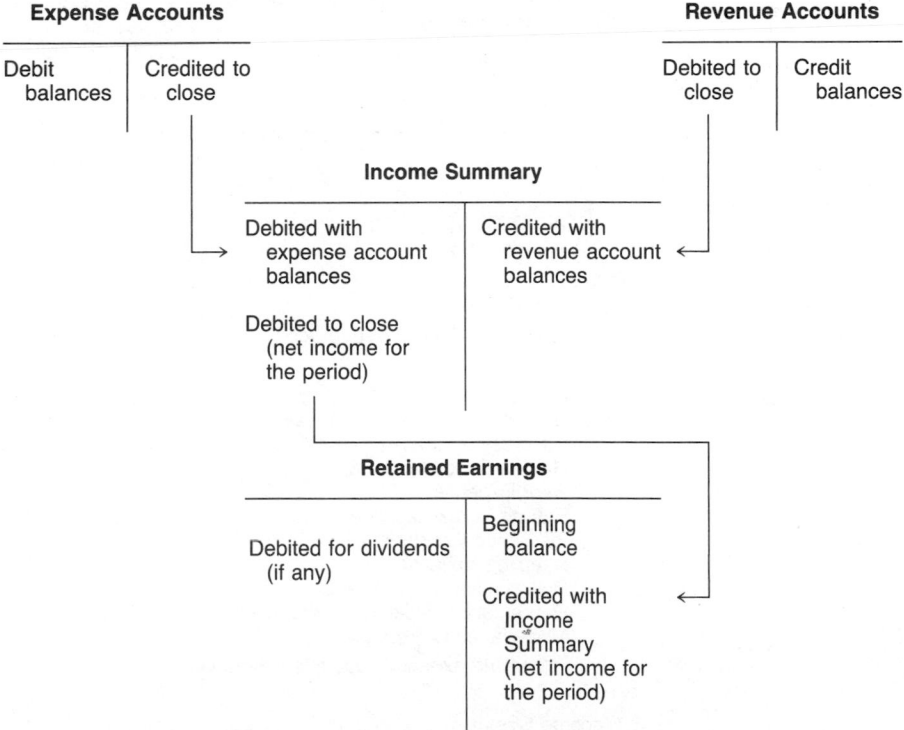

The **closing process** is (1) the act of transferring the balances in the revenue and expense accounts to a clearing account called Income Summary and then to Retained Earnings, and (2) the act of transferring the balance in the Dividends account (if it is used) to the Retained Earnings account. The closing process reduces revenue, expense, and Dividends account balances to zero so they will be ready to receive data for the next accounting period. Assume the income statement shown in Illustration 3.2 is for a company called Jane's, Inc. The accounts to be closed are all of the expense and revenue accounts shown in the income statement.

Illustration 3.2

JANE'S, INC.
Income Statement
For the Year Ended December 31, 1990

Sales		$145,000
Expenses:		
Salaries	$75,000	
Advertising	5,000	
Utilities	8,000	
Rent	12,000	
Payroll taxes	6,000	
Insurance	2,000	
Supplies	9,000	
Depreciation expense—Equipment	4,000	
Depreciation expense—Fixtures	2,000	
Miscellaneous	1,000	
Total expenses		124,000
Net income		$ 21,000

In journal form, the closing entries for Jane's, Inc. would read:

Sales	145,000	
Income Summary		145,000
To close the Sales revenue account.		

Income Summary	124,000	
Salaries Expense		75,000
Advertising Expense		5,000
Utilities Expense		8,000
Rent Expense.		12,000
Payroll Taxes Expense		6,000
Insurance Expense		2,000
Supplies Expense		9,000
Depreciation Expense—Equipment		4,000
Depreciation Expense—Fixtures.		2,000
Miscellaneous Expense		1,000
To close the expense accounts for the year.		

Income Summary	21,000	
Retained Earnings		21,000
To close net income for the year to Retained Earnings.		

When the entries are posted, each of the company's expense and revenue accounts will be reduced to a zero balance. Thus, they are ready to accumulate data on the operations for the year 1991. Note that Retained Earnings will have the same balance that it would have if all expenses and revenues had been entered directly in it. But the use of expense and revenue accounts permits classification of these elements and makes them readily available for reporting in the income statement.

The Use of a Work Sheet

The appendix to this chapter describes and illustrates how a work sheet could have been used in the above example involving Jane's, Inc. The use of such a work sheet is optional but often helpful.

The Financial Accounting Process Summarized

The steps involved in the operation of an accounting system are often referred to collectively as the accounting cycle. These steps include:

1. Journalizing transactions (and other events) in the journal.
2. Posting journal entries to ledger accounts.
3. Taking a trial balance of the accounts.
4. Journalizing the needed adjusting entries.
5. Posting the adjusting entries to the accounts.
6. Preparing the financial statements.
7. Journalizing the closing entries.
8. Posting the closing entries to the accounts.

THE CLASSIFIED BALANCE SHEET

Objective 6:
Prepare a classified
balance sheet

An **unclassified balance sheet** has only major categories labeled assets, liabilities, and stockholders' equity. A **classified balance sheet** subdivides at least some of the three major categories in order to provide useful information for interpretation and analysis by users of financial statements.

An example of a classified balance sheet is given in Illustration 3.3. It contains major categories of assets and liabilities. Accounts are then classified into these major categories. Notice that assets appear above liabilities and stockholders' equity in the Illustration. This vertical format is as appropriate as the horizontal format for either a classified or unclassified balance sheet. The horizontal format has assets on the left side and liabilities and stockholders' equity on the right side.

Included below are definitions and illustrations of accounts to be included under each major classification.

Current Assets

Current assets are cash and other assets that will be converted to cash or used up during a relatively short period of time, usually a year or less. Current assets are normally listed in the order of liquidity (how readily they can be converted to cash).

The current assets commonly found in a service-type business are as follows:

Cash includes deposits in banks available for current operations at the balance sheet date, plus cash on hand consisting of currency, undeposited checks, drafts, and money orders. Normally, cash is the first current asset to appear in a balance sheet.

Illustration 3.3
A CLASSIFIED BALANCE SHEET

WEST CORPORATION
Balance Sheet
June 30, 1990

Assets

Current assets:			
Cash		$ 40,000	
Accounts receivable		55,000	
Notes receivable		15,000	
Prepaid insurance		2,000	
Total current assets			$112,000
Property, plant, and equipment:			
Land		$114,000	
Building	$300,000		
Less: Accumulated depreciation	100,000	200,000	
Store equipment	$ 75,000		
Less: Accumulated depreciation	15,000	60,000	
Office equipment	$ 18,000		
Less: Accumulated depreciation	6,000	12,000	
Total property, plant, and equipment . . .			386,000
Total assets			$498,000

Liabilities and Stockholders' Equity

Current liabilities:			
Accounts payable		$ 25,000	
Notes payable		6,000	
Wages payable		800	
Unearned subscriptions revenue		1,100	
Total current liabilities			$ 32,900
Long-term liabilities:			
Notes payable, 10%, due in 2001			150,000
Total liabilities			$182,900
Stockholders' equity:			
Capital stock		$250,000	
Retained earnings		65,100	
Total stockholders' equity			315,100
Total liabilities and stockholders' equity			$498,000

Marketable securities are *temporary investments* made to earn a return on idle cash. The purpose of such investments is to earn additional money on cash that is not required in the business at the present time but will probably be needed in a short time.

An **account receivable** is an amount owed to a concern by a customer (debtor). The account receivable arises when a service (or merchandise) is sold and cash is not received immediately. Normally, no written evidence of indebtedness is given by the customer except by affixing his or her signature to the sales invoice or delivery ticket.

A *note* is an unconditional written promise to pay a definite sum of money at a certain or determinable date, usually with interest at a specified rate. A note is a *note receivable* on the balance sheet of the enterprise to which the note is given and is a *note payable* on the balance sheet of the promisor. A note receivable arises (*a*) when a sale is made and a note is taken from the customer, (*b*) when a customer gives a note for an amount due on open account, or (*c*) when money is loaned and a note is received as evidence.

Interest receivable arises when interest has been earned but not collected at the balance sheet date because the amount is not due until later. Items similar to interest receivable that are also current assets are rent receivable and royalties receivable.

Prepaid expenses are items that have been paid for in advance of their usage. Such items will be used up during the next accounting period. If they were not paid for in advance, they would require the disbursement of cash in the following period.

Long-Term Investments

A **long-term investment** usually consists of securities of another company or enterprise held with the intention of (*a*) obtaining control of another company, (*b*) securing a permanent source of income for the investor, or (*c*) establishing friendly business relations. The long-term investment classification in the balance sheet does not include those securities purchased for short-term purposes with temporarily unneeded cash. For most businesses, long-term investments may take the form of capital stock of other corporations or bonds of other entities. Occasionally long-term investments include funds accumulated for specific purposes, buildings that are rented to others, and plant sites for future use.

Property, Plant, and Equipment

Property, plant, and equipment are types of assets acquired for use in a business rather than for resale. Property, plant, and equipment also are termed *plant assets* or *fixed assets*. They are called fixed assets because they are to be used for long-term purposes. Several of the more common types of property, plant, and equipment are described below:

Land is ground upon which the business buildings of the enterprise are located.

Buildings that appear in the property, plant, and equipment section of a balance sheet are structures used to carry on the business; buildings owned as investments are not included as plant assets.

Machinery is heavy equipment used in manufacturing a product or performing a service for a customer. This item is not included in Illustration 3.3.

Store equipment, or **store fixtures,** includes items such as showcases, counters, tools, chairs, and cash registers.

Office equipment, or **office fixtures,** includes items such as file cabinets, calculators, typewriters, computers, desks, and chairs.

Delivery equipment, or trucks used in delivering goods to customers. This item is not included in Illustration 3.3.

Accumulated depreciation is a contra asset account to depreciable assets such as buildings, machinery, and equipment. It shows total depreciation taken to date on the assets.

Intangible Assets

Intangible assets consist of the noncurrent, nonphysical assets of a business. Costs of intangible assets must be charged to expense over the period benefited. Among the intangible assets are special grants by governmental bodies, such as leaseholds, copyrights, patents, and goodwill.

Leaseholds are rights to use rented properties, usually for a number of years.

A **copyright** is granted by the federal government and gives the owner the exclusive privilege of publication for a period of time.

A **patent** is a right granted by the federal government to an inventor or the owner of an invention whereby he or she alone has the authority to manufacture a product or to use a process for a period of time.

Goodwill is an intangible value that is attached to a business because its management has the ability to earn larger net income per dollar of stockholders' equity than earned by competitors in the same industry. The ability to produce superior profits is a valuable resource of a business. Normally, goodwill will be recorded only when it is purchased, and then only at the price paid for it.

Current Liabilities

A **current liability** is a debt—usually due within one year—the payment of which normally will require the use of current assets. Examples of current liabilities follow:

Accounts payable are amounts owed to creditors for items purchased from them. In the balance sheet, accounts payable are shown in one amount, which is the sum of the individual accounts payable.

Notes payable are unconditional written promises to pay a certain sum of money at a definite future date. The notes may arise from borrowing money from a bank, the purchase of assets, or the giving of a note in settlement of an account payable. Notes payable to banks are known as *nontrade notes;* those arising from purchases are known as *trade notes.* Generally, only notes payable due in one year or less are included as current liabilities.

Taxes withheld from employees are items such as federal income taxes, state income taxes, and social security taxes withheld from employees' paychecks. These amounts will be paid to the proper governmental agencies.

Interest payable is interest that has accumulated on indebtedness, such as notes or bonds. This accrued interest has not been paid at the balance sheet date because the amount is not due until later.

Dividends payable are amounts declared payable to stockholders and represent a distribution of income. These declared dividends have not been paid at the balance sheet date and consequently are a liability of the corporation.

Wages payable are amounts owed to employees for services rendered but for which payment has not been made at the balance sheet date. The wages have not been paid at the balance sheet date because they are not due until later.

Unearned revenues (revenues received in advance) result when payment is received for goods or services before it is earned, such as a subscription to a magazine. They represent a liability to return the asset received or to perform the agreed services or other contractual requirements, usually within the succeeding accounting period.

Long-Term Liabilities

Long-term liabilities are those not due for a relatively long period of time, usually more than one year. It is a good policy to show maturity dates in the balance sheet for all long-term liabilities.

Notes payable with maturity dates at least one year beyond the balance sheet date are long-term liabilities. **Bonds payable** are also long-term liabilities and are evidenced by formal printed certificates sometimes secured by liens (claims) on property, such as mortgages.

Stockholders' Equity

Stockholders' equity shows the owners' interest (equity) in the business. This interest is equal to the amount contributed plus the income left in the business.

Capital stock shows the capital paid into the company as the owners' investment.

Retained earnings show the cumulative income of the company less the amounts distributed to the owners in the form of dividends.

SUMMARY

Adjusting entries are made to include information on economic activity that has occurred but has not been recorded. They fall into two major classes; namely, those involving deferrals and those involving accruals.

Specific types of adjustments involving deferrals are for (1) asset/ expense and (2) liability/revenue items. Adjustments involving accruals are for (3) asset/revenue and (4) liability/expense items. In (1), the adjustment involves recognition of an expense as a result of the using up of a previously recorded asset; examples include insurance, rent, supplies, depreciation, and advertising. In (2), the adjustment involves recognition of the earning of revenue and the cancellation of a liability by providing services for which customers pay in advance; examples include delivery services, tickets, rent, and subscriptions. In (3), the adjustment involves recognition of the growth of an asset as a result of the rendering of services to customers; examples include interest and various kinds of services. In (4), the adjustment involves recognition of an expense and the corresponding obligation to pay as a result of the receipt of services; examples include salaries and interest. In all cases, adjusting entries involve changing account balances at the end of the period from what they presently contain to what they should contain for proper financial reporting.

At the end of the accounting period, after financial statements have been prepared, the expense and revenue accounts are closed. The closing process brings all the revenue and expense accounts to zero balances to be ready to receive information on the next period's activities.

A classified balance sheet shows the assets divided into categories such as current assets; long-term investments; property, plant and equipment; and intangible assets. The liabilities are divided into current and long-term categories.

In the next chapter, we move from accounting for service companies to accounting for merchandising companies. New accounts will be used in addition to the ones we have already used.

APPENDIX   THE WORK SHEET FOR A SERVICE COMPANY

Objective 7: Prepare a work sheet for a service company

In manually operated accounting systems containing large numbers of accounts, the accounting activities to be completed at the end of a financial reporting period may be organized and handled more efficiently through use of a work sheet. A **work sheet** is simply a sheet of paper containing a number of columns and lines for recording account titles, item descriptions, and dollar amounts. Since it is used internally only, it can take on a variety of forms. But to be of any real value, it will, as a minimum, contain columns for an unadjusted trial balance, adjusting entries, an income statement, and a balance sheet. An expanded version of a work sheet is presented in Illustration 3.4 and discussed below.

The Unadjusted Trial Balance Columns

Instead of preparing a separate trial balance, the open accounts in the ledger (assumed for Jane's, Inc.) are entered in the first pair of columns titled Unadjusted Trial Balance in the work sheet for the year ended December 31, 1990. The columns are summed, and the equality of the debits and credits in the ledger is shown by entering the totals ($187,000) immediately after the last item in the trial balance.

The Adjustments Columns

In the next pair of columns, all of the adjustments required to bring the accounts up to date prior to the preparation of financial statements are

Illustration 3.4

JANE'S, INC.
Work Sheet
For the Year Ended December 31, 1990

	Unadjusted Trial Balance Dr.	Unadjusted Trial Balance Cr.	Adjustments* Dr.	Adjustments* Cr.	Adjusted Trial Balance Dr.	Adjusted Trial Balance Cr.	Income Statement Dr.	Income Statement Cr.	Statement of Retained Earnings Dr.	Statement of Retained Earnings Cr.	Balance Sheet Dr.	Balance Sheet Cr.
Cash	5,000				5,000						5,000	
Supplies on hand	12,000			(a) 9,000	3,000						3,000	
Prepaid insurance	4,000			(b) 2,000	2,000						2,000	
Equipment	40,000				40,000						40,000	
Fixtures	20,000				20,000						20,000	
Accounts payable		2,000				2,000						2,000
Capital stock		30,000				30,000						30,000
Retained earnings, 12/31/89		10,000				10,000				10,000		
Dividends	2,000				2,000				2,000			
Sales		145,000				145,000		145,000				
Salaries expense	72,000		(e) 3,000		75,000		75,000					
Advertising expense	5,000				5,000		5,000					
Utilities expense	8,000				8,000		8,000					
Rent expense	12,000				12,000		12,000					
Payroll taxes expense	6,000				6,000		6,000					
Miscellaneous expense	1,000				1,000		1,000					
	187,000	187,000										
Supplies expense			(a) 9,000		9,000		9,000					
Insurance expense			(b) 2,000		2,000		2,000					
Depreciation expense—equipment			(c) 4,000		4,000		4,000					
Accumulated depreciation—equipment				(c) 4,000		4,000						4,000
Depreciation expense—fixtures			(d) 2,000		2,000		2,000					
Accumulated depreciation—fixtures				(d) 2,000		2,000						2,000
Salaries payable				(e) 3,000		3,000						3,000
			20,000	20,000	196,000	196,000	124,000	145,000				
Net income for 1990							21,000			21,000		
							145,000	145,000	2,000	31,000		
Retained earnings, December 31, 1990									29,000			29,000
									31,000	31,000	70,000	70,000

*These are keyed to the adjustments described in the chapter on pages 112–114.

entered. The adjustments for Jane's, Inc. are assumed to be based on the following data:

a. An inventory taken at year-end shows supplies on hand with a cost of $3,000.
b. The $4,000 balance in the Prepaid Insurance account represents the premium paid for insurance coverage for the years 1990 and 1991.
c. The equipment was acquired on January 1, 1990, and has an estimated useful life of 10 years with no scrap value.
d. The fixtures were acquired in January 1, 1990, and have an estimated useful life of 10 years with no scrap value.
e. There are $3,000 of unpaid salaries at year-end.

One advantage of a work sheet is that it assembles all of the accounts in one place, where they may easily be studied to determine the need for possible adjustment. As a result, entries are not likely to be overlooked.

After all of the adjusting entries are entered in the Adjustments columns, the two columns are totaled and their equality is noted as a partial check of the arithmetic accuracy of the work completed thus far.

The Adjusted Trial Balance Columns

After the adjustments have been entered, the adjusted balance of each account is determined and entered in the Adjusted Trial Balance columns.

Note carefully how the rules of debit and credit determine whether an entry increases or decreases the balance in the account. For example, Supplies on Hand has a debit balance of $12,000 which is decreased by a credit of $9,000 to a total of $3,000—the correct balance for financial reporting purposes.

The balances in the Adjusted Trial Balance columns are summed. The equality of the accounts with debit balances and those with credit balances is noted as a check upon the arithmetic accuracy of the work completed.

The Income Statement Columns

All of the accounts in the Adjusted Trial Balance columns that will appear in the Income Statement (the expense and revenue accounts) are now extended into the Income Statement columns—revenues as credits, expenses as debits. Each column is subtotaled, revealing revenues (credits) of $145,000 and expenses (debits) of $124,000. This means that the net income for the period amounted to $21,000. This amount is entered in the debit column to bring the two column totals into agreement. Note the similarity of the debit here to the debit in the Income Summary account to close or transfer net income to the Retained Earnings account. A net loss would, of course, be recorded in the opposite manner—that is, as a credit.

The Statement of Retained Earnings Columns

These columns contain the items that appear in the statement of retained earnings, namely: the $10,000 beginning balance of retained earnings as a credit, the $21,000 net income for the period as a credit, and the $2,000 of dividends as a debit. The columns are subtotaled, and the difference between the two subtotals, the ending balance of retained earnings, $29,000, is entered in the debit column in order to bring the two column totals into balance.

The Balance Sheet Columns

All of the asset, liability, and stockholders' equity accounts are extended into the Balance Sheet columns—assets as debits and the others as credits. Note that the ending $29,000 balance in Retained Earnings is carried into the credit column. Once again, to check the arithmetic accuracy of the work completed, the columns are totaled and their agreement is noted.

The Completed Work Sheet

Some accountants, in completing a work sheet, enter brief explanations keyed to the adjusting entries in the lower left-hand corner of the work sheet. Such a practice is useful for complicated adjustments, but is not necessary for the relatively routine adjustments illustrated here.

When the work sheet has been completed, all of the information needed to prepare the financial statements is readily available. It need only be recast into a more formal format.

Note, also, that it would be a relatively routine matter to journalize the adjusting and closing entries in the journal and then post them to the accounts. The adjusting entries can be readily prepared from information in the Adjustments columns and closing entries from the items in the Income Statement columns. But, since financial statements can be prepared from the work sheet, such entries are not likely to be entered formally in the journal and posted to the accounts at any time other than at the formal annual closing of the books. Thus, one of the real advantages of using a work sheet is that (monthly or quarterly) financial statements can be prepared without going through the work of journalizing and posting adjusting and closing entries.

The work sheet is a very convenient tool that assists in completing the accounting tasks at the end of the accounting period. While its use is optional, it is almost always used by accountants.

Objective 8: Define and use correctly the new terms in the glossary

NEW TERMS INTRODUCED IN CHAPTER 3

Accounting period   A time period normally of one month, one quarter, or one year into which an entity's life is arbitrarily divided for financial reporting purposes (89).

Accounting year (fiscal year)   An accounting period of one year. The accounting year may or may not coincide with the calendar year (89).

Accounts payable   Amounts owed to creditors for items purchased from them (110).

Accounts receivable   Amounts owed to a business by customers (debtors) (108).

Accrual basis of accounting   Recognizes revenues when sales are made or services are performed, regardless of when cash is received. Recognizes expenses as incurred whether or not cash has been paid out (89).

Accrued   A claim that comes into existence over time (101).

Accrued assets and liabilities   Assets and liabilities that exist at the end of an accounting period but have not yet been recorded; they represent rights to receive, or obligations to make, payments that are not legally due at the balance sheet date. Examples are accrued fees receivable and salaries payable (100–4).

Accrued items   See accrued assets and liabilities.

Accrued wages payable   Amounts owed to employees for services rendered (111).

Accumulated Depreciation account   A contra asset account that shows the total of all depreciation on the asset up to the balance sheet date (97, 110).

Adjusting entries   Journal entries made at the end of an accounting period to change the balance of certain accounts; they reflect economic activity that has taken place but has not yet been recorded. Adjusting entries are made to bring the accounts to their proper balances before financial statements are prepared (88).

Bonds payable   Written promises to pay a definite sum at a certain date as evidenced by formal printed certificates that are sometimes secured by liens on property, such as mortgages (111).

Book value   For depreciable assets, book value equals cost less accumulated depreciation (97).

Buildings   Structures in which business is carried out (109).

Calendar year   The normal year ending on December 31 (89).

Capital stock   Shows the capital paid in to the company as the stockholders' investment (111).

Cash   Includes deposits in banks available for current operations at the balance sheet date, plus cash on hand consisting of currency, undeposited checks, drafts, and money orders (107).

Cash basis of accounting   Recognizes revenues when cash is received and recognizes expenses when cash is paid out (88).

Classified balance sheet   Subdivides at least some of the major categories (assets, liabilities, and stockholders' equity) in order to provide useful information for interpretation and analysis by users of financial statements (107).

Closing process   The act of transferring the balances in the revenue and expense accounts to a clearing account called Income Summary and then to the Retained Earnings account. The balance in the Dividends account is also transferred to the Retained Earnings account (105).

Contra account   An account that is directly related to another account (97).

Contra asset account   An account shown as a deduction from the asset to which it relates in the balance sheet; used to give interested parties more complete financial information (97).

Copyright Grants the owner the exclusive privilege of publication of written material (110).

Current assets Cash and other assets that will be converted into cash or used up by the business during a relatively short period of time, usually a year or less (107).

Current liabilities Debts, usually due within one year, the payment of which normally will require the use of current assets (110).

Deferred items Those items involving data previously recorded in the accounts. Data are transferred from asset and liability accounts to expense and revenue accounts. Examples are prepaid expenses, depreciation, and unearned revenues (89).

Delivery equipment Trucks used to deliver goods to customers (110).

Depreciable asset A building, machine, vehicle, or equipment on which depreciation expense is recorded (96).

Depreciable cost The difference between an asset's cost and its estimated salvage value (96).

Depreciation accounting The process of recording depreciation expense (96).

Depreciation expense The amount of asset cost assigned as an expense to a particular time period (96).

Depreciation formula (straight-line)

$$\text{Annual depreciation} = \frac{\text{Asset cost} - \text{Estimated scrap value}}{\text{Number of years of useful life}} \quad (96)$$

Dividends payable Amounts declared payable to stockholders and represent a distribution of income (111).

Fiscal year An accounting year of 12 consecutive months that may or may not coincide with the calendar year. For example, a company may have an accounting or fiscal year that runs from April 1 of one year to March 31 of the next (89).

Goodwill An intangible value attaching to a business evidenced by the ability to earn larger net income per dollar of investment than that earned by competitors within the same industry (110).

Income Summary account A clearing account used only at the end of an accounting period to summarize revenues and expenses for the period (104).

Intangible assets Noncurrent, nonphysical assets of a business (110).

Interest payable Arises when interest has been incurred but not yet paid at the balance sheet date because the amount is not due until later (110).

Interest receivable Arises when interest has been earned but has not been collected at the balance sheet date (109).

Land Ground on which the business buildings of the company are located (109).

Leaseholds Rights to use leased properties (110).

Long-term investment Usually securities of another company which the owner expects to hold over long periods of time, usually more than one year (109).

Long-term liabilities Liabilities not due for a relatively long period of time, usually more than one year (111).

Machinery Heavy equipment used in manufacturing a product or performing a service for a customer (109).

Marketable securities Readily salable securities acquired with temporarily unneeded cash (108).

Matching principle An accounting principle requiring that expenses incurred in producing revenues be deducted from the revenues they generated during the accounting period (88).

Note payable An unconditional written promise to pay a definite sum of money at a certain or determinable date, usually with interest at a specified rate (110).

Office equipment (office fixtures) Items such as file cabinets, calculators, typewriters, computers, desks, and chairs (109).

Patent A right granted by the federal government to an inventor or the owner of an invention whereby he or she alone has the authority to manufacture a product or to use a process for a period of time (110).

Prepaid expense An asset that is awaiting assignment to expense. An example is prepaid insurance. Assets such as cash and accounts receivable are not prepaid expenses (91, 109).

Property, plant, and equipment They are acquired for use in a business rather than for resale; also called plant assets or fixed assets (109).

Retained earnings Show the cumulative income of the company less the amounts distributed to the owners in the form of dividends (111).

Scrap value (salvage value) The amount for which an asset can probably be sold at the end of its estimated useful life (96).

Service potential The benefits that can be obtained from assets. The future services that assets can render make assets "things of value" to a business (91).

Stockholders' equity Shows the owners' interest (equity) in the business (111).

Store equipment (store fixtures) Items such as showcases, counters, tools, chairs, and cash registers (109).

Taxes withheld from employees Income taxes and social security taxes withheld from employees (110).

Unclassified balance sheet Has only major categories labeled assets, liabilities, and stockholders' equity (107).

Unearned revenue Assets received from customers before services are performed for them. Since the revenue has not been earned, it is a liability, often called *revenue received in advance,* or *advances by customers* (99, 111).

Useful life The estimated number of periods that a company can make use of an asset (96).

Work sheet A columnar sheet of paper on which accountants have summarized information needed to make the adjusting and closing entries and to prepare the financial statements (112).

DEMONSTRATION PROBLEM 3–1

The trial balance of the Korman Company for December 31 of the current year includes, among other items, the following account balances:

	Debits	Credits
Office Supplies on Hand	$ 6,000	
Prepaid Rent	25,200	
Buildings	200,000	
Accumulated Depreciation—Buildings		$33,250
Salaries Expense	124,000	
Unearned Delivery Fees		4,000

Additional data:

1. Part of the supplies represented by the $6,000 balance of the Office Supplies on Hand account have been consumed. An inventory count of the supplies actually on hand at December 31 totaled to $2,400.
2. On May 1 of the current year, a rental payment of $25,200 was made for 12 months of rent; it was debited to Prepaid Rent.
3. The annual depreciation for the buildings is based on the cost shown in the Buildings account less an estimated scrap value of $10,000. The estimated useful lives of the buildings are 40 years each.
4. The salaries expense of $124,000 does not include $6,000 of unpaid salaries earned since the last payday.
5. One fourth of the unearned delivery fees have been earned by December 31.
6. Delivery services of $600 were performed for a customer, but a bill has not yet been sent.

Required:

a. Prepare the adjusting journal entries for December 31, assuming adjusting entries are prepared only at year-end.

b. Based on the adjusted balance shown in the Accumulated Depreciation—Building account, how many years has the Korman Company owned the building?

Solution to demonstration problem 3–1

a. See the general journal on page 120.

b. Eight years; computed as:

$$\frac{\text{Total accumulated depreciation}}{\text{Annual depreciation expense}} = \frac{\$33,250 + \$4,750}{\$4,750} = 8$$

KORMAN COMPANY
GENERAL JOURNAL

Date		Account Titles and Explanation	Post. Ref.	Debit	Credit
19—					
Dec.	31	Office Supplies Expense		3 6 0 0	
		Office Supplies on Hand			3 6 0 0
		To record office supplies expense			
		($6,000 − $2,400).			
	31	Rent Expense		1 6 8 0 0	
		Prepaid Rent			1 6 8 0 0
		To record rent expense ($25,200 × 8/12).			
	31	Depreciation Expense—Buildings		4 7 5 0	
		Accumulated Depreciation—Buildings			4 7 5 0
		To record depreciation			
		[($200,000 − 10,000) ÷ 40 years].			
	31	Salaries Expense		6 0 0 0	
		Salaries Payable			6 0 0 0
		To record accrued salaries.			
	31	Unearned Delivery Fees		1 0 0 0	
		Delivery Service Revenue			1 0 0 0
		To record delivery fees earned.			
	31	Accounts Receivable		6 0 0	
		Delivery Service Revenue			6 0 0
		To record delivery fees earned.			

QUESTIONS

1. Why are adjusting entries necessary? Why not treat every cash disbursement as an expense and every cash receipt as a revenue when the cash changes hands?

2. Give an example of each of the following:
   a. Equal growth of an expense and a liability.
   b. Earning of revenue that was previously recorded as unearned revenue.

    c. Equal growth of an asset and a revenue.

    d. Equal growth of an expense and decrease in an asset.

3. "Adjusting entries would not be necessary if the cash basis of accounting were followed (assuming no mistakes were made in recording cash transactions as they occurred). Under the cash basis, receipts that are of a revenue nature are considered revenue when received, and expenditures that are of an expense nature are considered expenses when paid. It is the use of the accrual basis of accounting, where an effort is made to match expenses incurred against the revenues they created, that makes adjusting entries necessary." Do you agree with this statement? Why?

4. Why don't accountants keep all the accounts at their proper balances continuously throughout the period so that adjusting entries would not have to be made before financial statements are prepared?

5. Identify the two major classes of adjusting entries and identify the types of adjusting entries that are included in each.

6. A fellow student makes the following statement: "It is easy to tell whether a company is using the cash or accrual basis of accounting. When an amount is paid for future rent or insurance services, a firm that is using the cash basis will debit an expense account while a firm that is using the accrual basis will debit an asset account." Is the student correct?

7. You notice that the Supplies on Hand account has a debit balance of $2,700 at the end of the accounting period. How would you determine the extent to which this account needs adjustment?

8. It may be said that some assets are converted into expenses as they expire and that some liabilities become revenues as they are earned. Give examples of asset and liability accounts for which the statement is true. Give examples of asset and liability accounts to which the statement does not apply.

9. What does the term *accrued liability* mean?

10. What is meant by the term *service potential*?

11. Give the depreciation formula for straight-line depreciation.

12. When assets are received before they are earned, what type of account is credited? As the amounts are earned, what type of account is credited?

13. The accountant often speaks of expired costs. Do costs literally expire?

14. What does the word *accrued* mean? Is there a conceptual difference between interest payable and accrued interest payable?

15. It is more difficult to match expenses incurred with revenues earned than it would be to match expenses paid with revenues received. Do you think that the effort is worthwhile?

16. What are closing entries? In general, why must they be made?

17. How is a classified balance sheet different from an unclassified balance sheet?

18. (Based on the Appendix.) Describe the purposes for which a work sheet is prepared.

EXERCISES

Prepare and post adjusting entry for insurance under two methods

1. a. A one-year insurance policy is purchased on August 1 for $3,600 and the following entry is made at that time:

Prepaid Insurance	3,600	
Cash		3,600

What adjusting entry is necessary at December 31, the end of the accounting year?

b. Give the adjusting entry that would be necessary if the entry to record the purchase of the policy on August 1 had been:

Insurance Expense	3,600	
Cash		3,600

c. Show by the use of T-accounts that the end result is the same under either (*a*) or (*b*).

Prepare adjusting entry for rent

2. Assume that rent of $9,000 was paid on September 1, 1990, to cover a one-year period from that date. Prepaid Rent was debited. If financial statements are prepared only on December 31 of each year, what adjusting entry is necessary on December 31, 1990, to bring the accounts involved to their proper balances?

Prepare adjusting entry for rent

3. If in Exercise 2 Rent Expense had been debited on September 1, 1990, what adjusting entry would have been necessary on December 31, 1990?

Determine date and entry for rent paid

4. At December 31, 1990, an adjusting entry was made as follows:

Rent Expense	6,000	
Prepaid Rent		6,000

You know that the gross amount of rent paid was $18,000, and it was to cover a one-year period. Determine:

a. The opening date of the year to which the $18,000 of rent applies.

b. The entry that was made on the date the rent was paid.

Prepare entries for purchase of supplies and adjustment at year-end

5. Office supplies were purchased for cash on May 2, 1990, for $3,000. Show two ways in which this entry could be recorded, then show the adjusting entry that would be necessary for each, assuming that $1,800 of the supplies remained at the end of the year.

Prepare adjusting entry for depreciation

6. Assume that a company acquires a building on January 1, 1990, at a cost of $1,800,000. The building has an estimated useful life of 40 years and an estimated scrap value of $200,000. What adjusting entry is needed on December 31, 1990, to record the depreciation for the entire year 1990?

Determine scrap value of building

7. A building is being depreciated by an amount of $27,000 per year. You know that it had an original cost of $300,000 and was expected to last 10 years. How must the $27,000 have been determined?

Prepare entries for receipt of subscription fees and adjustment at year-end

8. On September 1, 1990, the Rand Company received a total of $90,000 as payment in advance for a number of one-year subscriptions to a monthly magazine. By the end of the year, one third of the magazines paid for in advance had been delivered. Give the entries to record the receipt of the subscriptions fees and to adjust the accounts at December 31 assuming annual financial statements are prepared at year-end.

Prepare adjusting entry for accrued legal services

9. Guilty and Innocent, a law firm, performed legal services in late December 1990 for clients. The $19,000 of services will be billed to the clients in January 1991. Give the adjusting entry that is necessary on December 31, 1990, if financial statements are prepared at the end of each month.

Prepare adjusting entry for accrued salaries

10. Grill Company incurs sales salaries at the rate of $2,500 per day. The last payday in January is Friday, January 27. Salaries for Monday and Tuesday of the next week have not been recorded or paid as of January 31. Financial statements are prepared monthly. Give the necessary adjusting entry on January 31.

Determine effect on net income from failing to record adjusting entries

11. State the effect that each of the following would have on the amount of annual net income reported for 1990 and 1991.

    a. No adjustment was made for accrued salaries of $1,700 as of December 31, 1990.

    b. The collection of $1,400 for services yet unperformed as of December 31, 1990, was credited to a revenue account and not adjusted. The services are performed in 1991.

Prepare adjusting entry for accrued interest

12. A firm borrowed $35,000 on November 1. By December 31, $350 of interest had been incurred. Prepare the adjusting entry required on December 31.

Prepare closing entries

13. After adjustment, selected account balances of the Sleepy Campground are:

	Debits	Credits
Retained earnings		$ 80,000
Campsite rental revenue		120,000
Salaries expense	$42,000	
Depreciation expense	8,000	
Utilities expense.	26,000	
Dividends	4,000	

In T-account format, give the entries required to close the books for the period. Enter the above balances in the accounts before doing so. Key the postings from the first closing entry with the number (1), the second with the number (2), and so on.

PROBLEMS

Prepare adjusting entries, post to ledger accounts, and state the correct figures for the financial statements

3–1. The following data pertain to the Kraft Company:

Account Title	Trial Balance	Information for Adjustments
Case 1: Equipment	$80,000	The equipment has an estimated useful life of five years and an estimated scrap value of $20,000.
Accumulated Depreciation—		
Equipment	12,000	
Case 2: Salaries Expense	3,000	Unpaid salaries incurred amount to $400.
Case 3: Prepaid Insurance	16,800	Of the prepaid insurance in the trial balance, only $4,400 is for additional protection after December 31.

Required:

For each of the cases:

a. Prepare the adjusting journal entry, dating it December 31, 1990.

b. Set up ledger accounts showing debit, credit, and balance. Enter balances as given, if any, and post the adjusting entries made in part *(a)*.

c. State the correct figures for the balance sheet. Show related accounts in each case as they should appear on that statement.

d. State the correct figures for the income statement.

Prepare adjusting entries

3–2. The trial balance of the Pinkus Company at December 31 of the current year includes, among other items, the following account balances:

	Debits	*Credits*
Prepaid insurance	$ 7,296	
Buildings	158,000	
Accumulated depreciation—buildings		$31,600
Salaries expense	110,000	
Prepaid rent	24,000	

Additional data:

a. The debit balance in the Prepaid Insurance account is the advance premium for one year from September 1 of the current year.

b. The buildings are expected to last 25 years with no scrap value expected.

c. Salaries accrued and payable at December 31 amount to $6,400.

d. The debit balance in Prepaid Rent is for a one-year period that started March 1 of the current year.

Required:

Prepare the adjusting journal entries at December 31.

Prepare adjusting entries and post to ledger accounts

3–3. Among the account balances shown in the trial balance of the Jackson Company at December 31 of the current year are the following:

	Debits	*Credits*
Office supplies on hand	$ 3,480	
Prepaid insurance	4,800	
Buildings	84,000	
Accumulated depreciation—buildings		$19,500

Additional data:

a. The inventory of supplies on hand at December 31 amounts to $600.

b. The balance in the Prepaid Insurance account is for a two-year policy taken out June 1 of the current year.

c. Depreciation for the buildings is based on the cost shown in the Buildings account, less scrap value estimated at $9,000. When acquired, the lives of the buildings were estimated at 50 years each.

Required:

a. Prepare the adjusting journal entries at December 31.

b. Open ledger accounts for each of the accounts involved, enter the balances as shown in the trial balance, post the adjusting entries, and calculate balances.

Calculate correct net income

3–4. The reported net income amounts for the Adams Company were: 1990, $160,000; and 1991, $190,000. *No* annual adjusting entries were made at either year-end for any of the transactions given below:

Transactions:

a. A building was rented on April 1, 1990. Cash of $48,000 was paid on that date to cover a two-year period. Prepaid Rent was debited.

b. The balance in the Office Supplies on Hand account on December 31, 1990, was $8,000. An inventory of the supplies on December 31, 1990, revealed that only $5,000 was actually on hand at that date. No new supplies were purchased during 1990. At December 31, 1991, an inventory of the supplies revealed that $1,000 was on hand.

c. A building costing $1,000,000 and having an estimated useful life of 40 years and a salvage value of $200,000 was put into service on January 1, 1990.

d. Services were performed for a customer in December 1990. The $30,000 bill for these services was not sent until January 1991. The only transaction that was recorded was a debit to Cash and a credit to Service Revenue when payment was received in January.

Required:

Calculate the correct net income for 1990 and 1991. In your answer start with the reported net income amounts. Then show the effects of each correction (adjustment) using a plus or a minus to indicate whether reported income should be increased or decreased as a result of the correction. When the corrections are added to or deducted from the reported net income amounts, the result should be the correct net income amounts. The answer format should be as follows:

Explanation of Corrections	*1990*	*1991*
Reported net income	$160,000	$190,000
To correct error in accounting for:		
a. Prepaid rent:		
Correct expense in 1990	−18,000	
Correct expense in 1991		−24,000

Prepare adjusting entries

3–5. The Sancho Company occupies rented quarters on the main street of the city. In order to get this location, it was necessary for the company to rent a store larger than needed, so a portion of the area is subleased (rented) to Fredrick's Restaurant. The partial trial balance of the Sancho Company as of December 31, 1989, is as follows:

SANCHO COMPANY
Partial Trial Balance
December 31, 1989

	Debits	*Credits*
Cash	$80,000	
Prepaid insurance.	11,400	
Store equipment	88,000	
Accumulated depreciation—store equipment		$ 9,600
Notes payable		20,000
Service revenue		600,000
Supplies expense	10,800	
Rent expense	14,400	
Store salaries expense	98,000	
Rent revenue		4,400

Data to be considered:

a. Wages of the store clerks amount to $360 per day and were last paid through Wednesday, December 27. December 31 is a Sunday. The store is closed Sundays.

b. An analysis of the Store Equipment account disclosed:

Balance, January 1, 1989	$64,000
Addition, July 1, 1989	24,000
Balance, December 31, 1989, per trial balance . . .	$88,000

The company estimates that all equipment will last 20 years from the date it was acquired and that the scrap value will be zero.

c. The store carries one combined insurance policy which is taken out once a year effective August 1. The premium on the policy now in force amounts to $7,200 per year.

d. Unused store supplies on hand at December 31, 1989, have a cost of $720.

e. December's rent from Fredrick's Restaurant has not yet been received, $400.

Required:

Present the period-end entries required by the statements of fact presented above. Show your calculations of the amounts as explanations of your entries.

Prepare journal entries under cash basis and accrual basis and determine difference in net income

3–6. On June 1, 1990, Jeff Hanley opened a swimming pool cleaning and maintenance service business, Hanley Company. He vaguely recalled the process of making journal entries and establishing ledger accounts from a high school bookkeeping course he had taken some years ago. At the end of June, he prepared an income statement for the month of June, but he had the feeling that he had not proceeded correctly. He contacted his brother, Jay, a recent college graduate majoring in accounting, for assistance.

Jay immediately noted that his brother had kept his records on a cash basis, so he set about to bring the books to a full accrual basis.

Transactions:

June 1 Received cash of $18,000 from a motel chain in exchange for service agreements to clean and maintain their pools for the months of June, July, August, and September.
5 Paid rent for automotive and cleaning equipment to be used during the period June through September, $4,000. The payment covered the entire period.
8 Purchased a two-year liability insurance policy effective June 1 for $5,280 cash.
10 Received an advance of $5,000 from a Florida building contractor in exchange for an agreement to help service pools in his housing development during the months of October through May.
16 Paid wages for the first half of June, $5,600.
17 Paid $240 for advertising to be run in a local newspaper for two weeks in June and four weeks in July.
19 Paid the rent of $8,000 under a four-month lease on a building rented and occupied on June 1.
26 Purchased $3,600 of supplies for cash. (Only $600 of these supplies were used in June.)
29 Billed a customer for services rendered, $8,400.
30 Unpaid employee services received in the last half of June amounted to $5,200.
30 Received a bill for $400 for gas and oil used in June.

Required:

a. Prepare the entries for the transactions as Jeff must have recorded them under the cash basis of accounting.

b. Prepare the necessary adjusting entries as Jay must have prepared them to bring the books to a full accrual basis of accounting as of June 30.

c. Calculate the change in the net income for June brought about by changing from the cash to the accrual basis of accounting.

Prepare T-accounts, income statement, balance sheet, and closing entries required

3–7. The balances of all of the Paul Company accounts as of June 1, 1990, were as follows:

Cash	$16,800	Accounts payable	$ 8,000
Accounts receivable	17,200	Capital stock	24,000
		Retained earnings	2,000

The transactions (and certain other data) for the company for June were as follows:

1. Services rendered to a customer for cash, $16,000; on account, $32,000.
2. Paid rent for the six months ending November 30, $12,000. (Record entire amount as prepaid rent.)
3. Purchased equipment for cash, $19,200.
4. Supplies purchased on account, $3,200.
5. Received cash on account from a customer, $44,000.
6. Made payment on account to a supplier, $5,600.
7. Employee services received, $30,000; cash paid to employees, $26,000.
8. Paid utility bill of $800.
9. Paid dividend to stockholders, $1,200.
10. Equipment has an expected life of four years. It was acquired early in the month.
11. Adjust for prepaid rent that has expired.
12. Of the supplies purchased in (4), $2,800 were used by the end of the month.

Required:

a. Set up T-accounts and record the above data, including the beginning balances given above. (Ignore any possible federal income taxes.)
b. Prepare an income statement for the month of June.
c. Prepare a balance sheet as of June 30, 1990.
d. Enter in the T-accounts the closing entries that would be required if June 30, 1990, is the end of the accounting period. (Key these entries *a, b,* and *c* in the T-accounts.)

Prepare a corrected income statement

3–8. Randy Hall, president and sole stockholder of Hall's Service, Inc., prepared the following income statement for the company's second month of operations, May 1990.

Service revenues		$20,000
Wages expense	$11,200	
Oil and gasoline expense	2,000	
Other expenses	2,800	16,000
Net income		$ 4,000

In preparing the above income statement, Randy merely looked at the checkbook and treated deposits of receipts from customers as revenue and checks drawn in payment for expenses as the expenses for the month. Further analysis shows that, of the $20,000 collected from customers in May, $2,400 was for services rendered in April. Services were rendered in

May for which customers were billed $2,800, none of which was paid by the end of May. The $11,200 of wages paid included wages of $3,200 earned by employees in April. Wages earned in May but not paid by the end of May amounted to $1,200. A bill for $400 for gasoline and oil used in May remains unpaid at the end of May. The expenses shown above do not include depreciation on the equipment owned, which has a cost of $480,000, no scrap value, and an estimated life of 10 years.

Required:

Prepare a corrected income statement for May for Hall's Service, Inc.

Prepare closing entries and a classified balance sheet

3–9. You are given the following adjusted balances for the Isaac Company.

ISAAC COMPANY
Adjusted Trial Balance
December 31, 1990

	Debits	Credits
Cash	$117,200	
Accounts receivable	48,000	
Accrued interest receivable	400	
Notes receivable	20,000	
Prepaid insurance	2,400	
Supplies on hand	1,800	
Land	32,000	
Buildings	190,000	
Accumulated depreciation—buildings		$ 40,000
Office equipment	28,000	
Accumulated depreciation—office equipment		8,000
Accounts payable		38,000
Accrued salaries payable		8,500
Accrued interest payable		900
Notes payable (due 1993)		64,000
Capital stock		120,000
Retained earnings		42,800
Dividends	40,000	
Commissions and fees revenue		372,520
Advertising expense	14,000	
Commissions expense	75,440	
Travel expense	12,880	
Depreciation expense—building	8,500	
Salaries expense	88,400	
Depreciation expense—office equipment	2,800	
Supplies expense	3,800	
Insurance expense	3,600	
Building repair expense	1,900	
Utilities expense	3,400	
Interest expense	1,800	
Interest revenue		1,600
	$696,320	$696,320

Required:

a. Prepare the closing journal entries.

b. Prepare a classified balance sheet.

Prepare work sheet and closing entries

3–10. (Based on the appendix.) The trial balance and additional data given below are for the Wright Company:

WRIGHT COMPANY
Trial Balance
December 31, 1990

	Debits	Credits
Cash	$ 70,640	
Accounts receivable	139,520	
Notes receivable	170,000	
Stores supplies on hand	2,400	
Store equipment	88,000	
Accumulated depreciation—store equipment		$ 17,600
Accounts payable		78,800
Notes payable		24,000
Capital stock		300,000
Retained earnings		21,640
Service revenue		577,360
Interest revenue		1,000
Interest expense	600	
Sales salaries expense	138,400	
Advertising expense	78,000	
Store supplies expense	2,960	
General office expense	9,880	
Fire insurance expense	4,800	
Office salaries expense	80,800	
Officers' salaries expense	160,000	
Legal and auditing expenses	10,000	
Telephone expense	4,800	
Rent expense	57,600	
Dividends	2,000	
	$1,020,400	$1,020,400

Additional data as of December 31, 1990:

a. Fire insurance unexpired, $1,400.

b. Store supplies on hand, $1,700.

c. Prepaid rent expense (store only), $7,000.

d. The store equipment has a 10-year estimated life with no scrap value.

e. Accrued sales salaries, $4,000.

f. Accrued office salaries, $3,000.

Required:

a. Prepare a 12-column work sheet for the year ended December 31, 1990. (See chapter appendix for an illustration.)

b. Prepare the December 31, 1990, closing entries, in general journal form.

BUSINESS DECISION PROBLEM 3–1

Explain why adjusting entries are made and which accounts need adjustment

You have just been hired by the Taylor Company to help them prepare adjusting entries at the end of an accounting period. It becomes obvious to you that the management does not seem to have much of an understanding about the necessity for adjusting entries or which of the accounts might possibly need adjustment. The first step you take is to prepare the following unadjusted trial balance from the general ledger. It includes only those accounts from the ledger which had balances as of the end of the year.

	Debits	Credits
Cash	$ 60,000	
Accounts Receivable	18,000	
Office Supplies on Hand	3,000	
Prepaid Insurance	2,700	
Office Equipment	120,000	
Accumulated Depreciation—Office Equipment		$ 45,000
Building	360,000	
Accumulated Depreciation—Building		105,000
Accounts Payable		9,000
Bank Loan Payable		15,000
Unearned Brokerage Commissions		30,000
Capital Stock		150,000
Retained Earnings		69,300
Rental Commissions Revenue		270,000
Advertising Expense	6,000	
Salaries Expense	112,500	
Utilities Expense	7,500	
Miscellaneous Expense	3,600	
	$693,300	$693,300

Required:

a. Explain to management why adjusting entries in general are made.

b. Explain to management why some of the specific accounts appearing in the trial balance may need adjustment and what the nature of each adjustment might be (do not worry about specific dollar amounts).

4

SALES, COST OF GOODS SOLD, AND INVENTORIES

LEARNING OBJECTIVES

After studying this chapter, you should be able to:

1. Record journal entries for sales on account.
2. Describe accounting for inventories, returns and allowances, and cash discounts.
3. Prepare adjusting and closing entries.
4. Account for uncollectible accounts.
5. Calculate which costs are properly included in inventory.
6. Calculate cost of ending inventory, cost of goods sold, and effects on net income under the four major inventory costing methods.
7. Apply the lower-of-cost-or-market method to inventory.
8. Estimate cost of ending inventory using the gross margin and retail inventory methods.
9. Define and use correctly the new terms in the glossary.

As already noted, accountants seek to fulfill one of their most important tasks—the measurement of periodic net income—through a process of matching revenues and expenses by time periods. This chapter discusses accounting for the major source of revenue for most business firms—sales of a product—and a major element of expense—cost of the goods sold.

Attention is focused on cost of goods sold not only because it is a relatively large expense but, as we shall see, because measures of its periodic amount may differ, depending on which of several alternative accounting methods is used.

SALES, COST OF GOODS SOLD, AND GROSS MARGIN

Accounting for Sales Revenue

The revenue of a company engaged in selling merchandise is typically recorded at the time of the completion of the sale (which is assumed to occur when the goods are delivered) and at the price agreed upon in the sales contract. Thus, a sale of a machine on account at a price of $3,000 would be recorded when the machine was delivered as follows in journal entry and T-account form:

Objective 1: Record journal entries for sales on account

(a) Accounts Receivable	3,000	
Sales		3,000
To record sales on account.		

Accounts Receivable		Sales	
(a) 3,000			*(a)* 3,000

Recording revenue at the time of sale is usually considered appropriate because (1) the revenue has been earned; that is, the seller has completed its part of the contract; (2) the revenue is readily measurable—the actual selling price is known; (3) legal title to the goods has passed to the buyer; and (4) the revenue has been realized—a valid asset has been received in an exchange with an outsider. Furthermore, the actual sale of the goods may be the critical event in a series of events that end in a sale. As a practical matter, revenue from the sale of goods is usually recorded when the goods are delivered in a valid sales transaction. But goods delivered on a consignment basis should not be recorded as sold. Here the goods remain the property of the shipper until they are sold by the party to whom they are consigned—the consignee.

Cost of Goods Sold—Perpetual Procedure

Firms securing revenue from the sale of goods usually keep a supply of such goods on hand which is called **merchandise inventory.** If prior to the above sale the seller had purchased three identical machines on account at a price of $1,800 each, this purchase transaction would, under what is known as **perpetual inventory procedure,** be recorded as follows:

(b) Merchandise Inventory.	5,400	
Accounts Payable		5,400
To record purchase on account.		

Merchandise Inventory		Accounts Payable	
(b) 5,400			*(b)* 5,400

*Objective 2:
Describe
accounting for
inventories,
returns and
allowances, and
cash discounts*

Merchandise inventory is a current asset account, and accounts payable is a current liability. Under perpetual procedure, a second entry is required at the time of sale to record the *expense* incurred as a result of transferring an asset, part of the inventory, to the customer:

(c)	Cost of Goods Sold	1,800	
	Merchandise Inventory		1,800
	To record cost of merchandise sold.		

Merchandise Inventory				Cost of Goods Sold		
(b)	5,400	(c)	1,800	(c)	1,800	

The $1,800 in the above entry would be secured from supporting records called **stock cards** or **perpetual inventory cards.** These records show the dates, quantities, and prices of goods received and goods issued, and the quantities and prices of the goods on hand at any given time.

Assume that $500 of other expenses were incurred in the week ending July 18, 1990, in which the above sale was the company's only sale. The income statement for the week would be as follows:

Sales	$3,000
Cost of goods sold	1,800
Gross margin	$1,200
Other expenses	500
Net income	$ 700

The difference between sales and the cost of goods sold is called **gross margin** or **gross profit,** and the relationship between the gross margin and sales is often expressed as a percentage called the gross profit or gross margin rate—40 percent in this instance ($1,200 ÷ $3,000).

Perpetual inventory procedure is widely used in companies that sell merchandise of high individual unit value, such as furs, jewelry, and autos. Because each unit has a high value, management finds it especially useful to know which merchandise is selling and which is not. Promotional activity and purchasing can be planned. Also, inventory shortages can be determined by comparing amounts shown on perpetual records with physical counts of the items on hand. Thus, the benefits derived from keeping detailed perpetual records often exceed the cost of maintaining such records.

Cost of Goods Sold—Periodic Procedure

On the other hand, companies that sell goods with low unit values, such as greeting cards, nuts and bolts, and pencils, may find it too costly to maintain perpetual records for their merchandise. Such companies use **periodic inventory procedure.** Under this procedure, inventory is not updated in the accounts after every purchase and sale. Rather, the proper inventory balance is determined and recorded only after a physical count is taken of the goods on hand and the goods are properly priced. Such physical counts are usually taken once a year at a minimum. And the cost of goods sold is determined only after the physical inventory has been taken.

The Purchases account. Under periodic procedure, merchandise acquisitions are recorded in a separate Purchases account. A purchase of $40,000 of goods on account would then be recorded as follows:

```
(a)  Purchases . . . . . . . . . . . . . . . . . . . . . . . . .    40,000
         Accounts Payable  . . . . . . . . . . . . . . . . .             40,000
     Purchases of merchandise on account.
```

Purchases		Accounts Payable	
(a) 40,000		(a) 40,000

The **cost of goods sold** in any period is then determined as follows:

> Merchandise inventory (at beginning of period)
> + Purchases for the period
> = Cost of goods available for sale;
> − Ending inventory (goods on hand not sold)
> = Cost of goods sold (the expense for the period).

The computation of the cost of goods sold can be included in the income statement, if desired, as shown in Illustration 4.1. Future examples will illustrate this periodic procedure only.

Returns and Allowances

Whenever goods are sold, some of them may be returned by the buyer to the seller for any of a variety of reasons. For example, assume that goods have been sold to a buyer on account in the amount of $5,000. This transaction was recorded as a debit to Accounts Receivable and a credit to Sales of $5,000 by the seller, and as a debit to Purchases and a credit to

Illustration 4.1

X COMPANY Partial Income Statement For the Month Ended July 31, 1990		
Sales		$50,000
Cost of goods sold:		
Inventory, July 1	$15,000	
Purchases	40,000	
Cost of goods available for sale	$55,000	
Less: Inventory, July 31	22,000	
Cost of goods sold		33,000
Gross margin		$17,000

Accounts Payable of $5,000 by the buyer. Now goods with a sales price of $400 are returned. The entry on the seller's books would be:

(a) Sales Returns and Allowances   400
           Accounts Receivable   400
        To record return of goods by customer.

Sales Returns and Allowances		**Accounts Receivable**	
(a) 400		Beg. Bal. 5,000	(a) 400

The entry on the buyer's books would be:

(b) Accounts Payable   400
           Purchase Returns and Allowances   400
        To record return of goods to supplier.

Purchase Returns and Allowances		**Accounts Payable**	
	(b) 400	(b) 400	Beg. Bal. 5,000

The seller has credited the customer's account because the return has reduced the customer's obligation to pay. The customer (buyer) debited the vendor's account because the return reduced its obligation to the seller.

Occasionally, concessions will be granted from the originally agreed-upon price of a sale of merchandise because of blemishes, defects, or damage. Such price concessions are recorded in the same manner as returns.

Because sales returns and allowances represent actual cancellations of all or a part of a sale, they theoretically could be recorded directly as debits in the Sales account. For similar reasons, purchase returns and allowances could be recorded as credits in the Purchases account. But, returns and allowances are likely to be significant information to management and others, since the handling of returns can be costly to both buyers and sellers. Returns and allowances amount to as much as 15 percent of sales in some businesses; they are, therefore, recorded in separate accounts (called contra accounts) and often reported separately as deductions from sales and purchases to arrive at net sales and net purchases in the income statement.

Cash Discounts

Frequently, when goods are sold on a credit basis, the buyer is allowed a **cash discount** and is permitted to pay an amount less than the full invoice price of the goods if payment is made within a stated period of time. Thus, an invoice might state credit terms of "2/10, n/30"[1] (read as 2 10, net 30), which means that a 2% discount can be deducted from the total

---
[1]Some students believe the terms should read 2/10, g/30, since the *gross* amount is due in 30 days. But we will use the conventional terms, 2/10, n/30.

135

price of the goods if the invoice is paid within 10 days of the invoice date, and the gross amount is due within 30 days from date of purchase.

The gross price method. Under the **gross price method** merchandise purchases are recorded at the gross invoice price. Assume that goods are purchased at a $1,000 gross invoice price. If so, the original purchase and the ultimate payment within the discount period, under terms 2/10, n/30, would be recorded as follows:

Seller's Books

(a)	Accounts Receivable	1,000	
	Sales		1,000
	To record sales on account.		

(b)	Cash	980	
	Sales Discounts	20	
	Accounts Receivable		1,000
	To record receipt of payment within discount period.		

Accounts Receivable			**Sales**	
(a) 1,000	(b) 1,000			(a) 1,000

Cash		**Sales Discounts**	
(b) 980		(b) 20	

Buyer's Books

(c)	Purchases	1,000	
	Accounts Payable		1,000
	To record purchase on account.		

(d)	Accounts Payable	1,000	
	Cash		980
	Purchase Discounts		20
	To record payment made within discount period.		

Purchases		**Accounts Payable**	
(c) 1,000		(d) 1,000	(c) 1,000

Cash		**Purchase Discounts**	
Bal. xxx	(d) 980		(d) 20

The Sales Discounts and Purchase Discounts accounts are also contra accounts to the Sales and Purchases accounts, respectively. This treatment reflects the preferred theoretical view that such discounts are adjustments of recorded revenue and cost.

Transportation-In

The cost a buyer incurs to have merchandise delivered is part of the total cost of the goods. But because the total freight costs incurred may be significant information, the receipt of a freight bill usually results in an entry debiting **Transportation-In** and crediting Accounts Payable.

The partial income statement shown in Illustration 4.2 illustrates the financial reporting of returns, allowances, discounts, and transportation-in.

Adjusting and Closing Entries

Objective 3:
Prepare adjusting
and closing entries

The data in Illustration 4.2 can be used to show the adjusting and closing entries required in the accounts of a merchandising firm. First, an entry is needed to accumulate in one account (Cost of Goods Sold) all of the costs relating to the goods that were available for sale. Thus, the existing balances in the inventory, transportation-in, and the purchase-related accounts are transferred to the Cost of Goods Sold account as follows:

Cost of Goods Sold	85,000	
Purchase Returns and Allowances.	5,000	
Purchase Discounts	1,000	
Purchases		60,000
Transportation-In		3,000
Inventory		28,000

Illustration 4.2

FICTITIOUS COMPANY
Income Statement
For the Year Ended December 31, 1990

Sales			$100,000
Less: Sales returns and allowances	$ 4,000		
Sales discounts	1,000	5,000	
Net sales			$95,000
Cost of goods sold:			
Inventory, January 1		$ 28,000	
Purchases	$60,000		
Less: Purchase returns and allowances	$5,000		
Purchase discounts	1,000	6,000	
Net purchases	$54,000		
Transportation-in	3,000	57,000	
Cost of goods available for sale		$ 85,000	
Less: Inventory, December 31		21,000	64,000
Gross margin			$31,000
Operating expenses:			
Administrative expenses		$ 6,000	
Selling expenses		9,000	15,000
Net income			$16,000

The Cost of Goods Sold account (which started with a zero balance) now contains the cost of the goods available for sale. But not all of the goods have been sold. An inventory of $21,000 remains on hand. This must be set up as an asset and deducted from the balance in the Cost of Goods Sold account, which leads to the following entry:

Inventory	21,000	
Cost of Goods Sold		21,000

Now the revenue and revenue contra accounts can be closed to Income Summary:

Sales.	100,000	
Sales Returns and Allowances		4,000
Sales Discounts		1,000
Income Summary		95,000

The Cost of Goods Sold account would be closed in an entry involving a debit to Income Summary and a credit to Cost of Goods Sold, as follows:

Income Summary	64,000	
Cost of Goods Sold		64,000

The operating expenses would be closed in an entry involving a debit to Income Summary and a credit to the various expense accounts, as follows:

Income Summary	15,000	
Administrative Expenses		6,000
Selling Expenses		9,000

The net income of $16,000 would be closed to Retained Earnings, as follows:

Income Summary	16,000	
Retained Earnings		16,000

Work sheet. The appendix to this chapter illustrates a work sheet that may be used in preparing adjusting entries, closing entries, and the financial statements for a merchandising company.

UNCOLLECTIBLE ACCOUNTS

Objective 4: Account for uncollectible accounts

A seller doing business on a credit basis faces the virtual certainty that some customers' accounts will ultimately prove uncollectible. For example, assume that, because of past experience, a seller expects to collect only $95,000 out of $100,000 of accounts receivable outstanding at year-end. Normally, this would require the following entry:

Uncollectible Accounts Expense		Allowance for Uncollectible Accounts	
(a) 5,000		(a) 5,000	

This entry serves two purposes: (1) uncollectible accounts are charged as an expense in the year the sale giving rise to them was made; that is, a proper matching results when, say, uncollectible accounts arising from credit sales made in 1990 are charged as an expense in 1990, (2) the accounts receivable at year-end are properly valued at their *net realizable value*—the amount of cash expected to be collected.

The **Uncollectible Accounts Expense** (also called Bad Debts Expense) account is an operating expense a business incurs as a result of customers not paying their bills when the company sells on credit. The **Allowance for Uncollectible Accounts** (also called Allowance for Doubtful Accounts) is a contra account (reduction account) to Accounts Receivable; it reduces Accounts Receivable to their net realizable value. The Accounts Receivable account is not reduced directly because it is not known at this time which customers' accounts will actually prove uncollectible. The $100,000 of accounts receivable and the related allowance for uncollectible accounts of $5,000 are reported as follows in the current assets section of the balance sheet:

Accounts receivable	$100,000	
Less: Allowance for uncollectible accounts	5,000	$95,000

Estimation Methods

There are two basic methods of estimating the amount of uncollectible accounts to be charged to a given accounting period.

Percentage of sales method. The **percentage of sales method** involves calculating the amount that has proven uncollectible from credit sales in previous years. The ratio of uncollectible accounts to credit sales is then used in estimating the amount for the uncollectible accounts adjusting entry. If cash sales are small or are a fairly constant percentage of total sales, the entry may be based on total net sales.

To illustrate, assume that the Boulder Company has found that 1% of its net sales is uncollectible. On the basis of this experience, each period the company may charge an amount equal to 1% of the net sales for the period to Uncollectible Accounts Expense and add a like amount to the Allowance for Uncollectible Accounts. If net sales for 1990 are $400,000, the entry will read:

Uncollectible Accounts Expense	4,000	
Allowance for Uncollectible Accounts		4,000
To record uncollectible accounts expense.		

Assuming that the gross (total) amount of accounts receivable is $100,000 and there was no previous balance in the allowance account, net accounts receivable would appear as follows on the balance sheet:

Accounts receivable	$100,000	
Less: Allowance for uncollectible accounts	4,000	$96,000

Sometimes the Allowance for Uncollectible Accounts account has a balance before adjustment. Under the percentage of sales method, any existing balance in the allowance account will *not* influence the size of the uncollectible accounts adjusting entry.

This method is theoretically preferable because it bases the estimate of expense solely on the sales revenue of the same period and gives a more precise matching of expense and revenue than the alternative method.

Percentage of accounts receivable method. The **percentage of accounts receivable method** is designed to adjust the Allowance for Uncollectible Accounts balance to a certain percentage of accounts receivable. It may use one overall percentage or may use a different percentage for each age category of receivable. To illustrate the use of one overall percentage, assume that on the basis of past experience the Fox Company estimates that 5% of its outstanding receivables of $100,000 as of December 31, 1990, will ultimately prove to be uncollectible. The Allowance for Uncollectible Accounts already has a *debit* balance of $1,000. The journal entry to adjust the balance in the allowance account to its required $5,000 ($100,000 × 0.05) *credit* balance is as follows:

Uncollectible Accounts Expense	6,000	
Allowance for Uncollectible Accounts		6,000
To adjust allowance for possible uncollectible accounts.		

In T-account form, the effect of this entry can be shown as follows:

Uncollectible Accounts Expense		**Allowance for Uncollectible Accounts**	
Dec. 31 Adjustment 6,000		Beg. bal. 1,000	Dec. 31 Adjustment 6,000
			Bal. after adjustment 5,000

Thus, the percentage of accounts receivable method requires that you (1) determine what the balance of Allowance for Uncollectible Accounts should be and (2) determine the amount that needs to be recorded in a journal entry to bring the account to this required credit balance.

Aging schedule. Alternatively, an **aging schedule** may be used to apply a different percentage for each age category of receivable. An aging schedule is presented in Illustration 4.3, showing how the age of each customer's account is determined. As can be seen from Illustration 4.3, under this method the age of the accounts is the basis for estimating uncollectibility. For example, only 1% of the accounts not yet due (sales made less than 30 days prior to the end of the accounting period) is expected to be uncollectible. At the other extreme, 50% of all accounts 91 to 180 days past due is expected to become worthless. The journal entry amount is still affected by the amount already in the allowance account prior to adjustment. For instance, Illustration 4.3 shows that $33,150 is

Illustration 4.3
ACCOUNTS RECEIVABLE AGING SCHEDULE

			Number of Days Past Due			
Customer	Debit Balance	Not Yet Due	1–30	31–60	61–90	91–180
X	$ 8,000					$ 8,000
Y	16,000		$ 12,000	$ 4,000		
Z	4,000				$ 800	3,200
All others	800,000	$560,000	200,000	20,000	5,000	15,000
Totals	$828,000	$560,000	$212,000	$24,000	$5,800	$26,200
Estimated uncollectible percentage		1%	5%	10%	25%	50%
Amount uncollectible	$ 33,150	$ 5,600	$ 10,600	$ 2,400	$1,450	$13,100

ROGERS COMPANY
Analysis of Accounts Receivable
December 31, 1990

needed in the allowance account. If the account has a credit balance of $5,000 before adjustment, the adjusting entry would be made for $28,150.

Subsequent write-offs. Later, when an account is determined to be uncollectible, an entry is made debiting the Allowance for Uncollectible Accounts and crediting Accounts Receivable. Note that this entry has no effect on net income or on the valuation of the accounts receivable. The expense and the reduced valuation for the asset were recognized when the adjusting entry for estimated uncollectibles was made. The write-off entry merely gives recognition to an event that was anticipated when the allowance was established.

If, by chance, an error was made in writing off an individual customer's account (as shown by the collection of the account), an entry is made debiting Accounts Receivable and crediting the Allowance for Uncollectible Accounts for the full amount of the account previously written off. Then the cash collection is recorded as a debit to Cash and a credit to Accounts Receivable.

INVENTORY MEASUREMENT

Objective 5: Calculate which costs are properly included in inventory

A crucial step in the determination of net income is the measurement of the ending inventory of the period. This is true not only because it affects net income but also because it affects measurements of current assets, total assets, gross margin, retained earnings, and total stockholders' equity. How this happens will be explained later when questions of what to include as part of the cost of the inventory and which of several measurement methods should be used are discussed.

The Basic Rule

Chapter 4 of *Accounting Research Bulletin 43* states that "the primary basis of accounting for inventories is cost" and further stipulates that "a departure from the cost basis...is required when the utility of the goods is no longer as great as" their cost. Thus, inventories are usually reported in the balance sheet at a dollar amount described as *cost or market, whichever is lower.*

In applying this general or basic rule, several problems exist. As discussed below, these include:

1. Which costs should be included as part of the cost of the inventory?
2. What is the cost of the inventory when goods have been purchased at different unit costs?
3. What constitutes evidence of a decline in the utility of goods, and how is it measured?

Inventory Cost—Possible Inclusions

In principle, the cost of inventory includes all costs incurred, directly or indirectly, to acquire the goods and place them in position and condition for sale. Thus, cost includes the net invoice price of the goods plus insurance in transit; transportation charges; receiving, handling, and storage costs; and duties. But, as a practical matter, these related costs are often omitted from inventory cost because (1) they are not material in amount relative to the total cost of the goods purchased, or (2) there is no easy way to allocate these costs to individual units of merchandise. Also, because they are immaterial, purchase discounts are on occasion not deducted from the invoice price in determining inventory cost.

Inventory Costing Methods

Objective 6: Calculate cost of ending inventory, cost of goods sold, and effects on net income under the four major inventory costing methods

As already indicated, the cost of goods available for sale (beginning inventory plus purchases) must be apportioned between ending inventory and cost of goods sold. But how are these costs to be apportioned when goods have been acquired at different unit costs? For example, suppose that at the beginning of a month a retailer has three units of a product on hand, one acquired at $10, another at $11, and the third at $12. Suppose that during the month two units were sold. What is their cost? Is it $21, the cost of the first and second units? Or $22, the cost of the first and third units? Or $23, the cost of the second and third units? Or should it be $22 determined as two units at an average cost of $11? Four inventory costing methods have been developed to solve this type of problem. They are: (1) specific identification, (2) first-in, first-out (FIFO), (3) last-in, first-out (LIFO), and (4) weighted average. The cost-flow assumption used does not necessarily have to match the physical flow of the goods.

The data in Illustration 4.4 are assumed for the beginning inventory, purchases, and sales of a given product in order to illustrate the application of these four inventory costing methods.

Illustration 4.4
INVENTORY, PURCHASE, AND SALES DATA: PRODUCT X, MODEL 12

	Beginning Inventory and Purchases				Sales			
Date	Number of Units	Unit Cost	Total Cost	Date	Number of Units	Price	Total	
1/1 inventory	10	$10.00	$100.00	3/8	10	$15.00	$150.00	
3/2	10	10.40	104.00	7/5	10	15.00	150.00	
5/28	20	10.50	210.00	9/7	20	16.00	320.00	
8/12	10	11.00	110.00	11/27	20	16.00	320.00	
10/12.	20	10.90	218.00					
12/21.	10	11.20	112.00					
Total	80		$854.00		60		$940.00	

The total goods available for sale consisted of 80 units with a total cost of $854. Of the units available, 60 were sold, producing sales revenue of $940, and 20 units were left on hand in inventory. Our task now is to apportion the $854 between cost of goods sold (an expense) and ending inventory (an asset).

Specific identification. The **specific identification** method calls for the assignment of a known actual cost to a particular identifiable unit of product. The specific product involved is usually identifiable through the use of a serial number plate or an identification tag. The method is quite appropriately applied when large, readily identifiable units of product such as automobiles are purchased and sold.

To illustrate, assume that the 20 units of product on hand at the end of the year in Illustration 4.4 are definitely known to consist of 10 from the August 12 purchase and 10 from the December 21 purchase. The ending inventory then is shown in Illustration 4.5.

The cost of the ending inventory of $222 would be deducted from the total cost of goods available for sale of $854 to get the cost of goods sold of $632.

The specific identification method results in the cost of goods sold and the inventory being stated in terms of the actual cost of the actual units sold and on hand. Thus, costs are matched against revenues with a high degree of precision. The method is used most logically to account for "big

Illustration 4.5
ENDING INVENTORY UNDER SPECIFIC INDENTIFICATION

From Purchase of—	Number of Units	Cost Each	Total Cost
August 12	10	$11.00	$110.00
December 21	10	11.20	112.00
Total	20		$222.00

ticket" items, such as autos and trucks, because each unit tends to be unique. Also, the selling price of such items tends to be based on a markup over a specifically identified cost.

The method is criticized by some because it may result in two identical units of product being included in the inventory at different prices even if they have the same utility because they are identical. But supporters would contend that this is entirely logical and consistent with the cost basis of asset measurement. The method is also criticized by some as theoretically unacceptable because income may be manipulated when it is used. If higher income is desired, ship the units with the lower cost. If lower income is desired, ship the high-cost units.

But the major deficiency in the specific identification method is that it is simply too costly and too time consuming to apply in many situations. This would be true where large quantities of many different types of products with low unit costs are purchased and sold.

First-in, first-out (FIFO). Effective merchandising policy usually calls for moving the oldest goods first, if at all possible. In many businesses, the actual physical flow of goods *is* first-in, first-out to avoid substantial losses from spoilage, as in the case of dairy products and fresh produce.

The application of the **FIFO (first-in, first-out)** method results in the latest costs being included in inventory, while the older costs are charged to cost of goods sold. The method may be applied even in those circumstances in which goods do not flow in a first-in, first-out manner.

FIFO applied under periodic procedure. Under the FIFO method, the 20 units in ending inventory would be priced as shown in Illustration 4.6.

The ending inventory includes the costs of the latest purchases, and the balance of the cost of the goods available for sale (consisting of older costs) is charged to cost of goods sold. The ending inventory is $221, and this sum will be deducted from the total cost of goods available for sale of $854 to get the cost of goods sold of $633.

Last-in, first-out (LIFO). Under **LIFO (last-in, first-out),** the cost of the last goods purchased is charged against revenues as the cost of the goods sold, while the inventory is composed of the costs of the oldest goods acquired. Tax regulations provide that LIFO may be used for tax purposes only if it is used in general financial reports. Although the costs of the

Illustration 4.6
FIFO COST OF ENDING INVENTORY UNDER
PERIODIC PROCEDURE

From Purchase of—	Number of Units	Unit Price	Total Cost
December 21	10	$11.20	$112.00
October 12	10	10.90	109.00
Total	20		$221.00

goods purchased are assumed to flow in a last-in, first-out manner, this does not necessarily mean that the goods physically flow in this manner.

In order to determine the cost of the ending inventory, list the goods in the beginning inventory and continue listing subsequent purchases until enough units have been listed to equal the number in the ending inventory. Illustration 4.7 shows the determination of the ending inventory for the data listed in Illustration 4.4.

The cost of the ending inventory of $204 would be deducted from the cost of the goods available for sale of $854 to show a cost of goods sold of $650. Note that in this example the costs charged against revenues as the cost of the goods sold are all fairly current or recent costs while the inventory consists of a March 2 cost and the cost of the beginning inventory that may actually have been incurred many years ago.

FIFO and LIFO compared. Much has been written in recent years concerning the relative merits of FIFO and LIFO. LIFO's appeal can be tied directly to the long-run tendency toward rising prices experienced in this country since the early 1930s. An example will make this point clear.

Suppose that Company A has one unit of a given product on hand that cost $10. The unit is sold for $15, other expenses of sale amount to $3.50, the tax rate is assumed to be 50%, and the unit is replaced for $11 prior to the end of the accounting period. Under FIFO accounting, net income is computed as follows:

Net sales	$15.00
Cost of goods sold	10.00
Gross margin	$ 5.00
Expenses	3.50
Net operating margin	$ 1.50
Federal income taxes (50 percent rate)	0.75
Net income	$ 0.75

According to the above schedule the company is selling this product at a price sufficient to produce net income. But consider the following:

Cash secured from sale	$15.00
Expenses and taxes paid ($3.50 + $0.75)	4.25
Net cash available from sale	$10.75
Cash spent to replace unit sold	11.00
Additional cash that was required to replace inventory	$ 0.25

Illustration 4.7
LIFO COST OF ENDING INVENTORY

From Purchase of—	Number of Units	Unit Cost	Total Cost
Beginning inventory	10	$10.00	$100.00
March 2	10	10.40	104.00
Total	20		$204.00

Thus, Company A, which is reporting net income, finds itself unable to replace its inventory without securing additional cash. But note what happens when LIFO is used as the method of inventory pricing:

Net sales	$15.00
Cost of goods sold	11.00
Gross margin	$ 4.00
Expenses	3.50
Net operating income	$ 0.50
Federal income taxes	0.25
Net income	$ 0.25

The 25 cents of net income is matched by an increase in cash that is available for distribution as dividends or for other purposes:

Cash secured from sale	$15.00
Expenses and taxes ($3.50 + $0.25)	3.75
Net cash available from sale	$11.25
Cash spent to replace unit sold	11.00
Cash available for dividends (or other uses)	$ 0.25

Because the unit sold was replaced before the end of the year, the effect of using LIFO increased cost of goods sold $1.00 ($11.00 − $10.00). This, in turn, reduced taxable income by $1.00 and, with a 50 percent tax rate, reduced federal income taxes by 50 cents. Some of LIFO's popularity is due to its ability to minimize current tax payments in periods of rising prices, which is what has occurred in our economy over recent years.

But LIFO is supported on theoretical grounds in that it tends to match current revenues and current costs. The income statement reports sales and the most recent costs of making those sales when LIFO is used. Thus, the income reported reflects operating results and does not include gains from holding inventory in periods of rising prices—"inventory profits," as they are called. The inventory profit in the above example was $1—the difference between the cost to replace the unit sold at the time of sale ($11) and its actual cost ($10). LIFO is also supported by accountants who believe that selling prices are most likely to be based on replacement cost and that LIFO cost most closely approximates replacement cost.

On the other hand, FIFO advocates point out that LIFO matches the cost of *unsold* goods (because goods usually move in a first-in, first-out manner) against sales revenue. LIFO also tends to yield an inventory amount that, after a period of rising prices, is substantially below the inventory's current replacement cost. The net income reported under LIFO can also be manipulated to a certain extent by purchasing, or not purchasing, goods near the end of the accounting year when unit costs have changed. If smaller income is desired, increase the amount of purchases at current high costs, and, under LIFO, these high costs will be charged to cost of goods sold. If higher income is desired, delay making purchases and charge to cost of goods sold some of the older, lower costs in inventory.

Weighted-average method. Under the **weighted-average method** the total number of units purchased plus those on hand at the beginning of the year is divided into the total cost of the purchases plus the cost of the beginning inventory in order to derive a weighted-average unit cost. This unit cost is then multiplied by the number of units in the ending inventory to arrive at the cost of the inventory. Illustration 4.8 shows the application of this procedure.

Illustration 4.8
APPLICATION OF WEIGHTED-AVERAGE METHOD

Purchase Date	Number of Units Purchased	Unit Cost	Total Cost
1/1 inventory	10	$10.00	$100.00
3/2	10	10.40	104.00
5/28	20	10.50	210.00
8/12	10	11.00	110.00
10/12	20	10.90	218.00
12/21	10	11.20	112.00
Total	80		$854.00

Weighted-average unit cost is $854 ÷ 80, or $10.675.

Ending inventory, then, is $10.675 × 20.	213.50
Cost of goods sold	$640.50

Differences in cost methods summarized. Illustration 4.9 summarizes the cost of goods sold, ending inventories, and gross margins that will result from the application of the same data to the four basic cost methods of pricing ending inventory.

Illustration 4.9
SUMMARY OF EFFECTS OF EMPLOYING DIFFERENT INVENTORY METHODS WITH SAME BASIC DATA

	Specific Identification	FIFO	LIFO	Weighted-Average
Sales	$940.00	$940.00	$940.00	$940.00
Cost of goods sold:				
Beginning inventory	$100.00	$100.00	$100.00	$100.00
Purchases	754.00	754.00	754.00	754.00
Cost of goods available for sale	$854.00	$854.00	$854.00	$854.00
Ending inventory	222.00	221.00	204.00	213.50
Cost of goods sold	$632.00	$633.00	$650.00	$640.50
Gross margin	$308.00	$307.00	$290.00	$299.50

Note that each of the above methods produces a different inventory measurement and gross margin. As might be expected, since the trend of prices was upward during the period, LIFO shows the highest cost of goods sold and the lowest gross margin.

Which is the "correct" method? All of the above methods are considered acceptable, and no one of them can be considered the only "correct" one. Each method is attractive in particular circumstances. The application of LIFO results in matching current cost with current revenue and makes it more likely that any net income reported can be distributed as dividends without impairing the level of operations. LIFO is actually a partial answer to the problems encountered in accounting under inflationary conditions. LIFO also reduces the amount of taxes currently payable under these conditions.

On the other hand, LIFO often charges against revenues the cost of goods *not* sold. And it permits manipulation of net income simply by changing the time at which additional purchases of merchandise are made. If precision in the matching of *actual historical cost* with revenue is desired, FIFO or specific identification are preferred. But income may also be manipulated under the specific identification method, as it may be under the simple weighted-average method. Under the latter method the purchase of a large amount of goods at a relatively high price after the last sale of the period will change the average unit cost of the goods charged to the Cost of Goods Sold account. Only under FIFO is the manipulation of income *not* possible. But because net income under this method in periods of rising prices may have to be reinvested in inventory in order to maintain a given level of sales volume, this income is considered fictitious by many accountants and dubbed "paper profits."

There is also some evidence to suggest that companies have changed their method of inventory measurement simply to conform with other companies in their industry. And further, a company may employ different methods for different inventories.

Inventories at Less than Cost

As already noted, Chapter 4 of *Accounting Research Bulletin 43* requires a departure from the cost basis for inventories when the utility of the goods is less than their cost. Such loss of utility may be evidenced by damage or obsolescence or by a decline in the selling price of the goods.

Net realizable value. Damaged, obsolete, or shopworn goods are not to be carried in inventory or reported in the financial statements at an amount greater than their net realizable value. **Net realizable value** is defined as estimated selling price less costs to complete and dispose of the goods. For example, assume that an auto dealer has on hand one auto that has been used as a demonstrator. The auto was acquired at a cost of $7,200 and had an original sales price of $8,400. But, because it has been used and it is now late in the model year, the net realizable value of the auto is estimated at:

Estimated selling price	$7,000
Estimated maintenance and selling costs	600
Net realizable value	$6,400

The auto would be written down for inventory purposes from $7,200 to $6,400. In this way, the $800 would be treated as an expense in the period in which the decline in utility took place. If net realizable value exceeds cost, the item would of course be carried at cost. Accountants generally frown upon recognizing revenues before goods are sold.

Inventories at Lower-of-Cost-or-Market

Objective 7: Apply the lower-of-cost-or-market method to inventory

The **lower-of-cost-or-market (LCM) method** values inventory at the lower of its historical cost or its current market (replacement) cost. Pricing inventories at the lower of cost or market has a long history of acceptance in accounting. The method is based, in part, upon the assumption that, if the purchase price in the market in which the firm buys has fallen, the selling price has fallen or will fall. This is not always a valid assumption.

The term *market* as used in this context means replacement cost in terms of the quantity usually purchased. In the application of the method, it is still necessary to determine cost (by either the specific identification, FIFO, LIFO, or average method).

The method uses market values only to the extent that these values are less than cost. If the inventory at December 31, 1990, has a cost of $20,000 and a market value of $21,000, this increase in market value is not recognized. To do so would be to recognize revenue prior to the time of sale.

On the other hand, if market value is $19,400, the inventory may be written down to market value from cost and a $600 loss recognized since the inventory has lost some of its revenue-generating ability. Thus, the entry made anticipates a reduced selling price when the goods are actually sold.

Application of the method. As shown in Illustration 4.10, the lower-of-cost-or-market method may be applied to each item in the inventory, to

Illustration 4.10
APPLICATION OF LOWER–OF–COST–OR–MARKET METHOD

Item and Class	Quantity	Unit Cost	Unit Market	Total Cost	Total Market	Lower of Cost or Market	
						By Classes	By Units
Class A							
A1	100	$8.00	$6.90	$ 800	$ 690		$ 690
A2	200	5.00	4.25	1,000	850		850
				$1,800	$1,540	$1,540	
Class B							
B1	500	3.00	3.40	$1,500	$1,700		1,500
B2	300	4.00	3.90	1,200	1,170		1,170
				$2,700	$2,870	2,700	
				$4,500	$4,410	$4,240	$4,210

each class in the inventory or to the total inventory. Each method of application is considered acceptable, although tax regulations require application to individual items whenever feasible.

The inventory in Illustration 4.10 could be reported at $4,210, $4,240, or $4,410, and each of these measurements referred to as the lower of cost or market. When applied to each individual item, all possible losses are consistently anticipated. But this may be unduly conservative, since the inventory may be written down even though there has been an actual increase in its total market value.

Gross Margin Method of Estimating Inventory

Objective 8: Estimate cost of ending inventory using the gross margin method and retail inventory method

The **gross margin method** is a procedure for estimating inventory cost in which estimated cost of goods sold is deducted from the cost of goods available for sale to determine estimated ending inventory. The gross margin method is used to approximate the amount of an inventory for the following purposes:

1. To obtain an inventory at the end of each month of a fiscal period except the last. The inventory cost so computed is used in the monthly financial statements.
2. As a method of verifying a previously determined ending inventory amount.

The gross margin method is based on the assumption that the rate of gross margin realized is highly stable from period to period; the method is satisfactory only if this assumption is correct.

To illustrate the gross margin method of computing the inventory, assume that the Sweet Company has for several years maintained a rate of gross margin on sales of 40%. From this fact and the data given below, the approximate inventory of December 31, 1990, may be determined as shown in Illustration 4.11.

Inventory, January 1, 1990	$ 30,000
Purchases of merchandise in 1990	390,000
Sales of merchandise in 1990	600,000

Illustration 4.11
COMPUTATION OF THE INVENTORY, DECEMBER 31, 1990

Inventory, January 1, 1990		$ 30,000
Purchases		390,000
Cost of merchandise available for sale		$420,000
Less estimated cost of sales:		
Sales	$600,000	
Gross margin (40% of $600,000)	240,000	
Estimated cost of sales		360,000
Inventory, December 31, 1990		$ 60,000

Because the gross margin method is based on the assumption that the gross margin rate in the current period is the same as in prior periods, which, of course, may not be true, it is generally not an accurate enough method to be used for the year-end financial statements. One of the other methods described in this chapter should be used, preferably in conjunction with a physical inventory.

The Retail Method of Estimating Inventory

The **retail inventory method** is a procedure for estimating the cost of ending inventory by applying a cost/retail price ratio to ending inventory stated at retail prices. The method is used by a wide variety of companies that sell goods directly to the ultimate consumer. In such companies, each item of merchandise is usually marked or tagged with its retail or selling price. The result is that the goods are referred to and inventoried at their retail prices.

In skeletal form, the retail method consists first of determining the ending inventory at retail prices:

> Beginning inventory at retail prices
> + Purchases at retail prices
> = Goods available for sale at retail prices;
> − Sales (which are, of course, at retail prices)
> = Ending inventory at retail prices.

In order to convert the ending inventory at retail prices to cost, the relationship between cost and retail prices must be known. This requires that information on the beginning inventory and purchases be accumulated so that goods available for sale can be expressed in terms of cost and retail prices. Transportation-in is added to beginning inventory and net purchases in the cost column. This cost/retail price ratio is then applied to sales to determine cost of goods sold and to the ending inventory at retail to reduce it to cost. This procedure is shown in Illustration 4.12.

The $186,000 on the line entitled "Cost of goods sold and sales" is the amount of sales in the department for the month of January and is taken from the accounting records. The $111,600 is the cost of goods sold during

Illustration 4.12
INVENTORY CALCULATION USING THE RETAIL METHOD

	Cost	Retail Price
Inventory, January 1, 1990	$ 12,000	$ 20,000
Purchases, net	115,000	200,000
Transportation-in	5,000	−0−
Cost/retail price ratio:		
$132,000/$220,000, or 60%	$132,000	$220,000
Cost of goods sold and sales (cost is 60% of retail)	111,600	186,000
Inventory, January 31, 1990 (cost is 60% of retail)	$ 20,400	$ 34,000

the month, found by applying the cost/retail price ratio of 60 percent to the sales of $186,000. Deducting these two amounts, $111,600 and $186,000, from the $132,000 and $220,000 amounts on the preceding line—goods available for sale at cost and at retail—gives the January 31, 1990, inventory for the department at cost and at retail.

SUMMARY

Revenue generated by the selling activities of a business is usually recorded when the goods are delivered with the intent of making a sale. At that time, the revenue is measurable and has been earned and realized.

The major expense incurred in making sales to customers—the cost of the merchandise delivered—may be recorded at the time of sale (perpetual procedure) or at the end of the period (periodic procedure). The difference between sales revenue and the cost of the goods sold is called gross margin. Merchandise delivered may be returned or price concessions may be granted for any of a number of reasons. These returns and allowances are adjustments of recorded revenues or purchases and are recorded in separate contra accounts. Cash discounts are viewed and recorded similarly.

To obtain a proper matching of expense and revenue and to report a proper valuation for accounts receivable, the estimated uncollectible accounts arising from a year's sales are charged to uncollectible accounts expense and credited to an allowance for uncollectible accounts.

Inventory cost theoretically includes the net invoice price of the goods and the cost of transportation-in, insurance in transit, receiving, handling, storage, and duties. As a practical matter, invoice cost alone is often used.

The cost of the inventory may be determined by attaching known invoice costs to specifically identified goods or by assuming a pattern of cost flows—FIFO, LIFO, or weighted-average. Each method will yield different reported amounts for inventory and net income. Management faces the task of choosing the method it will use, and this choice may be influenced by many factors including the methods employed by other members of the industry. Generally, the method chosen will be used over a period of years because generally accepted accounting principles prohibit indiscriminate switching between methods. Such switching would open the door to manipulation of reported net income and would yield information lacking in consistency between years.

Generally accepted accounting principles usually require the write-down from cost to market value (replacement cost) of those goods for which selling prices have fallen or are expected to fall before the goods are sold. Damaged, obsolete, or shopworn goods should be inventoried at their net realizable value, if less than cost.

Inventories can, if necessary, be estimated by using the gross margin method or the retail inventory method.

In the next chapter you will learn about cash, another asset that is subject to theft and thus must be protected. The important topic of internal control introduces the chapter.

APPENDIX THE WORK SHEET FOR A MERCHANDISING COMPANY

The appendix in Chapter 3 illustrated the basic structure of a work sheet. It was prepared for a company providing services.

The purpose of this appendix is to show how a work sheet would be prepared for a merchandising company (see Illustration 4.13). The example is simplified to focus on the merchandise-related accounts.

The accounts which appear in the trial balance of a merchandising company that do not appear in the trial balance of a service company are Merchandise Inventory, Sales, Sales Returns and Allowances, Sales Discounts, Purchases, Purchase Returns and Allowances, Purchase Discounts, and Transportation-In. The balances in the Merchandise Inventory account (representing the beginning inventory), the Purchases account, and all of the purchase-related accounts (such as Transportation-In, Purchase Discounts, and Purchase Returns and Allowances) are transferred to the Cost of Goods Sold account in entry *(a)* in the work sheet. The entry made consists of debits to Cost of Goods Sold, Purchase Discounts, and Purchase Returns and Allowances; and credits to Merchandise Inventory, Purchases, and Transportation-In. The ending inventory (assumed to be $8,000) is established by debiting Merchandise Inventory and crediting Cost of Goods Sold in entry *(b)* in the work sheet. All of these debits and credits should appear in the Adjustments columns of the work sheet.

All revenue accounts in the work sheet are carried to the credit Income Statement column. All revenue contra accounts and all expense accounts, including the Cost of Goods Sold account, are carried to the debit Income Statement column.

The amount needed to balance the Income Statement columns is the net income or net loss amount for the period. It is carried to the credit (or debit, if loss) Statement of Retained Earnings column.

The beginning balance in retained earnings is carried to the credit Statement of Retained Earnings column. The dividends balance is carried to the debit Statement of Retained Earnings column. The amount needed to balance the Statement of Retained Earnings columns is the ending retained earnings balance. It is carried to the credit Balance Sheet column.

All assets are carried to the debit Balance Sheet column. All liabilities and stockholders' equity items are carried to the credit Balance Sheet column.

Illustration 4.13

HUNTLEY RETAIL STORE, INC.
Work Sheet
For the Month Ended January 31, 1990

Acct. No	Account Titles	Unadjusted Trial Balance Debit	Unadjusted Trial Balance Credit	Adjustments Debit	Adjustments Credit	Adjusted Trial Balance Debit	Adjusted Trial Balance Credit	Income Statement Debit	Income Statement Credit	Statement of Retained Earnings Debit	Statement of Retained Earnings Credit	Balance Sheet Debit	Balance Sheet Credit
1	Cash	18,663				18,663						18,663	
3	Accounts receivable	1,880				1,880						1,880	
4	Merchandise inventory, Jan. 1	7,000			(a) 7,000								
6	Accounts payable		700				700						700
7	Capital stock		15,000				15,000						15,000
8	Retained earnings		10,000				10,000				10,000		
9	Sales		13,600				13,600		13,600				
10	Sales returns and allowances	20				20		20					
11	Sales discounts	44				44		44					
12	Purchases	6,000			(a) 6,000								
13	Purchase returns and allowances		100	(a) 100									
14	Purchase discounts		82	(a) 82									
15	Transportation-in	75			(a) 75								
16	Sales salaries	650				650		650					
17	Rent expense	150				150		150					
18	Dividends	5,000				5,000				5,000			
		39,482	39,482										
	Cost of goods sold			(a) 12,893 (b) 8,000	(b) 8,000	4,893		4,893					
	Merchandise inventory, Jan. 31*			8,000		8,000						8,000	
				21,075	21,075	39,300	39,300	5,757	13,600				
	Net income for January							7,843			7,843		
								13,600	13,600	5,000	17,843	28,543	
	Retained earnings									12,843			12,843
										17,843	17,843	28,543	28,543

*If desired, the $8,000 in the adjustments column may be placed on the same line as the $7,000 beginning inventory figure.

154

NEW TERMS INTRODUCED IN CHAPTER 4

Aging schedule A means of classifying accounts receivable according to their age, used to determine the necessary balance in an Allowance for Uncollectible Accounts. A different uncollectibility rate is used for each age category (140).

Allowance for Uncollectible Accounts A contra asset account to the Accounts Receivable account; it reduces accounts receivable to their net realizable value. Also called Allowance for Doubtful Accounts or Allowance for Bad Debts (139).

Bad debts expense See uncollectible accounts expense.

Cash discount A deduction from the gross invoice price that can be taken only if the invoice is paid within a specified period of time: to the seller, it is a sales discount; to the buyer, it is a purchase discount (135).

Cost of goods sold Shows the cost to the seller of the goods sold to customers; under periodic procedure cost of goods sold is computed as Beginning inventory + Net cost of purchases − Ending inventory (134).

FIFO (first-in, first-out) A method of pricing inventory under which the costs of the first goods purchased are the first costs charged to cost of goods sold when goods are actually sold (144).

Gross margin Net sales − Cost of goods sold; identifies the number of dollars available to cover expenses; may be expressed as a percentage rate (133).

Gross margin method A procedure for estimating inventory cost in which estimated cost of goods sold (determined using an estimated gross margin) is deducted from the cost of goods available for sale to determine estimated ending inventory. The estimated gross margin is calculated using gross margin rates (in relation to net sales) of prior periods (150).

Gross price method The recording of merchandise purchases at gross invoice price (136).

Gross profit Net sales − Cost of goods sold (133).

LIFO (last-in, first-out) A method of pricing inventory under which the costs of the most recent purchases are the first costs charged to cost of goods sold when goods are actually sold (144).

Lower-of-cost-or-market (LCM) method An inventory pricing method that values inventory at the lower of its historical cost or its current market (replacement) cost (149).

Merchandise inventory The quantity of goods on hand and available for sale at any given time (132).

Net realizable value Estimated selling price of an item less the estimated costs that will be incurred in preparing the item for sale and selling it (148).

Percentage of accounts receivable method A method for determining the desired size of the Allowance for Uncollectible Accounts by basing the calculation on the Accounts Receivable balance at the end of the period (140).

Percentage of sales method A method of estimating uncollectible accounts from a given period's credit sales (139).

Periodic inventory procedure A method of accounting for merchandise acquired for sale to customers wherein the cost of merchandise sold and the cost of merchandise on hand are determined only at the end of the accounting period by taking a physical inventory (133).

Perpetual inventory procedure A method of accounting for merchandise acquired for sale to customers wherein the Merchandise Inventory account is debited for each purchase and credited for each sale so that the current balance is shown in the account at all times (132).

Retail inventory method A procedure for estimating the cost of the ending inventory by applying a cost/retail price ratio to ending inventory stated at retail prices (151).

Specific identification An inventory pricing method that attaches the actual cost to an identifiable unit of product (143).

Stock cards (perpetual inventory cards) Records that show the dates, quantities, and prices of goods received and goods issued, and the quantities and prices of the goods on hand at any given time (133).

Transportation-In account An account used under periodic inventory procedure to record transportation costs incurred in the acquisition of merchandise; a part of cost of goods sold (137).

Uncollectible Accounts Expense An operating (usually a selling) expense a business incurs as a result of customers not paying their bills when the company sells on credit (139).

Weighted-average method A method of pricing ending inventory using a weighted-average unit cost, determined by dividing the total number of units purchased plus those in beginning inventory into total cost of goods available for sale. Units in the ending inventory are carried at this per unit cost (146).

DEMONSTRATION PROBLEM 4–1

The following transactions occurred between Companies A and B in June of 1990.

Transactions:

June 20 Company A purchased merchandise from Company B, $40,000; terms 2/10, n/30.
   21 Company B incurred and paid freight of $600.
   24 Company A received an allowance of $2,000 from the gross invoice price because of damaged goods.
   27 Company A returned $4,000 of goods purchased because they were not the quality ordered.
   30 Company B received payment in full from Company A.

Required:

a. Journalize the transactions for Company A.

b. Journalize the transactions for Company B.

Solution to demonstration problem 4–1

a.

GENERAL JOURNAL

Date		Account Titles and Explanation	Post. Ref.	Debit	Credit
		Company A			
1990					
June	20	Purchases		4 0 0 0 0	
		Accounts Payable			4 0 0 0 0
		Purchased merchandise from Company B,			
		terms 2/10, n/30.			
	24	Accounts Payable		2 0 0 0	
		Purchase Returns and Allowances			2 0 0 0
		Received an allowance from Company B			
		for damaged goods.			
	27	Accounts Payable		4 0 0 0	
		Purchase Returns and Allowances			4 0 0 0
		Returned merchandise to Company B			
		because of improper quality.			
	30	Accounts Payable ($40,000 − $2,000 − $4,000)		3 4 0 0 0	
		Purchase Discounts ($34,000 × 0.02)			6 8 0
		Cash ($34,000 − $680)			3 3 3 2 0
		Paid the amount due to Company B.			

b.

GENERAL JOURNAL

Date		Account Titles and Explanation	Post. Ref.	Debit	Credit
		Company B			
1990					
June	20	Accounts Receivable		4 0 0 0 0	
		Sales			4 0 0 0 0
		Sold merchandise to Company A,			
		terms 2/10, n/30.			
	21	Delivery Expense		6 0 0	
		Cash			6 0 0
		Paid freight on sale of merchandise.			
	24	Sales Returns and Allowances		2 0 0 0	
		Accounts Receivable			2 0 0 0
		Granted an allowance to Company A			
		for damaged goods.			
	27	Sales Returns and Allowances		4 0 0 0	
		Accounts Receivable			4 0 0 0
		Merchandise returned from Company A			
		due to improper quality.			
	30	Cash ($34,000 − $680)		3 3 3 2 0	
		Sales Discounts ($34,000 × 0.02)		6 8 0	
		Accounts Receivable			
		($40,000 − $2,000 − $4,000)			3 4 0 0 0
		Received the amount due from Company A.			

DEMONSTRATION PROBLEM 4–2

The Best Company estimates its uncollectible accounts expense to be 1% of sales. Sales in 1990 were $750,000.

Required:

Prepare the journal entries for the following transactions:

Transactions:

1. The company prepared the adjusting entry for uncollectible accounts for the year 1990.
2. On January 15, 1991, the company decided that the account for James Ryan in the amount of $500 was uncollectible.
3. On February 12, 1991, James Ryan's check for $500 arrived.

Solution to demonstration problem 4–2

1. **1990**
   Dec. 31 | Uncollectible Accounts Expense . . . . | 7,500 |
   | Allowance for Uncollectible Accounts . . . . . . | | 7,500 |

   To record estimated uncollectible accounts for the year.

2. **1991**
   Jan. 15 | Allowance for Uncollectible Accounts . . . . | 500 |
   | Accounts Receivable—James Ryan . . . . . . | | 500 |

   To write off the account of James Ryan as uncollectible.

3. **1991**
   Feb. 12 | Accounts Receivable—James Ryan . . . . | 500 |
   | Allowance for Uncollectible Accounts . . . . . . | | 500 |

   To correct the write-off of James Ryan's account on January 15.

   12 | Cash . . . . | 500 |
   | Accounts Receivable—James Ryan . . . . . . | | 500 |

   To record the collection of James Ryan's account receivable.

DEMONSTRATION PROBLEM 4–3

Following are data related to the Jackson Company's beginning inventory and purchases of a given item of product for the year 1990:

	Units	Amount
Beginning inventory	6,250	@ $2.50
March 15	5,000	@ $2.60
May 10	8,750	@ $2.50
August 12	6,250	@ $2.90
November 20	3,750	@ $3.10

During the year, 25,000 units were sold.

Required:

Compute the ending inventory under each of the following methods:

a. Specific identification (assume ending inventory is taken equally from the August 12 and November 20 purchases).

b. FIFO.

c. LIFO.

d. Weighted-average.

Solution to demonstration problem 4–3

The ending inventory consists of:

	Units
Beginning inventory	6,250
Purchases	23,750
Goods available	30,000
Sales	25,000
Ending inventory	5,000

a. Ending inventory under specific identification:

Purchased	Units	Unit Cost	Total Cost
November 20	2,500	$3.10	$ 7,750
August 12	2,500	2.90	7,250
	5,000		$15,000

b. Ending inventory under FIFO:

Purchased	Units	Unit Cost	Total Cost
November 20	3,750	$3.10	$11,625
August 12	1,250	2.90	3,625
	5,000		$15,250

c. Ending inventory under LIFO:

	Units	Unit Cost	Total Cost
Inventory, January 1	5,000	$2.50	$12,500

d. Ending inventory under weighted-average:

Purchased	Units	Unit Cost	Total Cost
Inventory, January 1	6,250	$2.50	$15,625
March 15	5,000	2.60	13,000
May 10	8,750	2.50	21,875
August 12	6,250	2.90	18,125
November 20	3,750	3.10	11,625
	30,000		$80,250

Weighted-average unit cost is $80,250 ÷ 30,000, or $2.675.
Ending inventory cost is $2.675 × 5,000 = $13,375.

QUESTIONS

1. State several of the advantages of recording revenue at the time a credit sale is made. State one disadvantage of this practice.
2. Explain how perpetual procedure affords control over inventory.
3. Explain the meaning of the phrase "to take a physical inventory."
4. Why does an understated ending inventory understate net income (before income taxes) by the same amount?
5. In what respects are a purchase return and a purchase allowance similar? How do they differ?
6. What kind of an account is Sales Returns and Allowances? Why is such an account used?
7. Conceptually, what should the cost of inventory include?
8. What is the effect of a failure to include the cost of transportation, insurance in transit, and other handling and receiving costs in inventory?

9. What are the two basic ways of determining the necessary amount of the adjusting entry for uncollectible accounts expense?

10. Show how reported net income can be manipulated by a company using LIFO in pricing its inventory. Why is the same manipulation not possible under FIFO?

11. In what three ways can the lower-of-cost-or-market method of inventory measurement be applied?

12. Under what operating conditions will the gross margin method of computing an inventory produce approximately the correct amounts?

EXERCISES

Prepare entries for merchandise return and allowance on both buyer's and seller's books

1. **a.** The Young Company purchased merchandise from the Metro Company on account and, before paying its account, returned damaged merchandise with an invoice price of $1,500. Assuming use of periodic inventory procedure, prepare entries on both firms' books to record the return.

   b. Prepare the necessary entries, assuming that the Metro company granted an allowance of $800 on the damaged goods instead of accepting the return.

Prepare entries using gross price method

2. The Drew Corporation purchased goods for $14,000 on June 14 from Jones Company under the following terms: 2/10, n/30. The bill for the freight amounted to $300 and was paid by Drew Corporation in cash on June 14. Assume that the invoice was paid within the discount period, and prepare all of the entries required on Drew's books under the gross price method.

Prepare journal entries to record uncollectible accounts expense

3. The accounts of the Pond Company as of December 31, 1990, show Accounts Receivable, $360,000; Allowance for Uncollectible Accounts, $2,000 (credit); Sales, $2,160,000; and Sales Returns and Allowances, $40,000. Prepare journal entries to adjust for possible uncollectible accounts under each of the following assumptions:

   a. Uncollectible accounts expense is estimated at one half of 1% of net sales.

   b. The allowance is to be increased to 3% of accounts receivable.

Record write-off and subsequent recovery of account

4. On April 1, 1990, Doran Company, which uses the allowance method of accounting for uncollectible accounts, wrote off Bill Combs' account receivable of $745. On December 14, 1990, the company received a check for that amount from Combs marked "in full of account." Prepare the necessary entries for all of the above.

Use aging schedule to estimate Allowance for Uncollectible Accounts

5. Compute the required size of Allowance for Uncollectible Accounts for the following receivables:

Accounts Receivable	Age (Months)	Estimated Percentage Uncollectible
$200,000	Less than 1	5
80,000	1 to 3	20
40,000	3 to 6	30
10,000	6 to 12	60
2,000	12 and over	90

Compute ending inventory using FIFO and LIFO

6. The Grosse Company inventory records show:

Inventory:
Jan. 1 . . . . 500 units at $12.00 = $6,000
Purchases:
Feb. 14 . . . . 300 units at $10.80 = $3,240
Mar. 18 . . . . 800 units at $10.50 = $8,400
July 21 . . . . 600 units at $11.40 = $6,840
Sept. 27 . . . . 600 units at $10.80 = $6,480
Nov. 27 . . . . 200 units at $11.70 = $2,340
Dec. 31 Inventory . . . . 800 units

a. Present a short schedule showing the measurement of the ending inventory using the LIFO method.

b. Repeat using the FIFO method.

Determine effects on net income

7. The Miller Company's inventory of a certain product consisted of 8,000 units with a cost of $30 each on January 1, 1990. During 1990, numerous units of this product were purchased and sold. Also, during 1990 the purchase price to Miller of this product fell steadily until at year-end it was $22. The inventory at year-end consisted of 12,000 units. State which of the two methods of inventory measurement, LIFO or FIFO, would have resulted in the higher reported net income and explain briefly.

Compute cost of ending inventory and cost of goods sold using weighted-average

8. The following inventory data are for the Davis Company for 1990:

Jan. 1 Inventory, 100 units at $80 = $8,000.
Jan. 31 January sales were 20 units.
Feb. 28 February sales totaled 30 units.
Mar. 1 Purchased 50 units at $84.
Aug. 31 Sales for March through August were 40 units.
Sept. 1 Purchased 10 units at $96.
Dec. 31 September through December sales were 55 units.

Determine the cost of the December 31, 1990, inventory and the cost of goods sold for 1990, using the weighted-average method.

Determine net realizable value

9. Jimmy's Furniture Store has a stereo on hand at year-end that cost $900 and that it expected to sell for $1,200. But, since the stereo has been used as a display model, the estimated selling price is now only $800. Estimated reconditioning costs and selling commission amount to $100. At what dollar amount should this set be included in the year-end inventory? Why?

Compute value of ending inventory using LCM

10. Your assistant prepared the following schedule to assist you in pricing the inventory under the lower-of-cost-or-market method applied on an item basis. What is the dollar amount of ending inventory?

Item	Count	Unit Cost	Unit Market	Total Cost	Total Market
A	200	$36.00	$34.00	$ 7,200	$ 6,800
B	200	16.00	18.00	3,200	3,600
C	600	12.00	12.00	7,200	7,200
D	1,000	20.40	20.80	20,400	20,800
				$38,000	$38,400

Determine insurance settlement using gross margin method

11. Richie Company follows the practice of taking a physical inventory at the end of each calendar-year accounting period to establish the ending inventory amount for financial statement purposes. Its financial statements for the past few years indicate a normal gross margin of 20 percent. On July 25 a fire destroyed the entire store building and contents. The records were in a fire-proof vault and are intact. These records through July 24 show:

Merchandise inventory, January 1	$ 50,000
Merchandise purchases	1,350,000
Purchase returns	15,000
Transportation-in	85,000
Sales	1,550,000
Sales returns	50,000

The company was fully covered by insurance, and it asks you to determine the amount of its claim for loss of merchandise.

Determine ending inventory using retail inventory method

12. Using the retail inventory method, determine the ending inventory at cost from the following:

	Cost	Selling Price
Beginning inventory	$ 210,000	$ 390,000
Purchases	1,908,000	3,168,000
Purchase returns	24,000	45,000
Sales		2,448,000
Sales returns		12,000
Transportation-in	13,800	

PROBLEMS

Prepare and post journal entries using gross invoice amounts

4–1. Erickson Company, which uses periodic inventory procedure, purchased merchandise as follows:

(1) $25,000 from Lunt Company, terms 2/10, n/30.

(2) $18,000 from Andrews Company, terms 2/10, n/30.

The Lunt invoice was paid within the discount period. The Andrews invoice was paid late.

Required:

a. Prepare journal entries for the above transactions, assuming that the invoices were originally recorded at their gross invoice amounts.

b. Post the entries to T-accounts.

Prepare and post journal entries; prepare income statement

4–2. Following are selected, summarized transactions of the Drake Company (which uses periodic inventory procedure) for the year 1990:

1. Sales on account, $900,000; terms 2/10, n/30.
2. Sales returns and allowances totaled $22,000.
3. Customers remitted $794,800 in settlement of $800,000 of accounts after taking discounts offered.
4. Purchases on account, $800,000; terms 2/10, n/30.
5. Purchase returns and allowances amounted to $25,000.
6. Transportation-in costs incurred on account, $30,000.
7. Payments on account, $733,200, in settlement of $740,000 of invoices for merchandise after taking discounts offered.
8. Uncollectible accounts are estimated at 1% of sales, less sales returns and allowances.

Required:

a. Prepare journal entries for the above transactions using the gross price method (omit explanations).

b. Post the entries to T-accounts.

c. Assume that the inventory was $90,000 on January 1 and $145,000 on December 31 and that operating expenses and taxes amount to $90,000—including uncollectible accounts expense. Prepare an income statement for the year which includes the gross margin determination.

Prepare journal entries and post to T-accounts; determine cost of goods sold and gross margin and prepare an income statement

4–3. The following inventory data are for the Green Corporation for January 1990:

Jan. 1 Inventory on hand cost, $4,000.
12 Purchased on account from the Beatle Company goods costing $24,000; terms 2/10, n/30.
12 Paid transportation on goods purchased, $2,000 cash.
15 Returned to the Beatle Company goods costing $4,000.
21 Paid the Beatle Company the amount due.
25 Sale on account to Meyers Company was $28,000; terms n/30.
31 Partial collection of $12,000 was made on the receivable resulting from the sale.

The inventory on hand on January 31 cost $10,000. The operating expenses for the month were $8,000.

Required:

a. Prepare journal entries to record the transactions for the month of January using the gross price method (omit explanations).

b. Post the entries to T-accounts.

c. Determine the cost of goods sold in January.

d. Determine the gross margin for January.

e. Prepare an income statement for January.

Write off bad debt and record expense under alternative methods of estimation

4–4. Presented below are selected accounts of the Hertha Company as of December 31, 1990. Prior to closing the accounts, the $7,000 account of Pond Company is to be written off (this was a credit sale of February 12, 1990).

Accounts receivable	$ 490,000
Allowance for uncollectible accounts	8,000 Dr.
Sales	2,250,000
Sales returns and allowances	30,000

Required:

a. Prepare journal entries to record the above and to record the uncollectible accounts expense for the period, assuming the estimated expense is 2% of net sales.

b. Give the entry to record the estimated expense for the period if the allowance is to be adjusted to 5% of outstanding receivables instead of as in (a) above.

Prepare income statements using FIFO and LIFO inventory methods

4–5. The Butler Company began business on July 1, 1989, selling a single product. For the year ending June 30, 1990, 15,000 units were sold at $40 each. Purchases consisted of 10,000 units on July 1 at $16 and 10,000 units on December 18 at $20. Jim Johnson, the accountant for Butler Company, pre-

164

pared the following income statement for the year ended June 30, 1990, for presentation to the board of directors:

Sales	$600,000
Cost of goods sold	270,000
Gross margin	$330,000
Expenses	160,000
Net income before taxes	$170,000

At the board meeting, members of the board questioned Jim's use of the average cost method in determining the cost of goods sold and the cost of the ending inventory. One member indicated a preference for LIFO; another preferred FIFO; and yet another asked about the effects of using FIFO or LIFO and the direction of price changes. The board directed Jim to prepare the information desired by the various members and to report at the afternoon meeting of the board.

Required:

a. Using the above information, prepare two income statements similar to the one given, one using FIFO and the other using LIFO, for presentation to the board. Assume that Butler Company uses periodic inventory procedure.

b. Repeat *a*, using all of the same information, except assume that the July 1 purchases cost $20 each, while the December purchases cost $16 each.

c. What facts are revealed by the statements in *a* and *b* that should be brought to the board's attention?

Compute gross margin using FIFO and LIFO

4–6. The Crissy Corporation was organized on January 1, 1988, to sell a product whose resale price reacts promptly to changes in cost. Unit prices rose during the three years ended December 31, 1990. Selected data for 1988–90 follow:

Year Ended December 31	Inventory FIFO	Inventory LIFO	Annual Data Purchases	Annual Data Sales
1988	$ 6,400	$4,800	$28,800	$32,400
1989	8,000	5,600	24,000	38,000
1990	13,200	8,000	29,600	32,800

Required:

a. Compute the gross margin for each of the three years under FIFO and under LIFO.

b. Comment on your answer to *a*.

Compute ending inventory and cost of goods sold under FIFO, LIFO, and weighted-average methods

4–7. Following are data relating to the beginning inventory and purchases of the Ralph Company for the year 1990:

Jan. 1 inventory	2,800 @ $8.40
Purchases:	
Feb. 2	2,000 @ 8.00
Apr. 5	4,000 @ 6.96
June 15	2,400 @ 6.80
Sept. 20	2,800 @ 6.40
Nov. 28	3,600 @ 7.20

A physical count showed 4,400 units on hand at the end of the year.

Required:

Compute the cost of goods sold and the cost of the ending inventory under each of the following methods: (a) FIFO, (b) LIFO, and (c) weighted average.

Compute ending inventory, cost of goods sold, and gross margin under FIFO, LIFO, and weighted-average methods

4–8. The following data are related to the beginning inventory and purchases of the Swiss Corporation for 1990.

Jan. 1 inventory	1,000 @ $8.00
Purchases:	
Mar. 2	2,000 @ 8.20
June 5	5,000 @ 8.40
Aug. 12	2,000 @ 8.60

The Swiss Corporation sold 8,000 units at $20 each during 1990.

Required:

Compute the cost of the ending inventory, the cost of goods sold, and the gross margin under each of the following methods: (a) FIFO, (b) LIFO, and (c) weighted average.

Compute value of ending inventory using LCM applied on an item-by-item basis and a total inventory basis

4–9. Given below are data relating to the December 31, 1990, inventory of the Land Company:

Item	Quantity	Unit Cost	Unit Market
1	1,500	$ 9.00	$8.80
2	3,000	6.80	7.20
3	1,000	5.00	5.20
4	2,500	11.60	11.00
5	2,000	10.00	10.40
6	500	7.50	7.10

Required:

a. Compute the ending inventory, applying the lower-of-cost-or-market method to the total inventory.

b. Repeat a, applying the method to individual items.

c. What would be the effect on net income before income taxes of using the method applied to individual items rather than to total inventory?

Determine lowest ending inventory using cost or market dollar amount

4–10. You are the chief accountant of the Beacham Hardware Store, and your assistant has been applying the lower-of-cost-or-market method on an item basis to your company's December 31, 1990, inventory. Your assistant brings the following data to your attention:

Item	Units	Unit Cost
Product R: This item has been selling extremely well. Its retail price was recently raised 20% because replacement cost increased from $400 to $440 per unit	10	$400
Product S: The retail price of this item has been reduced because of a lack of demand. The cost to replace this item has also been reduced—from $120 to $100.	40	120

Item	Units	Unit Cost
Product T: The units on hand of this item are obsolete and damaged to such an extent that it will cost more to repair them than they can be sold for after repair	4	50
Product U: The cost of replacing this item has dropped 5%, but Beacham has a contract to sell all of these items at their regular selling price, which includes normal markup	100	20
Product V: This item is being discontinued. Its sales price is expected to be reduced from $100 to $50, with disposal costs of $4 each expected . .	50	100
Product W: This item was shipped to Beacham by Abrams on a consignment basis, with Beacham to pay only for units sold	20	150
Remainder: No problems encountered. Their dollar amount at lower of cost or market is $56,000.		

Required:

a. Compute the cost or market dollar amount, whichever is lower, for the ending inventory. State the amount assigned to each of the above items separately.

b. For the six items above, state the reason for the unit dollar amount you assigned in *a*.

Compute ending inventory under an alternative method and its effect on net income before taxes

4–11. The accountant for the Wilson Company prepared the following schedule of the company's December 31, 1990, inventory, and used the lower of total cost or total market in determining the cost of the goods sold for the year.

Item	Quantity	Unit Cost	Unit Market	Total Cost	Total Market
A	4,000	$12.00	$12.00	$ 48,000	$ 48,000
B	3,000	8.00	7.20	24,000	21,600
C	6,000	4.00	3.20	24,000	19,200
D	8,000	2.00	2.40	16,000	19,200
				$112,000	$108,000

Required:

a. State whether the method used is an accepted way of applying the lower-of-cost-or-market method.

b. Compute the dollar amount of the inventory under an alternative way of applying this method.

c. What would be the effect on net income before taxes of using the alternative method?

d. If the 3,000 units of product B are obsolete and shopworn so that they can be sold for an estimated $4 each, less total delivery charges of $150, at what amount should they be included in inventory?

Indicate estimation
methods for
inventory during
interim periods,
estimate inventory,
and prepare an
income statement

4–12. Rex Company recently asked Durant Company to sell merchandise to Rex on a credit basis. Durant asked for current financial statements before making a decision. Rex does not wish to incur the cost of taking a physical inventory, which it normally takes only at the end of its accounting year, December 31. Financial statements for the previous three years ending on December 31, 1989, show that Rex has consistently earned a gross margin on net sales of 40%. The accounts show, for the seven months ending on July 31, 1990, the following:

Expenses	$ 656,000
Sales	2,514,000
Purchases	1,452,000
Purchase returns	12,000
Sales returns	74,000
Inventory, January 1, 1990	184,000

Required:

a. Indicate in general terms how the cost of an inventory can be estimated for interim periods.

b. Estimate the July 31, 1990, inventory of Rex.

c. Prepare an income statement for Rex for the seven months ended July 31, 1990.

d. Upon what factor used in preparing the income statement in c does the accuracy of the statement depend very heavily? Explain.

4–13. (Based on the chapter appendix).

Required:

From the following trial balance and supplementary information for the Wells Company, prepare:

a. A 12-column work sheet for the year ended December 31, 1990. (See chapter appendix for illustration of form.)

b. The required closing entries.

Supplementary data:
(a) The building is to be depreciated at the rate of 2% per year.
(b) Depreciate the store fixtures 10% per year.
(c) The Allowance for Uncollectible Accounts is to be increased by one half of 1% of net sales. (Round amount to nearest full dollar.)
(d) Accrued interest on notes receivable is $300.
(e) Accrued interest on the mortgage note is $500.
(f) Accrued sales salaries are $1,400.
(g) Prepaid insurance is $400.
(h) Prepaid advertising is $1,000.
(i) Included in the cash on hand is a worthless check for $50 which was cashed for a former employee in 1990.
(j) Cost of merchandise inventory on hand December 31, 1990, is $55,500.

WELLS COMPANY
Trial Balance
December 31, 1990

	Debits	Credits
Cash	$ 17,200	
Accounts receivable	82,500	
Allowance for doubtful accounts		$ 1,700
Notes receivable	7,500	
Merchandise inventory, January 1, 1990	41,600	
Land	60,000	
Building	110,000	
Accumulated depreciation—building		33,000
Store fixtures	55,600	
Accumulated depreciation—store fixtures		11,120
Accounts payable		37,900
Mortgage note payable		50,000
Capital stock		100,000
Retained earnings		70,180
Sales		551,500
Sales returns and allowances	2,000	
Sales discounts	3,700	
Purchases	312,900	
Purchase returns and allowances		1,400
Purchase discounts		2,600
Transportation-in	7,300	
Sales salaries expense	64,000	
Advertising expense	12,000	
Transportation-out	4,600	
Officers' salaries expense	74,000	
Insurance expense	2,900	
Interest revenue		400
Interest expense	2,000	
	$859,800	$859,800

BUSINESS DECISION PROBLEM 4–1

Minimize income taxes and compute cost of goods sold and cost of ending inventory

The Lighthouse Company, which began operations on January 2, sells a single product, Product X. The following data relate to the purchases of Product X for the year:

	Units	Amount
January 2	250	@ $1.00
February 15	400	@ $1.00
April 8	500	@ $1.08
June 6	200	@ $1.13
August 19	400	@ $1.15
October 5	300	@ $1.25
November 22	250	@ $1.40

Periodic inventory procedure is used. On December 31, a physical inventory of Product X showed that 400 units were on hand.

Mr. Lighthouse is trying to decide which of the following inventory costing methods he should adopt: weighted-average, FIFO, or LIFO. Since Mr. Lighthouse is short of cash, he wants to minimize the amount of income taxes payable.

Required:

In this case, which of the three inventory costing methods will minimize the amount of income taxes payable? What will be the cost of goods sold and the cost of ending inventory under this method?

5 INTERNAL CONTROL AND THE CONTROL OF CASH

LEARNING OBJECTIVES

After studying this chapter, you should be able to:

1. Describe the necessity for and features of internal control.
2. Define cash and list the objectives sought by management in handling a company's cash.
3. Identify procedures for controlling cash receipts and disbursements.
4. Prepare a bank reconciliation statement and make necessary journal entries based on that statement.
5. Explain why a petty cash fund is used, describe its operation, and make the necessary journal entries.
6. Apply the net price method of handling purchase discounts.
7. Describe the operation of the voucher system.
8. Define and use correctly the new terms in the glossary.

So far in the text, the examples have been small corporations. In a small corporation, the president can make all the important decisions and usually can maintain a close watch over the affairs of the business. Often the president personally signs the checks. However, as the business grows and the need arises for additional employees, including other officers and managers, the president begins to lose total control and must trust employees to take over some of the affairs of the business. At this point, the president realizes that precautions must be taken to protect the company's interests. As a result, internal control measures are established.

This chapter discusses the internal control measures a company takes to protect its assets and to promote the accuracy of its accounting records.

You may think that internal control is used just to prevent theft and fraud. However, there is more to internal control. Company policies must be implemented, especially those policies that require compliance with federal law. Personnel must perform their assigned duties to promote efficiency of operations. Correct accounting records must be maintained so that accurate and reliable information is presented in the accounting reports. In this chapter you will learn how internal control is established through control of cash receipts and cash disbursements, proper use of the bank checking account, preparation of the bank reconciliation statement, protection of petty cash funds, and use of the net price method and the voucher system. The establishment of internal control is enhanced by hiring competent and trustworthy employees.

INTERNAL CONTROL

Objective 1: Describe the necessity for and features of internal control

An **internal control system** is defined as the plan of organization and all the procedures and actions taken by an entity to:

1. Protect its assets against theft and waste.
2. Ensure compliance with company policies and federal law.
3. Evaluate the performance of all personnel in the company so as to promote efficiency of operations.
4. Ensure accurate and reliable operating data and accounting reports.

Items 1 and 4 are considered to be "accounting controls," while items 2 and 3 are considered to be "administrative controls." Accounting and administrative controls together comprise the internal control system.

As you study the basic procedures and actions comprising an internal control system, you will realize that even a small corporation can benefit from the use of some internal control measures. Preventing theft and waste is only a part of internal control. In general terms, the purpose of internal control is to ensure the efficient operations of a business, thus making it possible for the business to effectively reach its goals.

Protection of Assets

Assets can be protected by (1) segregation of employee duties, (2) separation of employee functions, (3) rotation of employee job assignments, and (4) use of mechanical devices.

Segregation of employee duties. The **segregation of duties** is accomplished by having the person responsible for safeguarding an asset be someone other than the person who maintains the accounting records for that asset. Responsibility for related transactions should be divided among individuals so that the work of one person serves as a check on the work of others.

When the work of one person is such that it serves as a check on the work of others, then collusion between at least two persons would be necessary to steal assets and cover up the theft in the accounting records. For example, a person could not steal cash from a company and have it go undetected unless the cash records can be changed to cover the shortage. Changing the records can only be accomplished if the person stealing the cash maintains the cash records or is in collusion with the person who maintains the cash records.

Separate employee functions. When the responsibility for a particular work function is assigned to a specific person, that person is accountable for specific tasks. Then, in the event of a problem, the person responsible can be quickly identified.

It is relatively easy to trace lost documents or determine how a particular transaction is recorded when employees are given specific duties. The person responsible for a given task is the person best able to provide information about that task. With this division of responsibilities also goes a sense of pride and importance that tends to make people want to perform to the best of their ability.

Rotating employee's job assignments. When it is the company policy to rotate job assignments, this policy often discourages employees from engaging in long-term schemes to steal from the company. Employees realize that if they steal from the company, the theft may be discovered by the next employee assigned to that position.

Frequently, companies have the policy that all employees must take an annual vacation. This also discourages theft because many dishonest schemes collapse when the employee does not attend to the job on a daily basis.

Mechanical devices. Companies can use mechanical devices to help protect their assets. Devices such as check protectors (machines that perforate the check amount into the check), cash registers, and time clocks make it impossible for employees to alter certain company documents and records.

Compliance with Company Policies and Federal Law

To be effective, internal control policies must be followed by employees. To ensure that a company's internal control policies are carried out, the company must hire competent and trustworthy employees. The execution of effective internal control begins with the time and effort a company expends in hiring employees. Once the employees are hired, the company must train those employees and clearly communicate to them company policies, such as proper authorization before making a cash disbursement. Frequently, written job descriptions are effective in establishing the responsibilities and duties of employees. The initial training of employees should be such that they know exactly what they are expected to do, as well as how to do it.

In publicly held corporations, the company's internal control system must satisfy the requirements of federal law. In December 1977, the Foreign Corrupt Practices Act (FCPA) was enacted by Congress. Under this law, publicly held corporations are **required** to devise and maintain an effective system of internal control and to keep accurate accounting records. The responsibility for the establishment and the maintenance of internal control rests solely with management. Thus, a wise management team will show that an effective internal control system exists by documenting its features. The passage of this law came about partly because of the cover-ups in company accounting records of bribes and kickbacks made to foreign governments or government officials. The FCPA made this specific type of bribery illegal.

Evaluation of Personnel Performance

To evaluate how well company employees are doing their jobs, many companies have an internal auditing staff. **Internal auditing** consists of investigating and evaluating employees' compliance with the company's policies and procedures. Companies hire *internal auditors* to perform these audits; these individuals are trained regarding company policies and their own duties.

Internal auditors should encourage operating efficiency throughout the company and be constantly alert for breakdowns in the company's system of internal control. In addition, internal auditors make recommendations for the improvement of the company's internal control system when necessary. All companies can benefit from internal auditing; however, internal auditing is especially necessary in large organizations because the owner(s) cannot be personally involved with all aspects of the business.

Accuracy of Accounting Reports

Companies should maintain complete and accurate accounting records. The best method to ensure that this is done is to hire and train competent individuals. Periodically, supervisors should evaluate an employee's performance to make sure the employee is following company policies. Accounting records that are inaccurate or inadequate serve as an invitation to theft by dishonest employees because the theft can be easily concealed.

Almost all accounting transactions are supported by one or more business documents. These source documents are an integral part of the internal control system. For optimal control, source documents should be serially numbered. (Transaction documentation and related aspects of internal control will be presented throughout the text.)

Since source documents serve as documentation of business transactions, from time to time the validity of these documents should be checked. For example, to review a merchandise transaction, the documents used to record the transaction should be checked against the proper accounting records. When the accounting department records a merchandise transaction, it should receive copies of the following four documents:

1. Purchase requisition. A **purchase requisition** is a written request from an employee inside the company to the purchasing department to purchase certain items.
2. Purchase order. A **purchase order** is a document sent from the purchasing department to a supplier requesting that merchandise or other items be shipped to the purchaser.
3. Invoice. An **invoice** is the bill sent from the supplier to the purchaser requesting payment for the merchandise shipped.
4. Receiving report. A **receiving report** is a document prepared by the receiving department showing the descriptions and quantities of all items received from a supplier in a particular shipment.

These four documents together serve as authorization to pay for merchandise and should be checked against the accounting records. In the absence of these documents, a company might fail to pay a legitimate invoice, pay fictitious invoices, or pay an invoice more than once. Proper internal control can be accomplished only by periodically checking the source documents of business transactions with the accounting records of those transactions. Illustration 5.1 shows the flow of documents and goods in a merchandising transaction.

Unfortunately, even if a company implements all of the above features in its internal control system, theft may occur. If employees are dishonest, they can usually figure out a way to steal from a company, thus circumventing even the most effective internal control system. Therefore, it is advisable to carry adequate casualty insurance on assets. This insurance will reimburse the company for loss of a nonmonetary asset such as specialized equipment. Companies should also have **fidelity bonds** on employees handling cash and other negotiable instruments. These bonds will ensure that the company is reimbursed for losses due to theft of cash and other monetary assets. With both casualty insurance on assets and fidelity bonds on employees, a company can recover at least a portion of any loss that occurs.

Internal Control in a Computer Environment

The use of computers to maintain financial records makes it necessary to use the same internal control principles of separation of duties and control over access that are used in a manual accounting system. The exact control steps taken depend on whether you are using larger mainframe and minicomputers or small microcomputers.

Mainframe and minicomputers are used in the accounting environments of large corporations. Because of the size and complexity of these computers, specially trained persons are needed to keep these computer systems operating. Systems specialists operate the computer system it-

Illustration 5.1
FLOW OF DOCUMENTS AND GOODS IN A MERCHANDISING TRANSACTION

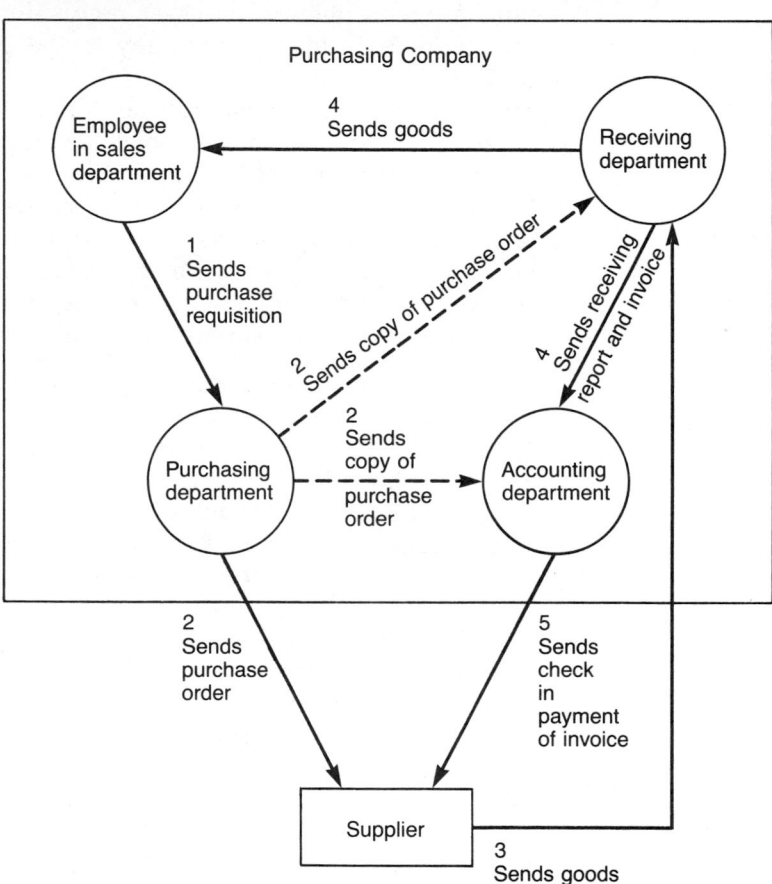

Steps:
1. Employee in sales department sends purchase requisition to purchasing department.
2. Purchasing department sends purchase order to supplier, with copies going to the receiving department and the accounting department.
3. Supplier sends goods and invoice to receiving department, which checks goods against purchase order and invoice.
4. Receiving department sends goods to sales department and sends receiving report and invoice to accounting department.
5. Accounting department sends check in payment of invoice to the supplier.

self, while programmers develop the programs that direct the computer to perform specific tasks. In a mainframe or minicomputer environment, internal control should include the following:

1. Computer access should be controlled by placing the computer in an easily secured room, and only persons authorized to operate the computer should be allowed to enter the room.

2. Systems specialists who operate the computer should not have programming experience, and programmers should not have access to the computer. This policy prevents a person from making unauthorized changes to certain programs.

3. Some programs, such as one used to print monthly accounts receivable statements to send to credit customers, should only be run at an authorized time. If programs and data are stored on magnetic tape, the tapes should be stored under lock and key and under the control of a "librarian." The librarian should be independent of the computer systems and programming function.

Internal control for a microcomputer environment is slightly different because smaller businesses often use microcomputers and usually are not able to hire a staff of specialists to run the computer. Thus, the programmers may run the computer. Also, the same microcomputer is often used by several persons.

In a microcomputer environment, the following controls can be useful:

1. The microcomputer should be kept under lock and key, and only persons authorized to use the computer should have a key.

2. Each computer user should have tight control over his or her diskettes on which programs and data are stored. Just as a single person maintains custody over a certain set of records in a manual system, in a computer system a single person maintains custody over diskettes containing a certain type of information (such as the account receivable subsidiary ledger). These diskettes should be locked up at night, and backup copies should be made.

The use of computers in accounting does not lessen the need for internal control. In fact, the access to a computer by an unauthorized person could result in accelerated theft in a shorter span of time.

CONTROLLING CASH

Objective 2: Define cash and list the objectives sought by management in handling a company's cash

In the preceding section you learned about some of the general principles of internal control. This section focuses specifically on the control of cash. Since cash is the most liquid of all assets, a business cannot survive and prosper if it does not have adequate control over its cash.

In accounting, **cash** includes coins; paper money; certain undeposited negotiable instruments such as checks, bank drafts, and money orders; amounts in checking and savings accounts; and demand certificates of deposit. A **certificate of deposit** is an interest-bearing deposit in a bank that can be withdrawn at will (demand CD) or at a fixed maturity date (time CD). Cash does not include postage stamps, IOUs, notes receivable, or time certificates of deposit.

In the general ledger, usually two cash accounts are maintained—Cash (bank checking account balance) and Petty Cash. The balances of these two accounts are combined into one amount and reported as "Cash" on the company's balance sheet.

Since many business transactions involve cash, it is a vital factor in the operation of a business. Of all the company's assets, cash is the most easily mishandled either through theft or carelessness. To protect its cash, companies should:

1. Account for all cash transactions accurately so that correct information will be available regarding cash flows and balances.
2. Make certain there is enough cash available to pay bills as they come due.
3. Avoid holding too much idle cash, because excess cash could be invested to generate income such as interest.
4. Prevent loss of cash due to theft or fraud.

The need to control cash is clearly evident. Although you might think first about how to protect cash from the greedy hands of a dishonest employee, as you can see from the list above there is more to controlling cash. Without the proper timing of cash flows and the protection of idle cash, a business cannot survive. This section discusses cash receipts and cash disbursements. Later in the chapter you will learn about the importance of preparing a bank reconciliation statement for each bank checking account, as well as controlling the petty cash fund. The net price method and voucher system are also described.

Controlling Cash Receipts

Objective 3: Identify procedures for controlling cash receipts and disbursements

When a merchandising company sells its merchandise, it may receive cash immediately or several days or weeks later. The cash that is received immediately "over the counter" usually is recorded and placed in a cash register. The presence of the customer as the sale is "rung up" usually ensures that the correct amount of the sale is entered in the cash register. At the end of each day, the cash in each cash register is reconciled with the cash register tape or computer printout for that register. When cash is received later, it is almost always in the form of checks. A record of the checks received should be prepared as soon as they are received. Some merchandising companies receive all their cash receipts on a delayed basis in the form of payments on accounts receivable (see the cash receipts cycle for merchandise transactions in Illustration 5.2).

Although the specific procedures for controlling cash receipts vary with each business, there are several basic principles:

1. A record of all cash receipts should be prepared as soon as cash is received. Most thefts of cash occur before a record is made of the receipt. Once a record is made, it is easier to trace a theft.
2. All cash receipts should be deposited on the day they are received or on the next business day. Undeposited cash is more susceptible to misappropriation.

Illustration 5.2
CASH RECEIPTS CYCLE FOR
MERCHANDISE TRANSACTIONS

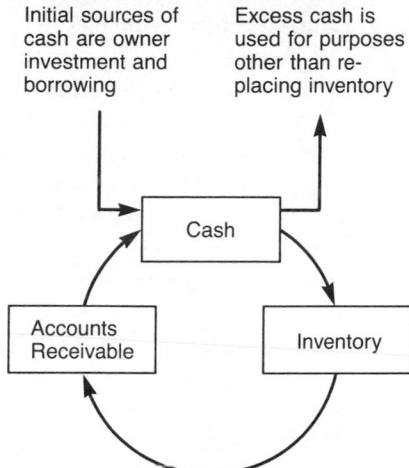

Initial sources of cash are owner investment and borrowing

Excess cash is used for purposes other than replacing inventory

Cash

Accounts Receivable

Inventory

Cash initially comes into the business from owner investment and borrowing. Cash is invested in inventory and other assets. When inventory is sold, cash may be received immediately, or receipt may be delayed and an account receivable is involved. The inventory generally is sold at more than cost so the company can make a profit. Each time the cycle is completed, the amount of cash grows and may be used for purposes other than replacing inventory.

3. The person who handles cash receipts should not also be the person who records the receipts in the accounting records. This control feature follows the general principle of "segregation of duties" given earlier in the chapter, as does item 4 below.
4. If possible, the person who receives the cash should not also be the person to disburse the cash. This control measure is possible in all but the smallest companies.

Controlling Cash Disbursements

Controls are also needed over cash disbursements. Since most of a firm's cash is spent by check, many of the internal controls for cash disbursements deal with checks and authorizations for cash payments. The basic principle of segregation of duties is also applied in controlling cash disbursements. Following are some basic control procedures for cash disbursements:

1. All disbursements should be made by check or from petty cash. Proper approval for all disbursements should be obtained, and a

permanent record of each disbursement should be created. In many retail stores, refunds for returned merchandise are made from the cash register. If this practice is followed, refund tickets should be prepared and approved by a supervisor before cash is refunded.

2. All checks should be serially numbered, and access to checks should be limited to employees authorized to write checks.
3. Preferably, two signatures should be required on each check so that one person alone cannot withdraw funds from the bank account.
4. If possible, the person who authorizes payment of a bill should not be allowed to sign checks. Otherwise, the checks could be written to "friends" in payment of fictitious invoices.
5. Approved documents should be required to support all checks issued.
6. The person authorizing cash disbursements should be certain that payment is for a legitimate purpose and is made out for the exact amount and to the proper party.
7. When liabilities are paid, the supporting documents should be stamped "paid," and the date and number of the check issued should be indicated. These procedures lessen the chance of paying the same debt more than once.
8. The person(s) who signs checks should not have access to canceled checks and should not prepare the bank reconciliation. This feature makes it more difficult to conceal a theft.
9. The bank reconciliation should be prepared each month, preferably by a person who has no other cash duties, so that errors and shortages will be quickly discovered.
10. All checks that are prepared incorrectly should be voided. Such checks should be physically marked "void" and retained to prevent their unauthorized use.
11. A voucher system (described later) may be needed in large firms for close control of cash.
12. Use of the net price method of recording purchases (described later in this chapter) helps avoid loss of purchase discounts through planned timing of cash payments.

Illustration 5.3 shows an overview of some of the internal control considerations relating to cash.

Almost without exception, companies use checking accounts to handle their cash transactions. The company deposits its cash receipts in a bank checking account and writes checks to pay its bills. The bank sends the company a statement each month. The company checks this statement against its records to determine if any corrections or adjustments are needed in either the company's balance or the bank's balance. You will learn how to do this later in the chapter when the bank reconciliation statement is discussed. In the next section you will learn about the bank checking account. If you have a personal checking account, some of this information will be familiar to you.

Illustration 5.3
SOME INTERNAL CONTROL CONSIDERATIONS
REGARDING CASH

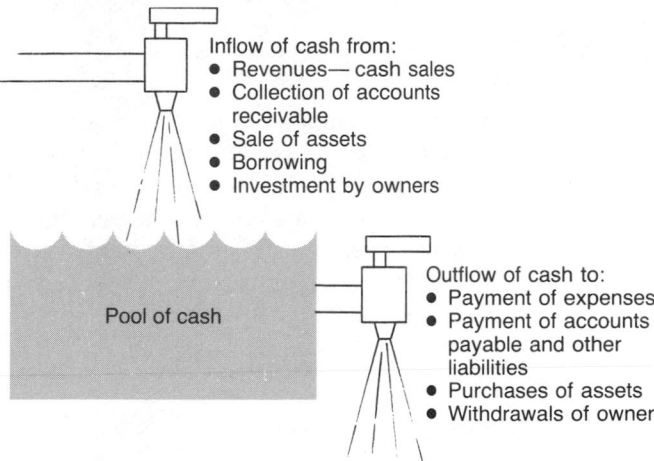

Inflow of cash from:
- Revenues— cash sales
- Collection of accounts receivable
- Sale of assets
- Borrowing
- Investment by owners

Pool of cash

Outflow of cash to:
- Payment of expenses
- Payment of accounts payable and other liabilities
- Purchases of assets
- Withdrawals of owner

Internal Control Considerations
- Are all cash receipts being properly recorded and actually going into the company's pool of cash, or are individuals siphoning off some of these receipts for their own use?
- Is the pool of cash protected from theft? Is the cash on hand managed so as to produce income for the company and yet be available when needed to make legitimate disbursements?
- Is there close control over cash disbursements to ensure that only legitimate disbursements are made in the proper amounts and on a timely basis?

THE BANK CHECKING ACCOUNT

Banks seek to earn income by providing a variety of services to individuals, businesses, and other entities such as churches, libraries, and so on. One of these services is the checking account. A **checking account** is a money balance maintained in the bank that is subject to withdrawal by the depositor, or owner of the money, on demand. To provide depositors with an accurate record of depositor funds received and disbursed, a bank uses the business documents discussed in this section.[1]

The Signature Card

A bank requires a new depositor to complete a **signature card,** which provides the signatures of persons authorized to sign checks drawn upon an account. The card is retained at the bank to identify signatures on checks

---

[1]Due to relaxed federal regulations, institutions other than banks—such as savings and loan associations and credit unions—now offer checking account services. All of these institutions function somewhat similarly, but for simplicity's sake only banks will be discussed here.

paid by the bank. The bank does not compare every check with this signature card; it usually makes the comparison only when the depositor disputes the validity of a check paid by the bank.

Deposit Ticket

When a bank deposit is made, the depositor prepares a deposit ticket or slip. A **deposit ticket** is a form that shows the date and the items that make up the deposit (see Illustration 5.4). The ticket is often preprinted to show the depositor's name, address, and account number for the account into which the deposit is made. Items comprising the deposit—cash and a list of checks—are entered on the ticket when the deposit is made. Upon making the deposit, the depositor is given a receipt showing the date and amount deposited.

Check

A **check** is a written order on a bank to pay a specific sum of money to the party designated as the payee by the party issuing the check. Thus, there are three parties to every check transaction: the bank, the **payee** (party to whom the check is made payable), and the **drawer** (depositor). Most checks are serially numbered and preprinted with information about the depositor, such as name, address, and telephone number. Often a business check will have an attached remittance advice. A **remittance advice** informs the payee why the drawer (or maker) of the check is making this payment; it is detached from the check before the check is cashed or deposited (see Illustration 5.5).

Illustration 5.4
DEPOSIT TICKET

Illustration 5.5
CHECK WITH ATTACHED REMITTANCE ADVICE

			No. 378

R.L. LEE COMPANY
1021 Roy Lane
East Lansing, Mich. 48823

May 4 ___ 19 91   74-992 / 724

PAY TO THE ORDER OF   K.F. Frazer Co. --- $ 1,250.00

One thousand two hundred fifty and no/100 ------------------------------------- DOLLARS

Brookfield Plaza Branch
East Lansing State Bank
WITH TRUST SERVICES
East Lansing, Michigan 48823

R.L. Lee

⑈072409927⑈   093061620⑈01 ⑈9531

Remittance advice (detach before depositing)

Date	P.O. No.	Description	Amount
5/4/91	R204	Payment in full of your invoice #4556	$1,250.00

Bank Statement

A **bank statement** is a statement issued (usually monthly) by a bank describing the activities in a depositor's checking account during the period. Illustration 5.6 shows a bank statement that includes the following data:

1. Deposits made to the checking account during the period.
2. Checks paid out of the depositor's checking account by the bank during the period. These checks have "cleared" the bank and are "canceled."
3. Other deductions from the checking account for items such as service charges, NSF (nonsufficient funds) checks, safe-deposit box rent, and check printing fees. **Service charges** are assessed by the bank on the depositor to cover the cost of handling the checking account, such as check clearing charges. An **NSF check** is a customer's check returned from the customer's bank because the customer's checking account balance was insufficient to cover the check. As a result, the check is returned to the depositor's bank, and the depositor's bank deducts the amount of the check from the depositor's checking account. Since the customer still owes the depositor money, the depositor will restore the amount of the NSF check to the account receivable for that customer in the company's books.
4. Other additions to the checking account for items such as proceeds of a note collected by the bank for the depositor and interest earned on the account.[2]

---

[2]Effective January 1, 1982, revised federal regulations permit banks to pay interest on a depositor's checking account balance.

Illustration 5.6
BANK STATEMENT

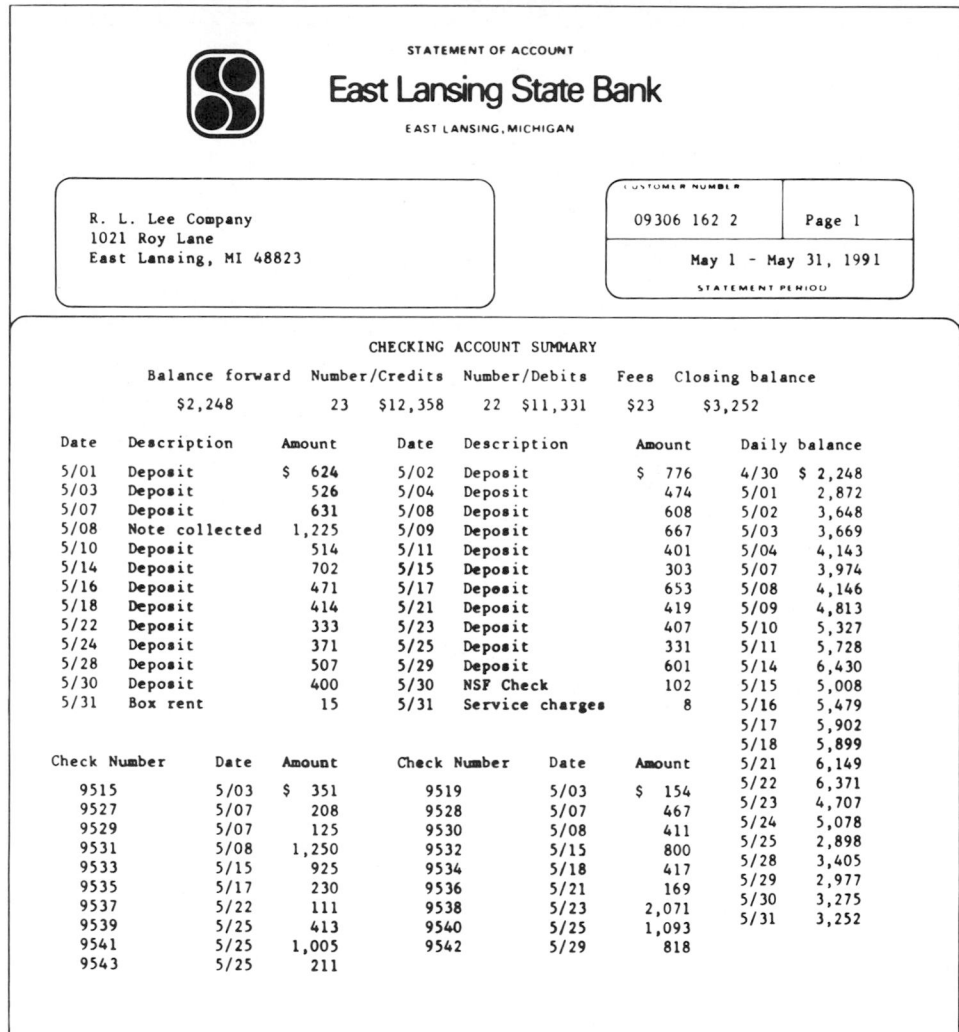

STATEMENT OF ACCOUNT

East Lansing State Bank

EAST LANSING, MICHIGAN

R. L. Lee Company
1021 Roy Lane
East Lansing, MI 48823

CUSTOMER NUMBER		
09306 162 2		Page 1
May 1 - May 31, 1991		
STATEMENT PERIOD		

CHECKING ACCOUNT SUMMARY

Balance forward	Number/Credits		Number/Debits		Fees	Closing balance
$2,248	23	$12,358	22	$11,331	$23	$3,252

Date	Description	Amount	Date	Description	Amount		Daily balance
5/01	Deposit	$ 624	5/02	Deposit	$ 776	4/30	$ 2,248
5/03	Deposit	526	5/04	Deposit	474	5/01	2,872
5/07	Deposit	631	5/08	Deposit	608	5/02	3,648
5/08	Note collected	1,225	5/09	Deposit	667	5/03	3,669
5/10	Deposit	514	5/11	Deposit	401	5/04	4,143
5/14	Deposit	702	5/15	Deposit	303	5/07	3,974
5/16	Deposit	471	5/17	Deposit	653	5/08	4,146
5/18	Deposit	414	5/21	Deposit	419	5/09	4,813
5/22	Deposit	333	5/23	Deposit	407	5/10	5,327
5/24	Deposit	371	5/25	Deposit	331	5/11	5,728
5/28	Deposit	507	5/29	Deposit	601	5/14	6,430
5/30	Deposit	400	5/30	NSF Check	102	5/15	5,008
5/31	Box rent	15	5/31	Service charges	8	5/16	5,479
						5/17	5,902
						5/18	5,899

Check Number	Date	Amount	Check Number	Date	Amount		Daily balance
9515	5/03	$ 351	9519	5/03	$ 154	5/21	6,149
9527	5/07	208	9528	5/07	467	5/22	6,371
9529	5/07	125	9530	5/08	411	5/23	4,707
9531	5/08	1,250	9532	5/15	800	5/24	5,078
9533	5/15	925	9534	5/18	417	5/25	2,898
9535	5/17	230	9536	5/21	169	5/28	3,405
9537	5/22	111	9538	5/23	2,071	5/29	2,977
9539	5/25	413	9540	5/25	1,093	5/30	3,275
9541	5/25	1,005	9542	5/29	818	5/31	3,252
9543	5/25	211					

In addition to the data shown in the bank statement in Illustration 5.6, bank statements also can show nonroutine deposits made to the depositor's checking account. Such deposits are not made directly by the depositor but, rather, by a third party. For example, the bank may have received a wire transfer of funds for the depositor.

A **wire transfer of funds** is an interbank transfer of funds by telephone. An interbank transfer of funds is often used by companies that operate in many widely scattered locations and therefore have checking accounts with several different local banks. These companies may set up special procedures to avoid accumulating too much idle cash in local bank accounts. One such procedure involves the use of special-instruction bank accounts. For example, **transfer bank accounts** may be set up so that local banks automatically transfer to a central bank (by wire or bank draft) all amounts on deposit in excess of a stated amount. In this way, funds not needed for local operations are sent quickly to company headquarters, where the funds can be used or invested as the company deems necessary.

Frequently, the bank returns canceled checks and original deposit tickets with the bank statement. Since it is expensive to sort, handle, and mail these items, banks are beginning to discontinue returning them. These documents are usually stored on microfilm at the bank, with photocopies available if needed. Most depositors need only a detailed bank statement, as shown in Illustration 5.6, and not the original documents to show what transactions occurred during a given period.

When banks debit or credit a depositor's checking account, they prepare debit and credit memos. These memos may also be returned with the bank statement. A **debit memo** is a form used by a bank to explain a deduction from the depositor's account; a **credit memo** explains an addition to the account. The terms *debit memo* and *credit memo* may seem reversed, but remember that the depositor's checking account is a liability—an account payable—of the bank. So, when the bank seeks to reduce a depositor's balance, a debit memo is prepared. To increase the balance, a credit memo is prepared. Examples of debit and credit memos are shown in Illustration 5.7. Banks are also trying to eliminate the mailing of these documents to the depositor and to rely instead on explanations on the bank statement.

Information the depositor did not know prior to receiving the bank statement (items 3 and 4 on page 183) requires new journal entries. After the entries have been made to record the new information, the balance in the Cash account is the actual cash available to the company. When the depositor has already received notice of NSF checks and other bank charges or credits, the needed journal entries may have been made earlier. In this chapter we assume no entries have been made for these items unless stated otherwise.

When a company receives its bank statement, the company must check the bank record of company cash with its own record. If you have a personal checking account, you also should check your bank statement with your checkbook. You can use the form on the back of the bank statement to record your checks that have not yet been paid by the bank and your deposits not yet shown on the bank statement. Some small businesses may also use this form. However, in addition they may prepare a bank reconciliation statement, which you will learn how to prepare in the next section.

Illustration 5.7
DEBIT MEMORANDUM (TOP) AND CREDIT MEMORANDUM (BOTTOM)

Debit memo

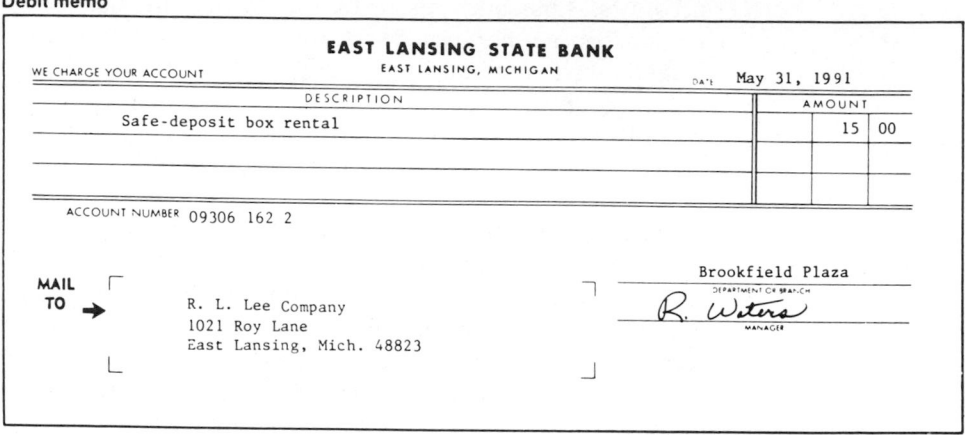

Credit memo

BANK RECONCILIATION STATEMENT

Objective 4:
Prepare a bank reconciliation state-ment and make necessary journal entries based on that statement

A **bank reconciliation statement,** often called a *bank reconciliation,* is a statement the company prepares to "reconcile," or explain, the difference between the cash balance shown on the bank statement and the cash balance shown on the company's books. The bank reconciliation is prepared to determine the company's actual cash balance. An example of a bank reconciliation statement is shown in Illustration 5.8.

The bank reconciliation statement is divided into two main sections. One section, on the left in Illustration 5.8, begins with the balance shown on the bank statement. The second section, on the right in Illustration 5.8, begins with the company's balance as shown on the company's books. Adjustments are made to both the "bank" and "book" balances; after these adjustments, both adjusted balances should be the same.

Illustration 5.8
BANK RECONCILIATION STATEMENT

R. L. LEE COMPANY
Bank Reconciliation Statement
May 31, 1990

Balance per bank statement, May 31, 1990	$3,252	Balance per ledger, May 31, 1990		$1,891
Add: Deposit in transit	452	Add: Note collected		1,225
	$3,704			$3,116
Less: Outstanding checks:				
No. 9544	$322	Less: NSF check	$102	
No. 9545	168	Safe-deposit box rent . .	15	
No. 9546	223 713	Service charges	8	125
Adjusted balance, May 31, 1990 . . .	$2,991	Adjusted balance, May 31, 1990 .		$2,991

The following steps are used in preparing the bank reconciliation statement:

1. *Deposits.* The deposits listed on the bank statement are compared with the deposits on the company's books. This can be done by placing check marks in the bank statement and in the company's books by the deposits that agree. Then the deposits in transit are determined. A **deposit in transit** is typically a day's cash receipts recorded in the depositor's books in one period but recorded as a deposit by the bank in the succeeding period. The most common deposit in transit is the deposit of the cash receipts of the last business day of the month. Normally, deposits in transit occur only near the end of the period covered by the bank statement. For example, a deposit made in a bank's night depository on May 31 would be recorded by the company on May 31 and by the bank on June 1. Thus, the deposit will not appear on a bank statement for the month ended May 31. The deposits in transit listed in last month's bank reconciliation should also be checked against the bank statement. Any missing deposit that does not involve a deposit made at the end of the period should be investigated immediately.

2. *Paid checks.* If canceled checks are returned with the bank statement, first compare them to the bank statement to be sure the amounts on the statement agree with the checks. Then sort the checks in numerical order. Next determine which checks are outstanding. **Outstanding checks** are checks issued by a depositor that have not yet been paid by the bank upon which they are drawn. The party receiving the check may not deposit it immediately. As a result, sometimes it takes several days or even weeks for checks written to clear the banking system. The outstanding checks are determined by a process of elimination. The check numbers that have cleared the bank are compared with a list of the check numbers of the checks issued by the company. Check marks are used in the company's record of checks issued to identify those checks returned by the

bank. Checks issued that have not yet been returned by the bank are the outstanding checks. If the bank does not return checks but provides only a listing of the cleared checks on the bank statement, the outstanding checks are determined by comparing this list with the company's record of checks issued.

Sometimes checks written long ago will still be outstanding. Checks outstanding as of the beginning of the month will appear on the prior month's bank reconciliation. Most of these will have cleared during the current month; those that have not cleared should be listed as still outstanding on the current month's reconciliation.

3. *Bank debit and credit memos.* Verify all debit and credit memos on the bank's statement. These are memos for such items as service charges, NSF checks, safe-deposit box rent, notes collected for the depositor by the bank, and so on. The bank debits and credits should be checked with the depositor's books to see if they have already been recorded. The accountant should make journal entries for any such items not in the company's books.

4. *Errors.* List any errors that have been found. A common error that occurs is when the depositor records a check in the accounting records at an amount that differs from the actual amount on the check. For example, a $47 check may be recorded at $74. The check will clear the bank at the amount written on the check ($47), but the depositor frequently does not catch the error until the bank statement or canceled checks are reviewed. Any error in the depositor's books will require an adjustment on the depositor's books.

Deposits in transit, outstanding checks, and bank service charges usually account for the difference between the company's Cash account and the bank balances. (This is also true in your personal checkbook record and the bank balance shown on your bank statement.) Remember that *all items shown on the bank reconciliation as adjustments of the book (ledger) balance will require journal entries to adjust the Cash account; items appearing on the bank side do not require entries by the depositor.* Any bank errors, of course, should be called to the bank's attention.

To illustrate the preparation of the bank reconciliation shown in Illustration 5.8, assume the following:

1. On May 31, 1990, R. L. Lee Company showed a balance in its Cash account of $1,891. On June 2, Lee received its bank statement for the month ended May 31, which showed an ending balance of $3,252.
2. A matching of debits to the Cash account on the books with deposits on the bank statement showed that the $452 of receipts of May 31 are included in Cash but not included as a deposit on the bank statement.
3. An examination of checks issued and checks cleared showed three checks outstanding:

No. 9544	$322
No. 9545	168
No. 9546	223
Total	$713

4. Included with the bank statement was a credit memo for $1,225 for collection of a note owed to Lee by Shipley Company. Lee did not earn interest on the note.[3] Such a note is called a noninterest-bearing note.
5. Included with the bank statement is a $102 debit memo for an NSF check written by R. Johnson and deposited by Lee.
6. Charges made to Lee's account include $15 for safe-deposit box rent and $8 for service charges.

After reconciling the book and bank balances, Lee Company finds that its actual cash balance is $2,991. The following entries are needed to record information from the bank reconciliation.

```
Cash . . . . . . . . . . . . . . . . . . . . . . . .    1,225
     Notes Receivable—Shipley Company . . . . . . . . . . . .           1,225
  To record note collected from Shipley Company.


Accounts Receivable—R. Johnson* . . . . . . . . . . . . .     102
     Cash . . . . . . . . . . . . . . . . . . . . . . . .                 102
  To charge NSF check back to customer, R. Johnson.


Bank Service Charges Expense . . . . . . . . . . . . . . .      23
     Cash . . . . . . . . . . . . . . . . . . . . . . . .                  23
  To record bank service charges.
```

* This debit would be posted to the Accounts Receivable control account in the general ledger and to R. Johnson's account in the accounts receivable subsidiary ledger.

The income statement for the period ending May 31, 1990, would include the $23 bank service charges as an expense. The May 31 balance sheet will show $2,991 cash, the actual cash balance.

The deposit in transit and the outstanding checks are already recorded in the depositor's books and will be handled routinely when they reach the bank. Since these items appear on the bank side of the reconciliation, they require no entry in the company's books. These items will be processed by the bank in the subsequent period.

When more than one checking account is maintained by a company, each account must be reconciled separately with the balance on the bank statement for that account. The depositor should then also check carefully to see that the bank did not make an error in keeping separate the transactions of the two accounts.

Certified and Cashier's Checks

To make sure a check will not "bounce" and become an NSF check, a payee may demand that the maker's check be a certified or cashier's check. Both certified checks and cashier's checks are liabilities of the bank rather than the depositor. As a result, these checks usually are accepted without question.

■ A **certified check** is a check written, or drawn, by a depositor and taken to the depositor's bank for certification. The bank will stamp

---

[3]Normally, interest is earned on notes, but we ignore this to simplify the discussion.

"certified" across the face of the check and insert the name of the bank and the date; the certification will be signed by a bank official. A check is certified only when the depositor's balance is large enough to cover the check. The amount of the check is deducted from the depositor's account at the time it is certified by the bank.

■ A **cashier's check** is a check drawn by a bank made out to either the depositor or a third party after deducting the amount of the check from the depositor's account or receiving cash from the depositor.

In this section you learned that all cash receipts should be deposited in the bank and all cash disbursements should be made by check. However, the next section explains that it is sometimes convenient to have small amounts of cash (petty cash) available for minor expenditures.

PETTY CASH FUNDS

Objective 5: Explain why a petty cash fund is used, describe its operation, and make the necessary journal entries

At times, every business finds it convenient to have small amounts of cash available for immediate payment of items such as delivery charges, postage stamps, taxi fares, supper money for employees working overtime, and other small items. To permit these disbursements to be made in cash and still maintain adequate control over the cash, companies frequently establish a **petty cash fund** of a round figure such as $100 or $500.

Usually one individual, called the petty cash custodian or cashier, is responsible for the operation of the fund, which includes the control of the petty cash and documenting the disbursements made from the fund. By assigning the responsibility for the fund to one individual, the company has internal control over the cash in the fund. In this section you will learn how to both establish and operate a petty cash fund.

Establishing the Fund

The petty cash fund is established by writing a check for, say, $100. The amount of a petty cash fund should be large enough to make disbursements for a reasonable period, such as a month.

For example, assume a $100 petty cash fund is to be established. A check in that amount is drawn, payable to cash or the petty cash custodian. The following entry is required:

```
Petty Cash . . . . . . . . . . . . . . . . . . . . . . . . . . . . . . .   100
    Cash . . . . . . . . . . . . . . . . . . . . . . . . . . . . . . . .          100
    To establish a petty cash fund.
```

The check is cashed, and the money is turned over to the petty cash custodian, who normally places the money in a small box that can be locked. The fund is now ready to be disbursed as needed.

Operating the Fund

One of the conveniences of the petty cash fund is that no journal entries are required when payments are made from the fund. Thus, using a petty cash fund avoids the need for making many entries for small amounts. Only when the fund is reimbursed will an entry be made in the journal.

When there is a need to disburse cash from the fund, a petty cash voucher is prepared by the petty cash custodian and should be signed by the person receiving the funds. A **petty cash voucher** (see Illustration 5.9) is a document or form that shows the amount of and reason for a petty cash disbursement. A voucher should be prepared for each disbursement from the fund. If an invoice for the expenditure is provided, the invoice should be stapled to the petty cash voucher. The person responsible for petty cash is at all times accountable for having cash and petty cash vouchers equal to the total amount of the fund.

Replenishing the Fund

When the petty cash fund becomes low, it should be replenished. The petty cash vouchers are presented to the person having authority to order that the fund be reimbursed. The vouchers are examined by that person, and, if all is in order, a check is drawn to restore the fund to its original amount.

To determine which accounts to debit, the petty cash vouchers are summarized according to the reasons for expenditure. The petty cash vouchers are then stamped or defaced to prevent reuse. The journal entry to record replenishing the fund would debit the various accounts indicated by the summary and credit Cash.

For example, assume the $100 petty cash fund currently has a money balance of $7.40. A summary of the vouchers shows payments of $22.75 for transportation-in, $50.80 for stamps, and $19.05 for an advance to an employee; these payments total $92.60. After the vouchers have been ex-

Illustration 5.9
PETTY CASH VOUCHER

PETTY CASH VOUCHER NO. 359			
To Local Cartage, Inc.		Date June 29, 1990	
EXPLANATION	ACCT. NO.	AMOUNT	
Freight on parts	27	2	27
APPROVED BY *a. E. S.*		RECEIVED PAYMENT *Ken Black*	

amined and approved, a check is drawn for $92.60 which, when cashed, restores the cash in the fund to its $100 balance. The journal entry to record replenishment is:

Transportation-In	22.75	
Postage Expense	50.80	
Advances to Employees	19.05	
Cash		92.60
To replenish petty cash fund.		

At the end of an accounting period, any petty cash disbursements for which the fund has not yet been replenished must be recorded. Since the fund has not been replenished, the credit would be to Petty Cash rather than Cash. Failure to make an entry at the end of an accounting period would cause errors in both the income statement and balance sheet. The easiest way to record these disbursements is to replenish the fund. Replenishing the fund at the end of an accounting period is handled exactly as at any other time.

If, after some experience, a petty cash fund is found to be larger than needed, the excess petty cash should be deposited in the company's checking account. The required entry debits Cash and credits Petty Cash for the amount returned and deposited. On the other hand, a petty cash fund may be too small, requiring replenishment every few days. The entry to record an increase in the size of the fund debits Petty Cash and credits Cash for the amount of the increase.

Cash Short and Over

Errors can be made in making change from the petty cash fund. In such cases, the amount of cash in the fund will be more or less than the amount of the fund less the total vouchers. When the fund is restored to its original amount, the credit to Cash is for the difference between the established amount and the actual cash in the fund. Debits are made for all vouchered items. Any discrepancy should be debited or credited to an account called Cash Short and Over. The Cash Short and Over account is an expense or a revenue, depending on whether it has a debit or credit balance.

To illustrate, assume in the preceding example that the balance in the fund was only $6.10 instead of $7.40. To restore the fund to $100, a check for $93.90 is needed. Since the petty cash vouchers total only $92.60, the fund is short $1.30. In this case, the entry for replenishment is:

Transportation-In	22.75	
Postage Expense	50.80	
Advances to Employees	19.05	
Cash Short and Over	1.30	
Cash		93.90
To replenish petty cash fund.		

Entries in the Cash Short and Over account may be entered from other change-making activities. For example, assume that a clerk accidentally short-changes a customer $1 and that total cash sales for the day are

$740.50. At the end of the day, actual cash will be $1 over the sum of the sales tickets or the total of the cash register tape. The journal entry to record the day's cash sales is:

```
Cash. . . . . . . . . . . . . . . . . . . . . . . . .   741.50
    Sales. . . . . . . . . . . . . . . . . . . . . .          740.50
    Cash Short and Over  . . . . . . . . . . . . .              1.00
  To record cash sales for the day.
```

In Chapter 4, you were shown how to record the purchases of the Hanson Retail Food Store using the gross invoice price method. You were also exposed briefly to the net price procedure for recording purchases. In the section below, the net price procedure is reviewed and explained in more detail. As you will see, the net price method has two advantages over the gross invoice price method.

NET PRICE METHOD

Objective 6: Apply the net price method of handling purchase discounts

Most well-managed companies take advantage of all the discounts made available to them by their suppliers. Effective internal control over cash disbursements makes certain that these discounts are taken. Even with today's high interest rates, a company may find it advisable to borrow cash to pay invoices within the discount period.

For example, assume goods are purchased for $10,000 under terms 2/10, n/30. The buyer is unable to pay at the end of 10 days but expects to be able to pay at the end of 30 days. To take the $200 discount offered, the buyer needs a $9,800 loan for 20 days, beginning on the last day of the 10-day discount period. The buyer would benefit if the interest cost of such a loan was less than $200. (Short-term loans and interest computations are discussed in Chapter 9.)

Some companies prefer to use the net price method because (1) the accounting theory behind the method is superior and (2) the method strengthens internal control. In the **net price method,** a purchase is recorded in Purchases and Accounts Payable "net" of the discount. Thus, the discount is deducted from the gross invoice price before entering the transaction in the accounts. To illustrate, assume a $1,500 purchase was made on May 14 under terms 2/10, n/30. The invoice was paid on May 24, and the discount taken. The entries comparing the net price method and gross price method are:

		Net		Gross	
May 14	Purchases	1,470		1,500	
	Accounts Payable		1,470		1,500
	Purchased goods under terms 2/10, n/30.				
24	Accounts Payable	1,470		1,500	
	Cash		1,470		1,470
	Purchase Discounts*				30
	Paid account within discount period.				

* This account would not appear in the net price entry.

193

Theoretically, the net price method is preferred over the gross price method because the goods are recorded at their actual cost. Thus, the cost principle of accounting is applied, goods are recorded at the total amount of resources given up to acquire them. Also, the liability is shown in the Accounts Payable account at the amount for which it could be settled.

Note that in the above net price example, discounts taken are not shown. If the invoice had not been paid within 10 days, there would have been an entry to **Discounts Lost.** For example, assume that the invoice in the above example was paid on May 28 instead of May 24. Then the entries for the payment comparing the net price and gross price methods are:

		Net	Gross
May 28	Accounts Payable	1,470	1,500
	Discounts Lost*	30	
	Cash		1,500
	Paid account after discount had expired.	1,500	1,500

* This account would not appear in the gross price entry.

Under the net price method, the only time discounts appear is when they are lost. When discounts of 2% or more are available, good cash management calls for internal control procedures ensuring that all invoices are paid within the discount period. The failure to take a discount highlights a deviation from company policy and directs management's attention to this deviation. The Discounts Lost account actually contains losses resulting from inefficiency, and it is reported among nonoperating expenses near the bottom of the income statement. Many companies prefer the net price method because it strengthens internal control over cash disbursements.

Companies also use the voucher system to strengthen internal control over cash disbursements. As shown in the next section, the nature of the voucher system is such that it provides a high level of internal control.

The Voucher System for Controlling Disbursements

Objective 7: Describe the operation of the voucher system

In very small companies where the owner has an intimate knowledge of all transactions and personally signs all checks, there need be no great concern over the proper handling of cash disbursements. In larger companies where the owners or top-management people have no direct part in the payment process, close control over this function should be provided via a formalized system of internal control.

With a **voucher system,** internal control over cash disbursements is achieved in the following way. Each transaction that will involve the payment of cash is entered on a voucher. A **voucher** is a form with spaces provided for data concerning the liability being set up (such as invoice number, invoice date, creditor's name and address, description of the goods or services, terms of payment, and amount due). It also has spaces for the signatures of those approving the obligation for payment. The voucher usually forms a "jacket" for the invoice and other supporting documents. Each voucher goes through a rigorous process of examination and eventual approval or disapproval. By the time a voucher is approved for payment, one can be quite certain that the liability for payment is legitimate, since various persons have attested to the propriety and accuracy of the claim.

After a voucher has been approved, it is returned to the accounting department and the proper accounts to be debited and credited are noted on the voucher. After a final review by an authorized person, the proper entry is made in the voucher register (debiting an expense or other type of account and crediting Vouchers Payable) and the voucher is filed in the unpaid voucher file. A **voucher register** is a multicolumn special journal used in a voucher system; it contains a record of all vouchers prepared, listed in order by date and voucher number. The **unpaid voucher file** contains all vouchers that have been prepared and approved as proper liabilities but have not yet been paid. In a voucher system the file of unpaid vouchers serves as the subsidiary accounts payable ledger. When payment is made, an entry is recorded in a check register debiting Vouchers Payable and crediting Cash. A **check register** is a special journal showing all checks issued by date and check number. The voucher is then moved from the unpaid vouchers file to the paid vouchers file. The **paid voucher file** is where paid vouchers are filed in numerical sequence.

The system of internal control is enhanced by a separation of duties. For instance, the person or persons who authorize the incurrence of liabilities should not also prepare and distribute checks. The receipt of assets or services resulting from a liability incurrence must be acknowledged and approved by *(a)* the receiving department or *(b)* others who do not have authority to prepare and distribute checks. The persons who have authority to sign checks should do so only when approved vouchers authorizing each check are presented. The possibilities of errors and of recording unauthorized liabilities or cash disbursements are minimized thereby.

SUMMARY

A system of internal control includes all procedures and actions taken to protect assets, ensure compliance with company policies, evaluate performance of personnel, and ensure accuracy and reliability in operating data and accounting reports. Management policies and various features of organization may be used to create a strong system of internal control.

Cash includes coins, paper money, certain undeposited negotiable instruments, amounts in checking or savings accounts at a bank, and demand certificates of deposit at a bank. Information on the company's cash position and cash movement supplied by the accounting system is used by management to fulfill its cash management function and by outsiders to appraise the overall financial position of the company.

Both cash receipts and cash disbursements must be adequately controlled to avoid theft and embezzlement. The bank checking account is a necessity in controlling cash.

The checking account balance on the monthly bank statement usually differs from the balance shown in the general ledger Cash account. This difference is caused by such items as deposits in transit, outstanding checks, and bank service charges that have not been recorded by the depositor. A bank reconciliation statement should be prepared reconciling these differences. Often entries are required in the company's records as a result of information gained by preparing the reconciliation.

To avoid writing checks for small expenditures such as taxi fares, stamps, and delivery charges, a petty cash fund may be established and maintained on a regular basis. One person is responsible for operating the fund. When the fund gets low, it is replenished by issuing a check to bring the fund up to its established figure.

Most well-managed companies take advantage of cash discounts. Companies use either the net price method of recording discounts or the gross price method illustrated in Chapter 4. The net price method has two advantages: (1) the accounting theory behind it is superior, and (2) it provides more efficient cash control.

The voucher system provides companies with a method of effectively controlling cash disbursements. Two special journals are used—the voucher register and the check register. A new account, called Vouchers Payable, is also used.

In the next chapter you will learn about plant assets. Most plant assets are consumed through use, and depreciation expense is recorded on them. Various depreciation methods may be used to assign a portion of the asset's cost to expense.

Objective 8: Define and use correctly the new terms in the glossary

NEW TERMS INTRODUCED IN CHAPTER 5

Bank reconciliation statement   A statement the depositor prepares to "reconcile," or explain, the difference between the cash balance shown on the bank statement and the cash balance on the depositor's books (186).

Bank statement   A statement issued (usually monthly) by a bank describing the activities in a depositor's checking account during the period (183).

Cash   Includes coins; paper money; certain undeposited negotiable instruments such as checks, bank drafts, and money orders; amounts in checking and savings accounts; and demand certificates of deposit (177).

Cashier's check   A check drawn by a bank made out to either the depositor or a third party after deducting the amount of the check from the depositor's account or receiving cash from the depositor (190).

Certificate of deposit   An interest-bearing deposit in a bank that can be withdrawn at will (demand CD) or at a fixed date (time CD) (177).

Certified check   A check written, or drawn, by a depositor and taken to the depositor's bank for certification. The check is deducted from the depositor's balance immediately and becomes a liability of the bank. Thus, it usually will be accepted without question (189).

Check   A written order on a bank to pay a specific sum of money to the party designated as the payee by the party issuing the check (182).

Check register A special journal showing all checks issued by date and check number (195).

Checking account A money balance maintained in the bank that is subject to withdrawal by the depositor, or owner of the money, on demand (181).

Credit memo A form used by a bank to explain an addition to the depositor's account (185).

Debit memo A form used by a bank to explain a deduction from the depositor's account (185).

Deposit in transit Typically a day's cash receipts recorded in the depositor's books in one period but recorded as a deposit by the bank in the succeeding period (187).

Deposit ticket A form that shows the date and the items that make up the deposit (182).

Discounts Lost account The account used to show the amount of discounts not taken when merchandise purchased is recorded at net invoice price (194).

Drawer The party (depositor) writing a check (182).

Fidelity bonds Insure an employer against loss up to a certain amount from fraud or theft by employees who are "bonded" (175).

Internal auditing Consists of investigating and evaluating compliance by employees with the company's policies and procedures. Internal auditing is performed by company personnel (174).

Internal control system The plan of organization and all the procedures and actions taken by an entity to (1) protect its assets against theft and waste, (2) ensure compliance with company policies and federal law, (3) evaluate the performance of all personnel in the company so as to promote efficiency of operations, and (4) ensure accurate and reliable operating data and accounting reports (172).

Invoice Bill sent from the supplier to the purchaser requesting payment for the merchandise shipped (175).

Net price method An accounting procedure in which purchases and accounts payable are initially recorded at net invoice price—gross price less discount offered for prompt payment. Records discounts lost rather than discounts taken (193).

NSF check A customer's check returned from the customer's bank because the customer's checking account balance was insufficient to cover the check (183).

Outstanding checks Checks issued by a depositor that have not yet been paid by the bank on which they are drawn (187).

Paid voucher file A permanent file used in a voucher system where paid vouchers are filed in numerical sequence (195).

Payee The party to whom a check is made payable (182).

Petty cash fund A nominal sum of money established as a separate fund from which minor cash disbursements for valid business purposes are made. The cash in the fund plus the vouchers covering disbursements must always equal the balance at which the fund was established and at which it is carried in the ledger accounts (190).

Petty cash voucher A document or form that shows the amount of and reason for a petty cash disbursement (191).

Purchase order   A document sent from the purchasing department to a supplier requesting that merchandise or other items be shipped to the purchaser (175).

Purchase requisition   A written request from an employee inside the company to the purchasing department to purchase certain items (175).

Receiving report   A document prepared by the receiving department showing the descriptions and quantities of all items received from suppliers (175).

Remittance advice   Informs the payee why the drawer (or maker) of the check is making this payment (182).

Segregation of duties   Having the person responsible for safeguarding an asset be someone other than the person who maintains the accounting records for that asset (172).

Service charges   Charges assessed by the bank on the depositor to cover the cost of handling the checking account (183).

Signature card   Provides the signatures of persons authorized to sign checks drawn on an account (181).

Transfer bank accounts   Bank accounts set up so that local banks automatically transfer to a central bank (by written bank draft) all amounts on deposit in excess of a stated amount (185).

Unpaid voucher file   Contains all vouchers that have been prepared and approved as proper liabilities but have not yet been paid. Serves as an accounts payable subsidiary ledger under a voucher system; unpaid vouchers are filed according to their due dates (195).

Voucher   A form with spaces provided for data about a liability that must be paid. The data include items such as creditor's name and address, description of the goods or services received, invoice number, terms of payment, due date, and amount due. The voucher also has spaces for signatures of those approving the liability for payment (194).

Voucher register   A multicolumn special journal used in a voucher system; it contains a record of all vouchers prepared, listed in order by date and voucher number. A brief explanation of each transaction also may be included. In addition to a credit column for Vouchers Payable, it normally has various columns for debits such as Merchandise Purchases, Salaries, and Transportation-In (195).

Voucher system   A set of procedures, special journals, and authorization forms designed to provide control over cash payments (194).

Wire transfer of funds   Interbank transfer of funds (in the form of accounting debits and credits) by telephone (184).

DEMONSTRATION PROBLEM 5–1

You are the manager of a restaurant that has an ice cream parlor as a separate unit. Your accountant comes in once a year to prepare financial statements and the tax return. In the current year you have a feeling that even though business seems good, net income is going to be lower. You ask the accountant to prepare condensed statements on a monthly basis. All sales are priced to yield an estimated gross margin of 40%. You, your accountant, and several of the accountant's assistants take physical inventories at the end of each of the four months indicated below. The resulting sales, cost of goods sold, and gross margins are:

	March		April		May		June	
	Restaurant	Ice Cream Parlor	Restaurant	Ice Cream Parlor	Restaurant	Ice Cream Parlor	Restaurant	Ice Cream Parlor
Sales	$72,600	$106,000	$78,100	$85,500	$76,200	$78,000	$82,500	$71,000
Cost of goods sold . .	46,550	63,000	47,600	62,000	45,950	61,500	51,000	62,250
Gross margin	$26,050	$ 43,000	$30,500	$23,500	$30,250	$16,500	$31,500	$ 8,750

Required:

What would you suspect after analyzing these reports? What sales control procedures would you recommend to correct the bad situation? All of the points covered in this problem were not specifically covered in the chapter, although the principles were. Use logic, common sense, and knowledge gained elsewhere in coming up with some of the control procedures.

Solution to demonstration problem 5–1

The gross margin percentages are as follows:

	March	April	May	June
Restaurant	35.88%	39.05%	39.70%	38.18%
Ice cream parlor . . .	40.57	27.49	21.15	12.32

Either cash or inventory is being stolen or given away in the ice cream parlor. It may be that cash is being pocketed by the employees or outsiders. Or the employees may be giving very liberal cones to friends or eating the ice cream themselves. There are several things that could be done to improve the sales control procedures:

1. The manager could hire an investigator to come in and watch the employees in action. If cash is being pocketed, the employees could be fired.
2. The prices of cones could be changed to odd amounts so that employees would not be as able to make change without going to the cash register. Also, the "No Sale" lever could be removed from the cash register.
3. The customers could be encouraged to ask for their cash register receipts by having a monthly drawing (for some prize) by cash register receipt number.
4. The cash register should be placed in a very prominent position so that each customer could see the amount recorded for each sale. The customer is not going to be willing to pay 65 cents when the employee rings up 50 cents.
5. The cash register tapes should be inaccessible to the employees. The manager (and possibly assistant manager) should have the only keys to the cash registers.
6. Mention to the employees the fact that you have a control system. They don't have to know what it is.
7. Pay the employees a competitive wage.
8. Require that all sales be rung up immediately after the sale.
9. The manager or assistant manager should reconcile the cash register tapes at the end of each day.

DEMONSTRATION PROBLEM 5–2

The following data pertain to the Nunn Company:

1. Balance per bank statement, dated March 31, 1990, is $8,900.
2. Balance of the Cash account on the company's books as of March 31, 1990, is $8,918.
3. The $2,600 deposit of March 31 was not shown on the bank statement.
4. Of the checks recorded as cash disbursements in March, some checks, totaling $2,100, have not yet cleared the bank.
5. Service and collection charges for the month were $20.
6. The bank erroneously charged the Nunn Company account for the $400 check of another company. The check was included with the canceled checks returned with the bank statement.
7. The bank credited the company's account with the $2,000 proceeds of a non-interest-bearing note that it collected for the company.
8. A customer's $150 check marked NSF was returned with the bank statement.
9. As directed, the bank paid and charged to the company's account a $1,015 noninterest-bearing note of the Nunn Company. This payment has not been recorded by the company.
10. An examination of the cash receipts and the deposit tickets revealed that the bookkeeper erroneously recorded a customer's check of $263 as $236.
11. The bank credited the company for $40 of interest earned on the company's checking account.

Required:

a. Prepare a bank reconciliation statement as of March 31, 1990.

b. Prepare the necessary journal entries to adjust the Cash account.

Solution to demonstration problem 5–2

a.

NUNN COMPANY
Bank Reconciliation Statement
March 31, 1990

Balance per bank statement, March 31, 1990		$ 8,900
Add: Deposit in transit	$2,600	
Check charged in error	400	3,000
		$11,900
Less: Outstanding checks		2,100
Adjusted balance, March 31, 1990		$ 9,800
Balance per ledger, March 31, 1990		$ 8,918
Add: Note collected	$2,000	
Interest earned on checking account	40	
Error in recording customer's check	27	2,067
		$10,985
Less: Service and collection charges	$ 20	
NSF check	150	
Nunn Company note charged against account	1,015	1,185
Adjusted balance, March 31, 1990		$ 9,800

b. 1990

Mar. 31   Cash   882
        Accounts Receivable   150
        Notes Payable   1,015
        Bank Service Charge Expense   20
            Notes Receivable   2,000
            Interest Revenue   40
            Accounts Receivable   27
        To record adjustments to Cash account.

Alternatively:

1990

Mar. 31   Cash   2,067
        Accounts Receivable   27
        Notes Receivable   2,000
        Interest Revenue   40
        To record additions to Cash account.

    31   Notes Payable   1,015
        Accounts Receivable   150
        Bank Service Charge Expense   20
            Cash   1,185
        To record deductions from Cash account.

DEMONSTRATION PROBLEM 5–3

The Blankenship Company uses a voucher system to control cash disbursements. Purchases are recorded at gross invoice prices. As of April 30, 1990, two vouchers are unpaid: Voucher No. 404 payable to Akers Company for $850 and Voucher No. 405 payable to Hanson Company for $50.

The Blankenship Company engaged in the following transactions affecting vouchers payable:

Transactions:

May 1   Prepared Voucher No. 406 payable to Carol Company for merchandise purchased; price on invoice dated April 30 is $400. Terms are 2/10, n/30, FOB destination.

     2   Issued Check No. 385 in payment of Voucher No. 405; no discount was offered on this purchase.

     4   Received a credit memo for $100 for merchandise returned to Akers Company. Purchase was originally recorded in Voucher No. 404. (Record in general journal with notation of return on Voucher No. 404.)

     5   Prepared Voucher No. 407 payable to Allen Brothers for merchandise with an invoice price of $950 on invoice dated May 3; terms are 2/10, n/30, FOB shipping point, freight prepaid. Supplier paid $50 freight bill and added $50 to the invoice for a total billing of $1,000.

     6   Prepared Voucher No. 408 payable to API, Inc. for cost incurred to deliver merchandise sold, $120; terms n/10.

     8   Issued Check No. 386 to pay Voucher No. 404, less return and less a 2% discount.

     9   Issued Check No. 387 to pay Voucher No. 406.

   12   Prepared Voucher No. 409 payable to Ames Insurance Company for $300, the three-year premium on an insurance policy. Issued Check No. 388 to pay Voucher No. 409.

   13   Issued Check No. 389 to pay Voucher No. 407.

   15   Prepared Voucher No. 410 payable to Cash for salaries of $2,000 for the first half of May. Issued Check No. 390 in payment of Voucher No. 410. Cashed the check and paid employees in cash.

   16   Issued Check No. 391 to pay Voucher No. 408.

23 Prepared Voucher No. 411 payable to Manders Company for merchandise with an invoice price of $300 on invoice dated May 22; terms are 2/10, n/30, FOB shipping point, freight collect.

24 Prepared Voucher No. 412 payable to Short-Lines, Inc. for $50 freight on merchandise purchased on May 23.

26 Prepared Voucher No. 413 payable to Bell Telephone Company for $125 for monthly telephone service.

28 Prepared Voucher No. 414 payable to We-Deliver, Inc. for costs incurred to deliver merchandise sold, $80; terms n/30.

31 Prepared Voucher No. 415 payable to Cash for salaries for the last half of May, $2,200. Issued Check No. 392 in payment of Voucher No. 415. Cashed the check and paid employees in cash.

Required:

a. Record the transactions above, using a voucher register, check register, and a general journal.

b. Prepare a Vouchers Payable account, and post the portions of the entries that affect this account.

c. Prepare a schedule (list) of unpaid vouchers to prove the accuracy of the balance in the Vouchers Payable account.

Solution to demonstration problem 5–3

a.

VOUCHER REGISTER* Page 12

Date 1990	Voucher No.	Payee	Paid Date	Paid Ck. No.	Vouchers Payable Cr.	Purchases Dr.	Freight-In Dr.	Delivery Expense Dr.	Salaries Expense Dr.	Other Accounts Dr. Account Name	Other Accounts Dr. Post Ref.	Other Accounts Dr. Amount Dr.
May 1	406	Carol Company	5/9	387	400	400						
5	407	Allen Brothers	5/13	389	1,000	950	50					
6	408	API, Inc.	5/16	391	120			120				
12	409	Ames Insurance Company	5/12	388	300					Prepaid Insurance		300
15	410	Cash	5/15	390	2,000				2,000			
23	411	Manders Company			300	300						
24	412	Short-Lines, Inc.			50		50					
26	413	Bell Telephone Company			125					Telephone Expense		125
28	414	We-Deliver, Inc.			80			80				
31	415	Cash	5/31	392	2,200				2,200			
					6,575	1,650	100	200	4,200			425

*A column for terms could have been included.

CHECK REGISTER *Page 5*

Date 1990		Payee	Voucher No.	Check No.	Vouchers Payable Dr.	Purchase Discounts Cr.	Cash Cr.
May	2	Hanson Company	405	385	50		50
	8	Akers Company	404	386	750	15	735
	9	Carol Company	406	387	400	8	392
	12	Ames Insurance Company	409	388	300		300
	13	Allen Brothers	407	389	1,000	19	981
	15	Cash	410	390	2,000		2,000
	16	API, Inc.	408	391	120		120
	31	Cash	415	392	2,200		2,200
					6,820	42	6,778

GENERAL JOURNAL *Page 17*

Date		Account Titles and Explanation	Post. Ref.	Debit	Credit
1990 May	4	Vouchers Payable		1 0 0	
		Purchase Returns and Allowances			1 0 0
		To record receipt of credit memo for			
		merchandise returned. Voucher No. 404.			

b.

GENERAL LEDGER

Vouchers Payable *Account No. 201*

Date		Explanation	Post. Ref.	Debit	Credit	Balance
1990 Apr.	30	Beginning balance				9 0 0 Cr.
May	4	Credit memo;				
		Voucher No. 404	J17	1 0 0		8 0 0 Cr.
	31		VR12		6 5 7 5	7 3 7 5 Cr.
	31		CR5	6 8 2 0		5 5 5 Cr.

c.
Blankenship Company
Schedule of Unpaid Vouchers
May 31, 1990

Voucher No.

411	Manders Company	$300
412	Short-Lines, Inc.	50
413	Bell Telephone Company	125
414	We-Deliver, Inc.	80
	Total	$555

QUESTIONS

1. What purposes does a system of internal control accomplish?

2. Identify some features which, if present, would strengthen the internal control system.

3. Name some control documents that are used in merchandise transactions.

4. What are the four objectives sought in effective cash management?

5. Cite some essential features in a system of internal control over cash receipts.

6. The bookkeeper of a given company was stealing remittances received from customers in payment of their accounts. To cover the theft, the bookkeeper made out false credit memoranda indicating returns and allowances made by or granted to the customers. What feature of a system of internal control, if operative, would have prevented this scheme?

7. Cite some essential features in a system of internal control over cash disbursements.

8. "The difference between a company's Cash ledger account balance and the balance in the bank statement is usually a matter of timing." Do you agree or disagree? Why?

9. Why might a company's management wish to determine the cash position daily?

10. Explain how the use of transfer bank accounts can bring about effective cash management.

11. Indicate the method of operation of a petty cash fund and the advantages obtained through its use. Indicate how control is maintained over petty cash transactions.

12. What is the advantage of recording purchases at the net invoice price?

13. Describe how the use of a voucher system provides close control over cash disbursements.

EXERCISES

Answer true-false questions about internal control

1. State whether each of the following statements about internal control is true or false:

    a. Those persons responsible for safeguarding an asset should maintain the accounting records for that asset.

b. Complete, accurate, and up-to-date accounting records should be maintained.

c. Whenever possible, responsibilities should be assigned and duties subdivided in such a way that only one person is responsible for a given function.

d. Employees should be assigned to one job and should remain in that job so that skill levels will be as high as possible.

e. The use of check protectors, check registers, and time clocks is recommended.

f. An internal auditing function should not be implemented because it leads the employees to believe that management does not trust them.

g. One of the best protections against theft is to hire honest, competent employees.

h. A foolproof system of internal control can be devised if management puts forth the effort.

Answer multiple choice question about internal control

2. Concerning internal control, which one of the following statements is correct? Explain.

a. Broadly speaking, internal control is only necessary in very large organizations.

b. The purposes of internal control are to check the accuracy of accounting data, safeguard assets against theft, promote efficiency of operations, and ensure that management's policies are being followed.

c. Once an internal control system has been established, it should be effective as long as the formal organization remains unchanged.

d. An example of internal control is having one individual count the day's cash receipts and compare the total with the total of the cash register tapes.

Determine available cash balance from bank statement and Cash account data

3. The Garber Company's Cash account balance was $260,550 at the end of August. The bank statement showed a balance of $257,400 for the same date. Checks outstanding totaled $88,000, and deposits in transit totaled $101,000. If these are the only pertinent data available to you, what was the correct amount of cash against which the Garber Company could have written checks as of the end of August?

Prepare bank reconciliation statement and specify cash available

4. From the following data, prepare a bank reconciliation statement and determine the correct available cash balance for the Burk Company as of October 31, 1990:

Balance per bank statement, October 31, 1990	$18,632
Ledger account balance	14,704
Note collected by bank not yet entered in ledger	4,000
Bank charges not yet entered by Burk Company	24
Deposit in transit	2,240
Outstanding checks:	
No. 527	512
No. 528	384
No. 529	960
No. 531	336

Prepare bank reconciliation statement and necessary journal entries

5. From the following information for the Higgins Company:

a. Prepare a bank reconciliation statement as of September 30, 1990.

b. Give the necessary journal entries to correct the Cash account.

Balance per bank statement, September 30, 1990	$65,200
Ledger account balance as of September 30, 1990 . . .	58,600
Note collected by bank	4,000
Bank charges	40
Deposits in transit	3,696
NSF check deposited and returned . . . . ._	336
Check of Brent Company deducted in error	200
Outstanding checks	6,872

Determine checks outstanding

6. As of March 1 of the current year the Davis Company had outstanding checks of $56,000. During March the company issued an additional $240,000 of checks. As of March 31 the bank statement showed that $224,000 of checks had cleared the bank during the month. What is the amount of outstanding checks as of March 31?

Determine deposits in transit

7. The Crowe Company's bank statement as of August 31, 1990, shows total deposits into the company's account of $92,680 and a total of 14 deposits. On July 31 deposits of $5,200 and $4,500 were in transit. The total cash receipts for August amounted to $94,240, and the company's records show 13 deposits made in August. What is the amount of deposits in transit at August 31?

Record reimbursement of petty cash fund

8. On August 31, 1990, the Dudley Company's petty cash fund contained:

Coin and currency	166.00
IOU from employee	20.00
Vouchers covering expenditures for:	
Postage	80.00
Taxi fares	34.00
Entertainment of a customer	92.00

The Petty Cash account shows a balance of $400. If financial statements are prepared for each calendar month, what journal entry is required on August 31?

Record reimbursement of petty cash fund

9. Use the data in Exercise 8 above. If the fund were replenished on August 31, 1990, what journal entry would be required? Which of the accounts debited would not appear in the income statement?

List the procedures to follow for processing an invoice up to the point of filing it in the unpaid vouchers file

10. You are the chief accountant of the Custer Company. An invoice has just been received from the Dunlop Company in the amount of $8,000, with terms of 2/10, n/30. List the procedures you would follow in processing this invoice up through the point of filing it in the unpaid vouchers file.

11. Elkins Company uses the net price method for handling purchase discounts. Prepare the journal entries necessary to record the following 1990 transactions:

Record purchases using net price method

Transactions:

Oct. 6 Purchased $300 of merchandise; terms 2/10, n/30.
     7 Purchased $1,000 of merchandise; terms 2/10, n/30.
   17 Paid the invoice for the October 7 purchase.
   31 Paid the invoice for the October 6 purchase.

PROBLEMS

Prepare bank reconciliation statement with necessary journal entries

5–1. The bank statement for the Holley Company's general checking account with the First National Bank for the month ended August 31, 1990, showed an ending balance of $21,236, service charges of $40, an NSF check returned of $840, and the collection of a $4,000 note plus interest of $40. Further investigation revealed that a wire transfer of $7,200 from the bank account maintained by a branch office of the company had not been recorded by the company as having been deposited in the First National Bank account. In addition, a comparison of deposits with receipts showed a deposit in transit of $8,400. Checks outstanding amounted to $6,024 while the cash ledger balance was $13,252.

Required:

a. Prepare a bank reconciliation statement for the Holley Company account for the month ended August 31, 1990.

b. Prepare all necessary journal entries.

Prepare bank reconciliation statement with necessary journal entries

5–2. The bank statement for Fulmer Company's account with the First National Bank for the month ended April 30, 1990, showed a balance of $43,544. On this date the company's Cash account balance was $38,108. Returned with the bank statement were (1) a debit memo for service charges of $40, (2) a debit memo for a customer's NSF check of $400, and (3) a credit memo for a $8,800 wire transfer of funds on April 14 from the State Bank, the local bank used by the company's branch office. Further investigation revealed that outstanding checks amounted to $5,200, the cash receipts of April 30 of $6,484 did not appear as a deposit on the bank statement, and the canceled checks included a check for $1,640 (drawn by the president of the company to cover travel expenses on a recent trip) which the company has yet to record.

Required:

a. Prepare a bank reconciliation statement for the month ended April 30, 1990.

b. Prepare any necessary journal entries.

Prepare bank reconciliation statement with necessary journal entries

5–3. The following data pertain to the Grant Company:

(1) Balance per the bank statement dated June 30, 1990, is $122,280.

(2) Balance of the Cash in Bank account on the company books as of June 30, 1990, is $35,940.

(3) Outstanding checks as of June 30, 1990, are $60,000.

(4) Bank deposit of June 30 for $9,420 was not included in the deposits per the bank statement.

(5) The bank had collected a $90,000, 6%, 30-day note and the interest of $450, which it credited to the Grant Company account. The bank charged the company a collection fee of $60 on the above note.

(6) The bank erroneously charged the Grant Company account for a $42,000 check of the Brant Company. The check was found among the canceled checks returned with the bank statement.

(7) Bank service charges for June, exclusive of the collection fee, amounted to $300.

(8) Among the canceled checks was one for $2,070 given in payment of an account. The bookkeeper had recorded the check at $2,880 in the company records.

(9) A check of Mr. Crosley, a customer, for $12,600, deposited on June 20, was returned by the bank marked NSF. No entry has been made to reflect the returned check on the company records.

(10) A check for $5,040 of Mr. Moran, a customer, which had been deposited in the bank, was erroneously recorded by the bookkeeper as $5,580.

Required:

Prepare a bank reconciliation statement as of June 30, 1990. Also prepare any necessary adjusting journal entries.

Prepare bank reconciliation statement with necessary journal entries

5–4. The following data pertain to the Flores Company. The reconciliation statement as of June 30, 1990, showed a deposit in transit of $5,400 and three checks outstanding:

No. 553	$2,400
No. 570	4,400
No. 571	3,200

During July the following checks were written and entered in the Cash account.

No. 572	$3,000	No. 578	$4,600
No. 573	3,300	No. 579	5,640
No. 574	5,640	No. 580	720
No. 575	2,540	No. 581	9,708
No. 576	5,052	No. 582	9,600
No. 577	3,380	No. 583	3,696

As of July 31, all of the checks written, except No. 578, had been mailed to the payees. Check No. 578 was kept in the vault pending receipt of a statement from the payee. Four deposits were made at the bank as follows:

July 7	$30,000
14	38,400
14	22,800
28	27,600

The bank statement, which was received on August 2, correctly included all deposits and showed a balance as of July 31 of $101,040. The following checks were returned: Nos. 570, 571, 572, 573, 574, 575, 576, 577, 580, and 581. With the paid checks there were three debit memoranda for:

(1) Fee of $16 for the collection on July 30 of a $4,400 noninterest-bearing note payable to the Flores Company for which a credit memorandum was enclosed.
(2) Monthly service charge of $20.
(3) Payment of a $3,000 noninterest-bearing note of the Flores Company.

The bank statement included a credit for $12,000 dated July 29. The bank telephoned the company on the morning of August 3 to explain that this credit was in error because it represented a transaction between the bank and the Florist Company.

The balance in the Cash account on the books of the Flores Company as of July 31 is $61,740.

Required:

Prepare a bank reconciliation statement for the Flores Company as of July 31, 1990. Also prepare any necessary adjusting entries.

Prepare bank reconciliation statement with necessary journal entries

5–5. The following information is taken from the books and records of the Massey Company:

Balance per bank statement, July 31, 1990	$91,556
Balance per ledger, July 31, 1990	92,968
Collections received on the last day of July and debited to Cash in Bank on books but not entered by bank until August	21,248

Debit memo for customer's check returned unpaid (uncollectible check is
  on hand, but no entry for the return has been made on the books) 2,000
Debit memo for bank service charge for July 60
Check issued but not paid by bank 20,136
Credit memo for proceeds of a note receivable which was left at the bank
  for collection but has not been recorded on the books as collected
  ($36 of this is interest revenue) 3,200
Check for an account payable entered on books as $1,920 but issued
  and paid by the bank in the correct amount of $3,360.

Required:

Prepare a bank reconciliation statement and the necessary journal entries to adjust the accounts.

Prepare bank reconciliation statement with necessary journal entries; comment on control of cash receipts

5–6. The following data for March 1990 are summarized from the accounts of Hall Company. The accountant also acts as cashier.

Cash Receipts		Cash Disbursements	
Mar. 2	$ 6,600	Check No. 911	$ 5,304
4	19,200	No. 912	7,356
5	7,800	No. 913	8,748
11	16,800	No. 914	5,328
13	21,000	No. 915	9,684
14	25,200	No. 916	14,400
19	6,000	No. 917	22,800
20	4,800	No. 918	16,200
27	360	No. 919	4,500
29	2,220	No. 920	4,200

At March 1 the checks outstanding were:

No. 209	. . . .	$ 540
No. 792	. . . .	9,600
No. 796	. . . .	3,348
No. 910	. . . .	7,572

There were no deposits in transit. The balance of the Cash in Bank account per books was $92,100 at March 31. The bank statement for the month of March is as follows:

BANK STATEMENT

Date	Checks	Deposits	Balance
Mar. 1			102,000
3		6,600	108,600
4	5,304		
4	7,356		95,940
6		27,000	122,940
9	9,684		
9	5,328		107,928
16		63,000	170,928
19	14,400		
19	16,200		140,328
24		10,800	151,128
25	3,348		
25	7,572		140,208
26	22,800		
26	6,000 NSF		111,408
27	6,000 DM		105,408
29		2,280	107,688
31	24 DM		107,664

The debit memoranda (DM) are for the payment of a company note and for the monthly service charge.

Required:

a. Prepare a bank reconciliation statement as of March 31, 1990.

b. Journalize the entry or entries necessary to correct the books.

c. Comment on the company's control of cash receipts.

Prepare necessary journal entries involving petty cash fund

5–7. Following are selected transactions of the Shell Company during 1990:

Mar. 1   Established a petty cash fund of $2,000 which will be under the control of the assistant office manager.

Apr. 3   Fund is replenished on this date. Prior to replenishment, the fund consisted of the following:

Coin and currency	$1,138.32
Payroll check issued by Shell Company to part-time office worker, Keri Kerr,	
properly endorsed by Kerr (cashed by the assistant office manager)	113.92
Petty cash vouchers indicating disbursements for:	
Postage stamps	280.00
Supper money for office employees working overtime	96.00
Office supplies	87.20
Window washing service	160.00
Flowers for wedding of employee	40.00
Flowers for hospitalized employee	40.00
Employee IOU	40.00

The employee's IOU is to be deducted from his next paycheck.

Required:

Present journal entries for the above transactions.

Prepare necessary journal entries involving petty cash fund

5–8. The following data pertain to the petty cash fund of the Longhorn Company:

Nov. 2   A $2,400 check is drawn and cashed, and the cash is placed in the care of the assistant office manager to be used as a petty cash fund.

Dec. 17   The fund is replenished. An analysis of the fund shows:

Coins and currency	$ 589.62
Petty cash vouchers for:	
Delivery expenses	693.90
Freight-in	1,044.48
Postage stamps purchased	60.00

31   The end of the accounting period falls on this date. The fund was not replenished. Its contents on this date consist of:

Coins and currency	$2,008.20
Petty cash vouchers for:	
Delivery expenses	126.60
Postage stamps	145.20
Employee's IOU	120.00

Required:

Present journal entries to record the above transactions.

BUSINESS DECISION PROBLEM 5–1

The outstanding checks of the Portnoy Company at November 30, 1990, were:

No. 237	$ 750,00
No. 271	816.75
No. 3686	509.25
No. 687	603.00
No. 3688	1,051.50

During the month, checks numbered 3689–3728 were issued, and all of these checks cleared the bank except Nos. 3727 and 2728 for $722.25 and $544.50, respectively. Check Nos. 3686, 3687, and 3688 also cleared the bank.

The bank statement on December 31 showed a balance of $17,958. Service charges amounted to $15, and two checks were returned by the bank, one marked NSF in the amount of $85.50 and the other marked "No account" in the amount of $1,500.

Hawker recently retired as the office manager-cashier-bookkeeper for the company and was replaced by Walker. Walker noted the absence of a system of internal control but was momentarily deterred from embezzling for lack of a scheme of concealment. Finally, Walker hit upon several schemes. The $1,500 check marked "No account" by the bank is the product of one scheme. Walker took cash receipts and replaced them with a check drawn upon a nonexistent account to make it appear that a customer had given the company a worthless check.

The other scheme was more subtle. Walker pocketed cash receipts to bring them down to an amount sufficient to prepare the following reconciliation statement:

Balance, Cash account, December 31, 1990		$20,420.10
Deduct:		
Worthless check	$1,500.00	
NSF check	85.50	
Service charges	15.00	1,600.50
Adjusted balance, December 31, 1990		$18,819.60
Balance per bank statement, December 31, 1990		$17,958.00
Add: Deposit in transit		2,128.35
		$20,086.35
Deduct: Outstanding checks:		
No. 3727	$ 722.25	
No. 3728	544.50	1,266.75
Adjusted balance, December 31, 1990		$18,819.60

Required:

a. State the nature of the second scheme used by Walker. How much in total does it appear Walker has stolen by use of the two schemes together?

b. Prepare a correct bank reconciliation statement as of December 31, 1990.

c. Suggest procedures which would have defeated the attempts of Walker to steal funds and conceal these actions.

6 PLANT ASSETS: ACQUISITION AND DEPRECIATION

LEARNING OBJECTIVES

After studying this chapter, you should be able to:

1. Recognize the characteristics of plant assets and identify the initial costs of acquiring plant assets.
2. Understand the various methods of calculating depreciation expense.
3. Distinguish between capital and revenue expenditures for plant assets.
4. Define and use correctly the new terms in the glossary.

Business assets are commonly classified as current or noncurrent assets, depending upon the amount of time that is expected to expire before they are converted into cash, consumed, or used up in the operations of the business. For many businesses, the noncurrent category of assets consists largely of plant assets (property, plant, and equipment), natural resources, and intangible assets. This chapter is the first of two on this important accounting and business topic. The acquisition of plant assets and their depreciation will be covered in this chapter.

NATURE OF PLANT ASSETS

Objective 1:
Recognize the characteristics of plant assets and identify the initial costs of acquiring plant assets

The term **plant assets** refers to tangible long-lived assets (assets whose useful lives are expected to exceed more than one period) obtained for use in business operations instead of for resale. Land, buildings, machinery, delivery equipment, and office equipment are typical examples of plant assets.

To be properly classified as a plant asset, an asset must be used in the production or sale of another asset or service. For example, a delivery truck or equipment held for sale by a dealer is classified as inventory, whereas the same truck or equipment used in producing or selling a product is classified as a plant asset. Once an asset is retired from service and held for sale or left idle, the asset is no longer classifiable as a plant asset.

Plant assets can be viewed as consisting of bundles of service potential that are consumed or used up over a period of time. For instance, a new delivery truck may represent 100,000 miles of transportation service. Likewise, a new building may represent 40 years of housing service. To match the revenues and the related expenses of a period as accurately and logically as possible, it is necessary to measure the part of the service potential of plant assets that expired during the period. While it is often difficult to determine the exact length of these assets' useful lives, some estimate must be made so that the amount of expense (the amount of the service expired) may be determined.

Types of Plant Assets

Plant assets can be broadly classified as land and depreciable property. Since land does not deteriorate with age or use, it is not depreciable. Farmland is an exception to this rule because it may lose its fertility or suffer from erosion.

All other plant assets are depreciable property. Their usefulness is reduced through wear and tear, or obsolescence.

The Cost of Plant Assets

Plant assets are usually recorded at cost. Cost includes all normal, reasonable, and necessary outlays to obtain and get the asset ready for use, such as invoice price, installation costs, and transportation. Traffic tickets or fines that must be paid as a result of hauling machinery to a new plant are not part of the cost of the machinery. Likewise, if the machinery is dropped and damaged while being unpacked, the cost of repairing the damage is not included in the cost of the machinery.

Land and land improvements.   The cost of land includes the purchase price; the option cost; real estate commissions; the cost of title search; fees for recording the title transfer; unpaid taxes assumed by the purchaser; the cost of surveying, clearing, grading, and landscaping; and local assessments for sidewalks, streets, sewers, and water mains. Sometimes land purchased as a building site contains an old building that must be removed. In such cases, the entire purchase price should be debited to the Land account. The Land account should also be debited for the cost of removing the old building, less any proceeds received from the sale of salvaged materials.

As stated above, land purchased as a building site is considered to have an unlimited life and is therefore not depreciable. But land improvements such as driveways, fences, parking lots, lighting systems, and sprinkler systems have limited lives and are therefore depreciable. Hence, the costs of land and land improvements should be recorded in two separate accounts.

Building. If a building is purchased, its cost includes the purchase price, the costs of repairing and remodeling the building for the purposes of the new owner, unpaid taxes assumed by the purchaser, legal costs, and real estate brokerage commissions. When land and buildings are purchased together, the total cost should be divided so that separate ledger accounts may be established for land and for buildings. An appraisal may be done by a competent appraiser and is needed in order to have a dollar amount on which to base the depreciation charges for the building.

If a building is constructed, the cost may be more difficult to determine. But its cost usually includes payments to contractors, architects' fees, building permits, taxes during construction, salaries of officers supervising construction, insurance during construction, and interest during construction. Miscellaneous revenues earned during construction reduce the cost of the building. For instance, if one floor is rented for some special purpose during construction the proceeds reduce the cost of the building.

To illustrate, assume that Collins Company purchased an old farm on the outskirts of Bridgeport, Connecticut, as a factory site. The company paid $300,000 for this property. In addition, the company agreed to pay taxes of prior years (called back taxes) of $12,000. Attorneys' fees and other legal costs related to the purchase of the farm amounted to $1,800. The farm buildings were demolished at a net cost of $20,000 (the cost of removal less the salvage value), and a building was constructed at a cost of $400,000. Building permits and architects' fees totaled $30,000. Interest incurred on a construction loan was $900. Finally, the company paid an assessment of $12,000 to the city for water mains, sewers, and street paving. The costs of the land and factory building are computed as follows:

	Land	Building
Cost of factory site	$300,000	
Back taxes	12,000	
Attorneys' fees and other legal costs	1,800	
Demolition	20,000	
Factory construction		$400,000
Building permits and architects' fees		30,000
Interest during construction		900
City assessment	12,000	
	$345,800	$430,900

All of the costs relating to the purchase of the farm and the razing of the old buildings are assignable to the land account because none of the old buildings purchased with the land are to be used. The real goal was to purchase the land, but the land was not available without taking the buildings also.

Instead of the situation described above, suppose that through a remodeling program one or more of the existing buildings had been adapted for use by Collins Company. Then it would have been necessary to determine what part of the cash purchase price of the farm, the back taxes, and the legal fees was allocable to such buildings and what part of the acquisition cost and the remodeling cost would be included in the cost of the new factory. These costs would have been allocated on the basis of appraised values. For instance, assume that the land was appraised at three fourths of the total value and the buildings at one fourth. Then three fourths of the acquisition cost would have been assigned to the land and one fourth to the buildings. The appraised values of any buildings to be demolished are added to the appraised value of the land in determining the allocation.[1]

Machinery. If machinery is purchased, its cost includes the net invoice price, transportation charges, insurance in transit, the cost of installation, the costs of any attachments or accessories, testing costs (if any), and other costs needed to put it into condition and location for use. If a company builds a machine for its own use, the cost includes material, labor, and an amount equal to the increase in factory costs caused by the construction of the machine. This cost of the machine should be recorded in the Machinery account (even if it is less than what the company would have paid if it had purchased the machine) since it represents recources sacrificed to acquire the machine.

To illustrate, assume that after pricing machinery of the type needed, the Dension Company decided to build its own machine. The cost of construction was $40,000. The shipping point price of a similar machine purchased from the usual source is $43,000, and transportation charges to the Dension Company's plant amount to another $1,000. The machine should be recorded in the accounts at $40,000—the amount of resources sacrificed to acquire it.

Delivery equipment. The cost of delivery equipment includes all costs necessary to place the equipment in use. Included in the cost are the net invoice purchase price, transportation charges, the cost of accessories, and special paint and decoration costs.

Office equipment. The cost of office equipment includes the net invoice purchase price and all costs necessary to place the equipment in condition and location for use.

Noncash Acquisitions and Gifts of Plant Assets

Plant assets are usually acquired by purchase for cash or on account. They may also be acquired through an exchange for securities or other assets or as gifts. When plant assets are acquired under these conditions, it is necessary to determine the amount at which they should be initially recorded. Several possible bases may be used, such as fair market value, appraised value, and book value.

Fair market value. **Fair market value** is the normal price that would be paid for an item in the normal course of business. If noncash assets are received in an exchange for securities or other noncash assets having a known market value, the cost of the assets received is considered equal to

---

[1]Some accountants merely ignore the appraised values of any buildings to be destroyed in determining the allocation.

the fair market value of the securities or assets given up. If the securities or assets given up do not have a known market value, the cash purchase price at which the assets received **could** have been acquired should be used as the cost of the acquired assets. Thus, the exchange should be recorded at the fair market value of the assets acquired or the securities or assets given up, whichever is more clearly evident.

Appraised value. Noncash assets are sometimes acquired as gifts. Although these assets do not cost the recipient anything, they are usually recorded in the accounts at their fair market value. If similar assets are not regularly traded and a fair market value cannot be determined for them, they may be recorded at an **appraised value** determined by a professional appraiser or by management.

Book value. **Book value** of an asset is its recorded cost less its accumulated depreciation. The book value of an asset given up is an acceptable basis for measuring a newly acquired asset only if a better basis is not available. This statement is true even if some cash is given or received in the exchange. The cost of an old asset is usually a poor and misleading indication of the economic importance of a new asset. When assets are received in a noncash exchange, it is the accountant's job to find the best measure of their value. The general rule followed is to use the fair market value of the assets received or of the assets given up, whichever is more clearly evident.

DEPRECIATION OF PLANT ASSETS

Objective 2:
Understand the various methods of calculating depreciation expense

Depreciation in accounting is an estimate, usually expressed in terms of cost, of the amount of an asset's service potential that expired in a given period. Major causes of depreciation are physical deterioration, inadequacy for future needs, and obsolescence.

Physical deterioration results from use, wear and tear, and the action of the elements. Even if a good maintenance and repair policy is in effect, a plant asset will eventually have to be discarded. If a company grows more rapidly than anticipated, existing plant assets suffer from **inadequacy.** In such a case, the company will not be able to meet all of the demands for its product or service. **Obsolescence** refers to the process of becoming out of date or obsolete because of technological progress. A machine may be in excellent physical condition yet also be obsolete because more efficient, economical, and higher-quality machines have become available. A good example of this would be in the computer industry. Computers generally become obsolete before they physically wear out. Both inadequacy and obsolescence are difficult to predict, but they must be taken into consideration in depreciation accounting.

Depreciation accounting distributes in a systematic and rational manner the cost of a depreciable plant asset, less its salvage value, over the asset's estimated useful life. *Thus, depreciation is a process of cost allocation and not of valuation.* Depreciation is recorded by debiting the Depreciation Expense account and crediting the Accumulated Depreciation account.

The later accounting treatment of the amounts of depreciation recorded depends upon the type of services which the asset provides. If the services received are classified as selling or administrative, the depreciation is usually expensed in the period recognized. If manufacturing services are received, the depreciation may be treated as a part of the manufacturing cost. In such an instance, it attaches to the units of product as part of the cost of the asset, inventory, and becomes an expense (as part of the cost of goods sold) only when the manufactured goods are sold to customers. The depreciation recorded on one asset may be considered part of the cost of another—for example, when a truck is used in the construction of a building.

Depreciation is one of the costs of operating a business. The cost of plant assets is recovered from customers by charging them enough for the product to cover all expenses, including depreciation. But note that the charge to expense by itself is not sufficient evidence that the cost has been recovered. Costs are recovered only when total revenue is at least equal to total expenses, which, of course, is the normal situation for firms that remain in business.

Factors affecting depreciation estimates. To estimate periodic depreciation the following three factors must generally be considered:

1. Cost.
2. Estimated salvage value. **Salvage** or **scrap value** is the amount estimated to be recoverable (less disposal cost) on the date that the asset will be disposed of or retired.
3. Estimated useful life. **Useful life** is the length of time the company holding a depreciable asset intends to use it. Useful life may be expressed in years, months, working hours, or units of production.

There are several methods of computing depreciation. When evaluating the various depreciation methods, it is important to remember the main causes of depreciation—physical deterioration, inadequacy, and obsolescence. These three factors should be taken into consideration in estimating salvage value and useful life as well as in selecting the appropriate depreciation method. For example, a machine may be capable of producing units for 20 years, but it is expected to be obsolete in 6 years. Thus, its estimated useful life is 6 years, not 20 years.

DEPRECIATION METHODS

The depreciation methods illustrated here are for financial reporting purposes. At one time, these same methods could be used for tax purposes. In 1981, a significant change in the tax laws occurred that allows very fast write-offs of depreciable assets for tax purposes. A discussion of depreciation for tax purposes is beyond the scope of this text.

Straight-Line Depreciation

The **straight-line method** assigns the same dollar amount of depreciation to expense each period. Under this method the passage of time is considered to be the main factor in allocating cost. The method assumes that wear, obsolescence, and deterioration of the plant assets are directly proportional to elapsed time. This assumption may not be true.

The formula for computing depreciation under the straight-line method is:

$$\frac{\text{Depreciation}}{\text{per period}} = \frac{(\text{Asset cost} - \text{Estimated salvage value})}{\text{Number of accounting periods in estimated life}}$$

To illustrate, for a machine costing $54,000 with an estimated life of 10 years and an estimated salvage value of $4,000, the depreciation per year is ($54,000 − $4,000) ÷ 10, or $5,000. The schedule in Illustration 6.1 presents the annual depreciation entries, the balance in the accumulated depreciation accounts, and the book (or carrying) value of this machine.

The entry to record depreciation at the end of year 1 is:

```
Depreciation Expense—Machinery  . . . . . . . . . . . . . .  5,000
    Accumulated Depreciation—Machinery  . . . . . . . . . .        5,000
    To record depreciation on machinery for year 1.
```

Depreciation expense is shown on the income statement, while accumulated depreciation is shown on the balance sheet as a deduction from the Machinery account. The balance in the Accumulated Depreciation account continues to grow year by year as shown in Illustration 6.1. The book value of the machinery at any point in time is equal to cost minus accumulated depreciation.

Illustration 6.1
DEPRECIATION SCHEDULE—STRAIGHT-LINE METHOD

End of Year	Depreciation Expense Dr.; Accumulated Depreciation Cr.	Total Accumulated Depreciation	Book Value (cost − accumulated depreciation)
			$54,000
1	$ 5,000	$ 5,000	49,000
2	5,000	10,000	44,000
3	5,000	15,000	39,000
4	5,000	20,000	34,000
5	5,000	25,000	29,000
6	5,000	30,000	24,000
7	5,000	35,000	19,000
8	5,000	40,000	14,000
9	5,000	45,000	9,000
10	5,000	50,000	4,000*
	$50,000		

* Estimated salvage value.

Units-of-Production Depreciation

The **units-of-production method** assigns an equal amount of depreciation for each unit of product manufactured or service rendered by an asset. If usage is the main factor causing the expiration of the asset, depreciation may be based on physical output. The depreciation charge per unit of output may be found by dividing the original cost of the asset, less any salvage value, by the estimated number of units to be produced during the asset's life. The periodic depreciation is then obtained by multiplying the rate per unit by the actual number of units produced during the period.

To illustrate, assume that on April 1, 1990, Lee Company purchased a machine at a total cost of $54,000. The machine is expected to have a 10-year useful life and a $4,000 salvage value. It is estimated that the machine will produce 5 million units of product throughout its useful life. The depreciation charge per unit of product produced is one cent, computed as follows:

$$\text{Depreciation per unit of product} = \frac{(\text{Asset cost} - \text{Estimated salvage value})}{\text{Estimated units of production}}$$

$$= \frac{(\$54,000 - \$4,000)}{5,000,000} = \$0.01$$

The formula for calculating total depreciation for a period is:

$$\text{Depreciation for the period} = \text{Depreciation per unit}$$
$$\times \text{ Number of units produced in the period}$$

Thus, if the machine produces 100,000 units in 1990, the depreciation charge under the units-of-production method will be $1,000 ($0.01 × 100,000). Similarly, if 250,000 units are produced in 1991, the depreciation charge will be $2,500 ($0.01 × 250,000).

Accelerated Depreciation

Accelerated depreciation methods permit larger amounts of depreciation to be recorded in the earlier years of an asset's life than in the later years. There is theoretical support for these methods. Their use seems especially appropriate when the service-rendering or revenue-producing ability of the asset declines over time, when the value of the asset declines more in the earlier years and less in the later years of its life, and when repairs and other maintenance costs increase over time.

Double-declining-balance method of depreciation. Under the **double-declining-balance (DDB) method** the straight-line rate of depreciation is doubled, and the doubled rate is applied to the declining balance of the asset—its net book value. Salvage value is ignored in the calculation but serves as a base below which the asset should not be depreciated. The formula for the double-declining-balance method is:

Illustration 6.2
DOUBLE-DECLINING-BALANCE METHOD DEPRECIATION SCHEDULE

End of Year	Depreciation Expense Dr.; Accumulated Depreciation Cr.		Total Accumulated Depreciation	Book Value
				$54,000.00
1 . . .	$10,800.00	(20% of $54,000)	$10,800.00	43,200.00
2 . . .	8,640.00	(20% of $43,200)	19,440.00	34,560.00
3 . . .	6,912.00	(20% of $34,560)	26,352.00	27,648.00
4 . . .	5,529.60	(20% of $27,648)	31,881.60	22,118.40
5 . . .	4,423.68	(20% of $22,118.40)	36,305.28	17,694.72
6 . . .	3,538.94	(20% of $17,694.72)	39,844.22	14,155.78
7 . . .	2,831.16	(20% of $14,155.78)	42,675.38	11,324.62
8 . . .	2,264.92	(20% of $11,324.62)	44,940.30	9,059.70
9 . . .	1,811.94	(20% of $9,059.70)	46,752.24	7,247.76
10 . . .	1,449.56*	(20% of $7,247.76)	48,201.80	5,798.20

* This amount could be $3,247.76 so as to reduce the book value down to the estimated salvage value of $4,000 if the salvage value is still expected to be $4,000. Also in practice, the amounts in this schedule would undoubtedly be rounded.

$$\text{(Asset cost } - \text{ Accumulated depreciation)} \times \left(\frac{100\%}{\text{Useful life}} \times 2 \right)$$

Illustration 6.2 gives an example of an asset costing $54,000 with an estimated life of 10 years and a salvage value of $4,000. In this example, the 10 percent straight-line rate of depreciation (100% ÷ 10 years = 10% per year) is doubled, giving a depreciation rate of 20%.

Under the double-declining-balance method, monthly depreciation is equal to 1/12 of the annual amount. For example, the depreciation per month in the first year for the asset in Illustration 6.2 is $900 ($10,800 ÷ 12). In the second year, it is $720 ($8,640 ÷ 12) per month.

Sum-of-the-years'-digits depreciation. The **sum-of-the-years'-digits (SYD) method** also produces larger depreciation charges in the early years of an asset's life. The years of estimated life of an asset are added together and used as the denominator in a fraction. The number of years of life remaining at the beginning of the accounting period is the numerator. Cost, less estimated salvage value, is then multiplied by this fraction to compute the periodic depreciation. The formula for the sum-of-the-years'-digits method is:

$$\text{(Asset cost } - \text{ Estimated salvage value)} \times \frac{\text{Remaining useful life as of beginning of period}}{\text{Sum-of-the-years'-digits}}$$

This method is illustrated below for a plant asset that costs $54,000 and has an estimated useful life of 10 years and a salvage value of $4,000.

Sum-of-the-years' digits: 1 + 2 + 3 + 4 + 5 + 6 + 7 + 8 + 9 + 10 = 55

Depreciation:
Year 1:	10/55 of $50,000	9,091
Year 2:	9/55 of $50,000	8,182
Year 3:	8/55 of $50,000	7,273
Year 4:	7/55 of $50,000	6,364
Year 5:	6/55 of $50,000	5,455
Year 6:	5/55 of $50,000	4,545
Year 7:	4/55 of $50,000	3,636
Year 8:	3/55 of $50,000	2,727
Year 9:	2/55 of $50,000	1,818
Year 10:	1/55 of $50,000	909
Total depreciation		$50,000

At the beginning of Year 1 there are 10 years of life remaining. Thus, the ratio used to compute the depreciation charge for Year 1 is 10/55.

The mathematical formula for finding the sum-of-the-years' digits for any given number of periods is:

$$S = \frac{n(n + 1)}{2},$$

where S is the sum-of-the-years' digits and n is the number of periods in the asset's life. Thus, the sum-of-the-years' digits for 10 years is 55, computed as follows:

$$\frac{10(10 + 1)}{2} = \frac{110}{2} = 55$$

Depreciation on Assets Acquired or Retired during an Accounting Period

When plant assets are acquired or retired during an accounting period, depreciation is usually computed to the nearest month. Thus, an asset purchased on or before the 15th day of the month is treated as if it had been purchased on the first day of the month. An asset purchased after the 15th of the month is treated as if it had been purchased on the first day of the following month. For instance, assume that a company that operates on a calendar year accounting period acquired a machine on March 14, 1990. The machine has a $52,000 cost, a $4,000 salvage value, and a 10-year estimated useful life. Under the straight-line method, the depreciation expense for 1990 would be $4,000 ($48,000 × 0.10 × 10/12). But if the machine had been purchased on March 16, the straight-line depreciation expense for 1990 would be $3,600 ($48,000 × 0.10 × 9/12).

When the double-declining-balance method is used the procedure is quite simple. For example, assume that a machine is acquired on July 1, 1990. The machine has an $80,000 cost, a $2,000 salvage value, and a 10-year estimated useful life. Double-declining-balance depreciation is used. For the year ending December 31, 1990, the depreciation expense is $8,000

($80,000 × 0.20 × 1/2). The 1991 depreciation expense would be $14,400, computed as follows:

$$($80,000 - $8,000) \times 0.20 = $14,400$$

But when the sum-of-the-years' digits method is used, the computation is more complex. Assume that an asset with a cost of $17,000, a salvage value of $2,000, and an estimated five-year life is acquired on July 1, 1990. Depreciation for 1990 is:

$$($17,000 - $2,000) \times 5/15 \times 1/2 = $2,500$$

Depreciation for 1991 is:

$$($17,000 - $2,000) \times 5/15 \times 1/2 = $2,500$$
$$($17,000 - $2,000) \times 4/15 \times 1/2 = \underline{2,000}$$

Total $\underline{\underline{$4,500}}$

Notice that the depreciation for 1991 includes one half of the first year of life of the asset and one half of the second year of its life.

Revisions of Life Estimates

When it is found that the estimate of the life of an asset is incorrect, the annual depreciation charge under the straight-line method may be changed as follows: the net book value (less salvage) of the asset at the beginning of the current period is divided by the estimated number of life periods remaining. The result is the revised annual depreciation charge applicable to the current and succeeding years.

For example, assume that a machine cost $60,000 and that it has an estimated salvage value of $6,000 and an estimated useful life of eight years. At the end of the fourth year of the machine's life, the balance in its accumulated depreciation account is $27,000. At the beginning of the fifth year, it is estimated that the asset will last six more years (the salvage value remains at $6,000). The revised annual depreciation charge is $4,500 [($60,000 - $27,000 - $6,000) ÷ 6].

Depreciation on the Financial Statements

When depreciation is recorded, a depreciation expense account is debited.[2] The depreciation expense appears in the income statement as one of the expenses of generating revenue. The periodic depreciation is credited to an accumulated depreciation account. The accumulated depreciation account is used so that the original cost of the asset will continue to be

---

[2]We have already noted that, in some instances, the depreciation recorded on one asset may be recorded as part of the cost of acquiring another asset, such as when a truck is used in constructing a building.

shown in the asset account. The ratio of the accumulated depreciation account to the asset's cost may give a hint as to the age of the asset. The total cost and accumulated depreciation will be shown separately on the balance sheet as follows:

Property, plant, and equipment:

Store equipment	$ 24,000	
Less: Accumulated depreciation	4,000	$ 20,000
Building	$200,000	
Less: Accumulated depreciation	40,000	160,000
Land		80,000
Total property, plant, and equipment		$260,000

The presentation of cost less accumulated depreciation may give the reader of financial statements a better understanding of the condition of a company's assets than does the mere presentation of undepreciated cost. For instance, it is one thing to report $200,000 of assets with $120,000 of accumulated depreciation and quite another to report $80,000 of new assets.

Some readers of financial statements mistakenly assume that the amount of accumulated depreciation represents funds available for replacing old assets with new assets. But accumulated depreciation is simply a measure of the cost of the portion of the asset that has expired and been charged to depreciation expense. Accumulated depreciation has a credit balance and is a contra asset account. An informed reader should realize that cash is required to replace assets and that the amount of cash a company holds is shown as a current asset on its balance sheet. There is no cash represented in the Accumulated Depreciation account.

Measurement of Plant Assets on the Balance Sheet

As stated above, plant assets are reported on the balance sheet at their undepreciated cost (cost less accumulated depreciation). The going concern concept is the justification for reporting undepreciated cost instead of market values. Under the *going concern concept*, it is assumed that the company will remain in business and will continue to use the plant assets in business operations instead of selling them. Thus, market values are not reported in the primary financial statements. Furthermore, the accounting requirement of *realization* does not allow recording market prices greater than cost until the asset is sold. It is also not proper to recognize a loss by writing down the asset to a market value lower than cost if the cost of the asset is expected to be fully recovered from the future revenues that the asset will produce.

Objective 3:
Distinguish between capital and revenue expenditures for plant assets

SUBSEQUENT EXPENDITURES ON PLANT ASSETS

It is often necessary to make expenditures for plant assets at times other than the time when they are acquired. The accounting treatment of such expenditures may consist of charging the amount to (1) an asset account, (2) an accumulated depreciation account, or (3) an expense account.

Expenditures that are added to the asset account or charged to the accumulated depreciation account are often called **capital expenditures.** These expenditures increase the net book value of the plant assets. On the other hand, expenditures recorded as expenses are called **revenue expenditures** because they help to produce revenues in the current period. The differences between these two are developed below.

Expenditures Capitalized in Asset Accounts

Expenditures for new or used assets, additions to existing assets, and betterments or improvements to existing assets are called capital expenditures. Such expenditures are properly chargeable to asset accounts because they add to the service-rendering ability of the assets. For example, assume that a used press cost the Day Company $50,000 in cash plus $900 in transportation costs, both of which were properly recorded in the company's Machinery account.

The Day Company then spent $7,900 to recondition the press and $1,700 to install it. These expenditures should also be charged to the Machinery account. They are part of the total costs incurred to obtain the services from the press throughout its entire life. They are capital expenditures.

Betterments are increases in the *quality* of the services an asset provides. For example, the air conditioner installed in an auto that did not have one previously is a betterment, and the cost should be debited to the asset account.

Expenditures Capitalized as Charges to Accumulated Depreciation

Occasionally, expenditures are made on a plant asset that extend its life or increase the *quantity* of output expected beyond the original estimate but not the quality of the services it produces. Because they will benefit future periods, these expenditures are properly capitalized. But because there is no visible, tangible addition to or improvement of the assets, such expenditures are often charged to the accumulated depreciation account. The expenditures are viewed as canceling a part of the accumulated depreciation.

Expenditures for major **extraordinary repairs** that do not extend the life of the asset beyond the original estimate are also often charged to accumulated depreciation (which increases future depreciation charges). This practice avoids the distortion of net income that might result if such expenditures were expensed in the year incurred. In this way the cost of major repairs is spread over a number of years.

To illustrate, assume that after operating its press for four years, the Day Company spent $7,500 to recondition it. The effect of the reconditioning is to increase the life of the press to a total of 14 years from an original estimate of 10 years. The journal entry to record the major repair is:

```
Accumulated Depreciation—Machinery  . . . . . . . . . . . .    7,500
    Cash (or Accounts Payable)  . . . . . . . . . . . . . . .          7,500
    Cost of reconditioning press.
```

When it was acquired, the press had an estimated life of 10 years with no expected salvage value. At the end of the fourth year, the balance in its Accumulated Depreciation account under the straight-line method is $24,200 [($60,500 ÷ 10) × 4]. After the $7,500 debit to the Accumulated Depreciation account, the balances in the Asset account and its related Accumulated Depreciation account are:

```
Cost of press . . . . . . . . . . . . . . . . .   $60,500
Accumulated depreciation . . . . . . . . . .       16,700
Net book value (end of four years)  . . . . . .   $43,800
```

The remaining book value of $43,800 is divided equally among the 10 remaining years in amounts of $4,380 per year under the straight-line method. The effect of the expenditure, then, is to increase the carrying amount of the asset by reducing its contra account, accumulated depreciation.

If the expenditure did not extend the life of the asset but, because of its size, was still charged to accumulated depreciation, the $43,800 would be spread over the remaining six years of life. The annual charges would be $7,300 ($43,800 ÷ 6) under the straight-line method.

Expenditures Charged to Expense

Recurring expenditures that neither add to the service-rendering abilities of the asset nor extend its life beyond the original estimate are treated as expenses. Thus, regular maintenance (lubricating a machine) and ordinary repairs (replacing a broken fan belt) are expensed immediately as revenue expenditures. For example, if the Day Company spends $380 to repair the press after using it for some time, the journal entry is:

```
Maintenance Expense . . . . . . . . . . . . . . . . . . . .    380
    Cash . . . . . . . . . . . . . . . . . . . . . . . . . .          380
    To record payment of repair cost on press.
```

SUMMARY

Noncurrent assets are those assets which are used in a business for an extended time period. These assets represent packages of service potential which are expected to yield future positive benefits. Noncurrent assets are usually referred to as plant assets. These assets may be divided into items which do not expire, for example, land used for a plant site, and assets which lose their service potentials over time, such as equipment. Proper accounting calls for allocating the costs of the assets for which service potentials expire to the periods benefiting from their use. Such allocation is referred to as depreciation of plant assets.

The proper method for allocating the cost of an asset to the periods benefited will depend on many factors including the nature of the revenue patterns, the expected useful life of the asset, and the maintenance policy of the firm. There are three main approaches to allocating the cost of an asset: (1) the straight-line method, in which the cost of the asset less its salvage value is allocated in equal amounts to each year of the expected life of the asset; (2) the units-of-production method, in which the cost allocated to each year is based upon the number of units produced; and (3) two accelerated methods (double-declining-balance and sum-of-the-years'-digits), in which decreasing portions of the cost are allocated to each year. Plant assets are generally reported on the balance sheet at cost less accumulated depreciation.

Expenditures made on plant assets after their acquisition may be either capital expenditures (capitalized) or revenue expenditures (expensed). Expenditures for new or used assets, additions to existing assets, and betterments or improvements are called capital expenditures. Capital expenditures are debited to the asset account if they increase the service-rendering ability of the asset or to the accumulated depreciation account if they simply extend the life of the asset. Expenditures recorded as expenses, such as regular maintenance and ordinary repairs, are called revenue expenditures.

The next chapter continues the discussion of plant assets. You will learn about accounting for plant asset disposals, natural resources, and intangible assets.

Objective 4: Define and use correctly the new terms in the glossary

NEW TERMS INTRODUCED IN CHAPTER 6

Accelerated depreciation methods   Record higher amounts of depreciation in the early years of an asset's life and lower amounts in later years (220).

Appraised values   The values assigned to assets by independent, professional appraisers (217).

Betterments (improvements)   Capital expenditures that are properly charged to asset accounts because they add to the service-rendering ability of the assets; they increase the quality of services that can be obtained from an asset (225).

Book value   An asset's recorded cost less its accumulated depreciation (217).

Capital expenditures   Expenditures that are debited to an asset account or to an accumulated depreciation account (225).

Depreciation   The amount of plant asset cost allocated to each period benefiting from the plant asset's use (217). The **straight-line depreciation** method charges an equal amount of plant asset cost to each period (219). The **units-of-production** method assigns an equal amount of depreciation for each unit of product manufactured or service rendered by an asset (220). The **sum-of-the-years'-digits (SYD)** (221) and the **double-declining-balance (DDB)** depreciation (220) methods assign decreasing amounts of depreciation to successive periods of time.

Depreciation accounting Distributes in a systematic and rational manner the cost of a depreciable plant asset, less its salvage value, over the asset's estimated useful life (217).

Extraordinary repairs Expenditures that are viewed as canceling a part of the existing accumulated depreciation because they increase the quantity of services expected from an asset (225).

Fair market value The normal price that would be paid for an item being sold in the normal course of business (not at a forced liquidation sale) (216).

Inadequacy The inability of a plant asset to produce enough products or provide enough services to meet current demands (217).

Obsolescence Decline in usefulness of an asset brought about by invention and technological progress (217).

Physical deterioration Results from use of the asset—wear and tear—and the action of the elements (217).

Plant assets Tangible long-lived assets obtained for use in business operations instead of for resale (213).

Revenue expenditures Expenditures (on a plant asset) that are immediately expensed (225).

Salvage (or scrap) value The amount of money the company expects to recover, less disposal costs, on the date a plant asset is scrapped, sold, or traded in. Also called residual value (218).

Useful life The length of time the company holding a depreciable asset intends to use it (218).

DEMONSTRATION PROBLEM 6–1

The Shorter Company acquired a machine on September 26, 1990, at a total cost of $90,200. The machine was estimated to have a useful life of 10 years and a salvage value of $2,200. It was also estimated that the machine would produce one million units of product during its life. The machine produced 99,000 units in 1990 and 137,500 units in 1991.

Required:

Compute the amounts of depreciation to be recorded in 1990 and 1991 under each of the following:

a. Straight-line method.
b. Units-of-production method.
c. Sum-of-the-years'-digits method.
d. Double-declining-balance method.

Solution to demonstration problem 6–1

a. Straight-line method:
1990: [($90,200 − $2,200) ÷ 10] × 3/12 = $2,200
1991: ($90,200 − $2,200) ÷ 10 = $8,800

b. Units-of-production method:

1990: [($90,200 − $2,200)/1,000,000] × 99,000 = $8,712

1991: [($90,200 − $2,200)/1,000,000] × 137,500 = $12,100

c. Sum-of-the-years'-digits method:

1990: ($90,200 − $2,200) × 10/55 × 3/12 = $4,000

1991: [($90,200 − $2,200) × 10/55 × 9/12]
    + [($90,200 − $2,200) × 9/55 × 3/12];
    $12,000 + $3,600 = $15,600

d. Double-declining-balance method:

1990: $90,200 × 20% × 3/12 = $4,510

1991: ($90,200 − $4,510) × 20% = $17,138

QUESTIONS

1. What is the main distinction between inventory and plant assets?

2. Which of the following items are properly classifiable as plant assets on the balance sheet?

    a. Future advertising paid to inform the public about new energy-saving programs at a manufacturing plant.

    b. A truck acquired by a manufacturing company to be used to deliver the company's products to wholesalers.

    c. An automobile acquired by an insurance company to be used by one of its salespersons.

    d. Calculators acquired by an office supply company to be resold to customers.

    e. The cost of constructing and paving a driveway that has a useful life of 10 years.

3. In any exchange of noncash assets, the accountant's task is that of finding the most appropriate valuation to assign to the assets received. What is the general rule for determining the most appropriate valuation in such a situation?

4. Why should periodic depreciation be recorded on all plant assets except land?

5. Howard Company is offered $200,000 for a tract of land carried in its accounts at $80,000. Should it accept the offer? Why or why not?

6. Define the terms *inadequacy* and *obsolescence* as used in accounting for plant assets.

7. What four factors must be known to compute depreciation on a plant asset?

8. What is the sum-of-the-years'-digits for a machine that has an estimated useful life of nine years?

9. The Lloyd Company has just acquired new factory machines and is trying to determine which depreciation method to use. List the relative merits of using each of the following methods:

    a. Straight-line.

    b. Units-of-production.

    c. Accelerated.

229

10. What does the balance in the accumulated depreciation account represent? Can this balance be used to replace the related plant asset at the end of its useful life?

11. Distinguish between capital expenditures and revenue expenditures.

12. For each of the following, state whether the expenditure made should be charged to an expense, an asset, or an accumulated depreciation account:

   a. Cost of installing air-conditioning equipment in a car that previously did not have air conditioning.

   b. Painting of an owned factory building every other year.

   c. Cost of replacing the roof on a 10-year-old building which was purchased new and has an estimated total life of 40 years. The replacement did not extend the life beyond the original estimate.

   d. Cost of repairing an electric motor.

EXERCISES

Determine cost of land

1. Cole Company recently bought a plot of land for $245,000 for construction of a new warehouse. Legal fees connected with the transaction were $2,400. Back taxes on the property amounted to $6,000, for which Cole Company assumed the liability. Demolition costs incurred to raze (destroy) the old warehouse on the property were $8,900. What is the cost of the land?

Determine cost of land and building when acquired together

2. Porter Company acquired real property consisting of a tract of land and two buildings for $480,000 cash. The company intended to raze (destroy) the old factory building and to remodel and use the old office building. To allocate the cost of the property acquired, the company had the property appraised. The appraised values were: land, $180,000; factory building, $180,000; and office building, $240,000. The factory building was demolished at a net cost of $24,000. The office building was remodeled at a cost of $48,000. The cost of a new identical office building was estimated to be $270,000. Present a schedule or schedules showing the determination of the amounts at which the assets acquired should be carried in the Porter Company accounts. Show calculations.

Determine cost of equipment

3. Dwight Company purchased an earthmover for $22,000, less a 2% cash discount. One of the company's employees drove the equipment to the company's storage lot. The company was fined $350 because the employee had failed to obtain a permit to drive the equipment on city streets. Break-in and testing costs totaled $3,000. What is the cost of the equipment?

Record cost of office furniture, depreciation thereon

4. The Roy Company purchased some office furniture on March 1, 1989, for $6,500 cash. Cash of $100 was paid for freight and cartage costs. The furniture is being depreciated over a four-year life under the straight-line method, assuming $360 of salvage value. The company employs a calendar-year accounting period and records depreciation for the full month in which an asset is installed. On July 1, 1990, $45 was spent to refinish the furniture. Prepare journal entries for the Roy Company to record all of the above data, including the annual depreciation adjustments, through 1990.

Compute difference in income taxes payable between DDB and straight-line

5. Keller Company purchased a new machine on January 2, 1989, at a cash cost of $180,000. The machine is estimated to have a life of five years, with no salvage value at the end of that time. If federal income taxes are levied at a rate of 50% of net income, how much would the income taxes payable for the years 1989

and 1990 be reduced if the company could choose the double-declining-balance method of computing depreciation rather than the straight-line method?

Compute SYD depreciation for two years

6. Coker Company acquired equipment costing $60,000 on April 1, 1989. The equipment has an estimated salvage value of $4,000 and an estimated useful life of seven years. The machine is being depreciated using the sum-of-the-years'-digits method. Compute the depreciation for the years ended December 31, 1989 and 1990.

Compute annual depreciation for two years under each of four different methods

7. On January 2, 1989, a new machine was acquired for $150,000. The machine has an estimated salvage value of $6,000 and an estimated useful life of 10 years. The machine is expected to produce a total of 500,000 units of product throughout its useful life. Compute depreciation for 1989 and 1990 using each of the following methods:

a. Straight-line.

b. Units-of-production (assume that 30,000 and 50,000 units were produced in 1989 and 1990, respectively).

c. Double-declining-balance.

d. Sum-of-the-years'-digits.

Compute straight-line depreciation given reduced estimated life

8. The Hart Company acquired a delivery truck on January 2, 1989, for $42,000. The truck has an estimated salvage value of $2,250 and an estimated useful life of eight years. The truck is being depreciated on a straight-line basis. At the beginning of 1992, it is estimated that the truck has a remaining useful life of seven years. What are the depreciation charges for 1989 and for 1992?

Determine whether expenditures are capital or revenue expenditures

9. Classify each of the following as either a capital expenditure or an expense:

a. Painting of office building at a cost of $1,700. The building is painted every year.

b. Addition of a new plant wing at a cost of $335,000.

c. Expansion of a paved parking lot at a cost of $90,000.

d. Replacement of a stairway with an escalator at a cost of $24,000.

e. Lubricating a machine at a cost of $300.

f. Replacing a broken fan belt at a cost of $185.

PROBLEMS

Determine building account balance, and prepare journal entry to record it

6–1. Lewis Company purchased land and a building having appraised values of $360,000 and $600,000, respectively. The terms of the sale were that Lewis would pay $489,000 in cash and assume responsibility for a $300,000 mortgage note, $15,000 of accrued interest, and $36,000 of unpaid property taxes. Lewis intends to use the building as an office building.

Required:

Prepare a journal entry to record the purchase.

Determine cost of land

6–2. The Meers Company purchased a two-square-mile farm from its owner under the following terms: cash paid, $386,500; mortgage note assumed, $193,000; and accrued interest on mortgage note assumed, $4,900. The company paid $42,000 for brokerage and legal services to acquire the property and secure clear title. It planned to subdivide the property into residential lots and to construct homes on these lots. Clearing and leveling costs of $17,000 were paid. Crops on the land were sold for $13,000. A house on the land, to be moved by the buyer, was sold for $11,200. The other buildings were razed at a cost of $15,000, and salvaged material was sold for $6,300. Approximately six acres of land were deeded to the township for roads, and another 10 acres were deeded to the local school district as the site for a future school. After the subdivision was completed, this land would have an approximate value of $5,800 per acre. The company secured a total of 1,200 salable lots from the remaining land.

Required:

Present a schedule showing in detail the composition of the cost of the 1,200 salable lots.

Determine correct valuations of assets

6–3. Hazel Company planned to erect a new factory building and a new office building in Atlanta, Georgia. Preliminary studies showed two possible sites as available and desirable. Further studies showed the second site to be preferable. A report on this property showed an appraised value of $600,000 for land and orchard and $400,000 for a building.

After considerable negotiation the company and the owner reached the following agreement. Hazel Company was to pay $520,000 in cash, assume a $300,000 mortgage note on the property, assume the accrued interest on the mortgage note of $6,400, and assume unpaid property taxes of $24,000. Hazel Company paid $66,000 cash for brokerage and legal services in acquiring the property.

Shortly after acquiring the property, Hazel Company sold the fruit on the trees for $8,800, remodeled the building into an office building at a cost of $128,000, and removed the trees from the land at a cost of $30,000. Construction of the factory building is to begin in a week.

Required:

Prepare schedules showing the proper valuation of the assets acquired by the Hazel Company.

Determine correct cost of equipment and place in T-account form

6–4. When you were hired as manager of the Ivy Street Company on January 1, 1990, the company bookkeeper gave you the following information regarding one of its equipment accounts (in T-account form):

Equipment—Machine C

1989			1989		
Jan. 1	Disposition cost of Machine B	3,000	Jan. 1	Cash from sale of Machine B	2,500
1	Material used in building Machine C	110,000	Dec. 31	Depreciation on Machine C for year ended 12/31/89 (10% of $213,300) . . .	21,330
1	Labor used in building Machine C	80,000			
1	Cost of installing Machine C	13,800			
1	Net income from building Machine C rather than purchasing it	12,000			

Required:

Construct the theoretically correct equipment account for Machine C.

Determine building account balance and prepare correcting entries

6–5. The Morton Company has the following entries in its Building account:

1989			Debits
May	5	Cost of land and building purchased	$800,000
	5	Broker fees incident to purchase	36,000
1990			
Jan.	3	Contract price of new wing added to south end of building	220,000
	15	Cost of new machinery, estimated life ten years	800,000
June	10	Real estate taxes for six months ending 6/30/90	18,000
Aug.	10	Cost of parking lot for employees in back of building	24,800
Sept.	6	Replacement of broken windows	800
Oct.	10	Repairs due to regular usage	9,200

1989			Credits
Dec.	31	Transfer to Land account, as per allocation of purchase cost authorized in minutes of board of directors	120,000
1990			
Jan.	5	Proceeds from lease of second floor for six months ended 12/31/89	20,000

The original property was acquired on May 5, 1989. The Morton Company immediately engaged a contractor to construct a new wing on the south end of the building. While the new wing was being constructed, the company leased the second floor as temporary warehouse space to the Joy Company. During this period (July 1 to December 31, 1989) the company installed new machinery costing $800,000 on the first floor of the building. Regular operations began on January 2, 1990.

Required:

a. Compute the correct balance for the Building account as of December 31, 1990. The building is expected to last 40 years. The company employs a calendar-year accounting period.

b. Prepare the necessary journal entries to correct the records of the Morton Company at December 31, 1990. No depreciation entries are required.

Compute depreciation for various assets using straight-line and units-of-production depreciation methods

6–6. The Neal Company's fiscal year ends May 31. The company has its own fleet of delivery vehicles. Included are the following:

Description	Date Acquired	Cost	Expected Life	Expected Salvage Value
Sedan No. 3	June 1, 1988	$ 32,000	4 years	$ 4,800
Truck No. 2	June 1, 1984	48,000	100,000 miles	4,000
Truck No. 5	Jan. 1, 1990	112,000	150,000 miles	11,200
Trailer No. 8	Apr. 1, 1987	64,000	400,000 miles	–0–

Speedometer readings at May 31 show the following:

	1989	1990	Total Mileage for Year Ended May 31, 1990
Sedan No. 3	15,000 miles	28,000 miles	13,000 miles
Truck No. 2	120,000	150,000	30,000
Truck No. 5	0	20,000	20,000
Trailer No. 8	50,000	75,000	25,000

233

Required:

Set up schedules showing in full detail the amount of depreciation to be recorded for the year ended May 31, 1990, on each of the above assets. Use the straight-line method for Sedan No. 3 and the units-of-production (number of miles driven) method for the other vehicles.

Compute deprecia-
tion for first year
under each of four
different methods

6–7. Crawford Company acquired a machine on July 1, 1989, at a cash cost of $144,000 and immediately spent $6,000 to install it. The machine was estimated to have a useful life of eight years and a scrap value of $9,000 at the end of this time. It was further estimated that the machine would produce 500,000 units of product during its life. In the first year, the machine produced 100,000 units.

Required:

Prepare journal entries to record depreciation for the fiscal year ended June 30, 1990, if the company used:

a. The straight-line method.

b. The units-of-production method.

c. The double-declining-balance method.

d. The sum-of-the-years'-digits method.

Compute deprecia-
tion for first year
under each of four
different methods

6–8. Garland Company acquired equipment on January 2, 1990, at a cash cost of $650,000. Transportation charges amounted to $8,000, and installation and testing costs totaled $20,000. The equipment was damaged while being installed, and the cost of repairing the damage was $4,000.

The equipment was estimated to have a useful life of nine years and a salvage value of $12,000 at the end of its life. It was further estimated that the equipment would be used in the production of 660,000 units of product during its life. During 1990, 220,000 units of product were produced.

Required:

Prepare journal entries to record depreciation for the year ended December 31, 1990, if the company used:

a. The straight-line method.

b. The units-of-production method.

c. The double-declining-balance method.

d. The sum-of-the-years'-digits method.

Compute first year
depreciation using
three methods;
assume life expec-
tancy change

6–9. Norcross Company purchased a machine on January 2, 1988, at an invoice price of $125,200. Transportation charges amounted to $1,400, and $3,000 was spent to install the machine. The costs of removing an old machine to make room for the new one amounted to $1,200; $400 was received for the scrap material from the old machine.

Required:

a. State the amount of depreciation that would be recorded on the machine for the first year on the straight-line basis, the double-declining-balance basis, and the sum-of-the-years'-digits basis, assuming an estimated life of eight years and no salvage value.

b. Give the journal entry needed at December 31, 1990, to record depreciation, assuming a revised total life expectancy of 12 years for the machine. Assume that depreciation has been recorded through December 31, 1989, on a straight-line basis.

Determine cost of machine; prepare entry for depreciation under DDB and assume change in estimated life

6–10. The Nill Corporation acquired a new computer on July 1, 1989. The computer had an invoice price of $144,000, but the company received a 3% cash discount by paying the bill at the date of acquisition. While transporting the computer to its new location, a Nill employee was fined $400 for speeding. Nill paid the fine. Installation and testing costs totaled $14,208. The computer is estimated to have a $5,600 salvage value and a seven-year useful life.

Required:

a. Prepare the journal entry to record the acquisition of the computer.

b. Prepare the journal entry to record depreciation for 1989 under the double-declining-balance method.

c. Assume that at the beginning of 1992 it is estimated that the computer will last another six years. Prepare the journal entry to record depreciation for 1992. Assume that depreciation has been recorded through 1991, on a straight-line basis and that the expected salvage value remains at $5,600.

Compute straight-line depreciation after major part is replaced

6–11. A machine belonging to the Dewey Company that cost $60,000 has an estimated life of 20 years. After 10 years, an extremely important machine part, representing about 40% of the original cost, is worn out and replaced. The replacement cost is $18,000, and the useful life of the new part is the same as the remaining useful life of the machine.

Required:

a. Prepare journal entries to record the replacement of the old part with the new part. Assume that depreciation has already been brought up to date.

b. Compute the annual depreciation charge after replacement, using the straight-line method.

Compute straight-line depreciation

6–12. Jarvis Company purchased a machine at a cash cost of $180,000. An electric motor was purchased for cash and attached to the machine at a total cost of $96,000. The machine was installed in a production center on the first floor at a cost of $36,000 on July 1, 1989. Its estimated life was 15 years, with no salvage value expected. On July 1, 1994, the machine and motor unit was moved from its first-floor location to the second floor and the entire unit was installed at a cost of $58,000. The estimated life of the unit in its second-floor location is 10 years, with no salvage value expected.

Required:

Compute the depreciation charge for the year ending June 30, 1995, using the straight-line method.

BUSINESS DECISION PROBLEM 6–1

Compute three years' depreciation using two methods; compute tax savings; and advise on which company to purchase

Blue Company and Green Company are quite similar except for the following: Blue Company uses double-declining-balance depreciation, whereas Green Company uses straight-line depreciation. On January 2, 1990, both companies acquired the following plant assets with the related costs, salvage values, and useful lives:

Plant Asset	Cost	Salvage Value	Useful Life
Building	$250,000	Negligible	40 years
Land	100,000	—	—
Machinery	200,000	Negligible	16 years

The companies reported the following net income for the years 1990, 1991, and 1992.

	Net Income	
Year	Blue Company	Green Company
1990	$47,500	$49,375
1991	50,000	51,250
1992	55,000	55,625

Mike Jernigan is interested in buying one of the companies. He notices that Green Company's income exceeds Blue Company's income each year. But Blue Company has more working capital (current assets minus current liabilities) than Green Company. Jernigan has engaged you to advise him on buying one of the companies.

Required:

a. Compute the amount of depreciation recorded by each of the companies in 1990, 1991, and 1992.

b. Compute the amount of tax savings Blue Company would obtain by using double-declining-balance depreciation instead of straight-line depreciation. (Assume a 40% tax rate and that this method can be used for tax purposes.)

c. Which company would you advise Mr. Jernigan to buy? Why?

7

PLANT ASSET DISPOSALS; NATURAL RESOURCES AND INTANGIBLE ASSETS

LEARNING OBJECTIVES

After studying this chapter, you should be able to:

1. Calculate and prepare entries for the sale, retirement, and destruction of plant assets.
2. Describe and record exchanges of dissimilar and similar plant assets.
3. Discuss the differences between accounting principles and tax rules in the treatment of gains and losses from the exchange of plant assets.
4. Determine the periodic depletion cost of a natural resource and calculate depreciation of plant assets on extractive industry property.
5. Prepare entries for the acquisition and amortization of intangible assets.
6. Define and use correctly the new terms in the glossary.

The study of long-term assets, which includes plant assets, natural resources, and intangible assets, began in Chapter 6. Discussion in that chapter focused on determining plant asset cost, computing depreciation, and distinguishing between capital and revenue expenditures. This chapter begins by discussing the disposal of plant assets. The next topic is accounting for natural resources such as ores, minerals, oil and gas, and timber. The final topic is accounting for intangible assets, such as patents, copyrights, franchises, trademarks and trade names, and leases.

Although several different long-term assets are discussed in this chapter, you will see that accounting for all long-term assets is basically the same. When a company purchases a long-term asset, the asset is recorded at cost. As the company receives benefits from the asset and the future service potential is reduced, the cost is transferred from an asset account to an expense account. Since the lives of long-term assets can extend for many years, the methods accountants use in reporting them can have a dramatic effect on the financial statements of many accounting periods.

DISPOSAL OF PLANT ASSETS

All plant assets except land eventually wear out or become inadequate or obsolete and must be sold, retired, or traded in on new assets. When a plant asset is disposed of, both the asset's cost and accumulated depreciation must be removed from the accounts. In this section you will learn how to account for the (1) sale of plant assets, (2) retirement of plant assets without sale, (3) destruction of plant assets, (4) exchanges of dissimilar and similar plant assets, and (5) costs of dismantling and removing an asset.

Sale of Plant Assets

*Objective 1:
Calculate and
prepare entries for
the sale, retirement,
and destruction of
plant assets*

Companies frequently dispose of plant assets by selling them. By comparing an asset's book value (cost less accumulated depreciation) with its sales price (or net amount realized if there are selling expenses), the company will show either a gain or loss. If the sales price is greater than the asset's book value, the company will show a gain. If the sales price is less than the asset's book value, the company will show a loss. Of course, if the sales price is equal to the asset's book value, there is no gain or loss.

To illustrate accounting for the sale of a plant asset, assume equipment costing $45,000 with accumulated depreciation of $14,000 is sold for $35,000. A gain of $4,000 is realized on the sale as computed below:

Equipment cost	$45,000
Accumulated depreciation	14,000
Book value	$31,000
Sales price	35,000
Gain realized	$ 4,000

The journal entry to record the sale is:

Cash	35,000	
Accumulated Depreciation—Equipment	14,000	
Equipment		45,000
Gain on Disposal of Plant Assets		4,000
To record sale of equipment at a price greater than book value.		

If, on the other hand, the equipment is sold for $28,000, a loss of $3,000 ($31,000 book value − $28,000 sales price) is realized and the journal entry to record the sale is:

```
Cash. . . . . . . . . . . . . . . . . . . . . . . . . . . . . .    28,000
Accumulated Depreciation—Equipment . . . . . . . . . . . .    14,000
Loss on Disposal of Plant Assets . . . . . . . . . . . . . .     3,000
    Equipment . . . . . . . . . . . . . . . . . . . . . . . .             45,000
        To record sale of equipment at a price less than book value.
```

If the equipment is sold for $31,000, there is no gain or loss, and the journal entry to record the sale is:

```
Cash. . . . . . . . . . . . . . . . . . . . . . . . . . . . . .    31,000
Accumulated Depreciation—Equipment . . . . . . . . . . . .    14,000
    Equipment . . . . . . . . . . . . . . . . . . . . . . . .             45,000
        To record sale of equipment at a price equal to book value.
```

Accounting for depreciation to date of disposition. When a plant asset is sold or otherwise disposed of, it is important to record the depreciation up to the date of sale or disposition. For example, if an asset is sold on April 1 and depreciation was last recorded on December 31, depreciation for three months (January 1–April 1) should be recorded. If depreciation is not recorded for the three months, operating expenses for that period will be understated, and the gain on the sale of the asset will be understated or the loss overstated.

To illustrate, assume that on August 1, 1990, Ray Company sold a machine for $1,500. The machine cost $12,000 and was being depreciated at the straight-line rate of 10% per year. As of December 31, 1989, after closing entries were made, the machine's accumulated depreciation account had a balance of $9,600. Before a gain or loss can be determined and before an entry can be made to record the sale, the following entry must be made to record depreciation for the seven months ended July 31, 1990:

```
July 31  Depreciation Expense—Machinery . . . . . . . . . . . .     700
             Accumulated Depreciation—Machinery . . . . . . . .             700
         To record depreciation for seven months
         ($12,000 × 0.10 × 7/12).
```

The $200 loss on the sale is computed as shown below:

```
Machine cost  . . . . . . . . . . . . . . . . . . . . . . . . . . . .    $12,000
Accumulated depreciation ($9,600 + $700) . . . . . . . . . . . . . . .     10,300
Book value  . . . . . . . . . . . . . . . . . . . . . . . . . . . . .    $ 1,700
Sales price  . . . . . . . . . . . . . . . . . . . . . . . . . . . . .      1,500
Loss realized  . . . . . . . . . . . . . . . . . . . . . . . . . . . .    $   200
```

The journal entry to record the sale is:

```
Cash. . . . . . . . . . . . . . . . . . . . . . . . . . . . . .     1,500
Accumulated Depreciation—Machinery. . . . . . . . . . . . .    10,300
Loss on Disposal of Plant Assets . . . . . . . . . . . . . .       200
    Machinery . . . . . . . . . . . . . . . . . . . . . . . .             12,000
        To record sale of machinery at a price less than book value.
```

Retirement of Plant Assets without Sale

When a plant asset is retired from productive service, the asset's cost and accumulated depreciation must be removed from the plant asset accounts. For example, Hayes Company would make the following journal entry when a fully depreciated machine that cost $15,000 and had no salvage value is retired:

Accumulated Depreciation—Machinery.	15,000	
Machinery		15,000
To record the retirement of a fully depreciated machine.		

Occasionally, a plant asset is continued in use after it has been fully depreciated. In such a case, the asset's cost and accumulated depreciation should not be removed from the accounts until the asset is sold, traded, or retired from service. Of course, no more depreciation can be recorded on a fully depreciated asset because total depreciation expense taken on an asset may never exceed the asset's cost.

Sometimes a plant asset is retired from service or discarded before it is fully depreciated. If the asset is to be sold as scrap (even if not immediately), its cost and accumulated depreciation should be removed from the asset and accumulated depreciation accounts. In addition, its estimated scrap value should be recorded in a Salvaged Materials account, and a gain or loss on disposal should be recognized. To illustrate, assume a machine with a $10,000 original cost and $7,500 of accumulated depreciation is retired. If the machine's estimated scrap value is $500, the following entry is required:

Salvaged Materials	500	
Accumulated Depreciation—Machinery.	7,500	
Loss on Disposal of Plant Assets	2,000	
Machinery		10,000
To record retirement of machinery, which will be sold for scrap at a later date.		

Destruction of Plant Assets

Plant assets are sometimes wrecked in accidents or destroyed by fire, flood, storm, or other causes. Losses are normally incurred in such situations. For example, assume that an *uninsured* building costing $40,000 with accumulated depreciation of $12,000 was completely destroyed by a fire. The journal entry is:

Fire Loss	28,000	
Accumulated Depreciation—Building.	12,000	
Building		40,000
To record fire loss.		

If the building was *insured*, only the amount of the fire loss exceeding the amount to be recovered from the insurance company would be debited to the Fire Loss account. To illustrate, assume that in the example above, the building was partially insured and that $22,000 is recoverable from the insurance company. The journal entry is:

Receivable from Insurance Company	22,000
Fire Loss	6,000
Accumulated Depreciation—Building	12,000
Building	40,000

To record fire loss and amount expected to be recovered from insurance company.

Exchanges of Plant Assets or Other Nonmonetary Assets

Nonmonetary assets are those items whose price may change over time, such as inventories, property, plant, and equipment. In accounting for the exchange of nonmonetary assets, ordinarily the recorded amount should be based on the fair value of the asset given up or the fair value of the asset received, whichever is clearly more evident.[1] If there is a gain or loss resulting from the exchange, the loss is always recognized; the gain may or may not be recognized, depending on whether the asset exchanged is similar or dissimilar in nature.

Similar assets are those of the same general type, that perform the same function, or that are employed in the same line of business. Examples of the exchange of similar assets include a building for a building, a delivery truck for a delivery truck, and equipment for equipment. Conversely, the exchange of dissimilar assets includes a building for land, and equipment for inventory.

In general, losses on nonmonetary assets are always recognized, regardless of whether the assets are similar or dissimilar in nature. Gains are recognized if the assets are dissimilar in nature because the earnings process related to those assets is considered to be completed. With one exception, gains are deferred on the exchange of similar nonmonetary assets. The exception occurs when monetary consideration (**boot**) is received in addition to the similar asset. In this case, a partial gain may be recognized when boot such as cash is received along with an asset. Because the specific details of monetary consideration are reserved for an intermediate text, assume in the examples given that cash has been paid, not received. Both gains and losses on the disposal of nonmonetary assets are computed by comparing the book value of the asset given up with the fair value of the asset given up.

The next two sections further illustrate the proper accounting for these different types of transactions.

Exchanges of Dissimilar Plant Assets

Objective 2: Describe and record exchanges of dissimilar and similar plant assets

Sometimes a machine is traded for a dissimilar plant asset such as a truck. Exchanges of dissimilar plant assets are accounted for by recording the new asset at the fair market value of the asset received or the asset(s) given up, whichever is more clearly evident. The cash price of the new asset may be stated; if so, the cash price should be used to record the new

---

[1]APB, "Accounting for Nonmonetary Transactions," *APB Opinion No. 29* (New York: AICPA, May 1973), par. 16.

asset. If the cash price is not stated, the fair market value of the old asset plus any cash paid is used to record the new asset. Thus, the asset received would normally be recorded at either (1) a stated cash price of the new asset or (2) a known fair value of the asset given up plus any cash paid.

The book value of the old asset is removed from the accounts by debiting accumulated depreciation and crediting the old asset. The Cash account is credited for any amount paid. If the amount at which the new asset is recorded exceeds the book value of the old asset plus any cash paid, a gain is recorded to balance the journal entry. If the situation is vice versa, a loss is recorded to balance the journal entry.

To illustrate such an exchange, assume that an old factory machine is exchanged for a new delivery truck. The machine cost $45,000 and had an accumulated depreciation balance of $38,000. The truck had a $55,000 cash price and was acquired by trading in the old machine with a fair value of $3,000 and paying $52,000 cash. The journal entry to record the exchange is:

Delivery Truck.	55,000	
Accumulated Depreciation—Factory Machinery	38,000	
Loss on Disposal of Plant Assets	4,000	
Factory Machinery.		45,000
Cash.		52,000
To record loss on exchange of dissimilar plant assets.		

The $4,000 loss on the exchange can also be computed as the book value of the old asset less the fair market value of the old asset. The calculation is as follows:

Machine cost	$45,000
Accumulated depreciation	38,000
Book value	$ 7,000
Fair market value of old asset (trade-in allowance)	3,000
Loss realized	$ 4,000

To illustrate the recognition of a gain from an exchange of dissimilar plant assets, assume that the fair market value of the above machine was $9,000 instead of $3,000, and that $46,000 was paid in cash. The gain would be $2,000 ($9,000 fair market value less $7,000 book value). The journal entry to record the exchange would be:

Delivery Truck	55,000	
Accumulated Depreciation—Factory Machinery	38,000	
Factory Machinery		45,000
Cash		46,000
Gain on Disposal of Plant Assets		2,000
To record gain on exchange of dissimilar plant assets.		

Remember, both gains and losses are always recognized on exchanges of dissimilar plant assets. As shown below, gains on exchanges of similar plant assets may or may not be recognized.

Exchanges of Similar Plant Assets

Plant assets such as automobiles, trucks, and office equipment are often exchanged by trading the old asset for a similar new one. In such cases, the company usually receives a trade-in allowance for the old asset,[2] and the balance is paid in cash. The cash price of the new asset is often stated. If not, the cash price is assumed to be the fair market value of the old asset plus the cash paid.

When similar assets are exchanged, the general rule that new assets are recorded at the fair market value of what is given up or received is modified slightly. The new asset is recorded at (1) the book value of the old asset plus the cash paid or (2) the cash price of the asset received, whichever is lower. When this rule is applied to exchanges of similar assets, *losses are recognized (or recorded), but gains are not.*

To illustrate the accounting for exchanges of similar plant assets, assume $50,000 cash and delivery truck No. 1, which cost $45,000 and had $38,000 accumulated depreciation, were exchanged for delivery truck No. 2. The new truck has a cash price (fair market value) of $55,000. A loss of $2,000 is realized on the exchange.

Cost of delivery truck No. 1	$45,000
Accumulated depreciation	38,000
Book value	$ 7,000
Fair market value of old asset (trade-in allowance)	5,000
Loss on exchange of plant assets	$ 2,000

The journal entry to record the exchange is:

Delivery Trucks (cost of No. 2)	55,000	
Accumulated Depreciation—Delivery Trucks	38,000	
Loss on Disposal of Plant Assets	2,000	
Delivery Trucks (cost of No. 1)		45,000
Cash		50,000
To record loss on exchange of similar plant assets.		

Note that exchanges of similar plant assets are recorded just like exchanges of dissimilar plant assets when a *loss* occurs from the exchange.

Accounting for any gain resulting from exchanges of similar assets is handled differently than a gain resulting from exchanges of dissimilar plant assets. To illustrate, assume that in the preceding example, delivery truck No. 1 and $45,000 cash were given in exchange for delivery truck No. 2. A gain of $3,000 is indicated on the exchange:

---

[2] Trade-in allowance is sometimes expressed as the difference between *list* price and cash paid, but we choose to define it as the difference between *cash* price and cash paid because this latter definition seems to agree with current practice for exchange transactions.

Cost of delivery truck No. 1.	$45,000
Accumulated depreciation	38,000
Book value	$ 7,000
Fair market value of old asset (trade-in allowance)	10,000
Gain indicated	$ 3,000

The journal entry to record the exchange is:

Delivery Trucks (cost of No. 2)	52,000	
Accumulated Depreciation—Delivery Trucks	38,000	
Delivery Trucks (cost of No. 1)		45,000
Cash		45,000
To record exchange of similar plant assets.		

When similar assets are exchanged, a gain is not recognized. The new asset is recorded at book value of the old asset ($7,000) plus cash paid ($45,000). The gain is deducted from the cost of the new asset ($55,000). Thus, the cost basis of the new delivery truck is equal to $55,000 less the $3,000 gain, or $52,000. This cost basis is used in recording depreciation on the truck and determining any gain or loss on its disposal.

The justification used by the Accounting Principles Board for not recognizing gains on exchanges of similar plant assets is "revenue should not be recognized merely because one productive asset is substituted for a similar productive asset but rather should be considered to flow from the production and sale of the goods or services to which the substituted productive asset is committed."[3] In effect, the gain on an exchange of similar plant assets is realized in the form of increased net income resulting from smaller depreciation charges on the newly acquired asset. In the preceding example, annual depreciation expense is less if it is based on the truck's $52,000 cost basis than if it is based on the truck's $55,000 cash price. Thus, future net income per year will be larger.

"Material" gains or losses are those that are large enough to affect the decisions of an informed user of the financial statements. When material gains or losses are recognized on the disposal of plant assets, they should be reported as a separate item on the income statement.

Objective 3: Discuss the differences between accounting principles and tax rules in the treatment of gains and losses from the exchange of plant assets

Tax Rules and Plant Asset Exchanges. The Internal Revenue Code does not allow recognition of gains or losses for income tax purposes when similar productive assets are exchanged. For income tax purposes, the cost basis of the new asset is the book value of the old asset plus any additional cash paid.

Accounting principles and income tax laws agree on the treatment of gains, but they disagree on the treatment of losses. Thus, the previous example involving a $2,000 loss on the exchange of delivery trucks must be recorded as follows for income tax purposes:

---

[3]*APB Opinion No. 29,* par. 16.

```
Delivery Trucks (cost of No. 2) ($7,000 + $45,000) . . . . . . .    52,000
Accumulated Depreciation—Delivery Trucks . . . . . . . . . . .    38,000
    Delivery Trucks (cost of No. 1) . . . . . . . . . . . . . .              45,000
    Cash. . . . . . . . . . . . . . . . . . . . . . . . . . .              45,000
```
To record exchange of similar plant assets using tax method.

Illustration 7.1 summarizes the rules for recording exchanges of plant assets, both for accounting purposes and for income tax purposes. Studying this illustration may help you to remember how to record these exchange transactions.

Because of differences between accounting principles and income tax laws, two sets of depreciation records must be kept if a material (relatively large) loss occurs on an exchange of similar plant assets. One set of depreciation records is based on the accounting valuation of the new asset (cash price of new asset or fair market value of old asset plus cash paid) and used to determine net income for financial reporting purposes; the second set is based on the tax valuation of the new asset (book value of old asset plus cash paid).

The **materiality concept** allows the accountant to treat immaterial items in a theoretically incorrect manner. Thus, two sets of accounting records do not have to be kept if the loss from an exchange is immaterial. Then the new asset is recorded at the cash price of the new asset (or book value of the old asset plus cash paid) for both income tax purposes and financial reporting purposes. For example, assume a company that earns approximately $1,000,000 per year suffers a $25 loss on an exchange of plant as-

Illustration 7.1
SUMMARY OF RULES FOR RECORDING EXCHANGES OF PLANT ASSETS

	Dissimilar Assets for Both Accounting and Tax Purposes	Similar Assets	
		For Accounting Purposes	For Tax Purposes
Recognize gains?	Yes	No	No
Recognize losses?	Yes	Yes	No
Record new asset at:	Cash price of new asset or fair market value of old asset plus cash paid	**If loss:** Cash price of new asset or fair market value of old asset plus cash paid **If gain:** Book value of old asset plus cash paid	Book value of old asset plus cash paid

sets. In relation to $1,000,000, $25 is immaterial, and the company need only keep one set of accounting records regarding the exchange.

Removal Costs

Removal costs are incurred to dismantle and remove a company's old plant asset. These costs are deducted from salvage proceeds to determine the asset's net salvage value. If removal costs exceed salvage proceeds, they increase the loss or reduce the gain recognized on disposal of the plant asset. Removal costs are associated with the old asset, not a new asset acquired to replace the old asset.

The next section discusses natural resources. Again you will note the underlying accounting principle of matching expenses of an accounting period with the revenues earned in that same accounting period.

NATURAL RESOURCES

Resources supplied by nature, such as ore deposits, mineral deposits, oil reserves, gas deposits, and timber stands, are known as **natural resources** or **wasting assets.** Natural resources represent inventories of raw materials that can be consumed (exhausted) through extraction or removal from their natural setting (e.g., removing oil from the ground).

On the balance sheet, natural resources are classified as a separate group of noncurrent assets within the property, plant, and equipment section; they are given headings such as "Timber stands" or "Oil reserves." Natural resources are typically recorded at their cost of acquisition plus exploration and development cost; they are reported on the balance sheet at total cost less accumulated depletion. (Accumulated depletion is similar to the accumulated depreciation used for plant assets.) When analyzing the financial condition of firms owning natural resources, caution must be exercised because the historical costs reported for the natural resources may only be a small fraction of their current value.

Depletion

Depletion is the exhaustion of a natural resource; it results from the physical removal of a part of the resource. In each accounting period, the depletion recognized is an estimate of the cost of the natural resource that was removed from its natural setting during the period. Depletion is recorded by debiting a depletion account and crediting an accumulated depletion account, which is a contra-asset account to the natural resource asset account.

By crediting the accumulated depletion account instead of the asset account, the original cost of the entire natural resource continues to be reported on the financial statements, and statement users can see the percentage of the resource that has been removed. This depletion cost is combined with other extraction, mining, or removal costs to determine the total cost of the resource available. This total cost is assigned to either the cost of natural resources sold or the inventory of the natural resource still on hand. Thus, it is possible that all, some, or none of the depletion and removal costs recognized in an accounting period will be expensed in that period, depending on the portion sold. If all of the resource is sold, all of the depletion and removal costs are expensed. The cost of any portion not yet sold will be part of the cost of inventory.

Objective 4: Determine the periodic depletion cost of a natural resource and calculate depreciation of plant assets on extractive industry property

Computing periodic depletion cost. Depletion charges usually are computed by using the units-of-production method. Total cost is divided by the estimated number of units—tons, barrels, or board feet—*that can be economically extracted* from the property. This calculation provides a per unit depletion cost. For example, assume that in 1989 a company paid $650,000 for a tract of land containing an ore deposit. The company spent $100,000 in exploration costs. The results indicated that approximately 900,000 tons of ore can be economically removed from the land, after which the land will be worth $50,000. Costs of $200,000 were incurred to develop the site, including the cost of running power lines and building roads. Total cost subject to depletion is the net cost assignable to the natural resource plus the exploration and development costs. Upon the purchase of the property, a journal entry is made to assign the purchase price to the two assets purchased—the natural resource and the land. The entry would be:

Land.	50,000	
Mineral Deposits.	600,000	
Cash.		650,000
To record purchase of land and mine.		

After the purchase, all other costs mentioned above are debited to the natural resource account. The entry would be:

Mineral Deposits ($100,000 + $200,000)	300,000	
Cash.		300,000
To record costs of exploration and development.		

The total cost of the mineral deposits is $900,000 ($600,000 + $300,000). The unit (per ton) depletion charge is $1 ($900,000/900,000 tons). If 100,000 tons are mined in 1989, the entry to record the depletion charge ($1 × 100,000) is:

Depletion of Mineral Deposits	100,000	
Accumulated Depletion—Mineral Deposits*		100,000
To record depletion for 1989.		

* Instead of crediting the accumulated depletion account, the Mineral Deposits account could have been credited directly. But for reasons indicated earlier, the credit is usually to an accumulated depletion account.

The depletion account contains the "in the ground" cost of the ore or natural resource mined. This cost is combined with other extractive costs to determine the total cost of the ore mined. To illustrate, assume that in addition to the $100,000 depletion cost, mining labor costs totaled $300,000, and other mining costs, such as depreciation, property taxes, power, and supplies, totaled $80,000. If 80,000 tons were sold and 20,000 remained on hand at the end of the period, the total cost of $480,000 would be allocated as follows:

Depletion cost	$100,000
Mining labor cost	300,000
Other mining costs	80,000
Total mining costs for 100,000 tons ($4.80 per ton)	$480,000
Less: Ore inventory (20,000 tons at $4.80)	96,000
Cost of ore sold	$384,000

The average cost per ton to mine 100,000 tons was $4.80 ($480,000/ 100,000). The income statement would show cost of ore sold of $384,000. There would be no separate reporting of depletion expense because depletion is included in cost of ore sold. The balance sheet would show inventory of ore on hand (a current asset) at $96,000 ($4.80 × 20,000). The balance sheet would also report the cost less accumulated depletion of the natural resource as follows:

Mineral deposits	$900,000
Less: Accumulated depletion	100,000
	$800,000

Depreciation of Plant Assets on Extractive Industry Property. Depreciable plant assets erected on extractive industry property are depreciated in the same manner as other depreciable assets. If such assets will be abandoned when the natural resource is exhausted, they should be depreciated over the shorter of the (*a*) physical life of the asset or (*b*) life of the natural resource. In some cases, periodic depreciation charges are computed using the units-of-production method. Using this method matches the life of the plant asset with the life of the natural resource. This method is recommended where the physical life of the plant asset equals or exceeds the life of the natural resource but its useful life is limited to the life of the natural resource.

Assume mining property is acquired and a building on the site is purchased for exclusive use in the mining operations. Also assume the units-of-production method is used for computing building depreciation. Relevant facts are:

Building cost	$310,000
Estimated physical life of building	20 years
Estimated salvage value of building (after mine exhausted)	$ 10,000
Capacity of mine	1,000,000 tons
Expected life of mine	10 years

Since the life of the mine (10 years or 1,000,000 tons) is shorter than the life of the building (20 years), the building should be depreciated over the life of the mine. In this case, the depreciation charge should be based on tons of ore rather than years because the mine's "life" could be longer or shorter than 10 years depending on how rapidly the ore is removed from the mine.

Suppose that during the first year of operations, 150,000 tons of ore are extracted. Building depreciation for the first year is $45,000, computed as follows:

$$\text{Depreciation per unit} = \frac{\text{Asset cost} - \text{Estimated salvage value}}{\text{Total tons of ore in mine}}$$

$$\text{Depreciation per unit} = \frac{\$310,000 - \$10,000}{1,000,000 \text{ tons}} = \$0.30 \text{ per ton}$$

$$\text{Depreciation for year} = \text{Depreciation per unit} \times \text{Units extracted}$$

$$\text{Depreciation for year} = \$0.30 \text{ per ton} \times 150,000 \text{ tons} = \$45,000$$

Depreciation on the building would be included on the income statement as part of the cost of ore that was sold and would be carried as part of inventory cost on the balance sheet for those tons of ore that were not sold during the period. Accumulated depreciation on the building would be reported on the balance sheet with the related asset account.

Plant assets and natural resources are tangible assets used by a company to produce revenues. A company may also acquire intangible assets to assist in producing revenues.

INTANGIBLE ASSETS

Intangible assets have no physical characteristics but are of value because of the advantages or exclusive privileges and rights they provide to a business. Intangible assets generally arise from two sources: (1) exclusive privileges granted by governmental authority or by legal contract, such as patents, copyrights, franchises, trademarks and trade names, and leases; and (2) superior entrepreneurial capacity or management know-how and customer loyalty, which is called goodwill.

All intangible assets are nonphysical, but not all nonphysical assets are classified as intangibles. For example, accounts receivable and prepaid expenses are nonphysical, but they are classified as current assets. Intangible assets are generally both nonphysical and noncurrent.

Acquisition of Intangible Assets

*Objective 5:
Prepare entries
for the acquisition
and amortization of
intangible assets*

Like most other assets, intangible assets are recorded initially at cost. However, computing an intangible asset acquisition cost is different from computing a plant asset acquisition cost. *Only outright purchase costs are included in the acquisition cost of an intangible asset;* the acquisition cost does *not* include cost of internal development or self-creation of the asset. If an intangible asset is internally generated in its entirety, none of its costs will be capitalized. Therefore, some companies have extremely valuable assets that may not even be recorded in their asset accounts. The reason for this practice can be understood by studying the history of accounting for research and development costs.

Research and development (R&D) costs are costs incurred in a planned search for new knowledge and in translating such knowledge into a new product or process. Prior to 1975, research and development costs were often capitalized as intangible assets when future benefits were expected from their incurrence. Since it was often difficult to determine the costs applicable to future benefits, many companies expensed all such costs as they were incurred. Other companies capitalized those costs that related to proven products and expensed the rest as incurred.

As a result of these varied accounting practices, the Financial Accounting Standards Board in *Statement No. 2* in 1974 ruled that all research and development costs, other than those directly reimbursable by government agencies and others, must be expensed when incurred. Immediate expensing is justified on the grounds that (1) the amount of costs applicable to the future cannot be measured with any high degree of precision; (2) doubt exists as to whether any future benefits will be received; and (3) even if benefits are expected, they cannot be measured. Thus, research and development costs no longer appear as intangible assets on the balance sheet. The same line of reasoning is applied to other costs associated with internally generated intangible assets, such as costs that are related to the development of a product which is subsequently patented, to prevent them from being capitalized and reported as intangible assets.

Amortization of Intangible Assets

Amortization is the systematic write-off of the cost of an intangible asset to expense. A portion of intangible asset cost is allocated to each accounting period in the economic (useful) life of the asset. All intangible assets are subject to amortization, which is similar to plant asset depreciation. Generally, amortization is recorded by debiting Amortization Expense and crediting the intangible asset account. An accumulated amortization account could be used to record amortization. However, usually the information gained from such accounting would not be significant because intangibles do not normally account for as significant an amount of total asset dollars as do plant assets.

Intangibles should be amortized over the shorter of (1) their economic life, (2) their legal life, or (3) 40 years. The 40-year limitation was established by the Accounting Principles Board. *APB Opinion No. 17* requires that an intangible asset acquired after October 1, 1970, be amortized over a period not to exceed 40 years. Straight-line amortization must be used unless another method of amortization (such as units-of-production) can be shown to be superior. Straight-line amortization is calculated in the same way as straight-line depreciation for plant assets.

Patents

A patent is a right granted by the federal government giving the owner the exclusive right to manufacture, sell, lease, or otherwise benefit from an invention. The real value of a patent lies in its ability to produce revenue. Patents have a legal life of 17 years. Protection for the patent owner begins at the time of patent application and lasts for 17 years from the date the patent is granted.

The purchase of a patent should be recorded in the Patents account at cost. The Patents account should also be debited for the cost of successfully defending the patent in lawsuits and for the cost of any competing patents that were purchased to ensure revenue-generating capability of the purchased patent.

The cost of a purchased patent should be amortized over the shorter of 17 years (or remaining legal life) or its estimated useful life. If a patent cost $40,000 and has a useful life of 10 years, the journal entry to record periodic amortization is:

```
Patent Amortization Expense . . . . . . . . . . . . . . . . . .    4,000
     Patents. . . . . . . . . . . . . . . . . . . . . . . . . . . . .          4,000
  To record patent amortization.
```

If the patent becomes worthless, the unamortized balance in the Patents account should be charged to expense.

As noted in the research and development cost section above, all such costs incurred in the internal development of a product, process, or idea that is later patented must be expensed rather than capitalized. In the above example, the cost of the purchased patent was amortized over its useful life of 10 years. If the patent had been the result of an internally generated product or process, its cost of $40,000 would have been expensed as incurred, in accordance with *Statement No. 2* of the Financial Accounting Standards Board.

Copyrights

A **copyright** is an exclusive right granted by the federal government giving the owner protection against the illegal reproduction by others of the owner's written works, designs, and literary productions. The copyright period is for the life of the creator plus 50 years. Since most publications have a limited life, the cost of the copyright may appropriately be charged to expense on a straight-line basis over the life of the first edition published or based on projections of the number of copies to be sold per year.

Franchises

A **franchise** is a contract between two parties granting the franchisee (the purchaser of the franchise) certain rights and privileges ranging from name identification to complete monopoly of service. In many instances, the two parties are both private businesses. For example, an individual who wishes to open a hamburger restaurant may purchase a McDonald's franchise; the two parties involved are the individual business owner and McDonald's Corporation. This franchise would allow the business owner to use the McDonald's golden arch, and would provide the owner with advertising and many other benefits.

The parties involved in a franchise arrangement are not always private businesses. A franchise may also be granted between a government agency and a private company. A city may give a franchise to a utility company, giving the utility the exclusive right to provide service to a particular area.

In addition to providing benefits, a franchise usually places certain restrictions on the franchisee. These restrictions are generally related to rates or prices charged; they may also be in regard to product quality or from whom supplies and inventory items must be purchased.

If periodic payments to the grantor of the franchise are required, they should be debited to a Franchise Expense account. If a lump-sum payment is made to obtain the franchise, the cost should be recorded in an asset account entitled Franchise and amortized over the shorter of the useful life of the franchise or 40 years.

Trademarks; Trade Names

A **trademark** is a symbol, design, or logo that is used in conjunction with a particular product or company. A **trade name** is a brand name under which a product is sold or a company does business. Many times trademarks and trade names are extremely valuable to a company, but if they have been internally developed, they will have no recorded asset cost. However, if such items are purchased by a business from an external source, they are recorded at cost and amortized over their economic life or 40 years, whichever is shorter.

Leases

A **lease** is a contract to rent property. The owner of the property is the grantor of the lease and is called the lessor. The person or company obtaining rights to possess and use the property is called the lessee. The rights granted under the lease are called a **leasehold.** The accounting for a lease depends upon whether it is a capital lease or an operating lease.

Capital Leases. In concept, a **capital lease** is a lease that transfers to the lessee virtually all rewards and risks that accompany ownership of property. A lease is a capital lease if, among other provisions, it (1) transfers ownership of the leased property to the lessee at the end of the lease term, or (2) contains a bargain purchase option that permits the lessee to buy the property at a price significantly below fair value at the end of the lease term.

A capital lease is a means of financing property acquisitions and has the same economic impact as a purchase made on an installment plan. Thus, the lessee in a capital lease must record the leased property as an asset and the lease obligation as a liability. Because it is an asset, the leased property is depreciated over its useful life to the lessee. A part of each lease payment is recorded as interest expense, with the balance viewed as a payment on the lease liability.

The proper accounting for capital leases for both lessees and lessors has been an extremely difficult problem. Further discussion of capital leases is left for an intermediate accounting text.

Operating Leases. If a lease does not qualify as a capital lease, it is an **operating lease.** A one-year lease on an apartment or a week's rental of an automobile are examples of operating leases. Such leases make no attempt to transfer any of the rewards and risks of ownership to the lessee. As a result, there may be no recordable transaction when a lease is signed.

In some situations, the lease may call for an immediate cash payment that must be recorded. Assume, for example, that a business signed a lease that required the immediate payment of the annual rent of $15,000 for the first and fifth years of a five-year lease. The lessee would record the payment as follows:

```
Prepaid Rent . . . . . . . . . . . . . . . . . . . . . . . . . . . .   15,000
Leasehold  . . . . . . . . . . . . . . . . . . . . . . . . . . . . .   15,000
     Cash. . . . . . . . . . . . . . . . . . . . . . . . . . . . .             30,000
     To record first and fifth years' rent on five-year lease.
```

Since the Leasehold account is actually a long-term prepaid rent account for the fifth year's annual rent, it is classified as an intangible asset until the beginning of the fifth year. Then the Leasehold account is reclassified as a current asset. Accounting for the balance in the Leasehold account depends on the terms of the lease. In the above example, the $15,000 in the Leasehold account will be charged to expense over the fifth year only. The balance in Prepaid Rent will be charged to expense in the first year. Thus, the entry for the first year, assuming the lease year and fiscal year coincide, is:

```
Rent Expense. . . . . . . . . . . . . . . . . . . . . . . . . . . .   15,000
     Prepaid Rent . . . . . . . . . . . . . . . . . . . . . . . . .             15,000
     To record rent expense.
```

The entry in the fifth year is:

```
Rent Expense. . . . . . . . . . . . . . . . . . . . . . . . . . . .   15,000
     Leasehold  . . . . . . . . . . . . . . . . . . . . . . . . . .             15,000
     To record rent expense.
```

The accounting for the second, third, and fourth years will be the same as for the first year. The rent will be set up in Prepaid Rent when paid in advance for the year and then expensed. The amount in the Leasehold account may be transferred to Prepaid Rent at the beginning of the fifth year by debiting Prepaid Rent and crediting Leasehold. If so, the credit in the above entry would have been to Prepaid Rent.

In some cases, when a lease is signed, a lump-sum payment is paid that does not cover a specific year's rent. If so, the payment is debited to the Leasehold account and amortized over the life of the lease. The straight-line method is required unless another method can be shown to be superior. Assume the $15,000 rent for the fifth year in the above example was, instead, a lump-sum payment on the lease in addition to the annual rent payments. An annual adjusting entry to amortize the $15,000 over five years is required. The entry would read:

```
Rent Expense. . . . . . . . . . . . . . . . . . . . . . . . . . .    3,000
    Leasehold  . . . . . . . . . . . . . . . . . . . . . . . . .           3,000
    To amortize leasehold.
```

In this example, the annual rental expense is $18,000: $15,000 annual cash rent plus $3,000 amortization of leasehold ($15,000/5).

Periodic rent may be based on current-year sales or usage rather than being a constant amount. For example, if a lease called for rent equal to 5% of current-year sales and sales were $400,000 in 1989, the rent for 1989 would be $20,000. The rent would either be paid or adjusted to the correct amount at the end of the year.

Leasehold Improvements

A **leasehold improvement** is any physical alteration made by the lessee to the leased property in which benefits are expected beyond the current accounting period. Leasehold improvements made by a lessee usually become the property of the lessor after the lease has expired. However, since leasehold improvements are an asset of the lessee during the lease period, they should be debited to a Leasehold Improvements account. Leasehold improvements are then amortized to expense over the period of time benefited by the improvements. The amortization period for leasehold improvements should be the shorter of the life of the improvements or the life of the lease. If the lease can (and probably will) be renewed at the option of the lessee, the option period should be included in the life of the lease.

As an illustration, assume that on January 2, 1989, Wolf Company leases a building for 20 years under a nonrenewable lease at an annual rental of $20,000, payable on each December 31. Wolf immediately incurs a cost of $80,000 for improvements to the building, such as interior walls for office separation, ceiling fans, and recessed lighting. The improvements have an estimated life of 30 years. The $80,000 should be amortized over the 20-year lease period, since that period is shorter than the life of the improvements, and Wolf will not be able to use the improvements beyond the life of the lease. If only annual financial statements are prepared, the following journal entry will properly record the rental expense for the year ended December 31, 1989:

```
Rent Expense (or Leasehold Improvement Expense)  . . . . . .    4,000
    Leasehold Improvements . . . . . . . . . . . . . . . . .           4,000
    To record leasehold improvement amortization.

Rent Expense. . . . . . . . . . . . . . . . . . . . . . . . . .   20,000
    Cash. . . . . . . . . . . . . . . . . . . . . . . . . . .          20,000
    To record annual rent.
```

Thus, the total cost to rent the building each year includes the $20,000 cash rent plus the amortization of the leasehold improvements.

Although leaseholds are intangible assets, leaseholds and leasehold improvements are sometimes shown in the property, plant, and equipment section of the balance sheet.

Goodwill

In accounting, **goodwill** is an intangible value attached to a company resulting mainly from the company's management skill or know-how and a favorable reputation with customers. A company's value may be greater than the total of the fair market values of its tangible and identifiable intangible assets. This greater value means that the company is able to generate an above-average rate of income on each dollar invested in the business. Thus, proof of the existence of goodwill for a company can be found only in its ability to generate superior earnings or income.

A Goodwill account will appear in the accounting records only if goodwill has been bought and paid for in cash or other property. Goodwill cannot be purchased by itself; an entire business or a part of a business must be purchased to obtain the accompanying intangible asset, goodwill.

For example, assume that Lenox Company purchased all of Martin Company's assets for $700,000. Lenox also agrees to assume responsibility for a $350,000 mortgage note payable owed by Martin. Goodwill is determined as the difference between the amount paid for the business ($1,050,000) and the fair market value of the assets purchased. Notice that fair market value rather than book value is used to determine the amount of goodwill. The following shows the computation for the amount of goodwill purchased by Lenox:

Cash paid		$ 700,000
Mortgage note payable assumed		350,000
Total price paid		$1,050,000
Less fair market values of individually identifiable assets:		
Accounts receivable	$ 95,000	
Inventories	100,000	
Land	240,000	
Buildings	275,000	
Equipment	200,000	
Patents	65,000	975,000
Goodwill		$ 75,000

The $75,000 is the amount of goodwill to be recorded as an intangible asset on the books of Lenox Company; all of the other assets will be recorded at fair market value, and the liability will be recorded at the amount due. Specific reasons for the existence of goodwill in a company might include good reputation, customer loyalty, product design, and superior human resources. Since these are not individually quantifiable, they are all grouped together and referred to as goodwill. The journal entry to record the above purchase is:

```
Accounts Receivable. . . . . . . . . . . . . . . . . . .    95,000
Inventories . . . . . . . . . . . . . . . . . . . . . .   100,000
Land . . . . . . . . . . . . . . . . . . . . . . . . .   240,000
Buildings . . . . . . . . . . . . . . . . . . . . . . .   275,000
Equipment . . . . . . . . . . . . . . . . . . . . . .   200,000
Patents . . . . . . . . . . . . . . . . . . . . . . . .    65,000
Goodwill . . . . . . . . . . . . . . . . . . . . . . .    75,000
    Cash . . . . . . . . . . . . . . . . . . . . . . . .          700,000
    Mortgage Note Payable . . . . . . . . . . . . . . .          350,000
    To record the purchase of Martin Company's assets and
    assumption of mortgage note payable.
```

Goodwill, like all other intangibles, must be amortized. There is no legal life for goodwill, and the useful life of goodwill cannot be reasonably estimated. If, for example, the new owner made substantial changes in the method of doing business, goodwill that existed at the purchase date could rapidly disappear. Therefore, current accounting practice requires the amortization of goodwill over a period not to exceed 40 years. This requirement is due to the fact that the value of purchased goodwill will eventually disappear. Other goodwill may be generated in its place, but the organization cannot record its internally created goodwill any more than it can record other internally generated intangible assets.

The entry to amortize the $75,000 goodwill over a 40-year period is:

```
Goodwill Amortization Expense . . . . . . . . . . . . . . . .    1,875
    Goodwill . . . . . . . . . . . . . . . . . . . . . . . . .          1,875
    To amortize goodwill ($75,000/40 years).
```

Reporting Amortization

Illustration 7.2 shows the frequencies of intangible assets being amortized by a sample of 600 companies for the years 1983–86.

Illustration 7.2
INTANGIBLE ASSETS HELD BY SAMPLE OF 600 COMPANIES

	Number of Companies			
	1986	1985	1984	1983
Goodwill.	322	301	279	270
Patents	63	60	55	50
Trademarks, brand names, copyrights .	39	30	26	21
Licenses, franchises, memberships . .	23	25	21	23
Other—described	27	16	10	11
Intangible assets	35	34	24	24

SOURCE: American Institute of Certified Public Accountants, *Accounting Trends & Techniques* (New York: AICPA, 1987), p. 163.

Amortization expense for most intangible assets discussed in this chapter appears among the operating expenses on the income statement. The account titles used are all of this type: "Amortization of Goodwill (or Patents, Copyrights, Franchises, Leaseholds) Expense." Periodic amortization of leaseholds and leasehold improvements is often reported as rent expense. The amortization of goodwill is an expense in determining accounting income, but is not a deductible item in determining taxable income.

SUMMARY

When plant assets are sold, retired from service, traded in, destroyed, or otherwise disposed of, the company must remove the assets' cost and accumulated depreciation from the accounts. On the sales of plant assets, both gains and losses may be recognized. Losses may also occur when assets that have not been fully depreciated are retired. When insured plant assets are destroyed, a company's losses are reduced by the amounts recoverable from insurance.

A nonmonetary asset is an item whose price may change over time, such as a building. In accounting for the exchanges of these assets, the recorded amount should be based on the fair value of the asset given up or the fair value of the asset received, whichever is clearly more evident. Depending on whether the assets exchanged are similar or dissimilar in nature, a gain may be recognized; a loss will be recognized for accounting purposes. However, income tax rules do not allow the recognition of either gains or losses on exchanges of similar assets.

When plant assets are exchanged for dissimilar plant assets, both losses and gains are recognized for both accounting and income tax purposes. When similar assets are exchanged, losses are recorded, but gains are not recorded for accounting purposes. Income tax rules do not allow recognition of either gains or losses on exchanges of similar assets.

Natural resources are usually recorded at the cost of acquisition and development. The gradual exhaustion of a natural resource resulting from its physical removal from its natural setting is called depletion. Charges for depletion are usually based on the number of physical units (pounds, tons, or barrels) involved. The depletion costs and removal costs are totaled and then assigned to either the cost of natural resources sold or the inventory of the natural resource still on hand. Plant assets located at a natural resource site are depreciated over their useful lives or the life of the resource, whichever is shorter.

All intangible assets are recorded at cost, but the cost of acquisition does not include cost of internal development or self-creation of the asset. Research and development costs are not assets and must be expensed as incurred unless directly reimbursable by government agencies or others. Intangible assets have limited lives and are subject to amortization.

Individually identifiable intangible assets grant exclusive privileges to the owner. Purchased intangible assets should be recorded at cost. All intangible assets should be amortized over the shorter of (1) their useful life, (2) their legal life, or (3) 40 years. Patents are usually amortized over their legal life of 17 years because their useful life would normally be longer than 17 years if protection were to continue. Copyright costs are usually amortized over their useful life because their useful life is normally less than 40 years. Franchises and trademarks purchased for a lump sum are often amortized over 40 years, since their useful life is often longer than 40 years.

Although leases are intangible assets, they are often listed with plant assets on the balance sheet. Under certain conditions, a lease may transfer virtually all risks and rewards of property ownership. These leases are known as capital leases and are capitalized as if the asset were purchased. Leases that do not transfer rewards and risks of ownership are operating leases and are not capitalized. Leasehold improvements are betterments made to a leased asset; they revert to the owner of the leased property at the end of the lease and are amortized by the lessee over the life of the lease or the life of the improvement, whichever is shorter.

Goodwill is the intangible value of an entity resulting from favorable reputation, customer loyalty, product design, or the capacity of its human resources to produce an above-average rate of return on investment. Goodwill is not an individually identifiable asset and is recorded only if purchased; it must be amortized over a period not to exceed 40 years.

Having concluded your study of accounting for long-term assets, in Chapter 8 you will learn about the proper accounting for stockholders' equity. Although many businesses, both large and small, use this particular type of capital structure, it is generally the least understood section of the financial statements, due in part to the accounting terminology involved.

Objective 6: Define and use correctly the new terms in the glossary

NEW TERMS INTRODUCED IN CHAPTER 7

Amortization   The term used to describe the systematic write-off of the cost of an intangible asset to expense (250).

Boot   The additional cash outlay made when one asset is traded for a similar asset (241).

Capital lease   A lease that transfers to the lessee virtually all of the rewards and the risks that accompany ownership of property (252).

Copyright   An exclusive right granted by the federal government giving the owner protection against the illegal reproduction by others of the owner's written works, designs, and literary productions (251).

Depletion   The exhaustion of a natural resource; an estimate of the cost of the resource that was removed during the period (246).

Franchise   A contract between two parties granting the franchisee (the purchaser of the franchise) certain rights and privileges ranging from name identification to complete monopoly of service (251).

Goodwill   An intangible value attached to a company resulting mainly from the company's management skill or know-how and a favorable reputation with customers. Evidenced by the ability to generate an above-average rate of income on each dollar invested in the business (255).

Intangible assets   Items that have no physical characteristics but are of value because of the advantages or exclusive privileges and rights they provide to a business (249).

Lease   A contract to rent property. Grantor of the lease is the lessor; the party obtaining the rights to possess and use property is the lessee (252).

Leasehold   The rights granted under a lease (252).

Leasehold improvement   Any physical alteration to leased property in which benefits are expected beyond the current accounting period (254).

"Material" gains or losses   Gains or losses large enough to affect the decisions of an informed user of the financial statements (244).

Materiality concept   Allows the accountant to deal with immaterial (unimportant) items in a theoretically incorrect manner (245).

Natural resources   Ore deposits, mineral deposits, oil reserves, gas deposits, and timber stands supplied by nature (246).

Nonmonetary assets   Items whose price may change over time, such as inventories, property, plant, and equipment (241).

Operating lease   A lease that does not qualify as a capital lease (253).

Patent   A right granted by a government giving the owner the exclusive right to manufacture, sell, lease, or otherwise benefit from an invention (250).

Research and development (R&D) costs   Costs incurred in a planned search for new knowledge and in translating such knowledge into a new product or process (250).

Trademark   A symbol, design, or logo that is used in conjunction with a particular product or company (252).

Trade name   A brand name under which a product is sold or a company does business (252).

Wasting assets   See Natural resources.

DEMONSTRATION PROBLEM 7–1

On September 1, 1990, Stephens Company sold a factory press for $10,000. The press cost $120,000 and was being depreciated on a straight-line basis of 10% a year. At December 31, 1989, the balance in the accumulated depreciation account was $96,000; no depreciation has been taken on the press for 1990.

Required:

a. Calculate and prepare the necessary journal entries to record the sale of the press.

b. Suppose that cash of $140,000 and the press is exchanged for another press with a fair market value of $150,000. Compute the gain or loss on the exchange and prepare the journal entry to record the transaction using generally accepted accounting principles.

Solution to demonstration problem 7–1

(a)

Stephens Company
General Journal

Sept. 1   Depreciation Expense—Factory Press   8,000

          Accumulated Depreciation—Factory Press   8,000

         To record depreciation for eight months

         ($120,000 × .10 × 8/12).

The $6,000 loss on the sale is computed as shown below:

Press cost	$120,000
Accumulated depreciation	
($96,000 + $8,000)	104,000
Book value	$ 16,000
Sales price	10,000
Loss realized	$ 6,000

The journal entry to record the sale is:

Sept. 1   Cash   10,000

         Accumulated Depreciation—Factory Press   104,000

         Loss on Disposal of Plant Assets   6,000

          Factory Press.   120,000

         To record sale of press at a price less than

         book value.

(b)

Press cost	$120,000
Accumulated depreciation	104,000
Book value	$ 16,000
Fair market value of old asset	
(trade-in allowance).	10,000
Loss on exchange of plant asset	$ 6,000

The journal entry to record the exchange is:

Sept. 1   Factory Press (cost of new press)   150,000

         Accumulated Depreciation—Factory Press   104,000

         Loss on Disposal of Plant Assets   6,000

          Factory Press (cost of old press)   120,000

          Cash   140,000

         To record loss on exchange of similar plant assets.

QUESTIONS

1. When depreciable plant assets are sold for cash, how is the gain or loss measured?

2. A plant asset that cost $15,000 and has a related accumulated depreciation account balance of $15,000 is still being used in business operations. Would it be appropriate to continue recording depreciation on this asset? Explain. When should the asset's cost and accumulated depreciation be removed from the accounting records?

3. Factory equipment and $10,000 cash are exchanged for a delivery truck. How should the cost basis (cash price) of the delivery truck be measured?

4. A plant asset is disposed of by exchanging it for a new asset of a similar type. How should the cost basis of the new asset be measured under generally accepted accounting principles?

5. A plant asset is exchanged for an asset of a similar type. What is the cost basis of the new asset for tax purposes?

6. **a.** Distinguish between depreciation, depletion, and amortization. Name two assets that are subject to depreciation; to depletion; to amortization.

   b. Distinguish between tangible and intangible assets, and classify the above-named assets accordingly.

7. A building with an estimated physical life of 40 years was constructed at the site of a coal mine. The coal mine is expected to be completely exhausted within 20 years. Over what length of time should the building be depreciated, assuming that it will be abandoned after all the coal has been extracted? Why?

8. You note that a certain store seems to have a steady stream of regular customers, a favorable location, courteous employees, high-quality merchandise, and a reputation for fairness in dealing with customers, employees, and suppliers. Does it follow automatically that this business has goodwill?

9. What is the difference between a leasehold (under an operating lease contract) and a leasehold improvement? Is there any difference in the accounting procedures applicable to each?

10. What reasons justify the immediate expensing of most research and development costs?

EXERCISES

Record sale of vehicle

1. A tow truck originally costing $15,000 was sold for $2,500 cash. Accumulated depreciation on the truck amounted to $13,500. Prepare the journal entry to record the sale of the truck.

Record destruction of machinery by fire—uninsured and insured asset

2. A machine costing $8,000, on which $6,000 of depreciation has been accumulated, is completely destroyed by fire. What journal entry should be made to record the machine's destruction and the resulting fire loss under each of the following unrelated assumptions:

   a. The machine is *not* insured.

   b. The machine *is* insured, and it is estimated that $1,500 will be recovered from the insurance company.

Update depreciation and record exchange of equipment

3. Farlee Company owns plant equipment acquired on December 31, 1987 at a cost of $65,000. At the time of purchase, the equipment was estimated to have a useful life of six years and a $2,000 salvage value. Depreciation of $21,000 has been recorded through December 31, 1989, on a straight-line basis. Because of technological changes, on August 31, 1990, the equipment is traded in for new equipment with a fair market value of $60,000. Cash of $25,000 is paid in addition to the old equipment. Prepare the journal entry to record the trade-in under generally accepted accounting principles.

Record variety of cases involving sale, retirement, or exchange of equipment

4. Equipment costing $22,000 which had been depreciated $15,000 was disposed of on January 2, 1989. What journal entries are required to record the equipment's disposition under each of the following unrelated assumptions?

a. The equipment was sold for $9,000 cash.

b. The equipment was sold for $5,800 cash.

c. The equipment was retired from service and hauled to the junk yard. No material was salvaged.

d. The equipment was exchanged for similar equipment having a cash price of $30,000. A trade-in allowance of $10,000 was received, and the balance was paid in cash.

e. The equipment was exchanged for similar equipment having a cash price of $30,000. A trade-in allowance of $5,000 was received, and the balance was paid in cash. (Record this transaction twice: first, for tax purposes, and second, for financial reporting purposes.)

Record exchanges of dissimilar plant assets

5. McGuire Company gave cash of $5,000 and traded a vehicle costing $14,500 with accumulated depreciation of $9,700 for an office computer. The computer had a cash price of $11,000. Prepare the journal entry to record the exchange. Assume that depreciation expense is up-to-date.

Determine depletion cost and expense

6. Spikes Company paid $1 million for the right to extract all of the mineral-bearing ore, estimated at 5 million tons, from a certain tract of land. During the first year, Spikes Company extracted 500,000 tons of the ore and sold 400,000 tons. What part of the $1 million should be charged to expense during the first year?

Calculate depreciation expense using the units-of-production method for plant assets on extractive industry property

7. Jenkins Drilling Company acquired mining property and purchased a building at the site for exclusive use in mining operations. Given the information below, determine the building depreciation expense using the units-of-production method.

Building cost	$230,000
Estimated salvage value	$ 20,000
Capacity of mine	2,000,000
Expected life of mine.	15 years
Units extracted during year	250,000 tons

Determine patent cost and periodic amortization

8. The Walter Company purchased a patent on January 1, 1973, at a total cost of $136,000. In January 1984 the company successfully defended a suit alleging infringement of another's patent rights. The legal fees amounted to $30,000. What will be the amount of patent cost amortized in 1989? (The useful life of the patent is the same as its legal life—17 years.)

Record leasehold; record rent accrued and leasehold amortization

9. Alvin Company leased a building under an operating lease for a 20-year period beginning January 1, 1989. The company paid $80,000 in cash and agreed to make annual payments equal to 1 percent of the first $500,000 of sales and one half of 1% of all sales over $500,000. Sales for 1989 amounted to $1,500,000. Payment of the annual amount will be made on January 12, 1990. Prepare journal entries to record the cash payment of January 1, 1989, and the proper expense to be recognized for the use of the leased building in 1989.

Prepare entry for a lump-sum payment under an operating lease (Refer to E-9)

10. Assume in Exercise 9 above that a lump-sum payment of $50,000 was made at the beginning of the lease term. Prepare the adjusting entry which would be required at the end of each year to amortize the payment.

Record franchise; accrued franchise fees, and record amortization

11. Bill Malone paid Sam's Sandwiches $30,000 for the right to operate a fast food restaurant using the Sam's Sandwiches name. The franchise agreement stated that Bill was to pay an operating fee of 1% of net sales for advertising and other services rendered by Sam's Sandwiches. Bill plans on operating the restaurant for about 15 years; operations began January 1, 1990. Net sales for the year were $400,000, with operating expenses of $70,000. Give the entries needed to record the payment of $30,000 and to record expenses relating to the franchise.

Determine amount of goodwill

12. On April 1, 1990, Athens Metal Company purchased all of the assets of Watkinsville Brick Company for $450,000, and agreed to accept responsibility for a $70,000 mortgage note payable. The book value of the assets was $300,000; the fair market value was $510,000. Determine the amount of goodwill purchased by Athens Metal Company.

PROBLEMS

Update depreciation and record sale of computer

7-1. Jackson Company purchased a personal computer on April 1, 1986 for $12,500. At the time of purchase, the computer had an expected life of six years and estimated salvage value of $800. The computer is being depreciated annually on a straight-line basis; accumulated depreciation through 1989 was $7,313. The computer was sold on June 1, 1990 for $4,000 cash.

Required:

Prepare journal entries to record the above data for 1990. Assume Jackson has a calendar-year accounting period.

Update depreciation and record exchange of autos under the tax method and generally accepted accounting principles

7-2. Watson Company purchased a new 1990 automobile on October 1, 1990. The cash price of the new car was $14,500; Watson paid $8,000 cash and received a trade-in allowance of $6,500 for a 1988 model. The 1988 model had been acquired on October 1, 1988 at a cost of $12,200. Depreciation of $3,031 had been recorded through December 31, 1989, on a straight-line basis, with four years of useful life expected. Salvage value was estimated to be $2,500. At the time of the trade-in, the 1988 automobile had a fair market value of $6,500.

Required:

Prepare journal entries to record the exchange of the automobiles under (a) the tax method, and (b) the theoretically correct accounting method.

Update depreciation and record six cases of asset disposal

7-3. On January 2, 1986, the Spengler Company purchased a delivery truck for $42,000 cash. The truck has an estimated useful life of six years and an estimated salvage value of $20,000. The double-declining-balance method of depreciation is being used.

Required:

a. Prepare a schedule which shows how the truck's book value on January 1, 1989, would be computed.

b. Assume that the truck is to be disposed of on July 1, 1989. What journal entry is required to record depreciation for the six months ended June 30, 1989?

c. Prepare the journal entries to record the disposition of the truck on July 1, 1989, under each of the following unrelated assumptions:

(1) The truck is sold for $6,000 cash.

(2) The truck is sold for $14,000 cash.

(3) The truck is retired from service, and it is expected that $3,000 will be received from the sale of salvaged materials.

(4) The truck and $40,000 cash are exchanged for office equipment having a cash price of $56,000.

(5) The truck and $44,000 cash are exchanged for a new delivery truck which has a cash price of $60,000.

(6) The truck is completely destroyed in an accident. Cash of $5,600 is expected to be recovered from the insurance company.

Record exchange of plant asset for a dissimilar asset under generally accepted accounting principles

7–4. On January 4, 1990, Martinez Company traded a delivery truck for an assortment of office equipment. The truck originally cost $12,500 and had accumulated depreciation of $7,500. The fair market value of the truck was $6,000. The cash value of the equipment was not known. In addition to the truck, Martinez paid $2,000 cash.

Required:

Prepare the journal entry to record the exchange of plant assets. Assume depreciation expense on the truck is up-to-date.

Determine depletion for period and depreciation on mining equipment; compute average cost per ton of ore mined

7–5. Shelton Company acquired a mine for $9 million. The mine contained an estimated 9 million tons of ore. It was also estimated that the land would have a value of $800,000 when the mine was exhausted and that only 8 million tons of ore could be economically extracted. A building was erected on the property at a cost of $1,200,000. The building has an estimated useful life of 35 years and no scrap value. Specialized mining equipment was installed at a cost of $1,650,000. This equipment has an estimated useful life of seven years and an estimated $42,000 salvage value. The company began operating on July 1, 1989. During the fiscal year ended June 30, 1990, 800,000 tons of ore were extracted. The company decided to use the units-of-production method to record depreciation on the building and the sum-of-the-years'-digits method to record depreciation on the equipment.

Required:

Prepare journal entries to record the depletion and depreciation charges for the fiscal year ended June 30, 1990. Show calculations.

Compute cost and amortization of patent

7–6. The Ken Company purchased a patent for $120,000 on January 2, 1989. The patent was estimated to have a useful life of 10 years. The $120,000 cost was properly charged to an asset account and amortized in 1989. On July 1, 1990, the company incurred legal and court costs of $36,000 in a successful defense of the patent in an infringement suit.

Required:

Compute the patent amortization cost for 1990.

Record leasehold amortization; record depreciation and trade-in

7–7. On July 1, 1990 the Danish Company had the following balances in its Plant Asset and Accumulated Depreciation accounts:

	Asset	Accumulated Depreciation
Land	$ 200,000	
Leasehold	150,000	
Buildings	1,876,000	$258,500
Equipment	816,000	260,000
Trucks	142,000	42,650

Additional information:

(1) The leasehold covers a plot of ground leased on July 1, 1985, for a period of 25 years.

(2) The office building is on the leased land and was completed on July 1, 1986, at a cost of $576,000. Its physical life is set at 40 years. The factory building is on the owned land and was completed on July 1, 1985, at a cost of $1,300,000. Its life is also set at 40 years. Neither building has any expected salvage value.

(3) Equipment is depreciated at 6⅔% per year on its cost.

(4) The company owns three trucks—A, B, and C. Truck A, purchased on July 1, 1988, at a cost of $32,000, has a life of three years and a scrap value of $2,000. Truck B, purchased on January 2, 1989, at a cost of $50,000, has a life of four years and a scrap value of $4,000. Truck C, purchased on January 2, 1990, at a cost of $60,000, has a life of five years and a scrap value of $6,000.

The following events occurred in the fiscal year ended June 30, 1991:

1990
July 1   Rent for July 1, 1990–June 30, 1991, on leased land is paid, $19,000.
Oct. 1   Truck A is traded in on Truck D. Cash price of the new truck is $64,000. Cash of $54,000 is paid. Truck D has a life of four years and a scrap value of $3,500.

1991
Feb. 2   Truck B is sold for $28,000 cash.
June 1   Truck C (uninsured) is completely demolished in an accident.

Required:

Prepare journal entries to record the above transactions and the necessary June 30, 1991, adjusting entries. Use the straight-line depreciation method.

Record amortization expense for a variety of intangible assets

7–8. Following are selected transactions and other data relating to the Willow Company for the year ended December 31, 1989:

a. The company rented the second floor of a building for five years on January 2, 1989, and paid the annual rent of $10,000 for the first and fifth years in advance.

b. In 1988 the company incurred legal fees of $30,000 in applying for a patent and paid a fee of $10,000 to a former employee who conceived of a device that substantially reduced the cost of manufacturing one of the company's products. The patent on the device has a market value of $300,000 and is expected to be useful for 10 years.

c. In 1988 the company entered into a 10-year operating lease on several floors of a building, paying $20,000 in cash immediately and agreeing to pay $10,000 at the end of each of the 10 years of life in the lease. It then incurred costs of $40,000 to install partitions, shelving, and fixtures. These items would normally last 25 years.

d. The company spent $12,000 promoting a trademark in a manner that it believed enhanced its value considerably. The trademark has an indefinite life.

e. Incurred costs amounting to $100,000 in 1988 and $130,000 in 1989 for research and development of new products that are expected to enhance the company's revenues for at least five years.

Required:

For each of the situations described above, prepare only the journal entries to record the expense applicable to 1989.

Calculate goodwill and prepare journal entry

7–9. On April 30, 1989, Cowan Company purchased all of the assets of Dean Company for $850,000, and assumed $55,000 of various liabilities owed by Dean Company. The fair market values of the assets purchased are as follows:

Accounts receivable	$ 75,000
Inventories	115,000
Land	250,000
Building	80,000
Equipment	270,000
Trademarks	80,000

Required:

a. Compute the amount of goodwill purchased by Cowan Company.

b. Give the entry to record the purchase of Dean Company's assets and assumption of liabilities.

BUSINESS DECISION PROBLEM 7–1:

Record exchange of similar assets; adjust accounts for errors in accounting for depreciable assets

Cheney Company acquired Machine T for $200,000 on January 2, 1988. Machine T had an estimated useful life of four years and no salvage value. The machine was depreciated on the straight-line basis. On January 2, 1990, Machine T was exchanged for Machine U. Machine U had a cash price of $240,000. In addition to Machine T, cash of $200,000 was given up in the exchange. The company recorded the exchange in accordance with income tax regulations instead of in accordance with generally accepted accounting principles. Machine U has an estimated useful life of five years and no salvage value. The machine is being depreciated using the straight-line method.

Required:

a. What journal entry did the Cheney Company make when it recorded the exchange of machines? (Show computations.)

b. What journal entry should the Cheney Company have made to record the exchange of machines in accordance with generally accepted accounting principles?

c. Assume the error is discovered on December 31, 1991, before adjusting journal entries have been made. What journal entry should be made to record depreciation for 1991? (Ignore income taxes.)

d. What effect did the error have on reported net income for 1990? (Ignore income taxes.)

e. How should Machine U be reported on the December 31, 1991, balance sheet?

BUSINESS DECISION PROBLEM 7–2:

Record purchase of two businesses and explain differences between the two; advise client as to which company should be purchased

Beth Anderson is trying to decide whether to buy Company X or Company Y. Both Company X and Company Y have assets with the following book values and fair market values:

	Book Value	Fair Market Value
Accounts receivable	$ 480,000	$ 480,000
Inventories	1,440,000	2,400,000
Land	1,200,000	2,160,000
Buildings	1,440,000	3,360,000
Equipment	576,000	960,000
Patents	384,000	480,000

Liabilities that would be assumed on the purchase of either company include accounts payable, $960,000, and notes payable, $240,000.

The only difference between Company X and Company Y is that Company X has net income that is about average for the industry, while Company Y has net income that is greatly above average for the industry.

Required:

a. Assume Anderson can buy Company X for $8,640,000 or Company Y for $11,040,000. Prepare the journal entry to record the acquisition of (1) Company X and (2) Company Y. What accounts for the difference between the purchase price of the two companies?

b. Assume Anderson can buy either company for $8,640,000. Which company would you advise Anderson to buy? Why?

8   STOCKHOLDERS' EQUITY

LEARNING OBJECTIVES

After studying this chapter, you should be able to:

1. Understand the advantages of a corporation.
2. Describe the various types of capital stock and recognize the differences between the types of stock.
3. Record capital stock issued for cash or other assets.
4. Record other transactions affecting paid-in capital and retained earnings.
5. Properly show extraordinary items, changes in accounting principle, and prior period adjustments in the financial statements.
6. Define and use correctly the new terms in the glossary.

Objective 1:
Understand the advantages of a corporation

A **corporation** is an entity recognized by law as possessing an existence separate and distinct from its owners. The corporation is the major form of business enterprise in terms of economic power. One of the reasons for this is that a corporation can raise huge amounts of capital by selling **shares of stock (capital stock)** to the public. Thus, the owners' interest in a corporation is usually called stockholders' or shareholders' equity. Other advantages of the corporation include the stockholders' limited liability and the ease of transferring ownership by selling the shares of stock owned. Limited liability means that a stockholder is not personally responsible (liable) for the debts of the corporation. The stockholder can lose only the amount invested.

The goals of accounting for stockholders' equity are to show the *sources of equity* capital and the *rights* of the various capital investors in the corporation. In addition to capital invested by owners, equity capital may be obtained by the retention of earnings in the corporation. The corporation may also obtain capital by issuing bonds or short-term debt. Accounting for this type of capital is discussed in another chapter, but it should be noted that the rights of equity capital holders rank below those of debt holders. This means that in times of economic hardship, all legal liabilities must be met before equity holders can share in the assets of the business. Thus, the major risks and rewards of a business lie with those who provide equity capital.

This chapter deals with accounting for various types of paid-in capital (including capital stock) and retained earnings. The chapter appendix discusses accounting for investments in the capital stock of other companies.

CAPITAL STOCK AUTHORIZED, ISSUED, AND OUTSTANDING

The corporate charter states the maximum number of shares and the par value, if any, per share of each class of stock that the corporation is authorized to issue—thus the term **capital stock authorized.** The total ownership interest in a corporation rests with the holders of its **capital stock outstanding**—that is, the shares authorized and issued and currently held by stockholders. If, for example, a corporation is authorized to issue 30,000 shares of common stock but has issued only 14,000 shares, the holders of the 14,000 shares are the sole owners of the corporation.

Each outstanding share of stock of a given class has identical rights and privileges with every other outstanding share of that class. Shares authorized but not yet issued are referred to as *unissued shares*. These shares possess no rights.

CLASSES OF CAPITAL STOCK

Common Stock

Objective 2: Describe the various types of capital stock and recognize the differences between the types of stock

Every corporation will have **common stock** outstanding. Investors purchase shares of stock so they can receive dividends and increases in market value of the shares. **Dividends** are distributions of assets (usually cash) that represent a withdrawal of earnings by the owners. The primary rights of the common stockholder include the right to (1) share in earnings when they are declared as dividends; (2) subscribe to additional offerings of the same stock in proportion to the amount currently held (preemptive right); (3) share in assets upon liquidation; (4) share in management through the election of a board of directors which guides the broad policy decisions of the business; and (5) dispose of the stock. The equity of the common stockholders is often referred to as the residual equity in a corporation, meaning that all other claims rank ahead of the claims of the common stockholders. The primary risks and rewards of ownership accrue to the common stockholder.

Preferred Stock

A corporation may need more equity capital than that provided by the common stockholders. Usually, the corporation will need to attract a different type of investor—one that is more interested in stable earnings on an investment. To do this, a class of stock granting certain preferences and called **preferred stock** may be issued. Usually, preferred stock is preferred as to dividends, although it can also be preferred as to assets in case of liquidation.

If stock is **preferred as to dividends,** its holders are entitled to a specified dividend per share before the payment of any dividend on the common stock. A stock preferred as to dividends is **cumulative** if all **dividends in arrears** (required dividends not paid in prior years) on this stock and the current dividend must be paid before dividends can be paid on the common stock. For example, assume that a company has $100,000 par value of 9% cumulative preferred stock outstanding, $100,000 par value of common stock outstanding, and $30,000 of retained earnings. No dividends have been paid for two years, including the current year. The preferred stockholders are entitled to dividends of $18,000 ($100,000 × .09 × 2 years) before any dividend can be paid to the common stockholders. If a preferred stock is **noncumulative,** a dividend that is not paid in any one year does not need to be paid in any future year. Because omitted dividends are lost forever, noncumulative preferred stocks hold little attraction for investors and are seldom issued.

Dividends in arrears are never shown as a liability of the corporation since dividends are not a legal liability until they have been declared by the board of directors. Because the amount of dividends in arrears may influence the decisions of users of a corporation's financial statements, such dividends should be and usually are disclosed in a footnote.

If stock is **preferred as to assets** in case of liquidation, its holders are entitled to receive par value or a larger specified amount per share (called liquidation value) before the common stockholders receive any distribution of assets. To illustrate the preference as to asset feature, assume that a corporation has $100,000 par value of preferred stock outstanding, $200,000 par value of common stock outstanding, and, after paying its liabilities, cash of $240,000 to distribute to its stockholders. If the preferred stock is preferred as to assets at par value and there are no dividends in arrears, the preferred stockholders will receive $100,000, with $140,000 being paid to common stockholders. If the preferred stock is not preferred as to assets, the $240,000 is prorated between the preferred and common stockholders in the ratio of the dollar total of the classes: $80,000 [($100,000/$300,000) × $240,000] to the preferred stockholders and $160,000 to the common stockholders.

The issuance of preferred stock may have other advantages for the corporation: (1) since preferred stocks usually have no voting rights, their issuance will not weaken the control of the common stockholders; and (2) the return (dividend) is usually fixed, thus giving financial leverage to the common stockholders.

Financial leverage. **Financial leverage** is the use of debt or preferred stock to increase (or perhaps decrease) earnings per share to common stockholders. Favorable financial leverage results when earnings per share (EPS) increase because of the issuance of preferred stock or debt. As an example of financial leverage, assume that the organizers of a corporation have two possible ways of getting capital: (1) issue 40,000 shares of $10 par value common stock for $400,000; or (2) issue 20,000 shares of $10 par value common stock for $200,000 and 2,000 shares of $100 par, 8% preferred stock for $200,000. Assume that net income of $80,000 per year is expected. The earnings to the common stockholders on a per share basis (net income, less preferred dividends, divided by number of common shares outstanding) and as a percentage of the original investment are shown in Illustration 8.1. Favorable leverage results when debt or preferred stock is used to increase the earnings per share of the common shareholders. In Illustration 8.1 the earnings per share of common stock are greater with preferred stock outstanding, and therefore, at that level of earnings there is favorable financial leverage. The result is earnings of $3.20 per share with the preferred stock and $2.00 per share without the preferred stock.

Financial leverage works in both directions. If net income in the above example should drop to $20,000, the corresponding earnings per common share would be $0.20 for the corporation with preferred stockholders and $0.50 for the all-common-stock corporation. Thus, in certain cases, the risks of financial leverage may offset the advantages. This is also true for long-term debt, which is another means of obtaining leverage.

Convertible preferred stock. In recent years, large amounts of new preferred stock have been issued in corporate mergers or acquisitions. The preferred stock issued was often **convertible preferred stock;** that is, the holder of the stock could exchange it when desired for shares of common stock of the same corporation at a conversion ratio stated in the preferred stock contract.

Convertible preferred stock is attractive to the investor because of (1) the stability of dividends and (2) the opportunity to participate in the growth of the corporation through the conversion privilege. Issuing preferred stock is also attractive to a corporation because it avoids the use of debt that will have to be repaid and that bears interest which must be paid regardless of the level of net income.

To illustrate this latter attraction, assume that the Olsen Company issued 2,000 shares of 8%, $100 par value convertible preferred stock at $100 per share. The stock can be converted at any time into four shares of

Illustration 8.1
ILLUSTRATION OF FAVORABLE FINANCIAL LEVERAGE

	With Preferred	Without Preferred
Net income	$80,000	$80,000
Preferred dividends	16,000	0
Net income to common stock	$64,000	$80,000
Number of common shares outstanding	20,000	40,000
Earnings per share of common stock	$3.20	$2.00

Olsen common stock which has a current market value of $25 per share. Assume further that in the next several years the company's net income increases sharply and that it increases the dividend of the common stock from $1.50 to $3.00 per share. The common stock now sells at $50 per share. The holder of one share of preferred stock could convert the stock into four shares of common stock and increase the annual dividend from $8 (from the preferred) to $12 (from the common). Or if one so desired, one could sell the preferred share at a substantial gain since the preferred stock would sell in the market for about $200—the market value of the four shares of common into which it is convertible. Or one may continue to hold the preferred stock in the expectation of realizing an even larger gain at a later date.

Virtually all preferred stocks, whether convertible or not, are callable by the issuing corporation. If a stock is callable, the issuing corporation may force the owners to surrender the stock for redemption. Holders of convertible preferred stock have the choice of either surrendering the stock or converting it into common shares. Preferred shares are usually callable at a small premium of 3 or 4% of the par value of the stock. If the stock is surrendered, the holder of record receives the par value, the call premium, any dividends in arrears, and a prorated portion of the current period's dividend. Assuming that there are no cumulative dividends in arrears and no current dividends to be prorated, the entry to record the call (and retirement) by the payment of $103 cash for a share of $100 par value preferred stock that was originally issued at par value, is:

Preferred Stock	100	
Retained Earnings	3	
Cash		103
To record the call and retirement of a share of preferred stock.		

Balance Sheet Presentation

As previously noted, the balance sheet should show the sources of capital and the rights of the various holders. It should also indicate the status of issued and unissued shares. To illustrate, assume that a corporation is authorized to issue (1) 20,000 shares of $100 par value, 8%, cumulative, convertible preferred stock, all of which have been issued and are outstanding; and (2) 400,000 shares of $10 par value common stock, of which 160,000 shares have been issued at par and are outstanding. The stockholders' equity section of the balance sheet (assuming $600,000 of retained earnings) would be:

Stockholders' equity:		
Preferred stock—$100 par value, 8% cumulative, convertible; authorized, issued, and outstanding, 20,000 shares	$2,000,000	
Common stock—$10 par value; authorized, 400,000 shares; issued and outstanding, 160,000 shares	1,600,000	$3,600,000
Retained earnings		600,000
Total stockholders' equity		$4,200,000

A footnote to the balance sheet would state the rate at which the preferred stock is convertible into common stock.

Recording Capital Stock Issued

Objective 3:
Record capital stock
issued for cash or
other assets

Each share of capital stock—common or preferred—will, according to the terms of the charter of the issuing corporation, be of par value or of no par value. The **par value,** if any, will be stated in the corporate charter and will be printed on the stock certificates. Par value may be of any amount.

Shares with par value. Par value serves two purposes. First, it is the amount per share that is recorded in the capital stock account for each share outstanding. Second, the par value of the outstanding shares is often the **legal** or **stated capital** of the corporation. A corporation is forbidden by law to declare dividends or to acquire its own stock if such action will reduce stockholders' equity below the legal capital of the corporation. If stock is issued at a discount from par, the stockholders may be liable to the creditors up to the total discount from par value.

Par value is not an indication of the amount of stockholders' equity per share (book value per share, as it is called) that is recorded in the accounting records of the corporation. The stockholders' equity consists of **paid-in** or **contributed capital** and **retained earnings,** and the latter may be either positive or negative. Nor does par value give any clue to the market value of the stock, because market value is based largely upon investors' expectations concerning future net income and dividends and general market prospects.

Stock is often issued through underwriters who guarantee the corporation a fixed price per share and make a commission by selling the stock to the public at a slightly higher price. To illustrate, assume that an underwriter guaranteed the sale of 300,000 shares at $20 per share net to the company and that its selling price to the public was $21. Assume further that shares are authorized and that their par value is $10 per share. The entry to record the receipt of the net proceeds would be:

Cash.	6,000,000	
Common Stock		3,000,000
Paid-in Capital in Excess of Par Value		3,000,000
To record the issuance of 300,000 shares of $10 par value common stock at $20 per share.		

After completion of the transaction, the stockholders' equity section of the balance sheet would be:

Stockholders' equity:	
Common stock—$10 par value; authorized, 500,000 shares;	
issued and outstanding, 300,000 shares	$3,000,000
Paid-in capital in excess of par value	3,000,000
Total stockholders' equity	$6,000,000

The computation is as follows:

Gross proceeds, 300,000 × $21	$6,300,000
Underwriter's charge	300,000
Proceeds to company.	$6,000,000
Par value, 300,000 × $10	3,000,000
Capital in excess of par	$3,000,000

Typically only $6 million is recorded as the capital received, since it represents the net proceeds to the company.

Shares without par value.   It is possible to have common stock without par value, called **no par stock.** Quite often, though, such stock will have a **stated value.** This stated value, like par value, may be set at any amount by the board of directors. The accounting treatment for par value stock and stated value stock is the same. The shares are carried in the capital account at either the par value or the stated value. Any proceeds in excess of par or stated value should be recorded in a separate paid-in capital account.

As an illustration, assume that the DeWitt Corporation, which is authorized to issue 20,000 shares of capital stock without par value, assigned a stated value of $15 per share to its stock. The 20,000 authorized shares were issued for cash at $20 per share. The entry would appear as follows:

Cash.	400,000	
Common Stock		300,000
Paid-in Capital in Excess of Stated Value		
(20,000 shares × $5)		100,000
To record the issuance of 20,000 shares of stock with a		
stated value of $15 at $20 per share.		

The stockholders' equity section of the balance sheet would be as follows:

Stockholders' equity:	
Common stock—no par value, stated value, $15; 20,000 shares	
authorized, issued, and outstanding	$300,000
Paid-in capital in excess of stated value.	100,000
Total stockholders' equity	$400,000

The $100,000 received over and above the stated value of $300,000 should be carried permanently as paid-in capital because it is a part of the capital originally contributed by the stockholders. But the stated capital of the DeWitt Corporation is $300,000—the stated value of the shares issued.

Shares without par or stated value.   If a corporation issues shares without par value to which no stated value is assigned or required by state law, the entire amount received is credited to the capital stock account. The entire amount received for such shares is the amount of stated capital.

In the above illustration of the DeWitt Corporation, if no stated value had been assigned to the shares, the entry would have been:

```
Cash. . . . . . . . . . . . . . . . . . . . . . . . . .   400,000
     Common Stock . . . . . . . . . . . . . . . . . . . .           400,000
     To record the issuance of 20,000 shares of stock at
     $20 per share.
```

The stockholders' equity section of the company's balance sheet would be:

```
Stockholders' equity:
  Common stock—no par or stated value; 20,000 shares
    authorized, issued, and outstanding  . . . . . . . . . . . .   $400,000
  Total stockholders' equity . . . . . . . . . . . . . . . . . .   $400,000
```

Sometimes capital stock is issued in exchange for noncash assets. In these situations, the transaction should be recorded at the fair market value of the stock or of the assets, whichever is more clearly determinable.

Values Associated with Capital Stock

Book value. The book value of a corporation is the total of its recorded net asset values, or simply total stockholders' equity. When only common stock is outstanding, **book value per share** is computed by dividing the stockholders' equity by the number of shares outstanding. For example, if a corporation has stockholders' equity consisting of capital stock of $100,000 and retained earnings of $50,000 and has 10,000 shares outstanding, the book value per share is $15 ($150,000 ÷ 10,000 shares).

When two or more classes of capital stock are outstanding, the computation of book value per share is more complex. The usual approach is to assume that the assets and liabilities are liquidated at book value. Preferred shareholders are typically entitled to at least par value plus cumulative dividends in arrears. The provision in the preferred stock contract will govern, and it may, for example, state specifically the amount that the holder of the preferred stock is entitled to receive in *liquidation* (the liquidation value) in addition to cumulative dividends, if any.

As an illustration, assume that the Celoron Company's stockholders' equity is as follows:

```
Stockholders' equity:
  Preferred stock—$50 par value, 8%, cumulative,
    8,000 shares. . . . . . . . . . . . . . . . . . . . . .   $  400,000
  Common stock—$10 par value, 400,000 shares . . . . . . .     4,000,000
  Paid-in capital in excess of par value—preferred . . . . . . .       40,000
  Retained earnings . . . . . . . . . . . . . . . . . . .         600,000
  Total stockholders' equity . . . . . . . . . . . . . . . . .   $5,040,000
```

Assume that the preferred stock has a liquidation value of $52 and that dividends on the preferred stock have not been paid this year. The book values for each class of stock are shown in Illustration 8.2.

Illustration 8.2
BOOK VALUE COMPUTATIONS

		Total	*Per Share*
Total stockholders' equity		$5,040,000	
Book value of preferred stock (8,000 shares):			
Liquidation value ($52 × 8,000)	$416,000		
Dividends (1 year at $32,000)	32,000	448,000	$56.00
Book value of common (400,000 shares)		$4,592,000	$11.48

Relationship of book value, par value, and market value. Par value and book value are related only to the extent that the par value of the stock is one element of the stockholders' equity—on which book value is computed. Book value and market value are related only to the extent that the market forces consider book value important. But market value is less dependent on book value than on (1) the company's future earnings power and possible dividend payments, (2) the present financial position of the company, and (3) the current state of the economy and other general stock market influences. Thus, a share of common or preferred stock may sell in a market for much more or much less than its book value or for more or less than its par value.

OTHER SOURCES OF PAID-IN (OR CONTRIBUTED) CAPITAL

Objective 4: Record other transactions affecting paid-in capital and retained earnings

The goal of paid-in capital accounts is to show the sources of capital. An account is usually established for each source of capital, for example, preferred stock, common stock, and capital in excess of par value from common stock issuances. The major source of capital is investment by stockholders. But sometimes a company may receive **donated capital.** This often happens when a city donates land and a building to a corporation to encourage it to locate there. Proper recording would show the source as Paid-in Capital—Donations. For example, assume that the Chamber of Commerce gave a building worth $300,000 and land worth $120,000 to a corporation. The entry required is:

Land	120,000	
Building	300,000	
Paid-in Capital—Donations		420,000
To record receipt of donated land and building.		

Other changes in the capital accounts might include: (1) capitalization of retained earnings through issuance of a stock dividend and (2) gains on treasury stock transactions (both of which are discussed later in this chapter).

The following stockholders' equity section of a balance sheet illustrates the reporting of capital:

Paid-in capital:
Preferred stock—$100 par value; authorized,
  issued, and outstanding, 4,000 shares . . . . . . $ 400,000
Common stock—no par value; stated value,
  $5 per share; authorized, issued, and
  outstanding, 200,000 shares 1,000,000 $1,400,000

Paid-in capital in excess of par or stated value:
From preferred stock issuances . . . . $ 40,000
From stock dividends   1,000,000
From donations   10,000   1,050,000

Total paid-in capital $2,450,000
Retained earnings   500,000
Total stockholders' equity $2,950,000

RETAINED EARNINGS

In general, the stockholders' equity in a corporation is made up of two elements: (1) paid-in (or contributed) capital and (2) retained earnings. **Retained earnings** is the term used to describe the increase in stockholders' equity resulting from profitable operation of the corporation. As such, it shows the source of assets received but not distributed to stockholders as dividends. Thus, both categories indicate the source of assets received by the corporation—actual investment by the stockholders and investment by the stockholders in the sense of dividends forgone. For now, the balance in the Retained Earnings account will be viewed as the difference between (1) the net income of the corporation during its existence to date and (2) the sum of the dividends declared during the same period.

When the Retained Earnings account has a negative (or debit) balance, a *deficit* exists. It is shown under that title as a negative amount in the stockholder's equity section of the balance sheet.

Dividends

As stated earlier, dividends are distributions of earnings by a corporation to its stockholders. The normal dividend is a cash dividend, but additional shares of the corporation's own capital stock may also be distributed as dividends.

Since dividends are the means whereby the owners of a corporation share in the earnings of the corporation, they usually are charged against retained earnings. They must be declared by the board of directors and recorded in the minutes book. The significant dates concerning dividends are the date of *declaration*, the date of *record*, and the date of *payment*. For example, the board of directors of the Clayton Corporation may declare on May 5, 1990, a cash dividend of $1.25 per share to stockholders of record on July 1, 1990, payable on July 10. The **date of declaration** is the date the board takes action in the form of a motion that dividends be paid.

This action creates the liability for dividends payable. The **date of record** is the date established by the board to determine who will receive the dividends. The stockholders on the date of record are determined from the corporation's records (a subsidiary stockholders' ledger). The **date of payment** is the date of actual payment of the dividend. Since a financial transaction occurs on the date of declaration (a liability is incurred) and on the date of payment (cash is paid), journal entries will be required on these dates. No journal entry is required on the date of record.

Cash dividends. **Cash dividends** are a cash distribution of earnings by a corporation to its stockholders. To illustrate the entries for cash dividends, consider the following example. On January 21, 1990, a corporation's board of directors declares a 2% (or $2,000) quarterly cash dividend on $100,000 of outstanding preferred stock (one fourth of the annual dividend on 1,000 shares of $100 par value, 8% preferred stock). The dividend will be paid on March 1, 1990, to stockholders of record on February 5, 1990. The entries at the declaration and payment dates are as follows:

```
1990
Jan. 21   Retained Earnings (or Dividends). . . . . . . . . . .   2,000
              Dividends Payable . . . . . . . . . . . . . . .            2,000
          Dividends declared: 2% on $100,000 of outstanding
          preferred stock, payable March 1, 1990, to
          stockholders of record on February 5, 1990.

Mar.  1   Dividends Payable . . . . . . . . . . . . . . . . .   2,000
              Cash . . . . . . . . . . . . . . . . . . . . . .            2,000
          Paid the dividends declared on January 21, 1990.
```

No entry is made on the date of record.

When a cash dividend is declared, some companies debit the Dividends account instead of Retained Earnings. The Dividends account is closed to Retained Earnings at the end of the year. A legally declared cash dividend is a current liability of the corporation, so Dividends Payable will be presented as a current liability on the balance sheet.

Stock dividends. A corporation may declare a **stock dividend,** which is a dividend that is payable in additional shares of the declaring corporation's capital stock. Stock dividend declarations usually provide that the distribution of additional shares be of the same class of stock as that held by the stockholders—for example, additional common stock to common stockholders. The usual accounting for a stock dividend distribution is to transfer a sum from retained earnings to permanent paid-in capital. The amount transferred per share for a stock dividend depends on the size of the stock dividend.

Stock dividends have no effect on the total amount of stockholders' equity. They merely decrease retained earnings and increase paid-in capital by an equal amount. Immediately after the declaration and distribution of a stock dividend, each share of similar stock has a lower book value per share. This is because more shares are outstanding with no increase in total stockholders' equity.

Stock dividends do not affect the individual stockholders' percentage of ownership in the corporation. For example, if a stockholder owns 1,000 shares in a corporation having 100,000 shares of stock outstanding, that stockholder owns 1% of the outstanding shares. After a 10% stock dividend, the stockholder will still own 1% of the outstanding shares—1,100 of 110,000 outstanding shares.

Reasons for declaring a stock dividend include:

1. Retained earnings may have become large relative to total stockholders' equity, or the corporation may simply desire a larger permanent capitalization.
2. The market price of the stock may have risen above a desirable trading range. A large stock dividend will generally reduce the per share market value of the company's stock.
3. The corporation may wish to have more stockholders and expects to increase their number by increasing the number of shares outstanding.
4. Stock dividends may be used to silence stockholders' demands for dividends from a corporation that does not have sufficient cash to pay cash dividends.

Recording small stock dividends. A stock dividend of less than 20 to 25% of the previously outstanding shares is assumed to have little effect on the market value of the shares. Thus, *the dividend should be accounted for at the present market value of the outstanding shares.*

Assume a corporation is authorized to issue 20,000 shares of $100 par value common stock, of which 8,000 shares are outstanding. Its board of directors now declares a 10% stock dividend (800 shares). The market price of the stock is $125 per share immediately before the stock dividend is announced. Since distributions of less than 20 to 25% of the previously outstanding shares are to be accounted for at market value, the entry for the declaration of the dividend is as follows (assuming the dividend was declared on August 10, 1990):

```
Aug. 10   Retained Earnings (or Stock Dividends)  . . . . . . .  100,000
              Stock Dividend Distributable—Common  . . . . .              80,000
              Paid-in Capital—Stock Dividend . . . . . . . . .              20,000
          To record the declaration of a 10 percent stock
          dividend; shares to be distributed on September 20,
          1990, to stockholders of record on August 31, 1990.
```

The entry to record the issuance of the shares is as follows:

```
Sept. 20  Stock Dividend Distributable—Common  . . . . . . .   80,000
              Common Stock  . . . . . . . . . . . . . . . . .              80,000
          To record distribution of 800 shares of common
          stock as authorized in stock dividends declared on
          August 10, 1990.
```

The **Stock Dividend Distributable—Common** account is a stockholders' equity account that is credited for the par or stated value of the shares distributable when recording the declaration of a stock dividend. Since a stock dividend distributable (payable) is not payable with assets, it is not a liability. If a balance sheet is prepared between the date of declaration of the 10% dividend and the date of issuance of the shares, the proper statement presentation of the effects of the stock dividend is as follows:

Stockholders' equity:
  Paid-in capital:
    Common stock, $100 par value; authorized, 20,000 shares;
      issued and outstanding, 8,000 shares $800,000
    Stock dividend distributable on September 20, 1990,
      800 shares at par value   80,000

    Total par value of shares issued and to be issued $880,000
    From capitalization of retained earnings through
      declaration of stock dividend   20,000

      Total paid-in capital . . . . $ 900,000
  Retained earnings   150,000
Total stockholders' equity $1,050,000

Recording large stock dividends. Stock dividends of over 20 to 25% of the previously outstanding shares are considered to be large stock dividends. One purpose of a large stock dividend is to reduce the market value of the stock; therefore, the old market value of the stock should not be used in the entry. *Such dividends are accounted for at their par or stated value rather than at their market value.* Stocks without par or stated value are accounted for at the amounts established by the laws of the state of incorporation or by the board of directors.

To illustrate the treatment of a stock dividend of over 20 to 25%, assume X Corporation has authorized capital of 10,000 shares of $10 par value common stock and has 5,000 shares issued and outstanding. X Corporation declares a 30% stock dividend (1,500 shares) on September 20, 1990, to be issued on October 15, 1990. The required entries are:

Sept. 20 Retained Earnings (or Stock Dividends)   15,000
           Stock Dividend Distributable   15,000
        To record the declaration of a 30% stock dividend.

Oct. 15 Stock Dividend Distributable   15,000
           Common Stock   15,000
        To record the issuance of the 30% stock dividend.

Note that, in contrast to the small stock dividend that was accounted for at market value, the 30% stock dividend was accounted for at par value (1,500 shares × $10 = $15,000). Because of the differences in accounting for large and small stock dividends, the relative size of the stock dividend must be determined before making any journal entries.

Stock splits. A **stock split,** as used in *Accounting Research Bulletin No. 43,* is a distribution of additional shares of the issuing corporation's stock for which the corporation receives no assets and for the purpose of causing a large reduction in the market price per share of the outstanding stock. The usual stock split is one in which the old shares are replaced by an increased number of new shares, with a corresponding reduction in the par value per share. A two-for-one split doubles the shares outstanding, a three-for-one split triples the shares, and so on. The par value per share is usually reduced at the time of the split so that the total dollar amount credited to the Common Stock account remains the same. For instance, in a two-for-one split, the par value per share is usually halved.

The entry to record a stock split depends on the particular circumstances. Usually, only the number of shares outstanding and the par or stated value need to be changed in the records. Thus, a two-for-one stock split in which the par value of the shares decreased from $20 to $10 and the number of shares originally outstanding was 5,000 would be recorded as follows:

Common Stock—$20 par value	100,000	
Common Stock—$10 par value		100,000
To record a two-for-one stock split, 5,000 shares of $20 par value common stock were replaced by 10,000 shares of $10 par value common stock.		

TREASURY STOCK

Nature of Treasury Stock

Treasury stock is capital stock, either preferred or common, that has been issued and reacquired by the issuing corporation. It has not been canceled, and it is legally available for reissuance. Treasury stock and unissued capital stock differ in that treasury stock has been issued at some time in the past, while unissued capital stock never has been issued.

Treasury stock may be acquired by purchase or in settlement of a debt. The corporation laws of most states consider treasury stock as issued but not outstanding. Treasury shares cannot be voted, and dividends are not paid on them.

Generally, as a matter of law, when a corporation acquires treasury stock at a cost (not as a gift), an equal amount of retained earnings is not available for dividends until the treasury stock is reissued or formally retired. As a result, the cost of treasury stock typically will not exceed the amount of retained earnings at the date of its acquisition. Thus, dividends plus treasury stock purchases must not impair the legal (or stated) capital of the corporation. If a corporation is subject to such a law, the retained earnings available for dividends are limited to the amount of retained earnings in excess of the cost of the treasury shares.

Treasury Stock in the Balance Sheet

The acquisition of treasury stock is normally recorded by a debit to a Treasury Stock account and a credit to Cash for its cost, as follows:

Treasury Stock	75,000	
Cash		75,000
To record acquisition of shares of the company's own stock.		

The treasury stock should not be reported as an asset on the balance sheet. Rather, it is reported as a deduction from the sum of the paid-in capital and retained earnings, as follows:

Stockholders' equity:

Common stock—authorized and issued, 40,000 shares; par value $10 per share, of which 5,000 shares are in the treasury	$400,000
Retained earnings (including $75,000 restricted by acquisition of treasury stock)	500,000
Total	$900,000
Less: Treasury stock at cost, 5,000 shares	75,000
Total stockholders' equity	$825,000

Treasury Stock Transactions

To illustrate the accounting for treasury stock, assume that the Hillside Corporation, with stockholders' equity consisting solely of capital stock and retained earnings, acquired 2,000 shares of its capital stock for $70,000. Two months later, when the market price of the stock was $40 per share, it issued 800 shares to officers and employees as bonuses. A year later, when it needed cash, it sold the rest of the shares at $30 each. The entries required are:

(1)	Treasury Stock (2,000 shares × $35)	70,000	
	Cash		70,000
	To record acquisition of 2,000 shares of the company's own stock.		
(2)	Salaries and Bonuses Expense (800 shares × $40)	32,000	
	Treasury Stock (800 shares × $35)		28,000
	Paid-in Capital—Treasury Stock Transactions		4,000
	To record issuance of 800 shares of treasury stock as bonuses.		
(3)	Cash (1,200 shares × $30)	36,000	
	Paid-in Capital—Treasury Stock Transactions	4,000	
	Retained Earnings	2,000	
	Treasury Stock (1,200 shares × $35)		42,000
	To record sale of 1,200 shares of treasury stock for cash.		

In T-account format these entries would appear as follows:

Cash				Treasury Stock				Paid-in Capital—Treasury Stock Transactions			
Bal.	xxx	(1)	70,000	(1)	70,000	(2)	28,000	(3)	4,000	(2)	4,000
(3)	36,000					(3)	42,000				

Salaries and Bonuses Expense				Retained Earnings			
Bal.	xxx			(3)	2,000	Bal.	xxx
(2)	32,000						

The acquisition of the shares is recorded at cost ($70,000). The issuance of the 800 shares as bonuses requires a debit to the Salaries and Bonuses Expense account for the market value of the shares, a credit to Treasury Stock for the cost of the shares, and a credit to a paid-in capital account for the excess of the fair value of the shares over their cost. When the remaining shares are issued, the deficiency of issue price from cost is charged against **Paid-in Capital—Treasury Stock Transactions** *until the credit balance in the account is exhausted.* The remaining deficiency is then charged to Retained Earnings.

If at the end of the fiscal year the Paid-in Capital—Treasury Stock Transactions account contained a positive (credit) balance, it would be reported in the balance sheet below capital stock as Paid-in Capital in Excess of Par (or Stated) Value. The gain on the transaction represents an increase in invested capital.

THE STATEMENT OF STOCKHOLDERS' EQUITY

Most corporations include four financial statements in their annual reports: a balance sheet, an income statement, a statement of stockholders' equity, and a statement of cash flows. A **statement of stockholders' equity** is a summary of the transactions affecting the accounts in the stockholders' equity section of the balance sheet during a stated period of time. These transactions include activities affecting both paid-in capital and retained earnings accounts. The columns reflect the major account titles within the stockholders' equity section: the types of stock issued and outstanding, paid-in capital in excess of par (or stated) value, retained earnings, and treasury stock. Each row indicates the effects of major transactions affecting one or more stockholders' equity accounts.

A typical statement of stockholders' equity is shown in Illustration 8.3. The first row indicates the beginning balances of each account in the stockholders' equity section. From this summary, it can be determined that Mathers Corporation issued 10,000 shares of common stock, declared a 5% stock dividend on common stock, repurchased 1,200 shares of treasury stock, earned net income of $185,000, and paid cash dividends on its preferred and common stock issues. After the transactions' effects are indicated within each row, each column's components are added or subtracted to determine the ending balance in each stockholders' equity account.

EXTRAORDINARY ITEMS, CHANGES IN ACCOUNTING PRINCIPLE, AND PRIOR PERIOD ADJUSTMENTS

In the determination of net income, more useful information is provided if revenues generated and expenses incurred in the normal operations of a business are reported separately from unusual, nonrecurring gains and losses. In addition, a more useful presentation results if certain corrections of accounting errors are reported in the retained earnings statement rather than the income statement.

Illustration 8.3
THE STATEMENT OF STOCKHOLDERS' EQUITY

MATHERS CORPORATION
Statement of Stockholders' Equity
For the Year Ended December 31, 1990

	$50 Par Value 6% Preferred Stock	$20 Par Value Common Stock	Paid-In Capital in Excess of Par Value	Retained Earnings	Treasury Stock	Total
Balance, January 1, 1990	$250,000	$300,000	$200,000	$500,000	($42,000)	$1,208,000
Issuance of 10,000 shares of common stock		200,000	100,000			300,000
5% stock dividend on common stock, 1,250 shares.		25,000	27,500	(52,500)		0
Purchase of 1,200 shares of treasury stock					(48,000)	(48,000)
Net income				185,000		185,000
Cash dividends						
Preferred stock				(15,000)		(15,000)
Common stock				(25,000)		(25,000)
Balance, December 31, 1990 . .	$250,000	$525,000	$327,500	$592,500	($90,000)	$1,605,000

Extraordinary Items

Abuses in the financial reporting of gains and losses as extraordinary items led to the issuance of *APB Opinion No. 30* (September 1973). In the *Opinion,* **extraordinary items** are defined as those events that are both unusual in nature *and* that occur infrequently. Note that both conditions must be met—unusual nature and infrequent occurrence. Whether an item is unusual and infrequent is to be determined in the light of the environment in which the firm operates. Examples include gains or losses that are the direct result of a major casualty (a flood), a confiscation of property by a foreign government, or a prohibition under a newly enacted law. Such items are to be included in the determination of periodic net income, but disclosed separately (net of their tax effects, if any) in the income statement. **Net-of-tax effect** is used for extraordinary items, changes in accounting principle, and prior period adjustments whereby items are shown at the dollar amounts remaining after deducting the effects on such items of the income taxes (federal and state, if any) payable currently. *FASB Statement No. 4* further directs that gains and losses from the early extinguishment of debt are extraordinary items. Income before extraordinary items and then income after extraordinary items must be reported as shown in Illustration 8.4. **Income before extraordinary items** is income from operations less applicable income taxes.

Gains or losses related to ordinary business activities are not extraordinary items regardless of their size. For example, litigation losses and material write-downs of uncollectible receivables, obsolete inventories, and intangible assets are not extraordinary items. But such items may be separately disclosed as part of net income from continuing activities.

Changes in Accounting Principle

A company's reported net income and financial position can be altered materially by changes in accounting principles. **Changes in accounting principle** (accounting changes) are changes in accounting data caused by changes in accounting principle such as a change in inventory valuation method (for example, from FIFO to LIFO) or a change in depreciation method (for example, from accelerated to straight-line). According to *APB Opinion No. 20*, a company should consistently apply the same accounting methods from one period to another. But a change may be made if the newly adopted method is preferable and if the change is adequately disclosed in the financial statements. In the period in which an accounting change is made, the nature of the change, its justification, and its effect on net income must be disclosed in the financial statements. Also, the cumulative effect of the change on prior years' income (net of tax) must be shown in the income statement for the year of change (see Illustration 8.4).

As an example of an accounting change, assume that Anson Company purchased a machine on January 2, 1988, for $30,000. The machine has a useful life of five years with no scrap value expected. Anson Company decided to depreciate the machine for financial reporting purposes using the sum-of-the-years'-digits method. At the beginning of 1990, the company decided to change to the straight-line method of depreciation. The cumulative effect of the change in accounting method is computed as follows:

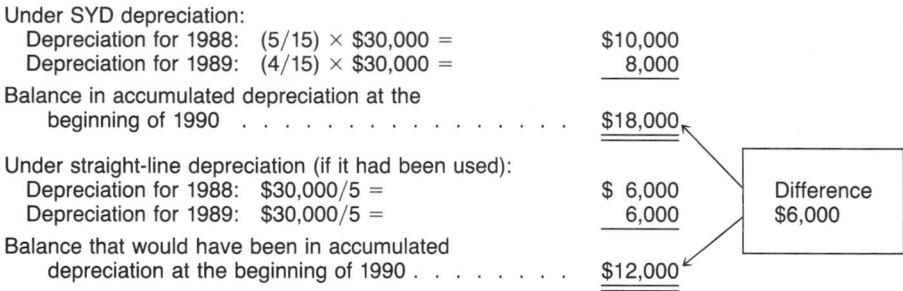

Under SYD depreciation:
Depreciation for 1988:   (5/15) × $30,000 = $10,000
Depreciation for 1989:   (4/15) × $30,000 =   8,000
Balance in accumulated depreciation at the
    beginning of 1990 . . . . $18,000

Under straight-line depreciation (if it had been used):
Depreciation for 1988: $30,000/5 = $ 6,000   Difference
Depreciation for 1989: $30,000/5 =   6,000 $6,000
Balance that would have been in accumulated
    depreciation at the beginning of 1990 . . . . $12,000

The accumulated depreciation account balance would have been $6,000 less under the straight-line method. Also, depreciation expense over the two years would have been $6,000 less. Therefore, Anson Company corrects the appropriate account balances by reducing the accumulated depreciation account balance by $6,000 and creating an account entitled Cumulative Effect of Change in Accounting Method, which will be closed to Retained Earnings during the normal closing process and thereby correct the previous years' misstated amounts of depreciation. The journal entry would be:

Accumulated Depreciation—Machinery   6,000
    Cumulative Effect of Change in Accounting Method   6,000
    To record the effect of changing from sum-of-the-years'-digits
    depreciation to straight-line depreciation on machinery.

Illustration 8.4
INCOME STATEMENT
Showing Extraordinary Item and a Change in Accounting Principle

ANSON COMPANY
Income Statement
For the Year Ended December 31, 1990

Net sales		$41,000,000
Other revenues		2,250,000
Total revenue		$43,250,000
Expenses:		
Cost of goods sold	$22,000,000	
Administrative, selling, and general expenses	12,000,000	34,000,000
Income before income taxes		$ 9,250,000
Federal income taxes (50%)		4,625,000
Income before extraordinary item and the		
cumulative effect of an accounting change		$ 4,625,000
Extraordinary item:		
Loss from flood damage	$ 40,000	
Less: tax effect	20,000	(20,000)
		$ 4,605,000
Change In accounting principle:		
Cumulative effect on prior years' income of		
changing to a different depreciation method . . .	$ 6,000	
Less: tax effect	3,000	3,000
Net income		$ 4,608,000
Earnings per share of common stock		
(1,000,000 shares outstanding):		
Income before extraordinary item and the		
cumulative effect of an accounting change		$ 4.625
Extraordinary item		(0.020)
Cumulative effect on prior years' income of changing		
to a different depreciation method		0.003
Net income		$ 4.608

The cumulative effect of changing to the straight-line depreciation method is reported in Illustration 8.4 at $3,000 since the assumed tax effect is 50%, ($6,000 × .5 = $3,000). (Income tax allocation procedures are covered in Chapter 21.)

Prior Period Adjustments

According to *FASB Statement No. 16,* **prior period adjustments** consist almost entirely of corrections of errors in previously published financial statements. Corrections of abnormal, nonrecurring errors that may have been caused by the improper use of an accounting principle or by mathematical mistakes are prior period adjustments.

To illustrate a prior period adjustment, assume that land costing $200,000 was expensed rather than capitalized. This caused a $100,000 underpayment of income taxes. The mistake subsequently was discovered and the following entry was made:

```
Land. . . . . . . . . . . . . . . . . . . . . . . . . . . . . . . .   200,000
    Federal Income Taxes Payable . . . . . . . . . . . . .              100,000
    Prior Period Adjustment—Correction of Error in
        Expensing Cost of Land . . . . . . . . . . . . . . .            100,000
    To correct an accounting error involving land.
```

In the **statement of retained earnings** (see Illustration 8.5), prior period adjustments are treated as adjustments of the opening balance of retained earnings.

Accounting for Tax Effects

Most extraordinary items, accounting changes, and prior period adjustments will affect the amount of income taxes payable, with the result that questions arise as to proper reporting procedure. To prevent distortions, *APB Opinion No. 9* recommends that extraordinary items and prior period adjustments be reported *net of their tax effects*, as shown in Illustrations 8.4 and 8.5. Changes in accounting principle are also reported net of their tax effects. The tax effect of an item may be shown separately (as for the flood loss and change in accounting principle in Illustration 8.4) or may be mentioned parenthetically with only the net amount shown (as for the correction of error in Illustration 8.5).

Illustration 8.5
STATEMENT OF RETAINED EARNINGS

ANSON COMPANY
Statement of Retained Earnings
For the Year Ended December 31, 1990

Retained earnings, January 1, 1990	$5,000,000
Prior period adjustment	
Correction of error of expensing land (net of tax effect of $100,000)	100,000
Adjusted retained earnings, January 1, 1990	$5,100,000
Add: Net income	4,608,000
	$9,708,000
Less: Dividends	500,000
Retained earnings, December 31, 1990	$9,208,000

EARNINGS PER SHARE

One final item needs to be discussed regarding corporations and income statement presentations, and that is earnings per share. A major item of interest to investors and potential investors is how much a company earned during the current year, both in total and for each share of stock outstanding. Earnings per share is calculated only for the residual or common shares of ownership. **Earnings per share** is computed as net income minus preferred stock dividends divided by the number of common shares outstanding. Income available to common stockholders is net income less any dividends on preferred stock.

Earnings per share (EPS) is usually calculated and presented for income before extraordinary items and the cumulative effect of accounting changes, extraordinary items, accounting changes, and net income. Notice in Illustration 8.4 the earnings per share amounts are reported at the bottom of the illustration.

Stockholders can compare the earnings per share of two companies more easily than total dollars of income. EPS is very useful in making decisions about the price to pay for stock and the return on that investment. Also, earnings per share is related to market price per share of stock in that if EPS increases, generally market price per share also increases.

SUMMARY

The goal in accounting for stockholders' equity is to show the sources of capital contributed to the corporation and to show the relevant claims held by the capital contributors. The corporation obtains equity capital (as opposed to debt capital) from three main sources: (1) common stockholders, (2) preferred stockholders, and (3) earnings retained in the business. Most of the risks and rewards of ownership lie with the holders of common stock. Preferred stock is often issued to attract potential investors who are more interested in stability of return. Recent preferred stock issues have been convertible into common stock in an attempt to make them more attractive.

Most stock issued will have either a par value or a stated value. If so, this amount is credited to a capital stock account. All proceeds in excess of par or stated value are recorded in separate capital in excess of par (or stated) value accounts.

Book value can be computed for common and preferred stock. Book value per share amounts usually differ from either the par value or the market value of the shares.

Dividends are distributions of assets (usually cash) and are charged to retained earnings. But it is quite common for companies to declare stock dividends in which additional shares are issued to the current holders. The issuance of small stock dividends (less than 20 to 25%) results in capitalizing a portion of retained earnings equal to the current market value of the shares issued. The issuance of a large stock dividend (more than 20 to 25%) often results in capitalizing retained earnings equal to the par value of the shares issued.

A stock split increases the number of shares outstanding and decreases the par or stated value of each share. It has no effect upon the stockholders' equity account balances.

Treasury stock is stock acquired by the issuing company. It is generally held for possible issuance to employees or for other reasons. The cost of the stock, if any, is considered a reduction of total equity and is shown as a deduction from total stockholders' equity—not as an asset.

The APB and the FASB have distinguished between extraordinary items (to be shown in the income statement) and prior period adjustments (which are, in a sense, corrections of the beginning retained earnings balance). Prior period adjustments consist almost solely of corrections of accounting errors. Such adjustments should be quite rare. Either a prior period adjustment or an extraordinary item should be shown at its **net-of-tax effect.**

When a change in accounting principle is made, the cumulative effect of the change on prior years' earnings must be shown on the income statement for the year of change, net of its tax effects.

Earnings per share (EPS) is usually calculated and presented for income before extraordinary items and the cumulative effect of accounting changes, extraordinary items, accounting changes, and net income.

In the next chapter you will learn about debt financing and bond investments. Both short-term and long-term debt are additional sources of equity capital.

APPENDIX   STOCK INVESTMENTS

Sometimes companies invest in the stocks of other companies. Such investments may actually consist of **marketable equity securities** in that the stocks may be readily marketable. But stocks are rarely purchased as temporary investments of idle cash. They are usually acquired either for long-term investment or in an attempt to speculate in the stock market.

The reasons for investing on a long-term basis in the securities of other companies include the desire to (1) establish an affiliation with another business, (2) acquire control over another business, or (3) secure a continuing stream of revenue from the investment over a period of years.

REPORTING SECURITIES IN THE BALANCE SHEET .

Determining how securities should be classified in the balance sheet depends on management's intent and may be summarized as follows:

1. If the securities held are readily marketable, they should be shown as current assets if they *will* be converted into cash in the normal operating cycle of the business. If they *will not* be converted, they should be considered noncurrent assets and reported in the investments section of the balance sheet.
2. If the securities are not readily marketable, they may not be classified as current assets unless they mature in the coming operating cycle and there is no doubt as to their redemption.

Valuation of Equity Securities

The FASB, in *Statement No. 12*, describes the method of accounting for marketable equity securities.[1] It requires the use of the lower-of-cost-or-market method for marketable equity securities (with certain limited exceptions). Marketable equity securities are to be carried at the lower of total cost or total market for all securities classified as *current*, taken as a group, and for securities classified as *noncurrent*, taken as a group.

Current Marketable Equity Securities

For the securities classified as current, any excess of total cost over total market is debited to an account such as Net Unrealized Loss on Current Marketable Equity Securities, which is shown in the income statement. The credit is to a current asset valuation allowance account such as Allowance for Market Decline of Current Marketable Equity Securities. The entry would appear as follows (assuming that the cost is $16,000 and the market is $15,500):

Net Unrealized Loss on Current Marketable Equity Securities	500	
Allowance for Market Decline of Current Marketable Equity Securities		500
To record write-down of current marketable equity securities to total market value.		

The balance sheet presentation would be as follows:

Current assets:		
Current marketable equity securities	$16,000	
Less: Allowance for market decline	500	$15,500

Any later recovery in the total market price (up to the amount of the original cost) would be debited to the asset valuation allowance and would be credited to an account such as Net Unrealized Gain on Current Marketable Equity Securities that would be shown in the income statement. The entry would appear as follows (assuming that the market recovered by $400):

Allowance for Market Decline of Current Marketable Equity Securities	400	
Net Unrealized Gain on Current Marketable Equity Securities		400
To record the $400 recovery of total market value of current marketable equity securities.		

The balance sheet presentation would now be:

Current assets:		
Current marketable equity securities	$16,000	
Less: Allowance for market decline	100	$15,900

---

[1] "Accounting for Certain Marketable Securities," *Statement of Financial Accounting Standards No. 12* (Stamford, Conn., 1975), p. 31.

Noncurrent marketable equity securities. Any "temporary" losses on noncurrent equity securities (long-term investments) are debited to a stockholders' equity account (but not deducted from net income) and credited to an asset valuation allowance account. The account debited might be entitled Net Unrealized Loss on Noncurrent Marketable Equity Securities. Thus, the entry might be as follows (assuming that the cost is $32,000 and the market price $31,000):

```
Net Unrealized Loss on Noncurrent Marketable Equity
    Securities  . . . . . . . . . . . . . . . . . . . . . . . . .   1,000
        Allowance for Market Decline of Noncurrent Marketable
            Equity Securities  . . . . . . . . . . . . . . . . .           1,000
    To record write-down of noncurrent marketable equity securities
    to total market value.
```

The balance sheet presentation would be:

```
Investments:
    Noncurrent marketable equity securities  . . . .   $32,000
    Less: Allowance for market decline  . . . . . .      1,000   $31,000
```

The Net Unrealized Loss on Noncurrent Marketable Equity Securities could be reported in the stockholders' equity section of the balance sheet as a deduction from the total of the par value of the stock outstanding plus any paid-in capital in excess of par value, or a deduction from total stockholders' equity.

Later recoveries in market value up to cost, but not above cost, would be debited to the allowance account and credited to the unrealized loss account as follows (assume that the market increases by $1,700):

```
Allowance for Market Decline of Noncurrent Marketable
    Equity Securities  . . . . . . . . . . . . . . . . . . . . .   1,000
        Net Unrealized Loss on Noncurrent Marketable Equity
            Securities  . . . . . . . . . . . . . . . . . . . . .           1,000
    To write the noncurrent marketable equity securities back up to
    original cost.
```

Thus, the entry would increase stockholders' equity by $1,000 (not $1,700) but would not increase reported income. If a loss on an individual noncurrent security is determined to be "permanent," it is recorded as a realized loss and deducted in measuring income. The entry would be (assuming a permanent loss of $1,400):

```
Realized Loss on Noncurrent Marketable Equity Securities  . . . .   1,400
    Investment in Noncurrent Marketable Equity Securities  . . . .           1,400
    To record the permanent loss of $1,400 on noncurrent marketable
    equity securities.
```

Any subsequent recovery in market value would be ignored until the security is sold.

The equity method. The equity method should be used for an investment in common stock that gives an investor the ability to exercise significant influence over a company's operating and financial policies (even though the investor holds less than 50% of the voting stock). In the absence of evidence to the contrary, holding 20% or more of the common stock indicates the ability to exercise significant influence, and holding less than 20% does not. In situations where there is the ability to exert significant influence, the investor is required to use the equity method of accounting for its investment.[2] Under the equity method, the investor initially records the investment at cost and then adjusts the carrying amount to recognize its share of the other company's earnings or losses after the date of acquisition. Dividends received are deducted from the investment. We shall not deal with this method further. In this appendix, we shall assume that investments in the common stock of other companies represent less than 20% of the outstanding shares.

Entry to Record Acquisition

When the common or preferred stocks of other corporations are acquired, they should be recorded at cost, which is the cash outlay or the fair value of the asset given in exchange. Since the stock acquired will usually be purchased from another investor through a broker, the cost will normally consist of the price paid for the stock plus a commission to the broker. For example, assume that Brewer Corporation purchased as a temporary investment 1,000 shares of Cowen Corporation common stock at $15 per share through a broker who charged $100 for services rendered in acquiring the stock. Brewer would record the transaction as follows:

Current Marketable Equity Securities	15,100	
Cash		15,100
To record purchase of 1,000 shares of Cowen common at $15 plus $100 broker's commission.		

Cash Dividends on Investments

The usual accounting for the receipt of dividends on stock investments is to debit Cash and credit Dividend Revenue when the cash dividend check is actually received. This accounting for dividends is acceptable for tax purposes and is widely followed by investors.

An alternative will be required when a dividend is declared in one accounting period which will not be paid until the following period. Assume that the Cowen Corporation declared a cash dividend of 20 cents per share on December 1, 1989, to stockholders of record as of December 20, 1989, payable on January 15, 1990. Under these circumstances an entry should be made either on December 20 or as an adjusting entry on December 31, as follows:

Dividends Receivable	200	
Dividend Revenue		200
To record dividend of 20 cents per share on Cowen common stock due January 15, 1990.		

---

[2]APB, "The Equity Method of Accounting for Investments in Common Stock," *APB Opinion No. 18* (New York: AICPA, 1971).

When the dividend is collected on January 15, the entry would be a debit to Cash and a credit to the Dividends Receivable account. In this manner the dividend is recorded as revenue in the period in which it is earned.

Stock Dividends and Stock Splits

A stock dividend consists of the distribution by a corporation of additional shares of its stock to its stockholders. Usually the distribution consists of additional common stock to common stockholders. Such a distribution is not considered to be a revenue-producing transaction to the holders of the stock. A stock dividend is viewed simply as having the effect of dividing the stockholders' equity into a larger number of smaller pieces. It simply increases the number of shares a stockholder holds, but it does not change his or her percentage of ownership of the outstanding shares.

Thus, the accounting for stock dividends consists only of a notation in the accounts of the number of shares received and a change in the average per share cost of the shares held. For example, if 100 shares of Company A common stock are held, which cost $22 per share, and Company A distributes a 10% stock dividend, the number of shares held is increased to 110 and the cost per share is now $20 ($2,200 ÷ 110 shares = $20 per share).

Similarly, when a corporation splits its stock, the only accounting entry required is a notation indicating the receipt of the additional shares. If Smith Company owned 1,000 shares of Jones Company common stock and Jones Company split its stock on a two-for-one basis, Smith would own 2,000 shares after the split, and the cost per share would be halved.

Sales of stock investments. When stock holdings are sold, the gain or loss on the sale is the difference between the net proceeds received and the carrying value of the shares sold. Assume, for example, that 100 shares of Thacker Company common stock were sold for $75 per share. The broker deducted his or her commission and other taxes and charges of $62 prior to making the remittance to the seller. If the seller's cost was $5,000, the required entry is:

Cash	7,438	
Current Marketable Equity Securities		5,000
Gain on Sale of Investments		2,438
To record gain on sale of investments.		

The realized gain on the sale of investments is shown in the income statement, regardless of whether the securities were classified as current or noncurrent equity securities.

Objective 6: Define and use correctly the new terms in the glossary

NEW TERMS INTRODUCED IN CHAPTER 8

Book value per share Stockholders' equity divided by the number of shares outstanding (276).

Capital stock Transferable units of ownership in a corporation (269).

Capital stock authorized   The number of shares of stock that a corporation is entitled to issue as designated in its charter (270).

Capital stock outstanding   The number of shares of authorized stock that have been issued and that are currently held by stockholders (270).

Cash dividends   Cash distributions of net income by a corporation to its stockholders (279).

Changes in accounting principle   Changes in accounting methods pertaining to such items as inventory and depreciation (286).

Common stock   Shares of stock representing the residual equity in the corporation. If only one class of stock is issued, it is known as common stock. All other claims rank ahead of common stockholders' claims (270).

Convertible preferred stock   Preferred stock that is convertible into common stock of the issuing corporation (272).

Corporation   An entity recognized by law as possessing an existence separate and distinct from its owners; that is, it is a separate legal entity. A corporation is granted many of the rights and placed under many of the obligations of a person. In any given state, all corporations organized under the laws of that state are domestic corporations; all others are foreign corporations (269).

Cumulative preferred stock   Preferred stock for which the right to receive a basic dividend accumulates if not paid; dividends in arrears must be paid before any dividends can be paid on the common stock (271).

Date of declaration (of dividends)   The date the board of directors takes action in the form of a motion that dividends be paid (278).

Date of payment (of dividends)   The date of actual payment of a dividend, or issuance of additional shares in the case of a stock dividend (279).

Date of record (of dividends)   The date established by the board to determine who will receive a dividend (279).

Dividend   A distribution of assets (usually cash) that represents a withdrawal of earnings by the owners. Dividends are similar in nature to withdrawals by sole proprietors and partners (270).

Dividends (cash)   See Cash dividends.

Dividends in arrears   Cumulative unpaid dividends, including passed quarterly dividends for the current year (271).

Dividends (stock)   See Stock dividends.

Donated capital   Results from donation of assets to the corporation, which increases stockholders' equity (277).

Earnings per share (EPS)   Earnings to the common stockholders on a per share basis, computed as net income available to common stockholders divided by the number of common shares outstanding (289).

Extraordinary items   Items that are unusual in nature and that occur infrequently; reported in the income statement net of their tax effects, if any (285).

Financial leverage   The use of debt or preferred stock to increase (or perhaps decrease) earnings per share to common stockholders (271).

Income before extraordinary items   Income from operations less applicable income taxes, if any (285).

Legal capital (stated capital)   An amount prescribed by law (often par value or stated value of shares outstanding) below which a corporation may not reduce stockholders' equity through the declaration of dividends or other payments to stockholders (274).

Marketable equity securities   Investments in the stocks of other companies that are readily marketable (290).

Net-of-tax effect   Used for extraordinary items, prior period adjustments, and changes in accounting principle, whereby items are shown at the dollar amounts remaining after deducting the effects of such items on income taxes, if any, payable currently (285).

Noncumulative preferred stock   Preferred stock on which the right to receive a dividend expires if the dividend is not declared (271).

No-par stock   Capital stock without par value, to which a stated value may or may not be assigned (275).

Paid-in (or contributed) capital   Amount of stockholders' equity that normally results from the cash or other assets invested by owners; it may also result from services provided for shares of stock and certain other transactions (274).

Paid-in Capital—Treasury Stock Transactions   The account credited when treasury stock is reissued for more than its cost; this account is debited to the extent of its credit balance when such shares are reissued at less than cost (284).

Par value   An arbitrary amount printed on each stock certificate that may be assigned to each share of a given class of stock, usually at the time of incorporation (274).

Preferred stock   Capital stock that carries certain features or rights not carried by common stock. Preferred stock may be preferred as to dividends, preferred as to assets, or preferred as to both dividends and assets. Preferred stock may be cumulative or noncumulative and participating or nonparticipating (271).

Prior period adjustments   Consist almost entirely of corrections of errors in previously published financial statements. Prior period adjustments are reported in the statement of retained earnings net of their tax effects, if any (287).

Retained earnings   The part of stockholders' equity resulting from net income; the account in which the results of corporate activity are reflected and to which dividends are charged (274–278).

Shares of stock   Units of ownership in a corporation (269).

Stated value   An arbitrary amount assigned by the board of directors to each share of a given class of no-par stock (275).

Statement of retained earnings   A formal statement showing the items causing changes in unappropriated and appropriated retained earnings during a stated period of time (288).

Stock Dividend Distributable—Common account   The stockholders' equity account that is credited for the par or stated value of the shares distributable when recording the declaration of a stock dividend (280).

Stock dividends   Dividends that are payable in additional shares of the declaring corporation's capital stock (279).

Stock preferred as to assets   Means that in liquidation the preferred stockholders are entitled to receive the par value (or a larger stipulated liquidation value) per share before any assets may be distributed to common stockholders (271).

Stock preferred as to dividends   Means that the preferred stockholders are entitled to receive a specified dividend per share before any dividend on common stock is paid (271).

Stock split A distribution of additional shares of the issuing corporation's stock for which the corporation receives no assets. The purpose of a stock split is to cause a large reduction in the market price per share of the outstanding stock (281).

Stock without par value See No-par stock.

Treasury stock Shares of capital stock issued and reacquired by the issuing corporation; they have not been formally canceled and are available for reissuance (282).

DEMONSTRATION PROBLEM 8–1

The King Company has been authorized to issue 200,000 shares of $5 par value common stock and 2,000 shares of 14%, cumulative preferred stock with a par value of $10.

Required:

Prepare the entries for the following transactions:

a. 100,000 shares of common stock are issued at $20 per share.

b. 1,500 shares of preferred stock are issued for cash at $15 per share.

c. 2,000 shares of common stock are issued for a machine with a cash price of $15,000.

Solution to demonstration problem 8–1

a. Cash	2,000,000	
Common Stock		500,000
Paid-In Capital in Excess of Par Value—Common. . .		1,500,000
To record issuance of 100,000 shares at $20 per share.		
b. Cash	22,500	
Preferred Stock		15,000
Paid-In Capital in Excess of Par Value—Preferred . .		7,500
To record the issuance of 1,500 shares for cash, at $15 per share.		
c. Machinery	15,000	
Common Stock		10,000
Paid-In Capital in Excess of Par Value—Common. . .		5,000
To record issuance of 2,000 shares in exchange for a machine.		

DEMONSTRATION PROBLEM 8–2

Following are selected transactions of the Inglis Company:

Transactions:

1. The company acquired 400 shares of its own $50 par value common stock for $20,600 cash.
2. One hundred of the treasury shares are reissued at $55 per share, cash.
3. One hundred forty of the treasury shares are reissued at $47.50 per share, cash.
4. Stockholders of the corporation donated 200 shares of their common stock to the company.
5. The 200 shares of treasury stock received by donation are reissued for $9,000.

Required:

Prepare the necessary journal entries to record the above transactions.

Solution to demonstration problem 8–2

1. Treasury Stock—Common 20,600
    Cash 20,600
    Acquired 400 shares at $20,600 ($51.50 per share).

2. Cash 5,500
    Treasury Stock—Common 5,150
    Paid-In Capital—Common Treasury Stock
        Transactions 350
    Reissued 100 shares at $55 per share.

3. Cash 6,650
    Paid-In Capital—Common Treasury Stock Transactions 350
    Retained Earnings 210
        Treasury Stock—Common 7,210
    Reissued 140 shares at $47.50 per share.

4. Stockholders donated 200 shares of common stock to the
   company.

5. Cash 9,000
    Paid-In Capital—Donations 9,000
    Reissued donated shares at $45 per share.

QUESTIONS

1. What are the basic rights associated with a share of capital stock, assuming that only one class of stock is outstanding?

2. A corporation has outstanding 5,000 shares of 8%, $50 par value, cumulative preferred stock. Dividends on this stock have not been declared for two years. Is the corporation liable to its preferred stockholders for these dividends? How should the dividends be shown in the balance sheet, if at all?

3. Assuming that no preferred stock is outstanding, how can the book value per share of common stock be determined? Of what significance is it? What is its relationship to market value per share?

4. What are the two parts of stockholders' equity in a corporation? Explain the difference between them. What does the balance in retained earnings mean to an investor? Why might a company with a $4 million credit balance in retained earnings need to raise additional capital to finance a $1 million plant?

5. The following dates are associated with a cash dividend of $100,000: July 15, July 31, and August 15. Identify each of the three dates. What is the accounting impact of each date?

6. What is the effect of each of the following on the total stockholders' equity of a corporation: *(a)* declaration of a cash dividend, *(b)* payment of a cash dividend, *(c)* declaration of a stock dividend, and *(d)* issuance of a stock dividend?

7. Distinguish between a small stock dividend and a large stock dividend. How is each accounted for?

8. What is treasury stock? Where does it appear on the balance sheet?

9. Distinguish between extraordinary items and prior period adjustments. Explain why it is important that the two be carefully distinguished.

10. (Based on the chapter appendix) Explain briefly the accounting for stock dividends and stock splits from the investor's point of view.

11. (Based on the chapter appendix) Carefully explain the main problem encountered in classifying marketable securities in the balance sheet.

EXERCISES

Prepare journal entries for declaration and payment of dividends

1. Smith Corporation's stockholders' equity consists of 6,000 authorized, issued, and outstanding shares of 5% preferred stock with a $50 par value and 300,000 authorized shares of $10 par value common stock, of which 240,000 shares are outstanding. Both classes of stock were issued at par. The retained earnings balance was $3,780,000 on January 1, 1989. During 1989, Smith had net income of $27,000. The preferred stock is preferred as to dividends. On December 24, 1989, Smith declared the annual preferred dividend and a 3% dividend on its common shares. All dividends were paid in cash on February 18, 1990. Give all necessary journal entries to record the dividend declaration and payment.

Prepare journal entry for conversion of common stock

2. Pearlie Corporation has outstanding 2,000 shares of $100 par value convertible preferred stock that were issued at par value. Each share is convertible into four shares of $20 stated value common stock. Give the entry to record conversion of all 2,000 preferred shares.

Journalize stock issuance and calling of preferred stock

3. Vancouver, Inc. called in all of its outstanding 1,200 shares of $200 par value preferred stock. The stock was cumulative, entitled to $200 per share plus cumulative dividends in liquidation, and callable at $210. Give the entry to record the calling of the preferred stock, assuming that it was originally issued at par. Give the entry that would have been required if the stock had originally been issued at $206. In both cases, assume that no unpaid cumulative dividends are in arrears and that there are no current dividends to be prorated.

Journalize stock issuance for three situations

4. Tramel Corporation has received $3 million in cash by issuing 20,000 shares of stock. Give the journal entry to record the issuance, assuming that:

a. The stock had a par value of $50 per share.

b. The stock had a stated value of $60 per share.

c. The stock had no par or stated value.

Journalize stock issuance for property

5. Two hundred shares of $100 par value common stock are issued to promoters of a corporation in exchange for land needed by the corporation for a plant site. Experienced appraisers have recently estimated the value of the land to be $34,000. At what amount should the land be recorded on the books?

Determine ending balance in retained earnings after declaration of a dividend

6. Randall Company has outstanding 4,000 shares of cumulative preferred stock with a $5 annual dividend per share and 20,000 shares of common stock without par or stated value. No dividends were paid in 1988 or 1989. At the beginning of 1990, the retained earnings account had a debit balance of $12,000. During 1990, Randall had net income of $185,000. If a dividend of $3 per share is declared on the common stock on December 31, 1990, what is the ending balance in retained earnings?

Prepare journal entry for small stock dividend and large stock dividend

7. Legrant Company has outstanding 400,000 shares of common stock, $10 par value, that were issued at an average price of $20 per share. Retained earnings total $2,600,000. The current market price of the common stock is $40 per share. The total authorized stock consists of 900,000 shares.

    a. Give the required journal entry to record the declaration of a 10% stock dividend.

    b. Give the required journal entry to record a 30% stock dividend.

Determine book value before and after stock dividend

8. Elene Corporation's balance sheet shows total assets of $1,600,000, liabilities of $600,000, and retained earnings of $600,000. Jim Ellis owns 400 shares of Elene's 40,000 outstanding shares of capital stock. Elene now declares and issues a 10% stock dividend. Compute the book value per share in total and of Jim's investment in Elene Corporation:

    a. Before the stock dividend.

    b. After the stock dividend.

Prepare journal entries for stock split and small stock dividend

9. Nelson Company's stockholders' equity consists of 80,000 authorized shares of $20 par value common stock, 40,000 of which have been issued at par, and retained earnings of $400,000. The company now splits its stock, two for one, by calling in the old shares and issuing new $10 par value shares.

    a. Give the required journal entry.

    b. Suppose instead that the company declared and later issued a 10% stock dividend. Give the required journal entries, assuming that the market value on the date of declaration was $25.00 per share.

Journalize treasury stock transaction for three situations

10. Fran Company has outstanding 200,000 shares of $5 stated value common stock, all issued at $6 per share, and retained earnings of $400,000. The company acquired 2,000 shares of its stock from the widow of a deceased stockholder for cash at book value.

    a. Give the entry to record acquisition of the stock.

    b. Give the entry to record the subsequent reissuance of this stock at $10 per share.

    c. Give the entry to record the reissuance of the stock at $7 per share instead of at $10 per share as in **b.**

Prepare journal entries for cash dividends

11. The stockholders' equity section of the balance sheet of Lakewood Corporation on December 31, 1989, shows 300,000 shares of authorized and issued $20 stated value common stock, of which 24,000 shares are held in the treasury. On this date, the board of directors declared a cash dividend of $2 per share to stockholders of record on January 10, payable January 21, 1990. Give the required dated journal entries.

Record stock purchase, stock sale, and receipt of dividends using T-accounts

12. (Based on the chapter appendix.) Black Company purchased as a temporary investment on July 1, 1990, 250 shares of Percy Company common stock at $28 per share plus a total commission of $150. Black received a cash dividend of $1 per share on August 12, 1990. On November 1, Black sold all of the above shares for $35 per share, less total commissions and taxes of $150. Record all of the above in Black Company's T-accounts.

PROBLEMS

Compute ending balance in retained earnings assuming declaration of dividends

8–1. Pall Company has outstanding 6,000 shares of cumulative preferred stock with a $4 annual dividend per share and 20,000 shares of no par value common stock. No dividends were paid in 1990 or 1991. At the beginning of 1992, the company had a deficit of $20,000. During 1992, it had net income of $150,000.

Required:

Assuming that a dividend of $2 per share was declared on the common stock, compute the December 31, 1992, balance in retained earnings.

Prepare stockholders' equity section; determine book values of stock

8–2. The Jennie Company issued all of its 10,000 shares of authorized preferred stock on July 1, 1989, at $210 per share. The preferred stock has a par value and a liquidation value of $200 per share and is entitled to a cumulative basic preference dividend of $16 per share. On July 1, 1989, Jennie also issued its 40,000 authorized shares of $30 stated value common stock at $80 per share.

On June 30, 1991, the end of the company's second fiscal year of operations, its retained earnings amounted to $380,000. No dividends have been declared or paid on either class of stock since the date of issue.

Required:

a. Prepare the stockholders's equity section of the Jennie Company's June 30, 1991, balance sheet.

b. Compute the book value per share of each class of stock.

Compute book values of a stockholder's preferred and common stock

8–3. Zeller Brothers, Inc., is a corporation in which all of the outstanding preferred and common stock is held by the four Zeller brothers. The brothers have an agreement stating that upon the death of one brother, the remaining brothers will purchase from his estate his holdings of stock in the company at book value. The agreement also stipulates that the land owned by the company be valued at fair market value, that inventory be valued at its current replacement cost, and that whatever other adjustments are needed to place the accounts on a sound accounting basis be made prior to computing book value.

The stockholders' equity accounts of the company on June 30, 1990, the date of James Zeller's death, show:

Stockholders' equity:	
Preferred stock—6%, $100 par value; $100 liquidation value; 12,000 shares authorized, issued, and outstanding	$1,200,000
Paid-in capital in excess of par—preferred	60,000
Common stock—no par value; stated value, $5; 180,000 shares authorized, issued, and outstanding	900,000
Paid-in capital from recapitalization	900,000
Retained earnings	120,000
Total stockholders' equity	$3,180,000

The fair market value of the land held by the company and carried in its accounts at $120,000 is $300,000, and the current replacement cost of the inventory is $96,000 more than the amount at which it is carried in the accounts, although no improper accounting is involved. It is also agreed by the three remaining brothers and the accountant representing Mrs. James Zeller that the accounts fail to include a proper accrual of $60,000 for pensions payable to employees. No dividends have been paid on the cumulative preferred stock in the last one-half year.

At the time of his death James Zeller held 6,000 shares of preferred stock and 30,000 shares of common stock.

Required:

Compute the amount which the remaining brothers must pay to the estate of James Zeller for the preferred and common stock which he held at the time of his death.

Prepare statement of retained earnings

8–4. The following information relates to the Ricardo Corporation for the year 1990 or on the dates indicated:

Net income for the year	$ 640,000
Dividends declared on common stock	80,000
Dividends paid on common stock during 1990	100,000
Dividends declared on preferred stock	32,000
Dividends received on investments	8,000
Retained earnings, January 1	1,620,000
Amount over par value received from preferred stock issued during the year	16,000

Required:

Prepare a statement of retained earnings for the year ended December 31, 1990.

Compute book value per share of common stock, compute book value assuming stock dividend, and determine value of investment

8–5. The stockholders' equity section of the Alden Company's June 30, 1990, balance sheet is

Capital stock—common, $50 par value; 15,000 shares authorized; 8,000 shares issued and outstanding	$400,000
Retained earnings	230,000
	$630,000

On June 30, 1990, the board of directors declared a $5 per share cash dividend to stockholders of record as of July 15, payable July 31.

Required:

a. Assuming no change in the amount of retained earnings except that caused by the dividend and no change in the number of shares outstanding between June 30 and July 31, compute the book value per share of common stock:
(1) Just prior to the declaration of the dividend.
(2) Just after the declaration of the dividend.
(3) Just after the payment of the cash dividend.

b. Assume that, instead of a cash dividend, a 5% stock dividend is issued on August 15 and is to be recorded at $70 per share (the market price on the declaration date). Show how this would affect the book value per share, assuming no change in retained earnings except that caused by the dividend.

Prepare stockholders' equity section assuming stock dividend and stock split

c. Assume that Jimmy Brown owned 300 shares of stock in the Alden Company before the stock dividend. Compute the book value of his investment before the stock dividend and after the stock dividend.

8–6. On January 1, 1990, the Lorenzo Corporation's stockholders' equity section appeared as follows:

Stockholders' equity:		
Paid-in capital:		
Preferred stock—$200 par value; authorized, issued, and outstanding, 10,000 shares	$2,000,000	
Common stock—$20 par value; authorized, 100,000 shares; issued and outstanding, 40,000 shares	800,000	$2,800,000
Retained earnings		1,200,000
Total stockholders' equity		$4,000,000

Required:

a. Prepare the stockholders' equity section on July 1, 1990, after the issuance of a 10% stock dividend to common stockholders. Market value per share at date of declaration was $130.

b. Ignore **a,** and prepare the stockholders' equity section on July 1, 1990, after a two-for-one common stock split. Market value per share before the split was $130.

Journalize stock transactions; prepare stockholders' equity section of balance sheet; determine book value

8–7. The stockholders' equity of the Colorado Company as of December 31, 1990, consisted of 35,000 shares of authorized and outstanding $10 par value common stock, paid-in capital in excess of par of $175,000, and retained earnings of $350,000.

Following are selected transactions for 1991:

May	1	Acquired 10,000 shares of its own common stock at $25.
June	1	Reissued 3,000 shares of $28.
Oct.	1	Declared a cash dividend of $1 per share payable to stockholders as of October 14.
Nov.	14	Reissued 4,500 shares at $23.
Dec.	1	Paid the cash dividend declared on October 1.

Net income for the year was $53,200. No other transactions affecting retained earnings occurred during the year.

Required:

a. Prepare journal entries to record the treasury stock and dividend transactions.

b. Prepare the stockholders' equity section of the December 31, 1991, balance sheet.

c. Compute the book value per share as of December 31, 1991.

Present stockholders' equity section of balance sheet

8–8. Selected account balances of the Atwood Company at December 31, 1990, are:

Bonds payable, 7%, due May 1, 1991	$1,200,000
Common stock—no par value; 200,000 shares authorized, issued, and outstanding; stated value of $20 per share	4,000,000
Retained earnings	1,140,000
Dividends payable (in cash, declared December 15 on preferred stock)	32,000
Accrued lawsuit damages	320,000
Preferred stock—8 percent, par value $200; 2,000 shares authorized, issued, and outstanding	400,000
Paid-in capital from donation of plant site	100,000
Paid-in capital in excess of par value—preferred	16,000

Required:

Present in good form the stockholders' equity section of the balance sheet.

Prepare income statement and statement of retained earnings

8–9. Selected accounts of the Claude Company for the year ended December 31, 1991, are:

Sales, net	$3,120,000
Interest expense	160,000
Cash dividends on common stock	320,000
Selling and administrative expense	480,000
Cash dividends on preferred stock	160,000
Rent revenue	880,000
Cost of goods sold	1,280,000
Flood loss (has never occurred before)	480,000
Interest revenue	160,000
Other revenue	240,000
Depreciation and maintenance on rental equipment	320,000
Stock dividend on common stock	800,000
Litigation loss	960,000
Cumulative effect on prior years' income of changing to a different depreciation method (credit)	80,000

Assume the applicable federal income tax rate is 50%. All of the above items of expense, revenue, and loss are includible in the computation of taxable income. The litigation loss resulted from a court award of damages for patent infringement on a product that the company produced and sold in 1988 and 1989 and discontinued in 1989. Retained earnings as of January 1, 1991, were $11.2 million. A total of 10,000 common stock shares were outstanding during the year.

Required:

Prepare an income statement and a statement of retained earnings for 1991.

Prepare income statement and statement of retained earnings

8–10. Selected accounts of the Glenn Corporation for the year ended December 31, 1990, are:

Sales, net	$24,900,000
Interest expense	1,200,000
Cash dividends on preferred stock	1,140,000
Cash dividends on common stock	4,200,000
Selling and administrative expense	1,260,000
Cost of goods sold	13,500,000
Loss from earthquake (extraordinary item).	2,700,000
Service revenue	1,980,000
Depreciation on equipment	2,100,000
Additional federal income taxes for 1987	300,000
Litigation loss	3,000,000

Assume the applicable federal income tax rate is 50%. All of the above items of expense, revenue, and loss are includible in the computation of income taxes payable. The litigation loss resulted from a court award for damages due to patent infringement on a product that Glenn produced in 1984 and 1985 and discontinued in 1986. Retained earnings as of December 31, 1990, were reported as $66 million. One million shares of common stock were outstanding during the year.

Required:

a. Prepare an income statement for 1990.

b. Prepare a statement of retained earnings for 1990.

Record stock transactions using T-accounts, and indicate place in balance sheet

8–11. (Based on the chapter appendix.) The Jenkins Company acquired as a temporary investment on July 15, 1990, 1,500 shares of Peyton Company $100 par value common stock at 98 plus a broker's commission of $350. On August 1, 1990, Jenkins Company received a cash dividend of 75 cents per share. On November 3, 1990, it sold 750 of these shares at $106, less a broker's commission of $270. On December 1, 1990, the Peyton Company issued the shares comprising a 100% stock dividend declared on its common stock on November 18.

Required:

a. Present entries in T-account format to record all of the above data.

b. If management now decides that the remaining shares are to be held for affiliation purposes—Peyton Company has become a major customer—indicate how they should be shown in the balance sheet. Assume that the market value is $67,500.

BUSINESS DECISION PROBLEM 8–1

Compute book values and determine amount of dividends received and effects on stock prices

The stockholders' equity section of the Noble Corporation's balance sheet for June 30, 1990, is shown below:

Paid-in capital:	
Common stock, $10 par value; authorized 240,000 shares;	
issued and outstanding 96,000 shares	$ 960,000
Paid-in capital in excess of par value	480,000
Total paid-in capital	$1,440,000
Retained earnings	600,000
Total stockholders' equity	$2,040,000

On July 1, 1990, the corporation's directors declared a 10% stock dividend distributable on August 2 to stockholders of record on July 16. On November 1, 1990, the directors voted a $1 per share annual cash dividend payable on December 2 to stockholders of record on November 16. For four years prior to 1990, the corporation had paid an annual cash dividend of $1.05.

Joe Fish owns 9,600 shares of Noble Corporation's common stock, which he purchased five years ago. The market value of his stock was $20 per share on July 1, 1990, and $18.18 per share on July 16, 1990.

Required:

a. What is the book value (total and per share) of Fish's shares on June 30, 1990, and on August 2, 1990 (after he receives his dividend shares)?

b. What amount of cash dividends will Fish receive in 1990? How does this amount differ from the amount of cash dividends Fish received in the previous four years?

c. For what logical reason did the price of the stock drop from $20.00 to $18.18 on July 16, 1990?

d. Is Fish better off as a result of the stock dividend and the $1 cash dividend than he would have been if he had just received the $1.05 dividend? Why?

9

DEBT FINANCING AND BOND INVESTMENTS

LEARNING OBJECTIVES

After studying this chapter, you should be able to:

1. Account for notes receivable and payable, including calculation of interest.
2. Record the discounting of a customer's note at a bank.
3. Describe the features of bonds and tell how bonds differ from shares of stock.
4. List the advantages and disadvantages of financing with long-term debt and prepare examples showing how financial leverage is employed.
5. Explain how interest rates affect bond prices and what causes a bond to sell at a premium or discount.
6. Apply the concept of present value to compute the price of a bond.
7. Prepare journal entries to account for bonds payable.
8. Prepare journal entries to account for bond investments.
9. Define and use correctly the new terms in the glossary.

In previous chapters you learned that corporations obtain cash for recurring business operations from stock issuances and profitable operations. Short-term borrowing can also be used to obtain cash. However, when situations arise that require large amounts of cash, such as the purchase of a building, corporations also raise cash from long-term borrowing, for example, by issuing bonds. The issuing of bonds results in a Bonds Payable account. After discussing short-term financing, the first part of this chapter discusses the issuing of bonds and accounting for bonds payable.

Since corporations are legal entities, they, like individuals, can invest in stocks and bonds issued by other corporations that are regularly traded on national exchanges. These types of investments can offer a rate of return substantially greater than a savings account. The second part of this chapter discusses bond investments.

SHORT-TERM FINANCING

Objective 1: Account for notes receivable and payable, including calculation of interest

Why would a business need short-term financing; that is, why would it need to use the bank's or some other creditor's money for short periods of time? A business usually expects the cash inflow from the sale of goods or services to exceed the cash outflow for the purchase of goods for resale or for the purchase of supplies, labor services, utilities, and so on. Also, some expenses, such as depreciation expense, do not involve an outflow of cash in the current period. But at certain times in the life of a business the inflow of cash may not be greater than the outflow of cash from operations. This can be caused by: (1) the delay in the receipt of cash due to giving customers credit terms on amounts due (though the business at least partly offsets this by the use of credit on its own purchases in order to delay the payment of cash); (2) the seasonal buildup of inventory, such as that which occurs in department stores just before the Christmas holidays; or (3) an expansion in operations caused by an expected future increase in sales. Some of the ways in which a business can obtain short-term financing are discussed below.

Short-Term Commercial Bank Loans

When a business needs additional financing it may go to a commercial bank to borrow on a short-term basis. When the loan is granted, the bank normally asks the borrower to sign a promissory note. A **promissory note** is an unconditional promise in writing made and signed by the borrower (the **maker**) obligating the borrower to pay the lender (the **payee**) or someone else who legally acquired the note a certain sum of money on demand or at a definite time. Normally, only the maker and the payee are parties to the instrument, but sometimes others who legally acquire the note or guarantee payment also become parties.

Nature of interest. Most notes bear an explicit (or stated) charge for interest. **Interest** is the fee charged for the use of money through time. It is an expense to the maker of the note and a revenue to the payee of the note. In commercial transactions interest is commonly figured on the basis of 360 days per year. The elapsed time in a fraction of a year between two stated days is computed by counting the exact number of days—omitting the day the money is borrowed but counting the day it is paid back. A note falling due on a Sunday or a holiday is due on the following business day.

Assume that we desire to calculate the interest on a $1,000 note with an interest rate of 6% and a life of 60 days. It can be done thus:

$$\text{Principal} \times \text{Rate of interest} \times \text{Time} = \text{Interest}$$

$$\$1,000 \times \frac{6}{100} \times \frac{60}{360} = \$10$$

Giving your own note to the bank. In instances in which a borrower presents his or her own noninterest-bearing note to a bank with a request for a loan, the bank computes the amount of interest on the face value of the note, deducts the amount computed from the face value, and gives the balance, the proceeds, to the borrower. The amount deducted is often called the bank discount or the **discount on notes payable,** and the process of computing the amount is referred to as discounting. To illustrate this process, assume that a bank discounts a customer's $20,000, 90-day, noninterest-bearing note at 12%. The calculation of interest is:

$$\$20,000 \times \frac{12}{100} \times \frac{90}{360} = \$600$$

The $600 interest is deducted from the $20,000, and the borrower receives $19,400. Assuming the above transaction occurred on December 1, 1990, it would be recorded by the borrower as follows:

Cash		Notes Payable—Discount		Notes Payable	
12/1 19,400		12/1 600			12/1 20,000

Note that the borrower does not receive $20,000, but $19,400. Since the borrower will pay $600 for the use of this sum for a period of 90 days, the rate of interest is actually higher than 12%. (If $600 is the interest on $20,000 at 12% for 90 days, then $600 is more than 12% on $19,400 for 90 days.) Note also that the bank must discount this note in order to introduce interest into the transaction. If the bank advanced $20,000 on this noninterest-bearing note, it would not earn any interest from this loan because at maturity it will receive only $20,000.

The Notes Payable—Discount account used above is a contra account to Notes Payable. Assuming that December 31, 1990, is the end of the borrower's accounting period, it would be necessary to record interest expense for the month of December as follows (the debit and credit are dated 12/31, and the debit balance of $600 shown in Notes Payable—Discount is the balance in the account *before* making the latest entry):

Interest Expense		Notes Payable—Discount	
12/31 200		Bal. 600	12/31 200

In the current liability section of the December 31, 1990, balance sheet, the note and the discount would appear as follows:

Notes payable $20,000
Less: Discount 400 $19,600

When the note is paid at maturity the accounts would be affected as follows (maturity date is March 1, 1991):

Cash				Notes Payable—Discount			
Bal.	xxx	3/1	20,000	Bal. after 12/31 adjustment	400	3/1	400

Notes Payable				Interest Expense			
3/1	20,000	Bal.	20,000	3/1	400		

In journal entry form this transaction would appear as follows:

Notes Payable 20,000
Interest Expense   400
    Cash. 20,000
    Notes Payable—Discount   400
To record payment of the note.

The above changes reduce the Notes Payable—Discount and Notes Payable accounts to zero balances. Notice that the difference in the cash paid out ($20,000) and that originally received ($19,400) is equal to the total interest expense ($600). The interest relates to a 90-day period, 30 days of which fall in the year ending December 31, 1990, and 60 days of which fall in the following year. Thus, the amount charged to interest expense should be $200 in 1990 and $400 in 1991.

An alternative approach the borrower may use in the loan arrangement with the bank is to compute interest on the amount requested, add this to the amount requested, and draw a note for the total of the two. Thus, the borrower would sign a 90-day, noninterest-bearing note for $20,600 and would receive $20,000. At the date of borrowing the entry would be:

Cash		Notes Payable—Discount		Notes Payable	
(a) 20,000		(a) 600			(a) 20,600

The borrower could use a second alternative loan arrangement by giving a $20,000, 90-day, 12% interest-bearing note. At the date of borrowing the required entry is:

Cash		Notes Payable	
(a) 20,000			(a) 20,000

At maturity the borrower pays both the face amount of the note and interest at the rate stated in the note on that face amount (a total of $20,600). The $600 paid over and above the $20,000 face of the note represents interest expense to the borrower.

Notes Arising from Business Transactions

A company may have notes receivable and/or notes payable arising from transactions with customers or suppliers. When a company is the maker of a note with a supplier as the payee, the company has *received* short-term financing from that supplier. When a company is the payee of a note and a customer is the maker, the company has *supplied* short-term financing to that customer. A note may result from the conversion of an overdue open account or directly from merchandise transactions. To illustrate, assume that on October 6, 1990, Fox Company, the payee, receives from Kent Company, the maker, a 60-day, $18,000 note. The interest rate is 12%, and the note results from the previous sale (on October 4) of merchandise by Fox Company to Kent Company. The interest will be earned over the life of the note and will not be paid until maturity, December 5, 1990. The entries for both the payee and the maker are:

FOX COMPANY, PAYEE

To record sale:

Accounts Receivable				Sales		
10/4	18,000				10/4	18,000

To record receipt of note:

Notes Receivable				Accounts Receivable		
10/6	18,000		Bal.	18,000	10/6	18,000

To record receipt of principal and interest:

Cash				Notes Receivable		
12/5	18,360		Bal.	18,000	12/5	18,000

Interest Revenue	
	12/5 360

KENT COMPANY, MAKER

To record purchase:

Purchases				Accounts Payable		
10/4	18,000				10/4	18,000

To record giving of note:

Accounts Payable				Notes Payable		
10/6	18,000	Bal.	18,000		10/6	18,000

To record payment of principal and interest:

Notes Payable				Cash		
12/5	18,000	Bal.	18,000	Bal. xxx	12/5	18,360

Interest Expense	
12/5	360

A note becomes a **dishonored note** if the maker fails to pay it at maturity. The payee of the note may debit either Accounts Receivable or Dishonored Notes Receivable and credit Notes Receivable for the face of the note. If interest is due, it should be debited to the same account to which the dishonored note is debited and credited to Interest Revenue. The maker should merely debit the amount of interest incurred to Interest Expense and credit Interest Payable. When a note cannot be paid at maturity, the maker sometimes either pays the interest on the original note or includes it in the face of a new note given to take the place of the old note.

Discounting Notes Receivable

Objective 2: Record the discounting of a customer's note at a bank

When a company issues its own note payable to a bank, it is directly liable to the bank at the maturity date of the loan. Such notes payable are shown in the balance sheet as liabilities.

Instead of borrowing directly, a company may use another method of obtaining short-term financing from a bank—**discounting a note receivable.** A note receivable held by the company may be endorsed and then sold to a bank. The bank discounts the note and gives the company cash in exchange for it. The company that sells the note receivable is contingently, instead of directly, liable to the lending bank; that is, the company must pay the bank the amount due at the **maturity date** only if the maker of the note fails to pay the obligation.

The cash proceeds from notes receivable discounted are computed as follows:

1. Determine the **maturity value** of the note (face value plus interest). This is the amount the bank will collect at maturity. For a noninterest-bearing note, the face of the note equals the maturity value. For an interest-bearing note, the face of the note plus interest for the life of the note equals the maturity value.
2. Determine the **discount period;** that is, count the exact number of days from the date of sale of the note to the date of maturity. Exclude

the date of sale but include the date of maturity in the count. The discount period, of course, can never be longer than the life of the note.
3. Using the **discount rate** charged by the bank, compute the discount on the maturity value (principal plus interest) for the discount period.
4. Deduct the bank discount from the maturity value to find the cash proceeds.

The contingent liability for the notes receivable discounted is usually shown in a note to the financial statements. If the original maker does not pay the bank at the maturity date, the company that sold the note to the bank will be held liable.

Example. Assume that on May 4, 1990, Carlson Company received a $10,000 note from Thomas (the maker). The note bears interest at 12% and matures in 60 days from May 4. On May 14, 1990, Carlson Company (the endorser) sold the note to the Michigan National Bank, which discounted the note at 14%. The discount and the cash proceeds are determined as follows:

Face value of note	$10,000.00
Add: Interest at 12% for 60 days	200.00
Maturity value	$10,200.00
Less: Bank discount on $10,200 at 14% for 50 days	198.33
Cash proceeds	$10,001.67

The entry for Carlson would be as follows:

Cash		Interest Revenue	
5/14 10,001.67			5/14 1.67

Notes Receivable	
5/4 10,000.00	5/14 10,000.00

If the book value of the note had exceeded the proceeds, the difference would have been debited to an Interest Expense account.

Balance sheet presentation of notes receivable discounted. In the above illustration a balance sheet prepared for Carlson Company as of December 31, 1990, should show a contingent liability in the amount of $10,000 for notes receivable discounted. Assume that the total of all notes receivable that have not been discounted is $60,000. An acceptable method of presenting this information in the balance sheet is:

Assets

Current assets:
Cash	$ xx,xxx
Accounts receivable	xx,xxx
Notes receivable (Note 1)	60,000

Note 1: At December 31, 1990, the company is contingently liable for a customer's $10,000 note receivable that it has endorsed and discounted at the local bank. This note is not included in the $60,000 of notes shown.

313

Although the contingent liability is actually for the note plus the accrued interest to maturity ($10,200), for convenience it is customarily shown only for the face value of the note ($10,000).

Discounted notes receivable paid by maker. When a note receivable has been sold, it is usually the duty of the endorsee (the holder) to present the note to the maker for payment at maturity. Sometimes the note designates the place of payment. If the maker pays the endorsee (the bank in the above illustrations) at maturity, the endorser is thereby relieved of contingent liability. If the note is not paid at maturity, the endorsee can collect from the endorser, who, in turn, can try to collect from the maker.

Assume that Thomas (above) pays his $10,000 note plus interest of $200 to the Michigan National Bank on July 3, 1990—the note's maturity date. Carlson Company, which sold the note to the bank, has been relieved of the possibility of being held liable for the note.

If Thomas dishonors the note at maturity instead of paying it, the Michigan National Bank will collect the principal ($10,000), interest ($200), and any protest fee (assume it is $5) from Carlson Company. Carlson Company will show the following changes in its accounts:

Accounts Receivable		Cash		
10,205		Bal.	xxx	10,205

Carlson Company will then try to collect $10,205 from Thomas. If this cannot be done, the $10,205 should be removed from the Accounts Receivable account and treated as a loss from uncollectible accounts.

LONGER-TERM FINANCING

Although it is conceivable that once a company begins operations it can finance the acquisition of additional long-term or plant assets out of operating cash flows, this is often not possible. It is quite common for companies to use long-term sources of financing to acquire such assets. Chapter 8 discussed the use of capital stock to acquire long-term funds. This chapter discusses some of the more common forms of long-term debt financing.

Notes Payable

Notes payable may be either short term or long term, but they are usually short term. Since these have been discussed earlier, we will not deal with them again in this section except to say that when payables (or receivables) have maturities exceeding approximately one year they are to be recorded at their present cash value.[1] The procedure is similar to that used in calcu-

---

[1]"Interest on Receivables and Payables," *APB Opinion No. 21* (New York: AICPA, 1971).

lating the proceeds of a discounted bank loan. To illustrate, assume that we are the maker of a $1,000 face value note bearing no explicit rate of interest, and the note is due one year from its date. (Even though this does not exceed "approximately one year" and technically would not have to be recorded at its present value, we will assume that the company chooses to do so). Assume also that the rate of interest to be used in reducing this note to its present value is 16%. To solve for the present value, we have to ask the question, "What amount, if invested at 16%, would grow to $1,000 one year from now?" If we let x equal that amount, our formula would be:

$$x + 0.16x = \$1,000$$

$$1.16x = \$1,000$$

$$x = \frac{\$1,000}{1.16}$$

$$x = \$862.07$$

Assuming that the note payable resulted from the purchase of a machine, it would be recorded as follows:

Machinery		Notes Payable—Discount		Notes Payable	
(a) 862.07		*(a)* 137.93			*(a)* 1,000

At the due date, $1,000 would be paid to the payee and $137.93 would be (or would have been) recorded as interest expense. The accounting for the interest in this type of transaction is quite similar to that used when a company discounts its own note at the bank.

Mortgage Notes Payable

Another form of long-term financing is a **mortgage note payable;** a note payable that is secured by a **mortgage**, that is, an obligation to give up certain property that has been pledged to the payee in case the maker defaults on the payments. Most of us become familiar with this form of financing when we purchase a home. Also, business firms sometimes use this method of financing when they acquire assets such as buildings.

This form of financing will be illustrated by assuming that a company acquires a small building. The company makes a constant lump-sum payment each month (exclusive of real estate taxes) which at first pays mostly interest and very little principal. Assume that the mortgage on the building (acquired in 1977) is $35,000, that the interest rate is 8%, and that the life of the note is 25 years. There are mortgage payment schedule books which indicate that the monthly payment for principal and interest is

$271. Here is how the first two months' and the last month's payments are applied:

	Monthly Payment	Interest at 8 Percent on Principal Balance	Payment on Principal ($271 Less Interest)	Principal Balance
Date of purchase				$35,000.00
1st month	$271	$233.33	$ 37.67	34,962.33
2nd month	271	233.08	37.92	34,924.41
300th month	271	2.00	269.00	0

Notice that interest is calculated on the latest principal balance. For instance, when the first $271 payment is made, interest is calculated as follows:

$$\frac{\$35,000 \times 0.08}{12} = \$233.33$$

It is necessary to divide by 12 because the interest rate is 8% per *year* and we are calculating the amount for one *month*. The excess of the payment over the interest is applied against the principal ($37.67 in the first payment above). Thus, the principal balance decreases slowly (but more rapidly each month) so that the last $271 payment at the end of 25 years pays interest (approximately $2) on the remaining principal balance (approximately $269) and then reduces the principal balance to zero.

Since the building is pledged (or mortgaged) as security for the loan, if the company does not keep up the payments, the party to which payment is due can foreclose on the mortgage and take over the building. As a practical matter, many lending institutions are quite lenient in allowing a few back payments to be made up rather than take this drastic step.

Bonds Payable

A **bond** is a long-term debt owed by its issuer. Physical evidence of the debt lies in a negotiable **bond certificate.** Long-term notes usually mature in 10 years or less, while bond maturities often run for 20 years or more. A bond derives its value primarily from two promises made by the borrower to the lender, or bondholder. The borrower promises to pay (1) the **face value** or **principal** amount of the bond on a specific maturity date in the future; and (2) periodic interest at a specified rate on face value at stated dates, usually semiannually, until the maturity date.

A bond issue generally consists of numerous $1,000 bonds, rather than one very large bond. For example, a company seeking to borrow $100,000 would issue one hundred $1,000 bonds, rather than one $100,000 bond. Investers with smaller amounts of cash to invest are able to purchase the bonds.

Comparing Bonds with Stock

*Objective 3:
Describe the
features of bonds
and tell how bonds
differ from shares
of stock*

A bond differs from a share of stock in several ways:

1. A bond is a debt or liability of the issuer, while a share of stock is a unit of ownership.
2. A bond has a maturity date when it must be paid. A share of stock does not mature; stock remains outstanding indefinitely unless the company decides to retire it.
3. Most bonds require stated periodic interest payments by the company. In contrast, dividends to stockholders are payable only when declared; even preferred dividends need not be paid in a particular period if the board of directors so decides.
4. Bond interest is deductible by the issuer in computing both net income and taxable income, while dividends are not deductible in either computation.

Selling (Issuing) Bonds

A company seeking to borrow millions of dollars generally will not be able to borrow from a single lender. In such an instance, the company will sell (issue) bonds to the public to secure the funds needed. Usually a bond issue is sold through an investment company or banker, called an **underwriter.** The underwriter performs many tasks for the issuer, such as advertising, selling, and delivering the bonds to the purchasers. The underwriter often guarantees the issuer a fixed price for the bonds, expecting to earn a profit by selling the bonds for more than the fixed price.

When bonds are sold to the public, many purchasers are involved. Rather than deal with each purchaser individually, the issuing corporation appoints a trustee to represent the bondholders. The **trustee** usually is a bank or trust company. The main duty of the trustee is to see that the borrower fulfills the provisions of the bond indenture. A **bond indenture** is the contract or loan agreement under which the bonds are issued. The indenture deals with matters such as the interest rate, maturity date and maturity amount, possible restrictions on dividends, repayment plans, and other provisions relating to the debt. If bond indenture provisions are not adhered to, the issuer is said to be in default. The trustee is expected to take action to force the issuer to comply with the indenture.

Characteristics of Bonds

All bonds have two common characteristics: (1) they promise to pay cash or other assets; and (2) they come due, or mature. In other respects, bonds may differ; they may be secured or unsecured bonds, registered or unregistered (bearer) bonds, and term or serial bonds. These differences and others are discussed below. Certain bond features are matters of legal necessity, such as the way interest is paid and ownership is transferred.

Such differences usually do not affect the issue price of the bonds. Other features, such as convertibility into common stock, are designed to make the bonds more attractive to potential purchasers. These added features, called "sweeteners," may increase the issue price of a bond.

Secured bonds. A **secured bond** is a bond for which specific property has been pledged to ensure its payment. Mortgage bonds are the most common type of secured bonds. A mortgage is a legal claim (lien) on a specific property which gives the bondholder the right to sell the pledged property if the company fails to make required payments.

Unsecured bonds. An **unsecured bond** is called a **debenture bond,** or simply a **debenture.** A debenture is a bond backed only by the general creditworthiness of the issuer, not by a lien on any specific property. A financially sound company will be able to issue debentures more easily than a company experiencing financial difficulty.

Registered bonds. A **registered bond** is a bond in which the owner's name appears on both the bond certificate and in the record of bond owners kept by the bond issuer or its agent, the registrar. Bonds may be registered as to principal (or face value of the bond) or as to both principal and interest. If a bond is registered as to both, interest on the bond is paid by check. Most bonds in our economy are registered as to principal only. Ownership of registered bonds is transferred by endorsing the bond and registering it in the new owner's name. Registered bonds are easily replaced if lost or stolen.

Unregistered (bearer) bonds. An **unregistered (bearer) bond** is assumed to be the property of its holder or bearer, since the owner's name does not appear on the bond certificate or in a separate record. Ownership is transferred by physical delivery of the bond.

Coupon bonds. A **coupon bond** is a bond not registered as to interest. A coupon bond carries detachable coupons for the interest it pays. At the end of each interest period, the coupon for the period is clipped and presented to a stated party, usually a bank, for collection.

Term bonds and serial bonds. A **term bond** is a bond that matures on the same date as all other bonds in a given bond issue. **Serial bonds** are bonds in a given bond issue with maturities spread over several dates. For instance, one fourth of the bonds may mature on December 31, 1991, another one fourth on December 31, 1992, and so on.

Callable bonds. A **callable bond** contains a provision that gives the issuer the right to call (buy back) the bond before its maturity date. The provision is similar to the call provision in some preferred stocks. A company might exercise this call right if outstanding bonds bear interest at a much higher rate than the company would have to pay if it issued new but similar bonds now. The exercise of the call provision normally requires the company to pay the bondholder a call premium of about $30 to $70 per $1,000 bond. A **call premium** is the price paid in excess of face value that the issuer of bonds is required to pay to redeem (call) bonds before their maturity date.

Convertible bonds. A **convertible bond** is a bond that may be exchanged, at the bondholder's option, for shares of stock of the issuing corporation. A convertible bond has a stipulated conversion rate of some number of shares for each $1,000 bond. Any type of bond may be convertible, but this feature usually is added to rather risky debenture bonds to make them more attractive to investors.

Bonds with stock warrants. A **stock warrant** allows the bondholder to purchase shares of common stock at a fixed price for a stated period of time. Warrants issued with long-term debt may be detachable or nondetachable. A bond with *nondetachable warrants* is virtually the same as a convertible bond; the holder must surrender the bond in order to acquire the common stock. *Detachable warrants* allow bondholders to keep their bonds and still purchase shares of stock through exercise of the warrants.

Advantages of Issuing Debt

Objective 4:
List the advantages and disadvantages of financing with long-term debt and prepare examples showing how financial leverage is employed

Several advantages come from raising cash by issuing bonds rather than stock. First, the current stockholders of a corporation do not have to dilute or surrender their control of the company if needed funds can be obtained by borrowing rather than issuing more shares of stock. It may also be less expensive to issue debt rather than additional stock because the interest payments made to bondholders are tax deductible while dividends are not. But probably the most important reason is that the use of debt may increase the earnings of stockholders through favorable financial leverage.

Favorable financial leverage. A company has **favorable financial leverage** when borrowed funds are used to increase earnings per share (EPS) of common stock. Increased EPS usually result from earning a higher rate of return than the rate of interest paid for the borrowed money. For example, suppose a company borrowed money at 10% and earned a 15% rate of return. The 5% difference increases earnings.

A more complex example of favorable financial leverage is provided in Illustration 9.1. The two companies in the illustration are identical in every respect except in the way they are financed. Company A issued only capital stock, while Company B issued equal amounts of 10% bonds and capital stock. Both companies have $20,000,000 of assets, and both earned $4,000,000 of income from operations. If we divide income from operations by assets ($4,000,000 ÷ $20,000,000), we see that both companies earned 20% on assets employed. Yet B's stockholders fared far better than A's. The ratio of net income to stockholders' equity is 18% for B, while it is only 12% for A.

Assume that both companies issued their stock at the beginning of 1990 at $10 per share. B's $1.80 EPS are 50% greater than A's $1.20 EPS. This EPS difference probably would cause B's shares to sell at a substantially higher market price than A's shares. B's larger EPS would also allow a larger dividend on B's shares.

Illustration 9.1
FAVORABLE FINANCIAL LEVERAGE

COMPANIES A AND B CONDENSED STATEMENTS
Balance Sheets
January 1, 1990

	Company A	Company B
Total assets	$20,000,000	$20,000,000
Bonds payable, 10%		$10,000,000
Stockholders' equity (capital stock)	$20,000,000	10,000,000
Total equities	$20,000,000	$20,000,000

Income Statements
For the Year Ended December 31, 1990

	Company A	Company B
Net income from operations	$ 4,000,000	$ 4,000,000
Interest expense		1,000,000
Net income before income taxes	$ 4,000,000	$ 3,000,000
Income taxes (40%)	1,600,000	1,200,000
Net income	$ 2,400,000	$ 1,800,000
Number of common shares outstanding	2,000,000	1,000,000
Earnings per share (EPS)	$1.20	$1.80
Rate of return on assets employed		
(both companies $4,000,000/$20,000,000)	20%	20%
Rate of return on stockholders' equity:		
Company A ($2,400,000/$20,000,000)	12%	
Company B ($1,800,000/$10,000,000)		18%

Company B, in the above illustration, is employing financial leverage, or is said to be **trading on the equity.** The company is using its stockholders' equity as a basis for securing funds on which a fixed return is paid. Company B expects to earn more from the use of such funds than their fixed after-tax cost, and as a result, Company B increases its rate of return on stockholders' equity and EPS.[2]

Disadvantages of Issuing Debt

Several disadvantages accompany the use of debt financing. First, the borrower has a fixed interest payment that must be met each period to avoid default. Use of debt also reduces a company's ability to sustain a major loss. For example, suppose that both Company A and Company B mentioned above sustain losses for 1990 of $11,000,000. At the end of 1990, Company A will still have $9,000,000 of stockholders' equity and can continue operations with a chance of recovery, as shown below. Company B, on the other hand, would have negative stockholders' equity of $1,000,000 (shown below), and the bondholders could force the company to liquidate if B could not make interest payments as they came due.

---

[2]Issuing bonds is only one method of using leverage. Other methods of using financial leverage include issuing preferred stock or long-term notes.

Partial Balance Sheets
December 31, 1990

	Company A	Company B
Stockholders' equity:		
Paid-in capital:		
Common stock.	$ 20,000,000	$ 10,000,000
Retained earnings	(11,000,000)	(11,000,000)
Total stockholders' equity	$ 9,000,000	$ (1,000,000)

Debt financing also causes a company to experience unfavorable financial leverage when income from operations falls below a certain level. **Unfavorable financial leverage** results when the cost of borrowed funds exceeds the revenue they generate; it is the opposite of favorable financial leverage. In the above example, if income from operations fell to $1,000,000, the rates of return on stockholders' equity would be 3% for A and zero for B, as shown in the schedule below:

Income Statements
For the Year Ended December 31, 1990

	Company A	Company B
Net income from operations	$1,000,000	$1,000,000
Interest expense		1,000,000
Net income before income taxes	$1,000,000	$ –0–
Income taxes (40%)	400,000	–0–
Net income	$ 600,000	$ –0–
Rate of return on stockholders' equity:		
Company A ($600,000/$20,000,000) . . .	3%	
Company B ($0/$10,000,000)		0%

Another disadvantage of issuing debt is that loan agreements often require the maintenance of a certain amount of working capital (Current assets − Current liabilities) and place limitations on dividends and additional borrowings.

Accounting for Bonds

When a company issues bonds, it incurs a long-term liability on which periodic interest payments must be made, usually twice a year. If interest dates fall on other than balance sheet dates, interest will need to be accrued in the proper periods. The following example illustrates the accounting for bonds issued at face value.

On December 31, 1990, Smith Company, with an accounting year ending on December 31, issued $100,000 face value of 10-year, 12% bonds for cash of $100,000. The bonds are dated December 31, 1990, call for semiannual interest payments on June 30 and December 31, and mature on December 31, 2000. Smith Company made all required cash payments when due. The entries for the 10 years are summarized below.

On December 31, 1990, the date of issuance:

```
1990
Dec. 31  Cash . . . . . . . . . . . . . . . . . . . . . . .   100,000
             Bonds Payable  . . . . . . . . . . . . . . . .          100,000
         To record bonds issued at face value.
```

On each June 30 and December 31 for 10 years, beginning June 30, 1991:

```
June 30
and
Dec. 31  Bond Interest Expense
             ($100,000 × 0.12 × 1/2) . . . . . . . . . . . .   6,000
             Cash . . . . . . . . . . . . . . . . . . .              6,000
         To record periodic interest payment.
```

On December 31, 2000, the maturity date:

```
2000
Dec. 31  Bonds Payable  . . . . . . . . . . . . . . . . .   100,000
             Cash . . . . . . . . . . . . . . . . . . . .          100,000
         To record bond redemption.
```

Note that no adjusting entries are needed when an interest payment date falls on the last day of the accounting period. The income statement for each of the 10 years 1991 to 2000 would show Bond Interest Expense of $12,000; the balance sheet at the end of each of the years 1990 to 98 would report Bonds Payable of $100,000 in long-term liabilities. At the end of 1999, the bonds would be reclassified as a current liability because they will be paid within the next year.

But the real world is seldom so uncomplicated. For example, Smith's fiscal year may end on October 31. If so, the June 30 entry remains unchanged, but an adjusting entry is needed on October 31 to accrue interest for the four months July through October. That entry would read:

```
1991
Oct. 31  Bond Interest Expense
             ($100,000 × 0.12 × 4/12) . . . . . . . . . . . .   4,000
             Bond Interest Payable . . . . . . . . . . . . .          4,000
         To accrue four months' interest expense.
```

The December 31 entry would then read:

```
1991
Dec. 31  Bond Interest Expense
             ($100,000 × 0.12 × 2/12)  . . . . . . . . . . .   2,000
             Bond Interest Payable  . . . . . . . . . . . . .   4,000
             Cash . . . . . . . . . . . . . . . . . . . . .          6,000
         To record semiannual interest payment.
```

Each year similar entries would be made for the semiannual payments and the fiscal year-end accrual. The $4,000 Bond Interest Payable account would be reported as a current liability on the October 31 balance sheet for each year.

Bonds issued at face value between interest dates.   Bonds are not always issued on the date they start to bear interest. An issue might be delayed several weeks or months for many reasons, such as expected changes in economic conditions. When bonds are issued between interest dates, the purchaser is required to pay for the interest accrued since the preceding interest date (or the date of the bonds if issued during the first interest period). This accrued interest payment is necessary because the issuer of outstanding bonds is required to pay investors a full six months' interest at each interest date. The bonds are reported to be selling at a stated price "plus accrued interest."

Suppose Smith Company issued its bonds on April 30, 1991, instead of on December 31, 1990. The entry required is:

```
1991
Apr. 30  Cash  . . . . . . . . . . . . . . . . . . . . .   104,000
               Bonds Payable . . . . . . . . . . . . . . .          100,000
               Bond Interest Payable
                 ($100,000 × 0.12 × 4/12) . . . . . . . . .            4,000
             To record bonds issued at face value plus
             accrued interest.
```

This entry records the cash received for the accrued interest as a liability. The entry required on June 30, 1991, when the full six months' interest is paid is:

```
1991
June 30  Bond Interest Expense . . . . . . . . . . . . . .    2,000
         Bond Interest Payable  . . . . . . . . . . . . . .    4,000
               Cash . . . . . . . . . . . . . . . . . . . .          6,000
             To record bond interest payment.
```

This entry records $2,000 interest expense on the $100,000 of bonds that were outstanding for two months. The $4,000 is the amount previously collected from the bondholders on April 30 as accrued interest and is now being returned to them.

Bond Prices and Interest Rates

Objective 5: Explain how interest rates affect bond prices and what causes a bond to sell at a premium or discount

The price of a bond issue sold to investors often differs from its face value. A difference between face value and price will exist whenever the market rate of interest differs from the contract rate of interest on the bonds. The **contract rate of interest** is stated in the bond indenture and printed on the face of each bond and is also called the **stated, coupon,** or **nominal rate.** The contract rate is used to determine the actual amount of cash that will be paid each interest period. The **market interest rate,** also called the **effective interest** or **yield rate,** is the minimum rate of interest investors are willing to accept on bonds of a particular risk category. The market rate fluctuates from day to day, responding to the supply and demand for money.

Contract and market rates of interest are likely to differ. The contract rate must be set before the bonds are actually sold to allow time for such things as printing the bonds. By the time the bonds are sold and the market rate becomes known, the established contract rate could be higher or lower than the fluctuating market rate. *If the contract rate is higher than the market rate, the bonds will sell for more than face value.* Investors will be attracted to bonds offering a contract rate greater than the market rate for such bonds and will bid up their price. *If the contract rate is lower than the market rate, the bonds will sell for less than face value.* Investors will not be interested in bonds bearing a contract rate less than the market rate unless the bonds' price falls. The amount a bond sells for above face value is called a **premium;** if sold for less than face value, the reduction is called a **discount.**

The effect of selling a bond at a premium or discount is to adjust the contract rate of interest on the bond to the market rate. To illustrate, using a short-term note, assume that you paid the Nance Company $9,800 for its $10,000, 10% note that matures in one year. The contract interest rate is 10%. But, if Nance pays the note at maturity, the effective rate of interest in the transaction is about 12.2%. Your actual interest earned is $1,200—the difference between the amount collected at the end of one year, $11,000 (principal plus interest), and the amount invested, $9,800. The effective rate of interest is 12.2% ($1,200/$9,800) per annum, simple interest.

Computing Bond Prices

Objective 6:
Apply the concept of present value to compute the price of a bond

Computing long-term bond prices is a more complex process than finding the effective rate of interest on a one-year note at simple interest. The process involves finding present values by using compound interest. The concept of present value is explained in the Appendix to this chapter. If you do not understand the present value concept, you should read the Appendix before continuing.

To compute the price investors will pay for a given bond issue, compute the present value of the bonds. Present value is computed by discounting promised cash flows in the bonds—principal and interest—using the market or effective interest rate. Market rate is used because the bonds must yield at least this rate or investors will invest in alternative investments. The life of the bonds is stated in terms of interest periods, which indicate how frequently interest is compounded. The interest rate used is the effective rate *per interest period*, which often is found by dividing the annual rate by the number of times interest is paid per year.

Bonds issued at face value. Specific steps involved in computing the price of a bond are illustrated by an example. Assume $100,000 face value of 12% bonds are issued by Rex Company to yield 12%. The bonds are dated and issued on July 1, 1990; call for semiannual interest payments; and mature on July 1, 1993. The bonds will sell at face value because they offer 12% and investors seek 12%. There is no reason to offer a premium or demand a discount. One way to prove the bonds would be sold at face value is by showing that their present value is $100,000:

	Present Value Factor	Present Value
Principal of $100,000 due in six periods multiplied by present value factor for 6% from Table II, Appendix C (end of text)	$100,000 × 0.70496 =	$ 70,496
Interest of $6,000 due at end of each of six periods multiplied by present value factor for 6% from Table III, Appendix C (end of text). . . .	$6,000 × 4.91732 =	29,504
Total price (present value)		$100,000

The schedule shows that if investors seek an effective rate of 6% per six-month period, they should pay $100,000 for these bonds. When the bonds are sold on July 1, 1990, the entry required debits Cash and credits Bonds Payable for $100,000.

Bonds issued at a discount. Assume the Rex Company bonds are sold to yield the market rate of 14%—actually 7% per semiannual period. The present value and selling price of the bonds is computed as follows:

	Present Value Factor	Present Value
Principal of $100,000 due in six periods multiplied by present value factor for 7% from Table II, Appendix C (end of text)	$100,000 × 0.66634 =	$66,634
Interest of $6,000 due at end of each of six periods multiplied by present value factor for 7% from Table III, Appendix C (end of text).	$6,000 × 4.76654 =	28,599
Total price (present value)		$95,233

Objective 7:
Prepare journal
entries to account
for bonds payable

Note that in computing present value of the bonds, the actual cash interest payments that will be made were used. The amount of cash flow does not change with changes in the market interest rate. Also, the market rate per semiannual period—7%—was used in finding interest factors in the tables. The journal entry to record issuance of the bonds is:

```
1990
July 1   Cash . . . . . . . . . . . . . . . . . . . . .     95,233
            Discount on Bonds Payable . . . . . . . . . . .      4,767
               Bonds Payable  . . . . . . . . . . . . .                  100,000
            To record bonds issued at a discount.
```

Note that in recording the bond issue, Bonds Payable is credited for the face value of the debt. The difference between face value and price received is debited to a contra account to Bonds Payable. Bonds Payable and the Discount on Bonds Payable are reported in the balance sheet as follows:

```
Long-term liabilities:
   Bonds payable, 12%, due July 1, 1993 . . . . .   $100,000
   Less: Discount on bonds payable . . . . . . . .      4,767   $95,233
```

The $95,233 is called the **carrying value** or **net liability** of the bonds.

Bonds issued at a premium. Assume that Rex Company issued the $100,000 face value of 12% bonds to yield 10%. The bonds would sell at a premium calculated as follows:

	Present Value Factor	Present Value
Principal of $100,000 due in six periods multiplied by present value factor for 5% from Table II, Appendix C (end of text)	$100,000 × 0.74622 =	$ 74,622
Interest of $6,000 due at end of each of six periods multiplied by present value factor for 5% from Table III, Appendix C (end of text)	$6,000 × 5.07569 =	30,454
Total price (present value)		$105,076

The journal entry to record the issuance of the bonds is:

```
1990
July 1  Cash . . . . . . . . . . . . . . . . . . . . . . . . .  105,076
            Bonds Payable . . . . . . . . . . . . . . . . .           100,000
            Premium on Bonds Payable . . . . . . . . . . .             5,076
          To record bonds issued at a premium.
```

Carrying value of these bonds at issuance is $105,076, consisting of face value of $100,000 and premium of $5,076. Premium is shown on the balance sheet as an addition to face value.

Discount/Premium Amortization

When bonds are issued at a discount or premium, total actual interest expense on the bonds differs from total interest paid periodically in cash. A discount increases and a premium decreases the cash interest to actual interest. For example, if $100,000 face value of Rex Company bonds were issued for $95,233, the total interest cost of borrowing would be $40,767: $36,000 (six payments of $6,000) plus the discount of $4,767. The $4,767 discount must be allocated (amortized) to the six periods that benefit from the use of borrowed money. *APB Opinion No. 21* recommends an amortization procedure called the **effective interest rate method,** or, simply, the **interest method.**

Under the interest method, *interest expense for any interest period is equal to the effective (market) rate of interest at date of issuance times the carrying value of the bonds at the beginning of that interest period.* Using the Rex Company example of $100,000 face value of 12% bonds sold to yield 14%, the carrying value at the beginning of the first interest period is the selling price of $95,233. The interest expense for the first semiannual period would be recorded in this way:

```
1991
Jan. 1  Bond Interest Expense ($95,233 × 0.14 × 1/2) . . . . . .  6,666
            Cash ($100,000 × 0.12 × 1/2) . . . . . . . . . . .             6,000
            Discount on Bonds Payable . . . . . . . . . . . . .               666
          To record discount amortization and interest payment.
```

Note that interest expense is calculated using the effective interest rate. The cash payment is calculated using the contract rate. The discount amortized for the period is the difference between the two amounts.

After the above entry, the carrying value of the bonds is $95,899. The balance in the discount account was reduced by $666 to $4,101. Assuming a fiscal year ending on June 30, the entry to accrue six months' interest at year-end is:

```
1991
June 30   Bond Interest Expense ($95,899 × 0.14 × 1/2)  . . . . .   6,713
               Bond Interest Payable . . . . . . . . . . . . . .            6,000
               Discount on Bonds Payable . . . . . . . . . . .               713
               To accrue six months' interest and discount amortization.
```

If the Rex Company bonds had been issued to yield 10%, the premium would be $5,076. But interest expense would be calculated in the same manner as for bonds sold at a discount, that is, carrying value times the effective interest rate. The entry would differ somewhat, showing a debit to the premium account. The entries for the first two interest periods are:

```
1991
Jan. 1    Bond Interest Expense ($105,076 × 0.10 × 1/2)  . . . .   5,254
          Premium on Bonds Payable . . . . . . . . . . . . .         746
               Cash . . . . . . . . . . . . . . . . . . . . .              6,000
               To record interest payment and premium amortization.
```

```
1991
June 30   Bond Interest Expense ($104,330 × 0.10 × 1/2)  . . . .   5,216
          Premium on Bonds Payable . . . . . . . . . . . . .         784
               Bond Interest Payable  . . . . . . . . . . . . .            6,000
               To accrue six months' interest expense and
               premium amortization.
```

Discount and premium amortization schedules. A discount amortization schedule (Illustration 9.2) and a premium amortization schedule (Illus-

Illustration 9.2
DISCOUNT AMORTIZATION SCHEDULE

(A) Interest Payment Date	(B) Interest Expense Debit (E × 0.14 × 1/2)	(C) Cash Credit ($100,000 × 0.12 × 1/2)	(D) Discount on Bonds Payable Credit (B − C)	(E) Carrying Value of Bonds Payable (E + D)
Issue price, 7/1/90				$ 95,233
1/1/91	$ 6,666	$ 6,000	$ 666	95,899
7/1/91	6,713	6,000	713	96,612
1/1/92	6,763	6,000	763	97,375
7/1/92	6,816	6,000	816	98,191
1/1/93	6,873	6,000	873	99,064
7/1/93	6,936*	6,000	936	100,000
	$40,767	$36,000	$4,767	

* Includes rounding difference.

Illustration 9.3
PREMIUM AMORTIZATION SCHEDULE

(A) Interest Payment Date	(B) Interest Expense Debit (E × 0.10 × 1/2)	(C) Cash Credit ($100,000 × 0.12 × 1/2)	(D) Premium on Bonds Payable Debit (C − B)	(E) Carrying Value of Bonds Payable (E − D)
Issue price, 7/1/90.				$105,076
1/1/91	$ 5,254	$ 6,000	$ 746	104,330
7/1/91	5,216	6,000	784	103,546
1/1/92	5,177	6,000	823	102,723
7/1/92	5,136	6,000	864	101,859
1/1/93	5,093	6,000	907	100,952
7/1/93	5,048	6,000	952	100,000
	$30,924	$36,000	$5,076	

tration 9.3) can be prepared to aid in preparing entries for interest expense. Companies usually prepare such schedules when bonds are first issued, often using standard computer programs. The schedules are then referred to whenever journal entries for interest are to be made. The schedules show the amount of the entries as if no adjusting entries were prepared the day before the interest date. The amounts may still be used in preparing the necessary adjusting entries. Note that, in each period, the amount of interest expense changes; expense gets larger when a discount is involved and smaller when a premium is involved. The reason is the carrying value to which a constant interest rate is applied changes at each interest payment date. With a discount, carrying value increases; with a premium, it decreases. But cash is always a constant amount determined by multiplying the face value by the contract rate per interest period.

Note that interest expense in Illustration 9.2 of $40,767 agrees with the earlier computation of total interest expense. In Illustration 9.3, total interest expense is shown as $30,924, which is equal to $36,000 (six $6,000 payments) *less* the $5,076 premium. In both illustrations, the carrying value of the bonds at the maturity date is the face value.

Adjusting entry for partial period. Illustration 9.3 can be used to obtain amounts needed if interest must be accrued for a partial period. Assume the fiscal year of the bond issuer ends on August 31. The adjusting entry needed on August 31, 1990, is:

```
1990
Aug. 31  Bond Interest Expense ($5,254 × 2/6) . . . . . . . . . .   1,751
            Premium on Bonds Payable ($746 × 2/6) . . . . . . .     249
            Bond Interest Payable ($6,000 × 2/6) . . . . . . .            2,000
         To record two months' accrued interest.
```

The entry records interest for two months, July and August, of the six-month interest period ending on January 1, 1991. The first line of Illustration 9.3 shows the interest expense and premium amortization for the six months. The above entry thus records two sixths (or one third) of the amounts for this six-month period. The remaining four months' interest is recorded when the first payment is made on January 1, 1991. That entry reads:

```
1991
Jan. 1  Bond Interest Payable . . . . . . . . . . . . . . . . .   2,000
        Bond Interest Expense ($5,254 × 4/6)  . . . . . . . . .   3,503
        Premium on Bonds Payable ($746 × 4/6) . . . . . . . .      497
            Cash . . . . . . . . . . . . . . . . . . . . . . .            6,000
        To record interest expense and interest payment.
```

Similar entries for August 31 and January 1 will be made in the remaining years of the life of the bonds. The amounts will differ from those in the above entry because the effective interest method of accounting for bond interest is being used.

The straight-line method. When applied to bond discount or premium, the **straight-line method of amortization** is a procedure that allocates an equal amount of discount or premium to each month the bonds are outstanding. The amount is calculated by dividing the discount or premium by the total number of months from date of issuance to maturity date. For example, if the $100,000 face value of Rex Company bonds were sold for $95,233, the $4,767 discount would be charged to interest expense at a rate of $132.42 ($4,767/36) per month. Interest expense for each six-month period then would be $6,795 [$6,000 + ($132.42 × 6)]. The entry to record the expense would have the same form as under the interest method.

The $5,076 premium on the $100,000 face value of bonds sold for $105,076 would be amortized at a rate of $141 ($5,076/36) per month. The entry for the first period's expense on bonds sold at a premium reads:

```
1991
Jan. 1  Bond Interest Expense . . . . . . . . . . . . . . . . .   5,154
        Premium on Bonds Payable ($141 × 6) . . . . . . . . .      846
            Cash . . . . . . . . . . . . . . . . . . . . . . .            6,000
        To record interest payment and premium amortization.
```

Interest expense is recorded at a *constant amount* under the straight-line method and at a *constant rate* under the interest method. Since the interest method is theoretically correct, *APB Opinion No. 21* states that the straight-line method may be used only when it does not differ materially from the interest method. In many cases, differences will not be material. In the premium example above, the difference in the first period's interest expense is only $100 ($5,254 − $5,154), and may not be material.

Redeeming Bonds Payable

Bonds may be paid at maturity, purchased in the market and retired, or called. Each of these actions is referred to as redemption of bonds or extinguishment of debt. If bonds are paid at maturity, any related discount or premium would have been amortized. The only entry required would debit Bonds Payable and credit Cash. More typical redemptions are discussed below.

An issuer may redeem some or all of its outstanding bonds before the maturity date by calling them. Or bonds may be purchased in the market and retired. In either case, the accounting is the same. Assume that on January 1, 1992, $10,000 face value of the bonds in Illustration 9.3 are called or purchased in the market at 103. Bond prices usually are quoted as percentages—the 103 means 103% of face value. For a $1,000 bond, the price is $1,030. A quote of 99.5 means a price of $995 for a $1,000 bond. In both cases, accrued interest, if any, will be added to the price. Assume that coupons for the interest due on this date have been detached so there is no accrued interest. A look at the last column on the line dated 1/1/92 in Illustration 9.3 reveals that the carrying value of the bonds is $102,723, which consists of Bonds Payable of $100,000 and Premium on Bonds Payable of $2,723. Since 10% of the bond issue is redeemed, 10% must be removed from each of these two accounts. A loss is incurred for the excess of the price paid for the bonds, $10,300, over their carrying value, $10,272. The required entry reads:

Bonds Payable	10,000	
Premium on Bonds Payable	272	
Loss on Bond Redemption	28	
Cash		10,300
To record bonds redeemed.		

According to *FASB Statement No. 4*, gains and losses from voluntary early retirement of bonds are extraordinary items, if material. Such gains and losses are reported in the income statement, net of their tax effects, as described in Chapter 8.

BOND INVESTMENTS

Objective 8: Prepare journal entries to account for bond investments

Bonds may be purchased as either short-term or long-term investments. A company makes short-term investments in bonds to earn income on what might otherwise be idle cash. Such investments may yield a higher return than available alternatives. Long-term investments in bonds usually are made for reasons other than a return on idle cash. A company may invest on a long-term basis in another company to guarantee needed raw materials, or one company could be a dealer or distributor of the other company's products. In any event, the most common reason is to establish a long-term relationship between two companies. If short-term bond investments are marketable (readily salable) and are considered a temporary use of cash available for operations, they are reported as current assets. All other bond investments are long term and are reported in the Investments section of the balance sheet below current assets, whether marketable or not.

Short-Term Bond Investments

Short-term bond investments are recorded in a single account at cost, which includes the price paid for the bonds and often includes a broker's commission. If bonds are purchased between interest dates, investors pay for accrued interest and collect the amount paid later when the semi-annual interest is received. *Premiums and discounts on short-term bond investments are not amortized because the length of time the bonds will be held is not known.*

To illustrate, assume that on May 31, 1990, Bay Company purchased as a short-term investment $10,000 face value, 12% bonds of Ace Company at 102, plus $100 of accrued interest from April 30. A $70 broker's commission was also paid. The entry required is:

```
1990
May 31   Temporary Investments (or Marketable Securities)
             ($10,200 + $70) . . . . . . . . . . . . . . . . . . .   10,270
         Bond Interest Receivable ($10,000 × 0.12 × 1/12) . . .        100
             Cash . . . . . . . . . . . . . . . . . . . . . .                 10,370
         To record bonds purchased.
```

On September 30, 1990, Bay sold the Ace bonds at 103.5, plus accrued interest of $500. A $70 broker's commission was charged on the sale. Before computing gain or loss on the sale, the broker's commission is deducted from selling price to compute net proceeds to the seller ($10,350 − $70 = $10,280). The gain or loss is the difference between net proceeds and cost. In this example, the gain is $10 ($10,280 − $10,270). Note that accrued interest does not affect the amount of gain or loss because it is paid for by the purchaser. The entry to record the sale is:

```
1990
Sept. 30   Cash ($10,350 + $500 − $70) . . . . . . . . . . .   10,780
               Temporary Investments . . . . . . . . . . . . .            10,270
               Bond Interest Receivable (from above entry) . . .             100
               Bond Interest Revenue ($10,000 × 0.12 × 4/12) . .             400
               Gain on Sale of Temporary Investments . . . . .               10
           To record sale of temporary investments.
```

The purchaser will receive the semiannual interest check from Ace Company to cover the $500 of accrued interest paid to Bay Company. Bay records only $400 of the $500 of interest received as interest revenue, since it held the bonds for only four months.

Long-Term Bond Investments

Long-term investments in bonds are recorded in a single account at cost that includes any discount or premium on the purchase. Although not set up in a separate account as it is for the issuing company, a discount or premium on long-term bond investments is amortized.

Bonds purchased at a discount. For example, assume that on July 1, 1990, Fenn Company purchased $100,000 face value of 12% bonds for $95,233, a price that yields 14%. These bonds were described in Illustration 9.2. The entry to record the purchase is:

```
Bond Investments . . . . . . . . . . . . . . . . . . . . . . . . . . . . .   95,233
    Cash . . . . . . . . . . . . . . . . . . . . . . . . . . . . . . . . .            95,233
    To record bonds purchased at a discount.
```

If a broker's commission was paid to acquire the bonds, it would be added to the Bond Investments account.

Since Fenn intends to hold the bonds to maturity, the discount is amortized over the remaining life of the bonds, using the effective interest method. Interest revenue and discount amortization on the bonds purchased by Fenn are computed the same way the issuer's expense and amortization are computed: multiply the bond price by the effective rate per period. The first period's interest revenue is $6,666 ($95,233 × 0.14 × 1/2). Discount amortized is $666 ($6,666 − $6,000). If Fenn has a calendar accounting year, the required adjusting entry is:

Dec. 31	Bond Interest Receivable	6,000	
	Bond Investments	666	
	Interest Revenue		6,666
	To record accrued interest revenue.		

Note that in the entry, the amount added to the Bond Investments account is equal to the discount amortized on the issuer's books. The discount is amortized even though it is not set up in a separate account on the investor's books. The original discount is $4,767, and this amount must be included in interest revenue on Fenn's books during the life of the bonds. Illustration 9.4 shows how the $4,767 is added to periodic Interest Revenue and to Bond Investments. The debits gradually increase the Bond Investments account balance to face value at the maturity date.

Fenn's December 31, 1990, balance sheet would show Bond Interest Receivable of $6,000, and Bond Investments of $95,899. If Fenn's fiscal year ended on November 30, the adjusting entry on that date would be the same as the December 31 entry, except all amounts would be five sixths of the December 31 amounts.

If the straight-line method is used, discount amortization would be $795 ($4,767/6) per period and interest revenue would be $6,795 ($6,000 + $795).

Bonds purchased at a premium. To illustrate accounting for bonds purchased at a premium, assume Big Company paid $105,076 for $100,000

Illustration 9.4
DISCOUNT AMORTIZATION SCHEDULE

(A) Interest Date	(B) Cash Debit ($100,000 × 0.12 × 1/2)	(C) Interest Revenue Credit (E × 0.14 × 1/2)	(D) Bond Investments Debit (C − B)	(E) Carrying Value of Bond Investments (E + D)
Purchase price, 7/1/90				$ 95,233
1/1/91	$ 6,000	$ 6,666	$ 666	95,899
7/1/91	6,000	6,713	713	96,612
1/1/92	6,000	6,763	763	97,375
7/1/92	6,000	6,816	816	98,191
1/1/93	6,000	6,873	873	99,064
7/1/93	6,000	6,936*	936	100,000
	$36,000	$40,767	$4,767	

* Includes rounding difference.

face value of 12% bonds, a price that yields 10%. These are the bonds in Illustration 9.3. The entry to record the purchase would debit Bond Investments and credit Cash for $105,076.

Interest revenue for the first interest period can be computed by multiplying the purchase price by the effective interest rate: $105,076 × 0.10 × 1/2 = $5,254. The required entry, assuming a fiscal year ended June 30, is:

```
1991
Jan. 1  Cash  . . . . . . . . . . . . . . . . . . . . . . .    6,000
             Bond Investments  . . . . . . . . . . . . . .              746
             Interest Revenue.  . . . . . . . . . . . . . .            5,254
          To record interest revenue collected.
```

The premium is amortized by crediting the Bond Investments account. If bonds are held to maturity, the balance in the Bond Investments account would be gradually decreased to the maturity value of $100,000 (Illustration 9.5). Interest revenue for the second six months can be read from Illustration 9.5. Or it can be computed: ($105,076 − $746) × 0.10 × 1/2 = $5,216. If the straight-line method were used, the periodic amortization of the premium would be $846 ($5,076/6). Interest revenue would be a constant amount each semiannual period of $5,154 ($6,000 − $846).

Sale of Bond Investments

When bond investments are sold, a gain or loss usually must be recorded. Gain or loss is computed as the difference between the price received and the carrying value of the bonds on the date sold. Suppose that on July 1, 1992, when their carrying value was $101,859 (Illustration 9.5), the Big Company sold all of its bonds for $102,500, less a $500 broker's commission. The required entry is:

```
Cash  . . . . . . . . . . . . . . . . . . . . . . . . . . .  102,000
        Bond Investments . . . . . . . . . . . . . . . . .            101,859
        Gain on Sale of Bond Investments  . . . . . . . . .                141
     To record sale of bond investments.
```

There was no accrued interest because the sale occurred on an interest payment date. If it had not been an interest payment date, an additional

Illustration 9.5
PREMIUM AMORTIZATION SCHEDULE

(A) Interest Date	(B) Cash Debit ($100,000 × 0.12 × 1/2)	(C) Interest Revenue Credit (E × 0.10 × 1/2)	(D) Bond Investments Credit (B − C)	(E) Carrying Value of Bond Investments (E − D)
Purchase price, 7/1/90				$105,076
1/1/91	$ 6,000	$ 5,254	$ 746	104,330
7/1/91	6,000	5,216	784	103,546
1/1/92	6,000	5,177	823	102,723
7/1/92	6,000	5,136	864	101,859
1/1/93	6,000	5,093	907	100,952
7/1/93	6,000	5,048	952	100,000
	$36,000	$30,924	$5,076	

entry would have been needed to record interest earned and discount or premium amortized to date of sale. The gain or loss on the sale of the investment is reported in the income statement.

Valuation of Bond Investments

Long-term bond investments are carried and reported at amortized cost. Amortized cost is equal to acquisition cost plus discount amortized or less premium amortized. An exception exists when a substantial, permanent decline in value occurs. Bond investments are then written down by debiting an account called Loss on Market Decline of Bond Investments and crediting Bond Investments.

Once bond investments have been written down, traditional accounting conservatism dictates that they may not be written up, not even to their original cost, if market price recovers. The written down amount serves as the basis for computing gain or loss when the bonds are sold.

SUMMARY

This chapter has been concerned with financing activities and investments in the financial obligations of other companies; it includes both short-term and long-term items.

When a company finds itself in a position in which cash outflows temporarily exceed cash inflows, it may have to seek short-term financing. It may decide to borrow from a commercial bank by giving its own note payable. The company may seek to borrow from suppliers by delaying the time of payment for goods purchased. (This often results in notes payable to those suppliers.) Or the company may decide to sell to a bank notes receivable which it obtained from customers. In the last instance, the company is contingently liable for the note; that is, if the maker of the note does not pay the bank at maturity, the company will have to pay the note.

Longer-term financing is sometimes necessary to acquire additional long-term assets such as property, plant, and equipment. Notes payable are sometimes used for this purpose. Long-term notes must be recorded at their present value (while short-term notes are usually recorded at their face value). Quite often these notes are secured by a mortgage on certain property. A mortgage is a conditional transfer of property which is actually transferred to the payee if the maker does not meet its obligations under the terms of the note. A common form of mortgage notes payable is that arising from the purchase of a home. Businesses sometimes use this same form of long-term financing. Bonds are one of the longest-term debt issues commonly used. Bonds may or may not be secured by a mortgage against specific property.

A bond is a long-term liability that derives its value from two promises made to the purchaser: the company will repay the principal at a specified later time and pay periodic interest charges until that time.

Interest is generally paid in semiannual amounts. If interest payment dates and balance sheet dates do not coincide, interest must be accrued into the proper periods. When bonds are issued between interest payment dates, investors must pay for the interest accrued since the preceding interest date. This accrued interest is refunded to them on the next interest date.

A bond may be issued at face value, at a discount, or at a premium. Discounts and premiums exist because of differences between the stated interest rate on a bond and the market rate of interest. If the market rate is greater than the stated rate, the bonds will be issued at a discount. If the market rate is less than the stated rate, the bond will be issued at a premium. The issue price of a bond is equal to the present value of the principal plus the present value of the interest payments. The rate of interest used in discounting to find the present value is the market rate.

If a bond is issued at a discount or premium, total interest expense differs from the amount of interest actually paid each period. The discount or premium is amortized over the life of the bond through a procedure called the interest method. Interest expense is then computed as the market rate of interest times the carrying value of the bonds at the beginning of the interest period. Interest actually paid is the contract rate of interest times the face (principal) of the bonds. The difference between these two amounts is the discount or premium to be amortized.

Bonds may be purchased as long-term investments. Long-term investments in bonds are recorded at cost, which includes any discount or premium. The discount or premium is amortized using the interest method. When bond investments are sold, a gain or loss is recorded as the difference between selling price and carrying value of the investment.

The next chapter discusses a new and very important financial statement—the statement of cash flows. The statement of cash flows must be published whenever an income statement and balance sheet are published.

APPENDIX FUTURE VALUE AND PRESENT VALUE

The concepts of interest, future value, and present value are widely applied in business decision making. Accountants may be better able to account properly for business activity if they understand how the concepts of interest, future value, and present value influence this activity.

Interest

Interest is the fee charged for the use of money through time; it is the cost incurred from borrowing money or the revenue earned from lending money. The cost or revenue typically is measured by comparing the amount loaned with the amount repaid. Thus, if $100 is borrowed and $110 is repaid one year later, the interest cost (revenue) is $10 and the interest rate is 10% per annum ($10/$100). But there is more to the concept of interest than the amount that is recorded as interest revenue or interest expense. The foregone opportunity to earn interest must be considered. If you have money and earn no interest on it, you have a cost in the sense of a revenue foregone.

The concept of the time value of money stems from the logical preference for a dollar today rather than a dollar at any future date. Most individuals would prefer having a dollar today rather than at some future date because: (1) the risk exists that the future dollar will never be received; and (2) if the dollar is on hand now, it can be invested resulting in an increase in total dollars possessed at that future date.

Most business decisions involve a comparison of cash flows in and out of the firm. To be useful in decision making, such comparisons must be in terms of dollars of the same point in time. That is, the dollars held now must be accumulated or rolled forward or future dollars must be discounted or brought back to today before comparisons are valid. Such comparisons involve future and present value concepts.

Future Value

The **future value** or **worth** of any investment is the amount to which a sum of money invested today will grow in a stated time period at a specified interest rate. The interest involved may be simple interest or compound interest. **Simple interest** is interest on principal only. For example, $1,000 invested today for two years at 12 percent simple interest will grow to $1,240 since interest is $120 per year. The principal of $1,000, plus $2 \times \$120$, is equal to $1,240. **Compound interest** is interest on principal and on interest of prior periods. For example, $1,000 invested for two years at 12% compounded annually will grow to $1,254.40. Interest for the first year is $120, ($1,000 × 0.12). For the second year, interest is earned on the principal plus the interest of the previous year, $120. Thus, the interest for the second year is $134.40, ($1,120 × 0.12). Future value at the end of year two is $1,254.40. The $1,254.40 is found by adding the second year's interest ($134.40) to the value at the beginning of the second year ($1,120). These computations of future value may be portrayed graphically (see Illustration 9.6).

Illustration 9.6 shows the growth of $1,000 to $1,254.40 when the interest rate is 12% compounded annually. The effect of compounding is $14.40—the interest in the second year that was based on the interest computed for the first year, or $120 × 0.12 = $14.40.

The task of computing the future value to which any invested amount will grow at a given rate for a stated period is aided by the use of interest tables. An example is Table I in Appendix C at the end of this text. To use the Appendix C tables, first determine the number of compounding periods involved. The compounding period tells how frequently interest is computed and added to the base upon which future interest calculations will be based. A compounding period may be any length of time, such as

Illustration 9.6
GRAPHIC ILLUSTRATION OF FUTURE VALUE

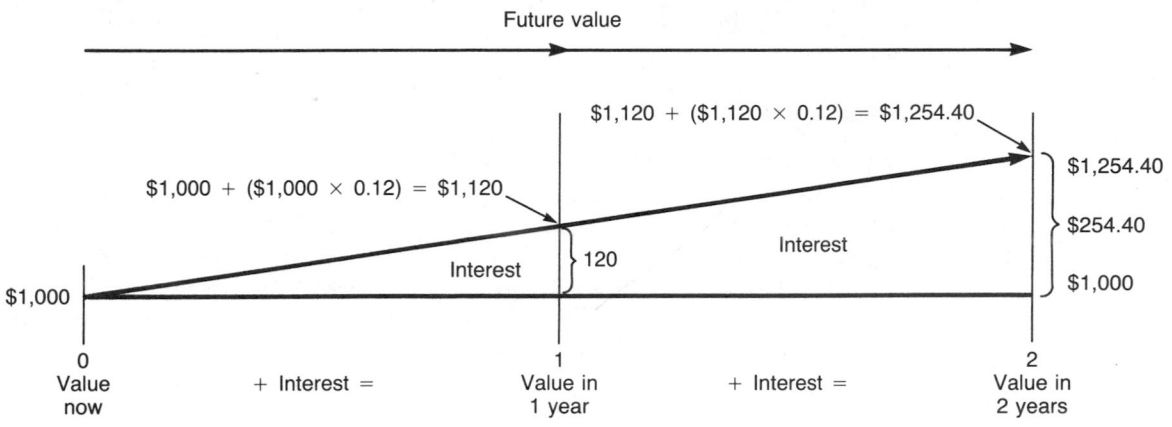

a day, a month, a quarter, a half-year, or a year, but normally not more than a year. The number of compounding periods is equal to the number of years in the life of the investment times the number of the compoundings in a year. Five years compounded annually is five periods, five years compounded quarterly is 20 periods, and so on.

Next, determine the interest rate per compounding period. Interest rates are usually quoted in annual terms. In fact, federal law requires statement of the interest rate in annual terms in certain situations. Divide the annual rate by the number of compounding periods per year to get the proper rate per period. Only with an annual compounding will the annual rate be the rate per period. All other cases involve a lower rate. For example, the rate per period will be 1% if the annual rate is 12% compounded monthly.

To use the table in a given situation, find the number of periods involved in the period row. Move across the table to the right, stopping in the column headed by the interest rate per period, which yields a number called a factor. The factor shows the amount to which an investment of $1 will grow for the periods and the rate involved. To compute future value of the investment, multiply the number of dollars in the given situation by this factor. For example, suppose your parents tell you that they will invest $8,000 at 12% for four years and give you the amount to which this investment will grow if you graduate from college in four years. How much will you receive at the end of four years if the interest rate is 12% compounded annually? How much will you receive if the interest rate is 12% compounded quarterly?

In Appendix C, Table I, in the 4 period row in the 12% column, you find the factor 1.57352. Multiply the factor by $8,000 to get $12,588.16 as the answer to the first question. Then look for 16 in the period row and under 3% for the needed factor to answer the second question. The factor is 1.60471, and the value of your investment is $12,837.68. The more frequent compounding would add $249.52 ($12,837.68 − $12,588.16) to the value of your investment. The reason for this difference in amounts is that 12% compounded quarterly is a higher rate than 12% compounded annually.

Present Value

Present value is the current worth of a future cash receipt and is essentially the reverse of future value. In future value, a sum of money is possessed now and its future worth must be calculated. In present value, rights to future cash receipts are possessed now and their current worth is to be calculated. Future cash receipts are discounted to find their present value. To discount future receipts is to deduct interest from them. If the proper interest rate is used, it should not matter to you whether you have cash in an amount equal to present value or have the rights to the larger amount of future receipts.

Assume that you have the right to receive $1,000 in one year. If the appropriate interest rate is 12% compounded annually, what is the present value of this $1,000 future cash receipt? You know that the present value is less than $1,000 because $1,000 due in one year is not worth $1,000 today. You also know that the $1,000 due in one year is equal to some amount, P, plus interest on P at 12% for one year. In other words, $P + 0.12P = \$1,000$, and $1.12P = \$1,000$. Dividing $1,000 by 1.12, you get $892.86. If the $1,000 was due in two years, you would find its present value by dividing $892.86 by 1.12 which equals $797.20. Portrayed graphically, present value looks very much like future worth, except for the direction of the arrows (Illustration 9.7).

Appendix C, Table II, contains present value factors for a number of periods and interest rates. Table II is used in the same manner as Table I. For example, the present value of $1,000 due in four years at 16% com-

Illustration 9.7
GRAPHIC ILLUSTRATION OF PRESENT VALUE OF A SINGLE AMOUNT

Present value

| Value now 0 | Value in 1 year 1 | Value in 2 years 2 |

$1,000

Interest $107.14   Interest

$202.80

$892.86

$797.20

$892.86 ÷ 1.12 = $797.20 $1,000 ÷ 1.12 = $892.86

$1,000

pounded annually is $552.29, computed as $1,000 × 0.55229. The 0.55229 is the present value factor found in the 4 period row in the 16% column.

As another example, suppose that you wish to have $4,000 in three years to pay for a vacation in Europe. If your investment will earn at a 20% rate compounded quarterly, how much should you invest now? To find the amount, you would use the present value factor found in Appendix C, Table II, 12 period row, 5% column. This factor is 0.55684, which means that an investment of about 55½ cents today would grow to $1 in 12 periods at 5% per period. To have $4,000 at the end of three years, you must invest 4,000 times this factor, or $2,227.36.

PRESENT VALUE OF AN ANNUITY

An **annuity** may be defined as a series of equal cash flows (often called rents) spaced equally in time. The semiannual interest payments on a bond form a frequently encountered annuity. The approach to valuing an annuity can be illustrated by finding the present value, at 6% per semiannual period, of an annuity calling for the payment of $100 at the end of each of the next three semiannual periods. It would be possible, by use of Appendix C, Table II, to find the present value of each of the $100 payments as follows:

Present value of $100 due in:
1 period is 0.94340 × $100 = $ 94.34
2 periods is 0.89000 × $100 =   89.00
3 periods is 0.83962 × $100 =   83.96
Total present value $267.30

Such a procedure could become quite tedious if the annuity consisted of 50 to 100 or more payments. Fortunately, tables are also available showing the present values of an annuity of $1 per period for varying interest rates and periods. See Appendix C, Table III. A single figure or factor can be obtained from the table that represents the present value of an annuity of $1 per period for three (semiannual) periods at 6% per (semiannual) period. The figure is 2.67301, and when multiplied by $100, the number of dollars in each payment, yields the present value of the annuity as $267.30. The present value of an annuity can be presented graphically (Illustration 9.8).

Illustration 9.8 shows that to find the present value of the three $100 cash flows, multiply the $100 by a present value of an annuity factor, 2.67301. The 2.67301 is equal to the sum of the present value factors for $1 due in one period, $1 in two periods, and $1 in three periods. Present value factors, such as the 2.67301, can be found in Appendix C, Table III, for varying periods and interest rates.

Suppose you won a prize in a lottery that awarded you your choice of $10,000 at the end of each of the next five years, or $35,000 cash immediately. You believe you can earn interest on invested cash at 15% per annum. Which option should you choose? To answer the question you

Illustration 9.8
GRAPHIC ILLUSTRATION OF PRESENT VALUE
OF AN ANNUITY

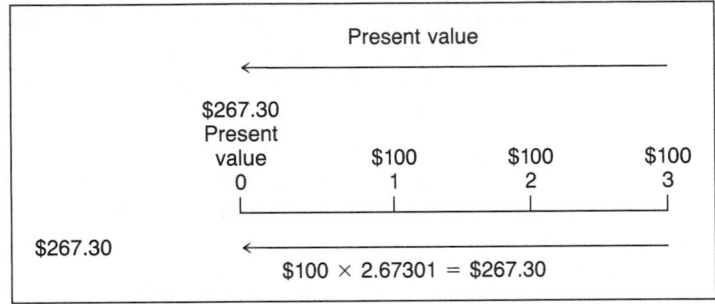

should compute the present value of an annuity of $10,000 per period for five years at 15%. The present value is $33,521.60, ($10,000 × 3.35216). You should accept the immediate payment of $35,000; since it is the larger present value.

Objective 9: Define and use correctly the new terms in the glossary

NEW TERMS INTRODUCED IN CHAPTER 9

Annuity   A series of equal cash flows spaced equally in time (339).

Bearer bond   See Unregistered bond.

Bond   A long-term debt owed by its issuer. A **bond certificate** is a negotiable instrument and is the formal, physical evidence of the debt owed (316).

Bond certificate   A negotiable instrument that represents physical evidence of the debt (316).

Bond indenture   The contract or loan agreement under which bonds are issued (317).

Call premium   The price paid in excess of face value that the issuer of bonds may be required to pay to redeem (call) bonds before their maturity date (318).

Callable bond   A bond that gives the issuer the right to call (buy back) the bond before its maturity date (318).

Carrying value (of bonds)   The face value of bonds minus any unamortized discount or plus any unamortized premium. Sometimes referred to as **net liability** on the bonds when used for bonds payable (325).

Compound interest   Interest calculated on the principal and on interest of prior periods (336).

Contract rate of interest   The interest rate printed on the bond certificates and specified on the bond indenture; also called the **stated, coupon,** or **nominal rate** (323).

Convertible bond   A bond that may be exchanged, at the bondholder's option, for shares of stock of the issuing corporation (319).

Coupon bond   A bond not registered as to interest; it carries detachable coupons that are to be clipped and presented for payment of interest due (318).

Debenture bond   An unsecured bond backed only by the general credit worthiness of its issuer (318).

Discount (on bonds)   Excess of face value over issue or selling price (324).

Discount on Notes Payable   A contra account used to reduce notes payable from face value to the net amount shown in the balance sheet (309).

Discount period   The exact number of days from the date of sale of a note to the date of maturity (312).

Discount rate   Rate of interest the bank charges on a discounted note receivable (313).

Discounting a note receivable   The act of selling a note receivable with recourse to a bank. With recourse means that the bank can collect from the company that sold the note to the bank if the maker does not pay at maturity (312).

Dishonored note   A note that the maker failed to pay at maturity (312).

Effective interest rate method (interest method)   A procedure for calculating periodic interest expense (or revenue) in which the first period's interest is computed by multiplying the carrying value of bonds payable (bond investments) by the market rate at the issue date. The difference between computed interest expense (revenue) and the interest paid (received), based on nominal rate times face value, is the discount or premium amortized for the period. Computations for subsequent periods are based on carrying value at the beginning of the period (326).

Face value   Principal amount of a bond (316).

Favorable financial leverage   An increase in EPS and rate of return on owners' equity resulting from earning a higher rate of return on borrowed funds than the fixed cost of such funds. **Unfavorable financial leverage** results when the cost of borrowed funds exceeds the income they generate, resulting in decreased income to owners (319).

Future value or worth   The amount to which a sum of money invested today will grow in a stated time period at a specified interest rate (336).

Interest   The fee charged for use of money through time (308).

Interest method   See Effective interest rate method.

Maker (of a note)   The party who prepares a note and is responsible for paying the note at maturity (308).

Market interest rate   The interest rate that an investor will earn on a bond investment by paying a specified price for it and the rate of interest expense a borrower will incur by issuing bonds at that price. Also called **effective interest** or **yield rate** (323).

Maturity date   The date on which a note becomes due and must be paid (312).

Maturity value   The amount that the maker must pay on a note on its maturity date (312).

Mortgage   A legal claim (lien) on a specific property that gives the bondholder the right to sell the pledged property if the company fails to make required payments. A bond secured by a mortgage is called a **mortgage bond** (315).

Mortgage note payable   A note that is secured by a pledge of certain property (315).

Payee (of a note)   The party who receives a note and will be paid cash at maturity (308).

Premium (on bonds)   Excess of selling or issue price over face value (324).

Present value   The current worth of a future cash receipt(s); computed by discounting future receipts at a stipulated interest rate (338).

Promissory note   An unconditional written promise by a borrower (maker) to pay a definite sum of money to the lender (payee) on demand or at a specific date (308).

Registered bond   A bond for which the owner's name appears on both the bond certificate and in the record of bond owners kept by the bond issuer or its agent, the registrar (318).

Secured bond   A bond for which specific property has been pledged to ensure its payment (318).

Serial bonds   Bonds in a given bond issue with maturities spread over several dates (318).

Simple interest   Interest on principal only (336).

Stock warrant   A right that allows the bondholder to purchase shares of common stock at a fixed price for a stated period of time. Warrants may be detachable or nondetachable (319).

Straight-line method of amortization   A procedure that, when applied to bond discount or premium, allocates an equal amount of discount or premium to each period in the life of a bond (329).

Term bond   A bond that matures on the same date as all other bonds in a given bond issue (318).

Trustee   Usually a bank or trust company appointed to represent the bondholders in a bond issue and to enforce the provisions of the bond indenture against the issuer (317).

Underwriter   An investment company that performs many tasks for the bond issuer in issuing bonds; may also guarantee the issuer a fixed price for the bonds (317).

Unfavorable financial leverage   Results when the cost of borrowed funds exceeds the revenue they generate; it is the opposite of **favorable financial leverage** (321).

Unregistered (bearer) bond   Ownership transfers by physical delivery (318).

Unsecured bond   A **debenture bond,** or simply a **debenture;** it is backed only by the general creditworthiness of the issuer, not by a lien on any specific property (318).

DEMONSTRATION PROBLEM 9–1

Jackson Company issued $100,000 face value of 15%, 20-year bonds on April 30, 1990. The bonds are dated April 30, 1990, call for semiannual interest payments on April 30 and October 31, and are issued to yield 16% (8% per period).

Required:

a. Compute the amount received for the bonds.

b. Prepare an amortization schedule. Enter data in the schedule for only the first two interest periods. Use the interest method.

c. Prepare journal entries to record issuance of the bonds, the first six months' interest expense on the bonds, the adjustment needed on December 31, 1990 (assuming Jackson's accounting year ends on that date), and the second six months' interest expense on April 30, 1991.

Solution to demonstration problem 9–1

a. Price received:

Present value of principal: $100,000 × .04603	$ 4,603
Present value of interest: $7,500 × 11.92461	89,435
Total	$94,038

b.

(A) Interest Payment Date	(B) Bond Interest Expense Debit (E × 0.16 × 1/2)	(C) Cash Credit ($100,000 × 0.15 × 1/2)	(D) Discount on Bonds Payable Credit (B − C)	(E) Carrying Value of Bonds Payable (previous balance in E + D)
Issue price				$94,038
10/31/90	$7,523	$7,500	$23	94,061
4/30/91	7,525	7,500	25	94,086

c.

JACKSON COMPANY
GENERAL JOURNAL

1990			
Apr. 30	Cash	94,038	
	Discount on Bonds Payable	5,962	
	Bonds Payable		100,000
	Issued $100,000 face value of 20-year, 15% bonds to yield 16%.		
Oct. 31	Bond Interest Expense	7,523	
	Discount on Bonds Payable		23
	Cash		7,500
	Paid semiannual bond interest expense.		
Dec. 31	Bond Interest Expense ($7,525 × 2/6)	2,508	
	Discount on Bonds Payable		8
	Bond Interest Payable ($7,500 × 2/6)		2,500
	To record accrual of two months' interest expense.		
1991			
Apr. 30	Bond Interest Payable	2,500	
	Bond Interest Expense ($7,525 × 4/6)	5,017	
	Discount on Bonds Payable		17
	Cash		7,500
	To record semiannual bond interest expense.		

DEMONSTRATION PROBLEM 9–2

On May 31, 1990, Martin Company purchased $10,000 face value of 8%, 10-year bonds issued by Shane Company. The bonds mature on May 31, 2000, call for semiannual interest payments on May 31 and November 30, and were issued for cash of $8,754, a price that yields an effective rate of 10%. The bonds are considered a long-term investment by Martin Company, which has a December 31 accounting year-end.

Required:

Prepare journal entries to record the investment in the Shane bonds, to record the interest collected on November 30, 1990, and to adjust the accounts on December 31, 1990. Use the effective interest rate method.

Solution to demonstration problem 9–2

MARTIN COMPANY
GENERAL JOURNAL

1990
May 31 Bond Investments 8,754
        Cash   8,754
        To record purchase of $10,000 face value of bonds.

Nov. 30 Cash ($10,000 × 0.08 × 1/2) 400
         Bond Investments   38
             Bond Interest Revenue ($8,754 × 0.10 × 1/2)   438
         To record semiannual interest revenue.

Dec. 31 Bond Interest Receivable ($10,000 × 0.08 × 1/12) 67
         Bond Investments   6
             Bond Interest Revenue
             [($8,754 + $38) × 0.10 × 1/12]   73
         To accrue one month's interest revenue.

QUESTIONS

1. Why might a business have need for short-term financing even when cash inflows are expected to exceed cash outflows?

2. How is interest calculated on a note?

3. How is interest introduced into a situation where a note is non-interest-bearing?

4. What does it mean for a note to be dishonored?

5. Describe the process of discounting a note receivable. What happens if the maker fails to pay the bank at maturity?

6. How are the cash proceeds determined when a note receivable is discounted?

7. What effect does the maturity date have on the carrying value of notes payable?

8. On a mortgage note payable, does the interest expense per period increase or decrease over time? Why?

9. What two promises are made by the issuer of a bond to the lender, or bondholder?

10. When bonds are issued between interest dates, why is it appropriate that the issuing corporation receive cash equal to the amount of accrued interest in addition to the issue price of the bonds?

11. Why would anyone be willing to pay more than face value for bonds?

12. Conceptually, how is the price at which a bond will sell computed?

13. What method(s) is (are) used to amortize discounts and premiums on bonds?

14. How are losses or gains from the early extinguishment of debt to be reported?

15. Describe the accounting for discounts and premiums on bonds purchased as short-term investments.

16. Describe the accounting for bonds purchased at a discount when they are to be held to maturity.

17. For long-term bond investments, in which account(s) is (are) premiums and discounts carried?

18. When bond investments are sold, what must be done regarding interest before recording the gain or loss?

19. (Based on the chapter appendix) Why isn't Table II used for finding the present value of an annuity?

EXERCISES

Use T-accounts to record short-term borrowing transactions

1. John Swift goes to the bank and asks to borrow $12,000 at 10-1/2% for a 60-day period. Using T-accounts, show how to record each of the following transactions:
   a. He signs a note for $12,000. Interest is deducted from the face amount in determining the proceeds.
   b. He receives $12,000 and signs a note for the interest plus the amount borrowed.
   c. He receives $12,000 and signs an interest-bearing note for that amount. The interest is to be paid at the maturity date.

Prepare journal entries for repayment of loan

2. Using T-accounts, give the entries at the maturity date for each of the alternatives given in 1, assuming that the loan is repaid. Also assume that repayment is made before the end of the accounting period.

Prepare entries for note

3. Hale gives his 90-day, $90,000, 12% note to Floyd in exchange for merchandise. Using T-accounts, give the entries each will make on the maturity date, assuming that payment is made.

Prepare entries for default

4. Referring to 3 above and using T-accounts, give the entries for each at the maturity date assuming that Hale defaults.

Prepare entries at date of discounting of note

5. Norris Company gave a 120-day, $30,000, 12% note to Forest Company on July 6, 1990. Forest Company sold the note to the bank on August 20, 1990. The rate of discount was 12%. Determine the entries each company would make on the date of discounting.

Prepare entries at maturity date

6. In Exercise 5, if Norris Company fails to make payment on the maturity date, what entry or entries are required on the books of each company?

Compute bond interest expense

7. On December 31, 1990, Apple Company issued $200,000 face value of 10-year, 8% bonds for cash of $164,150, a price to yield 11%. The bonds pay interest semiannually and mature December 31, 2000.

   a. State which was higher: the effective rate of interest or the nominal rate.

   b. Compute the bond interest expense for the first six months of 1991 using the interest method.

Record bond investment and first period's interest

8. Alex Company purchased $40,000 of the bonds issued by Apple Company (Exercise 7) as a long-term investment. Prepare a journal entry to record the investment. Prepare the entry to record the interest revenue earned on the bonds in the first six months of 1991 using the interest method.

Calculate interest using straight-line amortization

9. Compute the annual interest expense on the bonds in Exercise 7 and the interest revenue on the bonds in Exercise 8 assuming the bond discount is amortized under the straight-line method.

Prepare entry to record interest payment

10. After recording the payment of the interest coupon due on July 1, 1990, the accounts of the Brook Company showed Bonds Payable of $600,000 and Premium on Bonds Payable of $21,144. The $600,000 face value, five-year, 12% bonds, (interest payable semiannually on January 1 and July 1), were originally issued to yield 10%. Prepare the entry to accrue interest on December 31, 1990. Use the interest method.

Record interest received for six-month period given adjusting entry previously made

11. On April 30, 1990, the end of its fiscal year, Roxa Company prepared an adjusting entry to record $4,444 of accrued interest revenue earned on $100,000 face value of 12% bonds that were purchased on January 1, 1990, to yield 14%. The bonds are dated January 1, 1990, and call for semiannual interest payments on July 1 and January 1. Prepare the entry to record the interest revenue, the discount amortization, and the collection of interest on July 1, 1990.

Record call of bonds and payment of interest

12. On June 30, 1990 (a semiannual interest payment date), Paul Company redeemed all of its $600,000 face value of 10% bonds outstanding by calling them at 105. The bonds were originally issued on June 30, 1986, at 100. Prepare entries to record the payment of the interest and the redemption of the bonds on June 30, 1990.

Determine present value and specific worth (based on Appendix)

13. (Based on the Appendix) Conceptually, what is the present worth of a lump-sum payment of $400,000 due in five years? If the going market rate of interest on investments of this type is 10% per year and the present value of $1 due in five years at 10% is 0.62092, what is its specific worth?

Determine present value and a specific worth (based on Appendix)

14. (Based on the Appendix) Conceptually, what is the present worth of a series of semiannual payments of $50,000 due at the end of each six months of the next five years? If the going market rate of interest on investments of this type is 10% per year and the present value of an annuity of $1 for 10 periods at 5% is 7.72173, what is its specific worth?

PROBLEMS

Using T-accounts prepare journal entries to record discounting of company's own note

9–1. On November 1, 1990, the Chapman Company presented its own $114,000, 120-day, non-interest-bearing note to the B&D National Bank, which discounted it at 11%.

Required:

Using T-accounts, give the entries required on Chapman's books as of November 1, December 31 (the company's closing date), and the maturity date.

Prepare entries to record a number of note transactions, discounting of a note (customer's and own), adjusting entries for interest, and payment of notes

9–2. Following are selected transactions of the Cranwood Company:

Oct. 31   Presented its own 30-day, $60,000, non-interest-bearing note to the First State Bank, which discounted it at 11%.

Nov. 8   Received a $40,000, 30-day, 12% note from the Lively Company in settlement of an account receivable. The note is dated November 8.

   15   Purchased merchandise by issuing its own 60-day note for $24,000. The note is dated November 15 and bears interest at 12%.

   20   Sold the Lively Company note to the First State Bank, which discounted the note at 13%.

   30   The First State Bank notified the Cranwood Company that it had charged the note of October 31 against the company's checking account.

Required:

Assume that all notes falling due after November 30 were paid in full on their due dates by their respective makers. Give the journal entries required on Cranwood's books for each of the above transactions and each of the necessary adjustments assuming a fiscal year accounting period ending on November 30. Also give the journal entries required on Cranwood's books for payment of the notes due after November 30.

Compute two prices on bond issue and first period's interest

9–3. Hunter Company is seeking to issue $450,000 face value of 10%, 15-year bonds. The bonds are dated June 30, 1990; call for semiannual interest payments; and mature on June 30, 2004.

Required:

a. Compute the price investors should offer if they seek a yield of 8% on these bonds. Also, compute the first six months' interest assuming the bonds are issued at this price. Use the interest method.

b. Repeat part (a) assuming investors seek a yield of 12%.

Record bond interest expense payment, accrual for partial period, and mortgage note payment

9–4. On July 1, 1990, Green Corporation issued $300,000 face value of 10%, 10-year bonds. The bonds call for semiannual interest payments and mature on July 1, 2000. Green received cash of $265,590, a price that yields 12%.

   On September 30, 1990, Green also borrowed $150,000 on a 10-year mortgage note that called for 40 equal quarterly payments of $6,783. The note bears interest at 12% per year.

Required:

Assume that Green's fiscal year ended on March 31. Prepare entries to record the bond interest expense on January 1, 1991, and the adjustment needed on March 31, 1991, using the interest method. Also, prepare entries to record the first two quarterly payments on the mortgage note.

Compute issue price of bonds; prepare amortization schedule; journalize bond issuance; accrue interest

9–5. Allied Company issued $300,000 face value of 15%, 20-year bonds on October 1, 1990. The bonds are dated October 1, 1990, call for semiannual interest payments on April 1 and October 1, and are issued to yield 16% (8% per period).

Required:

a. Compute the amount received for the bonds.

b. Prepare an amortization schedule similar to that shown in Illustration 9.2. Enter data in the schedule for only the first two interest periods. Use the interest method.

c. Prepare journal entries to record issuance of the bonds, the first six months' interest expense on the bonds, and the adjustment needed on May 31, 1991, assuming Allied's fiscal year ends on that date.

Record bond investment, full and partial period's interest, and sale of bonds

9–6. Bowen Company purchased $30,000 face value of the Allied Company bonds (Problem 9–5) when they were issued on October 1, 1990, as a long-term investment.

Required:

a. Prepare entries to record purchase of the bonds, receipt of the first six months' interest, and the adjustment needed on June 30, 1991, assuming a fiscal year ended on that date. Use the interest method.

b. Assume that the Bowen Company sold all of these bonds on October 1, 1999, for cash of $29,850, after detaching the interest coupon due on this date. The bonds have a carrying value, properly adjusted to date, of $28,542. Prepare the journal entry to record the sale.

Compute price of bonds; prepare amortization schedule; journalize bond issuance, payment of first period's interest, and accrual of partial period's interest

9–7. Cook Company issued $200,000 face value of 18%, 20-year bonds on October 1, 1990. The bonds are dated October 1, 1990, call for semiannual interest payments on April 1 and October 1, and are issued to yield 16% (8% per period).

Required:

a. Compute the amount received for the bonds.

b. Prepare an amortization schedule similar to that shown in Illustration 9.3. Enter data in the schedule for only the first two interest periods. Use the interest method.

c. Prepare entries to record the issuance of the bonds, the first six months' interest on the bonds, and the adjustment needed on June 30, 1991, assuming Cook's fiscal year ends on that date.

Record bond investment, collection of full period's interest, accrual of partial period's interest, and call of bonds

9–8. Kent Corporation purchased $60,000 face value of the Cook bonds (Problem 9–7) when they were issued on October 1, 1990, as a long-term investment.

Required:

a. Prepare journal entries to record the purchase of the bonds, the receipt of the first six months' interest, and the adjustment needed on September 30, 1991, assuming a fiscal year ending on that date. Use the interest method.

b. Assume that on October 1, 2000, Cook called all of the bonds at 105. Kent received a check for $68,400, including $5,400 as payment of the semiannual interest due on this date. Prepare the entry to record the receipt of the $68,400. The properly adjusted carrying value of the bonds on this date was $65,918.

BUSINESS DECISION PROBLEM 9–1

Analyze two financing proposals; decide whether investment should be made

A company is trying to decide whether to invest $2,000,000 on plant expansion and $1,000,000 to finance a related increase in inventories and accounts receivable. The $3,000,000 expansion is expected to increase business volume substantially. Profit forecasts indicate that net income from operations will rise from $1,600,000 to $2,200,000. The income tax rate is assumed to be 40%. Net income last year was $915,000. Interest expense on debt now outstanding is $70,000 per year. There are 200,000 shares of capital stock currently outstanding.

The $3,000,000 needed can be obtained in two alternative ways:

1. Finance entirely by issuing additional shares of capital stock at an expected issue price of $75 per share.
2. Finance two thirds with bonds, one third with additional stock. The bonds would have a 20-year life, bear interest at 10%, and would sell at face value. The issue price of the stock would be $80 per share.

Required:

Should the investment be made? If so, which financing plan would you recommend? (Hint: Calculate earnings per share for last year and for future years under each of the alternatives.)

10 STATEMENT OF CASH FLOWS

LEARNING OBJECTIVES

After studying this chapter, you should be able to:

1. Understand the uses of the statement of cash flows.
2. Conceptually understand the statement of cash flows.
3. Prepare a statement of cash flows.
4. Understand the historical development from a statement of changes in financial position to a statement of cash flows.
5. Understand how to prepare a schedule of changes in working capital.
6. Define and use correctly the new terms in the glossary.

In your study of the statement of income and retained earnings (as separate statements or combined) and the balance sheet, you may have realized that these financial statements do not answer all the questions raised by users of financial statements. Such questions include: How much cash was generated by the company's operations? Why is such a profitable company only able to pay such small dividends? How much was spent for new plant and equipment, and where did the company get the cash for the expenditures? How was the company able to pay a dividend when it incurred a net loss for the year? The statement of cash flows answers these questions.

In this chapter you will first learn about the statement of cash flows. Finally, you will learn how to analyze changes in working capital.

In November 1987, the Financial Accounting Standards Board issued *Statement of Financial Accounting Standards No. 95*, "Statement of Cash Flows."[1] The statement is effective for annual financial statements for fis-

---

[1]FASB, "Statement of Cash Flows," *Statement of Financial Accounting Standards No. 95* (Stamford, Conn., 1987). Copyright by the Financial Accounting Standards Board, High Ridge Park, Stamford, Connecticut 06905, U.S.A. Quoted (or excerpted) with permission. Copies of the complete document are available from the FASB.

cal years ending after July 15, 1988. Thus, the statement of cash flows is now one of the major financial statements issued by a company.

The main purpose of a statement of cash flows is to report on the cash receipts and cash disbursements of an entity for a period. Cash is broadly defined to include both cash and "cash equivalents" such as treasury bills, commercial paper, and money market funds. A secondary purpose is to report on the entity's investing and financing activities for the period. To accomplish these purposes, the statement of cash flows reports the effects on cash during a period of its operating activities, investing activities, and financing activities. The effects of investing and financing activities that do not affect cash are also shown. A reconciliation of net income and cash flows from operating activities also should be provided.

USES OF THE STATEMENT OF CASH FLOWS

Objective 1: Understand the uses of the statement of cash flows

The **statement of cash flows** summarizes the effects on cash of the operating, financing, and investing activities of a company for a period; it reports on past management decisions on such matters as issuance of capital stock or sale of long-term bonds. This information is available only in bits and pieces from the other financial statements. Because cash flows are vital to a company's financial health, the statement of cash flows provides useful information to management and other interested parties, especially creditors and investors.

Management Uses

Since the statement of cash flows presents the effects on cash of all significant operating, financing, and investing activities, management can see the effects of its past major policy decisions in quantitative form by reviewing the statement. The statement may show a flow of cash from operating activities large enough to finance all projected capital needs internally rather than having to issue long-term debt or additional stock. Or, if the company has been experiencing cash shortages, management can use the statement to determine why such shortages are occurring. After reviewing the statement, management may decide to reduce dividends to conserve cash and reduce cash shortages.

Investor and Creditor Uses

The information in a statement of cash flows should help investors, creditors, and others to assess the:

1. Enterprise's ability to generate positive future net cash flows.
2. Enterprise's ability to meet its obligations.
3. Enterprise's ability to pay dividends.
4. Enterprise's need for external financing.
5. Reasons for differences between net income and associated cash receipts and payments.

6. Effects on an enterprise's financial position of both its cash and non-cash investing and financing transactions during the period (disclosed in a separate schedule).

INFORMATION IN THE STATEMENT OF CASH FLOWS

Objective 2:
Conceptually under-
stand the statement
of cash flows

The statement of cash flows classifies cash receipts and cash disbursements as operating, investing, and financing cash flows. Both inflows and out-flows are included within each category. Illustration 10.1 shows how activi-ties can be classified for purposes of preparing a statement of cash flows.

Operating activities generally include the cash effects of transactions and other events that enter into the determination of net income. Thus, cash inflows from operating activities include cash receipts from sales of goods or services, including receipts from collection or sale of accounts and both short- and long-term notes receivable from customers arising from those sales. Also, (because they are reported on the income state-ment) interest received from making loans and from other debt instru-ments of other entities and dividends received from investments in equity securities are included in cash inflows from operating activities. Other cash inflows include all other cash receipts that do not arise from transac-tions defined as investing or financing activities (such as amounts re-ceived to settle lawsuits, proceeds of certain insurance settlements, and refunds from suppliers). Cash outflows for operating activities generally in-

Illustration 10.1
RULES FOR CLASSIFYING ACTIVITIES IN THE STATEMENT OF CASH FLOWS

Operating Activities	*Investing Activities*	*Financing Activities*
Cash **received** from:	Cash **received** from:	Cash **received** from:
Sales of goods or services	Collections or sales of	Issuing equity instruments
Interest	loans	Sale of bonds,
Dividends	Sale of equity instru-	mortgages, notes, and
Other sources that are	ments of other	other borrowings
not from investing and	entities and returns of	Cash **paid** for:
financing activities.	investment in those	Cash dividends
Cash **paid** for:	instruments	Purchase of treasury
Raw materials or __	Sale of property, plant,	stock
Inventory	and equipment and	Repayments of amounts
Salaries and wages	other productive assets	borrowed
Taxes, duties, fines,	Cash **paid** for:	
penalties	Loans made by the	
Interest	enterprise and	
Other expenses not	payments to acquire	
considered investing	debt instruments of	
or financing activities	other entities	
	Purchase of equity	
	instruments of other	
	entities	
	Purchase of property,	
	plant, and equipment	
	and other productive	
	assets	

clude cash payments for expenses that appear on the income statement. Thus, cash outflows for operating activities include cash payments: (1) to acquire materials for manufacture or goods for resale (including principal payments on accounts and both short- and long-term notes payable to suppliers for those materials or goods); (2) to other suppliers and employees for other goods or services; (3) to governments for taxes, duties, fines, and other fees or penalties; (4) to lenders and other creditors for interest; and (5) all other cash payments that do not arise from transactions defined as investing or financing activities (such as payments to settle lawsuits, cash contributions to charities, and cash refunds to customers).

Investing activities generally include transactions involving the acquisition or disposal of noncurrent assets. Thus, investing activities include making and collecting loans and acquiring and dispensing of debt or equity instruments and acquiring and selling or disposing of property, plant, and equipment and other productive assets. Cash inflows from investing activities include cash received from collections or sales of loans made by the enterprise and of other entities' debt instruments that were purchased by the enterprise; cash received from the sale of equity instruments of other enterprises and from returns of investment in those instruments; and cash received from the sale of property, plant, and equipment and other productive assets. Cash outflows for investing activities include cash paid for loans made by the enterprise and payments to acquire debt instruments of other entities; cash paid to acquire equity instruments of other enterprises; and cash paid at the time of purchase or soon before or after purchase to acquire property, plant, or equipment and other productive assets.

Financing activities generally include transactions with creditors and owners. Thus, financing activities include obtaining resources from owners and providing them with a return *on* their investment and *of* their investment; borrowing money and repaying amounts borrowed, or otherwise settling the obligation; and obtaining and paying for other resources obtained from creditors on long-term credit. Cash inflows from financing activities include cash received from issuing equity instruments and bonds, mortgages, notes, and from other short- or long-term borrowing. Cash outflows for financing activities include payments of cash dividends or other distributions to owners (including cash paid to purchase treasury stock) and repayments of amounts borrowed. Payment of interest is not included because interest expense appears on the income statement and is therefore included in operating activities.

For both investing and financing activities, cash inflows and cash outflows for a particular item are shown at the gross amount. For instance, assume a company sold a building for $2,000,000 and purchased another building for $5,000,000. Both the inflow of $2,000,000 and the outflow of $5,000,000 must be shown, rather than showing only a net outflow of $3,000,000.

The *FASB Statement* also requires that investing and financing activities that do not involve cash flows be disclosed in a separate, accompanying schedule and may be in narrative form. Some transactions are part cash and part noncash. Only the cash portion should be reported in the statement of cash flows.

CASH FLOWS FROM OPERATING ACTIVITIES

The **cash flows from operating activities** can be calculated in two ways. The **direct method** deducts from cash sales only those operating expenses that consumed cash. Under this method, each item on the income statement is "directly" converted to a cash basis. Alternatively, the **indirect,** or **addback, method** starts with net income and "indirectly" adjusts net income for items that affected reported net income but did not involve cash. The FASB encourages the use of the direct method, but permits the use of the indirect method. We believe that the indirect method will be used more frequently in practice. Whenever a choice between the indirect and direct methods has been available in past situations, the indirect method has been used almost exclusively. Thus, we will emphasize the indirect method. But, we will discuss and illustrate the direct method also.

Under the direct method, each item in the income statement must be converted to a cash basis. (Thus, the name *direct method* is used.) For instance, assume sales are stated at $100,000 on an accrual basis. Accounts receivable was $25,000 at the beginning of the year and $20,000 at the end of the year. Thus, cash collections from customers were $105,000 ($100,000 + $25,000 − $20,000). All other items on the income statement are also converted to a cash basis. This process will be illustrated later.

Under the indirect method, net income is adjusted (rather than adjusting individual items in the income statement) for items that were included in net income but that did not affect cash. Thus, the name *indirect method* is used. The most common example of an operating expense that does not affect cash is depreciation expense. The journal entry to record depreciation requires a debit to an expense account and a credit to an accumulated depreciation account. This transaction has no effect on cash and therefore should not be included when measuring cash from operations. Because depreciation is deducted in arriving at net income, net income understates cash from operations. If net income is used as a starting point in measuring cash flows from operating activities, depreciation expense must be added back to net income.

Consider the following example. Company A had net income for the year of $20,000 after deducting depreciation of $10,000. Company B had a net loss for the year of $4,000 after deducting $10,000 of depreciation. Although Company B experienced a loss, the company has positive cash flows from operating activities as shown below:

	Company A	Company B
Net income (loss).	$20,000	$(4,000)
Add depreciation expense (which did not require use of cash) .	10,000	10,000
Positive cash flows from operating activities	$30,000	$ 6,000

Company B's loss would have had to exceed $10,000 for there to be negative cash flows from operating activities for the company.

There are other expenses and losses that are added back to net income because they do not actually use cash of the company; these addbacks are often called **noncash charges or expenses.** Besides depreciation, the items added back include amounts of depletion that were expensed, amortization of intangible assets such as patents and goodwill, amortization of discount on bonds payable, and losses from disposals of noncurrent assets.

To illustrate the addback of the losses from disposals of noncurrent assets, assume that Quick Company sold a piece of equipment for $6,000. The equipment had cost $10,000 and had accumulated depreciation of $3,000. The journal entry to record the sale is:

```
Cash. . . . . . . . . . . . . . . . . . . . . . . . . . . .      6,000
Accumulated Depreciation . . . . . . . . . . . . . . . . .       3,000
Loss on Sale of Equipment . . . . . . . . . . . . . . . .        1,000
     Equipment  . . . . . . . . . . . . . . . . . . . . .                10,000
   To record disposal of equipment at a loss.
```

The $6,000 inflow from the sale of the equipment will be shown as a positive cash flow from investing activities on the statement of cash flows. The loss amount ($1,000) was deducted in calculating net income but did not reduce cash. Thus, the loss must be added back to net income in converting net income to cash flows from operating activities.

Certain revenues and gains included in arriving at net income do not provide cash; these items are called **noncash credits or revenues.** These revenues and gains must be deducted from net income to compute cash flows from operating activities. Such items include gains from disposals of noncurrent assets, income from investments carried under the equity method, and amortization of premium on bonds payable.

To illustrate why the gain on the disposal of a noncurrent asset must be deducted from net income, assume that Quick Company sold the equipment mentioned above for $9,000. The journal entry to record the sale is:

```
Cash. . . . . . . . . . . . . . . . . . . . . . . . . . . .      9,000
Accumulated Depreciation  . . . . . . . . . . . . . . . .        3,000
     Equipment  . . . . . . . . . . . . . . . . . . . . .                10,000
     Gain on Sale of Equipment . . . . . . . . . . . . . .                 2,000
   To record disposal of equipment at a gain.
```

The $9,000 inflow from the sale of equipment is shown in the statement of cash as a positive cash flow from investing activities on the statement of cash flows. The gain does not affect cash, yet it was added in calculating net income. Thus, the gain must be deducted in converting net income to cash flows from operating activities.

STEPS IN PREPARING A STATEMENT OF CASH FLOWS

This section of the chapter covers the procedures followed to prepare a statement of cash flows. These procedures are illustrated using the finan-

Illustration 10.2
FINANCIAL STATEMENTS AND OTHER DATA

WELBY COMPANY
Balance Sheets
December 31, 1989, and 1990

	December 31	
	1990	*1989*
Assets		
Cash	$ 21,000	$ 10,000
Accounts receivable	30,000	20,000
Inventory	26,000	30,000
Plant assets	70,000	50,000
Accumulated depreciation	(10,000)	(5,000)
Total assets	$137,000	$105,000
Liabilities and Stockholders' Equity		
Accounts payable	$ 9,000	$ 15,000
Accrued liabilities	2,000	–0–
Common stock ($10 par value)	90,000	60,000
Retained earnings	36,000	30,000
Total liabilities and stockholders' equity	$137,000	$105,000

WELBY COMPANY
Income Statement
For the Year Ended December 31, 1990

Sales		$140,000
Cost of goods sold		100,000
Gross margin		$ 40,000
Operating expenses and taxes	$ 25,000	
Depreciation	5,000	30,000
Net income		$ 10,000

Additional data:
1. Plant assets purchased for cash during 1990 amounted to $20,000.
2. Common stock with a par value of $30,000 was issued at par for cash.
3. Cash dividends declared and paid in 1990 totaled $4,000.

cial statements and additional data for the Welby Company given in Illustration 10.2.

The first step is to calculate the cash flows from operating activities, using either the direct or indirect method. The second step is to analyze all of the noncurrent accounts for changes resulting from investing and financing activities. The third step is to arrange the information gathered in Steps 1 and 2 into the format required for the statement of cash flows.

Step 1: Determining Cash Flows from Operating Activities—
Direct Method

Under the direct method, the income statement in Illustration 10.2 is converted from the accrual basis to the cash basis as shown in Illustration 10.3.

The amount of sales is converted from an accrual to a cash basis by adding the beginning accounts receivable balance and deducting the ending

Illustration 10.3
CONVERSION OF INCOME STATEMENT FROM ACCRUAL BASIS TO CASH BASIS

			WELBY COMPANY			
			Income Statement			
			For the Year Ended December 31, 1990			
	Accrual Basis		Add	Deduct		Cash Basis
Sales		$140,000	$20,000[1]	$30,000[2]		$130,000
Cost of goods sold . .	$100,000		{26,000[3] {15,000[5]	{30,000[4] { 9,000[6]	$102,000	
Operating expenses and taxes	25,000		–0– [7]	2,000[8]	23,000	
Depreciation	5,000			5,000	–0–	
		130,000				125,000
Net income		$ 10,000				$ 5,000

[1] Beginning Accounts Receivable	[5] Beginning Accounts Payable
[2] Ending Accounts Receivable	[6] Ending Accounts Payable
[3] Ending Inventory	[7] Beginning Accrued Liabilities
[4] Beginning Inventory	[8] Ending Accrued Liabilities

accounts receivable balance. Cost of goods sold is the most complex conversion. First, ending inventory is added and beginning inventory is deducted. Then beginning accounts payable is added and ending accounts payable is deducted. The result is the cash outflow for goods acquired. Next, operating expenses are converted to a cash basis by adding the beginning accrued liabilities and deducting the ending accrued liabilities. Since depreciation does not involve cash flows, it is eliminated. Net income on a cash basis is $5,000 lower than net income on an accrual basis.

Alternative Step 1: Determining Cash Flows from Operating Activities—Indirect Method

Under the indirect method there are two types of adjustments in converting net income to cash flows from operating activities. The first type involves adding back or deducting from net income those items, such as depreciation, that did not use up or provide cash. The Welby Company only had one such item—depreciation in the amount of $5,000.

The second type includes changes that occurred in current accounts other than cash. Applying these two steps to the Welby Company financial statements and other data in Illustration 10.2 yields the following schedule:

Cash flows from operating activities:	
Net income	$ 10,000
Adjustments to reconcile net income to net cash provided by operating activities:	
Depreciation	5,000
Increase in accounts receivable	(10,000)
Decrease in inventory	4,000
Decrease in accounts payable	(6,000)
Increase in accrued liabilities	2,000
Net cash provided by operating activities	$ 5,000

The $10,000 increase in accounts receivable represents the difference between accrual basis sales revenue and cash collected from customers (sales revenue on a cash basis). An increase in accounts receivable indicates that accrual basis sales revenue was greater than cash basis sales revenue, and a decrease in accounts receivable indicates the opposite. Therefore, the $10,000 increase in accounts receivable must be deducted from accrual basis net income to convert it to cash basis income.

The changes in the balances of inventory and of accounts payable represent the difference between accrual basis cost of goods sold and cash paid for inventory purchases (cash basis cost of goods sold). We will first examine the effect of the change in inventory. If all the purchases had been for cash, then cost of goods sold on the cash basis would equal total purchases for the period. Total purchases were $96,000, computed as follows:

Ending inventory	$ 26,000
+Cost of goods sold	100,000
Cost of goods available for sale	$126,000
−Beginning inventory	30,000
Purchases	$ 96,000

Notice that the $4,000 decrease in inventory causes accrual basis cost of goods sold to be $4,000 greater than purchases. If we continue to assume that the total amount of purchases equals the amount of cash paid for purchases, then the higher cost of goods sold means that accrual basis income will be less than cash basis net income. Consequently, the $4,000 decrease in inventory must be added back to accrual basis net income to convert it to cash basis income.

However, not all purchases were made for cash. The $6,000 decrease in accounts payable represents the difference between purchases made on account and cash paid to suppliers during the period. A decrease in accounts payable means that more cash was paid than there were purchases, so cash basis cost of goods sold is greater than the amount of purchases. Thus, the $6,000 decrease in accounts payable must be deducted from accrual basis net income to convert it to cash basis income.

The correctness of the preceding analysis is demonstrated by the following computation:

Accounts payable, January 1.	$ 15,000
Purchases (from prior schedule)	96,000
Total	$111,000
Accounts payable, December 31	9,000
Cash paid to suppliers during the year	$102,000

Cash basis cost of goods sold is $102,000, or $2,000 more than the accrual basis amount. Net income on a cash basis is $2,000 less than the accrual basis amount. The $2,000 deduction agrees with the net amount of the individual analyses: $6,000 deducted for the decrease in accounts payable, and $4,000 added for the decrease in inventory nets out to a $2,000 deduction.

Accrued liabilities would be handled in a manner similar to accounts payable. Prepaid expenses would be treated the same as accounts receivable or inventory. Fortunately, you need not go through the above analysis every time you prepare a cash flow statement. Instead, the following table can be used to make the second type of adjustment.

For changes in these current assets and current liabilities:	Make these adjustments to convert accrual basis net income to cash basis net income:	
	Add	Deduct
Accounts receivable	Decrease	Increase
Inventory	Decrease	Increase
Prepaid expenses	Decrease	Increase
Accounts payable	Increase	Decrease
Accrued liabilities	Increase	Decrease

Notice in the above summary that all changes in current asset accounts are handled in a similar manner. Also, all changes in current liability accounts are handled in a similar manner, but that manner is exactly the opposite from the handling of the current asset changes. A more condensed table to use in making these adjustments is:

For Changes in:	Add the Change to Net Income	Deduct the Change from Net Income
Current assets	Decreases	Increases
Current liabilities	Increases	Decreases

In applying the rules given in the table, a decrease in a current asset is added to net income; an increase in a current asset is deducted from net income. For current liabilities, increases are added and decreases are deducted.

The complete adjustment or conversion procedure used in the following comprehensive example is summarized below:

Accrual basis net income
+ Expenses and losses not reducing cash
− Revenues and gains not producing cash
= Total
+ or − Changes in other current asset and current liability accounts
= Cash flows from operating activities

Step 2: Analyzing the Noncurrent Accounts

At first, it may seem quite unusual to seek the causes of the change in cash by looking at the noncurrent accounts. But bear in mind that when a transaction affects cash it also affects some other account. The changes in current assets and current liabilities have already been taken into consideration in Step 1. Now the noncurrent accounts must be analyzed. In the Welby Company example, there are four noncurrent accounts to analyze: Plant Assets, Accumulated Depreciation, Common Stock, and Retained Earnings.

1. Because of the importance of cash flows from operating activities, the analysis of the noncurrent accounts begins by reviewing the Retained Earnings account. Retained Earnings is the account to which net income or loss for the period was closed. The $6,000 increase in this account consists of $10,000 of net income less $4,000 of dividends paid. The net income amount can be found in the income statement. Both net income and dividends must be entered on the statement of cash flows using the indirect method in Illustration 10.5. The $10,000 net income is used as the starting figure in determining cash flows from operating activities. Thus, net income of $10,000 is entered on the statement in the "Cash flows from operating activities" section.

2. The Plant Assets account increased by $20,000 during the year. The additional data indicate that plant assets of $20,000 were purchased during the period. A purchase of plant assets is shown as a deduction in the section "Cash flows from investing activities."

3. The $5,000 increase in the Accumulated Depreciation account equals the amount of depreciation expense shown in the income statement for the period. Because depreciation does not affect or use up cash, under the addback method it must be added back to net income on the statement of cash flows to convert net income to a cash basis.

4. The $30,000 increase in common stock resulted from the issuance of stock at par value, as disclosed in the additional data (item 2). An issuance of stock is shown in the statement of cash flows as a positive amount in the section, "Cash flows from financing activities."

Step 3: Arranging Information into Statement of Cash Flows

After all the noncurrent accounts have been analyzed, the statement of cash flows can be prepared from the information generated in the last step. Illustration 10.4 presents the statement of cash flows for Welby Company using the direct method. Illustration 10.5 shows the statement of cash flows using the indirect method.

The completed statement of cash flows has three major sections: cash flows from operating activities, cash flows from investing activities, and cash flows from financing activities. The format in the "operating activities" section differs between the direct method and indirect method. The direct method adjusts each item in the income statement to a cash basis. The indirect method makes these same adjustments, but makes them to net income rather than to each item in the income statement. Both methods eliminate the effects of noncash items such as depreciation and also eliminate gains and losses on sales of plant assets.

The only item shown in the "Cash flows from investing activities" is the cash outflow of $20,000 for the purchase of plant assets. In a more complex example there could be several other items listed.

There are two items under the section headed, "Cash flows from financing activities." The issuance of common stock resulted in a cash inflow of $30,000. The payment of dividends resulted in a cash outflow of $4,000.

Illustration 10.4
STATEMENT OF CASH FLOWS—DIRECT METHOD

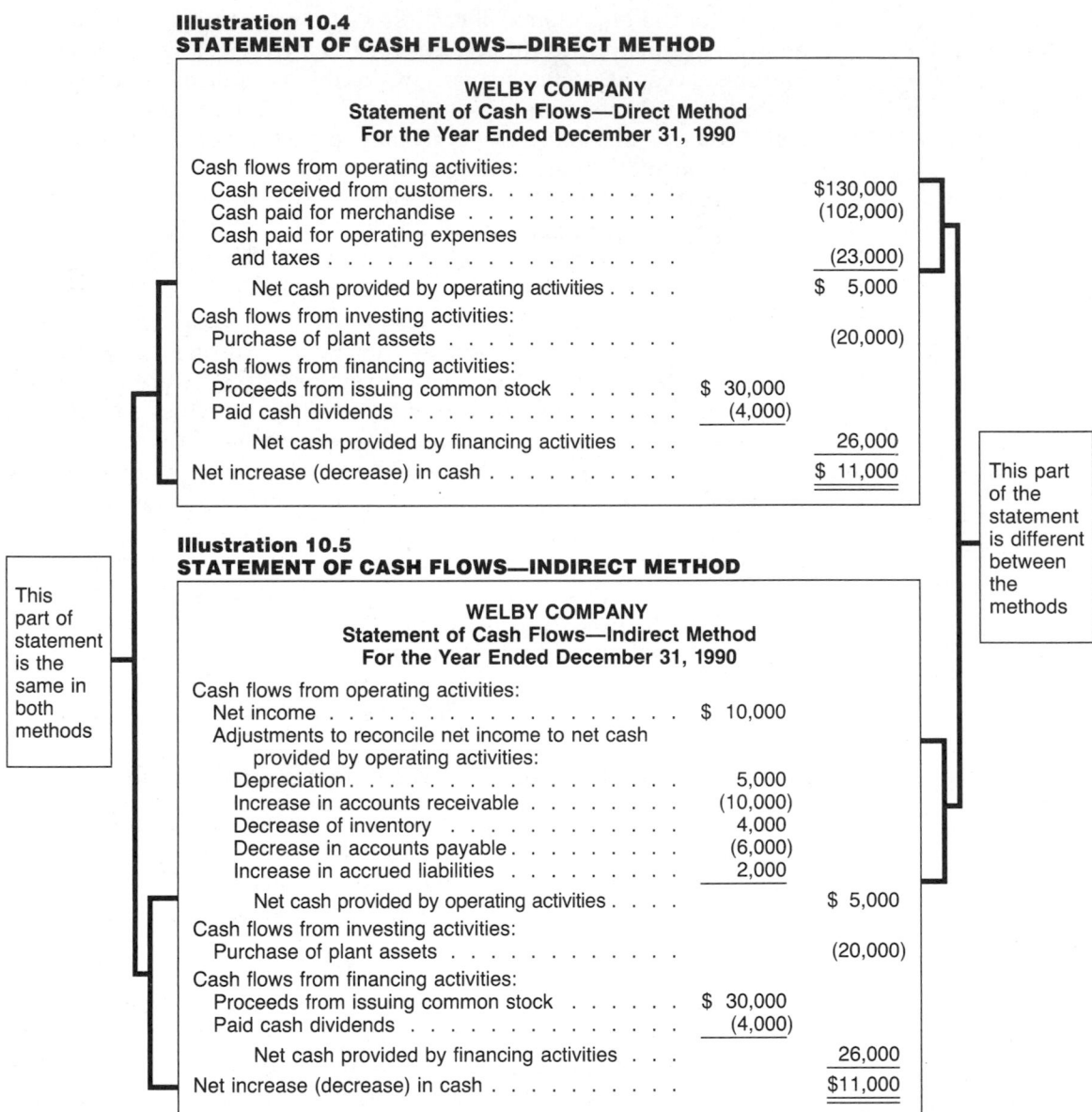

WELBY COMPANY
Statement of Cash Flows—Direct Method
For the Year Ended December 31, 1990

Cash flows from operating activities:
Cash received from customers. $130,000
Cash paid for merchandise . . . .   (102,000)
Cash paid for operating expenses
  and taxes . . . .   (23,000)

Net cash provided by operating activities . . . . $ 5,000

Cash flows from investing activities:
Purchase of plant assets . . . .   (20,000)

Cash flows from financing activities:
Proceeds from issuing common stock . . . . . . $ 30,000
Paid cash dividends . . . .   (4,000)

Net cash provided by financing activities . . .   26,000

Net increase (decrease) in cash . . . . $ 11,000

Illustration 10.5
STATEMENT OF CASH FLOWS—INDIRECT METHOD

WELBY COMPANY
Statement of Cash Flows—Indirect Method
For the Year Ended December 31, 1990

Cash flows from operating activities:
Net income . . . . $ 10,000
Adjustments to reconcile net income to net cash
  provided by operating activities:
  Depreciation.   5,000
  Increase in accounts receivable . . . .   (10,000)
  Decrease of inventory   4,000
  Decrease in accounts payable. . . . .   (6,000)
  Increase in accrued liabilities   2,000

Net cash provided by operating activities . . . . $ 5,000

Cash flows from investing activities:
Purchase of plant assets . . . .   (20,000)

Cash flows from financing activities:
Proceeds from issuing common stock . . . . . . $ 30,000
Paid cash dividends . . . .   (4,000)

Net cash provided by financing activities . . .   26,000

Net increase (decrease) in cash $11,000

This part of statement is the same in both methods

This part of the statement is different between the methods

The last line of the statement is the $11,000 increase in cash for the year. In other examples there could be a decrease in cash for the year.

COMPREHENSIVE ILLUSTRATION

Objective 3:
Prepare a statement of cash flows

Presented and discussed below is a more complete example of the procedures followed to prepare a statement of cash flows. A working paper (shown later in Illustration 10.8) is used to aid in preparing the statement.

This working paper is used for both the direct method and the indirect method. If the direct method is used, the information regarding cash flows from operations on the working paper is used to prepare the reconciliation of that figure with net income. An additional work paper is used to convert the income statement to a cash basis for use in the statement of cash flows.

The basic data for the example are found in Illustrations 10.6 and 10.7, which present the statement of income and retained earnings (combined) and comparative balance sheets of the United States Corporation.

Assume the following information about the noncurrent accounts is available:

1. There were no purchases of investments during the year. Investments with an $8,000 cost were sold for $9,700.
2. Land and buildings with a cost of $65,000 ($45,000 for the buildings and $20,000 for the land) were acquired, subject to a mortgage note of $35,000.

Illustration 10.6
STATEMENT OF INCOME AND RETAINED EARNINGS

<table>
<tr><td colspan="3" align="center">UNITED STATES CORPORATION
Statement of Income and Retained Earnings
For the Year Ended December 31, 1990</td></tr>
<tr><td>Net sales . . . .</td><td></td><td>$1,464,200</td></tr>
<tr><td>Cost of goods sold . . . .</td><td></td><td>871,150</td></tr>
<tr><td>Gross margin . . . .</td><td></td><td>$ 593,050</td></tr>
<tr><td>Operating expenses:</td><td></td><td></td></tr>
<tr><td>Salaries . . . .</td><td>$215,000</td><td></td></tr>
<tr><td>Depreciation ($3,250, buildings; $31,050, equipment) . .</td><td>34,300</td><td></td></tr>
<tr><td>Supplies . . . .</td><td>7,320</td><td></td></tr>
<tr><td>Advertising . . . .</td><td>90,000</td><td></td></tr>
<tr><td>Taxes, payroll and property . . . .</td><td>26,000</td><td></td></tr>
<tr><td>General and administrative expenses . . . .</td><td>123,780</td><td></td></tr>
<tr><td>Total operating expenses . . . .</td><td></td><td>$ 496,400</td></tr>
<tr><td>Income from operations . . . .</td><td></td><td>$ 96,650</td></tr>
<tr><td>Other revenue:</td><td></td><td></td></tr>
<tr><td>Interest revenue . . . .</td><td>$ 1,950</td><td></td></tr>
<tr><td>Gain on sale of long-term investments . . . .</td><td>1,700</td><td>3,650</td></tr>
<tr><td></td><td></td><td>$ 100,300</td></tr>
<tr><td>Other expenses:</td><td></td><td></td></tr>
<tr><td>Interest expense . . . .</td><td>$ 3,800</td><td></td></tr>
<tr><td>Loss on sale of equipment . . . .</td><td>900</td><td>4,700</td></tr>
<tr><td>Income before federal income taxes . . . .</td><td></td><td>$ 95,600</td></tr>
<tr><td>Deduct: Federal income taxes . . . .</td><td></td><td>45,250</td></tr>
<tr><td>Net income . . . .</td><td></td><td>$ 50,350</td></tr>
<tr><td>Retained earnings, January 1 . . . .</td><td></td><td>84,100</td></tr>
<tr><td></td><td></td><td>$ 134,450</td></tr>
<tr><td>Deduct: Dividends declared and paid . . . .</td><td></td><td>18,000</td></tr>
<tr><td>Retained earnings, December 31 . . . .</td><td></td><td>$ 116,450</td></tr>
</table>

Illustration 10.7
COMPARATIVE BALANCE SHEETS

UNITED STATES CORPORATION Comparative Balance Sheets December 31, 1989, and 1990	December 31, 1990	December 31, 1989	Increase/ (Decrease)
Assets			
Current assets:			
Cash	$ 46,300	$ 40,900	$ 5,400
Accounts receivable, net	112,160	101,000	11,160
Inventories	130,600	115,300	15,300
Prepaid advertising	3,100	4,700	(1,600)
Total current assets	$292,160	$261,900	$ 30,260
Investments	$ 17,000	$ 25,000	$ (8,000)
Property, plant, and equipment:			
Land	$100,000	$ 80,000	$ 20,000
Buildings	175,000	130,000	45,000
Accumulated depreciation— buildings	(29,750)	(26,500)	(3,250)
Equipment	198,000	175,000	23,000
Accumulated depreciation— equipment	(57,650)	(43,100)	(14,550)
Total property, plant, and equipment	$385,600	$315,400	$ 70,200
Total assets	$694,760	$602,300	$ 92,460
Liabilities and Stockholders' Equity			
Current liabilities:			
Accounts payable	$ 91,420	$ 86,870	$ 4,550
Accrued salaries	9,890	12,230	(2,340)
Federal income tax liability	12,000	14,100	(2,100)
Total current liabilities	$113,310	$113,200	$ 110
Long-term liabilities:			
Mortgage note payable, 10% (on land and buildings)	$ 35,000	$ –0–	$ 35,000
Bonds payable, 8%, due 1993 . . .	40,000	40,000	–0–
Total long-term liabilities . . .	$ 75,000	$ 40,000	$ 35,000
Total liabilities	$188,310	$153,200	$ 35,110
Stockholders' equity:			
Common stock, stated value, $50 per share	$390,000	$365,000	$ 25,000
Retained earnings	116,450	84,100	32,350
Total stockholders' equity . . .	$506,450	$449,100	$ 57,350
Total liabilities and stockholders' equity	$694,760	$602,300	$ 92,460

3. During the year, the corporation disposed of equipment that had an original cost of $20,000 and accumulated depreciation of $16,500. The equipment was sold for $2,600.
4. The common stock was sold for cash.

The working paper in Illustration 10.8 for the United States Corporation is used to analyze the transactions and prepare the statement of cash flows. The discussion that follows will describe the items and trace their effects in the entries made on the working paper.

The steps in preparing the working paper are described below:

1. Enter the account balances of all balance sheet accounts at the beginning of the period in the first column and enter the account balances at the end of the period in the fourth column. Notice that the debit items are listed first, followed by the credit items.
2. Total the debits and the credits in the first and fourth columns to make sure that debits equal credits in each column.
3. Write "Cash Flows from Operating Activities" immediately below the total of the credit items. Skip sufficient lines on which to record all adjustments to convert net income to cash flows from operating activities. Then write "Cash Flows from Investing Activities" and allow enough space for those items. Finally, write "Cash Flows from Financing Activities" and allow enough space for those items.
4. Entries for analyzing transactions are entered in the second and third columns. The entries, which may be made in any order, serve two functions: *(a)* they explain the change in each account, and *(b)* they classify the changes into operating, investing, and financing activities. These entries will be discussed individually.
5. Total the debits and credits in the second and third columns; they should be equal. There will be one pair of totals for the balance sheet items and another pair for the bottom portion of the working paper. The bottom portion of the working paper is used to prepare the statement of cash flows.

Completing the Working Paper

The working paper in Illustration 10.8 is completed by analyzing the change in each noncash balance sheet account. Remember that the focus of this working paper is on cash and that every change in cash is accompanied by a change in a noncash balance sheet account. After entries have been properly made to analyze all changes in noncash balance sheet accounts, the working paper will show all activities affecting cash flows. The explanations below are keyed by numbers to the entries on the working paper.

Entry (1). The beginning and ending cash balances are compared to determine the change for the year, which is a $5,400 increase. An entry is made on the working paper debiting Cash for $5,400 and crediting Increase in Cash for Year near the bottom of the schedule. This entry indicates that of the cash flowing into the company during the year, $5,400 was used to increase the Cash balance. The entry also sets out the change in cash that the statement seeks to explain. No further attention need be paid to cash in completing the working paper.

Illustration 10.8
WORKING PAPER FOR STATEMENT OF CASH FLOWS

UNITED STATES CORPORATION
Working Paper for Statement of Cash Flows
For the Year Ended, December 31, 1990

	Account Balances 12/31/89	Analysis of Transactions for 1990		Account Balances 12/31/90
		Debit	Credit	
Debits				
Cash	40,900	*(1)* 5,400		46,300
Accounts Receivable	101,000	*(10)* 11,160		112,160
Inventories	115,300	*(11)* 15,300		130,600
Prepaid Advertising	4,700		*(12)* 1,600	3,100
Investments	25,000		*(2)* 8,000	17,000
Land	80,000	*(3)* 20,000		100,000
Buildings	130,000	*(3)* 45,000		175,000
Equipment	175,000	*(5)* 43,000	*(4)* 20,000	198,000
Totals	671,900			782,160
Credits				
Accumulated Depreciation—Buildings	26,500		*(6)* 3,250	29,750
Accumulated Depreciation—Equipment	43,100	*(4)* 16,500	*(6)* 31,050	57,650
Accounts Payable	86,870		*(13)* 4,550	91,420
Salaries Payable	12,230	*(14)* 2,340		9,890
Federal Income Tax Liability	14,100	*(15)* 2,100		12,000
Mortgage Note Payable	–0–		*(3)* 35,000	35,000
Bonds Payable	40,000			40,000
Common Stock	365,000		*(7)* 25,000	390,000
Retained Earnings	84,100	*(9)* 18,000	*(8)* 50,350	116,450
Totals	671,900	178,800	178,800	782,160

continued

Attention is now directed toward changes in other balance sheet accounts. These accounts can be dealt with in any order. But, in order to group certain items, the noncurrent accounts are analyzed first.

Entry *(2)*. Investments is the first noncurrent account. The additional information disclosed that investments were sold at a gain, which was recorded in the following manner:

```
Cash . . . . . . . . . . . . . . . . . . . . . . . . . . . . .   9,700
    Investments . . . . . . . . . . . . . . . . . . . . . . .           8,000
    Gain on Sale of Investments . . . . . . . . . . . . . . .           1,700
```

Illustration 10.8 *(concluded)*

UNITED STATES CORPORATION
Working Paper for Statement of Cash Flows
For the Year Ended, December 31, 1990

	Account Balances 12/31/89	Analysis of Transactions for 1990		Account Balances 12/31/90
		Debit	**Credit**	
Cash Flows from Operating Activities:				
Net Income		(8) 50,350		
Gain on Sale of Investments			(2) 1,700	
Loss on Sale of Equipment		(4) 900		
Depreciation Expense—Buildings		(6) 3,250		
Depreciation Expense—Equipment		(6) 31,050		
Increase in Accounts Receivable			(10) 11,160	
Increase in Inventories			(11) 15,300	
Decrease in Prepaid Advertising		(12) 1,600		
Increase in Accounts Payable		(13) 4,550		
Decrease in Salaries Payable			(14) 2,340	
Decrease in Federal Income Tax Liability			(15) 2,100	
Cash Flows from Investing Activities:				
Proceeds from Sale of Investments		(2) 9,700		
Purchase of Land and Buildings (cash portion)			(3) 30,000	
Proceeds from Sale of Equipment		(4) 2,600		
Purchase of Equipment			(5) 43,000	
Cash Flows from Financing Activities:				
Proceeds from Issuing Common Stock		(7) 25,000		
Paid Cash Dividends			(9) 18,000	
Increase in Cash for Year			(1) 5,400	
Noncash Investing and Financing Activities:				
Mortgage Note Issued to Acquire Land and Buildings		(3) 35,000	(3) 35,000	
Totals		164,000	164,000	

Since cash changes and their causes are the focus of the working paper, the following entry is made on the working paper to show the source of cash.

```
Proceeds from Sale of Investments  . . . . . . . . . . . . . . . .   9,700
        Investments . . . . . . . . . . . . . . . . . . . . . . . .          8,000
        Gain on Sale of Investments . . . . . . . . . . . . . . . .          1,700
```

The working paper now shows that $9,700 cash resulted from the sale of investments. The entry also removes the $1,700 gain on sale of investments from cash flows from operating activities because this amount is already included as part of the cash resulting from sale of investments. If the $9,700 cash received from the sale is reported and the gain is not removed from cash flows from operating activities, the $1,700 gain is shown or counted twice. Note that the working paper entry is identical to the original journal entry for the sale, except for the $9,700 debit. Instead of debiting Cash, a properly described investing activity is debited. The activities affecting cash are shown in the lower section of the working paper. The $8,000 credit accounts fully for the change (decrease) in the Investments account balance; if it had not fully accounted for the change, there would have to be other transactions involving the Investments account to analyze and report.

Entry (3). The changes in the Land and Buildings accounts resulted from the following entry:

Land .	20,000	
Buildings .	45,000	
Cash .		30,000
Mortgage Note Payable		35,000

This transaction requires two entries on the working paper. First, Land and Buildings are debited for $20,000 and $45,000, respectively, and an item described as "Purchase of Land and Buildings" is credited for $30,000 in the "investing activity section" for the cash portion. Second, an entry labeled "Mortgage Note Issued to Acquire Land and Buildings" is entered at the bottom of the work sheet in both the debit and credit columns for the $35,000 noncash portion of the transaction. This item is listed on the work sheet so you will not forget to include it in a schedule that is separate from the statement of cash flows. This transaction is an example of a significant financing and investing activity that must be included in a separate schedule because part of it did not affect cash.

Entry (4). The Equipment account shows a net increase of $23,000 resulting from two transactions: a $43,000 purchase and a $20,000 retirement. The net change in the account must be analyzed to show both transactions.

Data relating to the $20,000 retirement were included in the additional information given. The computation of the loss on sale can be summarized as follows using data provided in the additional information:

Cost of equipment sold (given) .	$20,000
Less: Accumulated depreciation (given) .	16,500
Book value of equipment sold .	$ 3,500
Less: Cash received (given) .	2,600
Loss on sale (as shown in income statement) .	$ 900

The complete working paper entry for the sale of equipment is:

Sale of Equipment	2,600
Accumulated Depreciation—Equipment	16,500
Loss on Sale of Equipment	900
Equipment	20,000

This entry records the cash resulting from the sale of equipment under the "investing activities" section on the working paper and explains part of the changes in the Equipment and the Accumulated Depreciation— Equipment accounts. The loss is added back to net income because it is a noncash item that was deducted in arriving at net income. The loss has exactly the same effect as depreciation expense.

Entry (5). This entry debits the Equipment account and credits "Purchase of Equipment" in the "investing activities" section for the $43,000 cash spent to acquire new equipment. The $43,000 debit to Equipment along with the $20,000 credit to Equipment in entry (4) fully accounts for the $23,000 increase in the account.

Entry (6). This entry adds $3,250 building depreciation and $31,050 equipment depreciation back to net income and credits the respective accumulated depreciation accounts. The $31,050 credit to the accumulated depreciation account for equipment less the $16,500 debit to this account in entry (4) explains fully the increase in this account from $43,100 to $57,650.

Entry (7). This entry shows the $25,000 cash received from the sale of common stock as a "financing activity." The entry also explains completely the change in the Common Stock account. If stock had been sold for more than its stated value of $50 per share, the excess would be recorded in a separate Paid-In Capital in Excess of Stated Value account. But only the total amount of cash received from the issuance would have been reported on the statement of cash flows as a single figure because only the total amount received is significant.

Entry (8). The statement of income and retained earnings reveals that net income for 1989 was $50,350. Entry (8) records the $50,350 as the starting point in measuring cash flows from operating activities and credits Retained Earnings as a partial explanation of the change in that account.

Entry (9). This entry debits Retained Earnings and credits Payment of Cash Dividends for the $18,000 of dividends declared and paid. The entry also completes the explanation of the change in Retained Earnings ($84,100 + $50,350 − $18,000 = $116,450). Notice that on the statement of cash flows the dividends must be *paid* to be included as a cash outflow from financing activities.

If Retained Earnings had changed for reasons other than net income or cash dividends, the causes of the changes must be determined in order to decide whether they should be reported in the statement of cash flows. Transactions such as stock dividends and stock splits would not be reported on the statement of cash flows or in a separate schedule because they lack significance from an analytical viewpoint and because these items never affect cash. But an entry must be made on the working paper to explain the changes caused by a stock dividend or split, even if cash was not affected. All changes in all noncash accounts must be explained to show that a change affecting cash was not overlooked.

The next task is to analyze changes in current accounts other than Cash. All the current accounts of the United States Corporation are closely related to operations, and their changes are included in converting net income to net cash flows from operating activities. The changes in the current accounts are analyzed in the manner previously discussed (see pages 358–60).

Entry (10). The $11,160 increase in accounts receivable must be deducted from net income when converting it to cash flows from operating activities. If accounts receivable increased, sales to customers exceeded cash received from customers. To convert net income to a cash basis, the $11,160 must be deducted.

The working paper technique used makes the recording of these effects almost mechanical. Accounts Receivable must be debited for $11,160 to increase it from $101,000 to $112,160. If Accounts Receivable is debited, a credit must be entered for an item that can be entitled "Increase in Accounts Receivable." The increase is deducted from net income in converting it to cash flows from operating activities.

Entry (11) is virtually a duplicate of entry (10), except that it involves inventories rather than receivables.

Entry (12) is similar to the above two entries, except that it has the opposite effect because prepaid advertising decreased.

Entry (13) records the effect of an increase in accounts payable on net income in converting it to cash flows from operating activities.

Entries (14) and **(15)** record the effects of decreases in two other current liability accounts in converting net income to cash flows from operating activities.

The analysis of the noncash accounts is now complete. To be sure that a change has not been overlooked, the debits and credits in the middle two columns opposite the 1989 balances are added to or subtracted from those balances, line by line. If the working paper has been properly prepared, the results will be the 1990 balances listed in the fourth column. For example, the $43,000 debit is added to the beginning balance for Equipment, and the $20,000 credit deducted to get an ending balance of $198,000.

Next, the debits and credits for the balance sheet account entries and for the statement of cash flows are added to make sure that they are equal in both sections. Note that entries made in the working paper are used only to derive cash flows into and out of the company. These entries are not entered in the company's accounting system because the transactions that caused the cash flows have already been recorded.

Preparing the Statement of Cash Flows

The data in the lower section of the working paper are now used to prepare the statement of cash flows under the indirect method, shown in Illustration 10.9.

Information about all material investing and financing activities of an enterprise that do not result in cash receipts or disbursements in the period are to be reported in a separate schedule, rather than in the statement of cash flows. The disclosure may be in narrative form. United States Corporation had one such transaction, the issuance of a mortgage note to acquire land and buildings. A separate schedule might appear as follows:

> *Schedule of noncash financing and investing activities:*
> Mortgage note issued to acquire land and buildings $35,000

If the direct method is used, the information relating to the indirect method of calculating cash flows from operating activities in the bottom

Illustration 10.9
STATEMENT OF CASH FLOWS—INDIRECT METHOD

UNITED STATES CORPORATION Statement of Cash Flows For the Year Ended December 31, 1990		
Cash flows from operating activities:		
Net income	$ 50,350	
Adjustments to reconcile net income to net cash		
provided by operating activities:		
Gain on sale of investments	(1,700)	
Loss on sale of equipment	900	
Depreciation—buildings	3,250	
Depreciation—equipment	31,050	
Increase in accounts receivable	(11,160)	
Increase in inventories	(15,300)	
Decrease in prepaid advertising	1,600	
Increase in accounts payable	4,550	
Decrease in salaries payable	(2,340)	
Decrease in federal income tax liability	(2,100)	
Net cash provided by operating activities		$ 59,100
Cash flows from investing activities:		
Proceeds from sale of investments	$ 9,700	
Purchase of land and buildings (cash portion)	(30,000)	
Proceeds from sale of equipment	2,600	
Payment for purchase of equipment	(43,000)	
Net cash used by investing activities		(60,700)
Cash flows from financing activities:		
Proceeds from issuing common stock	$ 25,000	
Paid cash dividends	(18,000)	
Net cash provided by financing activities		7,000
Net increase in cash		$ 5,400

part of the working paper (Illustration 10.8) and in the top part of Illustration 10.9 would appear in a separate supporting schedule rather than in the statement of cash flows. Also, an additional working paper is needed if the direct method is used. This working paper converts the items in the income statement to a cash basis as shown in Illustration 10.10.

Notice that depreciation is eliminated when converting to a cash basis since it does not involve an outflow of cash in the current period. Also, the gain from sale of long-term investments and loss on sale of equip-

Illustration 10.10
WORKING PAPER TO CONVERT INCOME STATEMENT TO CASH BASIS

UNITED STATES CORPORATION
Income Statement
For the year ended December 31, 1990

	Accrual Basis	Add	Deduct	Cash Basis
Net sales	$1,464,200	$101,000[1]	$112,160[2]	$1,453,040
Cost of goods sold		130,600[3]	115,300[4]	
	871,150	86,870[5]	91,420[6]	881,900
Gross margin	$ 593,050			$ 571,140
Operating expenses:				
Salaries	$215,000	12,230[7]	9,890[8]	$217,340
Depreciation	34,300		34,300	–0–
Supplies	7,320			7,320
Advertising	90,000	3,100[9]	4,700[10]	88,400
Taxes, payroll and property . . .	26,000			26,000
General administrative				
expenses	123,780			123,780
Total operating expenses . .		496,400		462,840
Income from operations	$ 96,650			$ 108,300
Other revenues:				
Interest revenue	$ 1,950			$ 1,950
Gain on sale of long-term				
investments	1,700		1,700	–0–
	3,650			1,950
	$ 100,300			$ 110,250
Other expenses:				
Interest expense	$ 3,800			$ 3,800
Loss on sale of equipment . . .	900		900	–0–
	4,700			3,800
Income before federal				
income taxes	$ 95,600			$ 106,450
Deduct: Federal				
income taxes	45,250	14,100[11]	12,000[12]	47,350
Net income	$ 50,350			$ 59,100

[1] Beginning Accounts Receivable
[2] Ending Accounts Receivable
[3] Ending Inventory
[4] Beginning Inventory
[5] Beginning Accounts Payable
[6] Ending Accounts Payable
[7] Beginning Salaries Payable
[8] Ending Salaries Payable
[9] Ending Prepaid Advertising
[10] Beginning Prepaid Advertising
[11] Beginning Estimated Tax Liability
[12] Ending Estimated Tax Liability

Illustration 10.11
CASH FLOW STATEMENT—DIRECT METHOD

UNITED STATES CORPORATION
Statement of Cash Flows
For the Year Ended December 31, 1990

Cash flows from operating activities:

Cash received from customers.	$1,453,040	
Cash paid for merchandise for resale	(881,900)	
Cash paid to employees	(217,340)	
Cash paid for supplies	(7,320)	
Cash paid for advertising	(88,400)	
Taxes, payroll and property paid	(26,000)	
General administration expenses paid	(123,780)	
Interest received	1,950	
Interest paid	(3,800)	
Federal income taxes paid	(47,350)	
Net cash provided by operating activities		$59,100
Cash flows from investing activities:		
Proceeds from sale of investments	$ 9,700	
Purchase of land and buildings (cash portion)	(30,000)	
Proceeds from sale of equipment	2,600	
Payment for purchase of equipment	(43,000)	
Net cash used by investing activities	(60,700)	
Cash flows from financing activities:		
Proceeds from issuing common stock	$ 25,000	
Paid cash dividends	(18,000)	
Net cash provided by financing activities		7,000
Net increase in cash		$ 5,400

---

ment are eliminated since the proceeds of these transactions are reported in the section, "Cash flows from investing activities" in the statement of cash flows.

The statement of cash flows under the direct method is shown in Illustration 10.11. Notice that the only difference between the direct and indirect methods is in the section "Cash flows from operating activities."

WORKING CAPITAL OR CASH FLOWS

Objective 4:
Understand the historical development from a statement of changes in financial position to a statement of cash flows

Through the middle of 1988, a **statement of changes in financial position** was required to report on funds flows. This latter statement showed the sources and uses of funds as the two main categories rather than categorizing according to operating activities, investing activities, and financing activities. *Funds* were generally defined as either working capital or cash. **Working capital** is equal to current assets minus current liabilities. As can be seen in Illustration 10.12, the common practice before 1983 was to define funds as working capital.

Statements based on working capital were prepared for several reasons. Accurate information was needed about the flows of liquid assets (working capital) through a company because such flows are the lifeblood

Illustration 10.12
DEFINITIONS OF "FUNDS" IN STATEMENT
OF CHANGES IN FINANCIAL POSITION

	1986	1985	1984	1983	1982
Changes in working capital . . .	202	220	244	286	346
Changes in cash	398	380	356	314	254
Total	600	600	600	600	600

SOURCE: Based on American Institute of Certified Public Accountants, *Accounting Trends & Techniques* (New York: AICPA, 1987).

of a business. Yet constant changes in accounting principles yielded net income amounts that often were not good measures of such liquid asset flows from operations. In addition, attention focused on working capital rather than cash because little significance was attached to the composition of working capital, including how much of it was cash. In general, working capital usually turned over in a business quickly enough so that if not now in cash form, it would be shortly.

The Shift Toward Cash Flows

Beginning in 1983, more than half of a sample of 600 companies used the cash definition of funds. There were several reasons for this shift toward the cash definition of funds. Many companies experienced severe cash flow problems, not working capital problems. The FASB noted the importance of cash flows in the Conceptual Framework Project, stating "that the reporting of meaningful components of cash flows is generally more useful than reporting changes in working capital."[2] Shortly after the publication of this statement, the Financial Executives Institute (FEI) recommended that its members adopt the cash basis in preparing a statement of changes in financial position.[3] The FEI represents approximately 95% of the companies with securities traded on the New York Stock Exchange and the American Stock Exchange.

The shifting of attention from working capital flows to cash flows also is supported by developments in modern finance. The investment decision is seen more clearly as one in which cash outlays are compared with expected cash returns, appropriately discounted for time and risk. Management, investors, and creditors are all alike in that each "invests" cash to get future cash returns. Thus, information is needed to enable users to make predictions of the amounts, timing, and uncertainty surrounding expected cash receipts. Information also is needed to provide feedback on prior assessments of cash flow.

Information on prior *cash flows* provides a better basis for making predictions of cash flows than does information on prior *working capital flows*. Cash flows often differ sharply from working capital flows. For example, a rapidly expanding business that increases its working capital by ex-

[2]FASB, "Reporting Income, Cash Flows, and Financial Position of Business Enterprises," *Proposed Statement of Financial Accounting Concepts,* Exposure Draft (Stamford, Conn., 1981), p. xi.

[3]Financial Executives Institute, *Alert,* December 14, 1981.

panding inventories and accounts receivable may not have enough cash to meet current bills. Cash flow analysis, rather than working capital analysis, is required to reveal such problems.

The adoption of the statement of cash flows completed the shift from a working capital emphasis to a cash emphasis. The new statement of cash flows seems to provide information on cash flows in a much more useful and understandable format than did the old statement of changes in financial position. But an analysis of working capital can still provide useful information as illustrated in the next section.

Analysis of Working Capital

Objective 5: Understand how to prepare a schedule of changes in working capital

As stated earlier, **working capital** is equal to current assets minus current liabilities. A knowledge of the changes in total working capital and its composition can be helpful in judging a company's debt-paying ability. For instance, if working capital continues to decrease period after period, the time may come when current liabilities exceed current assets. Also, working capital may be composed of mostly slow-moving or obsolete inventory rather than cash or other "liquid" assets that will become cash within a short period of time. To assess the change in total working capital and changes in its composition over a period of time (such as a year), a **schedule of changes in working capital** is often prepared. Such a schedule lists all current assets and current liabilities, their beginning and ending balances, and the changes in these balances summarized into a single amount—the net change in working capital.

A schedule of changes in working capital for the Welby Company is presented in Illustration 10.13. Notice that increases in current assets

Illustration 10.13
SCHEDULE OF CHANGES IN WORKING CAPITAL

WELBY COMPANY				
Schedule of Changes in Working Capital				
For the Year Ended December 31, 1990				
	December 31		Working Capital	
	1990	1989	Increase	Decrease
Current assets:				
Cash	$21,000	$10,000	$11,000	
Accounts receivable	30,000	20,000	10,000	
Inventory	26,000	30,000		$ 4,000
Total current assets.	$77,000	$60,000		
Current liabilities:				
Accounts payable	$ 9,000	$15,000	6,000	
Accrued liabilities.	2,000	–0–		2,000
Total current liabilities.	$11,000	$15,000		
Working capital.	$66,000	$45,000		
Increase in working capital				21,000
			$27,000	$27,000

cause working capital to increase, while increases in current liabilities cause working capital to decrease. Decreases in current assets and current liabilities have just the opposite effect as increases in those accounts.

The $11,000 increase in cash, the $10,000 increase in accounts receivable, and the $6,000 decrease in accounts payable increased working capital. The $4,000 decrease in inventory and the $2,000 increase in accrued liabilities decreased working capital. Illustration 10.13 indicates that Welby's working capital increased $21,000 during the year. The company is in a stronger position to pay its short-term debts at the end of 1990 than it was at the end of 1989.

SUMMARY

The statement of cash flows is one of the major financial statements prepared by companies. The purpose of the statement of cash flows is analytical in that it attempts to explain how cash was acquired during a period, how cash was used, and what the net effect was on a company's cash position. Being an analytical tool, the statement of cash flows is an excellent means for assessing the quality of an organization's management.

The statement of cash flows focuses on cash flows into and out of an organization. Either the direct method or indirect method may be used to determine cash flows from operating activities. A key element in the preparation of the statement of cash flows under the direct method is the adjustment of the items in the income statement from an accrual basis to a cash basis. In this process, items such as depreciation and other noncash charges and credits are reduced to zero. Also, gains and losses from sales of plant assets are eliminated because the cash proceeds are reported in a separate section of the statement of cash flows. Under the indirect method these noncash charges and losses on sales of plant assets are *added back* to net income. Noncash credits and gains on sales of plant assets are *deducted* from net income. Then changes in current assets (other than cash) and current liabilities are added to, or deducted from, net income to arrive at cash flows from operating activities.

Next, changes in noncurrent balance sheet accounts are analyzed for their effects on cash. Finally, the resulting cash inflows and cash outflows are organized into a statement of cash flows. Significant investing and financing activities that did not result in cash flows are disclosed in narrative form or in a separate schedule.

This chapter illustrated the use of a working paper to help in preparing a statement of cash flows. The working paper helps to analyze changes in accounts and helps to format the final presentation of the statement of cash flows.

A schedule of changes in working capital may be prepared to help assess the debt-paying ability of a company. Such a schedule shows both the total change in working capital and changes in the composition of working capital over a period of time.

Now that you have studied the statement of cash flows, you should realize its importance in presenting a more complete picture of the business operations of a company. The next chapter discusses the important topic of financial statement analysis, where additional relationships between items in the financial statements are studied to evaluate the performance of the company and its management.

Objective 6: Define and use correctly the new terms in the glossary

NEW TERMS INTRODUCED IN CHAPTER 10

Direct method   Deducts from cash sales only those operating expenses that consumed cash (355).

Financing activities   Include obtaining resources from owners and providing them with a return on their investment and of their investment and obtaining resources from creditors and repaying or otherwise settling the debt (354).

Indirect method   A way of determining cash from operations that starts with net income and adjusts for expenses and revenues that do not affect cash or working capital. Also called the **addback** method (355).

Investing activities   Include lending money and collecting the principal on those loans; acquiring and selling or disposing of securities of other companies or entities; and acquiring and selling or disposing of property, plant, and equipment (354).

Cash flows from operating activities   The net amount of cash received or disbursed for a given period on items that normally appear on the income statement. Usually obtained by converting accrual basis net income to a cash basis amount (355).

Noncash charges or expenses   Expenses and losses that are added back to net income because they do not actually use cash of the company. The items added back include amounts of depletion that were expensed, amortization of intangible assets such as patents and goodwill, amortization of discount on bonds payable, and losses from disposals of noncurrent assets (356).

Noncash credits or revenues   Revenues and gains included in arriving at net income that do not provide cash; an example is a gain on the disposal of a noncurrent asset (356).

Operating activities   Generally include the cash effects of transactions and other events that enter into the determination of net income (353).

Schedule of changes in working capital   A schedule listing all current assets and current liabilities, their beginning and ending balances, and the changes in these balances summarized into a single amount—the net change in working capital (375).

Statement of cash flows   A statement that summarizes the effects on cash of the operating, investing, and financing activities of a company for a period. Both inflows and outflows are included in each category. The statement of cash flows must be prepared each time an income statement is prepared (352).

Statement of changes in financial position   A statement that reports the flows of cash or working capital into and out of a business in a given time period; it also shows significant financing and investing activities that do not involve cash or working capital flows (373).

Working capital   A possible definition of funds; equal to current assets minus current liabilities (373).

DEMONSTRATION PROBLEM 10–1

Given below are comparative balance sheets of the Dells Corporation as of June 30, 1989, and June 30, 1990. Also given are the income statement for the year ended June 30, 1990, and certain additional data.

DELLS CORPORATION
Comparative Balance Sheets
June 30, 1989, and 1990

	1990	1989	Increase (Decrease)
Assets			
Current assets:			
Cash	$ 30,000	$ 80,000	$ (50,000)
Accounts receivable	160,000	100,000	60,000
Inventory	100,000	70,000	30,000
Prepaid rent	20,000	10,000	10,000
Total current assets	$310,000	$260,000	$ 50,000
Property, plant, and equipment:			
Equipment	$400,000	$200,000	$ 200,000
Accumulated depreciation	(60,000)	(50,000)	(10,000)
Total property, plant, and equipment	$340,000	$150,000	$ 190,000
Total assets	$650,000	$410,000	$ 240,000
Liabilities and Stockholders' Equity			
Current liabilities:			
Accounts payable	$ 50,000	$ 40,000	$ 10,000
Notes payable—bank	–0–	50,000	(50,000)
Accrued salaries	10,000	20,000	(10,000)
Federal income tax payable	30,000	20,000	10,000
Total current liabilities	$ 90,000	$130,000	$ (40,000)
Stockholders' equity:			
Common stock, $10 par	$300,000	$100,000	$ 200,000
Paid-in capital in excess of par	50,000	–0–	50,000
Retained earnings	210,000	180,000	30,000
Total stockholders' equity	$560,000	$280,000	$ 280,000
Total liabilities and stockholders' equity	$650,000	$410,000	$ 240,000

DELLS CORPORATION
Statement of Income and Retained Earnings
For the Year Ended June 30, 1990

Sales		$1,000,000
Cost of goods sold	$600,000	
Salaries and wages	200,000	
Rent	40,000	
Depreciation	20,000	
Interest	3,000	
Loss on sale of equipment	7,000	870,000
Net income before federal income taxes		$ 130,000
Federal income taxes		60,000
Net income		$ 70,000
Retained earnings, July 1, 1989		180,000
		$ 250,000
Dividends		40,000
Retained earnings, June 30, 1990		$ 210,000

Additional data:

1. Equipment with a cost of $20,000, on which $10,000 of depreciation had been recorded, was sold for cash. Additional equipment was purchased.
2. Stock was issued for cash.

Required:

Using the data given for the Dells Corporation:

a. Prepare a working paper.

b. Prepare a statement of cash flows—indirect method.

c. Prepare a working paper to convert net income to a cash basis. Then prepare a partial statement of cash flows—direct method, showing only the section, "Cash flows from operating activities."

Solution to demonstration problem 10–1

a

DELLS CORPORATION
Working Paper for Statement of Cash Flows
For the Year Ended June 30, 1990

	Account Balances 6/30/90	Analysis of Transactions for 1990		Account Balances 6/30/90
		Debit	**Credit**	
Debits				
Cash	80,000		(1) 50,000	30,000
Accounts Receivable	100,000	(5) 60,000		160,000
Inventory	70,000	(6) 30,000		100,000
Prepaid Rent	10,000	(7) 10,000		20,000
Equipment	200,000	(11) 220,000	(4) 20,000	400,000
	460,000			710,000
Credits				
Accumulated Depreciation	50,000	(4) 10,000	(3) 20,000	60,000
Accounts Payable	40,000		(8) 10,000	50,000
Notes Payable-Bank	50,000	(13) 50,000		–0–
Accrued Salaries	20,000	(9) 10,000		10,000
Federal Income Tax Payable	20,000		(10) 10,000	30,000
Common Stock, $10 Par	100,000		(12) 200,000	300,000
Paid-In Capital in Excess of Par	–0–		(12) 50,000	50,000
Retained Earnings	180,000	(14) 40,000	(2) 70,000	210,000
	460,000	430,000	430,000	710,000

	Account Balances 6/30/90	Analysis of Transactions for 1990		Account Balances 6/30/90
		Debit	Credit	
Cash Flows from Operating Activities:				
Net Income		(2) 70,000		
Depreciation		(3) 20,000		
Loss on Sale of Equipment		(4) 7,000		
Increase in Accounts Receivable			(5) 60,000	
Increase in Inventory			(6) 30,000	
Increase in Prepaid Rent			(7) 10,000	
Increase in Accounts Payable		(8) 10,000		
Decrease in Accrued Salaries			(9) 10,000	
Increase in Federal Income Tax Payable		(10) 10,000		
Cash Flows from Investing Activities:				
Proceeds from Sale of Equipment		(4) 3,000		
Purchases of Property, Plant, and Equipment			(11) 220,000	
Cash Flows from Financing Activities:				
Proceeds from Issuing Common Stock		(12) 250,000		
Repayment of Bank Note			(13) 50,000	
Paid Cash Dividends			(14) 40,000	
Decrease in Cash		(1) 50,000		
		420,000	420,000	

b

DELLS CORPORATION
Statement of Cash Flows
For the Year Ended June 30, 1990

Cash flows from operating activities:
Net income . . . . $ 70,000
Adjustments to reconcile net income to net cash provided
   by operating activities:
   Depreciation 20,000
   Loss on sale of equipment. 7,000
   Increase in accounts receivable . . . . (60,000)
   Increase in inventory . . . . (30,000)
   Increase in prepaid rent . . . . (10,000)
   Increase in accounts payable 10,000
   Decrease in accrued salaries . . . . (10,000)
   Increase in federal income tax payable 10,000
      Net cash flow provided by operating activities. . . . . $ 7,000

Cash flows from investing activities:
   Proceeds from sale of equipment . . . . $ 3,000
   Purchases of property, plant, and equipment . . . . (220,000)
      Net cash used by investing activities. . . . . (217,000)

Cash flows from financing activities:
   Proceeds from issuing common stock. . . . . $ 250,000
   Repayment of bank note . . . . (50,000)
   Dividends paid . . . . (40,000)
      Net cash provided by financing activities 160,000
Net increase (decrease) in cash . . . . $ (50,000)

c

DELLS CORPORATION
Income Statement
For the Year Ended June 30, 1990

	Accrual Basis	Add	Deduct	Cash Basis
Sales	$1,000,000	$100,000[1]	$160,000[2]	$940,000
Cost of goods		{ 100,000[3]	{ 70,000[4]	
sold.	$600,000	{ 40,000[5]	{ 50,000[6]	$620,000
Salaries and wages.	200,000	20,000[7]	10,000[8]	210,000
Rent	40,000	20,000[9]	10,000[10]	50,000
Depreciation	20,000		20,000	–0–
Interest	3,000			3,000
Loss on sale of equipment.	7,000		7,000	–0–
Federal income taxes	60,000	20,000[11]	30,000[12]	50,000
	930,000			933,000
Net income	$ 70,000			$ 7,000

[1] Beginning Accounts Receivable
[2] Ending Accounts Receivable
[3] Ending Inventory
[4] Beginning Inventory
[5] Beginning Accounts Payable
[6] Ending Accounts Payable
[7] Beginning Accrued Salaries
[8] Ending Accrued Salaries
[9] Ending Prepaid Rent
[10] Beginning Prepaid Rent
[11] Beginning Federal Income Taxes Payable
[12] Ending Federal Income Taxes Payable

DELLS CORPORATION
Partial Statement of Cash Flows—Direct Method
For the Year Ended June 30, 1990

Cash flows from operating activities:	
Cash received from customers	$ 940,000
Cash paid for merchandise	(620,000)
Salaries and wages paid	(210,000)
Rent paid	(50,000)
Interest paid.	(3,000)
Federal income taxes paid	(50,000)
Net cash provided by operating activities	$7,000

QUESTIONS

1. What are the purposes of the statement of cash flows?

2. What are some of the uses of the statement of cash flows?

3. What information is contained in the statement of cash flows?

4. Which activities are generally included in operating activities?

5. Which activities are included in investing activities?

6. Which activities are included in financing activities?

7. Where should investing and financing activities that do not involve cash flows be reported?

8. Explain the difference between the direct and indirect methods for computing cash flows from operating activities.

9. What are noncash expenses? How are they treated in computing cash flows from operating activities?

10. Describe the treatment of a gain on the sale of equipment in preparing a statement of cash flows under the indirect method.

381

11. Depreciation is sometimes referred to as a source of cash. Is it a source of cash? Explain.

12. Why is it unlikely that cash flows from operating activities will be equal to net income for the same period?

13. If the net income for a given period is $25,000, does this mean that there is an increase of cash of the same amount? Why or why not?

14. Why might a company have positive cash flows from operating activity even though operating at a net loss?

15. Give two reasons why analysts seem to prefer cash flow statements to statements that report working capital flows.

16. Describe the schedule of changes in working capital.

EXERCISES

Report specific items on statement of cash flows

1. Indicate how the following data should be reported in a statement of cash flows. A company paid $30,000 cash for land. A building was acquired for $60,000 by assuming a mortgage on the building.

Report specific items on statement of cash flows

2. The following data are from the Automobile and the Accumulated Depreciation—Automobile accounts of a certain company:

Automobile

Date			Debit	Credit	Balance
Jan.	1	Balance brought forward			$8,000
July	1	Traded for new auto		$8,000	–0–
		New auto	$8,800		8,800

Accumulated Depreciation—Automobile

Date			Debit	Credit	Balance
Jan.	1	Balance brought forward			$6,000
July	1	One-half year's depreciation		$1,000	7,000
		Auto traded	$7,000		–0–
Dec. 31		One-half year's depreciation		1,100	1,100

The old auto was traded for a new one with the difference in values paid in cash. The income statement for the year shows a loss on the exchange of autos of $600.

Indicate the dollar amounts, the descriptions of these amounts, and their exact locations in a statement of cash flows—indirect method.

Compute cash used to purchase plant assets

3. Following are balance sheet data for the Cooper Corporation.

	December 31, 1991	December 31, 1990
Cash	$ 23,500	$ 13,000
Accounts receivable	70,500	67,000
Inventories	41,500	51,000
Prepaid expenses	4,500	5,500
Plant assets (net of accumulated depreciation) . . .	117,500	115,000
Accounts payable	61,000	63,500
Accrued expenses payable	20,000	20,500
Capital stock	150,000	150,000
Retained earnings	26,500	17,500

Assume that the depreciation recorded in 1991 was $7,500. Compute the cash spent to purchase plant assets assuming no assets were sold or scrapped in 1991.

4. Use the data in Exercise 3. Assume the net income for 1991 was $12,000, that depreciation was $7,500, and that dividends declared and paid were $3,000. Prepare a statement of cash flows—indirect method.

5. Cost of goods sold in the income statement for the year ended 1990 was $157,000. The balances in Inventory and Accounts Payable were:

	1/1/90	12/31/90
Inventory	$80,000	$85,000
Accounts Payable	22,000	18,000

Given only this information, calculate the amount of cash paid for merchandise for 1990.

6. The income statement of a company shows cost of goods sold of $525,000 and net income of $75,000; inventory on January 1 was $76,500 and on December 31 was $94,500; accounts payable for merchandise purchases were $57,000 on January 1 and $63,000 on December 31. Compute the cash flows from operating activities.

7. Dividends payable increased by $1,500 during the year in which total dividends declared were $30,000. What amount appears for dividends paid in the statement of cash flows?

8. Fill in the following chart showing how increases and decreases in these accounts affect the conversion of accrual basis income to cash basis income.

	Add	Deduct
Accounts receivable		
Inventories		
Prepaid expenses		
Accounts payable		
Accrued liabilities		

9. Using the data in Exercise 3, prepare a schedule of changes in working capital for 1991.

PROBLEMS

10–1. The information given below is related to the Rock Corporation.

ROCK CORPORATION
Comparative Balance Sheets
December 31, 1990, and 1991

	December 31	
	1991	1990
Assets		
Cash	$ 22,500	$ 30,000
Accounts receivable, net	84,000	60,000
Inventories	150,000	120,000
Equipment	412,500	315,000
Accumulated depreciation	(120,000)	(105,000)
Investments	75,000	15,000
Total assets	$ 624,000	$ 435,000

Liabilities and Stockholders' Equity

Accounts payable	$ 21,750	$ 18,750
Accrued liabilities	2,250	3,750
Capital stock—common—$10 par	375,000	300,000
Paid-in capital in excess of par	150,000	75,000
Retained earnings	75,000	37,500
Total liabilities and stockholders' equity	$ 624,000	$ 435,000

Additional data:

1. Net income was $67,500 for the year.
2. Fully depreciated equipment costing $15,000 was sold for $3,750, and equipment costing $112,500 was purchased for cash.
3. Depreciation expense for the year was $30,000.
4. Investments were purchased, $60,000.
5. An additional 7,500 shares of common stock were issued for cash at $20 per share.
6. Cash dividends of $30,000 were declared and paid.

Required:

Prepare a statement of cash flows under the indirect method. Try to do so without preparing a working paper.

Prepare statement of cash flows— indirect method

10–2. Given below are comparative balance sheets and other data of D & J, Inc.:

D & J, INC.
Comparative Balance Sheets
December 31, 1990, and 1991

	December 31	
	1991	1990
Assets		
Cash	$ 46,105	$ 21,000
Accounts receivable	26,075	24,250
Inventory	30,000	35,000
Supplies on hand	2,150	2,550
Prepaid insurance	1,000	1,200
Land	180,000	142,500
Equipment	270,000	300,000
Accumulated depreciation—equipment	(75,000)	(67,500)
Total assets	$480,330	$459,000
Liabilities and Stockholders' Equity		
Accounts payable	$ 15,330	$ 46,300
Salaries payable	4,000	2,000
Accrued liabilities	2,000	8,250
Long-term note payable	150,000	150,000
Common stock ($5 par)	185,000	165,000
Paid-in capital in excess of par	32,500	–0–
Retained earnings	91,500	87,450
Total liabilities and stockholders' equity	$480,330	$459,000

Additional data:

1. Dividends declared and paid in 1991 totaled $52,950.
2. Land was bought for cash.
3. Equipment costing $50,000 with accumulated depreciation of $30,000 was sold for a gain of $3,500, and equipment costing $20,000 was purchased for cash.
4. Common stock was issued for cash.
5. Depreciation expense for the year was $37,500.

Required:

Prepare a statement of cash flows under the indirect method. Try to do so without preparing a working paper.

Prepare working paper and statement of cash flows— direct method

10–3. The income statement for the Bow Company for the year ended December 31, 1991, shows:

Net sales.		$448,000
Cost of goods sold	$262,500	
Operating expenses.	70,000*	
Major repairs	35,000	
Interest expense	10,500	
Loss on sale of equipment	5,600	383,600
Net income before taxes		$ 64,400
Federal income taxes		33,600
Net income.		$ 30,800

* (including $14,000 of depreciation expense)

Comparative balance sheets for the company show:

BOW COMPANY
Comparative Balance Sheets
December 31, 1990, and 1991

	December 31	
	1991	1990
Assets		
Current assets:		
Cash	$ 33,600	$ 28,000
Accounts receivable, net	67,900	53,200
Inventories	147,000	126,000
Prepaid expenses	11,200	4,200
Total current assets.	$259,700	$211,400
Property, plant, and equipment:		
Buildings	$ 70,000	$ 70,000
Accumulated depreciation—buildings	(38,500)	(35,000)
Equipment.	129,500	91,000
Accumulated depreciation—equipment	(44,100)	(42,000)
Total property, plant, and equipment	$116,900	$ 84,000
Total assets	$376,600	$295,400

Liabilities and Stockholders' Equity

Current liabilities:

Accounts payable	$ 39,550	$ 57,750
Accrued expenses payable	11,550	10,150
Federal income taxes payable	33,600	31,500
Total current liabilities	$ 84,700	$ 99,400

Long-term liabilities:

Bonds payable, 15%	70,000	70,000
Total liabilities	$154,700	$169,400

Stockholders' equity:

Capital stock—$100 par	$175,000	$105,000
Paid-in capital in excess of par	17,500	–0–
Retained earnings	29,400	21,000
Total stockholders' equity	$221,900	$126,000
Total liabilities and stockholders' equity	$376,600	$295,400

Additional data:

1. Capital stock was issued for cash.
2. Accrued expenses payable and prepaid expenses relate solely to operating expenses.
3. Depreciation on equipment for the year amounted to $10,500. Equipment sold had an original cost of $21,000.
4. Dividends declared and paid during the year totaled $22,400.
5. Accounts payable arose solely from purchases of merchandise.

Required:

a. Prepare a working paper for a statement of cash flows.

b. Prepare a statement of cash flows under the indirect method.

c. Prepare a working paper to convert the income statement of a cash basis.

d. Prepare a statement of cash flows under the direct method.

Prepare working paper and statement of cash flows

10–4. The Bright Corporation comparative balance sheets at December 31, 1990, and 1991, and the statement of income and retained earnings for 1991 are presented below.

BRIGHT CORPORATION
Comparative Balance Sheets
December 31, 1990, and 1991

	December 31	
	1991	*1990*

Assets

Current assets:

Cash	$ 9,750	$ 13,000
Accounts receivable	82,550	63,700
Inventories	79,300	72,800
Prepaid insurance	1,950	2,600
Total current assets	$173,550	$152,100

Property, plant, and equipment:		
Land	$ 32,500	$ 19,500
Buildings	130,000	65,000
Accumulated depreciation—buildings	(16,250)	(13,000)
Equipment.	149,500	139,750
Accumulated depreciation—equipment	(81,250)	(65,000)
Total property, plant, and equipment	$214,500	$146,250
Total assets	$388,050	$298,350

Liabilities and Stockholders' Equity

Current liabilities:		
Accounts payable	$ 61,100	$ 58,500
Federal income taxes payable	23,400	19,500
Accrued salaries and wages payable	2,600	1,950
Accrued expenses payable	3,900	2,600
Total current liabilities	$ 91,000	$ 82,550
Long-term liabilities:		
Bonds payable, 9%.	65,000	65,000
Total liabilities	$156,000	$147,550
Stockholders' equity:		
Capital stock—common.	$195,000	$130,000
Paid-in capital in excess of par.	9,750	–0–
Retained earnings	27,300	20,800
Total stockholders' equity	$232,050	$150,800
Total liabilities and stockholders' equity	$388,050	$298,350

BRIGHT CORPORATION
Income Statement and Statement of Retained Earnings
For the Year Ended December 31, 1991

Sales, net		$585,000
Cost of goods sold.		390,000
Gross margin		$195,000
Salaries and wages	$97,500	
Depreciation	24,050	
Insurance.	1,300	
Other expenses (including interest)	32,500	
Loss on sale of equipment	650	156,000
Net income before federal income taxes		$ 39,000
Federal income taxes		16,900
Net income		$ 22,100
Retained earnings, December 31, 1990		20,800
		$ 42,900
Less: Dividends		15,600
Retained earnings, December 31, 1991		$ 27,300

Additional data:

1. Equipment having an original cost of $6,500 and on which $4,550 of depreciation was recorded was sold at a loss of $650. Equipment additions were for cash.
2. $3,250 of cash and all of the additional capital stock issued during the year were exchanged for land and a building.

387

Required:

a. Prepare a working paper for a statement of cash flows.

b. Prepare a statement of cash flows under the indirect method. Prepare a separate schedule of noncash investing and financing activities.

c. Prepare a working paper to convert the income statement to a cash basis.

d. Prepare a statement of cash flows under the direct method.

Prepare a schedule of changes in working capital and then comment

10–5. Refer to the balance sheets for the Bow Company in Problem 10–3.

Required:

Prepare a schedule of changes in working capital for the Bow Company for the year ended December 31, 1991. Comment on the possible future impact of the changes.

Prepare a schedule of changes in working capital and then comment

10–6. Refer to the balance sheets for the Bright Corporation in Problem 10–4.

Required:

Prepare a schedule of changes in working capital for the Bright Corporation for the year ended December 31, 1991. Comment on the possible future impact of the changes.

BUSINESS DECISION PROBLEM 10–1

Prepare a schedule showing net cash flow from operating activities

Following are comparative balance sheets for the Smith Company:

SMITH COMPANY
Comparative Balance Sheets
December 31, 1990, and 1991

	December 31	
	1991	*1990*
Assets		
Cash	$ 60,000	$ 37,500
Accounts receivable	60,000	45,000
Inventories	90,000	52,500
Land	67,500	60,000
Building	90,000	90,000
Accumulated depreciation—building	(30,000)	(27,000)
Equipment	285,000	225,000
Accumulated depreciation—equipment	(52,500)	(48,000)
Goodwill	120,000	150,000
Total assets	$690,000	$585,000
Liabilities and Stockholders' Equity		
Accounts payable	$ 75,000	$ 45,000
Accrued liabilities	30,000	22,500
Capital stock	315,000	300,000
Paid-in capital—stock dividends	75,000	67,500
Paid-in capital—land donations	15,000	–0–
Retained earnings	180,000	150,000
Total liabilities and stockholders' equity	$690,000	$585,000

An analysis of the Retained Earnings account for the year reveals the following:

Balance, December 31, 1990		$150,000
Add: Net income for the year		97,500
		$247,500
Less: Cash dividends	$45,000	
Stock dividends	22,500	67,500
Balance, December 31, 1991		$180,000

Additional data:

1. Equipment with a cost of $30,000 on which $27,000 of depreciation had been accumulated was sold during the year at a loss of $1,500. Included in net income is a gain on the sale of land of $9,000.
2. The president of the Smith company has set two goals for 1992: (1) increase cash by $40,000 and (2) increase cash dividends to $90,000. The company's activities in 1992 are expected to be quite similar to those of 1991 and no new fixed assets will be acquired.

Required:

Prepare a schedule showing cash flows from operating activities under the indirect method for 1991. Can the company meet its president's goals for 1992? Explain.

11 FINANCIAL STATEMENT ANALYSIS

LEARNING OBJECTIVES

After studying this chapter, you should be able to:

1. Describe and explain the objectives of financial statement analysis.
2. Calculate and explain changes in financial statements using horizontal analysis, vertical analysis, and trend analysis.
3. Perform ratio analysis on financial statements using liquidity ratios, long-term solvency ratios, profitability tests, and market tests.
4. Understand the considerations used in financial statement analysis.
5. Define and correctly use the new terms in the glossary.

As you will recall, the two primary objectives of every business are solvency and profitability. Solvency is the ability of a company to pay debts as they become due; it is reflected in the company's balance sheet. Profitability is the ability of a company to generate income; it is reflected in the company's income statement. Generally, all those interested in the affairs of a company are especially interested in a company's solvency and profitability.

This chapter discusses several common methods used to analyze and relate to one another the data in financial statements and, as a result, gain a clear picture of the solvency and profitability of a company. A company's financial statements are analyzed internally by management and externally by investors and creditors.

Management's analysis of financial statements primarily relates to *parts* of the company. Management conducts its analysis to plan, evaluate, and control operations within the company. The analysis by investors and creditors generally focuses on the company as a *whole*. Investors and creditors analyze financial statements to decide whether to invest in or extend credit to the company. In this chapter we discuss financial statement analysis as conducted by outside parties, such as investors and creditors, who rely primarily on a company's financial statements for their information.

OBJECTIVES OF FINANCIAL STATEMENT ANALYSIS

Objective 1: Describe and explain the objectives of financial statement analysis

Financial statement analysis consists of applying analytical tools and techniques to financial statements and other relevant data to obtain useful information. This information is shown as significant relationships between data and trends in those data assessing the company's past performance and current financial position. The information shows the results or consequences of prior management decisions. In addition, the information is used to make predictions that may have a direct effect on decisions made by many users of financial statements.

Present company investors and potential company investors are both interested in the future ability of a company to earn profits—its profitability. These investors wish to predict future dividends and changes in the market price of the company's common stock. Since both dividends and price changes are likely to be influenced by earnings, investors may seek to predict earnings. The company's past earnings record is the logical point in predicting future earnings.

Sometimes outside parties are interested in predicting a company's solvency rather than its profitability. Short-term solvency is affected by the liquidity of the company. **Liquidity** is the state of possessing liquid assets, such as cash and other assets that will soon be converted into cash. Short-term debts must be paid soon, so liquid assets must be available for their payment. A bank that is asked to extend a 90-day loan to a company would be interested in that company's projected short-term liquidity. The company's predicted ability to repay the loan is likely to be based, at least partially, on proven past ability to pay off debts.

Long-term creditors are interested in a company's long-term solvency. A company is generally considered to be solvent when its assets exceed its liabilities so that it has a positive stockholders' equity. The larger the assets are in relation to the liabilities, the greater the long-term solvency of the company. The company's assets could shrink significantly before its liabilities would exceed its assets.

FINANCIAL STATEMENT ANALYSIS

Several types of analysis can be performed on a company's financial statements. All these analyses rely on comparisons or relationships of data because comparisons enhance the utility, or practical value, of accounting information. For example, knowing that a company's net income last year was $100,000 is not, by itself, very useful information. Some usefulness is added when it is known that the prior year's net income was $25,000.

And even more useful information is gained if the amounts of sales and assets of the company are known. Such comparisons or relationships may be expressed as:

1. Absolute increases and decreases for an item from one period to the next.
2. Percentage increases and decreases for an item from one period to the next.
3. Trend percentages.
4. Percentages of single items to an aggregate total.
5. Ratios.

Items 1 and 2 make use of comparative financial statements. **Comparative financial statements** present the same company's financial statements for two or more successive periods in side-by-side columns. The calculation of dollar changes (see column 3 of Illustration 11.1 and column 9 of Illustration 11.2) or percentage changes (see column 4 of Illustration 11.1 and column 10 of Illustration 11.2) in the statement items or totals is known as **horizontal analysis.** This type of analysis helps detect changes in a company's performance and highlights trends.

Trend percentages (item 3) are similar to horizontal analysis except that a base year is selected and comparisons are made to the base year. Trend percentages are useful for comparing financial statements over several years because they disclose changes and trends occurring through time.

Information about a company can also be gained by the vertical analysis of the composition of a single financial statement, such as an income statement. **Vertical analysis** (item 4) consists of the study of a single financial statement in which each item is expressed as a percentage of a significant total. The use of vertical analysis is especially helpful in analyzing income statement data such as the percentage of cost of goods sold to sales or the gross margin percentage. For example, columns 11 and 12 of Illustration 11.2 show that in 1990, cost of goods sold was 65.4% of sales and decreased to 63.2% of sales in 1991. Vertical analysis is a useful tool in analyzing intercompany data.

Financial statements that show only percentages and no absolute dollar amounts are called **common-size statements.** All percentage figures in a common-size balance sheet are expressed as percentages of total assets (see columns 5 and 6 of Illustration 11.1). The use of common-size statements facilitates vertical analysis of a company's financial statements. For instance, looking at columns 11 and 12 of Illustration 11.2 gives you a better idea of the relationship of each item to sales than looking at columns 7 and 8.

Ratios (item 5) are expressions of logical relationships between certain items in the financial statements. The financial statements of a single period are generally used. Many ratios can be computed from the same set of financial statements. A ratio can show a relationship between two items on the same financial statement or between two items on different finan-

Illustration 11.1
COMPARATIVE BALANCE SHEETS

THE KNIGHT CORPORATION
Comparative Balance Sheets
December 31, 1990 and 1991   Exhibit A

	December 31		Increase or decrease* 1991 over 1990		Percent of total assets December 31	
	(1) 1991	(2) 1990	(3) Dollars	(4) Percent	(5) 1991	(6) 1990
Assets						
Current assets:						
Cash	$ 80,200	$ 55,000	$25,200	45.8	12.6	10.0
Accounts receivable, net	124,200	132,600	8,400*	6.3*	19.6	24.1
Notes receivable	55,000	50,000	5,000	10.0	8.7	9.1
Inventories	110,800	94,500	16,300	17.2	17.4	17.1
Prepaid expenses	3,600	4,700	1,100*	23.4*	0.6	0.9
Total current assets.	$373,800	$336,800	$37,000	11.0	58.8ᴿ	61.1ᴿ
Property, plant, and equipment:						
Land	$ 21,000	$ 21,000	$ –0–	–0–	3.3	3.8
Building	205,000	160,000	45,000	28.1	32.3	29.0
Less: Accumulated depreciation	(27,000)	(22,400)	(4,600)	21.0	(4.3)	(4.1)
Furniture and fixtures	83,200	69,800	13,400	19.2	13.1	12.7
Less: Accumulated depreciation	(20,800)	(14,100)	(6,700)	47.5	(3.3)	(2.6)
Total property, plant, and equipment . .	$261,400	$214,300	$47,100	22.0	41.2ᴿ	38.9ᴿ
Total assets	$635,200	$551,100	$84,100	15.3	100.0	100.0
Liabilities and Stockholders' Equity						
Current liabilities:						
Accounts payable	$ 70,300	$ 64,600	$ 5,700	8.8	11.1	11.7
Notes payable	20,000	15,100	4,900	32.5	3.1	2.7
Taxes accrued	36,800	30,200	6,600	21.9	5.8	5.5
Total current liabilties	$127,100	$109,900	$17,200	15.7	20.0	20.0ᴿ
Long-term liabilities:						
Mortgage notes payable, land and building, 12%, 1993.	43,600	60,800	17,200*	28.3*	6.9	11.0
Total liabilities	$170,700	$170,700	$ –0–	0.0	26.9	31.0
Stockholders' equity:						
Common stock, par value $10 per share	$240,000	$200,000	$40,000	20.0	37.8	36.3
Retained earnings	224,500	180,400	44,100	24.4	35.3	32.7
Total stockholders' equity	$464,500	$380,400	$84,100	22.1	73.1	69.0
Total liabilities and stockholders' equity . . .	$635,200	$551,100	$84,100	15.3	100.0	100.0

ᴿ Rounding difference.

cial statements (e.g., balance sheet and income statement). The choice of ratios to be prepared is limited only by the requirement that the items used to construct a ratio have a logical relationship to one another.

Illustration 11.2
COMPARATIVE STATEMENTS OF INCOME AND RETAINED EARN...

THE KNIGHT CORPORATION
Comparative Statements of Income and Retained E...
For the Years Ended December 31, 1990 and 199...

	Year ended December 31		Incr... decre... 1991 over...		Per... of net s...	
	(7) 1991	(8) 1990	(9) Dollars	(1.) Perce.	(11) 1991	(12. 1990
Net sales	$986,400	$765,500	$220,900	28.9	...0	100.0
Cost of goods sold	623,200	500,900	122,300	24.4	63...	65.4
Gross margin	$363,200	$264,600	$ 98,600	37.3	36...	\4.6
Operating expenses:						
Selling	$132,500	$ 84,900	$ 47,600	56.1	13.4	11.1
Administrative	120,300	98,600	21,700	22.0	12.2	12.9
Total operating expenses	$252,800	$183,500	$ 69,300	37.8	25.6	24.0
Net operating income	$110,400	$ 81,100	$ 29,300	36.0	11.2	10.6
Other expenses	3,000	2,800	200	7.1	0.3	0.4
Net income before federal income taxes	$107,400	$ 78,300	$ 29,100	37.2	10.9	10.2
Federal income taxes	48,300	31,700	16,600	52.4	4.9	4.1
Net income	$ 59,100	$ 46,600	$ 12,500	26.8	6.0	6.1
Retained earnings, January 1	180,400	146,300	34,100	23.3		
	$239,500	$192,900	$ 46,600	24.2		
Dividends declared	15,000	12,500	2,500	20.0		
Retained earnings, December 31	$224,500	$180,400	$ 44,100	24.4		

HORIZONTAL AND VERTICAL ANALYSIS: AN ILLUSTRATION

Objective 2: Calculate and explain changes in financial statements using horizontal analysis, vertical analysis, and trend analysis

Illustrations 11.1 and 11.2 show comparative financial statements of the Knight Corporation for the years ended December 31, 1990 and 1991. These statements will serve as a basis for a more complete illustration of horizontal and vertical analysis of a balance sheet and a statement of income and retained earnings.

Analysis of Balance Sheet

Imagine that you are a prospective investor of the Knight Corporatio...
have acquired the comparative balance sheets shown in Illustratio...
Columns 1, 2, and 3 in Illustration 11.1 show the absolute dollar...
for each item for December 31, 1990 and December 31, 1991, and...
for the year. If the change between the two dates is an increa...
to 1991, the change is shown as a positive figure. If the c...
crease, it is followed by an asterisk (*). A few of the c...
could make from your horizontal analysis of Illustratio...

Illustration 11.2
COMPARATIVE STATEMENTS OF INCOME AND RETAINED EARNINGS

THE KNIGHT CORPORATION
Comparative Statements of Income and Retained Earnings
For the Years Ended December 31, 1990 and 1991   Exhibit B

	Year ended December 31		Increase or decrease* 1991 over 1990		Percent of net sales	
	(7) 1991	(8) 1990	(9) Dollars	(10) Percent	(11) 1991	(12) 1990
Net sales	$986,400	$765,500	$220,900	28.9	100.0	100.0
Cost of goods sold	623,200	500,900	122,300	24.4	63.2	65.4
Gross margin	$363,200	$264,600	$ 98,600	37.3	36.8	34.6
Operating expenses:						
Selling	$132,500	$ 84,900	$ 47,600	56.1	13.4	11.1
Administrative	120,300	98,600	21,700	22.0	12.2	12.9
Total operating expenses	$252,800	$183,500	$ 69,300	37.8	25.6	24.0
Net operating income	$110,400	$ 81,100	$ 29,300	36.0	11.2	10.6
Other expenses	3,000	2,800	200	7.1	0.3	0.4
Net income before federal income taxes . . .	$107,400	$ 78,300	$ 29,100	37.2	10.9	10.2
Federal income taxes	48,300	31,700	16,600	52.4	4.9	4.1
Net income	$ 59,100	$ 46,600	$ 12,500	26.8	6.0	6.1
Retained earnings, January 1	180,400	146,300	34,100	23.3		
	$239,500	$192,900	$ 46,600	24.2		
Dividends declared	15,000	12,500	2,500	20.0		
Retained earnings, December 31	$224,500	$180,400	$ 44,100	24.4		

HORIZONTAL AND VERTICAL ANALYSIS: AN ILLUSTRATION

Objective 2: Calculate and explain changes in financial statements using horizontal analysis, vertical analysis, and trend analysis

Illustrations 11.1 and 11.2 show comparative financial statements of the Knight Corporation for the years ended December 31, 1990 and 1991. These statements will serve as a basis for a more complete illustration of horizontal and vertical analysis of a balance sheet and a statement of income and retained earnings.

Analysis of Balance Sheet

Imagine that you are a prospective investor of the Knight Corporation and have acquired the comparative balance sheets shown in Illustration 11.1. Columns 1, 2, and 3 in Illustration 11.1 show the absolute dollar amounts for each item for December 31, 1990 and December 31, 1991, and the change for the year. If the change between the two dates is an increase from 1990 to 1991, the change is shown as a positive figure. If the change is a decrease, it is followed by an asterisk (*). A few of the observations you could make from your horizontal analysis of Illustration 11.1 are:

1. Total current assets have increased $37,000, consisting largely of a $25,200 increase in cash, while total current liabilities have increased only $17,200.
2. Total assets have increased $84,100, while total liabilities have remained unchanged.
3. The increase in total assets has been financed by the sale of common stock, $40,000, and by the retention of earnings, $44,100.

Next, you study column 4 in Illustration 11.1, which expresses as a percentage the dollar change in column 3. Frequently, these percentage increases and decreases are more informative than absolute amounts, as is illustrated by the current asset and current liability changes. Although the absolute amount of current assets has increased more than twice the amount of current liabilities, the percentages reveal that current assets increased 11%, while current liabilities increased 15.7%. Thus, current liabilities are increasing at a rate faster than the current assets that will be used to pay them. But, in view of the substantial amount of cash possessed, the company is not likely to fail to pay its debts as they come due.

The percentages in column 4 lead you, the analyst, to several other observations. For one thing, the 28.3% decrease in mortgage notes payable indicates that interest charges will be lower; thus, this will tend to increase net income in the future. The 24.4% increase in retained earnings and the 45.8% increase in cash may indicate that higher dividends can be paid in the future.

Your vertical analysis of the Knight Corporation's balance sheet discloses each account's significance relative to total assets or equities. This comparison aids in assessing the importance of changes in each account. Columns 5 and 6 in Illustration 11.1 express the dollar amounts of each item in columns 1 and 2 as a percentage of total assets or equities. For example, although prepaid expenses declined $1,100 in 1991, a decrease of 23.4%, the account represents less than 1% of total assets and, therefore, probably does not have great significance. The vertical analysis also shows that total debt financing decreased by 4.1 percentage points, from 31% of total equities to 26.9% in 1991. At the same time, the percentage of stockholder financing to total assets of the company increased from 69.0% to 73.1%.

Analysis of Statement of Income and Retained Earnings

Illustration 11.2 provides you with the information to analyze the comparative statements of income and retained earnings of the Knight Corporation. Such a statement merely combines the income statement and the statement of retained earnings. Columns 7 and 8 in Illustration 11.2 show the dollar amounts for the years 1990 and 1991, respectively. Columns 9 and 10 show the absolute and percentage increase and decrease in each item from 1990 to 1991. The amounts and percentages in columns 11 and 12 are computed by dividing each item by net sales. Examination of the comparative statements of net income and retained earnings shows the following:

1. Sales increased 28.9% in 1991.
2. Gross margin increased 37.3% in 1991.
3. Selling expenses increased 56.1% in 1991.
4. Federal income taxes rose by 52.4% in 1991.
5. Net income increased 26.8%, while dividends increased 20.0%.
6. Net income per dollar of sales remained virtually constant over the two years (6.1% in 1990 and 6.0% in 1991).

Considering both horizontal and vertical analysis information, the analyst would conclude that an increase in the gross margin rate from 34.6% to 36.8%, coupled with a 28.9% increase in sales, resulted in a 37.3% increase in gross margin in 1991. The increase in net income was held to 26.8% because selling expenses increased 56.1% and income taxes increased 52.4%. Predicting net income for 1992 would be aided if you, the analyst, knew whether this increase in selling expenses is expected to recur. Other expenses remained basically the same, on a percentage-of-sales basis, over the two-year period.

Having completed the horizontal and vertical analysis of the balance sheet and statement of income and retained earnings of the Knight Corporation, you are ready to study trend percentages and ratio analysis. The last section in this chapter discusses some final considerations in financial statement analysis. Professional financial statement analysts use several tools and techniques to determine the solvency and profitability of companies.

TREND PERCENTAGES

Trend percentages are also referred to as index numbers and are used for the comparison of financial information over time to a base year. Trend percentages are calculated by:

1. Selecting a base year.
2. Assigning a weight of 100% to the amounts appearing on the base year financial statements.
3. Expressing the corresponding amounts shown on the other years' financial statements as a percentage of base-year amounts. The percentages are computed by dividing nonbase amounts by the corresponding base-year amounts and then multiplying the result by 100.

The following information is given to illustrate the calculation of trend percentages:

	1990	1991	1992	1993
Sales	$350,000	$367,500	$441,000	$485,000
Cost of goods sold	200,000	196,000	230,000	285,000
Gross margin	$150,000	$171,500	$211,000	$200,000
Operating expenses.	145,000	169,000	200,000	192,000
Net income before taxes. . .	$ 5,000	$ 2,500	$ 11,000	$ 8,000

If 1990 is the base year, trend percentages are calculated for each year by dividing sales by $350,000; cost of goods sold by $200,000; gross margin by $150,000; operating expenses by $145,000; and net income before income taxes by $5,000. After all divisions have been made, each result is multiplied by 100, and the resulting percentages that reflect trends appear as follows:

	1990	1991	1992	1993
Sales	100%	105%	126%	139%
Cost of goods sold	100	98	115	143
Gross margin	100	114	141	133
Operating expenses	100	117	138	132
Net income before taxes	100	50	220	160

Such trend percentages indicate changes that are taking place in an organization and highlight the direction of these changes. Percentages can provide clues to a user as to which items need further investigation or analysis. In reviewing trend percentages, a financial statement user should pay close attention to the trends in related items, such as the cost of goods sold in relation to sales. Trend analysis that shows a constantly declining gross margin rate may be a signal that future net income will decrease.

As useful as trend percentages are, they have one drawback. Expressing changes as percentages is usually straightforward as long as the amount in the base year is positive—that is, not zero or negative. A $30,000 increase in notes receivable cannot be expressed in percentages if the increase is from zero last year to $30,000 this year. Also, an increase from a loss last year of $10,000 to income this year of $20,000 cannot be expressed in percentage terms.

Proper analysis does not stop with the calculation of increases and decreases in amounts or percentages over several years. Such changes generally indicate areas worthy of further investigation. They are merely clues that may lead to significant findings. Accurate predictions depend on many factors including economic and political conditions; management's plans regarding new products, plant expansion, and promotional outlays; and the expected activities of competitors. Consideration of these factors in conjunction with horizontal analysis, vertical analysis, and trend analysis should provide a reasonable basis for predicting future performance.

RATIO ANALYSIS

Objective 3: Perform ratio analysis on financial statements using liquidity ratios, long-term solvency ratios, profitability tests, and market tests

Logical relationships exist between certain accounts or items in a company's financial statements. These accounts may appear on the same statement or they may appear on two different statements. The dollar amounts of the related accounts or items are set up in fraction form and called ratios. These ratios can be broadly classified as (1) liquidity ratios, (2) equity, or long-term solvency, ratios, (3) profitability tests, and (4) market tests.

Liquidity Ratios

Liquidity ratios are used to indicate a company's short-term debt-paying ability. Thus, these ratios are designed to show interested parties the company's capacity to meet maturing current liabilities.

Current, or working capital, ratio. Working capital is the excess of current assets over current liabilities. The ratio that relates current assets to current liabilities is known as the **current,** or **working capital, ratio.** The current ratio indicates the ability of a company to pay its current liabilities from current assets and, in this way, shows the strength of the company's working capital position.

The current ratio is computed by dividing total current assets by total current liabilities:

$$\text{Current ratio} = \frac{\text{Current assets}}{\text{Current liabilities}}$$

The ratio usually is stated in terms of the number of dollars of current assets to one dollar of current liabilities (although the dollar signs usually are omitted). Thus, if current assets total $75,000 and current liabilities total $50,000, the ratio is expressed as 1.5:1, meaning the company has $1.50 of current assets for each $1 of current liabilities.

The current ratio provides a better index of a company's ability to pay current debts than does the absolute amount of working capital. To illustrate, assume that Company A and Company B have current assets and current liabilities on December 31, 1990 as follows:

	Company A	Company B
Current assets (a)	$11,000,000	$200,000
Current liabilities (b)	10,000,000	100,000
Working capital (a − b).	$ 1,000,000	$100,000
Current ratio (a ÷ b).	1.1:1	2:1

Company A has 10 times as much working capital as Company B. But Company B has a superior debt-paying ability since it has $2 of current assets for each $1 of current liabilities. Company A has only $1.10 of current assets for each $1 of current liabilities.

Short-term creditors are particularly interested in the current ratio since the conversion of inventories and accounts receivable into cash is the primary source from which the company obtains the cash to pay short-term creditors. Long-term creditors are also interested in the current ratio because a company that is unable to pay short-term debts may be forced into bankruptcy. For this reason, many bond indentures, or contracts, contain a provision requiring that the borrower maintain at least a certain minimum current ratio.

A company must also guard against a current ratio that is too high, especially if caused by idle cash, slow-paying customers, and slow-moving inventory. Decreased net income can result when too much capital that could be used profitably elsewhere is tied up in current assets.

Refer back to the Knight Corporation data in column 4 of Illustration 11.1, which indicated that current liabilities are increasing more rapidly than current assets. This sort of observation can be made directly using changes in the current ratio. The Knight Corporation's current ratios for 1990 and 1991 are as follows:

	December 31		
			Amount of
	1991	1990	Increase
Current assets (a).	$373,800	$336,800	$37,000
Current liabilities (b).	127,100	109,900	17,200
Working capital (a − b)	$246,700	$226,900	$19,800
Current ratio (a ÷ b)	2.94:1	3.06:1	

Although Knight's working capital increased by $19,800, or 8.7%, its current ratio fell from 3.06 to 2.94, reflecting the fact that its current liabilities increased faster than its current assets.

Acid-test (or quick) ratio. The current ratio is not the only measure of a company's short-term debt-paying ability. Another measure, called the **acid-test (or quick) ratio,** is the ratio of quick assets (cash, marketable securities, and net receivables) to current liabilities. The formula for the acid-test ratio is:

$$\text{Acid-test ratio} = \frac{\text{Quick assets}}{\text{Current liabilities}}$$

Inventories and prepaid expenses are excluded from this computation because they might not be readily convertible into cash. Short-term creditors are interested particularly in this ratio since it relates the "pool" of cash and immediate cash inflows to immediate cash outflows.

The acid-test ratios for 1990 and 1991 for the Knight Corporation are:

	December 31		
			Amount of
	1991	1990	Increase
Quick assets (a)	$259,400	$237,600	$21,800
Current liabilities (b).	127,100	109,900	17,200
Net quick assets (a − b) . . .	$132,300	$127,700	$ 4,600
Acid-test ratio (a ÷ b).	2.04:1	2.16:1	

In deciding whether the acid-test ratio is satisfactory, it is necessary to consider the *quality* of the marketable securities and receivables. An accumulation of poor quality marketable securities or receivables, or both, could cause an acid-test ratio to appear deceptively favorable. Poor quality when referring to marketable securities means securities that are likely to generate losses upon sale; poor quality receivables are those that may be uncollectible or not collectible until long past due. The quality of receivables depends primarily on their age, which can be assessed by preparing an aging schedule or by calculating the accounts receivable turnover. (Refer to Chapter 4 for a discussion of an accounts receivable aging schedule.)

Accounts receivable turnover. **Turnover** is the relationship between the amount of an asset and some measure of its use. **Accounts receivable turnover** is the number of times per year that the average amount of receivables is collected. The ratio is calculated by dividing net credit sales by average net accounts receivable, that is, accounts receivable after deducting the allowance for uncollectible accounts:

$$\text{Accounts receivable turnover} = \frac{\text{Net credit sales (or net sales)}}{\text{Average net accounts receivable}}$$

When a ratio compares an income statement item (like net credit sales) with a balance sheet item (like accounts receivable) the balance sheet item should be an average. Ideally, average net accounts receivable should be computed by averaging the end-of-month balances or end-of-week balances of net accounts receivable outstanding during the period. The greater the number of observations used, the more accurate the resulting average. Often though, only the beginning-of-year and end-of-year balances are averaged because this information is easily obtainable from comparative financial statements. Sometimes a formula calls for the use of an average balance, but only the year-end amount is available. Then the analyst must use the year-end amount.[1]

In theory, only net credit sales should be used in the numerator of the accounts receivable turnover ratio because those are the only sales that generate accounts receivable. But, if cash sales are relatively small or their proportion to total sales remains fairly constant, reliable results can be obtained by using total net sales. In most cases, the analyst may have to use total net sales because the separate amounts of cash sales and credit sales are not reported on the income statement.

Accounts receivable turnover for the Knight Corporation is shown below. Since beginning-of-year data for 1990 are not provided in Illustration 11.1, assume net accounts receivable on January 1, 1990, totaled $121,200.

	1991	1990	Increase or Decrease*
Net sales *(a)*	$986,400	$765,500	$220,900
Accounts receivable:			
January 1	$132,600	$121,200	$ 11,400
December 31	124,200	132,600	8,400*
Total *(b)*	$256,800	$253,800	$ 3,000
Average accounts receivable *(c)* *(b ÷ 2 = c)*	$128,400	$126,900	
Turnover of accounts receivable *(a ÷ c)*	7.68	6.03	

The turnover ratio provides an indication of how quickly the receivables are being collected. For the Knight Corporation in 1991, the turnover ratio indicates that accounts receivable are collected, or "turned over," slightly more than seven times per year. This ratio may be better understood and more easily compared with a company's credit terms if it is converted into a number of days, as is illustrated in the next ratio.

---

[1] These general comments about the use of averages in a ratio apply to the other ratios involving averages discussed in this chapter.

Number of days' sales in accounts receivable. The **number of days' sales in accounts receivable** ratio, which also is called the **average collection period for accounts receivable,** is calculated as follows:

$$\text{Number of days' sales in accounts receivable (average collection period of accounts receivable)} = \frac{\text{Number of days in year (365)}}{\text{Accounts receivable turnover}}$$

The turnover ratios for the Knight Corporation given above can be used to show that the number of days' sales in accounts receivable decreased from about 61 days (365/6.03) in 1990 to 48 days (365/7.68) in 1991. The change means that the average collection period of the corporation's accounts receivable decreased from 61 to 48 days. Thus, the ratio measures the average liquidity of accounts receivable and gives an indication of their quality. Generally, the more rapid the collection period, the higher the quality of receivables. However, the average collection period will vary by industry; for example, they will be very rapid in utility companies and much slower in some retailing companies. A comparison of the average collection period with the credit terms extended customers by the company will provide further insight into the quality of the accounts receivable. For example, receivables arising under terms of 2/10, n/30 that have an average collection period of 75 days need to be investigated further. It is important to determine why customers are paying their accounts much later than expected.

Inventory turnover. A company's **inventory turnover** ratio shows the number of times its average inventory is sold during a period. Inventory turnover is calculated as follows:

$$\text{Inventory turnover} = \frac{\text{Cost of goods sold}}{\text{Average inventory}}$$

Inventory turnover relates a measure of sales volume to the average amount of goods on hand to produce this sales volume.

Assume the inventory on January 1, 1990, for the Knight Corporation was $85,100. The following schedule shows that the inventory turnover increased slightly from 5.58 times per year in 1990 to 6.07 times per year in 1991. These turnover ratios can be converted to the number of days it takes a company to sell its entire stock of inventory; this is done by dividing 365 by the inventory turnover. For the Knight Corporation, the average inventory was sold in about 60 days (365/6.07) in 1991 as contrasted to about 65 days (365/5.58) in 1990.

	1991	1990	Amount of Increase
Cost of goods sold (a)	$623,200	$500,900	$122,300
Inventories:			
January 1	$ 94,500	$ 85,100	$ 9,400
December 31	110,800	94,500	16,300
Total (b)	$205,300	$179,600	$ 25,700
Average inventory (c) (b ÷ 2 = c)	$102,650	$ 89,800	
Turnover of inventory (a ÷ c)	6.07	5.58	

Other things being equal, the management that is able to maintain the highest inventory turnover ratio is considered most efficient. Yet, other things are not always equal. For example, a company that achieves a high inventory ratio by keeping extremely small inventories on hand may incur larger ordering costs, lose quantity discounts, and lose sales due to lack of adequate inventory. In attempting to earn satisfactory income, management must balance the costs of inventory storage and obsolescence and the cost of tying up funds in inventory against possible losses of sales and other costs associated with keeping too little inventory on hand.

Total assets turnover. **Total assets turnover** shows the relationship between dollar volume of sales and average total assets used in the business and is calculated as follows:

$$\text{Total assets turnover} = \frac{\text{Net sales}}{\text{Average total assets}}$$

This ratio measures the efficiency with which a company uses its assets to generate sales. The larger the total assets turnover, the larger will be the income on each dollar invested in the assets of the business.

For the Knight Corporation, the total assets turnover ratios for 1991 and 1990 are shown below. Assume total assets as of January 1, 1990, were $510,200.

	1991	1990	Amount of Increase
Net sales *(a)*	$ 986,400	$ 765,500	$220,900
Total assets:			
January 1	$ 551,100	$ 510,200	$ 40,900
December 31	635,200	551,100	84,100
Total *(b)*	$1,186,300	$1,061,300	$125,000
Average total assets *(c)* (*b* ÷ 2 = *c*)	$ 593,150	$ 530,650	
Turnover of total assets (*a* ÷ *c*)	1.66:1	1.44:1	

In 1990, each dollar of total assets produced $1.44 of sales; and in 1991, each dollar of assets produced $1.66 of sales. In other words, between 1990 and 1991, the Knight Corporation had an increase of $0.22 of sales per dollar of investment in assets.

Equity, or Long-Term Solvency, Ratios

Equity, or long-term solvency, ratios show the relationship of debt and equity financing in a company.

Equity (or stockholders' equity) ratio. The two basic sources of assets in a business are owners (stockholders) and creditors, and the interests of both groups are referred to as total equities. But in ratio analysis, the term *equity* generally refers only to stockholders' equity. Thus, the **equity ratio** indicates the proportion of total assets (or total equities) that is provided by stockholders (owners) on any given date. The formula for the equity ratio is as follows:

$$\text{Equity ratio} = \frac{\text{Stockholders' equity}}{\text{Total assets (or total equities)}}$$

The Knight Corporation's liabilities and stockholders' equity, taken from Illustration 11.1, are given below. The Knight Corporation's equity ratio increased from 69.0% in 1990 to 73.1% in 1991. The schedule below shows that the company's stockholders increased their proportionate equity in the company's assets by additional investment in the company's common stock and by retention of income earned during the year.

	December 31, 1991		December 31, 1990	
	Amount	Percent	Amount	Percent
Current liabilities	$127,100	20.0	$109,900	20.0
Long-term liabilities	43,600	6.9	60,800	11.0
Total liabilities	$170,700	26.9	$170,700	31.0
Common stock	$240,000	37.8	$200,000	36.3
Retained earnings	224,500	35.3	180,400	32.7
Total stockholders' equity	$464,500	73.1	$380,400	69.0
Total equity (equal to total assets)	$635,200	100.0	$551,100	100.0

The equity ratio must be interpreted carefully. From a creditor's point of view, a high proportion of stockholders' equity is desirable. A high equity ratio indicates the existence of a large protective buffer for creditors in the event a company suffers a loss. But from an owner's point of view, a high proportion of stockholders' equity may or may not be desirable. If borrowed funds can be used by the business to generate income in excess of the net after-tax cost of the interest on such borrowed funds, a lower percentage of stockholders' equity may be desirable.

To illustrate the effect of higher leveraging (i.e., a larger proportion of debt), assume Knight Corporation could have financed its present operations with $40,000 of 12% bonds instead of 4,000 shares of common stock. The effect on income for 1991 would be as follows, assuming a federal income tax rate of 50%:

Net income as presently stated (Illustration 11.2)	$59,100
Deduct additional interest on debt (0.12 × $40,000)	4,800
	$54,300
Add reduced tax due to interest deduction (0.5 × $4,800)	2,400
Adjusted net income	$56,700

As shown, net income is reduced when leverage is increased by issuing bonds instead of common stock. But there are also fewer shares outstanding, so earnings per share (EPS) increase from $2.46 ($59,100/24,000 shares) to $2.84 ($56,700/20,000 shares). Since investors place heavy emphasis on EPS amounts, many companies in recent years have introduced large portions of debt into their capital structures in order to increase EPS.

It should be pointed out, though, that too low a percentage of owners' equity (too much debt) has its dangers. Financial leverage magnifies losses per share as well as EPS since there are fewer shares of stock over which to spread the losses. A period of business recession may result in operating losses and shrinkage in the value of assets, such as receivables and inventory, which in turn may lead to an inability to meet fixed payments for interest and principal on the debt. The result could be that the company may be forced into liquidation and the stockholders would lose their investments.

Stockholders' equity to debt ratio. The relative equities of owners and creditors may be expressed in several ways. To say that creditors hold a 26.9% interest in the assets of the Knight Corporation on December 31, 1991, is equivalent to saying stockholders hold a 73.1% interest. In many cases, this relationship is expressed as a ratio—**stockholders' equity to debt ratio.**

$$\frac{\text{Stockholders' equity}}{\text{to debt ratio}} = \frac{\text{Stockholders' equity}}{\text{Total debt}}$$

Such a ratio for the Knight Corporation would be 2.23:1 ($380,400/$170,700) on December 31, 1990, and 2.72:1 ($464,500/$170,700) on December 31, 1991. This ratio is sometimes inverted and called the **debt to equity ratio.** Some analysts use only long-term debt rather than total debt in calculating these ratios. The analysts do not consider short-term debt to be part of the capital structure since it will be paid within one year.

Profitability Tests

Profitability is a very important measure of a company's operating success. Generally, there are two areas of concern when judging profitability: (1) relationships on the income statement that indicate a company's ability to recover costs and expenses, and (2) relationships of income to various balance sheet measures that indicate the company's relative ability to earn income on assets employed.

Rate of return on operating assets. The best measure of earnings performance without regard to the sources of assets is the relationship of net operating income to operating assets, which is known as the **rate of return on operating assets.** This ratio is designed to show the earning power of the company as a bundle of assets. By disregarding both nonoperating assets and nonoperating income elements, the rate of return on operating assets measures the profitability of the company in carrying out its primary business functions. The ratio can be broken down into two elements—the operating margin and the turnover of operating assets.

Operating margin reflects the percentage of each dollar of net sales that becomes net operating income. Net operating income excludes **nonoperating income elements.** These elements include extraordinary items; nonoperating revenues, such as interest revenue; and nonoperating expenses, such as interest expense and income taxes. The formula for operating margin is:

$$\text{Operating margin} = \frac{\text{Net operating income}}{\text{Net sales}}$$

Turnover of operating assets shows the amount of sales dollars generated for each dollar invested in operating assets. Year-end operating assets typically are used, even though in theory an average would be better. **Operating assets** are all assets actively used in producing operating revenues. **Nonoperating assets** are assets owned but not used in producing operating revenues; they include items such as land held for future use, a factory building rented to another company, and long-term bond investments. Total assets should not be used in evaluating earnings performance because they include nonoperating assets that do not contribute to the generation of sales. The formula for the turnover of operating assets is:

$$\text{Turnover of operating assets} = \frac{\text{Net sales}}{\text{Operating assets}}$$

The rate of return on operating assets of a company is equal to operating margin multiplied by turnover of operating assets. The more a company earns per dollar of sales and the more sales it makes per dollar invested in operating assets, the higher will be the return per dollar invested. Rate of return on operating assets is expressed by the following formulas:

$$\text{Rate of return on operating assets} = \text{Operating margin} \times \text{Turnover of operating assets}$$

or

$$\text{Rate of return on operating assets} = \frac{\text{Net operating income}}{\text{Net sales}} \times \frac{\text{Net sales}}{\text{Operating assets}}$$

Since net sales appear in both ratios (once as a numerator and once as a denominator), it can be canceled out, and the formula for rate of return on operating assets becomes:

$$\text{Rate of return on operating assets} = \frac{\text{Net operating income}}{\text{Operating assets}}$$

It is, however, more useful for analytical purposes to leave the formula in the form that shows margin and turnover separately since it provides more information to analysts.

The rate of return on operating assets for the Knight Corporation for 1991 and 1990 are calculated below.

	1991	1990	Amount of Increase
Net operating income (a)	$110,400	$ 81,100	$ 29,300
Net sales (b)	$986,400	$765,500	$220,900
Operating assets* (c)	$635,200	$551,100	$ 84,100
Operating margin (a ÷ b)	11.19%	10.59%	
Turnover of operating assets (b ÷ c)	1.55:1	1.39:1	
Rate of return on operating assets (a ÷ c)	17.38%	14.72%	

*For the Knight Corporation there were no nonoperating assets, so total assets is used in the calculation.

Securing desired rate of return on operating assets. Companies that are to survive in the economy must attain some minimum rate of return on operating assets. But this minimum can be attained in many different ways. To illustrate, consider a grocery store and a jewelry store, each with a rate of return of 8% on operating assets. The grocery store normally would attain this rate of return with a low margin and a high turnover, while the jewelry store would have a high margin and a low turnover as shown below:

	Margin	×	Turnover	=	Rate of Return on Operating assets
Grocery store. . . .	1%	×	8.0 times		8%
Jewelry store. . . .	20%	×	0.4 times		8%

Net income to net sales. Another measure of a company's profitability is the **net income to net sales** ratio, calculated as follows:

$$\text{Net income to net sales} = \frac{\text{Net income}}{\text{Net sales}}$$

This ratio measures the proportion of the sales dollar that remains after the deduction of all expenses. The computations for the Knight Company are:

	1991	1990	Amount of Increase
Net income (a)	$ 59,100	$ 46,600	$ 12,500
Net sales (b).	$986,400	$765,500	$220,900
Ratio of net income to net sales (a ÷ b).	5.99%	6.09%	

Although the ratio of net income to net sales indicates the net amount of profit on each sales dollar, a great deal of care must be exercised in the use and interpretation of this ratio. The amount of net income includes all types of nonoperating items that may occur in a particular period; therefore, net income includes the effects of such things as extraordinary items and interest charges. Thus, a period that contains the effects of an extraordinary item will not be comparable to a period that contains no extraordinary items. Also, since interest expense is deductible in the determination of net income while dividends are not, net income is affected by the methods used to finance the firm's assets.

Net income to average stockholders' equity. From the stockholders' point of view, an important measure of the income-producing ability of a company is the relationship of **net income to average stockholders' equity,** also called the **rate of return on average stockholders' equity,** or simply the **return on equity (ROE).** Stockholders are interested in the ratio of operating income to operating assets as a measure of the efficient use of assets by management. But stockholders are even more interested in knowing what return is earned by the company on each dollar of stockholders' equity invested. The formula for net income to average stockholders' equity is:

$$\text{Net income to average} \atop \text{stockholders' equity} = \frac{\text{Net income}}{\text{Average stockholders' equity}}$$

The ratios for the Knight Company are shown below. Assume that total stockholders' equity on January 1, 1990, was $321,500.

	1991	1990	Amount of Increase
Net income (a)	$ 59,100	$ 46,600	$ 12,500
Total stockholders' equity:			
January 1	$380,400	$321,500	$ 58,900
December 31	464,500	380,400	84,100
Total (b)	$844,900	$701,900	$143,000
Average stockholders' equity (c) (b ÷ 2 = c) . . .	$422,450	$350,950	
Ratio of net income to stockholders' equity (a ÷ c). .	13.99%	13.28%	

The increase in the ratio from 13.28% to 13.99% would be regarded favorably by stockholders. This ratio indicates that for each average dollar of capital invested by a stockholder, the company earned nearly 14 cents in 1991.

Earnings per share. Probably the measure used most widely to appraise a company's operations is **earnings per share (EPS)** of common stock. EPS is equal to earnings available to common stockholders divided by the weighted-average number of shares of common stock outstanding. The financial press regularly publishes actual and forecasted EPS amounts for many corporations, together with period-to-period comparisons. The Accounting Principles Board noted the significance attached to EPS by requiring that such amounts be reported on the face of the income statement.[2]

The calculation of EPS may be fairly simple or highly complex, depending on the corporation's capital structure. A company has a simple capital structure if it has no outstanding securities (e.g., convertible bonds, convertible preferred stocks, warrants, or options) that can be exchanged for common stock. If a company has such securities outstanding, it has a complex capital structure.

A company with a simple capital structure reports a single EPS amount calculated as follows:

$$\text{EPS of common stock} = \frac{\text{Net income available to common stockholders}}{\text{Weighted-average number of common shares outstanding}}$$

Earnings available to common stockholders is equal to net income minus the current year's preferred dividends, whether such dividends have been declared or not.

Determining the weighted-average number of shares. The denominator in the EPS fraction is the weighted-average number of common shares out-

---

[2] Accounting Principles Board, "Reporting Earnings per Share," *Opinion No. 15* (New York; AICPA, 1969), par. 12.

standing for the period. If the number of shares outstanding did not change during the period, the weighted-average number of shares outstanding would, of course, be the number of shares outstanding at the end of the period. The balance in the common stock account of Knight Corporation (Illustration 11.1) was $200,000 on December 31, 1990, and the common stock has a $10 par value. Assuming that no shares were issued or redeemed during 1990, the weighted-average number of shares outstanding was 20,000 ($200,000/$10 per share).

If the number of shares changed during the period, such a change increases or decreases the capital invested in the company and should affect earnings available to shareholders. To compute the weighted-average number of shares outstanding, the change in the number of shares is weighted by the fractional portion of the year that those shares were outstanding. Shares are only considered outstanding during those periods that the related capital investment is available to produce income.

To illustrate, note that Knight Corporation's common stock balance increased by $40,000 (4,000 shares) during 1991. Assume that 3,000 of these shares were issued on April 1 and the other 1,000 shares were issued October 1. The computation of weighted-average shares outstanding would be as follows:

20,000 shares × 1 year.	20,000
3,000 shares × ¾ year (April–December).	2,250
1,000 shares × ¼ year (October–December)	250
Weighted-average number of shares outstanding	22,500

An alternate method looks at the total number of shares outstanding, weighted by the fractional portion of the year that the number of shares was outstanding, as follows:

20,000 shares × ¼ year (January–March)	5,000
23,000 shares × ½ year (April–September).	11,500
24,000 shares × ¼ year (October–December)	6,000
Weighted-average number of shares outstanding	22,500

Note that both methods give the same result.

Since the Knight Corporation had no preferred stock outstanding in either 1990 or 1991, EPS of common stock is computed as follows:

	1991	1990	Amount of Increase
Net income *(a)*	$59,100	$46,600	$12,500
Average number of shares of common stock outstanding *(b)*	22,500	20,000	2,500
EPS of common stock *(a ÷ b)*	$2.63	$2.33	

The better than 12% increase in EPS from $2.33 to $2.63 would probably be viewed quite favorably by the Knight Corporation's stockholders.

EPS and stock dividends or splits. Increases in shares outstanding as a result of a stock dividend or split do not require weighting for fractional periods. Such shares do not increase the capital invested in the business and therefore do not affect income. All that is required is to restate all prior calculations of EPS using the increased number of shares. For example, assume a company reported EPS for 1990 of $1 ($100,000/100,000 shares) and earned $150,000 in 1991. The only change in common stock over the two years was a two-for-one stock split on December 1, 1991, which doubled the shares outstanding to 200,000. EPS for 1990 would be restated at $0.50 ($100,000/200,000 shares) and would be $0.75 ($150,000/200,000 shares) for 1991.

Primary EPS and fully diluted EPS. In the merger wave of the 1960s, corporations often issued securities to finance their acquisitions of other companies. Many of the securities issued were "calls on common" or possessed "equity kickers." These terms mean that the securities were convertible into, or exchangeable for, shares of their issuers' common stock. As a result, many complex problems arose in computing EPS. *APB Opinion No. 15* provided guidelines for solving these problems. A company with a complex capital structure must present at least two EPS calculations, primary EPS and fully diluted EPS. Because of the complexities faced in the calculations, futher discussion of these two EPS amounts must be reserved for an intermediate accounting text.

Times interest earned ratio. Creditors, especially long-term creditors, want to know whether a borrower can meet its required interest payments when they become due. A ratio that provides some indication of this ability is the **times interest earned ratio,** or **interest coverage ratio.** It is computed as follows:

$$\text{Times interest earned ratio} = \frac{\text{Income before interest and taxes}}{\text{Interest expense}}$$

The ratio is a rough comparison of cash inflow from operations with cash outflow for interest on debt. **Income before interest and taxes (IBIT)** is used in the numerator since there would be no income taxes if interest expense is equal to or greater than IBIT. Analysts disagree on whether the denominator should be only interest on long-term debt or all interest expense. We prefer the latter since failure to make any required interest payment is a serious matter.

Assume that a company has IBIT of $100,000 and that the interest expense for the same period is $10,000. The times interest earned ratio is 10:1. The company earned enough during the period to pay its interest expense 10 times over. Very low or negative interest coverage ratios suggest that the borrower could default on required interest payments. A company is not likely to be able to continue interest payments over many periods if it fails to earn enough income to cover them. On the other hand, interest coverage of 10 to 20 times suggests the company is not likely to default on interest payments.

Times preferred dividends earned ratio. Preferred stockholders, like bondholders, must usually be satisfied with a fixed-dollar return on their investments. They are interested in the company's ability to make preferred dividend payments each year. This can be measured by computing the **times preferred dividends earned ratio.** It can be computed as follows:

$$\text{Times preferred dividends earned ratio} = \frac{\text{Net income}}{\text{Annual preferred dividends}}$$

Suppose a company has net income of $48,000 and has $100,000 ($100 par value) of 8% preferred stock outstanding. The number of time the annual preferred dividends are earned would be:

$$\frac{\$48,000}{\$8,000} = 6:1, \quad \text{or} \quad 6 \text{ times}$$

The higher this rate, the higher is the probability that the preferred stockholders will receive their dividends each year.

Market Tests

Certain ratios are computed using information from the financial statements and information about market price for the company's stock. These tests help investors and potential investors assess the relative merits of the various stocks in the marketplace.

The **yield** on a stock investment refers to either an earnings yield or a dividends yield.

Earnings yield on common stock. A company's **earnings yield on common stock** is calculated as follows:

$$\text{Earnings yield on common stock} = \frac{\text{EPS}}{\text{Current market price per share}}$$

Suppose, for example, that a company had common stock with an EPS of $2 and that the quoted market price of the stock on the New York Stock Exchange was $30. The earnings yield on common stock would be:

$$\frac{\$2}{\$30} = 6\frac{2}{3}\%$$

Price-earnings ratio. When inverted, the earnings yield on common stock is called the **price-earnings ratio.** In the case cited above, the price-earnings ratio is:

$$\text{Price-earnings ratio} = \frac{\text{Current market price per share}}{\text{EPS}} = \frac{\$30}{\$2} = 15:1$$

Investors would say that this stock is selling at 15 times earnings, or at a multiple of 15. These investors might have a specific multiple in mind as being the one that should be used to judge whether the stock is underpriced or overpriced. Different investors will have different estimates of the proper price-earnings ratio for a given stock and also different estimates of the future earnings prospects of the company. These different estimates are two of the factors that cause one investor to sell stock at a particular price and another investor to buy at that price.

Dividend yield on common stock. The dividend paid per share of common stock is also of much interest to common stockholders. When the current annual dividend per share is divided by the current market price per share, the result is called the **dividend yield on common stock.** If the company referred to immediately above paid a $1.50 per share dividend, the dividend yield would be:

$$\text{Dividend yield on common stock} = \frac{\text{Dividend per share}}{\text{Current market price per share}} = \frac{\$1.50}{\$30.00} = 5\%$$

Payout ratio. Using dividend yield, investors can compute the payout ratio on a stock. **Payout ratio** is computed as the dividend per share divided by EPS. The payout ratio for the above stock is:

$$\text{Payout ratio} = \frac{\text{Dividend per share}}{\text{EPS}} = \frac{\$1.50}{\$2.00} = 75\%$$

A payout ratio of 75% means that the company paid out 75% of the EPS in the form of dividends. Some investors are attracted by the stock of companies that pay out a large percentage of their earnings. Other investors are attracted by the stock of companies that retain and reinvest a large percentage of their earnings. The tax status of the investor has a great deal to do with this preference. Investors in very high tax brackets often prefer to have the company reinvest the earnings with the expectation that this will result in share price appreciation, which is taxed at capital gains rates when the shares are sold. Dividends are taxed at ordinary income rates, which have been much higher than capital gains rates.

Dividend yield on preferred stock. Preferred stockholders, as well as common stockholders, are interested in dividend yields. The computation of the **dividend yield on preferred stock** is similar to the common stock dividend yield computation. Suppose a company has 2,000 shares of $100 par value, 8% preferred stock outstanding that has a current market price of $110 per share. The dividend yield is computed as follows:

$$\text{Dividend yield on preferred stock} = \frac{\text{Dividend per share}}{\text{Current market price per share}} = \frac{\$8}{\$110} = 7.27\%$$

Through the use of dividend yield rates, different preferred stocks having different annual dividends and different market prices can be compared.

FINAL CONSIDERATIONS IN FINANCIAL STATEMENT ANALYSIS

Objective 4: Understand the considerations used in financial statement analysis

Standing alone, a single financial ratio may not be very informative. Greater insight can be obtained by computing and analyzing several related ratios for a company. The ratios presented in this chapter are summarized in Illustration 11.3.

Illustration 11.3
SUMMARY OF RATIOS

Ratio	Formula	Significance
Current ratio	Current assets ÷ Current liabilities	Test of debt-paying ability
Acid-test (quick) ratio	Quick assets (Cash + Marketable securities + Net receivables) ÷ Current liabilities	Test of immediate debt-paying ability
Accounts receivable turnover	Net credit sales (or net sales) ÷ Average net accounts receivable	Test of quality of accounts receivable
Number of days' sales in accounts receivable (average collection period of accounts receivable)	Number of days in year ÷ Accounts receivable turnover	Test of quality of accounts receivable
Inventory turnover	Cost of goods sold ÷ Average inventory	Test of whether or not a sufficient volume of business is being generated relative to inventory
Total assets turnover	Net sales ÷ Average total assets	Test of whether or not the volume of business generated is adequate relative to amount of capital invested in business
Equity ratio	Stockholders' equity ÷ Total assets (equities)	Index of long-run solvency and safety
Stockholders' equity to debt ratio	Stockholders' equity ÷ Total debt	Measure of the relative proportion of stockholders' and of creditors' equities
Rate of return on operating assets	Net operating income ÷ Operating assets or Operating margin × Turnover of operating assets	Measure of managerial effectiveness
Net income to net sales	Net income ÷ Net sales	Indicator of the amount of net profit on each dollar of sales
Net income to average stockholders' equity	Net income ÷ Average stockholders' equity	Measure of what a given company earned for its stockholders from all sources as a percentage of the stockholders' investment
EPS of common stock	Net income available to common stockholders ÷ Weighted-average number of common shares outstanding	Tends to have an effect on the market price per share
Times interest earned ratio	Income before interest and taxes ÷ Interest expense	Indicates likelihood that creditors will continue to receive their interest payments
Times preferred dividends earned ratio	Net income ÷ Annual preferred dividends	Indicates likelihood that preferred stockholders will receive their dividend each year
Earnings yield on common stock	EPS ÷ Current market price per share	Useful for comparison with other stocks
Price-earnings ratio	Current market price per share ÷ EPS	Index of whether a stock is relatively cheap or expensive based on ratio
Dividend yield on common stock	Dividend per share ÷ Current market price per share	Useful for comparison with other stocks
Payout ratio on common stock	Dividend per share ÷ EPS	Index of whether company pays out a large percentage of earnings as dividends or reinvests most of its earnings
Dividend yield on preferred stock	Dividend per share ÷ Current market price per share	Useful for comparison with other preferred stocks

413

Financial analysis relies heavily upon informed judgment. Percentages and ratios are guides to aid comparison and are useful in uncovering potential strengths and weaknesses. But the financial analyst should seek the basic causes behind changes and established trends.

Need for Comparable Data

Analysts must be sure that their comparisons are valid—especially when the comparison is of items for different periods or different companies. Consistent accounting practices must be followed if valid interperiod comparisons are to be made. Comparable intercompany comparisons are more difficult to secure. Accountants cannot do much more than disclose the fact that one company is using FIFO and another is using LIFO for inventory and cost of goods sold computations. Such a disclosure alerts analysts that intercompany comparisons of inventory turnover ratios, for example, may not be strictly comparable.

Also, when comparing a company's ratios to industry averages provided by an external source such as Dun & Bradstreet, the analyst must calculate the company's ratio in the same manner as the reporting service. Thus, if Dun & Bradstreet uses net sales (rather than cost of goods sold) to compute inventory turnover, so should the analyst. Net sales may be used because cost of goods sold amounts are not computed and reported in the same manner by all companies. Ratios based on net sales may lead to different conclusions from those obtained using cost of goods sold because gross margin rates may differ. For example, two companies, Company A and Company B, may both have $100 sales and $10 average inventory for an identical inventory turnover of 10 ($100/$10) based on sales. But, if Company A's gross margin rate is 40%, its inventory turnover based on cost of goods sold is 6 [($100 − $40)/$10]. If Company B's gross margin rate is 30%, its cost of goods sold is $70, and its inventory turnover is 7.

Influence of External Factors

Facts and conditions not disclosed by the financial statements may, however, affect their interpretation. A single important event may have been largely responsible for a given relationship. For example, a new product may have been unexpectedly put on the market by competitors, making it necessary for the company under study to sacrifice its inventory of a product suddenly rendered obsolete. Such an event would affect the percentage of gross margin to net sales severely. Yet there may be little or no chance that such an event will happen again.

General business conditions within the business or industry of the company under study must be considered. A corporation's downward trend in earnings, for example, is less alarming if the industry trend or the general economic trend is also downward.

Consideration should be given to the possible seasonal nature of the businesses under study. If the balance sheet date represents the seasonal peak in the volume of business, for example, the ratio of current assets to current liabilities may acceptably be much lower than if the balance sheet date is in a season of low activity.

The potential investor should realize that acquiring the ability to make informed judgments is a long process and does not occur overnight. Using ratios and percentages without thinking of underlying causes may lead to incorrect conclusions.

Impact of Inflation

The usefulness of conventional financial statements has been questioned in recent years more than ever before. There is one primary reason for this: financial statements fail to reveal the impact of inflation on the reporting entity. One of the primary rules to be followed in making comparisons is to be sure that the items being compared are comparable. The old adage is that one should not add apples and oranges and call the total either apples or oranges. Yet, the accountant does exactly this when dollars of different real worth are added or subtracted as if they were the same. The worth of a dollar declines during periods of inflation.

Considerable debate has existed over the proper response by accounting to inflation. Some argue that we should change our units of measure from the nominal, unadjusted dollar to a dollar of a constant purchasing power. Others maintain that only by adopting current cost as the attribute measured will the real effect of inflation on an entity be revealed. How each of these alternative approaches could be implemented is discussed in Appendix A at the end of the text.

Need for Comparative Standards

Relationships between financial statement items becomes more meaningful when standards are available for comparison. Comparison with standards provides a starting point for all the analyst's thinking and leads to further investigation and, ultimately, to conclusions and business decisions. Such standards consist of (1) those that the analyst has in his or her own mind as a result of experience and observations, (2) those provided by the records of past performance and position of the business under study, and (3) those provided about other enterprises. Examples of this last type of standard are data available through trade associations, universities, research organizations (such as Dun & Bradstreet and Robert Morris Associates), and governmental units (such as the Federal Trade Commission).

It is important in financial statement analysis to remember that standards for comparison vary by industry and financial analysis must be carried out with knowledge of specific industry characteristics. For example, a wholesale grocery company would have large inventories to be shipped to retailers and a relatively small investment in property, plant, and equipment, while an electric utility company would have no inventory (except for repair parts) and a large investment in property, plant, and equipment.

Even without an industry, specific variations may exist. Acceptable current ratios, gross margin percentages, debt-to-equity ratios, and so forth vary widely depending on unique conditions within an industry. Therefore, it is important to know the industry in order to make comparisons that have real meaning.

SUMMARY

The data contained in financial statements represent a quantitative summary of a company's operations and activities. If managers, investors, and creditors are skillful in using these financial statements, they can learn much about a company's strengths, weaknesses, problems, operating efficiency, solvency, and profitability.

Many analytical techniques are available to assist managers and others in using financial statements and in assessing the direction and importance of trends and changes that are taking place in a company. Three such techniques have been discussed—dollar and percentage changes in statements (horizontal and vertical analysis), trend analysis, and ratio analysis. In regard to ratio analysis, we have discussed (1) liquidity ratios, (2) equity, or long-term solvency, ratios, (3) profitability tests, and (4) market tests.

Ratios and other analytical techniques are not ends in themselves but rather represent a starting point in evaluating an organization. Once ratios are computed, the analyst should look for the basic causes behind the changes and trends that are observed. In interpreting the findings of ratio analysis and the other analytical techniques discussed in the chapter, the analyst may rely on various standards for comparison. The analyst must also be concerned about the comparability of data between companies or over periods of time, about the influence of external factors such as competitive conditions in the industry and general business conditions, and about the impact of inflation on financial statements.

Playing the role of an analyst, as you did in this chapter, should make you aware of some of the techniques used and decisions made by professional financial statement analysis. This chapter should improve your understanding of the uses of financial statements.

Having concluded your study of financial statement analysis, in Chapter 12 you will return to the accounting theory you were introduced to in Chapter 1. Chapter 12 also explains the effect international accounting has on financial reporting.

Objective 5: Define and correctly use the new terms in the glossary

NEW TERMS INTRODUCED IN CHAPTER 11

Accounts receivable turnover   Net sales divided by average net accounts receivable (400).

Acid-test (quick) ratio   Ratio of quick assets (cash, marketable securities, net receivables) to current liabilities (400).

Common-size statements Show only percentages and no absolute dollar amounts (393).

Comparative financial statements Present the same company's financial statements for two or more successive periods in side-by-side columns (393).

Current (working capital) ratio The ratio that relates current assets to current liabilities (399).

Debt to equity ratio Total debt divided by owners' equity (405).

Dividend yield on common stock Dividend per share divided by current market price per share of common stock (412).

Dividend yield on preferred stock Dividend per share divided by current market price per share of preferred stock (412).

Earnings per share (EPS) Usually computed for common stock; earnings available to common stockholders (which equals net income less preferred dividends) divided by weighted-average number of shares of common stock outstanding (408).

Earnings yield on common stock Ratio of current EPS to current market price per share (411).

Equity (stockholders' equity) ratio The ratio of stockholders' equity to total asset (or total equities) (403).

Horizontal analysis Analysis of a company's financial statements for two or more successive periods showing percentage and/or absolute changes from prior year. This type of analysis helps detect changes in a company's performance and highlights trends (393).

Income before interest and taxes (IBIT) Net income plus interest expense and taxes expense (410).

Inventory turnover Cost of goods sold divided by average inventory (402).

Liquidity State of possessing liquid assets, such as cash and other assets, that will soon be converted into cash (392).

Net income to average stockholders' equity Net income divided by average stockholders' equity; often called **rate of return on stockholders' equity,** or simply **return on equity** (ROE) (407).

Net income to net sales Net income divided by net sales (407).

Nonoperating assets Assets owned but not used in producing operating revenues (406).

Nonoperating income elements Elements that are excluded from net operating income because they are not directly related to operations; includes such elements as extraordinary items, interest revenue, interest expense, and income taxes (405).

Number of days' sales in accounts receivable The number of days in a year (365) divided by the accounts receivable turnover. Also called the **average collection period for accounts receivable** (402).

Operating assets All assets actively used in producing operating revenues (406).

Operating margin Net operating income divided by net sales (405).

Payout ratio (on common stock) The ratio of dividends per share divided by EPS (412).

Price-earnings ratio The ratio of current market price per share divided by the EPS of the stock (411).

Quick ratio Same as acid-test ratio.

Rate of return on operating assets (Net operating income ÷ Net sales) × (Net sales ÷ Operating assets). Result is equal to net operating income divided by operating assets (405).

Ratios They express the logical relationship between certain items in the financial statements (393).

Return on equity (ROE) Net income divided by average stockholders' equity (407).

Stockholders' equity to debt ratio Stockholders' equity divided by total debt; often used in inverted form and called the **debt to equity ratio** (405).

Times interest earned ratio A ratio computed by dividing income before interest expense and income taxes by interest expense (also called interest coverage ratio) (410).

Times preferred dividends earned ratio Net income divided by annual preferred dividends (411).

Total assets turnover Net sales divided by average total assets (403).

Trend percentages Similar to horizontal analysis except that a base year is selected and comparisons are made to the base year (393).

Turnover The relationship between the amount of an asset and some measure of its use. See accounts receivable turnover, inventory turnover, and total assets turnover (400).

Turnover of operating assets Net sales divided by operating assets (406).

Vertical analysis The study of a single financial statement in which each item is expressed as a percentage of a significant total; for example, percentages of sales calculations (393).

Working capital ratio Same as current ratio (399).

Yield (on stock) The yield on a stock investment refers to either an earnings yield or a dividend yield. Also see Earnings yield on common stock and Dividend yield on common stock and on preferred stock (411).

DEMONSTRATION PROBLEM 11–1

CLARK COMPANY
Comparative Income Statement
For the Years Ended December 31, 1990 and 1991

	1991	1990
Net sales	$1,370,000	$1,200,000
Cost of goods sold	808,300	690,000
Gross margin	$ 561,700	$ 510,000
Operating expenses	369,900	330,000
Net income before interest and taxes	$ 191,800	$ 180,000
Interest expense	20,550	19,200
Net income before income taxes	$ 171,250	$ 160,800
Income taxes	61,650	66,000
Net income	$ 109,600	$ 94,800

CLARK COMPANY
Comparative Balance Sheet
December 31, 1990 and 1991

	1991	1990
Assets		
Cash	$ 75,000	$ 60,000
Marketable securities	45,000	35,000
Accounts receivable, net	105,000	85,000
Inventory	225,000	150,000
Building, net	450,000	350,000
Total assets	$900,000	$680,000
Liabilities and Stockholders' Equity		
Accounts payable	$ 45,000	$ 35,000
Bank loans payable	15,000	20,000
Mortgage notes payable, due in 1993	60,000	60,000
Bonds payable, 10% due, December 31, 1995	150,000	150,000
Common stock, $100 par value	450,000	300,000
Retained earnings	180,000	115,000
Total liabilities and stockholders' equity	$900,000	$680,000

Required:

a. Prepare comparative common-size income statements for 1990 and 1991.

b. Perform a horizontal analysis of the comparative balance sheets.

c. Comment on the results of (a) and (b).

d. Compute the following ratios for 1991:

   1. Current ratio.
   2. Acid-test ratio.
   3. Accounts receivable turnover.
   4. Inventory turnover.
   5. Total assets turnover.
   6. Equity ratio.
   7. EPS of common stock (the new shares were issued for cash on May 1).
   8. Times interest earned ratio.

Solution to demonstration problem 11–1.

a.

CLARK COMPANY
Common-Size Comparative Income Statement
For the Years Ended December 31, 1990 and 1991

	1991	1990
Net sales	100.0	100.0
Cost of goods sold	59.0	57.5
Gross margin	41.0	42.5
Operating expenses	27.0	27.5
Net income before interest and taxes	14.0	15.0
Interest expense	1.5	1.6
Net income before income taxes	12.5	13.4
Income taxes	4.5	5.5
Net income	8.0	7.9

b.

CLACK COMPANY
Comparative Balance Sheet
December 31, 1990 and 1991

	1991	1990	Increase or Decrease* 1991 over 1990 Amount	Percent
Assets				
Cash	$ 75,000	$ 60,000	$ 15,000	25.0
Marketable securities	45,000	35,000	10,000	28.57
Accounts receivable, net	105,000	85,000	20,000	23.53
Inventory	225,000	150,000	75,000	50.00
Building, net	450,000	350,000	100,000	28.57
Total assets	$900,000	$680,000	$220,000	32.35
Liabilities and Stockholders' Equity				
Accounts payable	$ 45,000	$ 35,000	$ 10,000	28.57
Bank loans payable	15,000	20,000	5,000*	25.0*
Mortgage notes payable, due in 1993	60,000	60,000	–0–	–0–
Bonds payable, 10% due, December 31, 1995	150,000	150,000	–0–	–0–
Common stock, $100 par value	450,000	300,000	150,000	50.0
Retained earnings	180,000	115,000	65,000	56.52
Total liabilities and stockholders' equity	$900,000	$680,000	$220,000	32.35

c. The $170,000 increase in sales yielded only a $51,700 increase in gross margin because cost of goods sold increased from 57.5% to 59.0%. Although operating expenses increased from $330,000 to $369,900, they declined relatively from 27.5% to 27% of sales. This change together with the change in gross margin combined to hold net income to an increase of $14,800, which represents only a .10% increase in the rate of net income to sales. The significant change in the balance sheet was the 50% increase in inventory that was financed by the use of cash and accounts receivable and by increases in current liabilities and in retained earnings. Although the inventory increased heavily in 1991, the other current assets did not decline; therefore, the company is in a more liquid position at the end of 1991 than at the end of 1990.

d. 1. Current ratio:

$$\frac{\text{Current assets}}{\text{Current liabilities}} = \frac{\$450,000}{\$60,000} = 7.5:1$$

2. Acid-test ratio:

$$\frac{\text{Quick assets}}{\text{Current liabilities}} = \frac{\$225,000}{\$60,000} = 3.75:1$$

3. Accounts receivable turnover:

$$\frac{\text{Net sales}}{\text{Average net accounts receivable}} = \frac{\$1,370,000}{\$95,000} = 14.42 \text{ times}$$

4. Inventory turnover:

$$\frac{\text{Cost of goods sold}}{\text{Average inventory}} = \frac{\$808,300}{\$187,500} = 4.31 \text{ times}$$

5. Total assets turnover:

$$\frac{\text{Net sales}}{\text{Average total assets}} = \frac{\$1,370,000}{\$790,000} = 1.73 \text{ times}$$

6. Equity ratio:

$$\frac{\text{Stockholders' equity}}{\text{Total assets}} = \frac{\$630,000}{\$900,000} = 70\%$$

7. EPS of common stock:

$$\frac{\begin{array}{c}\text{Net income available}\\ \text{to common stockholders}\end{array}}{\begin{array}{c}\text{Weighted-average number of}\\ \text{common shares outstanding}\end{array}} = \frac{\$109,600}{3,500} = \$31.31$$

$$(3,000 \times 4/12 + 4,500 \times 8/12)$$

8. Times interest earned ratio:

$$\frac{\text{Income before interest and taxes}}{\text{Interest expense}} = \frac{\$191,800}{\$20,550} = 9.33 \text{ to } 1 \quad \text{or} \quad 9.33 \text{ times}$$

QUESTIONS

1. The higher the accounts receivable turnover rate, the better off the company is. Do you agree? Why?

2. Can you think of a situation where the current ratio is very misleading as an indicator of short-term debt-paying ability? Does the acid-test ratio offer a remedy to the situation you have described? Describe a situation where the acid-test ratio will not suffice either.

3. Before the Mitchell Company issued $10,000 of long-term notes (due more than a year from the date of issue) in exchange for a like amount of accounts payable, its acid-test ratio was 2 to 1. Will this transaction increase, decrease, or have no effect on the current ratio? The equity ratio?

4. Through the use of turnover rates, explain why a firm might seek to increase the volume of its sales even though such an increase can be secured only at reduced prices.

5. Indicate which of the relationships illustrated in the chapter would be best to judge:
   a. The short-term debt-paying ability of the firm. LIQUIDITY
   b. The overall efficiency of the firm without regard to the sources of assets.
   c. The return to owners of a corporation.
   d. The safety of long-term creditors' interest.
   e. The safety of preferred stockholders' dividends.

6. Indicate how each of the following ratios or measures is calculated:
   a. Payout ratio.
   b. Earnings per share of common stock.
   c. Price-earnings ratio.

    d. Yield on common stock.

    e. Yield on preferred stock.

    f. Times interest earned.

    g. Times preferred dividends earned.

    h. Return on stockholders' equity.

7. How is the rate of return on operating assets determined? Is it possible for two companies with "operating margins" of 5% and 1%, respectively, to both have a rate of return of 20% on operating assets? How? *p406*

8. Cite some of the possible deficiencies in accounting information, especially regarding its use in analyzing a particular company over a 10-year period.

EXERCISES

Prepare horizontal and vertical analysis and comment

1. Income statement data for Jones Company for 1990 and 1991 are:

	1991	1990
Net sales	$1,800,000	$1,426,000
Cost of goods sold	1,100,000	782,000
Operating expense	360,000	334,000
Administrative expense	250,000	230,000
Income taxes	34,000	30,000

Prepare a horizontal and vertical analysis of the above income data in a form similar to that in Illustration 11.2. Comment on the results of this analysis.

Compute current ratios.

2. Under each of the three conditions listed below, compute the current ratio after each of the transactions described. Current assets are now $400,000. (Consider each transaction independently of the others.) The current ratio before the transactions is:

    a. 1 to 1

    b. 2 to 1

    c. 1 to 2

Transactions:

1. Purchased $300,000 of merchandise on account.
2. Purchased $200,000 of machinery for cash.
3. Issued stock for $200,000 cash.

Compute accounts receivable ratios and comment

3. Smith Company has sales of $1,460,000 per year. Its average accounts receivable balance is $292,000.

    a. What is the average number of days an accounts receivable is outstanding?

    b. Assuming released funds can be invested at 10%, how much could the company earn by reducing the collection period of the accounts receivable to 30 days?

    c. What assumption must you make in order for this income calculation to be correct?

<table>
<tr><td>*Calculate inventory turnover*</td><td>**4.** From the following partial income statement calculate the inventory turnover for the period.</td></tr>
</table>

Net sales		$1,400,000
Cost of goods sold:		
Beginning inventory	$ 118,000	
Purchases	942,000	
Cost of goods available for sale	$1,060,000	
Less: Ending inventory	130,000	
Cost of goods sold.		930,000
Gross margin		$ 470,000
Operating expenses		250,000
Net operating income		$ 220,000

Calculate earnings per share

5. The Seaver Company had 190,000 shares of common stock outstanding on January 1, 1990. On August 31, 1990, it issued 30,000 additional shares for cash. The income available for common stockholders for 1990 was $500,000. What amount of earnings per share of common stock should the company report?

Compute times interest earned ratio

6. Auto Company paid interest of $10,000, incurred federal income taxes of $30,000 and had net income after taxes of $60,000. How many times was the interest earned?

Calculate times preferred dividends earned ratio and earnings yield on preferred stock

7. The Blue Company had 10,000 shares of $100 par value, 4%, preferred stock outstanding. Net income after taxes was $280,000. The market price per share was $64.

  a. How many times were the preferred dividends earned?

  b. What was the yield on the preferred stock assuming the regular preferred dividends were declared and paid?

Compute price-earnings ratio

8. A Company had 20,000 shares of $20 par value common stock outstanding. Net income was $70,000. Current market price per share is $84. Compute the price-earnings ratio.

Calculate rate of return on operating assets

9. Bay, Inc., had net sales of $1,510,000, gross margin of $805,000, and operating expenses of $495,000. Total assets (all operating) were $1,240,000. Compute Bay's rate of return on operating assets.

Compute weighted-average number of common shares outstanding

10. Dillon Company started 1990 with 125,000 shares of common stock outstanding. On March 31, it issued 15,000 shares for cash; and on September 1, it purchased 6,000 treasury shares for cash. Compute the weighted-average number of common shares outstanding for the year.

Determine rate of return on average stockholder's equity

11. Brick Company started 1990 with total stockholder's equity of $1,121,000. Its net income for 1990 was $316,000, and $30,000 of dividends were declared. Compute the rate of return on average stockholders' equity for 1990.

Calculate earnings per share and adjusted earnings per share

12. Mary Company reported EPS of $3 ($300,000/100,000 shares) for 1990, ending the year with 100,000 shares outstanding. In 1991, the Company earned net income of $451,500, issued 30,000 shares of common stock for cash on September 30, and distributed a 100% stock dividend on December 31, 1990. Compute EPS for 1991 and compute the adjusted EPS for 1990 that could be shown in the 1991 annual report.

PROBLEMS

Perform horizontal and vertical analysis

11–1. Presented below are Lake Company's comparative balance sheets at the end of 1990 and 1991. The comparative statements of income and retained earnings for the years ended December 31, 1990 and 1991 are also given.

LAKE COMPANY
Comparative Balance Sheet
December 31, 1990 and 1991

	1991	1990
Assets		
Current assets:		
Cash	$ 30,100	$ 16,352
Accounts receivable, net	84,882	83,512
Inventory	211,904	220,752
Total current assets	$326,886	$320,616
Plant assets, net	275,114	263,384
Total assets	$602,000	$584,000
Liabilities and Stockholders' Equity		
Current liabilities:		
Accounts payable and accruals	$ 83,678	$179,288
Notes payable	58,394	147,168
Total current liabilities	$142,072	$326,456
Long-term liabilities:		
Bonds payable	175,784	–0–
Total liabilities	$317,856	$326,456
Stockholders' equity:		
Common stock	$193,144	$184,544
Retained earnings	91,000	73,000
Total stockholders' equity	$284,144	$257,544
Total liabilities and stockholders' equity	$602,000	$584,000

LAKE COMPANY
Comparative Statement of Income and Retained Earnings
For the Years Ended December 31, 1990 and 1991

	1991	1990
Net sales	$832,400	$790,780
Cost of goods sold	532,736	514,007
Gross margin	$299,664	$276,773
Operating expenses:		
Selling	$120,698	$128,897
Administrative	112,374	102,801
Total operating expenses	$233,072	$231,698
Net operating income	$ 66,592	$ 45,075
Interest expense	20,810	10,280
Income before income taxes	$ 45,782	$ 34,795
Income taxes	20,810	14,234
Net income	$ 24,972	$ 20,561
Retained earnings, January 1	73,000	61,829
	$ 97,972	$ 82,390
Dividends	6,972	9,390
Retained earnings, December 31	$ 91,000	$ 73,000

Required:

Perform horizontal and vertical analysis of the above financial statements in a manner similar to that shown in Illustrations 11.1 and 11.2.

Prepare a statement showing trend percentages and comment

11–2.

	1990	1991	1992	1993
Sales	$700,000	$798,000	$840,000	$1,323,000
Cost of goods sold	500,000	540,000	650,000	1,075,000
Gross margin	$200,000	$258,000	$190,000	$ 248,000
Operating expenses	160,000	168,000	176,000	224,000
Net operating income	$ 40,000	$ 90,000	$ 14,000	$ 24,000

Required:

a. Prepare a statement showing the trend percentages for each of the above items, using 1990 as the base year.

b. Comment on the trends noted.

Compute various liquidity ratios

11–3. From the following data for the Wally Company compute the *(a)* working capital; *(b)* current ratio; and *(c)* acid-test ratio, all as of both dates; and *(d)* comment briefly on the company's short-term financial position.

	December 31 1991	December 31 1990
Notes payable (due in 90 days)	$192,300	$165,000
Merchandise inventory	780,275	708,200
Cash	287,400	324,500
Marketable securities	144,000	85,000
Accrued liabilities	55,000	56,600
Accounts receivable	478,025	457,360
Accounts payable	267,200	171,000
Allowance for doubtful accounts	60,500	42,400
Bonds payable, due 2001	380,000	402,000
Prepaid expenses	17,200	18,110

Determine the effects of transactions on working capital ratios

11–4. On December 31, 1990, the Time Company's current ratio was 3 to 1. Assume that the following transactions were completed on that date and indicate *(a)* whether the amount of working capital would have been increased, decreased, or unaffected by each of the transactions; and *(b)* whether the current ratio would have been increased, decreased, or unaffected by each of the transactions. (Consider each transaction independently of all the others.)

Transactions:

1. Purchased merchandise on account.
2. Paid a cash dividend declared on November 15, 1991.
3. Sold equipment for cash.
4. Temporarily invested cash in marketable securities.
5. Sold obsolete merchandise for cash (at a loss).
6. Issued 10-year bonds for cash.
7. Amortized goodwill.
8. Paid cash for inventory.

Prepare comparative income statements and balance sheets, schedule of current to total current assets, and compute standard ratios

11–5. The following are comparative balance sheets of the Davis Corporation on December 31, 1990 and 1991.

DAVIS CORPORATION
Comparative Balance Sheet
December 31, 1990 and 1991

	December 31, 1991	December 31, 1990
Assets		
Cash	$ 450,000	$ 510,000
Accounts receivable, net	390,000	450,000
Merchandise inventory	270,000	330,000
Plant assets, net	600,000	270,000
Total assets	$1,710,000	$1,560,000
Liabilities and Stockholders' Equity		
Accounts payable.	$ 210,000	$ 150,000
Notes payable	180,000	258,000
Common stock	660,000	660,000
Retained earnings	660,000	492,000
Total liabilities and stockholders' equity	$1,710,000	$1,560,000
Other Data		
Sales	$2,760,000	$2,400,000
Gross margin	1,140,000	1,020,000
Selling and administrative expenses	720,000	660,000
Interest expense	24,000	12,000
Cash dividends	228,000	90,000

During 1991, a note in the amount of $120,000 was given for equipment purchased at that price. Unlike the company's other notes, which are short-term, the $120,000 note matures in 2001.

Required:

a. Prepare comparative income statements that show percentage of net sales for each item.

b. Prepare comparative balance sheets that show percentage of total assets for each item.

c. Prepare a schedule that shows the percentage of each current asset to the total of current assets as of both year-end dates.

d. Compute the current ratios as of both dates.

e. Compute the acid-test ratios as of both dates.

f. Compute the percentage of stockholders' equity to total equity (or total assets) as of both dates.

Calculate various standard ratios

11–6. The following balance sheet and supplementary data are for the Sid Corporation for 1991.

SID CORPORATION
Balance Sheet
December 31, 1991

Assets

Current assets:		
Cash	$ 600,000	
Marketable securities	320,000	
Accounts receivable, net	520,000	
Inventory	440,000	$1,880,000

MINUS INV.

Financial Statement Analysis

Property, plant, and equipment:
Plant assets	$6,800,000	
Less: Accumulated depreciation	500,000	6,300,000
Total assets		$8,180,000

Liabilities and Stockholders' Equity

Current liabilities:
Accounts payable	$ 340,000	
Bank loans payable	140,000	$ 480,000

Long-term liabilities:
Mortgage notes payable, due in 2001	$ 180,000	
Bonds payable 6%, due December 31, 2001	860,000	1,040,000
Total liabilities		$1,520,000

Stockholders' equity
Common stock par value $50 per share	$4,400,000	
Appropriation for bond sinking fund	160,000	
Retained earnings	2,100,000	6,660,000
Total liabilities and stockholders' equity		$8,180,000

Supplementary data:
1. 1991 net income after taxes amounted to $600,000.
2. 1991 income before interest and taxes, $1,200,000.
3. 1991 cost of goods sold was $1,600,000.
4. 1991 net sales amounted to $3,000,000.
5. Inventory on December 31, 1990 was $300,000.
6. Interest expense for the year was $60,000 (some long-term liabilities were paid during the year).

Required:

Calculate the following ratios. Where you would normally use the average amount for an item in a ratio but the information is not available to do so, use the year-end balance. Show computations.

a. Current ratio.
b. Percentage of net income to stockholders' equity.
c. Turnover of inventory.
d. Average collection period of accounts receivable (there are 365 days in 1990).
e. Earnings per share of common stock.
f. Number of times interest was earned.
g. Stockholders' equity ratio.
h. Percentage of net income to total assets.
i. Turnover of total assets.
j. Acid-test ratio.

Calculate standard ratios and determine absolute changes

11–7. The following information is available about three companies:

	Operating Assets	Net Operating Income	Net Sales
Company 1	$ 450,000	$ 60,000	$ 660,000
Company 2	2,700,000	195,000	6,000,000
Company 3	12,000,000	1,575,000	11,250,000

427

Required:

a. Determine the operating margin, turnover of operating assets, and rate of return on operating assets for each company.

b. In the subsequent year the following changes took place (no other changes occurred):

Company 1 bought some new machinery at a cost of $75,000. Net operating income increased by $6,000 as a result of an increase in sales of $120,000.

Company 2 sold some equipment it was using that was relatively unproductive. The book value of the equipment sold was $300,000. As a result of the sale of the equipment, sales declined by $150,000 and operating income declined by $3,000.

Company 3 purchased some new retail outlets at a cost of $3,000,000. As a result, sales increased by $4,500,000 and operating income increased by $240,000.

Which company has the largest absolute change in:
 i.   Operating margin?
 ii. Turnover of operating assets?
 iii. Rate of return on operating assets?

Compute various profitability ratios and comment

11–8. The following information is available for the Channell Company:

	1991	1990
Net sales	$1,680,000	$1,040,000
Net income before interest and taxes	440,000	340,000
Net income after taxes	222,000	252,000
Interest expense	36,000	32,000
Stockholders' equity, December 31		
(on December 31, 1989, $800,000)	1,220,000	940,000
Common stock, par value $100, December 31	1,040,000	920,000

Additional shares of common stock were issued on January 1, 1991.

Required:

Compute the following for both 1990 and 1991:

a. Earnings per share of common stock.

b. Percentage of net income to net sales.

c. Rate of return on average stockholders' equity.

d. Number of times interest was earned.

Compare and comment.

Determine affects on ratios of change in accounting method (FIFO and LIFO)

11–9. The Dailey Company is considering switching from the FIFO method to the LIFO method of accounting for its inventory before its year-end financial statements are prepared. The January 1 inventory was $350,000. The following data is compiled from the adjusted trial balance at the end of the year.

Inventory, December 31 (FIFO) . . .	$ 550,000
Current assets	850,000
Current liabilities	425,000
Total assets (operating)	1,400,000
Net sales	3,000,000
Cost of goods sold	2,214,000
Operating expenses	436,000

If the change to LIFO takes place, the December 31 inventory would be $470,000.

Required:

a. Compute the current ratio, inventory turnover ratio, and the rate of return on operating assets using FIFO.

b. Repeat part **a** assuming the company adjusts its accounts to the LIFO inventory method.

BUSINESS DECISION PROBLEM 11–1

Compute net income, identify reason for cash increase, state main sources of financing, and indicate further analyses needed

Shown below are the comparative balance sheets of the Specter Corporation for December 31, 1990 and 1991.

SPECTER CORPORATION
Comparative Balance Sheets
December 31, 1990 and 1991

	December 31, 1991	December 31, 1990
Assets		
Cash	$286,000	$166,000
Accounts receivable, net	110,000	120,000
Inventory	164,000	162,000
Plant and equipment	98,000	100,000
Total assets	$658,000	$548,000
Liabilities and Stockholders' Equity		
Accounts payable	$ 14,000	$ 14,000
Common stock	200,000	200,000
Retained earnings	444,000	334,000
Total liabilities and stockholders' equity	$658,000	$548,000

Required:

a. What was the net income for 1991 assuming there were no dividend payments?

b. What was the primary source of the large increase in the cash balance from 1990 to 1991?

c. What are the two main sources of assets for the Specter Corporation?

d. What other comparisons and procedures would you use to complete the analysis of the balance sheet begun above?

BUSINESS DECISION PROBLEM 11–2

Compute turnover ratios for four years and number of days sales in accounts receivable; evaluate effectiveness of company's credit policy

The information below was obtained from the annual reports of the Lyle Manufacturing Company:

	Net Accounts Receivable	Net Sales
1989	$200,000	$1,800,000
1990	280,000	2,100,000
1991	400,000	2,500,000
1992	475,000	3,000,000

Required:

a. If cash sales account for 40% of all sales and credit terms are 1/15; n/45, determine all turnover ratios possible and the number of days' sales in accounts receivable at all possible dates. (The number of days' sales in accounts receivable should be based on year-end accounts receivable and net credit sales).

b. How effective is the company's credit policy?

BUSINESS DECISION PROBLEM 11–3

Analyze investment alternatives

Niles Gill is interested in investing in one of three companies (A, B, and C) by buying its common stock. The companies' shares are selling at about the same price. The long-term capital structure of the companies are as follows:

	Company A	Company B	Company C
Bond with an 8% interest rate			$ 600,000
Preferred stock with a 10% dividend rate		$ 650,000	
Common stock, $50 par value	$2,000,000	1,000,000	1,500,000
Retained earnings	125,000	125,000	125,000
Total long-term equity	$2,125,000	$1,775,000	$2,225,000
Number of common shares outstanding	40,000	20,000	30,000

Mr. Gill has consulted two investment advisers. One adviser believes that each of the companies will earn $75,000 per year before interest and taxes. The other believes that each of the companies will earn $180,000 per year before interest and taxes.

Required:

a. Compute each of the following, using the estimate made by the first adviser then the one made by the second adviser:
  i. Earnings available for common stockholders assuming a 40% tax rate.
  ii. EPS of common stock.
  iii. Rate of return on total stockholders' equity.

b. Which stock should Mr. Gill select if he believes the first adviser?

c. Are the stockholders as a group (common and preferred) better off with or without the use of long-term debt in the above companies?

12

ACCOUNTING THEORY AND INTERNATIONAL ACCOUNTING

LEARNING OBJECTIVES

After studying this chapter, you should be able to:

1. Identify and discuss the basic assumptions, principles, and modifying conventions of accounting.
2. Describe the Conceptual Framework Project of the Financial Accounting Standards Board.
3. Discuss the differences in international accounting among nations (Appendix).
4. Define and use correctly the new terms in the glossary.

In the preceding chapters you learned how accountants use the accounting process (or cycle) to account for the activities of a business. Only brief mention was made in Chapter 1 of the body of theory underlying accounting procedures. Theoretical concepts have also been mentioned in other chapters. In this chapter, accounting theory is discussed in greater depth. Now that you have learned some accounting procedures, you are better able to relate these theoretical concepts to accounting practice. **Accounting theory** is "a set of basic concepts and assumptions and related principles that explain and guide the accountant's actions in identifying, measuring, and communicating economic information."[1]

To some people, the word *theory* has the connotation of being abstract and "out of reach." In accounting, understanding the theory behind the

---

[1]American Accounting Association, *A Statement of Basic Accounting Theory* (Sarasota, Fla., 1966), pp. 1–2.

accounting process helps you make decisions in unusual accounting situations. Accounting theory provides a logical framework for accounting practice.

As businesses expand their operations beyond their own national boundaries, accountants must become aware of the accounting problems this presents. The Appendix to this chapter is devoted to international accounting.

UNDERLYING ASSUMPTIONS

Objective 1: Identify and discuss the basic assumptions, principles, and modifying conventions of accounting

The major underlying assumptions of accounting are (1) entity, (2) going concern (continuity), (3) money measurement, and (4) periodicity. In this section the effects of these assumptions on the accounting process are discussed.

Entity

Data gathered in an accounting system are assumed to relate to a specific business unit or entity. The business **entity** concept assumes that each business has an existence separate from its owners, creditors, employees, customers, other interested parties, and other businesses. For each business (such as a horse stable or a fitness center), the business, not the business owner, is the accounting entity. Financial statements are prepared for a particular business entity that must be identified on the statements. The content of the financial statements must be limited to reporting the activities, resources, and obligations of that entity.

A business entity may be made up of several different *legal* entities. For instance, a large business, such as General Motors Corporation, may consist of several separate corporations, each of which is a separate legal entity. But, because the corporations have a common ownership, they may be considered one business entity for reporting purposes.

Going Concern (Continuity)

Accountants record business transactions for an entity assuming the entity will continue to be a "going concern." The **going-concern (continuity) assumption** states that an entity will continue to operate indefinitely unless there is strong evidence that the entity will terminate. An entity is terminated by ceasing business operations and selling off its assets. The process of termination is called **liquidation.** If liquidation appears likely, the going-concern assumption can no longer be used.

The going-concern assumption is often cited to justify the use of historical costs, rather than market values, in measuring assets. Market values are thought to be of little or no significance to an entity that intends to use, rather than sell, its assets. On the other hand, if an entity is to be liquidated, liquidation values should be used to report assets.

The going-concern assumption permits the accountant to record certain items as assets. For example, printed advertising matter may be on hand to promote a special sale next month. This advertising material may have little, if any, value to anyone but its owner. But, because its owner is expected to continue operating long enough to benefit from it, the accountant classifies the expenditure as an asset, prepaid advertising, rather than as an expense.

Money Measurement

The economic activity of a business is normally recorded and reported in money terms. **Money measurement** is the use of a monetary unit of measurement, such as the dollar, instead of physical or other units of measurement. The use of a particular monetary unit provides accountants with a common unit of measurement to report economic activity. Without a monetary unit, it would be impossible to add such items as buildings, equipment, and inventory on a balance sheet.

The unit of measure (the dollar in the United States) is identified in the financial statements so the statement user can make valid comparisons of values. For example, it would be difficult to compare relative asset values or profitability of a company reporting in U.S. dollars with a company reporting in Japanese yen.

Stable dollar. In the United States, accountants make another assumption regarding money measurement—the stable dollar assumption. Under the **stable dollar** assumption, the dollar is accepted as a *reasonably stable* unit of measurement. Thus, no adjustments are made in the primary financial statements for the changing value of the dollar.

One of the difficulties that has developed as a result of following the stable dollar assumption occurs in depreciation accounting. Assume, for example, that a company acquired a building in 1960, and the 30-year depreciation on the building is computed without adjusting for any changes in the value of the dollar. Thus, the depreciation deducted in 1990 is the same as the depreciation deducted in 1960, and no adjustments are made for the difference in the values of the 1960 dollar and the 1990 dollar. Both dollars are treated as equal monetary units of measurement even though substantial price inflation has occurred over the 30-year period. Accountants and business executives have expressed concern over this inflation problem, especially since 1970. Today there is great interest in reflecting the effects of inflation on the financial statements. Inflation accounting is discussed in Appendix A at the end of this text.

Periodicity (Time Periods)

According to the **periodicity (time periods)** assumption, an entity's life can be subdivided into time periods (such as months or years) for purposes of reporting its economic activities. After subdividing an entity's life into time periods, accountants attempt to prepare accurate reports on the entity's activities for these periods—reports that will provide useful and timely financial information to investors and creditors. In fact, however, the financial reports may be inaccurate for certain of these time periods because accountants use estimates, such as depreciation expense and certain other adjusting entries.

Accounting reports cover relatively short periods of time. The time periods are usually of equal length so that valid comparisons can be made of a company's performance from period to period. The length of the accounting period must be stated in the financial statements.

Accrual basis and periodicity. In Chapter 3, you learned that financial statements more accurately reflect the financial status and operations of a company when prepared under the accrual basis of accounting rather than the cash basis. Under the cash basis of accounting, revenues are recorded when cash is received, and expenses are recorded when cash is paid. Under the accrual basis, however, revenues are recorded when services are rendered or products are sold and delivered, and expenses are recorded when incurred.

The periodicity assumption makes necessary the adjusting entries prepared under the accrual basis. Without the periodicity assumption, there would only be one time period running from the inception of the business to its termination. Then the concepts of cash basis and accrual basis accounting would be irrelevant because all revenues and expenses would be recorded in that one time period and would not have to be assigned to artificially short time periods of one year or less.

Approximation and judgment because of periodicity. To provide periodic financial information, estimates must often be made of such things as expected uncollectible accounts and useful lives of depreciable assets. Uncertainty about future events prevents precise measurement and makes estimates necessary in accounting. Estimates are often reasonably accurate when they are made by an informed accountant.

OTHER BASIC CONCEPTS

Other basic accounting concepts that affect the accounting for entities are (1) general-purpose financial statements, (2) substance over form, (3) consistency, (4) double-entry, and (5) articulation. These basic accounting concepts are discussed in the sections that follow.

General-Purpose Financial Statements

As you know, results of the financial accounting process are presented in financial statements. These are general-purpose financial statements that are prepared at regular intervals to meet many of the general information needs of external parties and top-level internal managers. In contrast, special-purpose financial information can be gathered for a specific decision, usually on a one-time basis. For example, management may need specific information to decide whether or not to purchase a new computer. Because special-purpose financial information must be specific, that information is best obtained from the detailed accounting records rather than from the financial statements.

Substance over Form

In some business transactions, the economic substance of the transaction may conflict with its legal form. For example, a contract that is legally a lease may, in fact, be equivalent to a purchase. A company may have a three-year contract to lease (rent) an auto at a stated monthly rental fee. At the end of the lease period, the company will receive title to the auto after paying a nominal sum (say, $1). The economic substance of this transaction is a purchase rather than a lease of the auto. Thus, under the substance-over-form concept, the auto should be carried as an asset on the balance sheet and should be depreciated rather than only reporting the lease fee as rent expense on the income statement. Accountants should record the *economic substance* of a transaction rather than be guided by the *legal form* of the transaction.

Consistency

When discussing inventories in Chapter 4, we introduced the consistency concept. **Consistency** generally requires a company to use the same accounting principles and reporting practices through time. This concept prohibits indiscriminate switching of principles or methods, such as changing inventory methods every year. However, consistency does not prohibit a change in principles if the information needs of financial statement users are better served by the change. When a change in principle is made, the following disclosures are required—nature of the change, reasons for the change, effect of the change on current net income, if significant, and the cumulative effect on past income.

Double Entry

Chapter 2 introduced the basic accounting principle of the double-entry method of recording transactions. Under the double-entry approach, every transaction has a two-sided effect on each company or party engaging in the transaction. Thus, to record each transaction, each company or party debits at least one account and credits at least one account. The total debits equal the total credits in each journal entry.

Articulation

When you learned how to prepare worksheets in Chapter 3, you also learned that financial statements are fundamentally related and *articulate* (interact) with each other. For example, the amount of net income is carried from the income statement to the statement of retained earnings. The ending balance on the statement of retained earnings is carried to the balance sheet to bring total assets and total equities into balance.

MEASUREMENT IN ACCOUNTING

In the Introduction of this text, accounting was defined as "the process of identifying, measuring, and communicating economic information to permit informed judgments and decisions by the users of the information."[2] In this section we focus on the *measurement* process of accounting.

The accountant seeks to measure the assets, liabilities, and stockholders' equity of a business entity and any changes that occur in them. The effects of these changes are assigned to particular time periods (periodicity) to find net income or net loss of the accounting entity.

Measuring Assets and Liabilities

Assets may be measured in different ways in accounting. Cash is measured at its specified amount. Claims to cash, such as notes and accounts receivable, are measured at their expected cash inflows, taking into consideration possible uncollectibles. Inventories, prepaid expenses, plant assets, and intangibles initially are measured at their historical costs. Some items, such as inventory, are later carried at the lower of cost or market value. Plant assets and intangibles are later carried at original cost less accumulated depreciation or amortization. Liabilities are measured in terms of cash that will be paid or the value of services that will be performed to satisfy the liabilities.

Measuring Changes in Assets and Liabilities

From the previous chapters, you have learned that some changes in assets and liabilities are easily measured by the accountant, such as the exchange of one asset for another of equal value, acquisition of an asset on credit, and payment of a liability. Other changes in assets and liabilities, such as those recorded in adjusting entries, are more difficult to measure because they often involve estimates and/or calculations. The accountant must determine when a change has taken place and the amount of the change. These decisions involve matching revenues and expenses and are guided by the principles discussed below.

THE MAJOR PRINCIPLES

As was mentioned in the Introduction to this text, generally accepted accounting principles (GAAP) set forth standards or methods for presenting financial accounting information. By having a standardized presentation format, it is easier for users to compare the financial information of different companies. Generally accepted accounting principles have been developed largely through accounting practice and have been established by authoritative organizations. Four major authoritative organizations that have contributed to the development of the principles are the American Institute of Certified Public Accountants (AICPA), Financial Accounting Standards Board (FASB), Securities and Exchange Commission (SEC), and the American Accounting Association (AAA).

---

[2]American Accounting Association, *A Statement of Basic Accounting Theory* (Evanston, Ill., 1966), p. 1.

In this section you will study the following principles:

1. Exchange-price (or cost) principle.
2. Matching principle.
3. Revenue recognition principle.
4. Expense and loss recognition principle.
5. Full disclosure principle.

Exchange-Price (or Cost) Principle

When a transfer of resources takes place between two parties, such as buying merchandise on account, the accountant must follow the exchange-price (or cost) principle when presenting that information. The **exchange-price (or cost) principle** requires that transfers of resources be recorded at prices agreed upon by the parties to the exchange at the time of exchange. This principle sets forth (1) what goes into the accounting system—transaction data; (2) when it is recorded—at the time of exchange; and (3) the amounts—exchange prices—at which assets, liabilities, stockholders' equity, revenues, and expenses are recorded.

As applied to most assets, this principle is often called the **cost principle,** meaning that purchased or self-constructed assets are initially recorded at historical cost. **Historical cost** is the amount paid, or the fair value of the liability incurred or other resources surrendered, to acquire an asset. The term *exchange-price principle* is preferred to *cost principle* because it seems inappropriate to refer to liabilities, stockholders' equity, and assets such as cash and accounts receivable as being measured in terms of cost.

Matching Principle

Using the **matching principle,** net income of a period is determined by associating or relating revenues earned in a period with expenses incurred to generate those revenues. The logic underlying this principle is that whenever economic resources are used, someone will want to know what was accomplished and at what cost. Every evaluation of economic activity will involve matching benefit with sacrifice. The application of the matching principle is discussed and illustrated below.

Revenue Recognition Principle

Revenue is not difficult to define or measure; it is the inflow of assets from the sale of goods and services to customers, measured by the amount of cash expected to be received from the customer. But *when* revenue should be recorded (credited to a revenue account) is a crucial question for the accountant. The general answer provided under the **revenue recognition principle** is that the revenue should be *earned* and *realized* before it is recognized (recorded).

The earning of revenue. All economic activities undertaken by a company to create revenues are part of the earning process. The actual receipt of cash from a customer may have been preceded by many activities, including (1) placing advertisements, (2) calling on the customer several times, (3) submitting samples, (4) acquiring or manufacturing goods, and (5) selling and delivering goods. Costs are incurred by the company for these activities. Although revenue was actually being earned by these activities, in most instances accountants do not recognize revenue until the time of sale because of the requirement that revenue be substantially earned before it is recognized (recorded). This requirement is referred to as the **earning principle.**

The realization of revenue. Under the **realization principle,** the accountant does not recognize (record) revenue until the seller acquires the right to receive payment from the buyer. The seller acquires the right to receive payment from the buyer at the time of sale for merchandise transactions, or when services have been performed in service transactions. Legally, a sale of merchandise occurs when title to the goods passes to the buyer. As a practical matter, accountants generally record revenue when goods are delivered.

The advantages of recognizing revenue at the time of sale are that (1) the actual transaction—delivery of goods—is an observable event; (2) revenue is easily measured; (3) risk of loss due to price decline or destruction of the goods has passed to the buyer; (4) revenue has been earned, or substantially so; and (5) because the revenue has been earned, expenses and net income can be determined. As discussed below, the disadvantage of recognizing revenue at the time of sale is that the revenue might not be recorded in the period during which most of the activity creating it occurred.

Exceptions to the realization principle. The following examples illustrate instances when practical considerations may cause accountants to vary the point of revenue recognition from the time of sale. These examples illustrate the effect that the business environment has on the development of accounting principles and standards.

Cash collection as point of revenue recognition. Some small firms record revenues and expenses at the time of cash collection and payment, which may not occur at the time of sale. This procedure is known as the *cash basis* of accounting. The cash basis is acceptable primarily in service enterprises that do not have substantial credit transactions or inventories, like with doctors or dentists.

Installment basis of revenue recognition. When the selling price of goods sold is to be collected in installments (such as monthly or annually) and considerable doubt exists as to collectibility, the installment basis of accounting may be used. This kind of sale is made in spite of the doubtful collectibility of the account because the margin of profit is high and the goods can be repossessed if the payments are not received. Under the **installment basis** the percentage of total gross margin (selling price of a good minus its cost) recognized in a period is equal to the percentage of total cash from a sale that is received in that period. In other words, the gross margin recognized in a period is equal to the amount of cash received times the gross margin percentage (gross margin divided by selling price). For example, assume the following facts concerning a stereo set:

Date of Sale	Selling Price	Cost	Gross Margin (Selling price − Cost)	Gross Margin Percentage (Gross margin ÷ Selling price)
October 1, 1990	$500	$300	($500 − $300) = $200	($200 ÷ $500) = 40%

The buyer makes 10 equal monthly installment payments of $50 each to pay for the set (10 × $50 = $500). If three monthly payments are received in 1990, the total amount of cash received in 1990 is $150 (3 × $50). The total gross margin to recognize or record in 1990 is computed as cash received times gross margin percentage, or $150 × 0.40 = $60.

The other installments are collected when due so that a total of $350 is received in 1991. The total gross margin to recognize in 1991 is $140 ($350 × 0.40). In summary, the total receipts and gross margin recognized in the two years are as follows:

	Total Amount of Cash Received	Gross Margin Recognized
1990	$150 (30%)	$ 60 (30%)
1991	350 (70%)	140 (70%)
Total	$500	$200

The installment basis of revenue recognition is no longer generally accepted for income tax purposes. Even for accounting purposes, since the installment basis delays revenue recognition beyond the time of sale, it is acceptable only when considerable doubt exists as to collectibility of the installments.

Revenue recognition on long-term construction projects. Revenue from a long-term construction project can be recognized under two different methods: (1) the completed-contract method or (2) the percentage-of-completion method. The **completed-contract method** does not recognize any revenue until the period in which the project is completed. At that point, all revenue is recognized even though the contract may have required three years to complete. Thus, the completed-contract method recognizes revenues at the time of sale, as is true for most sales transactions. Costs incurred on the project are carried forward in an inventory account (Construction in Process) and are charged to expense in the period in which the revenue is recognized.

Some accountants argue that it is unreasonable to wait so long to recognize any revenue. Revenue-producing activities have been performed during each year of construction, and revenue should be recognized in each year of construction even if estimates are needed. The **percentage-of-completion method** is a method of recognizing revenue based on the estimated stage of completion of a long-term project. The stage of completion is measured by comparing actual costs incurred in a period with the total estimated costs to be incurred on the project. The percentage-of-completion method is preferable when dependable estimates of costs can be obtained, both estimated and incurred.

To illustrate, assume that a firm has a contract to build a dam for $44 million. The estimated construction cost is $40 million. Estimated gross margin is calculated as follows:

Sales Price of Dam	Estimated Costs to Construct Dam	Estimated Gross Margin (Sales price − Estimated Costs)
$44 million	$40 million	($44 million − $40 million) = $4 million

Suppose that by the end of the first year (1990), the company had incurred actual construction costs of $30 million. The $30 million of construction costs is 75% of the total estimated construction costs ($30 million ÷ $40 million = 75%). Under the percentage-of-completion method, the 75% figure would be used to assign revenue to the first year. In 1991, another $4 million of construction cost is incurred. The amount of revenue to assign to each year is determined as follows:

Year	Ratio of Actual Construction Costs to Total Estimated Construction Costs	×	Agreed Price of Dam	=	Amount of Revenue to Recognize
1990 . . .	($30 million ÷ $40 million) = 75%	×	$44 million	=	$33 million
1991 . . .	($4 million ÷ $40 million) = 10%	×	$44 million	=	$4.4 million

The amount of gross margin in 1990 is equal to revenue of $33 million minus construction costs of $30 million. Thus, $3 million of gross margin is recognized in 1990. Gross margin in 1991 is equal to revenue of $4.4 million minus construction costs of $4 million, or $0.4 million ($400,000). Period costs, such as general and administrative expenses, would be deducted from gross margin to determine net income. For instance, assuming general and administrative expenses were $100,000 in 1991, net income would be $300,000 ($400,000 − $100,000).

Illustration 12.1 shows the frequencies of references to the methods of accounting for long-term contracts in the financial statements of a sample of 600 companies for the years 1983–86. The percentage-of-completion method seems to be the most widely used.

Illustration 12.1
METHOD OF ACCOUNTING FOR LONG-TERM CONTRACTS

	1986	1985	1984	1983
Percentage-of-completion	105	101	98	97
Completed contract	9	9	9	10
Not determinable	4	3	2	2
Referring to long-term contracts	118	113	109	109
Not referring to such contracts	482	487	491	491
Total companies	600	600	600	600

SOURCE: American Institute of Certified Public Accountants, *Accounting Trends & Techniques* (New York: AICPA, 1987), p. 314.

Revenue recognition at completion of production. Recognizing revenue at the time of completion of production or extraction is called the **production basis.** The production basis is considered acceptable procedure when accounting for many farm products such as wheat, corn, and soybeans and for certain precious metals (gold). Accountants justify recognizing revenue prior to sale for these products because (1) the products are homogeneous in nature, (2) they can usually be sold at their market prices, and (3) it is often difficult to determine unit production costs for these products.

Recognizing revenue upon completion of production or extraction is accomplished by debiting inventory (an asset) and crediting a revenue account for the expected selling price of the goods. All costs incurred in the period can then be treated as expenses. For example, assume that 1,000 ounces of gold are mined at a time when gold sells for $400 per ounce. The entry to record the extraction of 1,000 ounces of gold would be:

Inventory of Gold	400,000	
Revenue from Extraction of Gold		400,000
To record extraction of 1,000 ounces of gold. Selling price is		
$400 per ounce.		

If the gold is later sold at $400 per ounce, Cash is debited and Inventory of Gold is credited for $400,000 as follows:

Cash.	400,000	
Inventory of Gold		400,000
To record sale of 1,000 ounces of gold at $400 per ounce.		

If expenses in producing the gold amounted to $300,000, net income on the gold mined would be $100,000.

Expense and Loss Recognition Principle

Expense and loss recognition is closely related to, and is sometimes discussed as part of, the revenue recognition principle. An *expense* is the outflow or using up of assets in the generation of revenue. An expense is incurred *voluntarily* to produce revenue. For instance, the cost of a television set delivered by a dealer to a customer in exchange for cash is an asset "consumed" to produce revenue. Similarly, the cost of services such as labor are voluntarily incurred to produce revenue.

Losses also consume assets, but they are usually involuntary and do not create revenue. An example of an involuntary loss would be a loss resulting from destruction by fire of an uninsured building. A loss on the sale of a building may be "voluntary" if management decided to sell the building even though it meant incurring a loss.

The measurement of expense. Most assets used in operating a business are measured in terms of their historical costs. Therefore, expenses, such as depreciation, resulting from the consumption of those assets in producing revenues are measured in terms of the historical costs of those assets. Other expenses, such as wages, are paid for currently and are measured in terms of their current costs.

The timing of expense recognition. The matching principle implies that a relationship exists between expenses and revenues. For certain expenses, such as cost of goods sold, this relationship is easily seen. However, when a direct relationship cannot be seen, the costs of assets with limited lives may be charged to expense in the periods benefited on a systematic and rational allocation basis. Depreciation of plant assets is an example.

Product costs are costs incurred in the acquisition or manufacture of goods. Included as product costs for purchased goods are invoice, freight, and insurance-in-transit costs. For manufacturing companies, product costs include all costs of materials, labor, and factory operations necessary to produce goods. Product costs are assumed to attach to the goods purchased or produced and are carried in inventory accounts as long as the goods are on hand. Product costs are charged to expense when the goods are sold. The result is a precise matching of cost of goods sold expense to its related revenue.

Period costs are costs that cannot be traced to specific products and that are expensed in the period in which incurred. Selling and administrative costs are examples of period costs.

Full Disclosure Principle

Information that is important enough to influence the decisions of an informed user of the financial statements should be disclosed. Depending on its nature, this information should be disclosed either in the financial statements, in notes to the financial statements, or in supplemental statements. For instance, Appendix A at the end of the text illustrates how information regarding the effects of inflation may be disclosed in supplemental financial statements. The primary financial statements continue to ignore the effects of inflation. In judging whether or not to disclose information, it is better to err on the side of too much disclosure rather than too little. Many lawsuits against CPAs and their clients have resulted from inadequate or misleading disclosure of the underlying facts.

MODIFYING CONVENTIONS (OR CONSTRAINTS)

In certain instances, accounting principles are not strictly applied because of modifying conventions (or constraints). **Modifying conventions** are customs emerging from accounting practice that alter the results that would be obtained from a strict application of accounting principles. Three such modifying conventions are cost-benefit, materiality, and conservatism.

Cost-Benefit

The **cost-benefit consideration** involves deciding whether the benefits of including information in financial statements exceed the costs. Users tend to think information is cost free since they incur none of the costs of providing the information. Preparers realize that providing information is costly. The benefits of using information should exceed the costs of providing it. The measurement of benefits is nebulous and inexact, which makes application of this modifying convention difficult in practice.

Materiality

Materiality is a modifying convention that allows the accountant to deal with immaterial (unimportant) items in an expedient but theoretically incorrect manner. The fundamental question the accountant must ask in judging the materiality of an item is whether a knowledgeable user's decision would be different if the information was presented in the theoretically correct manner. If not, the item is immaterial and may be reported in a theoretically incorrect but expedient manner. For instance, small dollar amount items, like the cost of calculators, often do not make a difference in a statement user's decision to invest in the company; they are considered *immaterial* (unimportant) and may be expensed when purchased. Large dollar amount items, like the cost of mainframe computers, usually do make a difference in such a decision and are considered *material* (important) and should be recorded as an asset and depreciated. The accountant should record all material items in a theoretically correct way. Immaterial items may be recorded in a theoretically incorrect way simply because it is more convenient and less expensive to do so. For example, the purchase of a wastebasket may be debited to an expense account rather than an asset account even though the wastebasket has an expected useful life of 30 years. It simply is not worth the expense of recording depreciation expense on such a small item over its life.

There is more to materiality than relative size of dollar amounts. The very nature of the item may make it material. For example, it may be quite significant to know that a company is paying bribes or making illegal political contributions, even if the dollar amounts of such items are relatively small.

Conservatism

The accountant must be aware that a fine line exists between conservative and incorrect accounting. **Conservatism** means being cautious or prudent and making sure that net assets and net income are not overstated. Conservatism is the accountant's response to the uncertainty faced in the environment in which accounting is practiced. As we have seen in preceding chapters, many accounting measurements (such as depreciation expense) are estimates and involve the exercise of judgment. In such cases, conservatism tells the accountant to "play it safe." Playing it safe usually involves trying to avoid overstating net assets or net income.

Conservatism may be applied differently in various companies, causing decreased comparability among their financial statements. Conservative reporting may cause investors to act in a manner not in their best interest. Investors may, for example, dispose of their interest in a company because income of the company did not meet their expectations. Yet, this failure of income to reach expectations may have been due solely to a conservative measurement by the accountant of the company's inventories (e.g., last-in, first-out).

THE CONCEPTUAL FRAMEWORK PROJECT

Objective 2: Describe the Conceptual Framework Project of the Financial Accounting Standards Board

The exact nature of the basic concepts and related principles comprising accounting theory has been debated for years. The debate continues today even though numerous references can be found to "generally accepted accounting principles" (GAAP). To date, all attempts to present a concise statement of GAAP have received only limited acceptance.

Due to this limited success, many accountants suggest that the starting point in reaching a concise statement of GAAP is to seek agreement on the objectives of financial accounting and reporting. The belief is that if one (1) carefully studies the environment, (2) knows what objectives are sought, (3) can identify certain qualitative traits of accounting information, and (4) can define the basic elements of financial statements, one can discover the principles and standards that will lead to the attainment of the stated objectives. The FASB has taken the first three steps in "Objectives of Financial Reporting by Business Enterprises" and in "Qualitative Characteristics of Accounting Information."[3] The fourth step is represented by two concepts statements entitled "Elements of Financial Statements of Business Enterprises" and "Elements of Financial Statements."[4]

OBJECTIVES OF FINANCIAL REPORTING

Financial reporting objectives are the broad overriding goals sought by accountants engaging in financial reporting. According to the FASB, the first objective of financial reporting is to:

> provide information that is useful to present and potential investors and creditors and other users in making rational investment, credit, and similar decisions. The information should be comprehensible to those who have a reasonable understanding of business and economic activities and are willing to study the information with reasonable diligence.[5]

The term *other users* is interpreted broadly and includes employees, security analysts, brokers, and lawyers. Financial reporting should provide information to all who are willing to learn to use it properly.

---

[3]FASB, "Objectives of Financial Reporting by Business Enterprises," *Statement of Financial Accounting Concepts No. 1* (Stamford, Conn., 1978). FASB, "Qualitative Characteristics of Accounting Information," *Statement of Financial Accounting Concepts No. 2* (Stamford, Conn., 1980). Copyright © by the Financial Accounting Standards Board, High Ridge Park, Stamford, Connecticut 06905, U.S.A. Quoted (or excerpted) with permission. Copies of the complete document are available from the FASB.

[4]FASB, "Elements of Financial Statements of Business Enterprises," *Statement of Financial Accounting Concepts No. 3* (Stamford, Conn., 1980); and "Elements of Financial Statements," *Statement of Financial Accounting Concepts No. 6* (Stamford, Conn., 1985). Copyright © by the Financial Accounting Standards Board, High Ridge Park, Stamford, Connecticut 06905, U.S.A. Quoted (or excerpted) with permission. Copies of the complete documents are available from the FASB.

[5]FASB, "Objectives of Financial Reporting by Business Enterprises," p. viii.

The second objective of financial reporting is to:

provide information to help present and potential investors and creditors and other users in assessing the amounts, timing, and uncertainty of prospective cash receipts from dividends [owner withdrawals] or interest and the proceeds from the sale, redemption, or maturity of securities or loans. Since investors' and creditors' cash flows are related to enterprise cash flows, financial reporting should provide information to help investors, creditors, and others assess the amounts, timing, and uncertainty of prospective net cash inflows and to the related enterprise.[6]

This objective ties the cash flows of investors (owners) and creditors to the cash flows of the enterprise, a tie-in that appears entirely logical. Enterprise cash inflows are the source of cash for dividends (owner withdrawals), interest, and redemption of maturing debt.

Third, financial reporting should:

provide information about the economic resources of an enterprise, the claims to those resources (obligations of the enterprise to transfer resources to other entities and owners' equity), and the effects of transactions, events, and circumstances that change its resources and claims to those resources.[7]

A number of conclusions can be drawn from the three objectives and from a study of the environment in which financial reporting is carried out. Financial reporting should provide information about an enterprise's past performance because such information is used as a basis for prediction of future enterprise performance. Financial reporting should focus on earnings and its components, despite the emphasis in the objectives on cash flows. Earnings computed under the accrual basis provide a better indicator of ability to generate favorable cash flows than do statements prepared under the cash basis. Financial reporting does not seek to measure the value of a business, but to provide information that may be useful for doing so. Financial reporting does not seek to evaluate management's performance, predict earnings, assess risk, or estimate earning power, but should provide information to persons who wish to do so.

These conclusions are some of those reached in *Statement of Financial Accounting Concepts No. 1*. As the Board says, these statements "are intended to establish the objectives and concepts that the Financial Accounting Standards Board will use in developing standards of financial accounting and reporting."[8] How successful the Board will be in the approach adopted remains to be seen.

QUALITATIVE CHARACTERISTICS

Qualitative characteristics are those characteristics that accounting information should possess to be useful in decision making. This criterion is

---

[6]Ibid.

[7]Ibid.

[8]Ibid., p. i.

difficult to apply. The usefulness of accounting information in a given instance depends not only on information characteristics but also on the capabilities of the decision makers and their professional advisers, if any. Accountants cannot specify who the decision makers are, their characteristics, the decisions to be made, or the methods chosen to make the decisions; therefore, attention is directed to characteristics of accounting information. The FASB's graphic summarization of the problems faced is presented in Illustration 12.2.[9]

Illustration 12.2
A HIERARCHY OF ACCOUNTING QUALITIES

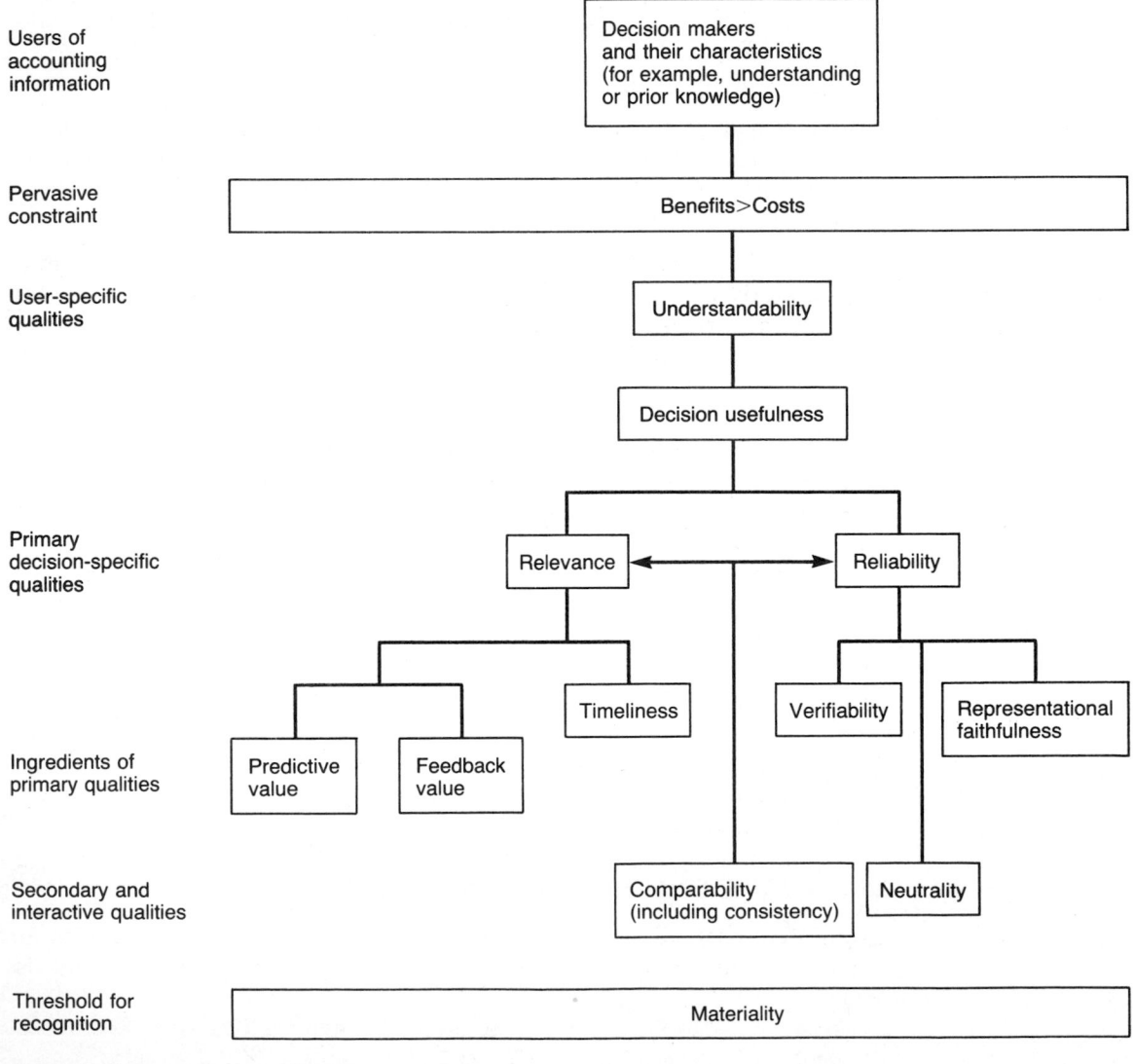

[9]FASB, "Qualitative Characteristics of Accounting Information," p. 15.

Relevance

For information to have **relevance,** it must be pertinent to or bear upon a decision. The information must "make a difference" to someone who does not already have the information. Relevant information is capable of making a difference in a decision either by affecting user predictions of outcomes of past, present, or future events or by confirming or correcting expectations.

Note that information need not be a prediction to be useful in developing, confirming, or altering expectations. Expectations are commonly based on the present or past. For example, any attempt to predict future earnings of a firm would quite likely start with a review of present and past earnings. Also, information that merely confirms prior expectations may be less useful, but is still relevant since it reduces uncertainty.

Certain types of accounting information have been criticized because of an alleged lack of relevance. For example, some would argue that a cost of $1 million paid for a tract of land 40 years ago and reported in the current balance sheet at that amount is irrelevant (except for possible tax implications) to users for decision making today. Such criticism has encouraged research into the types of information that are relevant to users. Suggestions have also been made that a different valuation basis, such as current cost, be used in reporting such assets.

Predictive value and feedback value. Because actions taken now can affect only future events, information is obviously relevant when it possesses **predictive value,** or improves users' abilities to predict outcomes of events. Information that reveals the relative success of users in predicting outcomes possesses **feedback value.** Because feedback reports on past activities, it can make a difference in decision making by (1) reducing uncertainty in a situation, (2) refuting or confirming prior expectations, and (3) providing a basis for further predictions. For example, a report on the first quarter's earnings of a company reduces the uncertainty surrounding the amount of such earnings, confirms or refutes the predicted amount of such earnings, and provides a possible basis on which to predict earnings for the full year. It is important to remember that although accounting information may possess predictive value, it does not consist of predictions. Making predictions is a function performed by the decision maker, not the accountant.

Timeliness. **Timeliness** requires that accounting information be provided at a time when it may be considered in reaching a decision. Utility of information decreases with age. It is much more useful to know what the net income for 1989 was in early 1990 than to receive this information a year later. If information is to be of any value in decision making, it must be available *before* the decision is made. If not, the information is useless. In determining what constitutes timely information, consideration must be given to the other qualitative characteristics and to the cost of gathering information. For example, a timely estimated amount for uncollectible accounts may be more valuable than a later, verified actual amount.

Timeliness alone cannot make information relevant, but otherwise relevant information might be rendered irrelevant by a lack of timeliness.

Reliability

In addition to being relevant, information must be reliable to be useful. Information has **reliability** when it faithfully depicts for users what it purports to represent. Thus, accounting information is reliable if users can depend on it to reflect the underlying economic activities of the organization. The reliability of information depends upon its representational faithfulness, verifiability, and neutrality. The information must also be complete and free of bias.

Representational faithfulness. Insight into this quality may be gained by considering a map. A map possesses representational faithfulness when it shows roads and bridges (among other things) where roads and bridges actually exist. There is correspondence between what is shown on the map and what is present physically. Similarly, there is **representational faithfulness** when accounting statements on economic activity correspond to the actual underlying activity. Where there is no correspondence, the cause may be bias or lack of completeness.

Effects of bias. Accounting measurements are biased if they are consistently too high or too low. Bias in accounting measurements may exist due to the choice of measurement method or to bias introduced either deliberately or through lack of skill by the measurer. These two types of bias are discussed below.

Completeness. To be free from bias, information must be sufficiently complete to ensure that it validly represents underlying events and conditions. **Completeness** means that all significant information must be disclosed in a way that aids understanding and does not mislead. Relevance of information also may be reduced if information that would make a difference to a user is omitted. Currently, full disclosure generally requires presentation of a balance sheet, an income statement, a statement of cash flows, and necessary notes to the financial statements and supporting schedules. A statement of changes in stockholders' equity is also required in annual reports. Such statements must be complete, with items properly classified and segregated (such as reporting sales revenue separately from other revenues). Required disclosures may be made in (1) the body of the financial statements, (2) the notes to such statements, (3) special communications, and (4) the president's letter or in other management reports in the annual report.

Another aspect of completeness is that full disclosure must be made of all changes in accounting principles and their effects.[10] Also disclosure should be made of unusual activities (loans to officers), changes in expectations (losses on inventory), depreciation expense for the period, long-term obligations entered into that are not recorded by the accountant (a 20-year lease on a building), new arrangements with certain groups (pen-

---

[10]APB, "Accounting Changes," *APB Opinion No. 20* (New York: AICPA, July 1971).

sion and profit-sharing plans for employees), significant events that occur after the date of the statements (loss of a major customer), and accounting policies (major principles and their manner of application) followed in preparing the financial statements.[11] Because of its emphasis on disclosure, this aspect of reliability is often called the full disclosure principle.

Verifiability. Financial information has **verifiability** when it can be substantially duplicated by independent measurers using the same measurement methods. Verifiability is directed toward eliminating measurer bias, rather than measurement method bias. The requirement that financial information be based on objective evidence is based on demonstrated needs of users for reliable, unbiased financial information. Unbiased information is needed especially when parties with opposing interests (credit seekers and credit grantors) rely on the same information. Reliability of information is enhanced if it is verifiable.

Financial information will never be free of subjective opinion and judgment; it will always possess varying degrees of verifiability. Some measurements can be supported by canceled checks and invoices. Others, such as periodic depreciation charges, can never be verified because of their very nature. Thus, financial information in many instances is verifiable only in that it represents a consensus as to what would be reported if the same procedures had been followed by other accountants.

Neutrality. **Neutrality** in accounting information means that the information should be free of measurement method bias. The primary concern should be relevance and reliability of the information that results from application of the principle, not the effect that the principle may have on a particular interest. Nonneutral accounting information is designed to favor one set of interested parties over others. For example, a particular form of measurement might favor owners over creditors, or vice versa. "To be neutral, accounting information must report economic activity as faithfully as possible, without coloring the image it communicates for the purpose of influencing behavior in *some particular direction.*"[12] Accounting standards should not be developed and used like certain tax regulations which seek deliberately to foster or restrain certain types of activity. Verifiability seeks to eliminate measurer bias; neutrality seeks to eliminate measurement method bias.

Comparability (and Consistency)

When **comparability** in financial information exists, reported differences and similarities in information are real and are not the result of differing accounting treatments. Comparable information will reveal relative strengths and weaknesses in a single company through time and between two or more companies at the same point in time.

---

[11]APB, "Disclosure of Accounting Policies,"*APB Opinion No. 22* (New York: AICPA, April 1971).

[12]FASB, "Qualitative Characteristics of Accounting Information," par. 100.

Consistency requires a company to use the same accounting principles and reporting practices through time. Consistency leads to comparability of financial information for a single company through time. Comparability between companies is more difficult to achieve because the same activities may be accounted for in different ways. For example, Company B may use one method of depreciation, while Company C accounts for an identical asset in similar circumstances using another method. A high degree of intercompany comparability in accounting information will not exist unless the same activities are required to be accounted for in the same manner across companies and through time.

Pervasive Constraints

As Illustration 12.2 shows, there are two pervasive constraints faced in providing useful information. First, benefits secured from the information must be greater than the cost of providing that information. Second, only material items need be disclosed and accounted for strictly in accordance with generally accepted accounting principles (GAAP).

Cost-benefit analysis. Accounting information is a commodity and, like all commodities, is desired only if it provides benefits greater than its cost. But, unlike most commodities, accounting information has no direct cost to users, since all costs are borne by the provider of the information. This fact has led users and authoritative organizations to demand ever greater amounts of financial information, which have often been answered with claims that the information desired costs more than it is worth. Such a contention was encountered frequently when the FASB proposed requiring disclosure of the impact of inflation upon financial statements. Complicating the issue is the fact that there is no agreed-upon method of measuring benefits of information and that even measurement of cost cannot be carried out without some disagreement. Yet, in the development of accounting standards, an attempt must be made to ensure that the benefits of required disclosures exceed the costs of providing the disclosures.

Materiality. As discussed earlier in the chapter, the basic idea inherent in materiality is that relatively large items must be accounted for in a theoretically correct way; relatively small, insignificant items need not be. Materiality has been defined by the FASB as "the magnitude of an omission or misstatement of accounting information that, in the light of surrounding circumstances, makes it probable that the judgment of a reasonable person relying on the information would have been changed or influenced by the omission or misstatement."[13] The term *magnitude* in this definition suggests that the materiality of an item may be assessed by looking at its relative size. A $10,000 error in an expense in a company with earnings of $30,000 is material. The same error in a company earning $30,000,000 may not be material.

---

[13]Ibid., p. xv.

THE BASIC ELEMENTS OF FINANCIAL STATEMENTS

Thus far we have discussed objectives of financial reporting and qualitative characteristics of accounting information. A third important task in developing a conceptual framework for any discipline is that of identifying and defining its basic elements. The basic elements of financial statements have been identified and defined by the FASB (First in *Concepts Statement No. 3* and then as replaced in *Concepts Statement No. 6*). Most of the terms were defined earlier in this text in a less precise way to convey a general understanding of the terms. The more technical definitions follow (these items are not repeated in the glossary):

Assets are probable future economic benefits obtained or controlled by a particular entity as a result of past transactions or events.

Liabilities are probable future sacrifices of economic benefits arising from present obligations of a particular entity to transfer assets or provide services to other entities in the future as a result of past transactions or events.

Equity or net assets is the residual interest in the assets of an entity that remains after deducting its liabilities. In a business enterprise, the equity is the ownership interest. In a not-for-profit organization, which has no ownership interest in the same sense as a business enterprise, net assets is divided into three classes based on the presence or absence of donor-imposed restrictions—permanently restricted, temporarily restricted, and unrestricted net assets.

Comprehensive income is the change in equity of a business enterprise during a period from transactions and other events and circumstances from nonowner sources. It includes all changes in equity during a period except those resulting from investments by owners and distributions to owners.

Revenues are inflows or other enhancements of assets of an entity or settlements of its liabilities (or a combination of both) from delivering or producing goods, rendering services, or other activities that constitute the entity's ongoing major or central operations.

Expenses are outflows or other using up of assets or incurrences of liabilities (or a combination of both) from delivering or producing goods, rendering services, or carrying out other activities that constitute the entity's ongoing major or central operations.

Gains are increases in equity (net assets) from peripheral or incidental transactions of an entity and from all other transactions and other events and circumstances affecting the entity except those that result from revenues or investments by owners.

Losses are decreases in equity (net assets) from peripheral or incidental transactions of an entity and from all other transactions and other events and circumstances affecting the entity except those that result from expenses or distributions to owners.

Investments by owners are increases in equity of a particular business enterprise resulting from transfers to it from other entities of something valuable to obtain or increase ownership interests (or equity) in it. Assets are most commonly received as investments by owners, but that which is received may also include services or satisfaction or conversion of liabilities of the enterprise.

Distributions to owners are decreases in equity of a particular business enterprise resulting from transferring assets, rendering services, or incurring liabilities by the enterprise to owners. Distributions to owners decrease ownership interest (or equity) in an enterprise.[14]

Note that the requirement that assets and liabilities be based upon past transactions normally rules out the recording of contracts that are mutual promises to do something, such as entering into an employment contract with an officer. On a similar basis, the accountant refuses to record an asset and a liability when a contract is signed whereby the entity agrees to purchase a certain number of units of a product over a coming period of time.

Recognition and Measurement in Financial Statements

In December 1984, the FASB issued *Statement of Financial Accounting Concepts No. 5*, "Recognition and Measurement in Financial Statements of Business Enterprises,"[15] describing recognition criteria and providing guidance as to the timing and nature of information to be included in financial statements. The recognition criteria established in the *Statement* are fairly consistent with those used in current practice. The *Statement* indicates, however, that when information that is more useful than currently reported information is available at a reasonable cost, it should be included in financial statements. A slightly modified income statement format is recommended.

The *Statement* may become a statement of earnings and comprehensive income. "Earnings" would generally be computed like income after extraordinary items (covered in Chapter 8) is presently calculated. Then cumulative account adjustments (such as changes in accounting principle) and other nonowner changes in equity would be added or deducted in arriving at "comprehensive income." The lower part of the statement would appear as follows:

---

[14]FASB, "Elements of Financial Statements," *Statement of Financial Accounting Concepts No. 6* (a replacement of *FASB Concepts Statement No. 3*) (Stamford, Conn., 1985). Copyright © by the Financial Accounting Standards Board, High Ridge Park, Stamford, Connecticut 06905, U.S.A. Quoted (or excerpted) with permission. Copies of the complete document are available from the FASB.

[15]FASB, "Recognition and Measurement in Financial Statements of Business Enterprises," *Statement of Accounting Concepts No. 5* (Stamford, Conn., 1984). Copyright © by the Financial Accounting Standards Board, High Ridge Park, Stamford, Connecticut 06905, U.S.A. Copies of the complete document are available from the FASB. (In case you are wondering why we do not mention *Statement of Financial Accounting Concepts No. 4*, it pertains to accounting for not-for-profit organizations and is, therefore, not relevant to this text.)

```
Earnings . . . . . . . . . . . . . . . . . . . . . . . . .      xx
+or−Cumulative account adjustments (e.g., cumulative
      effect of changes in accounting principle). . . . . . . . .   xx
+or−Other nonowner changes in equity (e.g., gains or
      losses on market changes in noncurrent
      marketable equity securities). . . . . . . . . . . . .       xx
Comprehensive income . . . . . . . . . . . . . . . . . .           xx
```

The *Statement* also indicates that a balance sheet does not show the value of a business, but when used in combination with other information and other financial statements, the balance sheet is helpful in estimating the value of an entity. The importance of cash flow information (covered in Chapter 10 of this text) is also mentioned.

SUMMARY

Accounting theory is a set of basic assumptions, concepts, and related principles. This theory explains and guides the accountant's actions in identifying, measuring, and communicating economic information. The underlying assumptions and concepts include entity, going concern, money measurement, and periodicity. Other basic concepts include general-purpose financial statements, substance over form, consistency, double entry, and articulation.

The accountant seeks to measure the assets, liabilities, and owner's equity of an accounting entity. Changes in these items are also measured and assigned to particular time periods to determine net income.

The major principles used in accounting include the exchange-price (cost), matching, revenue recognition, expense and loss recognition, and full disclosure principles. Exceptions are sometimes made in following these principles. For instance, in recognizing revenue sometimes the cash basis, installment basis, percentage-of-completion basis, or production basis is used.

Modifying conventions are customs emerging from accounting practice that alter results that would be obtained from a strict application of accounting principles. Three such modifying conventions are cost-benefit, materiality, and conservatism.

The Conceptual Framework Project consists of various FASB Statements. The Project identified the objectives of financial reporting, the qualitative characteristics of financial information, the elements of financial statements, and recognition and measurement in financial statements.

The objectives of financial reporting are the broad overriding goals sought by accountants in financial reporting. Qualitative characteristics are those characteristics that accounting information must possess to be useful in decision making. The primary qualitative characteristics are relevance and reliability. The basic elements are the terms and their definitions that comprise the content of financial statements. The standard on recognition and measurement in financial statements describes recognition criteria and provides guidance as to the timing and nature of information to be included in financial statements.

Thus far in the text we have discussed service and merchandising companies. The next chapter introduces accounting for a third type of company—a manufacturing company.

APPENDIX INTERNATIONAL ACCOUNTING*

WHY ACCOUNTING PRINCIPLES AND PRACTICES DIFFER AMONG NATIONS

Objective 3: Discuss the differences in international accounting among nations

In today's world we do not find it surprising to discover a British bank in Atlanta, Coca-Cola in Paris, and French airplanes in Zaire. German auto parts are assembled in Spain and sold in the United States. Japan buys oil from Saudi Arabia and sells cameras in Italy. Soviet livestock eat American grain, and the British sip tea from Sri Lanka and China. Business has become truly international, but accounting, often described as the language of business, does not cross borders so easily. Accounting principles and reporting practices differ from country to country, and international decision making is made more difficult by the lack of a common communication system. But, since business is practiced at an international level, accounting must find a way to provide its services at that level.

The problem is that accounting must first reflect the national economic and social environment in which it is practiced, and this environment is not the same in Bangkok as in Boston. Some economies, for example, are mainly agricultural. Others are based on manufacturing, trade, or service industries. Still others export natural resources, such as oil or gold, while a few derive most of their income from tourism. Accounting for inventories and natural resources, cost accounting techniques, and methods of foreign currency translation naturally have a different orientation, emphasis, and degree of refinement in these different economies.

Other accounting differences stem from the various legal or political systems of nations. In centrally controlled economies, for instance, the state owns all or most of the property. It makes little sense to prescribe full disclosure of accounting procedures to protect investors when there is little or no private ownership of property. Some of these countries standardize their accounting methods and incorporate them into law. But in market-oriented economies, the development of accounting principles and reporting practices is left mainly to the private sector. Where uniformity exists, it occurs more by general agreement or consensus of interested parties than by governmental decree. In market-oriented economies,

---

*The authors wish to express their appreciation to William P. Hauworth II, Partner, Arthur Andersen & Co., Chicago, Illinois, for updating this Appendix material on international accounting.

accounting principles and practices must be more flexible to serve the needs of business firms which differ widely in ownership, size, and complexity. In countries where business firms are predominately family owned, disclosure practices can be less complete than in countries where large, publicly held corporations dominate.

The degree of development of the accounting profession and the general level of education of a country also influence accounting practices and procedures. Nations that lack a well-organized accounting profession may adopt almost wholesale the accounting methods of other countries. Commonwealth countries, for example, tend to follow British accounting standards; the former French colonies of Africa use French systems; Bermuda follows Canadian pronouncements; and the influence of the United States is widespread. At the same time, levels of expertise vary. There is no point in advocating statistical accounting and auditing techniques in countries where there is little knowledge or understanding of statistics. Accounting systems designed for electronic data processing are not helpful in countries where few or no businesses use computers.

Even in advanced countries, genuine differences of opinion exist regarding accounting theory and appropriate accounting methods. American standards, for example, require the periodic amortization of goodwill to expense, but British, German, and Dutch standards do not. Accounting methods also differ within nations. Most countries, including the United States, permit several depreciation methods and two or more inventory costing methods. Such flexibility is essential if accounting is to serve a useful purpose in economic, political, and social environments that are not uniform.

ATTEMPTED HARMONIZATION OF ACCOUNTING PRACTICES

The question arises as to whether financial statements that reflect the economic and social environment of, say, France can also be useful to a potential American investor. Can some of the differences between French and American accounting be eliminated or at least explained so that French and American investors will understand each other's reports and find them useful when they make decisions?

Several organizations are working to achieve greater understanding and harmonization of different accounting practices. These include the United Nations Commission on Transnational Corporations, the Organization for Economic Cooperation and Development (OECD), the European Economic Community (EEC), the International Federation of Accountants (IFAC), and the International Accounting Standards Committee (IASC). These organizations study the information needs and accounting and reporting practices of different nations and issue pronouncements recommending specific practices and procedures for adoption by all members.

The IASC is making a significant contribution to the development of international accounting standards. It was founded in London in 1973 by the professional accountancy bodies of nine countries: Australia, Canada, France, Germany, Japan, Mexico, the Netherlands, the United Kingdom and Ireland, and the United States. The IASC selects a topic for study from lists of problems submitted by the profession all over the world. After research and discussion by special committees, the IASC issues an exposure draft of a proposed standard for consideration by the profession and the business and financial communities. After about six months' further study of the topic in light of the comments received, the IASC issues the final international accounting standard. To date, 26 standards have been issued on topics as varied as *Disclosure of Accounting Policies* (IAS 1), *Depreciation Accounting* (IAS 4), *Statement of Changes in Financial Position* (IAS 7), and *Revenue Recognition* (IAS 18, effective January 1, 1984). Setting international standards is not easy. If the standards are too detailed or rigid, then the flexibility needed to reflect different national environments will be lost. On the other hand, if pronouncements are vague and allow too many alternative methods, then there is little point in setting international standards.

One major problem is the enforcement of these standards. There is no organization, nor is there likely to be, to ensure compliance with international standards. Enforcement is left to national standard-setting bodies or legislatures, which may or may not adopt a recommended international standard. Generally, members commit themselves to support the objectives of the international body. The members promise to use their best endeavors to see that international standards are formally adopted by local professional accountancy bodies, by government departments or other authorities that control the securities markets, and by the industrial, business, and financial communities of their respective countries.

The American Institute of Certified Public Accountants (AICPA), for example, issued a revised statement in 1975 reaffirming its support for the implementation of international standards adopted by the IASC. The AICPA's position is that international accounting standards must be specifically adopted by the Financial Accounting Standards Board (FASB), which is not a member of the IASC, in order to achieve acceptance in the United States. But if there is no significant difference between an international standard and U.S. practice, compliance with U.S. generally accepted accounting principles (GAAP) constitutes compliance with the international standard. Where a significant difference exists, the AICPA publishes the IASC standard together with comments on how it differs from U.S. GAAP and undertakes to urge the FASB to give early consideration to harmonizing the differences.[16] Significant support for IASC standards has also resulted from a resolution adopted by the World Federation of Stock Exchanges in 1975. The resolution binds members to require conformance with IASC standards in securities listing agreements.[17]

---

[16] American Institute of Certified Public Accountants, *CPA Letter,* August 1975.
[17] *CA Magazine,* January 1975, p. 52.

Although these developments are important for international harmonization of accounting, ultimately the success of international pronouncements depends on the willingness of the members to support them. In some cases, national legislation is required and may be slow or difficult to pass. The EEC, for example, issues "Directives" which must be accepted as compulsory objectives by the 10 member states (Belgium, Denmark, France, Germany, Greece, Ireland, Italy, Luxembourg, the Netherlands, and the United Kingdom) but which are translated into national legislation at the discretion of each member state. The EEC's important *Fourth Directive* was adopted in 1978 to regulate the preparation, content, presentation, audit, and publication of the accounts and reports of companies. It applies to all limited-liability companies (corporations) registered in the EEC, except for banks and insurance companies. Under the directive, member states were to introduce legislation by July 1980 so that accounts in all EEC countries would conform to the directive as of the fiscal year beginning January 1, 1982. Yet by that date, only Belgium, Denmark, and the United Kingdom had passed the necessary legislation, although most of the other member countries were close to doing so.

The general movement toward international harmonization of accounting standards is increasing in other areas of society. The accounting profession, national standard-setting bodies, universities, academic societies, and multinational corporations have all shown an increased interest in international accounting problems in recent years. The AICPA has an International Practice Division as a formal part of its line organization. The American Accounting Association officially established an International Accounting Section in 1976. The University of Lancaster (England) and the University of Illinois have international accounting research centers that support research studies and conduct international conferences and seminars. Georgia State University received a Touche Ross & Co. grant to internationalize its accounting curriculum. Many universities currently offer courses in international business and accounting.

All this activity helps to increase the flow of information and our understanding of the accounting and reporting practices in other parts of the world. Greater understanding improves the likelihood that unnecessary differences will be eliminated and enhances the general acceptance of international standards.

The rest of this appendix gives examples of the accounting methods used in different countries and of the concepts that underlie them to illustrate the difficulty of achieving international harmonization.

FOREIGN CURRENCY TRANSLATION

Foreign currency translation is probably the most common problem in an international business environment. Foreign currency translation has two main components: accounting for transactions in a foreign currency and translating the financial statements of foreign enterprises into a different, common currency.

Accounting for Transactions in a Foreign Currency

Suppose an American automobile dealership imports vehicles from Japan and promises to pay for them in yen 90 days after receiving them. If there is no change in the dollar-yen exchange rate between the date the goods are received and the date the invoice is paid, there is no problem. Both the purchase and the payment will be recorded at the same dollar value. But if the yen appreciates against the dollar during the 90-day period, the importer must pay more dollars for the yen needed on the settlement date.[18] Which exchange rate should the importer use to record payment of the invoice—the rate in effect on the purchase date or on the payment date?

One approach to the problem is to regard the purchase of the automobiles and settlement of the invoice as two separate transactions and record them at two different exchange rates. The difference between the amount recorded in Accounts Payable on the purchase date and the cash paid on the settlement date is considered an exchange gain or loss. This approach, known as the "time-of-transaction" method, was the prescribed or predominant practice in 61 of 64 countries surveyed in 1979,[19] including the United States.[20] The time-of-transaction method is also the method recommended in the IASC's exposure draft, *Accounting for the Effects of Changes in Foreign Exchange Rates,* issued in March 1982.

Another approach, known as the "time-of-settlement" method, regards the transaction and its settlement as a single event. If this method is used, the amount recorded on the purchase date is regarded as an estimate of the settlement amount. Any fluctuations in the exchange rate between the purchase date and the settlement date are accounted for as part of the transaction and are not treated as a separate gain or loss. Consequently there is no effect on earnings.

Although the time-of-transaction method is widely used, the treatment of resulting exchange gains and losses is not uniform. If the gains or losses are realized, that is, if settlement is made within the same accounting period as the purchase, then most countries recognize such gains and losses in the income statement for that period. If the exchange gains or losses are unrealized, that is, if they result from translating Accounts Pay-

---

[18]This example ignores the possibility that the importer might obtain a forward exchange contract, a discussion of which is beyond the scope of this text.

[19]Price Waterhouse International *International Survey.* Data on the different methods used and on the number of countries using each method described in these examples are derived substantially from this publication.

[20]FASB *Statement of Financial Accounting Standards No. 8,* "Accounting for the Translation of Foreign Currency Transactions and Foreign Currency Financial Statements" (Stamford, Conn., 1975). The "time-of-transaction" method is also prescribed by FASB *Statement No. 52,* "Foreign Currency Translation" (Stamford, Conn., 1981) which supersedes FASB *Statement No. 8.*

able (or Accounts Receivable for the vendor) at the balance sheet date, the treatment varies. Recording losses unrealized was the prescribed or predominant practice in 54 countries in 1979. But only 40 countries similarly recognized exchange gains in income, the remaining nations preferring to defer them until settlement. In the United States, under the provisions of FASB *Statement No. 52,* both realized and unrealized transaction gains and losses are recognized in earnings of the period in which the exchange rate changes.

Translating Financial Statements

Financial statements of foreign subsidiaries are translated into a single common unit of measurement, such as the dollar, for purposes of consolidation. Considerable argument has arisen in recent years as to the correct way to do this; that is, which exchange rate should be used to translate items in the balance sheet and income statement, and what treatment is appropriate for any resulting exchange gains or losses? Items that translated at the historical rate cannot result in exchange gains or losses. But items that are translated at the exchange rate in effect on the balance sheet date, the **current rate,** can result in **exchange gains and losses** if the current rate differs from the rate in effect when those items were recorded (the **historical rate**). If the current rate is used, a related question arises: Should the resulting exchange gains or losses be recognized immediately in income or deferred in some way?

The methods used to translate financial statements fall basically into two groups: translation of all items at the current rate and translation of some items at the current rate and others at the historical rates. The two groups are based on different concepts of both consolidation and international business.

The current-rate approach. The **current-** (or **closing-**) **rate approach** translates all assets and liabilities at the current rate, the exchange rate in effect on the balance sheet date. The main advantage of this method is its simplicity; it treats all items uniformly. This approach is based on the view that a foreign subsidiary is a separate unit from the domestic parent company. The subsidiary's assets are viewed as being acquired largely out of local borrowing. Multinational groups, therefore, consist of entities that operate independently but which contribute to a central fund of resources. Consequently, in consolidation it is believed that stockholders of the parent company are interested primarily in the parent company's net investment in the foreign subsidiary.

The current/historical-rates approach. The **current/historical rates approach** regards the parent company and its foreign subsidiaries as a single business undertaking. Assets owned by a foreign subsidiary are viewed as indistinguishable from assets owned by the parent company. Foreign assets should, therefore, be reflected in consolidated statements in the same way that similar assets of the parent company are reported, that is, at historical cost in the parent company's currency.

Three translation methods are commonly used under this approach. The **current-noncurrent method** translates current assets and current liabilities at the current rate—the rate in effect on the balance sheet date—while noncurrent items are translated at their respective historical rates. The historical rate is the rate in effect when an asset or liability is originally recorded. Under the **monetary-nonmonetary method,** the current rate is used for monetary assets and liabilities—that is, for those that have a fixed, nominal value in terms of the foreign currency—while historical rates are applied to nonmonetary items. The **temporal method** is a variation of the monetary-nonmonetary method. Cash, receivables and payables, and other assets and liabilities carried at current prices (for example, marketable securities carried at current market value) are translated at the current rate of exchange. All other assets and liabilities are translated at historical rates.

Disagreement over the appropriate translation method seems likely to continue because of the different concepts of parent-subsidiary relations on which they are founded. In 1979, only six countries prescribed a single method. The temporal method was required in Austria, Canada, Bermuda, Jamaica, and the United States (under FASB *Statement No. 8*), while Uruguay required the current-rate method. Since that time the United States has changed to the current-rate method (FASB *Statement No. 52*), and Canada is reconsidering its position, a decision which will also affect Bermuda. Apart from these six nations, 24 countries, including most of Europe, Japan, and Australia, followed predominantly the current-rate approach, while in 25 countries, including Germany, South Africa, and most of Central and South America, some variation of the current/historical-rates approach was common practice.

The treatment of exchange gains and losses produced by translating items at the current rate varies and is not strictly related to the translation method used. In 1979, the predominant practice in 42 nations, including much of Europe, Latin America, Japan, and the United States, was to recognize all gains and losses immediately in income. Eighteen of these countries used the current-rate translation method and 23 followed one of the current/historical-rates methods. Alternative treatments of translation gains and losses included recording them directly in stockholders' equity (Australia), recognizing some of them immediately in income and deferring others (United Kingdom), and recognizing some in income and deferring and amortizing others over the remaining life of the items concerned (Canada and Bermuda).

Since the issuance of FASB *Statement No. 52*, the immediate recognition of translation gains and losses in income is not permitted in the United States. Instead, they are reported separately and accumulated in a separate component of stockholders' equity until the parent company's investment in the foreign subsidiary is sold or liquidated, at which time they are reported as part of the gain or loss on sale or liquidation of the investment.

INVENTORIES

Variations in accounting for inventories relate principally to the basis for determining cost, whether cost once determined should be increased or decreased to reflect the market value of the inventories, and whether the variable (direct) costing or the absorption (full) costing approach should be used to allocate overhead.

Determination of Cost

Although other methods are occasionally used in some countries, this text discusses the three principal bases for determining inventory cost: first-in, first-out (FIFO); last-in, first-out (LIFO); and average cost.

The most frequently used methods in 1979 were FIFO and average cost. Each of these methods was predominant in 31 countries, although no country required the use of one method to the exclusion of the other. FIFO was more common in Europe, although Austria, France, Greece, and Portugal used an average method. FIFO also predominated in Australia, Canada, South Africa, and the United States. The average method was generally followed in Latin America, Japan, and much of Africa. LIFO was the principal method in only one country — Italy — although it was a common minority method in Japan, the United States, most of Latin America, and several European countries. LIFO was considered an unacceptable method in Australia, Brazil, France, Ireland, Malawi, Norway, Peru, and the United Kingdom. IASC's Statement No. 2, *Valuation and Presentation of Inventories in the Context of the Historical Cost system*, supports the preference of the majority of countries and recommends the use of FIFO or average cost.

Market Value of Inventories

Only seven countries in 1979 did not require or predominantly follow the principle that inventories should be carried at the lower of cost or market value. Five of these countries, including Japan, used cost, even when cost exceeded market value. In the other two countries — Portugal and Switzerland — most enterprises wrote down inventories to amounts below both cost and market value, a practice permitted by law.

The main difference in the countries that did use the lower of cost or market approach was in the interpretation of "market value." Forty-eight countries equated it with net realizable value, meaning estimated selling price in the ordinary course of business less costs of completion and necessary selling expenses. This view was essentially required in 22 countries, including Australia, France, Ireland, South Africa, and the United Kingdom. IASC Statement No. 2 also requires this interpretation. Austria, Greece, Italy, and Venezuela interpreted market value as replacement cost — the current cost of replacing the inventories in their present condition and location.

The United States defines market value as replacement cost, with the stipulation that it cannot exceed net realizable value or fall below net realizable value reduced by the normal profit margin. In 1979, Chile, the Dominican Republic, Mexico, Panama, and the Philippines also used this interpretation of market value.

ACCOUNTING FOR THE EFFECTS OF CHANGING PRICES

The final example of international differences illustrates an opportunity for international harmonization that is almost unique. Accounting for the effects of inflation is still in its infancy, so it may be possible to achieve a general international approach to the problem before national practices become too varied and too entrenched.

In Appendix A at the end of the text, two approaches to accounting for the effects of inflation on business enterprises are discussed: general price-level accounting and current-cost accounting. The first approach attempts to reflect the effects of changes in general purchasing power on historical-cost financial statements, while the second is concerned with the impact of specific price changes. The United States at first required supplementary statements under both methods. Then it required only current-unit supplementary statements. Now it only recommends (but does not require) supplemental statements showing the effects of inflation.

A number of countries are concerned about the loss of relevance of historical-cost financial reporting in inflationary environments, and several have adopted one of the two standard approaches — constant dollar or current cost. Some countries, usually those with the longest history of severe inflation, have issued standards that are mandatory for all enterprises, or at least for large or publicly held entities. In other countries, the accounting profession recommends, but does not prescribe, a form of inflation-adjusted statements, usually as supplementary information. But few countries are prepared to abandon the historical-cost basis for their primary financial statements, at least until decision makers have had sufficient experience with inflation accounting to give an opinion on its utility. Exceptions to this view are Argentina, Brazil, and Chile, which now require incorporation of general price-level accounting in the primary financial statements of all enterprises.

The United Kingdom's standard prescribes the provision of current-cost information either in the primary financial statements or as supplementary statements or additional information. New Zealand requires a supplementary income statement and balance sheet on a current-cost basis. Australia and South Africa recommend, but do not yet require, similar supplementary current-cost statements. Germany recommends the incorporation of current-cost information in notes to the historical-cost financial statements, while in the Netherlands, some companies prepare the primary statements on a current-cost basis, and some provide only supplementary information.

The fact that the accountancy bodies of various nations are adopting neither a uniform approach nor a uniform application of any approach, even with something as relatively new as inflation accounting, highlights the difficulty of achieving international harmonization of accounting standards. Adoption of different approaches to inflation accounting by different countries will make the preparation of consolidated financial statements by multinational corporations especially difficult, while at the same time comparability of the financial reports of companies in different nations will be further reduced. But even if all countries adopted a similar approach, a major barrier to comparability would still remain: the price indices used in each country to compute adjustments for price changes are not comparable in composition, accuracy, frequency of publication, or timeliness.

Many accountants are reluctant to see inflation-adjusted statements replace historical-cost financial statements because they believe historical cost is the most objective basis of valuation. But business entities may be more likely to favor inflation accounting, once they become accustomed to it, because of its tax implications. Since inflation accounting generally leads to lower profit figures than those computed on the historical-cost basis, there is a strong incentive for companies to adopt inflation accounting in those countries where computation of the tax liability is based on reported net income. Governments, on the other hand, may decide to prohibit the use of inflation accounting for tax purposes when a decline in tax revenues becomes apparent.

The current trend in the use of inflation-accounting approaches appears to be toward current-cost accounting and away from general price-level accounting. It has been suggested that, of the two approaches, governments prefer current-cost accounting, and this preference may influence the decisions of the accounting profession in some countries. As one British writer has pointed out,

> No government wants to have the effects of its currency debasement measured by anyone—certainly not by every business enterprise in the country. Much better to point the finger at all those individual prices moving around because of the machinations of big business, big labour and big aliens.[21]

Whether current-cost accounting will become common practice or whether some combination of current-cost and general price-level accounting will gain favor should depend on the usefulness to decision makers of the information provided by each approach. One thing is clear: As inflation again becomes a problem, more countries will adopt some form of inflation accounting. The opportunity to achieve a higher level of international harmonization while national standards are still at the development stage should not be missed.

We have attempted in these few pages to provide a broad and general picture of the variety of accounting principles and reporting practices that

---

[21]P. H. Lyons, "Farewell to Historical Costs?" *CA Magazine*, February 1976, p. 23.

exist across the world. This variety is inevitable and necessary if accounting is to be useful within widely differing national business environments. At the same time, the information needs of international business must also be satisfied. It is a challenging problem and one that will receive increasing attention in the years to come.

SUMMARY

The appendix contains information on international accounting. Significant differences exist between accounting standards and procedures in the nations of the world. Some of these differences are caused by varying national economic and social environments. Differing legal or political systems also contribute to the problem.

There have been attempts at harmonization. But, to date, these efforts have had only limited success. Ultimately, the success of international pronouncements depends on the willingness of nations to support them.

NEW TERMS INTRODUCED IN CHAPTER 12

Objective 4:
Define and use
correctly the new
terms in the
glossary

Accounting theory "A set of basic concepts and assumptions and related principles that explain and guide the accountant's actions in identifying, measuring, and communicating economic information" (431).

Comparability A qualitative characteristic of accounting information; when information is comparable, it reveals differences and similarities that are real and are not the result of differing accounting treatments (449).

Completed-contract method A method of recognizing revenue on long-term projects in which no revenue is recognized until the period in which the project is completed; similar to recognizing revenue upon the completion of a sale (439).

Completeness A qualitative characteristic of accounting information; requires disclosure of all significant information in a way that aids understanding and does not mislead; sometimes called the full-disclosure principle (448).

Conservatism Being cautious or prudent and making sure that any errors in estimates tend to understate rather than overstate net assets and net income (443).

Consistency Requires a company to use the same accounting principles and reporting practices through time (435, 450).

Cost-benefit consideration Determining whether benefits exceed costs (442).

Cost principle See Exchange-price principle.

Current/historical-rates approach Regards the parent company and its foreign subsidiaries as a single business undertaking (459).

Current-noncurrent method Translates current assets and current liabilities at the current rate and noncurrent items at the historical rate (460).

Current rate Exchange rate in effect on the balance sheet date (459).

Current rate approach The current or **closing rate** approach translates all assets and liabilities at the exchange rate in effect on the balance sheet date (459).

Earning principle The requirement that revenue be substantially earned before it is recognized (recorded) (438).

Entity   The specific unit, such as a business, for which accounting information is gathered. Entities have a separate existence from owners, creditors, employees, customers, other interested parties, and other businesses (432).

Exchange gain or loss (Time of transaction method)   The difference between the amount recorded in Accounts Payable on the purchase date and the cash paid on the settlement date (459).

Exchange-price (or cost) principle   Transfers of resources are recorded at prices agreed on by the parties to the exchange at the time of the exchange (437).

Feedback value   A qualitative characteristic that information has when it reveals the relative success of users in predicting outcomes (447).

Financial reporting objectives   The broad overriding goals sought by accountants engaging in financial reporting (444).

Going-concern (continuity) assumption   The assumption that an entity will continue to operate indefinitely unless there is strong evidence that the entity will terminate (432).

Historical cost   The amount paid, or the fair value of a liability incurred or other resource surrendered, to acquire an asset (437).

Historical rate   The rate in effect when items were originally recorded (459).

Installment basis   A revenue recognition procedure in which the percentage of total gross margin recognized in a period on an installment sale is equal to the percentage of total cash from the sale that is received in that period (438).

Liquidation   Terminating a business by ceasing business operations and selling off the assets (432).

Losses   Asset expirations that are usually involuntary and do not create revenues (441).

Matching principle   The principle that net income of a period is determined by associating or relating revenues earned in a period with expenses incurred to generate the revenues (437).

Materiality   A modifying convention that allows the accountant to deal with immaterial (unimportant) items in a theoretically incorrect, expedient manner; also a qualitative characteristic specifying that financial accounting report only information significant enough to influence decisions or evaluations (443).

Modifying conventions   Customs emerging from accounting practice that alter the results that would be obtained from a strict application of accounting principles; conservatism is an example (442).

Money measurement   Use of a monetary unit of measurement, such as the dollar, instead of physical or other units of measurement—feet, inches, grams, and so on (433).

Monetary—nonmonetary method   The current rate is used for monetary assets and liabilities, while historical rates are applied to nonmonetary items (460).

Neutrality   A qualitative characteristic that requires accounting information to be free of measurement method bias (449).

Percentage-of-completion method   A method of recognizing revenue based on the estimated stage of completion of a long-term project. The stage of completion is measured by comparing actual costs incurred in a period with total estimated costs to be incurred in all periods (439).

Period costs Costs that cannot be traced to specific revenue and are expensed in the period in which incurred (442).

Periodicity (time periods) An assumption of the accountant that an entity's life can be subdivided into time periods for purposes of reporting its economic activities (433).

Predictive value A qualitative characteristic that information has when it improves users' abilities to predict outcomes of events (447).

Product costs Costs incurred in the acquisition or manufacture of goods. Product costs are accounted for as if they were attached to the goods, with the result that they are charged to expense when the goods are sold (442).

Production basis A method of revenue recognition used in limited circumstances that recognizes revenue at the time of completion of production or extraction (440).

Qualitative characteristics Characteristics that accounting information should possess to be useful in decision making (445).

Realization principle A principle directing that revenue is recognized only after the seller acquires the right to receive payment from the buyer (438).

Relevance A qualitative characteristic requiring that information be pertinent to or bear upon a decision (447).

Reliability A qualitative characteristic requiring that information faithfully depict for users what it purports to represent (448).

Representational faithfulness A qualitative characteristic requiring that accounting statements on economic activity correspond to the actual underlying activity (448).

Revenue recognition principle The principle that revenue should be earned and realized before it is recognized (recorded) (437).

Stable dollar An assumption that the dollar is a reasonably stable unit of measurement (433).

Temporal method Cash, receivables and payables, and other assets and liabilities carried at current prices are translated at current rate of exchange. All other assets and liabilities are translated to historical rates (460).

Timeliness A qualitative characteristic requiring that accounting information be provided at a time when it may be considered in reaching a decision (447).

Verifiability A qualitative characteristic of accounting information; information is verifiable when it can be substantially duplicated by independent measurers using the same measurement methods (449).

DEMONSTRATION PROBLEM 12–1

For each of the transactions or circumstances described below and the entries made, state which, if any, of the assumptions or concepts, principles, or modifying conventions of accounting have been violated. For the violations, give the entry to correct the improper accounting assuming the books have not been closed.

During the year, the Dorsey Company did the following:

1. Had its buildings appraised. They were found to have a market value of $410,000, although their book value was only $380,000. The accountant debited

the Buildings and Accumulated Depreciation—Buildings accounts for $15,000 each and credited Capital from Appreciation. No separate mention was made of this action in the financial statements.

2. Purchased a number of new electric pencil sharpeners for its offices at a total cost of $60. These were recorded as assets and are being depreciated over five years.

3. Produced a number of agricultural products at a cost of $26,000. These costs were charged to expense when the products were harvested. The products were set up in inventory at their net market value of $35,000, and the Farm Revenues Earned account was credited for $35,000.

Solution to demonstration problem 12–1

1. The realization principle and the modifying convention of conservatism may have been violated. Such write-ups simply are not looked upon with favor in accounting. To correct the situation, the entry made needs to be reversed:

Capital from Appreciation.	30,000	
Buildings		15,000
Accumulated Depreciation—Buildings		15,000

2. Theoretically, there were no violations unless there is one relating to the cost of compiling insignificant information. As a practical matter, the $60 could have been expensed on materiality grounds.

3. There were no violations. The procedures followed are considered acceptable for farm products that are interchangeable and readily marketable. No correcting entry is needed provided due allowance has been made for the costs to be incurred in delivering the products to the market.

QUESTIONS

1. Name the assumptions underlying generally accepted accounting principles. Comment on the validity in recent years of the stable unit of measurement assumption.

2. Why does the accountant assume the existence of an entity?

3. When is the going-concern assumption not to be used?

4. What is meant by the term *accrual basis of accounting?* What is its alternative?

5. What does it mean to say that accountants record substance rather than form?

6. If a company changes an accounting principle because the change better meets the information needs of users, what disclosures must be made?

7. What is the exchange price (or cost) principle? What is the significance of adhering to this principle?

8. What two requirements generally must be met before revenue will be recognized in a period?

9. Under what circumstances, if any, is the receipt of cash an acceptable time to recognize revenue?

10. What two methods may be used in recognizing revenues on long-term construction contracts?

11. Define expense. What principles guide the recognition of expense?

12. How does an expense differ from a loss?

13. What is meant by the accounting term *conservatism?* How does it affect the amounts reported in the financial statements?

14. Does materiality relate only to relative size of dollar amounts?

15. How might it be argued that a tax supposedly upon income is really a tax upon capital?

16. Identify the three major parts of the conceptual framework project that are included in the text.

17. In general, what are the qualitative characteristics? Which are the primary qualitative characteristics?

18. (Based on the Appendix) Why do differences exist in accounting standards and practices from nation to nation?

19. (Based on the appendix) How successful have efforts at harmonization been to date?

EXERCISES

Match theory terms with definitions

1. Match the items in Group A with the proper descriptions in Group B.

Group A

1. Going concern (continuity).
2. Consistency
3. Disclosure
4. Periodicity.
5. Conservatism.
6. Stable dollar.
7. Matching.
8. Materiality.
9. Exchange prices.
10. Entity.

Group B

a. An assumption relied on in the preparation of the primary financial statements that would be unreasonable when the inflation rate is high.

b. Concerned with relative dollar amounts.

c. The usual basis for the recording of assets.

d. Required if the accounting treatment differs from that previously accorded a particular item.

e. An assumption that would be unreasonable to use in reporting on a firm that had become insolvent.

f. None of these.

g. Requires a company to use the same accounting procedures and practices through time.

h. An assumption that the life of an entity can be subdivided into time periods for purposes of reporting.

i. Discourages undue optimism in measuring and reporting net assets and net income.

j. Requires separation of personal activity from business activity in the recording and reporting processes.

<table>
<tr><td>*Compute income under accrual basis and installment method*</td><td>

2. Smith Company sells its products on an installment sales basis. Data for 1989 and 1990 are as follows:

</td></tr>
</table>

	1989	1990
Installment sales	$100,000	$120,000
Cost of goods sold on installment . . .	70,000	90,000
Other expenses	15,000	20,000
Cash collected from 1989 sales	60,000	30,000
Cash collected from 1990 sales		80,000

a. Compute the net income for 1990 assuming use of the accrual (sales) basis of revenue recognition.

b. Compute the net income for 1990 assuming use of the installment method of recognizing gross margin.

Recognize revenue under percentage-of-completion method

3. A firm has a contract to build a ship at a price of $350 million and an estimated cost of $280 million. In 1990, costs of $70 million were incurred. Under the percentage-of-completion method how much revenue would be recognized in 1990?

Compute effect on financial statements of incorrectly expensing an asset

4. A company follows a practice of expensing the premium on its fire insurance policy when it is paid. In 1990, it charged to expense the $1,440 premium paid on a three-year policy covering the period July 1, 1990, to June 30, 1993. In 1987, a premium of $1,320 was charged to expense on the same policy for the period July 1, 1987, to June 30, 1990.

a. State the principle of accounting that was violated by this practice.

b. Compute the effects of this violation on the financial statements for the calendar year 1990.

c. State the basis upon which the company's practice might be justified.

Compute gross margin under GAAP and then comment on recognizing revenue as production is completed

5. Bates Company produces a product at a cost of $40 per unit that it sells for $60. The company has been very successful and is able to sell all of the units that it can produce. During 1990, the company manufactured 50,000 units, but because of a transportation strike, it was able to sell and deliver only 40,000 units.

a. Compute the gross margin for 1990 following the realization principle.

b. Describe any circumstances under which the realization principle is ignored and revenue is recognized as production is completed.

Match accounting qualities with proper descriptions

6. Using the following descriptions, match the accounting qualities with the proper descriptions. Some descriptions may be used more than once.

Descriptions:

a. Users of accounting information

b. Pervasive constraint

c. User-specific qualities

d. Primary decision-specific qualities

e. Ingredients of primary qualities

f. Secondary and interactive qualities

g. Threshold for recognition

Accounting qualities:

1. Relevance
2. Feedback value

3. Decision makers
4. Representational faithfulness
5. Reliability
6. Comparability
7. Benefits > costs
8. Predictive value
9. Timeliness
10. Decision usefulness
11. Verifiability
12. Understanding
13. Neutrality
14. Materiality

PROBLEMS

Compute income assuming revenues are recognized at time of sale and then assuming installment method is used

12–1. The Square-Deal Real Estate Sales Company sells lots in its development in Flash Flood Canyon under terms calling for small cash down payments with monthly installment payments spread over a few years. Following are data on the company's operations for its first three years:

	1988	1989	1990
Gross margin rate	45%	48%	50%
Cash collected in 1990 from sales of lots made in	$80,000	$100,000	$120,000

The total selling price of the lots sold in 1990 was $400,000, while general and administrative expenses (which are not included in the costs used to determine gross margin) were $100,000.

Required:

a. Compute the net income for 1990 assuming revenue is recognized upon the sale of a lot.

b. Compute net income for 1990 assuming use of the installment method of accounting for sales and gross margin.

Compute income assuming revenues are recognized at time of sale and then assuming installment method is used

12–2. Henco Video, Inc. sells video recorders under terms calling for a small down payment and monthly payments spread over three years. Following are data for the first three years of the company's operations:

	1989	1990	1991
Sales	$240,000	$360,000	$480,000
Cost of video sets sold	168,000	216,000	240,000
Gross margin	$ 72,000	$144,000	$240,000
Gross margin as a percentage of sales	30%	40%	50%
Cash collected in 1991:			
From 1989 sales			$ 72,000
From 1990 sales			96,000
From 1991 sales			156,000

General and selling expenses amounted to $144,000 in 1991.

Required:

a. Compute net income for 1991 assuming that revenues are recognized at the time of sale.

b. Compute net income for 1991 using the installment method of accounting for sales and gross margin.

Compute income under completed-contract and percentage-of-completion methods

12–3. Given below are the contract prices and construction costs relating to all of the Grady Company's long-term construction contracts (in millions of dollars):

		Costs Incurred		
	Contract Price	Prior to 1990	In 1990	Cost Yet to Be Incurred
On contracts completed in 1990	$16.0	–0–	$14.0	–0–
On incomplete contracts	48.0	$8.0	16.0	$16.0

General and administrative expenses for 1990 amounted to $600,000.

Required:

a. Compute net income for 1990 using the completed-contract method.

b. Compute net income for 1990 using the percentage-of-completion method. Assume that the general and administrative expenses are not to be treated as a part of the construction costs of the contracts.

Compute income under completed-contract and percentage-of-completion methods

12–4. The following data relate to the Craft Construction Company's long-term construction projects for the year 1991:

	Completed project	Incomplete projects
Contract price	$2,250,000	$12,000,000
Cost incurred prior to 1991	–0–	2,000,000
Costs incurred in 1991	1,850,000	4,000,000
Estimated costs to complete (at 12/31/91) . . .	–0–	4,000,000

General and administrative expenses incurred in 1991 amounted to $250,000, none of which is to be considered a construction cost.

Required:

a. Compute net income for 1991 under the completed-contract method.

b. Compute net income for 1991 using the percentage-of-completion method.

Match principles, assumptions, or concepts with certain accounting procedures followed

12–5. For each of the numbered items listed below, state the letter or letters of the principle(s), assumption(s), or concept(s) used to justify the accounting procedure followed:

A—Entity.
B—Conservatism.
C—Earning principle of revenue recognition.
D—Going concern (continuity).
E—Exchange-price principle.

F—Matching principle.

G—Period cost (or principle of immediate recognition of expense).

H—Realization principle.

I—Stable dollar assumption.

1. The estimated liability for federal income taxes was increased by $7,000 over the amount reported on the tax return to cover possible differences found by the Internal Revenue Service in determining the amount of income taxes payable.

2. A truck purchased in January was reported at 80% of its cost even though its market value at year-end was only 70% of its cost.

3. The collection of $14,000 of cash for services to be performed next year was reported as a current liability.

4. The president's salary was treated as an expense of the year even though he spent most of his time planning the next two years' activities.

5. No entry was made to record the company's receipt of an offer of $140,000 for land carried in its accounts at $84,000.

6. A stock of printed stationery, checks, and invoices with a cost of $2,800 was treated as a current asset at year-end even though it had no value to others.

7. A tract of land acquired for $49,000 was recorded at that price even though it was appraised at $56,000, and the company would have been willing to pay that amount.

8. The company paid and charged to expense the $2,100 paid to David Ross for rent of a truck owned by him. David Ross is owner of the company.

9. $16,800 of interest collected on $140,000 of 12% bonds was recorded as interest revenue even though the general level of prices increased 16% during the year.

BUSINESS DECISION PROBLEM 12–1

Indicate agreement or disagreement with accounting practices followed and comment

In each of the circumstances described below, the accounting practices followed may be questioned. You are to indicate whether you agree or disagree with the accounting employed and to state the assumptions, concepts, or principles on which you would rely to justify your position.

1. The cost of certain improvements to leased property having a life of five years was charged to expense because the improvements would revert to the lessor when the lease expires in three years.

2. The salaries paid to the top officers of the company were charged to expense in the period in which they were incurred, even though the officers spent over half of their time planning next year's activities.

3. A company spent over $8 million in developing a new product and then spent an additional $9 million promoting it. All of these costs were incurred and charged to expense this year even though future years would also benefit.

4. No entry was made to record the belief that the market value of the land owned (carried in the accounts at $58,000) increased.

5. No entry was made to record the fact that costs of $100,000 were expected to be incurred in fulfilling warranty provisions on products sold this year. The revenue from products sold was recognized this year.

6. The acquisition of a tract of land was recorded at the price paid for it of $108,000, even though the company would have been willing to pay $125,000.

7. A truck acquired at the beginning of the year was reported at year-end at 80 percent of its acquisition price, even though its market value then was only 65 percent of its original acquisition price.

13

ACCOUNTING FOR MANUFACTURING COMPANIES

LEARNING OBJECTIVES

After studying this chapter, you should be able to:

1. Describe the three basic components of manufacturing costs incurred in the production of a product.
2. Describe the difference between product costs and period costs and explain why proper classification is essential.
3. Describe the flow of costs of a manufacturing company under periodic inventory procedure and prepare journal entries.
4. Describe the difference in financial reporting between a merchandiser and a manufacturer and prepare a statement of costs of goods manufactured, an income statement, and a balance sheet for a manufacturer.
5. Describe the general pattern of the flow of costs of a manufacturing company under perpetual inventory procedure and prepare journal entries.
6. Define and use correctly the new terms in the glossary.

So far in this text, you have studied accounting as it pertains to service businesses and merchandising businesses (retailers and wholesalers). This chapter focuses on accounting for manufacturing businesses.

If you owned a retail appliance store, you would purchase appliances, such as refrigerators and ranges, and sell them to customers. To determine your profitability, the cost of purchasing the appliances would be accounted for and subtracted from your gross sales as cost of goods sold. However, if instead you owned the manufacturing company that made the appliances, your cost of goods sold would be based on manufacturing costs.

Accounting for manufacturing costs is more complex than accounting for costs of merchandise purchased that is ready for sale. This chapter explains and illustrates the procedures to account for manufacturing costs. Terms such as raw materials, work in process, finished goods, direct labor, indirect labor, and manufacturing overhead are part of manufacturing accounting. The basic accounting process discussed throughout the text also applies to manufacturing companies.

MERCHANDISER AND MANUFACTURER ACCOUNTING DIFFERENCES

Perhaps the most important accounting difference between merchandisers and manufacturers relates to the difference in the nature of their activities. A merchandiser purchases goods that are already in their finished state and ready to be sold. On the other hand, a manufacturer must purchase raw materials and use production equipment and employee labor to transform the raw materials into finished products. Thus, while a merchandiser has only one type of inventory—merchandise available for sale—a manufacturer has three types—unprocessed **materials,** partially complete **work in process,** and ready-for-sale **finished goods.** Three different inventory accounts (instead of one) are necessary to show the cost of inventory in various stages of production.

A comparison of a manufacturer's cost of goods sold section of the income statement with that of a merchandiser is shown in Illustration 13.1. There are two major differences in the cost of goods sold sections: (1) goods ready to be sold are referred to as *merchandise inventory* by a merchandiser and as *finished goods inventory* by a manufacturer, and (2) *cost of purchases* for a merchandiser is equivalent to *cost of goods manufactured* by a manufacturer.

Illustration 13.1
COST OF GOODS SOLD COMPARISON

Merchandiser		Manufacturer	
Cost of goods sold:		Cost of goods sold:	
Merchandise inventory, January 1	$ 25,000	Finished goods inventory, January 1	$ 40,000
Cost of purchases . . .	165,000	Cost of goods manufactured (from statement of cost of goods manufactured) . .	250,000
Cost of goods available for sale	$190,000		
Merchandise inventory, December 31	30,000	Cost of goods available for sale	$290,000
Cost of goods sold	$160,000	Finished goods inventory, December 31	50,000
		Cost of goods sold	$240,000

COST CLASSIFICATIONS

Cost is a financial measure of the resources used or given up to achieve a stated purpose. In manufacturing companies, costs can be classified as

(1) manufacturing or nonmanufacturing costs, (2) product costs or period costs, and (3) fixed or variable costs. Each of these classifications of costs will be discussed.

Manufacturing Costs

Objective 1: Describe the three basic components of manufacturing costs incurred in the production of a product

The total cost of manufacturing a product is referred to as manufacturing cost, factory cost, or product cost. **Manufacturing cost** includes three cost elements: (1) direct materials costs, (2) direct labor costs, and (3) manufacturing overhead costs.

Direct materials. **Direct materials** have three characteristics: (1) they are included in the finished product, (2) they are used only in the manufacture of the product, and (3) they are clearly and easily traceable to the product. For example, iron ore is a direct material to a steel company because the iron ore is clearly traceable to the finished product, steel. In turn, steel becomes a direct material to an automobile manufacturer.

The cost of direct materials includes the net invoice price of the actual quantity used plus delivery charges. Some companies also include storage and handling costs. Direct materials inventory may be accounted for using any of the inventory cost methods discussed in Chapter 4, including specific identification, FIFO, LIFO, or average cost.

Some materials (such as glue and thread used in manufacturing furniture) may become part of the finished product, but tracing those materials to the product would require great cost and effort. For this reason, these materials are referred to as indirect materials or supplies and are included in manufacturing overhead. **Indirect materials** are materials that are used in the manufacture of a product but cannot or will not, for practical reasons, be traced directly to the products being manufactured.

Direct labor. **Direct labor** costs include labor costs of all employees actually working on materials to convert them into finished goods. As with direct materials costs, direct labor costs of a product include only those labor costs that are clearly traceable to, or readily identifiable with, the finished product. Direct labor costs can be identified by showing that these costs vary in direct proportion to the number of units produced. Thus, the labor of machinists, assemblers, cutters, and painters can be classified as direct labor.

Direct labor cost is usually measured by multiplying the number of hours of direct labor by the hourly wage rate. Many employees receive fringe benefits—employer's payroll taxes, pension costs, paid vacations, etc. These fringe benefit costs can significantly increase the direct labor hourly wage rate. Although fringe benefit costs are occasionally accounted for as direct labor, they are normally included in manufacturing overhead because they can be traced to the product only at great cost and effort.

Some labor costs (for example, wages of materials handlers, custodial workers, and supervisors) tend to vary directly with the number of product units produced but are not accounted for as direct labor because the expense to trace these costs to product units would be too great. These labor costs are called indirect labor and are accounted for as manufacturing overhead. **Indirect labor** consists of the cost of services that cannot or will not, for practical reasons, be traced to the product being manufactured.

Manufacturing overhead. There are many alternative names for manufacturing overhead, including factory indirect costs, factory burden, and manufacturing expense. **Manufacturing overhead** is a "catchall" classification, since it includes all manufacturing costs except for those costs accounted for as direct materials and direct labor. Manufacturing overhead costs are manufacturing costs that must be incurred but that cannot or will not be traced directly to specific units produced. As noted earlier, manufacturing overhead may include certain materials and labor costs that could theoretically be accounted for as direct materials or direct labor.

Manufacturing overhead contains a number of other costs that are related to the manufacturing process, such as depreciation and maintenance on machines, supervisors' salaries, and factory utility costs. Illustration 13.2 summarizes most manufacturing overhead costs and details some examples of indirect materials and indirect labor.

Illustration 13.2
MANUFACTURING OVERHEAD COSTS

Repairs and maintenance on factory buildings and equipment	Payroll taxes and fringe benefits for manufacturing employees
Depreciation on factory buildings and equipment	Overtime wage premiums on direct labor
Insurance and taxes on factory property and inventories	Indirect labor:
Indirect materials:	Janitors
Lubricants	Supervisors
Adhesives	Engineers
Cleaners, etc.	Timekeepers
Write-off of hand tools	Toolroom personnel
Utilities for factory buildings	Materials storeroom personnel, etc.
	Cost accountant

Note from the illustration that overtime wage premiums on direct labor are commonly included in manufacturing overhead rather than in direct labor cost. The logic behind this practice is that the need for employees to work overtime normally results from an overall production backlog, not from the need to manufacture a given product line. For example, in a company that manufactures three products, employees may work overtime on any one of the three products, depending on the arbitrary scheduling by the production manager. In such situations, the need for overtime is due to the combined time requirements of all three products and should not be directly charged to any one product unless that product was clearly the sole cause of the overtime.

Manufacturing cost terminology. It is often useful for decision-making purposes to classify costs according to their relation to the finished product or the manufacturing process. For this reason, there are special terms to identify these classifications. The sum of direct materials costs and direct labor costs incurred to manufacture a product is called **prime cost.** The sum of direct labor costs and manufacturing overhead cost is called

conversion cost because these costs are incurred in the conversion of the direct materials into finished goods. The relationship of these cost terms is shown in Illustration 13.3.

Illustration 13.3
COST RELATIONSHIPS

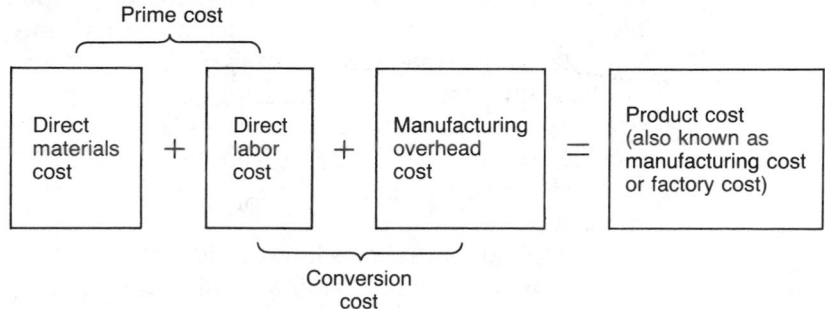

Nonmanufacturing Costs

Nonmanufacturing costs differ from manufacturing costs in that they relate to selling and administrative functions rather than to manufacturing. Nonmanufacturing costs are generally classified as either selling costs or administrative costs.

Selling costs. **Selling costs** are costs incurred to obtain customer orders and get the finished product into the customers' possession. Advertising, market research, sales salaries and commissions, and delivery and storage of finished goods are examples of selling costs. The costs of delivery and storage of finished goods are considered to be selling costs since they are incurred after production has been completed. Therefore, the costs of storing materials are included in manufacturing overhead, whereas the costs of storing finished goods are a part of selling costs. Keep in mind that retailers, wholesalers, manufacturers, and service organizations all have selling costs.

Administrative costs. **Administrative costs** are nonmanufacturing costs that include the costs of top administrative functions and various staff departments such as accounting, data processing, and personnel. Examples of administrative costs are executive salaries, clerical salaries, office expenses, office rent, donations, research and development costs, and legal costs. As with selling costs, all organizations have administrative costs.

Product and Period Costs

Objective 2: Describe the difference between product costs and period costs and the importance of proper classification

Costs in manufacturing companies can also be classified as product costs and period costs. This distinction is important for income determination purposes.

Product costs are costs incurred in the manufacture of products and are assigned to units of the product produced by a manufacturing company. These costs include costs of direct materials, direct labor, and manufacturing overhead.

Period costs are not assigned to units of a product; they are related more closely to periods of time rather than to products produced. These costs cannot be traced directly to the manufacture of a specific product. For this reason, period costs are expensed (deducted from revenues) in the period in which they are incurred. To illustrate, assume a company pays its sales manager a fixed salary. Even though the manager may be working on projects that will benefit the company in future accounting periods, the sales manager's salary is expensed in the period in which it is incurred because the expense cannot be traced to the production of a product. Thus, *all selling and nonfactory administrative costs are treated as period costs.*

Illustration 13.4 shows how product costs and period costs are reported in the financial statements of a manufacturing company. Note that product costs are not expensed when incurred but are expensed in the *period the goods are sold.* If product costs are incurred toward the end of period 1 and the goods are sold in period 2, the costs involved are expensed against revenues of period 2. In Illustration 13.4 finished products of $900,000 were sold to customers and expensed as costs of goods sold. The period costs, selling and administration expenses ($225,000), were expensed as incurred and deducted from gross margin on sales to compute income before taxes.

Illustration 13.4
STATEMENT ANALYSIS OF PERIOD AND PRODUCT COSTS

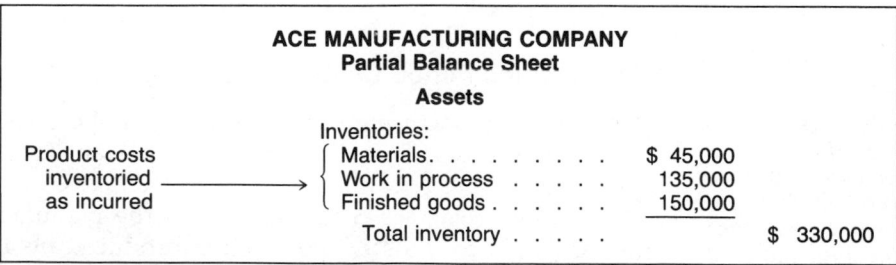

ACE MANUFACTURING COMPANY
Condensed Income Statement

Product costs expensed as finished goods are sold to customers →	Sales		$1,500,000
	Cost of goods sold		900,000
	Gross margin		$ 600,000
Period costs expensed → as incurred	Selling expenses	$100,000	
	Administrative expenses . . .	125,000	225,000
	Income before taxes		$ 375,000
	Federal income taxes ,. . . .		137,500
	Net income		$ 237,500

ACE MANUFACTURING COMPANY
Partial Balance Sheet

Assets

	Inventories:		
Product costs inventoried → as incurred	Materials.	$ 45,000	
	Work in process	135,000	
	Finished goods	150,000	
	Total inventory		$ 330,000

The ending inventories of a manufacturing company represent (1) materials, (2) work in process, and (3) finished goods. These three items are shown under "Inventories" in the balance sheet (see Illustration 13.4). These inventories are assets, and the product costs they contain are expensed in the period the goods are sold to customers. When items of finished goods inventory are sold, their costs are reported as an expense (cost of goods sold) on the income statement for the period of sale.

Fixed and Variable Costs

In addition to classifying costs by their relationships to the manufacturing process or to time periods, costs can be classified by how they respond to changes in the volume of manufacturing activity. Costs that are not affected in total amount by the volume of production activity are called fixed costs; costs that vary in total amount directly with changes in the volume of production activity are called variable costs.

Fixed costs. **Fixed costs** remain constant in total amount over wide variations in the level of manufacturing activity. For example, the annual license for an automobile may cost $50 whether the auto is driven 1,000 or 100,000 miles during the year. The same may hold true for the annual premium on an insurance policy for the auto. Property taxes, depreciation, rent, and executives' salaries are further examples of fixed costs. Fixed costs are basically time related, such as a one-year salary for the president, while variable costs are volume related, such as the total cost of motors necessary for some output of washing machines.

Fixed costs present a special problem in determining the unit cost of a product. Since total fixed costs do not change with the volume of production activity, cost *per unit* may vary widely if output varies. For example, assume that a company rents a factory building for $100,000 per year. The rental cost per ton of output is $1 if 100,000 tons are produced, $0.50 if 200,000 tons are produced, and only $0.10 if 1 million tons are produced. From this example you can see that *fixed cost per unit will decrease as the number of units produced increases and will increase as the number of units decreases.*

Variable costs. **Variable costs** are costs that vary directly in total amount with changes in the volume of production activity or output. Direct materials are a good example of a variable cost. For example, every washing machine produced by a manufacturer has one motor. If the motors cost $50 each, then the motor cost for one machine is $50; for two machines is $100; for three machines is $150; and so on. If profit plans call for the production of 10,000 washing machines, then the planned cost of the motors is $500,000. Similarly, the labor cost to install the motors is a variable cost.

Because fixed costs are basically time related, total fixed cost remains constant with volume changes, but fixed cost per unit varies inversely with the change in activity. Variable costs, on the other hand, remain constant on a per unit basis, but change in total in direct relation to the change in level of activity.

PERIODIC INVENTORY PROCEDURE

A manufacturer may use either periodic or perpetual inventory procedure. Recall from Chapter 4 that under periodic inventory procedure, accounts are brought to their proper balances only at the end of the accounting period by taking a physical inventory. Under perpetual inventory procedure, the inventory accounts are maintained at their proper balances throughout the period. This section discusses periodic inventory procedure applied in a manufacturing company. Perpetual inventory procedure is discussed in a later section in the chapter.

Accounts Used for Materials and Other Inventories

When a manufacturer uses periodic inventory procedure, the Materials Purchases, Transportation-In, Materials Purchase Returns and Allowances, and Materials Inventory accounts are used in the same manner as they are used by a retailer. Purchases during the period are debited to the Materials Purchases account. Transportation charges incurred on purchases are debited to Transportation-In. Returns of purchased materials and allowances granted on purchases are credits to Materials Purchase Returns and Allowances. Each of these accounts is closed through Manufacturing Summary to Income Summary at the end of the accounting period. The Materials Inventory account contains the beginning inventory amount until year-end, when the ending inventory is entered in the account during the closing process.

Since a manufacturer must account for unfinished goods still in various stages of production and completed goods that are yet to be sold, Work in Process Inventory and Finished Goods Inventory accounts are used. As with Materials Inventory, when a periodic inventory system is in use these inventory accounts will contain the beginning inventory amount until year-end, when a physical inventory is taken and the amount of ending inventory is entered in the accounts.

The following T-accounts show how the accounts are used by a manufacturer using a periodic inventory system:

Materials Purchases		Transportation-In	
Purchases of materials entered here	Closed through Manufacturing Summary to Income Summary at end of period	Freight charges incurred on purchases entered here	Closed through Manufacturing Summary to Income Summary at end of period

Materials Purchase Returns and Allowances	
Closed through Manufacturing Summary to Income Summary at end of period	Cost of materials returned to suppliers and amount of any allowances granted on purchases entered here

Materials Inventory	
Beginning balance xx Ending balance xx Ending balance is entered at end of period based on a physical inventory	Beginning balance is closed through Manufacturing Summary to Income Summary at end of period

Work in Process Inventory	
Beginning balance xx Ending balance xx Ending balance is entered at end of period based on a physical inventory	Beginning balance is closed through Manufacturing Summary to Income Summary at end of period

Finished Goods Inventory	
Beginning balance xx Ending balance xx Ending balance is entered at end of period based on a physical inventory	Beginning balance is closed to Income Summary at end of period

Estimation of Inventory Costs

When a manufacturer is using a periodic inventory system, inventory quantities are determined at year-end by making a physical count of the materials, work in process, and finished goods on hand. Once the *quantity* of these inventories has been established, their *cost* must be estimated.

Cost of the materials inventory on hand can be determined quite accurately by looking at purchase invoices to obtain purchase prices. Materials inventory cost is then calculated by multiplying the unit purchase price by the quantity of each type of item.

Estimating the cost of work in process or finished goods inventory is more complicated. For the average unit in work in process inventory and then for each unit in finished goods inventory, a manufacturer must estimate:

1. Direct materials cost contained in each unit.
2. Direct labor cost incurred for each unit.
3. Manufacturing overhead applicable to each unit.

The amounts of materials *may* differ, while the amounts of labor and overhead *will* differ, for units in work in process inventory and units in finished goods inventory. Materials may be added at the beginning of the process, uniformly throughout the process, or near the end of the process. Direct labor is incurred throughout the manufacturing process. The sum of the three cost elements represents the product cost per unit contained in each of the inventories. The relevant product costs are then multiplied by the number of units in the work in process inventory and the number of units in the finished goods inventory to obtain the total costs of these inventories.

Direct materials cost. Direct materials cost in each unit of work in process and in each unit in finished goods can be established by referring to a materials specification list to determine the quantity of materials contained in each product. A materials specification list indicates what types and quantities of materials are used in manufacturing a product. Also, one must know when the materials are added in the production process in order to estimate what proportion of the materials is in the average unit in work in process inventory. Of course, all of the materials are in each unit in finished goods inventory. The relevant quantities are multiplied by the purchase invoice unit price to obtain the direct materials cost per unit.

Direct labor cost. The direct labor cost in each unit of a product is typically based on observations made by management to determine the *normal* amount of time it takes workers to complete the product. This amount of time multiplied by the hourly wage rate gives the direct labor cost per unit. In the case of products still in production, management estimates the percentage of completion of the good and determines the amount of direct labor cost applicable to work in process based on this percentage. Direct materials and direct labor costs may be estimated in this manner because these costs are clearly traceable to the product.

Manufacturing overhead cost. Since manufacturing overhead costs are not clearly traceable, they must be allocated to the product based on a manufacturing overhead rate. The **manufacturing overhead rate** expresses manufacturing overhead costs in relation to some measure of manufacturing activity. Manufacturing overhead costs often vary almost proportionately with the amount of direct labor used. More direct labor usually requires more supervisors, more utilities to operate the plant, and more maintenance and repairs on machinery used in production. Recall that the costs of such items are classified as manufacturing overhead costs. Consequently, manufacturing overhead rates are frequently expressed as either (1) a percentage of direct labor cost or (2) a certain dollar amount per direct labor-hour.

To illustrate the computation of a manufacturing overhead rate and the cost of ending inventories of work in process and finished goods, assume the following information is available for a company:

Direct materials used (30,000 units)	$180,000
Direct labor (52,000 hours)	520,000
Manufacturing overhead	416,000
Ending inventories (determined by physical count):	
Work in process	8,000 units
Finished goods	2,000 units
Units sold during the period	20,000 units

The company manufactures only one product—product P. All direct materials are issued to production at the start of the manufacturing process. Each unit of product contains one unit of direct materials. Therefore, the direct material cost per unit is $180,000 ÷ 30,000 units = $6. The direct labor cost per hour is $520,000 ÷ 52,000 hours = $10. Management estimates that each completed unit of product contains two hours of direct labor, while each unit still in production contains an average of one hour of direct labor. Thus, the direct labor cost per unit is $20 for finished goods and $10 for work in process.

The manufacturing overhead rate expressed as a percentage of direct labor cost is computed as follows:

$$\frac{\text{Total manufacturing overhead cost}}{\text{Total direct labor cost}} = \text{Manufacturing overhead rate}$$

$$\frac{\$416,000}{\$520,000} = 0.80 = 80\%$$

This overhead rate can be interpreted as saying that for every $1 spent on direct labor, we spent $0.80 on manufacturing overhead.

The cost of the ending inventories of work in process and finished goods can now be determined as shown in Illustration 13.5.

THE WORK SHEET FOR A MANUFACTURING COMPANY USING PERIODIC PROCEDURE

Remember that the major accounting difference between merchandisers and manufacturers is that merchandisers have only one type of inventory (merchandise) while manufacturers have three types (materials, work in process, and finished goods). This difference is further complicated by the fact that Work in Process and Finished Goods inventories are each composed of direct materials, direct labor, and manufacturing overhead costs allocated to production. These factors contribute to the complexity of determining the periodic cost of goods sold for a manufacturer. For this reason, manufacturers prepare a statement of cost of goods manufactured to support the cost of goods sold figure on the income statement. To aid in preparing the statement of cost of goods manufactured (as well as adjusting and closing entries), a work sheet can be used. The work sheet for a manufacturing company has a pair of columns for the statement of cost of goods manufactured (manufacturing statement), as shown in Illustration 13.6. The example in Illustration 13.6 focuses on the production-related accounts.

Illustration 13.5
COMPUTATION OF WORK IN PROCESS AND FINISHED GOODS INVENTORIES OF PRODUCT P

Inventory	Direct Materials +	Direct Labor +	Manufacturing Overhead (80% of direct labor cost)	= Total	Total ×	Units in Inventory =	Total Ending Inventory Cost
Work in process	$6	$10	$ 8	$24	$24	8,000	$192,000
Finished goods	6	20	16	42	42	2,000	84,000

Column groups: *Estimated Cost per Unit* and *Estimated Total Inventory Cost*.

Illustration 13.6
MANUFACTURING WORKSHEET

JERNIGAN MANUFACTURING COMPANY
Work Sheet for the Year Ended December 31, 1990

Account Titles	Trial Balance		Adjustments		Manufacturing Statement		Income Statement		Balance Sheet	
	Debit	Credit	Debit	Credit	Debit	Credit	Debit	Credit	Debit	Credit
Cash	62,000								62,000	
Accounts Receivable	160,000								160,000	
Allowance for Uncollectible Accounts		500		(1) 1,500						2,000
Prepaid Insurance	7,500			(4) 6,500					1,000	
Inventories:										
Materials	40,000				40,000	38,000			38,000	
Work in Process	84,000				84,000	80,000			80,000	
Finished Goods	56,000						56,000	60,000	60,000	
Factory Building	400,000								400,000	
Accumulated Depreciation—Factory Building		40,000		(2) 20,000						60,000
Factory Equipment	460,000								460,000	
Accumulated Depreciation—Factory Equipment		92,000		(3) 46,000						138,000
Land	32,000								32,000	
Accounts Payable		60,000								60,000
Mortgage Payable, 10%		200,000								200,000
Common Stock—$5 Par Value		600,000								600,000
Retained Earnings, January 1		103,500								103,500
Sales		1,800,000						1,800,000		
Materials Purchases	480,000				480,000					

486

Account	Trial Balance Dr	Adjustments Dr	Adjustments Cr	Cost of Goods Manufactured Dr	Cost of Goods Manufactured Cr	Income Statement Dr	Income Statement Cr	Balance Sheet Dr	Balance Sheet Cr
Transportation-In	6,000			6,000					
Direct Labor	371,000	(5) 9,000		380,000					
Indirect Labor	62,500	(5) 2,500		65,000					
Supervisors' Salaries	127,000	(5) 3,000		130,000					
Maintenance and Repairs	17,000			17,000					
Utilities Expense	5,000			5,000					
Selling Expenses	199,500	(5) 500				200,000			
Administrative Expenses	184,500	(4) 500				185,000			
Interest Expense	20,000					20,000			
Factory Taxes Expense	15,000			15,000					
Income Tax Expense	107,000					107,000			
	2,896,000								
	2,896,000								
Uncollectible Accounts Expense		(1) 1,500				1,500			
Depreciation Expense—Factory Building		(2) 20,000		20,000					
Depreciation Expense—Factory Equipment		(3) 46,000		46,000					
Insurance Expense—Factory		(4) 6,000		6,000					
Accrued Payroll Payable			(5) 15,000						15,000
		89,000	89,000	1,294,000	118,000				
Manufacturing Summary (Cost of Goods Manufactured)					1,176,000	1,176,000			
				1,294,000	1,294,000	1,745,500	1,860,000		
Net Income						114,500			114,500
						1,860,000	1,860,000	1,293,000	1,293,000

(1) To record uncollectible accounts expense for the year.
(2) To record depreciation expense on factory building.
(3) To record depreciation expense on factory equipment.
(4) To record and distribute cost of expired insurance.
(5) To record and distribute cost of accrued payroll.

The Jernigan Manufacturing Company trial balance is taken from its ledger accounts at year-end. The administrative and selling expenses have been summarized in order to emphasize the company's production activities. The beginning-of-year inventory account balances for materials, work in process, and finished goods are $40,000, $84,000, and $56,000, respectively. The year-end inventory account balances are $38,000, $80,000, and $60,000, respectively.

Adjustments Columns

The required adjustments for the Jernigan Manufacturing Company appear in the Adjustments columns on the work sheet. The following information was used to prepare the adjustments:

1. The uncollectible accounts expense was estimated to be $1,500 for the year.
2. Depreciation on the factory building was $20,000.
3. Depreciation on the factory equipment was $46,000.
4. Insurance expiring during the year was $6,500. Of this amount, $6,000 applied to the factory building and equipment, and $500 applied to administrative offices (administrative expense).
5. Factory payroll accrued since the last payday was distributed as follows: direct labor, $9,000; supervisors' salary, $3,000; janitorial and maintenance, $1,800; materials storeroom personnel, $700; and finished goods storeroom personnel (selling expense), $500. Nonfactory employees were paid on December 31.

Based on the above information, the following adjusting entries need to be recorded on the work sheet of the Jernigan Manufacturing Company (see Illustration 13.6):

(1)	Uncollectible Accounts Expense	1,500	
	Allowance for Uncollectible Accounts		1,500
	To record uncollectible accounts expense for the year.		
(2)	Depreciation Expense—Factory Building	20,000	
	Accumulated Depreciation—Factory Building		20,000
	To record depreciation on factory building.		
(3)	Depreciation Expense—Factory Equipment	46,000	
	Accumulated Depreciation—Factory Equipment		46,000
	To record depreciation on factory equipment.		
(4)	Insurance Expense—Factory	6,000	
	Insurance Expense—Administrative	500	
	Prepaid Insurance		6,500
	To record and distribute cost of expired insurance.		
(5)	Direct Labor	9,000	
	Supervisors' Salaries	3,000	
	Indirect Labor	2,500	
	Selling Expenses	500	
	Accrued Payroll Payable		15,000
	To record and distribute cost of accrued payroll.		

Manufacturing Statement Columns

The Manufacturing Statement columns show the total of all manufacturing costs incurred during the period. This total is referred to as **cost to manufacture** for the period. The first element of total manufacturing cost is materials used in production. The beginning materials inventory plus materials purchases and related transportation costs represent the total cost of materials available for production. Therefore, Materials Inventory, Materials Purchases, and Transportation-In are included in the Manufacturing Statement debit column of the work sheet. Materials remaining in inventory at the end of the period were not used, so the ending balance in materials inventory is included in the Manufacturing Statement credit column in order to remove that amount from the cost of materials issued to production.

Direct labor incurred in production and all manufacturing overhead costs incurred during the period are included in the Manufacturing Statement debit column because these items increase the cost of goods produced during the period.

Cost to manufacture, the total of all manufacturing costs for the period, represent the costs added to production. **Cost of goods manufactured** represents the total cost of all goods completed during the period and removed from production.

To determine the cost of goods manufactured, add the beginning work in process inventory to total manufacturing costs for the period and subtract the ending work in process inventory. Thus, the beginning balance of Work in Process Inventory is included in the Manufacturing Statement debit column and the ending balance of Work in Process Inventory is included in the credit column. Note that *the excess of total debits over total credits represents the cost of goods manufactured and is the total cost of all goods completed during the period.*

THE CLOSING ENTRIES

Closing entries for a manufacturing company using periodic inventory procedure are slightly different from closing entries prepared for a merchandiser. This difference is due to the use of a Manufacturing Summary account, which records the cost of goods produced during the period. As shown below, all of the items in the Manufacturing Statement columns are closed to the Manufacturing Summary account first (this balance is the cost of goods manufactured); then all items in the Income Statement columns are closed to Income Summary. Finally, the Income Summary account is closed to Retained Earnings.

Closing the Accounts in the Manufacturing Statement Columns

The first closing entry closes all of the accounts appearing in the Manufacturing Statement debit column (Illustration 13.6) by crediting those accounts. The debit is to Manufacturing Summary for the subtotal of the Manufacturing Statement debit column ($1,294,000):

```
1990
Dec. 31   Manufacturing Summary  . . . . . . . . . .     1,294,000
                 Materials Inventory (beginning)  . . . . . .              40,000
                 Work in Process Inventory (beginning)  . . .              84,000
                 Materials Purchases . . . . . . . . . . .                480,000
                 Transportation-In . . . . . . . . . . . .                  6,000
                 Direct Labor . . . . . . . . . . . . . .                 380,000
                 Indirect Labor  . . . . . . . . . . . . .                 65,000
                 Supervisors' Salaries . . . . . . . . . .                130,000
                 Maintenance and Repairs . . . . . . . . .                 17,000
                 Utilities Expense . . . . . . . . . . . .                  5,000
                 Factory Taxes . . . . . . . . . . . . .                   15,000
                 Depreciation Expense—Factory Building  . .                20,000
                 Depreciation Expense—Factory
                     Equipment  . . . . . . . . . . . . .                  46,000
                 Insurance Expense—Factory  . . . . . . .                   6,000
          To close all accounts in the Manufacturing
          Statement debit column to Manufacturing
          Summary.
```

The second closing entry sets up the inventories that appear in the Manufacturing Statement credit column by debiting those accounts. The credit is to Manufacturing Summary for the subtotal of the Manufacturing Statement credit column ($118,000):

```
1990
Dec. 31   Materials Inventory (ending) . . . . . . . . . . .     38,000
          Work in Process Inventory (ending). . . . . . . . .     80,000
                 Manufacturing Summary  . . . . . . . . . . .              118,000
          To set up the ending inventories of materials and
          work in process.
```

At this point in the closing process, the Manufacturing Summary account has a debit balance of $1,176,000. This amount represents the cost of goods manufactured during the period.

Closing the Accounts in the Income Statement Columns

The third closing entry closes all of the accounts in the Income Statement debit column by crediting those accounts. The debit is to the Income Summary account for the subtotal of the Income Statement debit column, $1,745,500.

```
1990
Dec. 31   Income Summary  . . . . . . . . . . . . . .     1,745,500
                 Finished Goods Inventory (beginning)  . . .               56,000
                 Selling Expenses. . . . . . . . . . . . .                200,000
                 Administrative Expenses  . . . . . . . . .                185,000
                 Interest Expense . . . . . . . . . . . .                  20,000
                 Income Tax Expense . . . . . . . . . . .                 107,000
                 Uncollectible Accounts Expense . . . . . .                 1,500
                 Manufacturing Summary  . . . . . . . . .               1,176,000
          To close all accounts in the Income Statement
          debit column to Income Summary.
```

The fourth closing entry establishes the ending Finished Goods Inventory balance and closes the Sales account by debiting those accounts. The credit is to the Income Summary account for the subtotal of the Income Statement credit column, $1,860,000.

```
1990
Dec. 31   Finished Goods Inventory (ending) . . . . . . .    60,000
          Sales . . . . . . . . . . . . . . . . . . .      1,800,000
              Income Summary  . . . . . . . . . . . .                    1,860,000
          To set up the ending Finished Goods
          Inventory and close Sales to the Income
          Summary account.
```

At this point in the closing process the Income Summary account has a credit balance of $114,500, which is the amount of net income on the work sheet. The fifth (and last) closing entry closes the Income Summary account by debiting Income Summary and crediting Retained Earnings:

```
1990
Dec. 31   Income Summary  . . . . . . . . . . . . . . .   114,500
              Retained Earnings . . . . . . . . . . . . .                  114,500
          To close the Income Summary account to
          Retained Earnings.
```

FINANCIAL REPORTING BY MANUFACTURING COMPANIES

The major difference between a merchandiser and a manufacturer is in the types of inventories carried. Because inventories are reported on the balance sheet and also affect income (through cost of goods sold) on the income statement, the balance sheet and income statement of a merchandiser will differ from the balance sheet and income statement of a manufacturer.

The Statement of Cost of Goods Manufactured

Objective 4: Describe the difference in financial reporting between a merchandiser and a manufacturer and prepare a statement of cost of goods manufactured, an income statement, and a balance sheet for a manufacturer

The **statement of cost of goods manufactured** is used to support the cost of goods sold figure on the income statement. The two most important calculations on this statement are (1) the cost to manufacture and (2) the cost of goods manufactured. Careful attention should be given so that the terms *cost to manufacture* and *cost of goods manufactured* are not confused with one another or with *cost of goods sold*. The relationship between these terms is shown in Illustration 13.7. **Cost to manufacture** includes the costs of all *resources* put into production during the period. **Cost of goods manufactured** consists of the cost of all *goods completed* during the period; it includes "cost to manufacture" plus the beginning work in process inventory minus the ending work in process inventory. Cost of goods sold includes the cost of goods manufactured plus the beginning finished goods inventory minus the ending finished goods inventory.

Illustration 13.8 is the statement of cost of goods manufactured for the Jernigan Manufacturing Company for 1990. Note how the statement shows the costs incurred for materials, direct labor, and manufacturing

Illustration 13.7
RELATIONSHIP OF COST TO MANUFACTURE, COST OF GOODS MANUFACTURED, AND COST OF GOODS SOLD

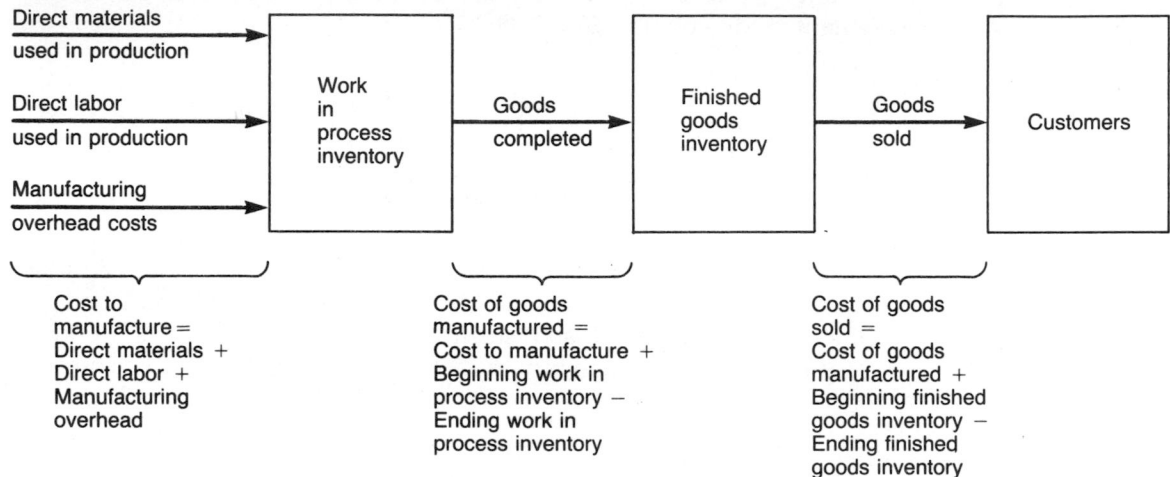

Cost to manufacture = Direct materials + Direct labor + Manufacturing overhead	Cost of goods manufactured = Cost to manufacture + Beginning work in process inventory − Ending work in process inventory	Cost of goods sold = Cost of goods manufactured + Beginning finished goods inventory − Ending finished goods inventory

Illustration 13.8
STATEMENT OF COSTS OF GOODS MANUFACTURED

JERNIGAN MANUFACTURING COMPANY
Statement of Cost of Goods Manufactured
For the Year Ended December 31, 1990

Materials:
Materials inventory, January 1	$ 40,000	
Materials purchases	480,000	
Transportation-in	6,000	
Materials available for use	$526,000	
Less: Materials inventory, December 31	38,000	
Materials used		$ 488,000
Direct labor		380,000

Manufacturing overhead:
Indirect labor	$ 65,000	
Supervisors' salaries	130,000	
Maintenance and repairs	17,000	
Utilities expense	5,000	
Factory taxes	15,000	
Depreciation expense—factory building	20,000	
Depreciation expense—factory equipment	46,000	
Insurance expense—factory	6,000	
Total manufacturing overhead		304,000
Cost to manufacture		$1,172,000
Add: Work in process inventory, January 1		84,000
		$1,256,000
Less: Work in process inventory, December 31		80,000
Cost of goods manufactured		$1,176,000

overhead; it describes the total of these three costs as **cost to manufacture** during the period. When beginning work in process inventory is added and ending work in process is deducted, we obtain cost of goods manufactured (completed). Cost of goods sold does not appear on the cost of goods manufactured statement but is shown on the income statement.

In this illustration, all materials (both direct and indirect) are included in the Materials Inventory account. Therefore, materials used consists of both direct materials and indirect materials. These amounts could have been separated and the amount of indirect materials could have been shown as a line item included under manufacturing overhead.

The Income Statement

Income statement preparation for a manufacturer may be considerably more complex than for a merchandiser. This is because a manufacturer incurs more types of costs than a merchandiser who buys goods that are ready for sale. In order to make the income statement more understandable to the readers of the financial statements, only the amount of cost of goods manufactured is shown on the income statement. A statement of cost of goods manufactured has already been prepared to support this amount. The income statement for the Jernigan Manufacturing Company is shown in Illustration 13.9. The data are taken directly from the work sheet in Illustration 13.6. Notice in Illustration 13.9 the relationship of the statement of cost of goods manufactured to the income statement. The cost of goods manufactured appears in the cost of goods sold section as

Illustration 13.9
INCOME STATEMENT OF A MANUFACTURER

JERNIGAN MANUFACTURING COMPANY Income Statement For the Year Ended December 31, 1990			
Operating revenues:			
Sales			$1,800,000
Cost of goods sold:			
Finished goods inventory, January 1		$ 56,000	
Cost of goods manufactured (see statement of			
cost of goods manufactured).		1,176,000	
Cost of goods available for sale		$1,232,000	
Less: Finished goods inventory, December 31, 1990 . .		60,000	
Cost of goods sold			1,172,000
Gross margin			$ 628,000
Operating expenses:			
Selling		$ 200,000	
Administrative		185,000	
Other operating expenses		1,500	
Total operating expenses			386,500
Income from operations			$ 241,500
Nonoperating revenues and expenses:			
Interest expense			20,000
Income before income taxes.			$ 221,500
Less: Income tax expense.			107,000
Net income			$ 114,500

an addition to the beginning inventory of finished goods to derive the cost of goods available for sale. Cost of goods manufactured is shown in the same place that purchases would be presented on a merchandiser's income statement. When financial statements are released to the public, it is common practice to include previous years' income statements alongside the current year's for comparison.

The Balance Sheet

Unlike the balance sheet for a merchandiser, which reports a single inventory amount, the balance sheet for a manufacturer typically shows materials, work in process, and finished goods inventories separately. Illustration 13.10 shows the balance sheet for the Jernigan Manufacturing Com-

Illustration 13.10
BALANCE SHEET OF A MANUFACTURER

JERNIGAN MANUFACTURING COMPANY			
Balance Sheet			
December 31, 1990			
Assets			
Current assets:			
Cash			$ 62,000
Accounts receivable		$160,000	
Less: Allowance for uncollectible accounts		2,000	158,000
Prepaid insurance			1,000
Inventories:			
Materials		$ 38,000	
Work in process		80,000	
Finished goods		60,000	178,000
Total current assets			$ 399,000
Property, plant, and equipment:			
Land			$ 32,000
Factory building		$400,000	
Less: Accumulated depreciation		60,000	340,000
Factory equipment		$460,000	
Less: Accumulated depreciation		138,000	322,000
Total property, plant, and equipment			$ 694,000
Total assets			$1,093,000
Liabilities and Stockholders' Equity			
Current liabilities:			
Accrued payroll payable		$ 15,000	
Accounts payable		60,000	$ 75,000
Long-term liabilities:			
Mortgage payable			200,000
Total liabilities			$ 275,000
Stockholders' equity:			
Common stock—$5 par value, 120,000 shares			
authorized, issued, and outstanding			$ 600,000
Retained earnings			218,000
Total stockholders' equity			$ 818,000
Total liabilities and stockholders' equity			$1,093,000

pany, using data taken from the work sheet in Illustration 13.6. A manufacturer's balance sheet may also show greater detail in the property, plant, and equipment section because of the significant investment in plant assets.

PERPETUAL INVENTORY PROCEDURE—THE GENERAL COST ACCUMULATION MODEL

Objective 5: Describe the general pattern of the flow of costs of a manufacturing company under perpetual inventory procedure and prepare journal entries

Periodic inventory systems are designed to determine the total cost of goods manufactured and the total cost of goods sold at the end of the accounting period so that financial statements can be prepared. But in many manufacturing companies, a primary accounting objective is to measure the cost of manufacturing a product line on a per unit basis during the period so that timely cost control and product pricing decisions can be made. Under perpetual procedure, unit product costs are determined during the period, rather than estimated at the end of the period, by transferring the cost of direct materials, direct labor, and manufacturing overhead to work in process and then to finished goods inventory accounts as goods are processed. Unit costs are available throughout the period because they can be obtained quickly without having to take a physical inventory. Before proceeding with an illustration of perpetual inventory procedure, it is important to first understand the basic pattern of cost accumulation under perpetual inventory procedure in a manufacturing environment.

Product and Cost Flows

Under perpetual procedure, accounting records are usually set up so that the flow of costs through the records will match the physical flow of products through the production process, as shown in Illustration 13.11.

The physical flow of the manufacturing process begins when materials are received from suppliers and placed in the materials storeroom. When needed for processing, the materials are moved from the materials storeroom to the production departments. During production, the materi-

Illustration 13.11
PRODUCT AND COST FLOWS

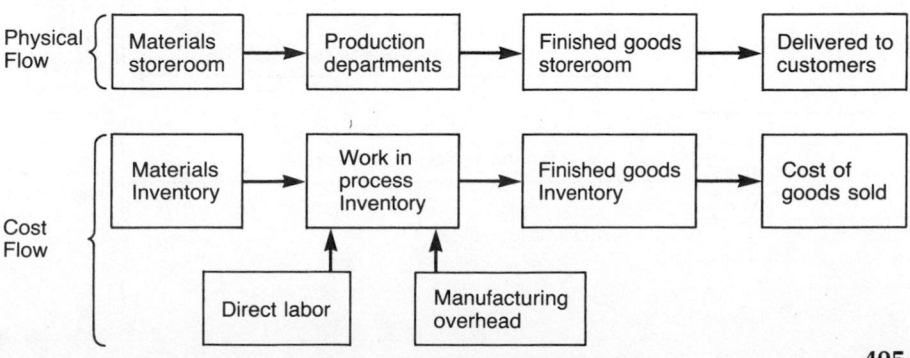

als are processed by laborers and machines and become partially manufactured products. At any time during production, these partially manufactured
products are collectively known as **work in process.** Eventually the products are completed, at which time they are known as **finished goods.** The
completed products are then moved to the finished goods storeroom for
later sale and delivery to customers.

The accounting flow of costs under perpetual procedure follows the
physical flow of the manufacturing process. The accounting records show
the flow of direct materials costs from Materials Inventory into Work in
Process Inventory. Here, the costs of direct labor and other factory services are added. When the products are completed and transferred to the
finished goods storeroom, their costs are removed from Work in Process
Inventory and assigned to Finished Goods Inventory. As the goods are
sold, the related costs are transferred from Finished Goods Inventory to
Cost of Goods Sold.

Illustration 13.12 shows the manufacturing cost flows along with the
selling, administrative, and financing costs of a company. These three ex-

Illustration 13.12
A MANUFACTURING COMPANY'S TOTAL OPERATIONS

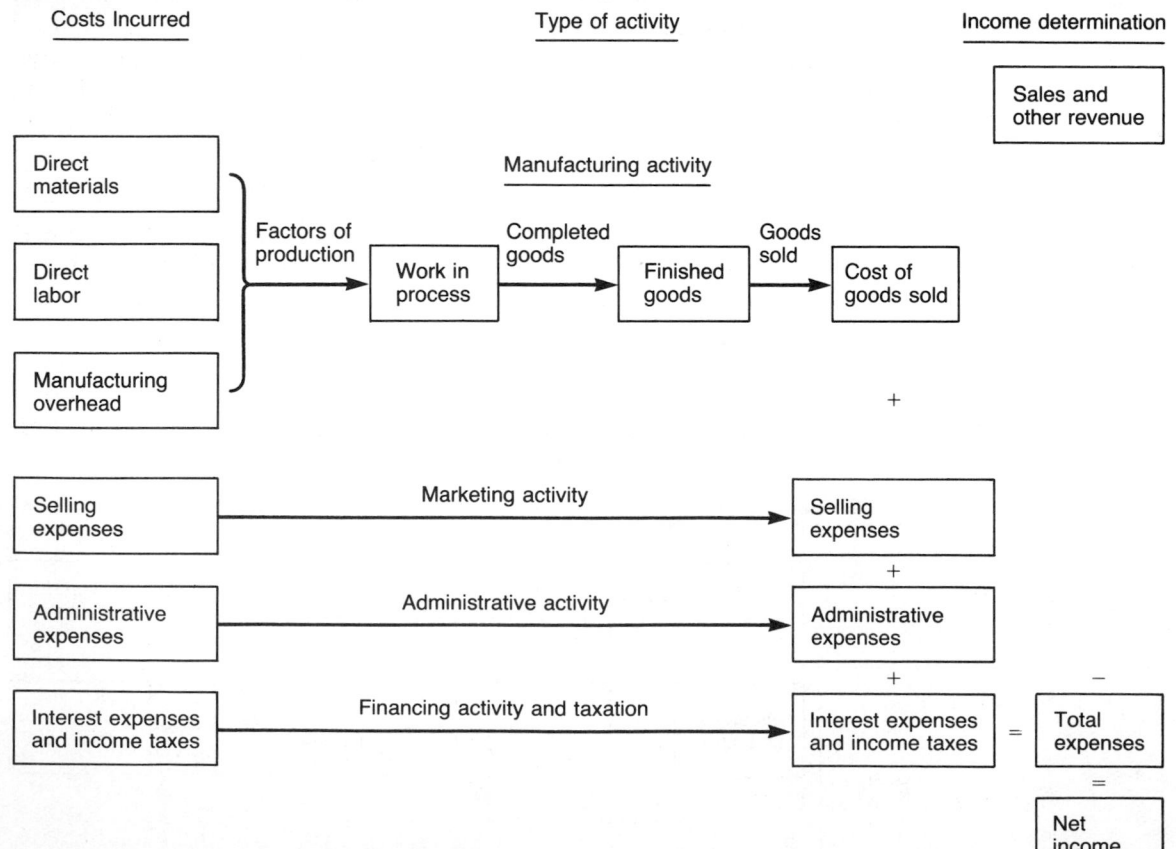

pense categories plus the cost of goods sold are the total expenses of the company and are deducted from sales to arrive at net income.

Manufacturing Cost Flows under Perpetual Inventory Procedure Illustrated

Illustration 13.13 uses T-accounts to trace the flow of materials, labor, and overhead costs through the production process to finished goods inventory. The sale of finished goods inventory to customers and the closing of the revenue and expense accounts for the year are then illustrated. Then the procedures followed in Illustration 13.13 are explained step by step, including examples of the journal entries necessary to record the transactions.

Flow of direct and indirect materials cost. During July, $40,000 of materials and supplies were purchased on account; $28,000 of direct materials and $2,000 of indirect materials (supplies) were issued to production from the storeroom. The required entries (keyed numerically to the entries in the T-accounts in Illustration 13.13, are:

(1)	Materials Inventory	40,000	
	Accounts Payable.		40,000
	To record purchases of materials and supplies on account.		
(2)	Work in Process Inventory	28,000	
	Manufacturing Overhead	2,000	
	Materials Inventory		30,000
	To record direct and indirect materials issued to production.		

Note that purchases of both direct and indirect materials (supplies) are debited to Materials Inventory. But when materials are issued to production, direct materials are debited to Work in Process Inventory, while indirect materials are recorded in Manufacturing Overhead because they are not easily traceable to specific products.

Flow of labor costs. Two kinds of labor costs must be accounted for in this procedure. *Payroll accounting* involves determining the total wages earned, the various deductions, and the net pay for each employee. *Labor costs accounting* involves determining which accounts are to be charged with what amount of labor costs. Under such a procedure, an account common to both groups is needed to tie together the separate accounting activities. This account is called Payroll Summary. The Payroll Summary account is a temporarily established (clearing) account that is debited when payrolls are prepared by the payroll department and credited when labor costs are distributed by the factory accounting department. Normally, the Payroll Summary account has a zero balance at the end of any accounting period. During the period, the account has a balance only because of the time lag between preparation of the payroll and classification of the payroll costs as direct or indirect labor.

The factory payrolls for July amounted to $75,000—direct labor of $60,000 and indirect labor of $15,000. Payroll withholdings amounted to

Illustration 13.13
COST AND REVENUE FLOWCHART (PERPETUAL INVENTORY SYSTEM)

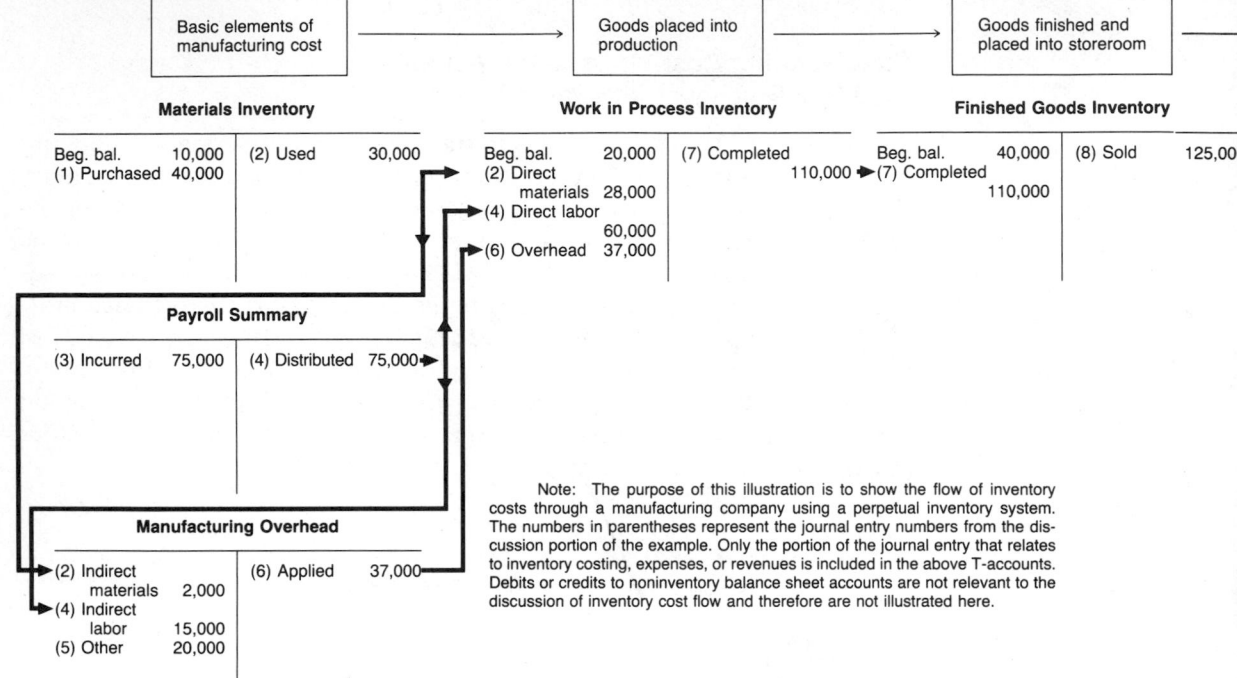

$3,500 social security taxes, $8,000 federal income taxes, and $500 union dues. The entries required are:

(3) Payroll Summary 75,000
     FICA Taxes Payable. 3,500
     Employees' Federal Income Taxes Payable 8,000
     Employees' Union Dues Payable 500
     Payroll Payable 63,000
    To record factory payroll and various withholdings.

(4) Work in Process Inventory 60,000
   Manufacturing Overhead. 15,000
     Payroll Summary 75,000
    To distribute labor costs for July.

Accrued payroll shown in entry *(3)* will be paid in cash to the employees, while the amounts withheld will be paid at a later date on the employees' behalf to the federal government (social security taxes and federal income taxes) and the labor union (union dues). Entry *(4)* adds to Work in Process Inventory all labor cost traceable to the products being manufactured (direct labor), while nontraceable labor costs (indirect labor) are transferred to Manufacturing Overhead.[1]

---

[1]Selling and administrative salaries are ignored since this chapter concentrates on aspects that are unique to a manufacturer.

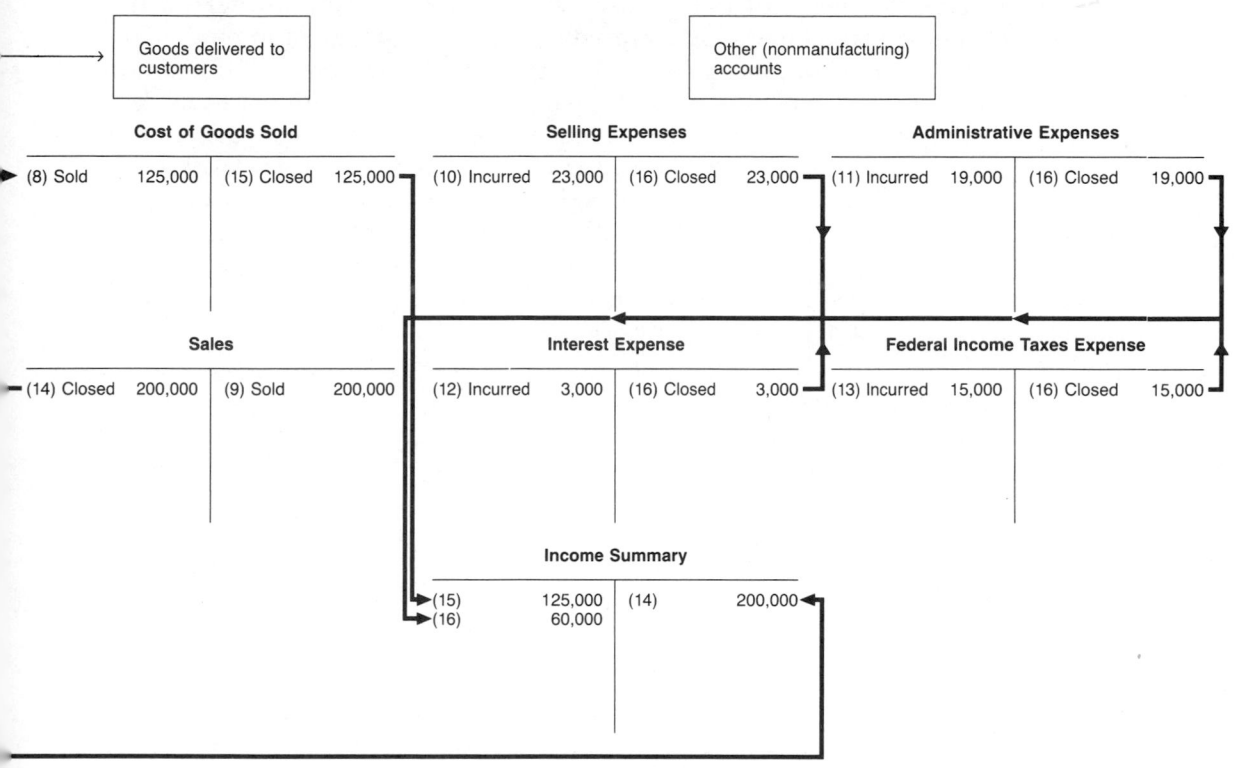

Flow of overhead costs. Indirect costs of operating the factory during the period included repairs of $1,000 paid in cash, property taxes of $1,500, expiration of prepaid equipment rent of $2,500, and insurance of $2,000, payroll taxes accrued of $3,500, utilities accrued of $4,000, and factory building depreciation of $5,500. Entry *(5)* below shows the recording of these indirect costs.

(5)	Manufacturing Overhead	20,000	
	Cash		1,000
	Property Taxes Payable		1,500
	Prepaid Rent		2,500
	Prepaid Insurance		2,000
	Payroll Taxes Payable		3,500
	Accounts Payable		4,000
	Accumulated Depreciation—Factory Building		5,500
	To record factory indirect costs for July.		

Manufacturing overhead costs are as much a part of a period's production cost as are the costs of direct materials and direct labor. Manufacturing overhead costs must, therefore, be added to the Work in Process Inventory account; this is done in entry *(6)* below:

(6)	Work in Process Inventory	37,000	
	Manufacturing Overhead		37,000
	To assign overhead to work in process.		

Manufacturing overhead costs are generally assigned to production using overhead rates. For purposes of this illustration however, it is assumed that all overhead incurred during July is assigned to production.

Flow of finished goods. As shown in Illustration 13.13 for product cost purposes Work in Process Inventory is charged with materials, labor, and overhead costs. When the goods are completed and transferred out of production, an entry is made to transfer their cost from Work in Process Inventory to Finished Goods Inventory. Assuming goods costing $110,000 were completed and transferred, the entry needed is:

(7)	Finished Goods Inventory	110,000	
	Work in Process Inventory		110,000
	To record transfer of completed goods.		

Now assume that goods costing $125,000 were sold on account for $200,000. Entries are required to transfer the cost of the inventory out of finished goods to cost of goods sold and to record the sale. The required entries are:

(8)	Costs of Goods Sold	125,000	
	Finished Goods Inventory		125,000
	To record cost of goods sold.		
(9)	Accounts Receivable	200,000	
	Sales		200,000
	To record sales on account.		

To complete the explanation of the entries in Illustration 13.13 assume that selling expenses of $23,000, administrative expenses of $19,000, interest expense of $3,000, and federal income taxes of $15,000 were incurred in July. The required entries are:

(10)	Selling Expenses	23,000	
	Various asset and liability accounts.		23,000
	To record selling expenses incurred in July.		
(11)	Administrative Expenses	19,000	
	Various asset and liability accounts		19,000
	To record administrative expenses incurred in July.		
(12)	Interest Expense.	3,000	
	Interest Payable		3,000
	To record interest expense incurred in July.		
(13)	Federal Income Taxes	15,000	
	Federal Income Taxes Payable		15,000
	To record estimated income taxes for July.		

Subsidiary records or accounts would be kept for the various types of selling and administrative expenses incurred. The credits in entries *(10)* and *(11)* would be to accounts such as Cash, Accounts Payable, Salaries Payable, Accumulated Depreciation and Prepaid Expenses.

Although the accounts are usually closed only at the end of the accounting year, entry *(14)* records the closing of the Sales revenue account for the month of July as an illustration of the annual entry:

(14) Sales. 200,000
        Income Summary   200,000
    To close Sales revenue account.

Entries *(15)* and *(16)* are required to close the expense accounts:

(15) Income Summary 125,000
        Cost of Goods Sold   125,000
    To close Cost of Goods Sold account.

(16) Income Summary 60,000
        Selling Expenses.   23,000
        Administrative Expenses   19,000
        Interest Expense.   3,000
        Federal Income Taxes Expense   15,000
    To close other expense account.

Entries *(15)* and *(16)* could be combined into one entry. Although it is not shown in Illustration 13.13 the closing process would be completed by transferring net income to the Retained Earnings account.

Income Summary 15,000
    Retained Earnings   15,000
    To close Income Summary.

Use of a Work Sheet under Perpetual Procedure

A manufacturing company using perpetual procedure can use the same work sheet as illustrated in Chapter 3. The work sheet has columns labeled Trial Balance, Adjustments, Adjusted Trial Balance, Income Statement, and Balance Sheet. Use of a set of columns for the Statement of Retained Earnings is optional. The amounts shown in the trial balance for materials inventory, work in process inventory, and finished goods inventory will be the end of period balances. The amounts would be carried to the Balance Sheet debit column. The cost of goods sold amount will be included with the other expenses in the trial balance. All other steps in preparing the work sheet are as described in Chapter 3 and will not be illustrated here.

SUMMARY

This chapter focused on accounting for inventory and cost of goods sold for a manufacturer. Unlike a merchandiser (retailer or wholesaler), who purchases and resells goods that are already in their finished state, a manufacturer purchases raw materials and uses equipment and labor to process those materials into products for sale. While the merchandiser has only one inventory—merchandise available for sale—a manufacturer has three inventories—unprocessed materials, partially complete work in process, and ready-for-sale finished goods.

Manufacturing costs can be divided into direct materials, direct labor, and manufacturing overhead. Direct materials are materials that are (1) included in the finished product, (2) used only in the manufacture of the product, and (3) clearly and easily traceable to the product. Direct labor is the cost of labor by employees actually working on materials to convert them into finished goods. Manufacturing overhead includes all other manufacturing costs, except those that are accounted for as direct material or direct labor. Prime cost is a term used to refer to the sum of direct materials cost and direct labor cost, and conversion cost refers to the sum of direct labor cost and manufacturing overhead cost.

Product costs are costs incurred in the manufacture of products. They are associated with products rather than with periods of time. Product costs are considered to be the cost of manufacturing inventory, and they are expensed only when the related inventory is sold. Period costs, on the other hand, are more closely related to periods of time than to products produced. Period costs are expensed in the period in which they are incurred. All selling and nonmanufacturing administrative costs are treated as period costs.

Costs that remain constant in total amount over a wide range of variations in the level of manufacturing activity are considered to be fixed costs. Variable costs, on the other hand, vary in total amount directly with changes in the level of manufacturing activity.

Like merchandisers, manufacturers can use either periodic or perpetual inventory procedure to account for inventory costs. When a manufacturer uses periodic inventory procedure, the Materials Purchases, Transportation-In, Materials Purchase Returns and Allowances, and Materials Inventory accounts are used in the same manner as they are by a merchandiser. In addition, the manufacturer has to account for work in process and finished goods inventories. Use of a work sheet aids in the preparation of the necessary adjusting and closing entries to compute ending inventories and cost of goods sold.

When a periodic inventory system is in use, inventory quantities are determined at year-end by making a physical count of the materials, work in process, and finished goods on hand. After the quantity of these inventories has been established, their cost must be determined. Cost of the raw materials inventory may be determined by multiplying purchase cost per unit of material by the amount of material on hand. To obtain the cost of the work in process and finished goods inventories, the manufacturer must estimate the per unit cost of direct materials used, direct labor used, and manufacturing overhead incurred in producing each unit. The amounts of materials may differ, while the amounts of labor and overhead will differ, for units in work in process inventory and units in finished goods inventory. Direct materials cost per unit can be established by referring to a materials specification list for the product and knowing when materials are added in the production process. Direct labor cost per unit is normally based on observations made by management to determine the normal amount of time it takes workers to complete the product. Manufacturing overhead costs must be allocated to the product based on a manufacturing overhead rate, which expresses overhead costs in relation to some measure of manufacturing activity.

Under perpetual inventory procedure, accounting records are set up so that the flow of costs through the records matches the physical flow of products through the production process. All materials purchases are debited to the Materials Inventory account. Materials issued to production are credited to Materials Inventory; direct materials are debited to the Work in Process Inventory account, and indirect materials are debited to the Manufacturing Overhead account. All labor costs are recorded in a Payroll Summary account. Direct labor costs are credited to Payroll Summary and debited to Work in Process Inventory, while indirect labor costs are credited to Payroll Summary and debited to Manufacturing Overhead. Other factory overhead costs are also debited to Manufacturing Overhead. Overhead applied to production is credited to Manufacturing Overhead and debited to Work in Process Inventory. The cost of goods completed is transferred from the Work in Process Inventory account to the Finished Goods Inventory account, and the cost of goods sold is transferred from Finished Goods Inventory to Cost of Goods Sold.

Perpetual inventory systems are superior to periodic inventory systems in their ability to provide information about manufacturing costs during the accounting period so that timely cost control and pricing decisions can be made. Under a periodic inventory system, total cost of goods manufactured and total cost of goods sold are determined only at the end of the accounting period, and the per unit production costs can only be estimated. A perpetual inventory system, by contrast, provides per unit production cost information throughout the period. A perpetual inventory system involves considerably more detailed accounting records.

The balance sheet and income statement of a manufacturer differ from those of a merchandiser. The statement of cost of goods manufactured is a statement used by a manufacturer to show cost to manufacture and cost of goods manufactured for the period. Only cost of goods manufactured is shown in the income statement in order to make the income statement more understandable to readers of the financial statements. The balance sheet for a manufacturer typically shows materials, work in process, and finished goods inventories separately. A manufacturer's balance sheet may also show greater detail in property, plant, and equipment because of the significant investment in plant assets.

In Chapters 14 and 15, you continue your study of manufacturing costs. Without efficient cost systems for accumulating manufacturing costs, manufacturing companies cannot evaluate past performance and adequately plan for the future.

Objective 6: Define and use correctly the new terms in the glossary

NEW TERMS INTRODUCED IN CHAPTER 13

Administrative costs Nonmanufacturing costs that include the costs of top administrative functions and various staff departments such as accounting, data processing, and personnel (479).

Conversion cost The sum of direct labor and manufacturing overhead costs (479).

Cost   A financial measure of the resources used or given up to achieve a stated purpose (476).

Cost of goods manufactured   Consists of the costs of all goods completed during the period; total manufacturing cost plus beginning work in process inventory minus ending work in process inventory (489, 491).

Cost to manufacture   Includes the costs of all resources put into production during the period (489, 491, 492).

Direct labor   Labor costs of all employees actually working on materials to convert them into finished goods (477).

Direct materials   Materials that are (1) included in the finished product, (2) used only in the manufacture of the product, and (3) clearly and easily traceable to the product (477).

Factory cost   See Manufacturing cost.

Finished goods   Completed manufactured products ready to be sold; also, Finished Goods Inventory is the title of an inventory account maintained for such products (476, 496).

Fixed costs   Costs that remain constant in total amount over wide variations in the level of manufacturing activity (481).

Indirect labor   The services of factory employees that cannot or will not, for practical reasons, be traced to the products being manufactured (478).

Indirect materials   Materials used in the manufacture of a product that cannot or will not, for practical reasons, be traced directly to the products being manufactured (477).

Manufacturing cost   The cost incurred to produce or create a product. It includes direct materials, direct labor, and manufacturing overhead costs (477).

Manufacturing overhead   All manufacturing costs except for those costs accounted for as direct materials or direct labor (478).

Manufacturing overhead rate   Expresses manufacturing overhead costs in relation to some measure of manufacturing activity (484).

Materials   Unprocessed items that will be used in the manufacturing process (476).

Period costs   Costs related more closely to periods of time than to products produced. Period costs cannot be traced directly to the manufacture of a specific product; they are expensed in the period in which they are incurred (480).

Prime cost   The sum of the direct materials costs and direct labor costs incurred to manufacture a product (478).

Product costs   (See also Manufacturing cost.) Costs incurred in the manufacture of products and assigned to units of the product produced by the manufacturing company. These costs include costs of direct materials, direct labor, and manufacturing overhead (479).

Selling costs   Costs incurred to obtain customer orders and get the finished product into the customer's possession (479).

Statement of cost of goods manufactured   An accounting report showing the cost to manufacture and the cost of goods manufactured (491).

Variable costs   Costs that directly vary in total amount with changes in the volume of production activity or output (481).

Work in process Partially manufactured products; also, Work in Process Inventory is the title of an inventory account maintained for such products (476, 496).

DEMONSTRATION PROBLEM 13–1

Data needed to prepare a work sheet of the David Manufacturing Company are given below. The company uses a periodic inventory system.

1. The December 31, 1990, trial balance was taken from the general ledger of the company. [The inventories in the trial balance are those of January 1, 1990.]

2. The only entry in the Retained Earnings account during the year ended December 31, 1990, was a debit of $27,000 for the declaration of cash dividends.

3. The inventories at December 31, 1990, were as follows:

   a. Materials inventory $36,000
   b. Work in process inventory 66,000
   c. Finished goods inventory 51,000

Adjustments were as follows:

1. The allowance for uncollectible accounts is to be adjusted to 5% of the accounts receivable.

2. Accrued wages and salaries are:

   Direct labor $3,600
   Sales salaries 6,000
   Office and officers' salaries 9,000

3. Interest on the mortgage bonds was last paid on July 1.

4. Factory supplies used, $3,300.

5. Factory insurance expired during the period, $1,800.

6. Accrued factory taxes, $2,100.

7. Depreciation of factory building, $6,000.

8. Depreciation of machinery and equipment, $34,500.

9. Depreciation of office equipment, $1,500.

The Trial Balance columns of the work sheet and the proper totals of other columns on the work sheet have already been completed (see pages 506–507).

Required:

Prepare the necessary adjusting entries for the work sheet, and extend the amounts in the work sheet Trial Balance columns (plus or minus) any adjustments to their proper columns.

Solution to demonstration problem 13–1

The adjusting entries for the David Manufacturing Company for the year ended December 31, 1990, are shown below:

(1)	Uncollectible Accounts Expense	5,700	
	Allowance for Uncollectible Accounts		5,700
	To increase allowance to 5% of outstanding accounts receivable:		
	0.05 × $120,000 = $6,000; $6,000 − $300 = $5,700.		

THE DAVID MANUFACTURING COMPANY
Work Sheet for the Year Ended December 31, 1990

Account Titles	Trial Balance Debit	Trial Balance Credit	Adjustments Debit	Adjustments Credit	Manufacturing Statement Debit	Manufacturing Statement Credit	Income Statement Debit	Income Statement Credit	Balance Sheet Debit	Balance Sheet Credit
Cash	46,500								46,500	
Accounts Receivable	120,000								120,000	
Allowance for Uncollectible Accounts		300		(1) 5,700						6,000
Prepaid Factory Insurance	2,700			(5) 1,800					900	
Materials Inventory	30,000				30,000	36,000			36,000	
Work in Process Inventory	63,000				63,000	66,000			66,000	
Finished Goods Inventory	42,000						42,000	51,000	51,000	
Factory Supplies on Hand	4,200			(4) 3,300					900	
Land	24,000								24,000	
Factory Building	300,000								300,000	
Accumulated Depreciation—Factory Building		30,000		(7) 6,000						36,000
Machinery and Equipment	345,000								345,000	
Accumulated Depreciation—Machinery and Equipment		69,000		(8) 34,500						103,500
Small Tools	1,050								1,050	
Office Equipment	27,000								27,000	
Accumulated Depreciation—Office Equipment		3,900		(9) 1,500						5,400
Accounts Payable		44,100								44,100
Income and FICA Taxes Withheld		3,900								3,900
Mortgage Bonds Payable, 3%		150,000								150,000
Common Stock		450,000								450,000
Retained Earnings		155,400								155,400
Sales		1,200,000						1,200,000		
Sales Discounts	6,000						6,000			
Materials Purchases	360,000				360,000					
Purchase Returns		3,000				3,000				
Transportation-In	4,500				4,500					
Direct Labor	276,000		(2) 3,600		279,600					
Supervisors' Salaries	96,000				96,000					

Account	Trial Balance Dr	Trial Balance Cr	Adjustments Dr	Adjustments Cr	Cost of Goods Manufactured Dr	Cost of Goods Manufactured Cr	Income Statement Dr	Income Statement Cr	Balance Sheet Dr	Balance Sheet Cr
Indirect Labor	24,000				24,000					
Building Maintenance and Repairs	3,300				3,300					
Maintenance of Machinery and Equipment	9,600				9,600					
Heat, Light, Power	3,600				3,600					
Factory Taxes Expense	14,700		(6) 2,100		16,800					
Small Tools Expense	4,650				4,650					
General Factory Expense	8,400				8,400					
Advertising and Sales Promotion	32,400						32,400			
Sales Salaries	90,000		(2) 6,000				96,000			
Sales Travel Expense	5,100						5,100			
Sales Office Expense	10,950						10,950			
Office and Officers' Salaries	135,000		(2) 9,000				144,000			
Stationery and Supplies Expense	3,300						3,300			
Office Taxes, Property, and Payroll	7,200						7,200			
Federal Income Tax Expense	12,600						12,600			
Mortgage Bond Interest Expense	2,250		(3) 2,250				4,500			
Gain on Sale of Plant Assets		5,400						5,400		
	2,115,000	2,115,000								
Uncollectible Accounts Expense			(1) 5,700				5,700			
Factory Insurance Expense			(5) 1,800		1,800					
Wages and Salaries Payable				(2) 18,600						18,600
Bond Interest Payable				(3) 2,250						2,250
Factory Supplies Used			(4) 3,300		3,300					
Taxes Payable				(6) 2,100						2,100
Depreciation Expense—Factory Building			(7) 6,000		6,000					
Depreciation Expense—Machinery and Equipment			(8) 34,500		34,500					
Depreciation Expense—Office Equipment			(9) 1,500				1,500			
			75,750	75,750	949,050	105,000	371,250	1,256,400	1,018,350	977,250
Manufacturing Summary (Cost of Goods Manufactured)						844,050	844,050			
					949,050	949,050	1,215,300	1,256,400		
Net Income							41,100			41,100
							1,256,400	1,256,400	1,018,350	1,018,350

(2)	Direct Labor	3,600	
	Sales Salaries	6,000	
	Office and Officers' Salaries	9,000	
	Wages and Salaries Payable		18,600
	To record accrual of salaries and wages.		

(3)	Mortgage Bond Interest Expense	2,250	
	Bond Interest Payable		2,250
	To record accrual of 6 months' interest on bonds ($150,000 × 0.03 × ½).		

(4)	Factory Supplies Expense	3,300	
	Factory Supplies on Hand		3,300
	To record factory supplies used.		

(5)	Factory Insurance Expense	1,800	
	Prepaid Factory Insurance		1,800
	To record expired factory insurance.		

(6)	Factory Taxes Expense	2,100	
	Taxes Payable		2,100
	To record the accrual of factory taxes.		

(7)	Depreciation Expense—Factory Building	6,000	
	Accumulated Depreciation—Factory Building		6,000
	To record depreciation on factory building.		

(8)	Depreciation Expense—Machinery and Equipment	34,500	
	Accumulated Depreciation—Machinery and Equipment . .		34,500
	To record depreciation on machinery and equipment.		

(9)	Depreciation Expense—Office Equipment	1,500	
	Accumulated Depreciation—Office Equipment		1,500
	To record depreciation on office equipment.		

The completed work sheet for the David Manufacturing Company for the year ended December 31, 1990, is shown on pages 506 and 507.

QUESTIONS

1. Identify the three broad classifications of costs incurred by manufacturing firms. Indicate why it is important that costs not be incorrectly classified.

2. Identify the three elements of cost incurred in manufacturing a product, and indicate the distinguishing characteristics of each.

3. Why might a firm claim that the total cost of employing a person is $10.30 per hour even though the employee's wage rate is $6.50 per hour? How should this difference be classified, and why?

4. In general, what is the relationship between cost flows in the accounts and the flow of physical products through a factory?

5. What is meant by the term *product cost*? State the general principle under which product costs are accumulated.

6. What is the general content of a statement of cost of goods manufactured and sold? What is its relationship to the income statement?

7. What is the typical accounting for the overtime wage premium paid a direct laborer? Why? Under what circumstances might an alternative accounting be considered preferable?

8. Why are certain costs referred to as period costs? What are the major types of period costs incurred by a manufacturer?

9. Why is the manufacturing overhead rate determined prior to the year in which it is used?

10. What is a manufacturing overhead rate? Why is the application of overhead to production through the use of such a rate almost an absolute necessity?

EXERCISES

Prepare journal entries for the issuance of materials

1. During a given week, $150,000 of direct materials and $30,000 of indirect materials were issued by the storeroom to the production department. Give the required journal entry or entries under perpetual inventory procedures.

Prepare journal entry for incurrence and distribution of labor costs

2. As prepared by the payroll department, the week's factory labor payroll amounted to $240,000, from which the following were withheld: social security taxes, $12,000; union dues, $3,500; and federal income taxes, $25,500. The payroll is to be paid next Friday. Analysis of the payroll shows that it consists of $200,000 of direct labor and the following wages and salaries: inspectors, $8,400; supervisors, $5,600; electricians, $7,200; timekeepers, $4,300; janitors, $6,800; and warehousemen, $7,700. Give the entry to record the incurrence of the above labor costs and their distribution to proper accounts.

Classify costs as direct materials, direct labor, manufacturing overhead, selling, or administrative

3. Given below are some costs incurred by an automobile manufacturer. Classify these costs as direct materials, direct labor, manufacturing overhead, selling, or administrative.
   a. Salary of the cost accountant.
   b. Cost of automobile radios installed in autos.
   c. Cost of stationery used in president's office.
   d. Supplies used in cost accountant's office.
   e. Wages of a factory inspector.
   f. Payroll taxes on assembly-line worker's wages.
   g. Repair parts used to repair factory machine.
   h. Cost of labor services to install radios in autos.
   i. Depreciation on automobiles driven by company's top executives.
   j. Cost of magazines purchased for the engineering department.

Indicate variable costs

4. Review the list of costs in Exercise 3, and indicate which of the costs listed are likely to vary directly with the number of autos produced.

Compute cost of goods manufactured and sold and prepare entry for transfer of completed goods

5. The following data pertain to the Horton Company for the year ended June 30, 1991:

Direct materials used	$ 600,000
Direct labor	1,200,000
Work in process, 7/1/90	120,000
Work in process, 6/30/91	180,000
Finished goods, 7/1/90	300,000
Finished goods, 6/30/91	420,000
Manufacturing overhead.	1,800,000

Compute the cost of goods manufactured and sold. Also, prepare one entry to summarize the transfer of completed goods for the year.

Determine the proper allocation of labor costs

6. Bobby Knight was paid for 46 hours of work as a plumber for Bill's Plumbing, Inc., for last week. His total wages amounted to $686—40 hours at $14 per hour plus 6 hours of Saturday work at $21 per hour (time and a half). He worked 30 hours of regular time on Job 113 and 10 hours of regular time and 5 hours of overtime on Job 114. He was idle one hour on Saturday, waiting for the customer to come home. Saturday work is common in the plumbing industry.

How much of the wages paid to Bobby Knight should be considered a cost of Job 113? Of Job 114? As manufacturing overhead? Explain.

Determine the proper allocation of purchase costs

7. Palmer Company sells 25-inch television sets which it assembles from purchased parts. In 1990 it purchased 10,000 picture tubes at $40 each. Of these 10,000 tubes, 30 were used by Palmer in testing their product life, 6 were used to replace burned-out tubes in display models, and 9,100 were issued to production. Of the 9,100 placed in production, 7,000 were in units completed, of which 5,900 were sold.

As of December 31, 1990, how much of the $400,000 cost of purchased picture tubes should appear in each of the following accounts:

a. Materials Inventory

b. Work in Process Inventory

c. Finished Goods Inventory

d. Manufacturing Overhead

e. Selling Expense

f. Cost of Goods Sold

Compute manufacturing overhead rate

8. Massey Company has total manufacturing overhead costs of $18,900 for the week ended April 19. The company received a total of 3,150 hours of direct labor services from its employees that were chargeable to specific units of the product. What is Massey's Manufacturing overhead rate for the week ended April 19?

Calculate estimated ending inventory costs

9. The following data pertain to the Click Company for the year ended December 31, 1990:

Estimated direct materials cost per unit included in work in process inventory for product X	$33
Estimated direct materials cost per unit included in finished goods inventory for product X	33
Estimated direct labor cost per unit included in work in process inventory for product X	25
Estimated direct labor cost per unit included in finished goods inventory for product X	48
Manufacturing overhead rate	75% of direct labor costs
Units of product X included in work in process inventory	450 units
Units of product X included in finished goods inventory	225 units

Compute the ending work in process inventory and finished goods inventory for product X.

*Prepare a cost and
revenue flowchart
under perpetual
inventory procedure*

10. The Hess Company uses perpetual inventory procedure. The following are data for the month of July:

1. Materials purchased on account, $117,000.
2. Direct materials issued, $135,000.
3. Repairs and maintenance on factory buildings, $13,500.
4. Factory depreciation, taxes, and utilities, $112,500.
5. Factory payroll for July, $81,000, including $7,200 of indirect labor.
6. Manufacturing overhead is assigned in full to production.
7. Cost of goods completed and transferred, $371,250.
8. Cost of goods sold, $360,000.
9. Sales for the month on account, $675,000.

The July 1 inventory account balances were:

Materials	$36,000
Work in process	90,000
Finished goods	27,000

Prepare a cost and revenue flowchart similar to the one in Illustration 13.13, incorporating the above data.

Prepare entries

11. Prepare journal entries to record transactions in Exercise 10.

*Prepare a statement
of cost of goods
manufactured*

12. The following data were taken from the completed work sheet of Marge's Corner Manufacturing Company at December 31, 1990:

Direct labor	$450,000	Materials purchases	$270,000
Indirect labor.	56,250	Transportation-in	13,500
Factory supervision. . . .	99,000	Insurance expense	
Factory supplies used . .	13,500	(70% applicable to	
Inventories, Jan. 1:		factory)	22,500
Materials	18,000	Payroll taxes (factory)	67,500
Work in process	45,000	Depreciation expense	
Finished goods.	40,500	(80% applicable to	
Inventories, Dec. 31:		factory)	90,000
Materials	27,000	Repairs and maintenance	
Work in process	56,250	expense.	3,375
Finished goods	49,500	Utilities expense	
		(70% applicable to	
		factory)	6,750

From the above data, prepare a statement of cost of goods manufactured for Marge's Corner Manufacturing Company.

PROBLEMS

*Identify variable,
fixed, direct
materials, direct
labor, and
manufacturing
overhead costs,
and comment*

13–1. A number of costs that would affect business decisions in the factory operations of different companies are listed below. These costs may be fixed or variable with respect to some measure of volume or output, and they may be classified as direct materials (DM), direct labor (DL), or manufacturing overhead (MO).

DM (1) Glue used to attach labels to bottles containing a patented medicine.
(2) Compressed air used in operating machines turning over products.
(3) Insurance on factory building and equipment.
(4) A production department supervisor's salary.

(5) Rent on factory machinery.
(6) Iron ore and coke in a steel mill.
(7) Oil, gasoline, and grease for forklift trucks.
(8) Services of painters in building construction.
(9) Cutting oils used in machining operations.
(10) Cost of food served in a factory employees' cafeteria.
(11) Payroll taxes and fringe benefits related to direct labor.
(12) The plant electricians' salaries.
(13) Sand for a glass manufacturer.
(14) Copy editor's salary for a book publisher.

Required:

a. List the numbers 1 through 14 down the left side of a sheet of paper. After each number, write the letters V (for variable) or F (for fixed) and either DM (for direct materials), DL (for direct labor), or MO (for manufacturing overhead) to show how you would classify the similarly numbered cost item given above.

b. With which of your own answers given for part (**a**) could you take issue? Discuss.

Compute manufacturing overhead costs and prepare journal entries for cost of goods completed and sold

13–2. Selected data for Furman Company for the month of April are as follows:

Materials issued (including $15,000 of indirect materials) . . .	$ 555,000
Factory payrolls (all direct labor except $30,000)	630,000
Finished goods inventory, April 1	210,000
Finished goods inventory, April 30	240,000
Total costs charged to Work in Process in April	1,740,000
Work in process, April 1	180,000
Work in process, April 30	210,000

Required:

a. Compute the manufacturing overhead assigned to production in April.

b. Prepare journal entries to record the cost of goods completed and sold.

Use T-accounts to analyze the flow of costs and revenues

13–3. The following data relate to the Pat Company for the month of July.

(1) Purchased materials on account, $210,000.
(2) Materials issued, $240,000, including $6,000 of indirect materials.
(3) Factory payroll for the month, $276,000.
(4) Payroll costs distributed; direct labor, $240,000; and indirect labor, $36,000.
(5) Other overhead costs incurred: factory depreciation, $210,000; property taxes, $48,000; repairs, $30,000; utilities, $24,000; and other, $18,000.
(6) Selling expenses incurred, $180,000; and administrative expenses incurred, $165,000.
(7) Actual overhead is assigned to production.
(8) Cost of goods completed and transferred, $780,000.
(9) Sales on account, $1,200,000.
(10) Cost of goods sold, $750,000.

July 1 inventory balances were:

Materials	$ 54,000
Work in process	66,000
Finished goods	126,000

Required:

Use T-accounts to analyze the above transactions.

Prepare statement of costs of goods manufactured and sold, an income statement and compute direct labor cost per unit

13–4. The production and revenue producing activities of the Claxton Company for the year ended December 31, 1990, are summarized below:

Sales	$1,200,000	Sales commission	$105,000
Factory maintenance	21,000	Interest expense	15,000
Factory depreciation	48,000	Direct labor cost	270,000
Factory insurance and taxes	24,000	Indirect materials	19,500
Indirect labor	45,000	Advertising expense	75,000
Payroll-related costs—factory	72,000	Administrative salaries	144,000
Other administrative expenses	36,000	Other selling expenses	45,000
Factory utilities	16,500	Work in process 1/1/90	60,000
Work in process, 12/31/90	63,000	Finished goods 1/1/90	45,000
Finished goods, 12/31/90	120,000	Direct materials	192,000

Federal income taxes are estimated at 40% of net income before such taxes. A total of 60,000 units was manufactured in 1990.

Required:

a. Prepare a statement of cost of goods manufactured and sold,

b. Prepare an income statement, and

c. Compute the direct labor cost per unit and the fixed overhead cost per unit.

Prepare a cost of goods manufactured statement and an income statement

13–5. The information given below was taken from a work sheet prepared by the Singletary Company on December 31, 1990:

Account Titles	Manufacturing Statement		Income Statement	
	Debit	Credit	Debit	Credit
Sales				1,387,500
Materials Purchases	178,125			
Materials Purchase Returns		9,375		
Transportation-In	1,875			
Inventories:				
Materials	22,500	18,750		
Work in Process	48,750	40,500		
Finished Goods			67,500	56,250
Direct Labor	210,000			
Indirect Materials	6,000			
Overtime Wages	12,000			
Payroll Taxes–Factory	63,750			
Utilities Expense	6,375			
Maintenance and Repairs	2,250			
Selling Expenses			225,000	
Administrative Expenses			337,500	
Property Taxes–Factory	1,650			
Income Tax Expense			75,000	
Insurance Expense–Factory	2,250			
Depreciation Expense–				
Factory Building	11,250			
Depreciation Expense–				
Factory Equipment	15,000			
	581,775	68,625		
Manufacturing Summary				
(Cost of goods manufactured)		513,150	513,150	
	581,775	581,775	1,218,150	1,443,750
Net Income			225,600	
			1,443,750	1,443,750

Required:

a. Prepare a statement of cost of goods manufactured for the Singletary Company for the year ended, December 31, 1990.

b. Prepare an income statement for the Singletary Company for the year ended December 31, 1990.

Prepare closing entries

13-6. Refer to the information given for the Singletary Company in Problem 13-5. Prepare all necessary entries to set up ending inventory balances and to close the books for 1990.

Compute manufacturing overhead rate and use rate to compute inventories; compute cost of goods manufactured and sold

13-7. The Whirl Company incurred the following manufacturing costs for the first quarter of 1990:

Materials used	$576,900
Direct labor	930,000
Manufacturing overhead	744,000

The work in process and finished goods inventories were $97,200 and $402,000, respectively, on January 1, 1990. The production department provided the following information relating to the cost of the work in process and finished goods inventories on March 31, 1990:

		Estimated Cost per Unit	
	Units in Inventory	Direct Materials	Direct Labor
Work in process:			
Product A	750	$12.00	$30.00
Product B	1,500	18.00	15.00
Finished goods:			
Product A	3,000	27.00	45.00
Product B	3,915	25.20	36.00

Required:

a. Compute the manufacturing overhead rate, based on direct labor cost.

b. Using the rate computed in (a), determine the cost of the inventories of work in process and finished goods at March 31, 1990.

c. Compute the cost of goods manufactured and the cost of goods sold during the first quarter of 1990. (Prepare a Statement of Cost of Goods Manufactured and Sold).

Prepare journal entries using perpetual inventory procedure and use T-accounts to analyze inventory balances

13-8. The Matthews Company uses perpetual inventory procedure. Assume inventories at August 1, 1990, were as follows:

Materials inventory	$46,200
Work in process inventory	67,200
Finished goods inventory	94,500

Transactions:

1. During August, $168,000 of raw materials were purchased on account and $136,500 were issued to production.

2. The factory payrolls (gross) for August were $199,500. Direct labor was $147,000, and indirect labor was $52,500. Payroll withholdings included $12,600 of FICA taxes, $37,800 of federal income taxes, and $3,150 of union dues.
3. The indirect costs of production included machinery repairs of $3,150, equipment rental of $6,300, utilities of $21,000, payroll taxes of $12,600, amortization of prepaid insurance of $8,400, and factory building depreciation of $6,720.
4. Overhead was assigned in full to production.
5. Goods costing $294,000 were completed and transferred to finished goods inventory.
6. Goods costing $315,000 were sold on account for $462,000.

Required:

a. Give the journal entries for the above transactions.

b. Using T-accounts, compute the balance in each of the three inventory accounts at August 31, 1990.

Prepare journal entries using perpetual, closing entries, and an income statement

13–9. The Courtney Manufacturing Company, which uses the perpetual inventory procedure, had the following transactions for the month of May 1990:

Transactions:

1. Materials and supplies purchased on account, $54,000.
2. Materials issued to production, $63,000; indirect materials issued, $4,500.
3. Repairs and maintenance on factory equipment, $3,375.
4. Recorded factory depreciation, $22,500; property taxes, $8,000; and utilities, $16,300.
5. Administrative salaries paid, $27,000.
6. Depreciation on administration building, $11,250.
7. Factory payroll (gross), $40,500; withholdings include $2,475 of FICA taxes and federal income taxes, $7,200.
8. Factory payroll distribution; direct labor, $36,900; indirect labor, $3,600.
9. Paid advertising expense, $1,125, and delivery expense, $780.
10. Sales salaries and commissions paid, $10,125.
11. Actual manufacturing overhead cost was assigned to production.
12. Cost of goods completed and transferred, $175,500.
13. Sales on account, $337,500; cost of goods sold, $180,000.
14. Other selling expenses, $630; other administrative expenses, $1,125; and interest expense, $90, paid in cash.
15. Federal income taxes were accrued at 40% of pretax income.

Required:

a. Prepare journal entries to record the May transactions.

b. Prepare an income statement for the Courtney Manufacturing Company for the month of May 1990.

c. Prepare closing entries as of May 31, 1990.

Classify costs as direct materials, labor, manufacturing overhead, selling, administrative, product, period, and variable

13–10. Given below are some costs incurred by an electrical appliance manufacturer.

a. President's salary.
b. Cost of electrical wire.
c. Cost of janitorial supplies.
d. Wages of assembly-line workers.
e. Cost of promotional displays.
f. Plant supervisor's salary.
g. Cost accountant's salary.
h. Research and development costs.
i. Cost of aluminum used for toasters.
j. Cost of market research survey.

Required:

a. Classify these costs as direct materials, direct labor, manufacturing overhead, selling, or administrative.

b. Classify the above costs as either product costs or period costs.

c. Which of the above costs are variable costs?

BUSINESS DECISION PROBLEM 13–1

Classify costs by behavior and type of production cost

A number of costs that would affect business decisions in manufacturing companies are listed below. These costs may be fixed or variable with respect to some measure of volume or output and may be classified as direct materials (DM), direct labor (DL), or manufacturing overhead (MO).

(1) Cellophane wrapping used to seal bottles containing a patented medicine.
(2) Gases used to carbonate beverages.
(3) Insurance on the factory and its equipment.
(4) A shift manager's supervisor salary.
(5) Rent on a temporary storage building.
(6) Trees at a lumber mill.
(7) Gas and oil for forklift trucks.
(8) Services of carpenters in building construction.
(9) Lubrications used in maintaining machinery.
(10) Cost of snacks supplied in a factory's break area.
(11) Payroll taxes and fringe benefits related to direct labor.
(12) The plant's janitorial salaries.
(13) Aluminum in a steel fabrication plant.
(14) Executive's secretary's salary.

Required:

a. List the numbers 1 through 14 down the left side of a sheet of paper. After each number, write the letters V (for variable) or F (for fixed) and either DM (for direct materials), DL (for direct labor), or MO (for manufacturing overhead) to show how you would classify the similarly numbered cost item given above.

b. Which of your own answers given for part (**a**) could you challenge? Discuss.

14 JOB ORDER COST SYSTEMS

LEARNING OBJECTIVES

After studying this chapter, you should be able to:

1. Define job order costing.
2. Describe where job order cost systems can be used.
3. Describe the documents used to accumulate product costs in a job order cost system.
4. Describe job order cost flows and record the proper journal entries beginning with initial materials requisition and ending with the sale of the final product.
5. Show how a predetermined overhead rate is computed and how it is used to assign overhead to production.
6. Transfer any overapplied or underapplied overhead to Cost of Goods Sold.
7. Define and use correctly the new terms in the glossary.

This chapter continues the discussion of perpetual inventory procedure begun in Chapter 13. Perpetual inventory procedure is used when a manufacturing company wants to determine the cost per unit of its products before taking a physical inventory at year-end.

A product unit cost figure depends on many factors, such as the inventory costing method (FIFO, LIFO, or weighted-average) used and the allocation procedure used to allocate indirect costs (manufacturing overhead) to products. The determination of product unit cost is always dependent on the type of cost accumulation system used by a company. For some decisions, information about future costs is more relevant than product unit cost information based on past costs.

There are two major types of cost accumulation systems under perpetual procedure—job order cost system and process cost system. This chapter discusses the job order cost system. Process cost systems are the topic of Chapter 15, but will be overviewed briefly in this chapter.

In each system, the goal is to *determine before year-end the unit costs of the products being manufactured.* These unit costs provide important data for management; they are used throughout the period to compute (1) cost of goods sold, (2) cost of work in process and finished goods ending inventories, (3) payments to be received under contracts based on "full" costs[1] and (4) selling prices.

Product costing is only feasible when the accounting system involved is able to clearly define what type of manufacturing costs to include in its analysis. It has been generally assumed that absorption costing is the concept used to define these manufacturing costs. Under absorption costing, all types of manufacturing costs (direct labor, direct materials, variable and fixed overhead) are assigned to individual products. This chapter and the next will show how the concept of absorption costing underlies the job order cost system and the process cost system.

PROCESS COST SYSTEMS

A **process cost system** is a cost accounting system in which costs incurred during production are accumulated according to the processes or departments a product goes through on its way to completion. Costs are not assigned to specific products or job orders. A process cost system is generally used for companies that produce a large quantity of similar products or that have a continuous production flow. The unit cost of the product produced is calculated by dividing the total manufacturing costs assigned to a particular department during the specified time period by the number of good units produced during that time period. Process costing is commonly used in the production of automobiles, soft drinks, and paint, to name a few industries.

JOB ORDER COST SYSTEMS

Objective 1: Define job order costing

Objective 2: Describe where job order cost systems can be used

A **job order cost system** is a cost accounting system in which the costs incurred to produce a product are accumulated for each individual job. A job order cost system is generally used when the products being manufactured can be separately identified or when goods are produced to meet a customer's particular needs. An example of the use of a job order cost system involves a shipbuilder who specifically designs ships for each customer. The costs incurred by the shipbuilder in the building of the ships are accumulated separately for each job. Other examples consist of a caterer accumulating the costs of each banquet separately, or a building contractor who accounts for the costs incurred in construction separately for each building. Job order costing is commonly used in construction, mo-

---

[1]A "full" cost contract basically guarantees the manufacturer total recovery of the costs incurred in producing the product (including overhead) and, usually, a specified profit margin.

tion pictures, printing, and other industries where many heterogeneous (dissimilar) products are produced.

Under job order costing, an up-to-date record of the costs incurred on a job is kept to provide management with timely cost data. Reports to management can be revised as often as desired, even daily, on such matters as materials used, labor costs incurred, manufacturing overhead assigned, goods completed, total production costs incurred, and budgeted and actual cost comparisons.

Up-to-date information for each job is made available by maintaining a job order cost sheet for each job. A **job order cost sheet** is a form used to summarize the costs of direct materials, direct labor, and manufacturing overhead incurred for a job. It is the *key document* in the system. The file of job order cost sheets for jobs not yet completed represents the subsidiary ledger for the Work in Process Inventory account.

Illustration 14.1 depicts the cost flows in a job order cost system.

Basic Records Used in Job Order Systems

Objective 3: Describe the documents used to accumulate product costs in a job order cost system

Illustration 14.2 shows the basic records or source documents used in a job order cost system:

1. The job order cost sheet summarizes all costs—direct materials, direct labor, and applied manufacturing overhead—of producing a given job or batch of products. One sheet is maintained for each job order. When goods are completed and transferred, the job order cost sheets are transferred to a completed jobs file. The number of units and their unit costs are recorded on inventory cards supporting the Finished Goods Inventory account. An example of a job order cost sheet is shown in Illustration 14.2.

2. A stores (or materials) card is kept for each type of direct and indirect material maintained in inventory. The stores card shows the quanti-

Illustration 14.1
COST FLOWS IN A JOB ORDER COST SYSTEM

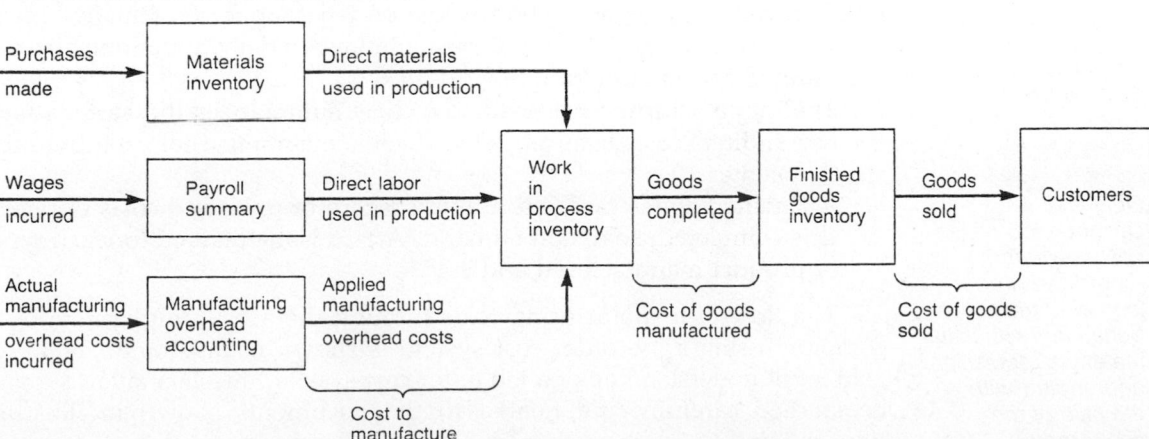

Illustration 14.2
BASIC RECORDS IN A JOB ORDER COST SYSTEM

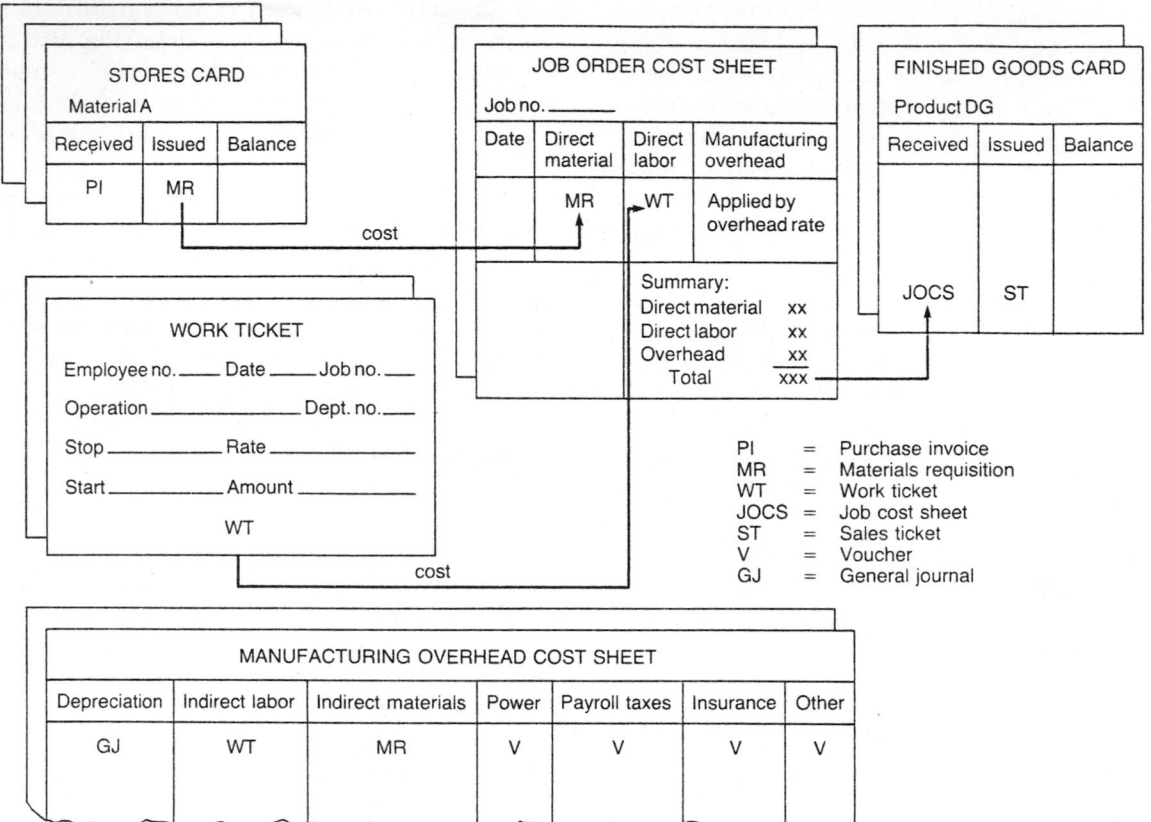

ties (and costs) of each type of material received, issued, and on hand for which the storekeeper is responsible. When a job is started, direct materials are ordered from the storeroom on a materials requisition, which shows the types and quantities of the materials ordered.

3. The work ticket shows who worked on what job for how many hours and at what wage rate. All of each employee's daily hours must be accounted for on one or more work tickets.

4. The manufacturing overhead cost sheet summarizes the various factory indirect costs incurred. One sheet is maintained for each production center.

*Objective 4:
Describe job order cost flows and record the proper journal entries beginning with initial materials requisition and ending with the sale of the final product*

5. A **finished goods card** is a running record of units and costs of products completed, sold, and on hand. A card is maintained for each type of product manufactured and sold.

The flow of manufacturing costs through the accounting system of a company using a job order cost system is shown in Illustration 14.3. To gain a full understanding of a job order cost system, this illustration should be studied carefully and related to the documents shown in Illustration 14.2 and to the journal entries in the following example.

Illustration 14.3
COST FLOWS IN A JOB ORDER SYSTEM

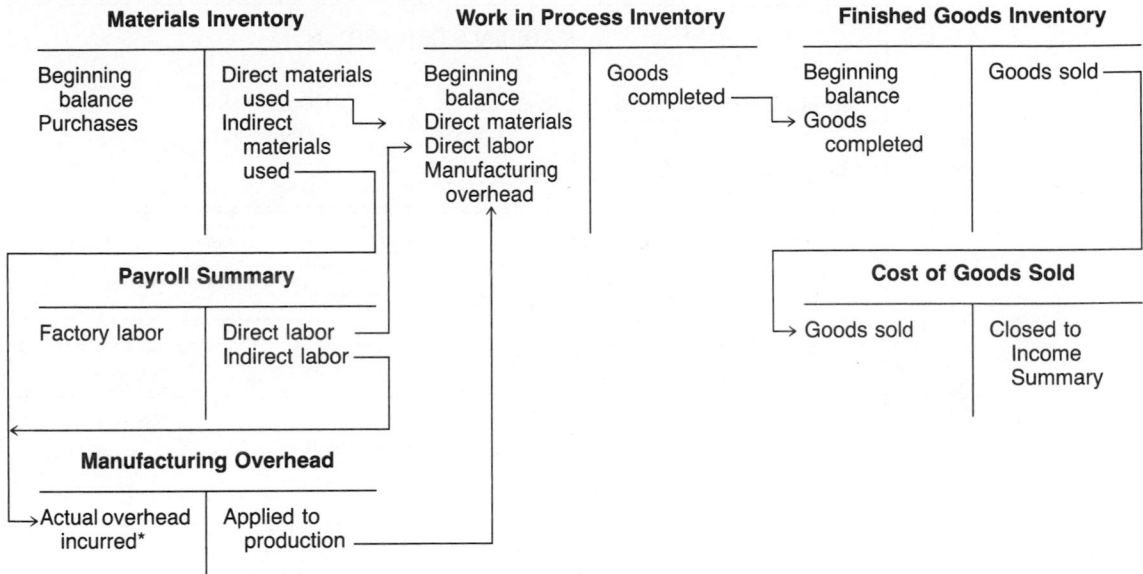

* Includes indirect materials, indirect labor, and other overhead.

The following section will explain the specific procedure followed in accounting for materials, labor, and manufacturing overhead costs in a job order cost system.

Accounting for Materials

As materials are received from vendors, they are placed in the materials storeroom. A **stores (or materials) card** is a perpetual inventory record that shows the quantities and costs of each type of material received, issued to a job, and left on hand. A card is kept for each type of direct and indirect material maintained in inventory. The file of these cards serves as the subsidiary ledger for the Materials Inventory account. When materials are needed in production, a supervisor fills out a materials requisition. A **materials requisition** is a written order directing the store's clerk to issue certain materials to a production center. The requisition shows the types, quantities, and costs of the materials ordered from the storeroom and identifies the job to which the cost of those materials is to be assigned (Illustration 14.4).

A **bill of materials** will typically be used for the requisition of materials in the cases where a job being worked on involves a product that is frequently manufactured. The bill of materials is basically a control sheet that shows the type and quantity of each item of material going into a completed unit.

The requisitions are accumulated by job number, and at the end of the day the amount of direct materials issued for each job is entered on

Illustration 14.4
MATERIALS REQUISITION

MATERIALS REQUISITION

Req. No. R4

Storekeeper: Issue Following to Bearer

Date 6/4/90

Dept. No. 1

Charge Job No. 201   **Dept. Assembly**

Item	Quantity	Stock No.	Cost	Amount
DG	8,000	16	$3.00	$24,000

Entered on
Job Order Cost Sheet

Signed:

J.H.R.

Inventory Stores Manager *J.B.S.* .

Production Manager *A.P.F.*

the job order cost sheet for that particular job order. When the material is-sued is classified by the company as indirect material, those requisitions are accumulated, and at the end of the day the total amount is charged to manufacturing overhead. Illustration 14.2 shows how the information from the materials requisition is used in the stores card, the job order cost sheet, and the manufacturing overhead cost sheet.

Accounting for Labor

A job order cost system requires that labor costs be accumulated and recorded for each job. As each employee works on a particular job assign-ment, that employee fills out a **work (labor time) ticket,** which is a form used to record labor costs. Information recorded on the work ticket in-cludes employee number, job number, number of hours worked, and any other important information. At the end of the day work tickets for each job are accumulated, and the total direct labor costs for each job are en-tered on the job order. A work ticket is shown in Illustration 14.2.

Work tickets are also used to accumulate and record indirect labor costs. When an employee is assigned work that is not directly related to any job (such as general maintenance work), this work is also recorded on a work ticket. Work not directly related to any job is indirect labor and is accounted for as part of manufacturing overhead. At the end of the day these tickets are accumulated, and the total indirect labor cost is recorded on the manufacturing overhead cost sheet.

The use of work tickets not only permits the accumulation and recording of direct labor costs for each job and indirect labor costs each day; it also provides control over the labor cost for each employee. Since each employee fills out a work ticket for each task performed, all of that employee's hours should be accounted for on one or more work tickets.

Cost Driver

Over the years, direct labor has become less of a factor in the cost of a number of products in certain industries. A reason for this is due in part to automation. Computers and robots are replacing many human-related tasks.

Thus, in the cases where direct labor is decreasing in importance, manufacturing overhead is increasing due to the depreciation of automated equipment and the development of new equipment (computers, robots, etc.).

Where operations are largely automated, direct labor probably has little to do with the incurrence of manufacturing overhead and may not be an appropriate base for computing overhead rates. A base should be used that acts as a **cost driver** in the occurrence of overhead cost. A cost driver is a measure of activity, such as machine-hours and computer time, that is a causal factor in the incurrence of cost in an organization. Use of a cost driver more appropriately and accurately computes overhead rates.

Direct labor is not decreasing in importance in all industries. In some industries, direct labor is still a significant factor. Therefore, every organization needs to analyze the effects of direct labor in their operations to determine if their overhead rates are accurate.

Accounting for Manufacturing Overhead

In order to exert some control over manufacturing overhead costs incurred, each production center or department must summarize its factory indirect costs. A **manufacturing overhead cost sheet** is the record used to summarize the various manufacturing overhead costs incurred. The file of manufacturing overhead cost sheets serves as the subsidiary ledger for the Manufacturing Overhead account. An example of a manufacturing overhead cost sheet was shown in Illustration 14.2.

Predetermined overhead rates. In most manufacturing operations, unit costs are computed at the time a job is completed. The costs of direct materials and direct labor have already been entered on the job order cost sheet as a result of posting information from materials requisitions and work tickets. Each job must then be assigned its share of the manufacturing overhead costs.

In the previous chapter, the manufacturing overhead rate was computed using actual overhead costs for the period. The formula for **actual overhead rate** is as follows:

$$\text{Actual overhead rate} = \frac{\text{Total manufacturing overhead}}{\text{Total manufacturing activity}}$$

Actual job order costing is simple, but it does produce results that are misleading. These misleading results are due to the fact that overhead rates may fluctuate in significant proportions from month to month, so that similar jobs done in different months have quite different amounts of overhead and total cost. These fluctuations could cause managers to reach incorrect conclusions about profitability. Because actual job order costing produces misleading results, it is not commonly used.

Most manufacturing companies prefer the use of a predetermined overhead rate rather than waiting to accumulate all overhead costs during a period and developing an actual manufacturing overhead rate. A **predetermined overhead rate** is calculated by dividing estimated total overhead costs for a period by an expected level of activity, such as total estimated machine-hours, total estimated direct labor-hours, or direct labor cost for the period. Predetermined overhead rates are set at the beginning of the year in which they will be used.

Reasons for using predetermined rates. Reasons for using a predetermined overhead rate in manufacturing operations include the following:

1. Overhead costs are seldom incurred uniformly throughout the year. For example, heating costs are larger during winter. No useful purpose is served by allocating less cost to a unit produced in the summer than to one produced in the winter. Use of a predetermined rate results in applying overhead based on direct labor cost, hours incurred, or some other measure of activity rather than on actual overhead incurred in a particular month.
2. Some overhead costs, like factory building depreciation, are fixed costs. Thus, if the volume of goods produced varies from month to month, there will be sharp fluctuations in average unit cost unless a predetermined rate is used.
3. Total unit costs of production are known sooner. Using a predetermined rate, overhead costs can be assigned to production when direct materials and direct labor costs are assigned. Without use of a predetermined rate, unit costs would not be known until the end of the month or even later if bills for costs had not arrived by then. For example, the electric bill for the month of July will probably not arrive until August. If actual overhead was used to compute unit cost, products produced in July could not be costed until August.

Objective 5: Show how a predetermined overhead rate is computed and how it is used to assign overhead to production

Computing predetermined overhead rates. Predetermined overhead rates are computed in the same basic manner as actual rates except that estimated rather than actual levels of activity and cost are used. As part of the budgeting process (discussed in Chapter 18), management estimates the level of manufacturing activity for the next year. This activity level is expressed in terms of some specified base, such as machine-hours, direct labor-hours, or direct labor costs. Next, expected overhead costs for the year are estimated, based on the expected level of activity. The overhead rate can then be calculated using the following formula:

$$\frac{\text{Estimated manufacturing overhead costs}}{\text{Expected level of activity (such as machine hours)}} = \frac{\text{Predetermined}}{\text{overhead rate}}$$

This process of estimating the expected level of activity and the expected overhead costs and then calculating the predetermined overhead rate may be done for the company as a whole (if the company desires a single, company-wide overhead rate), or it may be done separately for each production center (department) within the company.[2] To illustrate the calculation of a predetermined overhead rate for a single production center, assume that the expected level of activity in a certain production center is 60,000 machine-hours. Assume also that, at that level of activity, the estimated overhead costs are $540,000.

The predetermined overhead rate would be:

$$\frac{\$540,000}{60,000 \text{ hours}} = \$9 \text{ per machine-hour}$$

Since Work in Process Inventory must contain amounts for direct materials, direct labor, and manufacturing overhead, the predetermined overhead rate is used to apply overhead to Work in Process Inventory. Actual amounts for direct materials and direct labor will already be posted to the Work in Process Inventory account from the materials requisitions and the work tickets. In the above situation, overhead would be applied to Work in Process Inventory at the rate of $9 of overhead for each actual machine hour worked on a job. If 2,000 machine hours have been used, the journal entry to apply overhead is:

Work in Process Inventory	18,000	
Manufacturing Overhead		18,000

To apply overhead to Work in Process Inventory using a predetermined overhead rate of $9 per machine-hour.

Note that the credit in the above entry is to the Manufacturing Overhead account. Actual manufacturing overhead is accumulated in the Manufacturing Overhead account on the debit side. When overhead is applied to Work in Process Inventory, the Manufacturing Overhead account is credited. If the estimates used for overhead costs and expected level of activity are exactly the same as the actual amounts incurred for overhead and machine-hours, the Manufacturing Overhead account will have a zero balance at the end of the period.

Underapplied or overapplied overhead. Because it is highly unlikely that the estimates used in computing the predetermined overhead rate will be exactly equal to the actual overhead cost or machine-hours incurred, the Manufacturing Overhead account will normally have a debit or credit balance at the end of the period. A *debit* balance will remain if actual overhead exceeds the applied overhead for the period; we say that the overhead is underapplied (underabsorbed). **Underapplied overhead** is the amount by which actual overhead costs incurred in a period exceed the overhead applied to production in that period. In contrast, a *credit*

---

[2]Sometimes separate rates are computed for variable overhead and fixed overhead. Later chapters illustrate how these separate rates may be useful.

balance will remain if applied overhead exceeds actual overhead; we say that overhead is overapplied or overabsorbed. **Overapplied overhead** is the amount by which the overhead applied to production exceeds the actual overhead costs incurred in that same period. Remember that overhead is applied to Work in Process Inventory (production) using the *predetermined* overhead rate times the *actual* level of activity (such as machine-hours) incurred during the period.

To illustrate the use of a predetermined overhead rate during a period, consider the following facts:

Estimated manufacturing overhead for year	$48,000
Estimated level of activity for year	80,000 machine hours
Predetermined overhead rate ($48,000 ÷ 80,000 hours) . . .	$0.60 per machine hour
Actual overhead costs incurred during year	$45,000
Actual machine-hours	70,000 hours

The following journal entries are necessary to record the above information:

Manufacturing Overhead	45,000	
Various Accounts		45,000
To record actual manufacturing overhead costs incurred during period, machinery repair, indirect materials, etc.		
Work in Process Inventory	42,000	
Manufacturing Overhead		42,000
To apply manufacturing overhead to Work in Process Inventory at predetermined rate of $0.60 per machine-hour for 70,000 hours worked.		

In reality these entries are not made at a single point in time for the total amount. The accountant will record actual manufacturing overhead (the first entry above) continuously during the period as indirect materials are issued to production, as work tickets are accumulated for indirect labor, and as other circumstances require entries (machinery repair, utility bills, etc.). The second entry above, to record applied manufacturing overhead, will be recorded each time a job is completed (in order to properly compute the total cost of the job) or at the end of each period (so that financial statements containing proper balances can be prepared).

Based on these two entries, the Manufacturing Overhead account will appear as follows:

Manufacturing Overhead

Actual costs	45,000	Applied to production	42,000
Balance	3,000		

The $3,000 debit balance is the amount of underapplied overhead during the period.

Reasons for underapplied or overapplied manufacturing overhead. Two different factors are responsible for underapplied or overapplied overhead for the period. The first factor has to do with the difference between the amount of indirect manufacturing cost actually incurred and the amount management estimated for the period. The second factor relates to the difference between the estimated level of manufacturing activity (expected activity) used to set the predetermined overhead rate and the actual level of activity on which overhead is applied.

A difference between actual and estimated overhead costs can arise because unanticipated events cause overhead costs to be more or less than the budgeted amount. High heating bills caused by a severe winter, excess repairs to factory machinery, and increases in prices of supplies are all examples of events that cause actual overhead costs to exceed expected costs and tend to result in underapplied overhead. Unanticipated cost savings, on the other hand, tend to cause overapplied overhead.

Unanticipated events can also cause the estimated and actual levels of activity to differ. For example, a company could find itself without essential raw materials and have to cut back production, or, alternatively, a company could produce a product that becomes a "fad" and have to increase production in order to meet demand. Recall that in every manufacturing business some overhead costs are fixed costs that do not change with the level of manufacturing activity. As a result, total actual overhead costs do not vary in direct proportion to the actual level of activity. However, applied overhead costs do vary in direct proportion to the actual level of activity because applied overhead is being applied to Work in Process Inventory at a constant amount per actual unit of activity (such as machine-hours). Therefore, if actual operations are at a higher level of activity than that used to set the predetermined overhead rate, more overhead will be applied to Work in Process Inventory than originally anticipated and will tend to cause overapplied overhead. Operating at a lower level than originally estimated will tend to cause underapplied overhead.

Objective 6: Transfer any overapplied or underapplied overhead to Cost of Goods Sold

Disposition of underapplied or overapplied manufacturing overhead. An underapplied or overapplied manufacturing overhead balance can be carried forward in monthly or quarterly (interim) financial statements if the probability exists that it will be reduced or offset by operations for the remainder of the year. If a balance in overhead remains at year-end, it can be allocated (or disposed of) to Work in Process Inventory, Finished Goods Inventory, and Cost of Goods Sold. This disposition is done by re-computing the cost of production for the year using actual overhead rates and adjusting the three account balances to their appropriate actual amounts. As an alternative, underapplied overhead can be charged off as a loss of the period, particularly if it resulted from idle production capacity or from unusual circumstances.

As a practical matter, however, underapplied or overapplied overhead is usually transferred to Cost of Goods Sold. Little distortion of net income or of assets results from this treatment if the amount transferred is small or if most of the goods produced during the year were sold.

Thus, if the $3,000 of underapplied overhead in the previous example is a year-end balance, the journal entry to dispose of it will read:

```
Cost of Goods Sold . . . . . . . . . . . . . . . . . . . . . .    3,000
    Manufacturing Overhead . . . . . . . . . . . . . . . .            3,000
    To dispose of underapplied overhead.
```

Average cost per unit. When a job is finished, an **average cost per unit** of the job is computed. This average cost number is used to value the inventory on the balance sheet. Generally accepted accounting principles require that inventory be valued at cost. However, at times, the lower-of-cost-or-market rule will need to be applied where conditions in the market (such as obsolescence and changes in supply or demand) lower the market value below the cost of the inventory. In these situations, inventory would be valued at market value. But, one does need to know the cost of the inventory to apply this lower-of-cost-or-market rule.

Through the entire production process, manufacturing costs were recorded on a job order cost sheet. At the completion of the job, all costs are totaled. Then, to compute the average cost per unit, the following formula is used:

$$\text{Average cost per unit} = \frac{\text{Total manufacturing cost of job}}{\substack{\text{Total number of good (saleable)} \\ \text{finished units in job}}}$$

Job Order Costing—an Example

To illustrate a job order costing system in use, the following example includes nine transactions of the Casting Company for the month of July. On July 1, the Casting Company had beginning inventories as follows:

```
Materials inventory (material A, $10,000; material B, $6,000;
    various indirect materials, $4,000) . . . . . . . . . . . . . . . .   $20,000
Work in process inventory (Job No. 106: direct materials, $4,200;
    direct labor, $5,000; and overhead, $4,000) . . . . . . . . . . . .    13,200
Finished goods inventory (500 units of product AB at a cost of
    $11 per unit) . . . . . . . . . . . . . . . . . . . . . . . . . . .     5,500
```

Job No. 106 (Product DG), which was in process at the beginning of July, was completed in July. Of the two jobs started in July [Nos. 107 (Product XY) and 108 (Product OR)], only Job No. 107 was completed by the end of July.

The transactions and the journal entries to record these transactions are given below. You may want to refer back to Illustration 14.3 to follow the cost flows in a job order cost system.

1. Purchased $10,000 of material A and $15,000 of material B on account.

```
Materials Inventory . . . . . . . . . . . . . . . . . . . . . .   25,000
    Accounts Payable . . . . . . . . . . . . . . . . . . . . .         25,000
    To record purchase of direct materials.
```

2. Issued direct materials: material A to Job No. 106, $1,000; to Job No. 107, $8,000; to Job No. 108, $2,000; material B to Job No. 106, $2,000; to Job

No. 107, $6,000; to Job No. 108, $4,000. Indirect materials issued to all jobs, $1,000.

Work in Process Inventory	23,000	
Manufacturing Overhead	1,000	
Materials Inventory		24,000
To record direct and indirect materials issued.		

3. Factory payroll for the month, $25,000; FICA and income taxes withheld, $4,000.

Payroll Summary	25,000	
Various liability accounts for taxes withheld		4,000
Wages Payable		21,000
To record factory payroll for July.		

4. Factory payroll paid, $21,000.

Wages Payable	21,000	
Cash		21,000
To record cash paid to factory employees in July.		

5. Payroll costs assigned: direct labor, $20,000 (Job No. 106, $5,000; Job No. 107, $12,000; and Job No. 108, $3,000); and indirect labor, $5,000.

Work in Process Inventory	20,000	
Manufacturing Overhead	5,000	
Payroll Summary		25,000
To distribute factory labor costs incurred.		

6. Other indirect manufacturing costs incurred:

Payroll taxes accrued	$ 3,000
Repairs (on account)	1,000
Property taxes accrued	4,000
Heat, light, and power (on account)	2,000
Depreciation	5,000
	$15,000

Manufacturing Overhead	15,000	
Accounts Payable		3,000
Payroll Taxes Payable		3,000
Property Taxes Payable		4,000
Accumulated Depreciation		5,000
To record manufacturing overhead costs incurred.		

7. Manufacturing overhead applied to production (assume a predetermined rate of $4 per machine-hour, with 1,000 machine-hours on Job 106, 2,400 machine-hours on Job 107, and 600 machine-hours on Job 108.

Job No. 106, Product DG ($4 × 1,000)	$ 4,000
Job No. 107, Product XY ($4 × 2,400)	9,600
Job No. 108, Product OR ($4 × 600)	2,400
	$16,000

Work in Process Inventory	16,000	
Manufacturing Overhead		16,000
To record application of overhead to production.		

8. Jobs completed and transferred to finished goods storeroom (see Illustration 14.5 for details):

Job No. 106 (4,000 units of product DG @ $6.30)	$25,200	
Job No. 107 (10,000 units of product XY @ $3.56). . . .	35,600	
	$60,800	

Finished Goods Inventory	60,800	
Work in Process Inventory		60,800
To record completed production for July.		

9. Sales on account for the month: 500 units of product AB for $8,000, cost, $5,500; and 10,000 units of product XY for $62,000, cost, $35,600 (Job No. 107).

Accounts Receivable	70,000	
Sales		70,000
To record sales on account for July.		

Cost of Goods Sold	41,100	
Finished Goods Inventory		41,100
To record cost of goods sold in July.		

After the above entries have been posted, the Work in Process Inventory and Finished Goods Inventory accounts appear (in T-account form) as follows:

Work in Process Inventory

July 1 balance	13,200	Completed	60,800
Direct materials used	23,000		
Direct labor cost incurred	20,000		
Overhead applied	16,000		
July 31 balance	11,400		

Finished Goods Inventory

July 1 balance	5,500	Sold	41,100
Completed	60,800		
July 31 balance	25,200		

On July 31, the Work in Process Inventory account has a balance of $11,400, which agrees with the total costs charged thus far to Job No. 108, as shown in Illustration 14.5. The balance consists of direct materials, $6,000; direct labor, $3,000; and manufacturing overhead, $2,400. Finished Goods Inventory has a balance on July 31 of $25,200, supported by the finished goods inventory card for Job No. 106 (Illustration 14.5), which shows that the 4,000 units of product DG on hand have a total cost of $25,200.

Ledger account entries like the ones given above are often made from summaries of cost, and thus are recorded only at the end of the month. If,

Illustration 14.5
SUPPORTING INVENTORY CARDS AND JOB ORDER COST SHEETS

STORES CARD					STORES CARD		
Material A					Material B		
Received	Issued	Balance			Received	Issued	Balance
$10,000		$10,000			$15,000		$ 6,000
		20,000					21,000
	$1,000	19,000				$2,000	19,000
	8,000	11,000				6,000	13,000
	2,000	9,000				4,000	9,000

JOB ORDER COST SHEET (Product DG)   **Job No. 106**

Date	Direct Materials	Direct Labor	Manufacturing Overhead
July 1	$4,200	$ 5,000	$4,000
July	A: 1,000	5,000	4,000
	B: 2,000	$10,000	$8,000
	$7,200		

Job completed (4,000 units of product DG @ $6.30). Total cost, $25,200.

JOB ORDER COST SHEET (Product XY)   **Job No. 107**

Date	Direct Materials	Direct Labor	Manufacturing Overhead
July	A: $ 8,000	$12,000	$9,600
	B: 6,000		
	$14,000		

Job completed (10,000 units of product XY @ $3.56). Total cost, $35,600.

JOB ORDER COST SHEET (Product OR)   **Job No. 108**

Date	Direct Materials	Direct Labor	Manufacturing Overhead
July	A: $2,000	$3,000	$2,400
	B: 4,000		
	$6,000		

Job incomplete (1,000 units of product OR). Cost to date, $11,400.

FINISHED GOODS CARD				FINISHED GOODS CARD				FINISHED GOODS CARD		
Product AB				Product DG				Product XY		
Received	Issued	Balance		Received	Issued	Balance		Received	Issued	Balance
		$5,500		$25,200		$25,200		$35,600		$35,600
	$5,500	–0–							$35,600	–0–

on the other hand, management wants to be informed more frequently as costs are incurred, details of the various costs can be recorded more often, even daily.

The main advantage of using a predetermined overhead rate is shown in this example. Three jobs were worked on during the month. Job No. 106 was started last month and completed in July. Job No. 107 was started and completed in July. And Job No. 108 was started but not finished in July. Each required different amounts of direct materials and direct labor. Under these conditions, there is simply no timely way to apply overhead to products without the use of a predetermined rate based on some common level of activity. Note that the use of a predetermined overhead rate permits the computation of unit costs to be made for Job Nos. 106 and 107 at the time of their completion rather than waiting until the end of the month. But this advantage is secured only at the expense of keeping more detailed records of the costs incurred. As is discussed in the next chapter, the other major cost accumulation system—process cost—requires far less record-keeping, but the computation of unit costs is more complex.

This chapter has assumed that a single overhead rate has been used for a factory's operations. However, in large companies, multiple predetermined rates may be used, due to the single overhead rate's inability to equitably handle the overhead costs of all departments. A different activity base may exist for each department, because some departments may be more labor intensive, machine intensive, etc., than other departments. A rate is then developed for each department (or groups of departments) based on the needs of the department(s). As a product is moved along the production line, overhead is applied in each department according to various overhead rates that have been set. The total of all of these overhead applications represents the total overhead cost of the job.

SUMMARY

The job order cost system is one of two major types of cost accumulation systems under perpetual inventory cost procedure found in practice today. The goal of a cost accumulation system is to determine before year-end the unit costs of the products being manufactured. Unit costs may be used throughout the period to compute (1) cost of goods sold, (2) cost of work in process and finished goods inventories, (3) payments to be received under contracts based on "full" cost, and (4) selling prices.

A job order cost system is a cost accumulation system in which the costs incurred to produce a product are accumulated according to the individual job. A job order cost system is generally used when the products being manufactured can be grouped into separately identifiable jobs.

The key document in a job order cost system is the job order cost sheet, which summarizes the costs of direct materials, direct labor, and manufacturing overhead incurred for a job. The file of job order cost sheets for the incomplete jobs constitutes a subsidiary ledger for the Work in Process Inventory account. The actual costs of direct materials issued and of direct labor used for a particular job are recorded on the job order cost sheet. Overhead cost, however, is generally applied to the job through the use of a predetermined overhead rate.

A predetermined overhead rate is computed by dividing estimated overhead costs by the expected level of manufacturing activity. Overhead costs applied to production are debited to Work in Process Inventory and credited to the Manufacturing Overhead account. Actual overhead costs incurred are debited to Manufacturing Overhead and credited to Cash, Accounts Payable, or similar accounts. Since overhead is applied by a predetermined, estimated overhead rate, it is unlikely that the actual costs debited to Manufacturing Overhead will exactly equal the applied overhead that was credited to Manufacturing Overhead during the period. The debit balance (underapplied overhead) or credit balance (overapplied overhead) in the Manufacturing Overhead account can be allocated to Work in Process Inventory, Finished Goods Inventory, and Cost of Goods Sold, or it can simply be closed directly to Cost of Goods Sold.

Without accurate cost accounting information, a manufacturing company cannot determine its selling prices, prepare accurate financial statements, or determine the cost of its ending inventory. Chapter 15 discusses the second cost accumulation system—process costing.

NEW TERMS INTRODUCED IN CHAPTER 14

Objective 7: Define and use correctly the new terms in the glossary

Actual overhead rate Total manufacturing overhead divided by total manufacturing activity (523).

Average cost per unit Total manufacturing cost of a job divided by the total number of good finished units in the job (528).

Bill of materials A control sheet that shows the type and quantity of each item of material going into a completed unit (521).

Cost driver A measure of activity, such as machine-hours and computer time, that is a causal factor in the incurrence of cost in an organization (523).

Finished goods card A running record of units and costs of products completed, sold, and on hand (520).

Job order cost sheet A form used to summarize the costs of direct materials, direct labor, and manufacturing overhead incurred for a job. The job order cost sheets for all partially completed jobs form the subsidiary ledger for the Work in Process Inventory account (519).

Job order cost system (job costing) A cost accounting system in which the costs incurred to produce a product are accumulated according to the individual job, such as a building, dam, 1000 chairs, or 10 desks (518).

Manufacturing overhead cost sheet A record that summarizes the various manufacturing overhead costs incurred (523).

Materials requisition A written order directing the stores clerk to issue certain materials to a production center (521).

Overapplied (overabsorbed) overhead The amount by which the overhead applied to production exceeds the actual overhead costs incurred in that same period (526).

Predetermined overhead rate Calculated by dividing estimated total overhead costs for a period by the expected level of activity, such as direct labor-hours or machine-hours for the period (524).

Process cost system (process costing) A manufacturing cost system in which costs incurred to produce a product are accumulated according to the processes or departments a product goes through on its way to completion (518).

Stores (or materials) card A record that shows the quantities and costs of each type of material received, issued to a job, and left on hand (521).

Underapplied (underabsorbed) overhead The amount by which actual overhead costs incurred in a period exceeds the overhead applied to production in that period (525).

Work (labor time) ticket A form used to record labor costs. Information recorded on the work ticket includes employee number, job number, number of hours worked, and any other important information; may be prepared for both direct and indirect labor (522).

DEMONSTRATION PROBLEM 14–1

Mills Company employs a job order cost system. As of January 1, 1990, its records showed:

Materials and supplies	$120,000
Work in process	258,000
Finished goods (75,000 units at $4)	300,000

The work in process inventory consisted of two jobs:

No.	Materials	Labor	Manufacturing Overhead	Total
101	$45,000	$ 60,000	$30,000	$135,000
102	51,000	48,000	24,000	123,000
	$96,000	$108,000	$54,000	$258,000

Summarized below are manufacturing data for the company for 1990:

(1) Materials and supplies purchased on account, $495,000.

(2) Factory payrolls accrued, $1,020,000; FICA taxes withheld, $51,000; and federal income taxes withheld $90,000.

(3) Manufacturing overhead costs incurred; depreciation, $30,000; heat, light, and power, $12,000; and miscellaneous, $18,000.

(4) Direct materials and supplies requisitioned; Job No. 101, $78,000; Job No. 102, $144,000; Job No. 103, $240,000; and indirect labor requisitioned, $12,000.

(5) Payrolls distributed: direct labor—$120,000 for Job No. 101, $240,000 for Job No. 102, and $360,000 for Job No. 103; factory supervision, $120,000; and other indirect labor, $180,000.

(6) Overhead is assigned to work in process at $6 per machine-hour. Machine-hours were as follows: Job No. 101, 10,000; Job No. 102, 20,000; Job No. 103, 30,000.

(7) Job No. 101 and 102 were completed.

(8) Goods with a cost of $1,032,000 were sold for $1,350,000.

Required:

Prepare journal entries to record the above summarized data, as well as all closing entries for which you have sufficient information.

Solution to Demonstration Problem 14–1

MILLS COMPANY
General Journal

(1)	Materials Inventory	495,000	
	Accounts Payable.		495,000
	To record materials purchased on account.		
(2)	Payroll Summary	1,020,000	
	Employee's FICA Taxes Payable		51,000
	Employee's Federal Income Taxes Payable . . .		90,000
	Wages Payable.		879,000
	To record accrued factory payrolls.		
(3)	Manufacturing Overhead.	60,000	
	Accumulated Depreciation		30,000
	Accounts Payable (Liabilities Payable,		
	Cash, etc.)		30,000
	To record various manufacturing overhead costs.		
(4)	Work in Process Inventory	462,000	
	Manufacturing Overhead.	12,000	
	Materials Inventory		474,000
	To record requisitions of materials and supplies:		

Job No. 101	$ 78,000
Job No. 102	144,000
Job No. 103	240,000
Indirect Supplies	12,000
	$474,000

(5)	Work in Process Inventory	720,000	
	Manufacturing Overhead.	300,000	
	Payroll Summary		1,020,000
	To distribute labor costs:		

Job No. 101	$120,000	
Job No. 102	240,000	
Job No. 103	360,000	$ 720,000
Manufacturing overhead:		
Factory supervision	$120,000	
Other indirect labor	180,000	300,000
		$1,020,000

(6)	Work in Process Inventory	360,000	
	Manufacturing Overhead.		360,000
	Overhead assigned: Job No. 101, $60,000;		
	Job No. 102, $120,000; and Job No. 103, $180,000.		
(7)	Finished Goods Inventory	1,020,000	
	Work in Process Inventory		1,020,000

Completed and transferred jobs:

No. 101	$ 393,000	
No. 102	627,000	
	$1,020,000	

(8) Accounts Receivable   1,350,000
      Sales   1,350,000
    To record sales on account.

Cost of Goods Sold   1,032,000
      Finished Goods Inventory   1,032,000
    To record cost of goods sold.

(Closing Entries)

Cost of Goods Sold   12,000
      Manufacturing Overhead.   12,000
    To close underapplied manufacturing overhead.

Sales   1,350,000
      Income Summary   1,350,000
    To close Sales account.

Income Summary   1,044,000
      Cost of Goods Sold   1,044,000
    To close Cost of Goods Sold account.

QUESTIONS

1. What are the two major types of cost accumulation systems under perpetual procedure? What is the common goal of these systems, and why?

2. Define a job order cost system and give an example.

3. Briefly describe the basic records (source documents) used in a job order cost system.

4. What are the three major reasons for using predetermined manufacturing overhead rates?

5. What is the formula for computing a predetermined overhead rate? If the expected level of activity in a production center is 50,000 machine-hours, and the estimated overhead costs are $704,000, what is the predetermined overhead rate? Show calculation.

6. What is underapplied and overapplied overhead? What types of balances does each have in the manufacturing overhead account?

7. Explain why the manufacturing overhead account could have an underapplied or overapplied balance remaining at the end of the period.

8. What are the three alternative methods of disposing of overapplied or underapplied manufacturing overhead? Which alternative is normally used as a practical matter?

EXERCISES

Identify basic source documents

1. Indicate the source document which would most likely contain the following information:
   1. The receipt of a shipment of material.
   2. The amount of direct labor spent on a particular job.
   3. The amount of indirect labor incurred for the previous month.
   4. The power (electricity) used for the previous month.
   5. The manufacturing overhead applied to a particular job.

Compute cost of a job and give journal entry to record its completion

2. Job No. 501 has at the end of the second week in March, an accumulated total cost of $12,600. In the third week, $3,000 of direct materials were used on the job and 300 hours of direct labor were charged to the job at $15 per hour. Manufacturing overhead was applied on the basis of $8.50 per machine-hour for fixed overhead and $5 per machine hour for variable overhead, with six hundred machine-hours charged. Job No. 501 was the only job completed in the third week. Compute the cost of Job No. 501, and give the journal entry required to record its completion.

Compute job costs; prepare journal entries related to production activities

3. In July, Archer Company worked only on Job No. 801, completing it on July 31. During the month, the company purchased and used $7,500 of direct materials, incurred $11,250 of direct labor costs, and charged 1,300 machine-hours to the job. Assuming manufacturing overhead is applied at the rate of $10 per machine-hour, what is the total cost of Job No. 801? Prepare journal entries to assign the materials, labor, and manufacturing overhead costs to production and to record the transfer of Job No. 801 to finished goods inventory.

Compute job cost per unit; prepare journal entries to record transfer and sale

4. As of August 1, Job No. 110 had already accumulated $11,250 in total costs. During August, Job No. 110 required $15,750 of direct materials, $31,500 of direct labor, and 5,040 machine-hours. Manufacturing overhead is applied to production at the rate of $5 per machine-hour. Assuming completed Job No. 110 consisted of 1,200 units, what is the total cost per unit? Give the journal entries necessary to record the transfer of Job No. 110 to finished goods inventory and the ultimate sale of all 1,200 units at 150% of cost.

Prepare journal entries related to production; calculate unit cost

5. The Maxey Company builds desks to fit customers' specifications. It engaged in the following transactions during June:

Transactions:
   1. Purchased precut wood for desk tops, $22,500.
   2. Wood and other direct materials were issued to production, $15,750.
   3. Direct labor costs assigned to production, $11,250.
   4. Manufacturing overhead assigned to production, $13,500.
   5. Job No. 210 was completed and transferred. Job No. 210 was the only order worked on in June, and it consisted of 7,500 desks. The total cost assigned to Job No. 210 in May amounted to $10,125.

   a. Journalize the transactions listed above.
   b. Compute the cost per unit of Job No. 210.

Compute direct labor cost

6. a. Foster Company applied overhead to jobs at a rate of 120 percent of direct labor cost. When completed, Job No. 314 was charged with $5,400 of overhead. Compute the direct labor cost charged to the job.

   b. Custer Company applied overhead to jobs using a standard amount per machine-hour. In July, Job No. 720 was charged with $9,750 of overhead and used 6,500 machine-hours. Compute the predetermined overhead rate.

Compute total and unit cost of a job order

7. The Swift Company, which uses a job order cost system, has just completed a job for Lake Insurance Company—a special order for 300 gold-plated mechanical pencils. Machine-hours charged were 575; direct materials cost was $1,500; direct labor cost—300 hours at $15 per hour. Budgeted machine-hours for this year were 150,000; budgeted direct labor for this year was $1,200,000, and overhead was budgeted at $3,000,000.

   a. If the overhead rate is expressed as a percentage of direct labor cost, what is the total cost and the unit cost of the company's order?

   b. If the overhead rate is expressed as a rate per machine-hour, what is the total cost and the unit cost of the company's order?

Compute costs of three jobs

8. The Williams Company, which uses a job order cost system, engaged in the following activities during December:

   1. Three jobs were started: Nos. 102, 103, and 104.

   2. Direct materials issued:

To Job 102.	$3,750
To Job 103.	5,250
To Job 104.	3,000

   3. Direct labor costs incurred:

For Job 102	375 hours @ $10.00/hour
For Job 103	563 hours @ $9/hour
For Job 104	150 hours @ $12.80/hour

   4. Assume manufacturing overhead is applied at the rate of $2 per machine-hour.

For Job 102.	1,125 machine-hours
For Job 103.	1,689 machine-hours
For Job 104.	450 machine-hours

   Compute the cost of each job, and give the necessary journal entry to record the transfer of Job No. 103 to Finished Goods Inventory.

Prepare journal entry for disposition of overhead

9. Arnold Company estimated its manufacturing overhead for 1990 at $600,000. At the end of 1990, manufacturing overhead was overapplied by $2,250. Give the journal entry required to reflect a practical disposition of the manufacturing overhead balance.

Compute overhead rates and amount of overhead applied

10. The Hayes Company has the following estimated costs for the current year:

Estimated direct labor cost.	$135,000
Estimated factory overhead cost	$168,750
Estimated machine-hours	67,500

    The actual costs for the month of June:

Actual direct labor cost	$ 13,000
Actual factory overhead cost	$ 15,000
Actual machine-hours	3,750

    a. Compute the factory overhead rate assuming:

    (1) Factory overhead is applied to jobs on the basis of direct labor dollars.

    (2) Factory overhead is applied to jobs on the basis of machine-hours.

b. Compute the amount of overhead to be applied during the month of June using your answers to part (1) and (2).

Determine overapplied overhead and prepare journal entry (Refer to E-10)

11. Determine the amount of overapplied overhead in Exercise 10, part (1) and prepare the journal entry required to dispose of the overapplied amount. Assume the overapplied amount is considered small.

Determine underapplied overhead and prepare journal entry (Refer to E-10)

12. Determine the amount of underapplied overhead in Exercise 10, part (2), and prepare the journal entry required to dispose of the underapplied amount. Assume the underapplied amount is considered small.

PROBLEMS

Prepare journal entries in job order cost system

14–1. Pinson Company employs a job order cost system. As of January 1, 1990, its records showed:

Raw materials and supplies	$240,000
Work in process	516,000
Finished goods (75,000 units × $8)	600,000

The work in process inventory consists of two jobs:

No.	Materials	Labor	Manufacturing Overhead	Total
110 . . .	$ 90,000	$120,000	$ 48,000	$258,000
111 . . .	102,000	96,000	60,000	258,000
	$192,000	$216,000	$108,000	$516,000

Summaries below are manufacturing data for the company for 1990:

(1) Raw materials and supplies purchased on account, $990,000.

(2) Factory payrolls accrued, $2,040,000; social security taxes withheld, $102,000; and federal income taxes withheld, $180,000.

(3) Manufacturing overhead costs incurred: depreciation, $60,000; heat, light, and power, $24,000; and miscellaneous, $36,000.

(4) Direct materials and supplies requisitioned; for Job No. 110, $156,000; for Job No. 111, $288,000; and for Job No. 112, $480,000; and supplies requisitioned, $24,000.

(5) Payrolls distributed: direct labor—$240,000 for Job No. 110, $480,000 for Job No. 111, and $720,000 for Job No. 112; factory supervision, $240,000; and indirect labor, $360,000.

(6) Overhead is assigned to work in process at $8 per machine-hour. Machine-hours per job:

Job No. 110	15,000
Job No. 111	30,000
Job No. 112	45,000

(7) Jobs Nos. 110 and 111 were completed.

(8) The cost of goods sold for the year was $2,064,000.

Required:

Prepare general journal entries to record the above summarized data, as well as all closing entries for which you have sufficient information.

Compute total and per unit costs of four jobs; calculate ending work in process inventory

14–2. Ward Corporation employs a job order cost system. The company's manufacturing activities in July 1990, its first month of operation, are summarized as follows:

	Job Number			
	401	*402*	*403*	*404*
Direct materials. . . .	$12,000	$8,700	$18,900	$9,000
Direct labor cost . . .	$ 9,900	$9,000	$12,600	$3,600
Direct labor-hours. . .	1,650	1,500	2,100	600
Machine-hours	2,500	750	2,000	700
Units produced	300	150	1,500	450

Manufacturing overhead is applied at a rate of $3 per machine-hour for variable overhead, $4.50 per hour for fixed overhead.
Jobs Nos. 401, 402, and 403 were completed in July.

Required:

a. Compute the amount of overhead charged to each job.

b. Compute the total and unit cost of each completed job.

c. Prepare the entry, in general journal form, to record the transfer of completed jobs to Finished Goods.

d. Compute the balance in the July 31, 1990, Work in Process accounts and provide a schedule of the costs charged to each incomplete job to support this balance.

Compute predetermined overhead rate and total cost

14–3. a. The Benson Company has established the following budget for 1991:

	Assembly	*Packaging*
Manufacturing overhead	$ 750,000	$1,050,000
Direct labor cost	$1,350,000	$1,650,000
Direct labor-hours	112,500	165,000
Machine hours.	56,250	150,000

Benson Company uses predetermined rates to apply manufacturing overhead. These rates are based on machine-hours in assembly and on direct labor costs in packaging.

Required:

Compute the predetermined manufacturing overhead rate for each department.

b. During June, the job cost sheet for Job No. 104 showed the following:

	Assembly	*Packaging*
Direct materials used.	$18,000	$18,000
Direct labor cost	$13,500	$ 5,625
Direct labor-hours	1,125	562.5
Machine-hours.	562.5	375

Required:

Using the overhead rates computed in (**a**), compute the total manufacturing overhead cost of Job No. 104.

*Compute
predetermined
overhead rate and
under- or
overapplied
overhead*

14–4. Cloud Company applies overhead to production using a predetermined overhead rate based on machine-hours. Budgeted data for 1991 are:

Budgeted machine-hours 75,000
Budgeted manufacturing overhead $435,000

Required:

a. Compute the predetermined overhead rate.

b. Assume that in 1991, actual manufacturing overhead amounted to $498,750, and that 91,500 machine-hours were used. Compute the amount of underapplied or overapplied manufacturing overhead for 1991.

Compute predetermined overhead rate and overhead cost of one job

14–5. Maxwell Company uses a job order cost system, applying manufacturing overhead at predetermined rates based on direct labor-hours in Department A and machine-hours in Department B. Budgeted estimates for 1991 are:

	Department A	Department B
Manufacturing overhead . . .	$216,000	$288,000
Direct labor cost	$180,000	$198,000
Direct labor-hours	36,000	48,000
Machine-hours	24,000	72,000

Detailed cost records show the following for Job No. 105 which was completed in 1991:

	Department A	Department B
Materials used	$15,000	$750
Direct labor cost	$12,000	$900
Direct labor-hours	300	150
Machine-hours	75	120

Required:

a. Compute the predetermined overhead rates for 1991 for Department A and B.

b. Compute the amount of manufacturing overhead applied to Job No. 105 in each department.

Compute cost of ending inventories of materials, work in process, and finished goods

14–6. The Venus Company engaged in the following activities during 1991:

Materials purchased $292,500
Factory payroll incurred (all direct) $236,250

	Job No. 1	Job No. 2	Job No. 3
Direct materials	$ 76,500	$58,500	$90,000
Direct labor cost	$112,500	$90,000	$33,750
Machine-hours	65,000	42,000	16,000
Manufacturing overhead (applied at $2.50 per machine-hour)	?	?	?

Job No. 1 was completed and sold (at 150% of cost), Job No. 2 was completed but not sold, and Job No. 3 was not completed.

Required:

Compute the balance in each inventory account (Materials, Work in Process, and Finished Goods) at December 31, 1991.

*Prepare journal
entries in job order
cost system*

14–7. The Wright, Inc., general ledger on June 1, 1990, shows the following balances:

Sales	$12,000,000
Raw materials inventory	600,000
Work in process inventory	270,000
Finished goods inventory	750,000
Manufacturing overhead	3,000 Cr.
Accrued salaries and wages	12,000
Cost of goods sold	9,000,000
Selling expenses	900,000
Administrative expenses	1,200,000

The work in process inventory consists of the following:

Job No. 1500:	
Materials	$198,000
Labor	24,000
Overhead	48,000
	$270,000

Summarized, the transactions occurring in June 1990 were:

(1) Raw materials purchased on account, $780,000.
(2) Payroll for the month, $134,250; social security taxes withheld, $7,200; and federal income taxes withheld, $12,000.
(3) Materials issued during the month: direct, $330,000; and indirect, $48,000. Of the direct materials, $15,000 is assignable to Job No. 1500, the balance to Job No. 1501.
(4) The payroll for the month consisted of direct labor, $90,000 (Job No. 1500, $18,000; Job No. 1501, $72,000); factory supervision, $2,400; factory maintenance, $3,600; sales salaries, $14,250; and office and officers' salaries, $24,000.
(5) The manufacturing overhead rate of $5 per machine-hour. Machine-hours were charged as follows:

Job No. 1500	7,500
Job No. 1501	28,500

(6) Other costs incurred in June (on account or accrued except for depreciation and amortization):

Rent (60% factory, 40% administrative)	$60,000
Factory heat, light, and power	33,000
Factory machine repairs	11,400
Amortization of patents	22,200
Depreciation on factory machinery	27,000
Taxes on factory machinery	5,400
Various selling expenses	60,000

(7) Job No. 1500 was completed during the month.
(8) Sales for June, $1,800,000; cost of goods sold was $930,000.

Required:

a. Prepare journal entries to record the above summarized data.

b. Prepare any necessary adjusting and closing entries.

*Compute three
different overhead
rates and under-
or overapplied
manufacturing
overhead using
each rate; discuss
disposition of over-
or underapplied
overhead*

14–8. Holland Company intends to start a policy of using a predetermined rate to charge manufacturing overhead to production. Selected actual and budgeted production data and costs for 1991 follow:

	Budgeted	Actual
Manufacturing overhead	$450,000	$455,250
Direct labor-hours	56,250	57,000
Machine-hours	45,000	44,250
Units of production	150,000	146,250

Required:

a. Compute three possible rates by which the manufacturing overhead can be applied to production. Also compute the underapplied or overapplied manufacturing overhead for 1991 under each rate.

b. Theoretically, what disposition should be made for financial reporting of the underapplied or overapplied manufacturing overhead in part (**a**)?

*Prepare journal
entries for a job
order cost system;
calculate cost of
work in process
inventory*

14–9. The Jordan Company's general ledger showed the following balances as of January 1, 1991:

Materials inventory	$112,500
Work in process inventory	50,625
Finished goods inventory	184,500

The work in process inventory consisted of the following:

Job No. 1650:	
Material	$37,125
Labor	4,500
Manufacturing overhead	9,000
	$50,625

The following transactions took place in January:

Transactions:

(1) Materials purchased on account, $315,000.
(2) Materials issued during the month: direct, $225,000; indirect, $38,250. Of the direct materials issued, $31,500 were assigned to Job No. 1650, with the balance going equally to Job Nos. 1651 and 1652.
(3) Gross payroll for January was $168,750; FICA taxes withheld amounted to $9,000; federal income taxes withheld totaled $19,125.
(4) The $168,750 payroll consisted of $135,000 of direct labor (one third charged to each job) and $33,750 of indirect labor.
(5) Manufacturing overhead is applied at $12 per machine-hour. Machine-hours charged were 7,500 per job.
(6) Job No. 1650 was completed.

Required:

a. Prepare journal entries for the above transactions.

b. Compute the ending balance in Work in Process Inventory.

BUSINESS DECISION PROBLEM 14–1

The Chain Manufacturing Company produces one product, egg nog concentrate. The demand for this product is highly seasonal, and because of this, Chain adjusts its production schedule so that it is in line with demand (the concentrate is susceptible to spoilage). The president of Chain, Penny Daniels, has received complaints from the sales department that it is having difficulty in setting a stable price for the concentrate. It complains that the cost figures it receives from the production manager vary widely from quarter to quarter, which in turn cause the selling price to fluctuate. The sales department is under order from Ms. Daniels to set prices on the basis of "cost plus 40% of cost."

In an attempt to settle this dispute, Ms. Daniels calls the production manager, Eddie Robinson, into her office for a conference. Mr. Robinson reports that he has no choice but to change the cost every quarter, as to do otherwise would mean that a loss would result during periods of low demand. He tells Ms. Daniels that he has the numbers to back up these statements and reminds Ms. Daniels that figures don't lie. As proof, he offers the following information:

	1st Quarter	2nd Quarter	3rd Quarter	4th Quarter
Direct materials.	$ 28,000	$ 63,000	$ 70,000	$ 21,000
Direct labor	45,000	101,250	112,500	33,750
Variable manufacturing overhead	8,000	18,000	20,000	6,000
Fixed manufacturing overhead	180,000	180,000	180,000	180,000
Total	$261,000	$362,250	$382,500	$240,750
Number of gallons to be produced . . .	20,000	45,000	50,000	15,000
Cost per gallon	$13.05	$8.05	$7.65	$16.05

Ms. Daniels realizes that the root of the problem is manufacturing overhead. Manufacturing overhead costs cannot be reduced enough to make a difference during the periods of low demand. She asks Mr. Robinson to find a better way to allocate the manufacturing overhead costs to each gallon of concentrate produced in order to arrive at a more uniform cost figure per gallon.

Required:

a. How would you recommend to Mr. Robinson that manufacturing overhead costs be assigned to production? How would this differ from his present method?

b. What benefits would be gained by using your recommended solution?

c. To justify your recommendations made in (a) above, recalculate the per gallon cost of the concentrate using your recommendation.

15

PROCESS COSTING

LEARNING OBJECTIVES

After studying this chapter, you should be able to:

1. Describe the types of operations for which a process cost system is used.
2. Distinguish between process and job order costing systems.
3. Discuss the determination of unit costs and the concept of equivalent units in a process cost system.
4. Compute equivalent units of production under an average cost procedure.
5. Prepare a production cost report for a process cost system and discuss its relationship to the work in process inventory account.
6. Define and use correctly the new terms in the glossary.

This chapter continues the discussion of the two major types of cost accumulation systems under perpetual procedure. In the preceding chapter, job order costing was defined and illustrated. As stated in Chapter 14, a **job order cost system** is a cost accumulation system in which the costs incurred to produce a product are accumulated for each individual job. Job order costing is generally used when the products being manufactured can be separately identified or when goods are produced to meet a customer's particular needs. The other cost accumulation system, process costing, is the subject of this chapter.

PROCESS COST SYSTEMS

Objective 1: Describe the types of operations for which a process cost system is used

Many businesses manufacture huge quantities of a single product or similar products (paint, paper, chemicals, gasoline, rubber, and plastics) on a continuous basis over long periods of time. For these kinds of products, there is no separate job order; rather, production is ongoing over the year or even several years. A **process cost system (process costing)** is a manufacturing cost system in which costs incurred during production are accu-

mulated according to the processes or departments a product goes through on its way to completion. In these types of operations, costs must be accumulated for each process that a product undergoes. The processes or departments, known as **processing centers,** serve as "cost centers" where costs are accumulated for the entire period (usually a month). These costs are divided by the number of units produced (tons, pounds, gallons, or feet) to get an average unit cost. The cost system used under these circumstances is called a process cost system.

The two cost accumulation systems, job order costing and process costing, are similar in some ways, but also differ in other ways. Similarities between job order costing and process costing are:

1. Both cost systems have the same goal: to determine before year-end the unit cost of the products being manufactured.
2. Both cost systems have the same cost flows. Costs of the factors of production are first recorded in separate accounts for materials inventory, labor, and overhead. Costs are then transferred to a Work in Process Inventory account.
3. Both cost systems make use of a predetermined overhead rate (defined in Chapter 14) to apply manufacturing overhead.
4. Both cost systems use the same source documents to record direct/ indirect materials (a materials requisition) and direct/indirect labor (timecards).
5. Both cost systems record actual overhead as it is incurred.
6. Both cost systems measure over- or underapplied overhead at the end of a specified time period.

Job order costing and process costing also have their differences. The differences between these two systems are:

1. The products being accounted for. Under job order costing, many different jobs are worked on during each period, each job having different production requirements. Under process costing, a single product is produced, either on a continuous basis or for long periods of time. All products being produced are the same.
2. The cost accumulation procedures employed. Job order costing accumulates costs by individual jobs, while process costing accumulates costs by department.
3. The key documents used. Job order costing has job order cost sheets as its key documents, while process costing has the department production cost report.
4. The number of Work in Process Inventory accounts. Job order cost systems have only one Work in Process account. Process cost systems have a Work in Process account for each department or process.

Illustration 15.1 shows a process cost system in which products are processed in a specified sequential order; that is, the products are started

Illustration 15.1
COST FLOWS IN A PROCESS COST SYSTEM

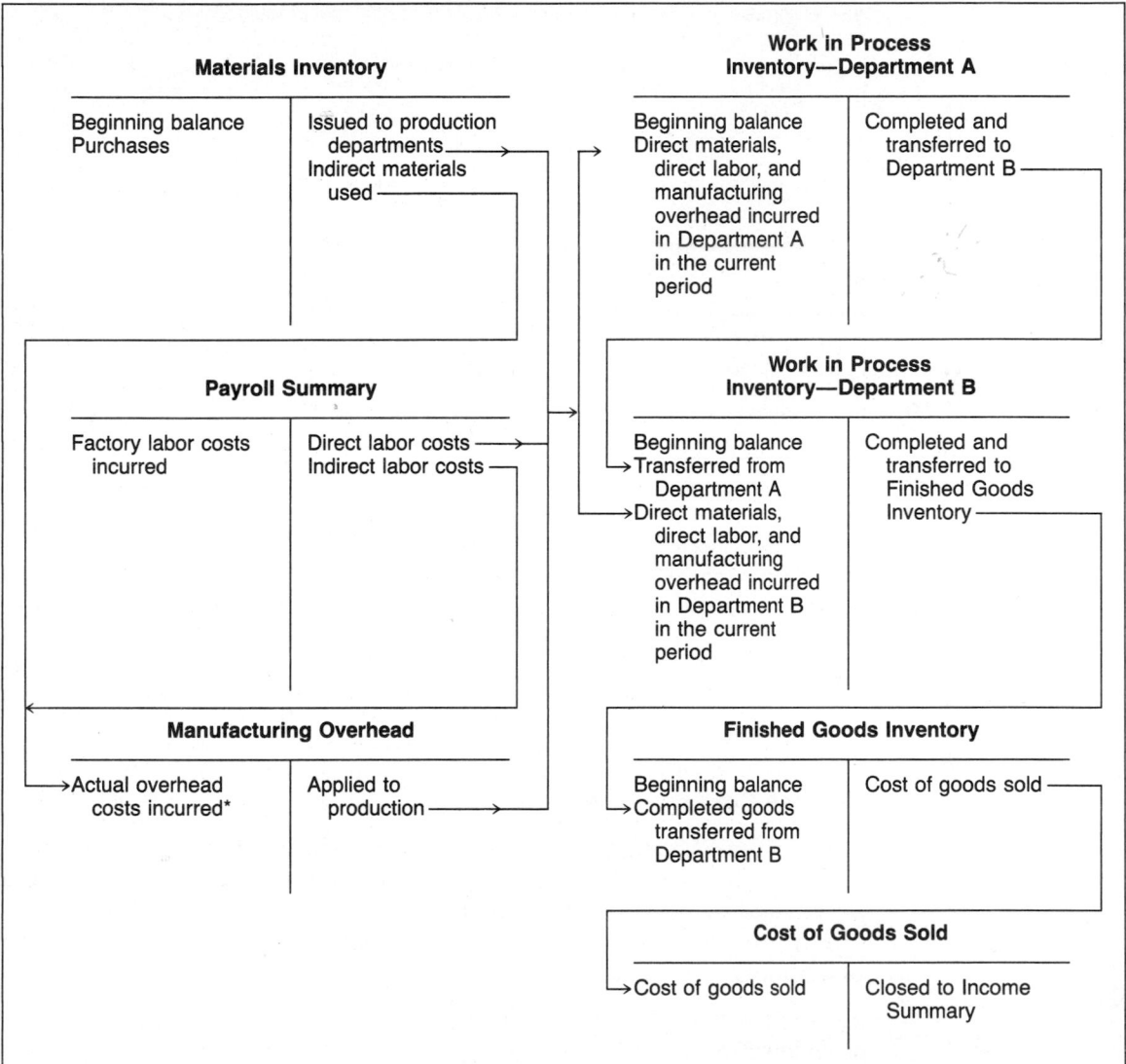

*Includes indirect materials, indirect labor, and other overhead.

and processed in Department A, transferred to Department B and processed further, and then transferred to Finished Goods Inventory. For illustration purposes, we will assume that all the process cost systems in this chapter are sequential; however, the student should be aware that many production flow combinations exist. Three different possibilities are presented in Illustration 15.2.

Illustration 15.2
POSSIBLE PRODUCTION FLOW COMBINATIONS

a. One product is processed sequentially, yielding one final product.

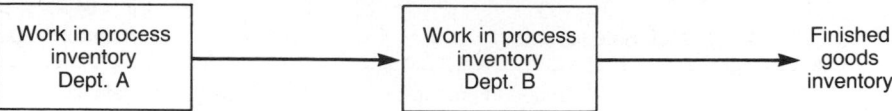

b. Two products are combined and then processed further to yield one final product.

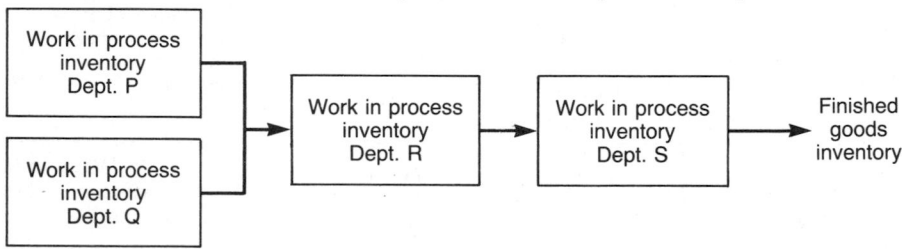

c. One product is further processed in two different manners, yielding two final products.

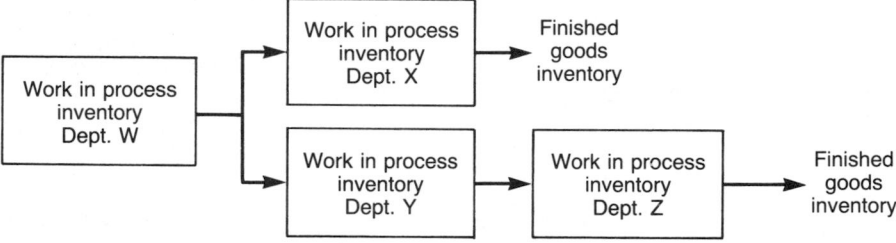

Process Costing Illustration

Assume that Ajax Company sells a chemical product that is processed in two departments. In Department A, basic materials are crushed, powdered, and blended. In Department B, the product is packaged and transferred to finished goods. This manufacturing process is shown in Illustration 15.3.

Production and cost data for Ajax Company for the month of June are as follows:

	Department A	Department B
Units started, completed, and transferred	11,000	9,000
Units on hand at June 30, partially completed	–0–	2,000
Beginning inventory	$ –0–	$ –0–
Direct materials	16,500	1,100
Direct labor	5,500	5,880
Actual manufacturing overhead	4,500	5,600
Applied manufacturing overhead	4,400	5,880

In Department A, manufacturing overhead is applied on the basis of a predetermined rate of 80% of direct labor cost. In Department B, manufacturing overhead is applied at the rate of 100% of direct labor cost.

Illustration 15.3
PRODUCT FLOWS IN A PROCESS COST SYSTEM
Ajax Company Example

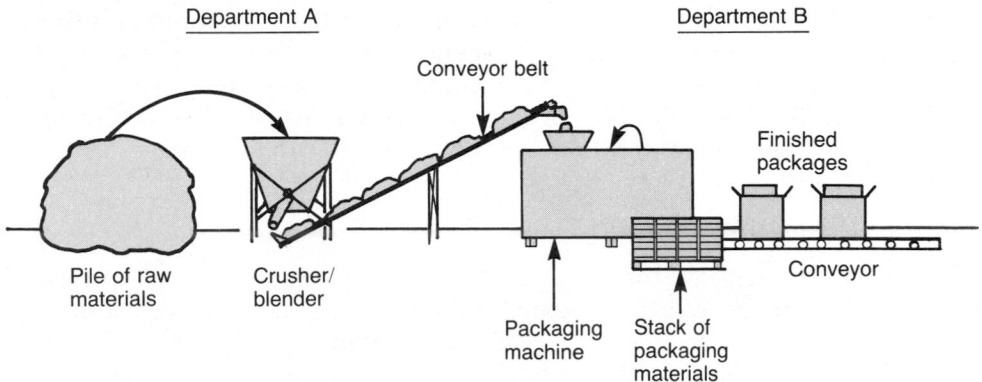

From these data, the Work in Process Inventory—Department A account can be constructed and summarized as follows:

Work in Process Inventory—Department A

Direct materials	16,500	Transferred to Department B—	
Direct labor	5,500	11,000 units @ $2.40	26,400
Applied overhead (80% of direct labor cost)	4,400		
Total	26,400		

Since all units started in June in Department A were completed and transferred to Department B, it follows that all costs assigned to those goods should also be transferred. The unit cost in Department A is computed by dividing $26,400 of total costs by the 11,000 units completed and transferred to get an average unit cost of $2.40.

Computations are seldom this simple. One complication is faced whenever partially completed inventories are present, as is true for Department B. Department B's Work in Process Inventory account for June is as follows before the cost of completed units is transferred out:

Work in Process Inventory—Department B

Transferred in from Department A	26,400
Direct material	1,100
Direct labor	5,880
Overhead (100% of direct labor)	5,880
Total	39,260

Recall that direct materials, direct labor, and manufacturing overhead are product costs, that is, they "attach" to the product. Thus the "Transferred in from Department A" line in the T-account above represents the material, labor, and overhead costs assigned to products in Department A. These costs have "followed" the physical units to Department B.

The task now faced is to divide the $39,260 total costs charged to Department B in June between the units transferred out and those remaining on hand in the department. The $39,260 cannot be divided by 11,000 to get an average unit cost because the 11,000 units are not alike; 9,000 are finished, and 2,000 are only partially finished. The problem is solved by using the concept of equivalent units of production.

EQUIVALENT UNITS

Objective 3: Discuss the determination of unit costs and the concept of equivalent units in a process cost system

Essentially, the concept of **equivalent units** involves expressing a given number of partially completed units as a smaller number of fully completed units. For example, 1,000 units brought to a 40% state of completion are equivalent to 400 units that are 100% complete. This concept is based on the fact that approximately the same amount of costs must be incurred to bring 1,000 units to a 40% level of completion as would be required to complete 400 units. The concept of equivalent units is presented pictorially in Illustration 15.4. In examining the diagram, think of the amount of water in the glasses as the costs which have already been incurred.

Objective 4: Compute equivalent units of production under an average cost procedure

The first step in computing equivalent units produced in Department B for the Ajax Company is to determine the stage of completion of the 2,000 unfinished units. These units are 100% complete as to **transferred-in costs** because if they were not, they would not have been transferred out of Department A. The units may have different stages of completion, however, as to the materials, labor, and overhead costs added in Department B. Assume that all materials are added at the beginning of the production

Illustration 15.4
THE CONCEPT OF EQUIVALENT UNITS

8 glasses of water 50% full

are equivalent to

4 glasses of water 100% full

process in Department B. Both ending inventory and units transferred out would be 100% complete as to materials; therefore, equivalent production for materials would be 11,000 units.

Units are usually assumed to be at the same stage of completion for both labor and overhead. The reason for this assumption is that overhead is often applied to work in process on a direct labor basis (recall that direct labor and overhead together are termed *conversion costs*). If we assume that the 2,000 units in ending inventory are, on the average, 40% complete as to conversion, equivalent production for labor and overhead would be 9,800 units—9,000 units transferred out fully completed and 2,000 brought to a 40% completion state, which is the equivalent of 800 fully completed units (2,000 × 40%).

Once the equivalent units of production are known, units costs of processing in Department B can be computed as follows:

	Transferred in	Materials	Conversion	Total
Costs to be accounted for:				
Charged to Department B	$26,400	$ 1,100	$11,760*	$39,260
Equivalent units	11,000	11,000	9,800†	
Unit costs	$2.40	$0.10	$1.20	$3.70

*Conversion costs consist of direct labor + overhead ($5,880 + $5,880).
†Units transferred out (9,000) + equivalent units in ending inventory (800).

Using the computed unit costs, the $39,260 of costs charged to Department B in June is divided between the costs associated with units completed and transferred out and the costs associated with the units remaining in the department's ending inventory:

	Transferred in (@ $2.40)	Materials (@ $0.10)	Conversion (@ $1.20)	Total
Costs accounted for:				
Units completed and transferred out (9,000 units).	$21,600	$ 900	$10,800	$33,300
Units remaining in ending inventory (2,000 units).	4,800	200	960*	5,960
Costs accounted for	$26,400	$1,100	$11,760	$39,260

*Equivalent units = 800 units.

The $33,300 total costs transferred out consists of $21,600 transferred in from Department A (9,000 × $2.40), $900 of materials costs (9,000 × $0.10), and $10,800 of conversion costs (9,000 × $1.20), or total costs of $3.70 per unit. The 2,000 units of ending inventory in Department B are fully complete as to materials and 40% complete as to conversion. Ending inventory cost is calculated as follows:

Costs from Department A (2,000 × $2.40)		$4,800
Costs added by Department B:		
Materials (2,000 × $0.10).	$200	
Conversion (800 equivalent units × $1.20)	960	1,160
Total cost of ending inventory		$5,960

The units transferred out of Department B will be carried in finished goods inventory at a cost of $3.70 each until they are sold, at which time the costs will be charged to Cost of Goods Sold.

The June journal entries for the above activities follow:

(1) Work in Process Inventory—Department A 16,500
    Work in Process Inventory—Department B 1,100
        Materials Inventory 17,600
    To record materials placed in production in June.

(2) Payroll Summary 11,380
        Various withholding accounts and
            wages payable 11,380
    To record factory payroll for June.

(3) Work in Process Inventory—Department A 5,500
    Work in Process Inventory—Department B 5,880
        Payroll Summary 11,380
    To distribute factory labor costs (assuming that all such costs are chargeable directly to production departments).

(4) Manufacturing Overhead 10,100
        Various accounts—cash, accounts payable, accruals,
           and accumulated depreciation 10,100
    To record actual overhead costs incurred in June.

(5) Work in Process Inventory—Department A 4,400
    Work in Process Inventory—Department B 5,880
        Manufacturing Overhead 10,280
    To apply overhead to production using predetermined rates based on direct labor cost: Department A, 80%; and Department B, 100%.

(6) Work in Process Inventory—Department B 26,400
        Work in Process Inventory—Department A 26,400
    To record transfer of goods from Department A to Department B.

(7) Finished Goods Inventory 33,300
        Work in Process Inventory—Department B 33,300
    To record transfer of completed goods from Department B to finished goods.

If 6,000 completed units were sold in June at a price of $10 per unit on account, the following entries would be required:

(8) Accounts Receivable 60,000
        Sales 60,000
    To record sales on account.

(9) Cost of Goods Sold 22,200
        Finished Goods Inventory 22,200
    To record cost of goods sold in June, 6,000 units @ $3.70.

Generally, the formula for equivalent production is:

$$\frac{\text{Equivalent}}{\text{production}} = \frac{\text{Units}}{\text{completed}} + \left(\frac{\text{Units in}}{\text{ending inventory}} \times \frac{\text{Percentage}}{\text{complete}} \right)$$

PRODUCTION COST REPORT

Objective 5:
Prepare a production cost report for a process cost system and discuss its relationship to the work in process inventory account

The key document in a process costing system is the production cost report. A **production cost report** shows both the flow of units and the flow of costs through a processing center. It also shows how these costs are divided between the cost of units completed and transferred out and the cost of units still in the processing center's ending inventory. This report is designed to make equivalent unit and unit cost computations easier.

To illustrate the preparation of a production cost report where there are partially completed beginning and ending inventories, assume the following data for Department 3 of the Storey Company, for the month of June 1990:

Units

Units in beginning inventory, complete as to materials, 60% complete as to conversion	6,000
Units transferred in from Department 2	18,000
Units completed and transferred out	16,000
Units in ending inventory, complete as to materials, 50% complete as to conversion	8,000

Costs

Cost of beginning inventory:		
Cost transferred in from preceding department in May	$12,000	
Materials added in May in Department 3	6,000	
Conversion costs (equal amounts of labor and overhead)	3,000	$21,000
Costs transferred in from preceding department in June		37,200
Costs added in Department 3 in June:		
Materials	$18,480	
Conversion (equal amounts of labor and overhead)	18,000	36,480
Total costs in beginning inventory and placed in production in Department 3 in June		$94,680

There are four steps in the preparation of the production cost report:

1. Tracing the physical flow of the units through the production department.
2. Converting actual units to equivalent units.
3. Computing unit costs for each cost element.
4. Distributing the total cost between the units completed and transferred and the units remaining in the ending inventory.

The production cost report for Department 3, shown in Illustration 15.5, is developed using the data for the month June. The first step in the preparation of a production cost report is to trace the physical flow of actual units into and out of the department. The section entitled "UNITS" in Illustration 15.5 shows that 6,000 units were in the June beginning inventory and that 18,000 units were transferred in from the previous department, making a total of 24,000 units that must be accounted for. Of these 24,000 units, 16,000 units were completed and transferred out (either to the next processing department or to finished goods), and 8,000 remained partially completed in Department 3 at the end of the month. These 8,000 units are the June ending inventory.

Illustration 15.5
PRODUCTION COST REPORT

STOREY COMPANY
Production Cost Report—Department 3
For the Month of June 1990

	Actual Units	Equivalent Units		
		Transferred In	Materials	Conversion
Units				
Units in beginning inventory	6,000			
Units transferred in from Department 2	18,000			
Units to be accounted for	24,000			
Units completed and transferred	16,000	16,000	16,000	16,000
Units in ending inventory*	8,000	8,000	8,000	4,000
Units accounted for.	24,000	24,000	24,000	20,000

* Inventory is complete as to materials added, 50% complete as to conversion.

	Transferred In	Materials	Conversion	Total
Costs				
Costs to be accounted for:				
Costs in beginning inventory.	$12,000	$ 6,000	$ 3,000	$21,000
Costs transferred in from Department 2	37,200			37,200
Costs added in Department 3		18,480	18,000	36,480
Costs to be accounted for	$49,200	$24,480	$21,000	$94,680
Equivalent units (as above)	24,000	24,000	20,000	
Unit costs (per equivalent unit).	$2.05	$1.02	$1.05	$4.12
Costs accounted for:				
Costs completed and transferred out	$32,800	$16,320	$16,800	$65,920
Costs remaining in ending inventory	16,400	8,160	4,200	28,760
Costs accounted for	$49,200	$24,480	$21,000	$94,680

The cost of production report illustrated uses an average cost procedure. Under an **average cost procedure,** the number of equivalent units for each cost element equals the number of units transferred out plus the number of equivalent units of that cost element in the ending inventory. (The number of units in beginning inventory and the degree of completion of the beginning inventory are not considered under the average cost methods.) In this example, the units in the ending inventory are fully complete as to cost transferred in and as to materials; therefore, the number of equivalent units for each of these cost elements is 24,000 (16,000 units completed and transferred + 8,000 units in the ending inventory × 100% complete for transferred-in cost and for materials). The units in ending inventory, however, were only 50% complete as to conversion; therefore, equivalent units for conversion costs are 20,000 [(16,000 units completed and transferred) + (8,000 units in the ending inventory × 50% complete as to conversion)].

Once equivalent units have been computed, unit costs must be calculated. Costs have been accumulated for each cost element of production—costs transferred in, materials, and conversion. Notice that the costs of beginning inventory and costs of the current month are totaled for each cost element. The total costs charged to the department are referred to as "costs to be accounted for." These costs have either been transferred out or will appear in the ending inventory of Department 3. To determine the cost per equivalent unit for each cost element, divide the total cost for each cost element by the equivalent units of production related to that cost element. (Since all costs for each cost element are totaled before the division, the unit costs computed are averaged across the current and the prior period.) As shown in Illustration 15.5, average per unit costs for June are as follows: transferred-in cost, $2.05; materials, $1.02; and conversion, $1.05. These costs are monitored closely by management for cost control purposes in the event that there are extreme fluctuations from one month to the next.

The last step is to allocate costs between the units completed and transferred out and the units remaining in ending inventory. The units that were transferred out were fully complete as to all elements of production. Therefore, the 16,000 units can be multiplied by $4.12, the total cost per unit. The result, $65,920, is the amount assigned to the next department as "costs transferred in" or to finished goods as the cost of completed current period production. The cost of ending inventory is computed as follows:

8,000 equivalent units transferred in @ $2.05	$16,400
8,000 equivalent units of materials costs @ $1.02	8,160
4,000 equivalent units of conversion costs @ $1.05.	4,200
Total cost of ending inventory	$28,760

The sum of the ending inventory cost and the cost of the units transferred out must equal the total costs to be accounted for. This built-in check determines whether the procedures of cost allocation have been properly followed. As shown in the production cost report, cost transferred out of $65,920 are added to ending inventory cost of $28,760, and the total equals costs to be accounted for ($94,680).

In some other textbooks, the production cost report is not used, but is replaced by three schedules. The first schedule is the schedule of equivalent production, which computes the equivalent units of production for the period for both materials and conversion costs. The second schedule is the unit cost analysis schedule, which sums all the costs charged to the Work in Process Inventory account of each department or production process and calculates the cost per equivalent unit for materials and conversion costs. The third schedule is the cost summary schedule, which makes use of the results of the preceding two schedules to distribute the total costs accumulated during the period among all the units of output. These three schedules are generally shown together in a process costs analysis report.

FIFO METHOD

The FIFO (first-in, first-out) procedure could have been used instead of the average cost procedure. Generally, the equivalent units number under FIFO consists of:

1. The work needed to complete the units in beginning inventory.
2. The work done on units started and completed during the period.
3. Work done on partially completed units in ending inventory.

Detailed discussion of the FIFO procedure is reserved for an advanced cost accounting course.

SUMMARY

Two major types of cost accumulation systems under perpetual inventory cost procedure are used by manufacturing companies—the job order cost system and the process cost system. In each system, the goal is to determine before year-end the unit costs of the products being manufactured. Unit costs may be used by management throughout the period to compute (1) cost of goods sold, (2) cost of work in process and finished goods inventories, (3) payments to be received under contracts based on "full" cost, and (4) selling prices.

A process cost system is a manufacturing cost system in which the costs incurred to produce a product are accumulated for each process or department a product goes through on its way to completion. Process cost systems are generally used where huge quantities of a single product or of similar products are manufactured on a continuous basis over long periods of time.

Before per unit cost of products can be calculated for a process cost system, the equivalent units of production for the period must be computed. Equivalent units must be determined for (1) costs transferred in (if the department receives products from another processing department), (2) costs of materials, and (3) costs of conversion. The costs of transferred in units (if any), materials, and conversion are then divided by the respective number of equivalent units to obtain cost per equivalent unit. Finally, the numbers of equivalent units (for transferred-in units, materials, and conversion costs) of units completed and transferred and ending work in process inventory are multiplied by their respective costs per equivalent unit to determine the total cost of the units completed and transferred and of the ending work in process inventory. This cost computation is performed in a production cost report, which is a key document in a process costing system.

Accurate accounting for product unit costs is important. Without accurate cost accounting information the management of a manufacturing company cannot determine selling prices, prepare accurate financial statements, or determine the cost of its ending inventory. Chapter 16 discusses ways that costs can be used to assess the efficiency of a manufacturing process.

NEW TERMS INTRODUCED IN CHAPTER 15

Average cost procedure A method of computing equivalent units where the number of equivalent units for each cost element equals the number of units transferred out plus the number of equivalent units of that element in the ending inventory (554).

Equivalent units A method of expressing a given number of partially completed units as a smaller number of fully completed units; for example, bringing 1,000 units to a 75% level of completion is the equivalent of bringing 750 units to a 100% level of completion (550).

Job order cost system A manufacturing cost system in which costs incurred to produce a product are accumulated for each individual job (545).

Process cost system (process costing) A manufacturing cost system in which costs incurred to produce a product are accumulated according to the processes or departments a product goes through on its way to completion (545).

Processing center An individual process or department in a process system which serves as a "cost center" where costs are accumulated for the entire period in question (546).

Production cost report A report that shows both the flow of units and the flow of costs through a processing center; it also shows how those costs are divided between the cost of units transferred out and the cost of units still in the processing center's ending inventory (553).

Transferred-in costs Costs, associated with physical units, which were accumulated in previous processing centers (550).

DEMONSTRATION PROBLEM 15–1

D. Holland, Inc. uses a process cost system to accumulate the costs it incurs to produce dead-bolt locks. The June 1 inventory consisted of 45,000 units, fully complete as to materials, 80% complete as to conversion. The beginning inventory cost of $360,000 consisted of $270,000 of costs transferred in from the molding department, $37,500 of finishing department material costs, and $52,500 of finishing department conversion costs. The costs incurred in the finishing department for the month of June appear below:

Costs from molding department		
(excluding costs in beginning inventory)		$ 900,000
Costs added in finishing department in June		
(excluding costs in beginning inventory):		
Materials	$ 79,500	
Conversion	164,220	243,720
		$1,143,720

The finishing department received 150,000 units from the molding department in June. During the month, 159,000 units were completed by the finishing department and transferred out. As of June 30, 36,000 units complete as to materials and 60% complete as to conversion, were left in inventory of the finishing department.

Required:

a. Prepare a production cost report for the finishing department for the month of June.

b. Compute the average unit cost for conversion in the finishing department in May.

Solution to demonstration problem 15–1

a.

D. HOLLAND, INC.
Finishing Department
Production Cost Report
For the Month Ending June 30

	Actual Units	Equivalent		
		Transferred In	Materials	Conversion
Units				
Units in June 1 inventory	45,000			
Units transferred in	150,000			
Units to be accounted for	195,000			
Units completed and transferred	159,000	159,000	159,000	159,000
Units in June 30 inventory*	36,000	36,000	36,000	21,600†
Units accounted for	195,000	195,000	195,000	180,600

* Inventory is complete as to materials, 60% complete as to conversion.
† (36,000 × .6 = 21,600).

	Transferred In	Materials	Conversion	Total
Costs				
Costs to be accounted for:				
Costs in June 1 inventory	$ 270,000	$ 37,500	$ 52,500	360,000
Costs transferred in	900,000			900,000
Costs added in department		79,500	164,220	243,720
Costs to be accounted for	$1,170,000	$117,000	$216,720	$1,503,720
Equivalent units (as above)	195,000	195,000	180,600	
Unit costs	$6.00	$0.60	$1.20	$7.80
Costs accounted for:				
Units completed and transferred out	$ 954,000	$ 95,400	$190,800	$1,240,200
Units remaining in June 30 inventory	216,000	21,600	25,920	263,520
Costs accounted for.	$1,170,000	$117,000	$216,720	$1,503,720

b. The unit cost of conversion in the finishing department in May was $1.46 [$52,500/(.8 × 45,000)].

QUESTIONS

1. How does a process cost system differ from a job order cost system? What factors should be taken into consideration in determining which type of system should be employed?

2. What is meant by the term *equivalent units*? Of what use is the computation of the number of equivalent units of production?

3. Distinguish between the number of units completed and transferred during a period and the equivalent units for the same period.

4. Under what circumstances would the number of equivalent units of materials differ from the equivalent units of labor and overhead in the same department in the same period? Under what circumstances would they be the same?

5. What is the basic information conveyed by a production cost report?

6. What is meant by average cost procedure?

7. Less effort is required to operate a job cost system than a process cost system. Do you agree or disagree? Explain.

EXERCISES

Compute equivalent units

1. Compute the equivalent production in each case given below:
   a. Units started in production during the month, 30,000; units completed and transferred, 22,000; and units in process at end of month (60% complete), 8,000.
   b. Units in process at beginning of month (30% complete), 5,000; units started during month, 20,000; and units in process at end of month (40% complete), 10,000.

Compute equivalent units

2. The 2,100 units of June ending inventory were 50% complete as to materials and 25% complete as to conversion. What are the equivalent units as to materials and conversion costs of the ending inventory?

Calculate equivalent units

3. In Department B, materials are added uniformly throughout processing. The beginning inventory was considered 50% complete, as was the ending inventory. Assume that there were 1,000 units in the beginning inventory and 3,000 in the ending inventory, and that 16,000 units were completed and transferred. If the average unit costs are to be computed, what is the equivalent production for the period?

Calculate costs of the units completed and transferred

4. If in Exercise 3 the total costs charged to the department amounted to $210,000, including the $6,030 cost of the beginning inventory, what is the cost of the units completed and transferred?

Calculate cost per equivalent unit; determine costs of units transferred and those remaining in ending inventory; determine change in conversion cost per unit

5. The following data relate to Department C, in which all material is added at the start of processing and in which the weight of the finished product is equal to the weight of the direct materials used:

Inventory, June 1:
Materials cost (400 pounds) $1,170
Conversion cost (20% complete) 165

Costs incurred during June:
Direct materials used (2,000 pounds at $3.015) . . . 6,030
Direct labor (300 hours at $6.60) 1,980
Overhead (at $3 per machine-hours;
990 machine-hours were incurred) 2,970

Inventory, June 30:
Materials cost (600 pounds, 100% complete)
Conversion cost (600 pounds, 2/3 complete)

Using the above data, compute:
a. The number of pounds transferred out of the department in June.
b. The unit cost per equivalent unit for materials and conversion (use the average method).

c. The cost of the product transferred out.

d. The cost of the ending inventory.

e. The change in the conversion cost per unit from May to June.

Calculate equivalent units

6. In Department T of the Cork Company, 50% of material cost are added at the beginning of the process and 50% are added just before units are sent to the next department. The October 31 ending inventory was 15% complete as to conversion costs. There were 3,150 units in beginning inventory, 2,850 units were started during October and 1,500 units remain in ending inventory. What are the equivalent units of production for materials and conversion costs for the month of October?

Compute equivalent units

7. The Batson Company manufactures golf balls. On March 31, Department M had ending inventory of 16,200 units 60% complete as to conversion. What are the equivalent units as to conversion costs of ending inventory?

Prepare journal entries for sales

8. The Cook Company manufactures cakes at a cost of $1.90 per cake and sells them for $4.50 each. In January, 9,750 cakes were sold. Prepare the required journal entries.

PROBLEMS

Prepare a production cost report; calculate average unit conversion cost

15–1. Marshall, Inc., uses a process cost system to accumulate the costs it incurs in producing steel transformers. The costs incurred in the finishing department are shown for the month of June. The June 1 inventory consisted of 30,000 units which were fully complete as to materials, 80% complete as to conversion. The inventory's total cost of $480,000 consisted of $360,000 of costs transferred in from the molding department, $50,000 of finishing department material costs, and $70,000 of conversion costs.

Costs from molding department (excluding costs in beginning inventory) . . .		$1,200,000
Costs added in finishing department in June (excluding costs in beginning inventory):		
Materials.	$106,000	
Conversion.	218,960	324,960
Total.		$1,524,960

The finishing department received 100,000 units from the molding department; 106,000 units were completed and transferred; and 24,000 units complete as to materials and 60% complete as to conversion, were left in the June 30, inventory.

Required:

a. Prepare a production cost report for the finishing department for the month of June.

b. Compute the average unit cost for conversion for May in the finishing department.

Calculate equivalent units, average unit costs, costs transferred, and cost of ending work in process inventory

15–2. The following data are for the initial processing center of the Walker Company for the month of June. All material is added at the beginning of the processing operation.

Work in process inventory, June 1 (15,000 pounds, 40% complete as to conversion):

Direct materials	$15,000
Direct labor	2,400
Manufacturing overhead (assigned at $2 per	
machine-hour; 2,400 machine-hours were	
incurred)	4,800
	$22,200

Added in June:

Direct materials (135,000 pounds)	$137,700
Direct labor (3,000 hours at $16)	48,000
Manufacturing overhead	96,000
	$281,700

The work in process inventory at June 30 consisted of 45,000 units (pounds), one third complete as to processing.

Required:

Compute the following:

a. Number of pounds completed and transferred out of the processing center.

b. The equivalent units of production for materials, labor, and overhead for June (assuming average unit costs are to be computed).

c. The average unit costs for June for materials, labor, and overhead.

d. The cost of the pounds transferred out in June.

e. The cost of the June 30 work in process inventory.

f. The average unit labor cost last month (May).

Prepare production cost report

15–3. Mauldin Company manufactures a product called Valem. The company uses a process cost system to determine product costs. Following are cost and production data for the Handle Department for the month of July:

	Units	Materials Costs	Conversion Costs
Inventory, July 1	30,000	$2,685	$ 3,300
Placed in production in July	90,000	8,115	14,340
Inventory, July 31	45,000	?	?

The July 1 inventory was complete as to materials and 50% complete as to conversion. The July 31 inventory was complete as to materials and 20% complete as to conversion.

Required:

Prepare a production cost report.

Prepare production cost report, calculate per unit conversion costs, and prepare journal entry

15–4. Smith Drug Company manufactures Stop-Sure, a cold remedy, in a blending department from which the remedy is transferred to the bottling department. Production and cost data for the bottling department for June are as follows:

Work in process, June 1 (60,000 pints):		
Transferred in costs (100% complete)	$ 60,000	
Bottling materials (100% complete)	24,000	
Conversion costs (50% complete)	12,000	
		$ 96,000
Added in June:		
Transferred in (180,000 pints).	184,800	
Bottling materials for 180,000 units	76,800	
Conversion costs	73,500	
		$335,100

All materials in the bottling department are added at the beginning of processing, and their amounts are determined by the number of pints in Stop-Sure transferred in. The ending inventory for June was 30,000 units, 100% complete as to materials and 50% complete as to conversion.

Required:

a. Prepare a production cost report for the bottling department for the month of June.

b. Compute the per unit conversion in the department for the prior month (May).

c. Give the journal entry needed to record the transfer of the units completed in the bottling department in June.

Prepare production cost report

15–5. Fraser Company uses a process cost system to account for the costs incurred in making its single product, a snack food called Potato Curls. This product is processed first in Department A and then in Department B. Materials are added in both departments. Production for May was as follows:

	Department A	Department B
Units started or transferred in.	225,000	168,750
Units completed and transferred out.	168,750	135,000
Stage of completion of May 31 inventory:		
Materials.	100%	80%
Conversion.	50%	40%
Direct materials cost.	$135,000	$ 24,300
Conversion costs	$393,750	$267,300

There was no May 1 inventory in either department.

Required:

a. Prepare a production cost report for Department A for May.

b. Prepare a production cost report for Department B for May.

Prepare production cost report

15–6. Collier Company manufactures a product called Bug and determines product costs using a process cost system. Materials costing $11,000 were introduced at the start of processing, and $9,700 of conversion costs were incurred. During the period, 20,000 units of product were started, and 19,000 were completed and transferred. At the end of the period, 1,000 units were still in process and were 40% complete as to conversion.

Required:

Prepare a production cost report using the average method.

*Calculate equivalent
units, costs per
equivalent unit,
cost of goods
transferred out, and
cost of ending
inventory*

15–7. The following data apply to Department D of the Felton Company:

Work in process inventory, April 1, 15,000 units.

Direct materials	$ 450,000
Direct labor	$ 150,000
Manufacturing Overhead (applied at $5 per machine-hour; 30,000 machine-hours were incurred)	$ 150,000
Units started in April, 45,000	
Costs incurred in April	
Direct materials	1,425,000
Direct labor	393,750
Manufacturing Overhead applied (75,000 machine-hours were incurred.)	?

Ending inventory of 7,500 units was 100% complete as to materials, 25% complete as to conversion.

Required: Compute the following:

a. Units completed and transferred out.

b. Equivalent units of production for materials and conversion costs using the average method.

c. Cost per equivalent unit.

d. Cost of units transferred out.

e. Cost of ending inventory.

*Prepare production
cost report*

15–8. The following information relates to the Hayes Company:

Units in beginning inventory	2,250
Cost of units in beginning inventory:	
Materials.	$ 22,500
Conversion.	$ 10,500
Units placed in production	60,000
Costs incurred during current period:	
Materials.	$133,125
Conversion.	$119,910
Units remaining in ending inventory (100% complete as to materials, 50% complete as to conversion).	3,750

Required:

Prepare a production cost report using the average method.

BUSINESS DECISION PROBLEM 15–1

*Determine how
production costs
should be allocated.*

The Tops Manufacturing Company manufactures thousands of tabletops every year. While the company has developed a per unit cost for its tabletops, it has not been able to accurately break down its costs in each of its three departments: cutting, assembling, and packing. Ted Gurnee, the production manager, has been concerned with cost overruns during the month of July in the assembling department.

On July 1, the assembly department had 5,000 units in its work in process inventory. These units were 100% complete as to materials and 40% complete as to conversion. The department had incurred $10,000 in materials costs and $78,000 in conversion costs in processing these 5,000 units.

The department handled 25,000 units during the month, including the 5,000 units on July 1. At the end of the month, the department's work in process included 3,000 units which were 100% complete as to materials and 30% complete as to conversion. The month's costs were allocated based on the number of units processed during the month as follows:

	Materials	Conversion
Costs	$49,000	$227,500
Units handled during month	25,000	25,000
Cost per unit	$1.96	$9.10

The $11.06 of per-unit costs was systematically allocated and resulted in the following costs:

	Beginning Work in Process	Work Started and Completed	Ending Work in Process
Costs transferred in	$ 88,000		
Costs incurred during the month:			
5,000 units × $11.06	55,300		
17,000 units × $11.06		$188,020	
3,000 units × $11.06			$33,180
Total costs	$143,300	$188,020	$33,180
Per unit costs	$28.66	$11.06	$11.06

Mr. Gurnee realizes that this per-unit cost allocation is incorrect because the beginning work in process has too high a per-unit cost. He asks you to develop a better method of allocating these costs for the month of July.

Required:

a. How would you recommend to Mr. Gurnee that July's costs be assigned to the units produced? How would this differ from his present method?

b. To justify your recommendation, recalculate July's costs using your recommendation.

16

CONTROL
THROUGH
STANDARD COSTS

LEARNING OBJECTIVES

After studying this chapter, you should be able to:

1. Discuss the nature of standard costs, including how standards are set.
2. Discuss the advantages of using standard costs.
3. Calculate the six variances from standard, and determine if each variance is favorable or unfavorable.
4. Discuss what each of the six variance accounts shows, and prepare journal entries to record the variances.
5. Discuss the three selection guidelines used to investigate variances from standard.
6. Discuss the theoretical and practical methods for disposing of variances from standard.
7. Discuss how standard costs are applied in both job order and process cost systems (covered in Appendix).
8. Define and use correctly the new terms in the glossary.

You will recall that the job order and process cost systems discussed in Chapters 14 and 15 are based on actual historical cost data. Because these data say little about how efficiently operations were conducted, many companies find it helpful to introduce standard costs into their cost systems. Standard costs can be used in both job order and process cost systems as shown in the Appendix to this chapter.

Standard and actual cost systems differ in that an actual cost system collects *actual* costs for materials, labor, and manufacturing overhead, while a standard cost system gathers both actual costs and *standard* costs for these elements of production. The standard costs flow through the accounting system to determine a standard, or "normal," cost for finished goods inventory. Actual costs incurred during the period are then compared with standard costs to assist management in decision making and to determine whether proper control is being maintained over production costs.

This chapter discusses the nature of standard costs and how to compute the difference between an actual cost and a standard cost, which is called a variance. The variances discussed are: materials variances, labor variances, and overhead variances. As you work with variances you will become aware of how important variances are in controlling costs.

STANDARD COSTS

Possibly you have set goals in your own life that you have sought to achieve. These goals could well have been called standards. Periodically, you might measure your actual performance against these standards and analyze the differences. Similarly, management sets goals, such as standard costs, and compares actual costs with these goals to identify possible problems.

Nature of Standard Costs

Objective 1: Discuss the nature of standard costs, including how standards are set

A **standard cost** is a carefully predetermined measure of what a cost should be under stated conditions. A standard cost is not merely an estimate of what a cost will be; it represents a goal. If a standard is properly set, achieving it represents a reasonably efficient level of performance.

Standards are set in many ways, but to be of any real value they should be more than estimates found by extending historical trends into the future. Usually, engineering studies and time and motion studies are undertaken to determine the amounts of materials, labor, and other services required to produce a product. General economic conditions should also be considered in setting standards because economic conditions affect the cost of materials and other services that must be purchased by a manufacturing company. A standard cost is found for each manufactured unit of product by determining the standard costs of direct materials, direct labor, and manufacturing overhead needed to produce that unit.

Standard direct materials cost per unit is made up of the standard amount of material required to produce that unit multiplied by the standard price of the material. It is extremely important to distinguish between the terms *standard price* and *standard cost*. Standard price usually refers to the price per unit of inputs into the production process. For example, the price per pound of raw materials is a standard price. Standard cost, on the other hand, is the product of the standard quantity of an input required per unit of output times the standard price per unit of that input. For example, if the standard price of cloth is $3 per yard and the standard quantity of material required to produce a dress is 3 yards, then the standard direct materials cost of the dress is $9 (3 yards × $3 per yard). Similarly, the standard direct labor cost per unit for a product is computed as the standard number of hours needed to produce one unit multiplied by the standard labor or wage rate.

The standard manufacturing overhead cost of a unit is determined as follows. First, the expected level of output is determined for the year. This level of output is called the **standard level of output.** Next, the total budgeted manufacturing overhead cost at the standard level of output is determined. The total budgeted overhead cost includes both fixed and variable components. Total fixed cost is the same at every level of output. Variable overhead varies in direct proportion to the number of units produced. Finally, the standard manufacturing overhead cost per unit is computed by dividing the budgeted manufacturing overhead cost by the standard level of output. The result is an overhead cost (or rate) per unit of output. Sometimes accountants find the standard overhead cost (or rate) per direct labor-hour instead of per unit. To find the cost per unit, merely multiply the direct labor-hours per unit times the standard overhead cost per direct labor-hour. For instance, if the standard overhead cost per direct labor-hour is $5 and the standard number of direct labor-hours is two hours per unit, the standard overhead cost per unit is $10 ($5 × 2 hours).

ADVANTAGES OF USING STANDARD COSTS

Objective 2. Discuss the advantages of using standard costs

A number of benefits result from the use of a standard cost system. These include:

1. Improved cost control.
2. More useful information for managerial planning and decision making.
3. More reasonable inventory measurements.
4. Cost savings in record-keeping.
5. Possible reductions in production costs incurred.

Improved cost control. Cost control is gained mainly by setting standards for each type of cost incurred and then highlighting exceptions, or variances—instances where things are not going as planned. Variances provide a starting point for judging the effectiveness of managers in controlling the costs for which they are held responsible.

Assume, for example, that in a certain production center, actual direct materials cost was $52,015 and exceeded standard cost by $6,015. Knowing that actual direct materials cost exceeded standard cost by $6,015 is more useful than merely knowing actual direct materials cost amounted to $52,015. Now the cause of the excess of actual cost over standard cost can be investigated and action can be taken. Further investigation will show whether the exception was caused by factors under management's control. The exception (variance) may be caused by inefficient use of materials, or it may be the result of higher prices due to inflation. In either case, the standard cost system has served as an early warning system by highlighting a potential hazard for management.

More useful information for managerial planning and decision making. When management develops appropriate cost standards and succeeds in controlling production costs, then future actual costs should be fairly close to standard. As a result, standard costs can be used in preparing more accurate budgets and in estimating costs for bidding on jobs. A standard cost system can be valuable in top management planning and decision making.

More reasonable inventory measurements. A standard cost system provides a more logical inventory valuation than an actual cost system. Unit costs for batches of identical products may differ widely under an actual cost system. This difference may be caused by a machine malfunction during the production of a given batch that resulted in more labor and overhead being charged to that batch. Under a standard cost system such costs would not be included in inventory. Rather, they would be charged to variance accounts after comparing actual costs to standard costs. Thus, in a standard cost system, all units of a given product are carried in inventory at the same unit cost. Logically, identical physical units produced in a given time period should be recorded at the same cost.

Cost savings in record-keeping. Although a standard cost system may seem to require more detailed record-keeping than an actual cost system, the reverse is true. For example, in a job order system, detailed records must be kept of various types of materials used on each job as well as the various types and quantities of labor services received. In a standard cost system, standard cost sheets may be printed in advance showing quantities, unit costs, and total costs for the materials, labor, and overhead needed to produce a given amount of a certain product.

Possible reductions in production costs incurred. A standard cost system may lead to cost savings. The use of standard costs may cause employees to become more cost conscious and thus seek improved methods of completing their tasks. Only when employees become active in reducing costs can companies really become successful in cost control.

COMPUTING VARIANCES

Objective 3: Calculate the six variances from standard, and determine if each variance is favorable or unfavorable

As stated earlier, standard costs represent *goals*. Standard cost is the amount that a cost should be under a given set of circumstances. The accounting records, however, contain information regarding *actual* costs. The amount by which actual cost differs from standard cost is called a **variance**. A variance is designated as favorable when actual costs are less than standard, and unfavorable when actual costs exceed standard. But it does not automatically follow that favorable and unfavorable variances should be equated with good and bad. As you will see, such an appraisal should only be made after the causes of the variance are known.

The following section explains how to compute the dollar amount of variances, a process called *isolating variances,* using data for the Beta Company. Beta Company manufactures and sells a single product, each unit of which has the following standard costs:

Materials—5 sheets at $6 . . . . $30
Direct labor—2 hours at $10   20
Manufacturing overhead—2 direct labor-hours at $5   10
Total standard cost per unit $60

Additional data regarding the production activities of the company will be presented as needed.

Materials Variances

The standard materials cost of any product is simply the standard quantity of materials that should be used multiplied by the standard price that should be paid for those materials. Actual costs may differ from standard costs for materials because the price paid for the materials and/or the quantity of materials used varied from the standard amounts management had set. These two factors are accounted for by isolating two variances for materials—a price variance and a usage variance.

There are several reasons for isolating two materials variances. First, different individuals may be responsible for each—a purchasing agent for the price variance and a production manager for the usage variance. Second, materials might not be purchased and used in the same period. The variance associated with the purchase should be isolated in the period of purchase, and the variance associated with usage should be isolated in the period of use. As a general rule, the sooner a variance can be isolated, the greater its value in cost control. Finally, it is unlikely that a single materials variance—the difference between the standard cost and the actual cost of the materials used—would be of any real value to management for effective cost control. A single variance would not show management what caused the difference, or one variance might simply offset another and make the total difference appear immaterial.

Materials price variance. In a manufacturing company, the standard price for materials meeting certain engineering specifications is usually set by the purchasing and accounting departments. Consideration is given to factors such as market conditions, vendors' quoted prices, and the optimum size of a purchase order when setting a standard price. The **materials price variance (MPV)** is caused by paying a higher or lower price than the standard price set for materials. Materials price variance (MPV) is the difference between actual price paid (AP) and standard price allowed (SP) multiplied by the actual quantity of materials purchased (AQ). In equation form, the materials price variance is:

Materials price variance =

(Actual price − Standard price) × Actual quantity purchased

To illustrate, assume that a new foreign supplier entered the market and the Beta Company was able to purchase 60,000 sheets of material from this supplier at a price of $5.90 each. Since the standard price set by management is $6 per sheet, the materials price variance is computed as:

Materials price variance =

$\qquad$ (Actual price − Standard price) × Actual quantity purchased

Materials price variance = ($5.90 − $6.00) × 60,000

Materials price variance = $−0.10 × 60,000

Materials price variance = $−6,000 (favorable)

$\qquad$ The materials price variance of $6,000 is considered favorable since the materials were acquired for a price less than standard. (Why it is expressed as a negative amount will be explained later.) If the actual price had exceeded the standard price, the variance would be unfavorable because more costs would have been incurred than allowed by the standard.

$\qquad$ In T-account form, the entry to record the purchase of the materials is:

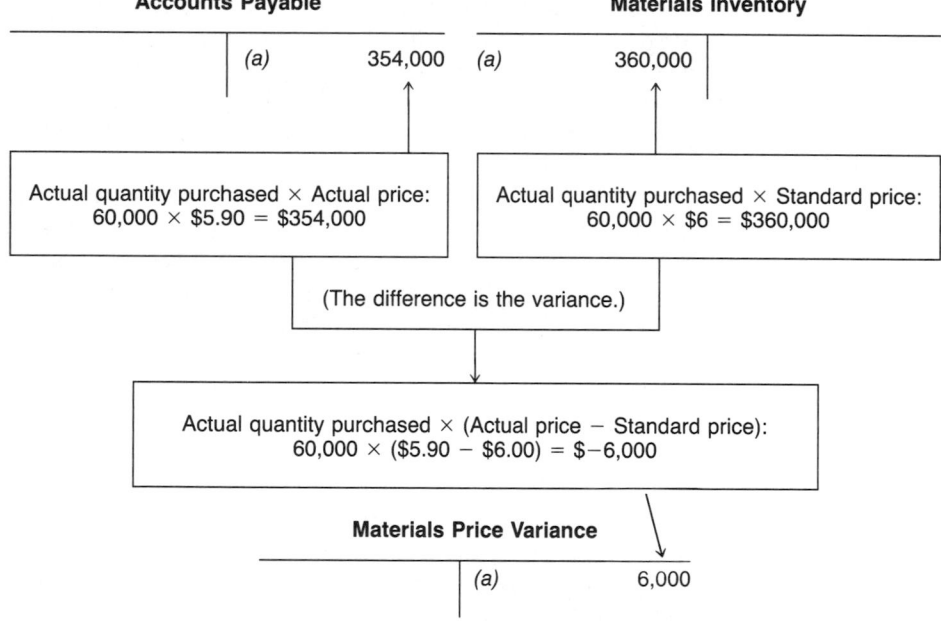

Objective 4:
Discuss what each
of the six variance
accounts shows,
and prepare journal
entries to record the
variances

The general journal entry to record the purchase of materials is:

```
a.  Materials Inventory. . . . . . . . . . . . . . . . . . . . .   360,000
        Materials Price Variance . . . . . . . . . . . . . .                6,000
        Accounts Payable . . . . . . . . . . . . . . . . . .              354,000
      To record the purchase of materials at less than
      standard cost.
```

Note that the Accounts Payable account shows the actual debt owed to suppliers, while the Materials Inventory account shows the standard price of the actual quantity of materials purchased. The Materials Price Variance account shows the difference between actual price and standard price multiplied by the actual quantity purchased.

Materials usage variance. Since the standard quantity of materials to be used in making a product is largely a matter of physical requirements or product specifications, it is usually set by the engineering department. But if the quality of materials used varies with price, the accounting and purchasing departments may take part in special studies to find the "right" quality.

The **materials usage variance (MUV)** is caused by using more or less than the standard amount of materials to produce a product or complete a process. The variance shows only differences from standard caused by the quantity of materials used; it does not include any effect of variances in price. Thus, the materials usage variance (MUV) is equal to actual quantity used (AQ), minus standard quantity allowed (SQ), multiplied by standard price (SP):

Materials usage variance =

> (Actual quantity used − Standard quantity) × Standard price

To illustrate, assume that the Beta Company used 55,500 sheets of materials to produce 11,000 units of a product for which the standard quantity allowed is 55,000 sheets (5 × 11,000). Since the standard price of the material is $6 per sheet, the materials usage variance of $3,000 would be computed as follows:

Materials usage variance =

> (Actual quantity used − Standard quantity) × Standard price

Materials usage variance = (55,500 − 55,000) × $6

Materials usage variance = 500 × $6

Materials usage variance = $3,000 (unfavorable)

The variance is unfavorable because more materials were used than the standard amount allowed to complete the job. If the standard quantity allowed had exceeded the quantity actually used, the materials usage variance would have been favorable.

The following T-accounts record the use of materials:

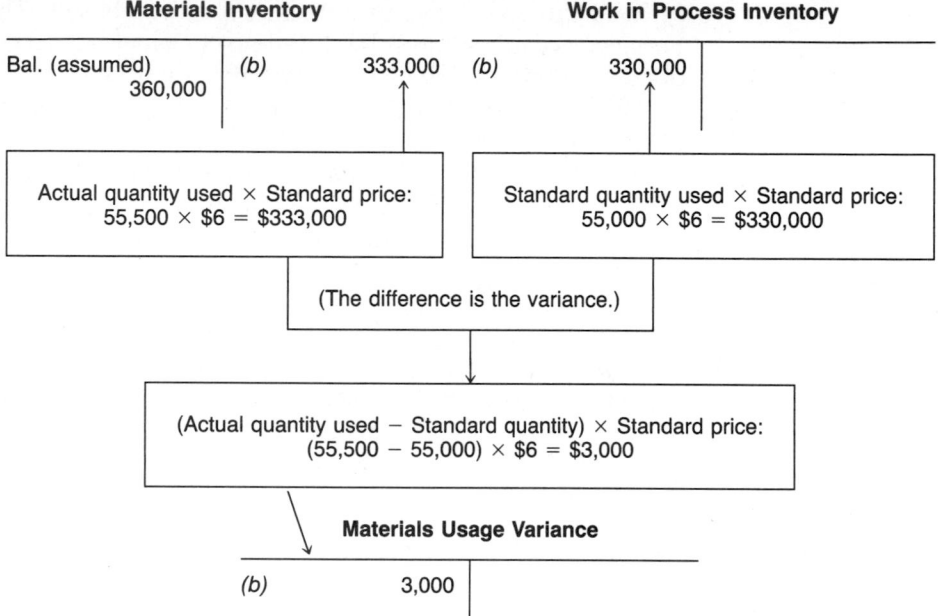

Materials Inventory		Work in Process Inventory	
Bal. (assumed) 360,000	*(b)* 333,000	*(b)* 330,000	

Actual quantity used × Standard price:
55,500 × $6 = $333,000

Standard quantity used × Standard price:
55,000 × $6 = $330,000

(The difference is the variance.)

(Actual quantity used − Standard quantity) × Standard price:
(55,500 − 55,000) × $6 = $3,000

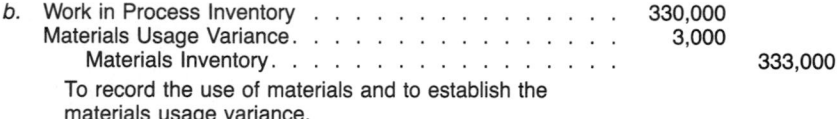

Materials Usage Variance

(b) 3,000

The general journal entry to record the use of materials is:

```
b.  Work in Process Inventory  . . . . . . . . . . . . . . . .   330,000
    Materials Usage Variance.  . . . . . . . . . . . . . .       3,000
        Materials Inventory.  . . . . . . . . . . . . . . . .              333,000
    To record the use of materials and to establish the
    materials usage variance.
```

The Materials Usage Variance shows the standard cost of the excess materials used. Note also that the Work in Process Inventory account contains both standard quantities and standard prices.

The equations for both of the above materials variances were expressed so that positive amounts were unfavorable variances and negative amounts were favorable variances. Unfavorable variances are debits in variance accounts because they add to the costs incurred, which are recorded as debits. Similarly, favorable variances are shown as negative amounts because they are reductions in costs. Thus, favorable variances are recorded in variance accounts as credits. This format will be used in this text, but a word of caution is in order. Far greater understanding is achieved if a variance is determined to be favorable or unfavorable by reliance upon reason or logic. If more materials were used than standard, or if a price greater than standard was paid, the variance is unfavorable. If the reverse is true, the variance is favorable.

Labor Variances

The standard labor cost of any product is equal to the standard quantity of labor time allowed multiplied by the wage rate that should be paid for this time. Here again it follows that the actual labor cost may differ from standard labor cost because of the wages paid for labor, the quantity of labor used, or both. Thus, there are two variances—a rate variance and an efficiency variance.

Labor rate variance. The **labor rate variance (LRV)** is caused by paying a higher or lower rate of pay than standard to produce a product or complete a process. The labor rate variance is similar to the materials price variance.

The labor rate variance (LRV) is computed by multiplying the difference between the actual direct labor-hour rate paid (AR) and the standard direct labor-hour rate allowed (SR) by the actual hours of direct labor services required (AH):

Labor rate variance = (Actual rate − Standard rate) × Actual hours

To continue the Beta Company example, assume that the direct labor payroll of the company consisted of 22,200 hours at a total cost of $233,100 (an average actual hourly rate of $10.50). Since management has set a standard direct labor-hour rate of $10 per hour, the labor rate variance is:

Labor rate variance = (Actual rate − Standard rate) × Actual hours

Labor rate variance = ($10.50 − $10.00) × 22,200

Labor rate variance = $0.50 × 22,200

Labor rate variance = $11,100 (unfavorable)

The variance is positive and unfavorable because the actual rate paid exceeded the standard rate allowed. If the reverse were true, the variance would be favorable.

Labor efficiency variance. The standard amount of direct labor time (hours or minutes) needed to complete a product is usually set by the company's engineering department. The direct labor time standard may be based on time and motion studies, or it may be the subject of bargaining with the employees' union. The **labor efficiency variance (LEV)** is caused by using more or less than the standard amount of direct labor-hours to produce a product or complete a process. The labor efficiency variance is similar to the materials usage variance.

The labor efficiency variance (LEV) is computed by multiplying the difference between the actual direct labor-hours required (AH) and the standard direct labor-hours allowed (SH) by the standard direct labor-hour rate per hour (SR):

Labor efficiency variance =

(Actual hours − Standard hours) × Standard rate

To illustrate, assume that the 22,200 hours of direct labor time worked by Beta Company employees resulted in 11,000 units of production. These 11,000 units have a standard direct labor time of 22,000 hours (11,000 units at 2 hours per unit). Since the standard direct labor rate is $10 per hour, the labor efficiency variance is $2,000, computed as follows:

Labor efficiency variance =
(Actual hours − Standard hours) × Standard rate

Labor efficiency variance = (22,200 − 22,000) × $10

Labor efficiency variance = 200 × $10

Labor efficiency variance = $2,000 (unfavorable)

The variance is unfavorable since more hours than standard were required to complete the period's production. If the reverse were true, the variance would be favorable.

Illustration 16.1 shows the relationship between standard and actual direct labor cost and the computation of the labor variances; it is based on the following data relating to the Beta Company:

Standard direct labor time per unit	2 hours
Equivalent units produced in period.	11,000 units
Standard labor rate per direct labor-hour	$10
Total direct labor wages paid (at average rate of $10.50 per hour)	$233,100
Actual direct labor hours worked	22,200 hours

The standard direct labor time allowed for the period's output is 22,000 hours (11,000 units at 2 hours per unit). The standard direct labor cost is $10 per hour; therefore, the standard direct labor cost for the output achieved is $220,000. The $220,000 is the amount of direct labor costs that will be assigned to inventory, regardless of the actual direct labor cost.

The unfavorable labor rate variance is the above-standard wages paid ($10.50 − $10.00 = $0.50 per hour) times the actual direct labor-hours worked (22,200), or $11,100. The labor rate variance is shown in Illustration 16.1 by the area within the rectangle *a b c d*. Note that the labor rate variance includes the above-standard wages paid on the 200 extra (above-standard) direct labor-hours used to secure the production—the lightly

Illustration 16.1
COMPUTATION OF LABOR VARIANCE

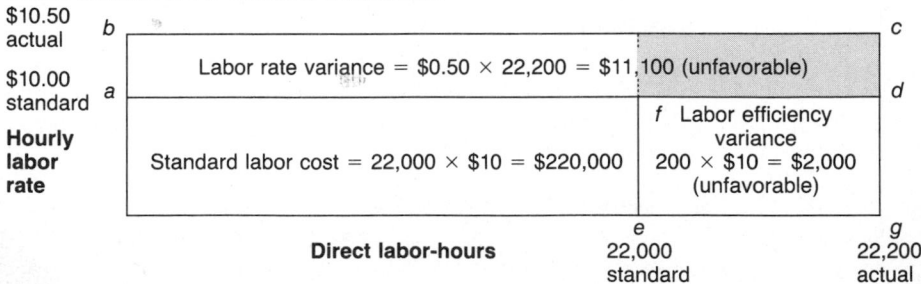

shaded area in the upper right-hand corner of Illustration 16.1. This variation from standard is actually caused by both extra hours and above-standard wages. But, as shown, it is included in the labor rate variance. The labor efficiency variance is the standard cost of the extra hours of direct labor required [(22,200 − 22,000) × $10 = $2,000]. This variance is unfavorable because more hours of direct labor were used than are allowed by the standard.

The charging of Work in Process Inventory with direct labor cost and the recording to the two labor variances for the Beta Company is shown in the T-accounts below. The labor efficiency variance is shown in Illustration 16.1 by the rectangle *e f d g*.

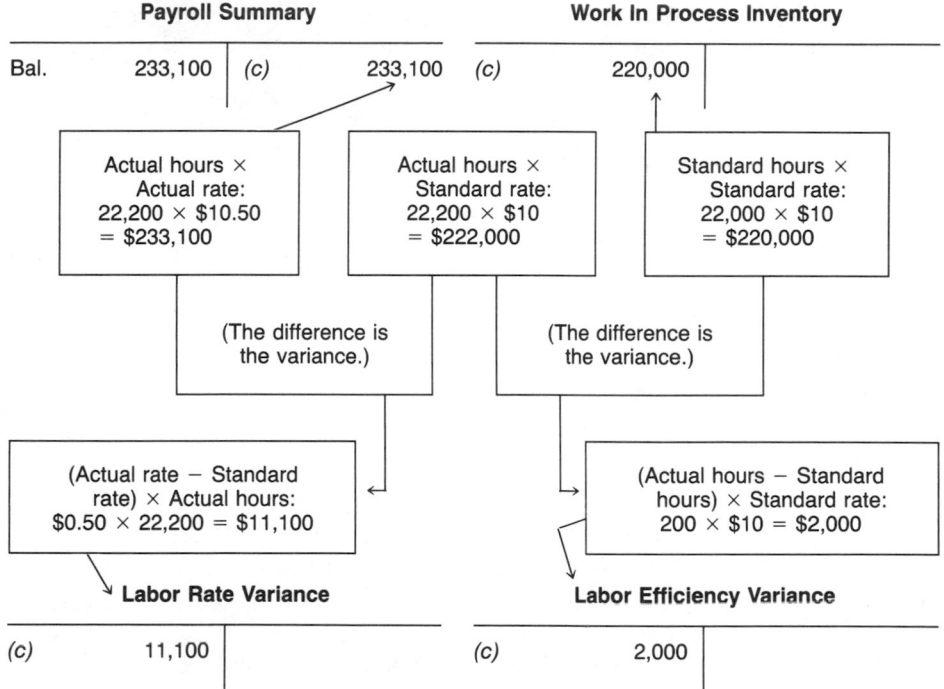

The general journal entry to charge the direct labor cost to work in process is:

c. Work in Process Inventory 220,000
  Labor Rate Variance 11,100
  Labor Efficiency Variance 2,000
    Payroll Summary. 233,100
  To charge work in process with direct labor and to
  establish the two labor variances.

With the above entry, gross wages earned by direct-production employees ($233,100) are distributed as follows: $220,000 (the standard labor cost of production) to Work in Process Inventory and the balance to the two labor variance accounts. The unfavorable labor rate variance is not necessarily caused by paying employees more wages than they are entitled to receive. A more probable reason is either that more highly skilled employees (with higher wage rates) worked on production than originally anticipated, or that employee wage rates increased after the standard was developed and the standard was not revised. Favorable rate variances, on the other hand, could be caused by using less skilled (cheaper) labor in the production process. Typically, the hours of labor employed are more likely to be under management's control than the rates that are paid. For this reason, labor efficiency variances are generally watched more closely than labor rate variances.

Summary of labor variances. The accuracy of the two labor variances can be checked by comparing their sum with the difference between actual and standard labor cost for a period. In the Beta Company illustration, this difference was:

Actual labor cost incurred (22,200 hours × $10.50)	$233,100
Standard labor cost allowed (22,000 hours × $10)	220,000
Total labor variance (unfavorable)	$ 13,100

This $13,100 is made up of two labor variances, both unfavorable:

Labor efficiency variance (200 × $10) . . .	$ 2,000
Labor rate variance (22,200 × $0.50) . . .	11,100
Total labor variance (unfavorable)	$13,100

Overhead Variances

In a standard cost system, manufacturing overhead is applied to the goods produced by means of a standard overhead rate. The rate is set prior to the start of the period by dividing the budgeted manufacturing overhead cost by a standard level of output or activity. Total budgeted manufacturing overhead will vary at different levels of standard output, but, since some overhead costs are fixed, total budgeted manufacturing overhead will not vary in direct proportion with output.

A **flexible budget** is used in isolating overhead variances and may be used in setting the standard overhead rate. A flexible budget shows the budgeted amount of manufacturing overhead for various levels of output.

The flexible budget for the Beta Company for the period is shown in Illustration 16.2. Note that it shows the variable and fixed manufacturing overhead costs expected to be incurred at three levels of activity: 90%, 100%, and 110% of capacity. For product costing purposes, the expected level of activity must be estimated in advance and a rate set based on that level. The level chosen is called the *standard volume of output*. This standard volume of output (or activity) may be expressed in terms of any of the activity bases that can be used in setting overhead rates. These activity bases include percent of capacity, units of output, and direct labor-hours, among others. In our example, standard volume is assumed to be 100% of capacity. At this level of operation, 10,000 units are expected to be pro-

Illustration 16.2
FLEXIBLE MANUFACTURING OVERHEAD BUDGET

BETA COMPANY Flexible Manufacturing Overhead Budget			
Percent of capacity.	90%	100%	110%
Direct labor-hours	18,000	20,000	22,000
Units of output	9,000	10,000	11,000
Variable overhead:			
Indirect materials.	$ 7,200	$ 8,000	$ 8,800
Power.	9,000	10,000	11,000
Royalties	1,800	2,000	2,200
Other	18,000	20,000	22,000
Total variable overhead	$36,000	$ 40,000	$ 44,000
Fixed overhead:			
Insurance	$ 4,000	$ 4,000	$ 4,000
Property taxes	6,000	6,000	6,000
Depreciation.	20,000	20,000	20,000
Other	30,000	30,000	30,000
Total fixed overhead	$60,000	$ 60,000	$ 60,000
Total manufacturing overhead	$96,000	$100,000	$104,000
Standard overhead rate ($100,000 ÷ 20,000 hours) . . .		$5	

duced and 20,000 direct labor-hours of services are expected to be used. Assume that Beta Company applies manufacturing overhead using a rate based on direct labor-hours. According to the flexible manufacturing overhead budget, the expected manufacturing overhead cost at the standard volume (20,000 direct labor-hours) is $100,000, so the standard overhead rate is $5 per direct labor-hour ($100,000 ÷ 20,000 direct labor-hours).

Knowing the separate rates for variable and fixed overhead is sometimes useful. The variable overhead rate is $2 ($40,000 ÷ 20,000 hours) per hour, and the fixed overhead rate is $3 ($60,000 ÷ 20,000 hours) per hour. If the expected volume had been 18,000 direct labor-hours (90% of capacity), the standard overhead rate would have been $5.33 ($96,000 ÷ 18,000 hours). If the standard volume had been 22,000 direct labor-hours (110% of capacity), the standard overhead rate would have been $4.73 ($104,000 ÷ 22,000 hours). Note that the difference in rates is due solely to dividing fixed overhead by a different number of units. That is, the variable overhead cost per unit stays constant ($2 per direct labor-hour) regardless of the number of units expected to be produced, and only the fixed overhead cost per unit changes.

Continuing with the Beta Company illustration, assume that the company incurred $108,000 of actual manufacturing overhead costs in a period during which 11,000 units of product were produced. The actual costs would be debited to Manufacturing Overhead and credited to a variety of accounts such as Accounts Payable, Accumulated Depreciation, Prepaid Insurance, Property Taxes Payable, and so on. According to the flexible budget, the standard number of direct labor-hours allowed for 11,000 units of production is 22,000 hours. Therefore, $110,000 of manufacturing overhead is applied to production ($5 per direct labor-hour times 22,000 hours) by debiting Work in Process Inventory and crediting Manufacturing Overhead for $110,000.

The entry, in T-account form, to record the application of $110,000 of manufacturing overhead to production (22,000 hours at $5 per hour) would be:

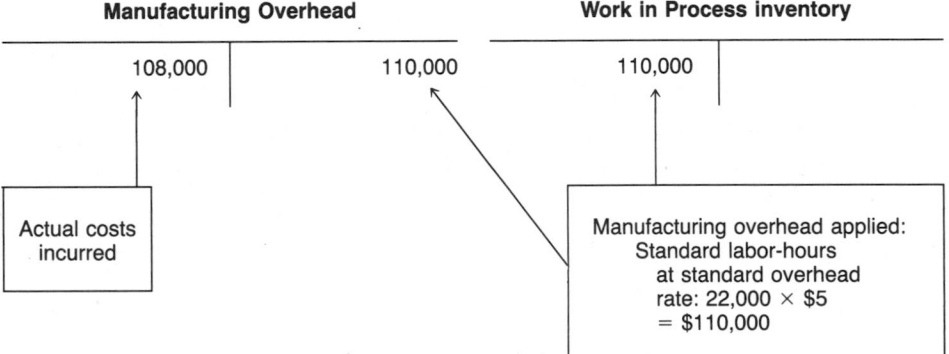

The general journal entry to apply manufacturing overhead to production would be:

Work in Process.   110,000
    Manufacturing Overhead   110,000
To apply manufacturing overhead to production (22,000
hours at $5 per hour).

The above accounts show that manufacturing overhead has been overapplied to production by the $2,000 credit balance in the Manufacturing Overhead account. Manufacturing overhead will tend to be overapplied when actual production is greater than standard production.

The rate of $5 (which was based on output of 10,000 units) was used to apply manufacturing overhead when actual output was 11,000 units. The $5 is a predetermined rate set at the beginning of the year, when management expected to produce 10,000 units. Actual production achieved is not known until year-end.

Although various complex computations can be made for overhead variances, a simple approach will be used in this text. In this approach, known as the two-variance approach to overhead variances, only two variances are calculated—an overhead budget variance and an overhead volume variance.

The overhead budget variance. The **overhead budget variance (OBV)** (also called the spending or controllable variance) shows in one amount how economically overhead services were purchased and how efficiently they were used. This overhead variance is similar to a combined price and usage variance for materials or labor. The overhead budget variance (OBV) is equal to the difference between total actual overhead costs (Actual OH) and total budgeted overhead costs (BOH) for the actual output attained.

Total budgeted overhead costs are calculated as the variable overhead rate times the standard direct labor-hours allowed for production achieved, plus the constant amount of fixed overhead. For the Beta Company, this would be $2 variable overhead times 22,000 hours (11,000 units × 2 hours per unit), or $44,000 variable overhead plus $60,000 of fixed overhead—a total of $104,000. Since the total actual overhead was $108,000 and the total budgeted overhead was $104,000, then the overhead budget variance is computed as follows:

Overhead budget variance = Actual overhead − Budgeted overhead

Overhead budget variance = $108,000 − $104,000

Overhead budget variance = $4,000 (unfavorable)

The variance is unfavorable because actual overhead costs were $108,000, while, according to the flexible budget, they should have been $104,000.

Overhead volume variance. The **overhead volume variance (OVV)** is caused by producing at a level other than that used in setting the standard overhead application rate. The OVV shows whether plant assets produced more or fewer goods than expected. Because fixed overhead is not constant on a per unit basis, any deviation from planned production will cause the overhead application rate to be incorrect. The OVV is the difference between the budgeted amount of overhead for the actual volume achieved (BOH) and the applied overhead (Applied OH):

Overhead volume variance = Budgeted overhead − Applied overhead

In the Beta Company illustration, the 11,000 units produced in the period have a standard labor allowance of 22,000 hours. Budgeted overhead was calculated when we computed the overhead budget variance. The flexible budget in Illustration 16.2 shows that the budgeted overhead for 22,000 direct labor-hours is $104,000. Overhead is applied to work in process on the basis of standard hours allowed for a particular amount of production, in this case 22,000 hours at $5 per hour. The overhead volume variance then is:

Overhead volume variance = Budgeted overhead − Applied overhead

Overhead volume variance = $104,000 − $110,000

Overhead volume variance = $−6,000 (favorable)

Note that the amount of the overhead volume variance is related solely to fixed overhead. As Illustration 16.2 shows, fixed overhead at all levels of activity is $60,000. Since Beta Company used 100% of capacity, or 20,000 direct labor-hours, as its standard, the fixed overhead rate is $3 per direct labor-hour. Beta worked 2,000 (22,000 − 20,000) more standard hours than was expected. The overhead volume variance can also be calculated as follows:

$$
\begin{pmatrix} \text{Number of hours} \\ \text{used in setting} \\ \text{predetermined} \\ \text{overhead rates} \end{pmatrix} - \begin{pmatrix} \text{Number of standard} \\ \text{hours allowed} \\ \text{for production} \\ \text{level achieved} \end{pmatrix} \times \begin{matrix} \text{Fixed over-} \\ \text{head rate} \\ \text{per hour} \end{matrix} = \begin{matrix} \text{Overhead} \\ \text{volume} \\ \text{variance} \end{matrix}
$$

$$
(20{,}000 \quad - \quad 22{,}000) \quad \times \quad \$3 \quad = \quad \$-6{,}000 \\ \text{(favorable)}
$$

The variance is favorable since the company achieved a higher level of production than was expected.

Recording overhead variances. Formal entries are made in the accounts showing the two parts of the $2,000 net overhead variance. The T-account entries for the Beta Company would be as follows (the debits and credits are keyed with the letter [*f*]):

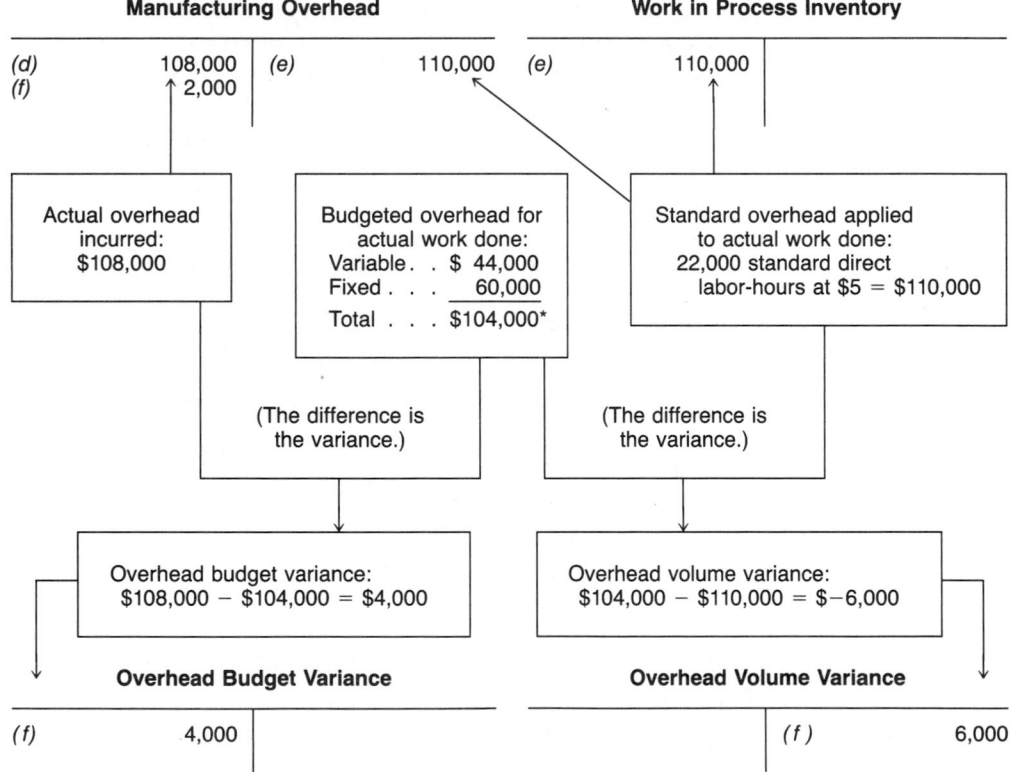

*From flexible budget. See Illustration 16.2.

The general journal entries related to overhead are as follows:

d. Manufacturing Overhead 108,000
      Various Accounts 108,000
    To record actual manufacturing overhead.

e. Work in Process   110,000
      Manufacturing Overhead   110,000
      To record the application of manufacturing overhead
      to work in process.

f. Manufacturing Overhead   2,000
   Overhead Budget Variance   4,000
      Overhead Volume Variance   6,000
      To record the variances related to overhead and close
      the Manufacturing Overhead account.

The first entry records the actual manufacturing overhead costs incurred during the period by Beta Company. The second entry applies manufacturing overhead to Work in Process at the rate of $5 per standard direct labor-hour (22,000). The final entry reduces the Manufacturing Overhead account balance to zero and recognizes the two variances calculated for overhead; these two variance accounts analyze the causes of the overapplied manufacturing overhead for the period.

Summary of overhead variances. The accuracy of the two overhead variances can be easily determined by comparing the sum of the budget and volume variances with the difference between the costs of actual manufacturing overhead and applied manufacturing overhead (the amount of over- or underapplied overhead). For the Beta Company example, the difference between actual and applied manufacturing overhead was:

Actual manufacturing overhead incurred $108,000
Applied manufacturing overhead allowed
   (22,000 direct labor-hours × $5 per hour)   110,000
Total overhead variance (favorable) . . . . $ −2,000

This difference is made up of the two overhead variances:

Overhead budget variance—Unfavorable ($108,000 − $104,000) . . . . $ 4,000
Overhead volume variance—Favorable [$104,000 − (22,000 × $5)] . . . . . .   −6,000
Total overhead variance (favorable) . . . . $−2,000

Illustration 16.3 provides a quick summary review of the six variances from standard covered in this chapter.

Illustration 16.3
SUMMARY OF VARIANCES FROM STANDARD

Materials price variance = (Actual price − Standard price) × Actual quantity purchased
Materials usage variance = (Actual quantity used − Standard quantity) × Standard price
Labor rate variance = (Actual rate − Standard rate) × Actual hours
Labor efficiency variance = (Actual hours − Standard hours) × Standard rate
Overhead budget variance = Actual overhead − Budgeted overhead
Overhead volume variance = Budgeted overhead − Applied overhead

GOODS COMPLETED AND SOLD

To complete the standard cost system example using the Beta Company, assume that 11,000 units were completed and transferred to finished goods, 10,000 units were sold on account at a price equal to 160% of standard cost, there was no beginning or ending work in process inventory, and there was no finished goods beginning inventory. In the T-accounts below, entry *(g)* shows the transfer of the standard cost of the units completed, $660,000 (11,000 × $60), from Work in Process Inventory to Finished Goods Inventory. Entry *(h)* records the sales for the period, $960,000 (160% × $60 × 10,000). Entry *(i)* records the cost of goods sold, $600,000 (10,000 × $60).

Work in Process Inventory

(b) Materials	330,000	*(g)* Completed	660,000
(c) Labor	220,000		
(e) Manufacturing			
overhead	110,000		

Finished Goods Inventory

(g) Completed	660,000	*(i)* Sold	600,000

Accounts Receivable		**Cost of Goods Sold**	
(h) 960,000		*(i)* Sold 600,000	

Sales

	(h) 960,000	

In journal entry form, entries *(g)*, *(h)*, and *(i)* are:

g. Finished Goods Inventory.   660,000
     Work in Process Inventory   660,000
    To record the transfer of completed units to finished
    goods inventory.

h. Accounts Receivable.   960,000
     Sales.   960,000
    To record sales for the period.

i. Cost of Goods Sold   600,000
    Finished Goods Inventory.   600,000
    To record cost of goods sold for the period.

Work in Process Inventory has been debited with the standard cost of materials, labor, and manufacturing overhead for units put into production. Therefore, the entry recording the transfer of the standard cost of the completed units, $660,000 (11,000 × $60), reduces Work in Process Inventory to a zero balance. Note that Finished Goods Inventory is debited with the standard cost of goods completed and credited with the standard cost of goods sold. Thus, ending finished goods inventory consists of the units actually on hand (1,000) at their standard cost of $60 each, or $60,000. Sales for the period amount to 10,000 units at $96 each (160% of $60). It is fairly common practice to base selling prices at least partially on standard costs.

INVESTIGATING VARIANCES FROM STANDARD

Objective 5: Discuss the three selection guides used to investigate variances from standard

Once all variances have been computed, management must decide which ones should be investigated further. Since numerous variances will occur, not all of them can be investigated. Management needs some selection guides. Possible guides include (1) amount of the variance; (2) size of the variance relative to cost incurred; and (3) controllability of the cost associated with the variance—that is, whether it is considered controllable or noncontrollable. Statistical analysis may also be used in deciding which variances to investigate. For instance, the average value of actual costs could be determined for a period of time so that only those variances deviating from the average by more than a certain amount or percentage would be investigated. To decide which selection guides are most useful, management should seek the opinions of knowledgeable operating personnel.

Any analysis of variances is likely to disclose some variances that are controllable within the company and others that are not. For instance, quantities used are generally controllable internally. Prices paid for materials purchased may or may not be controllable. Management may discover that the purchasing agent is not getting competitive bids; therefore, the price paid for materials would have been controllable by seeking competitive bids. On the other hand, a raw materials shortage may exist which drives the price upward, and the price paid is beyond the buyer's control.

Another point to remember about the analysis of variances is that separate variances are not necessarily independent. For example, an unfavorable labor rate variance may result from using higher paid employees in a certain task. However, higher paid employees may be more productive, resulting in a favorable labor efficiency variance. These employees may also be more highly skilled and may waste less material, resulting in a favorable materials usage variance. Therefore, significant variances, both favorable and unfavorable, should be investigated.

DISPOSING OF VARIANCES FROM STANDARD

Objective 6: Discuss the theoretical and practical methods for disposing of variances from standard

At the end of the year, variances from standard must be disposed of in the accounting records. The variances may be (1) viewed as losses due to inefficiency and closed to Income Summary; (2) allocated as adjustments to the recorded cost of Work in Process Inventory, Finished Goods Inventory, and Cost of Goods Sold; or (3) closed to Cost of Goods Sold. Theoretically, the alternative chosen should depend upon whether the standards set were reasonably attainable and whether the variances were controllable by company employees. For instance, an unfavorable materials usage or labor efficiency variance caused by carelessness or inefficiency may be considered a loss and closed to Income Summary because the standard was attainable and the variance was controllable. An unfavorable materials price variance caused by an unexpected price change may be considered an added cost and allocated to the inventory accounts and Cost of Goods Sold because the standard was unattainable and the variance was uncontrollable. As a practical matter, and especially if they are small, variances are usually closed to the Cost of Goods Sold account rather than allocated to the inventory accounts and to Cost of Goods Sold.

Entry (j) in the T-accounts below reflects this practical disposition of the variances in the continuing example of the Beta Company.

Materials Price Variance				Labor Rate Variance				Overhead Budget Variance			
(j)	6,000	(a)	6,000	(c)	11,100	(j)	11,100	(f)	4,000	(j)	4,000

Materials Usage Variance				Labor Efficiency Variance				Overhead Volume Variance			
(b)	3,000	(j)	3,000	(c)	2,000	(j)	2,000	(j)	6,000	(f)	6,000

Cost of Goods Sold		
(i)	600,000	
(j)	8,100	

In general journal entry form, entry (j) is

```
j.  Materials Price Variance. . . . . . . . . . . . . . . . . . . .    6,000
    Overhead Volume Variance . . . . . . . . . . . . . . . . .    6,000
    Cost of Goods Sold. . . . . . . . . . . . . . . . . . . . .    8,100
         Materials Usage Variance . . . . . . . . . . . . . . .           3,000
         Labor Rate Variance . . . . . . . . . . . . . . . . . .          11,100
         Labor Efficiency Variance . . . . . . . . . . . . . . .           2,000
         Overhead Budget Variance . . . . . . . . . . . . . .           4,000
    To close the variance accounts.
```

Variances are not reported separately in financial statements released to the public, but are simply included in the reported cost of goods sold amount. In reports prepared for internal use, the variances may be listed separately after cost of goods sold is shown at standard cost.

SUMMARY

A standard cost system gathers information about manufacturing costs incurred and the efficiency of manufacturing operations during the accounting period. A standard cost system can be used in both job order and process cost systems.

Standard costs are carefully predetermined measures of what costs should be under stated conditions. For each type of product manufactured, standard costs are established for *direct materials, direct labor,* and *manufacturing overhead.* The standard cost for each product unit produced is the sum of its standard direct materials cost, standard direct labor cost, and standard manufacturing overhead cost.

The amount by which the actual cost of a product unit differs from the standard cost of the unit is an exception or variance. A standard cost system highlights these variances. Six different types of variances are normally computed: materials price variance, materials usage variance, labor rate variance, labor efficiency variance, overhead budget variance, and overhead volume variance. Once variances are computed, management must decide which variances should be investigated further to determine the underlying causes of the variances.

Three inventory accounts—Materials Inventory, Work in Process Inventory, and Finished Goods Inventory—are carried at standard cost. Variances from standard are recorded separately in the respective variance accounts. At the end of the accounting period, variances must be disposed of in the accounting records. The variances may be (1) considered as losses due to inefficiency and closed to Income Summary; (2) allocated as adjustments to the recorded cost of Work in Process Inventory, Finished Goods Inventory, and Cost of Goods Sold; or (3) closed to Cost of Goods Sold. Theoretically, the alternative chosen by management to dispose of the variances should depend on whether the standards set were reasonably attainable and whether the variances were controllable by company employees. In actual practice, variances are usually closed to Cost of Goods Sold.

By using standard costs to control actual costs, management assumes responsibility for reducing the production costs of its products. In Chapter 17, you will learn about responsibility accounting in a broader sense. Many successful companies rely on responsibility accounting to make their business operations profitable.

APPENDIX   APPLYING STANDARD COSTS IN JOB ORDER AND PROCESS COST SYSTEMS

STANDARD COSTS IN A JOB ORDER COST SYSTEM

Objective 7: Discuss how standard costs are applied in both job order and process cost systems

In a job order cost system, production quantities are known in advance. Thus, some variances can be isolated much earlier than in a process cost system (in which equivalent production is known only at the end of a period). This early isolation of variances is illustrated in the following example.

Assume that Company A accounts for the manufacture of its products in a job order cost system using standard costs. Its flexible budget shows that at the standard level of output, variable overhead is $24,000 and fixed overhead is $16,000 per month. At the standard activity level of 8,000 direct labor-hours, these figures yield a standard overhead rate of $5 per direct labor-hour. The variable portion of this rate is $3 ($24,000 ÷ 8,000 hours), and the fixed portion is $2 ($16,000 ÷ 8,000 hours).

Company A had no work in process inventory as of June 1. The standard specifications for the two jobs started during June are given below:

	Job 101	Job 102
Direct materials	$20,000	$50,000
Direct labor:		
2,000 hours at $4	8,000	
5,000 hours at $4		20,000
Overhead:		
2,000 hours at $5	10,000	
5,000 hours at $5		25,000
Total standard cost	$38,000	$95,000

Company A's activities for June 1990 are summarized as follows:

a. Materials with a standard cost of $79,500 were purchased on account at an actual price of $80,150.

b. Standard direct materials were issued for both jobs. In addition, excess materials were requisitioned: Job No. 101, $400; and Job No. 102, $700.

c. Analysis of the factory payrolls debited to Payroll Summary shows they consisted of $10,000 of indirect labor ($4,000 variable and $6,000 fixed), and 6,000 hours of direct labor (Job No. 101, 1,980 hours and Job No. 102, 4,020 hours) at a cost of $24,600.

d. Various overhead costs were incurred: variable, $14,500; and fixed, $10,200.

e. Standard overhead was assigned to production: Job No. 101, $10,000 (2,000 hours at $5 per hour), and Job No. 102, $20,100 (4,020 hours at $5 per hour). Even though Job No. 102 was incomplete at the end of the month, overhead needs to be assigned to it for proper valuation of Work in Process Inventory on the balance sheet.

f. Job No. 101 was completed and transferred to the finished goods storeroom.

g. Sales for the month—all units in Job No. 101 at a total price of $60,000.

The entries to record the above information and isolate the variances follow:

a.	Materials Inventory.	79,500	
	Materials Price Variance	650	
	Accounts Payable		80,150
	To record purchase of materials and to isolate materials price variance.		
b.	Work in Process Inventory	70,000	
	Materials Usage Variance.	1,100	
	Materials Inventory.		71,100
	To charge standard materials to production and to charge excess materials requisitioned to a variance account.		

c. Work in Process Inventory 24,080
    Manufacturing Overhead 10,000
    Labor Rate Variance 600
          Labor Efficiency Variance 80
          Payroll Summary. 34,600
    To distribute labor costs and to isolate labor variances.

          Job No. 101 (2,000 hours at $4) . . . . $ 8,000
          Job No. 102 (4,020 hours at $4) 16,080

          Total labor to Work in Process Inventory. $24,080

          Labor efficiency variance on Job No. 101: (1,980
          actual hours − 2,000 standard hours) × $4 = $−80
          (favorable). Labor rate variance: ($4.10 actual
          wage rate − $4.00 standard rate) × 6,000 hours =
          $600 (unfavorable).

d. Manufacturing Overhead 24,700
          Accounts Payable (and various other accounts) 24,700
    To record incurrence of overhead costs.

e. Work in Process Inventory 30,100
          Manufacturing Overhead 30,100
    To apply standard overhead to production: Job No. 101—
    $10,000 (standard amount, job completed); Job No. 102—
    4,020 hours at $5 = $20,100 (based on standard labor,
    job incomplete).

f. Finished Goods Inventory. 38,000
          Work in Process Inventory 38,000
    To record transfer of completed Job No. 101 at standard.

g. Accounts Receivable 60,000
          Sales 60,000
    To record sales for the month.

    Cost of Goods Sold 38,000
          Finished Goods Inventory 38,000
    To record cost of goods sold (Job No. 101, $38,000).

Note that in the above entries the materials and labor variances are isolated rather routinely in the recording process. But the overhead variances must be computed separately at the end of the period, unless standard production for the period is known earlier. For Company A, the overhead variances are computed as follows:

Overhead budget variance:
  Actual overhead (entries [c] and [d] above) $34,700
  Budgeted overhead (from flexible budget)
    (6,020* standard hours at $3 variable overhead +
    $16,000 fixed overhead). 34,060
        Unfavorable overhead budget variance . . . . $ 640
Overhead volume variance:
  Budgeted overhead [(6,020* hours × $3) + $16,000]. $34,060
  Standard overhead applied to production
    (6,020* hours at $5). 30,100
        Unfavorable overhead volume variance 3,960
Total unfavorable overhead variance $4,600

*6,020 hours are used in the calculations because standard hours allowed for Job No. 101 are 2,000 and standard hours allowed this far on Job No. 202 are 4,020 for a total of 6,020 hours.

The following entry isolates the two overhead variances in the accounts:

Overhead Budget Variance	640	
Overhead Volume Variance	3,960	
Manufacturing Overhead		4,600

    To set up separate overhead variance accounts.

Note that the credit to Manufacturing Overhead of $4,600 reduces that account to a zero balance (for previous entries to the account, see entries *[c]*, *[d]* and *[e]* above), thus proving the accuracy of the computations.

Typically, the overhead variances and the materials and labor variances are summarized in a report prepared periodically for internal management. Such a report could be called a "Summary of Variances from Standard."

STANDARD COSTS IN A PROCESS COST SYSTEM

To provide a brief illustration of how standard costs might be incorporated into a process cost system, assume that Company P manufactures a product for which the standard specifications are:

Materials—2 pounds at $2 per pound	$4.00
Direct labor—0.5 hours at $4 per hour	2.00
Overhead—0.5 hours at $3 per hour	1.50
Total standard cost	$7.50

The fixed overhead included in the standard cost is based on a monthly budget that shows budgeted variable overhead of $120,000 and budgeted fixed overhead of $60,000 at a standard activity level of 60,000 standard direct labor-hours. Thus, the variable overhead rate is $2 per direct labor-hour ($120,000 ÷ 60,000 hours), and the fixed overhead rate is $1 per direct labor-hour ($60,000 ÷ 60,000 hours). Since each unit only requires one-half hour to produce, total overhead assignable per unit is $1.50 ($3 per hour × 1/2 hour).

This example makes one change in the standard cost system illustrated earlier in the chapter: Work in Process will be charged with actual quantities and actual costs rather than standard quantities and standard costs, as shown previously. The variances will be calculated and placed in variance accounts at the end of the month. Alternatively, the materials price variance could be recorded when materials are purchased, and the labor rate variance could be recorded when direct labor is charged to Work in Process Inventory.

The entries to the Work in Process Inventory account for the month of May are summarized below:

Direct materials (180,500 at $2.02)	$364,610
Direct labor (40,100 hours at $3.95)	158,395
Actual fixed overhead	58,700
Actual variable overhead	80,500
Total cost put into production	$662,205
Standard cost of units completed and transferred	
(70,000 at $7.50)	525,000
Balance, May 31, 1989	$137,205

Production records show that 70,000 units were completed and transferred and that 20,000 units of the product remain in process at the end of the month. These units are complete as to materials and 50% complete as to conversion. From this information, the equivalent production for the period in terms of standard units of product can be computed as follows:

	Materials	Labor and Overhead (conversion)
Units started and finished	70,000	70,000
Equivalent units in ending inventory	20,000	10,000
Equivalent production.	90,000	80,000

We now have enough information to calculate all of the variances presented in the "Summary of Variances from Standard" shown in Illustration 16.4.

Since the actual price paid for materials was $0.02 per pound above standard, the materials price variance is the actual usage of 180,500 pounds multiplied by $0.02 ($3,610). Since the standard materials allowed for 90,000 equivalent units is 180,000 pounds (90,000 × 2), the materials usage variance is $1,000 (500 pounds × $2). Both variances are unfavorable.

The average wage rate paid employees was $0.05 less than standard, resulting in a favorable rate variance of this amount multiplied by actual hours of 40,100. The standard labor-hours allowed for the production of the period (80,000 × 0.5 hours) is 100 hours less than the actual direct labor-hours used. Hence, an unfavorable labor efficiency variance was experienced.

Fixed overhead costs were $1,300 ($58,700 − $60,000) less than their budgeted amount, while variable overhead costs exceeded their budgeted

Illustration 16.4
SUMMARY OF VARIANCES FROM STANDARD

COMPANY P Summary of Variances from Standard Month Ended May 31, 1990		
Materials:		
Price variance (180,500 pounds × $0.02)	$ 3,610	
Usage variance (500 pounds × $2)	1,000	
Total unfavorable materials variance		$ 4,610
Labor:		
Rate variance (40,100 hours × $−0.05)	$−2,005	
Efficiency variance (100 hours × $4)	400	
Net favorable labor variance		−1,605
Overhead:		
Budget variance [fixed ($58,700 − $60,000) + variable ($80,500 − $80,000*)]	$ −800	
Volume variance ($140,000 − $120,000)	20,000	
Net unfavorable overhead variance.		19,200
Total variance from standard for the month		$22,205

*(40,000 hours × $2).

amount for the actual production in May by $500 [$80,500 − (40,000 × $2)]. Together, these costs yield a net favorable variance of $800. Because the standard overhead applied to production of $120,000 (40,000 standard direct labor-hours × $3) is less than the budgeted overhead for the month of $140,000 [(40,000 standard direct-labor hours × $2) + $60,000], there is an unfavorable volume variance of $20,000. These variances amount to a net unfavorable overhead variance of $19,200. Added together, the materials, labor, and overhead variances amount to $22,205, the total variance (unfavorable) from standard for the month.

The variances shown in Illustration 16.4 can be formally recorded in the accounts by the following entry, thus removing the month's variances from Work in Process Inventory:

Materials Price Variance	3,610	
Materials Usage Variance.	1,000	
Labor Efficiency Variance.	400	
Overhead Volume Variance	20,000	
Labor Rate Variance		2,005
Overhead Budget Variance		800
Work in Process Inventory		22,205
To set up variances from standard for the month.		

Subtracting the $22,205 from the previously given balance of $137,205 in the Work in Process Inventory account leaves a balance of $115,000, which is equal to the standard cost of the ending inventory. The standard cost of the ending inventory can be separately computed as follows:

Direct materials (20,000 units, 100% complete, unit cost $4)	$ 80,000
Direct labor (20,000 units, 50% complete, unit cost $2)	20,000
Overhead (20,000 units, 50% complete, unit cost $1.50).	15,000
Total standard cost of ending inventory	$115,000

NEW TERMS INTRODUCED IN CHAPTER 16

Objective 8: Define and use correctly the new terms in the glossary

Flexible budget   A budget that shows the expected amount of overhead for various levels of output; used in isolating overhead variances and setting standard overhead rates (576).

Labor efficiency variance (LEV)   A variance from standard caused by using more or less than the standard amount of direct labor-hours to produce a product or complete a process; computed as (Actual direct labor-hours − Standard direct labor-hours) × Standard rate per hour (573).

Labor rate variance (LRV)   A variance from standard caused by paying a higher or lower average rate of pay than standard to produce a product or complete a process; computed as (Actual rate per hour − Standard rate per direct labor-hour) × Actual direct labor-hours worked (573).

Materials price variance (MPV)   A variance from standard caused by paying a higher or lower price than standard for materials purchased; computed as (Actual price − Standard price) × Actual quantity purchased (569).

Materials usage variance (MUV) A variance from standard caused by using more or less than the standard amount of materials to produce a product or complete a process; computed as (Actual quantity used − Standard quantity allowed) × Standard price (571).

Overhead budget variance (OBV) A variance from standard caused by incurring more or less than the standard manufacturing overhead for the actual production volume achieved, as shown by a flexible budget; computed as Actual overhead − Budgeted overhead at actual production volume level (578).

Overhead volume variance (OVV) A variance from standard caused by producing at a level other than that used in setting the standard overhead rates; computed as Budgeted overhead − Applied overhead (579).

Standard cost A carefully predetermined measure of what a cost should be under stated conditions (566).

Standard level of output A carefully predetermined measure of what the expected level of output should be for a specified period of time, usually one year (567).

Variance The amount by which actual cost differs from standard cost; may be favorable or unfavorable. That is, actual costs may be less than or more than standard costs. Variances may relate to materials, labor, or manufacturing overhead (568).

DEMONSTRATION PROBLEM 16–1

The Samone Company produces a perfume called Rapture. The standard cost for one bottle of Rapture is:

Direct materials:	
6.2 ounces at $0.25	$1.55
Direct labor (1 hour at $6)	6.00
Overhead:	
Fixed ($22,000 ÷ 70,000 units)	.31
Variable.	.35
	$8.21

The standard overhead rate is based on a volume of 70,000 units per month. In August, 60,000 units were manufactured. Detailed data relative to production are summarized below:

Materials purchased: 150,000 ounces at $0.28.
Materials used: 365,000 ounces.
Direct labor: 59,500 hours at $5.90.
Fixed manufacturing overhead: $22,500.
Variable manufacturing overhead: $25,000.

Required:

From the above data, compute the six variances from standard for the month of August.

Solution to demonstration problem 16–1

Matrials price variance:		
($0.28 − $0.25) × 150,000	$ 4,500 (unfavorable)	
Materials usage variance:		
(365,000 − 372,000*) × $0.25	−1,750 (favorable)	
Net materials variance		$ 2,750 (unfavorable)
Labor rate variance:		
($5.90 − $6.00) × 59,500	$−5,950 (favorable)	
Labor efficiency variance:		
(59,500 − 60,000) × $6.00	−3,000 (favorable)	
Net labor variance		$−8,950 (favorable)

Overhead budget variance:			
Actual ($22,500 + $25,000)	$47,500		
Budgeted [$22,000 + (60,000 × $0.35)]	43,000		
Overhead budget variance		$ 4,500 (unfavorable)	
Overhead volume variance:			
Budgeted − Applied [$43,000 − (60,000 × $0.66)] . .		3,400 (unfavorable)	
Total overhead variance			$ 7,900 (unfavorable)
Total variance for month			$ 1,700 (unfavorable)

*60,000 units × 6.2 ounces per unit

QUESTIONS

1. Is a standard cost an estimated cost? What is the primary objective of employing standard costs in a cost system? What are some of the other advantages of using standard costs?

2. Describe how the materials price and usage variances would be computed from the following data:

> Standard—1 unit of material at $20 per unit.
> Purchases—1,200 units of material at $20.25; used—995 units.
> Production—1,000 units of finished goods.

3. When might a given company have a substantial favorable materials price variance and a substantial unfavorable materials usage variance?

4. What is the usual cause of a favorable or unfavorable labor rate variance? What other labor variance is isolated in a standard cost system? Of the two variances, which is more likely to be under the control of management? Explain.

5. Identify the type of variance indicated by each situation below and indicate whether it is favorable or unfavorable.

   a. The cutting department of a company during the week ending July 15 cut 12 size-S cogged wheels out of three sheets of 12-inch high-tempered steel. Usually three wheels of such size are cut out of each sheet.

   b. A company purchased and installed an expensive new cutting machine to handle expanding orders. This purchase and the related depreciation had not been anticipated when the overhead rate was set.

   c. Edwards, the band saw operator, was on vacation last week. Lands took his place for the normal 40-hour week. Edwards' wage rate is $5.40 per hour, while Land's is $5.20 per hour. Production was at capacity last week and the week before.

6. Theoretically, how should an accountant dispose of variances from standard? How does an accountant typically dispose of variances?

7. Would you expect the normal overhead volume variance to be favorable or unfavorable? Explain.

8. How do standards help in controlling production costs?

EXERCISES

Compute materials variances

1. During the month of July a department completed 2,000 units of a product which had a standard material cost of 4,000 square feet at $0.80 per square foot. The actual material purchased and used consisted of 4,050 square feet at a cost of $3,321. Compute the materials usage and materials price variances, and indicate clearly whether each is favorable or unfavorable.

Compute materials variances

2. During December, the machining department completed 1,500 units of a product that had a standard materials cost of 2 square feet per unit at $1.50 per square foot. The actual material purchased consisted of 2,550 square feet at $1.40 per square foot, for a total cost of $3,570. The actual material used in December was 2,420 square feet. Compute the materials price and usage variances and indicate whether each is favorable or unfavorable.

Compute materials variances

3. Daniel Products, Inc. manufactures a number of consumer items, including a chopping board. During June, the company manufactured 6,000 boards, purchasing and using 19,400 board feet of hardwood which cost $26,500. The standard amount set for one cutting board is 3.4 board feet of hardwood, at a cost of $1.45 per board foot. Determine what the cost should have been for the 6,000 chopping boards and compute the materials price and materials usage variances.

Compute labor variances

4. Compute the labor variances under the following circumstances:

Actual direct labor payroll (19,800 hours)	$162,360
Standard labor allowed per unit, 4 hours at $8	32
Equivalent production for the month (in units)	5,000

Compute labor variances

5. During March, 100 units of a given product were produced. These units have a standard labor cost of one hour at $8 per hour in Process A and of two hours at $7.00 per hour in Process B. Assume that James worked 95 hours on Process A during the month, for which he earned $836, and that Brown worked 205 hours on Process B, for which he earned $1,394. Compute the labor cost variances for each process.

Compute labor variances; evaluate labor foreman

6. The Stonewall Company manufactures roofing shingles that have a standard direct labor cost of two hours at $7 per hour. In producing 8,200 shingles, the foreman used a different crew than usual, which resulted in a total labor cost of $112,700 for 17,000 hours. Compute the labor variances, and comment on the foreman's decision to use a different crew.

Compute overhead budget and volume variances

7. The following relate to the manufacturing activities of the Towers Company for the month of May 1989:

Standard activity (units)	50,000
Actual production (units).	40,000
Budgeted fixed overhead	$ 60,000
Variable overhead rate (per unit)	$ 4.00
Actual fixed overhead	$ 60,800
Actual variable overhead	$156,600

Compute the overhead budget variance and the overhead volume variance.

Compute overhead volume variance

8. In Exercise 7, if the actual production had been 65,000 units, what would the overhead volume variance have been?

Compute materials and labor variances

9. Toyo Toys, Inc. produces a toy called Tyler-Talk. The company has recently established a standard cost system to help control costs. The following standards for Tyler-Talk have been established:

> Direct materials: 7 pieces per toy at $0.60 per piece
> Direct labor: 1.5 hours per toy at $10.00 per hour

During the month of April, 1991, 4,200 Tyler-Talk toys were produced. Production data for April was:

> Direct materials: 28,000 pieces were purchased at a cost of $0.55 per piece.
> 1,000 pieces remained in inventory at April 30th.
> Direct labor: 6,200 direct labor-hours were worked at a total cost of $64,976.

Compute the materials price and usage variances and the labor rate and efficiency variances.

Set-up T-accounts: prepare journal entry

10. The standard cost variance accounts of the Tory Company at the end of its fiscal year had the following balances:

Materials price variance (unfavorable)	$10,000
Materials usage variance (unfavorable)	8,000
Labor rate variance (favorable)	−6,000
Labor efficiency variance (unfavorable)	22,000
Overhead budget variance (favorable)	−2,000
Overhead volume variance (unfavorable)	12,000

Set up T-accounts for the above variances; enter the above balances in these accounts; then prepare one journal entry to record the closing of these variance accounts in the manner in which they are usually disposed of in practice.

PROBLEMS

Prepare journal entries for purchase and issuance of materials

16–1. During the month of February, the cutting department of the Clancy Company completed 4,800 units of a product that had a standard material cost of 5,800 square feet at $0.50 per square foot. The actual materials used consisted of 5,900 square feet at an actual cost of $2,900. The actual purchase of this material amounted to 9,500 square feet at a total cost of $3,420.

Required:

a. Using T-accounts, prepare entries for (1) the purchase of the materials and (2) the issuance of materials to production.

b. Make the necessary journal entries for (1) and (2) from part (**a**).

Determine and record labor variances

16–2. The welding department of the Republic Company produced 40,000 units during the month of November. The standard direct labor per unit is two hours. The standard rate per hour is $18. During the month, 82,000 direct labor-hours were worked at a cost of $1,508,800.

Required:

a. Draw a diagram similar to Illustration 16.1 showing the determination of the two labor variances.

b. Record the labor data in a journal entry and post the entry to T-accounts.

Compute overhead variances

16–3. The monthly budgeted fixed overhead of the Houston plant of the RLA Company is absorbed into production, using a rate based upon a standard volume of output of 100,000 units per month. The flexible overhead budget for the month allows $150,000 for fixed overhead and $2 per unit of output for variable overhead. The actual overhead for the month consisted of $151,200 of fixed overhead and the actual variable overhead given below.

Required:

Compute the overhead budget variance and the overhead volume variance, assuming that the actual production in units and the actual variable overhead in dollars were:

a. 75,000 units and $152,000.

b. 110,000 units and $225,400.

Compute overhead variances

16–4. The Wilder Company manufactures and sells two similar table lamps, each of which is assembled and packaged in Department IV. The expected volume of activity for Department IV is 120,000 direct labor-hours, at which level budgeted fixed overhead is $160,000, while variable overhead is budgeted at $2.60 per direct labor-hour. In March, a total of 83,300 direct labor-hours was worked in the department, 1,500 of which were in excess of the standard labor allowed for the month's production. The actual overhead for March consisted of $141,400 of fixed overhead and $198,600 of variable overhead.

Required:

Compute the two overhead variances for the month of March, showing your computations.

Compute materials, labor, and overhead variances

16–5. Based on a standard volume of output of 80,000 units per month, the standard cost of the product manufactured by the Dexter Company is:

Direct materials (0.25 pounds)	$ 2.00
Direct labor (0.5 hours)	4.00
Variable overhead	3.50
Fixed overhead	1.50
	$11.00

During the month of May, 82,000 units were produced and the following costs were incurred:

Direct materials purchased and used (20,650 pounds at $8.20)	$169,330
Direct labor (41,080 hours at $7.80)	320,424
Variable overhead	289,400
Fixed overhead	121,040

Required:

Compute the materials price and usage variances, the labor rate and efficiency variances, and the overhead budget and volume variances.

Compute materials, labor, and overhead variances; prepare journal entries to record the variances

16–6. The Colby Company, Inc. has determined the standard production volume to be 80,000 units per month. The standard costs associated with this level of output were determined to be:

Direct materials (10 units)	$ 6.00
Direct labor (1 hour)	12.00
Variable overhead	5.25 per unit produced
Fixed overhead	
(240,000 ÷ 80,000 units)	3.00 per unit produced
	$26.25

During April, 77,000 units were produced and the following costs were incurred.

Direct materials purchased and used (775,000 units at $0.68)	$527,000
Direct labor (85,000 hours at $11.75)	998,750
Variable overhead.	426,400
Fixed overhead	214,800

Required:

a. Compute the materials price and usage variances, the labor rate and efficiency variances, and the overhead budget and volume variances. Indicate whether each variance is favorable or unfavorable.

b. Prepare journal entries to record the variances and an entry to close out the variances assuming that they are not material.

Prepare journal entries for various transactions; compute overhead variances

16–7. (Based on the chapter appendix.) The Baker Manufacturing Company employs a job order standard cost accounting system. The standard cost of the material used is $1.60 per square foot, while the standard labor cost is $8 per hour. Overhead is assigned to jobs at the rate of $6 per standard direct labor-hour. Based upon a standard volume of activity of 60,000 direct labor-hours, the flexible budget allows $120,000 of fixed overhead and $4 of variable overhead per direct labor-hour for the month of June 1990.

Work in process is charged with standard quantities and standard prices. On June 1, 1990, one job (No. 301) was in process, to which the following standard costs have already been assigned:

Material (2,500 square feet)	$4,000
Labor (400 direct labor-hours)	3,200
Manufacturing overhead ($6 per standard direct-labor hour)	2,400
Total.	$9,600

When completed, the standard quantities for Job No. 301 are 4,000 square feet of material and 500 hours of direct labor.

During the month of June 1990, the following transactions and events occurred:

(1) Purchased 600,000 square feet of materials at $1.56 per square foot.

(2) Materials issued:

Job No.	Actual Quantity	Standard Quantity
301.	1,600 sq. ft.	1,500 sq. ft.
All others . . .	420,000 sq. ft.	421,200 sq. ft.
	421,600 sq. ft.	422,700 sq. ft.

(3) The direct labor costs and hours for the month were:

Incurred on:	Actual Hours	Standard Hours	Actual Cost
Job No. 301.	104	100	$ 868
All other jobs	51,096	51,000	413,932
	51,200	51,100	$414,800

(4) The appropriate amount of overhead was assigned to the jobs.

(5) The actual overhead incurred during the month was $310,000.

(6) Job No. 301 was completed during the month. Other production also completed during the month has a standard cost of $1,040,000.

Required:

a. Prepare general journal entries for each of the numbered transactions given above.

b. Compute and prepare general journal entries to record the overhead budget variance and the overhead volume for the month.

Compute materials, labor, and overhead variances, and prepare journal entries

16–8. (Based on the chapter appendix.) The Markov Company employs a process cost system with standard costs to account for the product it manufactures in a two-step process through Departments A and B. The standard cost of this product in Department A is:

Direct materials (10 units at $16)	$160
Direct labor (5 hours at $12)	60
Variable overhead (5 hours at $8)	40
Fixed overhead (5 hours at $4)	20
	$280

The flexible overhead budget, based on 60,000 direct labor-hours as a standard volume of activity, allows $240,000 of fixed overhead plus $8 per direct labor-hour. Materials price variances are isolated at the time of purchase, labor rate variances when payrolls are distributed. Materials usage and labor efficiency variances are isolated at the end of the month, when production is known. Standard overhead is assigned to production and overhead variances isolated at the end of the month, when production and actual costs are known.

There was no work in process inventory as of July 1, 1990, in Department A. Selected, summarized data for the month are:

(1) Purchased 121,000 units of raw material for $1,926,320.

(2) Direct materials requisitioned by Department A, 110,580 units.

(3) Of the payroll costs for the month, 49,900 hours with a total cost of $599,520 are chargeable to Department A.

(4) Total overhead costs incurred by the department for the month consist of $241,800 of fixed overhead and $402,200 of variable overhead.

(5) A total of 9,000 units was completed during the month, and 2,000 units remain in process, 100% complete as to materials and 50% complete as to labor and overhead.

(6) Overhead is assigned to production on the basis of standard labor hours.

Required:

a. Prepare journal entries to record the above summarized data. (In the illustration in the chapter appendix, all variances were isolated at the end of the period. Use logic to isolate them as required in this problem.)

b. Compute the materials usage variance and the labor efficiency variance, and prepare journal entries to remove them from Work in Process Inventory.

c. Compute and prepare journal entries to record the overhead budget variance and the overhead volume variance.

d. Assuming the variances isolated are for the year ending July 31, 1990, prepare an entry that represents a practical disposition of these variances.

BUSINESS DECISION PROBLEM 16–1

Discuss possible causes for variances

For each of the variances listed below, give a possible reason for its existence.

Materials price variance (unfavorable)	$5,000
Materials usage variance (unfavorable)	2,800
Labor rate variance (favorable)	3,150
Labor efficiency variance (unfavorable)	6,650
Overhead budget variance (favorable)	800
Overhead volume variance (unfavorable)	3,200

BUSINESS DECISION PROBLEM 16–2

Analyze situation where actual costs differ from standard costs; evaluate the two managers involved

Randy Ellis, the president of the Dark Company, has a problem. The problem does not involve substantial dollar amounts but does involve the important question of responsibility for variances from standard costs. He has just received the following report:

Standard materials at standard price for the production of July	$53,250
Unfavorable materials price variance ($8.20 − $7.50) × 8,000 pounds	5,600
Unfavorable materials usage variance (8,000 pounds − 7,100 pounds) × $7.50	6,750
Total actual materials costs for the month of May	$65,600

Ellis has discussed the unfavorable price variance with Terry Quaid, the purchasing officer. She agrees that under the circumstances she should be held responsible for most of the materials price variance. But she objects to the inclusion of $630 (900 pounds of excess materials used at $0.70 per pound). This, she argues, is the responsibility of the production department. If it had not been so inefficient in the use of materials, she would not have had to purchase the extra 900 pounds.

On the other hand, Scott Tate, the production manager, agrees that he is basically responsible for the excess quantity of materials used. But he does not agree that the above materials usage variance should be revised to include the $630 of unfavorable price variance on the excess materials used. "That's Terry's responsibility," he says. Ellis now turns to you for help. Specifically, he wants you to tell him:

1. Who is responsible for the $630 in dispute?

2. If responsibility cannot be clearly assigned, in which materials variance account should the accounting department include the variance?

3. Are there likely to be other circumstances where materials variances cannot be considered the responsibility of the manager most closely involved with them? Explain.

Required:

Prepare written answers to the three questions asked by Ellis.

17

RESPONSIBILITY ACCOUNTING AND SEGMENTAL ANALYSIS

LEARNING OBJECTIVES

After studying this chapter, you should be able to:

1. Explain responsibility accounting and its use in a business entity.
2. Prepare responsibility accounting reports.
3. Prepare a segmental income statement using the contribution margin format.
4. Calculate return on investment, margin, and turnover for a segment.
5. Calculate the residual income of a segment.
6. Define and correctly use the new terms in the glossary.

When a business is small, the owner usually oversees many different activities in the business. As a business grows, responsibility for some of these activities must be given to other persons. Obviously, the success of a business depends to a great extent on the persons responsible for these activities.

In this chapter you will learn about delegating authority to lower-level managers for managing various business activities and holding these lower-level managers responsible for the activities under their control. You will also learn how to assess the performance of these managers. The activities in a company are grouped into responsibility centers. The manager in charge of each center is responsible for controlling certain expenses. Sometimes the manager also has some control over revenues. The performance of each manager is measured in terms of the items of revenue and expense over which that manager has control. Various types of responsibility centers are discussed and illustrated. The chapter ends with a discussion of return on investment, which directly relates to the profitability of a company.

RESPONSIBILITY ACCOUNTING

Objective 1: Explain responsibility accounting and its use in a business entity

The term **responsibility accounting** refers to an accounting system that collects, summarizes, and reports accounting data relating to the responsibilities of individual managers. A responsibility accounting system provides information to evaluate each manager on revenue and expense items over which that manager has primary control (authority to influence). A responsibility accounting report contains only those items that are controllable by the responsible manager. If, however, both controllable *and uncontrollable* items are included in the report, the categories should be clearly separated. The identification of controllable items is a fundamental task in responsibility accounting and reporting.

To implement responsibility accounting in a company, the business entity must be organized so that responsibility is assignable to individual managers. The various company managers and their lines of authority (and the resulting levels of responsibility) should be fully defined. The organization chart in Illustration 17.1 demonstrates lines of authority and responsibility that could be used as a basis for responsibility reporting. If clear lines of authority and resulting levels of responsibility cannot be determined, it is very doubtful that responsibility accounting can be implemented effectively.

To identify the items over which each manager has control, the lines of authority should follow a specified path. For example, Illustration 17.1 shows that a plant supervisor may report to a plant manager, who reports to a vice president of manufacturing, who reports to the president. The president is ultimately responsible to stockholders and their elected representatives, the board of directors. In a sense, the president is responsible for all revenue and expense items of the company, since at the presidential level all items are controllable over some period of time. The president cannot delegate responsibility so as to avoid personal responsibility. But, the president will usually delegate authority to lower-level managers since the president cannot keep fully informed of the day-to-day operating details of all areas of the business.

The manager's level in the organization also affects identification of the items over which that manager has control. The president is usually considered a first-level manager. Managers who report directly to the president are second-level managers. Notice on the organization chart in Illustration 17.1 that individuals at a specific management level are on a horizontal line across the chart. But not all managers at that level necessarily have equal authority and responsibility. The degree of a manager's authority will vary from company to company.

While the president may delegate much decision-making power, there are some revenue and expense items that will remain exclusively

Illustration 17.1
A CORPORATE FUNCTIONAL ORGANIZATION CHART INCLUDING FOUR LEVELS OF MANAGEMENT
(Illustrates Only Manufacturing Function from Level Three)

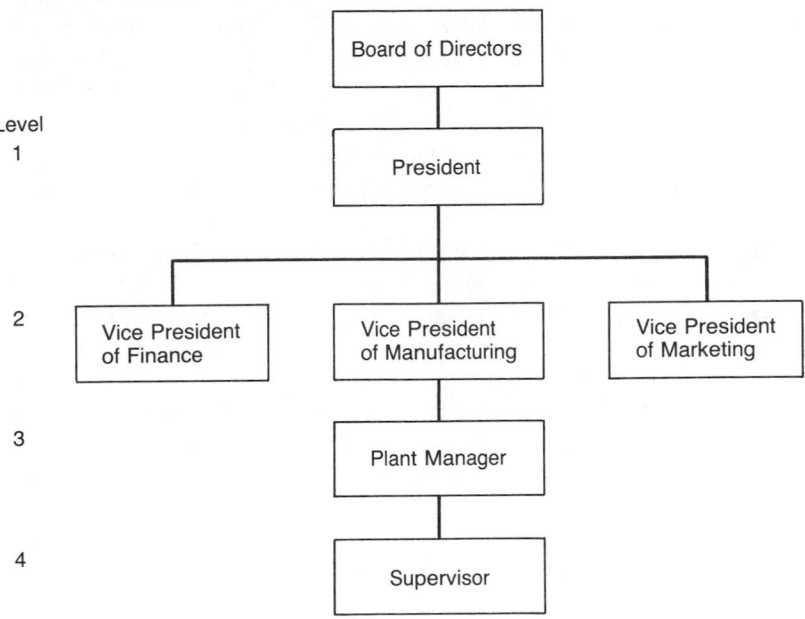

under the president's control. For example, in some companies, large capital (plant and equipment) expenditures may be approved only by the president. Depreciation, property taxes, and other related expenses should not, therefore, be designated as a plant manager's responsibility since these costs are not primarily under that manager's control.

The controllability criterion is crucial to the content of performance reports for each manager. For example, at the supervisor level, perhaps only direct materials and direct labor cost control are appropriate for measuring performance. A plant manager, however, has the authority to make decisions regarding many other costs that are not controllable at the supervisory level (such as salaries of supervisors); these other costs would be included in the performance evaluation of the plant manager, but not the supervisor.

THE CONCEPT OF CONTROL

Theoretically, a manager should have absolute control over an item to be held responsible for it. Unfortunately, absolute controllability is rare. Frequently, external or internal factors beyond a manager's control may affect revenues or expenses under that manager's responsibility. For example, the imposition of a 10% excise tax by a governmental agency may cause the price of the product to go up and thereby decrease sales of certain

601

items in a specific segment. Although a particular manager may have the authority and responsibility for that segment of the company's sales, such a decline in revenues is beyond that manager's control. Another example would be the excessive use of raw materials in a production process under the control of a particular manager. Although the manager has the authority to control such expenses, that manager should not be held responsible for excess costs if the purchasing department bought low-quality materials that created an unusual amount of spoilage.

Therefore, the theoretical requirement that a manager should have absolute control over items for which that manager is held responsible often must be compromised, since most revenue and expense items have some degree of noncontrollability in them. The manager is, thus, usually held responsible for items over which that manager has relative control. **Relative control** means that the manager has control over most of the factors that influence a given budget item. The use of relative control as a basis for evaluation may lead to some motivational problems in a company, since the manager is evaluated on results that may not reflect that manager's actual efforts. Nevertheless, most budget plans assign control on a relative basis in order to develop and use segmental budgets.

RESPONSIBILITY REPORTS

Objective 2: Prepare responsibility accounting reports

A unique feature of a responsibility accounting system is the varying amount of detail included in the reports issued to different levels of management. Although the amount of detail varies, reports issued under a responsibility accounting system are interrelated. Totals from the report on one level of management are carried forward in the report to the management level immediately above. For example, a performance report to a supervisor would include actual and budgeted dollar amounts of all revenue and expense items under that supervisor's control. The responsibility report issued to a supervisor's plant manager would show only totals from all the supervisors' performance reports and any additional items under the plant manager's control, such as plant administrative expenses. The vice president of manufacturing's report would contain totals from all the plant manager's reports plus any additional items under the vice president's control. Because a responsibility accounting system selectively condenses data, the report to the president includes summary totals of the subordinate levels plus any additional items under the president's control. In effect, the president's report should include all revenue and expense items in summary form since the president is responsible for controlling the profitability of the entire company.

The condensation of data as information flows upward to increasingly higher levels of management may seem to be a hindrance to performance analysis. Actually, this lack of detail results in "management by exception." **Management by exception** is the principle that upper-level management does not need to examine operating details at lower levels unless there appears to be a problem. Since businesses are becoming increasingly complex, it has become necessary to filter and condense accounting data so that these data may be analyzed quickly. Most executives do not have time to study detailed accounting reports and search for problem areas. Reporting only summary totals highlights those areas that need attention so that the executive can make more efficient use of available time.

The condensation of data that occurs in successive levels of management reports is justified on the basis that the appropriate manager will take the necessary corrective action. Thus, specific performance details need not be reported to superiors. For example, if direct labor cost has been excessively high in a particular department, that departmental supervisor should seek to find and correct the cause of the problem. When the plant manager questions the unfavorable budget variance of the department, the supervisor can inform the manager that corrective action was taken. Hence, it is not necessary to report to the vice president of manufacturing that a particular department within one of the plants is not operating satisfactorily, since the matter has already been resolved. Alternatively, if a manager's entire plant has been performing poorly, *summary* totals reported to the vice president of manufacturing will disclose this situation, and an investigation of the plant manager's problems may be indicated.

In preparing responsibility accounting reports, two basic methods are used to handle revenue or expense items. In the first approach, only those items over which a manager has direct control are included in the responsibility report for that management level. Any revenue and expense items that cannot be directly controlled are not included. The second approach is to include all revenue and expense items that can be traced directly or allocated indirectly to a particular manager, whether or not they are controllable. This second method represents a full-cost approach, which means all costs of a given area are disclosed in a single report. When this approach is used, care must be taken to separate controllable from noncontrollable items in order to differentiate those items for which a manager can and should be held responsible.

Features of Responsibility Reports

For accounting reports to be of maximum benefit, they must be *timely*. That is, reports should be prepared as soon as possible after the end of the performance measurement period. Timely reporting allows prompt corrective action to be taken. Reports that are delayed excessively lose their effectiveness as control devices. For example, a report on the previous month's operations that is not received until the end of the current month is virtually useless for analyzing poor performance areas and taking corrective action.

Reports should also be issued *regularly* so that trends can be spotted. Appropriate management action can be initiated before major problems occur. Regularity is also important so that managers will rely on the reports and become familiar with their contents.

603

The format of responsibility reports should be relatively simple and easy to read. Confusing terminology should be avoided. Results should be expressed in physical units where appropriate, since these may be more familiar and understandable to some managers. To assist management in quickly spotting budget variances, both budgeted (expected) and actual amounts should be reported. A **budget variance** is the difference between the budgeted and actual amounts of an item. Because variances highlight problem areas (exceptions), they are helpful in applying the management-by-exception principle. To help management evaluate performance to date, responsibility reports often include both a current period and a year-to-date analysis.

RESPONSIBILITY REPORTS—AN ILLUSTRATION

The following illustration is designed to show how responsibility accounting reports in an organization are interrelated. In this example the organization has four management levels as shown in Illustration 17.2. The representative managers we will focus on are the president, vice president of manufacturing, plant manager, and supervisor. For each management level a responsibility report will be prepared as shown in Illustration 17.3.

Illustration 17.2
ORGANIZATION CHART

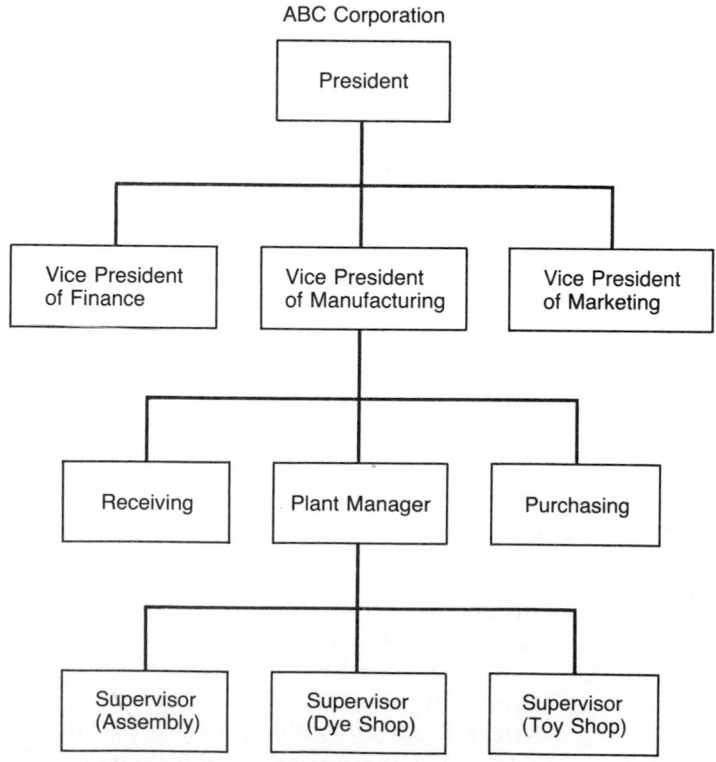

Illustration 17.3
RESPONSIBILITY REPORTS

ABC Corporation

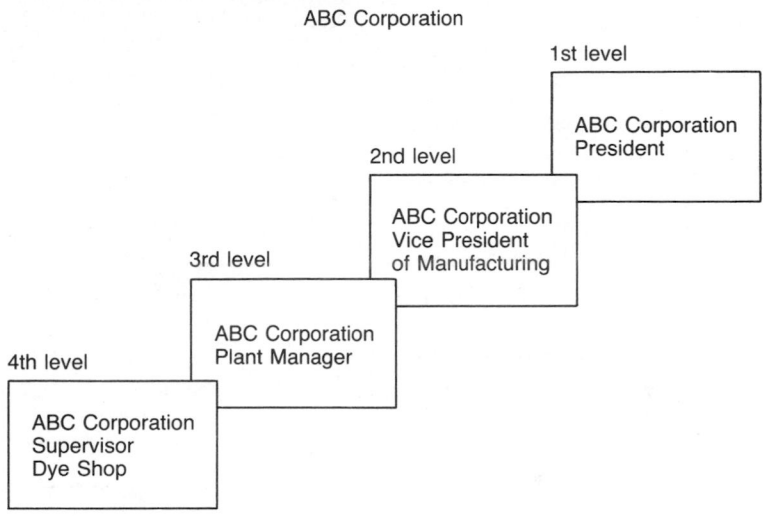

1st level

ABC Corporation
President

2nd level

ABC Corporation
Vice President
of Manufacturing

3rd level

ABC Corporation
Plant Manager

4th level

ABC Corporation
Supervisor
Dye Shop

Illustration 17.4 shows the detailed information included in the responsibility reports for each manager. Only the individual manager's controllable expenses are contained in these reports. Notice that only totals from the dye shop supervisor's report are included in the plant manager's report. In turn, only totals from the plant manager's report are included in the report to the vice president, and so on. In this way, detailed data from the lower levels are summarized (condensed) and reported at the next higher level. You can see that at each level, more and more costs become controllable. Also, controllable costs that were not included on lower-level reports are introduced into the reports for levels 3, 2, and 1. The only plant cost that is not included at the plant manager's level is the plant manager's salary, because it is noncontrollable by that plant manager. This cost is, however, controllable by the plant manager's supervisor, the vice president of manufacturing, and is included at that level of responsibility reporting.

Based on an analysis of these reports, the dye shop supervisor probably will take immediate action to see why supplies and overtime were significantly over budget this month. The plant manager may ask the supervisor what the problems were and whether they are now under control. The vice president may ask the same question of the plant manager. The president may ask each vice president why the budget was exceeded this month and what corrective action has been taken.

RESPONSIBILITY CENTERS

A **segment** is a fairly autonomous unit or division of a company defined according to function or product line. Traditionally, companies have been organized along functional lines. The segments or departments organized

Illustration 17.4
RESPONSIBILITY REPORTS FOR ABC CORPORATION

First Level

ABC CORPORATION
President

Controllable Expenses	Amount This Month	Amount Year to Date	Over or (Under) Budget This Month	Over or (Under) Budget Year to Date
President's office expense	$ 1,000	$ 5,000	$ 100	$ 200
Manufacturing vice president's costs	**18,800**	**93,000**	**600**	**800**
Vice president, sales	8,700	19,000	400	800
Vice president, finance	4,000	15,000	800	900
Vice presidents' salaries.	9,000	45,000	–0–	–0–
Total	$41,500	$177,000	$1,900	$2,700

Second Level

Vice President of Manufacturing

Controllable Expenses	Amount This Month	Amount Year to Date	Over or (Under) Budget This Month	Over or (Under) Budget Year to Date
Vice president's office expense.	$ 2,840	$ 9,500	$ (50)	$ (800)
Plant manager's costs	**7,880**	**43,000**	**250**	**500**
Purchasing	380	2,500	100	200
Receiving	700	3,000	300	900
Salaries of plant manager and heads of purchasing and receiving	7,000	35,000	–0–	–0–
Total (include in report for next higher level)	$18,800	$ 93,000	$ 600	$ 800

Third Level

Plant Manager

Controllable Expenses	Amount This Month	Amount Year to Date	Over or (Under) Budget This Month	Over or (Under) Budget Year to Date
Plant manager's office expense	$ 800	$ 9,100	$ (50)	$ (100)
Dye shop costs	**680**	**2,600**	**160**	**230**
Toy shop costs.	1,000	5,000	80	130
Assembly	400	1,300	60	240
Salaries of supervisors	5,000	25,000	–0–	–0–
Total (include in report for next higher level)	$ 7,880	$ 43,000	$ 250	$ 500

Fourth Level

Supervisor, Dye Shop

Controllable Expenses	Amount This Month	Amount Year to Date	Over or (Under) Budget This Month	Over or (Under) Budget Year to Date
Repairs and maintenance	$ 200	$ 1,000	$ 10	$ 40
Supplies.	180	850	80	95
Tools	100	300	(10)	81
Overtime	200	450	80	14
Total (include in report for next higher level)	$ 680	$ 2,600	$ 160	$ 230

along functional lines perform a specified function (e.g., marketing, finance, purchasing, production, or shipping). Recently, large companies have tended to organize segments according to product lines (e.g., electrical products division, shoe department, or food division).

A **responsibility center** is a segment of an organization for which a particular executive is responsible. There are three types of responsibility centers—expense (or cost) centers, profit centers, and investment centers. It is very important in designing a responsibility accounting system to examine the characteristics of each segment and the extent of the responsible manager's authority. Care must be taken to ensure that the basis for evaluating performance (i.e., expense center, profit center, or investment center) matches the characteristics of the segment and the authority of the segment's manager. The following sections of the chapter will discuss the characteristics of each of these types of centers and the appropriate bases for evaluating the performance of each type.

Expense Centers

An **expense center** is a responsibility center incurring only expense items and producing no direct revenue from the sale of goods or services. Examples of expense centers are service centers (e.g., the maintenance department or accounting department) or intermediate production facilities that produce parts for assembly into a finished product. *Managers of expense centers are held responsible only for specified expense items.*

The appropriate goal of an expense center is the long-run minimization of expenses. Short-run minimization of expenses may not be appropriate. For example, a production supervisor could eliminate maintenance costs for a short period of time, but in the long run, total costs might be higher due to more frequent machine breakdowns.

Profit Centers

A **profit center** is a responsibility center having both revenues and expenses. Since segmental earnings are usually defined as segmental revenues minus related expenses, the manager must be able to control both of these categories. The manager must have the authority to control selling price, sales volume, and all reported expense items. The manager's authority over all of these measured items is essential to proper performance evaluation. **Controllable profits of a segment** are shown when expenses under a manager's control are deducted from revenues under that manager's control.

Today, many companies are organizing segments as profit centers, including those that were normally considered expense centers. For example, consider the intermediate production facility mentioned in the last section which only produced output that becomes part of the final assembly in another segment. To enable the producing division to become a profit center rather than an expense center, a transfer price can be established.

Transfer prices. A **transfer price** is an artificial price used when goods or services are transferred from one segment to another segment within the same company. The transfer price is recorded as a revenue of the producing segment and as a cost, or expense, of the receiving segment. In using transfer prices, no cash actually changes hands between the segments. Instead, the transfer price is recorded as an internal accounting transaction.

Ideally, a transfer price should be the amount a part or service would cost if purchased from an outside party. Because such a "market" price might not be available, transfer prices often are determined on a cost-plus-profit-margin basis. In other cases, transfer prices are negotiated between the two segments, possibly with the help of an internal arbitration board.

No matter how the transfer price is determined, it is essential that the manufacturing segment manager have some degree of control over setting the price. If the manager does not have any control over the transfer price and output volume, the use of a profit center may not be a motivator.

Investment Centers

Closely related to the profit center concept is an investment center. An **investment center** is a responsibility center having revenues, expenses, and an appropriate investment base. When a segment is considered an investment center, it is evaluated according to the rate of return that it can earn on its investment base. **Return on investment (ROI),** also called rate of return, is computed by dividing segmental income by the appropriate investment base. For example, if a segment earns $500,000 on an investment base of $5,000,000, its ROI is 10%.

Determining the investment base to be used in the ROI calculation is a tricky matter. Normally, the assets available for use by the division make up the investment base of the division. But accountants disagree on whether depreciable assets should be included in the ROI calculation at original cost, original cost less accumulated depreciation, or current replacement cost. **Original cost** is the price paid to acquire an asset. **Original cost less accumulated depreciation** is the book value of the asset—the amount paid less total depreciation taken. **Current replacement cost** is the cost of replacing the present assets with similar assets in the same condition as those now in use. A different rate of return results from each of these measures. Therefore, management must select and agree upon an appropriate measure of investment base prior to making ROI calculations or interdivision comparisons.

Even after the investment base is defined, problems may still remain since many segment managers have limited control over some of the items included in the investment base of their segment. For instance, capital expenditure decisions for major plant assets are often made by top-level management rather than at the segment level. Therefore, the segment manager may have little control over the plant assets used by the segment. Another problem area may exist if the company has a centralized credit and collection department. In this case, the segment manager may have little or no control over the amount of accounts receivable included as segment assets since the manager cannot change the credit-granting or collection policies of the company.

Usually the above problems are overcome by realizing that if all segments are treated in the same manner, the inclusion of noncontrollable items in the investment base may have negligible effects. Comparisons of the ROI for all segments will then be based on a consistent treatment of items. It is important, though, that the segment managers agree to this treatment to avoid adverse reactions or decreased motivation.

Companies prefer to evaluate segments as investment centers because the ROI criterion facilitates performance comparisons between segments. Segments with more resources should produce more profits than segments with fewer resources, so it is difficult to compare the performance of segments of different sizes on the basis of profits alone. However, when ROI is used as a performance measure, performance comparisons take into account the differences in the sizes of the segments. The segment with the highest percentage ROI is presumably the most effective in using whatever resources it has.

Typical investment centers are large, autonomous segments of large companies. The centers are often separated from one another by location, types of products, functions, and/or necessary management skills. Segments such as these often seem to be separate companies to an outside observer. But the investment center concept can be applied even in relatively small companies in which the segment managers have control over the revenues, expenses, and assets of their segments.

SEGMENTAL ANALYSIS

So far, this chapter has described only the fundamentals of responsibility accounting. This section focuses specifically on segmental analysis.

Decentralization is the dispersion of decision-making authority among individuals at lower levels of the organization. In other words, the extent of decentralization refers to the degree of control that segment managers have over the revenues, expenses, and assets of their segments. When a segment manager has control over these three elements, the investment center concept can be applied to the segment. Thus, the more decentralized the decision making is in an organization, the more applicable is the investment center concept to the segments of the company. The more centralized the decision making is, the more likely one is to find responsibility centers established as expense centers. Some of the advantages of decentralized decision making are:

1. Increased control over their segments train managers for high-level positions in the company. The added authority and responsibility also

represents "job enlargement" and often increase job satisfaction and motivation.

2. Top management can be more removed from day-to-day decision making at lower levels of the company and can manage by exception. When top management is not involved with routine problem solving, it can devote more time to long-range planning and to the company's most significant problem areas.

3. Decisions can be made at the point where problems arise. It is often difficult for members of top management to make appropriate decisions on a timely basis when they are not intimately involved with the problem they are trying to solve.

4. Since decentralization permits use of the investment center concept, performance evaluation criteria such as ROI and residual income can be used.

CONCEPTS USED IN SEGMENTAL ANALYSIS

The concepts of variable cost, fixed cost, direct cost, indirect cost, net income of a segment, and contribution to indirect expenses are used in segmental analysis. Each concept will be described, except for variable cost and fixed cost, which were discussed in Chapter 13.

Direct Cost and Indirect Cost

Costs may be either directly or indirectly related to a particular cost objective. A **cost objective** is a segment, product, or other item for which costs may be accumulated. In other words, a cost is not "direct" or "indirect" in and of itself. It is only "direct" or "indirect" in relation to a given cost objective.

A **direct cost (expense)** is specifically traceable to a given cost objective. An **indirect cost (expense)** is not traceable to a given cost objective but has been allocated to it. A particular cost (expense) can only be designated as direct or indirect by reference to a given cost objective, and a cost that is direct to one cost objective may be indirect to another. For instance, the salary of a segment manager may be a direct cost of a given manufacturing segment but an indirect cost of one of the products manufactured by that segment. In this example the segment and the product are two distinct cost objectives.

Since a direct cost is traceable to a cost objective, the cost is likely to be eliminated if the cost objective is eliminated. For instance, if the plastics segment of a business is closed down, the salary of the manager of that segment probably will be eliminated. Sometimes a direct cost would remain even if the cost objective were eliminated, but this is the exception rather than the rule.

An indirect cost is not traceable to a particular cost objective; therefore, it only becomes an expense of the cost objective through an allocation process. For example, consider the depreciation expense on the company headquarters building that is allocated to each of the segments of the company. The depreciation expense is a direct cost for the company headquarters, but it is an indirect cost to each segment. If a segment of the company is eliminated, the indirect cost for depreciation assigned to that segment will not disappear; the cost will simply be allocated among the remaining segments. In a given situation, it may be possible to identify an indirect cost that would be eliminated if the cost objective were eliminated, but this would be the exception to the general rule.

Since direct costs of a segment are clearly identified with that segment, these costs are often controllable by the segment manager. Since indirect costs become segment costs only through allocation, most indirect costs are noncontrollable by the segment manager. But care must be taken not to equate direct costs with controllable costs. For example, the salary of a segment supervisor may be direct to that segment and yet noncontrollable by that supervisor because supervisors cannot specify their own salaries.

NET INCOME OF A SEGMENT—EVALUATION CRITERIA FOR A PROFIT CENTER

Objective 3: Prepare a segmental income statement using the contribution margin format

When preparing internal reports on the performance of segments of a company, management often finds it important to classify expenses as fixed or variable and as direct or indirect to the segment. These classifications may be more useful to management than the traditional classifications of cost of goods sold, operating expenses, and nonoperating expenses that are used for external reporting in the company's financial statements. As a result, many companies prepare (for internal use) an income statement with the format shown in Illustration 17.5.

This format is called the **contribution margin format** for the income statement because it shows the contribution margin. **Contribution margin** is defined as sales revenue less variable expenses. Notice in Illustration 17.5 that all variable expenses are direct expenses of the segment.

Illustration 17.5
CONTRIBUTION MARGIN FORMAT INCOME STATEMENT—
ALL EXPENSES ALLOCATED

	Segment A	Segment B	Total
Sales	$2,500,000	$1,500,000	$4,000,000
Less: Variable expenses (all direct expenses)	700,000	650,000	1,350,000
Contribution margin.	$1,800,000	$ 850,000	$2,650,000
Less: Direct fixed expenses	450,000	550,000	1,000,000
Contribution to indirect expenses.	$1,350,000	$ 300,000	$1,650,000
Less: Indirect fixed expenses	270,000	330,000	600,000
Net income	$1,080,000	$ (30,000)	$1,050,000

The second subtotal shown in the contribution margin format income statement (Illustration 17.5) is the segment's contribution to indirect expenses. **Contribution to indirect expenses** is defined as sales revenue less all direct expenses of the segment (both variable direct expenses and fixed direct expenses). The final total in the income statement is **segmental net income,** defined as segmental revenues less all expenses (direct expenses and allocated indirect expenses).

Earlier we stated that the performance of a profit center is evaluated on the basis of the segment's profits. It is tempting to use segmental net income to make this evaluation since total net income is used to evaluate the performance of the entire company. The problem with using segmental net income to evaluate performance is that segmental net income includes certain indirect expenses that have been allocated to the segment but are not directly related to it or its operations. Because segmental contribution to indirect expenses includes only revenues and expenses that are directly related to the segment, this amount is often more appropriate for evaluation purposes.

Given the facts in Illustration 17.5, if management relied on segmental net income to judge segmental performance, management might conclude that Segment B should be eliminated since it shows a loss of $30,000. But this action would reduce overall company profits by $300,000, as shown below:

Reduction in corporate revenues		$1,500,000
Reduction in corporate expenses		
Variable expenses	$650,000	
Direct fixed expenses	550,000	1,200,000
Reduction in corporate income		$ 300,000

Notice that the elimination of Segment B would not eliminate the $330,000 of allocated fixed costs. These costs would need to be allocated to Segment A if Segment B no longer existed.

To stress the importance of a segment's contribution to indirect expenses, many companies prefer the contribution margin income statement format presented in Illustration 17.6 rather than the format used in Illustration 17.5. The difference is that indirect fixed costs are not allocated to individual segments. Indirect fixed expenses are only shown in the total column for the computation of net income for the entire company. The computation for each segment stops with the segment's contribution to indirect expenses; this is the appropriate figure to use for evaluating the earnings performance of a segment. Only for the company as a whole is net income (revenues minus all expenses) computed; this is, of course, the appropriate figure to use for evaluating the company as a whole.

Arbitrary allocations of indirect fixed expenses. As stated above, indirect fixed expenses, such as depreciation on the corporate administration building or on the computer facility maintained at company headquarters, can only be allocated to segments on some arbitrary basis. There are two

Illustration 17.6
CONTRIBUTION MARGIN FORMAT INCOME STATEMENT—INDIRECT FIXED EXPENSES NOT ALLOCATED

	Segment A	Segment B	Total
Sales	$2,500,000	$1,500,000	$4,000,000
Less: Variable expenses	700,000	650,000	1,350,000
Contribution margin.	$1,800,000	$ 850,000	$2,650,000
Less: Direct fixed expenses	450,000	550,000	1,000,000
Contribution to indirect expenses.	$1,350,000	$ 300,000	$1,650,000
Less: Indirect fixed expenses			600,000
Net income			$1,050,000

basic guidelines for allocating indirect fixed expenses—by the benefit received and by the responsibility for incurrence of the expense.

Allocation can be made on the basis of benefit received for certain indirect expenses. For instance, assume a corporate computer was used for a total of 10,000 hours by the entire company. If Segment K used 4,000 hours, it could be charged with (allocated) 40% of the computer's depreciation for the period, since Segment K received 40% of the total benefits for the period.

For certain other indirect expenses, allocation is based on responsibility for incurrence. For instance, assume that Segment M contracts with a magazine to run an advertisement that will benefit both Segment M and various other segments of the company. Many companies would allocate the entire cost of the advertisement to Segment M since it was responsible for incurring the advertising expense.

To further illustrate the allocation of indirect expenses based on a measure of benefit or responsibility for incurrence, assume that Daily Company operates two segments, X and Y. It allocates the following indirect expenses to its two segments using these designated allocation bases:

Expense	Allocation Base
Home office building occupancy expense, $50,000	Net sales
Insurance expense, $35,000	Cost of segmental plant assets
General administrative expenses, $40,000	Number of employees

The following additional data are provided:

	Segment X	Segment Y	Total
Sales (net)	$400,000	$500,000	$900,000
Segmental plant assets. . . .	$250,000	$400,000	$650,000
Number of employees	50	80	130

The allocation of indirect expenses is as shown in the following expense allocation schedule:

	Segment X	Segment Y	Total
Home office building occupancy expense	$22,222[1]	$27,778[2]	$50,000
Insurance expense	13,462[3]	21,538[4]	$35,000
General administrative expenses	15,385[5]	24,615[6]	$40,000

$[1]\dfrac{\$400,000}{\$900,000} \times \$50,000 = \$22,222$ $[4]\dfrac{\$400,000}{\$650,000} \times \$35,000 = \$21,538$

$[2]\dfrac{\$500,000}{\$900,000} \times \$50,000 = \$27,778$ $[5]\dfrac{50}{130} \times \$40,000 = \$15,385$

$[3]\dfrac{\$250,000}{\$650,000} \times \$35,000 = \$13,462$ $[6]\dfrac{80}{130} \times \$40,000 = \$24,615$

When neither "benefit" nor "responsibility" can be used to allocate indirect fixed expenses, some other reasonable, but arbitrary, basis must be found. Often, for lack of a better approach, indirect expenses are allocated based on net sales. For instance, if segment X's net sales were 60% of total company sales, then 60% of the indirect expenses would be allocated to Segment X. Allocating expenses based on sales is not recommended because it reduces the incentive of a segment manager to increase sales, since this would result in more indirect expenses being allocated to that segment.

Having covered some basic concepts essential to segment analysis, some specific procedures for performance evaluation will be presented.

INVESTMENT CENTER ANALYSIS

Objective 4: Calculate return on investment, margin, and turnover for a segment

To this point, the segmental analysis discussion has concentrated on the contribution to indirect expenses and segmental net income approaches. Now we will introduce the investment base concept into the analysis. Two criteria that include the concept of investment base in the analysis are ROI (return on investment) and RI (residual income).

Return on Investment (ROI)

A segment that has a large amount of assets will usually earn more in an absolute sense than will a segment that has a small amount of assets. Therefore, absolute amounts of segmental income cannot be used to compare the performance of different segments. To measure the relative effectiveness of segments, a company must use **return on investment** (ROI), which calculates the return (income) as a percentage of the assets employed (investment). The formula for return on investment is:

$$ROI = \frac{Income}{Investment}$$

To illustrate the difference between using absolute amounts and using percentages in evaluating a segment's performance, consider the data shown in Illustration 17.7 for a company with three segments. If absolute dollars of income are used to evaluate performance, Segment 2 appears to be doing twice as well as Segment 3. But the use of ROI as a criterion for

Illustration 17.7
COMPUTATION OF RETURN ON INVESTMENT (ROI)

		Segment 1	Segment 2	Segment 3	Total
a.	Income	$ 250,000	$1,000,000	$ 500,000	$1,750,000
b.	Investment.	2,500,000	5,000,000	2,000,000	9,500,000
	Return on investment				
	a ÷ b	10%	20%	25%	18.42%

evaluating the segments indicates that Segment 3 is really performing the best (25%), Segment 2 is the next best (20%), and Segment 1 is performing the worst (10%). ROI is therefore a more useful indicator of the relative performance of segments than absolute income.

Although ROI appears to be a quite simple and straightforward computation, there are several alternative methods for making the calculation. These alternatives focus on what is meant by "income" and "investment." Illustration 17.8 shows various definitions and applicable situations for each type of computation.

As discussed earlier in the chapter, alternative valuation bases include original cost, cost less accumulated depreciation, and current replacement cost. Each of the valuation bases has merits and drawbacks, as you will now see.

Cost less accumulated depreciation is probably the most widely used valuation base and is easily determined. But since there are many types of depreciation methods, comparisons between segments or companies may

Illustration 17.8
POSSIBLE DEFINITIONS OF "INCOME " AND "INVESTMENT"

Situation	Definition of Income	Definition of Investment
1. Evaluation of the earning power of the company. Do not use for segments or segment managers due to inclusion of noncontrollable expenses.	Net income of the company.*	Total assets of the company.†
2. Evaluation of rate of income contribution of segment. Do not use for segment managers due to inclusion of noncontrollable expenses.	Contribution to indirect expenses.	Assets directly used by and identified with the segment.
3. Evaluation of income performance of segment manager.	"Controllable" income. This would begin with contribution to indirect expenses and would eliminate any revenues and direct expenses not under the control of the segment manager.	Assets under the control of the segment manager.

*Often *net operating income* is used; this is defined as income before interest and taxes.
†*Operating assets* are often used in the calculation. This definition excludes assets not used in normal operations.

be difficult. Also, as book value decreases, a constant income results in a steadily increasing ROI even though the segment's performance is unchanged. The use of original cost eliminates the problem of decreasing book value but has its own drawback. The investment in (cost of) old assets will be much less than an investment in new assets, so a segment with old assets can earn less than a segment with new assets and still realize the same ROI. Current replacement cost is difficult to use because replacement cost figures often are not available, but this base does eliminate some of the problems caused by the other two methods. Whichever valuation basis is adopted, all ROI calculations that are used for comparative purposes should be made consistently.

Expanded form of ROI computation. The ROI formula can be broken into two component parts as follows:

$$\text{ROI} = \frac{\text{Income}}{\text{Sales}} \times \frac{\text{Sales}}{\text{Investment}}$$

The first part of the formula, Income/Sales, is called margin or return on sales. The **margin** refers to the percentage relationship of income or profits to sales. This percentage shows the number of cents of profit that are generated by each dollar of sales. The second part of the formula, Sales/Investment, is called turnover. **Turnover** shows the number of dollars of sales generated by each dollar of investment. Turnover measures how effectively each dollar of assets was used.

There are several ways to increase ROI:

1. A manager can concentrate on increasing profit margin while holding turnover constant. Pursuing this strategy means keeping selling prices constant and making every effort to increase efficiency and thereby reduce expenses.
2. A manager can concentrate on increasing turnover by reducing the investment in assets while holding income and sales constant. For example, working capital could be decreased, thereby reducing the investment in assets.
3. A manager can take actions that affect both margin and turnover. For example, disposing of nonproductive depreciable assets would decrease investment while also increasing income (through the reduction of depreciation expense). Thus, both margin and turnover would increase. An advertising campaign would probably increase sales and income. In this case, turnover would increase, and margin might increase or decrease depending on the relative amounts of the increases in income and sales.

Illustration 17.9 shows possible outcomes of some of these strategies to increase ROI.

Illustration 17.9
STRATEGIES FOR INCREASING ROI

Know!

Past year return on investment:

$$ROI = Margin \times Turnover$$

$$ROI = \frac{Income}{Sales} \times \frac{Sales}{Investment}$$

$$ROI = \frac{\$100,000}{\$2,000,000} \times \frac{\$2,000,000}{\$1,000,000}$$

$$ROI = 5\% \times 2 \text{ times}$$

$$ROI = 10\%$$

1. Increase margin through reducing expenses by $40,000; no effect on sales or investment.

$$ROI = \frac{\$140,000}{\$2,000,000} \times \frac{\$2,000,000}{\$1,000,000}$$

$$ROI = 7\% \times 2 \text{ times}$$

$$ROI = 14\%$$

2. Increase turnover through reducing investment in assets by $200,000; no effect on sales or income.

$$ROI = \frac{\$100,000}{\$2,000,000} \times \frac{\$2,000,000}{\$800,000}$$

$$ROI = 5\% \times 2.5 \text{ times}$$

$$ROI = 12.5\%$$

3(a). Increase margin and turnover by disposing of nonproductive depreciable assets; income increased by $10,000; investment decreased by $200,000.

$$ROI = \frac{\$110,000}{\$2,000,000} \times \frac{\$2,000,000}{\$800,000}$$

$$ROI = 5.5\% \times 2.5 \text{ times}$$

$$ROI = 13.75\%$$

3(b). Increase margin and turnover through increased advertising; sales increased by $500,000 and income by $50,000; no effect on investment.

$$ROI = \frac{\$150,000}{\$2,500,000} \times \frac{\$2,500,000}{\$1,000,000}$$

$$ROI = 6\% \times 2.5 \text{ times}$$

$$ROI = 15\%$$

3(c). Increase turnover through increased advertising; sales increased by $500,000 and income by $12,500; no effect on investment.

$$ROI = \frac{\$112,500}{\$2,500,000} \times \frac{\$2,500,000}{\$1,000,000}$$

$$ROI = 4.5\% \times 2.5 \text{ times}$$

$$ROI = 11.25\%$$

Residual Income

Objective 5: Calculate the residual income of a segment

The use of ROI as the sole criterion for evaluating performance can result in what is termed suboptimization. **Suboptimization** occurs when a segment manager takes an action that is in the segment's best interest (i.e., raises that segment's ROI), but is not in the best interest of the company as a whole.

To prevent suboptimization, companies sometimes use the concept of residual income. **Residual income (RI)** is defined as the amount of income a segment has in excess of a desired minimum ROI. Each company sets its minimum ROI based on many factors, including expected growth rate, debt coverage, industry technology, and desired returns to stockholders. The formula for residual income is:

Residual Income (RI) = Income − (Investment × Desired minimum ROI)

When RI is used to evaluate performance, the segment rated as the best is the segment with the greatest amount of RI rather than the one with the highest ROI.

To illustrate the value of using residual income to measure performance, assume the manager of Segment 3 in Illustration 17.10 has an opportunity to take on a project involving an investment of $100,000 that is estimated to return $22,000, or 22%, on the investment. Since the segment's ROI is currently 25%, the manager may decide to reject the project. However, from a company standpoint, ROI will increase from 18.89% to 18.96% if the project is accepted. The decision to reject the project is a valid decision from the manager's point of view because to accept the project will cause the segment's ROI to decline. But from a company standpoint, ROI is 18.89%, and accepting the project would increase the overall company ROI.

The project opportunity for Segment 3 could earn in excess of the desired minimum ROI of 10%. In fact, it has residual income of $12,000 [$22,000 − (10% × $100,000)]. If residual income (RI) were applied as the basis for evaluating segmental performance, the manager of Segment 3 would accept the project because doing so would improve his or her segment's performance. That choice would also be beneficial to the entire company.

Critics of the residual income method complain that larger segments are likely to have the highest residual income. In a given situation it may be advisable to look at both ROI and RI in assessing performance.

Since it is always assumed that a manager will make choices that improve his or her segment's performance, the challenge is to select evaluation bases for segments that will result in managers making choices that benefit the entire company. When performance is evaluated on RI, choices that improve a segment's performance are more likely to be good for the entire company as well.

When calculating RI for a *segment,* the income and investment definitions are "contribution to indirect expenses" and "assets directly used by

Illustration 17.10
COMPUTATION OF RESIDUAL INCOME (RI)

Before acceptance of the project by Segment 3, the amounts are as follows:

	Segment 1	Segment 2	Segment 3	Total Company
a. Income	$ 100,000	$ 500,000	$ 250,000	$ 850,000
b. Investment	1,000,000	2,500,000	1,000,000	4,500,000
c. Rate of return on investment (ROI)	10%	20%	25%	18.89%
d. Desired minimum ROI (10%)	$ 100,000	$ 250,000	$ 100,000	*
e. Residual income	–0–	250,000	150,000	*

*The RI concept is generally not used for evaluating an entire company, since the problem of suboptimization by definition, does not exist.

With acceptance of the project by Segment 3, the amounts would be as follows:

	Segment 1	Segment 2	Segment 3	Total Company
a. Income	$ 100,000	$ 500,000	$ 272,000*	$ 872,000
b. Investment	1,000,000	2,500,000	1,100,000†	4,600,000
c. Rate of return on investment (ROI)	10%	20%	24.7%	18.96%
d. Desired minimum ROI (10%)	$ 100,000	$ 250,000	$ 110,000	
e. Residual income	–0–	250,000	162,000	

*$250,000 + (22% of $100,000).
†$1,000,000 original investment + $100,000 new investment.

and identified with the segment." When calculating RI for a *manager* of a segment, the income and investment definitions should be "income controllable by the segment manager" and "assets under the control of the segment manager."

In evaluating the performance of a segment or a segment manager, comparisons should be made with (1) the current budget, (2) other segments or managers within the company, (3) past performance of that segment or manager, and (4) similar segments or managers in other companies. Consideration must be given to general economic conditions, market conditions for the product being produced, and so on. A superior segment in Company A may be considered superior because it is earning a return of 12%, which is above similar segments in other companies but below other segments in Company A. But segments in Company A may be more profitable because of market conditions and the nature of the company's products rather than because of the performance of the segment managers. Careful judgment must be used whenever performance is evaluated.

SEGMENTAL REPORTING IN EXTERNAL FINANCIAL STATEMENTS

Formerly, segmental information was reported only to management for internal decision-making purposes. In December 1976, the Financial Accounting Standards Board issued *Statement of Financial Accounting Standards*

No. 14, "Financial Reporting for Segments of a Business Enterprise." This *Statement* requires publicly held companies to publish certain segmental information in their annual financial statements. Thus, external users of financial statements now have segmental information to aid them in their decisions regarding these companies. However, fewer details are presented in these external statements than in reports intended for management.

SUMMARY

A responsibility accounting system provides information to evaluate each manager on revenue and expense items over which that manager has primary control. Responsibility accounting reports contain only those items controlled by the responsible manager, or if noncontrollable items are included, the reports should clearly separate controllable from noncontrollable items. The identification of controllable items is a fundamental task in responsibility accounting and reporting.

Management by exception is the concept that upper-level management does not need to be concerned with operating details of subordinate levels unless there appears to be a problem. To accomplish management by exception, responsibility reports contain details only of activities immediately under the manager's control; only summary information of results from subordinate levels is presented. Also, responsibility reports should present both budgeted and actual results, as well as budget variances and year-to-date totals.

A responsibility center is a segment of an organization for which a particular executive is responsible. There are three types of responsibility centers—expense centers, profit centers, and investment centers.

A responsibility center having only expense items and producing no revenue from the sale of goods or services is properly accounted for as an expense center. Managers of expense centers are held responsible only for specified expense items.

A profit center has both revenues and expenses, so it is possible to calculate segmental income. A profit center manager is evaluated on controllable profits of the segment, the difference between revenue items under the manager's control and expense items under the manager's control. When a profit center sells its output only to other segments of the same company, controllable profits of the profit center are strongly influenced by the transfer price that is established for the "sale." It is essential that the manufacturing segment (profit center) manager have some control over setting the transfer price.

An investment center is a responsibility center that has revenues, expenses, and a specified investment base. Performance of an investment center and of an investment center's manager can be evaluated on the basis of return on investment (ROI). ROI is computed by dividing segmental income by the appropriate investment base.

A direct cost of a given cost objective can be traced directly to that cost objective. An indirect cost cannot be traced directly to a cost objective; it can be assigned to the cost objective only through a cost allocation process. A cost that is direct to one cost objective may be indirect with regard to another.

Segment contribution margin is the difference between net sales and variable expenses of a segment. Segment contribution to indirect expenses is the amount remaining after all direct expenses of the segment are deducted from the revenues generated by the segment. Segmental net income is the amount that remains after all of a segment's expenses (direct and indirect) are deducted from the segment's revenues. Since a segment's contribution to indirect expenses includes only items that are directly related to the segment, this amount indicates the effect on company profits if the segment were eliminated. Consequently, contribution to indirect expenses is often considered more appropriate than segmental net income for evaluation purposes.

Two different criteria exist for evaluating the performance of investment centers. Return on investment (ROI) directly compares segmental income to the segment's investment base. Both segmental income and the segment's investment base may be defined in a number of ways, any of which may be appropriate depending on the circumstances. The ROI computation can also be expanded to consider separately the effects of margin and turnover. The other criterion for evaluating investment center performance is residual income (RI), the amount by which segmental income exceeds a minimum desired ROI. Use of the RI criterion for segmental evaluation reduces the tendency toward suboptimization that can occur when managers are evaluated on ROI alone. Possibly both ROI and RI should be used in evaluating performance.

Chapter 18 discusses budgeting. Companies, like individuals, should plan for the future. A budget is one method of planning. Just as you may use a budget in managing your personal finances, budgets are an important tool of company management.

Objective 6: Define and correctly use the new terms in the glossary

NEW TERMS INTRODUCED IN CHAPTER 17

Budget variance   The difference between the budgeted and actual amounts of an item (604).

Contribution margin   Sales revenue less variable expenses (611).

Contribution margin format   An income statement format that shows the contribution margin (Sales − Variable expenses) for a segment (611).

Contribution to indirect expenses   The income of a segment remaining after direct expenses are deducted from segmental revenues (612).

Controllable profits of a segment   Profit of a segment when expenses under a manager's control are deducted from revenues under that manager's control (607).

Cost objective   A segment, product, or other item for which costs may be accumulated (610).

Current replacement cost The cost of replacing the present assets with similar assets in the same condition as those now in use (608).

Decentralization The dispersion of decision-making authority among individuals at lower levels of the organization (609).

Direct cost (expense) A cost that is directly traceable to a given cost objective (610).

Expense center A responsibility center producing only expense items and producing no direct revenue from the sale of goods or services. Examples include the accounting department and the maintenance department (607).

Indirect cost (expense) A cost that is not traceable to a given cost objective but has been allocated to it (610).

Investment center A responsibility center having revenues, expenses, and an appropriate investment base (608).

 Management by exception The principle that upper-level management does not need to examine operating details at lower levels unless there appears to be a problem (an exception) (602).

 Margin (as used in ROI) The percentage relationship of income (or profits) to sales.

$$\text{Margin} = \frac{\text{Income}}{\text{Sales}} \ (616).$$

Original cost The price paid to acquire an asset (608).

Original cost less accumulated depreciation The book value of an asset—the amount paid less total depreciation taken (608).

Profit center A responsibility center having both revenue and expense items (607).

Relative control Means the manager has control over most of the factors that influence a given budget item (602).

Residual income (RI) The amount of income a segment has in excess of a desired minimum ROI. Residual income is equal to Income − (Investment × Desired minimum ROI) (618).

 Responsibility accounting Refers to an accounting system that collects, summarizes, and reports accounting data according to the responsibilities of the individual managers. A responsibility accounting system provides information to evaluate each manager on revenue and expense items over which that manager has primary control (600).

Responsibility center A segment of an organization for which a particular executive is responsible (607).

 Return on investment (ROI) Calculates the return (income) as a percentage of the assets employed (investment).

$$\frac{\text{Return on}}{\text{investment}} = \frac{\text{Income}}{\text{Investment}} \ \text{or} \ \frac{\text{Income}}{\text{Sales}} \times \frac{\text{Sales}}{\text{Investment}} \ (608, 614).$$

Segment A fairly autonomous unit or division of a company defined according to function or product line (605).

Segmental net income Final total in the income statement; segmental revenues less all expenses (direct expenses and allocated indirect expenses) (612).

Suboptimization A situation that occurs when a segment manager takes an action that is in the segment's best interest but is not in the best interest of the company as a whole (618).

Transfer price An artificial price used when goods or services are transferred from one segment to another segment within the same company (608).

Turnover (as used in ROI) The number of dollars of sales generated by each dollar of investment.

$$\text{Turnover} = \frac{\text{Sales}}{\text{Investment}} \quad (616).$$

DEMONSTRATION PROBLEM 17–1

The Brandon Company has two segments. Results of operations for 1990 follow:

	Segment 1	Segment 2	Total
Sales	$35,000	$90,000	$125,000
Variable expenses	15,000	55,000	70,000
Fixed expenses:			
Direct	7,000	10,000	17,000
Indirect			18,000

The company has total operating assets of $195,000; $150,000 of these assets are identified with particular segments as follows:

	Segment 1	Segment 2
Assets directly used by and identified with the segment	$50,000	$100,000

Required:

a. Prepare a statement showing the contribution margin, contribution to indirect expenses for each segment, and the total income for the Brandon Company.

b. Calculate the return on investment for each segment and then for the entire company.

c. Comment on the results of (a) and (b).

Solution to demonstration problem 17–1

a.

BRANDON COMPANY
Income Statement Showing Segmental
Contributions to Indirect Expenses
For the year ended December 31, 1990

	Segment 1	Segment 2	Total
Sales	$35,000	$90,000	$125,000
Less: Variable expenses.	15,000	55,000	70,000
Contribution margin	$20,000	$35,000	$ 55,000
Less: Direct fixed expenses	7,000	10,000	17,000
Contribution to indirect expenses . . .	$13,000	$25,000	$ 38,000
Less: Indirect fixed expenses			18,000
Net income	13,000	25,000	$ 20,000

b. **1.** $\text{ROI} = \dfrac{\text{Contribution to indirect expenses}}{\substack{\text{Assets directly used by and} \\ \text{identified with segment}}}$

Segment 1	*Segment 2*
$\text{ROI} = \dfrac{\$13,000}{\$50,000} = 26\%$	$\text{ROI} = \dfrac{\$25,000}{\$100,000} = 25\%$

2. $\text{ROI} = \dfrac{\text{Net operating income}}{\text{Operating assets}} = \dfrac{\$20,000}{\$195,000} = 10.3\%$

c. In part (**a**), Segment 2 showed a higher contribution to indirect expenses. But in (**b**), Segment 1 showed a higher return on investment. The difference between these calculations shows that when a segment is evaluated as a profit center, the center with the highest investment base will usually show the best results. But when the segment is evaluated as an investment center, the segment with the highest investment base will not necessarily show the highest return. The computations in (**b**) also demonstrate that the return on investment for the company as a whole will be lower than the segments because of the increased investment base.

QUESTIONS

1. What is the fundamental principle of responsibility accounting?

2. How soon after the end of the performance measurement period should accounting reports be prepared? Explain.

3. Compare and contrast an expense center and an investment center.

4. Differentiate between a direct cost and an indirect cost of a segment. What happens to each category if the segment to which it is related is eliminated?

5. Indicate how each of the following is calculated for a segment:
  a. Gross margin.
  b. Contribution margin.
  c. Contribution to indirect expenses (under the two different formulas).
  d. Net income.

6. Give the general formula for return on investment (ROI). How may this formula be split into two components?

7. How is residual income determined?

8. If the residual income for Segment Manager A is $40,000, while the residual income for Segment Manager B is $90,000, does this necessarily mean that B is a better manager than A?

EXERCISES

Prepare a responsibility report for a given management level

1. The following information refers to the card shop of the Hallway Company for the month of June:

	June Amount	Over or (Under) Budget
Supplies	$ 45,000	$(15,000)
Repairs & maintenance	225,000	22,000
Overtime	110,000	14,000
Salary of supervisor	40,000	(5,000)
Salary of plant manager	55,000	0
Allocation of company accounting costs	33,000	10,000
Allocation of depreciation	26,000	(7,000)

[handwritten annotations: Variable, Fixed, Variable, Fixed]

Using the above information, prepare a responsibility report for the supervisor of the card shop for the month of June. (Ignore year-to-date expenses.)

Prepare an income statement for a segment in a contribution margin format

2. Present the following information for Segment S in the contribution margin format:

Sales	$1,220,000
Variable selling & administrative expenses	80,000
Fixed direct manufacturing expenses	33,000
Variable manufacturing expenses	325,000
Fixed direct selling & administrative expenses	105,000

Prepare an income statement for a segment using the contribution margin format; determine effect of elimination of segment on company income

3. Given the following data, prepare a schedule which shows contribution margin, contribution to indirect costs, and net income of the segment:

Direct fixed expenses	$ 67,000
Indirect fixed expenses	48,000
Sales	320,000
Variable expenses	165,000

What would be the effect on company earnings if the segment was eliminated?

Allocate expenses to various segments using a specified allocation base

4. Three segments (M, N, and O) of the Thomas Company have net sales of $800,000, $600,000, and $400,000, respectively. A decision is made to allocate the pool of $120,000 of administrative overhead expenses of the home office to the segments, based on net sales.

   a. How much should be allocated to each of the segments?

   b. If Segment O is eliminated, how much would be allocated to M and N?

Calculate ROI, margin, and turnover for a segment

5. Two segments (tires and batteries) showed the following data for the most recent year:

	Tires	Batteries
Contribution to indirect expenses	$ 55,000	$ 124,000
Assets directly used by and identified with the segment	265,000	700,000
Sales	1,500,000	1,650,000

   a. Calculate return on investment (ROI) for each segment in the most direct manner.

   b. Calculate return on investment (ROI) utilizing the margin and turnover components.

Determine the effect on margin, turnover, and ROI when the variables are altered

6. Determine the effect of each of the following on the margin, turnover, and ROI of the tire segment in Exercise 5. Consider each change independently of the others.

   a. Direct variable expenses were reduced by $5,000, and indirect expenses were reduced by $7,500. Sales and assets were unaffected.

b. Assets used by the segment were reduced by $50,000, while income and sales were unaffected.

c. An advertising campaign increased sales by $100,000 and income by $16,000. Assets directly used by the segment remained unaffected.

Determine residual income in evaluating segments

7. The Carver Company has three segments: Red, Blue, and White. Data concerning "income" and "investment" are as follows:

	Red	Blue	White
Contribution to indirect expenses	$ 30,000	$ 55,000	$ 80,000
Assets directly used by and identified with the segment	100,000	295,000	720,000

Assuming that the minimum desired return on investment is 10%, calculate the residual income of each of the segments. Do the results indicate that any of the segments should be eliminated?

PROBLEMS

Prepare responsibility reports for various levels of management

17–1. You were given the following information for the McMillan Company for the year ended December 31, 1990:

Controllable Expenses	Plant Manager		Vice President of Manufacturing		President	
	Budget	Actual	Budget	Actual	Budget	Actual
Office expense	$ 3,200	$ 5,500	$ 8,500	$12,500	$ 16,500	$12,000
Printing shop	2,500	2,500				
Iron shop	1,750	1,050				
Toaster shop	10,000	10,000				
Purchasing.			11,500	13,000		
Receiving			6,000	8,500		
Inspection			11,000	9,050		
Sales Manager					110,000	95,000
Controller					85,000	70,000
Treasurer					70,000	45,000
Personnel Manager . .					20,000	30,000

Required:

Prepare the responsibility accounting reports for three levels of management—plant manager, vice president of manufacturing, and president.

Evaluate responsibility centers as profit centers and investment centers

17–2. The Turner Corporation has three production plants, A, B, and C. These plants are treated as responsibility centers. The following summarizes the results for the month of October 1990:

Plant	Revenue	Expenses	Investment Base (gross assets)
A	$ 950,000	$450,000	$18,000,000
B	1,650,000	725,000	8,000,000
C	3,750,000	975,000	26,000,000

Required:

a. If the plants are treated as profit centers, which plant manager appears to have done the best job?

b. If the plants are treated as investment centers, which plant manager appears to have done the best job? (Assume that plant managers are evaluated in terms of ROI on gross assets.)

c. Do the results of profit center analysis and investment center analysis give different findings? If so, why?

Allocate indirect expenses to illustrate the arbitrary nature of expense allocation

17–3. Calhoun, Inc., allocates expenses and revenues to the two segments, R and S, that it operates. It extends credit to customers under a revolving charge plan whereby all account balances not paid within 30 days are charged interest at a rate of 1-1/2% per month.

Given below are selected revenue and expense accounts and some additional data needed to complete the allocation of the one revenue amount and the expenses.

Revenue and Expenses (allocation bases)

Revolving charge service revenue (net sales)	$ 40,000
Home office building occupancy expense (net sales)	30,000
Buying expenses (net purchases)	100,000
General administrative expenses (number of employees in department)	50,000
Insurance expense (relative average inventory plus cost of equipment and fixtures in each department)	12,000
Depreciation expense on home office equipment (net sales)	20,000

Additional data:

	Segment R	Segment S	Total
Number of employees	6	14	20
Sales (net)	$200,000	$400,000	$600,000
Purchases (net)	160,000	240,000	400,000
Average inventory	40,000	80,000	120,000
Cost of equipment and fixtures	60,000	120,000	180,000

Required:

Prepare a schedule showing allocation of the above items to Segments R and S.

Prepare a schedule showing contribution margin and contribution to indirect expenses using contribution margin format; prepare segmental income statements

17–4. Davis, Inc., is a company with two segments, 1 and 2. Its revenues and expenses for 1990 are as follows:

	Segment 1	Segment 2	Total
Sales (net)	$150,000	$280,000	$430,000
Direct expenses:*			
Cost of goods sold	65,000	140,000	205,000
Selling	17,400	13,000	30,400
Administrative:			
Uncollectible accounts.	5,500	2,000	7,500
Insurance	3,750	2,500	6,250
Interest	1,400	850	2,250
Indirect expenses (all fixed):			
Selling			25,600
Administrative			43,000

*All direct expenses are variable except insurance and interest, which are fixed.

Required:

a. Prepare a schedule showing the contribution margin, the contribution to indirect expenses of each segment, and net income for the company as a whole. Do not allocate indirect expenses to the segments.

b. Assume that indirect selling expenses are to be allocated on the basis of net sales and that indirect administrative expenses are to be allocated on the basis of direct administrative expenses. Prepare a statement (starting with the contribution to indirect expenses) which shows the net income of each segment.

c. Comment on the appropriateness of the "income" amounts shown in parts (a) and (b) for determining the earnings contribution of the segments.

Prepare an income statement for two segments using the contribution margin format; calculate the ROI for (1) the entire company, (2) each segment, and (3) each manager

17–5. The Barry Corporation has three segments. Results of operations for 1990 were as follows:

	Segment 1	Segment 2	Segment 3	Total
Sales	$27,000,000	$13,500,000	$9,500,000	$50,000,000
Variable expenses	16,000,000	9,500,000	7,750,000	33,250,000
Fixed expenses:				
Direct	3,000,000	1,250,000	1,000,000	5,250,000
Indirect				2,500,000

The following direct fixed expenses were not under the control of the segment manager: segment 1, $350,000; segment 2, $275,000; and segment 3, $300,000.

For the company's total operating assets of $70,000,000, the following facts exist:

	Segment 1	Segment 2	Segment 3
Assets directly used by and identified with the segment	$35,000,000	$20,000,000	$10,000,000
Assets under the "control" of the segment manager	30,000,000	16,000,000	8,000,000

Required:

a. Prepare a statement showing the contribution margin and the contribution to indirect expenses for each segment and the total income of the Barry Corporation.

b. Determine the ROI for evaluating (1) the earning power of the entire company, (2) the rate of income contribution of each segment, and (3) the earnings performance of each segment manager.

Calculate ROI and RI for each segment and segment manager

17–6. The Scott Company operates with three segments, X, Y, and Z. Data regarding the segments are as follows:

	Segment X	Segment Y	Segment Z
Contribution to indirect expenses	$ 180,000	$100,000	$ 80,000
Earnings controllable by the manager	250,000	150,000	128,000
Assets directly used by and identified with the segment	1,000,000	800,000	400,000
Assets under the "control" of the segment manager	880,000	710,000	360,000

Required:

a. Calculate the ROI for each segment and each segment manager. Rank them from highest to lowest.

b. Assume that the minimum desired rates of return are 12% for a segment and 20% for a segment manager. Calculate the residual income for each segment and each manager. Rank them from highest to lowest.

c. Repeat part (**b**), but now assume the desired minimum rates of return are 17% for a segment and 25% for a segment manager. Rank them from highest to lowest.

d. Comment on the rankings achieved.

Determine margin turnover, and ROI for a segment and the effect on each when the variables are changed

17–7. The Grape segment of the Beverage Corporation reported the following data for 1990:

Contribution to indirect expenses	$ 3,900,000
Assets directly used by and identified with the segment . . .	15,400,000
Sales	32,000,000

Required:

a. Determine the margin, turnover, and ROI for the segment in 1990.

b. Determine the effect on margin, turnover, and ROI of the segment in 1991 if each of the following changes were to occur. Consider each one separately, and assume that any items not specifically mentioned remain the same as in 1990.

(1) A new labor contract with the union increased expenses by $500,000 for 1991.

(2) A strike in early 1991 shut down operations for two months. Sales decreased by $8,000,000, cost of goods sold by $5,000,000, and other direct expenses by $1,500,000.

(3) Introduction of a new product caused sales to increase by $11,000,000, cost of goods sold by $7,500,000, and other direct expenses by $800,000. Assets increased by $1,500,000.

(4) An advertising campaign was launched. As a result, sales increased by $2,500,000, cost of goods sold by $1,700,000, and other direct expenses by $800,000.

BUSINESS DECISION PROBLEM 17–1

Allocate unusual expenses to departments; determine controllable and noncontrollable expenses

a. The Davies Company manufactures scuba gear. The company's business is highly seasonal, and between December and March, 15 skilled manufacturing employees are usually "laid off." In order to improve morale, the financial vice-president suggests that these 15 employees not be laid off in the future. Instead it was suggested that they work in general labor from December to March but still be paid their manufacturing wages of $10 per hour. General labor personnel earn $5 per hour. What are the implications of this plan for the assignment of costs to the various segments?

b. The Parker Company constructs office buildings. Talmadge is in charge of the construction department. Among other responsibilities, Talmadge hires and supervises the electricians and other workers who build the homes. The Parker Company does not do its own foundation work. The construction of foundations is done by subcontractors hired by Hines of the procurement department.

To start the development of an office park, Hines hired the Wendt Company to build the foundations for the homes. On the day construction was to begin, the Wendt Company went out of business. Consequently, construction was delayed eight weeks while Hines hired a new subcontractor. Which department should be charged with the delay in construction? Why?

c. Gordon Jackson is supervisor of Department 27 of the Michaels Company. The annual budget for the department is as follows:

Depreciation, building	$ 9,200
Depreciation, machinery	8,000
Direct labor	40,200
Direct materials	13,750
Property insurance	3,000
Property taxes	1,000
Set up	4,200
Small tools	8,000
Supervision	30,000
Supplies	10,600
	$127,950

Jackson's salary of $20,000 is included in supervision. The remaining $10,000 in supervision is the salary of the assistant supervisor who is directly responsible to Jackson. Identify the budget items that are controllable by Jackson.

18

THE BUDGET—FOR PLANNING AND CONTROL

LEARNING OBJECTIVES

After studying this chapter, you should be able to:

1. Define a budget and name several kinds of budgets.
2. List several benefits of a budget.
3. List five general principles of budgeting.
4. Prepare a planned operating budget and its supporting budgets, such as the sales budget, production and purchases budgets, and other expense budgets.
5. Prepare flexible operating budgets.
6. Prepare a financial budget and its supporting budgets.
7. Define and use correctly the new terms in the glossary.

In planning the management of your personal finances, you may have only a general notion of the inflows and outflows of cash that will occur for a period. If the outflows exceed the inflows, you may have to borrow to cover the difference. If the inflows exceed the outflows, you may have excess cash to place in a bank or to invest.

At times, especially if you find that your cash position is tight, you may be tempted to prepare a written plan detailing your anticipated cash flows so that you may better control your finances. Such a written plan is a budget.

Companies usually prepare budgets so that they may plan for and then control their revenues (inflows) and expenses (outflows). Failure to prepare a budget could lead to significant cash flow problems or even financial disaster for a company. In fact, one of the leading causes of failure in small businesses is failing to plan and control operations through the use of budgets.

THE BUDGET—FOR PLANNING AND CONTROL

Objective 1: Define a budget and name several kinds of budgets

Time and wealth are scarce resources to all individuals and organizations, and use of these resources requires planning. But planning alone is insufficient. Control is also necessary to ensure that feasible plans are actually carried out. A tool widely used in planning and controlling the use of scarce resources is a budget.

There are many types of budgets. Responsibility budgets, which were examined in the preceding chapter, are designed to judge the performance of an individual segment or manager. Capital budgets, covered in Chapter 20, evaluate long-term capital projects such as the addition of equipment or the relocation of a plant. This chapter examines the **master budget,** which consists of a planned operating budget and a financial budget. The **planned operating budget** helps plan future earnings and results in a projected income statement. The **financial budget** helps management plan the financing of assets and results in a projected balance sheet.

Purposes of Budgets

The budgeting process involves planning for future profitability. The ultimate objective of operating a company is to earn a reasonable return on the resources used. A company must devise some method for how it will handle the uncertainty that the future holds. If a company chooses to do no planning whatsoever, then it has chosen to deal with the future by default and can only react to events as they occur. Most businesses, however, devise some blueprint for the actions they will take given the alternative events that may occur.

Objective 2: List several benefits of a budget

A **budget** is a plan showing the company's objectives and how management intends to acquire and use resources to attain those objectives. A budget also shows how management intends to control the acquisition and use of resources in the coming period(s). A budget formalizes management's plans in quantitative terms. It also forces all levels of management to think ahead, anticipate results, and take action to remedy possible poor results.

Budgets may also be used to motivate individuals so that they strive to achieve stated goals. Budget-to-actual comparisons may be used to evaluate individual performance. For instance, the standard variable cost of producing a given part in a given cost center is a budget figure with which actual cost can be compared to help evaluate the performance of that cost center's manager. This type of comparison was illustrated in Chapter 17.

The preparation and use of budgets result in many other benefits. Business activities are better coordinated; managers become aware of other managers' plans; employees may become cost conscious and try to conserve resources; the organizational plan of the company may be reviewed more often and changed where necessary; and a breadth of vision, which might not otherwise be developed, is fostered. The planning process that results in a formal budget provides an opportunity for various levels of management to think through and commit future plans to writing. In addition, a properly prepared budget will allow management to follow the management-by-exception principle by devoting attention to activities that deviate significantly from planned levels. For all these reasons, the expected results, which are reflected in the budget, must be clearly stated.

Considerations in Preparing a Budget

Being uncertain about future developments is a poor excuse for failing to budget. In fact, the less stable the conditions, the more necessary and desirable is budgeting, although the process becomes more difficult. Obviously, stable operating conditions permit greater reliance on past experience as a basis for budgeting. But it must be emphasized that budgets are based on more than past results. Future plans must also be considered. The current year's expected activities as expressed in the budget are based on current conditions. As a result, budgeted performance is more useful than past performance as a basis for judging actual results.

A budget should describe management's assumptions relating to (1) the state of the economy over the planning horizon; (2) plans for adding, deleting, or changing product lines; (3) the nature of the industry's competition; and (4) the effects of existing or possible government regulations. If assumptions change during the budget period, the effects of the changes should be analyzed and included in the evaluation of performance.

Budgets are quantitative plans for the future. But they are based mainly on past experience adjusted for future expectations. Thus, accounting data related to the past play an important part in budget preparation. The accounting system and the budget are closely related. The details of the budget must agree with the company's ledger accounts. In turn, the accounts must be designed to assist in preparing the budget, financial statements, and interim financial reports to facilitate operational control.

Accounting data and budgeted projections should be compared often during the budget period, and any differences should be investigated. Yet budgeting is not a substitute for good management. Rather, the budget is an important tool of managerial control. Managers make decisions in budget preparation that serve as a plan of action.

Some General Principles of Budgeting

Objective 3: List five general principles of budgeting

Budgeting involves the coordination of financial and nonfinancial planning to satisfy organizational goals and objectives. Although there is no foolproof method for preparing an effective budget, the following aspects should be carefully considered.

1. Top management support. All management levels must be aware of the budget's importance to the company. Plans must be clearly stated. Overemphasis on the mechanics of the budget process should be avoided. Overall broad objectives for the corporation must be decided upon and communicated throughout the organization.

2. Participation in goal setting. It is generally believed that employees are more likely to strive toward organizational goals if they participate in setting them. Employees may have significant information that would help the budget process. Also, the employees can be made aware of the interrelationships among budget items.

3. Responsibility accounting. Individuals should be informed of management's expectations. Only those costs over which an individual has predominant control should be used in evaluating that individual's performance. As noted in the previous chapter, responsibility reports often contain budget-to-actual comparisons.

4. Communication of results. People should be informed of their progress promptly and clearly. Effective communication implies (1) timeliness, (2) reasonable accuracy, and (3) understandability. Results should be communicated so that any necessary adjustments to performance can be made.

5. Flexibility. If the basic assumptions underlying the budget change during the year, the budget should be restated. In this way, performance at the actual level of operations can be compared to expected performance at that level.

Behavioral Implications of Budgets

The term *budget* has negative connotations for many employees who feel they are subjected to a budget. Often in the past, management has imposed a budget without considering the opinions and feelings of the personnel affected. Such a dictatorial process may result in resistance to the budget. A number of reasons may underlie such resistance, including lack of understanding of the program, concern for status, and an expectation of increased pressure to perform. Employees may believe that the performance evaluation method is unfair or that the goals are unrealistic and unattainable. They may lack confidence in the way accounting figures are generated or may prefer a less formal communication and evaluation system. Often these fears are completely unfounded, but if an employee believes these problems exist, it will be very difficult to accomplish the objectives of budgeting.

Problems encountered with such imposed budgets have led accountants and management to participatory budgeting. **Participatory budgeting** means that all levels of management responsible for actual performance actively participate in setting operating goals for the coming period. Managers are more likely to understand, accept, and pursue goals if they are involved in formulating them.

Where do accountants fit into a participatory budgeting process? Accountants should be compilers or coordinators of the budget, not preparers. They should be on hand during the preparation process to present and explain significant fianancial data. Accountants must identify the relevant cost data that will enable management's objectives to be quantified in dollars, and they are responsible for meaningful budget reports. Accountants must continually strive to make the accounting system more responsive to managerial needs. That responsiveness, in turn, will increase confidence in the system.

Although budget participation has been used successfully in many companies, it does not always work. Studies have shown that in many organizations budget participation failed to make employees more motivated to achieve budgeted goals. Whether or not participation works depends on management's leadership style and on the organization's size and structure. Participation is not the answer to all the problems of budget preparation. It is one way to achieve better results in organizations that are receptive to that philosophy of participation.

THE MASTER BUDGET

A **master budget** consists of a projected income statement (planned operating budget) and a projected balance sheet (financial budget) showing the organization's objectives and proposed ways of attaining them. The remainder of this chapter will concentrate on how to prepare a master budget. The master budget is emphasized mainly because of its prime importance to financial planning and control in a business entity.

The budgeting process starts with management's plans and objectives for the next period. Managers and other individuals within individual segments and divisions of the company usually set plans and goals for their individual unit that are in agreement with overall company goals and objectives. Then these goals and objectives are translated into budgets. The budgets from the individual units are then aggregated into an overall company budget.

In the process of preparing a master budget, various policy decisions involving such factors as selling prices, distribution network, and advertising expenditures must be made. Also, environmental influences affecting sales forecasts for the period must be considered.

Illustration 18.1 shows a flowchart of the financial planning process. The sales budget in dollars is prepared by taking forecasted unit sales and multiplying by sales prices. Projected cost of goods sold is based on expected units of sales, modified by inventory policy. Thus, units of production may be larger or smaller than expected units of sales. Selling and administrative expenses and other expenses (including taxes) are considered. Some of these expenses vary directly with sales or production and some are determined by company policy. The resulting projected income statement and balance sheet from the budgeting process incorporate elements from all budgets and schedules prepared by individual segments or divisions. The projected balance sheet is prepared using information contained in the planned operating budget; it is also influenced by policy

Illustration 18.1:
A FLOWCHART OF THE FINANCIAL PLANNING PROCESS

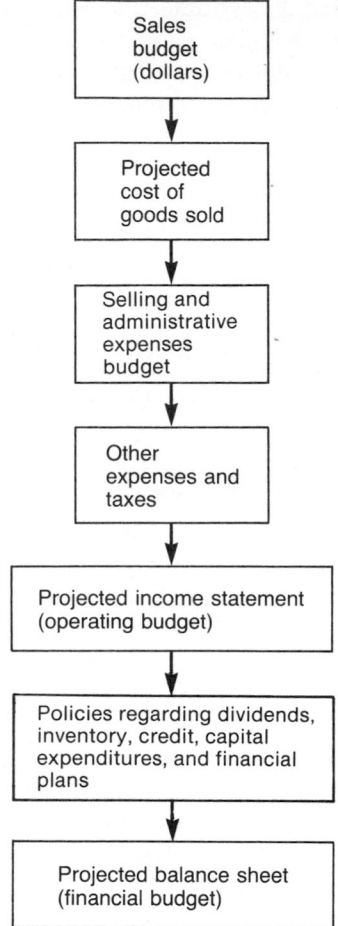

decisions pertaining to dividends, inventory, credit, capital expenditures, and financial plans. The planning of capital expenditures will be described in Chapter 20. Financing by debt or stock issuances was discussed in earlier chapters.

This chapter cannot cover all areas of budgeting in detail; whole books are devoted to the subject. But the following presentation provides an overview of a budgeting procedure that has been used successfully by many business enterprises.

Preparing the Planned Operating Budget at the Expected Level of Operations

Since the projected balance sheet, or **financial budget,** depends on many items in the projected income statement, the logical starting point in preparing a master budget is the projected income statement, or **planned**

operating budget. However, since the planned operating budget shows the net effect of many interrelated activities, several supporting budgets (sales, production, and purchases, to name a few) must be prepared before preparing the planned operating budget. The process begins with the sales budget.

The sales budget. The cornerstone of the budgeting process is the sales budget because if it is not properly prepared, the entire operating budget would be useless. The sales budget involves estimating or forecasting how much demand exists for a company's goods and then determining if a realistic, attainable profit can be achieved based on this demand. This sales forecasting can either be formal or informal.

Formal sales forecasting usually involves the use of some statistical model that uses one or more independent variables to predict sales—the dependent variable. For instance, an economic indicator, such as the Gross National Product or Personal Income could be used to predict the trend and approximate the amount of sales. Examples of other independent variables that could be included in given situations are population growth, per capita income, new construction, and population migration.

To use this method to forecast sales, a relationship must exist between the independent variable(s) and the dependent variable—sales. The statistical models usually indicate to what extent sales are "fixed" and to what extent they vary with changes in the independent variable(s). The models can be used to predict sales for the entire industry or for an individual company.

Informal sales forecasting involves the use of intuition or judgment instead of statistical models. Management may simply project next year's sales at the same amount as last year's sales. But the economic environment may have changed. The economy may be headed toward a recession, which could cause sales to decline. Allowances must be made for varying conditions that affect consumers, products, and competitors. For example, the effect of any changes in the expected level of advertising by this company or its competitors must be estimated.

Quite often companies begin the sales forecasting process by using a formal statistical model to approximate estimated sales. Then informal considerations are taken into account to refine the estimate. Based on consideration of all relevant factors, an overall projection of sales is made. Then quotas may be set by territory and salesperson to "meet" the overall plan.

The sales manager is usually responsible for the sales budget, which is prepared first in units and then in dollars by multiplying the units by their selling price. The remaining budgets that support the operating budget are based on the sales budget in units.

The production budget. The **production budget** takes into account the units in the sales budget and the company's inventory policy. The production budget is first developed in units, but unit costs cannot be developed until production volume is known. Determining production volume is an important task. Careful scheduling is needed to maintain certain minimum quantities of inventory on hand while avoiding excessive inventory accumulation. The cost of carrying inventory on hand must be compared with the higher unit costs frequently encountered in producing relatively small batches of a product. *The principal objective of the production budget is to coordinate (in terms of time and quantity) the production and sale of goods.*

The production budget is often subdivided into budgets for materials, labor, and manufacturing overhead. Usually materials, labor, and some elements of manufacturing overhead will vary directly with production within a given relevant range of production. Fixed manufacturing overhead costs do not vary directly with production but are constant in total within a relevant range of production. For example, fixed manufacturing overhead costs may be $15,000 when production ranges from 60,000 to 80,000 units. However, when production is 80,001 to 95,000 units, the fixed manufacturing overhead costs might be $25,000. Management will need to determine which level of production will be the "relevant range" to accurately determine fixed manufacturing overhead costs.

Selling, administrative, and other expense budgets (schedules). Departmental personnel and expenditure forecasts are used to budget the amounts of selling and administrative expenses. Other expenses such as interest expense, income tax expense, and research and development expenses are also estimated.

Preparing the Financial Budget

Preparing a projected balance sheet, or financial budget, involves analyzing every balance sheet account. The beginning balance for each account is the amount shown on the balance sheet prepared at the end of the preceding period. Then, the effects of any planned activities on each account are considered. Many accounts will be affected by items appearing in the operating budget and by either cash inflows or outflows. Cash inflows and outflows are usually shown in a cash budget, which will be discussed later in the chapter.

The complexities encountered in preparing the financial budget often require the preparation of detailed schedules. These schedules analyze such things as planned accounts receivable collections and balances, planned material purchases, planned inventories, changes in all accounts affected by operating costs, and the amount of federal income taxes payable. Dividend policy, inventory policy, financing policy and constraints, credit policy, and planned capital expenditures also affect amounts shown in the financial budget.

THE MASTER BUDGET ILLUSTRATED

The first part of this chapter discussed some general concepts relating to the preparation of a master budget. This section illustrates step by step how to prepare a master budget for 1990 for the Leed Company.

Preparing the Planned Operating Budget in Units for the Leed Company

Objective 4: Prepare a planned operating budget and its supporting budgets, such as the sales budget, production and purchases budget, and other expense budgets

The planned operating budget is developed first in units rather than dollars. Because revenues and many expenses vary with volume, they can be forecasted more easily after sales and production quantities are established.

To illustrate this step, assume that Leed's management forecasts sales for the year 1990 at 100,000 units. Quarterly sales are expected to be 20,000, 35,000, 20,000, and 25,000 units. We will assume that the company's policy is to stabilize production, so that 100,000 units will be produced uniformly throughout the year. Therefore, production will be at the rate of 25,000 units per quarter (100,000 units/four quarters). To simplify our example, assume there are no beginning or ending work in process inventories (although it would be equivalent and more realistic to assume that work in process inventories would remain at a constant amount throughout the year). Finished goods inventory on January 1, 1990, is 10,000 units. From these data, a schedule of budgeted sales and production in units is prepared, as shown in Illustration 18.2.

Illustration 18.2
LEED COMPANY'S PLANNED PRODUCTION AND SALES FOR FIRST TWO QUARTERS OF 1990 (in units)

	Quarter Ending	
	March 31, 1990	June 30, 1990
Beginning finished goods inventory	10,000*	15,000
Add: Planned production	25,000	25,000
Units available for sale	35,000	40,000
Less: Sales forecast	20,000	35,000
Ending finished goods inventory	15,000	5,000

*Actual on January 1.

Notice that the above ending inventory must be allowed to fluctuate if sales vary and a stable production policy is maintained. Thus, the finished goods inventory is affected by the difference between production and sales. When establishing inventory policy, management has decided that it is less costly to deal with fluctuating inventories than with fluctuating production.

In Illustration 18.2 sales and production data were given for each period, and we had to solve for ending inventory. Sometimes we are given sales and ending inventory data (described as a certain percentage of the next period's sales), and we have to calculate the required level of production. Assume Leed Company wishes to have ending inventory equal to 50% of the next month's sales in units (30,000 units). In this latter instance, the following format may be used to calculate planned production.

Sales forecast (units)—current month	20,000
Add: Planned ending finished goods inventory	15,000*
Total units required for the period	35,000
Deduct: Beginning finished goods inventory	10,000
Planned production (units)	25,000

*50% × 30,000.

When management states that ending finished goods inventory must be a specified percentage of future sales, a constant production policy cannot be maintained unless sales each period are constant.

Preparing the Planned Operating Budget in Dollars

Next, dollars must be introduced into the analysis. A forecast of expected selling prices must be made and costs must be analyzed. The forecasted selling price and costs are shown in Illustration 18.3. Note that costs are classified according to whether they are variable or fixed and are budgeted accordingly. As noted earlier, **variable costs** vary in total directly with production or sales. **Fixed costs** are unaffected in total by the relative level of production or sales. Thus, variable costs are budgeted as a constant dollar amount *per unit* while fixed costs are budgeted only in total.

Illustration 18.3
BUDGET ESTIMATE OF SELLING PRICE AND COSTS

LEED COMPANY Budget Estimates of Selling Price and Costs For the Quarters Ending March 31, and June 30, 1990	
Forecasted selling price	$ 20
Manufacturing costs:	
Variable (per unit manufactured):	
Direct materials	2
Direct labor	6
Manufacturing overhead.	1
Fixed overhead (total each quarter)	75,000
Selling and administrative expenses:	
Variable (per unit sold)	2
Fixed (total each quarter)	100,000

Management must now prepare a schedule to forecast cost of goods sold, the next major amount on the planned operating budget. This schedule is shown in Illustration 18.4. Notice that the beginning finished goods inventory amount for the quarter ending March 31 is the amount shown on the December 31, 1989, year-end balance sheet. Cost of goods manufactured is calculated using the variable costs of production from Illustration 18.3 plus an allocated amount of fixed manufacturing overhead ($75,000/25,000 units). The amount of ending finished goods inventory is the number of units determined to be in ending inventory (from Illustration 18.2) times the cost per unit manufactured during the period.

Illustration 18.4
SCHEDULE OF PLANNED COST OF GOODS SOLD

LEED COMPANY		
Planned Cost of Goods Sold		
		Quarter ending
	March 31, 1990	*June 30, 1990*
Beginning finished goods inventory	$130,000*	$180,000
Cost of goods manufactured:		
Direct materials (25,000 × $2)	$ 50,000	$ 50,000
Direct labor (25,000 × $6)	150,000	150,000
Variable manufacturing overhead (25,000 × $1)	25,000	25,000
Fixed manufacturing overhead (per Illustration 18.3)	75,000	75,000
Cost of goods manufactured (25,000 units at $12)	$300,000	$300,000
Goods available for sale	$430,000	$480,000
Ending finished goods inventory:		
(15,000 at $12)[†]	180,000	
(5,000 at $12)		60,000
Cost of goods sold	$250,000	$420,000

*Actual on January 1 (10,000 at $13); see balance sheet Illustration 18.9.
[†]First-in, first-out procedure assumed.

After cost of goods sold has been forecasted, a separate budget is prepared for all selling and administrative expenses. Several support schedules may be involved for items such as advertising expense, office expense, and payroll department expense. The schedules to support budgeted selling and administrative expenses are not illustrated here, but the total selling and administrative expenses for each of the first two quarters is entered into the planned operating budget in Illustration 18.5.

The Planned Operating Budget Illustrated

Illustration 18.5 shows the resulting planned operating budget for the Leed Company. All of the items appearing in the planned operating budget except the income tax accrual have been discussed and explained. Income taxes are budgeted for Leed Company at an assumed rate of 40% of net income before taxes.

If the planned operating budget does not show the desired net income, new operating plans will have to be formulated, and a new budget will be developed. The purpose of preparing a planned operating budget is to gain some knowledge of the results of a period's activities before they actually occur.

Flexible Operating Budgets

Objective 5:
Prepare flexible
operating budgets

Early in the chapter you learned that a budget should be adjusted for changes in assumptions or variations in the level of operations. A technique known as flexible budgeting, which was introduced in Chapter 16,

Chapter 18

Illustration 18.5
PLANNED OPERATING BUDGETS

LEED COMPANY Planned Operating Budgets For Quarters Ending March 31 and June 30, 1990		
	Quarter ending	
	March 31, *1990*	*June 30,* *1990*
Forecasted sales (20,000 and 35,000 at $20) (per Illustrations 18.2 and 18.3)	$400,000	$700,000
Cost of goods sold (per Illustration 18.4)	250,000	420,000
Gross margin	$150,000	$280,000
Selling and administrative expenses:		
Variable (20,000 and 35,000 at $2) (per Illustration 18.3) . .	$ 40,000	$ 70,000
Fixed (per Illustration 18.3)	100,000	100,000
Total selling and administrative expenses	$140,000	$170,000
Income before income taxes	$ 10,000	$110,000
Estimated federal income taxes (assumed to be 40%)	4,000	44,000
Net income	$ 6,000	$ 66,000

is used to deal with budgetary adjustments. A **flexible operating budget** is a special kind of budget that provides detailed information about budgeted expenses (and revenues) at various levels of output.

Illustration 18.6 shows a flexible budget for Leed Company's manufacturing overhead costs at various levels of output. In this example, supplies are considered a strictly variable cost, increasing $200 each time production increases by 10% of capacity. In actuality, however, there are probably few costs that vary in an exact linear relationship with output. Power is a mixed (or semivariable) cost in this example. A mixed cost

Illustration 18.6
FLEXIBLE BUDGET FOR MANUFACTURING OVERHEAD

LEED COMPANY Flexible Budget for Manufacturing Overhead				
Element of *manufacturing* *overhead*	*Volume (percent of capacity)**			
	70%	*80%*	*90%*	*100%*
Supplies	$ 1,400	$ 1,600	$ 1,800	$ 2,000
Power	7,600	8,400	9,200	10,000
Insurance	4,500	4,500	5,000	5,000
Maintenance	5,800	6,200	7,200	8,000
Depreciation	40,000	40,000	40,000	40,000
Supervision	35,000	35,000	35,000	35,000
	$94,300	$95,700	$98,200	$100,000

*Capacity is 100,000 units per period.

642

varies with volume, but not in direct proportion to the changes in volume. In the case of power cost, there is a fixed amount that Leed Company must pay, plus an additional $800 for each 10% increase in volume. Insurance and maintenance are considered step variable costs in this example since they increase in "steps" as volume increases. Depreciation and supervision, on the other hand, are completely fixed costs in this example since they are constant over the entire relevant range of activity.

A similar flexible budget could be prepared for selling and administrative expenses with supporting schedules for each expense item. Variable expenses are calculated for various levels of sales volume, while fixed costs remain constant within the relevant range.

Budget variances. When management uses a flexible budget to appraise a department's performance, the evaluation is based on the amounts budgeted for the level of activity actually experienced. The difference between actual costs incurred and the budgeted amount for that same level of operations is called a **budget variance.** Budget variances can indicate a department's or company's degree of efficiency, since they emerge from a comparison of "what was" with "what should have been."

To illustrate the computation of budget variances, assume that Leed Company prepared an overhead budget based on an expected volume of 100%. At this level of production, the budgeted amount for supplies is $2,000, or $0.02 per unit. By the end of the period, $1,900 of supplies has been used. The first impression is that a favorable variance of $100 exists. But if actual production for the period was only 90,000 units (90% of capacity), there is actually an unfavorable variance of $100. This is because, according to the flexible operating budget, at 90% of capacity only $1,800 of supplies should have been used. Consequently, there appears to have been an inefficient use of supplies.

To give another example using the data in Illustration 18.6, maintenance may have been budgeted at $6,200 for a given period assuming the company planned to produce 80,000 units (80% of operating capacity). However, actual maintenance costs may have been $6,800 for the period. This result does not necessarily mean that an unfavorable variance of $600 was incurred. The variance depends on actual production volume. Assume once again that 90,000 units were produced during the period; maintenance costs are budgeted at $7,200 for that level of production. Therefore, there would actually be a favorable variance of $400 ($7,200 − $6,800).

Flexible budgets often show budgeted amounts for every 10% change in the level of operations, such as at the 70%, 80%, 90%, 100%, and 110% levels of capacity. But actual production may fall somewhere between levels, say, at 84%. When actual production falls between the levels shown in the flexible budget, the budgeted amounts at that level of operations must be calculated. The only kind of cost that does not have to be recalculated is a fixed cost since, by definition, it does not vary over the relevant range. For directly variable costs, the expected cost can be computed easily at any level since the cost is constant per unit of output. For mixed costs (partially fixed and partially variable), the budgeted amount for any operating level other than those presented can be computed using the following formula, assuming the relationship between costs and volume above a minimum level of costs is linear.

Budgeted amount = Fixed portion of costs +

(Variable portion of cost per unit × Units of output)

Step variable costs may change only when a sufficiently large increase in production occurs, such as when one additional inspector must be added for every 20% increase in capacity used. Such step variable costs usually can be read directly from the flexible budget.

Flexible operating budget and budget variances illustrated. As stated above, a flexible operating budget provides detailed information about budgeted expenses at various levels of activity. The main advantage of using a flexible operating budget along with a planned operating budget is that performance can be appraised on two levels. First, comparison of the deviation of the actual results with the planned operating budget permits analysis of actual output from expected output. Then, given the actual level of operations, actual costs can be compared with expected costs for that level of output, shown on the flexible operating budget. The use of flexible operating budgets gives a valid basis for comparison when actual production or sales volume differs from expectations.

A detailed planned operating budget and flexible operating budget for the Leed Company for the quarter ended March 31, 1990, are presented in Illustrations 18.7 and 18.8. The planned operating budget and flexible operating budget have been prepared using the data from Illustration 18.3. The planned operating budget was based on a sales forecast of 20,000 units and a production forecast of 25,000 units, while the actual results for the period, reported in Illustrations 18.7 and 18.8, show actual sales of 19,000 units and actual production of 25,000 units. The actual selling price was $20 per unit, the same price that had been forecast.

Illustration 18.7 shows the comparison of the actual results with the planned operating budget. Comparison of actual results with the planned operating budget yields some useful information, for it shows where actual performance deviated from planned performance. For example, sales were 1,000 units lower than expected, sales revenue was $20,000 less than expected, gross margin was $12,500 less than expected, and net income was $2,400 more than expected. However, the comparison of actual results with the planned operating budget does not provide a basis for evaluating whether or not management performed efficiently at the actual level of operations. For example, Illustration 18.7 shows that cost of goods sold was $7,500 less than expected. But the meaning of this difference is not clear since the actual cost of goods sold relates to the 19,000 units actually sold, while the planned cost of goods sold relates to the 20,000 units that were expected. The planned operating budget projected sales revenue, cost of goods sold, and selling and administrative expenses based on a sales forecast of 20,000 units, but only 19,000 units were actually sold. The

Illustration 18.7
COMPARISON OF PLANNED OPERATING BUDGET AND ACTUAL RESULTS

LEED COMPANY
Comparison of Planned Operating Budget and Actual Results
For Quarter Ended March 31, 1990

	Budget	Actual
Sales (budgeted 20,000 units, actual 19,000 units)	$400,000	$380,000
Cost of goods sold:		
Beginning finished goods inventory	$130,000	$130,000
Cost of goods manufactured (25,000 units):		
Direct materials	$ 50,000	$ 62,500
Direct labor	150,000	143,750
Variable manufacturing overhead	25,000	31,250
Fixed manufacturing overhead	75,000	75,000
Cost of goods manufactured	$300,000	$312,500
Goods available for sale	$430,000	$442,500
Ending finished goods inventory	180,000	200,000
Cost of goods sold	$250,000	$242,500
Gross margin	$150,000	$137,500
Selling and administrative expenses:		
Variable	$ 40,000	$ 28,500
Fixed	100,000	95,000
Total selling and administrative expenses	$140,000	$123,500
Income before income taxes	$ 10,000	$ 14,000
Estimated federal income taxes (40%)	4,000	5,600
Net income	$ 6,000	$ 8,400

levels of activity are not the same, so the comparisons do not give valid information for expense control.

A valid analysis for expense control purposes can be made only by comparing actual results with a flexible operating budget that is based on the same level of sales and production that actually occurred. That is the comparison shown in Illustration 18.8. The flexible budget shown in Illustration 18.8 is made up of several pieces. The flexible budget amounts for sales revenue and selling and administrative expenses come from a flexible sales budget (not illustrated) for 19,000 units of sales, and the flexible budget amounts for production costs come from a flexible production budget (also not illustrated) for 25,000 units of production. Since the actual level of production (25,000 units) in this case was the same as the planned level, the production costs shown in the planned operating budget and the flexible operating budget are the same.

In comparisons such as these, if the number of units produced is equal to the number sold, beginning and ending inventories often are not shown. Instead, the flexible operating budget may show the number of units actually sold multiplied by the budgeted unit cost of direct materials, direct labor, and manufacturing overhead. The actual costs for direct

Illustration 18.8
COMPARISON OF FLEXIBLE OPERATING BUDGET AND ACTUAL RESULTS

LEED COMPANY
Comparison of Flexible Operating Budget and Actual Results
For Quarter Ended March 31, 1990

	Budget	Actual	Budget Variance Over/(Under)
Sales (19,000 units)	$380,000	$380,000	$ –0–
Cost of goods sold:			
Beginning finished goods inventory	$130,000	$130,000	$ –0–
Cost of goods manufactured (25,000 units):			
Direct materials	$ 50,000	$ 62,500	$ 12,500
Direct labor	150,000	143,750	(6,250)
Variable manufacturing overhead	25,000	31,250	6,250
Fixed manufacturing overhead	75,000	75,000	–0–
Cost of goods manufactured	$300,000	$312,500	$ 12,500
Goods available for sale	$430,000	$442,500	$ 12,500
Ending finished goods inventory.	192,000	200,000	8,000
Cost of goods sold (19,000 units)	$238,000	$242,500	$ 4,500
Gross margin	$142,000	$137,500	$ (4,500)
Selling and administrative expenses:			
Variable	$ 38,000	$ 28,500	$ (9,500)
Fixed	100,000	95,000	(5,000)
Total selling and administrative expenses	$138,000	$123,500	$(14,500)
Income before income taxes	$ 4,000	$ 14,000	$ 10,000
Estimated federal income taxes (40%)	1,600	5,600	4,000
Net income	$ 2,400	$ 8,400	$ 6,000

materials, direct labor, and manufacturing overhead are also shown for the number of units sold.

The comparison of the actual results with the flexible operating budget (Illustration 18.8) reveals some inefficiencies for items in the costs of goods manufactured section. For instance, direct materials cost was $2.50 per unit ($62,500/25,000) instead of the $2 expected. Direct labor cost was only $5.75 per unit ($143,750/25,000) instead of the $6 expected. Variable overhead was $1.25 per unit ($31,250/25,000) instead of the $1 expected.

Net income was $6,000 more than expected at a sales level of 19,000 units. The main reason for the increase in net income was the lower than expected amounts of selling and administrative expenses. Variable selling and administrative expenses were only $1.50 per unit ($28,500/19,000) instead of the $2 expected; fixed selling and administrative expenses were only $95,000 instead of the $100,000 expected.

Preparing the Financial Budget for the Leed Company

Objective 6:
Prepare a financial budget and its supporting budgets

To prepare a projected balance sheet, each balance sheet account must be analyzed. First, the beginning balance is taken from the balance sheet at the end of the preceding period. The Leed Company balance sheet as of

Illustration 18.9
BALANCE SHEET AT BEGINNING OF PERIOD

LEED COMPANY
Balance Sheet
December 31, 1989

Assets

Current assets:

Cash			$ 130,000
Accounts receivable			200,000
Inventories:			
Materials		$ 40,000	
Finished goods		130,000	170,000
Prepaid expenses			20,000
Total current assets			$ 520,000

Property, plant, and equipment:

Land			$ 60,000
Buildings		$1,000,000	
Less: Accumulated depreciation		400,000	600,000
Equipment		$ 600,000	
Less: Accumulated depreciation		180,000	420,000
Total property, plant, and equipment			$1,080,000
Total assets			$1,600,000

Liabilities and Stockholders' Equity

Current liabilities:

Accounts payable			$ 80,000
Accrued liabilities			160,000
Federal income taxes payable			100,000
Total current liabilities			$ 340,000

Stockholders' equity:

Capital stock (100,000 shares of $10 par value)			$1,000,000
Retained earnings			260,000
Total stockholders' equity			$1,260,000
Total liabilities and stockholders' equity			$1,600,000

December 31, 1989, is shown in Illustration 18.9. Management must consider the effects of planned activities on these balances. Many accounts will be affected by items shown in the planned operating budget, by cash inflows and outflows, and by policy decisions of the company. The planned operating budget shown in Illustration 18.5 and other illustrations previously given will be used to prepare Leed Company's financial budget for the first two quarters of 1990.

Accounts receivable. To prepare a financial budget, several new schedules must be prepared. The first of these schedules is the accounts receivable schedule shown in Illustration 18.10. We will assume that 60% of the current quarter's sales for Leed Company will be collected in that quarter, and the remaining 40% will be collected in the following quarter. Thus, collections for the first quarter will be $440,000; that is 60% of bud-

Illustration 18.10
PLANNED ACCOUNTS RECEIVABLE COLLECTIONS AND BALANCES

LEED COMPANY Planned Accounts Receivable Collections and Balances	Quarter Ending	
	March 31, 1990	June 30, 1990
Planned balance at beginning of quarter	$200,000*	$160,000
Planned sales for period (per Illustration 18.5)	400,000	700,000
Total	$600,000	$860,000
Projected collections during quarter (per discussion in text)	440,000	580,000
Planned balance at end of quarter	$160,000	$280,000

*Actual on January 1.

geted sales of $400,000 for the first quarter plus the uncollected sales of the previous quarter [0.6($400,000) + $200,000]. Second quarter collections will be $580,000 [0.6($700,000) + $160,000]. Several other assumptions have been made to simplify this schedule; for example, there are no sales returns or allowances, no discounts, and no uncollectible accounts. All sales are assumed to be on a credit basis.

Inventories. A schedule of planned materials purchases and inventories must also be prepared. Planned usage and cost per unit of materials are taken from the planned cost of goods sold schedule (Illustration 18.4). Assuming no work in process inventories, there will be only materials and finished goods inventories.

Illustration 18.11 shows a schedule of planned purchases and inventories of materials for the Leed Company. Materials inventory is normally maintained at a level of one half of next quarter's planned usage. The $40,000 beginning inventory was greater than normal because of a strike

Illustration 18.11
PLANNED MATERIALS PURCHASES AND INVENTORIES

LEED COMPANY Planned Materials Purchases and Inventories	Quarter Ending	
	March 31, 1990	June 30, 1990
Planned usage (25,000 × $2) (per Illustration 18.4)	$50,000	$50,000
Planned ending inventory (1/2 × 25,000 × $2) (per discussion in text)	25,000	25,000
Planned material available for use	$75,000	$75,000
Inventory at beginning of quarter	40,000*	25,000
Planned purchases for the quarter	$35,000	$50,000

*Actual on January 1.

threat in the supplier company. This threat has now passed, and the materials inventory will be reduced at the end of the first quarter to the normal planned level.

The calculation of planned ending finished goods inventories is included in Illustration 18.4.

Accounts affected by operating costs. Individual schedules could be prepared for each of the accounts affected by operating costs. But for illustrative purposes a schedule will be prepared combining the analyses of all the accounts affected by materials purchases or operating costs.

1. All purchases of materials are made on account.
2. Direct labor incurred is credited to accrued liabilities.
3. Manufacturing overhead incurred is credited to the following accounts:

	Quarter Ending	
	March 31	June 30
Accounts Payable	$ 16,000	$ 13,000
Accrued Liabilities	60,000	64,000
Prepaid Expenses	6,000	5,000
Accumulated Depreciation—Building	5,000	5,000
Accumulated Depreciation—Equipment	13,000	13,000
Total	$100,000	$100,000

4. Selling and administrative expenses incurred are credited to the following accounts:

	Quarter Ending	
	March 31	June 30
Accounts Payable	$ 5,000	$ 10,000
Accrued Liabilities	130,000	154,000
Prepaid Expenses	2,000	3,000
Accumulated Depreciation—Building	1,000	1,000
Accumulated Depreciation—Equipment	2,000	2,000
Total	$140,000	$170,000

5. Planned cash payments are as follows:

	Quarter Ending	
	March 31	June 30
Accounts Payable	$ 80,000	$ 56,000
Accrued Liabilities	330,000	354,000
Prepaid Expenses	–0–	10,000
Total	$410,000	$420,000

Illustration 18.12 shows analyses of the accounts credited as a result of the above data. The illustration provides a considerable amount of information needed in constructing financial budgets for the quarters ended March 31, 1990, and June 30, 1990. The balances on both dates for Accounts Payable, Accrued Liabilities, Prepaid Expenses (the only debit

Illustration 18.12
ANALYSES OF ACCOUNTS CREDITED FOR MATERIALS PURCHASES AND OPERATING COSTS

LEED COMPANY
Analyses of Accounts Credited for Materials Purchases and Operating Costs

	Total Debits	Accounts Payable	Accrued Liabilities	Prepaid Expenses	Accumulated Depreciation Building	Accumulated Depreciation Equipment
Purchases or operating costs, quarter ending March 31 (credits made to accounts shown at right):						
Direct materials (per Illustration 18.11)	$ 35,000*	$ 35,000				
Direct labor (per Illustration 18.4)	150,000*		$150,000			
Manufacturing overhead (per Illustration 18.4)	100,000*	16,000	60,000	$ 6,000	$ 5,000	$ 13,000
Selling and administrative expenses (per Illustration 18.5)	140,000*	5,000	130,000	2,000	1,000	2,000
Total	$425,000*	$ 56,000	$340,000	$ 8,000	$ 6,000	$ 15,000
Beginning balances (per Illustration 18.9)		80,000	160,000	20,000*	400,000	180,000
Total		$136,000	$500,000	$12,000*	$406,000	$195,000
Planned cash payments (debits made to accounts shown)		80,000*	330,000*			
Planned balances, March 31, 1990 . .		$ 56,000	$170,000	$12,000*	$406,000	$195,000
Purchases or operating costs, quarter ending June 30 (credits made to accounts shown at right):						
Direct materials (per Illustration 18.11)	$ 50,000*	$ 50,000				
Direct labor (per Illustration 18.4)	150,000*		$150,000			
Manufacturing overhead (per Illustration 18.4)	100,000*	13,000	64,000	$ 5,000	$ 5,000	$ 13,000
Selling and administrative expenses (per Illustration 18.5)	170,000*	10,000	154,000	3,000	1,000	2,000
Total	$470,000	$ 73,000	$368,000	$ 8,000	$ 6,000	$ 15,000
Total including March 31 balances		$129,000	$538,000	$ 4,000*	$412,000	$210,000
Planned cash payments (debits made to accounts shown)		56,000*	354,000*	10,000*		
Planned balances, June 30, 1990 . .		$ 73,000	$184,000	$14,000*	$412,000	$210,000

*Debits or debit balances.

balance account shown), Accumulated Depreciation—Building, and Accumulated Depreciation—Equipment are computed in the schedule.

Federal income taxes payable. A separate schedule could be prepared showing the changes in the Federal Income Taxes Payable account, but in this example, a brief discussion will suffice. Balances reported in the financial budgets assume that one half of the $100,000 liability shown in the December 31, 1989, balance sheet is paid in each of the first two quarters of 1990 (shown in Illustration 18.15 later in the chapter). The accrual for the current quarter is added (Illustration 18.5). Thus, the balance on March 31, 1990, is $54,000 ($100,000 − $50,000 + $4,000). The balance on June 30, 1990, is $48,000 ($54,000 − $50,000 + $44,000). On June 30, the balance equals the accrual for the current year, $4,000 for the first quarter and $44,000 for the second quarter.

Cash budget. After the above analyses have been prepared, sufficient information is available to prepare the cash budget and compute the balance in the cash account on March 31 and June 30, 1990. To prepare a cash budget, information about cash receipts and cash disbursements is required.

Cash receipts. The cash receipts schedule can be prepared from the information used to compute the accounts receivable schedule (Illustration 18.10). A schedule of planned cash receipts for the Leed Company is shown in Illustration 18.13.

Cash disbursements. Cash is needed to pay for purchases, wages, rent, interest, income taxes, cash dividends, and most other expenses. The amount of each cash disbursement may be obtained from other budgets or schedules. Illustration 18.14 shows the cash disbursements schedule

Illustration 18.13
PLANNED CASH RECEIPTS

LEED COMPANY
Planned Cash Receipts

	Quarter Ending	
	March 31, 1990	*June 30, 1990*
Collections on accounts receivable:		
From preceding quarter's sales	$200,000	$160,000
From current quarter's sales	240,000 (0.6 × $400,000)	420,000 (0.6 × $700,000)
Total cash receipts (per Illustration 18.10)	$440,000	$580,000

Illustration 18.14
PLANNED CASH DISBURSEMENTS

LEED COMPANY
Planned Cash Disbursements

	Quarter Ending	
	March 31, 1990	*June 30, 1990*
Payment of accounts payable (per Illustration 18.12)	$ 80,000	$ 56,000
Payment of accrued liabilities (per Illustration 18.12)	330,000	354,000
Payment of federal income tax liability	50,000	50,000
Payment of dividends	20,000	40,000
Expenses prepaid (per Illustration 18.12)	–0–	10,000
Total cash disbursements	$480,000	$510,000

for the Leed Company. The illustration shows where the information came from, except for the payment of federal income taxes and dividends. Income taxes, discussed earlier, are assumed to be 40% of net income before taxes. It is assumed that $20,000 of dividends will be paid in the first quarter and $40,000 in the second quarter.

Once cash receipts and disbursements have been determined, a cash budget can be prepared for the Leed Company, as shown in Illustration 18.15. The **cash budget** is a plan indicating expected inflows and outflows of cash. This cash budget helps management to decide whether enough cash will be available for short-term needs. If the cash budget indicates a cash shortage at a certain date, the company may need to borrow money on a short-term basis. If the expected cash balance appears to be higher than necessary, the company may wish to invest the extra funds for short periods to earn interest rather than leave the cash idle. Knowing of possible shortages or excess cash balances in advance will allow management sufficient time to plan for such occurrences.

Illustration 18.15
PLANNED CASH FLOWS AND CASH BALANCES

LEED COMPANY		
Planned Cash Flows and Cash Balances		
	Quarter Ending	
	March 31, 1990	*June 30, 1990*
Planned balance at beginning of quarter	$130,000*	$ 90,000
Planned cash receipts:		
Collections of accounts receivable (per Illustration 18.13) . .	440,000	580,000
	$570,000	$670,000
Planned cash disbursements:		
Payment of accounts payable (per Illustration 18.12)	$ 80,000	$ 56,000
Payment of accrued liabilities (per Illustration 18.12)	330,000	354,000
Payment of federal income tax liability	50,000	50,000
Payment of dividends.	20,000	40,000
Expenses prepaid (per Illustration 18.12)	–0–	10,000
Total cash disbursements	$480,000	$510,000
Planned balance at end of quarter	$ 90,000	$160,000

*Actual on January 1.

The Financial Budget Illustrated

The preparation of the financial budget for the quarters ending March 31, 1990, and June 30, 1990, shown in Illustration 18.16 completes the master budget. Management now has information to help appraise the policies it has adopted before implementing them. If the results of these policies, as shown by the master budget, are unsatisfactory, the policies can be changed before serious problems arise. For example, the Leed Company

Illustration 18.16
PROJECTED BALANCE SHEET

LEED COMPANY
Projected Balance Sheet

	March 31, 1990	June 30, 1990
Assets		
Current assets:		
Cash (per Illustration 18.15)	$ 90,000	$ 160,000
Accounts receivable (per Illustration 18.10)	160,000	280,000
Inventories:		
Materials (per Illustration 18.11)	25,000	25,000
Finished goods (per Illustration 18.4)	180,000	60,000
Prepaid expenses (per Illustration 18.12)	12,000	14,000
Total current assets	$ 467,000	$ 539,000
Property, plant, and equipment:		
Land (per Illustration 18.9)	$ 60,000	$ 60,000
Buildings ($1,000,000 less accumulated depreciation of $406,000 and $412,000)		
(per Illustrations 18.9 and 18.12)	594,000	588,000
Equipment ($600,000 less accumulated depreciation of $195,000 and $210,000)		
(per Illustrations 18.9 and 18.12)	405,000	390,000
Total property, plant, and equipment	$1,059,000	$1,038,000
Total assets	$1,526,000	$1,577,000
Liabilities and Stockholders' Equity		
Current liabilities:		
Accounts payable (per Illustration 18.12)	$ 56,000	$ 73,000
Accrued liabilities (per Illustration 18.12)	170,000	184,000
Federal income taxes payable (per discussion on page 650)	54,000	48,000
Total current liabilities	$ 280,000	$ 305,000
Stockholders' equity:		
Capital stock (100,000 shares of $10 par value) (per Illustration 18.9).	$1,000,000	$1,000,000
Retained earnings (see below).	246,000*	272,000†
Total stockholders' equity	$1,246,000	$1,272,000
Total liabilities and stockholders' equity	$1,526,000	$1,577,000

*$260,000 (per Illustration 18.9) + Income of $6,000 − Dividends of $20,000.
†$246,000 + Income of $66,000 − Dividends of $40,000.

management had a policy of stable production each period. The master budget shows that production can be stabilized even though sales fluctuate widely. But the planned ending inventory at June 30 may be considered somewhat low in view of the fluctuations in sales. Management now knows this in advance and can take corrective action if necessary.

Purchases Budget for a Merchandising Company

Throughout this chapter, discussion has centered on the preparation of operating and financial budgets for a manufacturer. Suppose a budget is being prepared for a retail merchandising business, such as a dress shop or a furniture store. In this case, a purchases budget will be prepared instead of a production budget. To compute the purchases for each quarter, the cost of the goods to be sold during the quarter and the inventory required at the end of the quarter must be estimated.

The purchases budget can be derived from the sales budget and the company's inventory policy. Using the Strobel Furniture Company as an example, suppose a sales budget was prepared as shown in Illustration 18.17. Assume that the company likes to maintain sufficient inventory to cover one half of the next quarter's sales. Cost of goods sold is 55% of sales. The ending inventory on December 31, 1989, was $8,250. The purchases budget can now be prepared, as shown in Illustration 18.18. For the first quarter of 1990, notice that the ending inventory is one half of the second quarter's cost of goods sold $[0.5 \times (55\% \text{ of } \$80,000) = \$22,000]$.

The Strobel Company would use the information in the purchases budget in preparing the cost of goods sold section of the planned operating budget, the cash disbursements schedules, and the inventory and accounts payable amounts on the financial budget.

Illustration 18.17
SALES BUDGET

STROBEL FURNITURE COMPANY
Sales Budget

Quarter Ending

March 31, 1990	June 30, 1990	September 30, 1990	December 31, 1990	March 31, 1991
$30,000	$80,000	$50,000	$90,000	$40,000

Illustration 18.18
PURCHASES BUDGET

STROBEL FURNITURE COMPANY
Purchases Budget

Quarter Ending

	March 31, 1990	June 30, 1990	September 30, 1990	December 31, 1990
Ending inventory desired*.	$22,000	$13,750	$24,750	$11,000
Cost of goods sold (55% of sales)	16,500	44,000	27,500	49,500
Total	$38,500	$57,750	$52,250	$60,500
Less: Beginning inventory	8,250	22,000	13,750	24,750
Purchases required . . .	$30,250	$35,750	$38,500	$35,750

*Next period's sales × 55% × 50%.

SUMMARY

A budget is one of management's most useful tools for planning and controlling income, cash flow, and other aspects of a business. A well-prepared budget forces management to think ahead, anticipate results, and take action when actual results differ from expected results. Used effectively, a budget can motivate employees. Used ineffectively, a budget can cause employee disenchantment and possible disruption of operations.

Participation in the preparation of budgets generally improves the motivational aspects of budgeting. Participation gives the people who have responsibility for performance a voice in setting the goals for the forthcoming period.

The preparation of an effective budget requires top management support and timely communication of results. The accountant should strive to design the accounting system to reflect the operations of the business and at the same time to facilitate responsibility reporting.

There are several types of budgets. The two budgets discussed in this chapter are the planned operating budget and the financial budget. The planned operating budget (a projected income statement) helps management plan future earnings. The financial budget (a forecast balance sheet) helps management plan the financing of assets. Together, the planned operating budget and the financial budget are referred to as the master budget.

The preparation of the master budget begins with detail budgets that support the planned operating budget. First, a sales forecast is made to project the number of units to be sold in the upcoming year. Based on this sales forecast, the expected price, and the projected selling expenses, a sales budget can be proposed showing expected sales revenue and selling expenses. Next, management uses that sales forecast and the company's inventory policy to decide the number of units to produce in the next year. Once the level of operations is established, management can use production cost information to project the cost to manufacture, cost of goods manufactured, and cost of goods sold for the year. This information is presented in the production budget. Finally, budgets for administrative and other expenses are established, based on the levels of sales and of production established in the sales and production budgets. Collectively, these subsidiary budgets provide enough information for a projected income statement, which is the planned operating budget.

A budget variance is a deviation between actual performance and the expected performance for the actual level of operations. A flexible operating budget is a series of budgets, each of which corresponds to a different level of operations. A flexible operating budget amount shown for the actual level of operations serves as a standard for comparing a department's actual results with the expected results.

The use of a flexible operating budget along with a planned operating budget permits performance appraisal on two levels. First, comparison of the actual results with the planned operating budget permits the deviation from expected output to be analyzed. Then, given the actual level of operations, actual costs can be compared with expected costs for that level of output, shown on the flexible operating budget.

Preparing a projected balance sheet (or financial budget) involves analyzing every balance sheet account in light of the planned activities expressed in the income statement. A separate cash budget is usually prepared to show sources of, uses of, and net changes in cash for the period. The complexities involved in preparing the financial budget often require the preparation of supplemental schedules for various accounts on the balance sheet.

You must realize by now that the terms *management* and *decision making* go hand in hand. Under normal economic conditions, poor decision making by management is usually the cause of business failures. In Chapter 19 short-term decision making is discussed.

Objective 7: Define and use correctly the new terms in the glossary

NEW TERMS INTRODUCED IN CHAPTER 18

Budget A plan showing a company's objectives and proposed ways of attaining the objectives. Two major types of budgets are the (1) master budget and (2) control, or responsibility, budget (632).

Budgeting The coordination of financial and nonfinancial planning to satisfy an organization's goals (633).

Budget variance The difference between an actual cost incurred (or revenue earned) at a certain level of operations and the budgeted amount for that same level of operations (643).

Cash budget A plan indicating expected inflows (receipts) and outflows (disbursements) of cash; it helps management decide whether enough cash will be available for short-term needs (652).

Financial budget The projected balance sheet portion of a master budget (632, 636).

Fixed costs Costs that are unaffected by the relative levels of production or sales (640).

Flexible operating budget Provides detailed information about budgeted expenses and revenues at various levels of output (642).

Master budget The projected income statement and projected balance sheet showing the organization's objectives and proposed ways of attaining them; includes supporting budgets for such areas as cash, sales, costs, and production. It is the overall plan of the enterprise and ideally consists of all of the various segmental budgets (632, 635).

Participatory budgeting A method of preparing the budget that includes the participation of all levels of management responsible for actual performance (634).

Planned operating budget The projected income statement portion of a master budget (632, 636).

Production budget Takes into account the units in the sales budget and the company's inventory policy (637).

Variable costs Costs that vary directly with production or sales and are a constant dollar amount per unit of output over different levels of output or sales (640).

DEMONSTRATION PROBLEM 18–1

During January 1990, the Phoenix Company plans to sell 20,000 units of its product at a price of $20 per unit. Selling expenses are estimated to be $40,000 plus 2% of sales revenue. General and administrative expenses are estimated to be $30,000 plus 1% of sales revenue. Income tax expense is estimated to be 40% of net income before taxes.

Phoenix plans to produce 25,000 units during January with estimated variable costs per unit as follows: $2 for material, $5 for labor, and $3 for variable overhead. The fixed overhead cost is estimated at $20,000 per month. The finished goods inventory at January 1, 1990 is 4,000 units with a cost per unit of $10. The company uses FIFO inventory procedure.

Required:

Prepare a projected income statement for January 1990.

Solution to demonstration problem 18–1

PHOENIX COMPANY
Projected Income Statement
For January 1990

Sales (20,000 × $20)		$400,000
Cost of goods sold (see Schedule 1)		212,800
Gross margin		$187,200
Selling expenses:		
Fixed	$ 40,000	
Variable (0.02 × $400,000)	8,000	
General and administrative expenses:		
Fixed	30,000	
Variable (0.01 × $400,000)	4,000	82,000
Income before taxes		$105,200
Income taxes (40%)		42,080
Net income		$ 63,120

Schedule 1   **PHOENIX COMPANY**
Planned Cost of Goods Sold

Beginning finished goods inventory (4,000 × $10)		$ 40,000
Cost of goods manufactured:		
Direct materials (25,000 × $2)	$ 50,000	
Direct labor (25,000 × $5)	125,000	
Variable manufacturing overhead (25,000 × $3)	75,000	
Fixed manufacturing overhead	20,000	
Cost of goods manufactured (25,000 × $10.80)		270,000
Cost of goods available for sale		$310,000
Ending finished goods inventory (9,000 × $10.80)		97,200
Cost of goods sold		$212,800

QUESTIONS

1. What are the three main objectives of budgeting?

2. What is meant by the term management by exception? How does the concept relate to budgeting?

3. What are five basic principles which, if followed, should improve the possibilities of preparing a meaningful budget? Why is each important?

4. What is the difference between an "imposed" budget and a "participatory" budget?

5. Define and explain a budget variance. A budget variance implies the use of what kind of budget?

6. What are the two major budgets in the master budget? Which should be prepared first? Why?

7. Distinguish between master and responsibility budgets.

8. What is a flexible budget?

9. The budget established at the beginning of a given period carried an item for supplies in the amount of $40,000. At the end of the period, the supplies used amounted to $44,000. Can it be concluded from these data that there was inefficient use of supplies or that care was not exercised in purchasing the supplies?

10. Management must make certain assumptions about the business environment when preparing a budget. What areas should be considered?

11. Why is budgeted performance better than past performance as a basis for judging actual results?

EXERCISES

Prepare a schedule of planned sales and production

1. The Davis Shoe Company has decided to produce 110,000 pairs of shoes at a uniform rate throughout 1990. The sales department of the Davis Shoe Company has estimated sales for 1990 according to the following schedule:

First quarter	22,000
Second quarter	16,000
Third quarter	20,000
Fourth quarter	32,000
Total for 1990	90,000

If the December 31, 1989, inventory is estimated to be 10,000 pairs of shoes, prepare a schedule of planned sales and production in units for the first two quarters of 1990.

Prepare a flexible production budget

2. Labor and materials of Alan Corp. are considered to be variable costs. Expected production for the year is 100,000 units. At that level of production, labor cost is budgeted at $750,000 and materials cost is expected to be $330,000. Prepare a flexible budget for labor and materials for possible production levels of 70,000, 80,000, and 90,000 units of production.

Compute budget variances

3. Assume that in Exercise 2, actual production was 80,000 units and materials cost was $270,000, while labor cost was $594,000. What is the budget variance?

Prepare a schedule of planned collections and ending balance for accounts receivable

4. The following data apply to the collection of accounts receivable for the Miles Company.

Current balance, February 28—$400,000 (of which $240,000 relates to February sales).
Planned sales for March—$500,000.

Assumptions:

70% of sales are collected in the month of the sales; 20% in the following month; and the remaining 10% in the second month after the sales. Prepare a schedule of planned collections and ending balance for accounts receivable as of March 31, 1990.

Prepare an operating budget

5. The Tenner Company expects to sell 30,000 units of Whisbees during the next quarter at a price of $20 per unit. Production costs (all variable) are $7.00 per unit. Selling and administrative expenses are: variable, $5.00 per unit; fixed, $160,000 in total. What is the budgeted net income? (Do not consider taxes.)

Compute the budget variance for operations

6. Fixed production costs for the Harrison Company are budgeted at $140,000 assuming 25,000 units of production. Actual sales for the period were 20,000 units, while actual production was 25,000 units. Actual fixed costs used in computing the cost of goods sold were $112,000. What is the budget variance?

PROBLEMS

Prepare a projected income statement

18–1. During January 1990, the Sunset Company plans to sell 30,000 units at a price of $50 per unit. Selling expenses are estimated to be $120,000 plus 2% of sales revenue. General and administrative expenses are estimated to be $90,000 plus 1% of sales revenue. Income tax expense is estimated to be 40% of net operating income.

Sunset Company plans to produce 35,000 units during January, with estimated variable costs per unit as follows: $5 for materials; $11 for labor, and $7 for variable overhead. The fixed overhead cost is estimated at $60,000 per month. The finished goods inventory at January 1, 1990, is 6,000 units, with a cost per unit of $24. The company uses FIFO inventory procedure.

Required:

Prepare a projected income statement for January 1990.

Prepare a schedule of budgeted production; prepare a schedule of budgeted cost of goods sold

18–2. The Thomas Company prepares monthly operating and financial budgets. Estimates of sales (in units) are made for each month. Production is scheduled at a level high enough to take care of current needs and to carry into each month one half of that month's unit sales. Raw materials, direct labor, and variable overhead are estimated at $4, $8, and $2 per unit, and fixed overhead is budgeted at $154,000 per month. Sales for April, May, June, and July are estimated at 50,000, 60,000, 80,000, and 60,000 units. The inventory at April 1 consists of 25,000 units with a cost of $16.40 per unit.

Required:

a. Prepare a schedule showing the budgeted production in units for April, May, and June 1990.

b. Prepare a schedule showing the budgeted cost of goods sold for the same three months, assuming that the FIFO method is used for inventories.

Prepare budget reports

18–3. Net operating income for the Baker Company for 1990 was as follows:

Sales		$4,000,000
Cost of goods sold:*		
Raw materials	$800,000	
Direct labor	600,000	
Fixed overhead	400,000	
Variable overhead	240,000	2,040,000
Gross margin		$1,960,000
Selling expenses:		
Variable	$240,000	
Fixed	360,000	600,000
		$1,360,000
General and administrative expenses:		
Variable	$320,000	
Fixed	480,000	800,000
Net operating income.		$ 560,000

*Since production was equal to sales, beginning and ending inventories may be ignored.

An operating budget is prepared for 1991, with sales forecast at a 20% increase solely from volume. Raw materials, direct labor, and all costs labeled variable above are completely variable. Fixed costs are expected to continue as above, except for a $40,000 increase in fixed general and administrative costs. Assume that production was equal to sales so that beginning and ending inventories may be ignored in parts (a) and (b) below.

The actual operating data for 1991 are:

Sales	$4,600,000
Raw materials	940,000
Direct labor	700,000
Fixed overhead	410,000
Variable overhead	270,000
Variable selling expense	276,000
Fixed selling expense	364,000
Variable general and administrative expense . . .	380,000
Fixed general and administrative expense	540,000

Required:

a. Prepare a budget report comparing the 1991 planned operating budget with the actual 1991 data.

b. Prepare a budget report which would be useful in appraising the performance of the various persons charged with responsibility for providing satisfactory earnings. (Hint: Prepare budget data on a flexible basis.)

c. Comment on the difference revealed by the two reports.

Prepare a planned operating budget; analyze the efficiency of operations

18–4. The following data are presented for the T. K. Anderson Company for use in preparing its 1990 operating budget:

Plant capacity	500,000 units
Expected sales	450,000 units
Expected production	450,000 units
Forecast sales price	$10.00 per unit

Manufacturing costs:
Variable:

Raw material	$4.00
Direct labor	$2.00
Overhead	$1.00
Fixed	$225,000

Selling and administrative expenses:

Variable	$0.50
Fixed	$200,000

Assume no beginning inventory. Taxes are assumed to be 40% of pretax earnings. The actual sales price was $9.50 per unit. The actual production in units was equal to the actual sales in units. Thus, beginning and ending inventories may be ignored.

Required:

a. Prepare a planned operating budget for the year ended December 31, 1990.

b. The actual results for the T. K. Anderson Company for the year ended December 31, 1990, were as follows:

Sales		$4,750,000
Costs of goods sold:		
Materials	$1,900,000	
Direct labor	1,050,000	
Variable overhead	600,000	
Fixed overhead	225,000	3,775,000
		$ 975,000
Selling and administrative expense:		
Variable	$ 250,000	
Fixed	200,000	450,000
Income before taxes		$ 525,000
Income tax at 40%		210,000
Net income		$ 315,000

Using a flexible budget, analyze the efficiency of operations and the company's sales policy. Comment on the results for 1990.

Prepare detailed expense budget

18–5. The Holly Company is in the process of preparing its master budget for the year ended December 31, 1990. Management is interested in the responsibility budget to be prepared for the sales department. The sales manager and the general manager have met with all department heads and have given you the following estimates relating to next year's expectations:

(1) At present, the company employs 40 full-time salesmen with a base salary of $350 per month. In addition, it has eight regional managers with a base salary of $15,000 per year, while the one sales manager draws $30,000 per year.

(2) Sales for the current year are estimated at $9 million. The 40 full-time salesmen are given 5% sales commissions on about 70% of total sales and 3% sales commissions on 20% of sales, while the remaining 10% of sales are not subject to commission. Approximately one third of the sales are made in the first three months of the year.

(3) Advertising commitments have been made with major magazines. These commitments are for $15,000 per month.

(4) The company is planning a special in-store promotion during January–February–March. Special incentives are given to the retailers in the form of supplies, aids, and advertising assistance up to 2% of total gross sales during the month. Past history has shown that the retailers take advantage of about three fourths of these incentives.

(5) A supplementary advertising campaign will also be used during the first quarter of 1990 and will average $30,000 for January and $20,000 during each of the next two months.

(6) Salesmen's travel allowances average $150 per month for each of the 40 salesmen.

(7) Selling supplies average 1% of gross sales.

(8) Sales department clerical salaries are set at $2,500 per month. Rent for sales offices is $6,000 per month.

(9) The sales department will conduct a special market test of a new product during the first quarter. Nonrecurring expenses of $45,000 associated with this test are expected to be incurred.

Required:

Prepare a detailed expense budget for the sales department for the first quarter of 1991.

Prepare a schedule of planned cost of goods manufactured and sold

18–6. The MDA Manufacturing Company is in the process of preparing a schedule of the planned cost of goods sold and the ending inventory for the quarters ended March 31, 1990 and June 30, 1990. The following data relate to expected activity for the two quarters:

(1) Expected sales:

March quarter	$200,000
June quarter	$150,000
September quarter	$300,000

(2) The selling price per unit is $20.

(3) The company policy is to carry an end-of-the-period inventory equal to 20% of the next period's requirements. The beginning inventory at January 1, 1990, was 1,000 units valued at $12.50 per unit.

(4) Cost of production is estimated as follows:

Materials	$3 per unit
Direct labor	$7 per unit
Variable overhead	$2 per unit
Fixed overhead	$19,000 per quarter

(5) There is no work in process inventory at the beginning or end of any period.

(6) Inventory is computed on a FIFO basis.

Required:

Prepare a schedule of Planned Cost of Goods Manufactured and Sold for the quarters ended March 31, and June 30, 1990. (Hint: Prepare the production schedule in units first.)

Prepare a planned operating budget; prepare a financial budget

18–7.

A & K CORPORATION
Post-Closing Trial Balance
December 31, 1990

	Debits	Credits
Cash	$ 20,000	
Accounts receivable	40,000	
Allowance for doubtful accounts		$ 3,000
Inventories	50,000	
Prepaid expenses	6,000	
Land	50,000	
Buildings and equipment	150,000	
Accumulated depreciation—buildings and equipment		20,000
Accounts payable		30,000
Accrued liabilities (including income taxes) . . .		20,000
Capital stock		200,000
Retained earnings		43,000
	$316,000	$316,000

The A & K Corporation, whose post-closing trial balance at December 31, 1990 appears above, is a rapidly expanding company. Sales amounted to $200,000 in the last quarter of 1990 and are projected at $250,000 and $400,000 for the first two quarters of 1991. This expansion has created a very tight cash position. Management is especially concerned about the probable cash balance at March 31, 1991 since payment in the amount of $30,000 for some new equipment must be made upon delivery on April 2. The current cash balance of $20,000 is considered to be the minimum workable balance.

Additional data:

(1) Purchases, all on account, are to be scheduled so that the inventory at the end of any quarter is equal to one third of the goods expected to be sold in the coming quarter. The cost of goods sold averages 60% of sales.

(2) Selling expenses are budgeted at $10,000 fixed plus 8% of sales; $2,000 is expected to be incurred on account, $24,000 accrued, $2,800 from expired prepayments, and $1,200 from allocated depreciation.

(3) Purchasing expenses are budgeted at $7,000 fixed plus 5% of purchases; $1,000 will be incurred on account, $13,000 accrued, $1,100 from expired prepayments, and $900 from allocated depreciation.

(4) Administrative expenses are budgeted at $12,500 fixed plus 3% of sales; $2,000 will be incurred on account, $11,000 accrued, $1,100 from expired prepayments, and $900 from allocated depreciation, while bad debts expense is equal to 2% of current sales.

(5) Federal income taxes are budgeted at 50% of net operating earnings before taxes and are accrued in Accrued Liabilities. Payments on these taxes are included in the payments on Accrued Liabilities discussed below.

(6) All December 31, 1990, Accounts Payable plus 80% of current credits to this account will be paid in the current quarter. All of the December 31, 1990, accrued liabilities will be paid in the current quarter except for $6,000. Of the current quarter's accrued liabilities, all but $24,000 will be paid during the quarter.

(7) Cash outlays for various expenses normally prepaid will amount to $8,000 during the quarter.

(8) All sales are made on account, and 80% of the sales are collected in the quarter in which they are made, and all of the remaining sales are collected in the following quarter, except for 2% which are never collected. The allowance for uncollectible accounts shows the estimated amount of accounts receivable at December 31, 1990 arising from 1990 sales which will not be collected.

Required:

a. Prepare a planned operating budget for the quarter ending March 31, 1991. Supporting schedules for planned purchases and operating expenses should be included.

b. Prepare a financial budget for March 31, 1991. Include supporting schedules analyzing accounts credited for purchases and expenses, showing planned cash flows and the planned cash balance, and showing planned collections on and the planned balance of accounts receivable.

c. Will sufficient cash be on hand April 2 to pay for the new equipment?

BUSINESS DECISION PROBLEM 18–1:

Prepare a cash budget

The Maharis Company has applied at a local bank for a short-term loan of $200,000 starting on April 1. The loan will be repaid with interest at 12% on June 30. The bank's loan officer has requested a cash budget from the company for the quarter ending June 30. The following budget information is needed to prepare the cash budget:

Sales	$800,000
Purchases	480,000
Salaries and wages to be paid	140,000
Rent payments	10,000
Supplies (payments for)	8,000
Insurance payments	2,000
Other cash payments	67,000

A cash balance of $60,000 is planned for April 1. Accounts receivable are expected to be $75,000 on April 1. All of these accounts will be collected in the quarter ending June 30. In general, sales are collected as follows: 80% in the quarter of sale and 20% in the quarter after sale. Accounts payable will be $500,000 on April 1 and will be paid during the quarter ending June 30. All purchases are paid for in the quarter after purchase.

Required:

a. Prepare a cash budget for the quarter ending June 30. Assume that the $200,000 loan will be made on April 1 and will be repaid with interest at 12% on June 30.

b. Will the company be able to repay the loan on June 30? If the company desires a minimum cash balance of $50,000, will the company be able to repay the loan as planned?

19

SHORT-TERM DECISION MAKING

LEARNING OBJECTIVES

After studying this chapter, you should be able to:

1. Explain and describe the different cost behavior patterns.
2. Calculate the break-even point for a company.
3. List the assumptions underlying cost-volume-profit analysis.
4. Calculate the various applications of cost-volume-profit analysis.
5. Explain differential analysis and describe its various components.
6. Calculate the various applications of differential analysis.
7. Compare and contrast absorption costing and direct costing.
8. Define and use correctly the new terms introduced in the chapter.

In making decisions, management must frequently distinguish between short-run decision making and long-run decision making. The term **short run** describes a time frame during which a company's management cannot change the effects of certain past decisions. The short-run time frame is often considered to be one year or less. In the short run, many costs, such as depreciation expense, are assumed to be fixed and unchangeable. Because of this assumption, short-run decision making uses different criteria than long-run decision making, under which all costs are subject to change.

In this chapter you will be introduced to some of the analytical tools that can be used to make short-run decisions. The chapter begins with a discussion of cost behavior patterns because the classification of costs as fixed or variable is the first step in using the analytical tools.

COST BEHAVIOR PATTERNS

Objective 1: Explain and describe the different cost behavior patterns

Illustration 19.1 shows four basic cost behavior patterns: variable, fixed, mixed (semivariable), and step. As discussed in earlier chapters, **variable costs** vary directly with changes in volume of production or sales. Direct

Illustration 19.1
FOUR COST PATTERNS

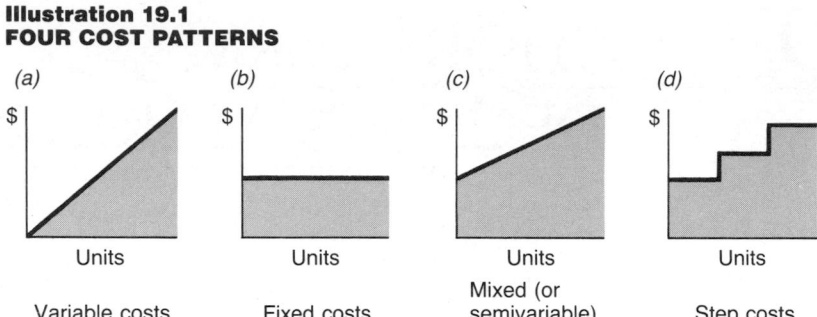

materials, direct labor, and sales commissions are examples of variable costs. In contrast, **fixed costs** remain constant over some relevant range of output, and are often described as time-related costs. Depreciation, insurance, property taxes, and administrative salaries are examples of fixed costs.

Mixed and step costs demonstrate both fixed and variable characteristics. A **mixed cost** contains a fixed portion of cost that will be incurred even when the plant is completely idle and a variable portion that will increase directly with production volume. An example of a mixed cost is electricity. A certain amount of cost is incurred in order for the company to have electrical service. As the plant operates, each additional kilowatt-hour of usage generates an additional amount of cost. A mixed cost may be separated into its fixed and variable components, as shown in Illustration 19.2.

Illustration 19.2
SEPARATION OF A MIXED COST

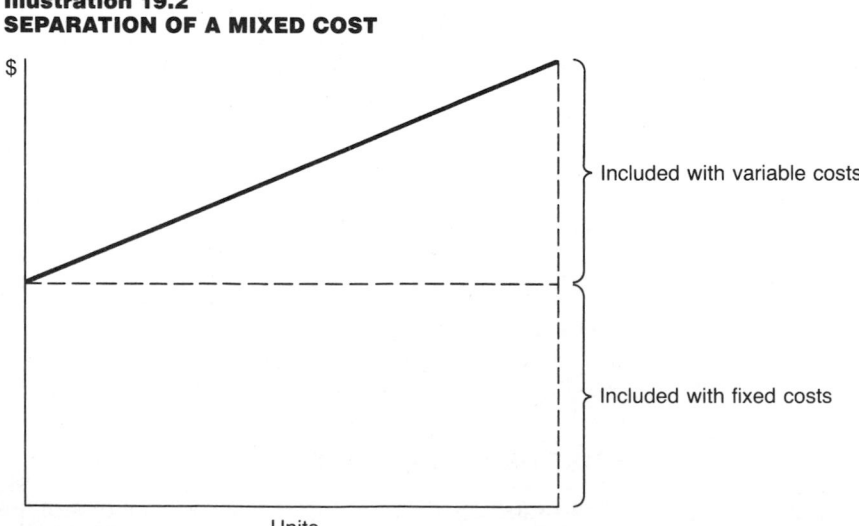

A **step cost** remains constant in total over a range of output (or sales) but then increases in steps at certain points. A step cost may be either a step variable or a step fixed cost. The major difference between the two types is the size of the "steps." In both cases, there are fixed and variable components of the cost. An example of a step variable cost is the cost of water. The utility company charges a flat fee for providing water (fixed component) and an additional amount depending on the quantity of water used (variable component). Unlike the variable charge for electricity, which is on an hour-by-hour basis, the charge for water may be stated in increments as follows: $10 for the first 1,000 gallons or less; $5 additional for use of 1,001 to 5,000 gallons; $8 additional for use of 5,001 to 10,000 gallons; and so on. This type of cost is shown in Illustration 19.3.

Supervisors' salaries are an example of a step fixed cost. At any level of production from 1 unit to 40,000 units, one supervisor is necessary at a salary of $20,000 per year. If the company produces at a level over 40,000 units but below 100,000 units, a second supervisor is needed at an additional cost of $20,000. A step fixed cost for supervisors' salaries is shown in Illustration 19.4.

For decision making, management must separate mixed and step costs into their fixed and variable components. A mixed cost can be easily

Illustration 19.3
SEPARATION OF A STEP VARIABLE COST

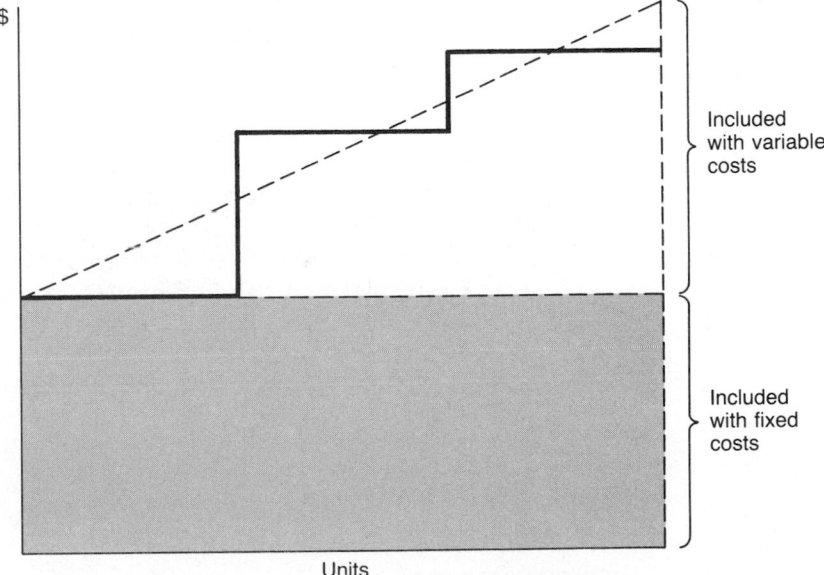

Even though step variable costs do not vary directly with changes in volume, they can be treated for planning purposes as though they are directly variable costs. The slanted dashed line represents the smoothing of the step variable cost into a directly variable cost.

Illustration 19.4
A STEP FIXED COST

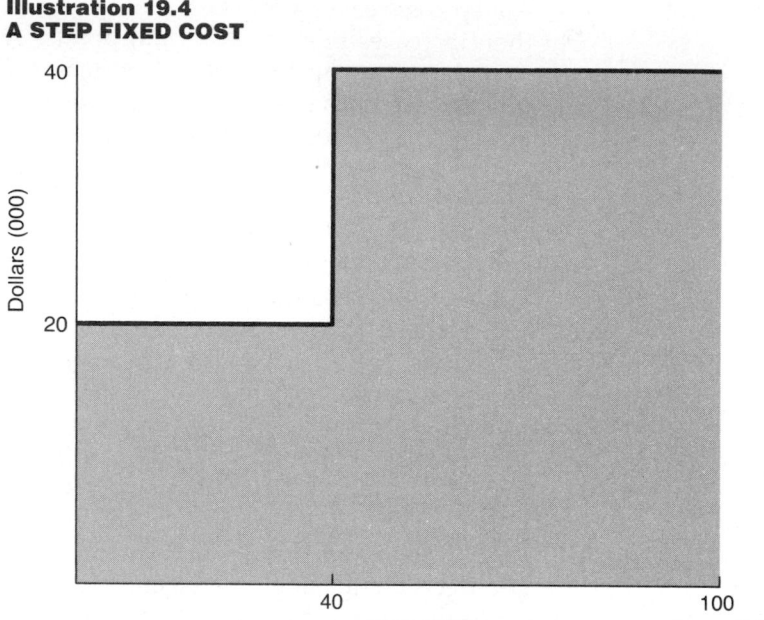

broken down into these two components. The fixed portion of a mixed cost is included with other fixed costs, while the variable element is shown as directly changing with volume. A step variable cost is treated in the same manner as a mixed cost. The fixed portion of a step variable cost is treated as a fixed cost, and the remaining cost is treated as entirely variable.

Since a step fixed cost is fixed over a relatively wide range of activity, it is treated as entirely fixed for decision-making purposes. This is done by estimating the level of operations and then treating the step fixed cost expected at that level of operations as a fixed cost for decision making.

Thus, even though there are four different types of cost patterns, it has been shown that two basic categories—variable and fixed—may be used to include all of them. Before we proceed, one other comment is in order. Some variable costs do not vary in a strictly linear relationship with volume. Rather, they vary in a curvilinear pattern—a 10% increase in volume may yield an 8% change in costs at lower output levels and an 11% change in costs at higher output levels. A curvilinear relationship is diagrammed in Illustration 19.5. But, in the remainder of this chapter, variable costs are assumed to vary in a linear relationship with volume. The need for this assumption will become more evident as you proceed through the chapter.

Methods for Analyzing Costs

There are several methods available for breaking down a mixed or a step variable cost into its fixed and variable cost components. Three of these

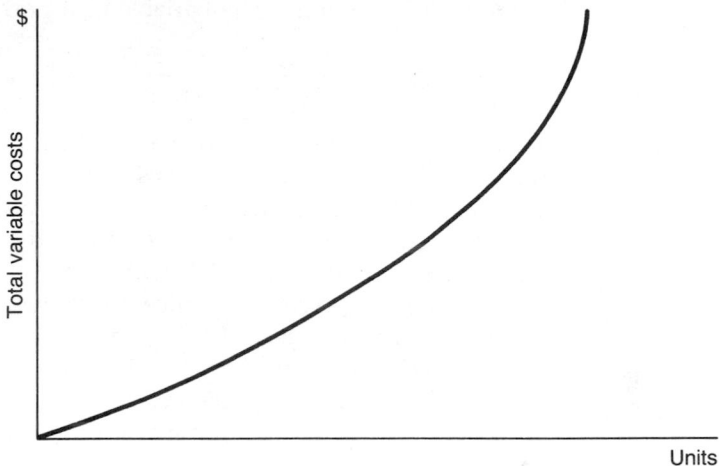

Illustration 19.5
CURVILINEAR COST PATTERN

procedures are the scatter diagram, the least-squares method, and the high-low method.

The scatter diagram.   A **scatter diagram** shows plots of actual costs incurred for various levels of output or sales. The dots on the scatter diagram in Illustration 19.6 represent total actual maintenance costs for a company's fleet of delivery trucks at various levels of past activity. A line is drawn through what appears visually to be the center of the pattern formed by the dots. In Illustration 19.6, the fixed element of the mixed

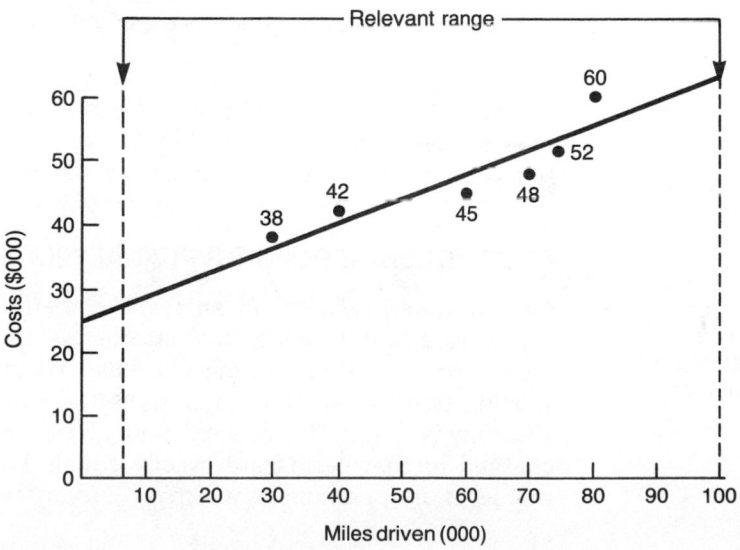

Illustration 19.6
SCATTER DIAGRAM

costs is $23,000, since that is the amount of cost at zero volume of output. The line (called a regression line) rises from $23,000 to $63,000 over the range of 100,000 units. The variable cost portion can be computed as:

$$\frac{\$63,000 - \$23,000}{100,000 \text{ units}} = \$0.40 \text{ per unit}$$

The data in the chart suggest that the company's truck maintenance costs can be estimated at $23,000 plus 40 cents for every mile driven.

The least-squares method. A more sophisticated technique called the least-squares method is used to draw the regression line and divide mixed costs into their fixed and variable portions. The least-squares method is more precise, but since it involves statistical analysis, it will not be presented in this text.

The high-low method. The high-low method is also widely used to identify the behavior of mixed costs. The **high-low method** uses only the highest and lowest points on a scatter diagram to draw a line representing a total mixed cost.

To illustrate, the lowest point in Illustration 19.6 is $38,000 of expense at 30,000 units of output, and the highest point is $60,000 at 80,000 units of output. The amount of variable cost per unit is found as follows:

$$\frac{\text{Change in cost}}{\text{Change in units}} = \frac{\$60,000 - \$38,000}{80,000 \text{ units} - 30,000 \text{ units}}$$

$$= \frac{\$22,000}{50,000 \text{ units}} = \$0.44 \text{ per unit}$$

The fixed portion is then found as follows:

Total cost at 80,000 units of output	$60,000
Less: Variable cost at that level of output	
(80,000 × $0.44)	35,200
Fixed cost at all levels of output within the	
relevant range.	$24,800

The high-low method is less precise than the scatter diagram since it uses only two data points in the computation. Either or both points may not be representative of the data as a whole.

COST-VOLUME-PROFIT (CVP) ANALYSIS

*Objective 2:
Calculate the
break-even point
for a company*

Cost-volume-profit (CVP) analysis (sometimes called **break-even analysis**) is used to determine what effects any changes in a company's selling prices, costs, and/or volume will have on income in the short run. The starting point of such an analysis is the company's break-even point. A company is said to "break even" for a given period if sales revenue and costs charged to that period are exactly equal. Thus, the **break-even point** is that level of operations at which a company realizes no net income or loss.

A careful and accurate cost-volume-profit (CVP) analysis requires knowledge of costs and their behavior (i.e., fixed or variable) as volume changes. The types and quantities of cost data accumulated depend on the costs of obtaining the data compared to the benefits of having more refined information. Within this constraint, it is desirable to compute break-even points for each area of decision making within the company. Some important classifications of cost data for break-even analysis are by product, territory, salesperson, or class of customer.

A break-even point may be expressed in dollars of sales revenue or number of units produced or sold. No matter how the break-even point is expressed, it is still the point of zero income or loss.

To illustrate the calculation of a break-even point, assume the Muffet Manufacturing Company produces a single product that sells for $20. Fixed costs per period total $40,000, while variable cost is $12 per unit. The **variable cost rate,** which expresses variable cost as a percentage of sales, is 60% ($12 ÷ $20). That is, for each dollar of sales, the company incurs $0.60 of variable cost. The sales revenue needed to break even would be calculated as that point at which all costs are covered, but no income is generated. Therefore, the break-even point can be expressed as:

$$\text{Sales} = \text{Fixed costs} + \text{Variable costs}$$

or

$$S = FC + VC$$

Substituting the Muffet Company amounts of fixed costs and the variable cost rate in the formula gives the following:

$$S = \$40,000 + 0.60S$$
$$S - 0.60S = \$40,000$$
$$0.40S = \$40,000$$
$$S = \$40,000 \div 0.40$$
$$S = \$100,000$$

Sales revenue at the break-even point is $100,000. To compute the break-even point in units, simply divide the $100,000 of sales by the $20 selling price per unit. This gives a break-even point of 5,000 units.

If desired, the break-even point can be expressed in terms of capacity. Newspaper reports often refer to the break-even point of the steel industry, or of a company in that industry, as being a stated percentage of capacity, for example, 65%. If in the example presented above the output capacity of the plant was 25,000 units, the break-even point in terms of plant capacity is 20% (5,000 ÷ 25,000).

Alternatively, the break-even point in units could be calculated first. The break-even point in units involves a concept known as contribution margin. **Contribution margin** is the amount by which revenue exceeds variable costs of producing that revenue; it can be calculated on a per unit or total sales volume basis. On a per unit basis, the contribution margin for Muffet Company is $8, which equals the selling price of $20 less the variable cost per unit of $12. Contribution margin indicates the amount of money remaining after variable cost is covered. This remainder contributes to the coverage of fixed costs and to the generation of net income. The break-even point in units is computed by dividing total fixed costs by the contribution margin per unit.

$$\mathrm{BEP}_{\text{units}} = \frac{\text{Fixed costs}}{\text{Contribution margin per unit}}$$

$$\mathrm{BEP}_{\text{units}} = \frac{\$40,000}{\$8 \text{ per unit}}$$

$$= 5,000 \text{ units}$$

If the Muffet Company's production capacity is 20,000 units, then the break-even point is equal to 25% of capacity (5,000/20,000 = 25%).

An alternative method of finding the break-even point in sales dollars is to divide the total fixed costs by the contribution margin rate. The **contribution margin rate** expresses the contribution margin as a percentage of sales and is calculated by dividing the contribution margin per unit by the selling price per unit. The Muffet Company's contribution margin rate is:

$$\frac{\text{Contribution margin per unit}}{\text{Selling price per unit}} = \frac{\$20 - \$12}{\$20} = \frac{\$8}{\$20} = 0.40$$

Using this rate, the Muffet Company's break-even point in sales dollars is calculated as follows:

$$\mathrm{BEP}_{\text{dollars}} = \frac{\text{Fixed costs}}{\text{Contribution margin rate}}$$

$$\mathrm{BEP}_{\text{dollars}} = \frac{\$40,000}{0.40}$$

$$= \$100,000$$

Break-Even Chart

A **break-even chart** is a graph that shows the relationships between sales, costs, volume, and profit and also shows the break-even point. Illustration 19.7 presents the break-even chart for the Muffet Company. Each break-even chart or calculation is valid only for a specified relevant range of volume. The **relevant range** is the range of production or sales volume over which the basic cost behavior assumptions will hold true. For volumes outside these ranges, costs will behave differently and will alter the assumed relationships. For example, if more than 10,000 units were produced by the Muffet Company, it might be necessary to increase plant capacity (thus incurring additional fixed costs) or to work extra shifts (thus incurring overtime charges and other inefficiencies). In either case, the

Illustration 19.7
THE BREAK-EVEN CHART

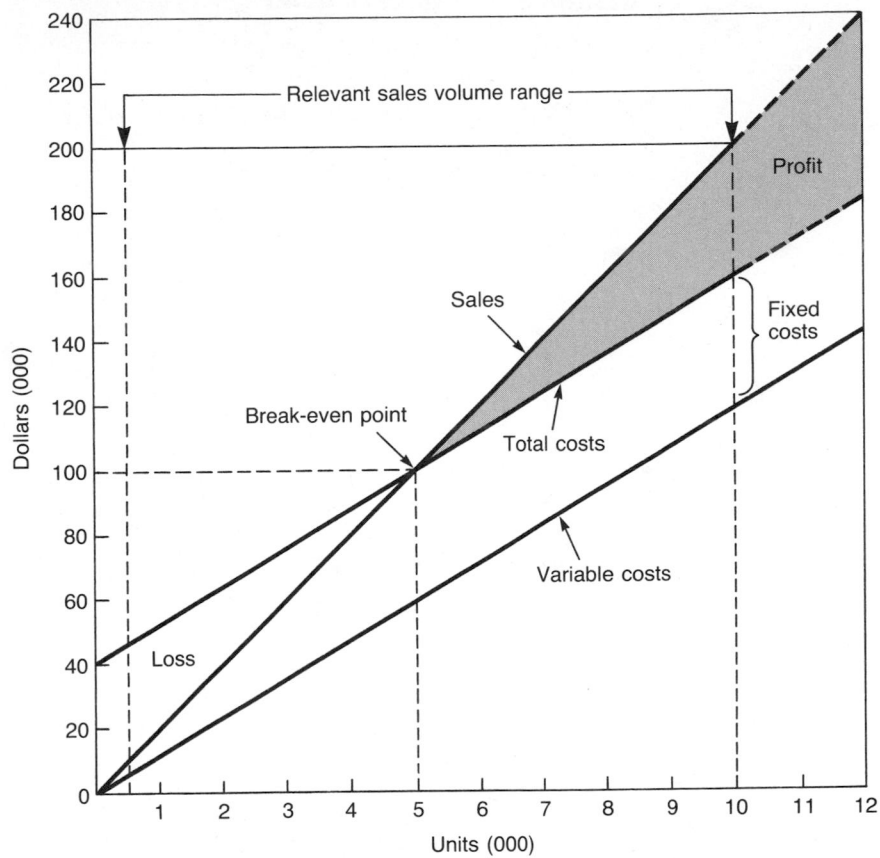

cost relationships first assumed are no longer valid. Illustration 19.7 is based on cost data for Muffet Company in a relevant range of output from 500 to 10,000 units.

The chart in Illustration 19.7 shows that the break-even volume of sales is $100,000 (5,000 units at $20 per unit). At this level of sales, fixed costs and variable costs are exactly equal to sales revenue, as shown:

Revenues	$100,000
Less: Variable costs	60,000
Contribution margin	$ 40,000
Less: Fixed costs	40,000
Net income	$ –0–

The break-even chart could also be re-labeled to indicate contribution margin, as shown in Illustration 19.8.

The break-even charts show that a period of complete idleness will produce a loss of $40,000 (the amount of fixed costs), while output of

Illustration 19.8
**BREAK-EVEN CHART SHOWING THAT FIXED COSTS EQUAL CONTRIBUTION
MARGIN AT BREAK-EVEN POINT**

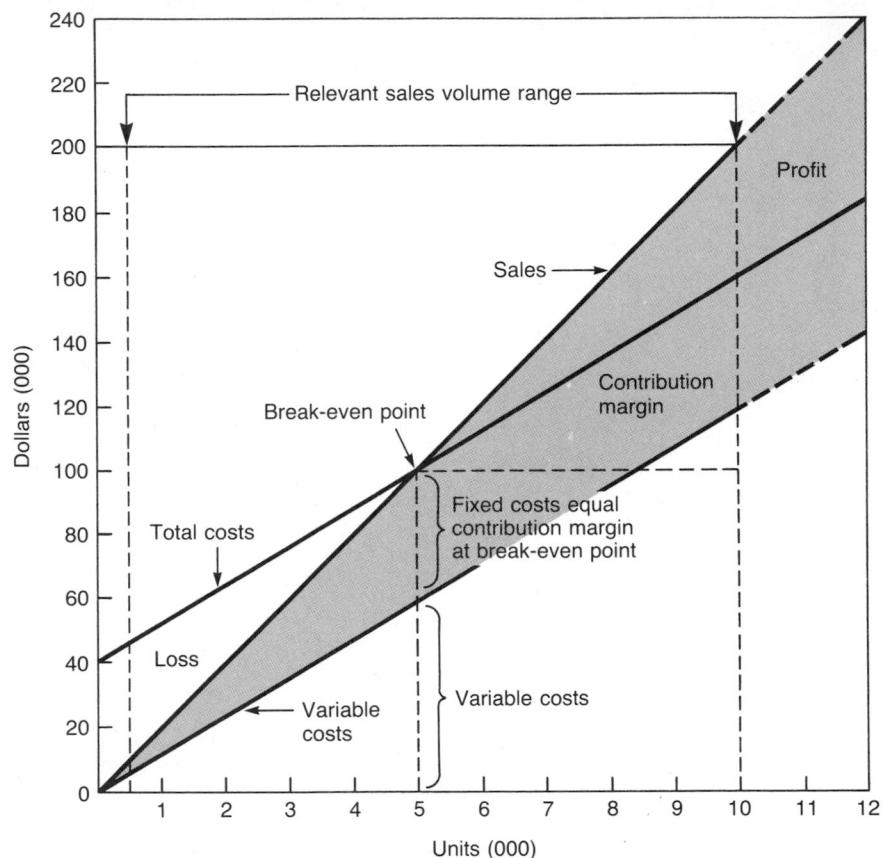

10,000 units will produce net income of $40,000. Other points on the graph show that sales of 7,500 units will result in $150,000 of revenue. At that point, total costs amount to $130,000, leaving net income of $20,000. The charts also show that net income at any level of output can be found by multiplying the contribution margin per unit by the number of units sold and subtracting total fixed costs from the result.

Changing the Break-Even Point

A break-even point can be lowered or raised by changing selling price, variable cost per unit, or fixed costs. Lowering the break-even point means that the company can earn income at a lower volume of operations. If the selling price is increased or the variable cost per unit is decreased, the break-even point will be lower because the contribution margin per unit is larger. A larger contribution margin means that more of the selling price of each unit can be used to cover fixed costs. Similarly, if fixed costs are decreased, it takes fewer units sold to cover the smaller amount of fixed costs. These actions in reverse will create a higher break-even point. That is, lowering the selling price, increasing the variable cost per unit, or increasing fixed costs will raise the break-even point.

To illustrate the effects of changing the (1) selling price, (2) variable cost, or (3) fixed cost to lower the break-even point, assume that a company currently has a single product that sells for $60. Variable cost per unit is $15, or 25% of selling price, and fixed costs are $27,000. The break-even point is $36,000 of sales revenue, computed as follows:

$$S = FC + VC$$
$$S = \$27,000 + 0.25S$$
$$0.75S = \$27,000$$
$$S = \$36,000$$

As shown below, companies have a great deal of flexibility in the means of adjusting their break-even points. Companies attempt to operate at a level of operations above the break-even point in order to make a profit.

Increase selling price. If the company can increase its selling price to $75 while keeping variable costs and fixed costs the same, the variable cost rate becomes 20%, ($15 ÷ $75). The break-even point will then decrease by $2,250:

$$S = FC + VC$$
$$S = \$27,000 + 0.20S$$
$$0.80S = \$27,000$$
$$S = \$33,750$$

If the company incurs $5,000 higher fixed costs at the same time it increases its selling price, the break-even point would be:

$$S = \$32,000 + .20S$$
$$.80S = \$32,000$$
$$S = \$40,000$$

Reduce variable cost. If the company can reduce the variable cost per unit to $13.20 and thus reduce the variable cost rate to 22% of selling price, ($13.20 ÷ $60) the break-even point can be lowered:

$$S = FC + VC$$
$$S = \$27,000 + 0.22S$$
$$0.78S = \$27,000$$
$$S = \$34,615$$

Reduce fixed costs. If the company can reduce its fixed costs by $3,000 to $24,000, the break-even point is again reduced:

$$S = FC + VC$$
$$S = \$24,000 + 0.25S$$
$$0.75S = \$24,000$$
$$S = \$32,000$$

Margin of Safety

If a company's current sales are above its break-even point, then the company is said to have a margin of safety equal to current sales less break-even sales. The **margin of safety** is the amount by which sales can decrease before a loss will be incurred. For example, assume a company currently has sales of $250,000 and its break-even sales are $200,000. The margin of safety is $50,000, computed as follows:

$$\text{Margin of safety} = \text{Current sales} - \text{Break-even sales}$$

$$\$50,000 = \$250,000 - \$200,000$$

The margin of safety is sometimes expressed as a percentage, called the margin of safety rate. The **margin of safety rate** is equal to (Current sales − Break-even sales) ÷ Current sales. Using data from the company just discussed, the margin of safety rate would be computed as follows:

$$\text{Margin of safety rate} = \frac{\text{Current sales} - \text{Break-even sales}}{\text{Current sales}}$$

$$= \frac{\$250,000 - \$200,000}{\$250,000} = 20\%$$

This means that sales volume could drop by 20% before a loss would be incurred.

Assumptions Made in Cost-Volume-Profit Analysis

Objective 3: List the assumptions underlying cost-volume-profit analysis

Certain assumptions are made in CVP analysis:

1. Selling price, variable cost per unit, and total fixed costs remain constant throughout the relevant range. This means that more or fewer units could be sold at the same price and that there is no change in technical efficiency as volume changes.
2. The number of units produced equals the number of units sold.
3. In multiproduct situations, the product mix is known in advance. (Multiproduct situations are covered later in this chapter.)
4. Costs can be accurately classified into their fixed and their variable portions.

Although these assumptions are sometimes criticized as being unrealistic, they are necessary in order to make the calculations.

Cost-Volume-Profit Analysis Illustrated

Objective 4: Calculate the various applications of cost-volume-profit analysis

CVP analysis has many applications, several of which are illustrated below using data regarding an airline.

Calculating the break-even point. A major airline wishes to know the number of seats that must be sold on a certain flight for the flight to break even. To solve this problem, costs must first be identified and separated into fixed and variable categories.

The fixed costs are the same regardless of the number of seats filled. Fixed costs include items such as the fuel required to fly the plane and crew (with no passengers) to its destination; depreciation on the plane used on the flight; and salaries of required crew members, gate attendants, and maintenance and refueling personnel. The variable costs will vary directly with the number of passengers. Variable costs include meals and beverages provided to passengers, baggage handling costs, and the cost of the additional fuel required to fly the plane with passengers to its destination. Each variable cost should be expressed on a per person basis.

Assume that after the various costs have been analyzed and classified as fixed or variable, the fixed costs for a given flight are $12,000. Variable costs are $25 per passenger, and tickets are sold at $125; thus the variable cost rate is 20% ($25 ÷ $125). This rate yields a contribution margin per ticket of $100 ($125 − $25). The contribution margin rate is 80% [($125 − $25) ÷ $125].

The break-even point can be expressed in sales revenue (dollars) or in number of passengers. The sales revenue needed to break even is computed as follows:

$$Sales = Fixed\ costs + Variable\ costs$$
$$S = FC + VC$$
$$S = \$12{,}000 + 0.20S$$
$$0.80S = \$12{,}000$$
$$S = \$15{,}000$$

The break-even point in dollars can also be computed as follows:

$$BEP_{dollars} = \frac{Fixed\ costs}{Contribution\ margin\ rate} = \frac{\$12{,}000}{0.80} = \$15{,}000$$

The break-even point in number of passengers (units) may be found by dividing fixed costs by the contribution margin per unit:

$$BEP_{units} = \frac{Fixed\ costs}{Contribution\ margin\ per\ unit} = \frac{\$12{,}000}{\$125 - \$25} = 120\ passengers$$

Calculating sales volume needed for desired net income. With a simple adjustment in the break-even formulas, CVP analysis can also show the sales volume needed to generate some desired level of net income. This adjustment is made by adding the desired income amount to the total costs that need to be covered. Management can then determine the necessary sales volume in dollars or units. For example, if the airline discussed above wishes to earn $8,000 of income on its flight, the company can calculate the amount of necessary sales revenue by the following formula:

$$\text{Sales} = \text{Fixed costs} + \text{Variable costs} + \text{Desired net income}$$

or
$$S = FC + VC + NI$$
$$S = \$12{,}000 + 0.20S + \$8{,}000$$
$$0.80S = \$20{,}000$$
$$S = \$25{,}000$$

If the airline wants to know how many passenger tickets must be sold in order to earn $8,000, a similar modification of another form of the break-even point formula will yield the desired calculation. Remembering that the contribution margin per ticket is $100, the number of tickets to be sold is computed as follows:

$$\text{Number of units} = \frac{\text{Fixed costs} + \text{Desired net income}}{\text{Contribution margin per unit}}$$

$$= \frac{\$12{,}000 + \$8{,}000}{\$100} = \frac{\$20{,}000}{\$100} = 200 \text{ passengers}$$

Calculating the effect on net income of changing price. The break-even formula can also be used to determine the results if the price used in the formula is changed. To illustrate, assume that the flight normally carries 150 passengers (sales of $18,750 and net income of $3,000) and that a decision is made to increase ticket prices by 5%. If variable and fixed costs remain constant and passenger load does not change, net income will rise from $3,000 to $3,937.50 as shown:

$$S = FC + VC + NI$$
$$\$18{,}750(1.05) = \$12{,}000 + 0.20(\$18{,}750) + NI$$
$$\$19{,}687.50 = \$12{,}000 + \$3{,}750 + NI$$
$$\$19{,}687.50 = \$15{,}750 + NI$$
$$NI = \$3{,}937.50$$

We assume that variable costs would remain constant at 20% of original sales in the above illustration because a change in selling price has no effect on the variable costs associated with providing flight service. Income would rise by the entire amount of the price increase ($19,687.50 − $18,750 = $937.50) because all variable and fixed costs are already being covered by the original selling price.

Calculating sales needed to maintain net income when costs change. The break-even formula has yet another application; it can be used to calculate the sales needed to maintain income when costs change. For example, if the price of gasoline rises, both fixed and variable costs will increase for the airline. Assume that fixed costs are increased by $4,000, and variable costs are increased by $6.25 per passenger. Variable costs are now 25% ($31.25/$125) of sales price. In order to maintain the current net income of $3,000 (on $18,750 of sales), the airline will need to increase sales revenue to $25,333 as shown below.

$$S = FC + VC + NI$$
$$S = \$16,000 + 0.25S + \$3,000$$
$$0.75S = \$19,000$$
$$S = \$25,333 \text{ (or 203 passengers)}$$

Other uses of CVP analysis. Management can also use its knowledge of CVP relationships to determine whether to increase sales promotion costs in an effort to increase sales volume or to accept an order at a lower-than-usual price. In general, the careful study of break-even charts helps management plan future courses of action. Indeed, it has been said that to be successful, management must become "break-even minded."

Calculating Break-Even for a Multiproduct Company

When computing the break-even point for a multiproduct company, only dollars of sales are used. In a multiproduct company, a given product mix is assumed to be constant for CVP purposes. **Product mix** refers to the proportion of the company's total sales attributable to each type of product sold. To illustrate the computation of the break-even point for a multiproduct company, assume the following historical data:

| | Products | | | | | | | |
| | 1 | | 2 | | 3 | | Total | |
	Amount	Percent	Amount	Percent	Amount	Percent	Amount	Percent
Sales	$60,000	100	$30,000	100	$10,000	100	$100,000	100
Less: Variable costs . .	40,000	67	16,000	53	4,000	40	60,000	60
Contribution margin . .	$20,000	33	$14,000	47	$ 6,000	60	$ 40,000	40

The relationships shown in the Total column are used to compute the break-even point. Variable costs are 60% ($60,000/$100,000) of total sales. If the product mix is assumed to remain constant and fixed costs for the company are $50,000, break-even sales are $125,000:

$$S = FC + VC$$
$$S = \$50,000 + 0.60S$$
$$0.40S = \$50,000$$
$$S = \$125,000$$

The $125,000 sales can be specified by product by multiplying total sales dollars by the percent of product mix of each of the three products. The product mix for products 1, 2, and 3 is 60:30:10, respectively; that is, out of the $100,000 total sales, there were $60,000 sales of product 1, $30,000 sales of product 2, and $10,000 sales of product 3. Therefore, the company will have to sell $75,000 (0.6 × $125,000) of product 1, $37,500

$(0.3 \times \$125,000)$ of product 2, and $\$12,500$ $(0.1 \times \$125,000)$ of product 3 in order to break even.

If there is any change in the mix of products sold, the break-even point will also change. The break-even point changes because each product has a different contribution margin. Also, if historical patterns of selling prices or variable costs are not expected to hold true in the future, projected sales and variable expenses should be used to determine expected percentages of variable expenses to total sales.

To illustrate the effects of such changes, assume that the product mix for products 1, 2, and 3 is expected to change to 20:30:50 in the upcoming period, as shown in the following chart. Also assume that total sales are $\$100,000$ and that the variable costs for product 3 are expected to fall to 33% of the selling price. To compute the new break-even point, we again use the relationships shown in the Total column.

	Products							
	1		2		3		Total	
	Amount	Percent	Amount	Percent	Amount	Percent	Amount	Percent
Sales	$20,000	100	$30,000	100	$50,000	100	$100,000	100
Less: Variable costs . .	13,333	67	16,000	53	16,667	33	46,000	46
Contribution margin . .	$ 6,667	33	$14,000	47	$33,333	67	$ 54,000	54

As shown in the Total column, variable costs are expected to fall to 46% of total sales in the upcoming period. The new break-even point will be $\$92,593$ computed as follows:

$$S = FC + VC$$
$$S = \$50,000 + 0.46S$$
$$0.54S = \$50,000$$
$$S = \$92,593$$

Notice that the new break-even point is lower than the old one. Sales shifted from the lowest contribution margin product (product 1) to the highest contribution margin product (product 3), thereby increasing the contribution margin dollars available to cover fixed costs.

DIFFERENTIAL ANALYSIS

Objective 5: Explain differential analysis and describe its various components

Another analytical tool of short-term decision making is differential analysis. **Differential analysis** involves analyzing the different costs and benefits that would arise from alternative solutions to a particular situation. **Relevant revenues or costs** in a given situation are future revenues or costs that differ depending on which alternative course of action is selected. **Differential revenue** is defined as the difference in revenues between two alternatives. **Differential cost or expense** is the difference between relevant costs for two alternatives.[1] Future costs that do not differ between alternatives are irregular and may be ignored since they will affect both alternatives similarly. Past costs, also known as **sunk costs,** are also not relevant in decision making because the costs have already been incurred and, therefore, cannot be changed no matter which alternative is selected.

For certain decisions, revenues do not differ between alternatives. Under those circumstances, management should select the alternative with the least cost. In other situations, costs do not differ between alternatives. Accordingly, the alternative that results in the greatest revenue should be selected. But many times both future costs and revenues differ between alternatives. In these situations, the alternative that results in the greatest positive difference between future revenues and expenses (costs) should be selected.

To illustrate relevant, differential, and sunk costs, assume that Jack Bennett had invested $400 in a tiller so that he could till gardens to earn $1,500 during the summer. He is now offered the opportunity of working at a horse stable feeding horses and cleaning stalls for a salary of $1,200 for the summer. The costs that he would incur in tilling are $100 for transportation and $150 for supplies. The costs he would incur at the horse stable are $100 for transportation and $50 for supplies. If Jack works at the stable, he would still have the tiller, and it would be used by his parents and loaned to friends at no charge. The tiller cost of $400 is not relevant to the decision because it is a sunk cost. The transportation cost of $100 is also not relevant because it is the same for both alternatives. The relevant costs and revenues are shown below:

	Performing Tilling Service	Working at Horse Stable	Differential
Revenues.	$1,500	$1,200	$300
Costs	150	50	100
Net benefit in favor of tilling service			$200

Based on this differential analysis, Jack Bennett should perform his tilling service rather than work at the stable.

In many situations, total variable costs differ between alternatives while total fixed costs do not. But one cannot assume that variable costs are always differential costs and fixed costs are never differential costs. For example, the differential cost between operating at a production level of 40,000 units versus a production level of 60,000 units might include increases in both variable and fixed costs. This increase in fixed costs could be the result of a step fixed cost, such as that related to the number of supervisors necessary for a particular production level.

---

[1]Some authors equate relevant cost and differential cost. This text uses the term *relevant* to identify which costs should be considered in a situation and the term *differential* to identify the amount by which these costs differ.

The Nature of Fixed Costs

Up to this point in our discussion, fixed costs have been treated as if they were all alike. But two types of fixed costs should be identified. They are committed fixed costs and discretionary fixed costs.

Committed fixed costs. **Committed fixed costs** relate to the basic facilities and organization structure that a company must have to continue operations. These costs are not changed in the short run without seriously disrupting operations. Examples of committed fixed costs are depreciation on buildings and equipment and salaries of key executives. In the short run, costs such as these are viewed as not being subject to the discretion or control of management. They result from past decisions that "committed" the company for a period of several years. For instance, once a company constructs a building to house production operations, it is committed to the use of the building for many years. Thus, the depreciation on that building is not as subject to control by management as are some other types of fixed costs.

Discretionary fixed costs. In contrast to committed fixed costs, **discretionary fixed costs** are subject to management control from year to year. Each year management decides how much to spend on advertising, research and development, and employee training and development programs. Since these decisions are made each year, they are said to be under the "discretion" of management. Management is not locked in or committed to a certain level of expense for any more than one budget period. The next period it may change the level of expense or may eliminate it completely.

The philosophy of management can affect to some extent which fixed costs are committed and which are discretionary. For instance, during the recession of the mid-1970s, some companies terminated persons in the upper levels of management, while other companies kept their "management team" intact. Thus, in some companies the salaries of top-level managers were discretionary while in others they were committed.

The discussion of committed fixed costs and discretionary fixed costs is relevant to CVP analysis. If a company's fixed costs are almost all committed fixed costs, it is going to have a more difficult time in reducing its break-even point for the next budget period than if most of its fixed costs are discretionary in nature. A company with a large proportion of discretionary fixed costs may be able to reduce fixed costs dramatically in a recessionary period. By doing this, it may be able to "run lean" and show some income even when economic conditions are difficult. Its chances of long-run survival may be enhanced.

Opportunity Cost

Another cost concept relevant to decision making is opportunity cost. An **opportunity cost** is the potential benefit that is forgone from *not* following the next best alternative course of action. For instance, assume that the two best uses of a plot of land are as a mobile home park (annual income of $100,000) and as a golf driving range (annual income of $60,000). The opportunity cost of utilizing the land as a mobile home park is $60,000, while the opportunity cost of utilizing the land as a driving range is $100,000. Opportunity costs are not recorded in the accounting records since they are the costs of not following a certain alternative. However, opportunity cost is a relevant cost in many decision problems because it represents a real sacrifice that comes about because one alternative is chosen instead of another.

Applications of Differential Analysis

Objective 6:
Calculate the various applications of differential analysis

To illustrate the application of differential analysis to specific decision problems, we will now consider five types of decisions: (1) setting prices of products; (2) accepting or rejecting special orders; (3) eliminating products, segments, or customers; (4) processing or selling joint products; and (5) deciding to make or buy. These five types of decisions are not the only applications of differential analysis, but they represent typical short-term business decisions to which differential analysis can properly be applied.

Setting prices of products. When differential analysis is applied to pricing decisions, each possible price for a given product represents an alternative course of action. The sales revenues for each alternative and the costs that differ between alternatives are the relevant amounts in these decisions. Total fixed costs usually remain the same between pricing alternatives and, if so, may be ignored. In selecting a price for a product, the goal is to select the price at which total future revenues will exceed total future variable costs by the greatest amount or, in other words, the price that will result in the greatest total contribution margin.

A high price is not necessarily the price that will maximize income. There may be many substitutes for the product. If a high price is set, the number of units sold may decline substantially as customers switch to lower-priced competitive products. Thus, in the maximization of income, the expected volume of sales at each price is as important as the contribution margin per unit of product sold. In making any pricing decision, management should seek the combination of price and volume that will produce the largest total contribution margin. This combination is often difficult to identify in an actual situation since management may have to estimate the number of units that can be sold at each price.

For example, assume that a company has fixed costs of $10,000 and variable production costs of $5 per unit. Estimates of product demand are:

Choice	Demand
1	20,000 units at $4 per unit
2	15,000 units at $6 per unit
3	10,000 units at $8 per unit
4	5,000 units at $10 per unit

What price should be set for the product? Based on the calculations shown below, the company should select a price of $8 per unit (choice 3) since this will result in the greatest total contribution margin ($30,000).

Choice	Contribution Margin per Unit*	×	Number of Units	=	Total Contribution Margin
1	$-1		20,000		$-20,000
2	1		15,000		15,000
3	3		10,000		30,000
4	5		5,000		25,000

*Sales price—Variable cost.

Accepting or rejecting special orders. Sometimes management is faced with the opportunity to sell its product in two or more markets at two or more different prices. Price discrimination is unlawful under the Robinson-Patman Act unless it is justified by differences in costs of delivery or selling. Since such cost differences often exist, a single product may be marketed at more than one selling price. Differential analysis can be used to determine if special orders (orders at a price different from the norm) should be accepted.

The desirability of keeping physical facilities and personnel working at capacity is obvious. Good business management requires keeping the cost of idleness at a minimum. When operations are at a level less than full capacity, additional business should be sought. Such additional business may be accepted at prices lower than average unit costs because the only relevant costs are the future additional costs that will be incurred. For the most part, the relevant costs will be variable costs, such as direct materials and direct labor.

To illustrate, assume that a given company produces and sells a single product that has a variable cost of $8 per unit. Annual capacity is 10,000 units, and annual fixed costs total $48,000. The selling price is $20 per unit, and production and sales are budgeted at 5,000 units. Thus, budgeted net income before taxes is $12,000, computed as follows:

Sales (5,000 units at $20)		$100,000
Costs:		
Fixed	$48,000	
Variable (5,000 units at $8)	40,000	88,000
Net income before taxes		$ 12,000

Assume an order for 3,000 units is received from a foreign distributor at a price of $10 per unit. This $10 price is only half of the regular selling price per unit and is also less than the average cost per unit of $17.60 ($88,000 ÷ 5,000 units). But the $10 price offered exceeds the variable cost per unit by $2. If the order is accepted, net income will be $18,000, computed as follows:

Sales (5,000 units at $20, 3,000 units at $10)		$130,000
Costs:		
Fixed	$48,000	
Variable (8,000 units at $8)	64,000	112,000
Net income before taxes		$ 18,000

To continue to operate at 50% capacity (producing 5,000 units) would produce net income of only $12,000. A contribution margin of $2 per unit on the new units will result from acceptance of the order; thus, net income will increase by $6,000. Because the regular market is unlikely to be affected by the export of the product at a sharply reduced price, the order should be accepted assuming it does not violate international trade agreements.

Differential analysis would provide the following calculations:

	(1) Accept Order	(2) Reject Order	Differential
Revenues	$130,000	$100,000	$30,000
Costs	64,000	40,000	24,000
Net benefit in favor of accepting order . .			$ 6,000

In summary, variable costs set a floor for the selling price in cost analyses. Even if the price exceeds variable costs only slightly, the additional business may make a contribution to income. But "contribution pricing" of marginal business often brings only short-term increases in income. Such pricing should be appraised in light of the long-range effects on company and industry price structures. In the long run, full costs must be covered.

Eliminating products, segments, or customers. Periodically, management has to decide whether to eliminate or retain certain products, segments, or customers. Differential analysis can be useful in this type of decision making. Since the income statement does not automatically associate costs with given products, segments, or customers, costs must be reclassified as those that *would be changed* by the elimination and those that *would not*. In effect, one must simply assume elimination and compare the reduction in revenues with the eliminated costs.

Usually costs such as direct materials, direct labor, and other variable costs would be eliminated and, therefore, become part of differential costs. The fixed costs will normally remain unaffected and, if so, are not relevant to the decision. If revenues lost from discontinuing the product, segment, or customer exceed the costs that would be eliminated, then that item is making a positive contribution to profits and should, therefore, be retained unless a more profitable opportunity exists.

To illustrate, assume that the elimination of product R is being considered. Product R provides revenues of $100,000 annually and incurs costs of $110,000, $80,000 variable and $30,000 fixed. Therefore, product R creates an apparent annual loss of $10,000. But careful cost analysis reveals that if product R were dropped, the reduction in costs would be $80,000. The $30,000 fixed costs would continue to be incurred and would need to be covered by the remaining products of the company. The analysis is as follows:

	(1) Retain Product R	(2) Drop Product R	Differential
Revenues	$100,000	$–0–	$100,000
Costs	80,000	–0–	80,000
Net benefit of retaining product R . . .			$ 20,000

This illustration shows that product R, even though it produces no net income itself, has been contributing $20,000 ($100,000 revenues − $80,000 variable costs) annually to covering the fixed costs of the business. In other words, product R has a contribution to indirect expenses of $20,000. Consequently, its elimination could be a costly mistake unless there is a more profitable use for the released facilities.

If there is a profitable alternative use for those facilities, the potential income from that alternative represents an opportunity cost of retaining product R. Assume, for example, that those facilities could be used to manufacture a product that would contribute $30,000 to the company's income. In this case, the relevant costs in the decision to retain product R are $110,000 ($80,000 of variable manufacturing costs and $30,000 of opportunity cost), while the relevant revenues are still $100,000. Therefore, the net advantage of keeping product R is $−10,000, meaning that product R should not be retained. Similarly, when analyzing the decision to replace product R with the alternative, the $20,000 contribution to indirect expenses that is foregone if product R is replaced becomes an opportunity cost of the alternative product.

Processing or selling joint products. In some manufacturing situations, several products result from a common raw material or manufacturing process; these products are called **joint products.** For instance, when crude oil is manufactured, a wide variety of fuels, solvents, lubricants, and residual petrochemicals are derived. Some of these products can be processed further or sold in their existing condition. Management can use differential analysis to decide whether to process a joint product further or to sell it in its present condition. **Joint costs** are those costs incurred up to the point where the joint products split off from each other. These costs are sunk costs in deciding whether to process a joint product further before selling it or to sell it in its condition at split-off.

The following example will illustrate the issue of whether to process or sell joint products. Assume that Company Y manufactures two products, A and B, from a common manufacturing process. Each of the products could be sold in its present form or could be processed further and sold at a higher price. Data for both products are given below:

Product	Selling Price per Unit at Split-Off Point	Cost per Unit of Further Processing	Selling Price per Unit after Further Processing
A	$10	$6	$21
B	12	7	18

The differential revenues and costs of further processing of the two products are as follows:

Product	Differential Revenue of Further Processing	Differential Cost of Further Processing	Net Advantage (Disadvantage) of Further Processing
A	$11	$6	$ 5
B	6	7	(1)

Based on this analysis, product A should be processed further since it will increase income by $5 per unit sold. Product B should not be processed further, for doing so would decrease income by $1 per unit sold.

This same form of differential analysis should also be used in deciding whether **by-products,** the waste materials that result from the production of a product, should be discarded or processed further to be made saleable. If the differential revenue of further processing exceeds the differential cost, then further processing should be done. If not, the waste material should be discarded.

Deciding to make or buy. Differential analysis can also be applied to make-or-buy decisions. A **make-or-buy decision** concerns whether to manufacture or purchase a part or material used in the manufacture of another product. The price that would be paid for the part if it were purchased is compared with the additional costs that would be incurred if the part were manufactured. If almost all of the manufacturing costs are fixed and would exist in any case, it is likely that manufacture rather than purchase of the part or material would be more economical.

To illustrate the application of differential analysis to a make-or-buy decision, assume that a company manufactures parts costing $6 each for use in its final product. Cost components are materials, $3; labor, $1.50; fixed overhead costs, $1.05; and variable overhead costs, $0.45. The part could be purchased for $5.25. Since fixed overhead would presumably continue even if the part were purchased, manufacture of the part should be continued. The added costs of manufacturing amount to only $4.95 ($3.00 + $1.50 + $0.45). This amount is 30 cents per unit less than the purchase price of the part, as shown in the following analysis:

	(1) Make	(2) Buy	Differential
Costs	$4.95	$5.25	$0.30
Net advantage of making			$0.30

The opportunity cost of not utilizing the space for some other purpose should also be considered. If the opportunity cost of not using this space in its best alternative use is more than 30 cents per unit times the number of units produced, then the part should be purchased.

In some manufacturing situations, it is possible to avoid a portion of fixed costs by buying from an outside source. For example, if the part was no longer produced, a segment supervisor's salary (a fixed cost) could be eliminated, thereby reducing fixed costs by the amount of that salary. In such a situation, these fixed costs should be treated the same as variable costs in the analysis, since they would then be relevant costs.

It is also possible that the cost to manufacture may be only slightly less than the cost of purchasing the part or material. In this case, other factors should be considered, such as the competency of existing personnel to undertake manufacture of the part or material, the availability of working capital, and the cost of any loans that may be necessary.

ABSORPTION VERSUS DIRECT COSTING

Objective 7: Compare and contrast absorption costing and direct costing

As the final consideration in short-term decision making, a new form of income statement and product costing will be introduced. Currently, the most commonly accepted theory and method of product costing is called absorption or full costing. Under **absorption (or full) costing,** all production costs, including fixed manufacturing overhead, are accounted for as product costs and are allocated to the units of product produced during a period. Absorption costing is the theory on which the discussion of product costing in Chapters 14 and 15 was based. Another method, **direct (or variable) costing,** on the other hand, includes only variable manufacturing costs as product costs. All fixed manufacturing overhead costs are charged to expense in the period in which they are incurred. The difference between the income statements under the two methods is that absorption costing focuses on gross margin, while direct costing focuses on contribution margin.

The differences between absorption and direct costing can be seen by comparing the income statements that would result from applying each technique to the same data. Assume the Bradley Company had the following data related to manufacturing and sales activities for May 1990.

BRADLEY COMPANY
May 1990

Beginning inventory (units)	–0–	Variable costs (per unit):	
Production (units)	10,000	Direct materials	$2.00
Sales (units)	9,000	Direct labor	1.00
		Manufacturing overhead	0.30
		Total	$3.30
Fixed costs:			
Manufacturing overhead	$ 6,000	Variable selling expenses	
Selling expenses	15,000	(per unit)	$0.20
Administrative expenses	12,000	Selling price (per unit)	$8.00

Absorption Costing

Under absorption costing, fixed manufacturing overhead costs would be applied to the units of production at the rate of $0.60 per unit ($6,000/10,000 units). Therefore, the cost per unit of inventory is $3.90, the total of the direct materials, direct labor, and variable and fixed manufacturing overhead. All selling and administrative expenses are period costs. Illustration 19.9 contains the income statement for the Bradley Company prepared under absorption costing.

Generally, variable and fixed manufacturing costs do not appear as separate line items on the income statement; they are presented this way simply to illustrate that the fixed manufacturing costs are included as part of product cost and that some of these costs are included in ending inventory. Ending inventory is priced at "full cost" of $3.90 per unit ($39,000/10,000). Also, no distinction is made between fixed and variable selling expenses. These are totaled and shown under operating expenses of the period.

Absorption costing is required for external financial statement presentation and also for tax purposes. But, as shown throughout this chapter, a

Illustration 19.9
INCOME STATEMENT UNDER ABSORPTION COSTING

BRADLEY COMPANY
Income Statement
For the Period Ending May 31, 1990

Sales (9,000 units at $8)		$72,000
Cost of goods sold:		
Variable costs of production (10,000 units at $3.30)	$33,000	
Fixed overhead costs.	6,000	
Total costs of producing 10,000 units	$39,000	
Less: Ending inventory (1,000 units at $3.90)	3,900	35,100
Gross margin on sales		$36,900
Operating expenses:		
Selling ($15,000 fixed plus 9,000 at $0.20 each)	$16,800	
Administrative	12,000	28,800
Net income before taxes		$ 8,100

"full" cost approach is not necessarily the best approach for internal management decision making. Management often needs information on contribution margin rather than gross margin to calculate break-even points and make decisions regarding special-order pricing. Direct costing presents this information in a more obvious and prominent form.

Direct Costing

Under direct costing, all *variable* costs of production (direct materials, direct labor, and variable manufacturing overhead) are treated as product costs. Product costs attach to the product and only become an expense (cost of goods sold) when the products are sold. All *fixed* manufacturing overhead costs are considered period costs and are charged to expense in the period received. The logic behind this expensing of fixed manufacturing overhead is that such costs would be incurred whether there was production or whether the plant was idle; therefore, these fixed costs do not specifically relate to the manufacture of products. The direct costing income statement for Bradley Company for May 1990 is presented in Illustration 19.10.

Notice in the direct cost income statement that the goods in inventory are carried at $3.30 per unit rather than at the $3.90 full cost. All variable costs are shown separately at the top of the statement as deductions from sales to disclose contribution margin for the month. All fixed costs are classified as period costs no matter what the source of the cost (manufacturing, selling, or administrative).

Comparing the Two Methods

Comparing the two income statements, there is a $600 difference in net income before taxes for the month and a $600 difference in ending inventory valuation. These differences are due to the treatment of fixed

Illustration 19.10
INCOME STATEMENT UNDER DIRECT COSTING

BRADLEY COMPANY
Income Statement
For the Period Ending May 31, 1990

Sales (9,000 units at $8)		$72,000
Variable costs:		
Variable production costs incurred (10,000 units at $3.30) . .	$33,000	
Less: Ending inventory (1,000 units at $3.30)	3,300	29,700
Manufacturing margin		$42,300
Variable selling expenses (9,000 units at $0.20)		1,800
Contribution margin		$40,500
Fixed costs:		
Manufacturing overhead	$ 6,000	
Selling expenses	15,000	
Administrative expenses	12,000	33,000
Net income before taxes		$ 7,500

---

manufacturing overhead costs. Under absorption costing, each unit in ending inventory carries $0.60 of fixed overhead cost as part of product cost. There are 1,000 units in inventory at the end of the month; therefore, ending inventory under absorption costing includes $600 of fixed manufacturing overhead costs ($0.60 × 1,000 units) and is valued at $600 more than under direct costing. Under direct costing, all the fixed manufacturing overhead costs are charged off during the period rather than being deferred and carried forward to the next period as part of inventory cost. Therefore, $6,000 of fixed manufacturing overhead costs appear on the direct costing income statement as an expense, rather than $5,400 ($6,000 fixed manufacturing overhead costs −$600 fixed manufacturing overhead included in inventory) under absorption costing. Consequently, net income before taxes under direct costing is $600 less than under absorption costing because more expense is charged off during the period.

As a final point of emphasis, recognize that the difference between the two methods is solely in the treatment of fixed manufacturing overhead costs and income statement presentation. Selling and administrative expenses are treated as period costs under both methods. The only difference in regard to these costs is their placement on the income statement and the segregation of variable and fixed selling and administrative expenses. Variable selling and administrative expenses are not part of product cost under either method.

The analysis is slightly more complicated when both beginning and ending inventories are involved. The difference in net income before taxes is found by determining whether the amount of fixed manufacturing overhead costs included in inventory cost under absorption costing increased or decreased from the beginning to the end of the period. If that amount increased, net income before taxes under direct costing will be less than under absorption costing. If the amount of fixed manufacturing overhead costs included in inventory decreased during the period, net income before taxes under direct costing will be greater than under absorption costing. (Demonstration Problem 19–2 illustrates how to determine net income before taxes when both beginning and ending inventories are involved.)

As a general rule, the difference in net income before taxes under the two methods can be related to the change in inventories. Assuming a relatively constant level of production, if inventories increase during the year, then production exceeded sales, and reported net income before taxes will be less under direct costing than under absorption costing. Conversely, if inventories decreased, then sales exceeded production, and net income before taxes will be larger under direct costing than under absorption costing.

Direct costing is not currently considered acceptable for income measurement, inventory valuation, or tax purposes. Currently accepted practice requires that all costs of producing a product be attached to that product and treated as expenses only when the product is sold. But the type of information accumulated under direct costing, especially the classification of costs as fixed and variable, is very useful to management in understanding relationships between costs, volume, and profits. Since direct costing is such a valuable management tool, its use is likely to increase.

SUMMARY

The short term (or short run) is defined as that period of time in which the effects of certain past decisions cannot be changed. As a result, some costs are fixed in the short run, while others vary with changes in the level of activity. For purposes of short-term decision making, management must attempt to classify all costs as fixed or variable to understand how total costs will react to changes in the volume of production or sales.

There are four basic types of cost behavior patterns—variable costs, fixed costs, mixed (or semivariable) costs, and step costs. Various techniques exist for analyzing actual cost data to identify the underlying cost patterns. These techniques include the scatter diagram, the high-low method, and sophisticated statistical techniques like the least squares method.

The chapter discusses three topics related to short-term decision making—cost-volume-profit (CVP) analysis, differential analysis, and direct costing. CVP analysis is a technique used to estimate the relationship between selling prices, costs, the company's volume of operations, and net income in the short run. The starting point for CVP analysis is the company's break-even point, which means the level of operations at which revenues and costs are equal. Once that is determined, management can look at the changes in income that would result if selling prices, fixed costs, or variable costs were changed. In addition, management can compute the level of operations required to produce a certain amount of income.

Differential analysis is another tool of short-term analysis. In differential analysis, a particular set of alternatives is analyzed by looking at the revenues and costs or expenses that will differ in the future, depending on which alternative is chosen. Such revenues and costs are designated as relevant revenues and relevant costs for differential analysis. Differential revenue is the amount by which relevant revenues differ between alternatives. Differential cost or expense is the amount by which total expense differs between alternatives. In differential analysis, the preferred alternative is the one that provides the largest positive difference between differential revenue and differential expense. A number of specific types of decisions can be addressed through differential analysis including the following: setting prices of products; accepting or rejecting special orders; eliminating products, segments, or customers; processing or selling joint products; and deciding to make or buy.

Under absorption (or full) costing all manufacturing costs are treated as product costs. Under direct (or variable) costing only variable manufacturing costs are treated as product costs; fixed manufacturing overhead costs are considered to be period costs. Absorption costing is required for financial reporting purposes. Direct costing, however, provides cost information that is useful to management for many decision-making purposes, including CVP analysis and differential analysis. As a general rule, the difference in the net income before taxes computed under each of the methods is related to the change in inventories over the period. If there is no change in inventories, both methods give the same net income before taxes amount.

In this chapter you studied the importance of short-run planning. Chapter 20 discusses long-range planning regarding the acquisition of capital assets. All businesses must establish long-range goals and must plan for the future to be successful.

Objective 8:
Define and use
correctly the new
terms introduced
in the chapter

NEW TERMS INTRODUCED IN CHAPTER 19

Absorption (or full) costing   A concept of costing under which all production costs, including fixed manufacturing overhead, are accounted for as product costs and allocated to the units produced during a period (688).

Break-even analysis   See Cost-volume-profit analysis.

Break-even chart   A graph that shows the relationships between sales, costs, volume, and profit and also shows the break-even point (672).

Break-even point   That level of operations at which revenues for a period are equal to the costs assigned to that period so that there is no net income or loss (670).

By-products   The waste materials (which sometimes have a small market value compared to the main product) that result from the production of a product or products (687).

Committed fixed costs Costs relating to the basic facilities and organization structure that a company must have to continue operations. An example is depreciation on the factory building (682).

Contribution margin The amount by which revenue exceeds the variable costs of producing that revenue (671).

Contribution margin rate Contribution margin per unit divided by selling price per unit (672).

Cost-volume-profit (CVP) analysis An analysis of the effects that any changes in a company's selling prices, costs, and/or volume will have upon income (profits) in the short run. Also called break-even analysis (670).

Differential analysis An analysis of the different costs and benefits that would arise from alternative solutions to a particular problem (680).

Differential cost or expense The difference between the amounts of relevant costs for two alternatives (680).

Differential revenue The difference between the amounts of relevant revenues for two alternatives (680).

Direct (or variable) costing A concept of costing under which only variable manufacturing costs are accounted for as product costs and charged to the units produced during a period. All fixed manufacturing overhead is charged to expense in the period in which it is incurred (688).

Discretionary fixed costs Fixed costs that are subject to management control from year to year. An example is advertising expense (682).

Fixed costs Costs that remain constant (in total) over some relevant range of output (666).

High-low method A method used in dividing mixed costs into their fixed and variable portions. The high plot and low plot of actual costs are used to draw a line representing a total mixed cost (670).

Joint costs Those costs incurred up to the point where joint products split off from each other (686).

Joint products Two or more products resulting from a common raw material or manufacturing process (686).

Make-or-buy decision Concerns whether to manufacture or purchase a part or material used in the manufacture of another product (687).

Margin of safety Amount by which sales can decrease before a loss will be incurred (676).

Margin of safety rate Margin of safety expressed as a percentage; is equal to (Current sales − Break-even sales) ÷ Current sales (676).

Mixed cost Contains a fixed portion of cost that will be incurred even when the plant is completely idle and a variable portion that will increase directly with production volume (666).

Opportunity cost The potential benefit that is foregone from not following the next best alternative course of action (682).

Product mix The proportion of the company's total sales attributable to each type of product sold. Product mix may be defined either in terms of sales dollars or in terms of the number of units sold (679).

Relevant revenues or costs Revenues or costs that will differ in the future depending on which alternative course of action is selected (680).

Relevant range The range of production or sales volume over which the basic cost behavior assumptions will hold true (672).

Scatter diagram A diagram that shows plots of actual costs incurred for various levels of output or sales; it is used in dividing mixed costs into their fixed and variable portions (669).

Short run (short term) The period of time over which it is assumed that plant capacity and certain costs are fixed; often determined to be one year or less (665).

Step cost A cost that remains constant in total over a range of output (or sales) but then increases in steps at certain points (667).

Sunk costs Past costs about which nothing can be done; they are not relevant in decision making because the costs have already been incurred (681).

Variable costs Costs that vary (in total) directly with changes in volume (665).

Variable cost rate Variable costs expressed as a percentage of sales; used to find the break-even point (671).

DEMONSTRATION PROBLEM 19–1

The Miles Company has fixed costs of $325,000 per year and variable costs of $9 per unit. Its product sells for $15 per unit. Full capacity is 200,000 units. Variable costs are 60% of sales ($9/$15).

Required:

a. Compute the break-even point in (1) sales dollars, (2) units, and (3) percentage of capacity.

b. Compute the number of units the company must sell if it wishes to have net income of $200,000.

Solution to demonstration problem 19–1

a. (1) Sales (S) = Fixed costs (FC) + Variable costs (VC)

$$S = \$325,000 + .60S$$
$$.40S = \$325,000$$
$$S = \$325,000 \div .40$$
$$S = \underline{\underline{\$812,500}}$$

(2) Break-even point in units = $812,500 ÷ $15 = $\underline{\underline{54,167}}$ or $\dfrac{\$325,000}{\$15 - \$9} = \underline{\underline{54,167}}$

(3) Break-even point as percentage of capacity = 54,167 ÷ 200,000 = $\underline{\underline{27.1\%}}$

b. Number of units $= \dfrac{\text{Fixed cost} + \text{Desired net income}}{\text{Contribution margin}}$

$$= \dfrac{\$325,000 + \$200,000}{\$15 - \$9}$$

$$= \dfrac{\$525,000}{\$6}$$

$$= \$87,500$$

DEMONSTRATION PROBLEM 19–2

The Atlanta Division of the Curtis Company produces a single product that it sells for $18 each. Production costs include $3 per unit variable costs and $360,000 per year of fixed manufacturing overhead costs. Normal activity for fixed manufacturing overhead cost absorption is 150,000 units per year. Thus, fixed manufacturing overhead costs are applied at $2.40 per unit. Selling and administrative expenses are $30,000 plus $0.60 per unit sold.

On December 31, 1990, the division's finished goods inventory consisted of 60,000 units with a total cost of $324,000 ($180,000, variable; $144,000, fixed). Sales and production data for 1991 are:

Sales in units	120,000
Dollars of sales	$2,160,000
Production in units	150,000
Variable production costs	$ 450,000

Required:

a. Prepare an income statement for the division for 1991 under absorption costing.

b. Prepare an income statement for the division for 1991 under direct costing.

Solution to demonstration problem 19–2

a. Income statement under absorption costing:

CURTIS COMPANY (Atlanta Division)
Income Statement
For the Year Ended December 31, 1991

Sales (120,000 units at $18)			$2,160,000
Cost of goods sold:			
Beginning finished goods inventory (absorption cost $5.40 per unit)		$324,000	
Variable production costs ($3 per unit)	$450,000		
Fixed manufacturing overhead costs absorbed ($2.40 per unit)	360,000		
Cost of goods manufactured		810,000	
Ending finished goods inventory (absorption cost $5.40 per unit)		(486,000)	
Cost of goods sold			648,000
Gross margin on sales			$1,512,000
Selling and administrative expenses			102,000
Net income			$1,410,000

b. Income statement under direct costing:

CURTIS COMPANY (Atlanta Division)
Income Statement
For the Year Ended December 31, 1991

Sales (120,000 units at $18)		$2,160,000
Cost of goods sold:		
Beginning finished goods inventory		
(direct cost $3 per unit)	$ 180,000	
Direct cost of goods manufactured ($3 per unit)	450,000	
Ending finished goods inventory		
(direct cost of $3 per unit)	(270,000)	
Cost of goods sold		360,000
Manufacturing margin		$1,800,000
Variable selling and administrative expenses		72,000
Contribution margin		$1,728,000
Period costs:		
Fixed manufacturing overhead	$ 360,000	
Fixed selling and administrative expenses	30,000	390,000
Net income		$1,338,000

QUESTIONS

1. Name and describe the four types of cost patterns.

2. What is meant by the term *break-even point*? What factors must be taken into consideration in determining the break-even point?

3. What are the different ways in which the break-even point may be expressed?

4. Why is break-even analysis considered appropriate only for short-run decisions?

5. Why might a business wish to lower its break-even point? How would it go about lowering the break-even point? What effect would you expect the mechanization and automation of production processes to have upon the break-even point?

6. What is a committed fixed cost? Give some examples.

7. What is a discretionary fixed cost? Give some examples.

8. Identify some types of decisions that can be made using differential analysis.

9. What essential feature distinguishes direct costing from absorption costing?

10. Under what specific circumstances would you expect net income to be larger under direct costing than under absorption costing? What is the specific reason for this difference?

EXERCISES

Compute break-even point in sales dollars

1. Compute the break-even point for a company in which fixed costs amount to $425,000 and variable costs are 60 percent of sales.

Analyze mixed cost using high-low method

2. The Williams Company uses the high-low method in determining the cost line for a mixed cost. Assume that the low and high plots are as follows:

Volume	Cost
8,000	$10,000
20,000	16,000

Determine the variable cost per unit and the amount of total fixed costs.

3. The King Company sells each unit it produces for $12, with fixed costs of $75,000 and variable cost of $7 per unit. Find the break-even point in units.

4. Butler Company is currently producing and selling 10,000 units of a given product at $12 per unit. Its average cost of production and sale is $8 per unit. It is contemplating an attempt to sell 40,000 units at $9 each. At this level, the average cost per unit will be $7.50. At which level should it seek to operate?

5. If a given company has fixed costs of $125,000 and variable costs of production of $11.50 per unit, how many units would the company have to sell at a price of $17.50 each in order to break-even? How many units would it have to sell in order to earn $55,000? If 200,000 units represents 100 percent of capacity, what percentage of capacity does this latter level of operations represent?

6. Using the data in Exercise 5, what would be the effect on the break-even point if (consider each separately):

a. The price per unit were increased to $19.50?

b. Fixed costs were lowered by $20,000?

c. Variable costs were reduced to $10 per unit?

7. The Tucker Company sells three products. Last year's sales were $80,000 for product X, $95,000 for product Y, and $60,000 for product Z. Variable costs were X, $55,000; Y, $65,000; and Z, $33,000. Fixed costs were $35,000. Determine the break-even point.

8. Assume you had invested $120 in a lawn mower to set up a lawn mowing business for the summer. During the first week, you are presented with two opportunities. You can mow the grounds at a housing development for $150, or you can help paint a garage for $125. The additional costs you will incur are $25 and $10, respectively. These costs include $2 under each alternative for a pair of gloves that will last the entire summer. Prepare a schedule showing:

a. The relevant revenues and expenses (costs).

b. The differential revenue and expense.

c. The net benefit or advantage of selecting one alternative over the other.

9. Department 3 of the Harris Company has revenues of $200,000, variable expenses of $80,000, direct fixed expenses of $40,000, and allocated, indirect fixed expenses of $100,000. If the department is eliminated, what will be the effect on net income before taxes?

10. The Craig Company manufactures two joint products. At the split-off point, they have sales values of:

Product 1:	$14/unit
Product 2:	$10/unit

After further processing costing $8 and $6, respectively, they can be sold for $30 and $14, respectively. Should further processing be done on these products? Why?

Compute net income
before taxes under
direct and
absorption costing

11. The following data are for Top Company for the year 1990:

Sales (40,000 units)	$600,000
Direct materials used (48,000 units @ $2.25)	108,000
Direct labor cost incurred	72,000
Manufacturing overhead incurred:	
Variable	21,600
Fixed	28,800
Selling and administrative expenses:	
Variable	36,000
Fixed	120,000

Assume that one unit of direct materials goes into each unit of finished goods. There is a beginning inventory of finished goods of 4,000 units, and there are no other beginning or ending work in process inventories. The variable and fixed overhead rates (based on normal activity of 48,000 units) are $0.45 and $0.60, respectively. Compute the net income before taxes under (*a*) absorption costing and (*b*) direct costing.

PROBLEMS

Determine
break-even point;
determine projected
net income

19–1. The Tucker Company is operating at almost 100% of capacity. The company expects the demand for its product to increase by 25% next year (1991). In order to satisfy the demand for its product, the company is considering two alternatives. The first alternative involves a capital outlay which will increase fixed costs by 15%, but will have no effect on variable costs. The second alternative will not affect fixed costs, but will cause variable costs to increase to 60% of the selling price of the company's product.

The Tucker Company's condensed income statement for 1990 is shown below:

Sales		$5,000,000
Costs:		
Variable	$2,500,000	
Fixed	800,000	3,300,000
Net income before taxes		$1,700,000

Required:

a. Determine the break-even point for 1991 under each of the alternatives.

b. Determine the projected net income before taxes for 1991 under each of the alternatives.

c. Which alternative would you recommend? Why?

Prepare a break-
even chart; compute
break-even point by
using the equation;
determine units
needed to be sold
to reach desired
income level

19–2. The Caldwell Corporation has a plant capacity of 100,000 units. The variable costs amount to $400,000 at 100% capacity. The fixed costs amount to $300,000, but management thinks that this is probably only true between 20,000 and 80,000 units.

Required:

a. Prepare a break-even chart for the Caldwell Corporation, assuming that its product sells for $10 per unit. Be sure to indicate the relevant range, contribution margin, and net income on the chart.

b. Compute the break-even point by using the equation to verify your chart.

c. How many units must be sold to have net income (ignoring taxes) of $30,000?

Compute break-even point; prepare condensed operating statements

19–3. Following is a summary of operations in 1990 for two companies:

	Company A		Company B	
Sales		$300,000		$300,000
Expenses:				
Fixed	$ 75,000		$200,000	
Variable	200,000		75,000	
Total expenses		275,000		275,000
Net operating income . . .		$ 25,000		$ 25,000

Required:

a. Compute the break-even point for each company.

b. Assume that without changes in selling prices, the sales of each company decreased by 25%. Prepare condensed operating statements, similar to the ones above, which show the effect of the decrease in sales on the operating income of each company.

Determine net income and break-even under different conditions

19–4. **a.** In 1990, the Widner Company's sales were $187,500 and its variable costs amounted to $46,875. The company's break-even point is at a sales volume of $200,000. Determine the amount of its fixed costs. What was the net income for 1990?

b. What would have been the net income of the Widner Company in part (**a**) above if the 1990 sales volume had been 10% higher but selling prices had remained unchanged?

c. What would have been the net income of the Widner Company in part (**a**) above if the 1990 variable costs had been 10% lower?

d. What would have been the net income of the Widner Company in part (**a**) above if the fixed costs in 1990 had been 10% lower?

e. Determine the break-even point for the Widner Company on the basis of the data given in both part (**c**) above and part (**d**) above.

Determine the break-even point assuming different sales mixes

19–5. The Spencer Company has fixed costs of $80,000. It sells four products. Its sales and variable costs during 1990 were as follows:

	Products			
	A	B	C	D
Sales	$60,000	$30,000	$70,000	$40,000
Variable costs . . .	40,000	25,000	35,000	15,000

Required:

a. Determine the break-even point for 1991, assuming that the sales mix will remain the same as it was in 1990.

b. Determine the break-even point for 1991, assuming that the sales mix is expected to be in the ratio of 10-30-15-45.

Determine fixed and variable costs using the high-low method

19–6. The Ellis Company has identified the variable and fixed costs in its operations. There is a mixed cost which needs to be divided into its fixed and variable portions. The actual data pertaining to this cost are as follows:

Year	Units	Cost
1990	5,200	$6,400
1991	5,000	6,000
1992	5,500	6,700
1993	6,400	6,400
1994	7,100	6,500
1995	7,500	6,900
1996	8,200	7,100
1997	8,900	7,600
1998	9,400	8,000
1999	10,000	8,600

Required:

Using the high-low method, determine the total amount of fixed costs and the amount of variable cost per unit. Draw the cost line.

Prepare an income statement under variable costing; prepare an income statement under absorption costing; explain differences

19–7. Fowler Company employs an absorption cost system in accounting for the single product it manufactures. Following are selected data for the year 1990:

Sales	$1,200,000
Direct materials used (24,000 units @ $18)	432,000
Direct labor cost incurred	144,000
Variable manufacturing overhead	43,200
Fixed manufacturing overhead	57,600
Variable selling and administrative expenses . . .	72,000
Fixed selling and administrative expenses	240,000

One unit of direct materials goes into each unit of finished goods. Overhead rates are based on a capacity of 24,000 units and are $1.80 and $2.40 per unit for variable and fixed overhead, respectively. The only beginning or ending inventory is the 8,000 units of finished goods on hand at the end of 1990.

Required:

a. Prepare an income statement for 1990 under variable costing.

b. Prepare an income statement for 1990 under absorption costing.

c. Explain the reason for the difference in net income before taxes between (**a**) and (**b**).

BUSINESS DECISION PROBLEM 19–1:

Compute break-even point; determine point at which factory should shut down rather than produce

When the plant of the Davis Company is completely idle, fixed costs amount to $400,000. When the plant operates at levels of 50% of capacity and below, its fixed costs are $650,000; at levels above 50% of capacity, its fixed costs are $750,000. The company's variable costs at full capacity (150,000 units) amount to $1,575,000.

Required:

a. Assuming that the company's product sells for $30.00 per unit, what is the company's break-even point in sales dollars?

b. Using only the data given, at what level of sales would it be more economical to close the factory than to operate it? In other words, at what level will operating losses approximate the losses incurred if the factory is closed down completely?

c. Assume that when the Davis Company is operating at half of its capacity, it decides to reduce the selling price from $30 per unit to $20 per unit in order to increase sales. At what percentage of capacity must the company operate in order to break even at the reduced sales price?

BUSINESS DECISION PROBLEM 19–2:

Decide whether to make or buy a part; find variable cost and calculate cost to manufacture part

The Mead Company has recently been awarded a contract to sell 100,000 units of its product to the federal government. Mead manufactures the components of the product rather than purchasing them. When the news of the contract was released to the public, the president of Mead, Mike George, received a call from the president of the Martin Corporation, Jack Martin. Mr. Martin offered to sell to Mead 100,000 units of one of the needed components, part Y, for $9.75. After receiving the offer, Mr. George calls you into his office and assigns you the task of providing him a recommendation (along with any supporting information) on whether to accept or reject Mr. Martin's offer.

You first go to the company's records and obtain the following information concerning the production of part Y:

	Costs at Current Level of Production (900,000 units)
Direct labor	$4,500,000
Direct materials	1,260,000
Manufacturing overhead	1,350,000
Total cost	$7,110,000

You calculate the unit cost of part Y to be $7.90 ($7,110,000/900,000). But you suspect that this unit cost may not hold true at all production levels. To find out, you consult the production manager. She tells you that in order to meet the increased production needs, equipment will have to be rented and the production workers will have to work some overtime. She estimates the machine rental to be $200,000 and the total overtime premiums to be $250,000. She provides you with the following cost information:

	Costs at Increased Level of Production (1,000,000 units)
Direct labor	$5,000,000
Direct materials	1,400,000
Manufacturing overhead	1,900,000
Total cost	$8,300,000

The production manager advises you to reject Martin's offer, since the unit cost of part Y will only rise to $8.30 ($8,300,000/1,000,000) even with the additional costs of equipment rental and overtime premiums. This is much less than the $9.75 offered by Mr. Martin. You are still undecided, so you return to your office to consider the matter further.

Required:

a. Using the high-low method, compute the variable cost portion of manufacturing overhead. (Remember that the costs of equipment rental and overtime premiums are included in manufacturing overhead. Subtract these amounts before performing the calculation).

b. Compute the total costs to manufacture the additional units of part Y. (Note: Include overtime premiums as a part of direct labor).

c. Compute the unit cost to manufacture the additional units of part Y.

d. Should Mr. George accept or reject Mr. Martin's offer?

20 CAPITAL BUDGETING: LONG-RANGE PLANNING

LEARNING OBJECTIVES

After studying this chapter, you should be able to:

1. Define capital budgeting and explain the effects of making poor capital-budgeting decisions.
2. Determine the net cash inflows, after taxes, for both an asset addition and an asset replacement.
3. Evaluate projects using the payback period.
4. Evaluate projects using the unadjusted rate of return.
5. Evaluate projects using the net present value.
6. Evaluate projects using the profitability index.
7. Evaluate projects using the time-adjusted rate of return.
8. Determine, for project evaluation, the effect of an investment in working capital.
9. Define and correctly use the new terms in the glossary.

In your personal life you make many short-run decisions (such as where to go on vacation this year) and many long-run decisions (such as whether to buy a home). The quality of these decisions determines to a large extent the success of your life. Businesses also face short-run and long-run decisions.

In Chapter 19, you studied how accountants help management make short-run decisions, such as what prices to charge for their products this year. Accountants also play an important role in advising management on long-range decisions, such as investing in new buildings and equipment, that will benefit the company for many years. Long-run decisions have a great impact on the long-run success of a company. Incorrect long-run decisions can threaten the survival of a company.

Whereas short-run decisions involve items such as selling prices, costs, volume, and profits in the current year, long-run decisions involve investments in capital assets, such as buildings and equipment, affecting the current year and many future years. Planning for these investments is referred to as capital budgeting. This chapter discusses the general concepts behind capital budgeting.

CAPITAL BUDGETING DEFINED

Objective 1: Define capital budgeting and explain the effects of making poor capital-budgeting decisions

Capital budgeting is the process of considering alternative capital projects and selecting those alternatives that provide the most profitable return on available funds, within the framework of company goals and objectives. A **capital project** is any long-range endeavor to purchase, build, lease, or renovate buildings, equipment, or other major items of property. Such decisions usually involve very large sums of money and usually bring about a large increase in fixed costs for a number of years in the future. Once a company builds a plant or undertakes some other capital expenditure, it becomes less flexible.

Poor capital-budgeting decisions can be very costly because of the large sums of money and relatively long time periods involved. If a poor capital-budgeting decision is implemented, the company can lose all or part of the funds originally invested in the project and not realize expected benefits. In addition, other actions taken within the company regarding the project, such as finding suppliers of raw materials, are wasted if the capital-budgeting decision must later be revoked. Poor capital-budgeting decisions may also harm the company's competitive position because the company will not have the most efficient productive assets needed to compete in world markets.

Investment of funds in a poor alternative can create other problems as well. Workers who were hired for the project might be laid off if the project fails, creating morale and unemployment problems. Many of the fixed costs will still remain even if a plant is closed or is not producing. Advertising efforts will have been wasted. Stock prices could be affected by the decline in income.

On the other hand, failure to invest enough funds in a good project can also be costly. Ford's Mustang is an excellent example of this. If, at the time of the original capital-budgeting decision, Ford had correctly projected the Mustang's popularity, the company would have expended more funds on the project. Because of an undercommitment of funds, Ford found itself short on production capacity, which caused lost and postponed sales of the automobile.

Finally, the amount of funds available for investment is limited. Thus, once a capital investment decision is made, alternative investment opportunities are lost. The benefits or returns lost by rejecting the best alternative investment are the **opportunity cost** of a given project.

For all these reasons, companies must be very careful in their analyses of capital projects. Capital expenditures do not occur as often as ordinary expenditures (such as payroll or inventory purchases) but involve substantial sums of money that are then committed for a long period of time. Therefore, the means by which companies evaluate capital expenditure decisions need to be much more formal and detailed than would be necessary for ordinary purchase decisions.

PROJECT SELECTION: A GENERAL VIEW

Making capital-budgeting decisions involves analyzing cash inflows and outflows. This section identifies benefits and costs that are relevant to capital-budgeting decisions.

Time Value of Money

Money received today is worth more than the same amount of money received at a future date, such as a year from now. This principle is known as the time value of money. Money has a time value because of investment opportunities, not because of inflation. For example, $100 today is worth more than $100 to be received one year from today because the $100 received today may be invested and will grow to some amount greater than $100 in one year. Future value and present value concepts are extremely important in assessing the desirability of long-term investments (capital budgeting). These concepts were covered in the Appendix to Chapter 9. If you need to review these concepts, refer back to the Chapter 9 Appendix before continuing with this chapter.

Net Cash Inflow

Objective 2: Determine the net cash inflows, after taxes, for both an asset addition and an asset replacement

The **net cash inflow** (as used in capital budgeting) is the net cash benefit expected from a project in a period. The net cash inflow is the difference between the periodic cash inflows and the periodic cash outflows for a proposed project.

Asset acquisition. Assume, for example, that a company is considering the purchase of new equipment for $120,000. The equipment is expected to have a useful life of 15 years and no salvage value. The equipment is expected to produce cash inflows (revenue) of $75,000 per year and cash outflows (costs) of $50,000 per year. Ignoring depreciation and taxes, the annual net cash inflow is computed as follows:

Cash inflows	$75,000
Cash outflows	50,000
Net cash flow	$25,000

***

Depreciation and taxes. The computation of the net cash inflow usually includes the effects of depreciation and taxes. Although depreciation does not involve a cash outflow, it is deductible in arriving at federal taxable income. Thus, depreciation reduces the amount of cash outflow for income taxes. This reduction is a tax savings made possible by a depreciation tax shield. A **tax shield** is the amount by which taxable income is reduced due to the deductibility of an item. In order to simplify the illustration, we assume the use of straight-line depreciation for tax purposes throughout the chapter. Straight-line depreciation can be elected for tax purposes, even under the new tax law. Thus, if depreciation is $8,000, the tax shield is $8,000.

The tax shield results in a tax savings. The amount of the tax savings can be found by multiplying the tax rate by the amount of the depreciation tax shield. The formula is shown below:

Tax rate × Depreciation tax shield = Tax savings

Using the data in the previous example and assuming straight-line depreciation of $8,000 per year and a 40% tax rate, the amount of the tax savings is $3,200 (40% × $8,000 depreciation tax shield). Now, considering taxes and depreciation, the annual net cash inflow from the $120,000 of equipment is computed as follows:

	Change in Net Income	Change in Cash Flow
Cash inflows	$75,000	$75,000
Cash outflows	50,000	50,000
Net cash inflow before taxes	$25,000	$25,000
Depreciation	8,000	
Net income before taxes	$17,000	
Tax at 40%	6,800	6,800
Net income after taxes	$10,200	
Net cash inflow (after taxes)		$18,200

If there were no depreciation tax shield, income tax would have been $10,000 ($25,000 × 40%), and the net after-tax cash inflow from the investment would have been $15,000 ($25,000 − $10,000), or [$25,000 × (1 − 40%)]. The depreciation tax shield, however, reduces income tax by $3,200 ($8,000 × 40%) and increases the investment's after-tax net cash inflow by the same amount. Therefore, the following formula can also be used to determine the after-tax net cash inflow from an investment:

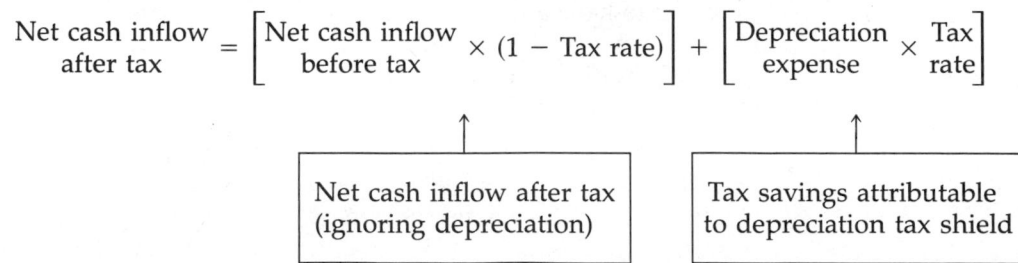

$$\begin{matrix}\text{Net cash inflow} \\ \text{after tax}\end{matrix} = \left[\begin{matrix}\text{Net cash inflow} \\ \text{before tax}\end{matrix} \times (1 - \text{Tax rate})\right] + \left[\begin{matrix}\text{Depreciation} \\ \text{expense}\end{matrix} \times \begin{matrix}\text{Tax} \\ \text{rate}\end{matrix}\right]$$

Net cash inflow after tax (ignoring depreciation)

Tax savings attributable to depreciation tax shield

706

Asset replacement. Sometimes a company must decide whether or not it should replace existing plant assets. Such replacement decisions often occur when faster and more efficient machinery and equipment appear on the market.

The computation of the net cash inflow is more complex for a replacement decision than for an acquisition decision because cash inflows and outflows for two items (the asset being replaced and the new asset) must be considered. To illustrate, assume that a company operates two machines that were purchased four years ago at a cost of $18,000 each. The estimated useful life of each machine is 12 years (with no salvage value). Each machine will produce 30,000 units of product per year. The annual cash operating expenses (labor, repairs, etc.) for the two machines together total $14,000. After the old machines have been used for four years, a new machine becomes available. The new machine can be acquired for $28,000 and has an estimated useful life of eight years (with no salvage value). The new machine will produce 60,000 units annually and will entail annual cash operating expenses of $10,000.

A $28,000 cash outflow is required in the first year to acquire the new machine. In addition to this initial outlay, the annual net cash inflow from replacement is computed as follows:

Annual cash operating expenses:		
Old machines		$14,000
New machine		10,000
Annual net cash inflow (savings) before tax		$ 4,000
1 − Tax rate		×60%
Annual net cash inflow (savings)* after tax		
(ignoring depreciation) (1)		$ 2,400
Annual depreciation expense:		
Old machines	$3,000	
New machine	3,500	
Additional annual depreciation expense	$ 500	
Tax rate	×40%	
Additional depreciation tax savings (2)		200
Net cash inflow after tax (1) + (2)		$ 2,600

*Cash savings are considered to be cash inflows.

Notice that the above figures concentrated only on the differences in costs for each of the two alternatives. Two other items are also relevant to the decision. First, the purchase of the new machine will create a $28,000 cash outflow immediately upon acquisition. Second, the two old machines can probably be sold, and the selling price or salvage value of the old machines will create a cash inflow in the period of disposal. Also, the above example used straight-line depreciation. If the Capital Cost Recovery (modified ACRS) method had been used, the tax shield would have been larger in the early years and smaller in the later years of the asset's life.

Out-of-pocket and sunk costs. A distinction between out-of-pocket costs and sunk costs needs to be made for capital-budgeting decisions.

An **out-of-pocket cost** is one that requires a future outlay of resources, usually cash; it can be avoided or changed in amount. Future labor and repair costs are examples of out-of-pocket costs.

Sunk costs are costs that have already been incurred. Nothing can be done about sunk costs at the present time; they cannot be avoided or changed in amount. The price paid for a machine becomes a sunk cost the minute the purchase has been made (before that moment it was an out-of-pocket cost). The amount of that past outlay cannot be changed regardless of whether the machine is scrapped or used. Thus, depreciation is a sunk cost because it represents a past cash outlay. Depletion and amortization of assets such as ore deposits and patents are also sunk costs.

A sunk cost is a past cost, while an out-of-pocket cost is a future cost. Only the out-of-pocket costs (the future cash outlays) are relevant to capital-budgeting decisions. Sunk costs are not relevant, except for any effect they have on the cash outflow for taxes.

Initial cost and salvage value. Any cash outflows necessary to acquire an asset and place it in a position and condition for use are part of the **initial cost of the asset.** If an investment has a salvage value, that value should be treated as a cash inflow in the year of the asset's disposal.

The cost of capital. The cost of capital is important in project selection. Certainly any acceptable proposal should offer a return that exceeds the cost of the funds used to finance it. **Cost of capital,** usually expressed as a rate, is the cost of all sources of capital (debt and equity) employed by a company. For convenience, most current liabilities, such as accounts payable and federal income taxes payable, are treated as being without cost. Every other item on the right (equity) side of the balance sheet has a cost. The subject of determining the cost of capital is a controversial topic in the literature of accounting and finance and will not be discussed here. Assumed rates for the cost of capital will be given in the remainder of the chapter.

PROJECT SELECTION: PAYBACK PERIOD

*Objective 3:
Evaluate projects
using the payback
period*

The next few sections of this chapter examine specific techniques used to evaluate capital projects. The first of these is the payback period. The **payback period** is the period of time it takes for the cumulative sum of the annual net cash inflows from a project to equal the initial net cash outlay. In effect, the payback period answers the question: How long will it take the capital project to recover, or pay back, the initial investment? If the net cash inflows each year are a constant amount, the formula for the payback period is:

$$\text{Payback period} = \frac{\text{Initial cash outlay}}{\text{Annual net cash inflows (or benefits)}}$$

The payback period for the two assets discussed previously can be computed as follows. The purchase of the $120,000 equipment discussed on page 705 will create an annual net cash inflow after taxes of $18,200, so the payback period is 6.6 years, computed as follows:

$$\text{Payback period} = \frac{\$120,000}{\$18,200} = 6.6 \text{ years}$$

The payback period for the replacement machine mentioned on page 707, with a $28,000 cash outflow in the first year and an annual net cash inflow of $2,600, is 10.8 years, computed as follows:

$$\text{Payback period} = \frac{\$28,000}{\$2,600} = 10.8 \text{ years}$$

Remember that the payback period indicates how long it will take the machine to pay for itself. The replacement machine being considered has a payback period of 10.8 years, but a useful life of only 8 years. Therefore, since the investment cannot pay for itself within its useful life, the machine should not be purchased to replace the two old machines.

In each of the two examples above, the projected net cash inflow per year was uniform. When the annual returns are uneven, a cumulative calculation must be used to determine payback period, as shown in the following situation.

The Neil Company is considering a capital investment project that costs $40,000 and is expected to last 10 years. The projected annual net cash inflows are as follows:

Year	Investment	Annual Net Cash Inflow	Cumulative Net Cash Inflows
0	$40,000	—	—
1	—	$8,000	$ 8,000
2	—	6,000	14,000
3	—	7,000	21,000
4	—	5,000	26,000
5	—	8,000	34,000
6	—	6,000	40,000
7	—	3,000	43,000
8	—	2,000	45,000
9	—	3,000	48,000
10	—	1,000	49,000

The payback period in this example is six years—the time it takes to recover the $40,000 original investment.

When the payback period analysis is used to evaluate investment proposals, management may use one of the following rules to decide on project selection:

1. Select the investments with the shortest payback periods.
2. Select only those investments that have a payback period of less than a specified number of years.

Both decision rules focus on the rapid return of invested capital. If capital can be recovered rapidly, it can be invested in other projects, thereby generating more cash inflows or profits.

Payback period analysis is used extensively in capital-budgeting decisions due to its simplicity and because cash flow is critical in many businesses. However, this type of analysis has two important limitations:

1. Payback period analysis ignores the time period beyond the payback period. For example, assume the Allen Company is considering two alternative investments that each requires an initial outlay of $30,000. Proposal Y will return $6,000 per year for five years, while proposal Z will return $5,000 per year for eight years. The payback period for Y is five years ($30,000/$6,000) and for Z is six years ($30,000/$5,000). But, if the goal is to maximize income, proposal Z should be selected rather than proposal Y, even though Z has a longer payback period. This is because Z will return a total of $40,000, while Y simply recovers the initial $30,000 outlay.

2. Payback analysis also ignores the time value of money. For example, assume the following net cash inflows are expected in the first three years from two capital projects:

	Net Cash Inflows	
	Project A	Project B
First year	$15,000	$ 9,000
Second year	12,000	12,000
Third year	9,000	15,000
Total	$36,000	$36,000

Assume that both projects have the same net cash inflows each year beyond the third year. If the cost of each project is $36,000, then each has a payback period of three years. But common sense indicates that the projects are not equal because money has a time value and can be reinvested to increase income. Since larger amounts of cash are received earlier under project A, it is the preferable project.

PROJECT SELECTION: UNADJUSTED RATE OF RETURN

Objective 4: Evaluate projects using the unadjusted rate of return

The unadjusted rate of return is another method used in evaluating investment projects. The **unadjusted rate of return** is an approximation of the rate of return on investment of a capital project. It is computed by dividing the average annual income after taxes by the average amount of investment in the project. The *average investment* is the original cash outlay divided by 2. The formula for the unadjusted rate of return is:

$$\text{Unadjusted rate of return} = \frac{\text{Average annual income after taxes}}{\text{Average amount of investment}}$$

Notice that annual *income* rather than net cash inflow is used in the calculation.[1]

To illustrate the use of the unadjusted rate of return, assume the Thomas Company is considering two capital project proposals that both

---

[1]Some formulas use the initial investment as the denominator instead of the average investment.

have useful lives of three years. The company does not have enough funds to undertake both projects. Information relating to the projects is shown below:

Proposal	Initial Cost	Average Annual Before-Tax Net Cash Inflow	Average Depreciation
1	$72,000	$45,000	$24,000
2	90,000	55,000	30,000

Assuming a 40% tax rate, the unadjusted rate of return for each project is determined as follows:

		Proposal 1	Proposal 2
Average investment:			
Original outlay ÷ 2	(1)	$36,000	$45,000
Annual net cash inflow (before taxes)		$45,000	$55,000
Annual depreciation		24,000	30,000
Annual income (before taxes)		$21,000	$25,000
Income taxes at 40%		8,400	10,000
Average annual net income from investment	(2)	$12,600	$15,000
Rate of return (2) ÷ (1)		35%	33⅓%

From these calculations, if Thomas Company makes an investment decision solely on the basis of unadjusted rate of return, Proposal 1 would be selected since it has a higher rate.

The unadjusted rate of return can also be computed with the following formula:

$$\text{Rate of return} = \frac{\left(\begin{array}{c}\text{Average annual before-} \\ \text{tax net cash inflow}\end{array} - \begin{array}{c}\text{Average annual} \\ \text{depreciation}\end{array}\right) \times (1 - \text{Tax rate})}{\text{Average investment}}$$

For Proposal 1 above, the computation is as follows:

$$\text{Rate of return} = \frac{(\$45,000 - \$24,000) \times (1 - 0.4)}{(\$72,000/2)} = \frac{(\$21,000) \times (0.6)}{\$36,000}$$

$$= \frac{\$12,600}{\$36,000} = 35\%$$

For Proposal 2 above, the computation is as follows:

$$\text{Rate of return} = \frac{(\$55,000 - \$30,000) \times (1 - 0.4)}{(\$90,000/2)} = \frac{(\$25,000) \times (0.6)}{\$45,000}$$

$$= \frac{\$15,000}{\$45,000} = 33\frac{1}{3}\%$$

Sometimes information is provided on the average annual after-tax net cash inflow. Average annual after-tax net cash inflow is equal to annual before-tax cash inflow minus taxes. Given this information, the depreciation can be deducted to arrive at average net income. For instance, for Proposal 2 above, average net income would be computed as follows:

After-tax net cash inflow ($55,000 − $10,000)	$45,000
Less: Depreciation	30,000
Average net income	$15,000

The unadjusted rate of return, like payback period analysis, has several limitations:

1. The length of time over which the return will be earned is not considered.
2. The rate allows a sunk cost, depreciation, to enter into the calculation. Since depreciation can be calculated in so many different ways, the rate of return can be manipulated by simply changing the method of depreciation used for the project.
3. The timing of cash flows is not considered. Thus, the time value of money is ignored.

PROJECT SELECTION: NET PRESENT VALUE METHOD AND THE PROFITABILITY INDEX

Unlike the two project selection methods just illustrated, the net present value method and the profitability index take into account the time value of money in the analysis. Because of their computational similarities, the net present value method and the profitability index will both be discussed in this section. For purposes of these methods we assume that all net cash inflows occur at the end of the year. This assumption is often used in capital-budgeting analysis and makes the calculation of present values less complicated than if we assume the cash flows occurred at some other time.

A major issue in acknowledging the time value of money in capital-budgeting decisions is determining an appropriate discount rate to use in computing the present value of cash flows. Management requires some minimum rate of return on its investments. This rate should be the company's cost of capital, but that rate is difficult to determine. Therefore, management often selects a target rate that it believes to be at or above the company's cost of capital, and then that rate is used as a basis for present value calculations.

Net Present Value Method

Objective 5:
Evaluate projects using the net present value

Under the net present value method, all expected after-tax cash inflows and outflows from the proposed investment are discounted to their present values using the company's required minimum rate of return as a discount rate. The **net present value** of the proposed investment is the difference between the present value of the annual net cash inflows and the present value of the required cash outflows. In many projects, the only cash outflow is the initial investment, and since it occurs immediately, the initial investment does not need to be discounted. Therefore, in such projects, the net present value of the proposed project may be computed as the present value of the annual net cash inflows minus the initial investment. Other types of projects require that additional investments, like a major repair, be made at later dates in the life of the project. In those cases, the cash outflows must be discounted to their present value before they are compared to the present value of the net cash inflows.

To illustrate the net present value method, assume the Morris Company is considering a capital investment project that will cost $25,000. Net cash inflows after taxes for the next four years are expected to be $8,000, $7,500, $8,000, and $7,500, respectively. Management requires a minimum rate of return of 14% and wants to know if the project is acceptable. The following analysis is developed, using the tables in Appendix C at the end of the text:

	Annual Net Cash Inflow (after taxes)	Present Value of $1 at 14% (from Table II)	Total Present Value
First year.	$8,000	0.87719	$ 7,018
Second year	7,500	0.76947	5,771
Third year	8,000	0.67497	5,400
Fourth year.	7,500	0.59208	4,441
Present value of net cash inflows			$22,630
Cost of investment			25,000
Net present value			$ (2,370)

Since the present value of the net cash inflows, $22,630, is less than the initial outlay of $25,000, the project is not acceptable. The net present value for the project is equal to the present value of its net cash inflows less the present value of its cost (the investment amount), which in this instance is $−2,370 ($22,630 − $25,000).

In general, a proposed capital investment is acceptable if it has a positive net present value. In the previous example, if the expected net cash inflows from the investment had been $10,000 per year for four years, the present value of the benefits would have been (from Appendix C, Table III):

$$\$10,000 \times 2.91371 = \$29,137$$

This yields a net present value of $4,137 ($29,137 − $25,000). Since the net present value is positive, the investment proposal is acceptable. But there may be a competing project that has an even higher net present value. When the net present value method is used to screen alternative projects, the higher a project's net present value, the more desirable the project.

Profitability Index

Objective 6:
Evaluate projects
using the
profitability index

When investment projects costing different amounts are being compared, the net present value method does not provide a valid means by which to rank the projects in order of contribution to income or desirability under limited financial resources. A **profitability index** provides this additional information to management. A profitability index is the ratio of the present value of the expected net cash benefits (after taxes) divided by the initial cash outlay (or present value of cash outlays if future outlays are required). The profitability index formula is:

$$PI = \frac{\text{PV of net cash inflows}}{\text{Initial outlay (or present value of cash}}$$
$$\text{outlays if future outlays are required)}$$

Only those proposals having a profitability index greater than or equal to 1.00 should be considered by management. Proposals with a profitability index of less than 1.00 will not yield the minimum rate of return because the present value of the projected cash inflows will be less than the initial cost.

To illustrate use of the profitability index, assume that a company is considering two alternative capital outlay proposals that have the following initial costs and expected net cash inflows after taxes:

	Proposal X	*Proposal Y*
Initial cost	$7,000	$9,500
Expected net cash inflow (after taxes):		
Year 1	$5,000	$9,000
Year 2	4,000	6,000
Year 3	6,000	3,000

Management's minimum desired rate of return is 20%.

The net present values and profitability indexes can be computed as follows (using Appendix C, Table II):

	Present Value	
	Proposal X	*Proposal Y*
Year 1 (net cash inflow in year 1 × 0.83333)	$ 4,167	$ 7,500
Year 2 (net cash inflow in year 2 × 0.69444)	2,778	4,167
Year 3 (net cash inflow in year 3 × 0.57870)	3,472	1,736
Present value of net cash inflows	$10,417	$13,403
Initial outlay	7,000	9,500
Net present value	$ 3,417	$ 3,903

	Proposal X	*Proposal Y*
Profitability index:	$\frac{\$10,417}{\$7,000} = 1.49$	$\frac{\$13,403}{\$9,500} = 1.41$

When net present values are compared, Proposal Y appears to be more favorable than X because its net present value is higher. But after computing the profitability indexes, Proposal X is found to be a more desirable investment because it has the higher profitability index. The higher the profitability index, the more profitable the project per dollar of investment. Proposal X is earning a higher rate of return on a smaller investment than Proposal Y.

PROJECT SELECTION: THE TIME-ADJUSTED RATE OF RETURN

Another technique for evaluating capital projects that accounts for the time value of money is the time adjusted rate of return. The **time-adjusted rate of return,** also called the discounted or internal rate of return, equates the present value of expected after-tax net cash inflows from an investment with the cost of the investment by finding the rate at which the net present value of the project is zero. If the time-adjusted rate of return equals or exceeds the cost of capital or target rate of return, then the investment should be considered further. But if the proposal's time-adjusted rate of return is less than the minimum rate, the proposal should be rejected. Ignoring other considerations, the higher the time-adjusted rate of return, the more desirable the project.

Present value tables can be used to approximate the time-adjusted rate of return. To illustrate, assume the Young Company is considering a $90,000 investment that is expected to last 25 years with no salvage value. The investment will yield a $15,000 annual after-tax net cash inflow. This $15,000 is referred to as an **annuity,** which is a series of equal cash inflows.

The first step in computing rate of return is to determine the payback period. In this case, payback period is six years ($90,000 ÷ $15,000). Next, examine Appendix C, Table III (present value of an annuity) to find the present value factor that is nearest in amount to the payback period of 6. Since the investment is expected to yield returns for 25 years, look at that row in the table. In that row, the factor nearest to 6 is 5.92745, which appears under the 16.5% interest column. If the annual return of $15,000 is multiplied by the 5.92745 factor, the result is $88,912, which is just below the $90,000 cost of the project. Thus, the actual rate of return is slightly less than 16.5%. It is less than 16.5% but more than 16% because, as interest rates increase, present values decrease since less investment is needed to generate the same income.

The above example involves uniform net cash inflows from year to year. What happens when net cash inflows are not uniform? In such instances, a trial and error procedure is necessary. For example, assume that a company is considering a $200,000 project that will last four years and will yield the following returns:

Year	Net Cash Inflow (after taxes)
1	$ 20,000
2	40,000
3	80,000
4	150,000
Total . . .	$290,000

The average annual net cash inflow is $72,500 ($290,000 ÷ 4). Based on this average net cash inflow, the payback period is 2.76 years ($200,000 ÷ $72,500). Looking in the four-year row of Appendix C, Table III, we find that the factor 2.77048 is nearest to the payback period of 2.76.

But in this case, cash flows are not uniform. The largest returns will occur in the later years of the asset's life. Since the early returns have the largest present value, it is likely that the rate of return will be less than the 16.5% rate that corresponds to the present value factor of 2.77048. If the returns had been greater during the earlier years of the asset's life, the correct rate of return would have been higher than 16.5%. To find the specific discount rate that yields a present value closest to the initial outlay, or $200,000, several interest rates less than 16% are tried out. By trial and error the rate of return is found; the following computation reveals the rate to be slightly higher than 12%:

	Return	Present Value Factor at 12%	Present Value of Net Cash Inflows
Year 1	$ 20,000	0.89286	$ 17,857
Year 2	40,000	0.79719	31,888
Year 3	80,000	0.71178	56,942
Year 4	150,000	0.63553	95,330
			$202,017

Since the cost of capital is not a precise percentage, some financial theorists argue that the time-adjusted rate of return method is better than the net present value method. Under the time-adjusted rate of return method, the cost of capital is used only as a cutoff point in deciding which projects are acceptable for more consideration. Under the net present value method, the cost of capital is used in the calculation of the present value of the benefits. Thus, if the cost of capital percentage is wrong, the ranking of the projects will be affected. As a result, management may select projects that are really not as profitable as other projects.

No matter which time value of money concept is considered "better," these methods are both theoretically superior to the payback and unadjusted rate of return methods. But the time value of money methods are more difficult to compute. In reality, no single method should be used by itself to make capital-budgeting decisions. All aspects of the investment should be considered, including nonquantitative factors, such as employee morale (layoff of workers due to higher efficiency of a new machine) and company flexibility (versatility of production of one machine over another). The company will be committed to its investment in a capital project for a long period of time and should use the best selection techniques and judgment available.

INVESTMENTS IN WORKING CAPITAL

Objective 8: Determine, for project evaluation, the effect of an investment in working capital

An investment in a capital asset usually must be supported by an investment in working capital, such as accounts receivable and inventory. For example, an investment in a capital project often is expected to increase sales. Increased sales usually bring about an increase in accounts receivable from customers and an increase in inventory to support the higher sales level. The increases in the current assets—accounts receivable and inventory—are investments in working capital that usually are recovered in full at the end of a capital project's life. Such working capital investments should be considered in capital-budgeting decisions.

To illustrate, assume that a company is considering a capital project that will involve a $50,000 investment in machinery and a $40,000 investment in working capital. The machine, which will be used to produce a new product, has a useful life of eight years and has no salvage value. The annual cash inflow (before taxes) is estimated at $25,000, with annual cash outflow (before taxes) of $5,000. The annual net cash inflow from the project is computed below (assuming straight-line depreciation and a 40% tax rate):

Cash inflows	$25,000
Cash outflows	5,000
Net cash inflow before tax	$20,000
1 − Tax rate	×60%
Net cash inflow after tax (ignoring depreciation) (1)	$12,000
Depreciation tax shield ($50,000 ÷ 8 years)	$ 6,250
Tax rate	×40%
Depreciation tax savings (2)	$ 2,500
Annual net cash inflow (years 1–8) (1) + (2)	$14,500

The annual net cash inflow from the machine is $14,500 each year for eight years. However, the working capital investment needs to be considered. First, the investment of $40,000 in working capital at the start of the project is an additional outlay that must be made when the project is started. The $40,000 will be tied up every year until the project is finished, or in this case, until the end of the life of the machine. At that point, the working capital will be released, and the $40,000 can be used for other investments. Therefore, the $40,000 is a cash outlay at the start of the project and a cash inflow at the end of the project.

The net present value of the project is computed as follows (assuming a 14% minimum desired rate of return):

Net cash inflow, years 1–8 ($14,500 × 4.63886)	$67,263
Recovery of investment in working capital ($40,000 × 0.35056)	14,022
Present value of net cash inflows	$81,285
Initial cash outlay ($50,000 + $40,000)	90,000
Net present value	$ (8,715)

The discount factor for the cash inflows, 4.63886, comes from Appendix C, Table III, since the cash inflows in this example are a series of equal payments—an annuity. The recovery of the investment in working capital is assumed to represent a single lump sum that is received at the end of the project's life. As such, it is discounted using a factor (0.35056) that comes from Appendix C, Table II.

The investment is not acceptable because it has a negative net present value. If the working capital investment had been ignored, the proposal would have had a rather large positive net present value of $17,263 ($67,263 − $50,000). Thus, it should be obvious that investments in working capital must be considered if correct capital-budgeting decisions are to be made.

THE POSTAUDIT

The last step in the capital-budgeting process is a postaudit review that should be performed by a person not involved in the capital-budgeting decision-making process. Such a person can provide an impartial judgment on the project's worthiness. This step should be performed early in the project's life, but enough time should have passed for any operational "bugs" to have been worked out. Actual operating costs and revenues should be determined and compared with those estimated when the project was originally reviewed and accepted.

The postaudit review performs these functions:

1. Lets management know if the projections were accurate and if the particular project is performing as expected regarding cash inflows and outflows.
2. May identify additional factors for management to consider in upcoming capital-budgeting decisions, such as cash outflows that were forgotten in a particular project.
3. Provides a review of the capital-budgeting process to determine how effectively and efficiently it is working. The postaudit provides information that allows management to compare the actual results of decisions with the expectations it had during the planning and selection phases of the capital-budgeting process.

SUMMARY

A capital project is any long-term endeavor to purchase, lease, or renovate buildings, equipment, or other major items of property. Capital budgeting is the process of considering alternative capital projects and selecting those alternatives that provide the most profitable return on available funds, within the framework of company goals and objectives.

Several concepts are important to capital-budgeting decisions. The time value of money concept states that money received today is worth more than money received in the future. The time value of money is considered by discounting future cash flows to their present values. The net cash inflow is the difference between the periodic cash inflows and the periodic cash outflows expected from a project. The net cash inflow is usually computed after considering the tax effect of depreciation. Out-of-pocket costs require future outlays of resources, usually cash, while sunk costs have already been incurred. The initial cost of the project includes any cash outlays necessary to acquire the asset and to place it in a position and condition for use. The expected salvage value represents an expected future cash inflow at the end of the asset's life. The cost of capital, usually expressed as a rate of return, includes the cost of all the company's sources of capital. Management often selects as a discount rate a minimum required rate of return that it believes to be at or above the company's cost of capital.

Various capital project selection techniques are discussed in the chapter. Payback period analysis compares the project's initial investment to its annual net cash inflows and asks how many years it will be before the sum of the net cash inflows equals, or pays back, the initial investment. The unadjusted rate of return compares the project's average annual net income after tax (rather than its net cash inflows) to its average investment and computes an approximate rate of return. Neither of these methods considers the time value of money.

The other techniques examined in the chapter do consider the time value of money. The net present value method involves calculating the difference between the present value of the net cash inflows and the initial investment (or the present value of the cash outlays if future outlays are required). The profitability index, on the other hand, computes the ratio of the present value of the net cash inflows to the initial investment (or the present value of the cash outlays if future outlays are required). Finally, the time-adjusted rate of return method computes the project's rate of return by examining the amount and timing of the net cash inflows and the required cash outlay(s). The resulting rate can then be compared directly to the company's required rate of return to judge the acceptability of the investment.

When preparing a capital-budgeting proposal, management must be careful to include not only the cost of buildings and equipment but also the cost of working capital necessary to operate the project. Such a commitment of resources is part of the overall investment in the project.

The postaudit review is the last step in the capital-budgeting process. The postaudit provides management an opportunity to compare actual results with the projections on which the selection decision was based. This review provides feedback to permit management to revise the current project if necessary and to help management improve future capital-budgeting decisions.

Objective 9: Define and correctly use the new terms in the glossary

NEW TERMS INTRODUCED IN CHAPTER 20

Annuity   A series of equal cash inflows (715).

Capital budgeting   Process of considering alternative capital projects and selecting those alternatives that provide the most profitable return on available funds, within the framework of company goals and objectives (704).

Capital project   Any long-range endeavor to purchase, build, lease, or renovate buildings, equipment, or other major items of property (704).

Cost of capital   The cost of all sources of capital (debt and equity) employed by a company (708).

719

Initial cost of an asset   Any cash outflows necessary to acquire an asset and place it in a position and condition for its intended use (708).

Net cash inflow   The periodic cash inflows from a project less the periodic cash outflows related to the project (705).

Net present value   A project selection technique that discounts all expected after-tax cash inflows and outflows from the proposed investment to their present values using the company's minimum rate of return as a discount rate. If the amount obtained by this process exceeds or equals the investment amount, the proposal is considered acceptable for further consideration (712).

Opportunity cost   The benefits or returns lost by rejecting the best alternative investment (705).

Out-of-pocket cost   A cost requiring a future outlay of resources, usually cash (708).

Payback period   The period of time it takes for the cumulative sum of the annual net cash inflows from a project to equal the initial net cash outlay (708).

Profitability index   The ratio of the present value of the expected net cash inflows (after taxes) divided by the initial cash outlay (or present value of cash outlays if future outlays are required) (713).

Sunk costs   Costs that have already been incurred. Nothing can be done about sunk costs at the present time; they cannot be avoided or changed in amount (708).

Tax shield   The total amount by which taxable income is reduced due to the deductibility of an item (706).

Time-adjusted rate of return   A project selection technique that finds a rate of return that will equate the present value of future expected net cash inflows (after taxes) from an investment with the cost of the investment (715).

Unadjusted rate of return   The rate of return computed by dividing average annual income after taxes from a project by the average amount of the investment (710).

DEMONSTRATION PROBLEM 20–1

The Logue Company is considering three different investments. Listed below are some data related to these investments:

Investment	Initial Cash Outlay	Expected After-Tax Net Cash Inflow per Year	Expected Life of Proposals
A	$100,000	$20,000	10 years
B	120,000	17,600	15
C	150,000	21,000	20

Management requires a minimum return on investments of 14%.

Required:

Rank these proposals using the following selection techniques. (Ignore income taxes and salvage value.)

a. Payback period.

b. Unadjusted rate of return.

c. Profitability index.

d. Time-adjusted rate of return.

Solution to demonstration problem 20–1

a. Payback period:

		(a)	(b) Annual After-Tax	(a)/(b)
Proposal		Investment	Cash Inflow	Payback Period
A	. . . . .	$100,000	$20,000	5.00 years
B	. . . . .	120,000	17,600	6.82
C	. . . . .	150,000	21,000	7.14

The proposals in order of desirability are A, B, and C.

b. Unadjusted rate of return:

	(a) Average Investment	(b) Average Annual After-Tax Net Cash Inflow	(c) Average Depreciation	(d) = (b) − (c) Average Annual Income	(d)/(a) Rate of Return
Proposal					
A	$50,000	$20,000	$10,000	$10,000	20%
B	60,000	17,600	8,000	9,600	16
C	75,000	21,000	7,500	13,500	18

The proposals in order of desirability are A, C, and B.

c. Profitability index:

	(a) Annual After-Tax Net Cash Inflow	(b) Present Value Factor at 14%	(c) = (a) × (b) Present Value of Annual Net Cash Inflow	(d) Initial Cash Outlay	(c)/(d) Profitability Index
Proposal					
A	$20,000	5.21612	$104,322	$100,000	1.04
B	17,600	6.14217	108,102	120,000	0.90
C	21,000	6.62313	139,086	150,000	0.93

The proposals in order of desirability are A, C, and B. (But neither B nor C should be considered acceptable since each has a profitability index of less than one.)

d. Time-adjusted rate of return.

Proposal	Rate	How Found
A . . .	15% (slightly above)	($100,000 ÷ $20,000) = Factor of 5 in 10-period row
B . . .	12 (slightly below)	($120,000 ÷ $17,600) = Factor of 6.82 in 15-period row
C . . .	13 (slightly below)	($150,000 ÷ $21,000) = Factor of 7.14 in 20-period row

The proposals in order of desirability are A, C, and B. (But neither B nor C earns the minimum rate of return.)

QUESTIONS

1. How do capital expenditures differ from ordinary expenditures?

2. What effects can capital-budgeting decisions have on a firm?

3. What effect does depreciation have on cash flow?

4. Give an example of an out-of-pocket cost and a sunk cost by describing a situation in which both are encountered.

5. A machine currently is being considered for purchase. The salesperson attempting to sell the machine says that it will pay for itself in five years. What is meant by this statement?

6. Discuss the limitations of the payback method.

7. What is the profitability index and of what value is it?

8. What is the time-adjusted rate of return of a capital investment?

9. What role does the cost of capital play in the time-adjusted rate of return method and in the net present value method?

10. What is the purpose of a postaudit? When should a postaudit be performed?

EXERCISES

Determine estimated income and net cash inflow for an asset addition

1. The Barclay Athletic Club is considering investing $150,000 in some new sports equipment with an estimated useful life of 10 years and no salvage value. The equipment is expected to produce $60,000 in cash inflows and $40,000 in cash outflows annually. Assume straight-line depreciation is used by the company, and a 40% tax rate applies. Determine the annual estimated income and net cash inflow.

Determine additional cash inflow for an asset replacement

2. The Classic Manufacturing Company is considering replacing a four-year-old machine with a new, advanced model. The old machine was purchased for $30,000, has a useful life of 10 years with no salvage value, and has annual maintenance costs of $7,500. The new machine would cost $22,500 and would produce the same output as the old machine. But annual maintenance costs would be only $3,000. The new machine would have a useful life of 10 years with no salvage value. Using straight-line depreciation and a 40% tax rate, compute the additional annual cash inflow if the old machine is replaced.

Compute payback period for a new machine

3. Given the following annual costs, compute the payback period for a new machine if its net cost is $280,000. (Ignore income taxes.)

	Old Machine	New Machine
Depreciation	$ 24,000	$ 56,000
Labor	96,000	84,000
Repairs	28,000	6,000
Other costs	16,000	4,800
	$164,000	$150,800

Compute unadjusted rate of return for a new machine

4. The Washington Company is considering investing $32,000 in a new machine. The machine is expected to last eight years and to have no salvage value. Annual after-tax net cash inflow from the machine is expected to be $9,500. Calculate the unadjusted rate of return. (Ignore tax effect of depreciation.)

Compute profitability index for two projects and rank projects

5. Compute the profitability index for each of the following two proposals assuming a desired minimum rate of return of 20%. Based upon the profitability indices, which proposal is better?

	Proposal R	Proposal T
Initial outlay	$16,000	$20,600
Cash flow (after taxes):		
First year	$10,000	$12,000
Second year	9,000	12,000
Third year	6,000	8,000
Fourth year	–0–	5,000
Total.	$25,000	$37,000

Rank projects using payback and unadjusted rate of return

6. The Sparky Company is considering three alternative investment proposals. Using the information presented below, rank the proposals in order of desirability using (a) the payback method and (b) the unadjusted rate of return method. (Ignore tax effect of depreciation.) Assume the net cash inflows occur evenly throughout each year.

	Proposal J	Proposal K	Proposal L
Initial outlay	$ 80,000	$ 80,000	$ 80,000
Net cash inflow			
(after taxes):			
First year	–0–	$ 20,000	$ 20,000
Second year	$ 40,000	50,000	40,000
Third year	40,000	30,000	55,000
Fourth year	20,000	40,000	85,000
Total.	$100,000	$140,000	$200,000

Determine acceptability of a project using net present value

7. The Andrew Company is considering the purchase of a new machine. The machine can be bought for $45,000. The machine is expected to save $9,000 cash per year for 10 years, has an estimated useful life of 10 years, and an estimated salvage value of zero. Management will not make any investment unless at least an 18% rate of return can be earned.

Using the net present value method, determine if the proposal is acceptable.

Compute time-adjusted rate of return

8. Assume the same situation described in Exercise 7. Calculate the time-adjusted rate of return. (Ignore income taxes.)

Rank projects using payback, net present value, and time-adjusted rate of return

9. Rank the following investments in order of their desirability using (a) the payback method, (b) the net present value method, and (c) the time-adjusted rate of return method. Management requires a minimum rate of return of 14%.

Investment	Initial Outlay	Expected After-Tax Net Cash Inflow per Year	Expected Life of Proposal
A	$40,000	$ 6,000	8
B	50,000	8,750	20
C	80,000	16,000	10

PROBLEMS

Determine net after-tax cash inflow; determine payback period

20–1. Courtney Company is considering purchasing a new machine that would cost $250,000 and have a useful life of 10 years with no salvage value. The new machine is expected to have annual cash inflows of $125,000 and annual cash outflows of $50,000. The machine will be depreciated using straight-line depreciation, and the tax rate is assumed to be 40%.

Required:

a. Determine the net after-tax cash inflow for the new machine.

b. Determine the payback period for the new machine.

Determine annual additional after-tax cash inflow

20-2. The Abilene Company currently uses four machines to produce 200,000 units annually. The machines were bought three years ago for $50,000 each and have a useful life of 10 years with no salvage value. They cost a total of $28,000 a year to repair and maintain.

The company is considering replacing the four machines with one technologically superior machine that is capable of producing the 200,000 units annually by itself. The machine would cost $140,000 and have a useful life of seven years with no salvage value. Annual repair and maintenance costs are estimated at $14,000.

Required:

Assuming straight-line depreciation and a 40% tax rate, determine the annual additional after-tax cash inflow if the new machine is acquired.

Use payback method and net present value method to evaluate alternatives

20-3. The Alma Manufacturing Company owns five spinning machines that it uses in its manufacturing operations. Each of the machines was purchased four years ago at a cost of $90,000. Each machine has an estimated life of 10 years with no expected salvage value. A new machine has become available. One new machine has the same productive capacity as the five old machines combined. The new machine will cost $444,000, is estimated to last six years, and will have a salvage value at the end of that time of $60,000. A trade-in allowance of $28,000 is available for each of the old machines. The new machine can produce 450,000 units each year.

Operating costs per unit are compared below:

	Five Old Machines	New Machine
Repairs	$0.453	$0.057
Depreciation	0.100	0.160
Power	0.126	0.069
Other operating costs	0.108	0.033
Operating costs per unit	$0.787	$0.319

Required:

Ignore income taxes. Use the payback method for parts **(a)** and **(b)**.

a. Do you recommend replacing the old machines? Support your answer with computations. Disregard all factors except those reflected in the data given above.

b. If the old machines were already fully depreciated, would your answer be different? Why?

c. Using the net present value method with a discount rate of 20%, present a schedule showing whether or not the new machine should be acquired.

Compute time-
adjusted rate of
return

20–4. The Columbia Canning Company has used a particular canning machine for several years. The machine has a zero salvage value. The company is considering buying a technologically improved machine at a cost of $58,000. The new machine will save $12,500 per year after taxes in cash operating costs. If the company decides not to buy the new machine, it can use the old machine for an indefinite period of time by incurring heavy repair costs. The new machine will have a useful life of eight years.

Required:

a. Compute the time-adjusted rate of return for the new machine.

b. Management thinks the estimated useful life of the new machine may be more or less than eight years. Compute the time-adjusted rate of return for the new machine if its useful life is (1) 5 years, and (2) 12 years, instead of eight years.

c. Suppose the new machine's useful life is eight years but the annual after-tax cost savings are only $10,000. Compute the time-adjusted rate of return.

d. Assume the annual after-tax cost savings from the new machine will be $11,000 and its useful life will be 10 years. Compute the time-adjusted rate of return.

Rank alternative
proposals using
various techniques

20–5. The Cougar Company is considering three different investments involving depreciable assets with no salvage value. Listed below are some data related to these investments:

Investment	Initial Outlay	Expected After-Tax Net Cash Inflow per Year	Expected Life of Proposal
1.	$140,000	$28,000	10 years
2.	240,000	48,000	20
3.	360,000	68,000	10

Management requires a minimum return on investments of 12%.

Required:

Rank these proposals using the following selection techniques. (Ignore income taxes and salvage value.)

a. Unadjusted rate of return. (Ignore tax effect of depreciation.)

b. Payback period.

c. Time-adjusted rate of return.

d. Profitability index.

Determine whether
to lease or purchase
equipment

20–6. The Scottsdale Company has decided to computerize its accounting system. The company has two alternatives—it can lease a computer under a three-year contract, or it can purchase a computer outright.

If the computer is leased, the lease payment will be $18,000 each year. The first lease payment will be due on the day the lease contract is signed. The other two payments will be due at the end of the first and second years. All repairs and maintenance will be provided by the lessor.

If the computer is purchased outright, the following costs will be incurred:

Acquisition cost	$42,000
Repairs and maintenance:	
First year	$ 1,200
Second year	1,000
Third year	1,400

The computer is expected to have only a three-year useful life because of obsolescence and technological advancements. The computer will have no salvage value and will be depreciated on a double-declining-balance basis. The Scottsdale Company's cost of capital is 16%.

Required:

Show whether the Scottsdale Company should lease or purchase the computer. (Ignore income taxes.)

Using net present value method, decide whether or not to add a new line of products

20–7. The Prescott Sports Company is trying to decide whether or not to add tennis equipment to its existing line of football, baseball, and basketball equipment. Market research studies and cost analyses have provided the following information:

1. Additional machinery and equipment will be needed to manufacture the tennis equipment. The machines and equipment will cost $800,000 total, will each have a 10-year useful life, and total salvage value will be $40,000.
2. Sales of tennis equipment for the next 10 years have been projected as follows:

1	$120,000
2	170,000
3	245,000
4	270,000
5	295,000
6–10 (each year)	320,000

3. Variable costs are 60% of selling price, and fixed costs and straight-line depreciation will total $156,000 per year.
4. The company will need to advertise its new product line to gain rapid entry into the market. Its advertising campaign costs will be:

1–3	$120,000 (each year)
4–10	70,000 (each year)

5. The company requires a 14% minimum rate of return on investments.

Required:

Using the net present value method, decide whether or not the Prescott Sports Company should add the tennis equipment to its line of products. (Ignore income taxes.)

Evaluate an investment using net present value method

20–8. The Woodruff Company is considering purchasing new equipment that will cost $600,000. It is estimated that the useful life of the equipment will be five years and that there will be a salvage value of $200,000. The company uses straight-line depreciation. It is estimated that the new equipment will have a net cash inflow (before taxes) of $86,000 annually. Assume a tax rate of 40% and that management requires a minimum return of 14%.

Required:

Using the net present value method, determine whether the equipment is an acceptable investment.

Determine whether to sell or keep equipment

20–9. The Holland Company has an opportunity to sell some equipment for $10,000. Such a sale will result in a tax-deductible loss of $1,000. If it is not sold, the equipment is expected to produce net cash inflows after taxes of $3,000 for the next 10 years. In 10 years, it is expected that the equipment can be sold for its book value of $1,000. The company's management feels that currently it has other opportunities that will yield 18%. Assume a 40% tax rate.

Required:

Should the company sell the equipment? Prepare a schedule to support your conclusion.

BUSINESS DECISION PROBLEM 20–1

Compute net present value of several proposals; rank proposals in order of acceptability

The Rice Company wishes to invest $1,000,000 in capital projects that have a minimum expected rate of return of 15%. Six proposals are being evaluated. Acceptance of one proposal does not preclude acceptance of any of the other proposals. The company's criterion is to select proposals that meet its minimum required rate of return (15%).

The relevant information related to the six proposals is presented below:

Investment	Initial Cash Outlay	Expected After-Tax Net Cash Inflow per Year	Expected Life of Proposal
A	$675,000	$131,000	10
B	250,000	46,000	5
C	400,000	73,000	10
D	600,000	130,000	12
E	175,000	34,000	10
F	200,000	60,000	6

Required:

a. Compute the net present value of each of the six proposals.
b. Which projects should be undertaken? Why? Rank them in order of desirability.

BUSINESS DECISION PROBLEM 20–2

Evaluate bookkeeper's computation of a project's net present value; determine acceptability of project

The Trapp Company is considering a capital project that will involve a $300,000 investment in machinery and a $60,000 investment in working capital. The machine has a useful life of 15 years and no salvage value. The annual cash inflows (before taxes) are estimated at $100,000 with annual cash outflows (before taxes) of $25,000. The company uses straight-line depreciation. The income tax rate is assumed to be 40%.

The company's new bookkeeper computed the net present value of the project using a minimum required rate of 18% (the company's cost of capital). The bookkeeper's computations are as follows:

Cash inflows	$100,000
Cash outflows	25,000
Net cash inflow	$ 75,000
Present value factor at 18%	× 5.0915
Present value of net cash inflow	$381,863
Initial cash outlay	300,000
Net present value	$ 81,863

Required:

a. Are the bookkeeper's computations correct? If not, compute the correct net present value.

b. Is this capital project acceptable to the company? Why or why not?

BUSINESS DECISION PROBLEM 20–3

Determine whether to purchase or lease a new machine

The Smith Company is trying to decide whether to purchase or lease a new factory machine. If the machine is purchased, the following costs will be incurred:

Acquisition cost	$500,000
Repairs and maintenance:	
Years 1–5	$ 15,000
Years 6–15	20,000

The machine will be depreciated on a straight-line basis and will have no salvage value. If the machine is leased, the lease payment will be $65,000 each year for 15 years. The first lease payment will be due on the day the lease contract is signed. All repairs and maintenance will be provided by the lessor. The Smith Company's cost of capital is 15%.

Required:

Do you recommend that the company purchase or lease the machine? Show computations to support your answer (ignore income taxes).

21 PERSONAL AND CORPORATE INCOME TAXES

LEARNING OBJECTIVES

After studying this chapter, you should be able to:

1. Compute gross income, adjusted gross income, and taxable income for personal tax returns.
2. Compute the tax liability on personal returns.
3. Compute the tax liability for corporations.
4. Illustrate the use of tax loss carrybacks and carryforwards.
5. Calculate the depreciation allowance for tax purposes using modified ACRS (Accelerated Cost Recovery System).
6. Identify the nature of permanent and temporary differences between taxable income and accounting pre-tax income.
7. Account for temporary differences using interperiod allocation.
8. Define and correctly use the new terms in the glossary.

In 1913, the ratification of the 16th Amendment established the constitutionality of the federal income tax in the United States. Without a doubt, you can expect to file income tax forms as long as you have any significant income.

Income taxes play an important role in both personal and business decisions. Whenever a person or a company considers financial opportunities, the tax consequences of those opportunities should be noted and weighed.

The purpose of this chapter is to provide an introductory understanding of federal income taxes, both personal and corporate. This chapter can only provide a general overview of these taxes due to their complexity and the constantly changing nature of tax laws. Coverage in this chapter is based on tax laws in effect as of the end of 1987. Provisions of major tax legislation such as the Tax Reform Act of 1986 are included. Recognize that some changes may have been made to the tax law since this chapter was revised. The tax rates in effect for 1988 will be used in this chapter unless otherwise stated.

PERSONAL FEDERAL INCOME TAXES

Objective 1: Compute gross income, adjusted gross income, and taxable income for personal tax returns

The first part of this chapter develops the concept of taxable income and illustrates the measurement of the tax liability for individual taxpayers.

Who Must File a Return

In general, all U.S. citizens and resident aliens must file a federal tax return. More specifically, the determination of who must file a return depends on filing status and income level. For examples, the income levels at which a tax return must be filed in 1988 are $4,950 for a single person; $5,700 if age 65 or older; $8,900 for a married couple filing a joint return; $9,500 if one spouse is age 65 or older; and $10,100 if both are age 65 or older. After 1988 all of the minimum income levels at which a tax return must be filed are subject to change because of the indexing of various items in the IRS code.

Filing status. There are four basic filing statuses that can be used in filing an income tax return—single, married filing jointly, married filing separately, and head of household. All of these are self-explanatory except **head of household,** who typically is an unmarried or legally separated person who maintains a residence for someone who qualifies as a dependent of the taxpayer.

Gross Income

Illustration 21.1 contains a general model of the determination of taxable income. The model starts with gross (total) income. **Gross income** includes all of a taxpayer's income from whatever source derived, except for those items specifically excluded, such as inheritances. Gross income includes wages, interest (but not interest earned on an IRA), dividends, tips, bonuses, gambling winnings, gains from property sales, and prizes (including noncash prizes). Even income generated illegally, such as by theft, must be included in gross income. The general rule is that every income item, unless specifically exempted by law, must be included in gross income.

Exclusions from Gross Income

Income items specifically excluded are interest on certain state and municipal bonds, social security benefits, workers' compensation insurance benefits, and several employee "fringe" benefits, such as employer-paid health insurance premiums. Also, gifts, inheritances, certain disability benefits, scholarships, and the proceeds from life insurance policies are excluded.

Illustration 21.1
DETERMINATION OF TAXABLE INCOME
FOR AN INDIVIDUAL TAXPAYER

GROSS (TOTAL) INCOME

Includes all income from whatever source derived except for a few specifically excluded items. Includes such items as wages, dividends, interest, proprietorship earnings, taxpayer's share of partnership earnings, net rents.

less

DEDUCTIONS FOR ADJUSTED GROSS INCOME

Consists of business expenses, payments to an individual retirement arrangement, and a few other minor items.

equals

ADJUSTED GROSS INCOME

less

STANDARD OR ITEMIZED PERSONAL DEDUCTIONS

Deduct the higher of the standard deduction ($3,000 for an unmarried person, or $5,000 for a couple filing jointly in 1988, plus an additional $750 if unmarried, or $600 if married, for each individual over 65 or blind) or itemized personal deductions. Itemized deductions consist of contributions, mortgage interest, certain taxes levied directly against the taxpayer, limited casualty and theft losses, limited medical expenses, and certain "nonbusiness" expenses.

less

EXEMPTIONS

One fixed amount (e.g., $1,950 in 1988) for taxpayer, one for spouse, and one for each dependent.

equals

TAXABLE INCOME

Adjusted Gross Income

Taxpayers are allowed to deduct certain items from gross income in arriving at **adjusted gross income. Deductions for adjusted gross income** include business expenses (only 80% of meals and entertainment), payments by certain individuals to individual retirement accounts (IRA) or payments to Keogh retirement plans, and alimony paid to a former spouse.

Employees can deduct from gross income contributions to an individual retirement account (IRA) if neither the taxpayer nor the taxpayer's spouse is an active participant in an employer-sponsored retirement plan. An IRA is a retirement savings account usually set up in a bank, savings and loan association, insurance company, mutual fund, or brokerage firm. The annual deduction is limited to the lesser of 100% of earnings or $2,000 for an individual, $4,000 for a married couple if both spouses have jobs, and $2,250 for a married couple if only one spouse has earned income. Deductions can only be based on earned income, not "passive" income, such as interest and dividends. The maximum amount will be phased out, however, where adjusted gross income (before the IRA deduction) is over $40,000 on a joint return or $25,000 for an unmarried individual. The deduction will be eliminated when adjusted gross income reaches $50,000 on a joint return or $35,000 for an unmarried person. Employees may also be eligible to contribute to certain other retirement savings plans, including tax-sheltered annuities, government plans, or qualified cash or deferred arrangements (so-called Sec. 401(k) plans).

Because self-employed individuals are not covered by company-established retirement plans, they are allowed to establish their own retirement plan called a Keogh plan (pronounced Key-oh). Keogh plans are available only to self-employed individuals. A self-employed individual (e.g., a consultant) may contribute annually the lesser of $30,000 or 20% of earned income to a defined contribution Keogh plan under the 1986 Tax Reform Act. Additional details concerning IRAs and Keogh plans are left to more advanced textbooks.

Taxable Income

Taxpayers are allowed certain additional deductions and exemptions in arriving at **taxable income.** The **deductions from adjusted gross income** are specified by law and consist of two categories: (1) standard or (2) itemized personal deductions. The **standard deduction amount** in 1988 is $3,000 for single persons, $4,400 for persons filing as head of household, $5,000 for married couples filing a joint return, and $2,500 for married couples filing separate returns. The standard deduction may be increased for each individual or spouse by an additional $600 ($750 for an unmarried individual) for each case of being over 65 or blind. Individuals may use either the standard deduction or the **itemized deductions,** whichever is higher. A taxpayer will itemize deductions only if they exceed the standard deduction.

Itemized deductions. The more common itemized deductions include:

1. Taxes. Real estate taxes, personal property taxes, and state and local income taxes are deductible. License fees, state sales taxes, and federal excise taxes are not deductible.

2. Interest. Interest paid on mortgages on the principal residence and a second residence is generally deductible. The interest must be attributable to loans not exceeding the original purchase price plus the cost of any house improvements (unless the excess mortgage is incurred for educational or medical expenses).

3. Charitable contributions. Gifts to educational, religious, scientific, and charitable organizations are deductible to the extent they do not exceed 50% of adjusted gross income. Donations to individuals, labor unions, and organizations that are established primarily to influence legislation are not deductible.

4. Medical expenses. Within certain limits, unreimbursed health insurance premiums and hospital, medical, and dental expenses incurred by taxpayers and their dependents are deductible. Only that amount of medical costs that exceeds 7.5% of adjusted gross income is deductible. The entire cost of prescription drugs and insulin can be included in medical costs. The cost of other drugs and medicines cannot be included.

To clarify the treatment of medical expenses, assume that in 1988 a taxpayer with an adjusted gross income of $20,000 paid $550 of health insurance premiums, incurred other medical expenses of $700, and incurred prescription drug costs of $400. The medical deduction is:

Health insurance premiums	$ 550
Other unreimbursed medical expenses	700
Medicine costs	400
	$1,650
Less: 7.5% of adjusted gross income (0.075 × $20,000)	1,500
Medical deduction	$ 150

5. Personal casualty losses. Casualty losses are sudden and unexpected losses resulting from theft, accidents, storms, fires, and similar events. Personal casualty losses (that is, casualty losses in property other than for trade or business or for transactions entered for profit) are deductible to the extent that *each* casualty loss exceeds $100 *and* that the total of all unreimbursed casualty losses for the year exceeds 10% of adjusted gross income. Thus, to compute the deduction, first subtract $100 from the dollar amount of *each* loss (ignore losses of less than $100) to obtain an adjusted casualty loss. Then, from the sum of all of the adjusted casualty losses, subtract 10% of adjusted gross income. The positive difference is the personal casualty loss deduction. To illustrate, assume a taxpayer had adjusted gross income of $50,000 and suffered two personal casualty losses during the year—a fire loss of $9,000 and a theft loss of $12,000. The casualty loss deduction is computed as follows:

Adjusted fire loss ($9,000 − $100)	$ 8,900
Adjusted theft loss ($12,000 − $100)	11,900
Total	$20,800
Less 10% of adjusted gross income	5,000
Casualty loss deduction	$15,800

6. Other deductions. In general, this category consists of expenses related to the taxpayer's business or profession that are not deductible from gross income. Included are the costs of professional publications and dues, union dues, safe-deposit box rentals, income tax preparer's fees, business entertainment, and job-related clothing and tools. These miscellaneous deductions are only deductible to the extent that they exceed 2% of adjusted gross income.

Exemptions

The final step in determining taxable income is to deduct exemptions. The dollar amount of exemptions is determined by multiplying the number of **exemptions** allowed the taxpayer by $1,950 in 1988. The exemption allowance increases to $2,000 in 1989 and will increase again in the future because of indexing for inflation. Thus, if a taxpayer has two exemptions in 1988, the dollar amount would be $3,900 ($1,950 × 2). Married persons filing jointly are both considered taxpayers and are allowed one exemption each even though only one spouse has income. An additional exemption may be taken for each dependent.

A dependent for tax purposes is a person who (1) is closely related to the taxpayer or who lived as a member of the taxpayer's family for the entire year; (2) had an income of less than $1,950; (3) received more than half of his or her support from the taxpayer; and (4) who, if married, did not file a joint return with a spouse for the taxable year. An individual to be claimed as a dependent on another taxpayer's return may not deduct any amount as a personal exemption. Beginning in 1988, personal exemptions will be phased out for certain high-income taxpayers.

Computing Tax Liability

Objective 2: Compute the tax liability on personal returns

Once taxable income has been determined, the tax liability can be computed using the rates given in Illustration 21.2. To illustrate the use of these rates, assume Mr. and Mrs. Olson, who have no dependents, file a joint return showing taxable income of $46,280. Their tax liability is computed as follows:

$$\$29,750 \times 0.15 = \$4,462.50$$
$$(\$46,280 - \$29,750) \times 0.28 = \underline{4,628.40}$$
$$\underline{\underline{\$9,090.90}}$$

Marginal and effective tax rates. The tax rates in Illustration 21.2 are progressive on taxable incomes through the range to which the 33% rates apply. Progressive tax rates increase with successively higher amounts of taxable income.

The taxable income of a single taxpayer between $17,850 and $43,150 is taxed at a 28% rate. These percentages are called **marginal tax rates**. A marginal tax rate is the rate applied to the next dollar of taxable income or each incremental amount of income. Such rates are important in decision

Illustration 21.2
TAX RATES

	1988 Tax rate schedules						
	Married filing jointly		**Head of household**		**Single**		
Dependents	*Taxable Income*	*Rate*	*Taxable Income*	*Rate*	*Taxable Income*	*Rate*
0	$0–$29,750	15%			$0–$17,850	15%
	$29,750–$71,900	28	Not available		$17,850–$43,150	28
	$71,900–$171,090	33			$43,150–$100,480	33
	Over $171,090	28			Over $100,480	28
1	$0–$9,750	15%	$0–$23,900	15%	$0–$17,850	15%
	$29,750–$71,900	28	$23,900–$61,650	28	$17,850–$43,150	28
	$71,900–$182,010	33	$61,650–$145,630	33	$43,150–$111,400	33
	Over $182,010	28	Over $145,630	28	Over $111,400	28
2	$0–$29,750	15%	$0–$23,900	15%	$0–$17,850	15%
	$29,750–$71,900	28	$23,900–$61,650	28	$17,850–$43,150	28
	$71,900–$192,930	33	$61,650–$156,550	33	$43,150–$122,320	33
	Over $192,930	28	Over $156,550	28	Over $122,320	28
3	$0–$29,750	15%	$0–$23,900	15%	$0–$17,850	15%
	$29,750–$71,900	28	$23,900–$61,650	28	$17,850–$43,150	28
	$71,900–$203,850	33	$61,650–$167,470	33	$43,150–$133,240	33
	Over $203,850	28	Over $167,470	28	Over $133,240	28

Note: The top figure for the 33% bracket will increase by $10,920 in 1988 for each exemption in addition to two (joint) or one (single) included in the tables.

making because they show the marginal effect of a decision. For example, assume that Joe Hardy, a single taxpayer in the 28% tax bracket, could earn $400 on a plumbing job if he would work on Sunday. But being in the 28% bracket, Joe would have to pay $112 ($400 × 0.28) more income taxes if he takes the job, which means that he would net only $288 from the job. Joe may decide he would rather watch a football game or go fishing. This type of analysis illustrates the correct use of the marginal tax rate.

The effective tax rate rather than the marginal rate should be used as a measure of total taxes to be paid. The **effective tax rate** is the average rate of taxation for a given amount of taxable income. For example, if Joe Hardy earns $34,600 for the year, he is in the 28% marginal tax bracket. But he does not pay $9,688 ($34,600 × 0.28) per year in taxes. Joe actually pays taxes at a 21.3% effective tax rate computed as follows:

$$\frac{\text{Effective}}{\text{(average) tax rate}} = \frac{\text{Total taxes paid}}{\text{Total taxable income}}$$

$$\text{Effective tax rate} = \frac{(\$17,850 \times 0.15) + [0.28 \times (\$34,600 - \$17,850)]^*}{\$34,600}$$

$$\text{Effective tax rate} = \frac{\$7,367.50}{\$34,600} = 21.3\%$$

*These rates were taken from Illustration 20.2 for a single taxpayer.

Capital Gains and Losses

Capital assets are all items of property other than inventories, receivables, copyrights, certain governmental obligations, and real and depreciable property used in a trade or business. Investments in capital stocks and bonds are examples of capital assets. A gain is an excess of selling price over cost. Some capital gains escape taxation. For example, a taxpayer age 55 or older may exclude from gross income up to $125,000 ($62,500 on a separate return) of any gain on the sale of the taxpayer's home. All other capital gains are taxed at the same rates as ordinary income. The tax law relative to net losses is more complex, containing certain limitations. Discussion of losses is left for a more advanced course.

Tax Credits

A **tax credit** is a direct deduction from the amount of taxes to be paid, resulting largely from certain expenditures made by the taxpayer. Because tax credits reduce the amount of taxes to be paid dollar for dollar, they are much more valuable to the taxpayer than deductions. A tax credit of $100 saves $100 of cash; a $100 deduction, on the other hand, is worth only $100 times the taxpayer's marginal tax rate. The maximum value, then, of any deduction is 33% of the amount of the deduction since the highest tax rate in 1988 is 33%.

There are tax credits for persons with low earned income levels, for the elderly, for child and dependent care expenses, and for income taxes paid to foreign countries.

Filing the Tax Return

Personal tax returns for a calendar year must be filed by April 15 of the following year. Extensions may be filed, but payment of any tax liability is still due on April 15. Most taxpayers are also employees and, therefore, taxes are withheld by employers under our pay-as-you-go tax system. Also, taxpayers having income above a prescribed amount that is not subject to withholding must pay an **estimated tax.** This estimated tax must be paid in four installments. The taxes withheld and the estimated taxes paid are entered as offsets to the total tax liability on the tax return. Any remaining unpaid taxes are paid to the Internal Revenue Service when the return is filed. In some cases, tax withholdings and estimated taxes paid may have exceeded tax liability, and the taxpayer can claim a refund.

COMPREHENSIVE ILLUSTRATION—PERSONAL INCOME TAXES

An actual tax return consists of a number of preprinted forms that are filled out by the taxpayer. Most taxpayers will file either Form 1040A, often called the short form, or Form 1040, the long form. A taxpayer who intends to itemize deductions cannot file a short form, 1040A. A taxpayer who uses the long form generally must attach various schedules to it.

Two common schedules included in the long form are Schedule A and Schedule B. Schedule A shows the itemized deductions, while Schedule B lists all dividends and interest income when dividend and interest income exceeds $400. One copy of the taxpayer's Form W-2 is attached to the tax return. The W-2 is issued by the employer and shows wages earned and taxes withheld during the period of these wages.

Illustration 21.3 shows a brief summary schedule of the 1988 tax return items for Lee and Dora Bowman, who are married and file a joint return. Lee is chief engineer for a manufacturing company; Dora is a full-time homemaker. Both taxpayers are under age 65; they have two dependent children, ages 13 and 15. Dora owns a number of bonds and shares of stock, some of which she sold during the year, realizing $10,000 of capital gains and $1,000 of capital losses. Total income taxes withheld during the year amounted to $12,400. In addition, Lee and Dora paid estimated taxes of $800. Other information needed to compute the Bowman's tax liability and tax refund are shown in the illustration. The income tax of $12,975 is computed using the tax rate schedule in Illustration 21.2.

Illustration 21.3
JOINT TAX RETURN COMPUTATIONS

Salary		$58,000
Interest income		4,000
Dividend income		6,000
Capital gain ($10,000) less capital loss ($1,000)		9,000
Total		$77,000
Contribution to an individual retirement account		–0–
Adjusted gross income		$77,000
Itemized deductions:		
Medical expense ($5,925 − $5,775; total medical cost less 7.5% of adjusted gross income)	$ 150	
Charitable contributions	2,240	
Taxes (real estate on home, state income)	5,670	
Casualty loss ($8,350 − $100 − $7,700; total personal casualty loss less $100 exclusion and 10% of adjusted gross income)	550	
Miscellaneous (professional dues, subscriptions, etc.) [$1,980 − ($77,000 × 0.02)]	440	
	$ 9,050	
Standard deduction amount	$ 5,000	
Higher of itemized versus standard deduction		9,050
		$67,950
Exemptions (4 × $1,950)		7,800
Taxable income		60,150
Income tax (0.15 × $29,750) + (0.28 × $30,400)		12,975
Less: Applicable tax credits		–0–
Total tax liability		12,975
Income taxes withheld	$12,400	
Estimated taxes paid	800	13,200
Income taxes refund due		$ 225

CORPORATE FEDERAL INCOME TAXATION

Objective 3: Compute the tax liability for corporations

Business managers strive to maximize income in a company, while at the same time attempting to minimize taxes. In a sole proprietorship or partnership, business earnings flow directly to the owner or owners and thus affect personal tax returns. In contrast, the corporation itself is considered a taxpayer by law and, therefore, is the only form of business organization that pays federal income taxes.

Taxable Income

Corporate income taxes are based on the amount of taxable income shown on IRS Form 1120. Corporation taxable income is computed by subtracting all allowable deductions from the corporation's gross income. Corporate gross income is calculated much like the calculation for personal gross income; it basically includes all revenues from sales, services, or investments of the company. Allowable deductions from a corporate standpoint must meet four criteria; such deductions must be business related, ordinary, necessary, and reasonable in amount.

Tax Rates

Once taxable income is determined, a tax rate is applied to find the amount of tax liability. The graduated tax rates applicable to corporations for 1988 are as shown in Illustration 21.4.

Illustration 21.4
CORPORATE TAX RATES

Corporate Taxable Income	Tax Rate
$0–$ 50,000	15%
$ 50,000–$ 75,000	25
$ 75,000–$100,000	34
$100,000–$335,000	39
A corporation with taxable income over $335,000 will pay a flat rate of 34% on all taxable income.	

To illustrate, using these rates, a corporation with taxable income of $110,000 will have a tax liability of $26,150, computed as follows:

Tax on first $50,000 (at 15%)	$ 7,500
Tax on next $25,000 (at 25%).	6,250
Tax on next $25,000 (at 34%)	8,500
Tax on remaining $10,000 (at 39%)	3,900
	$26,150

Whereas a corporation with taxable income of $500,000 will have a tax liability of $170,000 ($500,000 × 34%).

The tax law requires that an alternative minimum tax be calculated and paid by the corporation if it is higher than the ordinary tax. The tax will be calculated at 20% of taxable income adjusted by adding back a number of the tax breaks allowed to arrive at taxable income and reduced, in some cases, by an exemption of up to $40,000.

Tax Loss Carrybacks and Carryforwards

*Objective 4:
Illustrate the use of
tax loss carrybacks
and carryforwards*

If a corporation suffers a net loss in a given year, it of course owes no income tax in that year. The tax law also provides that the corporation can apply this loss to its taxable income from prior years and recover some or all of the taxes paid during those years. This provision is called **tax loss carryback**. If the corporation elects to carry the loss back, it may carry the loss back three years. The loss must be applied first to the oldest year, then to the next oldest year, and so on until the loss is used up or until there is no more prior year income that may be affected. The corporation may then carry the remaining, unused loss forward for up to 15 years to reduce its taxable income in those future years. This is called a **tax loss carryforward.**

To illustrate the application of this provision, assume that a corporation had the amounts of taxable income (or loss) shown below (assume that the 1988 rates were in effect for all years):

Year	Taxable Income (or Loss)	Taxes Paid	Taxes Recovered
1985 . . .	$ 15,000	$ 2,250	$2,250
1986 . . .	20,000	3,000	3,000
1987 . . .	5,000	750	750
1988 . . .	(100,000)	–0–	–0–
1989 . . .	40,000	–0–	–0–
1990 . . .	10,000	–0–	–0–
1991 . . .	30,000	3,000	–0–
1992 . . .	50,000	7,500	–0–
1993 . . .	60,000	10,000	–0–

The loss of $100,000 in 1988 would first be offset against the $15,000 of income in 1985, then the $20,000 in 1986, and next the $5,000 in 1987. The company would recover the $6,000 taxes previously paid. At this point it would have a $60,000 loss carryforward. It would apply $40,000 of the loss toward taxable income in 1989; the result is a taxable income of $0 for 1989. This leaves $20,000 of loss carryforward remaining; $10,000 would be used to offset income in the next year (1990), and the other $10,000 would be used to reduce 1991 taxable income. The taxes paid for 1991 are ($30,000 − $10,000) × 0.15 = $3,000. If a corporation decides not to apply the loss to its taxable income from prior years, it can still carry the loss forward to future years. If the loss carryforward is not "used up" by the end of the 15th year, the remaining portion is lost.

Accounting Methods Used for Tax Purposes

Accrual method. The method of accounting affects when revenues and expenses are recognized. Most corporations and large businesses use the accrual method. Under this method revenues are generally recognized when earned. The earning of revenue normally occurs when services are rendered or when goods are delivered. When payment has been received before the revenue has been earned, an exception may require recognition of income at the time payment is received.

Expenses are generally recognized when liabilities are established for payment of goods or services received. Costs of assets are deferred and charged to expense in the period in which the assets are used or consumed.

Modified cash method. Sole proprietorship, partnerships, and certain small corporations may use a modified cash method. This method is described as a "modified" (rather than a "pure") cash method, because long-term assets cannot be charged to expense when purchased nor can all prepaid expenses (such as a three-year insurance premium) be deducted when paid. Also, revenues must be reported when *constructively received* even though the cash is not yet in the possession of the business. For instance, a check received at the end of the year is considered to be revenue even though it has not been cashed. If inventories are a substantial factor in producing income, the company must use the accrual basis for recognizing sales, cost of goods sold, and related asset (inventory and accounts receivable) and liability (accounts payable) accounts.

Accounting for inventories. There are several different methods of accounting for inventories. Each method assumes a different flow of costs and thus results in a different taxable income if used for tax purposes. In recent years many firms have adopted LIFO (last-in, first-out), in which the last goods purchased are assumed to be the first ones sold. Under this method, during periods of rising prices, the most recent higher costs are charged against revenues and the asset, inventory, is shown at lower earlier costs. The result is lower net income and lower taxes. The tax law generally requires that a company may only use the LIFO methods for tax purposes if it uses it for financial statement purposes.

Depreciation Methods Used for Tax Purposes

Objective 5: Calculate the depreciation allowance for tax purposes using modified ACRS

Tax depreciation is substantially different from depreciation used for accounting purposes. In accounting, depreciation methods are designed to match the expense of a capital investment against the revenue the investment produces. The depreciable period or useful life used for tax purposes is based on tax law and has no relationship to the actual useful life of the asset; thus, no attempt is made to match revenues and expenses.

Prior to 1981, several depreciation methods were available for tax purposes, including the sum-of-the-years'-digits method and the uniform-rate-on-declining-balance method. The Economic Recovery Tax Act of 1981 introduced a new depreciation system known as the Accelerated Cost Recovery System (ACRS). However, generally effective January 1, 1987, the Tax Reform Act of 1986 substantially modified the ACRS rules. For purposes of this textbook, we shall refer to these rules as **modified ACRS.**

Depreciable assets are grouped into one of eight different classes (see Illustration 21.5). Each class has an assigned life over which costs of the assets (not reduced by salvage) are depreciated.

Illustration 21.5
MODIFIED ACRS

Class of Investment	Kinds of Assets
3 years	Investments in some short-lived assets.
5 years	Automobiles, light-duty trucks, machinery, and equipment used in research and development.
7 years	All other machinery and equipment, such as dies, drills, presses, etc., furniture, and fixtures.
10 years	Some longer-lived equipment.
15 years	Sewage treatment plants and telephone distribution plants.
20 years	Sewer pipes and very long-lived equipment.
27.5 years	Residential rental property.
31.5 years	Nonresidential real estate.

Depreciable assets in the 3-, 5-, 7-, and 10-year classes may be depreciated by using the 200% declining-balance method. Assets in the 15- and 20-year classes may be depreciated by using the 150% declining-balance method. Assets in the 27.5- and 31.5-year classes must be depreciated by using straight-line depreciation. The declining-balance methods result in faster write-offs in the first few years of an investment's life. Cash saved from reduced taxes in the early years of the life of the assets can be invested in new productive assets or can be applied to the replacement of the old assets when they become obsolete or worn out.

Once the asset has been classified, the depreciation schedule for the life of the asset can be completed. To illustrate a depreciation schedule, assume that Bigwig Company acquired and placed in service a depreciable asset on January 1, 1988, for $10,000. The asset falls into the three-year class under the new tax law. The depreciation schedule for the asset would be as follows:

Year	Recovery Percentage*		Original Cost	Depreciation Expense	Total Accumulated Depreciation	Book Value
1988	33.33%	×	$10,000	$3,333	$ 3,333	$6,667
1989	44.45	×	10,000	4,445	7,778	2,222
1990	14.81	×	10,000	1,481	9,259	741
1991	7.41	×	10,000	741	10,000	0

*These cost recovery percentages are from IRS Revenue Procedure 87–57.

Tax depreciation is very desirable since it decreases taxable income and hence decreases the corporation's tax liability. However, it is sometimes beneficial for taxpayers to spread out depreciation rather than bunching it in earlier years of the asset's life. For this reason the law provides an alternative. The taxpayer may elect to use the straight-line method rather than the accelerated method.

INCOME TAX ALLOCATION

Objective 6: Identify the nature of permanent and temporary differences between taxable income and accounting pre-tax income

Taxable income and net income before income taxes (for simplicity, pre-tax income) for a corporation may differ sharply for a number of reasons. In fact, the tax return may show a loss, while the income statement shows positive pre-tax income. This difference raises a question about the amount of federal income tax expense to be shown on the income statement. The answer lies in the nature of the items causing the difference between taxable income and pre-tax income. Some items create permanent differences, while others create temporary (or timing) differences. Both kinds of differences are discussed on the following pages.

Permanent Differences

Certain types of revenues and expenses included in the computation of net income for book purposes are excluded from the computation of taxable income. **Permanent differences** between taxable income and financial statement pre-tax income are caused by tax law provisions that exclude an item of expense, revenue, gain, or loss as an element of taxable income. For instance, interest earned on certain state, county, or municipal bonds is included in book net income but is not subject to tax and therefore is not included in determining taxable income. The same is true for life insurance proceeds received by a corporation. Other items that are expensed for book purposes are not deductible for tax purposes, such as premiums paid for officers' life insurance, costs of attempting to influence legislation, and amortization of goodwill. These are only a few of the numerous items for which the tax treatment is completely different from the accounting treatment. These differences in treatment never change or reverse themselves. Therefore they are called permanent differences. Such differences cause no accounting problem—the estimated actual amount of income tax expense for the year is shown on the income statement even if this results in reporting only $1,000 of income tax expense on $100,000 of pre-tax income.

Temporary Differences

Other items of revenue and expense often are recognized for tax purposes at times different from those for financial reporting purposes. Such temporary differences between taxable income and financial statement pre-tax income are caused by items that affect both taxable income and pre-tax income, but in different periods.

A **temporary difference** is the difference between taxable income and financial statement income caused by items that affect both taxable income and pre-tax income, but in different periods.

For example, interpretations of the tax code generally have held that revenue received in advance is taxable when received and that current expenses based on estimates of future costs (such as costs of performance under service contracts) are not deductible until incurred. Temporary differences can also result from using accounting methods for tax purposes that are different from the ones used for financial reporting purposes. For example, a corporation may use straight-line depreciation for book purposes and modified ACRS depreciation for tax purposes. Eventually these revenues and expenses are recognized in computing both accounting income and taxable income. Therefore, these variations between taxable income and net income are called temporary differences.

A sample reconciliation between income before taxes and taxable income for a corporation appears below:

Net income before taxes per income statement		$74,000
Add:		
Life insurance premiums paid	$ 700	
Service revenue received in advance	5,000	
Estimated expenses under service contracts	1,000	6,700
		$80,700
Deduct:		
Interest on New York State bonds	$3,000	
Difference in depreciation for tax purposes ($8,000)		
and for book purposes ($6,000)	2,000	5,000
Taxable income		$75,700

As discussed above, temporary differences include items that will be included in both taxable income and pre-tax income, but in different periods. The items involved will thus have a tax effect. When there are temporary differences, generally accepted accounting principles require application of tax allocation procedures. Under **interperiod income tax allocation** the tax effect of an element of expense or revenue, or of loss or gain, that will affect taxable income is allocated to the period in which the item is recognized for accounting purposes, regardless of the period in which the element is recognized for tax purposes.

In the preceding reconciliation between net income before taxes and taxable income, the life insurance premiums paid (for which the corporation is beneficiary of the policy) are *never deductible* for income tax purposes, and the interest on New York State bonds is *never* taxable. These are permanent differences and therefore involve no income tax allocation. The other reconciling items are temporary differences for which income tax allocation procedures are required.

Objective 7: Account for temporary differences using interperiod allocation

Income tax allocation illustrated. To illustrate the tax allocation procedure required for temporary differences, assume that:

1. A firm acquired a depreciable asset on Janaury 1, 1988, for $10,000 that has an estimated life of 3 years with no expected scrap value.
2. The firm uses the straight-line depreciation method for financial reporting purposes and the new modified ACRS method for tax pur-

poses (the asset falls into the three-year class for which depreciation has been previously calculated).

3. Net income before depreciation and income taxes is $10,000 for each year of the asset's life.
4. There are no other items that cause differences between pre-tax income and taxable income.
5. The tax rate is 15% (to simplify the illustration).

The federal income tax liability for each year would be as shown in Illustration 21.6.

The federal income tax expense for each year for financial reporting purposes would be as shown in Illustration 21.7.

Illustration 21.6
CALCULATION OF FEDERAL INCOME TAX LIABILITY

	1988	1989	1990	1991	Total
Income before depreciation and income taxes	$10,000	$10,000	$10,000	$10,000	$40,000
Depreciation for tax purposes . . .	3,333	4,445	1,481	741	10,000
Taxable income	$ 6,667	$ 5,555	$ 8,519	$ 9,259	$30,000
Federal income tax payable (15% of taxable income)	$ 1,000	$ 833	$ 1,278	$ 1,389	$ 4,500

Illustration 21.7
CALCULATION OF FEDERAL INCOME TAX EXPENSE

	1988	1989	1990	1991	Total
Income before depreciation and income taxes	$10,000	$10,000	$10,000	$10,000	$40,000
Depreciation (straight-line method) (rounded)	3,333	3,333	3,334	–0–	10,000
Pre-tax income	$ 6,667	$ 6,667	$ 6,666	$10,000	$30,000
Federal income tax expense (15% of pre-tax income)	$ 1,000	$ 1,000	$ 1,000	$ 1,500	$ 4,500
Net income	$ 5,667	$ 5,667	$ 5,666	$ 8,500	$25,500

Note that for 1989, tax depreciation ($4,445, Illustration 21.6) exceeds the book expense for depreciation ($3,333, Illustration 21.7) by $1,112, but that effect is reversed during 1990 through 1991 so that depreciation at the end of 1991 is the same ($10,000) in both cases. Since the effects reverse over time, they constitute temporary differences which result in debits or credits to the Deferred Federal Income Tax Payable account. Because tax and book depreciation happen to be the same for 1988, no deferred income tax is recorded for that year. The required entries for 1988 and 1989 to record income taxes and to set up deferred income taxes for the temporary difference for excess of tax depreciation over financial depreciation are:

	1988		1989	
Federal Income Tax Expense	1,000		1,000	
Federal Income Tax Payable		1,000		833
Deferred Federal Income Tax Payable		–0–		167
To record income tax expense.				

The required entries for 1990 and 1991 to record income taxes and to adjust the Deferred Federal Income Tax Payable account to its proper balance are:

	1990		1991	
Federal Income Tax Expense	1,000		1,500	
Deferred Federal Income Tax Payable	278			111
Federal Income Tax Payable		1,278		1,389
To record income tax expense.				

Note again that the amount of federal income tax expense recognized for the three years the asset is depreciated for book purposes (i.e., 1988–1990) remains constant at $1,000 even though the federal income tax liability varies from $833 for 1989 to $1,278 for 1990. The normalizing of the tax expense for each year is accomplished by making entries in the Deferred Federal Income Tax Payable account. The tables clearly show that the tax expense for the four years is $4,500 and that the tax payments for the four years also sum to $4,500. The only difference is that the tax expense charged to each year is not the same amount as the actual liability for each year.

In this simplified example, the Deferred Federal Income Tax Payable account has a zero balance at the end of four years. But actual business experience has shown that once a Deferred Federal Income Tax Payable account is established, it is seldom decreased or reduced to zero. The reason is that most businesses acquire new depreciable assets, usually at higher prices. The result is that depreciation for tax purposes continues to be greater than depreciation for financial reporting purposes, and the balance in the Deferred Federal Income Tax Payable account also continues to grow. For this reason, many accountants seriously question the validity of tax allocation in circumstances such as those described above. Also, some accountants question whether a company can have a liability at a reporting date for income taxes for tax years that have not yet started. But discussion of these controversial issues must be left to more advanced textbooks. In the above example, the Deferred Federal Income Tax Payable account would be reported as a long-term liability on the balance sheet because the asset causing its existence is classified as a long-term asset.

SUMMARY

Income taxes play a significant role in both personal and business decisions. Whenever a company or a person considers financial opportunities, the tax consequences of those opportunities need to be considered.

There are a number of steps in the determination of taxable income for an individual taxpayer. The general rule is that all income from all sources is included in gross income unless the item is specifically excluded. Among items specifically excluded are interest on state and municipal bonds, certain social security benefits, and workmen's compensation insurance benefits.

Certain deductions are subtracted from gross income to arrive at adjusted gross income. These deductions, called deductions for adjusted gross income, consist primarily of business expenses, certain contributions to IRA and Keogh retirement plans, and other specified items. A second set of deductions is subtracted from adjusted gross income. These deductions, called itemized deductions, include items such as taxes, interest expense, medical expenses, and charitable contributions. In addition to the itemized deductions, the taxpayer is permitted to subtract from adjusted gross income a certain amount of income that is exempt from taxation. One exemption is available for each taxpayer and each qualifying dependent. After the greater of itemized deductions or the standard deduction and the exemptions are subtracted from adjusted gross income, the result is taxable income.

The amount of tax due is determined by comparing the taxpayer's taxable income with either the tax table or the tax rate schedule that is appropriate for the taxpayer's filing status—single, married filing jointly, married filing separately, or head of household. The marginal tax rate is the tax rate that is applied to the next dollar of taxable income. The effective tax rate, on the other hand, is the average rate of tax paid on the taxpayer's total income. Capital gains no longer receive more favorable tax treatment than does ordinary income. Capital gains are taxed at ordinary income rates.

Tax credits directly reduce the taxpayer's tax liability. Among the more common of the tax credits allowed to individual taxpayers are the child and dependent care tax credit and the low earned-income tax credit.

Personal income tax returns for a calendar tax year must be filed by April 15 of the following year. All taxpayers earning more than specified minimum amounts of income must file a tax return. Because of tax withholding requirements, most taxpayers will have paid most, if not all, of their income taxes for the year during the tax year.

Computing gross income for a corporation is much like computing gross income for an individual. Computing gross income for a corporation involves adding revenues from sales, services, and investments of the company. The computation of taxable income for a corporation involves subtracting allowable deductions from gross income; allowable deductions are expenses that are business related, ordinary, necessary, and reasonable in amount. Once taxable income is determined, a tax rate is applied to find the amount of the tax liability. As noted with personal tax returns, tax credits are also available for corporations.

Corporations that suffer net losses for a taxable year may apply the loss to taxable income from the three prior years and recover some or all of the taxes paid during those years. This provision is known as a tax loss carryback. The corporation may then carry the loss forward and apply it to taxable income in future years, a provision known as a tax loss carry-forward.

Tax depreciation is substantially different from depreciation used for accounting purposes. Modified ACRS is a depreciation system that is used for tax purposes. The system classifies depreciable assets into various classes and provides depreciation schedules for each of those classes of assets.

Certain types of revenues and expenses included in the computation of net income for book purposes are excluded from the computation of taxable income. These items give rise to permanent differences between taxable income and financial statement pre-tax income. Certain other revenue and expense items are recognized for tax purposes at different times than they are recognized for financial statement purposes. Those differences are referred to as temporary differences. Interperiod tax allocation is a procedure whereby the effects of an element of expense or revenue, or loss or gain, that will affect taxable income are allocated to the period in which the item is recognized for accounting purposes, regardless of the period in which it is recognized for tax purposes.

Objective 8: Define and correctly use the new terms in the glossary

NEW TERMS INTRODUCED IN CHAPTER 21

Adjusted gross income Gross income less deductions for adjusted gross income such as business expenses, certain payments to an individual retirement account (IRA), and certain other deductions (731).

Capital assets All items of property other than inventories, trade accounts and notes receivable, copyrights, government obligations due within one year and issued at a discount, and real or depreciable property used in a trade or business. Examples include investments in capital stocks and bonds (736).

Deductions for adjusted gross income Expenses of carrying on a trade, business, or practice of a profession, certain payments to an IRA or Keogh plan, and alimony paid (731).

Deductions from adjusted gross income Specified by law; either standard deduction amount or itemized deductions (732).

Effective tax rate Average rate of taxation for a given amount of taxable income (735).

Estimated tax A tax that must be paid in four installments by persons having amounts of income above a certain level that are not subject to withholding (736).

Exemptions A fixed amount, $1,950 in 1988 and $2,000 in 1989 due to indexing, that a taxpayer may deduct from adjusted gross income for the taxpayer, the spouse, and one more for each dependent (734).

Gross income All items of income from whatever source derived, except for those items specifically excluded by law (730).

Head of household Certain unmarried or legally separated persons who maintain a residence for a relative or dependent (730).

Interperiod income tax allocation A procedure whereby the tax effects of an element of expense, revenue, loss or gain, that will affect taxable income is allocated to the period in which the item is recognized for accounting purposes, regardless of the period in which the element is recognized for tax purposes (743).

Itemized deductions Deductions from adjusted gross income for items such as contributions, mortgage interest paid, taxes, casualty losses, limited medical expenses, and other employment related expenses (732).

Marginal tax rate The tax rate that will be levied against the next dollar of taxable income (734).

Modified ACRS A tax method of depreciation that assigns assets into particular groups that have specified lives for depreciation purposes. The 1986 Tax Reform Act modified the Accelerated Cost Recovery System (740).

Permanent differences Differences between taxable income and financial statement pre-tax income caused by tax law provisions that exclude an item of expense, revenue, gain, or loss as an element of taxable income (742).

Standard deduction amount An amount that can all be taken in lieu of itemized deductions. For 1988 the amount is $3,000 for single persons, $4,400 for head of households, and $5,000 for married persons filing joint returns. An additional $750 (or $600 if married) is allowed for each individual over 65 or blind (732).

Tax credit A direct reduction from the amount of taxes to be paid, resulting largely from certain expenditures made (736).

Tax loss carryback Provisions in tax law permitting corporations to apply a loss to their taxable income from three prior years and recover some or all of the taxes paid during those years (739).

Tax loss carryforward Provisions in tax law permitting corporations to carry any remaining, unused loss forward for up to 15 years to reduce their taxable income for future years (739).

Taxable income Adjusted gross income less deductions and exemptions (732).

Temporary (or timing) differences Differences between taxable income and financial statement pre-tax income caused by items that affect both taxable income and pre-tax income, but in different periods (742).

Total (gross) income See Gross income.

DEMONSTRATION PROBLEM 21–1

Bob Smith is a CPA employed by a CPA firm at an annual salary of $45,000. He is single and has no dependents. Other information concerning his 1988 finances follows:

Gain on sale of stock acquired in 1982	$ 6,000
Loss on sale of stock purchased in November 1985	600
Interest received	1,500
Dividends received	2,440
Interest paid on mortgage	690
Taxes paid:	
State income	1,800
Property	750
Professional dues and subscriptions to professional journals	1,562
Business entertainment expenses	300
Charitable contributions	388
Health insurance premiums	500
Drugs and medicine	700
Other medical and dental expenses	3,470
Income taxes withheld	12,000

Required:

a. Compute the taxable income for Mr. Smith (Prepare a schedule similar to Illustration 21.3.)

b. Using the 1988 tax rates in Illustration 21.2, compute the additional taxes due the IRS or the refund due Mr. Smith.

Solution to demonstration problem 21–1

a.
Salary			$45,000
Interest income			1,500
Dividend income			2,440
Capital gain ($6,000) less capital loss ($600)			5,400
			$54,340
Itemized deductions:			
Interest paid		$ 690	
Taxes paid (state income, property)		2,550	
Miscellaneous business expenses (entertainment, professional dues, journal subscriptions) ($1,862 − $1,087)		775	
Charitable contributions		388	
Health care:			
Health insurance premiums	$ 500		
Other medical and dental expenses	3,470		
Drugs and medicine	700		
	$4,670		
Less 7.5% of adjusted gross income	4,076		
Medical deduction		594	
		$4,997	
Standard deduction		$2,540	
Higher of itemized versus standard deduction			4,997
			$49,343
Exemptions (1 × $1,950)			1,950
Taxable income			$47,393

b.
Income tax ($17,850 × 0.15) + ($5,400* × 0.28) + ($24,143 × 0.28)		10,949.54
Income taxes withheld		12,000.00
Tax refund		$ 1,050.46

*Net capital gain taxed at a maximum of 28%.

DEMONSTRATION PROBLEM 21–2

The records of the LaVista Corporation show the following for the calendar year 1988:

Sales	$385,000
Interest earned on—	
State of New Jersey bonds	3,000
City of Miami bonds	1,500
Essex County, Ohio, School District No. 2 bonds	375
Costs of goods sold and other expenses	315,000
Allowable extra depreciation under modified ACRS	4,500
Dividends declared	15,000
Revenue received in advance, considered taxable income this year	3,000
Contribution to influence legislation (included in "other expenses")	300

Required:

a. Present a schedule showing the computation of taxable income.

b. Compute the amount of the corporation's tax that is payable for the current year. (Use the rates given in the textbook.)

c. Prepare the adjusting entry necessary to recognize federal income tax expense assuming income tax allocation procedures are followed. The only permanent differences are the contribution to influence legislation and the nontaxable interest.

Solution to demonstration problem 21–2

a.

LAVISTA CORPORATION
Computation of Taxable Income and Income Taxes
For the Year 1988

Sales	$385,000
Cost of goods sold and other expenses	315,000
Reported income from operations	$ 70,000
Add: Revenue received in advance	3,000
Contribution to influence legislation	300
	$ 73,300
Less: Allowable additional depreciation	4,500
Taxable income	$ 68,800

b.

Computation of tax liability:

15% of the first $50,000	$ 7,500	
25% of the next $18,800	4,700	
Total tax payable	$12,200	

c.

Federal Income Tax Expense*	12,575	
Federal Income Taxes Payable		12,200
Deferred Federal Income Taxes Payable		375

*Federal income tax expense is computed as follows:

Reported income from operations	$70,000
Add back permanent difference—contribution to influence legislature . .	300
Base for computing tax expense	$70,300

Computation of tax expense:

$50,000 at 15%	$ 7,500
$20,300 at 25%	5,075
Tax on $70,300 (tax expense)	$12,575

DEMONSTRATION PROBLEM 21–3

On January 1, 1988, the Warble Corporation purchased new equipment for $20,000. The equipment falls into the three-year class under modified ACRS, but will be depreciated for accounting purposes over four years using the straight-line method.

Required:

a. Using the cost recovery percentages in the table following Illustration 21.5 (page 741), compute the depreciation for tax purposes for 1988, 1989, 1990, and 1991.

b. Assuming that there are no other temporary differences and that net income before depreciation and income taxes is $80,000 for each of the four years, prepare a schedule showing taxable income and income taxes payable. Use a 40% rate.

c. Prepare a schedule showing net income and income tax expense for each of the four years.

d. Give the required adjusting journal entry at year-end to record income tax expense for each of the four years.

Solution to demonstration problem 21–3

a.
$$1988: \$20,000 \times 33.33\% = \$6,666$$
$$1989: \$20,000 \times 44.45\% = \$8,890$$
$$1990: \$20,000 \times 14.81\% = \$2,962$$
$$1991: \$20,000 \times \ 7.41\% = \$1,482$$

b.

	1988	1989	1990	1991
Income before depreciation and income taxes	$80,000	$80,000	$80,000	$80,000
Depreciation	6,666	8,890	2,962	1,482
Taxable income	$73,334	$71,110	$77,038	$78,518
Income taxes payable (40%)	$29,334	$28,444	$30,815	$31,407

c.

	1988	1989	1990	1991
Income before depreciation and income taxes	$80,000	$80,000	$80,000	$80,000
Depreciation	5,000	5,000	5,000	5,000
Pre-tax income	$75,000	$75,000	$75,000	$75,000
Income tax expense (40%)	30,000	30,000	30,000	30,000
Net income	$45,000	$45,000	$45,000	$45,000

d. 1988

Federal Income Tax Expense	30,000	
Deferred Federal Income Taxes Payable		666
Federal Income Tax Payable		29,334
To record federal income tax expense.		

1989

Federal Income Tax Expense	30,000	
Deferred Federal Income Taxes Payable		1,556
Federal Income Tax Payable		28,444
To record federal income tax expense.		

1990

Federal Income Tax Expense	30,000	
Deferred Federal Income Taxes Payable	815	
Federal Income Taxes Payable		30,815
To record federal income tax expense.		

1991

Federal Income Tax Expense	30,000	
Deferred Federal Income Taxes Payable	1,403	
Federal Income Taxes Payable		31,403
To record federal income tax expense.		

QUESTIONS

1. What is the general rule for determining whether a particular cash receipt should be included in gross income? Name several items that might be considered income that are excluded from gross income. Why are they excluded?

2. Define the term *adjusted gross income* as it is used for personal income tax purposes.

3. For what kinds of expenditures may personal (itemized) deductions be taken on a personal income tax return?

4. What are exemptions, and by how much does one exemption reduce taxable income?

5. What is a tax credit? Give an example of tax credits.

6. Which is the most valuable to a taxpayer: *(a)* a tax credit of $1,000, *(b)* a $1,000 allowed deduction for a contribution to an IRA, or *(c)* an additional exemption which is currently worth $1,000? In your answer, rank the three items according to their probable value to a taxpayer.

7. What does a person mean when making the statement, "I'm in the 28% bracket"?

8. What is an estimated tax? How is it levied and paid?

9. Hud Corporation has suffered a loss for the current year. How can the corporation treat this loss for tax purposes?

10. How is depreciation for accounting purposes different from tax depreciation?

11. Distinguish between permanent differences and temporary differences. List two items that might be a cause of each type of difference.

12. When is interperiod tax allocation used?

13. A classmate states: "Why all the fuss about deferring revenue and recognizing expenses sooner for tax purposes? All net taxable income is taxed eventually anyway. It is only a matter of putting off the payment. I don't think these manipulations are worth the effort." Comment.

14. Classified among the long-term liabilities of Corporation A is an account entitled "Deferred Federal Income Taxes Payable." Explain the nature of this account.

EXERCISES

Determine number of exemptions allowed

1. T. J. Mex is 65 years old; his wife is 65 years old and blind. They have three sons, ages 22, 24, and 30. The son who is 22 is a full-time student in law school and earns $1,000 per year. His parents contribute $8,000 annually toward his living expenses. The other two sons are fully self-supporting. How many exemptions are T. J. Mex and his wife entitled to claim on their joint return?

Compute tax liability

2. Bud Webb has gross income of $250,000, deductions for adjusted gross income of $25,000, and itemized deductions of $60,000. He files a joint return with his wife who has no separate income. Both are under 65, and they have three dependents. Using the 1988 tax rates in Illustration 21.2 for married taxpayers filing jointly, compute their tax liability.

Identify items included in gross income

3. Identify those items listed below that would be included in gross income:

   a. Tips received while working as a beautician.

   b. Golf clubs won as a door prize while attending a conference.

c. A check received as reimbursement for medical expenses paid earlier this year.

d. Cash received from an uncle's estate.

e. Cash received from the proceeds of a life insurance policy on an aunt.

f. Gain on the sale of a personal asset, a sailboat.

g. Interest earned on an IRA.

Calculated adjusted gross income

4. Using the following data, calculate the adjusted gross income for the joint return of Lana and Jim Tipper:

Interest on State of Virginia bonds	$ 4,700
Salary of Jim	54,000
Dividend income—Jim	400
Dividend income—Lana	100
Irish Sweepstakes prize	500
Capital gain on sale of stock	10,000
Cash received as personal award for injury suffered in auto accident	1,000

Compute amount of tax due or refund claimable

5. The following data are for Alice Stenbeck, a single taxpayer:

Salary	$25,000
Contribution to an IRA	2,000
Itemized personal expenses	2,790
Income taxes withheld from salary	4,500

Using the 1988 tax rates in Illustration 21.2, compute the amount of tax due or refund claimable.

Compute taxable income

6. Genie Flip has three exemptions even though she is unmarried. Her adjusted gross income is $20,100. Her itemized personal expenses amount to $3,100, and she files as head of household. Compute her taxable income.

Determine amount of federal income taxes

7. Ruthless Corporation had taxable income of $15,000, $30,000, and $65,000 in its first three years of operation. Determine the amount of federal income taxes it will incur each year assuming the first year of operation is 1988.

Compute tax liability

8. U-Be Corporation had taxable income of $130,000 in 1988. Compute the tax liability of U-Be Corporation.

Determine the amount of taxes recoverable due to a loss carryback

9. Lou Company suffered a $60,000 loss in its fifth year of operations. Information from Lou's previous tax returns is given below:

Year	Taxable Income	Taxes Paid
1	$30,000	$4,500
2	35,000	5,250
3	15,000	2,250
4	25,000	3,750

Assuming that Lou elects to carry the loss back, determine the amount of taxes that can be recovered for each of the previous years.

Prepare journal entry to record income tax chargeable and tax liability for year

10. The pre-tax income of the Jay Corporation for a given year amounts to $200,000, while its taxable income is only $160,000. The difference is attributable entirely to additional depreciation taken for tax purposes. If the current income tax rate is 40%, give the entry to record the income tax expense and income tax liability for the year.

PROBLEMS

Note: Use the 1988 rates for all personal income tax problems unless otherwise directed.

Compute amount of tax due or refund claimable

21–1. June Reddy is a professional model and is considered self-employed for tax purposes. She is single and has no dependents. She gathered the following information for your use in preparing her 1988 income tax return:

Income	$50,000
Royalties received	2,000
Interest received (including $100 on New York City bonds)	1,300
Capital gains	5,000
Contribution to a retirement account (Keogh plan)	7,000
Medical and dental expenses including $400 medical insurance premiums paid and $200 of nonprescription lotions	3,896
Property taxes on residence	2,690
State income tax	4,200
Mortgage interest paid	6,500
Contributions to church and charitable organizations	2,800
Theft loss, excess over $100	2,100
Political contributions	200
Estimated taxes paid and income taxes withheld	8,000

Required:

Using the 1988 tax rates in Illustration 21.2, compute the additional income taxes due or the refund claimable.

Prepare a schedule showing computation of additional taxes due or refund claimable

21–2. Arthur Ross is a systems analyst for a computer company at an annual salary of $50,000. He also provides consulting services from which he derived $16,000 of income in 1988 after deducting related expenses. Arthur is single and has no dependents. Other data for 1988 include:

Interest received	$ 2,500
Capital gain from sale of securities	2,500
Contribution to a retirement (Keogh) plan	2,400
Interest paid on mortgage	1,000
Medical and dental expenses, including medical insurance premium paid of $450 and prescription drugs and medicine of $200	2,463
Taxes:	
State income	2,600
Property taxes on residence	2,200
Contributions to charitable organizations	600
Professional dues, subscriptions to professional publications, business entertainment, safe-deposit box rentals, etc.	1,762
Casualty loss ($550 damage loss to automobile, less $200 reimbursement)	350
Income taxes withheld	10,200
Estimated taxes paid	8,000

Required:

Using the 1988 tax rates for a single taxpayer in Illustration 21.2 present a schedule similar to Illustration 21.3 showing the computation of the additional taxes due or the refund claimable.

Prepare a schedule showing computation of additional taxes due or refund claimable

21–3. Jill and Ernest Young, who are married and are the parents of two school-age children, file a joint tax return. They provide almost all of the support for Jill's mother, aged 66, who lives with them. In 1988, Ernest earns a salary of $53,000. They earned $800 of taxable interest during the year. They received $500 of dividends and realized a capital gain of $5,000. Ernest invested $2,000 in an IRA. Other data for the year are:

State income taxes paid	$1,900
State sales taxes paid	350
Property taxes paid on residence	2,080
Contributions (including $200 of clothing donated to neighbors who suffered a loss from fire)	660
Interest paid (on mortgage, $4,500; on auto loan, $1,000)	5,500
Medical expenses paid (including health insurance premium of $500 and prescription drugs and medicine of $300	2,452
Miscellaneous expenses paid (all deductible)	1,386
Income tax withheld	8,000

Required:

Prepare a schedule similar to Illustration 21–3 showing the additional taxes due or refund claimable.

Prepare a schedule showing computation of taxable income; compute the tax liability

21–4. The records of the Bonanza Corporation show the following for the year 1988:

Sales	$750,000
Interest earned on—	
State of New York bonds	6,000
City of Detroit bonds	3,000
Howard County, Ohio, School District No. 1 bonds	750
Cost of goods sold and other expenses	630,000
Loss on sale of asset	6,000
Gain on sale of asset	15,000
Allowable extra depreciation deduction for tax purposes	9,000
Dividends declared	30,000
Revenue received in advance, considered taxable income of this year	6,000
Contribution made to influence legislation (included in the $630,000 listed above)	600

Required:

a. Present a schedule showing the computation of taxable income.

b. Compute the corporation's tax for the current year using the tax rates given in this chapter.

Prepare a table showing taxes due or refund claimable

21–5. Buck and Jane Rogers file a joint return. They have three children; the oldest is Dave, who is 20 and a full-time student. Although Dave earned $1,000 in the current year, he still gets most of his support from his parents. Buck earned a salary of $34,000 in 1988. He also received $500 income from interest and $80 from dividends. He sold some bonds at a gain of $3,000 and also sold some stock at a loss of $500. Jane received $330 of interest on City of Detroit bonds and $420 of dividends. Total income taxes withheld were $3,800. Among the personal expenditures of the Rogers family are the following:

Investment in an IRA.	$2,000
State income taxes.	1,300
Social security taxes withheld	2,212
Property taxes on residence.	2,040
Charitable contributions.	700
Mortgage interest paid	1,200
Medical costs, including $400 of health insurance premiums and cost of prescription drugs and medicine of $500 . . .	2,638
Miscellaneous items consisting of subscriptions, and fee paid for income tax return preparation.	970

Required:

Prepare a schedule similar to Illustration 21.3 showing the taxes due or refund claimable.

Compute taxable income; calculate the tax liability for year

21–6. The following information relates to the activities of the Parade Company for 1988:

Sales.	$900,000
Interest income—	
State of Alabama Bonds	8,000
ABC Corporation Bonds	9,000
Cost of goods sold	675,000
Other expenses	125,000
Extra depreciation allowed for tax purposes	15,000
Amortization of goodwill, included in "other expenses" . .	1,100

Required:

a. Compute the taxable income for Parade Company.

b. Calculate the tax liability for the current year using the tax rates given in the chapter (Illustration 21.2).

Calculate tax liability making various assumptions about a loss carryback

21–7. The Allen Company had the following amounts of taxable income (loss) in the years indicated:

1988	$30,000
1989	20,000
1990	60,000
1991 (see parts [a], [b], and [c] below)	
1992	40,000
1993	10,000
1994	50,000
1995	70,000
1996	80,000
1997	65,000

Assume that the rates for 1988 are in effect for the entire period.

Required:

a. If the loss in 1991 is $110,000 and is carried back, how much would the company recover in back taxes?

b. If the loss in 1991 is $180,000 and is first carried back, how much would the company have to pay in taxes for the period 1992–97?

c. If the loss in 1991 is $400,000 and is carried back, how much would the company have to pay in taxes for the period 1992–97?

d. If there is an unused carryforward at the end of 15 years, what happens to it?

Prepare a schedule showing taxable income, income taxes due, and income tax allocation; prepare year-end entries to recognize income tax expense

21–8. On January 1, 1988, Cleo Corporation acquired a depreciable asset for $100,000 that is expected to have a four-year life and no salvage value. The company uses the modified ACRS (three-year class) method of depreciation for tax purposes and the straight-line method for book purposes. There are no other temporary differences. Net income before depreciation and income taxes is $100,000 for each of the four years.

Assume that the recovery percentages are 33.33%, 44.45%, 14.81%, and 7.41% for each of the four years, respectively.

Required:

a. Prepare a schedule showing taxable income and income taxes due for each of the four years using a 40% tax rate.

b. Prepare a schedule showing income tax expense assuming that income tax allocation procedures are used.

c. Prepare the year-end adjusting entry required at the end of each of the four years to recognize federal income tax expense.

Calculate tax liability making various assumptions about a loss carryback

21–9. The Harris Company had the following amounts of taxable income (loss) in the years indicated:

1988	$40,000
1989	50,000
1990	30,000
1991 (see parts [a], [b], and [c] below)	
1992	15,000
1993	45,000
1994	20,000
1995	50,000
1996	75,000
1997	90,000

Assume that the rates for 1988 are in effect for the entire period.

Required:

a. If the loss in 1991 is $120,000 and is carried back, what amount of back taxes would Harris be eligible to recover?

b. Assuming that the loss in 1991 is $210,000 and is first carried back, what amount of taxes would Harris be required to pay for the years 1992–1997?

c. If the 1991 loss is $350,000 and is carried back, what amount of taxes would be paid for the years 1992–1997?

d. If, after 15 years, there is an unused carryforward remaining, what happens to it?

BUSINESS DECISION PROBLEM 21–1

Determine whether a project is acceptable by using net present value

Cross Enterprises is considering whether or not to invest in new depreciable assets, thereby expanding into a new business area for the company. Erik Allan, president of Cross Enterprises, estimates that the assets will generate a net cash inflow before income taxes of $180,000 per year for three years. The assets would cost $300,000 and would have an estimated useful life of four years. The assets will be classified as three-year property under modified ACRS tax regulations.

Assume that the recovery percentages are 33.33%, 44.45%, 14.81%, and 7.41% for each of the four years, respectively.

Required:

Assume the company is subjected to a 40% tax rate and that all cash flows, except the $300,000 cost, fall at the end of the year. Show whether this project is acceptable, assuming the company requires a minimum return of 18%. (Hint: Use the net present value method of appraising alternative investment projects.)

APPENDIX A

INFLATION

ACCOUNTING

After studying this appendix, you should be able to:

1. Describe how inflation affects information presented in conventional financial statements.
2. Apply the two basic approaches to income statement adjustment under inflationary conditions.
3. Discuss the FASB requirements regarding inflation accounting.
4. Define and use correctly the new terms in the glossary.

INFLATION—A SERIOUS REPORTING PROBLEM

Objective 1: Describe how inflation affects information presented in conventional financial statements

Until recent years, no attempt has been made to include the impact of inflation on the results of operations and financial position of the reporting company. A serious problem faced by accountants—how to account for and report financial data in periods of inflation—is discussed in this section.

A **period of inflation** is a time during which prices in general are rising, while a **period of deflation** occurs when prices in general are falling. Only in periods of high inflation, like in the 1970s, has the historical cost approach to recording accounting data been severely criticized. During times of inflation, the historical cost approach often reports a positive net income when the economic value of the owner's investment has not even been maintained.

There are two widely recommended accounting approaches to the problem of inflation. One approach is current cost accounting. The current cost accounting approach shows the current cost or value of items in the financial statements. The other approach is constant dollar accounting, also known as general price-level adjusted accounting. The constant dollar accounting approach shows financial statement historical cost figures as adjusted for changes in the general price level.

759

The Nature and Measurement of Inflation

In a **period of inflation,** the "real value" of the dollar—its ability to purchase goods and services—falls. In a **period of deflation,** the real value of the dollar rises.

Changes in the general level of prices are measured by means of a general price index such as the consumer price index (CPI). A **price index** is a weighted average of prices for various goods and services. A base year is chosen and assigned a value of 100 for comparative purposes. If the index stands at 108 a year later, this means that prices in general rose 8% during the year. An index of 200 would mean that prices on the average doubled. Because the index is an average, prices of individual types of items may change at different rates and may, in some cases, actually decline. For example, the CPI shows that prices for a "basket" of selected consumer goods doubled in the decade of the 1970s. But during that same decade, gasoline prices quadrupled, while the price of electronic hand-held calculators declined very sharply.

The real value or purchasing power of the dollar relative to that of the base year is shown by the reciprocal of the price index; the ratio is simply inverted. For example, if the index for 1990 is 200 and for 1980 is 100, the price index is 200/100, meaning that prices have doubled since 1980. Alternatively, the reciprocal of the price index is 100/200, meaning that the value of the dollar in 1990 has dropped to one half, or 50%, of its purchasing power in 1980.

Because accounting measurements consist largely of dollars of historical cost, financial reports are inadequate in periods of inflation. **Historical cost accounting** measures accounting transactions in terms of the actual dollars expended or received. Such a measurement system has worked well in periods of stable prices. But the system does not work well when the dollar, in terms of its purchasing power, is a sharply changing unit of measure.

To illustrate, assume that a tract of land was purchased for $2,000 and held several years before being sold for $2,500. While the land was held, a general price index rose from 100 to 140. Historical cost accounting would report the recovery of the $2,000 cost and income of $500 as a gain on the sale of the land. But if we measure this transaction in terms of dollars of constant purchasing power, a far different result is obtained. To get back the purchasing power originally invested in the land, the land would have to be sold for $2,800 ($2,000 × 140/100). Since only $2,500 was received, no real income has been earned because the cost has not been recovered. In fact, a loss of $300 of current purchasing power was incurred.

Consequences of Ignoring Effects of Inflation

As shown in the example above, transactions and, therefore, financial statements that have not been adjusted for the effects of inflation may yield misleading information. Such information may make comparisons between companies difficult. Suppose Company A acquired a tract of land for $100,000 several years ago. Now Company B acquires a virtually identical tract of land for $150,000, paying the higher price because prices in general have risen 50% since Company A bought its land. Both companies immediately sold their land for $150,000 each. Company A would appear to have the more efficient management because it was able to earn $50,000 on the sale of the land, while Company B earned nothing. In reality, the two companies are in the same position relative to the sale of the land because they have the same number of dollars of current purchasing power. The financial statement difference is caused by recording and continuing to carry the land at its historical cost.

As another example of the consequences of ignoring the effects of inflation, assume the above land was instead a depreciable asset, such as a building. Company A and Company B earn exactly the same number of dollars of revenues and incur, except for depreciation, exactly the same number of dollars of expenses. If both companies had assumed a 10-year useful life on the asset and apply straight-line depreciation to the building, Company A will have a larger net income than Company B simply due to the fact that the historical cost of its asset and, therefore, its recorded depreciation expense is lower than Company B's.

Failure to adjust for the impact of inflation may lead to conclusions that are not valid. A five-year summary of sales may show that sales dollars have increased 50% over the period. If sales prices have increased 60% over the five years, physical sales volume has actually declined.

There are other consequences that flow from a failure to adjust financial reports for the effects of inflation. Companies are paying taxes on "income" when in reality, costs may not have been covered. Also, financial reports that fail to reflect the impact of inflation may be misleading to individual decision makers, causing them to make decisions that are not in their best interest.

Accounting Responses to Changing Prices

Objective 2:
Apply the two basic approaches to income statement adjustment under inflationary conditions

Specific price-level changes relate to changes in the price of a particular good or service, such as calculators or computers. General price-level changes relate to the changes in the economy as a whole, such as those reflected by the Consumer Price Index. A specific price-level change may change in the same, or opposite, direction as the general price-level, and at the same or a different rate. Because of this, there are two types of price changes (specific and general) and two recommended approaches to accounting for changing prices. These recommended approaches are:

1. Change the basis of measurement from historical cost to current cost or value; this approach is called **current cost accounting.**
2. Change the basis of measurement from the actual historical (nominal) dollar to a dollar of constant purchasing power; this approach is referred to as **constant dollar accounting.**

An example of these two approaches is necessary before turning to a more detailed illustration. Assume the following facts regarding the purchase and resale of 1,000 units of a product:

Date	Transaction	Amount	Price-Level Index
January 1, 1990	Purchased 1,000 units	$3,000	100
December 31, 1990	Sold 1,000 units	5,000	120

The current cost of the units on December 31, 1990, was $3,900. The company incurred $800 of expenses to sell the units.

Under conventional (historical cost) accounting, net income from operations for 1990 would be:

Sales		$5,000
Cost of goods sold	$3,000	
Other expenses	800	3,800
Income from continuing operations*		$1,200

*Income from continuing operations in most cases is the same as income from operations. The technical difference between these terms is covered in intermediate accounting.

The $1,200 of income results from deducting the historical cost of the goods sold as well as the other expenses from sales revenue. The company appears to be better off after the transactions because it has not only recovered the original dollar investment in the goods, together with the expenses incurred, but also has an additional $1,200. The fact that current replacement cost of the goods sold exceeds their historical cost by $900 ($3,900 − $3,000) is ignored. Also, no attention is paid to the fact that the dollars recovered do not have the same purchasing power as those originally invested.

Using the preceding example, Illustration A.1 compares income from continuing operations under historical cost and each of the two inflation accounting methods.

Illustration A.1
ALTERNATIVE REPORTING APPROACHES—STATEMENT OF INCOME FROM CONTINUING OPERATIONS

Statement of Income from Continuing Operations			
	Historical Cost Accounting	Current Cost Accounting	Constant Dollar Accounting
Sales	$5,000	$5,000	$5,000
Cost of goods sold	$3,000	$3,900	$3,600
Other expenses	800	800	800
Total expenses . . .	$3,800	$4,700	$4,400
Income from continuing operations	$1,200	$ 300	$ 600

The second set of columns in Illustration A.1 shows the income from continuing operations using the current cost method. The **current cost** of an asset is the amount that would have to be paid currently to acquire the asset. In the column headed "Current cost accounting," income from continuing operations is computed by deducting the current cost of replacing the goods sold and the other expenses from current revenues. No adjustments are made for general price-level changes. Calculating income from continuing operations in this manner is supported on the grounds that the sale of an inventory item leads directly to a further action—replenishment of the inventory—if the company is to remain a going concern. A better picture of a company's ability to compete in its markets may also be provided by comparing current revenues with current costs rather than with outdated historical costs. In addition, we can say that only the $300 represents "disposable" income. Only $300 or less can be distributed to owners without reducing the scale of operations since the remainder of the funds is necessary to replace inventory sold and to maintain productive facilities at their present level.

In Illustration A.1, in the column headed "Constant dollar accounting," cost of goods sold is restated in end-of-1990 dollars by use of a ratio of the current price index to the old price index: $3,000 × 120/100 = $3,600. The $3,600 is the amount of purchasing power invested in the goods expressed in the end-of-1990 dollars. Thus, the $3,600 is restated into the same dollars in which the sales revenue is expressed. The $800 of other expenses is assumed to be selling expenses incurred at point of sale (such as sales commissions), which are already stated in end-of-1990 dollars. All dollar amounts are now expressed in comparable terms—end-of-1990 dollars. The company is better off because it has increased its purchasing power by $600. Under constant dollar accounting, net income is a measurement of increased purchasing power—the entity's increased ability to acquire goods and services.

The next two sections illustrate the current cost and constant dollar accounting methods applied to the income statement of a hypothetical company—the Carol Company.

CURRENT COST ACCOUNTING

In the past, inflation adjusted statements generally have been recommended, not required, as supplementary information to conventional financial statements. In 1979, the FASB issued a standard that required certain large, publicly held corporations to present certain supplementary information about the effects of inflation.[1]

---

[1]FASB, "Financial Reporting and Changing Prices," *Statement of Financial Accounting Standards No. 33* (Stamford, Conn., 1979). Copyright © by Financial Accounting Standards Board, High Ridge Park, Stamford, Connecticut 06905, U.S.A. Quoted (or excerpted) with permission. Copies of the complete document are available from the FASB.

To illustrate a statement from continuing operations prepared on a current cost basis, we use the data from the historical cost income statement of the Carol Company in Illustration A.2.

Management has determined that the cost of goods sold in terms of current cost is $146,000, and the current cost of the plant assets was $160,000 on December 31, 1989, and $180,000 on December 31, 1990. There were no additions or retirements of plant assets in 1990. Carol Company depreciates its plant assets over a 20-year life, or an annual rate of 5% on a straight-line basis.

Current cost depreciation for 1990 can be computed by multiplying the average current cost of the plant assets for the year by the annual depreciation rate of 5%. The amount is:

$$\frac{\$160,000 + \$180,000}{2} \times 5\% = \$8,500$$

The $146,000 current cost of goods sold and $8,500 current cost depreciation are shown in an income statement prepared under current cost accounting. There is no need to adjust sales or other expenses since they are already expressed at current cost for the year.

Illustration A.3 shows the amounts that would be reported in the historical cost and current cost income statements shown for the Carol Company.

Current Cost Accounting—Pro and Con

The advantages of current cost accounting include:

1. Specific current costs incurred by a company are shown.

Illustration A.2
STATEMENT OF INCOME FROM CONTINUING OPERATIONS— HISTORICAL COST BASIS

CAROL COMPANY		
Statement of Income from Continuing Operations		
For the Year Ended December 31, 1990		
Sales		$200,000
Cost of goods sold:		
Inventory, January 1, 1990	$ 20,000	
Purchases	160,000	
Goods available for sale	$180,000	
Inventory, December 31, 1990	40,000	
Cost of goods sold		140,000
Gross margin		$ 60,000
Expenses:		
Depreciation	$ 4,000	
Other expenses	46,000	50,000
Income from continuing operations		$ 10,000

Illustration A.3
COMPARISON OF HISTORICAL COST AND CURRENT COST
INCOME STATEMENTS

CAROL COMPANY Statements of Income from Continuing Operations For the Year Ended December 31, 1990	Historical Cost	Current Cost
Sales	$200,000	$200,000
Cost of goods sold	$140,000	$146,000
Depreciation expense	4,000	8,500
Other expenses	46,000	46,000
Total	$190,000	$200,500
Income (loss) from continuing operations	$ 10,000	$ (500)

2. Current costs, rather than historical costs, are deducted from current revenues to calculate net income; this provides for a more meaningful matching of effort and accomplishment.
3. If owner withdrawals are limited to an amount equal to or less than current cost income from continuing operations, the economic capital of the company is maintained.

The disadvantages of current cost accounting include:

1. Current costs may be subjective.
2. Current costs may be difficult and costly to determine.

CONSTANT DOLLAR ACCOUNTING

As already discussed briefly, historical dollar amounts in an income statement may be converted or restated into a number of constant dollars that have an equivalent amount of purchasing power. When adjusted for inflation, conventional financial statements are called constant dollar or general price-level adjusted financial statements.

To illustrate an income statement prepared on a constant dollar basis, we again refer to Illustration A.2 for the Carol Company.

To convert historical dollars into constant end-of-year dollars, the formula is:

$$\text{Historical dollars} \times \frac{\text{Price index at end of current period}}{\text{Price index at date of historical transaction}} = \text{Constant dollars}$$

In order to convert the income statement of the Carol Company, certain assumptions must be made or information provided. These data follow:

1. The general price-level index stood at 100 on December 31, 1989, and at 108 on December 31, 1990.

2. Sales, purchases, other expenses, and taxes were incurred uniformly throughout the year. This means that, on the average, these items were incurred when the price index was 104.
3. Inventories are costed on a FIFO basis. The beginning inventory was acquired when the price index was 98, and the ending inventory was acquired when the index stood at 106.
4. The price index was 54 when the plant assets were acquired.

The procedure for converting the Carol Company income statement in Illustration A.2 to constant dollars is as follows. First, all revenues, purchases, and expenses were assumed to occur uniformly throughout the year; therefore, these items are converted by multiplying their historical amounts by a ratio of 108/104. Beginning inventory is converted using a ratio of 108/98, while ending inventory is converted using a 108/106 ratio. Since depreciation is calculated on the historical costs of the related assets that were acquired when the index stood at 54, depreciation expense is converted using a ratio of 108/54. Illustration A.4 shows the restated income statement for the Carol Company. Purchasing power gains and losses are discussed in the next section.

Purchasing power gains and losses. Purchasing power gains and losses result from holding monetary assets and liabilities during inflation or deflation. **Monetary items** are cash and other assets and liabilities that represent fixed claims to cash, such as accounts and notes receivable and payable. **Nonmonetary items** include all items on the balance sheet other

Illustration A.4
INCOME STATEMENT—CONSTANT DOLLAR BASIS (end-of-year dollars)

CAROL COMPANY
Restated Income for the Year Ended December 31, 1990
(in constant end-of-year 1990 dollars)

	Historical Dollars		Conversion Ratio		Constant Dollars
Sales	$200,000	×	108/104	=	$207,692
Cost of goods sold:					
Inventory, January 1, 1990	$ 20,000	×	108/98	=	$ 22,041
Purchases.	160,000	×	108/104	=	166,154
Goods available for sale	$180,000				$188,195
Inventory, December 31, 1990	40,000	×	108/106	=	40,755
Cost of goods sold	$140,000				$147,440
Gross margin	$ 60,000				$ 60,252
Expenses:					
Depreciation.	$ 4,000	×	108/54	=	$ 8,000
Other expenses	46,000	×	108/104	=	47,769
Total expenses	$ 50,000				$ 55,769
Income from continuing operations	$ 10,000				$ 4,483
Purchasing power gain on monetary items					2,625
Net income	$ 10,000				$ 7,108

than monetary items. A **purchasing power gain** results from holding monetary liabilities during inflation or monetary assets during deflation. A **purchasing power loss** results from holding monetary assets during inflation or monetary liabilities during deflation.

Assume that Bill Allen holds $1,000 of cash during a year in which prices in general rose 25%. Even though Bill still has his $1,000 at year-end, he has less purchasing power than he did at the beginning of the year. Bill needs to have $1,250 ($1,000 × 125/100) at year-end to be as well off as he was at the start of the year. Therefore, during the year, Bill has sustained a purchasing power loss of $250.

Conversely, a gain results from being in debt during inflation. Assume that Kathy Rice owes $600 during a year in which prices rise 40%. The original debt has a year-end purchasing power equivalent of $840 ($600 × 140/100). Kathy can satisfy the debt by paying $600 currently. Thus, she has experienced a purchasing power gain of $240.

Assume that the Carol Company, in Illustration A.4, experienced a purchasing power gain of $2,625 during 1990. This amount would be added to net income from continuing operations on the restated income statement. Carol Company has net income on a constant dollar basis of $7,108, which is nearly 30% less than the net income shown on the conventional (historical cost) income statement.

Constant Dollar Accounting—Pro and Con

The advantages of constant dollar accounting include the following:

1. Measurement of the impact of inflation on a company is objective because adjustments made to convert the statements to a constant dollar basis are based on historical cost.
2. Comparability of the financial statements between companies is improved because of the use of the same procedures and the same index numbers for each firm.
3. There is greater comparability of the financial statements of a single company through time since effects of price-level changes are removed by stating all amounts in dollars of the same purchasing power.

The disadvantages of constant dollar accounting include:

1. Benefits resulting from the use of such statements have not been shown to be in excess of the cost of preparing these statements.
2. The assumption that the impact of inflation affects all companies equally is not true.
3. Only one deficiency—the changing value of the measuring unit—is corrected; the effects of specific price changes are ignored. This is undoubtedly the most significant limitation of constant dollar accounting.

Illustration A.5 shows a comparison of all three income statements for the Carol Company.

Illustration A.5
INFLATION IMPACT DISCLOSURES

CAROL COMPANY
Statement of Income Adjusted for Changing Prices
For the Year Ended December 31, 1990

	Historical Cost	Current Cost	Constant Dollar (end-of-year dollars)
Sales	$200,000	$200,000	$207,692
Cost of goods sold	$140,000	$146,000	$147,440
Expenses:			
Depreciation expense	4,000	8,500	8,000
Other expenses	46,000	46,000	47,769
Total	$190,000	$200,500	$203,209
Income (loss) from continuing operations . .	$ 10,000	$ (500)	$ 4,483
Purchasing power gain on monetary items . .			2,625
Net income	$ 10,000	$ (500)	$ 7,108

Which method of adjusting for inflation is correct? There is no simple answer. Each method is correct if one accepts the definitions of cost and income assumed under the method. A much more important question is: Which method is more useful to users of the financial reports? The answer to this question has been of considerable concern to many people, including members of the FASB and the staff of the SEC.

THE FASB REQUIREMENTS

Objective 3: Discuss the FASB requirements regarding inflation accounting

FASB Statement No. 33 called for disclosure by companies in their annual reports of both the impact of specific price changes and of general inflation on earnings and other selected items. The *Statement* did not require full, completely adjusted financial statements, nor did it affect the way in which the basic (primary) financial statements were prepared, since all required disclosures appeared as supplementary information. The *Statement* applied only to publicly held companies (1) with total assets in excess of $1 billion (after deducting accumulated depreciation) or (2) having $125 million (before deducting accumulated depreciation) of inventories and property, plant, and equipment. Thus, about 1,200 to 1,400 large, publicly held companies were directly affected. The FASB also encouraged all companies to report the effects of inflation by applying the methods described in *FASB Statement No. 33*.

For fiscal years ended on or after December 25, 1979, affected companies initially had to report as supplementary information:

  a. Net income on a current cost basis.

b. Net income on a constant dollar basis (historical cost adjusted for the effects of general inflation).
c. Purchasing power gain or loss on monetary items.[2]

Other disclosure requirements, including a five-year summary of selected financial data, also existed.

Uncertainty over whether constant dollar information or current cost information is preferable caused the FASB to initially require both types. This uncertainty was shown in responses sent to the FASB by various users when the proposed statement was circulated. Some knowledgeable persons preferred current cost information, while others preferred constant dollar information.

Since *FASB Statement No. 33* was released in 1979, companies and financial statement users have had several years of experience with both approaches. In 1984, the FASB indicated its preference for current cost information over constant dollar information. In *FASB Statement No. 82*, the FASB eliminated the requirement for reporting constant dollar information in supplemental financial statements to reduce the cost incurred in preparing financial statements.[3] Under *FASB Statement No. 82*, the reporting of current cost information was still required. However, a company could substitute constant dollar information for current cost information. In 1986, the FASB issued *FASB Statement No. 89* that *encourages*, but *does not require*, companies to disclose supplementary information on the effects of changing prices.[4]

SUMMARY

Inflation represents a serious reporting problem. In periods of high inflation, the use of historical cost in financial statements has been criticized. Accountants have developed two approaches to report the effects of inflation. One approach is the current cost approach, which shows the current cost of items in the financial statements. The other approach is constant dollar accounting, also called general price-level adjusted accounting. This approach shows historical cost amounts adjusted for changes in the general price level.

In 1979, the FASB issued *FASB Statement No. 33*, which required certain large, publicly held corporations to present certain supplementary information about the effects of inflation. These companies had to report

---

[2]*FASB Statement No. 33*, pars. 29–35.

[3]FASB, "Financial Reporting and Changing Prices: Elimination of Certain Disclosures," *Statement of Financial Accounting Standards No. 82* (Stamford, Conn., 1984). Copyright © by Financial Accounting Standards Board, High Ridge Park, Stamford, Connecticut, 06905, U.S.A.

[4]FASB, "Financial Reporting and Changing Prices," *Statement of Financial Accounting Standards No. 89* (Stamford, Conn., 1987). Copyright © by Financial Accounting Standards Board, High Ridge Park, Stamford, Connecticut, 06905, U.S.A.

both current cost and constant dollar information. However, in 1984, the FASB indicated its preference for current cost information over constant dollar information. As of 1985, these companies were no longer required to report constant dollar information. As of 1987 inflation accounting became optional.

Objective 4: Define and use correctly the new terms in the glossary

NEW TERMS INTRODUCED IN APPENDIX A

Constant dollar accounting A recommended approach to deal with the problem of accounting for inflation by changing the unit of measure from the actual historical (nominal) dollar to a dollar of constant purchasing power (761).

Current cost The amount that would have to be paid currently to acquire an asset (763).

Current cost accounting A recommended approach to deal with the problem of accounting for inflation by showing current cost or value of items in the financial statements (761).

Deflation (period of) Exists when prices in general are falling (759, 760).

Historical cost accounting Conventional accounting in which accounting measurements are in terms of the actual dollars expended or received (760).

Inflation (period of) Exists when prices in general are rising (759, 760).

Monetary items Cash and other assets and liabilities that represent fixed claims to cash, such as accounts and notes receivable and payable (766).

Nonmonetary items All items on the balance sheet other than monetary items; examples are inventories, plant assets, capital stock, and owner's equity (766).

Price index A weighted average of prices for various goods and services. A base year is chosen and assigned a value of 100 for comparative purposes (760).

Purchasing power gain The gain that results from holding monetary liabilities during inflation or monetary assets during deflation (767).

Purchasing power loss The loss that results from holding monetary assets during inflation or monetary liabilities during deflation (767).

DEMONSTRATION PROBLEM A–1

Duncan Book Company's financial statements included the following partial income statement:

DUNCAN BOOK COMPANY
Partial Income Statement
For the Year Ended December 31, 1990

Sales.		$250,000
Cost of goods sold.	$180,000	
Depreciation	3,000	
Other expenses	15,000	198,000
Income from continuing operations.		$ 52,000

Sales were made uniformly throughout the year. The cost of goods sold consisted of books acquired when the general price index stood at 105. This same index ended the year at 120 and averaged 110 for the year. The current cost of the goods sold was $200,000.

The $3,000 depreciation reported is on a delivery truck that cost $12,000 when the general price index stood at 100. The truck had a current cost of $14,000 at the beginning of 1990 and a current cost of $16,000 at the end of 1990. The other expenses were incurred uniformly throughout the year, were paid in cash, and are substantially equal to their current cost at time of incurrence.

Assume that Duncan Company experienced a purchasing power gain of $1,500 during 1990.

Required:

a. Prepare a statement showing current cost income from continuing operations for the year ended December 31, 1990.

b. Prepare a statement showing constant dollar income in December 31, 1990, dollars for the year then ended.

Solution to demonstration problem A–1

a.

DUNCAN BOOK COMPANY
Statement of Current Cost Income from Continuing Operations
For the Year Ended December 31, 1990

Sales.		$250,000
Cost of goods sold	$200,000	
Depreciation ($14,000 + $16,000)/2 × 0.25 . .	3,750	
Other expenses	15,000	218,750
Income from continuing operations		$ 31,250

b.

DUNCAN BOOK COMPANY
Statement of Constant Dollar Income
In End-of-Year Dollars
For the Year Ended December 31, 1990

Sales ($250,000 × 120/110)		$272,727
Cost of goods sold ($180,000 × 120/105) . .	$205,714	
Depreciation ($3,000 × 120/100)	3,600	
Other expenses ($15,000 × 120/110)	16,364	225,678
Income from continuing operations		$ 47,049
Purchasing power gain on monetary items . .		1,500
Net income		$ 48,549

QUESTIONS

1. How might it be argued that a tax supposedly on income is really a tax on capital?

2. What are the two basic approaches that might be used to reveal the impact of inflation on financial statements?

3. When items in a set of financial statements are all converted into constant dollars, what do they have in common?

4. If an index of the general level of prices rose 15% in a period, what is the effect upon the value or real worth of the dollar?

5. How is the dollar amount for land adjusted under constant dollar accounting?

6. Explain the typical adjustment of sales and most expenses under constant dollar accounting.

7. Identify whether each of the following items is a monetary or nonmonetary item:

   a. Cash.

   b. Equipment.

   c. Notes receivable.

   d. Merchandise inventory.

   e. Accounts receivable.

   f. Patents.

   g. Common stock.

   h. Land.

   i. Accounts payable.

   j. Buildings.

8. What are purchasing power gains and losses? When do purchasing power gains occur? When do purchasing power losses occur?

9. If supplementary disclosures are made, how are the effects of inflation shown?

10. What is the major deficiency in constant dollar accounting?

EXERCISES

Compute income under historical cost accounting, constant dollar accounting, and current cost accounting

1. Assume the following facts regarding the purchase and sale of 100 units of a product:

Date	Transaction	Amount	Price-level Index
January 1, 1990	Purchased 100 units	$18,000	100
December 31, 1990.	Sold 100 units	30,000	110

The company incurred $3,600 of expenses to sell the units. The replacement cost of the units on December 31, 1990, was $21,000. Prepare a schedule showing net income from continuing operations under historical cost accounting, current cost accounting, and constant dollar accounting.

Convert cost of goods sold section of income statement to constant dollar amounts

2. The cost of goods sold section of the conventional (historical cost) income statement for the Howard Company appears below:

Cost of goods sold:	
Inventory, January 1, 1990	$ 36,000
Purchases	108,000
Goods available for sale	$144,000
Inventory, December 31, 1990	18,000
Cost of goods sold	$126,000

The general price-level index was 100 on December 31, 1989, and 110 on December 31, 1990. The FIFO inventories were acquired when the index stood at

96 for the beginning inventory and 108 for the ending inventory. Purchases were incurred uniformly throughout the year. Convert the cost of goods sold section of the income statement to end-of-year constant dollar amounts.

Compute current cost depreciation

3. R Company's plant assets at December 31, 1989, had a historical cost of $50,000 and accumulated depreciation of $20,000 (10% annual depreciation rate). There were no additions or retirements in 1990. The current cost of the plant assets on December 31, 1989, was $65,000 and on December 31, 1990, was $75,000. Compute the current cost depreciation for 1990.

Determine purchasing power gain or loss

4. In each of the situations given, determine the amount of purchasing power gain or loss:

a. You hold cash of $10,000 during a year in which prices in general rose 10%.

b. You are in debt $5,000 during a year in which prices in general rose 8%.

PROBLEMS

Compute income on both current cost and constant dollar basis

A–1. A partial income statement for the Knight Company for the year ended December 31, 1990, in terms of historical dollars is given below:

KNIGHT COMPANY
Partial Income Statement
For the Year Ended December 31, 1990

Sales		$630,000
Cost of goods sold	$405,600	
Depreciation	24,000	
Other expenses	126,000	555,600
Income from continuing operations		$ 74,400

The sales were made rather uniformly throughout the year. Other expenses were also incurred rather uniformly throughout the year and largely on a cash basis. The depreciation reported relates to a machine acquired at a cost of $240,000 that is being depreciated over a 10-year life on a straight-line basis.

The current cost of the goods sold was $450,000 at the time of their sale. The current cost (gross) of the machine was $390,000 at the beginning of 1990 and $450,000 at the end of the year. An index of the general level of prices stood at 80 when the machine was acquired, at 100 at the beginning of 1990, averaged 105 for 1990, and ended the year at 110. This same index stood at 104 when the goods sold were acquired.

Required:

a. Prepare a statement showing current cost income from continuing operations for the year ended December 31, 1990.

b. Prepare a statement showing constant dollar income from continuing operations in end-of-year dollars for the year ended December 31, 1990.

Compute income on both current cost and constant dollar basis

A–2. A partial income statement for the Q Company for the year ended December 31, 1990, in terms of historical dollars follows:

Q COMPANY
Partial Income Statement
For the Year Ended December 31, 1990

Sales		$220,000
Cost of goods sold	$126,000	
Depreciation	12,000	
Other expenses	24,200	162,200
Income from continuing operations		$ 57,800

The sales were made uniformly throughout the year. The cost of goods sold consisted of goods acquired when the general price index stood at 105. This same index ended the year at 120 and averaged 110 for the year. The current cost of the goods sold was $150,000.

The $12,000 of depreciation reported is on a machine that cost $60,000 when the general price index stood at 90. The machine had a current cost of $100,000 at the beginning of 1990 and a current cost of $120,000 at the end of 1990.

The other expenses were incurred uniformly throughout the year, were paid in cash, and are substantially equal to their current cost at time of incurrence.

Required:

a. Prepare a statement showing current cost income from continuing operations for the year ended December 31, 1990.

b. Prepare a statement showing income from continuing operations in constant end-of-year 1990 dollars.

Prepare income statement in constant dollars

A–3. Osborn Company was organized on December 31, 1989. The company immediately paid a year's rent of $12,000 in advance on a building, purchased $6,000 of supplies, and purchased $20,000 of cleaning equipment. The company began operations on January 1, 1990.

During 1990, services were rendered for customers, and other expenses were incurred uniformly throughout the year. An index of the general level of prices stood at 80 at the beginning of the year, averaged 100 for the year, and ended the year at 120. The income statement for the year follows:

OSBORN COMPANY
Income Statement
For the Year Ended December 31, 1990

Service revenue		$50,000
Supplies expense	$ 4,000	
Rent expense	12,000	
Depreciation expense	5,000	
Other expenses	20,000	41,000
Net income		$ 9,000

Required:

Prepare a schedule converting the income statement for 1990 into constant end-of-year 1990 dollars. The purchasing power loss on net monetary items was $7,000.

Prepare income statement in constant dollars

A–4. Lumpkin Company began business on January 2, 1990, with $128,000 of inventory and $96,000 of equipment. An index of the general level of prices stood at 100 on January 2, 1990. This index rose uniformly throughout the year, averaging 125 for the year, and ending at 150. Lumpkin's income statement for the year in historical dollars is given below.

LUMPKIN COMPANY
Income Statement
For the Year Ended December 31, 1990

Sales		$160,000
Cost of goods sold		80,000
Gross margin		$ 80,000
Depreciation	$16,000	
Other expenses	32,000	48,000
Net income		$ 32,000

In 1990, Lumpkin sold goods out of the beginning inventory with a cost of $80,000 for $160,000 cash. Expenses in the amount of $32,000 were incurred uniformly throughout the year and were paid in cash. No new equipment was purchased during the year.

Required:

Prepare an income statement for 1990 with all amounts expressed in constant end-of-year 1990 dollars. The purchasing power loss on net monetary items was $1,600.

Compute income on both current cost and constant dollar basis

A–5. The following is a partial income statement for the McIntyre Corporation for the year ended June 30, 1991:

McINTYRE CORPORATION
Partial Income Statement
For the Year Ended June 30, 1991

Sales		$748,000
Cost of goods sold	$428,400	
Depreciation	40,800	
Other expenses.	82,280	551,480
Income from continuing operations		$196,520

Sales were made uniformly throughout the year, while cost of goods sold consisted of goods acquired when the general price index stood at 105. This index was 120 on June 30, 1991, and had averaged 110 for the preceding 12 months. The current cost of the goods sold was $493,000.

The depreciation reported is on a machine that cost $204,000 when the general price index stood at 90. The machine had a current cost of $340,000 on June 30, 1990; and on June 30, 1991, its current cost was $408,000. All other expenses were incurred uniformly throughout the year, were paid in cash, and were basically equal to their current cost at time of incurrence.

Required:

a. Prepare a current cost statement of income from continuing operations for the year ended June 30, 1991.

b. Prepare a statement showing constant dollar income from continuing operations in end-of-year dollars for the year ended June 30, 1991.

*Compute income on
both current cost
and constant dollar
basis*

A–6. Following is a partial income statement for Britt Home Furnishings for the year ended December 31, 1990:

BRITT HOME FURNISHINGS
Partial Income Statement
For the Year Ended December 31, 1990

Sales		$210,000
Cost of goods sold	$135,200	
Depreciation	8,000	
Other expenses.	42,000	185,200
Income from continuing operations		$ 24,800

Sales were made uniformly throughout the year. Other expenses were also incurred rather uniformly throughout the year and largely on a cash basis. Thus, their historical cost is substantially equal to their current cost. The depreciation reported relates to a machine acquired at a cost of $80,000 that is being depreciated over a 10-year life on a straight-line basis.

The current cost of the goods sold was $150,000 at the time of sale. The current (gross) cost of the machine was $130,000 at the beginning of 1990 and $150,000 at the end of the year. An index of the general level of prices stood at 80 when the machine was acquired, stood at 100 at the beginning of 1990, averaged 105 for 1990, and ended the year at 110. The index stood at 104 when the goods sold were acquired.

Required:

a. Prepare a statement showing current cost income from continuing operations for the year ended December 31, 1990.

b. Prepare a statement showing constant dollar income from continuing operations in end-of-year dollars for the year ended December 31, 1990.

BUSINESS DECISION PROBLEM A–1

*Prepare income
statement in
constant dollars,
evaluate profitability
of the company, and
decide if inflation
accounting basis
used is appropriate*

Oakland Cleaning Company was organized on December 31, 1989. The company immediately paid a year's rent of $18,000 in advance on a building, purchased $9,000 of supplies, and purchased $30,000 of cleaning equipment. The company began operations on January 1, 1990.

Revenues were earned and expenses were incurred evenly throughout 1990. An index of the general level of prices was 95 at the beginning of the year, averaged 110 for the year, and rose to 125 at year-end. The conventional income statement for the year follows:

OAKLAND CLEANING COMPANY
Income Statement
For the Year Ended December 31, 1990

Service revenue		$75,000
Supplies expense	$ 6,000	
Rent expense	18,000	
Depreciation expense	7,500	
Other expenses	30,000	61,500
Net income		$13,500

Required:

a. Prepare a schedule converting the income statement into constant December 31, 1990, dollars. The purchasing power loss on net monetary items was $7,084.

b. Assuming you are evaluating this company, what would you conclude about its income performance?

APPENDIX B
FINANCIAL STATEMENTS CONTAINED IN THE ANNUAL REPORT OF AMR CORPORATION (AMERICAN AIRLINES)

Presented in this appendix are 13 pages of the 1987 Annual Report of AMR Corporation (parent of American Airlines) and its consolidated subsidiaries. Included are (1) Consolidated Statement of Operations (Income); (2) Consolidated Balance Sheet; (3) Consolidated Statement of Cash Flows; (4) Consolidated Statement of Non-Redeemable Preferred Stock, Common Stock, and Other Stockholders' Equity; (5) Notes to Financial Statements; and (6) Report of Certified Public Accountants. These items illustrate the financial reporting practices of a modern business corporation to its stockholders and to other external parties.

Particular attention should be paid to the rather substantial amounts of additional information and explanation presented in the Notes to Consolidated Financial Statements. For example, Note 1 discloses the accounting policies followed in developing the amounts reported in the various statements.

A strong trend has developed in recent years toward making more informative disclosures in corporate annual reports. Many of these added disclosures result from FASB and SEC requirements.

AMR CORPORATION

Consolidated Statement of Operations

(in thousands, except per share amounts)

	Year ended December 31,		
	1987	1986	1985
Revenues			
Passenger	$6,150,884	$4,960,513	$4,985,565
Other	1,047,090	1,057,662	1,145,463
Total operating revenues	7,197,974	6,018,175	6,131,028
Expenses			
Wages, salaries and benefits (Note 10)	2,452,619	2,157,864	2,115,027
Aircraft fuel	1,008,557	837,280	1,141,848
Other operating expenses (Notes 4 and 11)	3,275,734	2,612,108	2,337,520
Total operating expenses	6,736,910	5,607,252	5,594,395
Operating Income	461,064	410,923	536,633
Other Income (Expense)			
Interest income	83,763	107,149	131,898
Interest expense	(213,365)	(177,840)	(152,888)
Interest capitalized	25,824	24,685	19,726
Gain from sale of subsidiaries (Note 13)	—	60,312	—
Miscellaneous — net (Notes 6 and 12)	(34,812)	(6,567)	(16,323)
	(138,590)	7,739	(17,587)
Earnings Before Income Taxes	322,474	418,662	519,046
Provision for income taxes (Note 7)	124,067	139,530	173,206
Net Earnings	$ 198,407	$ 279,132	$ 345,840
Earnings Per Common Share			
Primary (Note 8)	$ 3.28	$ 4.63	$ 5.94
Fully diluted	$ 3.28	$ 4.63	$ 5.88

The accompanying notes are an integral part of these financial statements.

AMR CORPORATION
Consolidated Balance Sheet
(in thousands)

ASSETS	December 31,	
	1987	1986
Current Assets		
Cash	$ 44,763	$ 21,573
Short-term investments (Notes 2, 3 and 6)	967,566	1,061,857
Receivables, less allowances for uncollectible accounts		
(1987 — $14,549; 1986 — $17,458)	729,244	690,282
Inventories, less allowances for obsolescence		
(1987 — $82,985; 1986 — $71,831)	299,423	262,525
Other current assets	105,299	73,170
Total current assets	2,146,295	2,109,407
Equipment and Property (Notes 3 and 6)		
Flight equipment, at cost	4,836,284	4,225,666
Less accumulated depreciation	1,547,238	1,328,638
	3,289,046	2,897,028
Purchase deposits for flight equipment	67,936	144,726
	3,356,982	3,041,754
Other equipment and property, at cost	1,612,617	1,322,707
Less accumulated depreciation	704,202	591,869
	908,415	730,838
	4,265,397	3,772,592
Equipment and Property Under Capital Leases (Note 4)		
Flight equipment	1,515,104	1,147,068
Other equipment and property	190,042	175,547
	1,705,146	1,322,615
Less accumulated amortization	382,641	353,797
	1,322,505	968,818
Other Assets		
Funds held by bond trustees (Note 3)	201,677	277,431
Other (Note 5)	487,475	399,721
	689,152	677,152
	$8,423,349	$7,527,969

The accompanying notes are an integral part of these financial statements.

LIABILITIES AND STOCKHOLDERS' EQUITY	December 31, 1987	1986
Current Liabilities		
Accounts payable	$ 560,407	$ 514,444
Accrued salaries and wages	261,256	241,087
Other accrued liabilities	467,237	440,568
Air traffic liability and customers' deposits	577,001	510,771
Notes payable to banks (Note 6)	77,902	156,519
Current maturities of long-term debt	77,131	79,554
Current obligations under capital leases	50,073	42,048
Total current liabilities	2,071,007	1,984,991
Long-Term Debt, less current maturities (Note 6)	1,235,217	1,228,739
Obligations Under Capital Leases, less current obligations (Note 4)	1,546,869	1,183,288
Other Liabilities		
Deferred federal income tax (Note 7)	573,516	483,100
Other liabilities and deferred credits (Note 10)	165,686	138,955
	739,202	622,055
Commitments, Leases and Contingencies (Notes 3 and 4)		
Redeemable Preferred Stock (Note 8)	—	24,000
Non-Redeemable Preferred Stock, Common Stock and Other Stockholders' Equity (Notes 6, 8 and 9)		
Non-redeemable preferred stock	150,000	—
Common stock — $1 par value; 100,000 shares authorized; shares issued and outstanding:		
1987 — 58,816; 1986 — 58,747	58,816	58,747
Additional paid-in capital	1,060,388	1,058,480
Retained earnings	1,561,850	1,367,669
	2,831,054	2,484,896
	$8,423,349	$7,527,969

AMR CORPORATION

Consolidated Statement of Cash Flows

(in thousands)

	Year ended December 31,		
	1987	**1986**	**1985**
Cash Flow from Operating Activities:			
Net earnings	$ 198,407	$ 279,132	$ 345,840
Adjustments to reconcile net earnings to net cash provided by operating activities:			
Depreciation and amortization	485,931	388,688	336,876
Deferred federal income tax	90,416	183,382	58,334
Gain from sale of subsidiaries	—	(60,312)	—
Change in assets and liabilities, net of effects from purchase of AirCal and sale of subsidiaries:			
Increase in receivables	(16,710)	(71,669)	(38,174)
Increase in inventories	(36,824)	(55,011)	(2,499)
Increase in other current assets	(22,540)	(23,711)	(15,547)
Increase in accounts payable and accrued liabilities	36,274	26,141	125,640
Increase in air traffic liability and customers' deposits	36,656	58,564	69,787
Change in other liabilities and deferred credits	(8,906)	(54,356)	(2,157)
Other, net	29,063	(20,872)	28,912
Net cash provided by operating activities	791,767	649,976	907,012
Cash Flow from Investing Activities:			
Capital expenditures	(1,181,478)	(1,556,910)	(1,208,432)
Acquisition of AirCal, net of cash acquired	(139,954)	(83,646)	—
Disposal of equipment and property	41,617	19,391	32,820
Purchases of short-term investments	(24,785,986)	(13,838,493)	(9,584,011)
Maturities and sales of short-term investments	24,908,979	14,109,267	9,576,207
Proceeds from sale of subsidiaries, net	—	159,388	—
Acquisition of other assets	(25,927)	(36,511)	(26,346)
Net cash used for investing activities	(1,182,749)	(1,227,514)	(1,209,762)
Cash Flow from Financing Activities:			
Proceeds from issuance of long-term debt	128,229	360,556	64,618
Proceeds from sale-leaseback transactions	403,049	219,680	136,394
Proceeds from issuance of capital stock and common stock warrants	148,500	35,640	196,810
Reimbursements from funds held by bond trustees	71,244	39,362	25,830
Payments on long-term debt and capital lease obligations	(230,007)	(159,539)	(117,147)
Proceeds (payments) on notes payable to banks	(78,617)	156,519	—
Redemption of redeemable preferred stock	(24,000)	(74,244)	—
Payment of dividends on preferred stock	(4,226)	(3,248)	(8,226)
Net cash provided by financing activities	414,172	574,726	298,279
Net increase (decrease) in cash	23,190	(2,812)	(4,471)
Cash at beginning of year	21,573	24,385	28,856
Cash at end of year	$ 44,763	$ 21,573	$ 24,385
Cash Payments (Refunds) for:			
Interest (net of amounts capitalized)	$ 163,206	$ 147,319	$ 106,960
Income taxes	(17,168)	17,969	79,286
Financing and Investing Activities Not Affecting Cash:			
Capital lease obligations incurred	$ 249,771	$ 120,630	$ 79,168
Debt proceeds held by bond trustees for capital expenditures	—	—	110,655
Debt issued in exchange for preferred stock	—	—	33,997
Issuance of common stock upon conversion of preferred stock	—	—	124,920

The accompanying notes are an integral part of these financial statements.

AMR CORPORATION

Consolidated Statement of Non-Redeemable Preferred Stock, Common Stock and Other Stockholders' Equity

(in thousands, except share amounts)

	Non-Redeemable Preferred Stock	Common Stock	Additional Paid-In Capital	Retained Earnings	Total
Balance at January 1, 1985	$125,000	$48,453	$ 709,632	$ 755,322	$1,638,407
Net earnings	—	—	—	345,840	345,840
Dividends on preferred stock	—	—	—	(8,226)	(8,226)
Issuance of 5,000,000 shares of common stock	—	5,000	191,810	—	196,810
Issuance of 5,022,618 shares upon conversion of convertible preferred stock	(125,000)	5,022	119,898	—	(80)
Issuance of 205,979 shares pursuant to stock option and restricted stock incentive plans	—	206	6,629	—	6,835
Other	—	—	2,154	(826)	1,328
Balance at December 31, 1985	—	58,681	1,030,123	1,092,110	2,180,914
Net earnings	—	—	—	279,132	279,132
Dividends on preferred stock	—	—	—	(3,248)	(3,248)
Redemption of redeemable preferred stock	—	—	(9,298)	—	(9,298)
Issuance of 200,000 common stock warrants	—	—	35,640	—	35,640
Issuance of 66,570 shares pursuant to stock option and restricted stock incentive plans	—	66	2,015	—	2,081
Other	—	—	—	(325)	(325)
Balance at December 31, 1986	—	58,747	1,058,480	1,367,669	2,484,896
Net earnings	—	—	—	198,407	198,407
Dividends on preferred stock	—	—	—	(4,226)	(4,226)
Issuance of 300 shares of preferred auction rate stock	150,000	—	(1,500)	—	148,500
Issuance of 69,185 shares pursuant to stock option and restricted stock incentive plans	—	69	3,408	—	3,477
Balance at December 31, 1987	$150,000	$58,816	$1,060,388	$1,561,850	$2,831,054

The accompanying notes are an integral part of these financial statements.

AMR CORPORATION
Notes to Financial Statements

1. SUMMARY OF ACCOUNTING POLICIES

Basis of Consolidation and Business

The consolidated financial statements include the accounts of AMR Corporation (AMR) and its wholly owned subsidiaries, except for AMR Leasing Corporation, a finance subsidiary, which is accounted for by the equity method and which is insignificant with respect to total consolidated assets, liabilities, revenues and expenses. Flagship International, Inc. (Flagship), AMR Energy Corporation and American Airlines Training Corporation have been included in the consolidated financial statements through the dates of sale (see Note 13). All significant intercompany transactions have been eliminated.

American Airlines, Inc. (American), AMR's principal subsidiary accounting for approximately 99% of its operating revenues and expenses, is one of the largest United States airlines, serving 149 airports in 42 states, the District of Columbia, Bermuda, Canada, the Caribbean, Great Britain, France, Switzerland, West Germany, Mexico, Puerto Rico, Japan and Venezuela. American's revenues are primarily derived from the common carriage of passengers in scheduled airline service. See the Eleven-Year Comparative Summary (page 51) for the operating results of the airline.

Statement of Cash Flows

As of December 31, 1987, AMR adopted Statement of Financial Accounting Standards No. 95, "Statement of Cash Flows," which requires a statement of cash flows in place of a statement of changes in financial position. The consolidated statement of changes in financial position for the years ended December 31, 1986 and 1985 have been restated to conform with the 1987 presentation.

Short-term investments, without regard to original maturity, are not considered cash equivalents for purposes of the accompanying consolidated statement of cash flows.

Inventories

Spare parts, materials and supplies relating to flight equipment are carried at average cost and are expensed when used in operations. Allowances for obsolescence are provided, over the estimated useful life of the related aircraft and engines, for spare parts expected to be on hand at the date aircraft are retired from service.

Equipment and Property

The provision for depreciation of operating equipment and property is computed on the straight-line method applied to each unit of property, except that spare assemblies are depreciated on a group basis. The estimated useful lives and residual values used for the principal depreciable asset classifications are as follows:

	Estimated Useful Life	Residual Value
Boeing 727-200 aircraft and engines	December 31, 1994*	5%
Boeing 737-200 aircraft and engines	December 31, 1994*	5%
Boeing 747SP aircraft and engines	December 31, 1999*	5%
Boeing 767-200 aircraft and engines	20 years	5%
MD-80 aircraft and engines	20 years	5%
DC-10-10 aircraft and engines	December 31, 1999*	5%
DC-10-30 aircraft and engines	December 31, 1999*	5%
Commuter aircraft and engines	5-15 years	10%
Major rotable parts, avionics and assemblies	Life of equipment to which applicable	None
Improvements to leased flight equipment	Term of lease	None
Buildings and improvements (principally on leased land)	10 to 30 years or term of lease, whichever is shorter	None
Other equipment	3 to 15 years	None

*Common retirement date.

In addition to the above, American operates 37 fully depreciated Boeing 727 aircraft.

Equipment and property under capital leases are amortized over the term of the lease. Lease terms vary but are generally 12 to 25 years for aircraft and from 7 to 40 years for other leased equipment and property.

Excess of Purchase Price Over Net Assets Acquired

Excess of purchase price over the fair value of the net assets acquired, aggregating $197,000,000 at December 31, 1987, net of accumulated amortization of $12,719,000, is being amortized on a straight-line basis over 40 years. This excess results primarily from the merger in 1971 of Trans Caribbean Airways, Inc. into American and the acquisition in 1987 of ACI Holdings, Inc. (AirCal).

Passenger Revenues

Passenger ticket sales are initially recorded as a current liability. Revenue derived from the sale is recognized at the time transportation is provided.

Income Taxes

AMR and its subsidiaries file a consolidated federal income tax return. Provision is made for federal income taxes that are currently payable and amounts that are deferred to future periods. The deferred amounts result from the fact that, under the applicable tax statutes and regulations, some items of income and expense are not recognized in the same year for tax reporting purposes as for financial statement purposes. AMR follows the "flow through" method in recognizing benefit of investment tax credits.

Earnings Per Common Share

Primary earnings per common share computations are based upon earnings applicable to common shares and the average number of shares of common stock outstanding and dilutive common stock equivalents (stock options and warrants) and assume the tendering of American's debt to exercise warrants for the purchase of common stock. Earnings applicable to common shares were increased to reflect the elimination of interest (less tax effect) on the assumed tendered debt. The number of shares used in the computations for the years ended December 31, 1987, 1986 and 1985, was 60,483,000, 60,433,000 and 56,994,000, respectively.

Fully diluted earnings per common share are determined on the basis of the average number of shares of common stock and dilutive common stock equivalents outstanding and assumes the tendering of American's debt to exercise warrants for the purchase of common stock and in 1985 assumes the conversion of outstanding convertible preferred stock into common stock. Earnings applicable to common shares were increased to reflect the elimination of interest (less tax effect) on the assumed tendered debt.

2. SHORT-TERM INVESTMENTS

Short-term investments consisted of the following (in thousands):

	December 31,	
	1987	1986
Certificates of deposit	$380,004	$ 876,652
Commercial paper	289,336	175,067
Tax-exempt securities	276,008	—
Other	22,218	10,138
	$967,566	$1,061,857

Short-term investments are carried at cost, which approximates market value.

3. COMMITMENTS AND CONTINGENCIES

American has on order one Boeing 767-200 aircraft scheduled for delivery in 1988 and 62 McDonnell Douglas MD-80 aircraft scheduled for delivery through 1989. Deposits of $67,936,000 have been made towards the purchase of these aircraft. Future payments, including estimated amounts for price escalation through anticipated delivery dates, for these aircraft and related equipment will be approximately $752,000,000 and $482,000,000 in 1988 and 1989, respectively.

Additional expenditures of approximately $1,065,000,000 for aircraft modifications, spare parts, additional airport and office facilities and equipment have been authorized, of which an estimated $946,000,000 will be expended during 1988.

In March 1987, American signed agreements to acquire 25 Airbus A300-600 aircraft and 15 Boeing 767-300 aircraft for delivery in 1988 and 1989. The agreements entitle American to return the aircraft to the manufacturer at any time during the first ten years. American will account for these agreements as operating leases.

At December 31, 1987, American was contingently liable with respect to approximately $219,200,000 of guarantees relating to certain aircraft lease agreements and certain hotel interests sold. Should a default occur requiring American to make payment, American has certain remedies, including the right to reduce subsequent payments under the related leases and the right to reacquire control of the hotel interests.

From 1983 through 1985, $887,800,000 of special facility revenue bonds were issued by certain municipalities, primarily to purchase equipment and improve airport facilities that are leased by American. From these proceeds, $162,500,000 in 1985 and $86,300,000 in 1984 were loaned to American and are included in long-term debt. In certain circumstances, American may be required to purchase the special facility revenue bonds prior to maturity, in which case American has the right to resell the bonds or to use the bonds to offset its lease or debt obligations. For certain bond issues aggregating $412,600,000, American may borrow the purchase price under standby letter of credit agreements. At American's option, these letters of credit are secured by funds held by bond trustees and by approximately $270,000,000 of short-term investments.

4. LEASES

AMR's subsidiaries lease various types of equipment and property, including aircraft, passenger terminals, ground equipment and various other facilities.

The future minimum lease payments required under capital leases (together with the present value of net minimum lease payments) and future minimum lease payments required under operating leases that have an initial or remaining non-cancellable lease term in excess of one year as of December 31, 1987, were as follows (in thousands):

Notes to Financial Statements, Continued

Year ending December 31,	Capital Leases	Operating Leases
1988	$ 149,616	$ 275,550
1989	154,393	372,952
1990	170,776	302,688
1991	163,849	216,763
1992	159,720	215,314
1993 and subsequent	2,305,453	3,657,473
	3,103,807(a)	5,040,740(a)
Less minimum sublease rentals	—	155,271
		$4,885,469
Less amount representing interest	1,506,865	
Present value of net minimum lease payments	$1,596,942(b)	

(a) Future minimum payments required under capital leases and operating leases include $357,965 and $720,849, respectively, guaranteed by AMR relating to special facility revenue bonds issued by municipalities. Minimum sublease rentals relative to capital leases are $29,391.

(b) Includes $155,379 guaranteed by American.

Other operating expenses for 1987, 1986 and 1985 include rent expense of $269,200,000, $195,000,000 and $191,400,000, respectively. American has 44 McDonnell Douglas MD-80 aircraft, 6 BAe 146 aircraft, 2 Boeing 727 aircraft and 23 Boeing 737 aircraft under operating leases.

5. ACQUISITION OF AIRCAL

In November 1986, American and AirCal signed a definitive merger agreement which provided that American would acquire AirCal for $15.00 per common share. As of December 31, 1986, American had acquired approximately 6,700,000 common shares, representing approximately 65% of AirCal's then outstanding common stock, and placed substantially all of these shares in a voting trust pending regulatory approval of the merger agreement. American had also purchased approximately 1,000,000 shares of AirCal's convertible preferred stock. This investment, aggregating approximately $116,000,000 at December 31, 1986, was accounted for by the cost method through March 30, 1987, when the Department of Transportation approved the merger agreement. Accordingly, results of operations of AMR include the results of AirCal from the date of approval. Results of operations of AMR for 1986 and 1987 would not have been significantly impacted by the results of AirCal if the acquisition of AirCal were assumed to have occurred on January 1, 1986, and therefore, pro forma financial information is not presented.

The acquisition cost of approximately $225,000,000 (a portion of which was paid in 1986) exceeded the fair value of assets acquired ($245,000,000, less liabilities assumed of $170,000,000) by approximately $150,000,000.

6. LONG-TERM DEBT

Long-term debt (excluding amounts maturing within one year) consisted of the following (in thousands):

	December 31, 1987	1986
Senior debt:		
4¼%-15.63% promissory notes and bonds due through 2025 (net of unamortized discount of $9,699 and $14,117, respectively)	$ 537,231	$ 550,394
8.95%-10½% equipment trust certificates due through 1998	174,757	200,800
Floating rate notes due through 2024 (4.87%-7.23% at December 31, 1987)	111,574	136,300
8⅝% debentures due 2017 (net of unamortized discount of $1,949), 8.81% effective interest rate	98,051	—
9% debentures due 2016 (net of unamortized discount of $3,184 and $3,206, respectively), 9.32% effective interest rate	96,816	96,794
Other	24,873	21,006
	1,043,302	1,005,294
Subordinated debentures:		
4¼% subordinated debentures due 1992	21,349	21,349
5¼% subordinated debentures due 1998	2,070	1,986
6¼% subordinated debentures due 1996 (net of unamortized discount of $31,504 and $34,034, respectively), 9.03% effective interest rate	168,496	165,966
10¼% subordinated debentures due 2006 (net of unamortized discount of $5,359), 12.18% effective interest rate	—	34,144
	191,915	223,445
Long-term debt, less current maturities	$ 1,235,217	$ 1,228,739

Maturities of long-term debt (including sinking fund requirements) for the next five years are: 1988 — $77,131,000; 1989 — $77,591,000; 1990 — $94,544,000; 1991 — $60,038,000; 1992 — $81,543,000.

Certain senior debt is secured by aircraft, engines, equipment and other assets having a net book value of approximately $772,000,000 at December 31, 1987, and by $2,900,000 of certificates of deposit.

American has an interest rate swap agreement with an international bank, maturing in 1994, which effectively converts $100,000,000 of its floating rate debt into 6.91% fixed-rate debt.

During 1985, AMR exchanged $39,502,950 of new 10¼% subordinated debentures due April 1, 2006 for 1,580,118 shares of its $2.1875 cumulative redeemable preferred stock. As a result of the exchange, $1,676,000, representing the difference between the carrying value of the preferred stock and the fair market value of the debentures, net of issuance cost, was credited to additional paid-in capital. During 1987, AMR redeemed these debentures with an outstanding balance of $39,502,950 at a loss of $5,329,000.

AMR has 100,000 warrants outstanding to purchase at par $100,000,000 of 9.10% debentures due 2016. The warrants are exercisable at any time on or prior to May 1, 1989.

American has a $500,000,000 note placement and short-term advance facility agreement with a group of banks which expires in 1992. American also has an additional $500,000,000 short-term advance facility agreement, which expires in 1992 but is extendable to 1995. Interest on these agreements is calculated at a floating rate based upon the London Interbank Offering Rate. At December 31, 1986, $130,000,000 in short-term advances were outstanding at a rate of 7.50%. Such advances were repaid in January 1987.

During 1982, $82,453,000 of foreign currency denominated 9.2% promissory notes were issued. Approximately $26,151,000 of this amount has been hedged with a forward exchange contract resulting in an interest rate of 14.4%. Unrealized foreign currency exchange losses of $32,310,000, $20,512,000 and $15,674,000 on the unhedged portion of the notes are included in Miscellaneous — net for the years ended December 31, 1987, 1986 and 1985, respectively.

The debt agreements of American contain certain restrictive covenants, including limitations on indebtedness and the declaration of dividends on shares of its capital stock. Such restrictions could affect AMR's ability to pay dividends. At December 31, 1987, under the most restrictive provisions of those debt agreements, approximately $1,431,000,000 of American's retained earnings was available for payment of cash dividends to AMR.

The indentures for AMR's debentures contain certain restrictive covenants, including a limitation on the declaration of dividends on shares of capital stock. At December 31, 1987, under the terms of such indentures, all of AMR's retained earnings were available for the payment of dividends.

7. INCOME TAXES

The provision for income taxes is as follows (in thousands):

| | Year ended December 31, | | |
	1987	1986	1985
Federal, current	$ 32,177	$ (47,373)	$100,989
Federal, deferred	90,416	183,382	58,334
State and local	641	2,935	13,216
Foreign	833	586	667
	$124,067	$139,530	$173,206

The provision for income taxes varies from the tax computed at the U.S. statutory rate principally due to the utilization of investment tax credits (ITC) of approximately $10,900,000, $102,000,000 and $96,700,000 in 1987, 1986 and 1985, respectively, partially offset by the reduction in tax basis of assets for ITC. The current federal tax benefit for 1986 represents primarily the carryback of ITC for tax purposes.

The sources of deferred federal income tax and the tax effect of each are as follows (in thousands):

| | Year ended December 31, | | |
	1987	1986	1985
Accelerated depreciation and amortization	$145,480	$136,677	$68,005
Expenses deductible for tax purposes in a year different from the year accrued	(13,543)	3,339	(29,825)
Unrealized foreign currency exchange loss	(12,924)	(9,436)	(7,210)
Capital leases	(18,643)	(8,297)	(6,777)
Alternative minimum tax	(11,469)	—	—
Capitalized interest	9,344	11,355	9,063
Reduction in tax basis of assets for ITC	4,354	45,373	18,129
Tax benefit transfers	(6,532)	(4,663)	(4,729)
Disposal of equipment and property	(345)	(966)	3,708
Other	(5,306)	10,000	7,970
	$ 90,416	$183,382	$58,334

At December 31, 1987, AMR has available for federal income tax purposes approximately $9,000,000 in alternative

Notes to Financial Statements, Continued

minimum tax (AMT) credit carryforwards and, as a result of the acquisition of AirCal, approximately $45,000,000 of preacquisition operating loss carryforwards for regular tax purposes and approximately $3,000,000 of preacquisition ITC carryforwards. The AMT carryforward is available for an indefinite period while the remaining carryforwards expire in the years 1995 through 2001 if not used. For financial reporting purposes, the tax effect of the AirCal preacquisition carryforwards will reduce the excess of purchase price over net assets acquired to the extent used in future periods.

See Management Discussion and Analysis for the potential effects of adoption of Statement of Financial Accounting Standards No. 96, "Accounting for Income Taxes."

8. REDEEMABLE AND NON-REDEEMABLE PREFERRED STOCK AND COMMON STOCK RIGHTS

AMR has authorized 20,000,000 shares of preferred stock of which 300 shares are outstanding.

During 1987, AMR issued 300 shares, at $500,000 per share, of no par preferred auction rate stock in three series of $50,000,000 each, having an aggregate liquidation value of $150,000,000. The dividends are based on the results of an auction every 49 days with the maximum rate payable limited to a percentage premium over the AA composite commercial paper rate. The average dividend rate for the year ended December 31, 1987, was approximately 5.39%.

In July 1986, AMR redeemed the 2,969,762 outstanding shares of $2.1875 cumulative redeemable preferred stock (with a carrying value of $64,946,000) for $74,244,000.

During 1985, 4,997,580 shares of AMR's $2.125 convertible preferred stock were converted into 5,022,618 shares of AMR's common stock and the remaining shares were redeemed at $26.70 per share. If the conversion and redemption were assumed to have occurred on January 1, 1985, the primary earnings per share for the year ended December 31, 1985 would have been $5.88.

During 1984, a wholly owned subsidiary of American authorized and issued 960 shares of $1 par cumulative redeemable preferred stock which was redeemed at its carrying value of $24,000,000 in 1987. This redeemable preferred stock accrued dividends at a rate which was adjusted monthly, resulting in an effective dividend rate for the year ended December 31, 1987 of 4.26%. Dividends were charged to expense as accrued.

During 1986, the Board of Directors of AMR declared a dividend of one preferred share purchase right for each outstanding share of its common stock. Each right will entitle stockholders to purchase 1/100th of a share of newly authorized Series A Junior Participating Preferred Stock, without par value, at a price of $200 per right. The rights will not be exercisable until a party either acquires beneficial ownership of 20% of AMR's common stock or makes a tender offer for at least 30% of its common stock. The rights expire on February 29, 1996. The rights do not have voting rights and may be redeemed by AMR at 5¢ per right at any time prior to the public announcement of the acquisition of 20% of its common stock. If AMR is acquired in a merger or business combination, each right can be used to purchase the common stock of the surviving company having a market value of twice the exercise price of each right. As a result, the Board has reserved 610,000 shares of preferred stock for possible conversion of these rights.

9. STOCK AWARDS, OPTIONS AND WARRANTS

The 1979 Stock Option Plan, as amended, provides for the granting to officers and key employees of AMR and its subsidiaries non-qualified stock options and stock appreciation rights. Options may be granted for a maximum of 200,000 shares in any calendar year. However, if fewer than 200,000 options are granted in any year, the difference will be available for grant in any subsequent year. The 1979 Plan will terminate no later than December 31, 1989. Options are exercisable at the market value of the stock at the date of grant, generally becoming exercisable in equal annual installments over one to five years following the date of grant and expiring 10 years from date of grant. In addition, stock appreciation rights may be granted either in conjunction with a specific stock option or at any time prior to the exercise of such option and the exercise of either serves to cancel the other. At December 31, 1987, 500,900 stock appreciation rights were outstanding. Stock option activity for the year ended December 31, 1987, is summarized as follows:

Outstanding at January 1	571,584
Granted	360,000
Exercised	(15,020)*
Cancelled	(112,000)**
Outstanding at December 31	804,564

*At prices ranging from $9.125 to $43.875.
**Includes 88,700 options cancelled upon exercise of stock appreciation rights.

The aggregate purchase price of outstanding options at December 31, 1987, was approximately $36,443,000. At December 31, 1987, 168,664 options outstanding were exercisable and 22,775 options were available for grant.

There are 109,375 warrants outstanding, entitling the holder to purchase an equal number of shares of AMR common stock at a subscription price of $40 per share. These warrants will expire by March 15, 1991. Under the terms of the agreement, the holder may not sell, assign or transfer the warrants.

In conjunction with subordinated debentures issued in 1986, AMR issued 200,000 warrants, each entitling the holder to purchase 16.19 shares of common stock at an exercise price of $61.766. If not exercised, these warrants will expire on March 1, 1996. Warrants may be exercised by payment of cash, surrender of the debentures or a combination thereof. As of December 31, 1987, no warrants had been exercised.

AMR has adopted a restricted stock incentive plan, pursuant to which officers and key employees may be awarded, through 1995, shares of its common stock at no cost. In connection with the plan, 250,000 shares have been authorized for issuance, and at December 31, 1987, 96,000 of these shares are available for future award. Vesting of the shares occurs generally over a five year period.

At December 31, 1987, 4,470,714 shares of AMR's common stock were reserved for the exercise of options and warrants and for restricted stock.

In January 1988, AMR adopted the 1988 long-term incentive plan (the 1988 Plan), subject to stockholder approval, pursuant to which officers and key employees of AMR and its subsidiaries may be granted stock options, stock appreciation rights, restricted stock, deferred stock, stock purchase rights and/or other stock-based awards. The total number of common shares reserved and available for distribution under the 1988 Plan shall be 4,500,000 shares plus 7.65% of any increase (other than any increase due to awards under this plan or other plans, including the 1979 Plan) in the number of authorized and issued shares of common stock outstanding at December 31, 1987. The 1988 Plan will terminate no later than May 18, 1998. In connection with the 1988 Plan, 355,000 shares of deferred stock have been awarded at no cost, and such shares will vest generally over an eight year period.

10. RETIREMENT BENEFITS

Substantially all employees of American are eligible to participate in retirement benefit plans. The defined benefit plans provide benefits for certain employees based on years of service and average compensation for a specified period of time before retirement. Airline pilots and flight engineers also participate in defined contribution plans for which company contributions are determined as a percentage of participant earnings.

Pension costs for all retirement plans were approximately $100,200,000, $86,700,000 and $102,900,000 in 1987, 1986 and 1985, respectively.

During 1986, AMR adopted, effective January 1, 1986, Statement of Financial Accounting Standards (SFAS) No. 87, "Employers' Accounting for Pensions," and SFAS No. 88, "Employers' Accounting for Settlements and Curtailments of Defined Benefit Pension Plans and for Termination Benefits." The adoption of SFAS No. 87 resulted in a decrease in pension cost of approximately $46,400,000 in 1986.

American also recognized additional expense of $19,500,000 and $14,800,000 in 1987 and 1986, respectively, in accordance with SFAS No. 88 as a result of early retirement programs temporarily offered to certain groups of employees.

Net periodic pension cost of the defined benefit plans for 1987 and 1986 was as follows (in thousands):

	1987	1986
Service cost-benefits earned during the period	$ 62,843	$ 44,311
Interest cost on projected benefit obligation	172,246	155,711
Loss (return) on assets	76,756	(301,395)
Net amortization and deferral	(258,221)	127,258
	$ 53,624	$ 25,885

Plan assets consist primarily of government and corporate debt securities, marketable equity securities and money market funds.

**Notes to Financial
Statements,
Continued**

The following table sets forth the funded status and actuarial present value of benefit obligations of the plans at December 31, 1987 and 1986 (in thousands):

	1987	1986
Plan assets at fair value	$1,558,866	$1,677,134
Accumulated benefit obligation, including vested benefits of $1,140,755 and $1,411,512, respectively	1,401,527	1,472,685
Effect of projected future salary increases	276,584	259,921
Projected benefit obligation	1,678,111	1,732,606
Plan assets less than projected benefit obligation	(119,245)	(55,472)
Unrecognized net loss	165,297	93,073
Unrecognized prior service cost	12,732	—
Unrecognized transition net asset	(136,963)	(149,070)
Accrued pension cost*	$ 78,179	$ 111,469

*AMR's funding policy is to make contributions annually equal to, or in excess of, the minimum funding requirements of the Employee Retirement Income Security Act of 1974. In certain years the amount funded has been less than the amount of pension costs, and as a result, accrued pension costs of $23,900 and $21,200 are included in non-current liabilities at December 31, 1987 and 1986, respectively.

The projected benefit obligation was calculated using weighted average discount rates of 11.25% and 10.25% and rates of increase for compensation of 4.75% and 4.56% at December 31, 1987 and 1986, respectively. The weighted average expected long-term rate of return on assets was 10.25% in 1987 and 11.5% in 1986.

Pension costs for defined contribution plans were $45,700,000 and $44,700,000 in 1987 and 1986, respectively.

In addition to providing pension benefits, certain health care and life insurance benefits are also provided to retired employees. Employees may become eligible for those benefits if they satisfy the eligibility requirements while working for certain AMR subsidiaries. The cost of providing such benefits is recognized by expensing the health care claims incurred and the annual life insurance premiums. The cost was approximately $20,900,000, $16,400,000 and $16,400,000 for 1987, 1986 and 1985, respectively.

11. DEPRECIATION

As a result of a comprehensive review of its fleet plan, effective April 1, 1987, American changed the estimated useful lives of its Boeing 767-200 and McDonnell Douglas MD-80 aircraft and engines from 16 to 20 years. Estimated residual value for these aircraft and engines was also changed from 10% to 5%. The effect of these changes was to decrease depreciation expense for 1987 by approximately $12,600,000. Effective January 1, 1986, American changed the estimated useful lives of its Boeing 727-200 and McDonnell Douglas DC-10 aircraft and engines to reflect common retirement dates of December 31, 1994 and 1999, respectively. The estimated residual value for these aircraft and engines was also changed from 10% to 5%. The effect of these changes was to decrease depreciation expense for 1986 by approximately $42,000,000.

12. OTHER INCOME AND EXPENSE ITEMS

Miscellaneous — net in 1987 and 1986 includes gains of $14,600,000 and $14,800,000, respectively, resulting from the sale of certain property rights.

13. GAIN FROM SALE OF SUBSIDIARIES

In 1986, AMR sold three of its wholly owned subsidiaries, Flagship and American Airlines Training Corporation at gains and AMR Energy Corporation at a loss, and wrote off certain assets of AMR Energy Corporation not included in that sale. These transactions resulted in a pre-tax gain of $60,312,000.

Revenues of the former subsidiaries included in the consolidated statement of operations were $104,000,000 and $262,000,000 in 1986 and 1985, respectively, and operating income was $8,000,000 and $20,000,000 for the respective years.

14. QUARTERLY FINANCIAL DATA (UNAUDITED)

Unaudited summarized financial data by quarter for 1987 and 1986 are as follows (in thousands, except per share amounts):

	Operating Revenues	Operating Income	Net Earnings (Loss)	Earnings (Loss) Per Common Share Primary	Fully Diluted
1987					
First Quarter	$1,509,335	$ 72,154	$ 19,915	$ .34	$ .34
Second Quarter	1,831,143	161,830	92,167	1.51	1.51
Third Quarter	1,975,441	161,481	87,130	1.41	1.41
Fourth Quarter	1,882,055	65,599	(805)	(.05)	(.05)
1986					
First Quarter	$1,455,098	$ 36,573	$ 13,828	$ .20	$ .20
Second Quarter	1,517,742	124,908	137,979	2.23	2.23
Third Quarter	1,546,770	168,559	120,756	1.98	1.98
Fourth Quarter	1,498,565	80,883	6,569	.11	.11

Results for the second, third and fourth quarters of 1987 include the effect ($4,200,000 in each quarter) of a change in the depreciable lives and residual values of certain aircraft and engines (see Note 11). Results for the second quarter also include a gain of $14,600,000 from the sale of certain property rights. Results for the third quarter also include the cost ($19,500,000) of an early retirement program. Results for the fourth quarter also include a $23,100,000 unrealized exchange loss relating to debt denominated in a foreign currency and an additional tax provision of $9,800,000 resulting from changes during the quarter which impacted the effective tax rate for the year.

Results for the second and third quarters of 1986 include pre-tax gains of $56,945,000 and $3,367,000, respectively, on the sale of certain subsidiaries (see Note 13). Results for the fourth quarter of 1986 include a gain of $14,800,000 from the sale of certain property rights, a $38,900,000 increase in income taxes due to the retroactive provisions of the Tax Reform Act of 1986 related to investment tax credits, and the effect of a change in the annual effective tax rate.

REPORT OF CERTIFIED PUBLIC ACCOUNTANTS

The Board of Directors and Stockholders
AMR Corporation

We have examined the accompanying consolidated balance sheets of AMR Corporation at December 31, 1987 and 1986, and the related consolidated statements of operations, non-redeemable preferred stock, common stock and other stockholders' equity, and cash flows for each of the three years in the period ended December 31, 1987. Our examinations were made in accordance with generally accepted auditing standards and, accordingly, included such tests of the accounting records and such other auditing procedures as we considered necessary in the circumstances.

In our opinion, the statements mentioned above present fairly the consolidated financial position of AMR Corporation at December 31, 1987 and 1986, and the consolidated results of operations and cash flows for each of the three years in the period ended December 31, 1987, in conformity with generally accepted accounting principles applied on a consistent basis during the period, except for the change, with which we concur, in the method of accounting for pension costs, as described in Note 10.

Arthur Young & Company
ARTHUR YOUNG & COMPANY

2121 San Jacinto
Dallas, Texas 75201
February 12, 1988

REPORT OF MANAGEMENT

The management of AMR Corporation is responsible for the integrity and objectivity of the accompanying financial statements, which have been prepared in conformity with generally accepted accounting principles and reflect certain estimates and judgments of management as to matters set forth therein.

AMR maintains a system of internal controls which, in the opinion of management, provides reasonable assurance that its financial records can be relied upon in the preparation of financial statements and that its assets are safeguarded against loss or unauthorized use. The system of internal controls provides for appropriate division of responsibility and is documented by written policies and procedures that are communicated to employees with significant roles in the financial reporting process and updated as necessary. Management continually monitors the system for compliance. AMR maintains a strong internal auditing program that independently assesses the effectiveness of the internal controls and recommends possible improvements thereto.

The Audit Committee of the Board of Directors, composed entirely of directors who are not employees of AMR, meets periodically and privately with AMR's independent accountants, and its internal auditors, as well as with AMR's management, to review accounting, auditing, internal control and financial reporting matters.

ROBERT L. CRANDALL
Chairman, President and
Chief Executive Officer

DONALD J. CARTY
Senior Vice President and
Chief Financial Officer

Report of Certified Public Accountants and Report of Management

APPENDIX C
FUTURE
AND PRESENT
VALUE TABLES

Table I
FUTURE VALUE OF $1 AT COMPOUND INTEREST: 0.5%–10%

$$F_{1,n} = (1 + i)^n$$

Period	.5%	1%	1.5%	2%	2.5%	3%	3.5%	4%	4.5%	5%
1	1.00500	1.01000	1.01500	1.02000	1.02500	1.03000	1.03500	1.04000	1.04500	1.05000
2	1.01003	1.02010	1.03023	1.04040	1.05063	1.06090	1.07123	1.08160	1.09203	1.10250
3	1.01508	1.03030	1.04568	1.06121	1.07689	1.09273	1.10872	1.12486	1.14117	1.15762
4	1.02015	1.04060	1.06136	1.08243	1.10381	1.12551	1.14752	1.16986	1.19252	1.21551
5	1.02525	1.05101	1.07728	1.10408	1.13141	1.15927	1.18769	1.21665	1.24618	1.27628
6	1.03038	1.06152	1.09344	1.12616	1.15969	1.19405	1.22926	1.26532	1.30226	1.34010
7	1.03553	1.07214	1.10984	1.14869	1.18869	1.22987	1.27228	1.31593	1.36086	1.40710
8	1.04071	1.08286	1.12649	1.17166	1.21840	1.26677	1.31681	1.36857	1.42210	1.47746
9	1.04591	1.09369	1.14339	1.19509	1.24886	1.30477	1.36290	1.42331	1.48610	1.55133
10	1.05114	1.10462	1.16054	1.21899	1.28008	1.34392	1.41060	1.48024	1.55297	1.62889
11	1.05640	1.11567	1.17795	1.24337	1.31209	1.38423	1.45997	1.53945	1.62285	1.71034
12	1.06168	1.12683	1.19562	1.26824	1.34489	1.42576	1.51107	1.60103	1.69588	1.79586
13	1.06699	1.13809	1.21355	1.29361	1.37851	1.46853	1.56396	1.66507	1.77220	1.88565
14	1.07232	1.14947	1.23176	1.31948	1.41297	1.51259	1.61869	1.73168	1.85194	1.97993
15	1.07768	1.16097	1.25023	1.34587	1.44830	1.55797	1.67535	1.80094	1.93528	2.07893
16	1.08307	1.17258	1.26899	1.37279	1.48451	1.60471	1.73399	1.87298	2.02237	2.18287
17	1.08849	1.18430	1.28802	1.40024	1.52162	1.65285	1.79468	1.94790	2.11338	2.29202
18	1.09393	1.19615	1.30734	1.42825	1.55966	1.70243	1.85749	2.02582	2.20848	2.40662
19	1.09940	1.20811	1.32695	1.45681	1.59865	1.75351	1.92250	2.10685	2.30786	2.52695
20	1.10490	1.22019	1.34686	1.48595	1.63862	1.80611	1.98979	2.19112	2.41171	2.65330
21	1.11042	1.23239	1.36706	1.51567	1.67958	1.86029	2.05943	2.27877	2.52024	2.78596
22	1.11597	1.24472	1.38756	1.54598	1.72157	1.91610	2.13151	2.36992	2.63365	2.92526
23	1.12155	1.25716	1.40838	1.57690	1.76461	1.97359	2.20611	2.46472	2.75217	3.07152
24	1.12716	1.26973	1.42950	1.60844	1.80873	2.03279	2.28333	2.56330	2.87601	3.22510
25	1.13280	1.28243	1.45095	1.64061	1.85394	2.09378	2.36324	2.66584	3.00543	3.38635
26	1.13846	1.29526	1.47271	1.67342	1.90029	2.15659	2.44596	2.77247	3.14068	3.55567
27	1.14415	1.30821	1.49480	1.70689	1.94780	2.22129	2.53157	2.88337	3.28201	3.73346
28	1.14987	1.32129	1.51722	1.74102	1.99650	2.28793	2.62017	2.99870	3.42970	3.92013
29	1.15562	1.33450	1.53998	1.77584	2.04641	2.35657	2.71188	3.11865	3.58404	4.11614
30	1.16140	1.34785	1.56308	1.81136	2.09757	2.42726	2.80679	3.24340	3.74532	4.32194

5.5%	6%	6.5%	7%	7.5%	8%	8.5%	9%	9.5%	10%
1.05500	1.06000	1.06500	1.07000	1.07500	1.08000	1.08500	1.09000	1.09500	1.10000
1.11303	1.12360	1.13423	1.14490	1.15563	1.16640	1.17723	1.18810	1.19903	1.21000
1.17424	1.19102	1.20795	1.22504	1.24230	1.25971	1.27729	1.29503	1.31293	1.33100
1.23882	1.26248	1.28647	1.31080	1.33547	1.36049	1.38586	1.41158	1.43766	1.46410
1.30696	1.33823	1.37009	1.40255	1.43563	1.46933	1.50366	1.53862	1.57424	1.61051
1.37884	1.41852	1.45914	1.50073	1.54330	1.58687	1.63147	1.67710	1.72379	1.77156
1.45468	1.50363	1.55399	1.60578	1.65905	1.71382	1.77014	1.82804	1.88755	1.94872
1.53469	1.59385	1.65500	1.71819	1.78348	1.85093	1.92060	1.99256	2.06687	2.14359
1.61909	1.68948	1.76257	1.83846	1.91724	1.99900	2.08386	2.17189	2.26322	2.35795
1.70814	1.79085	1.87714	1.96715	2.06103	2.15892	2.26098	2.36736	2.47823	2.59374
1.80209	1.89830	1.99915	2.10485	2.21561	2.33164	2.45317	2.58043	2.71366	2.85312
1.90121	2.01220	2.12910	2.25219	2.38178	2.51817	2.66169	2.81266	2.97146	3.13843
2.00577	2.13293	2.26749	2.40985	2.56041	2.71962	2.88793	3.06580	3.25375	3.45227
2.11609	2.26090	2.41487	2.57853	2.75244	2.93719	3.13340	3.34173	3.56285	3.79750
2.23248	2.39656	2.57184	2.75903	2.95888	3.17217	3.39974	3.64248	3.90132	4.17725
2.35526	2.54035	2.73901	2.95216	3.18079	3.42594	3.68872	3.97031	4.27195	4.59497
2.48480	2.69277	2.91705	3.15882	3.41935	3.70002	4.00226	4.32763	4.67778	5.05447
2.62147	2.85434	3.10665	3.37993	3.67580	3.99602	4.34245	4.71712	5.12217	5.55992
2.76565	3.02560	3.30859	3.61653	3.95149	4.31570	4.71156	5.14166	5.60878	6.11591
2.91776	3.20714	3.52365	3.86968	4.24785	4.66096	5.11205	5.60441	6.14161	6.72750
3.07823	3.39956	3.75268	4.14056	4.56644	5.03383	5.54657	6.10881	6.72507	7.40025
3.24754	3.60354	3.99661	4.43040	4.90892	5.43654	6.01803	6.65860	7.36395	8.14027
3.42615	3.81975	4.25639	4.74053	5.27709	5.87146	6.52956	7.25787	8.06352	8.95430
3.61459	4.04893	4.53305	5.07237	5.67287	6.34118	7.08457	7.91108	8.82956	9.84973
3.81339	4.29187	4.82770	5.42743	6.09834	6.84848	7.68676	8.62308	9.66836	10.83471
4.02313	4.54938	5.14150	5.80735	6.55572	7.39635	8.34014	9.39916	10.58686	11.91818
4.24440	4.82235	5.47570	6.21387	7.04739	7.98806	9.04905	10.24508	11.59261	13.10999
4.47784	5.11169	5.83162	6.64884	7.57595	8.62711	9.81822	11.16714	12.69391	14.42099
4.72412	5.41839	6.21067	7.11426	8.14414	9.31727	10.65277	12.17218	13.89983	15.86309
4.98395	5.74349	6.61437	7.61226	8.75496	10.06266	11.55825	13.26768	15.22031	17.44940

Table I *(concluded)*
FUTURE VALUE OF $1 AT COMPOUND INTEREST: 10.5%–20%

Period	10.5%	11%	11.5%	12%	12.5%	13%	13.5%	14%	14.5%	15%
1	1.10500	1.11000	1.11500	1.12000	1.12500	1.13000	1.13500	1.14000	1.14500	1.15000
2	1.22103	1.23210	1.24323	1.25440	1.26563	1.27690	1.28822	1.29960	1.31102	1.32250
3	1.34923	1.36763	1.38620	1.40493	1.42383	1.44290	1.46214	1.48154	1.50112	1.52088
4	1.49090	1.51807	1.54561	1.57352	1.60181	1.63047	1.65952	1.68896	1.71879	1.74901
5	1.64745	1.68506	1.72335	1.76234	1.80203	1.84244	1.88356	1.92541	1.96801	2.01136
6	1.82043	1.87041	1.92154	1.97382	2.02729	2.08195	2.13784	2.19497	2.25337	2.31306
7	2.01157	2.07616	2.14252	2.21068	2.28070	2.35261	2.42645	2.50227	2.58011	2.66002
8	2.22279	2.30454	2.38891	2.47596	2.56578	2.65844	2.75402	2.85259	2.95423	3.05902
9	2.45618	2.55804	2.66363	2.77308	2.88651	3.00404	3.12581	3.25195	3.38259	3.51788
10	2.71408	2.83942	2.96995	3.10585	3.24732	3.39457	3.54780	3.70722	3.87307	4.04556
11	2.99906	3.15176	3.31149	3.47855	3.65324	3.83586	4.02675	4.22623	4.43466	4.65239
12	3.31396	3.49845	3.69231	3.89598	4.10989	4.33452	4.57036	4.81790	5.07769	5.35025
13	3.66193	3.88328	4.11693	4.36349	4.62363	4.89801	5.18736	5.49241	5.81395	6.15279
14	4.04643	4.31044	4.59037	4.88711	5.20158	5.53475	5.88765	6.26135	6.65697	7.07571
15	4.47130	4.78459	5.11827	5.47357	5.85178	6.25427	6.68248	7.13794	7.62223	8.13706
16	4.94079	5.31089	5.70687	6.13039	6.58325	7.06733	7.58462	8.13725	8.72746	9.35762
17	5.45957	5.89509	6.36316	6.86604	7.40616	7.98608	8.60854	9.27646	9.99294	10.76126
18	6.03283	6.54355	7.09492	7.68997	8.33193	9.02427	9.77070	10.57517	11.44192	12.37545
19	6.66628	7.26334	7.91084	8.61276	9.37342	10.19742	11.08974	12.05569	13.10039	14.23177
20	7.36623	8.06231	8.82058	9.64629	10.54509	11.52309	12.58686	13.74349	15.00064	16.36654
21	8.13969	8.94917	9.83495	10.80385	11.86323	13.02109	14.28608	15.66758	17.17573	18.82152
22	8.99436	9.93357	10.96597	12.10031	13.34613	14.71383	16.21470	17.86104	19.66621	21.64475
23	9.93876	11.02627	12.22706	13.55235	15.01440	16.62663	18.40369	20.36158	22.51781	24.89146
24	10.98233	12.23916	13.63317	15.17863	16.89120	18.78809	20.88818	23.21221	25.78290	28.62518
25	12.13548	13.58546	15.20098	17.00006	19.00260	21.23054	23.70809	26.46192	29.52141	32.91895
26	13.40971	15.07986	16.94910	19.04007	21.37793	23.99051	26.90868	30.16658	33.80202	37.85680
27	14.81772	16.73865	18.89824	21.32488	24.05017	27.10928	30.54135	34.38991	38.70331	43.53531
28	16.37359	18.57990	21.07154	23.88387	27.05644	30.63349	34.66443	39.20449	44.31529	50.06561
29	18.09281	20.62369	23.49477	26.74993	30.43849	34.61584	39.34413	44.69312	50.74101	57.57545
30	19.99256	22.89230	26.19667	29.95992	34.24330	39.11590	44.65559	50.95016	58.09846	66.21177

15.5%	16%	16.5%	17%	17.5%	18%	18.5%	19%	19.5%	20%
1.15500	1.16000	1.16500	1.17000	1.17500	1.18000	1.18500	1.19000	1.19500	1.20000
1.33402	1.34560	1.35722	1.36890	1.38063	1.39240	1.40422	1.41610	1.42802	1.44000
1.54080	1.56090	1.58117	1.60161	1.62223	1.64303	1.66401	1.68516	1.70649	1.72800
1.77962	1.81064	1.84206	1.87389	1.90613	1.93878	1.97185	2.00534	2.03926	2.07360
2.05546	2.10034	2.14600	2.19245	2.23970	2.28776	2.33664	2.38635	2.43691	2.48832
2.37406	2.43640	2.50009	2.56516	2.63164	2.69955	2.76892	2.83976	2.91211	2.98598
2.74204	2.82622	2.91260	3.00124	3.09218	3.18547	3.28117	3.37932	3.47997	3.58318
3.16706	3.27841	3.39318	3.51145	3.63331	3.75886	3.88818	4.02139	4.15856	4.29982
3.65795	3.80296	3.95306	4.10840	4.26914	4.43545	4.60750	4.78545	4.96948	5.15978
4.22493	4.41144	4.60531	4.80683	5.01624	5.23384	5.45989	5.69468	5.93853	6.19174
4.87980	5.11726	5.36519	5.62399	5.89409	6.17593	6.46996	6.77667	7.09654	7.43008
5.63617	5.93603	6.25045	6.58007	6.92555	7.28759	7.66691	8.06424	8.48037	8.91610
6.50977	6.88579	7.28177	7.69868	8.13752	8.59936	9.08528	9.59645	10.13404	10.69932
7.51879	7.98752	8.48326	9.00745	9.56159	10.14724	10.76606	11.41977	12.11018	12.83918
8.68420	9.26552	9.88300	10.53872	11.23487	11.97375	12.75778	13.58953	14.47167	15.40702
10.03025	10.74800	11.51370	12.33030	13.20097	14.12902	15.11797	16.17154	17.29364	18.48843
11.58494	12.46768	13.41346	14.42646	15.51114	16.67225	17.91480	19.24413	20.66590	22.18611
13.38060	14.46251	15.62668	16.87895	18.22559	19.67325	21.22904	22.90052	24.69575	26.62333
15.45460	16.77652	18.20508	19.74838	21.41507	23.21444	25.15641	27.25162	29.51143	31.94800
17.85006	19.46076	21.20892	23.10560	25.16271	27.39303	29.81035	32.42942	35.26615	38.33760
20.61682	22.57448	24.70839	27.03355	29.56618	32.32378	35.32526	38.59101	42.14305	46.00512
23.81243	26.18640	28.78527	31.62925	34.74026	38.14206	41.86043	45.92331	50.36095	55.20614
27.50335	30.37622	33.53484	37.00623	40.81981	45.00763	49.60461	54.64873	60.18134	66.24737
31.76637	35.23642	39.06809	43.29729	47.96327	53.10901	58.78147	65.03199	71.91670	79.49685
36.69016	40.87424	45.51433	50.65783	56.35684	62.66863	69.65604	77.38807	85.94045	95.39622
42.37713	47.41412	53.02419	59.26966	66.21929	73.94898	82.54240	92.09181	102.69884	114.47546
48.94559	55.00038	61.77318	69.34550	77.80767	87.25980	97.81275	109.58925	122.72511	137.37055
56.53216	63.80044	71.96576	81.13423	91.42401	102.96656	115.90811	130.41121	146.65651	164.84466
65.29464	74.00851	83.84011	94.92705	107.42321	121.50054	137.35111	155.18934	175.25453	197.81359
75.41531	85.84988	97.67373	111.06465	126.22227	143.37064	162.76106	184.67531	209.42916	237.37631

Table II
PRESENT VALUE OF $1 AT COMPOUND INTEREST: 0.5%–7%

$$P_{1,n} = \frac{1}{(1+i)^n}$$

Period	.5%	1%	1.5%	2%	2.5%	3%	3.5%	4%	4.5%	5%	5.5%	6%	6.5%	7%
1 ...	0.99502	0.99010	0.98522	0.98039	0.97561	0.97087	0.96618	0.96154	0.95694	0.95238	0.94787	0.94340	0.93897	0.93458
2 ...	0.99007	0.98030	0.97066	0.96117	0.95181	0.94260	0.93351	0.92456	0.91573	0.90703	0.89845	0.89000	0.88166	0.87344
3 ...	0.98515	0.97059	0.95632	0.94232	0.92860	0.91514	0.90194	0.88900	0.87630	0.86384	0.85161	0.83962	0.82785	0.81630
4 ...	0.98025	0.96098	0.94218	0.92385	0.90595	0.88849	0.87144	0.85480	0.83856	0.82270	0.80722	0.79209	0.77732	0.76290
5 ...	0.97537	0.95147	0.92826	0.90573	0.88385	0.86261	0.84197	0.82193	0.80245	0.78353	0.76513	0.74726	0.72988	0.71299
6 ...	0.97052	0.94205	0.91454	0.88797	0.86230	0.83748	0.81350	0.79031	0.76790	0.74622	0.72525	0.70496	0.68533	0.66634
7 ...	0.96569	0.93272	0.90103	0.87056	0.84127	0.81309	0.78599	0.75992	0.73483	0.71068	0.68744	0.66506	0.64351	0.62275
8 ...	0.96089	0.92348	0.88771	0.85349	0.82075	0.78941	0.75941	0.73069	0.70319	0.67684	0.65160	0.62741	0.60423	0.58201
9 ...	0.95610	0.91434	0.87459	0.83676	0.80073	0.76642	0.73373	0.70259	0.67290	0.64461	0.61763	0.59190	0.56735	0.54393
10 ...	0.95135	0.90529	0.86167	0.82035	0.78120	0.74409	0.70892	0.67556	0.64393	0.61391	0.58543	0.55839	0.53273	0.50835
11 ...	0.94661	0.89632	0.84893	0.80426	0.76214	0.72242	0.68495	0.64958	0.61620	0.58468	0.55491	0.52679	0.50021	0.47509
12 ...	0.94191	0.88745	0.83639	0.78849	0.74356	0.70138	0.66178	0.62460	0.58966	0.55684	0.52598	0.49697	0.46968	0.44401
13 ...	0.93722	0.87866	0.82403	0.77303	0.72542	0.68095	0.63940	0.60057	0.56427	0.53032	0.49856	0.46884	0.44102	0.41496
14 ...	0.93256	0.86996	0.81185	0.75788	0.70773	0.66112	0.61778	0.57748	0.53997	0.50507	0.47257	0.44230	0.41410	0.38782
15 ...	0.92792	0.86135	0.79985	0.74301	0.69047	0.64186	0.59689	0.55526	0.51672	0.48102	0.44793	0.41727	0.38883	0.36245
16 ...	0.92330	0.85282	0.78803	0.72845	0.67362	0.62317	0.57671	0.53391	0.49447	0.45811	0.42458	0.39365	0.36510	0.33873
17 ...	0.91871	0.84438	0.77639	0.71416	0.65720	0.60502	0.55720	0.51337	0.47318	0.43630	0.40245	0.37136	0.34281	0.31657
18 ...	0.91414	0.83602	0.76491	0.70016	0.64117	0.58739	0.53836	0.49363	0.45280	0.41552	0.38147	0.35034	0.32189	0.29586
19 ...	0.90959	0.82774	0.75361	0.68643	0.62553	0.57029	0.52016	0.47464	0.43330	0.39573	0.36158	0.33051	0.30224	0.27651
20 ...	0.90506	0.81954	0.74247	0.67297	0.61027	0.55368	0.50257	0.45639	0.41464	0.37689	0.34273	0.31180	0.28380	0.25842
21 ...	0.90056	0.81143	0.73150	0.65978	0.59539	0.53755	0.48557	0.43883	0.39679	0.35894	0.32486	0.29416	0.26648	0.24151
22 ...	0.89608	0.80340	0.72069	0.64684	0.58086	0.52189	0.46915	0.42196	0.37970	0.34185	0.30793	0.27751	0.25021	0.22571
23 ...	0.89162	0.79544	0.71004	0.63416	0.56670	0.50669	0.45329	0.40573	0.36335	0.32557	0.29187	0.26180	0.23494	0.21095
24 ...	0.88719	0.78757	0.69954	0.62172	0.55288	0.49193	0.43796	0.39012	0.34770	0.31007	0.27666	0.24698	0.22060	0.19715
25 ...	0.88277	0.77977	0.68921	0.60953	0.53939	0.47761	0.42315	0.37512	0.33273	0.29530	0.26223	0.23300	0.20714	0.18425
26 ...	0.87838	0.77205	0.67902	0.59758	0.52623	0.46369	0.40884	0.36069	0.31840	0.28124	0.24856	0.21981	0.19450	0.17220
27 ...	0.87401	0.76440	0.66899	0.58586	0.51340	0.45019	0.39501	0.34682	0.30469	0.26785	0.23560	0.20737	0.18263	0.16093
28 ...	0.86966	0.75684	0.65910	0.57437	0.50088	0.43708	0.38165	0.33348	0.29157	0.25509	0.22332	0.19563	0.17148	0.15040
29 ...	0.86533	0.74934	0.64936	0.56311	0.48866	0.42435	0.36875	0.32065	0.27902	0.24295	0.21168	0.18456	0.16101	0.14056
30 ...	0.86103	0.74192	0.63976	0.55207	0.47674	0.41199	0.35628	0.30832	0.26700	0.23138	0.20064	0.17411	0.15119	0.13137
31 ...	0.85675	0.73458	0.63031	0.54125	0.46511	0.39999	0.34423	0.29646	0.25550	0.22036	0.19018	0.16425	0.14196	0.12277
32 ...	0.85248	0.72730	0.62099	0.53063	0.45377	0.38834	0.33259	0.28506	0.24450	0.20987	0.18027	0.15496	0.13329	0.11474
33 ...	0.84824	0.72010	0.61182	0.52023	0.44270	0.37703	0.32134	0.27409	0.23397	0.19987	0.17087	0.14619	0.12516	0.10723
34 ...	0.84402	0.71297	0.60277	0.51003	0.43191	0.36604	0.31048	0.26355	0.22390	0.19035	0.16196	0.13791	0.11752	0.10022
35 ...	0.83982	0.70591	0.59387	0.50003	0.42137	0.35538	0.29998	0.25342	0.21425	0.18129	0.15352	0.13011	0.11035	0.09366
36 ...	0.83564	0.69892	0.58509	0.49022	0.41109	0.34503	0.28983	0.24367	0.20503	0.17266	0.14552	0.12274	0.10361	0.08754
37 ...	0.83149	0.69200	0.57644	0.48061	0.40107	0.33498	0.28003	0.23430	0.19620	0.16444	0.13793	0.11579	0.09729	0.08181
38 ...	0.82735	0.68515	0.56792	0.47119	0.39128	0.32523	0.27056	0.22529	0.18775	0.15661	0.13074	0.10924	0.09135	0.07646
39 ...	0.82323	0.67837	0.55953	0.46195	0.38174	0.31575	0.26141	0.21662	0.17967	0.14915	0.12392	0.10306	0.08578	0.07146
40 ...	0.81914	0.67165	0.55126	0.45289	0.37243	0.30656	0.25257	0.20829	0.17193	0.14205	0.11746	0.09722	0.08054	0.06678
41 ...	0.81506	0.66500	0.54312	0.44401	0.36335	0.29763	0.24403	0.20028	0.16453	0.13528	0.11134	0.09172	0.07563	0.06241
42 ...	0.81101	0.65842	0.53509	0.43530	0.35448	0.28896	0.23578	0.19257	0.15744	0.12884	0.10554	0.08653	0.07101	0.05833
43 ...	0.80697	0.65190	0.52718	0.42677	0.34584	0.28054	0.22781	0.18517	0.15066	0.12270	0.10003	0.08163	0.06668	0.05451
44 ...	0.80296	0.64545	0.51939	0.41840	0.33740	0.27237	0.22010	0.17805	0.14417	0.11686	0.09482	0.07701	0.06261	0.05095
45 ...	0.79896	0.63905	0.51171	0.41020	0.32917	0.26444	0.21266	0.17120	0.13796	0.11130	0.08988	0.07265	0.05879	0.04761
46 ...	0.79499	0.63273	0.50415	0.40215	0.32115	0.25674	0.20547	0.16461	0.13202	0.10600	0.08519	0.06854	0.05520	0.04450
47 ...	0.79103	0.62646	0.49670	0.39427	0.31331	0.24926	0.19852	0.15828	0.12634	0.10095	0.08075	0.06466	0.05183	0.04159
48 ...	0.78710	0.62026	0.48936	0.38654	0.30567	0.24200	0.19181	0.15219	0.12090	0.09614	0.07654	0.06100	0.04867	0.03887
49 ...	0.78318	0.61412	0.48213	0.37896	0.29822	0.23495	0.18532	0.14634	0.11569	0.09156	0.07255	0.05755	0.04570	0.03632
50 ...	0.77929	0.60804	0.47500	0.37153	0.29094	0.22811	0.17905	0.14071	0.11071	0.08720	0.06877	0.05429	0.04291	0.03395
51 ...	0.77541	0.60202	0.46798	0.36424	0.28385	0.22146	0.17300	0.13530	0.10594	0.08305	0.06518	0.05122	0.04029	0.03173
52 ...	0.77155	0.59606	0.46107	0.35710	0.27692	0.21501	0.16715	0.13010	0.10138	0.07910	0.06178	0.04832	0.03783	0.02965
53 ...	0.76771	0.59016	0.45426	0.35010	0.27017	0.20875	0.16150	0.12509	0.09701	0.07533	0.05856	0.04558	0.03552	0.02771
54 ...	0.76389	0.58431	0.44754	0.34323	0.26358	0.20267	0.15603	0.12028	0.09284	0.07174	0.05551	0.04300	0.03335	0.02590
55 ...	0.76009	0.57853	0.44093	0.33650	0.25715	0.19677	0.15076	0.11566	0.08884	0.06833	0.05262	0.04057	0.03132	0.02420
56 ...	0.75631	0.57280	0.43441	0.32991	0.25088	0.19104	0.14566	0.11121	0.08501	0.06507	0.04987	0.03827	0.02941	0.02262
57 ...	0.75255	0.56713	0.42799	0.32344	0.24476	0.18547	0.14073	0.10693	0.08135	0.06197	0.04727	0.03610	0.02761	0.02114
58 ...	0.74880	0.56151	0.42167	0.31710	0.23879	0.18007	0.13598	0.10282	0.07785	0.05902	0.04481	0.03406	0.02593	0.01976
59 ...	0.74508	0.55595	0.41544	0.31088	0.23297	0.17483	0.13138	0.09886	0.07450	0.05621	0.04247	0.03213	0.02434	0.01847
60 ...	0.74137	0.55045	0.40930	0.30478	0.22728	0.16973	0.12693	0.09506	0.07129	0.05354	0.04026	0.03031	0.02286	0.01726

Period	.5%	1%	1.5%	2%	2.5%	3%	3.5%	4%	4.5%	5%	5.5%	6%	6.5%	7%
61	0.73768	0.54500	0.40325	0.29881	0.22174	0.16479	0.12264	0.09140	0.06822	0.05099	0.03816	0.02860	0.02146	0.01613
62	0.73401	0.53960	0.39729	0.29295	0.21633	0.15999	0.11849	0.08789	0.06528	0.04856	0.03617	0.02698	0.02015	0.01507
63	0.73036	0.53426	0.39142	0.28720	0.21106	0.15533	0.11449	0.08451	0.06247	0.04625	0.03428	0.02545	0.01892	0.01409
64	0.72673	0.52897	0.38563	0.28157	0.20591	0.15081	0.11062	0.08126	0.05978	0.04404	0.03250	0.02401	0.01777	0.01317
65	0.72311	0.52373	0.37993	0.27605	0.20089	0.14641	0.10688	0.07813	0.05721	0.04195	0.03080	0.02265	0.01668	0.01230
66	0.71952	0.51855	0.37432	0.27064	0.19599	0.14215	0.10326	0.07513	0.05474	0.03995	0.02920	0.02137	0.01566	0.01150
67	0.71594	0.51341	0.36879	0.26533	0.19121	0.13801	0.09977	0.07224	0.05239	0.03805	0.02767	0.02016	0.01471	0.01075
68	0.71237	0.50833	0.36334	0.26013	0.18654	0.13399	0.09640	0.06946	0.05013	0.03623	0.02623	0.01902	0.01381	0.01004
69	0.70883	0.50330	0.35797	0.25503	0.18199	0.13009	0.09314	0.06679	0.04797	0.03451	0.02486	0.01794	0.01297	0.00939
70	0.70530	0.49831	0.35268	0.25003	0.17755	0.12630	0.08999	0.06422	0.04590	0.03287	0.02357	0.01693	0.01218	0.00877
71	0.70179	0.49338	0.34746	0.24513	0.17322	0.12262	0.08694	0.06175	0.04393	0.03130	0.02234	0.01597	0.01143	0.00820
72	0.69830	0.48850	0.34233	0.24032	0.16900	0.11905	0.08400	0.05937	0.04204	0.02981	0.02117	0.01507	0.01074	0.00766
73	0.69483	0.48366	0.33727	0.23561	0.16488	0.11558	0.08116	0.05709	0.04023	0.02839	0.02007	0.01421	0.01008	0.00716
74	0.69137	0.47887	0.33229	0.23099	0.16085	0.11221	0.07842	0.05490	0.03849	0.02704	0.01902	0.01341	0.00947	0.00669
75	0.68793	0.47413	0.32738	0.22646	0.15693	0.10895	0.07577	0.05278	0.03684	0.02575	0.01803	0.01265	0.00889	0.00625
76	0.68451	0.46944	0.32254	0.22202	0.15310	0.10577	0.07320	0.05075	0.03525	0.02453	0.01709	0.01193	0.00835	0.00585
77	0.68110	0.46479	0.31777	0.21766	0.14937	0.10269	0.07073	0.04880	0.03373	0.02336	0.01620	0.01126	0.00784	0.00546
78	0.67772	0.46019	0.31308	0.21340	0.14573	0.09970	0.06834	0.04692	0.03228	0.02225	0.01536	0.01062	0.00736	0.00511
79	0.67434	0.45563	0.30845	0.20921	0.14217	0.09680	0.06603	0.04512	0.03089	0.02119	0.01456	0.01002	0.00691	0.00477
80	0.67099	0.45112	0.30389	0.20511	0.13870	0.09398	0.06379	0.04338	0.02956	0.02018	0.01380	0.00945	0.00649	0.00446
81	0.66765	0.44665	0.29940	0.20109	0.13532	0.09124	0.06164	0.04172	0.02829	0.01922	0.01308	0.00892	0.00609	0.00417
82	0.66433	0.44223	0.29497	0.19715	0.13202	0.08858	0.05955	0.04011	0.02707	0.01830	0.01240	0.00841	0.00572	0.00390
83	0.66102	0.43785	0.29062	0.19328	0.12880	0.08600	0.05754	0.03857	0.02590	0.01743	0.01175	0.00794	0.00537	0.00364
84	0.65773	0.43352	0.28632	0.18949	0.12566	0.08350	0.05559	0.03709	0.02479	0.01660	0.01114	0.00749	0.00504	0.00340
85	0.65446	0.42922	0.28209	0.18577	0.12259	0.08107	0.05371	0.03566	0.02372	0.01581	0.01056	0.00706	0.00473	0.00318
86	0.65121	0.42497	0.27792	0.18213	0.11960	0.07870	0.05190	0.03429	0.02270	0.01506	0.01001	0.00666	0.00445	0.00297
87	0.64797	0.42077	0.27381	0.17856	0.11669	0.07641	0.05014	0.03297	0.02172	0.01434	0.00948	0.00629	0.00417	0.00278
88	0.64474	0.41660	0.26977	0.17506	0.11384	0.07419	0.04845	0.03170	0.02079	0.01366	0.00899	0.00593	0.00392	0.00260
89	0.64154	0.41248	0.26578	0.17163	0.11106	0.07203	0.04681	0.03048	0.01989	0.01301	0.00852	0.00559	0.00368	0.00243
90	0.63834	0.40839	0.26185	0.16826	0.10836	0.06993	0.04522	0.02931	0.01903	0.01239	0.00808	0.00528	0.00346	0.00227
91	0.63517	0.40435	0.25798	0.16496	0.10571	0.06789	0.04369	0.02818	0.01821	0.01180	0.00766	0.00498	0.00324	0.00212
92	0.63201	0.40034	0.25417	0.16173	0.10313	0.06591	0.04222	0.02710	0.01743	0.01124	0.00726	0.00470	0.00305	0.00198
93	0.62886	0.39638	0.25041	0.15856	0.10062	0.06399	0.04079	0.02606	0.01668	0.01070	0.00688	0.00443	0.00286	0.00185
94	0.62573	0.39246	0.24671	0.15545	0.09816	0.06213	0.03941	0.02505	0.01596	0.01019	0.00652	0.00418	0.00269	0.00173
95	0.62262	0.38857	0.24307	0.15240	0.09577	0.06032	0.03808	0.02409	0.01527	0.00971	0.00618	0.00394	0.00252	0.00162
96	0.61952	0.38472	0.23947	0.14941	0.09343	0.05856	0.03679	0.02316	0.01462	0.00924	0.00586	0.00372	0.00237	0.00151
97	0.61644	0.38091	0.23594	0.14648	0.09116	0.05686	0.03555	0.02227	0.01399	0.00880	0.00555	0.00351	0.00222	0.00141
98	0.61337	0.37714	0.23245	0.14361	0.08893	0.05520	0.03434	0.02142	0.01338	0.00838	0.00526	0.00331	0.00209	0.00132
99	0.61032	0.37341	0.22901	0.14079	0.08676	0.05359	0.03318	0.02059	0.01281	0.00798	0.00499	0.00312	0.00196	0.00123
100	0.60729	0.36971	0.22563	0.13803	0.08465	0.05203	0.03026	0.01980	0.01226	0.00760	0.00473	0.00295	0.00184	0.00115
101	0.60427	0.36605	0.22230	0.13533	0.08258	0.05052	0.03098	0.01904	0.01173	0.00724	0.00448	0.00278	0.00173	0.00108
102	0.60126	0.36243	0.21901	0.13267	0.08057	0.04905	0.02993	0.01831	0.01122	0.00690	0.00425	0.00262	0.00162	0.00101
103	0.59827	0.35884	0.21577	0.13007	0.07860	0.04762	0.02892	0.01760	0.01074	0.00657	0.00403	0.00247	0.00152	0.00094
104	0.59529	0.35529	0.21258	0.12752	0.07669	0.04623	0.02794	0.01693	0.01028	0.00626	0.00382	0.00233	0.00143	0.00088
105	0.59233	0.35177	0.20944	0.12502	0.07482	0.04488	0.02699	0.01627	0.00984	0.00596	0.00362	0.00220	0.00134	0.00082
106	0.58938	0.34828	0.20635	0.12257	0.07299	0.04358	0.02608	0.01565	0.00941	0.00567	0.00343	0.00208	0.00126	0.00077
107	0.58645	0.34484	0.20330	0.12017	0.07121	0.04231	0.02520	0.01505	0.00901	0.00540	0.00325	0.00196	0.00118	0.00072
108	0.58353	0.34142	0.20029	0.11781	0.06947	0.04108	0.02435	0.01447	0.00862	0.00515	0.00308	0.00185	0.00111	0.00067
109	0.58063	0.33804	0.19733	0.11550	0.06778	0.03988	0.02352	0.01391	0.00825	0.00490	0.00292	0.00174	0.00104	0.00063
110	0.57774	0.33469	0.19442	0.11324	0.06613	0.03872	0.02273	0.01338	0.00789	0.00467	0.00277	0.00165	0.00098	0.00059
111	0.57487	0.33138	0.19154	0.11101	0.06451	0.03759	0.02196	0.01286	0.00755	0.00445	0.00262	0.00155	0.00092	0.00055
112	0.57201	0.32810	0.18871	0.10884	0.06294	0.03649	0.02122	0.01237	0.00723	0.00423	0.00249	0.00146	0.00086	0.00051
113	0.56916	0.32485	0.18592	0.10670	0.06140	0.03543	0.02050	0.01189	0.00692	0.00403	0.00236	0.00138	0.00081	0.00048
114	0.56633	0.32164	0.18318	0.10461	0.05991	0.03440	0.01981	0.01143	0.00662	0.00384	0.00223	0.00130	0.00076	0.00045
115	0.56351	0.31845	0.18047	0.10256	0.05845	0.03340	0.01914	0.01099	0.00633	0.00366	0.00212	0.00123	0.00072	0.00042
116	0.56071	0.31530	0.17780	0.10055	0.05702	0.03243	0.01849	0.01057	0.00606	0.00348	0.00201	0.00116	0.00067	0.00039
117	0.55792	0.31218	0.17518	0.09858	0.05563	0.03148	0.01786	0.01016	0.00580	0.00332	0.00190	0.00109	0.00063	0.00036
118	0.55514	0.30908	0.17259	0.09665	0.05427	0.03056	0.01726	0.00977	0.00555	0.00316	0.00180	0.00103	0.00059	0.00034
119	0.55238	0.30602	0.17004	0.09475	0.05295	0.02967	0.01668	0.00940	0.00531	0.00301	0.00171	0.00097	0.00056	0.00032
120	0.54963	0.30299	0.16752	0.09289	0.05166	0.02881	0.01611	0.00904	0.00508	0.00287	0.00162	0.00092	0.00052	0.00030

Table II *(continued)*
PRESENT VALUE OF $1 AT COMPOUND INTEREST: 7.5%–14%

Period	7.5%	8%	8.5%	9%	9.5%	10%	10.5%	11%	11.5%	12%	12.5%	13%	13.5%	14%
1 ...	0.93023	0.92593	0.92166	0.91743	0.91324	0.90909	0.90498	0.90090	0.89686	0.89286	0.88889	0.88496	0.88106	0.87719
2 ...	0.86533	0.85734	0.84946	0.84168	0.83401	0.82645	0.81898	0.81162	0.80436	0.79719	0.79012	0.78315	0.77626	0.76947
3 ...	0.80496	0.79383	0.78291	0.77218	0.76165	0.75131	0.74116	0.73119	0.72140	0.71178	0.70233	0.69305	0.68393	0.67497
4 ...	0.74880	0.73503	0.72157	0.70843	0.69557	0.68301	0.67073	0.65873	0.64699	0.63553	0.62430	0.61332	0.60258	0.59208
5 ...	0.69656	0.68058	0.66505	0.64993	0.63523	0.62092	0.60700	0.59345	0.58026	0.56743	0.55493	0.54276	0.53091	0.51937
6 ...	0.64796	0.63017	0.61295	0.59627	0.58012	0.56447	0.54932	0.53464	0.52042	0.50663	0.49327	0.48032	0.46776	0.45559
7 ...	0.60275	0.58349	0.56493	0.54703	0.52979	0.51316	0.49712	0.48166	0.46674	0.45235	0.43846	0.42506	0.41213	0.39964
8 ...	0.56070	0.54027	0.52067	0.50187	0.48382	0.46651	0.44989	0.43393	0.41860	0.40388	0.38974	0.37616	0.36311	0.35056
9 ...	0.52158	0.50025	0.47988	0.46043	0.44185	0.42410	0.40714	0.39092	0.37543	0.36061	0.34644	0.33288	0.31992	0.30751
10 ...	0.48519	0.46319	0.44229	0.42241	0.40351	0.38554	0.36845	0.35218	0.33671	0.32197	0.30795	0.29459	0.28187	0.26974
11 ...	0.45134	0.42888	0.40764	0.38753	0.36851	0.35049	0.33344	0.31728	0.30198	0.28748	0.27373	0.26070	0.24834	0.23662
12 ...	0.41985	0.39711	0.37570	0.35553	0.33654	0.31863	0.30175	0.28584	0.27083	0.25668	0.24332	0.23071	0.21880	0.20756
13 ...	0.39056	0.36770	0.34627	0.32618	0.30734	0.28966	0.27308	0.25751	0.24290	0.22917	0.21628	0.20416	0.19278	0.18207
14 ...	0.36331	0.34046	0.31914	0.29925	0.28067	0.26333	0.24713	0.23199	0.21785	0.20462	0.19225	0.18068	0.16985	0.15971
15 ...	0.33797	0.31524	0.29414	0.27454	0.25632	0.23939	0.22365	0.20900	0.19538	0.18270	0.17089	0.15989	0.14964	0.14010
16 ...	0.31439	0.29189	0.27110	0.25187	0.23409	0.21763	0.20240	0.18829	0.17523	0.16312	0.15190	0.14150	0.13185	0.12289
17 ...	0.29245	0.27027	0.24986	0.23107	0.21378	0.19784	0.18316	0.16963	0.15715	0.14564	0.13502	0.12522	0.11616	0.10780
18 ...	0.27205	0.25025	0.23028	0.21199	0.19523	0.17986	0.16576	0.15282	0.14095	0.13004	0.12002	0.11081	0.10235	0.09456
19 ...	0.25307	0.23171	0.21224	0.19449	0.17829	0.16351	0.15001	0.13768	0.12641	0.11611	0.10668	0.09806	0.09017	0.08295
20 ...	0.23541	0.21455	0.19562	0.17843	0.16282	0.14864	0.13575	0.12403	0.11337	0.10367	0.09483	0.08678	0.07945	0.07276
21 ...	0.21899	0.19866	0.18029	0.16370	0.14870	0.13513	0.12285	0.11174	0.10168	0.09256	0.08429	0.07680	0.07000	0.06383
22 ...	0.20371	0.18394	0.16617	0.15018	0.13580	0.12285	0.11118	0.10067	0.09119	0.08264	0.07493	0.06796	0.06167	0.05599
23 ...	0.18950	0.17032	0.15315	0.13778	0.12402	0.11168	0.10062	0.09069	0.08179	0.07379	0.06660	0.06014	0.05434	0.04911
24 ...	0.17628	0.15770	0.14115	0.12640	0.11326	0.10153	0.09106	0.08170	0.07335	0.06588	0.05920	0.05323	0.04787	0.04308
25 ...	0.16398	0.14602	0.13009	0.11597	0.10343	0.09230	0.08240	0.07361	0.06579	0.05882	0.05262	0.04710	0.04218	0.03779
26 ...	0.15254	0.13520	0.11990	0.10639	0.09446	0.08391	0.07457	0.06631	0.05900	0.05252	0.04678	0.04168	0.03716	0.03315
27 ...	0.14190	0.12519	0.11051	0.09761	0.08626	0.07628	0.06749	0.05974	0.05291	0.04689	0.04158	0.03689	0.03274	0.02908
28 ...	0.13200	0.11591	0.10185	0.08955	0.07878	0.06934	0.06107	0.05382	0.04746	0.04187	0.03696	0.03264	0.02885	0.02551
29 ...	0.12279	0.10733	0.09387	0.08215	0.07194	0.06304	0.05527	0.04849	0.04256	0.03738	0.03285	0.02889	0.02542	0.02237
30 ...	0.11422	0.09938	0.08652	0.07537	0.06570	0.05731	0.05002	0.04368	0.03817	0.03338	0.02920	0.02557	0.02239	0.01963
31 ...	0.10625	0.09202	0.07974	0.06915	0.06000	0.05210	0.04527	0.03935	0.03424	0.02980	0.02596	0.02262	0.01973	0.01722
32 ...	0.09884	0.08520	0.07349	0.06344	0.05480	0.04736	0.04096	0.03545	0.03070	0.02661	0.02307	0.02002	0.01738	0.01510
33 ...	0.09194	0.07889	0.06774	0.05820	0.05004	0.04306	0.03707	0.03194	0.02754	0.02376	0.02051	0.01772	0.01532	0.01325
34 ...	0.08553	0.07305	0.06243	0.05339	0.04570	0.03914	0.03355	0.02878	0.02470	0.02121	0.01823	0.01568	0.01349	0.01162
35 ...	0.07956	0.06763	0.05754	0.04899	0.04174	0.03558	0.03036	0.02592	0.02215	0.01894	0.01621	0.01388	0.01189	0.01019
36 ...	0.07401	0.06262	0.05303	0.04494	0.03811	0.03235	0.02748	0.02335	0.01987	0.01691	0.01440	0.01228	0.01047	0.00894
37 ...	0.06885	0.05799	0.04888	0.04123	0.03481	0.02941	0.02487	0.02104	0.01782	0.01510	0.01280	0.01087	0.00923	0.00784
38 ...	0.06404	0.05369	0.04505	0.03783	0.03179	0.02673	0.02250	0.01896	0.01598	0.01348	0.01138	0.00962	0.00813	0.00688
39 ...	0.05958	0.04971	0.04152	0.03470	0.02903	0.02430	0.02036	0.01708	0.01433	0.01204	0.01012	0.00851	0.00716	0.00604
40 ...	0.05542	0.04603	0.03827	0.03184	0.02651	0.02209	0.01843	0.01538	0.01285	0.01075	0.00899	0.00753	0.00631	0.00529
41 ...	0.05155	0.04262	0.03527	0.02921	0.02421	0.02009	0.01668	0.01386	0.01153	0.00960	0.00799	0.00666	0.00556	0.00464
42 ...	0.04796	0.03946	0.03251	0.02680	0.02211	0.01826	0.01509	0.01249	0.01034	0.00857	0.00711	0.00590	0.00490	0.00407
43 ...	0.04461	0.03654	0.02996	0.02458	0.02019	0.01660	0.01366	0.01125	0.00927	0.00765	0.00632	0.00522	0.00432	0.00357
44 ...	0.04150	0.03383	0.02761	0.02255	0.01844	0.01509	0.01236	0.01013	0.00832	0.00683	0.00561	0.00462	0.00380	0.00313
45 ...	0.03860	0.03133	0.02545	0.02069	0.01684	0.01372	0.01119	0.00913	0.00746	0.00610	0.00499	0.00409	0.00335	0.00275
46 ...	0.03591	0.02901	0.02345	0.01898	0.01538	0.01247	0.01012	0.00823	0.00669	0.00544	0.00444	0.00362	0.00295	0.00241
47 ...	0.03340	0.02686	0.02162	0.01742	0.01405	0.01134	0.00916	0.00741	0.00600	0.00486	0.00394	0.00320	0.00260	0.00212
48 ...	0.03107	0.02487	0.01992	0.01598	0.01283	0.01031	0.00829	0.00668	0.00538	0.00434	0.00350	0.00283	0.00229	0.00186
49 ...	0.02891	0.02303	0.01836	0.01466	0.01171	0.00937	0.00750	0.00601	0.00483	0.00388	0.00312	0.00251	0.00202	0.00163
50 ...	0.02689	0.02132	0.01692	0.01345	0.01070	0.00852	0.00679	0.00542	0.00433	0.00346	0.00277	0.00222	0.00178	0.00143
51 ...	0.02501	0.01974	0.01560	0.01234	0.00977	0.00774	0.00615	0.00488	0.00388	0.00309	0.00246	0.00196	0.00157	0.00125
52 ...	0.02327	0.01828	0.01438	0.01132	0.00892	0.00704	0.00556	0.00440	0.00348	0.00276	0.00219	0.00174	0.00138	0.00110
53 ...	0.02164	0.01693	0.01325	0.01038	0.00815	0.00640	0.00503	0.00396	0.00312	0.00246	0.00194	0.00154	0.00122	0.00096
54 ...	0.02013	0.01567	0.01221	0.00953	0.00744	0.00582	0.00455	0.00357	0.00280	0.00220	0.00173	0.00136	0.00107	0.00085
55 ...	0.01873	0.01451	0.01126	0.00874	0.00680	0.00529	0.00412	0.00322	0.00251	0.00196	0.00154	0.00120	0.00094	0.00074
56 ...	0.01742	0.01344	0.01037	0.00802	0.00621	0.00481	0.00373	0.00290	0.00225	0.00175	0.00137	0.00107	0.00083	0.00065
57 ...	0.01621	0.01244	0.00956	0.00736	0.00567	0.00437	0.00338	0.00261	0.00202	0.00157	0.00121	0.00094	0.00073	0.00057
58 ...	0.01508	0.01152	0.00881	0.00675	0.00518	0.00397	0.00305	0.00235	0.00181	0.00140	0.00108	0.00083	0.00065	0.00050
59 ...	0.01402	0.01067	0.00812	0.00619	0.00473	0.00361	0.00276	0.00212	0.00162	0.00125	0.00096	0.00074	0.00057	0.00044
60 ...	0.01305	0.00988	0.00749	0.00568	0.00432	0.00328	0.00250	0.00191	0.00146	0.00111	0.00085	0.00065	0.00050	0.00039

Period	7.5%	8%	8.5%	9%	9.5%	10%	10.5%	11%	11.5%	12%	12.5%	13%	13.5%	14%
61 ..	0.01214	0.00914	0.00690	0.00521	0.00394	0.00299	0.00226	0.00172	0.00131	0.00099	0.00076	0.00058	0.00044	0.00034
62 ..	0.01129	0.00847	0.00636	0.00478	0.00360	0.00271	0.00205	0.00155	0.00117	0.00089	0.00067	0.00051	0.00039	0.00030
63 ..	0.01050	0.00784	0.00586	0.00439	0.00329	0.00247	0.00185	0.00140	0.00105	0.00079	0.00060	0.00045	0.00034	0.00026
64 ..	0.00977	0.00726	0.00540	0.00402	0.00300	0.00224	0.00168	0.00126	0.00094	0.00071	0.00053	0.00040	0.00030	0.00023
65 ..	0.00909	0.00672	0.00498	0.00369	0.00274	0.00204	0.00152	0.00113	0.00085	0.00063	0.00047	0.00035	0.00027	0.00020
66 ..	0.00845	0.00622	0.00459	0.00339	0.00250	0.00185	0.00137	0.00102	0.00076	0.00056	0.00042	0.00031	0.00023	0.00018
67 ..	0.00786	0.00576	0.00423	0.00311	0.00229	0.00169	0.00124	0.00092	0.00068	0.00050	0.00037	0.00028	0.00021	0.00015
68 ..	0.00732	0.00534	0.00390	0.00285	0.00209	0.00153	0.00113	0.00083	0.00061	0.00045	0.00033	0.00025	0.00018	0.00014
69 ..	0.00680	0.00494	0.00359	0.00262	0.00191	0.00139	0.00102	0.00075	0.00055	0.00040	0.00030	0.00022	0.00016	0.00012
70 ..	0.00633	0.00457	0.00331	0.00240	0.00174	0.00127	0.00092	0.00067	0.00049	0.00036	0.00026	0.00019	0.00014	0.00010
71 ..	0.00589	0.00424	0.00305	0.00220	0.00159	0.00115	0.00083	0.00061	0.00044	0.00032	0.00023	0.00017	0.00012	0.00009
72 ..	0.00548	0.00392	0.00281	0.00202	0.00145	0.00105	0.00075	0.00055	0.00039	0.00029	0.00021	0.00015	0.00011	0.00008
73 ..	0.00510	0.00363	0.00259	0.00185	0.00133	0.00095	0.00068	0.00049	0.00035	0.00026	0.00018	0.00013	0.00010	0.00007
74 ..	0.00474	0.00336	0.00239	0.00170	0.00121	0.00086	0.00062	0.00044	0.00032	0.00023	0.00016	0.00012	0.00009	0.00006
75 ..	0.00441	0.00311	0.00220	0.00156	0.00111	0.00079	0.00056	0.00040	0.00028	0.00020	0.00015	0.00010	0.00008	0.00005
76 ..	0.00410	0.00288	0.00203	0.00143	0.00101	0.00071	0.00051	0.00036	0.00026	0.00018	0.00013	0.00009	0.00007	0.00005
77 ..	0.00382	0.00267	0.00187	0.00131	0.00092	0.00065	0.00046	0.00032	0.00023	0.00016	0.00012	0.00008	0.00006	0.00004
78 ..	0.00355	0.00247	0.00172	0.00120	0.00084	0.00059	0.00041	0.00029	0.00021	0.00014	0.00010	0.00007	0.00005	0.00004
79 ..	0.00330	0.00229	0.00159	0.00110	0.00077	0.00054	0.00038	0.00026	0.00018	0.00013	0.00009	0.00006	0.00005	0.00003
80 ..	0.00307	0.00212	0.00146	0.00101	0.00070	0.00049	0.00034	0.00024	0.00017	0.00012	0.00008	0.00006	0.00004	0.00003
81 ..	0.00286	0.00196	0.00135	0.00093	0.00064	0.00044	0.00031	0.00021	0.00015	0.00010	0.00007	0.00005	0.00004	0.00002
82 ..	0.00266	0.00182	0.00124	0.00085	0.00059	0.00040	0.00028	0.00019	0.00013	0.00009	0.00006	0.00004	0.00003	0.00002
83 ..	0.00247	0.00168	0.00115	0.00078	0.00054	0.00037	0.00025	0.00017	0.00012	0.00008	0.00006	0.00004	0.00003	0.00002
84 ..	0.00230	0.00156	0.00106	0.00072	0.00049	0.00033	0.00023	0.00016	0.00011	0.00007	0.00005	0.00003	0.00002	0.00002
85 ..	0.00214	0.00144	0.00097	0.00066	0.00045	0.00030	0.00021	0.00014	0.00010	0.00007	0.00004	0.00003	0.00002	0.00001
86 ..	0.00199	0.00134	0.00090	0.00060	0.00041	0.00028	0.00019	0.00013	0.00009	0.00006	0.00004	0.00003	0.00002	0.00001
87 ..	0.00185	0.00124	0.00083	0.00055	0.00037	0.00025	0.00017	0.00011	0.00008	0.00005	0.00004	0.00002	0.00002	0.00001
88 ..	0.00172	0.00114	0.00076	0.00051	0.00034	0.00023	0.00015	0.00010	0.00007	0.00005	0.00003	0.00002	0.00001	0.00001
89 ..	0.00160	0.00106	0.00070	0.00047	0.00031	0.00021	0.00014	0.00009	0.00006	0.00004	0.00003	0.00002	0.00001	0.00001
90 ..	0.00149	0.00098	0.00065	0.00043	0.00028	0.00019	0.00013	0.00008	0.00006	0.00004	0.00002	0.00002	0.00001	0.00001
91 ..	0.00139	0.00091	0.00060	0.00039	0.00026	0.00017	0.00011	0.00008	0.00005	0.00003	0.00002	0.00001	0.00001	0.00001
92 ..	0.00129	0.00084	0.00055	0.00036	0.00024	0.00016	0.00010	0.00007	0.00004	0.00003	0.00002	0.00001	0.00001	0.00001
93 ..	0.00120	0.00078	0.00051	0.00033	0.00022	0.00014	0.00009	0.00006	0.00004	0.00003	0.00002	0.00001	0.00001	0.00001
94 ..	0.00112	0.00072	0.00047	0.00030	0.00020	0.00013	0.00008	0.00005	0.00004	0.00002	0.00002	0.00001	0.00001	0.00000
95 ..	0.00104	0.00067	0.00043	0.00028	0.00018	0.00012	0.00008	0.00005	0.00003	0.00002	0.00001	0.00001	0.00001	0.00000
96 ..	0.00097	0.00062	0.00040	0.00026	0.00016	0.00011	0.00007	0.00004	0.00003	0.00002	0.00001	0.00001	0.00001	0.00000
97 ..	0.00090	0.00057	0.00037	0.00023	0.00015	0.00010	0.00006	0.00004	0.00003	0.00002	0.00001	0.00001	0.00000	0.00000
98 ..	0.00084	0.00053	0.00034	0.00021	0.00014	0.00009	0.00006	0.00004	0.00002	0.00002	0.00001	0.00001	0.00000	0.00000
99 ..	0.00078	0.00049	0.00031	0.00020	0.00013	0.00008	0.00005	0.00003	0.00002	0.00001	0.00001	0.00001	0.00000	0.00000
100 ..	0.00072	0.00045	0.00029	0.00018	0.00011	0.00007	0.00005	0.00003	0.00002	0.00001	0.00001	0.00000	0.00000	0.00000
101 ..	0.00067	0.00042	0.00026	0.00017	0.00010	0.00007	0.00004	0.00003	0.00002	0.00001	0.00001	0.00000	0.00000	0.00000
102 ..	0.00063	0.00039	0.00024	0.00015	0.00010	0.00006	0.00004	0.00002	0.00002	0.00001	0.00001	0.00000	0.00000	0.00000
103 ..	0.00058	0.00036	0.00022	0.00014	0.00009	0.00005	0.00003	0.00002	0.00001	0.00001	0.00001	0.00000	0.00000	0.00000
104 ..	0.00054	0.00033	0.00021	0.00013	0.00008	0.00005	0.00003	0.00002	0.00001	0.00001	0.00000	0.00000	0.00000	0.00000
105 ..	0.00050	0.00031	0.00019	0.00012	0.00007	0.00005	0.00003	0.00002	0.00001	0.00001	0.00000	0.00000	0.00000	0.00000
106 ..	0.00047	0.00029	0.00018	0.00011	0.00007	0.00004	0.00003	0.00002	0.00001	0.00001	0.00000	0.00000	0.00000	0.00000
107 ..	0.00044	0.00027	0.00016	0.00010	0.00006	0.00004	0.00002	0.00001	0.00001	0.00001	0.00000	0.00000	0.00000	0.00000
108 ..	0.00041	0.00025	0.00015	0.00009	0.00006	0.00003	0.00002	0.00001	0.00001	0.00000	0.00000	0.00000	0.00000	0.00000
109 ..	0.00038	0.00023	0.00014	0.00008	0.00005	0.00003	0.00002	0.00001	0.00001	0.00000	0.00000	0.00000	0.00000	0.00000
110 ..	0.00035	0.00021	0.00013	0.00008	0.00005	0.00003	0.00002	0.00001	0.00001	0.00000	0.00000	0.00000	0.00000	0.00000
111 ..	0.00033	0.00019	0.00012	0.00007	0.00004	0.00003	0.00002	0.00001	0.00001	0.00000	0.00000	0.00000	0.00000	0.00000
112 ..	0.00030	0.00018	0.00011	0.00006	0.00004	0.00002	0.00001	0.00001	0.00001	0.00000	0.00000	0.00000	0.00000	0.00000
113 ..	0.00028	0.00017	0.00010	0.00006	0.00004	0.00002	0.00001	0.00001	0.00000	0.00000	0.00000	0.00000	0.00000	0.00000
114 ..	0.00026	0.00015	0.00009	0.00005	0.00003	0.00002	0.00001	0.00001	0.00000	0.00000	0.00000	0.00000	0.00000	0.00000
115 ..	0.00024	0.00014	0.00008	0.00005	0.00003	0.00002	0.00001	0.00001	0.00000	0.00000	0.00000	0.00000	0.00000	0.00000
116 ..	0.00023	0.00013	0.00008	0.00005	0.00003	0.00002	0.00001	0.00001	0.00000	0.00000	0.00000	0.00000	0.00000	0.00000
117 ..	0.00021	0.00012	0.00007	0.00004	0.00002	0.00001	0.00001	0.00000	0.00000	0.00000	0.00000	0.00000	0.00000	0.00000
118 ..	0.00020	0.00011	0.00007	0.00004	0.00002	0.00001	0.00001	0.00000	0.00000	0.00000	0.00000	0.00000	0.00000	0.00000
119 ..	0.00018	0.00011	0.00006	0.00004	0.00002	0.00001	0.00001	0.00000	0.00000	0.00000	0.00000	0.00000	0.00000	0.00000
120 ..	0.00017	0.00010	0.00006	0.00003	0.00002	0.00001	0.00001	0.00000	0.00000	0.00000	0.00000	0.00000	0.00000	0.00000

Table II *(concluded)*
PRESENT VALUE OF $1: 14.5%–20%

Period	14.5%	15%	15.5%	16%	16.5%	17%	17.5%	18%	18.5%	19%	19.5%	20%
1	0.87336	0.86957	0.86580	0.86207	0.85837	0.85470	0.85106	0.84746	0.84388	0.84034	0.83682	0.83333
2	0.76276	0.75614	0.74961	0.74316	0.73680	0.73051	0.72431	0.71818	0.71214	0.70616	0.70027	0.69444
3	0.66617	0.65752	0.64901	0.64066	0.63244	0.62437	0.61643	0.60863	0.60096	0.59342	0.58600	0.57870
4	0.58181	0.57175	0.56192	0.55229	0.54287	0.53365	0.52462	0.51579	0.50714	0.49867	0.49038	0.48225
5	0.50813	0.49718	0.48651	0.47611	0.46598	0.45611	0.44649	0.43711	0.42796	0.41905	0.41036	0.40188
6	0.44378	0.43233	0.42122	0.41044	0.39999	0.38984	0.37999	0.37043	0.36115	0.35214	0.34339	0.33490
7	0.38758	0.37594	0.36469	0.35383	0.34334	0.33320	0.32340	0.31393	0.30477	0.29592	0.28736	0.27908
8	0.33850	0.32690	0.31575	0.30503	0.29471	0.28478	0.27523	0.26604	0.25719	0.24867	0.24047	0.23257
9	0.29563	0.28426	0.27338	0.26295	0.25297	0.24340	0.23424	0.22546	0.21704	0.20897	0.20123	0.19381
10	0.25819	0.24718	0.23669	0.22668	0.21714	0.20804	0.19935	0.19106	0.18315	0.17560	0.16839	0.16151
11	0.22550	0.21494	0.20493	0.19542	0.18639	0.17781	0.16966	0.16192	0.15456	0.14757	0.14091	0.13459
12	0.19694	0.18691	0.17743	0.16846	0.15999	0.15197	0.14439	0.13722	0.13043	0.12400	0.11792	0.11216
13	0.17200	0.16253	0.15362	0.14523	0.13733	0.12989	0.12289	0.11629	0.11007	0.10421	0.09868	0.09346
14	0.15022	0.14133	0.13300	0.12520	0.11788	0.11102	0.10459	0.09855	0.09288	0.08757	0.08258	0.07789
15	0.13120	0.12289	0.11515	0.10793	0.10118	0.09489	0.08901	0.08352	0.07838	0.07359	0.06910	0.06491
16	0.11458	0.10686	0.09970	0.09304	0.08685	0.08110	0.07575	0.07078	0.06615	0.06184	0.05782	0.05409
17	0.10007	0.09293	0.08632	0.08021	0.07455	0.06932	0.06447	0.05998	0.05582	0.05196	0.04839	0.04507
18	0.08740	0.04081	0.07474	0.06914	0.06399	0.05925	0.05487	0.05083	0.04711	0.04367	0.04049	0.03756
19	0.07633	0.07027	0.06471	0.05961	0.05493	0.05064	0.04670	0.04308	0.03975	0.03670	0.03389	0.03130
20	0.06666	0.06110	0.05602	0.05139	0.04715	0.04328	0.03974	0.03651	0.03355	0.03084	0.02836	0.02608
21	0.05822	0.05313	0.04850	0.04430	0.04047	0.03699	0.03382	0.03094	0.02831	0.02591	0.02373	0.02174
22	0.05085	0.04620	0.04199	0.03819	0.03474	0.03162	0.02879	0.02622	0.02389	0.02178	0.01986	0.01811
23	0.04441	0.04017	0.03636	0.03292	0.02982	0.02702	0.02450	0.02222	0.02016	0.01830	0.01662	0.01509
24	0.03879	0.03493	0.03148	0.02838	0.02560	0.02310	0.02085	0.01883	0.01701	0.01538	0.01390	0.01258
25	0.03387	0.03038	0.02726	0.02447	0.02197	0.01974	0.01774	0.01596	0.01436	0.01292	0.01164	0.01048
26	0.02958	0.02642	0.02360	0.02109	0.01886	0.01687	0.01510	0.01352	0.01211	0.01086	0.00974	0.00874
27	0.02584	0.02297	0.02043	0.01818	0.01619	0.01442	0.01285	0.01146	0.01022	0.00912	0.00815	0.00728
28	0.02257	0.01997	0.01769	0.01567	0.01390	0.01233	0.01094	0.00971	0.00863	0.00767	0.00682	0.00607
29	0.01971	0.01737	0.01532	0.01351	0.01193	0.01053	0.00931	0.00823	0.00728	0.00644	0.00571	0.00506
30	0.01721	0.01510	0.01326	0.01165	0.01024	0.00900	0.00792	0.00697	0.00614	0.00541	0.00477	0.00421
31	0.01503	0.01313	0.01148	0.01004	0.00879	0.00770	0.00674	0.00591	0.00518	0.00455	0.00400	0.00351
32	0.01313	0.01142	0.00994	0.00866	0.00754	0.00658	0.00574	0.00501	0.00438	0.00382	0.00334	0.00293
33	0.01147	0.00993	0.00861	0.00746	0.00648	0.00562	0.00488	0.00425	0.00369	0.00321	0.00280	0.00244
34	0.01001	0.00864	0.00745	0.00643	0.00556	0.00480	0.00416	0.00360	0.00312	0.00270	0.00234	0.00203
35	0.00875	0.00751	0.00645	0.00555	0.00477	0.00411	0.00354	0.00305	0.00263	0.00227	0.00196	0.00169
36	0.00764	0.00653	0.00559	0.00478	0.00410	0.00351	0.00301	0.00258	0.00222	0.00191	0.00164	0.00141
37	0.00667	0.00568	0.00484	0.00412	0.00352	0.00300	0.00256	0.00219	0.00187	0.00160	0.00137	0.00118
38	0.00583	0.00494	0.00419	0.00355	0.00302	0.00256	0.00218	0.00186	0.00158	0.00135	0.00115	0.00098
39	0.00509	0.00429	0.00362	0.00306	0.00259	0.00219	0.00186	0.00157	0.00133	0.00113	0.00096	0.00082
40	0.00444	0.00373	0.00314	0.00264	0.00222	0.00187	0.00158	0.00133	0.00113	0.00095	0.00080	0.00068
41	0.00388	0.00325	0.00272	0.00228	0.00191	0.00160	0.00134	0.00113	0.00095	0.00080	0.00067	0.00057
42	0.00339	0.00282	0.00235	0.00196	0.00164	0.00137	0.00114	0.00096	0.00080	0.00067	0.00056	0.00047
43	0.00296	0.00245	0.00204	0.00169	0.00141	0.00117	0.00097	0.00081	0.00068	0.00056	0.00047	0.00039
44	0.00259	0.00213	0.00176	0.00146	0.00121	0.00100	0.00083	0.00069	0.00057	0.00047	0.00039	0.00033
45	0.00226	0.00186	0.00153	0.00126	0.00104	0.00085	0.00071	0.00058	0.00048	0.00040	0.00033	0.00027
46	0.00197	0.00161	0.00132	0.00109	0.00089	0.00073	0.00060	0.00049	0.00041	0.00033	0.00028	0.00023
47	0.00172	0.00140	0.00114	0.00093	0.00076	0.00062	0.00051	0.00042	0.00034	0.00028	0.00023	0.00019
48	0.00150	0.00122	0.00099	0.00081	0.00066	0.00053	0.00043	0.00035	0.00029	0.00024	0.00019	0.00016
49	0.00131	0.00106	0.00086	0.00069	0.00056	0.00046	0.00037	0.00030	0.00024	0.00020	0.00016	0.00013
50	0.00115	0.00092	0.00074	0.00060	0.00048	0.00039	0.00031	0.00025	0.00021	0.00017	0.00014	0.00011
51	0.00100	0.00080	0.00064	0.00052	0.00041	0.00033	0.00027	0.00022	0.00017	0.00014	0.00011	0.00009
52	0.00088	0.00070	0.00056	0.00044	0.00036	0.00028	0.00023	0.00018	0.00015	0.00012	0.00009	0.00008
53	0.00076	0.00061	0.00048	0.00038	0.00031	0.00024	0.00019	0.00015	0.00012	0.00010	0.00008	0.00006
54	0.00067	0.00053	0.00042	0.00033	0.00026	0.00021	0.00017	0.00013	0.00010	0.00008	0.00007	0.00005
55	0.00058	0.00046	0.00036	0.00028	0.00022	0.00018	0.00014	0.00011	0.00009	0.00007	0.00006	0.00004
56	0.00051	0.00040	0.00031	0.00025	0.00019	0.00015	0.00012	0.00009	0.00007	0.00006	0.00005	0.00004
57	0.00044	0.00035	0.00027	0.00021	0.00017	0.00013	0.00010	0.00008	0.00006	0.00005	0.00004	0.00003
58	0.00039	0.00030	0.00023	0.00018	0.00014	0.00011	0.00009	0.00007	0.00005	0.00004	0.00003	0.00003
59	0.00034	0.00026	0.00020	0.00016	0.00012	0.00009	0.00007	0.00006	0.00004	0.00003	0.00003	0.00002
60	0.00030	0.00023	0.00018	0.00014	0.00010	0.00008	0.00006	0.00005	0.00004	0.00003	0.00002	0.00002

Period	14.5%	15%	15.5%	16%	16.5%	17%	17.5%	18%	18.5%	19%	19.5%	20%
61	0.00026	0.00020	0.00015	0.00012	0.00009	0.00007	0.00005	0.00004	0.00003	0.00002	0.00002	0.00001
62	0.00023	0.00017	0.00013	0.00010	0.00008	0.00006	0.00005	0.00003	0.00003	0.00002	0.00002	0.00001
63	0.00020	0.00015	0.00011	0.00009	0.00007	0.00005	0.00004	0.00003	0.00002	0.00002	0.00001	0.00001
64	0.00017	0.00013	0.00010	0.00007	0.00006	0.00004	0.00003	0.00003	0.00002	0.00001	0.00001	0.00001
65	0.00015	0.00011	0.00009	0.00006	0.00005	0.00004	0.00003	0.00002	0.00002	0.00001	0.00001	0.00001
66	0.00013	0.00010	0.00007	0.00006	0.00004	0.00003	0.00002	0.00002	0.00001	0.00001	0.00001	0.00001
67	0.00011	0.00009	0.00006	0.00005	0.00004	0.00003	0.00002	0.00002	0.00001	0.00001	0.00001	0.00000
68	0.00010	0.00007	0.00006	0.00004	0.00003	0.00002	0.00002	0.00001	0.00001	0.00001	0.00001	0.00000
69	0.00009	0.00006	0.00005	0.00004	0.00003	0.00002	0.00001	0.00001	0.00001	0.00001	0.00000	0.00000
70	0.00008	0.00006	0.00004	0.00003	0.00002	0.00002	0.00001	0.00001	0.00001	0.00001	0.00000	0.00000
71	0.00007	0.00005	0.00004	0.00003	0.00002	0.00001	0.00001	0.00001	0.00001	0.00000	0.00000	0.00000
72	0.00006	0.00004	0.00003	0.00002	0.00002	0.00001	0.00001	0.00001	0.00000	0.00000	0.00000	0.00000
73	0.00005	0.00004	0.00003	0.00002	0.00001	0.00001	0.00001	0.00001	0.00000	0.00000	0.00000	0.00000
74	0.00004	0.00003	0.00002	0.00002	0.00001	0.00001	0.00001	0.00000	0.00000	0.00000	0.00000	0.00000
75	0.00004	0.00003	0.00002	0.00001	0.00001	0.00001	0.00001	0.00000	0.00000	0.00000	0.00000	0.00000
76	0.00003	0.00002	0.00002	0.00001	0.00001	0.00001	0.00000	0.00000	0.00000	0.00000	0.00000	0.00000
77	0.00003	0.00002	0.00002	0.00001	0.00001	0.00001	0.00000	0.00000	0.00000	0.00000	0.00000	0.00000
78	0.00003	0.00002	0.00001	0.00001	0.00001	0.00000	0.00000	0.00000	0.00000	0.00000	0.00000	0.00000
79	0.00002	0.00002	0.00001	0.00001	0.00001	0.00000	0.00000	0.00000	0.00000	0.00000	0.00000	0.00000
80	0.00002	0.00001	0.00001	0.00001	0.00000	0.00000	0.00000	0.00000	0.00000	0.00000	0.00000	0.00000
81	0.00002	0.00001	0.00001	0.00001	0.00000	0.00000	0.00000	0.00000	0.00000	0.00000	0.00000	0.00000
82	0.00002	0.00001	0.00001	0.00001	0.00000	0.00000	0.00000	0.00000	0.00000	0.00000	0.00000	0.00000
83	0.00001	0.00001	0.00001	0.00000	0.00000	0.00000	0.00000	0.00000	0.00000	0.00000	0.00000	0.00000
84	0.00001	0.00001	0.00001	0.00000	0.00000	0.00000	0.00000	0.00000	0.00000	0.00000	0.00000	0.00000
85	0.00001	0.00001	0.00000	0.00000	0.00000	0.00000	0.00000	0.00000	0.00000	0.00000	0.00000	0.00000
86	0.00001	0.00001	0.00000	0.00000	0.00000	0.00000	0.00000	0.00000	0.00000	0.00000	0.00000	0.00000
87	0.00001	0.00001	0.00000	0.00000	0.00000	0.00000	0.00000	0.00000	0.00000	0.00000	0.00000	0.00000
88	0.00001	0.00000	0.00000	0.00000	0.00000	0.00000	0.00000	0.00000	0.00000	0.00000	0.00000	0.00000
89	0.00001	0.00000	0.00000	0.00000	0.00000	0.00000	0.00000	0.00000	0.00000	0.00000	0.00000	0.00000
90	0.00001	0.00000	0.00000	0.00000	0.00000	0.00000	0.00000	0.00000	0.00000	0.00000	0.00000	0.00000
91	0.00000	0.00000	0.00000	0.00000	0.00000	0.00000	0.00000	0.00000	0.00000	0.00000	0.00000	0.00000
92	0.00000	0.00000	0.00000	0.00000	0.00000	0.00000	0.00000	0.00000	0.00000	0.00000	0.00000	0.00000
93	0.00000	0.00000	0.00000	0.00000	0.00000	0.00000	0.00000	0.00000	0.00000	0.00000	0.00000	0.00000
94	0.00000	0.00000	0.00000	0.00000	0.00000	0.00000	0.00000	0.00000	0.00000	0.00000	0.00000	0.00000
95	0.00000	0.00000	0.00000	0.00000	0.00000	0.00000	0.00000	0.00000	0.00000	0.00000	0.00000	0.00000
96	0.00000	0.00000	0.00000	0.00000	0.00000	0.00000	0.00000	0.00000	0.00000	0.00000	0.00000	0.00000
97	0.00000	0.00000	0.00000	0.00000	0.00000	0.00000	0.00000	0.00000	0.00000	0.00000	0.00000	0.00000
98	0.00000	0.00000	0.00000	0.00000	0.00000	0.00000	0.00000	0.00000	0.00000	0.00000	0.00000	0.00000
99	0.00000	0.00000	0.00000	0.00000	0.00000	0.00000	0.00000	0.00000	0.00000	0.00000	0.00000	0.00000
100	0.00000	0.00000	0.00000	0.00000	0.00000	0.00000	0.00000	0.00000	0.00000	0.00000	0.00000	0.00000
101	0.00000	0.00000	0.00000	0.00000	0.00000	0.00000	0.00000	0.00000	0.00000	0.00000	0.00000	0.00000
102	0.00000	0.00000	0.00000	0.00000	0.00000	0.00000	0.00000	0.00000	0.00000	0.00000	0.00000	0.00000
103	0.00000	0.00000	0.00000	0.00000	0.00000	0.00000	0.00000	0.00000	0.00000	0.00000	0.00000	0.00000
104	0.00000	0.00000	0.00000	0.00000	0.00000	0.00000	0.00000	0.00000	0.00000	0.00000	0.00000	0.00000
105	0.00000	0.00000	0.00000	0.00000	0.00000	0.00000	0.00000	0.00000	0.00000	0.00000	0.00000	0.00000
106	0.00000	0.00000	0.00000	0.00000	0.00000	0.00000	0.00000	0.00000	0.00000	0.00000	0.00000	0.00000
107	0.00000	0.00000	0.00000	0.00000	0.00000	0.00000	0.00000	0.00000	0.00000	0.00000	0.00000	0.00000
108	0.00000	0.00000	0.00000	0.00000	0.00000	0.00000	0.00000	0.00000	0.00000	0.00000	0.00000	0.00000
109	0.00000	0.00000	0.00000	0.00000	0.00000	0.00000	0.00000	0.00000	0.00000	0.00000	0.00000	0.00000
110	0.00000	0.00000	0.00000	0.00000	0.00000	0.00000	0.00000	0.00000	0.00000	0.00000	0.00000	0.00000
111	0.00000	0.00000	0.00000	0.00000	0.00000	0.00000	0.00000	0.00000	0.00000	0.00000	0.00000	0.00000
112	0.00000	0.00000	0.00000	0.00000	0.00000	0.00000	0.00000	0.00000	0.00000	0.00000	0.00000	0.00000
113	0.00000	0.00000	0.00000	0.00000	0.00000	0.00000	0.00000	0.00000	0.00000	0.00000	0.00000	0.00000
114	0.00000	0.00000	0.00000	0.00000	0.00000	0.00000	0.00000	0.00000	0.00000	0.00000	0.00000	0.00000
115	0.00000	0.00000	0.00000	0.00000	0.00000	0.00000	0.00000	0.00000	0.00000	0.00000	0.00000	0.00000
116	0.00000	0.00000	0.00000	0.00000	0.00000	0.00000	0.00000	0.00000	0.00000	0.00000	0.00000	0.00000
117	0.00000	0.00000	0.00000	0.00000	0.00000	0.00000	0.00000	0.00000	0.00000	0.00000	0.00000	0.00000
118	0.00000	0.00000	0.00000	0.00000	0.00000	0.00000	0.00000	0.00000	0.00000	0.00000	0.00000	0.00000
119	0.00000	0.00000	0.00000	0.00000	0.00000	0.00000	0.00000	0.00000	0.00000	0.00000	0.00000	0.00000
120	0.00000	0.00000	0.00000	0.00000	0.00000	0.00000	0.00000	0.00000	0.00000	0.00000	0.00000	0.00000

Table III
PRESENT VALUE OF AN ORDINARY ANNUITY OF $1 PER PERIOD: 0.5%–7%

$$P_{A_{1,n}} = \frac{1 - \dfrac{1}{(1-i)^n}}{i}$$

Period	.5%	1%	1.5%	2%	2.5%	3%	3.5%	4%	4.5%	5%	5.5%	6%	6.5%	7%
1	0.99502	0.99010	0.98522	0.98039	0.97561	0.97087	0.96618	0.96154	0.95694	0.95238	0.94787	0.94340	0.93897	0.93458
2	1.98510	1.97040	1.95588	1.94156	1.92742	1.91347	1.89969	1.88609	1.87267	1.85941	1.84632	1.83339	1.82063	1.80802
3	2.97025	2.94099	2.91220	2.88388	2.85602	2.82861	2.80164	2.77509	2.74896	2.72325	2.69793	2.67301	2.64848	2.62432
4	3.95050	3.90197	3.85438	3.80773	3.76197	3.71710	3.67308	3.62990	3.58753	3.54595	3.50515	3.46511	3.42580	3.38721
5	4.92587	4.85343	4.78264	4.71346	4.64583	4.57971	4.51505	4.45182	4.38998	4.32948	4.27028	4.21236	4.15568	4.10020
6	5.89638	5.79548	5.69719	5.60143	5.50813	5.41719	5.32855	5.24214	5.15787	5.07569	4.99553	4.91732	4.84101	4.76654
7	6.86207	6.72819	6.59821	6.47199	6.34939	6.23028	6.11454	6.00205	5.89270	5.78637	5.68297	5.58238	5.48452	5.38929
8	7.82296	7.65168	7.48593	7.32548	7.17014	7.01969	6.87396	6.73274	6.59589	6.46321	6.33457	6.20979	6.08875	5.97130
9	8.77906	8.56602	8.36052	8.16224	7.97087	7.78611	7.60769	7.43533	7.26879	7.10782	6.95220	6.80169	6.65610	6.51523
10	9.73041	9.47130	9.22218	8.98259	8.75206	8.53020	8.31661	8.11090	7.91272	7.72173	7.53763	7.36009	7.18883	7.02358
11	10.67703	10.36763	10.07112	9.78685	9.51421	9.25262	9.00155	8.76048	8.52892	8.30641	8.09254	7.88687	7.68904	7.49867
12	11.61893	11.25508	10.90751	10.57534	10.25776	9.95400	9.66333	9.38507	9.11858	8.86325	8.61852	8.38384	8.15873	7.94269
13	12.55615	12.13374	11.73153	11.34837	10.98318	10.63496	10.30274	9.98565	9.68285	9.39357	9.11708	8.85268	8.59974	8.35765
14	13.48871	13.00370	12.54338	12.10625	11.69091	11.29607	10.92052	10.56312	10.22283	9.89864	9.58965	9.29498	9.01384	8.74547
15	14.41662	13.86505	13.34323	12.84926	12.38138	11.93794	11.51741	11.11839	10.73955	10.37966	10.03758	9.71225	9.40267	9.10791
16	15.33993	14.71787	14.13126	13.57771	13.05500	12.56110	12.09412	11.65230	11.23402	10.83777	10.46216	10.10590	9.76776	9.44665
17	16.25863	15.56225	14.90765	14.29187	13.71220	13.16612	12.65132	12.16567	11.70719	11.27407	10.86461	10.47726	10.11058	9.76322
18	17.17277	16.39827	15.67256	14.99203	14.35336	13.75351	13.18968	12.65930	12.15999	11.68959	11.24607	10.82760	10.43247	10.05900
19	18.08236	17.22601	16.42617	15.67846	14.97889	14.32380	13.70984	13.13394	12.59329	12.08532	11.60765	11.15812	10.73471	10.33560
20	18.98742	18.04555	17.16864	16.35143	15.58916	14.87747	14.21240	13.59033	13.00794	12.46221	11.95038	11.46992	11.01851	10.59401
21	19.88798	18.85698	17.90014	17.01121	16.18455	15.41502	14.69797	14.02916	13.40472	12.82115	12.27524	11.76408	11.28498	10.83553
22	20.78406	19.66038	18.62082	17.65805	16.76541	15.93692	15.16712	14.45112	13.78442	13.16300	12.58317	12.04158	11.53520	11.06124
23	21.67568	20.45582	19.33086	18.29220	17.33211	16.44361	15.62041	14.85684	14.14777	13.48857	12.87504	12.30338	11.77014	11.27219
24	22.56287	21.24339	20.03041	18.91393	17.88499	16.93554	16.05837	15.24696	14.49548	13.79864	13.15170	12.55036	11.99074	11.46933
25	23.445C4	22.02316	20.71961	19.52346	18.42438	17.41315	16.48151	15.62208	14.82821	14.09394	13.41393	12.78336	12.19788	11.65358
26	24.32402	22.79520	21.39863	20.12104	18.95061	17.87684	16.89035	15.98277	15.14661	14.37519	13.66250	13.00317	12.39237	11.82578
27	25.19803	23.55961	22.06762	20.70690	19.46401	18.32703	17.28536	16.32959	15.45130	14.64303	13.89810	13.21053	12.57500	11.98671
28	26.06769	24.31644	22.72672	21.28127	19.96489	18.76411	17.66702	16.66306	15.74287	14.89813	14.12142	13.40616	12.74648	12.13711
29	26.93302	25.06579	23.37608	21.84438	20.45355	19.18845	18.03577	16.98371	16.02189	15.14107	14.33310	13.59072	12.90749	12.27767
30	27.79405	25.80771	24.01584	22.39646	20.93029	19.60044	18.39205	17.29203	16.28889	15.37245	14.53375	13.76483	13.05868	12.40904
31	28.65080	26.54229	24.64615	22.93770	21.39541	20.00043	18.73628	17.58849	16.54439	15.59281	14.72393	13.92909	13.20063	12.53181
32	29.50328	27.26959	25.26714	23.46833	21.84918	20.38877	19.06887	17.87355	16.78889	15.80268	14.90420	14.08404	13.33393	12.64656
33	30.35153	27.98969	25.87895	23.98856	22.29188	20.76579	19.39021	18.14765	17.02286	16.00255	15.07507	14.23023	13.45909	12.75379
34	31.19555	28.70267	26.48173	24.49859	22.72379	21.13184	19.70068	18.41120	17.24676	16.19290	15.23703	14.36814	13.57661	12.85401
35	32.03537	29.40858	27.07559	24.99862	23.14516	21.48722	20.00066	18.66461	17.46101	16.37419	15.39055	14.49825	13.68696	12.94767
36	32.87102	30.10751	27.66068	25.48884	23.55625	21.83225	20.29049	18.90828	17.66604	16.54685	15.53607	14.62099	13.79057	13.03521
37	33.70250	30.79951	28.23713	25.96945	23.95732	22.16724	20.57053	19.14258	17.86224	16.71129	15.67400	14.73678	13.88786	13.11702
38	34.52985	31.48466	28.80505	26.44064	24.34860	22.49246	20.84109	19.36786	18.04999	16.86789	15.80474	14.84602	13.97921	13.19347
39	35.35309	32.16303	29.36458	26.90259	24.73034	22.80822	21.10250	19.58448	18.22966	17.01704	15.92866	14.94907	14.06499	13.26493
40	36.17223	32.83469	29.91585	27.35548	25.10278	23.11477	21.35507	19.79277	18.40158	17.15909	16.04612	15.04630	14.14553	13.33171
41	36.98729	33.49969	30.45896	27.79949	25.46612	23.41240	21.59910	19.99305	18.56611	17.29437	16.15746	15.13802	14.22115	13.39412
42	37.79830	34.15811	30.99405	28.23479	25.82061	23.70136	21.83488	20.18563	18.72355	17.42321	16.26300	15.22454	14.29216	13.45245
43	38.60527	34.81001	31.52123	28.66156	26.16645	23.98190	22.06269	20.37079	18.87421	17.54591	16.36303	15.30617	14.35884	13.50696
44	39.40823	35.45545	32.04062	29.07996	26.50385	24.25427	22.28279	20.54884	19.01838	17.66277	16.45785	15.38318	14.42144	13.55791
45	40.20720	36.09451	32.55234	29.49016	26.83302	24.51871	22.49545	20.72004	19.15635	17.77407	16.54773	15.45583	14.48023	13.60552
46	41.00219	36.72724	33.05649	29.89231	27.15447	24.77545	22.70092	20.88465	19.28837	17.88007	16.63292	15.52437	14.53543	13.65002
47	41.79322	37.35370	33.55319	30.28658	27.46748	25.02471	22.89944	21.04294	19.41471	17.98102	16.71366	15.58903	14.58725	13.69161
48	42.58032	37.97396	34.04255	30.67312	27.77315	25.26671	23.09124	21.19513	19.53561	18.07716	16.79020	15.65003	14.63592	13.73047
49	43.36350	38.58808	34.52468	31.05208	28.07137	25.50166	23.27641	21.34147	19.65130	18.16872	16.86275	15.70757	14.68161	13.76680
50	44.14279	39.19612	34.99969	31.42361	28.36231	25.72976	23.45562	21.48218	19.76201	18.25593	16.93152	15.76186	14.72452	13.80075
51	44.91820	39.79814	35.46767	31.78785	28.64616	25.95123	23.62862	21.61749	19.86795	18.33898	16.99670	15.81308	14.76481	13.83247
52	45.68975	40.39419	35.92874	32.14495	28.92308	26.16624	23.79576	21.74758	19.96933	18.41807	17.05848	15.86139	14.80264	13.86212
53	46.45746	40.98435	36.38300	32.49505	29.19325	26.37499	23.95726	21.87267	20.06634	18.49340	17.11705	15.90697	14.83816	13.88984
54	47.22135	41.56866	36.83054	32.83828	29.45683	26.57766	24.11330	21.99296	20.15918	18.56515	17.17255	15.94998	14.87151	13.91573
55	47.98145	42.14719	37.27147	33.17479	29.71398	26.77443	24.26405	22.10861	20.24802	18.63347	17.22517	15.99054	14.90282	13.93994
56	48.73776	42.71999	37.70588	33.50469	29.96486	26.96546	24.40971	22.21982	20.33303	18.69854	17.27504	16.02881	14.93223	13.96256
57	49.49031	43.28712	38.13387	33.82813	30.20962	27.15094	24.55045	22.32675	20.41439	18.76052	17.32232	16.06492	14.95984	13.98370
58	50.23911	43.84863	38.55554	34.14523	30.44841	27.33101	24.68642	22.42957	20.49224	18.81954	17.36712	16.09898	14.98577	14.00346
59	50.98419	44.40459	38.97097	34.45610	30.68137	27.50583	24.81780	22.52843	20.56673	18.87575	17.40960	16.13111	15.01011	14.02192
60	51.72556	44.95504	39.38027	34.76089	30.90866	27.67556	24.94473	22.62349	20.63802	18.92929	17.44985	16.16143	15.03297	14.03918

Period	.5%	1%	1.5%	2%	2.5%	3%	3.5%	4%	4.5%	5%	5.5%	6%	6.5%	7%
61 ...	52.46324	45.50004	39.78352	35.05969	31.13040	27.84035	25.06738	22.71489	20.70624	18.98028	17.48801	16.19003	15.05443	14.05531
62 ...	53.19726	46.03964	40.18080	35.35264	31.34673	28.00034	25.18587	22.80278	20.77152	19.02883	17.52418	16.21701	15.07458	14.07038
63 ...	53.92762	46.57390	40.57222	35.63984	31.55778	28.15567	25.30036	22.88729	20.83399	19.07508	17.55847	16.24246	15.09350	14.08447
64 ...	54.65435	47.10287	40.95785	35.92141	31.76369	28.30648	25.41097	22.96855	20.89377	19.11912	17.59096	16.26647	15.11127	14.09764
65 ...	55.37746	47.62661	41.33779	36.19747	31.96458	28.45289	25.51785	23.04668	20.95098	19.16107	17.62177	16.28912	15.12795	14.10994
66 ...	56.09698	48.14516	41.71210	36.46810	32.16056	28.59504	25.62111	23.12181	21.00572	19.20102	17.65096	16.31049	15.14362	14.12144
67 ...	56.81291	48.65857	42.08089	36.73343	32.35177	28.73305	25.72088	23.19405	21.05811	19.23907	17.67864	16.33065	15.15833	14.13219
68 ...	57.52529	49.16690	42.44423	36.99356	32.53831	28.86704	25.81727	23.26351	21.10824	19.27530	17.70487	16.34967	15.17214	14.14223
69 ...	58.23411	49.67020	42.80219	37.24859	32.72030	28.99712	25.91041	23.33030	21.15621	19.30981	17.72974	16.36762	15.18511	14.15162
70 ...	58.93942	50.16851	43.15487	37.49862	32.89786	29.12342	26.00040	23.39451	21.20211	19.34268	17.75330	16.38454	15.19728	14.16039
71 ...	59.64121	50.66190	43.50234	37.74374	33.07108	29.24604	26.08734	23.45626	21.24604	19.37398	17.77564	16.40051	15.20872	14.16859
72 ...	60.33951	51.15039	43.84467	37.98406	33.24008	29.36509	26.17134	23.51564	21.28808	19.40379	17.79682	16.41558	15.21945	14.17625
73 ...	61.03434	51.63405	44.18194	38.21967	33.40495	29.48067	26.25251	23.57273	21.32830	19.43218	17.81689	16.42979	15.22953	14.18341
74 ...	61.72571	52.11292	44.51422	38.45066	33.56581	29.59288	26.33092	23.62762	21.36680	19.45922	17.83591	16.44320	15.23900	14.19010
75 ...	62.41365	52.58705	44.84160	38.67711	33.72274	29.70183	26.40669	23.68041	21.40363	19.48497	17.85395	16.45585	15.24788	14.19636
76 ...	63.09815	53.05649	45.16414	38.89913	33.87584	29.80760	26.47989	23.73116	21.43888	19.50950	17.87104	16.46778	15.25623	14.20220
77 ...	63.77926	53.52127	45.48191	39.11680	34.02521	29.91029	26.55062	23.77996	21.47262	19.53285	17.88724	16.47904	15.26407	14.20767
78 ...	64.45697	53.98146	45.79498	39.33019	34.17094	30.00999	26.61896	23.82689	21.50490	19.55510	17.90260	16.48966	15.27142	14.21277
79 ...	65.13132	54.43709	46.10343	39.53940	34.31311	30.10679	26.68498	23.87201	21.53579	19.57628	17.91716	16.49968	15.27833	14.21755
80 ...	65.80231	54.88821	46.40732	39.74451	34.45182	30.20076	26.74878	23.91539	21.56534	19.59646	17.93095	16.50913	15.28482	14.22201
81 ...	66.46996	55.33486	46.70672	39.94560	34.58714	30.29200	26.81041	23.95711	21.59363	19.61568	17.94403	16.51805	15.29091	14.22617
82 ...	67.13428	55.77709	47.00170	40.14275	34.71916	30.38059	26.86996	23.99722	21.62070	19.63398	17.95643	16.52646	15.29663	14.23007
83 ...	67.79531	56.21494	47.29231	40.33603	34.84796	30.46659	26.92750	24.03579	21.64660	19.65141	17.96818	16.53440	15.30200	14.23371
84 ...	68.45304	56.64845	47.57863	40.52552	34.97362	30.55009	26.98309	24.07287	21.67139	19.66801	17.97932	16.54188	15.30704	14.23711
85 ...	69.10750	57.07768	47.86072	40.71129	35.09621	30.63115	27.03680	24.10853	21.69511	19.68382	17.98987	16.54895	15.31178	14.24029
86 ...	69.75871	57.50265	48.13864	40.89342	35.21582	30.70986	27.08870	24.14282	21.71781	19.69887	17.99988	16.55561	15.31622	14.24326
87 ...	70.40668	57.92342	48.41246	41.07198	35.33251	30.78627	27.13884	24.17579	21.73953	19.71321	18.00936	16.56190	15.32040	14.24604
88 ...	71.05142	58.34002	48.68222	41.24704	35.44635	30.86045	27.18728	24.20749	21.76032	19.72687	18.01835	16.56783	15.32431	14.24864
89 ...	71.69296	58.75249	48.94800	41.41867	35.55741	30.93248	27.23409	24.23797	21.78021	19.73987	18.02688	16.57342	15.32800	14.25106
90 ...	72.33130	59.16088	49.20985	41.58693	35.66577	31.00241	27.27932	24.26728	21.79924	19.75226	18.03495	16.57870	15.33145	14.25333
91 ...	72.96647	59.56523	49.46784	41.75189	35.77148	31.07030	27.32301	24.29546	21.81746	19.76406	18.04261	16.58368	15.33470	14.25545
92 ...	73.59847	59.96557	49.72201	41.91362	35.87462	31.13621	27.36523	24.32256	21.83489	19.77529	18.04987	16.58838	15.33774	14.25743
93 ...	74.22734	60.36195	49.97242	42.07218	35.97524	31.20021	27.40602	24.34861	21.85156	19.78599	18.05675	16.59281	15.34060	14.25928
94 ...	74.85307	60.75441	50.21913	42.22762	36.07340	31.26234	27.44543	24.37367	21.86753	19.79619	18.06327	16.59699	15.34329	14.26101
95 ...	75.47569	61.14298	50.46220	42.38002	36.16917	31.32266	27.48350	24.39776	21.88280	19.80589	18.06945	16.60093	15.34581	14.26262
96 ...	76.09522	61.52770	50.70168	42.52943	36.26261	31.38122	27.52029	24.42092	21.89742	19.81513	18.07531	16.60465	15.34818	14.26413
97 ...	76.71166	61.90862	50.93761	42.67592	36.35376	31.43808	27.55584	24.44319	21.91140	19.82394	18.08086	16.60816	15.35040	14.26555
98 ...	77.32503	62.28576	51.17006	42.81953	36.44269	31.49328	27.59018	24.46461	21.92479	19.83232	18.08612	16.61147	15.35249	14.26687
99 ...	77.93536	62.65917	51.39907	42.96032	36.52946	31.54687	27.62337	24.48520	21.93760	19.84031	18.09111	16.61460	15.35445	14.26810
100 ...	78.54264	63.02888	51.62470	43.09835	36.61411	31.59891	27.65543	24.50500	21.94985	19.84791	18.09584	16.61755	15.35629	14.26925
101 ...	79.14691	63.39493	51.84700	43.23368	36.69669	31.64942	27.68640	24.52404	21.96158	19.85515	18.10032	16.62033	15.35802	14.27033
102 ...	79.74817	63.75736	52.06601	43.36635	36.77726	31.69847	27.71633	24.54234	21.97281	19.86205	18.10457	16.62295	15.35964	14.27133
103 ...	80.34644	64.11619	52.28178	43.49642	36.85586	31.74609	27.74525	24.55995	21.98355	19.86862	18.10860	16.62542	15.36117	14.27228
104 ...	80.94173	64.47148	52.49437	43.62394	36.93255	31.79232	27.77318	24.57687	21.99382	19.87488	18.11241	16.62776	15.36260	14.27315
105 ...	81.53406	64.82325	52.70381	43.74896	37.00736	31.83720	27.80018	24.59315	22.00366	19.88083	18.11603	16.62996	15.36394	14.27398
106 ...	82.12344	65.17153	52.91016	43.87153	37.08035	31.88078	27.82626	24.60879	22.01307	19.88651	18.11946	16.63204	15.36521	14.27474
107 ...	82.70989	65.51637	53.11346	43.99170	37.15156	31.92308	27.85146	24.62384	22.02208	19.89191	18.12271	16.63400	15.36639	14.27546
108 ...	83.29342	65.85779	53.31375	44.10951	37.22104	31.96416	27.87581	24.63831	22.03070	19.89706	18.12579	16.63585	15.36750	14.27613
109 ...	83.87405	66.19583	53.51108	44.22501	37.28882	32.00404	27.89933	24.65222	22.03894	19.90196	18.12872	16.63759	15.36855	14.27676
110 ...	84.45180	66.53053	53.70550	44.33824	37.35494	32.04276	27.92206	24.66560	22.04684	19.90663	18.13148	16.63924	15.36953	14.27735
111 ...	85.02666	66.86191	53.89704	44.44926	37.41946	32.08035	27.94402	24.67846	22.05439	19.91108	18.13411	16.64079	15.37045	14.27789
112 ...	85.59867	67.19001	54.08576	44.55810	37.48240	32.11684	27.96523	24.69082	22.06162	19.91531	18.13659	16.64226	15.37131	14.27840
113 ...	86.16783	67.51486	54.27168	44.66480	37.54380	32.15227	27.98573	24.70272	22.06853	19.91934	18.13895	16.64364	15.37212	14.27888
114 ...	86.73416	67.83649	54.45486	44.76941	37.60371	32.18667	28.00554	24.71415	22.07515	19.92318	18.14119	16.64494	15.37289	14.27933
115 ...	87.29767	68.15494	54.63533	44.87197	37.66216	32.22007	28.02467	24.72514	22.08148	19.92684	18.14331	16.64617	15.37360	14.27975
116 ...	87.85838	68.47024	54.81313	44.97252	37.71918	32.25250	28.04316	24.73571	22.08754	19.93033	18.14531	16.64733	15.37428	14.28014
117 ...	88.41630	68.78242	54.98831	45.07110	37.77481	32.28398	28.06103	24.74588	22.09334	19.93364	18.14722	16.64843	15.37491	14.28050
118 ...	88.97144	69.09150	55.16089	45.16775	37.82908	32.31454	28.07829	24.75565	22.09889	19.93680	18.14902	16.64946	15.37550	14.28084
119 ...	89.52382	69.39753	55.33093	45.26250	37.88203	32.34421	28.09496	24.76505	22.10420	19.93981	18.15073	16.65043	15.37606	14.28116
120 ...	90.07345	69.70052	55.49845	45.35539	37.93369	32.37302	28.11108	24.77409	22.10929	19.94268	18.15235	16.65135	15.37658	14.28146

Table III *(continued)*
PRESENT VALUE OF AN ORDINARY ANNUITY OF $1 PER PERIOD: 7.5%–14%

Period	7.5%	8%	8.5%	9%	9.5%	10%	10.5%	11%	11.5%	12%	12.5%	13%	13.5%	14%
1	0.93023	0.92593	0.92166	0.91743	0.91324	0.90909	0.90498	0.90090	0.89686	0.89286	0.88889	0.88496	0.88106	0.87719
2	1.79557	1.78326	1.77111	1.75911	1.74725	1.73554	1.72396	1.71252	1.70122	1.69005	1.67901	1.66810	1.65732	1.64666
3	2.60053	2.57710	2.55402	2.53129	2.50891	2.48685	2.46512	2.44371	2.42262	2.40183	2.38134	2.36115	2.34125	2.32163
4	3.34933	3.31213	3.27560	3.23972	3.20448	3.16987	3.13586	3.10245	3.06961	3.03735	3.00564	2.97447	2.94383	2.91371
5	4.04588	3.99271	3.94064	3.88965	3.83971	3.79079	3.74286	3.69590	3.64988	3.60478	3.56057	3.51723	3.47474	3.43308
6	4.69385	4.62288	4.55359	4.48592	4.41983	4.35526	4.29218	4.23054	4.17029	4.11141	4.05384	3.99755	3.94250	3.88867
7	5.29660	5.20637	5.11851	5.03295	4.94961	4.86842	4.78930	4.71220	4.63704	4.56376	4.49230	4.42261	4.35463	4.28830
8	5.85730	5.74664	5.63918	5.53482	5.43344	5.33493	5.23919	5.14612	5.05564	4.96764	4.88205	4.79877	4.71774	4.63886
9	6.37889	6.24689	6.11906	5.99525	5.87528	5.75902	5.64632	5.53705	5.43106	5.32825	5.22848	5.13166	5.03765	4.94637
10	6.86408	6.71008	6.56135	6.41766	6.27880	6.14457	6.01477	5.88923	5.76777	5.65022	5.53643	5.42624	5.31952	5.21612
11	7.31542	7.13896	6.96898	6.80519	6.64730	6.49506	6.34821	6.20652	6.06975	5.93770	5.81016	5.68694	5.56786	5.45273
12	7.73528	7.53608	7.34469	7.16073	6.98384	6.81369	6.64996	6.49236	6.340: 1	6.19437	6.05348	5.91765	5.78666	5.66029
13	8.12584	7.90378	7.69095	7.48690	7.29118	7.10336	6.92304	6.74987	6.58348	6.42355	6.26976	6.12181	5.97943	5.84236
14	8.48915	8.24424	8.01010	7.78615	7.57185	7.36669	7.17018	6.98187	6.80133	6.62817	6.46201	6.30249	6.14928	6.00207
15	8.82712	8.55948	8.30424	8.06069	7.82818	7.60608	7.39382	7.19087	6.99671	6.81086	6.63289	6.46238	6.29893	6.14217
16	9.14151	8.85137	8.57533	8.31256	8.06226	7.82371	7.59622	7.37916	7.17194	6.97399	6.78479	6.60388	6.43077	6.26506
17	9.43396	9.12164	8.82519	8.54363	8.27604	8.02155	7.77939	7.54879	7.32909	7.11963	6.91982	6.72909	6.54694	6.37286
18	9.70601	9.37189	9.05548	8.75563	8.47127	8.20141	7.94515	7.70162	7.47004	7.24967	7.03984	6.83991	6.64928	6.46742
19	9.95908	9.60360	9.26772	8.95011	8.64956	8.36492	8.09515	7.83929	7.59644	7.36578	7.14652	6.93797	6.73946	6.55037
20	10.19449	9.81815	9.46334	9.12855	8.81238	8.51356	8.23091	7.96333	7.70982	7.46944	7.24135	7.02475	6.81890	6.62313
21	10.41348	10.01680	9.64363	9.29224	8.96108	8.64869	8.35376	8.07507	7.81149	7.56200	7.32565	7.10155	6.88890	6.68696
22	10.61719	10.20074	9.80980	9.44243	9.09688	8.77154	8.46494	8.17574	7.90269	7.64465	7.40058	7.16951	6.95057	6.74294
23	10.80669	10.37106	9.96295	9.58021	9.22089	8.88322	8.56556	8.26643	7.98447	7.71843	7.46718	7.22966	7.00491	6.79206
24	10.98297	10.52876	10.10410	9.70661	9.33415	8.98474	8.65662	8.34814	8.05782	7.78432	7.52638	7.28288	7.05279	6.83514
25	11.14695	10.67478	10.23419	9.82258	9.43758	9.07704	8.73902	8.42174	8.12361	7.84314	7.57901	7.32998	7.09497	6.87293
26	11.29948	10.80998	10.35409	9.92897	9.53203	9.16095	8.81359	8.48806	8.18261	7.89566	7.62578	7.37167	7.13213	6.90608
27	11.44138	10.93516	10.46460	10.02658	9.61830	9.23722	8.88108	8.54780	8.23552	7.94255	7.66736	7.40856	7.16487	6.93515
28	11.57338	11.05108	10.56645	10.11613	9.69707	9.30657	8.94215	8.60162	8.28298	7.98442	7.70432	7.44120	7.19372	6.96066
29	11.69617	11.15841	10.66033	10.19828	9.76902	9.36961	8.99742	8.65011	8.32554	8.02181	7.73717	7.47009	7.21914	6.98304
30	11.81039	11.25778	10.74684	10.27365	9.83472	9.42691	9.04744	8.69379	8.36371	8.05518	7.76638	7.49565	7.24153	7.00266
31	11.91664	11.34980	10.82658	10.34280	9.89472	9.47901	9.09271	8.73315	8.39795	8.08499	7.79234	7.51828	7.26126	7.01988
32	12.01548	11.43500	10.90008	10.40624	9.94952	9.52638	9.13367	8.76860	8.42866	8.11159	7.81541	7.53830	7.27864	7.03498
33	12.10742	11.51389	10.96781	10.46444	9.99956	9.56943	9.17074	8.80054	8.45619	8.13535	7.83592	7.55602	7.29396	7.04823
34	12.19295	11.58693	11.03024	10.51784	10.04526	9.60857	9.20429	8.82932	8.48089	8.15656	7.85415	7.57170	7.30745	7.05985
35	12.27251	11.65457	11.08778	10.56682	10.08699	9.64416	9.23465	8.85524	8.50304	8.17550	7.87036	7.58557	7.31934	7.07005
36	12.34652	11.71719	11.14081	10.61176	10.12511	9.67651	9.26213	8.87859	8.52291	8.19241	7.88476	7.59785	7.32982	7.07899
37	12.41537	11.77518	11.18969	10.65299	10.15992	9.70592	9.28700	8.89963	8.54072	8.20751	7.89757	7.60872	7.33904	7.08683
38	12.47941	11.82887	11.23474	10.69082	10.19171	9.73265	9.30950	8.91859	8.55670	8.22099	7.90895	7.61833	7.34718	7.09371
39	12.53899	11.87858	11.27625	10.72552	10.22074	9.75696	9.32986	8.93567	8.57103	8.23303	7.91906	7.62684	7.35434	7.09975
40	12.59441	11.92461	11.31452	10.75736	10.24725	9.77905	9.34829	8.95105	8.58389	8.24378	7.92806	7.63438	7.36065	7.10504
41	12.64596	11.96723	11.34979	10.78657	10.27146	9.79914	9.36497	8.96491	8.59541	8.25337	7.93605	7.64104	7.36621	7.10969
42	12.69392	12.00670	11.38229	10.81337	10.29357	9.81740	9.38006	8.97740	8.60575	8.26194	7.94316	7.64694	7.37111	7.11376
43	12.73853	12.04324	11.41225	10.83795	10.31376	9.83400	9.39372	8.98865	8.61502	8.26959	7.94947	7.65216	7.37543	7.11733
44	12.78003	12.07707	11.43986	10.86051	10.33220	9.84909	9.40608	8.99878	8.62334	8.27642	7.95509	7.65678	7.37923	7.12047
45	12.81863	12.10840	11.46531	10.88120	10.34904	9.86281	9.41727	9.00791	8.63080	8.28252	7.96008	7.66086	7.38258	7.12322
46	12.85454	12.13741	11.48877	10.90018	10.36442	9.87528	9.42739	9.01614	8.63749	8.28796	7.96451	7.66448	7.38554	7.12563
47	12.88794	12.16427	11.51038	10.91760	10.37847	9.88662	9.43656	9.02355	8.64349	8.29282	7.96846	7.66768	7.38814	7.12774
48	12.91902	12.18914	11.53031	10.93358	10.39130	9.89693	9.44485	9.03022	8.64887	8.29716	7.97196	7.67052	7.39043	7.12960
49	12.94792	12.21216	11.54867	10.94823	10.40301	9.90630	9.45235	9.03624	8.65369	8.30104	7.97508	7.67302	7.39245	7.13123
50	12.97481	12.23348	11.56560	10.96168	10.41371	9.91481	9.45914	9.04165	8.65802	8.30450	7.97785	7.67524	7.39423	7.13266
51	12.99982	12.25323	11.58119	10.97402	10.42348	9.92256	9.46529	9.04653	8.66190	8.30759	7.98031	7.67720	7.39580	7.13391
52	13.02309	12.27151	11.59557	10.98534	10.43240	9.92960	9.47085	9.05093	8.66538	8.31035	7.98250	7.67894	7.39718	7.13501
53	13.04474	12.28843	11.60882	10.99573	10.44055	9.93600	9.47588	9.05489	8.66850	8.31281	7.98444	7.68048	7.39839	7.13597
54	13.06487	12.30410	11.62103	11.00525	10.44799	9.94182	9.48043	9.05846	8.67130	8.31501	7.98617	7.68184	7.39947	7.13682
55	13.08360	12.31861	11.63229	11.01399	10.45478	9.94711	9.48456	9.06168	8.67382	8.31697	7.98771	7.68304	7.40041	7.13756
56	13.10103	12.33205	11.64266	11.02201	10.46099	9.95191	9.48829	9.06457	8.67607	8.31872	7.98907	7.68411	7.40124	7.13821
57	13.11723	12.34449	11.65222	11.02937	10.46666	9.95629	9.49166	9.06718	8.67809	8.32029	7.99029	7.68505	7.40198	7.13878
58	13.13231	12.35601	11.66104	11.03612	10.47183	9.96026	9.49472	9.06954	8.67990	8.32169	7.99137	7.68589	7.40262	7.13928
59	13.14633	12.36668	11.66916	11.04231	10.47656	9.96387	9.49748	9.07165	8.68152	8.32294	7.99232	7.68663	7.40319	7.13972
60	13.15938	12.37655	11.67664	11.04799	10.48088	9.96716	9.49998	9.07356	8.68298	8.32405	7.99318	7.68728	7.40369	7.14011

Future and Present Value Table

Period	7.5%	8%	8.5%	9%	9.5%	10%	10.5%	11%	11.5%	12%	12.5%	13%	13.5%	14%
61	13.17152	12.38570	11.68354	11.05320	10.48482	9.97014	9.50225	9.07528	8.68429	8.32504	7.99394	7.68786	7.40413	7.14044
62	13.18281	12.39416	11.68990	11.05798	10.48842	9.97286	9.50430	9.07683	8.68546	8.32593	7.99461	7.68837	7.40452	7.14074
63	13.19331	12.40200	11.69576	11.06237	10.49171	9.97532	9.50615	9.07822	8.68651	8.32673	7.99521	7.68882	7.40487	7.14100
64	13.20308	12.40926	11.70116	11.06640	10.49471	9.97757	9.50783	9.07948	8.68745	8.32743	7.99574	7.68922	7.40517	7.14123
65	13.21217	12.41598	11.70614	11.07009	10.49745	9.97961	9.50935	9.08061	8.68830	8.32807	7.99621	7.68958	7.40544	7.14143
66	13.22062	12.42221	11.71073	11.07347	10.49996	9.98146	9.51072	9.08163	8.68906	8.32863	7.99663	7.68989	7.40567	7.14160
67	13.22848	12.42797	11.71496	11.07658	10.50224	9.98315	9.51196	9.08255	8.68974	8.32913	7.99701	7.69017	7.40588	7.14176
68	13.23580	12.43330	11.71885	11.07943	10.50433	9.98468	9.51309	9.08338	8.69035	8.32958	7.99734	7.69042	7.40606	7.14189
69	13.24260	12.43825	11.72245	11.08205	10.50624	9.98607	9.51411	9.08413	8.69090	8.32999	7.99764	7.69063	7.40622	7.14201
70	13.24893	12.44282	11.72576	11.08445	10.50798	9.98734	9.51503	9.08480	8.69139	8.33034	7.99790	7.69083	7.40636	7.14211
71	13.25482	12.44706	11.72881	11.08665	10.50957	9.98849	9.51586	9.08541	8.69183	8.33066	7.99813	7.69100	7.40648	7.14221
72	13.26030	12.45098	11.73162	11.08867	10.51102	9.98954	9.51662	9.08595	8.69222	8.33095	7.99834	7.69115	7.40659	7.14229
73	13.26539	12.45461	11.73421	11.09052	10.51235	9.99050	9.51730	9.08644	8.69257	8.33121	7.99852	7.69128	7.40669	7.14236
74	13.27013	12.45797	11.73660	11.09222	10.51356	9.99135	9.51792	9.08688	8.69289	8.33143	7.99869	7.69140	7.40678	7.14242
75	13.27454	12.46108	11.73880	11.09378	10.51467	9.99214	9.51848	9.08728	8.69318	8.33164	7.99883	7.69150	7.40685	7.14247
76	13.27864	12.46397	11.74083	11.09521	10.51568	9.99285	9.51899	9.08764	8.69343	8.33182	7.99896	7.69160	7.40692	7.14252
77	13.28246	12.46664	11.74270	11.09653	10.51660	9.99350	9.51945	9.08797	8.69366	8.33198	7.99908	7.69168	7.40698	7.14256
78	13.28601	12.46911	11.74443	11.09773	10.51744	9.99409	9.51986	9.08826	8.69387	8.33213	7.99918	7.69175	7.40703	7.14260
79	13.28931	12.47140	11.74601	11.09883	10.51821	9.99463	9.52024	9.08852	8.69405	8.33226	7.99927	7.69181	7.40707	7.14263
80	13.29238	12.47351	11.74748	11.09985	10.51892	9.99512	9.52057	9.08876	8.69422	8.33237	7.99935	7.69187	7.40711	7.14266
81	13.29524	12.47548	11.74883	11.10078	10.51956	9.99556	9.52088	9.08897	8.69436	8.33247	7.99942	7.69192	7.40715	7.14268
82	13.29790	12.47729	11.75007	11.10163	10.52015	9.99597	9.52116	9.08916	8.69450	8.33257	7.99949	7.69197	7.40718	7.14270
83	13.30037	12.47897	11.75122	11.10241	10.52068	9.99633	9.52141	9.08934	8.69462	8.33265	7.99955	7.69201	7.40721	7.14272
84	13.30267	12.48053	11.75228	11.10313	10.52117	9.99667	9.52164	9.08949	8.69472	8.33272	7.99960	7.69204	7.40723	7.14274
85	13.30481	12.48197	11.75325	11.10379	10.52162	9.99697	9.52185	9.08963	8.69482	8.33279	7.99964	7.69207	7.40725	7.14275
86	13.30680	12.48331	11.75415	11.10440	10.52202	9.99724	9.52203	9.08976	8.69490	8.33285	7.99968	7.69210	7.40727	7.14277
87	13.30865	12.48455	11.75497	11.10495	10.52240	9.99749	9.52220	9.08987	8.69498	8.33290	7.99972	7.69212	7.40729	7.14278
88	13.31037	12.48569	11.75574	11.10546	10.52274	9.99772	9.52235	9.08998	8.69505	8.33294	7.99975	7.69214	7.40730	7.14279
89	13.31197	12.48675	11.75644	11.10593	10.52305	9.99793	9.52249	9.09007	8.69511	8.33299	7.99978	7.69216	7.40731	7.14280
90	13.31346	12.48773	11.75709	11.10635	10.52333	9.99812	9.52262	9.09015	8.69517	8.33302	7.99980	7.69218	7.40732	7.14280
91	13.31485	12.48864	11.75768	11.10675	10.52359	9.99829	9.52273	9.09023	8.69522	8.33306	7.99982	7.69219	7.40733	7.14281
92	13.31614	12.48948	11.75823	11.10711	10.52383	9.99844	9.52283	9.09029	8.69526	8.33309	7.99984	7.69221	7.40734	7.14282
93	13.31734	12.49026	11.75874	11.10744	10.52404	9.99859	9.52293	9.09036	8.69530	8.33311	7.99986	7.69222	7.40735	7.14282
94	13.31846	12.49098	11.75921	11.10774	10.52424	9.99871	9.52301	9.09041	8.69534	8.33314	7.99988	7.69223	7.40736	7.14283
95	13.31949	12.49165	11.75964	11.10802	10.52442	9.99883	9.52309	9.09046	8.69537	8.33316	7.99989	7.69224	7.40736	7.14283
96	13.32046	12.49227	11.76004	11.10827	10.52458	9.99894	9.52315	9.09050	8.69540	8.33318	7.99990	7.69225	7.40737	7.14283
97	13.32136	12.49284	11.76040	11.10851	10.52473	9.99903	9.52322	9.09054	8.69543	8.33319	7.99991	7.69225	7.40737	7.14284
98	13.32219	12.49337	11.76074	11.10872	10.52487	9.99912	9.52327	9.09058	8.69545	8.33321	7.99992	7.69226	7.40738	7.14284
99	13.32297	12.49386	11.76105	11.10892	10.52500	9.99920	9.52332	9.09061	8.69547	8.33322	7.99993	7.69226	7.40738	7.14284
100	13.32369	12.49432	11.76134	11.10910	10.52511	9.99927	9.52337	9.09064	8.69549	8.33323	7.99994	7.69227	7.40738	7.14284
101	13.32437	12.49474	11.76160	11.10927	10.52522	9.99934	9.52341	9.09067	8.69551	8.33324	7.99995	7.69227	7.40739	7.14284
102	13.32499	12.49513	11.76184	11.10942	10.52531	9.99940	9.52345	9.09069	8.69552	8.33325	7.99995	7.69228	7.40739	7.14285
103	13.32557	12.49549	11.76207	11.10956	10.52540	9.99945	9.52348	9.09071	8.69553	8.33326	7.99996	7.69228	7.40739	7.14285
104	13.32611	12.49582	11.76227	11.10969	10.52548	9.99950	9.52351	9.09073	8.69555	8.33327	7.99996	7.69228	7.40739	7.14285
105	13.32662	12.49613	11.76246	11.10981	10.52555	9.99955	9.52354	9.09075	8.69556	8.33328	7.99997	7.69229	7.40739	7.14285
106	13.32709	12.49642	11.76264	11.10991	10.52562	9.99959	9.52357	9.09077	8.69557	8.33328	7.99997	7.69229	7.40740	7.14285
107	13.32752	12.49668	11.76280	11.11001	10.52568	9.99963	9.52359	9.09078	8.69558	8.33329	7.99997	7.69229	7.40740	7.14285
108	13.32793	12.49693	11.76295	11.11010	10.52573	9.99966	9.52361	9.09079	8.69558	8.33329	7.99998	7.69229	7.40740	7.14285
109	13.32831	12.49716	11.76309	11.11019	10.52578	9.99969	9.52363	9.09080	8.69559	8.33330	7.99998	7.69230	7.40740	7.14285
110	13.32866	12.49737	11.76322	11.11026	10.52583	9.99972	9.52365	9.09082	8.69560	8.33330	7.99998	7.69230	7.40740	7.14285
111	13.32898	12.49756	11.76333	11.11033	10.52587	9.99975	9.52366	9.09082	8.69560	8.33330	7.99998	7.69230	7.40740	7.14285
112	13.32929	12.49774	11.76344	11.11040	10.52591	9.99977	9.52368	9.09083	8.69561	8.33331	7.99999	7.69230	7.40740	7.14285
113	13.32957	12.49791	11.76354	11.11046	10.52595	9.99979	9.52369	9.09084	8.69561	8.33331	7.99999	7.69230	7.40740	7.14285
114	13.32983	12.49807	11.76363	11.11051	10.52598	9.99981	9.52370	9.09085	8.69562	8.33331	7.99999	7.69230	7.40740	7.14286
115	13.33008	12.49821	11.76371	11.11056	10.52601	9.99983	9.52371	9.09085	8.69562	8.33332	7.99999	7.69230	7.40740	7.14286
116	13.33030	12.49834	11.76379	11.11060	10.52603	9.99984	9.52372	9.09086	8.69563	8.33332	7.99999	7.69230	7.40740	7.14286
117	13.33051	12.49846	11.76386	11.11065	10.52606	9.99986	9.52373	9.09086	8.69563	8.33332	7.99999	7.69230	7.40740	7.14286
118	13.33071	12.49858	11.76393	11.11069	10.52608	9.99987	9.52374	9.09087	8.69563	8.33332	7.99999	7.69230	7.40741	7.14286
119	13.33089	12.49868	11.76399	11.11072	10.52610	9.99988	9.52374	9.09087	8.69563	8.33332	7.99999	7.69230	7.40741	7.14286
120	13.33106	12.49878	11.76405	11.11075	10.52612	9.99989	9.52375	9.09088	8.69563	8.33332	7.99999	7.69230	7.40741	7.14286

Table III *(concluded)*
PRESENT VALUE OF AN ORDINARY ANNUITY OF $1 PER PERIOD: 14.5%–20%

Period	14.5%	15%	15.5%	16%	16.5%	17%	17.5%	18%	18.5%	19%	19.5%	20%
1	0.87336	0.86957	0.86580	0.86207	0.85837	0.85470	0.85106	0.84746	0.84388	0.84034	0.83682	0.83333
2	1.63612	1.62571	1.61541	1.60523	1.59517	1.58521	1.57537	1.56564	1.55602	1.54650	1.53709	1.52778
3	2.30229	2.28323	2.26443	2.24589	2.22761	2.20958	2.19181	2.17427	2.15698	2.13992	2.12309	2.10648
4	2.88410	2.85498	2.82634	2.79818	2.77048	2.74324	2.71643	2.69006	2.66412	2.63859	2.61346	2.58873
5	3.39223	3.35216	3.31285	3.27429	3.23646	3.19935	3.16292	3.12717	3.09208	3.05763	3.02382	2.99061
6	3.83600	3.78448	3.73407	3.68474	3.63645	3.58918	3.54291	3.49760	3.45323	3.40978	3.36721	3.32551
7	4.22358	4.16042	4.09876	4.03857	3.97979	3.92238	3.86631	3.81153	3.75800	3.70570	3.65457	3.60459
8	4.56208	4.48732	4.41451	4.34359	4.27449	4.20716	4.14154	4.07757	4.01519	3.95437	3.89504	3.83716
9	4.85771	4.77158	4.68789	4.60654	4.52746	4.45057	4.37578	3.30302	4.23223	4.16333	4.09627	4.03097
10	5.11591	5.01877	4.92458	4.83323	4.74460	4.65860	4.57513	4.49409	4.41538	4.33893	4.26466	4.19247
11	5.34140	5.23371	5.12951	5.02864	4.93099	4.83641	4.74479	4.65601	4.56994	4.48650	4.40557	4.32706
12	5.53834	5.42062	5.30693	5.19711	5.09098	4.98839	4.88918	4.79322	4.70037	4.61050	4.52349	4.43922
13	5.71034	5.58315	5.46055	5.34233	5.22831	5.11828	5.01207	4.90951	4.81044	4.71471	4.62217	4.53268
14	5.86056	5.72448	5.59355	5.46753	5.34619	5.22930	5.11666	5.00806	4.90333	4.80228	4.70474	4.61057
15	5.99176	5.84737	5.70870	5.57546	5.44747	5.32419	5.20567	5.09158	4.98171	4.87586	4.77384	4.67547
16	6.10634	5.95423	5.80840	5.66850	5.53422	5.40529	5.28142	5.16235	5.04786	4.93770	4.83167	4.72956
17	6.20641	6.04716	5.89472	5.74870	5.60878	5.47461	5.34589	5.22233	5.10368	4.98966	4.88006	4.77463
18	6.29381	6.12797	5.96945	5.81785	5.67277	5.53385	5.40075	5.27316	5.15078	5.03333	4.92055	4.81219
19	6.37014	6.19823	6.03416	5.87746	5.72770	5.58449	5.44745	5.31624	5.19053	5.07003	4.95443	4.84350
20	6.43680	6.25933	6.09018	5.92884	5.77485	5.62777	5.48719	5.35275	5.22408	5.10086	4.98279	4.86958
21	6.49502	6.31246	6.13868	5.97314	5.81532	5.66476	5.52101	5.38368	5.25239	5.12677	5.00652	4.89132
22	6.54587	6.35866	6.18068	6.01133	5.85006	5.69637	5.54980	5.40990	5.27628	5.14855	5.02638	4.90943
23	6.59028	6.39884	6.21704	6.04425	5.87988	5.72340	5.57430	5.43212	5.29644	5.16685	5.04299	4.92453
24	6.62907	6.43377	6.24852	6.07263	5.90548	5.74649	5.59515	5.45095	5.31345	5.18223	5.05690	4.93710
25	6.66294	6.46415	6.27577	6.09709	5.92745	5.76623	5.61289	5.46691	5.32780	5.19515	5.06853	4.94759
26	6.69252	6.49056	6.29937	6.11818	5.94631	5.78311	5.62799	5.48043	5.33992	5.20601	5.07827	4.95632
27	6.71836	6.51353	6.31980	6.13636	5.96250	5.79753	5.64084	5.49189	5.35014	5.21513	5.08642	4.96360
28	6.74093	6.53351	6.33749	6.15204	5.97639	5.80985	5.65178	5.50160	5.35877	5.22280	5.09324	4.96967
29	6.76064	6.55088	6.35281	6.16555	5.98832	5.82039	5.66109	5.50983	5.36605	5.22924	5.09894	4.97472
30	6.77785	6.56598	6.36607	6.17720	5.99856	5.82939	5.66901	5.51681	5.37219	5.23466	5.10372	4.97894
31	6.79288	6.57911	6.37755	6.18724	6.00734	5.83709	5.67576	5.52272	5.37738	5.23921	5.10771	4.98245
32	6.80601	6.59053	6.38749	6.19590	6.01489	5.84366	5.68150	5.52773	5.38175	5.24303	5.11106	4.98537
33	6.81747	6.60046	6.39609	6.20336	6.02136	5.84928	5.68638	5.53197	5.38545	5.24625	5.11386	4.98781
34	6.82749	6.60910	6.40354	6.20979	6.02692	5.85409	5.69054	5.53557	5.38856	5.24895	5.11620	4.98984
35	6.83623	6.61661	6.40999	6.21534	6.03169	5.85820	5.69407	5.53862	5.39119	5.25122	5.11816	4.99154
36	6.84387	6.62314	6.41558	6.22012	6.03579	5.86171	5.69708	5.54120	5.39341	5.25312	5.11980	4.99295
37	6.85054	6.62881	6.42041	6.22424	6.03930	5.86471	5.69965	5.54339	5.39528	5.25472	5.12117	4.99412
38	6.85637	6.63375	6.42460	6.22779	6.04232	5.86727	5.70183	5.54525	5.39686	5.25607	5.12232	4.99510
39	6.86146	6.63805	6.42823	6.23086	6.04491	5.86946	5.70368	5.54682	5.39820	5.25720	5.12328	4.99592
40	6.86590	6.64178	6.43136	6.23350	6.04713	5.87133	5.70526	5.54815	5.39932	5.25815	5.12408	4.99660
41	6.86978	6.64502	6.43408	6.23577	6.04904	5.87294	5.70660	5.54928	5.40027	5.25895	5.12475	4.99717
42	6.87317	6.64785	6.43643	6.23774	6.05068	5.87430	5.70775	5.55024	5.40107	5.25962	5.12532	4.99764
43	6.87613	6.65030	6.43847	6.23943	6.05208	5.87547	5.70872	5.55105	5.40175	5.26019	5.12579	4.99803
44	6.87872	6.65244	6.44024	6.24089	6.05329	5.87647	5.70955	5.55174	5.40232	5.26066	5.12618	4.99836
45	6.88098	6.65429	6.44176	6.24214	6.05433	5.87733	5.71026	5.55232	5.40280	5.26106	5.12651	4.99863
46	6.88295	6.65591	6.44308	6.24323	6.05522	5.87806	5.71086	5.55281	5.40321	5.26140	5.12679	4.99886
47	6.88467	6.65731	6.44423	6.24416	6.05598	5.87868	5.71137	5.55323	5.40355	5.26168	5.12702	4.99905
48	6.88618	6.65853	6.44522	6.24497	6.05664	5.87922	5.71180	5.55359	5.40384	5.26191	5.12721	4.99921
49	6.88749	6.65959	6.44608	6.24566	6.05720	5.87967	5.71217	5.55389	5.40409	5.26211	5.12738	4.99934
50	6.88864	6.66051	6.44682	6.24626	6.05768	5.88006	5.71249	5.55414	5.40429	5.26228	5.12751	4.99945
51	6.88964	6.66132	6.44746	6.24678	6.05809	5.88039	5.71275	5.55436	5.40447	5.26242	5.12762	4.99954
52	6.89052	6.66201	6.44802	6.24722	6.05845	5.88068	5.71298	5.55454	5.40461	5.26254	5.12772	4.99962
53	6.89128	6.66262	6.44850	6.24760	6.05876	5.88092	5.71318	5.55469	5.40474	5.26264	5.12780	4.99968
54	6.89195	6.66315	6.44892	6.24793	6.05902	5.88113	5.71334	5.55483	5.40484	5.26272	5.12786	4.99974
55	6.89253	6.66361	6.44928	6.24822	6.05924	5.88131	5.71348	5.55494	5.40493	5.26279	5.12792	4.99978
56	6.89304	6.66401	6.44959	6.24846	6.05944	5.88146	5.71360	5.55503	5.40500	5.26285	5.12797	4.99982
57	6.89348	6.66435	6.44987	6.24868	6.05960	5.88159	5.71370	5.55511	5.40507	5.26290	5.12801	4.99985
58	6.89387	6.66466	6.45010	6.24886	6.05974	5.88170	5.71379	5.55518	5.40512	5.26294	5.12804	4.99987
59	6.89421	6.66492	6.45030	6.24902	6.05987	5.88180	5.71386	5.55524	5.40516	5.26297	5.12807	4.99989
60	6.89451	6.66515	6.45048	6.24915	6.05997	5.88188	5.71393	5.55529	5.40520	5.26300	5.12809	4.99991

Period	14.5%	15%	15.5%	16%	16.5%	17%	17.5%	18%	18.5%	19%	19.5%	20%
61	6.89477	6.66534	6.45063	6.24927	6.06006	5.88195	5.71398	5.55533	5.40523	5.26303	5.12811	4.99993
62	6.89499	6.66552	6.45076	6.24937	6.06014	5.88200	5.71403	5.55536	5.40526	5.26305	5.12812	4.99994
63	6.89519	6.66567	6.45088	6.24946	6.06020	5.88206	5.71406	5.55539	5.40528	5.26307	5.12814	4.99995
64	6.89536	6.66580	6.45098	6.24953	6.06026	5.88210	5.71410	5.55542	5.40530	5.26308	5.12815	4.99996
65	6.89551	6.66591	6.45106	6.24960	6.06031	5.88214	5.71413	5.55544	5.40532	5.26309	5.12816	4.99996
66	6.89565	6.66601	6.45114	6.24965	6.06035	5.88217	5.71415	5.55546	5.40533	5.26310	5.12816	4.99997
67	6.89576	6.66609	6.45120	6.24970	6.06039	5.88219	5.71417	5.55547	5.40534	5.26311	5.12817	4.99998
68	6.89586	6.66617	6.45125	6.24974	6.06042	5.88222	5.71419	5.55548	5.40535	5.26312	5.12818	4.99998
69	6.89595	6.66623	6.45130	6.24978	6.06045	5.88224	5.71420	5.55549	5.40536	5.26313	5.12818	4.99998
70	6.89602	6.66629	6.45134	6.24981	6.06047	5.88225	5.71421	5.55550	5.40537	5.26313	5.12819	4.99999
71	6.89609	6.66634	6.45138	6.24983	6.06049	5.88227	5.71422	5.55551	5.40537	5.26314	5.12819	4.99999
72	6.89615	6.66638	6.45141	6.24986	6.06050	5.88228	5.71423	5.55552	5.40538	5.26314	5.12819	4.99999
73	6.89620	6.66642	6.45144	6.24988	6.06052	5.88229	5.71424	5.55552	5.40538	5.26314	5.12820	4.99999
74	6.89624	6.66645	6.45146	6.24989	6.06053	5.88230	5.71425	5.55553	5.40539	5.26314	5.12820	4.99999
75	6.89628	6.66648	6.45148	6.24991	6.06054	5.88231	5.71425	5.55553	5.40539	5.26315	5.12820	4.99999
76	6.89632	6.66650	6.45150	6.24992	6.06055	5.88231	5.71426	5.55554	5.40539	5.26315	5.12820	5.00000
77	6.89635	6.66653	6.45151	6.24993	6.06056	5.88232	5.71426	5.55554	5.40539	5.26315	5.12820	5.00000
78	6.89637	6.66654	6.45153	6.24994	6.06057	5.88232	5.71427	5.55554	5.40540	5.26315	5.12820	5.00000
79	6.89640	6.66656	6.45154	6.24995	6.06057	5.88233	5.71427	5.55554	5.40540	5.26315	5.12820	5.00000
80	6.89642	6.66657	6.45155	6.24996	6.06058	5.88233	5.71427	5.55555	5.40540	5.26315	5.12820	5.00000
81	6.89643	6.66659	6.45156	6.24996	6.06058	5.88234	5.71427	5.55555	5.40540	5.26315	5.12820	5.00000
82	6.89645	6.66660	6.45157	6.24997	6.06058	5.88234	5.71428	5.55555	5.40540	5.26315	5.12820	5.00000
83	6.89646	6.66661	6.45157	6.24997	6.06059	5.88234	5.71428	5.55555	5.40540	5.26316	5.12820	5.00000
84	6.89647	6.66661	6.45158	6.24998	6.06059	5.88234	5.71428	5.55555	5.40540	5.26316	5.12820	5.00000
85	6.89648	6.66662	6.45158	6.24998	6.06059	5.88234	5.71428	5.55555	5.40540	5.26316	5.12820	5.00000
86	6.89649	6.66663	6.45159	6.24998	6.06059	5.88235	5.71428	5.55555	5.40540	5.26316	5.12820	5.00000
87	6.89650	6.66663	6.45159	6.24998	6.06060	5.88235	5.71428	5.55555	5.40540	5.26316	5.12820	5.00000
88	6.89651	6.66664	6.45159	6.24999	6.06060	5.88235	5.71428	5.55555	5.40540	5.26316	5.12820	5.00000
89	6.89651	6.66664	6.45160	6.24999	6.06060	5.88235	5.71428	5.55555	5.40540	5.26316	5.12820	5.00000
90	6.89652	6.66664	6.45160	6.24999	6.06060	5.88235	5.71428	5.55555	5.40540	5.26316	5.12820	5.00000
91	6.89652	6.66665	6.45160	6.24999	6.06060	5.88235	5.71428	5.55555	5.40540	5.26316	5.12820	5.00000
92	6.89652	6.66665	6.45160	6.24999	6.06060	5.88235	5.71428	5.55555	5.40540	5.26316	5.12820	5.00000
93	6.89653	6.66665	6.45160	6.24999	6.06060	5.88235	5.71428	5.55555	5.40540	5.26316	5.12820	5.00000
94	6.89653	6.66665	6.45160	6.24999	6.06060	5.88235	5.71428	5.55555	5.40540	5.26316	5.12820	5.00000
95	6.89653	6.66666	6.45161	6.25000	6.06060	5.88235	5.71428	5.55555	5.40540	5.26316	5.12820	5.00000
96	6.89654	6.66666	6.45161	6.25000	6.06060	5.88235	5.71428	5.55555	5.40541	5.26316	5.12820	5.00000
97	6.89654	6.66666	6.45161	6.25000	6.06060	5.88235	5.71428	5.55555	5.40541	5.26316	5.12820	5.00000
98	6.89654	6.66666	6.45161	6.25000	6.06060	5.88235	5.71428	5.55556	5.40541	5.26316	5.12820	5.00000
99	6.89654	6.66666	6.45161	6.25000	6.06060	5.88235	5.71429	5.55556	5.40541	5.26316	5.12821	5.00000
100	6.89654	6.66666	6.45161	6.25000	6.06060	5.88235	5.71429	5.55556	5.40541	5.26316	5.12821	5.00000
101	6.89654	6.66666	6.45161	6.25000	6.06060	5.88235	5.71429	5.55556	5.40541	5.26316	5.12821	5.00000
102	6.89654	6.66666	6.45161	6.25000	6.06061	5.88235	5.71429	5.55556	5.40541	5.26316	5.12821	5.00000
103	6.89655	6.66666	6.45161	6.25000	6.06061	5.88235	5.71429	5.55556	5.40541	5.26316	5.12821	5.00000
104	6.89655	6.66666	6.45161	6.25000	6.06061	5.88235	5.71429	5.55556	5.40541	5.26316	5.12821	5.00000
105	6.89655	6.66666	6.45161	6.25000	6.06061	5.88235	5.71429	5.55556	5.40541	5.26316	5.12821	5.00000
106	6.89655	6.66666	6.45161	6.25000	6.06061	5.88235	5.71429	5.55556	5.40541	5.26316	5.12821	5.00000
107	6.89655	6.66666	6.45161	6.25000	6.06061	5.88235	5.71429	5.55556	5.40541	5.26316	5.12821	5.00000
108	6.89655	6.66666	6.45161	6.25000	6.06061	5.88235	5.71429	5.55556	5.40541	5.26316	5.12821	5.00000
109	6.89655	6.66667	6.45161	6.25000	6.06061	5.88235	5.71429	5.55556	5.40541	5.26316	5.12821	5.00000
110	6.89655	6.66667	6.45161	6.25000	6.06061	5.88235	5.71429	5.55556	5.40541	5.26316	5.12821	5.00000
111	6.89655	6.66667	6.45161	6.25000	6.06061	5.88235	5.71429	5.55556	5.40541	5.26316	5.12821	5.00000
112	6.89655	6.66667	6.45161	6.25000	6.06061	5.88235	5.71429	5.55556	5.40541	5.26316	5.12821	5.00000
113	6.89655	6.66667	6.45161	6.25000	6.06061	5.88235	5.71429	5.55556	5.40541	5.26316	5.12821	5.00000
114	6.89655	6.66667	6.45161	6.25000	6.06061	5.88235	5.71429	5.55556	5.40541	5.26316	5.12821	5.00000
115	6.89655	6.66667	6.45161	6.25000	6.06061	5.88235	5.71429	5.55556	5.40541	5.26316	5.12821	5.00000
116	6.89655	6.66667	6.45161	6.25000	6.06061	5.88235	5.71429	5.55556	5.40541	5.26316	5.12821	5.00000
117	6.89655	6.66667	6.45161	6.25000	6.06061	5.88235	5.71429	5.55556	5.40541	5.26316	5.12821	5.00000
118	6.89655	6.66667	6.45161	6.25000	6.06061	5.88235	5.71429	5.55556	5.40541	5.26316	5.12821	5.00000
119	6.89655	6.66667	6.45161	6.25000	6.06061	5.88235	5.71429	5.55556	5.40541	5.26316	5.12821	5.00000
120	6.89655	6.66667	6.45161	6.25000	6.06061	5.88235	5.71429	5.55556	5.40541	5.26316	5.12821	5.00000

APPENDIX D:
THE USE OF THE
MICROCOMPUTER
IN ACCOUNTING*

The use of the microcomputer in American business has greatly increased in recent years due to decreasing computer prices and significant technological advances in both computer hardware and software. Microcomputers now frequently cost under $5,000 and have as much power as computers that would have cost millions of dollars and filled several large rooms only a short time ago. The microcomputer is especially useful in the accounting field because of the great need for fast and accurate information processing when dealing with large volumes of financial data. In order to further our understanding of the microcomputer and its use in accounting, we will discuss the following topics: computerized accounting systems, computer spreadsheets, database management systems, and the use of microcomputers in public accounting.

COMPUTERIZED ACCOUNTING SYSTEMS

Numerous accounting system packages for microcomputers are currently available on the market, and most of them cost from just under $100 to $2,500. These packages are designed for use by small businesses, and they can provide many advantages over manual accounting systems. Companies can greatly reduce the clerical work performed by their accounting staff and can also substantially reduce clerical errors in the financial data by changing from a manual to a computerized accounting system. Computerized systems also allow companies to gather information and produce reports much more efficiently than is possible under manual systems. The proper implementation of one of these accounting system packages can result in a company having a computerized accounting system that is both more efficient and less expensive than a manual system.

---

*Written by Gary Fayard, Senior Manager in the Atlanta Office of Ernst & Whinney, and Dana R. Hermanson, Senior Accountant in the Atlanta Office of Ernst & Whinney.

Now that we understand the potential advantages of using an accounting system package, let us examine the typical characteristics of a package on the market today. One basic characteristic of all effective systems is that some type of control exists over who can use the computer to make journal entries. Many packages have a password that must be used in order to get into the accounting system, while other packages are protected by physically locking up the terminals when they are not being used by authorized personnel. The importance of this control cannot be overstated.

Another common characteristic of most accounting packages today is that they are menu driven. This means that the program user selects an option listed on the screen to access the part of the accounting system that he or she wishes to use. For example, when the user first turns on the computer and enters the proper password, a screen similar to this may appear:

```
                    XYZ  Company

          1>  General  Ledger
          2>  Accounts  Receivable
          3>  Accounts  Payable
          4>  Inventory  Management
          5>  Payroll
          6>  Invoicing
          7>  End  Session
```

If the user wanted to access the Accounts Payable section of the program, he or she would type a "3" into the computer and hit "ENTER." The user would then have access to the Accounts Payable section, and another menu would appear that would provide the user with several options within that section. The menu system is designed to make accounting packages much more "user friendly."

The final characteristic to be discussed is the typical organization or format of a computerized accounting package. Most packages are divided into the modules shown on the screen above—General Ledger, Accounts Receivable, Accounts Payable, Inventory Management, Payroll, and Invoicing. Let us now briefly discuss the function of each module.

The General Ledger module contains all of a company's accounts and their balances. General Journal entries are made in this section, and these entries include all entries not made in one of the other system modules. For example, an entry relating to accounts receivable would be made in the Accounts Receivable module; however, an entry to record the borrowing of cash from a bank does not fit into any of the specific modules and would be made in the General Ledger module as a General Journal entry. Adjusting entries would also be entered in the General Ledger module. One other function performed in the General Ledger module is the printing of a company's financial statements. Most accounting packages will automatically make all the necessary closing entries before printing out the financial statements.

The Accounts Receivable module is used to record sales on credit to various customers and amounts received from customers. This module serves as the Accounts Receivable Subsidiary Ledger, and the Accounts Receivable control account in the General Ledger module is usually automatically updated when entries are made in the Accounts Receivable module.

The Accounts Payable module is used to record credit purchases from various vendors as well as payments made to these vendors. This module also acts as the subsidiary ledger for Accounts Payable, and the control account is usually automatically updated when entries are made in the Accounts Payable module.

The Inventory Management module is designed to keep the perpetual inventory, and all purchases and sales of inventory are reflected in this module. The Inventory Management module interfaces with the Accounts Receivable and Accounts Payable modules in order to keep track of the receivables and payables from sales and purchases.

The Payroll module is used to record all of the payroll entries. The totals from the Payroll module are often automatically posted to the appropriate General Ledger accounts, although this automatic posting is not always available.

The Invoicing module is simply used to print the sales invoices that are sent to customers. Sometimes this Invoicing module is combined with the Accounts Receivable module.

COMPUTER SPREADSHEETS

Another type of computer program that has become extremely popular during the last decade is the electronic spreadsheet. Two of the most popular spreadsheet programs are 1–2–3® from Lotus® and SuperCalc®. These programs have numerous applications in business and specifically in accounting. Spreadsheets are ideal for creating large schedules and performing great volumes of calculations. Their specific uses in accounting range from performing depreciation calculations to creating trial balances and other schedules. Other specific uses of spreadsheets will be discussed in the section on the use of the microcomputer in public accounting.

Let us now examine the basics of the electronic spreadsheet. An electronic spreadsheet is simply a large blank "page" on the computer screen that is made up of rows and columns. The spreadsheet is so large that only a very small percentage of the sheet can be seen on the screen at one time. The blocks created by the intersection of the rows and columns are called cells, and each cell can hold a word, a number, or the product of a mathematical formula. This is what a typical blank spreadsheet looks like:

```
          A  B  C  D  E  F  G
       1
       2 ////  (Cursor)
       3
       4                 (Cell C4)
       5
       6
       7
       8
       9
      10
      A2>  (Type appears here)
      (Cursor location)
```

The cursor indicates the cell on the screen in which information can be entered at a given time. For example, on the above screen, the user can now enter a word, number, or formula into cell A2. Note that the information will appear at the bottom (on some programs, at the top) of the screen next to the cursor location until the user presses the ENTER key to transfer the information to its cell. The user can move the cursor around the screen by pressing different cursor control keys.

By going through the following example we can gain a better understanding of how the electronic spreadsheet actually works. Assume you are an accountant in Burke Company and you wish to create an income statement for 1990 and a projected income statement for 1991 like those shown below:

```
           A                    B                  C            D
    1  ////                   BURKE CO
    2                     INCOME STATEMENT      PROJECTED
    3                    YEAR ENDED 12/31/90     12/31/91
    4
    5  Sales                 1,000,000          1,100,000
    6  Cost of Sales           600,000            660,000
    7  Gross Profit            400,000            440,000
    8  Other Expenses          100,000            110,000
    9  Net Income              300,000            330,000
   10
   A1>
```

The first step in creating these statements is to set up the proper headings. In cell B1 we would enter BURKE CO by moving the cursor to B1, typing in the words BURKE CO, and pressing the ENTER key to transfer the words to cell B1. Likewise, the appropriate headings would be entered into cells B2, B3, C2, and C3. The second step is to enter the income statement items in column A, and these would be placed in cells A5 through A9 in the same way that the other headings were entered.

Now that all of the headings and titles have been entered, let us begin to enter the financial figures into the 1990 Income Statement. Cell B5 will contain the Sales figure of $1,000,000, and B6 will hold the $600,000 Cost of Goods Sold figure. These numbers will be entered in the same manner that the headings and titles were entered. Cell B7 will not hold a specific word or number; however, it will contain the result of a mathematical formula (B5 − B6). By moving the cursor to B7, typing +B5 − B6, and pressing the ENTER key, the result of this formula is entered into B7. Finally, $100,000 will be entered in cell B8. The result of +B7 − B8 will be entered in cell B9.

The final step in constructing this spreadsheet is to complete cells C5 through C9, which will show the projected Income Statement figures for 1991. If we assume that Sales, Cost of Goods Sold, and Other Expenses will increase by 10% from 1990 to 1991, then we can enter the following formulas for cells C5, C6, and C8. Cell C5 will contain the number resulting from the formula +B5*1.1. Cells C6 and C8 will show the results of +B6*1.1 and +B8*1.1, respectively. Finally, C7 and C9 will hold the results of +C5 − C6 and +C7 − C8, respectively. Our spreadsheet is now complete, as it presents the 1990 Income Statement for Burke Company as well as a projected Income Statement for 1991.

We have only used a few of the columns and rows available in a typical spreadsheet. Most spreadsheets contain many columns and rows. For instance, Lotus 1–2–3 contains 256 columns and 8,192 rows.

While the Income Statement just constructed is a simple example of spreadsheet use, it is important to note several more advanced functions that spreadsheets can perform. First, when showing a current schedule and projections of that schedule far into the future, the user can play "what if" games by changing various numbers or formulas in the spreadsheet, and the program will recalculate all of the schedules based on the changes made. Second, many spreadsheet programs allow the user to construct various types of graphs showing the data contained in spreadsheet schedules. Finally, the schedules that appear on the user's computer screen can be printed out on paper for use by other people.

The computerized spreadsheet is a powerful tool, but the potential for inefficient use of spreadsheets is great. To promote better use of spreadsheets, Ernst & Whinney has developed the following tips for its staff:

1. Spend time on planning. Planning how to design, organize, and construct your spreadsheet can ensure that the spreadsheet meets your requirements, reduce errors, and make the spreadsheet easier to use.
2. Keep the overall design simple. Spreadsheet design should aim at producing clear and concise analyses. Quality is more important than quantity.

3. Organize the spreadsheet to make it easy to understand. Separate data input areas from reports. Include instructions and a table of contents to make the spreadsheet understandable to other people.
4. Use simple formulas to make your printed output more understandable and to make errors easier to detect.
5. Use validation tests to alert you if errors occur.
6. Test the spreadsheet before use. Always check spreadsheet calculations before using the results.
7. Use graphics to highlight patterns or trends in your data and to make your spreadsheets more interesting and understandable.
8. Document the spreadsheet. Both users and reviewers need adequate documentation of spreadsheet logic and design. Proper headings and descriptions, as well as other documentation, are important for a well-designed spreadsheet.
9. Use the "protect" command to safeguard the spreadsheet and identify where data should be entered.
10. Make regular backups. Maintain up-to-date copies of spreadsheet files to avoid losing important data and development work.

DATABASE MANAGEMENT SYSTEMS

In many accounting systems the various applications have been developed independently. As a result, for example, although inventory, purchasing, sales, and production all use part numbers to identify inventory items, that piece of information would have to be stored in each file for each application. The same data stored in separate files could vary as far as accuracy and timeliness are concerned. This can result in inefficiencies (data redundancy) and inaccuracies (data inconsistency). A database management system helps solve these problems by storing related data together independent of the application. Many of today's modern accounting systems have integrated applications through the use of a database management system. This means in the above example that the inventory part number is stored in only one file but is used by all the applications.

Database management software is frequently used on microcomputers. Two of the most popular microcomputer database management systems are dBASE III® and R:BASE®. These systems can be used to develop integrated accounting systems and are useful for many single applications also. With database software, you can easily enter data into a microcomputer and then analyze, sort, and print the information using English-like commands. The advantage of using the database management system for a single application over writing the application in a programming language (i.e., BASIC, PASCAL) is that the database management system takes care of data file access for you.

Let us look at an example of a database application. The database file can be any organized collection of related information, such as monthly sales information. The information is kept in records, with each record consisting of a series of fields. A field is the part of a record that holds a particular item of information. An example of a record might be all information related to a salesperson. The fields in the record might include the salesperson's name, address, city, state, and ZIP code.

Suppose you are a sales manager and you need to maintain information relative to your salespersons, your customers, and your company's products. You could use a database management system to help you keep up with this information. In this case, you would probably have three database files—one for salespersons, one for customers, and one for products—however, all of this information would be interrelated by the database management system. The salespersons are related to the customers, the customers to the products, and so on. Once this information has been defined to the database management system you can use English-like commands to help answer such questions as: What products have been sold? Who are the customers? What are the amounts of sales by salespersons? You would also be able to sort and print a customer list sorted by ZIP code, alphabetical order, or salesperson.

USE OF MICROCOMPUTERS IN PUBLIC ACCOUNTING

Microcomputers are having far-reaching effects in all areas of accounting. The following discussion explains some of the uses of microcomputers in public accounting.

Auditing

Auditing involves performing an examination of the financial statements of a company to enable the certified public accountant to express an opinion on the financial statements. The examination of the financial statements involves many different types of tests. Many times statistical sampling techniques are used to test the details of account balances. The microcomputer is very useful in helping both to plan and select the sample and to evaluate the results of the sample.

A typical example of microcomputer-based statistical sampling is the selection of random numbers for a test of cash disbursements. You enter the sequences of the checks written during the year, and the statistical sampling package will select a random sample of the checks to be tested. After the test is completed, the results of the test are entered to determine the statistical results (i.e., confidence level and upper precision limit) of the test.

The microcomputer has had a tremendous impact on the auditing profession in the areas of analytical review and trial balance/financial statement preparation. Microcomputer packages are available that enable the auditor to enter the client's general ledger information and post adjusting journal entries. These packages will print analytical review information, such as percentage increases in expense accounts as compared with the prior year or current and quick ratios. They will also consolidate the financial statements of several related companies and print consolidated financial statements. Another benefit of some of these packages is that they will print the financial information in a way to facilitate income tax return preparation.

Other uses of the microcomputer in auditing are calculations of present/ future values, amortization schedules for debt, depreciation schedules for fixed assets, and flowcharting of accounting systems.

Computer spreadsheets are used extensively both for their ease of use and their capability to quickly change and recalculate computations. Use of a computer spreadsheet to calculate the income tax provision is a typical example. The calculation of the income tax provision can be a complicated computation and is subject to change if adjustments to the financial statements are made as a result of the audit. The use of the computer spreadsheet allows the auditor to quickly reflect the adjusted amounts and recalculate the income tax provision.

Tax

The microcomputer has also had a dramatic impact on the tax practice of public accounting firms. Microcomputers are used to prepare tax returns and are used extensively in income and estate tax planning. Specialized tax programs and computer spreadsheets are both used to perform tax planning. Use of the microcomputer allows the tax professional to ask "what if" questions and quickly see the results of different tax strategies.

Another important use of the microcomputer is in the area of tax research. Through the use of a modem, research databases can be accessed over the phone lines. These databases have current tax law, tax cases, and revenue rulings that can be quickly searched and the information found can be downloaded to the microcomputer for review and printing.

Management Consulting Services

Management consultants, as the name implies, work with clients in a variety of areas. These areas include advising on acquisitions of computer hardware and software, implementing accounting systems, analyzing staffing needs, reviewing manufacturing procedures and cost systems, and performing financial modeling tasks.

Financial modeling is the process of taking historical financial information and projecting the results based on various scenarios. Financial modeling can be performed by use of a computer spreadsheet; however, most large, complicated models are performed by use of microcomputer financial modeling packages.

The following are examples of the uses of financial modeling.

1. A manufacturer needs help in overcoming a seasonal cash shortage. Because of the nature of the business, the company annually builds up large inventories, which result in dramatic increases in payables. Using a financial model, the company is able to anticipate its cash requirements and avert an annual cash crisis.

2. A manufacturer wants to expand its business by acquiring the manufacturing capabilities of existing companies. Using a financial model, the company can develop a series of projections of the anticipated results of various acquisitions and the impact on the company's debt service and borrowing capabilities.

3. A privately held company has plans to go public. A key ingredient to a successful public offering is a well-conceived business plan that allows underwriters to make an objective initial assessment of the company's current situation and future potential. A financial model can be used to prepare projections of the company's financial statements. These projected financial statements would be included in the business plan to allow the underwriters to assess the company's future potential.

YOUR FUTURE AND THE MICROCOMPUTER

The microcomputer is now firmly established as a valuable tool in the accounting field. As computer technology continues to progress, accountants will find more and more ways in which to use these powerful machines.

Future applications of the computer in public accounting will involve the use of "expert systems" and artificial intelligence. Expert systems are software programs designed to duplicate the decisions of an "expert," given certain facts and circumstances. For instance, the program might be able to predict whether or not a client is a going concern with the same success rate as an expert on this topic could. These programs are extremely expensive and time consuming to develop.

Artificial intelligence is a much broader concept than expert systems. The field of artificial intelligence is devoted to making the computer think like a human being by being able to interact with humans and adapt to unstructured situations. In the distant future we may have computers that think and respond like humans.

Your success as an accountant in the future may depend greatly on your ability to use microcomputers efficiently. We hope this appendix has alerted you to the need for an understanding of the uses of the microcomputer in accounting.

APPENDIX E
THE COMPUTER—
BASIC CONCEPTS

THE COMPUTER

The search for greater speed, accuracy, and storage capacity in an accounting system has presented a persistent challenge to both the accounting profession and the designers of information systems. This challenge has been met over the years through the increasing use of more sophisticated devices. The most recent sophisticated device has been the computer. The computer has permitted human participation in the processing of data to be limited to the preparation of the input (transaction) data and the program, or set of instructions, telling the computer how to process these data. If properly programmed, the computer is capable of journalizing and posting transactions with great speed and a high degree of accuracy.

The distinguishing features of a computer are its abilities to accept instructions on the processing of transaction data, store these instructions, and execute them any number of times precisely in the desired sequence. The computer uses elementary logic to alter the sequence of instructions by observing the outcome of a numeric or alphabetic comparison. For example, the computer can be instructed to test whether the cash balance is zero before each transaction and to continue processing cash disbursements only if the balance is greater than zero. Use of such techniques allows the computer to perform functions that are most time consuming when performed manually.

The advantages of a computerized accounting system are many. Computers remain exceedingly accurate at very high calculating speeds. Since sets of operating instructions can be given to the computer at the outset, human effort is conserved. The performance of repetitive tasks, routine numerical decision making, and certain types of logical decision making can be taken over by the computer. The time will come when almost every business uses a computerized system of accounting.

COMPUTER COMPONENTS

The computer consists of three basic components—storage unit, arithmetic unit, and control unit.

The **storage unit** (sometimes called core storage) of a computer is its internal memory system; it records and retains data until they are required by and transferred to other areas of the computer. This unit is the most expensive component of the computer. To determine the optimum size of the storage unit, speed and cost factors must be considered. Generally, the greater the speed and storage required, the greater the cost. Storage space can be added to the computer by utilizing peripheral devices such as disks, drums, or tape units for temporary external storage.

The **arithmetic unit** of a computer performs simple computations and comparisons. Mathematical operations such as addition, subtraction, multiplication, and division are handled through the arithmetic unit. This unit is also the logic unit of the computer.

The **control unit** of a computer is the unit that interprets the **program** (the set of **instructions** submitted to the computer that specifies the operations to be performed and the correct sequence), assigns storage space, and alters the sequence of operations if so instructed by the program. If the unit encounters a situation for which no explicit instructions are given, it will instruct the computer to halt operations. The computer operator can then find and correct the problem situation and restart the processing by means of a console. The **console** allows the operator to exercise control over the computer when necessary.

Peripheral equipment can be attached to the computer and used mainly to feed unprocessed information into the computer and receive the output of processed information. Examples of peripheral equipment are tape drives, card readers, and printers. The manner in which this peripheral equipment is connected and controlled varies from computer to computer.

Illustration E-1 shows a schematic design of a simple computer system. The control unit controls operation of the system. The peripheral equipment is not part of the computer but is used to transmit data into and out of the computer as directed by the control unit. The control unit sends the data to the storage unit until there is time available to process the data. At that time, the data are recalled from storage and transferred to the arithmetic unit, where the required arithmetic operations are performed. On completion, processed data are sent by the control unit either to the peripheral equipment or, if there is more processing to be done using the data, back to storage. The peripheral equipment will display the processed output in a predefined format.

APPLICATIONS OF ELECTRONIC DATA PROCESSING TO ACCOUNTING

Early electronic data processing applications in accounting were in the areas of payroll, accounts receivable, accounts payable, and inventory. Now programs exist for all phases of accounting, including manufacturing operations and total integration of other accounting programs with the general ledger. Nearly all applications of data processing, and particu-

Illustration E-1
MAIN ELEMENTS OF A COMPUTER

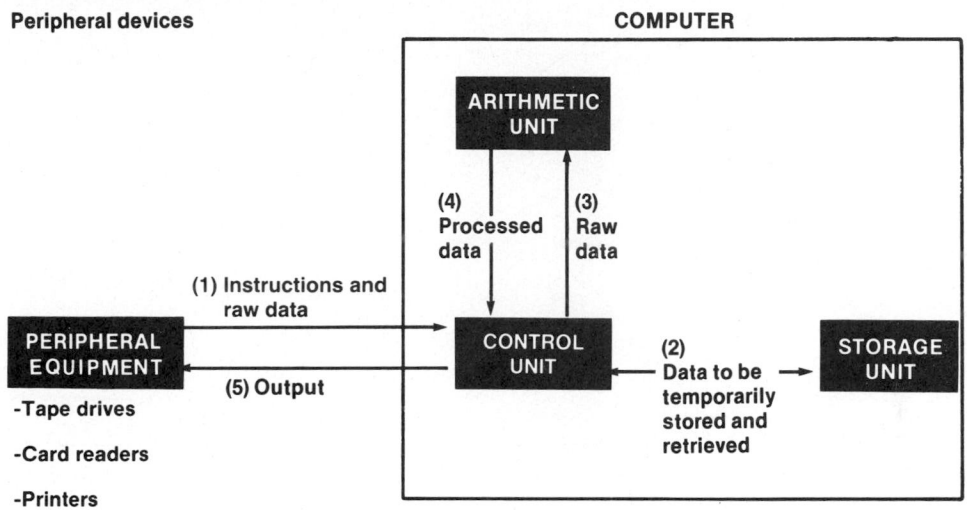

Peripheral devices   COMPUTER

larly those that involve the accounting process, have made considerable use of files.

A **file** is a grouping of similar data arranged in an identifiable order. For example, the accounts receivable ledger is a file. The data in this file are the individual account balances, invoices, and payments received. These data may be stored by customer number. As transactions with customers occur, processing is undertaken to update this file; the end result is a new, updated accounts receivable file created by the computer.

Files also exist for accounts payable and inventory. Recently, an effort has been made to create one large database for a company that would include all of the data in these files in addition to other information regarding company operations and the current status of resources. The database can be used for many purposes, including accounting functions. Developments in the hardware and software areas will have a significant impact on how accounting tasks will be performed in the future.

INDEX

835